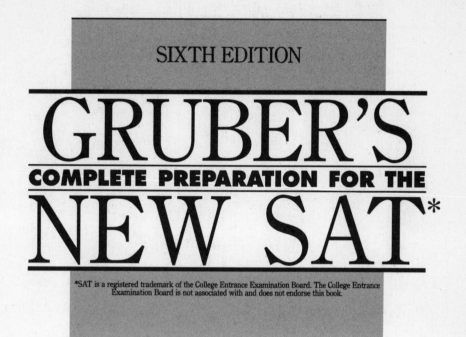

SIXTH EDITION

GRUBER'S
COMPLETE PREPARATION FOR THE
NEW SAT*

SIXTH EDITION

GRUBER'S
COMPLETE PREPARATION FOR THE
NEW SAT*

*SAT is a registered trademark of the College Entrance Examination Board. The College Entrance Examination Board is not associated with and does not endorse this book.

By Gary R. Gruber, Ph.D.

Featuring
CRITICAL THINKING SKILLS

 HarperPerennial
A Division of HarperCollins*Publishers*

GRUBER'S COMPLETE PREPARATION FOR THE NEW SAT. Copyright © 1993 by Gary R. Gruber. All rights reserved. Printed in the United States of America. No part of this book may be used or reproduced in any manner whatsoever without written permission except in the case of brief quotations embodied in critical articles and reviews. For information address HarperCollins Publishers, Inc., 10 East 53rd Street, New York, NY 10022.

HarperCollins books may be purchased for educational, business or sales promotional use. For information, please write: Special Markets Department, Harper-Collins Publishers, Inc., 10 East 53rd Street, New York, NY 10022.

FIRST EDITION

Designed by Marsha Cohen/Parallelogram Graphics

ISBN 0-06-463738-7
ISSN 1068-7262

94 95 96 97 98 PS/CK 10 9 8 7 6 5 4 3

Flash

In March 1994 the SAT changed! BUYER BEWARE! This book is the most up-to-date book on the new SAT. EVERY EXAM is patterned after the NEW SAT, and *all* the strategies and techniques deal with the new SAT. The new SAT incorporates all the Gruber Critical Thinking Strategies.

PBS [Public Broadcasting System] has claimed that Gruber is the originator of the critical-thinking methods necessary for standardized tests like the SAT. PBS chose Dr. Gruber to train the nation's teachers on how to prepare students for the SAT through a national satellite teleconference and videotape.

This book was written by the leading authority on the SAT, who knows more than anyone else in the test-prep market on exactly what is being tested for in the new exam. In fact the procedures to answer the New SAT questions rely more heavily on the Gruber Thinking Strategies than ever before and it is the only book that has the exact thinking strategies you need to use to maximize your SAT score. Gruber's SAT books are used more than any other books by the nation's school districts and proved to get the highest documented school district SAT scores. For example, the New York City Board of Education uses the Gruber SAT book for all their classroom SAT courses.

Important: The changes on the new SAT are very subtle, and many books can be misleading in reflecting the new SAT questions. Don't practice with questions misrepresenting the actual questions on the new SAT. For example, the math questions created by the test makers are now oriented to allow someone to solve many problems with a calculator as fast as without one and some faster without a calculator. This book reflects the new SAT more accurately than any other commercial book, and the strategies contained in it are exactly those needed to be used on the new SAT. It is said that only Dr. Gruber has the expertise and ability to reflect the exam far more closely than any competitor! Don't trust your future with less than the best material.

Note on the New 1994 SAT

General

The test will incorporate the need for more critical-thinking strategies.

Verbal Section

- **Analogy questions** and **Sentence completions** (same as current SAT, except more emphasis will be on vocabulary).

- **Reading comprehension questions** involving longer passages (with more questions and more questions per passage involving critical thinking). Some vocabulary questions will be presented in "context" in the reading passages. There will be one double passage (like a pro–con or passages that deal with similar subjects), and about a fourth of the questions will ask about both passages.

- **Antonyms** (Vocabulary opposite questions) will be deleted, but it will still be important for you to know vocabulary as it will appear in the Analogies, Sentence Completion, and Reading.

Math Section

- Some of the Regular Math questions will be oriented to more real-life situations, and many will rely on deeper thinking. More data interpretation questions, such as those involving graphs, charts, and tables, will be given.

- Ten of the questions will not have multiple choices, but will require that the student "grid" in an answer.

- The Quantitative Comparison questions will remain the same.

- The use of calculators will be allowed, but questions can be solved without a calculator.

If you're planning on taking the new 1994 SAT and use this book, the Critical Thinking methods and problems and practice tests in this book will prepare you better and faster than those in any other book.

The Author Has Something Important to Tell You About How to Raise Your SAT Score

What Are Critical Thinking Skills?

First of all, I believe that intelligence can be taught. Intelligence, simply defined, is the aptitude or ability to reason things out. I am convinced that *you can learn to think logically* and figure things out better and faster, *particularly in regard to SAT Math and Verbal problems*. But someone must give you the tools. Let us call these tools *strategies*. And that's what Critical Thinking Skills are all about—*strategies*.

Learn the Strategies to Get More Points

The Critical Thinking Skills (beginning on page 164) will sharpen your reasoning ability so that you can increase your score up to 300 points on each part of the Scholastic Aptitude Test.

These Critical Thinking Skills—5 General strategies, 25 Math strategies, and 22 Verbal strategies—course right through this book. The Explanatory Answers for the 5 Practice Tests in the book direct you to those strategies that may be used to answer specific types of SAT questions. We can readily prove that the strategies in Part 2 of this book are usable for more than 90 percent of the questions that will appear on your new SAT. *Each additional correct answer gives you approximately 10 points.* It is obvious, then, that your *learning* and *using* the 52 easy-to-understand strategies in this book will very likely raise your SAT score substantially.

Are the Practice Tests in This Book Like an Actual New SAT?

If you compare any one of the 5 Practice Tests in this book with an actual new SAT, you will find the book test very much like the *actual* test in regard to *format, question types*, and *level of difficulty*. Compare our book tests with one of the official tests, published by the College Board!

Documentary evidence is readily available to prove conclusively that no other commercial SAT book has Practice Tests that follow the actual SAT as closely as the 5 Practice Tests in this book.

Building Your Vocabulary Can Make a Big Difference on Your Test

Although Antonyms no longer appear on the SAT, vocabulary will still be tested, especially on the Analogies, Sentence Completions, and Reading Comprehension. This book includes four vital sections to build your vocabulary:

1. 3,400-Word List
2. 100 Vocabulary Tests
3. 366 Latin and Greek roots, prefixes, and suffixes
4. The 291 Most Frequently Used Words on the new SAT

If you have time, it is important for you to study this word-building instructional material. You will find that *many, many words* in the 3,400-Word List will actually show up in the Analogies, Sentence Completion, and Reading Comprehension sections of the Verbal part of your SAT. We repeat that each additional correct answer adds approximately 10 points to your score. Knowing the meanings of the words in the 3,400-Word List will, therefore, help you considerably to "rake in" those precious points.

Study the 366 Latin and Greek Roots, Prefixes, and Suffixes

We have developed a list of roots, prefixes, and suffixes which contains the 50 prefixes and roots that give you the meaning of more than 150,000 words. Learning all 366 will increase your vocabulary immensely.

Study the 291 Most Frequently Used Words on the New SAT

We have developed a list of most frequently used words and their opposites related to specific categories for easy memorization. Study these words.

The Explanatory Answers to Questions Are Keyed to Specific Strategies and Basic Skills

The Explanatory Answers in this book are far from skimpy—so unlike those of other SAT books. Our detailed answers will direct you to the strategy that will help you to arrive at a correct answer quickly. In addition, the Math solutions in the book refer directly to the 150-page Math Refresher section, particularly useful in case your Math skills are "rusty."

Lift That SAT Score—Don't Follow the Down-Trend

You have probably read or heard about the latest College Board statistics that alarmingly reveal that the average score on the Verbal section of the SAT has dropped to 424 from 478, while the average score on the Math section has fallen to 478 from 502. You can reverse that down-trend for yourself. How? Simply do what this book directs you to do. You'll never regret it.

—Gary Gruber

Contents

INTRODUCTION XV

PART 1

DIAGNOSTIC SAT PRE-TEST 1

PART 2

STRATEGY DIAGNOSTIC TEST FOR THE NEW SAT 93

PART 6

MINI-MATH REFRESHER   281

PART 7

COMPLETE NEW SAT MATH REFRESHER   291

PART 10

THE SAT-II WRITING TEST   917

INTRODUCTION

I. Important Facts about the New SAT

What Is the New SAT?

The new "Scholastic Aptitude Test" (formerly called the SAT) is now called the Scholastic Assessment Test (SAT-I Reasoning Test). It is still a three-hour college entrance test, but it now has 7 sections, 5 of which are timed 30 minutes each and 2 of which are timed 15 minutes each. The new test contains 60 counted math questions in three math sections and 78 counted verbal questions in three verbal sections. One section is experimental and does not count toward any score.

The SAT-II tests, which are primarily used for college placement, don't count toward the SAT-I score. For example, the new SAT-II Writing Test is used by most colleges for college first-year English class placement. At the end of this book is a section explaining the new SAT-II Writing Test with practice examples and strategies for the new Essay. You may want to look at this section, although preparation for this Writing Test will not increase your SAT-I Reasoning Test score. For most of the colleges that use the test for placement only, you may not want to overstudy for this SAT-II test in order to be more accurately placed in an English class geared to your current level. You would then not risk being matched up in the English class with students way above your level.

How Is the SAT Scored?

The SAT is scored from 200 to 800 on both parts, verbal and math.

What Is the National Average Score?

The average national SAT score for the 1992–93 school year was 424 for the verbal and 478 for the math.

How Much Is Each Question Worth in SAT Points?

On the SAT you get a *raw* score (the number of correct answers minus a small penalty for incorrect ones). You also get a *scaled* score, which is derived from the raw score. This scaled score is your actual SAT score. Each additional question you get right can increase your score by about 10 more points.

What Verbal Background Must I Have?

The reading and vocabulary level is at a 10th- to 12th-grade level, but strategies presented here will help you even if you are at a lower grade level.

What Math Background Must I Have?

The SAT includes questions related to only first-year elementary algebra and plane geometry. However, if you use common sense and rely on just a handful of geometric formulas, you really don't need to have taken a full course in geometry. If you have not taken algebra you should still be able to answer many of the math questions using the strategies presented.

When Is Guessing Advisable?

There is a penalty of approximately 2.5 SAT points for each wrong answer in a 5-choice type question, and about a 3.3 SAT points penalty for each wrong answer in a 4-choice type question. Guessing is advisable if you can eliminate one or more choices. However, if you cannot eliminate any choices, and you guess, because you have a 1 in 5 chance (with 5 choice questions) and a 1 in 4 chance (for 4 choice questions), the effective penalty is not 2.5–3.5 points, but more like 0.5–0.8 points. It is sometimes thought advisable not to leave any answer blank so that you don't risk mismarking your answer sheet, even if you have to guess at an answer.

Should I Take an Administered Actual SAT for Practice?

Yes, but only if you will learn from your mistakes by seeing what strategies you should have used on your exam. Taking the SAT merely for its own sake is a waste of time and may in fact reinforce bad methods and habits.

What's on the New 1994 SAT?

This is what the new Spring 1994 SAT will contain:

Verbal Section

- **Analogy questions** and **Sentence completions** (same as current SAT)

- **Reading comprehension questions** involving longer passages and more questions involving critical thinking. Some vocabulary questions will be presented in "context" in the reading passages.

- **Antonyms** (Vocabulary opposite questions) will be *deleted*, but it will still be important for you to know vocabulary as it will appear in the Analogies, Sentence Completion, and Reading.

Math Section

- The Regular Math questions will be oriented to more real-life situations and rely on deeper thinking.

- Ten of the questions will not have multiple choices, but will require the student to "grid" in an answer.

- The Quantitative Comparison questions will remain the same.

- Calculators will be allowed, but every question can be solved *without* a calculator.

Can I Get Back the SAT with My Answers and the Correct Ones After I Take It? How Can I Make Use of This Service?

The SAT is disclosed (sent back to the student on request with a $10.00 payment) 3 of the 7 times it is given through the year. Very few people take advantage of this fact or use the disclosed SAT to see what mistakes they've made and what strategies they could have used on the questions.

Check in your SAT information bulletin for the dates this Question and Answer Service is available.

To receive an order form for test results, write: College Board, ATP, P.O. Box 6203, Princeton, NJ 08541–6203.

How Do Other Exams Compare with the SAT? Can I Use the Strategies in This Book?

Most other exams are modeled after the SAT, and so the strategies used here are definitely useful when taking them. For example, the GRE (Graduate Records Examination, for entrance into graduate school) has questions that use the identical strategies used on the SAT. The questions are just worded at a slightly higher level. The ACT (American College Testing Program), another college entrance exam, was changed in the fall of 1989 to reflect strategies that are used on the SAT.

How Does the Gruber Preparation Method Differ from Other Programs?

Many other SAT programs try to use "quick fix" methods or subscribe to rote memorization. So-called "quick fix" methods can be detrimental to effective preparation because the SAT people constantly change questions to prevent "gimmick" approaches. Rote memorization methods do not enable you to answer the variety of questions that appear in the SAT exam. In more than twenty-five years of experience writing preparation books for the SAT, we have developed and honed the critical-thinking skills and strategies that are based on all standardized test construction. So, while this method immediately improves your performance on the SAT, it also provides you with the confidence to tackle problems in all areas of study for the rest of your life.

II. Are Men Better Than Women on the SAT?

These are questions that women found significantly more difficult than men. However, *after* learning the strategies in this book, women scored as high as men, with both increasing SAT scores significantly.

Note this was based on the previous SAT format.

Verbal

Antonyms (*no longer given on the new SAT*)

Choose the word or phrase that is most nearly *opposite* in meaning to the word in capital letters.

1. EXPULSION:

    (A) admission
    (B) relentlessness
    (C) impulsive behavior
    (D) relief from pain
    (E) suppression of information

2. BECLOUD:

    (A) clarify
    (B) beckon
    (C) rescue
    (D) becalm
    (E) recount

3. OBSTREPEROUS:

    (A) quiet and docile
    (B) round and pudgy
    (C) old and venerable
    (D) exotic and unfamiliar
    (E) loyal and honest

Analogies

Each question below consists of a related pair of words or phrases, followed by five lettered pairs of words or phrases. Select the lettered pair that best expresses a relationship similar to that expressed in the original pair.

4. THIMBLE : FINGER : :

    (A) armor : body
    (B) crown : head
    (C) torso : waist
    (D) earring : ear
    (E) stocking : leg

5. BUILDING : CHURCH : :

    (A) dance : ballet
    (B) poetry : sonnet
    (C) museum : relics
    (D) song : hymn
    (E) morality : ethics

Sentence Completion

Choose the word or set of words that, when inserted in the sentence, best fits the meaning of the sentence as a whole.

6. The most _____ means of transportation in the world is the bicycle; indeed, no powered vehicle requires less energy to move as much mass over the same distance.

    (A) grandiose
    (B) infallible
    (C) efficient
    (D) engrossing
    (E) unstable

7. The artistry of cellist Yo Yo Ma is essentially _____; the melodic line rises _____, imbued with feeling and totally lacking in apparent calculation.

    (A) carefree / stiffly
    (B) reserved / involuntarily
    (C) lyrical / passionately
    (D) detached / carefully
    (E) deliberate / methodically

Math

1. Carol has twice as many books as Beverly has. After Carol gives Beverly five books, she still has 10 more books than Beverly has. How many books did Carol have originally?

   (A) 20
   (B) 25
   (C) 30
   (D) 35
   (E) 40

2.
$$\begin{array}{r} 5\,\Delta\,2 \\ \times\quad 9 \\ \hline 5,\,2\,\square\,8 \end{array}$$

   In the correctly computed multiplication problem above, if Δ and $\square$ are different digits, then $\Delta =$

   (A) 1
   (B) 5
   (C) 6
   (D) 7
   (E) 8

3. If s equals ½ percent of t, what percent of s is t?

   (A) 2%
   (B) 200%
   (C) 2,000%
   (D) 20,000%
   (E) 200,000%

4. Which of the following could be the product of 65,218 and 384?

   (A) 25,043,715
   (B) 25,043,714
   (C) 25,043,713
   (D) 25,043,712
   (E) 25,043,711

Answer:

  A *if the quantity in Column A is greater;*
  B *if the quantity in Column B is greater;*
  C *if the two quantities are equal;*
  D *if the relationship cannot be determined from the information given.*

AN E RESPONSE WILL NOT BE SCORED

5.

Column A	Column B
$\sqrt{5} + \sqrt{11}$	$\sqrt{16}$

6.
$$xy = 6$$
$$x^2 + y^2 = 13$$

$(x + y)^2$	18

Answers, Strategy, and Page in Book for questions

Verbal

Answer	Strategy	Page
1. A	Vocabulary 1	275
2. A	Vocabulary 3	279
3. A	Vocabulary 2	277
4. A	Analogy 4	240
5. D	Analogy 4	240
6. C	Sentence Completion 1	245
7. C	Sentence Completion 2,4	246, 249

Math

Answer	Strategy	Page
1. E	Math 2	176
2. E	Math 8	193
3. D	Math 2 and 7	176, 191
4. D	Math 12	201
5. A	Math D	227
6. A	Math 4	183

Source: The College Entrance Examination Board and Gruber research studies.

III. A Four-Hour Study Program for the SAT

For those who have only a few hours to spend in SAT preparation, I have worked on a *minimum* study program to get you by. It tells you what basic math skills you need to know, what vocabulary practice you need, and the most important strategies you need from the 52 in this book.

General

Study general strategies, pages 165–166.

Verbal

Study the following verbal strategies beginning on page 236: (first 3 questions).

Analogy strategy 1, page 236
Analogy strategy 4, page 240
Sentence Completion strategies 1, 2, pages 245, 246
Vocabulary strategies 1, 2, and 3, pages 275–278
Reading Comprehension strategies 1 and 2, pages 260–264
Study the 291 Most Important SAT Words and Their Opposites, page 475

Math

Study the "Mini-Math Refresher" beginning on page 281
Study the following math strategies beginning on page 174* (first 3 questions)

Strategy 2, page 176
Strategy 4, page 183
Strategy 8, page 193
Strategy 12, page 201
Strategy 13, page 203
Strategy 14, page 205
Strategy 17, page 212
Strategy 18, page 215
Strategy A, page 221
Strategy B, page 223
Strategy C, page 224
Strategy D, page 227

If you have time, take Practice Test 1 starting on page 9. Do sections 1–7. Check your answers with the explanatory answers starting on page 52, and look again at the strategies and basic skills that apply to the questions you missed.

*Make sure you read pages 167–173 before you study math strategies.

IV. Longer-Range Study Program and Helpful Steps for Using This Book

1. Learn the Five General Strategies for test-taking on pages 165–166.
2. Take the Strategy Diagnostic SAT Test on page 93 and follow the directions for diagnosis in (3).
3. Take the Diagnostic SAT Pre-Test on page 1 and score yourself according to the instructions.
4. For those problems or questions that you answered incorrectly or were uncertain of, see the explanatory answers beginning on page 52 and make sure that you learn the strategies keyed to the questions, beginning on page 163. For complete strategy development it is a good idea to study *all* the strategies beginning on page 163, Part V the Strategy Section, and learn how to do all the problems within each strategy.
5. Take the 101 Basic Skills Math Questions Diagnostic test on page 131 and follow the directions for diagnosis.
6. The advanced student should take the "19 Questions That Predict Top College Entry" test and follow the directions for diagnosis. Part III, page 121.

For Vocabulary Building

7. Learn the special Latin and Greek prefixes, roots, and suffixes beginning on page 468. This will significantly build your vocabulary.
8. Study 100 words per day from the 3,400-Word List, page 479.
9. Optional: Take the Vocabulary tests beginning on page 531.
10. Study the 291 Most Important SAT Words and Their Opposites beginning on page 475.

For Math-Area Basic Skills Help

11. For the basic math skills keyed to the questions, study the SAT Math Refresher beginning on page 291, or for quicker review look at the Bird's Eye Math Refresher, beginning on page 281.

Now

12. Take the remaining four practice SAT tests beginning on page 599, score yourself, and go over your answers with the explanatory answers. Always refer to the associated strategies and basic skills for questions you answered incorrectly or were not sure how to do.

FORMAT OF THE 1994 SAT
(Beginning with March 1994)

Total time for "counted" (not experimental) VERBAL: 75 minutes—78 questions
Total time for "counted" (not experimental) MATH: 75 minutes—60 questions
Total time for experimental, pre-test items: 30 minutes

Note: The following represents the form of a new SAT. However, the SAT has many different forms, so the order of the sections may vary and the experimental section may not be the last section as we have here.

7 Sections of the SAT*	Number of Questions	Number of Minutes
Section 1: VERBAL	**30 or 31 total**	**30**
Sentence Completions	9	
Analogies	6	
Reading Comprehension (2 passages)	15–16	
Passage 1–400–550 words (500)	6 (or 4–8)	
Passage 2–550–700 words (650)	9 (or 7–9)	
Section 2: MATH	**23–25 total**	**30**
Regular Math	23–25	
Section 3: VERBAL	**35–36 total**	**30**
Sentence Completions	10	
Analogies	13	
Reading Comprehension (1 passage)	12 or 13	
700–900 wds		
OR Reading Comprehension Double reading passage about 450 words each	12 or 13	
Section 4: MATH	**25 total**	**30**
Quantitative Comparison	15	
Student Produced ("grid type")	10	
Section 5: VERBAL	**12 or 13 total**	
Reading Comprehension		**15**
Double reading passage about 450 words each OR	12 or 13	
Reading Comprehension (1 passage) 700–900 words	12 or 13	

Section 6: MATH Regular Math	*10–12 total* 10–12	*15*
Section 7: ***EXPERIMENTAL USED FOR PRE-TEST PURPOSES** *(Format can be any one of the preceding six sections)*	*23–36 total*	*30*

TOTAL MINUTES = 180
(3 Hours)

* The order of the sections on the actual test varies since the SAT has several different forms.
 There will be one passage on Humanities, one on Social Sciences, one on Natural Sciences, and one Narrative (fiction or nonfiction). Total number of Reading Questions will be 40.

1 passage—400–550 words
  4–8 questions
	1 passage—700–850 words
	  12–13 questions

1 passage—550–700 words
  7–9 questions
	1 double passage @ 700–850 words
	  12–13 questions

** One of the seven sections is experimental. An experimental section does *not* count in your SAT score. You cannot tell which of the seven sections of the test is experimental.

FORMAT OF THE NEW PSAT

Given two times in October of each year.   Note: The order of the sections may vary.

4 Sections of the PSAT	Number of Questions	Number of Minutes
Section 1: VERBAL ABILITY Sentence Completions Reading Comprehension (Critical reading) (2 passages or 1 passage + 1 "double" passage)	16 ⎱ **29 or** 13 or⎰ **30** 14	30
Section 2: MATH ABILITY Regular Math	25	30
Section 3: VERBAL ABILITY Analogies Reading Comprehension (Critical reading) (2 passages or 1 passage + 1 "double" passage)	12 ⎱ **28 or** 16 or⎰ **29** 17	30
Section 4: MATH ABILITY Quantitative Comparison Grid-Type (Student-produced response questions)	15 ⎱ **25** 10 ⎰	30

Important Note: The PSAT is identical to the SAT in question types, level of difficulty, and strategies used. There is also a penalty for wrong answers, similar to the SAT penalties. Every single strategy for the SAT applies to the PSAT is used for determining National Merit Scholarships among other uses.

PART 1

DIAGNOSTIC SAT PRE-TEST

To See How You'd Do on
an SAT and What You
Should Do to Improve.
Don't Waste Any Time!
Take This SAT Pre-Test
Before You Do
Anything Else!

This SAT Pre-Test is very much like the actual SAT. It follows the genuine SAT very closely. Taking this Diagnostic Pre-Test is like taking the actual SAT. Following is the purpose of taking this Pre-Test:

1. to find out what you are *weak* in and what you are *strong* in;
2. to know where to concentrate your efforts in order to be fully prepared for the actual test.

Taking this Pre-Test will prove to be a very valuable TIME SAVER for you. Why waste time studying what you already know? Spend your time profitably by studying what you *don't* know. That is what this Pre-Test will tell you.

In this book, we do not waste precious pages. We get right down to the business of helping you to increase your SAT scores.

Other SAT preparation books place their emphasis on drill, drill, drill. We do not believe that drill work is of primary importance in preparing for the SAT exam. Drill has its place. In fact, this book contains a great variety of drill material—2,500 SAT-type multiple-choice questions (Verbal and Math), practically all of which have explanatory answers. But drill work must be coordinated with learning Critical Thinking Skills. These skills will help you to think clearly and critically so that you will be able to answer many more SAT questions correctly.

After you finish the Pre-Test, you will come to Part 5 of this book—"Using Critical Thinking Skills to Score High on the SAT," beginning on page 164.

Ready? Start taking the Pre-Test. It's just like the real thing.

Answer Sheet—Practice Test 1 (Diagnostic SAT Pre-Test)

Make each mark a dark mark that completely fills the oval and is as dark as all your other marks. If you erase, do so completely. Incomplete erasures may be read as intended responses.

Use a No. 2 pencil only. Be sure each mark is dark and completely fills the intended oval. Completely erase any errors or stray marks.

Start with number 1 for each new section. If a section has fewer questions than answer spaces, leave the extra answer spaces blank.

SECTION 1

1 Ⓐ Ⓑ Ⓒ Ⓓ Ⓔ	11 Ⓐ Ⓑ Ⓒ Ⓓ Ⓔ	21 Ⓐ Ⓑ Ⓒ Ⓓ Ⓔ	31 Ⓐ Ⓑ Ⓒ Ⓓ Ⓔ
2 Ⓐ Ⓑ Ⓒ Ⓓ Ⓔ	12 Ⓐ Ⓑ Ⓒ Ⓓ Ⓔ	22 Ⓐ Ⓑ Ⓒ Ⓓ Ⓔ	32 Ⓐ Ⓑ Ⓒ Ⓓ Ⓔ
3 Ⓐ Ⓑ Ⓒ Ⓓ Ⓔ	13 Ⓐ Ⓑ Ⓒ Ⓓ Ⓔ	23 Ⓐ Ⓑ Ⓒ Ⓓ Ⓔ	33 Ⓐ Ⓑ Ⓒ Ⓓ Ⓔ
4 Ⓐ Ⓑ Ⓒ Ⓓ Ⓔ	14 Ⓐ Ⓑ Ⓒ Ⓓ Ⓔ	24 Ⓐ Ⓑ Ⓒ Ⓓ Ⓔ	34 Ⓐ Ⓑ Ⓒ Ⓓ Ⓔ
5 Ⓐ Ⓑ Ⓒ Ⓓ Ⓔ	15 Ⓐ Ⓑ Ⓒ Ⓓ Ⓔ	25 Ⓐ Ⓑ Ⓒ Ⓓ Ⓔ	35 Ⓐ Ⓑ Ⓒ Ⓓ Ⓔ
6 Ⓐ Ⓑ Ⓒ Ⓓ Ⓔ	16 Ⓐ Ⓑ Ⓒ Ⓓ Ⓔ	26 Ⓐ Ⓑ Ⓒ Ⓓ Ⓔ	36 Ⓐ Ⓑ Ⓒ Ⓓ Ⓔ
7 Ⓐ Ⓑ Ⓒ Ⓓ Ⓔ	17 Ⓐ Ⓑ Ⓒ Ⓓ Ⓔ	27 Ⓐ Ⓑ Ⓒ Ⓓ Ⓔ	37 Ⓐ Ⓑ Ⓒ Ⓓ Ⓔ
8 Ⓐ Ⓑ Ⓒ Ⓓ Ⓔ	18 Ⓐ Ⓑ Ⓒ Ⓓ Ⓔ	28 Ⓐ Ⓑ Ⓒ Ⓓ Ⓔ	38 Ⓐ Ⓑ Ⓒ Ⓓ Ⓔ
9 Ⓐ Ⓑ Ⓒ Ⓓ Ⓔ	19 Ⓐ Ⓑ Ⓒ Ⓓ Ⓔ	29 Ⓐ Ⓑ Ⓒ Ⓓ Ⓔ	39 Ⓐ Ⓑ Ⓒ Ⓓ Ⓔ
10 Ⓐ Ⓑ Ⓒ Ⓓ Ⓔ	20 Ⓐ Ⓑ Ⓒ Ⓓ Ⓔ	30 Ⓐ Ⓑ Ⓒ Ⓓ Ⓔ	40 Ⓐ Ⓑ Ⓒ Ⓓ Ⓔ

SECTION 2

1 Ⓐ Ⓑ Ⓒ Ⓓ Ⓔ	11 Ⓐ Ⓑ Ⓒ Ⓓ Ⓔ	21 Ⓐ Ⓑ Ⓒ Ⓓ Ⓔ	31 Ⓐ Ⓑ Ⓒ Ⓓ Ⓔ
2 Ⓐ Ⓑ Ⓒ Ⓓ Ⓔ	12 Ⓐ Ⓑ Ⓒ Ⓓ Ⓔ	22 Ⓐ Ⓑ Ⓒ Ⓓ Ⓔ	32 Ⓐ Ⓑ Ⓒ Ⓓ Ⓔ
3 Ⓐ Ⓑ Ⓒ Ⓓ Ⓔ	13 Ⓐ Ⓑ Ⓒ Ⓓ Ⓔ	23 Ⓐ Ⓑ Ⓒ Ⓓ Ⓔ	33 Ⓐ Ⓑ Ⓒ Ⓓ Ⓔ
4 Ⓐ Ⓑ Ⓒ Ⓓ Ⓔ	14 Ⓐ Ⓑ Ⓒ Ⓓ Ⓔ	24 Ⓐ Ⓑ Ⓒ Ⓓ Ⓔ	34 Ⓐ Ⓑ Ⓒ Ⓓ Ⓔ
5 Ⓐ Ⓑ Ⓒ Ⓓ Ⓔ	15 Ⓐ Ⓑ Ⓒ Ⓓ Ⓔ	25 Ⓐ Ⓑ Ⓒ Ⓓ Ⓔ	35 Ⓐ Ⓑ Ⓒ Ⓓ Ⓔ
6 Ⓐ Ⓑ Ⓒ Ⓓ Ⓔ	16 Ⓐ Ⓑ Ⓒ Ⓓ Ⓔ	26 Ⓐ Ⓑ Ⓒ Ⓓ Ⓔ	36 Ⓐ Ⓑ Ⓒ Ⓓ Ⓔ
7 Ⓐ Ⓑ Ⓒ Ⓓ Ⓔ	17 Ⓐ Ⓑ Ⓒ Ⓓ Ⓔ	27 Ⓐ Ⓑ Ⓒ Ⓓ Ⓔ	37 Ⓐ Ⓑ Ⓒ Ⓓ Ⓔ
8 Ⓐ Ⓑ Ⓒ Ⓓ Ⓔ	18 Ⓐ Ⓑ Ⓒ Ⓓ Ⓔ	28 Ⓐ Ⓑ Ⓒ Ⓓ Ⓔ	38 Ⓐ Ⓑ Ⓒ Ⓓ Ⓔ
9 Ⓐ Ⓑ Ⓒ Ⓓ Ⓔ	19 Ⓐ Ⓑ Ⓒ Ⓓ Ⓔ	29 Ⓐ Ⓑ Ⓒ Ⓓ Ⓔ	39 Ⓐ Ⓑ Ⓒ Ⓓ Ⓔ
10 Ⓐ Ⓑ Ⓒ Ⓓ Ⓔ	20 Ⓐ Ⓑ Ⓒ Ⓓ Ⓔ	30 Ⓐ Ⓑ Ⓒ Ⓓ Ⓔ	40 Ⓐ Ⓑ Ⓒ Ⓓ Ⓔ

Use a No. 2 pencil only. Be sure each mark is dark and completely fills the intended oval. Completely erase any errors or stray marks.

Start with number 1 for each new section. If a section has fewer questions than answer spaces, leave the extra answer spaces blank.

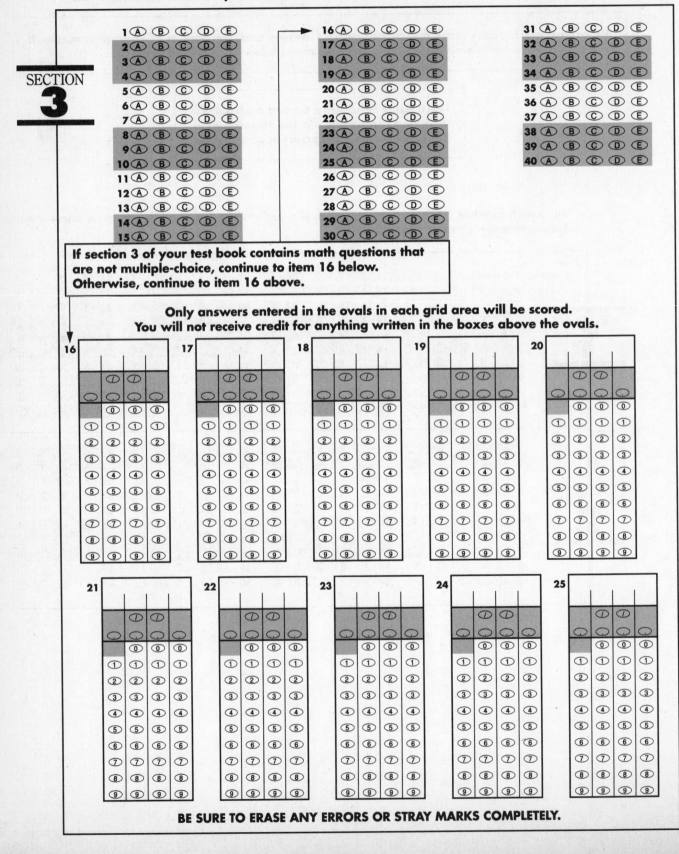

SECTION
3

If section 3 of your test book contains math questions that are not multiple-choice, continue to item 16 below. Otherwise, continue to item 16 above.

Only answers entered in the ovals in each grid area will be scored.
You will not receive credit for anything written in the boxes above the ovals.

BE SURE TO ERASE ANY ERRORS OR STRAY MARKS COMPLETELY.

Use a No. 2 pencil only. Be sure each mark is dark and completely fills the intended oval. Completely erase any errors or stray marks.

Start with number 1 for each new section. If a section has fewer questions than answer spaces, leave the extra answer spaces blank.

SECTION
4

If section 3 of your test book contains math questions that are not multiple-choice, continue to item 16 below.
Otherwise, continue to item 16 above.

Only answers entered in the ovals in each grid area will be scored.
You will not receive credit for anything written in the boxes above the ovals.

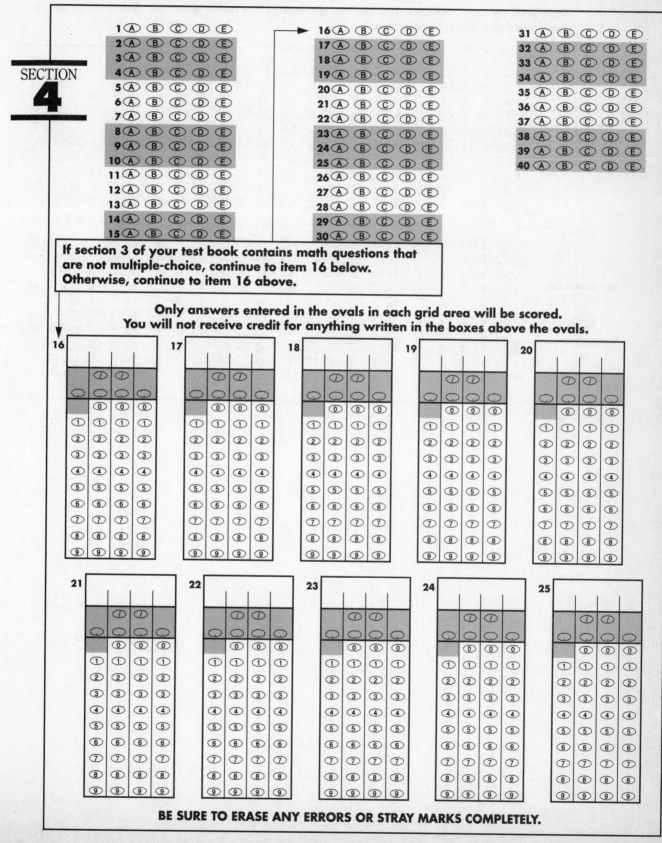

BE SURE TO ERASE ANY ERRORS OR STRAY MARKS COMPLETELY.

Use a No. 2 pencil only. Be sure each mark is dark and completely fills the intended oval. Completely erase any errors or stray marks.

Start with number 1 for each new section. If a section has fewer questions than answer spaces, leave the extra answer spaces blank.

SECTION 5

1 Ⓐ Ⓑ Ⓒ Ⓓ Ⓔ 11 Ⓐ Ⓑ Ⓒ Ⓓ Ⓔ 21 Ⓐ Ⓑ Ⓒ Ⓓ Ⓔ 31 Ⓐ Ⓑ Ⓒ Ⓓ Ⓔ
2 Ⓐ Ⓑ Ⓒ Ⓓ Ⓔ 12 Ⓐ Ⓑ Ⓒ Ⓓ Ⓔ 22 Ⓐ Ⓑ Ⓒ Ⓓ Ⓔ 32 Ⓐ Ⓑ Ⓒ Ⓓ Ⓔ
3 Ⓐ Ⓑ Ⓒ Ⓓ Ⓔ 13 Ⓐ Ⓑ Ⓒ Ⓓ Ⓔ 23 Ⓐ Ⓑ Ⓒ Ⓓ Ⓔ 33 Ⓐ Ⓑ Ⓒ Ⓓ Ⓔ
4 Ⓐ Ⓑ Ⓒ Ⓓ Ⓔ 14 Ⓐ Ⓑ Ⓒ Ⓓ Ⓔ 24 Ⓐ Ⓑ Ⓒ Ⓓ Ⓔ 34 Ⓐ Ⓑ Ⓒ Ⓓ Ⓔ
5 Ⓐ Ⓑ Ⓒ Ⓓ Ⓔ 15 Ⓐ Ⓑ Ⓒ Ⓓ Ⓔ 25 Ⓐ Ⓑ Ⓒ Ⓓ Ⓔ 35 Ⓐ Ⓑ Ⓒ Ⓓ Ⓔ
6 Ⓐ Ⓑ Ⓒ Ⓓ Ⓔ 16 Ⓐ Ⓑ Ⓒ Ⓓ Ⓔ 26 Ⓐ Ⓑ Ⓒ Ⓓ Ⓔ 36 Ⓐ Ⓑ Ⓒ Ⓓ Ⓔ
7 Ⓐ Ⓑ Ⓒ Ⓓ Ⓔ 17 Ⓐ Ⓑ Ⓒ Ⓓ Ⓔ 27 Ⓐ Ⓑ Ⓒ Ⓓ Ⓔ 37 Ⓐ Ⓑ Ⓒ Ⓓ Ⓔ
8 Ⓐ Ⓑ Ⓒ Ⓓ Ⓔ 18 Ⓐ Ⓑ Ⓒ Ⓓ Ⓔ 28 Ⓐ Ⓑ Ⓒ Ⓓ Ⓔ 38 Ⓐ Ⓑ Ⓒ Ⓓ Ⓔ
9 Ⓐ Ⓑ Ⓒ Ⓓ Ⓔ 19 Ⓐ Ⓑ Ⓒ Ⓓ Ⓔ 29 Ⓐ Ⓑ Ⓒ Ⓓ Ⓔ 39 Ⓐ Ⓑ Ⓒ Ⓓ Ⓔ
10 Ⓐ Ⓑ Ⓒ Ⓓ Ⓔ 20 Ⓐ Ⓑ Ⓒ Ⓓ Ⓔ 30 Ⓐ Ⓑ Ⓒ Ⓓ Ⓔ 40 Ⓐ Ⓑ Ⓒ Ⓓ Ⓔ

SECTION 6

1 Ⓐ Ⓑ Ⓒ Ⓓ Ⓔ 11 Ⓐ Ⓑ Ⓒ Ⓓ Ⓔ 21 Ⓐ Ⓑ Ⓒ Ⓓ Ⓔ 31 Ⓐ Ⓑ Ⓒ Ⓓ Ⓔ
2 Ⓐ Ⓑ Ⓒ Ⓓ Ⓔ 12 Ⓐ Ⓑ Ⓒ Ⓓ Ⓔ 22 Ⓐ Ⓑ Ⓒ Ⓓ Ⓔ 32 Ⓐ Ⓑ Ⓒ Ⓓ Ⓔ
3 Ⓐ Ⓑ Ⓒ Ⓓ Ⓔ 13 Ⓐ Ⓑ Ⓒ Ⓓ Ⓔ 23 Ⓐ Ⓑ Ⓒ Ⓓ Ⓔ 33 Ⓐ Ⓑ Ⓒ Ⓓ Ⓔ
4 Ⓐ Ⓑ Ⓒ Ⓓ Ⓔ 14 Ⓐ Ⓑ Ⓒ Ⓓ Ⓔ 24 Ⓐ Ⓑ Ⓒ Ⓓ Ⓔ 34 Ⓐ Ⓑ Ⓒ Ⓓ Ⓔ
5 Ⓐ Ⓑ Ⓒ Ⓓ Ⓔ 15 Ⓐ Ⓑ Ⓒ Ⓓ Ⓔ 25 Ⓐ Ⓑ Ⓒ Ⓓ Ⓔ 35 Ⓐ Ⓑ Ⓒ Ⓓ Ⓔ
6 Ⓐ Ⓑ Ⓒ Ⓓ Ⓔ 16 Ⓐ Ⓑ Ⓒ Ⓓ Ⓔ 26 Ⓐ Ⓑ Ⓒ Ⓓ Ⓔ 36 Ⓐ Ⓑ Ⓒ Ⓓ Ⓔ
7 Ⓐ Ⓑ Ⓒ Ⓓ Ⓔ 17 Ⓐ Ⓑ Ⓒ Ⓓ Ⓔ 27 Ⓐ Ⓑ Ⓒ Ⓓ Ⓔ 37 Ⓐ Ⓑ Ⓒ Ⓓ Ⓔ
8 Ⓐ Ⓑ Ⓒ Ⓓ Ⓔ 18 Ⓐ Ⓑ Ⓒ Ⓓ Ⓔ 28 Ⓐ Ⓑ Ⓒ Ⓓ Ⓔ 38 Ⓐ Ⓑ Ⓒ Ⓓ Ⓔ
9 Ⓐ Ⓑ Ⓒ Ⓓ Ⓔ 19 Ⓐ Ⓑ Ⓒ Ⓓ Ⓔ 29 Ⓐ Ⓑ Ⓒ Ⓓ Ⓔ 39 Ⓐ Ⓑ Ⓒ Ⓓ Ⓔ
10 Ⓐ Ⓑ Ⓒ Ⓓ Ⓔ 20 Ⓐ Ⓑ Ⓒ Ⓓ Ⓔ 30 Ⓐ Ⓑ Ⓒ Ⓓ Ⓔ 40 Ⓐ Ⓑ Ⓒ Ⓓ Ⓔ

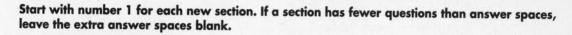
Use a No. 2 pencil only. Be sure each mark is dark and completely fills the intended oval. Completely erase any errors or stray marks.

Start with number 1 for each new section. If a section has fewer questions than answer spaces, leave the extra answer spaces blank.

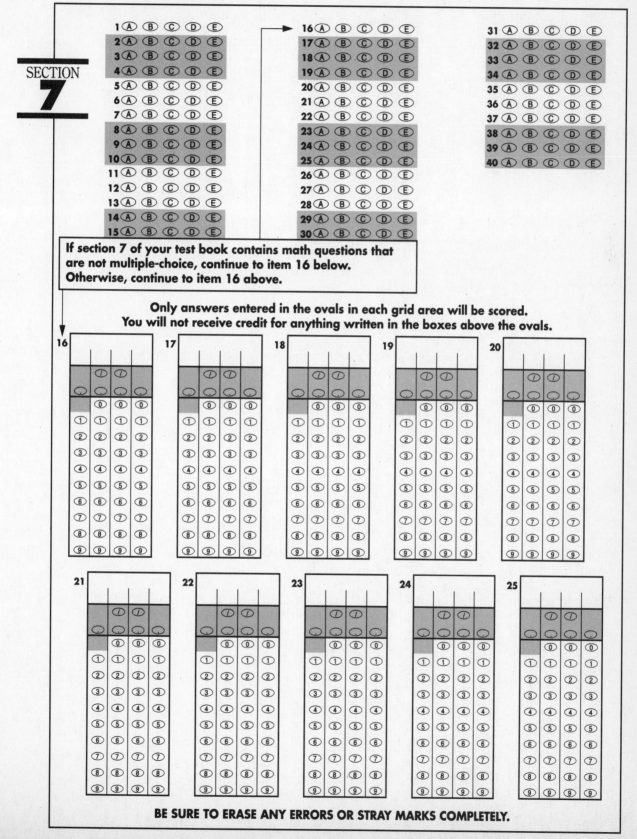

SECTION
7

If section 7 of your test book contains math questions that are not multiple-choice, continue to item 16 below. Otherwise, continue to item 16 above.

Only answers entered in the ovals in each grid area will be scored. You will not receive credit for anything written in the boxes above the ovals.

BE SURE TO ERASE ANY ERRORS OR STRAY MARKS COMPLETELY.

New SAT Practice Test 1
[Full-Length Diagnostic Pre-Test]

Time: 30 Minutes—For each question in this section, select the best answer from among the choices given and fill in
30 Questions   the corresponding oval on the answer sheet.

Each of the following sentences has one or two blanks, each blank indicating that something has been omitted. Following the sentence are five lettered words or sets of words labeled A through E. Choose the word or set of words that, when inserted in the sentence, *best* fits the meaning of the sentence as a whole.

Example:

Medieval kingdoms did not become constitutional republics overnight; on the contrary, the change was _____.

(A) unpopular
(B) unexpected
(C) advantageous
(D) sufficient
(E) gradual

(A) (B) (C) (D) ●

1 Because the majority of the evening cable TV programs available dealt with violence and sex, the parents decided that the programs were _____ for the children to watch.

(A) exclusive   (B) acceptable
(C) instructive   (D) inappropriate
(E) unnecessary

2 The novel *Uncle Tom's Cabin*, which effectively _____ the unfairness toward black people, was a major influence in _____ the anti-slavery movement.

(A) portrayed . . . strengthening
(B) attacked . . . pacifying
(C) glamorized . . . launching
(D) viewed . . . appraising
(E) exposed . . . condemning

3 Having written 140 books to date, he may well be considered one of the most _____ novelists of the century.

(A) eccentric   (B) controversial
(C) easygoing   (D) unheralded
(E) prolific

4 The articles that he wrote ran the gamut from the serious to the lighthearted, from objective to the _____, from the innocuous to the _____.

(A) constant . . . evil
(B) casual . . . realistic
(C) ridiculous . . . remote
(D) argumentative . . . hostile
(E) incapacitated . . . conditioned

5 Because auto repair places have such _____ rates, many community colleges have _____ courses in automotive mechanics.

(A) shattering . . . planned
(B) exorbitant . . . instituted
(C) impertinent . . . discussed
(D) reasonable . . . introduced
(E) intolerable . . . discontinued

6 Though Socrates was _____ by his students who found truth in his teachings, his philosophy constituted _____ to the existent government.

(A) accepted . . . a benefit
(B) denied . . . an innovation
(C) appraised . . . an exception
(D) slighted . . . a challenge
(E) revered . . . a threat

7 The quotation was erroneously _____ to a British poet.

(A) resolved
(B) attributed
(C) activated
(D) relegated
(E) vitiated

8 Mindful that his hardworking parents _____ to give him an education, Lopez, now wealthy, contributes _____ to scholarship funds for the needy.

(A) planned . . . needlessly
(B) skimped . . . profitably
(C) squandered . . . sparingly
(D) struggled . . . generously
(E) regaled. . . regretfully

9 He tried his hardest to maintain his _____ in the face of the threatening mob.

(A) synthesis
(B) analogy
(C) fraternity
(D) umbrage
(E) composure

GO ON TO THE NEXT PAGE

Each of the following questions consists of a related pair of words or phrases, followed by five pairs of words or phrases labeled A through E. Select the pair that *best* expresses a relationship similar to that expressed in the original pair.

Example:

CRUMB : BREAD ::
(A) ounce : unit
(B) splinter : wood
(C) water : bucket
(D) twine : rope
(E) cream : butter

Ⓐ ⬤ Ⓒ Ⓓ Ⓔ

10 COT : BED ::

(A) hotel : motel
(B) tissue : handkerchief
(C) lesson : composition
(D) hand : finger
(E) tea : lemon

11 PARAGRAPH : ESSAY ::

(A) question : response
(B) saddle : horse
(C) act : play
(D) performance : applause
(E) author : book

12 PROVERB : PITHY ::

(A) novel : acclaimed
(B) poem : ribald
(C) accident : tragic
(D) wedding : humorous
(E) snowflake : white

13 SCOLD : DENOUNCE ::

(A) mutter : jabber
(B) advocate : support
(C) squander : spend
(D) exhaust : refresh
(E) injure : maim

14 INTEGRITY : CORRUPTED ::

(A) disguise : recognized
(B) accusation : freed
(C) appearance : seen
(D) simplicity : admired
(E) nonchalance : bored

15 VIRTUOUS : TRUST ::

(A) kindly : avoid
(B) honest : encounter
(C) intellectual : study
(D) shady : suspect
(E) simple : greet

GO ON TO THE NEXT PAGE →

Each passage below is followed by questions based on its content. Answer the questions following each passage on the basis of what is <u>stated</u> or <u>implied</u> in that passage and in any introductory material that may be provided.

Questions 16–21 are based on the following passage.

The following passage tracks the career of the famous artist Vincent van Gogh, and his encounter with another famous artist, Paul Gauguin.

It was at Arles, the small city in the south of France where he stayed from early in 1888 to the spring of 1889, that Vincent van Gogh had his first real bout with madness. After a quarrel with Paul Gauguin, he cut off part of his own ear. Yet
5 Arles was also the scene of an astonishing burst of creativity. Over the short span of 15 months, van Gogh produced some 200 paintings and more than 100 drawings and watercolors, a record that only Picasso has matched in the modern era. Orchards and wheatfields under the glowing
10 sun, neighbors and townspeople, interiors of the Yellow House where he lived, were all subjects of his frenetic brush. The Arles canvases, alive with color—vermilion, emerald green, Prussian blue and a particularly brilliant yellow—have intensity of feeling that mark the high point of his
15 career, and deeply affected the work of artists to follow, notably the Fauves and the German Expressionists.

Van Gogh went to Arles after two years in Paris, where his beloved younger brother Theo, who supported him psychologically and financially for most of his adult life, was an
20 art dealer. In Paris, Vincent had met Gauguin, and other important artists—Lautrec, Degas, Pissarro, and Seurat. Like the last two, he worked in the Neo-Impressionist or Pointillist style—applying color in tiny dots or strokes that "mixed" in the viewer's eye to create effects of considerable
25 intensity. But he wanted "gayer" colors than Paris provided, the kind of atmosphere evoked by the Japanese prints he so admired. Then, too, the French capital had exhausted him, mentally and physically. He felt that in Arles, not exactly a bustling arts center, he might find serenity, and even estab-
30 lish an artistic tradition.

It was van Gogh's hope of founding a new artists' colony in the south that made him eager to have Gauguin, whose talent van Gogh readily recognized, join him at Arles. The plan, on Vincent's part, was for Gauguin to stay in Arles
35 for maybe a year, working and sharing with him the small living quarters and studio he had found for himself and dubbed the Yellow House. At first, the two men got along well. But they did not at all agree on judgments of other artists. Still, Gauguin had an influence on van Gogh. Gauguin
40 began pushing the younger artist to paint from memory rather than actuality.

Before the year was up, whether because of Gauguin's attempts to change van Gogh's style, or what, the two men had apparently begun to get on each other's nerves. Gauguin
45 wrote to Theo that he felt he had to return to Paris, citing his and Vincent's "temperamental incompatibility." A letter from Vincent to Theo followed, noting that Gauguin was "a little out of sorts with the good town of Arles, and especially with me."
50 But then, the two apparently made up—but not for long. Gauguin returned to Paris and never saw van Gogh again, although they later had friendly correspondence.

16 Which of the following is the best title for the passage?

(A) Where van Gogh's Art Reached Its Zenith
(B) An Unfortunate Mismatch Between Two Great Artists
(C) Another Tale of a Genius Unable to Adjust to Society
(D) A Prolific Painter Whose Art Will Live On
(E) Van Gogh's Frustration in His Hope to Found a New Artists' Colony

17 According to the passage, which of the following statements is *not* true?

(A) Fauvism is a movement in painting typified by vivid colors.
(B) Gauguin was an older man than Theo.
(C) Pissarro was a painter associated with the Neo-Impressionist school.
(D) Van Gogh's work began to deteriorate after Gauguin's departure from Arles.
(E) Van Gogh's behavior was, at times, quite abnormal.

GO ON TO THE NEXT PAGE

18 For which of the following reasons did van Gogh decide to leave Paris and go to Arles?

I. He sought a different environment for the kind of painting he wished to do.
II. He had hopes of forming a new artists' colony.
III. He wanted a more peaceful location where there was less stress.

(A) II only
(B) III only
(C) I and II only
(D) I and III only
(E) I, II, and III

19 The word "frenetic" in line 11 most nearly means

(A) colorful
(B) smooth
(C) bright
(D) rapid
(E) frantic

20 Gauguin's attitude toward van Gogh is best described in the passage as one of

(A) gentle ridicule
(B) unallayed suspicion
(C) tolerant acceptance
(D) open condescension
(E) resentful admiration

21 Aside from his quarrel with Gauguin, we may infer that a major contributory reason for van Gogh's going to the extreme of cutting off part of his ear was his

(A) concern about being able to support himself financially
(B) inability to get along with Gauguin
(C) failure to form an artists' colony in Arles
(D) mental and emotional instability
(E) being upset by Gauguin's attempts to change his style

GO ON TO THE NEXT PAGE

Questions 22–30 are based on the following passage.

The following passage is excerpted from the essay *Self-Reliance* by the American writer Ralph Waldo Emerson.

Infancy conforms to nobody: all conform to it, so that one babe commonly makes four or five out of the adults who prattle and play to it. So God has armed youth and puberty and manhood no less with its own piquancy and charm, and
5 made it enviable and gracious and its claims not to be put by, if it will stand by itself. Do not think the youth has no force, because he cannot speak to you and me. Hark! in the next room his voice is sufficiently clear and emphatic. It seems he knows how to speak to his contemporaries. Bashful or bold,
10 then, he will know how to make us seniors very unnecessary.

The nonchalance of boys who are sure of a dinner, and would disdain as much as a lord to do or say aught to conciliate one, is the healthy attitude of human nature. A boy is in the parlor what the pit is in the playhouse; independent,
15 irresponsible, looking out from his corner on such people and facts as pass by, he tries and sentences them on their merits, in the swift, summary way of boys, as good, bad, interesting, silly, eloquent, troublesome. He lumbers himself never about consequences, about interests; he gives an inde-
20 pendent, genuine verdict. You must court him: he does not court you. But the man is, as it were, clapped into jail by his consciousness. As soon as he has once acted or spoken with eclat, he is a committed person, watched by the sympathy or the hatred of hundreds, whose affections must now enter
25 into his account. There is no Lethe for this. Ah, that he could pass again into his neutrality.

These are the voices which we hear in solitude, but they grow faint and inaudible as we enter into the world. Society everywhere is in conspiracy against the manhood of every
30 one of its members. Society is a joint-stock company, in which the members agree, for the better securing of his bread to each shareholder, to surrender the liberty and culture of the eater. The virtue in most request is conformity. Self-reliance is its aversion. It loves not realities and creators,
35 but names and customs.

Whoso would be a man must be a nonconformist. He who would gather immortal palms must not be hindered by the name of goodness, but must explore if it be goodness. Nothing is at last sacred but the integrity of your own mind.
40 No law can be sacred to me but that of my nature. Good and bad are but names very readily transferable to that or this; the only right is what is after my constitution, the only wrong what is against it. A man is to carry himself in the presence of all opposition as if every thing were titular and
45 ephemeral but he. I am ashamed to think how easily we capitulate to badges and names, to large societies and dead institutions. Every decent and well-spoken individual affects and sways me more than is right. I ought to go upright and vital, and speak the rude truth in all ways.
50 I shun father and mother and wife and brother, when my genius calls me. I would write on the lintels of the doorpost, *Whim.* I hope it is somewhat better than whim at

last, but we cannot spend the day in explanation. Expect me not to show cause why I seek or why I exclude company.
55 Then, again, do not tell me, as a good man did to-day, of my obligation to put all poor men in good situations. Are they *my* poor? I tell thee, thou foolish philanthropist, that I grudge the dollar, the dime, the cent, I give to such men as do not belong to me and to whom I do not belong. There is a
60 class of persons to whom by all spiritual affinity I am bought and sold; for them I will go to prison, if need be; but your miscellaneous popular charities; the education at college of fools; the building of meeting-houses to the vain end to which many now stand; alms to sots; and the thousandfold
65 Relief Societies;—though I confess with shame I sometimes succumb and give the dollar, it is a wicked dollar which by and by I shall have the manhood to withhold.

For nonconformity the world whips you with its displeasure. And therefore a man must know how to estimate a
70 sour face. The by-standers look askance on him in the public street or in the friend's parlor. If this aversion had its origin in contempt and resistance like his own, he might well go home with a sad countenance; but the sour faces of the multitude, like their sweet faces, have no deep cause, but are
75 put on and off as the wind blows and an newspaper directs. Yet is the discontent of the multitude more formidable than that of the senate and the college.

The other terror that scares us from self-trust is our consistency; a reverence for our past act or word, because
80 the eyes of others have no other data for computing our orbit than our past acts, and we are loath to disappoint them.

But why should you keep your head over your shoulder? Why drag about this corpse of your memory, lest you contradict somewhat you have stated in this or that public
85 place? Suppose you should contradict yourself; what then?

A foolish consistency is the hobgoblin of little minds, adored by little statesmen and philosophers and divines. With consistency a great soul has simply nothing to do. He may as well concern himself with his shadow on the wall.
90 Speak what you think now in hard words; and to-morrow speak what to-morrow thinks in hard words again, though it contradict everything you said to-day.—"Ah, so you shall be sure to be misunderstood."—Is it so bad, then, to be misunderstood? Pythagoras was misunderstood, and Socrates,
95 and Jesus, and Luther, and Copernicus, and Galileo, and Newton, and every pure and wise spirit that ever took flesh. To be great is to be misunderstood.

GO ON TO THE NEXT PAGE

22 The main theme of the selection is best expressed as follows:

(A) "A foolish consistency is the hobgoblin of little minds."
(B) "Eternal youth means eternal independence."
(C) "Whoso would be a man must be a nonconformist."
(D) "Colleges are designed to educate fools."
(E) "Infancy conforms to nobody."

23 We are most nonconformist during our period of

(A) infancy
(B) puberty
(C) youth
(D) manhood
(E) old age

24 According to the author, "To be great is to be misunderstood" means that

(A) one should never say exactly what one means
(B) to be misunderstood is to be great
(C) all great men have always been misunderstood
(D) a man should not hesitate to change his mind if he sees the need to, even at the risk of being considered inconsistent
(E) nice people seldom succeed

25 The refusal of young people to cater to accepted public opinion is, according to the author,

(A) characteristic of the rebelliousness of youth
(B) a healthy attitude of human nature
(C) a manifestation of deep-seated immaturity
(D) simply bad manners
(E) part of growing up

26 From the selection, one may infer that the "pit in the playhouse" was

(A) a section containing the best seats in the theater
(B) favored by independent, outspoken, unself-conscious playgoers
(C) an underground theater
(D) a generally staid, quiet section of the theater, favored by young people only
(E) the actors' dressing rooms

27 "Society is a joint-stock company etc." is one way in which the author shows

(A) that the public is anti-culture
(B) society is highly organized and structured
(C) how society rejects self-reliance
(D) that there is no room for solitude in our world
(E) the public's interest in the stock market

28 The word "eclat" (line 23), as used in this selection, means

(A) fun-loving and luxury
(B) violence and force
(C) disrespect and resistance
(D) reason and logic
(E) spirit and enthusiasm

29 "I would write on the lintels of the doorpost, *Whim.*" By this, the author means

(A) that one should renounce his immediate family
(B) that signposts have an important educational function in our society
(C) that an impulsive action may have a subsequent rational explanation
(D) that one must never be held responsible for what one says and does
(E) that everyone should do foolish things occasionally

30 The statement that best sums up the spirit and sense of this selection is

(A) "Nothing is at last sacred but the integrity of your own mind."
(B) "With consistency, a great soul has simply nothing to do."
(C) "Do not think the youth has no force, because he cannot speak to you and me."
(D) "The virtue in most request is conformity."
(E) "A man must know how to estimate a sour face."

IF YOU FINISH BEFORE TIME IS CALLED, YOU MAY CHECK YOUR WORK ON THIS SECTION ONLY. DO NOT TURN TO ANY OTHER SECTION IN THE TEST.

STOP

Time: 30 Minutes   In this section solve each problem, using any available space on the page for scratchwork.
25 Questions   Then decide which is the best of the choices given and fill in the corresponding oval on the
                    answer sheet.

Notes:

1. The use of a calculator is permitted. All numbers used are real numbers.
2. Figures that accompany problems in this test are intended to provide information useful in solving the problems. They are drawn as accurately as possible EXCEPT when it is stated in a specific problem that the figure is not drawn to scale. All figures lie in a plane unless otherwise indicated.

Reference Information

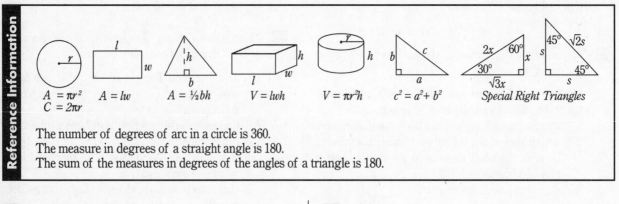

$A = \pi r^2$ $A = lw$ $A = \frac{1}{2}bh$ $V = lwh$ $V = \pi r^2 h$ $c^2 = a^2 + b^2$ *Special Right Triangles*
$C = 2\pi r$

The number of degrees of arc in a circle is 360.
The measure in degrees of a straight angle is 180.
The sum of the measures in degrees of the angles of a triangle is 180.

1 If a and b are positive integers and $ab = 64$, what is the smallest possible value of $a + b$?

(A) 65
(B) 34
(C) 20
(D) 16
(E) 8

2 Find the value of $x + x^3 + x^5 + x^6$ if $x = -1$.

(A) -4
(B) -2
(C) 1
(D) 2
(E) 4

GO ON TO THE NEXT PAGE

3

AB
+BA
‾‾‾‾
66

If $0 < A < 6$ and $0 < B < 6$ in the addition problem above, how many different integer values of A are possible?

(A) Two
(B) Three
(C) Four
(D) Five
(E) Six

4 At 8:00 A.M. the outside temperature was −15°F. At 11:00 A.M. the temperature was 0°F. If the temperature continues to rise at the same uniform rate, what will the temperature be at 5:00 P.M. on the same day?

(A) −15°F
(B) −5°F
(C) 0°F
(D) 15°F
(E) 30°F

Questions 5–6 refer to the following chart.

Number of Shirts	Total Price
1	$12.00
Box of 3	$22.50
Box of 6	$43.40

5 Which of the following is the closest approximation of the lowest cost per shirt, when a box of shirts is purchased?

(A) $7.10
(B) $7.20
(C) $7.30
(D) $7.40
(E) $7.50

6 If exactly 11 shirts are to be purchased, what is the minimum amount of money that must be spent?

(A) $65.90
(B) $89.90
(C) $91.50
(D) $103.40
(E) $132.00

GO ON TO THE NEXT PAGE

7 If $5x^2 - 15x = 0$ and $x \neq 0$, find the value of x.

(A) -10
(B) -3
(C) 10
(D) 5
(E) 3

9 If $55{,}555 = y + 50{,}505$ find the value of $50{,}505 - 10y$.

(A) -5.05
(B) 0
(C) 5
(D) 5.05
(E) 50.5

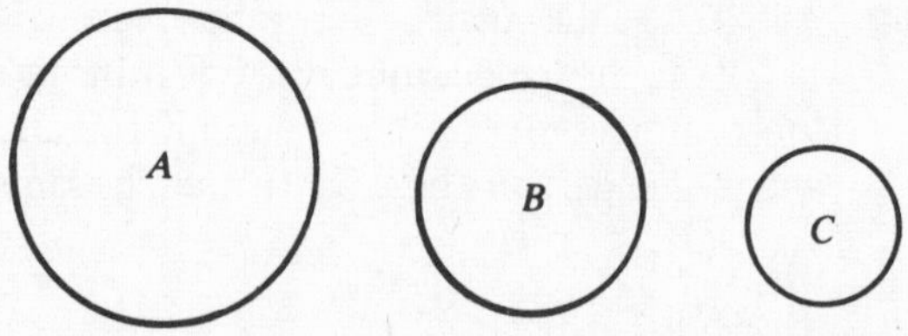

8 The chickens on a certain farm consumed 600 pounds of feed in half a year. During that time the total number of eggs laid was 5,000. If the feed cost $1.25 per pound, then the feed cost per egg was

(A) $0.0750
(B) $0.1250
(C) $0.15
(D) $0.25
(E) $0.3333

10 In the figure above, there are three circles, A, B, and C. The area of A is three times that of B, and the area of B is three times that of C. If the area of B is 1, find the sum of the areas of A, B, and C.

(A) 3
(B) 3⅓
(C) 4⅓
(D) 5
(E) 6⅓

GO ON TO THE NEXT PAGE

11 $[(3a^3b^2)^3]^2 =$

(A) $27a^9b^6$
(B) $54a^9b^6$
(C) $729a^9b^6$
(D) $729a^{18}b^{12}$
(E) $729a^{54}b^{16}$

13 Given that $\left(\dfrac{3}{10}\right)^2$ is equal to p hundredths, find the value of p.

(A) 5
(B) 6
(C) 9
(D) 12
(E) 32

Note: Figure not drawn to scale.

12 In the figure above, two concentric circles with center P are shown. PQR, a radius of the larger circle, equals 9. PQ, a radius of the smaller circle, equals 4. If a circle L (not shown) is drawn with center at R and Q on its circumference, find the radius of circle L.

(A) 13
(B) 5
(C) 4
(D) 2
(E) It cannot be determined from the information given.

14 Find the circumference of a circle that has the same area as a square that has perimeter 2π.

(A) $2\sqrt{2}$
(B) $\pi\sqrt{\pi}$
(C) $\dfrac{\pi}{2}$
(D) $\dfrac{\sqrt{2}}{\pi}$
(E) 2

GO ON TO THE NEXT PAGE

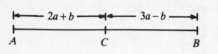

15 Given *ACB* is a straight line segment, and *C* is the midpoint of *AB*. If the two segments have the lengths shown above, then

(A) $a = -2b$

(B) $a = -\frac{2}{5}b$

(C) $a = \frac{2}{5}b$

(D) $a = b$

(E) $a = 2b$

17 Bus A averages 40 kilometers per gallon of fuel. Bus B averages 50 kilometers per gallon of fuel. If the price of fuel is $3 per gallon, how much less would an 800-kilometer trip cost for Bus B than for Bus A?

(A) $18

(B) $16

(C) $14

(D) $12

(E) $10

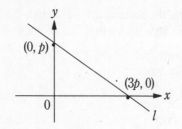

Note: Figure not drawn to scale.

16 What is the slope of line *l* in the above figure?

(A) -3

(B) $-\frac{1}{3}$

(C) 0

(D) $\frac{1}{3}$

(E) 3

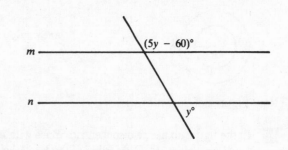

18 $m \| n$ in the figure above. Find *y*.

(A) 10

(B) 20

(C) 40

(D) 65

(E) 175

GO ON TO THE NEXT PAGE

19 Given 4 percent of $(2a+b)$ is 18 and a is a positive integer. What is the *greatest* possible value of b?

(A) 450
(B) 449
(C) 448
(D) 43
(E) 8

21 Using the formula $C=\frac{5}{9}(F-32)$, if the Celsius (C) temperature increased 35°, by how many degrees would the Fahrenheit (F) temperature be increased?

(A) $19\frac{4}{9}°$

(B) 31°
(C) 51°
(D) 63°
(E) 82°

20 A square has an area of R². An equilateral triangle has a perimeter of E. If r is the perimeter of the square and e is a side of the equilateral triangle, then, in terms of R and E, $e+r=$

(A) $\dfrac{E + R}{7}$

(B) $\dfrac{4R + 3E}{3}$

(C) $\dfrac{3E + 4R}{12}$

(D) $\dfrac{12E + R}{3}$

(E) $\dfrac{E + 12R}{3}$

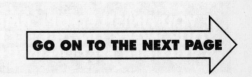

22 Equilateral polygon ABCDEF is inscribed in the circle. If the length of arc BAF is 14π, find the length of the diameter of the circle.

(A) 7
(B) 14
(C) 7π
(D) 21
(E) 42

GO ON TO THE NEXT PAGE

23 If $\frac{a}{b} = \frac{1}{4}$, where a is a positive integer, which of the following is a possible value of $\frac{a^2}{b}$?

   I. $\frac{1}{4}$

   II. $\frac{1}{2}$

   III. 1

(A) None
(B) I only
(C) I and II only
(D) I and III only
(E) I, II, and III

24 A plane left airport A and has traveled x kilometers per hour for y hours. In terms of x and y, how many kilometers from airport A had the plane traveled $\frac{2}{3}y$ hours ago?

(A) $\frac{xy}{6}$

(B) $\frac{xy}{3}$

(C) xy

(D) $\frac{3xy}{2}$

(E) $\frac{xy}{12}$

25 The average (arithmetic mean) of k scores is 20. The average of 10 of these scores is 15. Find the average of the remaining scores in terms of k.

(A) $\frac{20k + 150}{10}$

(B) $\frac{20k - 150}{10}$

(C) $\frac{150 - 20k}{10}$

(D) $\frac{150 - 20k}{k - 10}$

(E) $\frac{20k - 150}{k - 10}$

IF YOU FINISH BEFORE TIME IS CALLED, YOU MAY CHECK YOUR WORK ON THIS SECTION ONLY. DO NOT TURN TO ANY OTHER SECTION IN THE TEST.

Time: 30 Minutes—For each question in this section, select the best answer from among the choices given and fill in
35 Questions   the corresponding oval on the answer sheet.

Each of the following sentences has one or two
blanks, each blank indicating that something has
been omitted. Beneath the sentence are five words
or sets of words labeled A through E. Choose the
word or set of words that, when inserted in the
sentence, best fits the meaning of the sentence as a
whole.

Example:

Medieval kingdoms did not become constitutional republics overnight; on the contrary, the
change was _____.

(A) unpopular
(B) unexpected
(C) advantageous
(D) sufficient
(E) gradual

Ⓐ Ⓑ Ⓒ Ⓓ ●

1 The low-cost apartment buildings, new and well
managed, are _____ to those accustomed to living in
tenements _____ by shady characters.

(A) a boon . . . haunted
(B) a specter . . . inhabited
(C) an exodus . . . frequented
(D) an example . . . viewed
(E) a surprise . . . approached

2 Before the inflation _____, one could have had a
complete meal in a restaurant for a dollar, including
the tip, whereas today a hot dog, coffee, and dessert
would _____ add up to two or three times that
much.

(A) spiral . . . indubitably
(B) cancellation . . . rapidly
(C) problem . . . improbably
(D) abundance . . . consequently
(E) incidence . . . radically

3 Although the death of his dog had saddened him
markedly, his computer designing skills remained
completely _____.

(A) twisted
(B) unaffected
(C) incapable
(D) repaired
(E) demolished

4 A sense of fairness _____ that the punishment
should fit the crime; yet, in actual practice, judicial
decisions _____ greatly for the same type of criminal offense.

(A) assumes . . . coincide
(B) relegates . . . deviate
(C) accumulates . . . simplify
(D) insists . . . compromise
(E) dictates . . . vary

5 The guerrillas were so _____ that the general had to
develop various strategies to trap them.

(A) distant
(B) wild
(C) unreasonable
(D) elusive
(E) cruel

6 The typist made no effort to be _____; she double-
spaced the first and third letter, then single-spaced
the second, fourth, and fifth letters.

(A) consistent
(B) prompt
(C) amicable
(D) courteous
(E) considerate

GO ON TO THE NEXT PAGE

7 As an outstanding publisher, Alfred Knopf was able to make occasional _____, but his bad judgment was tolerated in view of his tremendous _____.

(A) appearances ... energy
(B) mistakes ... success
(C) remarks ... connections
(D) enemies ... audacity
(E) conferences ... patience

8 Their married life was not _____ since it was fraught with bitter fighting and arguments.

(A) nubile
(B) tranquil
(C) obvious
(D) cogent
(E) imminent

9 Because of his _____ driving, the other car was forced to turn off the road or be hit.

(A) perceptive
(B) negligent
(C) resourceful
(D) placid
(E) exemplary

10 The _____ in the Bible are both entertaining and instructive.

(A) syllables
(B) abatements
(C) milestones
(D) parables
(E) utilities

GO ON TO THE NEXT PAGE

Each of the following examples consists of a related pair of words or phrases, followed by five pairs of words or phrases labeled A through E. Select the pair that *best* expresses a relationship similar to that expressed in the original pair.

Example:

CRUMB : BREAD ::

(A) ounce : unit
(B) splinter : wood
(C) water : bucket
(D) twine : rope
(E) cream : butter

Ⓐ ● Ⓒ Ⓓ Ⓔ

11 PIONEER : WEST ::

(A) astronaut : moon
(B) pilgrim : shrine
(C) admiral : navy
(D) Indian : reservation
(E) invalid : obstacle

12 ANIMAL : HIDE ::

(A) sailor : uniform
(B) child : blanket
(C) floor : carpet
(D) head : hat
(E) person : skin

13 CARAVAN : DESERT ::

(A) library : books
(B) safari : jungle
(C) worship : temple
(D) casino : betting
(E) boat : cruise

14 HOBO : HOME ::

(A) professional : team
(B) citizen : country
(C) orphan : parent
(D) dreamer : hope
(E) philosopher : follower

15 ECOLOGY : ENVIRONMENT ::

(A) petrology : rocks
(B) meteorology : heavenly bodies
(C) botany : animal life
(D) etymology : insects
(E) physiology : motion

16 DISORGANIZED : SYSTEM ::

(A) greedy : money
(B) traitorous : loyalty
(C) athletic : intelligence
(D) conservative : party
(E) retired : hope

17 FRUSTRATE : DRIVE ::

(A) supervise : penalty
(B) guide : goal
(C) alert : warning
(D) reprimand : offense
(E) swindle : property

18 REBEL : CHANGE ::

(A) soldier : conflict
(B) gambler : profit
(C) coach : advice
(D) baby : attention
(E) architect : blueprint

19 INFERENCES : DISCERNING ::

(A) successes : enterprising
(B) insults : obnoxious
(C) agreements : competitive
(D) observations : social-minded
(E) warnings : suspicious

20 INTREPID : FEARFUL ::

(A) infallible : meaningful
(B) impotent : powerful
(C) wealthy : unscrupulous
(D) unemployed : slothful
(E) callow : unwise

GO ON TO THE NEXT PAGE

21 PEDANTIC : KNOWLEDGE ::

(A) truthful : innocence
(B) grandiloquent : speech
(C) virtuous : reward
(D) pungent : taste
(E) assertive : egotism

22 GELID : COOL ::

(A) abortive : normal
(B) sultry : warm
(C) dismal : transparent
(D) tepid : moderate
(E) thermal : frigid

23 INTRACTABLE : CONTROL ::

(A) judicious : decide
(B) pacific : instill
(C) indicted : arrest
(D) nullified : forget
(E) cryptic : decipher

The passage below is followed by questions based on its content. Answer the questions on the basis of what is stated or implied in the passage and in any introductory material that may be provided.

Questions 24–35 are based on the following passage.

The following passage discusses advanced technological institutions and their relation to the work force with social implications.

A second major hypothesis would argue that the most important dimension of advanced technological institutions is the social one; that is, the institutions are agencies of highly centralized and intensive social control. Technology con-
5 quers nature, as the saying goes. But to do so it must first conquer man. More precisely, it demands a very high degree of control over the training, mobility, and skills of the work force. The absence (or decline) of direct controls or of coercion should not serve to obscure from our view the reality
10 and intensity of the social controls which are employed (such as the internalized belief in equality of opportunity, indebtedness through credit, advertising, selective service channeling, and so on).

Advanced technology has created a vast increase in
15 occupational specialties, many of them requiring many, many years of highly specialized training. It must motivate this training. It has made ever more complex and "rational" the ways in which these occupational specialties are combined in our economic and social life. It must win passivity
20 and obedience to this complex activity. Formerly, technical rationality had been employed only to organize the production of rather simple physical objects, for example, aerial bombs. Now technical rationality is increasingly employed to organize all of the processes necessary to the utilization of
25 physical objects, such as bombing systems, maintenance, intelligence and supply systems. For this reason it seems a mistake to argue that we are in a "post-industrial" age, a concept favored by the *laissez innover* school. On the contrary, the rapid spread of technical rationality into organiza-
30 tional and economic life and, hence, into social life is more aptly described as a second and much more intensive phase of the industrial revolution. One might reasonably suspect that it will create analogous social problems.

Accordingly, a third major hypothesis would argue that
35 there are very profound social antagonisms or contradictions not less sharp or fundamental than those ascribed by Marx to the development of nineteenth-century industrial society. The general form of the contradictions might be described as follows: a society characterized by the employ-
40 ment of advanced technology requires an ever more socially disciplined population, yet retains an ever declining capacity to enforce the required discipline.

One may readily describe four specific forms of the same general contradiction. Occupationally, the work force
45 must be over-trained and under-utilized. Here, again, an anal-
ogy to classical industrial practice serves to shorten and simplify the explanation. I have in mind the assembly line. As a device in the organization of the work process the assembly line is valuable mainly in that it gives management a
50 high degree of control over the pace of the work and, more to the point in the present case, it divides the work process into units so simple that the quality of the work performed is readily predictable. That is, since each operation uses only a small fraction of a worker's skill, there is a very great
55 likelihood that the operation will be performed in a minimally acceptable way. Alternately, if each operation taxed the worker's skill there would be frequent errors in the operation, frequent disturbance of the work flow, and a thoroughly unpredictable quality to the end product. The
60 assembly line also introduces standardization in work skills and thus makes for a high degree of interchangeability among the work force.

For analogous reasons the work force in advanced technological systems must be relatively over-trained or, what is
65 the same thing, its skills relatively under-used. My impression is that this is no less true now of sociologists than of welders, of engineers than of assemblers. The contradiction emerges when we recognize that technological progress requires a continuous increase in the skill levels of its work
70 force, skill levels which frequently embody a fairly rich scientific and technical training, while at the same time the advance of technical rationality in work organization means that those skills will be less and less fully used.

Economically, there is a parallel process at work. It is
75 commonly observed that the work force within technologically advanced organizations is asked to work not less hard but more so. This is particularly true for those with advanced training and skills. Brzezinski's conjecture that technical specialists undergo continuous retraining is off the
80 mark only in that it assumes such retraining only for a managing elite. To get people to work harder requires growing incentives. Yet the prosperity which is assumed in a technologically advanced society erodes the value of economic incentives (while of course, the values of craftsman-
85 ship are "irrational"). Salary and wage increases and the goods they purchase lose their overriding importance once necessities, creature comforts, and an amply supply of luxuries are assured. As if in confirmation of this point, it has been pointed out that among young people one can already
90 observe a radical weakening in the power of such incentives as money, status, and authority.

GO ON TO THE NEXT PAGE

24 The term "technical rationality" is used in conjunction with

(A) a 20th-century euphemism for the industrial revolution
(B) giving credibility to products of simple technology
(C) the incorporation of unnecessary skills into economic social living
(D) effective organization of production processes
(E) safeguarding against technological over-acceleration

25 The author states that advanced technological institutions exercise control by means of

(A) assembly-line work process
(B) advertising, selective service channeling, etc.
(C) direct and coercive pressures
(D) salary incentives
(E) authoritarian managerial staffs

26 The word "taxed" in line 56 means

(A) a burdensome or excessive demand on the worker
(B) a financial obstacle the worker must endure
(C) the speed at which the worker must complete the job
(D) the efficiency of the worker's performance on the job
(E) the standardization in work skills of the work force

27 The passage indicates that technologically advanced institutions

(A) fully utilize worker skills
(B) fare best under a democratic system
(C) necessarily overtrain workers
(D) find it unnecessary to enforce discipline
(E) are operated by individuals motivated by traditional work incentives

28 The value of the assembly line is that it

I. minimizes the frequency of error
II. allows for interchangeability among the work force
III. allows for full utilization of workers' skills

(A) I and III only
(B) I and II only
(C) II and III only
(D) I, II, and III
(E) I only

29 Technologies cannot conquer nature unless

(A) there is unwavering worker allegiance to the goals of the institutions
(B) there is strict adherence to a *laissez innover* policy
(C) worker and management are in concurrence
(D) there is another more intense, industrial revolution
(E) the institutions have control over the training, mobility, and skills of the work force

30 The article states that the work force within the framework of a technologically advanced organization is

(A) expected to work less hard
(B) segregated into levels defined by the degree of technical training
(C) familiarized with every process of production
(D) expected to work harder
(E) isolated by the fact of its specialization

31 From the tone of the article, it can be inferred that the author is

(A) an eloquent spokesman for technological advancement
(B) in favor of increased employee control of industry
(C) a social scientist objectively reviewing an industrial trend
(D) vehemently opposed to the increase of technology
(E) skeptical of the workings of advanced technological institutions

GO ON TO THE NEXT PAGE

32 According to the author, economic incentives

(A) are necessary for all but the managerial elite
(B) are bigger and better in a society made prosperous by technology
(C) cease to have importance beyond a certain level of luxury
(D) are impressive only to new members of the work force
(E) are impressive to all but the radical young

33 The "managing elite" in line 81 refers to

(A) all the "blue" collar workers
(B) the assembly-line workers only
(C) the craftsman only
(D) the owners of the organizations
(E) the top technical specialists

34 According to the article, technological progress requires

  I. increasing skill levels of work force
 II. less utilization of work skills
III. rich scientific and technical training

(A) I and II only
(B) II and III only
(C) I and III only
(D) III only
(E) I, II, and III

35 The article states that money, status, and authority

(A) will always be powerful work incentives
(B) are not powerful incentives for the young
(C) are unacceptable to radical workers
(D) are incentives that are a throwback to 19th-century industrial society
(E) are incentives evolving out of human nature

Time: 30 Minutes   This section contains two types of questions. You have 30 minutes to complete both types. You
25 Questions   may use any available space for scratchwork.

Notes:

1. The use of a calculator is permitted. All numbers used are real numbers.
2. Figures that accompany problems in this test are intended to provide information useful in solving the
   problems. They are drawn as accurately as possible EXCEPT when it is stated in a specific problem that the
   figure is not drawn to scale. All figures lie in a plane unless otherwise indicated.

Reference Information

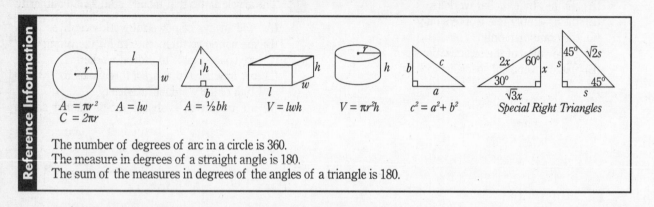

$A = \pi r^2$ $A = lw$ $A = \frac{1}{2}bh$ $V = lwh$ $V = \pi r^2 h$ $c^2 = a^2 + b^2$ *Special Right Triangles*
$C = 2\pi r$

The number of degrees of arc in a circle is 360.
The measure in degrees of a straight angle is 180.
The sum of the measures in degrees of the angles of a triangle is 180.

Directions for Quantitative Comparison Questions

Questions 1–15 each consist of two quantities in boxes, one in Column A and one in Column B. You are to compare the two quantities and on the answer sheet fill in oval

A if the quantity in Column A is greater;
B if the quantity in Column B is greater;
C if the two quantities are equal;
D if the relationship cannot be determined from the information given.

AN E RESPONSE WILL NOT BE SCORED.

Notes:

1. In some questions, information is given about one or both of the quantities to be compared. In such cases, the given information is centered above the two columns and is not boxed.
2. In a given question, a symbol that appears in both columns represents the same thing in Column A as it does in Column B.
3. Letters such as x, n, and k stand for real numbers.

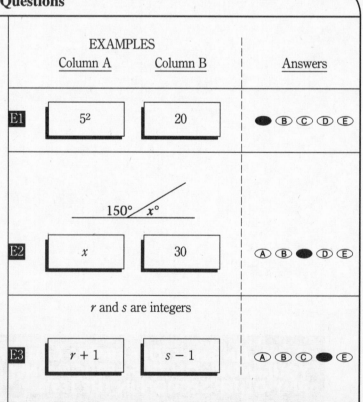

EXAMPLES

Column A	Column B	Answers
E1 5^2	20	● ⒷⒸⒹⒺ

150° $x°$

| E2 x | 30 | ⒶⒷ●ⒹⒺ |

r and *s* are integers

| E3 $r + 1$ | $s - 1$ | ⒶⒷⒸ●Ⓔ |

GO ON TO THE NEXT PAGE

SECTION 4

4 4 4 4

SUMMARY DIRECTIONS FOR COMPARISON QUESTIONS

Answer: A if the quantity in Column A is greater;
B if the quantity in Column B is greater;
C if the two quantities are equal;
D if the relationship cannot be determined from the information given.

AN E RESPONSE WILL NOT BE SCORED.

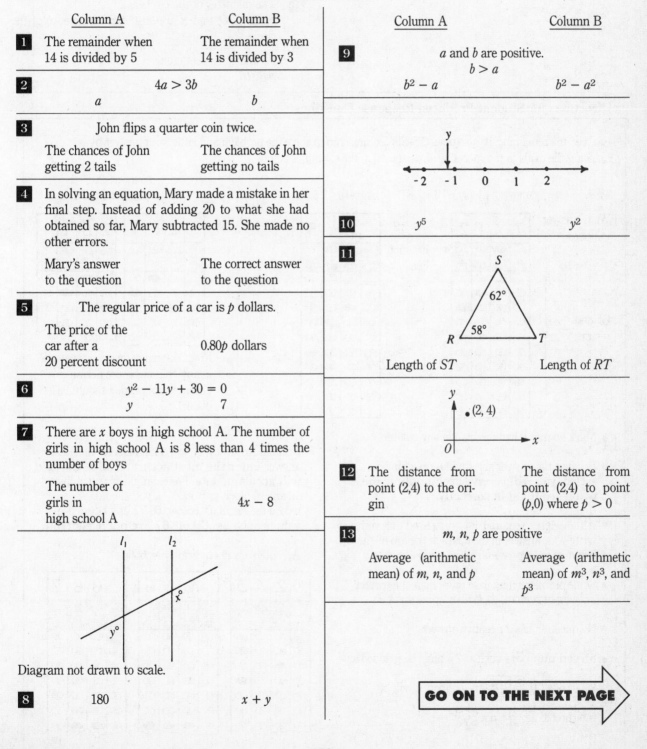

	Column A	Column B
1	The remainder when 14 is divided by 5	The remainder when 14 is divided by 3
2	$4a > 3b$	
	a	b
3	John flips a quarter coin twice.	
	The chances of John getting 2 tails	The chances of John getting no tails
4	In solving an equation, Mary made a mistake in her final step. Instead of adding 20 to what she had obtained so far, Mary subtracted 15. She made no other errors.	
	Mary's answer to the question	The correct answer to the question
5	The regular price of a car is p dollars.	
	The price of the car after a 20 percent discount	$0.80p$ dollars
6	$y^2 - 11y + 30 = 0$	
	y	7
7	There are x boys in high school A. The number of girls in high school A is 8 less than 4 times the number of boys	
	The number of girls in high school A	$4x - 8$

Diagram not drawn to scale.

	Column A	Column B
8	180	$x + y$

	Column A	Column B
9	a and b are positive. $b > a$	
	$b^2 - a$	$b^2 - a^2$
10	y^5	y^2
11	Length of ST	Length of RT
12	The distance from point (2,4) to the origin	The distance from point (2,4) to point $(p,0)$ where $p > 0$
13	m, n, p are positive	
	Average (arithmetic mean) of $m, n,$ and p	Average (arithmetic mean) of $m^3, n^3,$ and p^3

GO ON TO THE NEXT PAGE ➡

33

Column A   Column B

14 $\boxed{x}$ is the greatest integer less than or equal to x

$\boxed{xy}$ $\boxed{x}$ $\boxed{y}$

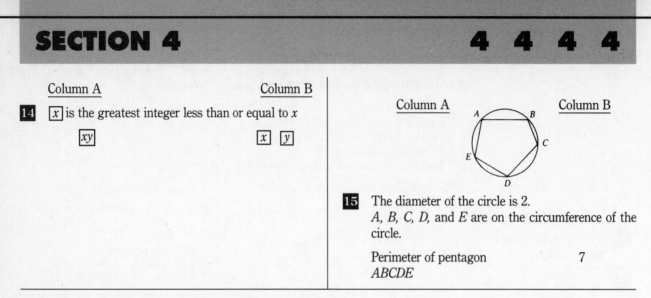

Column A   Column B

15 The diameter of the circle is 2.
A, B, C, D, and E are on the circumference of the circle.

Perimeter of pentagon   7
$ABCDE$

Directions for Student-Produced Response Questions

Each of the remaining 10 questions (16–25) requires you to solve the problem and enter your answer by marking the ovals in the special grid, as shown in the examples below.

Answer: $\frac{7}{12}$ or 7/12   Answer: 2.5   Answer: 201
                                                             Either position is correct.

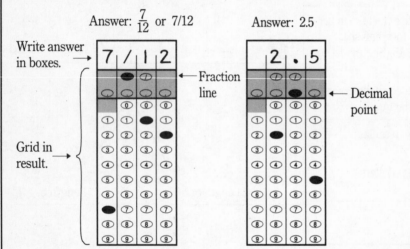

Write answer in boxes. → Fraction line ← Decimal point

Grid in result.

Note: You may start your answers in any column, space permitting. Columns not needed should be left blank.

- Mark no more than one oval in any column.

- Because the answer sheet will be machine-scored, **you will receive credit only if the ovals are filled in correctly.**

- Although not required, it is suggested that you write your answer in the boxes at the top of the columns to help you fill in the ovals accurately.

- Some problems may have more than one correct answer. In such cases, grid only one answer.

- No question has a negative answer.

- **Mixed numbers** such as $2\frac{1}{2}$ must be gridded as 2.5 or 5/2. (If $\boxed{2\frac{1}{2}}$ is gridded, it will be interpreted as $\frac{21}{2}$, not $2\frac{1}{2}$.)

- Decimal Accuracy: If you obtain a decimal answer, **enter the most accurate value the grid will accommodate.** For example, if you obtain an answer such as 0.6666 ... , you should record the result as .666 or .667. **Less accurate values such as .66 or .67 are not acceptable.**

Acceptable ways to grid $\frac{2}{3}$ = .6666 ...

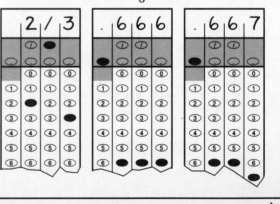

GO ON TO THE NEXT PAGE →

16 If $\frac{1}{4} < x < \frac{1}{3}$, find one value of x.

17 Given $3x + y = 17$ and $x + 3y = -1$, find the value of $3x + 3y$.

Note: Figure not drawn to scale.

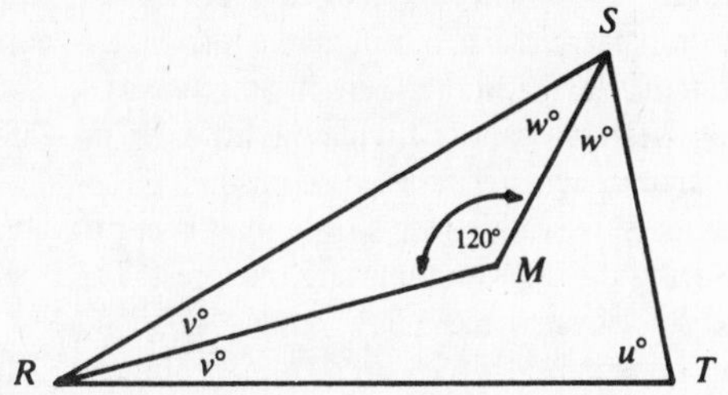

18 If $< RST = 80\,°$, find u.

19 There are 22 people on an island. A tram can carry at most 4 people at a time. What is the least number of trips that the tram must make to the mainland to get all the people to the mainland?

20 Let us define the operation $\odot$ as
$a \odot b = (a + b)^2 - (a - b)^2$
Find the value of $\sqrt{18} \odot \sqrt{2}$.

21 How many ordered pairs of *integers* (x,y) satisfy $x^2 + y^2 < 9$?

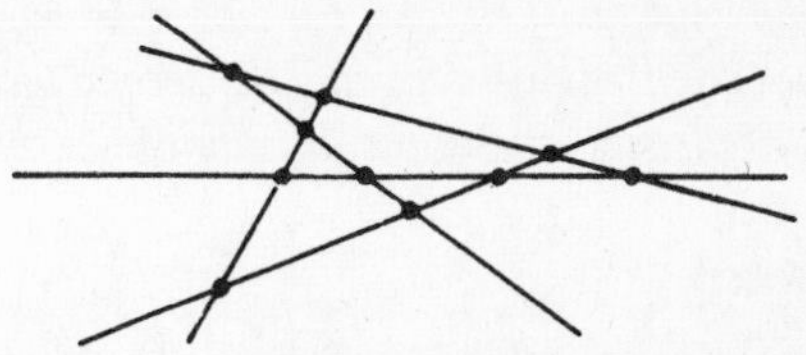

22 The figure above demonstrates that 5 straight lines can have 10 points of intersection. What is the maximum number of points of intersection of 4 straight lines?

23 A boy planned to buy some chocolate bars at 50 cents each but instead decided to purchase 30-cent chocolate bars. If he originally had enough money to buy 21 of the 50-cent bars, how many of the less expensive ones did he buy?

24 Let d be the least integer greater than 96,666 such that four of d's digits are identical. Find the value of $d - 96,666$.

25 Find 25 percent of 25 percent of 2.

IF YOU FINISH BEFORE TIME IS CALLED, YOU MAY CHECK YOUR WORK ON THIS SECTION ONLY. DO NOT TURN TO ANY OTHER SECTION IN THE TEST.

STOP

Time: 15 Minutes—For each question in this section, select the best answer from among the choices given and fill in
13 Questions   the corresponding oval on the answer sheet.

The two passages below are followed by questions based on their content and on the relationship between the two
passages. Answer the questions on the basis of what is <u>stated</u> or <u>implied</u> in the passages and in any introductory
material that may be provided.

Questions 1–13 are based on the following Passages.

The following two passages are about science. The first describes science in general, and the second focuses on the subject of physics, one of the disciplines of science.

PASSAGE A

Science, like everything else that man has created, exists, of course, to gratify certain human needs and desires. The fact that it has been steadily pursued for so many centuries, that it has attracted an ever-wider extent of attention, and that it

5 is now the dominant intellectual interest of mankind, shows that it appeals to a very powerful and persistent group of appetites. It is not difficult to say what these appetites are, at least in their main divisions. Science is valued for its practical advantages, it is valued because it gratifies

10 curiosity, and it is valued because it provides the imagination with objects of great aesthetic charm. This last consideration is of the least importance, so far as the layman is concerned, although it is probably the most important consideration of all to scientific men. It is quite obvious, on

15 the other hand, that the bulk of mankind value science chiefly for the practical advantages it brings with it.

   This conclusion is borne out by everything we know about the origin of science. Science seems to have come into existence merely for its bearings on practical life.

20 More than two thousand years before the beginning of the Christian era both the Babylonians and the Egyptians were in possession of systematic methods of measuring space and time. They had a rudimentary geometry and a rudimentary astronomy. This rudimentary science arose to

25 meet the practical needs of an agricultural population. Their geometry resulted from the measurements made necessary by the problems of land surveying. The cultivation of crops, dependent on the seasons, made a calendar almost a necessity. The day, as a unit of time, was, of course, imposed

30 by nature. The movement of the moon conveniently provided another unit, the month, which was reckoned from one new moon to the next. Twelve of these months were taken to constitute a year, and the necessary adjustments were made from time to time by putting in extra months.

PASSAGE B

35 Let's be honest right at the start. Physics is neither particularly easy to comprehend nor easy to love, but then again, *what*—or for that matter, *who*—is? For most of us it is a new vision, a different way of understanding with its own scales, rhythms, and forms. And yet, as with *Macbeth,*

40 *Mona Lisa,* or *La Traviata*, physics has its rewards. Surely you have already somehow prejudged this science. It's all too easy to compartmentalize our human experience: science in one box, music, art, and literature in other boxes.

   The Western mind delights in little boxes—life is

45 easier to analyze when it's presented in small pieces in small compartments (we call it specialization). It is our traditional way of seeing the trees and missing the forest. The label on the box for physics too often reads "Caution: Not for Common Consumption" or "Free from Sentiment." If you

50 can, please tear off that label and discard the box or we will certainly, sooner or later, bore each other to death. There is nothing more tedious than the endless debate between humanist and scientist on whose vision is truer; each of us is less for what we lack of the other.

55 It is pointless and even worse to separate physics from the body of all creative work, to pluck it out from history, to shear it from philosophy, and then to present it pristine pure, all-knowing, and infallible. We know nothing of what will be with absolute certainty. There is no scientific tome of

60 unassailable, immutable truth. Yet what little we do know about physics reveals an inspiring grandeur and intricate beauty.

GO ON TO THE NEXT PAGE

1 According to Passage A,

(A) the Babylonians and the Egyptians were the first to use scientific methods
(B) the Christians were the first to have a calendar
(C) a 12-month calendar was first used by the Egyptians or Babylonians
(D) the Christians preceded the Babylonians and Egyptians
(E) scientists are probably more attracted to the charm of science than to its practical benefits

2 The author of Passage A implies that scientists are generally

(A) sociable   (B) imaginative   (C) practical
(D) philosophical   (E) arrogant

3 The main idea of Passage A is that

(A) science originated and developed because of the practical advantages it offers
(B) the Egyptians and the Babylonians used scientific methods to meet the practical needs of feeding their people
(C) the use of geometry and astronomy are very important for agricultural development
(D) science has a different value for scientists than it does for the rest of the population
(E) science is valued not only for its practical contributions to mankind but also for its potential to stir the imagination

4 In line 13, the phrase "seeing the trees and missing the forest" means

(A) putting experiences into categories
(B) viewing the world too narrowly
(C) analyzing scientific discoveries
(D) making judgments too hastily
(E) ignoring the beauty of natural surroundings

5 According to the author of Passage B, what does the label on the box for physics suggest about physics?

(A) It is a dangerous area of study.
(B) It is a cause for great excitement.
(C) It is uninteresting and pointless.
(D) It is too scholarly for the ordinary person.
(E) It is a subject that should be elective but not required.

6 What statement does the author of Passage B make about physics?

(A) It should be recognized for its unique beauty.
(B) It is a boring course of study.
(C) It appeals only to the Western mind.
(D) It is superior to music, art, and literature.
(E) It is unpopular with people who are romantic.

7 What is the main idea of Passage B?

(A) Scientists contribute more to mankind than do humanists.
(B) The Western mind is more precise than other minds.
(C) Complete vision needs both the scientist and the humanist.
(D) Humanists and scientists share no common ground.
(E) Physics is as important as other science.

8 In which manner does the author of Passage B address his audience?

(A) affectionately
(B) arrogantly
(C) humorously
(D) cynically
(E) frankly

9 The word "rudimentary" in line 23 means

(A) sophisticated
(B) flawed
(C) unworkable
(D) basic
(E) coarse

10 The author of Passage B leaves out an important aspect of the subject that, however, is contained in Passage A. This aspect is the

(A) reaction of laymen to physics
(B) the specialization in science
(C) the purity of physics
(D) the practical applications of physics
(E) the arguments between the humanists and scientists

GO ON TO THE NEXT PAGE

11 Which device or method does the author of Passage B use that is not used by the author of Passage A?

(A) analogy through objects
(B) critique
(C) contrast with respect to perceived values
(D) historical referencing
(E) examples to support a claim

12 Which subject is not directly mentioned in either passage?

(A) agriculture
(B) astronomy
(C) art
(D) philosophy
(E) chemistry

13 The word "intricate" in line 61 means

(A) eloquent
(B) complicated
(C) devastating
(D) uninteresting
(E) pointless

Time: 15 Minutes   In this section solve each problem, using any available space on the page for scratchwork.
10 Questions   Then decide which is the best of the choices given and fill in the corresponding oval on the answer sheet.

Notes:

1. The use of a calculator is permitted. All numbers used are real numbers.
2. Figures that accompany problems in this test are intended to provide information useful in solving the problems. They are drawn as accurately as possible EXCEPT when it is stated in a specific problem that the figure is not drawn to scale. All figures lie in a plane unless otherwise indicated.

Reference Information

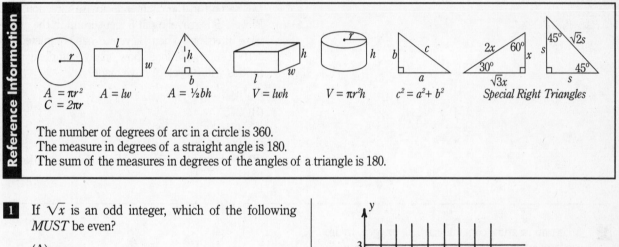

$A = \pi r^2$ $A = lw$ $A = \frac{1}{2}bh$ $V = lwh$ $V = \pi r^2 h$ $c^2 = a^2 + b^2$ *Special Right Triangles*
$C = 2\pi r$

The number of degrees of arc in a circle is 360.
The measure in degrees of a straight angle is 180.
The sum of the measures in degrees of the angles of a triangle is 180.

---

1 If $\sqrt{x}$ is an odd integer, which of the following *MUST* be even?

(A) x
(B) $3\sqrt{x}$
(C) $\sqrt{2x}$
(D) $2\sqrt{x}$
(E) x^2

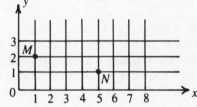

2 If a rectangle is drawn on the grid above with $\overline{MN}$ as one of its diagonals, which of the following could be the coordinates of another vertex of the rectangle?

(A) (1,0)
(B) (2,0)
(C) (3,3)
(D) (4,3)
(E) (5,2)

3 The degree measures of the four angles of a quadrilateral are w, x, y, and z respectively. If w is the average (arithmetic mean) of x, y, and z, then $x + y + z =$

(A) 45°
(B) 90°
(C) 120°
(D) 180°
(E) 270°

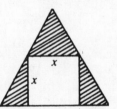

Bicycle B Bicycle A

5 In the figure above, two bicycles are being pedaled in opposite directions around a circular race track of circumference = 120 feet. Bicycle A is traveling at 5 feet/second in the counterclockwise direction, and Bicycle B is traveling at 8 feet/second in the clockwise direction. When Bicycle B has completed exactly 600 revolutions, how many complete revolutions will Bicycle A have made?

(A) 180
(B) 375
(C) 475
(D) 960
(E) It cannot be determined from the given information.

4 A certain mixture contains carbon, oxygen, hydrogen, and other elements in the percentages shown in the graph below. If the total mixture weighs 24 pounds, which number represents the closest number of pounds of carbon that is contained in the mixture?

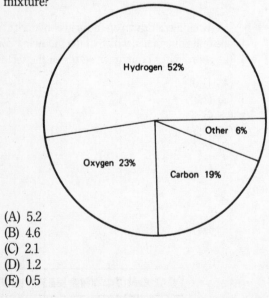

Hydrogen 52%

Other 6%

Oxygen 23%

Carbon 19%

(A) 5.2
(B) 4.6
(C) 2.1
(D) 1.2
(E) 0.5

6 A square of side x is inscribed inside an equilateral triangle of area $x^2\sqrt{3}$. If a rectangle with width x has the same area as the shaded region shown in the figure above, what is the length of the rectangle in terms of x?

(A) $\sqrt{3}x - 1$
(B) $x\sqrt{3}$
(C) $\sqrt{3} - x$
(D) $x(\sqrt{3} - 1)$
(E) $x^2\sqrt{3} - x^2$

GO ON TO THE NEXT PAGE

7 If p is the average of x and y, and if q is the average of y and z, and if r is the average of x and z, then what is the average of x, y, and z?

(A) $\dfrac{p + q + r}{3}$

(B) $\dfrac{p + q + r}{2}$

(C) $\dfrac{2}{3}(p + q + r)$

(D) $p + q + r$

(E) $\dfrac{3}{2}(p + q + r)$

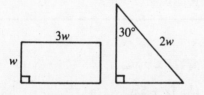

8 The length and width of a rectangle are $3w$ and w respectively. The length of the hypotenuse of a right triangle, one of whose acute angles is 30°, is $2w$. What is the ratio of the area of the rectangle to that of the triangle?

(A) $2\sqrt{3} : 1$

(B) $\sqrt{3} : 1$

(C) $1 : \sqrt{3}$

(D) $1 : 2\sqrt{3}$

(E) $1 : 6$

9 At a certain college, the number of freshmen is three times the number of seniors. If $\frac{1}{4}$ of the freshmen and $\frac{1}{3}$ of the seniors attend a football game, what fraction of the total number of freshmen and seniors attends the game?

(A) $\dfrac{5}{24}$

(B) $\dfrac{13}{48}$

(C) $\dfrac{17}{48}$

(D) $\dfrac{11}{24}$

(E) $\dfrac{23}{48}$

10 At Jones College, there are a total of 100 students. If 30 of the students have cars on campus, and 50 have bicycles, and 20 have both cars and bicycles, then how many students have neither a car nor a bicycle on campus?

(A) 80

(B) 60

(C) 40

(D) 20

(E) 0

IF YOU FINISH BEFORE TIME IS CALLED, YOU MAY CHECK YOUR WORK ON THIS SECTION ONLY. DO NOT TURN TO ANY OTHER SECTION IN THE TEST.

Time: 30 Minutes
25 Questions

In this section solve each problem, using any available space on the page for scratchwork. Then decide which is the best of the choices given and fill in the corresponding oval on the answer sheet.

Notes:

1. The use of a calculator is permitted. All numbers used are real numbers.
2. Figures that accompany problems in this test are intended to provide information useful in solving the problems. They are drawn as accurately as possible EXCEPT when it is stated in a specific problem that the figure is not drawn to scale. All figures lie in a plane unless otherwise indicated.

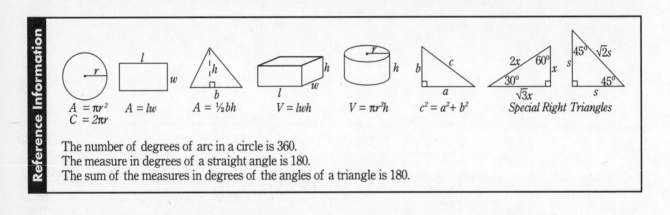

$A = \pi r^2$ $A = lw$ $A = \frac{1}{2}bh$ $V = lwh$ $V = \pi r^2 h$ $c^2 = a^2 + b^2$ *Special Right Triangles*
$C = 2\pi r$

The number of degrees of arc in a circle is 360.
The measure in degrees of a straight angle is 180.
The sum of the measures in degrees of the angles of a triangle is 180.

1 Tommy and Bobby like to watch their school's baseball team play. Tommy watched ⅔ of all the games the team played last season. Bobby watched 28 games. If Tommy watched more games than Bobby did last season, which of the following could be the number of games the team played last season?

(A) 33
(B) 36
(C) 39
(D) 42
(E) 45

2 $3x(4x + 2y) =$

(A) $7x + 5xy$
(B) $12x + 6xy$
(C) $12x^2 + 2y$
(D) $12x^2 + 6xy$
(E) $12x^2 + 6x$

GO ON TO THE NEXT PAGE

Box Number	Height of Box (in millimeters)
A	1700
B	2450
C	2735
D	1928
E	2130

3 Exactly how many of the boxes listed in the table above are more than 20 decimeters high?
(1 decimeter = 100 millimeters)

(A) Zero
(B) One
(C) Two
(D) Three
(E) Four

4 If $a - 3 = 7$, then $2a - 14 =$

(A) -6
(B) -4
(C) 2
(D) 4
(E) 6

5 An athlete runs 90 laps in 6 hours. This is the same as how many laps per minute?

(A) $\frac{1}{15}$

(B) $\frac{1}{9}$

(C) $\frac{1}{4}$

(D) $\frac{1}{2}$

(E) 1

6 $\frac{7}{10} + \frac{7}{100} + \frac{77}{1000} =$

(A) .0091
(B) .7777
(C) .784
(D) .847
(E) .854

GO ON TO THE NEXT PAGE

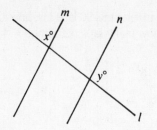

7 Parallel lines m and n are intersected by line l as shown. Find the value of $x + y$.

(A) 180
(B) 150
(C) 120
(D) 90
(E) It cannot be determined from the information given.

Item	Value
1	P
2	$P \times 3$
3	$(P \times 3) \div 2$
4	$[(P \times 3) \div 2] + 12$
5	$[(P \times 3) \div 2] + 12 - 1$

8 According to the table above, which item has the greatest value when $P = 12$?

(A) 1
(B) 2
(C) 3
(D) 4
(E) 5

9 If $\frac{3x}{4} = 9$, find $6x$.

(A) 12
(B) 18
(C) 27
(D) 36
(E) 72

10 If 8 people share a winning lottery ticket and divide the cash prize equally, what percent of the prize do 2 of them together receive?

(A) 8%
(B) 10%
(C) 20%
(D) 25%
(E) 40%

GO ON TO THE NEXT PAGE

11 Given $8r + 3s = 12$ and $7r + 2s = 9$, find the value of $5(r + s)$.

(A) 5
(B) 10
(C) 15
(D) 20
(E) 25

13 The operation $\boxdot$ is defined for all numbers x and y by the following: $x \boxdot y = 3 + xy$. For example, $2 \boxdot 7 = 3 + 2(7) = 17$. If $y \neq 0$ and x is a number such that $x \boxdot y = 3$, then find x.

(A) 0

(B) $-\dfrac{3}{y}$

(C) $-y + 3$

(D) $\dfrac{3}{y}$

(E) $y + 3$

12 Paul's average (arithmetic mean) for 3 tests was 85. The average of his scores for the first 2 tests was also 85. What was his score for the third test?

(A) 80
(B) 85
(C) 90
(D) 95
(E) It cannot be determined from the information given.

Note: Figure not drawn to scale.

14 In the figure above, each pair of intersecting segments is perpendicular with lengths as shown. Find the length of the dash line segment.

(A) 7
(B) $6\sqrt{3}$
(C) $4\sqrt{2}$
(D) $\sqrt{46}$
(E) $\sqrt{59}$

GO ON TO THE NEXT PAGE

15 For how many two-digit positive numbers will tripling the tens digit give us a two-digit number that is triple the original number?

(A) None
(B) One
(C) Two
(D) Three
(E) Four

17 At one instant, two meteors are 2,500 kilometers apart and traveling toward each other in straight paths along the imaginary line joining them. One meteor has a velocity of 300 meters per second while the other travels at 700 meters per second. Assuming that their velocities are constant and that they continue along the same paths, how many seconds elapse from the first instant to the time of their collision? (1 kilometer = 1000 meters)

(A) 250
(B) 500
(C) 1,250
(D) 2,500
(E) 5,000

16 If A is the least positive 5-digit integer with *nonzero* digits, none of which is repeated, and B is the greatest of such positive integers, then $B - A =$

(A) 2,468
(B) 66,666
(C) 86,420
(D) 86,424
(E) 89,999

18 Let $x = \sqrt{\dfrac{1}{9} + \left(\dfrac{1}{3} + \dfrac{1}{9} + \dfrac{1}{27} + \dfrac{1}{81} \right)}$

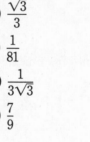

An equivalent expression for x is

(A) $\dfrac{1}{9}$

(B) $\dfrac{\sqrt{3}}{3}$

(C) $\dfrac{1}{81}$

(D) $\dfrac{1}{3\sqrt{3}}$

(E) $\dfrac{7}{9}$

GO ON TO THE NEXT PAGE

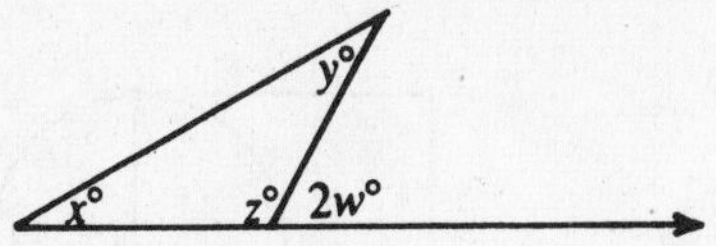

19 In the figure above, one side of a triangle has been extended. What is the value of $w + x + y$?

(A) $3w$
(B) $3z$
(C) $2x + y$
(D) $2x + 2y$
(E) $2w + z$

Questions 20–21 refer to the following game.

A computer generates numbers. Points are assigned as described in the following table each time any of the four number pairs given appears in a number.

Number Pair	Number of Points
"33"	11
"34"	6
"43"	4
"44"	3

20 As an example, the number 4,347 is assigned 4 points for "43" and 6 points more for "34," giving a total of 10 points. Which of the following numbers would be assigned the most points?

(A) 934,432
(B) 464,457
(C) 834,415
(D) 437,934
(E) 336,283

21 If a certain number has 13 points assigned to it, which of the following statements must be true?

   I. 33 is not in the number.
  II. 34 and 43 are both in the number.
 III. 43 is in the number.

(A) I only
(B) II only
(C) III only
(D) I and III only
(E) I, II, and III

22 Given the volume of a cube is 8 cubic meters. Find the distance from any vertex to the center point inside the cube.

(A) $1\,m$
(B) $\sqrt{2}\,m$
(C) $2\sqrt{2}\,m$
(D) $2\sqrt{3}\,m$
(E) $\sqrt{3}\,m$

GO ON TO THE NEXT PAGE

23 The ratio of Sue's age to Bob's age is 3 to 7. The ratio of Sue's age to Joe's is 4 to 9. The ratio of Bob's age to Joe's is

(A) 28 to 27
(B) 7 to 9
(C) 27 to 28
(D) 10 to 13
(E) 13 to 10

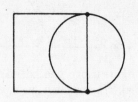

25 The square in the figure above has two sides tangent to the circle. If the area of the circle is $9a^2\pi^2$, find the area of the square.

(A) $12a^2\pi^2$
(B) $36a^2\pi$
(C) $36a^2\pi^2$
(D) $18a^4\pi^2$
(E) It cannot be determined from the information given.

24 The sum of r consecutive positive integers will always be divisible by 2 if r is a multiple of

(A) 6
(B) 5
(C) 4
(D) 3
(E) 2

IF YOU FINISH BEFORE TIME IS CALLED, YOU MAY CHECK YOUR WORK ON THIS SECTION ONLY. DO NOT TURN TO ANY OTHER SECTION IN THE TEST.

How Did You Do on This Test?

Step 1. Go to the Answer Key on page 50.

Step 2. For your "raw score," calculate it using the directions on page 87.

Step 3. Get your "scaled score" for the test by referring to the Raw Score/Scaled Score Conversion Tables on page 90.

THERE'S ALWAYS ROOM FOR IMPROVEMENT!

Answer Key for Practice Test 1 (Diagnostic SAT Pre-test)

Section 1—Verbal

1. D	6. E	11. C	16. A	21. D	26. B
2. A	7. B	12. E	17. D	22. C	27. C
3. E	8. D	13. E	18. E	23. A	28. E
4. D	9. E	14. A	19. E	24. D	29. C
5. B	10. B	15. D	20. C	25. B	30. A

Section 2—Math

1. D	6. B	11. D	16. B	21. D
2. B	7. E	12. B	17. D	22. E
3. D	8. C	13. C	18. C	23. E
4. E	9. C	14. B	19. C	24. B
5. B	10. C	15. E	20. E	25. E

Section 3—Verbal

1. A	6. A	11. A	16. B	21. B	26. A	31. E
2. A	7. B	12. E	17. E	22. B	27. C	32. C
3. B	8. B	13. B	18. B	23. E	28. B	33. E
4. E	9. B	14. C	19. A	24. D	29. E	34. E
5. D	10. D	15. A	20. B	25. B	30. D	35. B

Section 4—Math

1. A	6. B	11. B	16. $\frac{7}{24}$ or a number	19. 6	24. 333
2. D	7. C	12. D	between .025 and	20. 24	25. $\frac{1}{8}$ or .125
3. C	8. D	13. D	.3333 . . .	21. 25	
4. B	9. D	14. D	17. 12	22. 6	
5. C	10. B	15. B	18. 60	23. 35	

Section 5—Verbal

1. A	3. B	5. C	7. C	9. D	11. A	13. B
2. E	4. B	6. A	8. E	10. D	12. E	

Section 6—Math

1. D	3. E	5. B	7. A	9. B
2. E	4. B	6. D	8. A	10. C

Section 7—Math

1. E	6. D	11. C	16. C	21. D
2. D	7. A	12. B	17. D	22. E
3. D	8. B	13. A	18. E	23. A
4. E	9. E	14. C	19. A	24. C
5. C	10. D	15. D	20. A	25. B

Explanatory Answers for Diagnostic SAT Pre-test (Practice Test 1)

Section 1: Verbal Ability

As you read these Explanatory Answers, you are advised to refer to "Using Critical Thinking Skills in Verbal Questions" (beginning on page 236) whenever a specific Strategy is referred to in the answer. Of particular importance are the following Master Verbal Strategies:

Sentence Completion Master Strategy 1—page 245.
Sentence Completion Master Strategy 2—page 246.
Analogies Master Strategy 1—page 236.
Reading Comprehension Master Strategy 2—page 263.

1. Choice D is correct. **See Sentence Completion Strategy 4.** The first word, "Because," is a *result indicator.* We can then expect some action to take place after the information about what the evening cable TV programs deal with. The expected action is that parents will consider such programs "inappropriate." Accordingly, only Choice D is correct.

2. Choice A is correct. See **Sentence Completion Strategy 2.** Examine the first word of each choice. Choice (C) glamorized . . . and Choice (D) viewed . . . do *not* make good sense because a word does not effectively glamorize or effectively view unfairness. Now consider the other choices. Choice (A) portrayed . . . strengthening is the only choice which has a word pair that makes sentence sense.

3. Choice E is correct. See **Sentence Completion Strategy 1.** The word "prolific" (meaning "producing abundant works or results") completes the sentence so that it makes good sense. The other choices do *not* do that.

4. Choice D is correct. Although this is a two-blank question, we should use **Sentence Completion**

Strategy 1 (primarily used for one-blank questions). Note that we have a set of three opposites: from the "serious" to the "lighthearted," from the "objective" to the "argumentative," and from the "innocuous" (meaning *harmless, innocent*) to the "hostile." The other choices do *not* have this opposite pattern.

5. Choice B is correct. See **Sentence Completion Strategy 2.** Examine the first word of each choice. Choice (A) shattering . . . and Choice (C) impertinent . . . do *not* make sense because rates at a repair place are not aptly called shattering or impertinent. Now consider the other choices. Choices D and E do *not* make sense in the sentence. Choice (B) exorbitant . . . instituted *does* make sense.

6. Choice E is correct. See **Sentence Completion Strategy 2.** Examine the first word of each choice. Choice (B) denied . . . and Choice (D) slighted . . . do *not* make sense because students who found truth in Socrates' teachings would not deny or slight him. Now consider the other choices. Choice (A) accepted . . . a benefit and Choice (C) appraised . . . an exception do not make sense in the sentence. Choice

(E) revered . . . a threat *does* make sense in the sentence.

7. Choice B is correct. See **Sentence Completion Strategy 1.** Try each of the choices. The only one that fits is choice B: The quotation was erroneously *ascribed,* or *credited to,* a British poet.

8. Choice D is correct. See **Sentence Completion Strategy 2.** Examine the first words of each choice. We eliminate Choice (C) squandered and Choice (E) regaled because hardworking parents do *not* squander (spend money recklessly) or regale (entertain) to give their son an education. Now consider the other choices. The word pairs of Choice A and Choice B do *not* make sense in the sentence. Choice (D) struggled . . . generously *does* make good sense.

9. Choice E is correct. See **Sentence Completion Strategy 1.** Try each choice. He tried his hardest to maintain his *calm,* or *poise.*

10. **(B)** Choice B is correct. A cot is used instead of a bed. A tissue is used instead of a handkerchief.

    (Purpose relationship)

11. **(C)** Choice C is correct. A paragraph is a necessary part of the whole essay. An act is a necessary part of the whole play. You might have chosen Choice (B) saddle : horse, which is incorrect because a saddle is *not* a necessary or indispensable part of the horse. Also see **Analogy Strategy 4.**

    (Part-Whole relationship)

12. **(E)** Choice E is correct. It is a characteristic of a proverb to be pithy—that is, short and to the point. It is a characteristic of snow to be white. The other choices do not have this characteristic or association relationship *consistently.* Also see **Analogy Strategy 4.**

    (Association relationship)

13. **(E)** Choice E is correct. The word "scold" means to reprimand or to find fault with another person. The word "denounce" means to speak out strongly against or condemn another person openly. Therefore, "denounce" is a stronger form than "scold." To maim means to injure seriously. Therefore, to maim is a stronger form than to injure. We have in this question a Degree relationship. Note that there is also a Degree relationship in Choice C since to squander means to spend recklessly. But Choice C

is incorrect because the order of words is reversed. If the choice were spend : squander, this choice would also be correct. See **Analogy Strategy 3.**

(Degree relationship)

14. **(A)** Choice A is correct. A person's integrity would prevent him from being corrupted. A person's disguise would prevent him from being recognized. We have here an opposite relationship and also cause-and-effect relationship in a negative way. Choice C sounds correct, but it is *not* correct. A person's simplicity might cause him to be admired, but we do not have the negative situation that we have in the capitalized pair and in the correct Choice A. See **Analogy Strategy 4.**

(Opposite and Cause and Effect relationship)

15. **(D)** Choice D is correct. One is likely to trust a person who is virtuous. One is likely to suspect a person who is shady. Also see **Analogy Strategy 5.**

(Association relationship)

Note: If you don't know the meaning of the word "virtuous," you can use **Analogy Strategy 6,** The Context Method for Unfamiliar Words.

You either trust someone or don't trust someone, so let's assume that "virtuous" means trustworthy or *not* trustworthy. Now look at the choices:
Here's the sentence to use, working backward: You would *trust* (or if you thought "virtuous" meant not trustworthy, you would not *trust*) a *virtuous* person. Choice D fits best: You would *suspect* a *shady* person.

16. Choice A is correct. The passage deals mainly with van Gogh's 15-month stay in Arles. It was in this small French town that his art, in fact, did reach its zenith. See lines 4–9: "Yet Arles . . . in the modern era." Although Choices B, C, D, and E have some association with the passage, none of these choices represents the best title for the passage as a whole. Therefore, these choices are incorrect.

17. Choice D is *not* stated nor is it implied in the passage. Therefore, it is the correct choice. First see lines 42–45: "Before the year was up . . . had to return to Paris." Note that Gaugin had stayed in Arles *less* than a year. Now see lines 4–9: "Yet Arles was also the scene . . . in the modern era." Choice A is true—therefore an incorrect choice. See lines 12–16: "The Arles canvases, alive with color . . . notably the Fauves." Choice B is true—therefore an incorrect

choice. First see lines 17–20: "Van Gogh went to Arles . . . beloved younger brother Theo . . . an art dealer." Now see lines 39–41: "Gaugin had an influence on van Gogh . . . pushing the younger artist . . . than actuality." Choice C is true—therefore an incorrect choice. See lines 20–23: "In Paris . . . Neo-Impressionist . . . style." Choice E is true—therefore incorrect. See lines 1–4: "It was at Arles . . . cut off part of his own ear."

18. Choice E is correct. Let us consider each of the three Roman numeral items. Item 1 is true. See lines 25–27: "But he wanted 'gayer' colors . . . Japanese prints he so admired."

   Item II is true. First see lines 28–30: "He felt that in Arles . . . establish an artistic tradition." Now see lines 31–33: "It was van Gogh's hope . . . join him at Arles."

   Item III is true. See lines 27–30: "Then, too, the French capital . . . an artistic tradition."

   Accordingly, Choice E is the only correct choice.

19. In the context in the sentence ". . . under the glowing sun . . . ," it would appear that the word "frenetic" should mean "frantic." Choice A is incorrect because the author would not be likely to repeat the word "colorful" in the next sentence.

20. Choice C is correct. Gauguin's attitude of tolerant acceptance of van Gogh is indicated in the following lines of the passage. Lines 37–41: "At first . . . rather than actuality." Lines 44–49: "Gauguin wrote to Theo . . . especially with me." Lines 50–52: "But then . . . they later had friendly correspondence."

   Choices A, B, D, and E are incorrect because the passage does not give evidence of the attitudes mentioned in these choices.

21. Choice D is correct. The passage indicates that there was a buildup of stresses and strains on van Gogh that he was eventually unable to cope with because of his mental and emotional instability. This condition led him to such acts as cutting off a piece of his ear. Finally—though the passage does not include this fact—van Gogh committed suicide in Paris on July 29, 1890, by shooting himself in the chest. The following lines in the passage are related to van Gogh's mental and emotional instaiblity. Lines 1–3: "It was at Arles . . . had his first real bout with madness." Lines 17–20: "Van Gogh went to Arles . . . supported him psychologically and financially . . . art dealer." Lines 44–46: "Gauguin wrote to Theo . . . 'temperamental incompatability.' "

Choices B and E are incorrect because these were not the basic reasons for van Gogh's extreme action. The basic reason was van Gogh's mental and emotional instability (Choice A). Choice C is incorrect because the passage mentions nothing about van Gogh's failure to form an artists' colony in Arles.

22. Choice C is correct. The theme of this essay, *Self-Reliance,* by the American writer Ralph Waldo Emerson (1803–1882), is expressed in various other ways throughout the essay. For example: in referring to the independence of opinion that one loses with one's loss of early youth; in condemning our surrender of the freedom of solitude to the group actions of society at large; and in encouraging us not to fear the consequences of being inconsistent and misunderstood.

23. Choice A is correct. The infant can be, and is expected to be, completely irresponsible. "Infancy conforms to nobody: all conform to it, so that one babe commonly makes four or five out of the adults who prattle and play to it."

24. Choice D is correct. "Speak what you think now in hard words; and to-morrow speak what you think in hard words again, though it contradict everything you said to-day." The misunderstanding will occur because what you say may be the opposite of conventional opinion, or may be ahead of its time. But the risk is worth it.

25. Choice B is correct. It is a natural prerogative of youth to give "an independent, genuine verdict." He naturally cares very little about what older people may think because "It seems he knows how to speak to his contemporaries. Bashful or bold, then, he will know how to make us seniors very unnecessary."

26. Choice B is correct. The "pit" or gallery in a theater usually contains the least expensive seats. Consequently, it is favored by those less economically endowed, and, according to the author, less committed to conventional manners and highly dignified behavior. In effect, these are the people who go to the theater to see, rather than to be seen.

27. Choice C is correct. When people desert solitude (or individual action) to join society (group action), they surrender a large part of individual freedom in exchange for a livelihood. They thus become more reliant and dependent on others than on themselves. The metaphor of the joint-stock company is a good one because such a company is faceless and without identity. No one member stands out above any other member.

28. Choice E is correct. "Spirit and enthusiasm" are something individualistic and definite. To be spirited and enthusiastic is to be spontaneous, natural, and uninhibited. One must (according to the author) be committed and courageous "As soon as he has once acted or spoken with eclat. . . ."

29. Choice C is correct. To act out of whim is to act impulsively and in an unpremeditated, spontaneous (and generally sincere) manner. The author, however, is not endorsing *whimsical* action simply because it is uninhibited ("I hope it is somewhat better than whim at last, but we cannot spend the day in explanation"), but because it is a way of speaking freely, and usually with complete honesty.

30. Choice A is correct. The essence of true self-reliance and genuine nonconformity is, as Shakespeare put it, "To thine own self be true." If one is dishonest with oneself, one will be dishonest with others; if one is honest with oneself, one will be honest with others.

Explanatory Answers for Practice Test 1 (continued)

Section 2: Math Ability

As you read these solutions, you are advised to do two things if you answered the Math question incorrectly:

1. When a specific Strategy is referred to in the solution, study that strategy, which you will find in "Using Critical Thinking Skills in Math Questions" (beginning on page 174).

2. When the solution directs you to the "Math Refresher" (beginning on page 291)—for example, Math Refresher #305—study the 305 Math principle to get a clear idea of the Math operation that was necessary for you to know in order to answer the question correctly.

---

1. Choice D is correct.

   Given: $ab = 64$ and a and b are
   positive integers   ☐1

   (Use Strategy 7: Use numerics to help find the answer.)

   If $a = 64$, $b = 1$, then ☐1 is satisfied
   and $a + b = 65$ ☐2
   If $a = 32$, $b = 2$, then ☐1 is satisfied
   and $a + b = 34$ ☐3
   If $a = 16$, $b = 4$, then ☐1 is satisfied
   and $a + b = 20$ ☐4
   If $a = 8$, $b = 8$, then ☐1 is satisfied
   and $a + b = 16$ ☐5

   The only other pairs of values that satisfy ☐1 are each of the above pairs of values reversed for a and b. Thus ☐5, $a + b = 16$, is the smallest value of $a + b$.

   (Math Refresher #431)

2. Choice B is correct.

   Given: $x + x^3 + x^5 + x^6$ ☐1
   $x = -1$ ☐2

Substitute ☐2 into ☐1. We get

$$-1 + (-1)^3 + (-1)^5 + (-1)^6 =$$
$$-1 - 1 - 1 + 1 \qquad = -2$$

   (Math Refresher #431)

3. Choice D is correct.

   Given: AB $0 < A < 6$ ☐1
   $+ \underline{\text{BA}}$ $0 < B < 6$ ☐2
   66   ☐3

   (Use Strategy 17: Use the given information effectively.) From ☐3 we see that

$$B + A = 6 \qquad ☐4$$

   (Use Strategy 7: Use numerics to help find the answer.) Conditions ☐1, ☐2 and ☐4 can be satisfied when:

   $A = 1, B = 5$
   $A = 2, B = 4$
   $A = 3, B = 3$
   $A = 4, B = 2$
   $A = 5, B = 1$

   Thus, there are five possible values of A.

   (Math Refresher #431)

4. Choice E is correct.

Given: Temperature at 11:00 A.M. =   0°F [1]
           Temperature at 8:00 A.M. = −15°F [2]
Let x = Temperature at 5:00 P.M.   [3]

    y = Temperature rise   [4]

(Use Strategy 13: Find unknowns by subtracting.) Subtract [2] from [1]. We get

Temperature rise in 3 hours = 15°F [5]
Subtract the times in [1] and [3]. We get

Time change = 6 hours [6]

Use [4], [5] and [6] to find temperature rise from 11:00 A.M. to 5:00 P.M. We get

$$\frac{3 \text{ hours}}{6 \text{ hours}} = \frac{15°F}{y}$$

$$3y = 6 \times 15°F$$
$$y = 30°F$$

Use [1], [3] and [7] to find the final temperature.

$$x = 0°F + 30°F$$
$$x = 30°F$$

(Math Refresher #120)

5. Choice B is correct.

Number of Shirts	Total Price
1	$12.00
Box of 3	$22.50
Box of 6	$43.40

From the chart above, we know

6 shirts = $43.40 [1]

(Use Strategy 13: Find unknowns by division.) Dividing [1] by 6, we get

$$\frac{6 \text{ shirts}}{6} = \frac{\$43.40}{6}$$
1 shirt = $ 7.23$\overline{3}$
Cost per shirt ≈ $7.20

(Math Refresher #406)

6. Choice B is correct. [See chart in Question 5 above.]

(Use Strategy 17: Use the given information effectively.) From the chart above, we see

Box of 6 shirts = $43.40
Price per shirt = $\frac{\$43.40}{6}$ = 7.23$\overline{3}$ [1]

Box of 3 shirts = $22.50
Price per shirt = $\frac{\$22.50}{3}$ = $7.50 [2]

1 shirt   = $12.00
Price per shirt = $12.00 [3]

From [1], [2] and [3] we see the best price per shirt is for a box of 6; then a box of 3; and finally a single shirt. To buy exactly 11 shirts at *minimum* cost we need

1 Box of 6   = $43.40 [4]
1 Box of 3   = $22.50 [5]
2 single shirts = $\begin{cases} \$12.00 \\ \$12.00 \end{cases}$ [6] [7]

(Use Strategy 13: Find unknowns by adding.)

Adding [4], [5], [6] and [7], we get

Minimum cost of exactly 11 shirts = $89.90

(Math Refresher #406)

7. Choice E is correct.

Given: $5x^2 - 15x = 0$ [1]
         $x \neq 0$ [2]

Factoring [1], we get

$$5x(x - 3) = 0$$
$$5x = 0 \text{ or } x - 3 = 0$$
$$x = 0 \text{ or } x = 3 \quad [3]$$

Applying [2] to [3], we get

$$x = 3$$

(Math Refresher #407)

8. Choice C is correct. **(Use Strategy 2: Translate words to algebra.)** In $\frac{1}{2}$ year, 600 pounds of feed were used at a rate of $1.25 per pound. Thus (600 pounds) × ($1.25 per pound) was spent or $750 was spent. Hence,

$$\text{Feed cost per egg} = \frac{\text{Total cost for feed}}{\text{number of eggs}}$$

$$= \frac{\$750}{5,000 \text{ eggs}}$$

(Use Strategy 19: Factor and reduce.)

$$= \frac{\$75 \times 10}{500 \times 10 \text{ eggs}}$$

$$= \frac{\$25 \times 3}{25 \times 20 \text{ eggs}}$$

$$= \frac{\$3}{20} \text{ per egg}$$

$$= \$0.15 \text{ per egg}$$

(Math Refresher #200 and #601)

9. Choice C is correct. **(Use Strategy 17: Use the given information effectively.)**

Given: $55,555 = y + 50,505$
$5,050 = y$ ☐1

We need: $50,505 - 10y$ ☐2

Substitute ☐1 into ☐2. We get

$$50,505 - 10(5,050) =$$
$$50,505 - 50,500 \ =$$
$$5$$

(Math Refresher #406)

10. Choice C is correct. **(Use Strategy 2: Translate from words to algebra.)**

Given: Area B = 1 ☐1
Area A = 3(Area B) ☐2
Area B = 3(Area C) ☐3

Substitute ☐1 into ☐2. We get

Area A = 3(1) = 3 ☐4

Substitute ☐1 into ☐3. We get

$$1 = 3(\text{Area C})$$

$$\frac{1}{3} = \text{Area C} \qquad \boxed{5}$$

Using ☐1, ☐4 and ☐5, we have

Sum of areas A, B and C = $3 + 1 + \frac{1}{3}$
Sum of areas A, B and C = $4\frac{1}{3}$

(Math Refresher #200)

11. Choice D is correct. **(Use Strategy 17: Use the given information effectively.)**

$$[(3a^3b^2)^3]^2 =$$
$$(3a^3b^2)^6 = 3^6a^{18}b^{12}$$

Checking the choices, we find only Choice D has $a^{18}b^{12}$ and must be correct.
Note: We did not have to calculate 3^6!

(Math Refresher #429)

12. Choice B is correct.

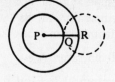

Given: PQR = 9 ☐1
PQ = 4 ☐2

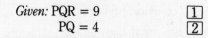

(Use Strategy 3: The whole equals the sum of its parts.) From the diagram, we see that

PQR = PQ + QR ☐3

Substitute ☐1 and ☐2 into ☐3. We get

$$9 = 4 + QR$$
$$5 = QR$$

QR is the radius of a circle with center R and Q on its circumference. (See dot circle in diagram.)

(Math Refresher #524)

13. Choice C is correct. **(Use Strategy 17: Use the given information effectively.)**

$$\left(\frac{3}{10}\right)^2 = \frac{9}{100}$$

Thus $\left(\frac{3}{10}\right)^2 = 9$ hundredths.

(Math Refresher #429)

14. Choice B is correct. **(Use Strategy 2: Translate from words to algebra.)**

Given: Square has perimeter 2π ☐1
Let S = side of square.
We know Perimeter of a square = 4S ☐2

Substitute ☐1 into ☐2. We get

$$\text{Perimeter of square} = 4S$$
$$2\pi = 4S$$
$$\frac{2\pi}{4} = S$$
$$\frac{\pi}{2} = S \qquad \boxed{3}$$

We are given that:
area of circle = ☐4
area of square
We know that:
area of circle = πr^2 ☐5
area of square = S^2 ☐6

Substituting ☐5 and ☐6 into ☐4, we get

$$\pi r^2 = S^2 \qquad \boxed{7}$$

Substitute $\boxed{3}$ into $\boxed{7}$. We get

$$\pi r^2 = \left(\frac{\pi}{2}\right)^2$$

$$\pi r^2 = \frac{\pi^2}{4}$$

$$r^2 = \frac{\pi^2}{4\pi}$$

$$r^2 = \frac{\pi}{4}$$

$$r = \sqrt{\frac{\pi}{4}} = \frac{\sqrt{\pi}}{2} \qquad \boxed{8}$$

We know the circumference of a circle $= 2\pi r$
Substitute $\boxed{8}$ into $\boxed{9}$. We have

$$\text{Circumference} = 2\pi\left(\frac{\sqrt{\pi}}{2}\right)$$

$$\text{Circumference} = \pi\sqrt{\pi}$$

(Math Refresher #303 and #310)

15. Choice E is correct.

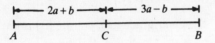

Given: C is the midpoint of AB
Thus, AC = CB $\qquad \boxed{1}$
Substitute the lengths from the diagram into $\boxed{1}$. We have

$$2a + b = 3a - b$$
$$b = a - b$$
$$2b = a$$

(Math Refresher #431)

16. Slope is defined as $\frac{y_2 - y_1}{x_2 - x_1}$ where (x_1, y_1) is a point on the line and (x_2, y_2) is another point on the line. We are given that one point is $(0, p)$ and the other point is $(3p, 0)$ so,

$$\frac{y_2 - y_1}{x_2 - x_1} = \frac{p - 0}{0 - 3p} = \frac{p}{-3p} = -\frac{1}{3}$$

(Math Refresher #416)

17. Choice D is correct.

Given: Bus A averages $\frac{40\text{km}}{\text{gallon}}$ $\qquad \boxed{1}$
Bus B averages $\frac{50\text{km}}{\text{gallon}}$ $\qquad \boxed{2}$
Trip distance = 800 km $\qquad \boxed{3}$
Fuel cost = $\frac{\$3}{\text{gallon}}$ $\qquad \boxed{4}$

(Use strategy 10: Know how to use units.)
Divide $\boxed{3}$ by $\boxed{1}$. We get

$\frac{800\text{km}}{40\text{km}} = \frac{800}{40}$ gallons = 20 gallons used by Bus A $\qquad \boxed{5}$

Divide $\boxed{3}$ by $\boxed{2}$. We get

$\frac{800\text{km}}{50\text{km}} = \frac{800}{50}$ gallons = 16 gallons used by Bus B $\qquad \boxed{6}$

Multiply $\boxed{5}$ by $\boxed{4}$. We get

20 gallons $\times \frac{\$3}{\text{gallon}}$ = \$60 cost for fuel for Bus A $\qquad \boxed{7}$

Multiply $\boxed{6}$ by $\boxed{4}$. We get

16 gallons $\times \frac{\$3}{\text{gallon}}$ = \$48 cost for fuel for Bus B $\qquad \boxed{8}$

(Use Strategy 13: Find unknowns by subtracting.)

Subtract $\boxed{8}$ from $\boxed{7}$. We get \$60 − \$48 = \$12 difference in the fuel costs between Bus A and Bus B for an 800 km trip.

(Math Refresher #202)

18. Choice C is correct.

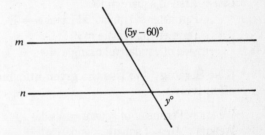

(Use Strategy 17: Use the given information effectively.)

Given: $m \| n$ $\qquad \boxed{1}$
From $\boxed{1}$ we know that the two angles are supplementary. Thus,

$$(5y - 60)° + y° = 180°$$
$$6y - 60 = 180°$$
$$6y = 240°$$
$$y = 40°$$

(Math Refresher #504)

19. Choice C is correct. **(Use Strategy 2: Translate from words to algebra.)**

We have: $\frac{4}{100} \times (2a + b) = 18$ $\qquad \boxed{1}$

(Use Strategy 13: Find unknowns by multiplication.) Multiply $\boxed{1}$ by $\frac{100}{4}$. We get

$$\frac{100}{4}\left(\frac{4}{100} \times (2a + b)\right) = \frac{100}{4}\left(18\right)$$

(Use Strategy 19: Factor and reduce.)

$$2a + b = \frac{\cancel{4} \times 25}{\cancel{4}}\left(18\right)$$
$$2a + b = 450$$
$$b = 450 - 2a \qquad \boxed{2}$$

(Use Strategy 17: Use the given information effectively.)

b will be greatest when a is smallest. $\qquad \boxed{3}$
Given: a is a positive integer $\qquad \boxed{4}$

Applying $\boxed{4}$ to $\boxed{3}$, we get

$$a = 1$$

Substituting $\boxed{5}$ into $\boxed{2}$, we have

$$b = 450 - 2(1)$$
$$= 450 - 2$$
$$b = 448$$

(Math Refresher #406)

20. Choice E is correct.

Given: Area of square = R^2 $\qquad \boxed{1}$
Perimeter of equilateral triangle = E $\qquad \boxed{2}$
Perimeter of square = r $\qquad \boxed{3}$
Side of equilateral triangle = e $\qquad \boxed{4}$

(Use Strategy 17: Use the given information effectively.)

We know Perimeter of square = 4(side) $\qquad \boxed{5}$
We know Area of square = (side)^2 $\qquad \boxed{6}$
Substituting $\boxed{1}$ into $\boxed{6}$, we get

$$R^2 = (\text{side})^2$$
$$R = \text{side} \qquad \boxed{7}$$

Substituting $\boxed{7}$ and $\boxed{3}$ into $\boxed{5}$, we have

$$r = 4(R)$$
$$r = 4R \qquad \boxed{8}$$

We know Perimeter of
equilateral triangle = 3(side) $\qquad \boxed{9}$

Substituting $\boxed{2}$ and $\boxed{4}$ into $\boxed{9}$, we get

$$E = 3(e)$$
$$E = 3e$$
$$\frac{E}{3} = e \qquad \boxed{10}$$

We need $e + r$ $\qquad \boxed{11}$

(Use Strategy 13: Find unknowns by addition.) Add $\boxed{8}$ and $\boxed{10}$ to get $\boxed{11}$. We have

$$e + r = \frac{E}{3} + 4R$$
$$= \frac{E}{3} + 4R\left(\frac{3}{3}\right)$$
$$\frac{E}{3} + \frac{12R}{3}$$
$$e + r = \frac{E + 12R}{3}$$

(Math Refresher #303 and #308)

21. Choice D is correct.

Given: $C = \frac{5}{9}(F - 32)$ $\qquad \boxed{1}$

Call the number of degrees that the Fahrenheit temperature (F°) increases, x.

(Now use Strategy 17: Use the given information effectively.)

The Centigrade temperature (C°) is given as

$$C = \frac{5}{9}(F - 32) \qquad \boxed{1}$$

When the Centigrade temperature increases by 35°, the Fahrenheit temperature increases by x°, so we get:

$$C + 35 = \frac{5}{9}[(F + x) - 32]$$
$$C + 35 = \frac{5}{9}F + \frac{5}{9}x - \frac{5}{9}(32) \qquad \boxed{2}$$

(Now use Strategy 13: Find unknowns by subtraction.)

Subtract $\boxed{1}$ from $\boxed{2}$:

$$C + 35 = \frac{5}{9}F + \frac{5}{9}x - \frac{5}{9}(32) \qquad \boxed{2}$$
$$- \qquad C \;\; = \frac{5}{9}F - \frac{5}{9}(32) \qquad \boxed{1}$$
$$\overline{}$$
$$35 = \frac{5}{9}x \qquad \boxed{3}$$

Multiply $\boxed{3}$ by 9:

$$35 \times 9 = 5x \qquad \boxed{4}$$

(Use Strategy 19: Don't multiply when reducing can be done first.)

Divide $\boxed{4}$ by 5:

$$\frac{35 \times 9}{5} = x \qquad \boxed{5}$$

Now reduce $\frac{35}{5}$ to get 7 and we get for $\boxed{5}$

$$7 \times 9 = x$$
$$63 = x$$

(Math Refresher #406)

22. Choice E is correct.

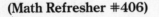

Given: $\overset{\frown}{BAF} = 14\pi$ $\qquad \boxed{1}$
ABCDEF is equilateral $\qquad \boxed{2}$

From $\boxed{2}$ we know that all 6 sides are = $\qquad \boxed{3}$
From $\boxed{3}$ we know that all 6 arcs are equal. $\qquad \boxed{4}$
From $\boxed{1}$ and $\boxed{4}$ we find

$$\overset{\frown}{AB} = \overset{\frown}{BC} = \overset{\frown}{CD} = \overset{\frown}{DE} = \overset{\frown}{EF} = \overset{\frown}{FA} = 7\pi \qquad \boxed{5}$$

(Use Strategy 3: The whole equals the sum of its parts.)

Circumference of circle =

$6 \times 7\pi$ (since there are 6 arcs) $\qquad \boxed{6}$

We know circumference = $2\pi r$ $\qquad \boxed{7}$

Using $\boxed{6}$ and $\boxed{7}$, we get

$$2\pi r = 6 \times 7\pi$$
$$2\pi r = 42\pi$$
$$2r = 42 \qquad \boxed{8}$$
We know diameter = $2 \times$ radius $\qquad \boxed{9}$
So diameter = 42

(Math Refresher #310 and #524)

23. Choice E is correct.

Given: $\dfrac{a}{b} = \dfrac{1}{4}$ $\qquad \boxed{1}$

(Use Strategy 13: Find unknowns by multiplying.) Cross-multiply $\boxed{1}$. We have

$$4a = b \qquad \boxed{2}$$

Substituting $4a = b$ in the given $\dfrac{a^2}{b}$, we get

$$\frac{a^2}{b} = \frac{a^2}{4a} = \frac{a}{4} \qquad \boxed{3}$$

(Use Strategy 7: Use numerics to help find the answer.) If $a = 1$ is substituted into $\boxed{3}$ we have

$$\frac{a^2}{b} = \frac{a}{4} = \frac{1}{4}$$

Thus, Choice I is satisfied. If $a = 2$ is substituted into $\boxed{3}$, we get

$$\frac{a^2}{b} = \frac{a}{4} = \frac{2}{4} = \frac{1}{2}$$

Thus, Choice II is satisfied. If $a = 4$ is substituted into $\boxed{3}$, we have

$$\frac{a^2}{b} = \frac{a}{4} = \frac{4}{4} = 1$$

Thus Choice III is satisfied.

(Math Refresher #111 and #112)

24. Choice B is correct. **(Use Strategy 2: Translate from words to algebra.)**

Given: Rate of plane = x $\dfrac{\text{km}}{\text{hour}}$ $\qquad \boxed{1}$

Time of flight = y hours $\qquad \boxed{2}$

Need: Distance plane had flown $\frac{2}{3}y$ hours ago $\qquad \boxed{3}$

Subtracting $\boxed{3}$ from $\boxed{2}$, we get

Time plane had flown $\frac{2}{3}y$ hours ago = $y - \frac{2}{3}y$

Time plane had flown $\frac{2}{3}y$ hours ago = $\qquad \boxed{4}$
$\frac{1}{3}y$ hours

(Use Strategy 9: Know the rate, time, and distance relationship.)

We know: Rate × Time = Distance $\qquad \boxed{5}$
Substitute $\boxed{1}$ and $\boxed{4}$ into $\boxed{5}$. We get

$$x \frac{\text{km}}{\text{hour}} \times \frac{1}{3}y \text{ hours} = \text{Distance}$$
$$\frac{xy}{3} = \text{Distance plane had flown } \frac{2}{3}y \text{ hours ago.}$$

(Math Refresher #201 and #202)

25. Choice E is correct.

(Use Strategy 5: Average =

$$\frac{\text{Sum of values}}{\text{Total number of values}})$$

We know that Average =

$$\frac{\text{Sum of values}}{\text{Total number of values}} \qquad \boxed{1}$$

Given: Average of k scores is 20 $\qquad \boxed{2}$

Substitute $\boxed{2}$ into $\boxed{1}$. We get

$$20 = \frac{\text{Sum of } k \text{ values}}{k}$$

$$20k = \text{Sum of } k \text{ values} \qquad \boxed{3}$$

Given: Average of 10 of these scores is 15. $\qquad \boxed{4}$

Substitute $\boxed{4}$ into $\boxed{1}$. We have

$$15 = \frac{\text{Sum of 10 scores}}{10}$$

$$150 = \text{Sum of 10 scores} \qquad \boxed{5}$$

There are $k - 10$ scores remaining. $\qquad \boxed{6}$

(Use Strategy 3: The whole equals the sum of its parts.)

We know: Sum of 10 scores + Sum of remaining scores

$$= \text{Sum of } k \text{ scores} \qquad \boxed{7}$$

Substituting $\boxed{3}$ and $\boxed{5}$ into $\boxed{7}$, we get

$$150 + \text{Sum of remaining scores} = 20k$$
$$\text{Sum of remaining scores} = 20k - 150$$

Substituting $\boxed{6}$ and $\boxed{8}$ into $\boxed{1}$, we get

$$\text{Average of remaining scores} = \frac{20k - 150}{k - 10}$$

(Math Refresher #601)

Explanatory Answers for Practice Test 1 (continued)

Section 3: Verbal Ability

As you read these Explanatory Answers, you are advised to refer to "Using Critical Thinking Skills in Verbal Questions" (beginning on page 236) whenever a specific Strategy is referred to in the answer. Of particular importance are the following Master Verbal Strategies:

Sentence Completion Master Strategy 1—page 245.
Sentence Completion Master Strategy 2—page 246.
Analogies Master Strategy 1—page 236.
Reading Comprehension Master Strategy 2—page 263.

1. Choice A is correct. See **Sentence Completion Strategy 2.** Examine the first word of each choice. Choice (B) a specter . . . and Choice (C) an exodus . . . do *not* make sense because a nice apartment building is not a specter (ghost) or an exodus (a departure). Now consider the other choices. Choice (A) a boon . . . haunted is the only choice that makes sense in the sentence. The word "haunted" here means "visited frequently."

2. Choice A is correct. See **Sentence Completion Strategy 2.** Examine the first word of each choice. Choice (B) cancellation . . . and Choice (D) abundance . . . do *not* make sense because we do not refer to an inflation cancellation or an inflation abundance. Now consider the other choices. Choice (A) spiral . . . indubitably (meaning unquestionably, certainly) is the only choice which has a word pair that makes sentence sense.

3. Choice B is correct. See **Sentence Completion Strategy 4.** The first word, "although," is an *opposition indicator.* After the subordinate clause "although . . . markedly," we can expect an opposing idea in the main clause that follows and completes

the sentence. Choice (B) unaffected gives us the word that brings out the opposition thought that we expect in the sentence. Choices A, C, D, and E do not give us a sentence that makes sense.

4. Choice E is correct. See **Sentence Completion Strategy 2.** Examine the first word of each choice. Choice (B) relegates (meaning to banish or to assign to a lower position) . . . and Choice (C) accumulates . . . do *not* make sense since we do not say that a sense of fairness relegates or accumulates. Now consider the other choices. Choice (E) dictates . . . varies, is the only choice that makes sentence sense.

5. Choice D is correct. See **Sentence Completion Strategy 1.** The word "elusive" means "cleverly or skillfully; able to avoid being caught." Therefore, Choice (D) elusive is the only correct choice.

6. Choice A is correct. See **Sentence Completion Strategy 1.** The typist's inconsistency is obvious in the manner in which she typed the five letters. Choices B, C, D, and E are incorrect because they do not make good sense in the sentence.

7. Choice B is correct. See **Sentence Completion Strategy 2.** Let us first examine the first words of each choice. We can then eliminate Choice (C) remarks ... and Choice (E) conferences ... because an outstanding publisher's being able to make occasional remarks or occasional conferences does not make good sense. Now we go on to the three remaining choices. When you fill in the two blanks of Choice A and of Choice D, the sentence does not make sense. So these two choices are also incorrect. Filling in the two blanks of Choice B makes the sentence meaningful.

8. Choice B is correct. See **Sentence Completion Strategy 1 and 4.** Try each choice being aware that "since" is a *result indicator.* Their married life was not *smooth and content.*

9. Choice B is correct. See **Sentence Completion Strategy 1 and 4.** Try each choice, being aware that "because" is a *result indicator.* This happened because of his *careless, indifferent* driving.

10. Choice D is correct. See **Sentence Completion Strategy 1.** Try each choice. Parables are *stories* or fables that illustrate a moral or ethical point while relating a simple incident.

11. Choice A is correct. The pioneers made history by being the first white men to live and settle in the West. The American astronauts made history by being the first human beings to land on the moon.

    (Association and Place relationship)

12. Choice E is correct. The natural covering of an animal is its hide. The natural covering of a person is his skin. We have here a PURPOSE relationship. The coverings referred to in the second word of Choices A, B, C, and E also show a purpose. However, the coverings in each of these four choices are *not* natural coverings. So these choices are incorrect. See **Analogy Strategy 4.**

    (Purpose relationship)

13. Choice B is correct. A caravan is a group of travelers who journey through a desert. A safari is a group of hunters who hunt usually in a jungle.

    (People-Place relationship)

14. Choice C is correct. A hobo does *not* have a home. An orphan does *not* have a parent.

    (Opposite relationship)

15. Choice A is correct. Ecology is the study of environment. Petrology is the study of rocks.

    (Association relationship)

16. Choice B is correct. A disorganized person is without system. A traitorous person is without loyalty.

    (Opposite relationship)

17. Choice E is correct. When we frustrate a person, we deprive him of drive—in this case, meaning motivation, initiative, aggressiveness. When we swindle a person, we deprive him of property or money. Also see **Analogy Strategy 5.**

    (Cause and Effect relationship)

18. Choice B is correct. A rebel's purpose is to bring about a change—in government, for example. A gambler's purpose is to bring about a profit—by winning money in a card game, for example. Also see **Analogy Strategy 5.**

    (Purpose relationship)

19. Choice A is correct. Inferences are likely to be made by the person who is discerning. Successes are likely to be scored by the person who is enterprising.

    (Association relationship)

20. Choice B is correct. One who is intrepid is *not* fearful. One who is impotent is *not* powerful.

    (Opposite relationship)

21. Choice B is correct. One who is pedantic shows off knowledge. One who is grandiloquent shows off speech.

    (Characteristic relationship)

22. Choice B is correct. Gelid is extremely cool. Sultry is extremely warm.

    (Degree relationship)

23. Choice E is correct. A person who is intractable is difficult to control. Something that is cryptic is difficult to understand.

    (Association relationship)

    Note: If you don't know the meaning of the word "intractable," you can use **Analogy Strategy 6,** The Context Method for Unfamiliar Words.

You could either have control or not have control. The "in" in "intractable" signifies an OPPOSITE. So assume that "intractable" means the opposite of "control." Now look for OPPOSITE choices. Choice E fits the bill.

24. Choice D is correct. See paragraph 2: "Formerly, technical rationality had been employed only to organize the production of rather simple physical objects . . . Now technical rationality is increasingly employed to organize all of the processes necessary to the utilization of physical objects . . ."

25. Choice B is correct. See paragraph 1: "The absence of direct controls or of coercion should not serve to obscure from our view the . . . social controls which are employed (such as . . . advertising, selective service channeling, and so on)."

26. Choice A is correct. It can be seen from the context of the sentence: ". . . there would be frequent errors . . ." Choice A is correct.

27. Choice C is correct. See paragraph 5: "The force must be relatively over-trained . . ."

28. Choice B is correct. See paragraph 4: "The assembly line also introduced standardization in work skills and thus makes for a high degree of interchangeability among the work force . . . If each operation taxed the worker's skill there would be frequent errors . . ."

29. Choice E is correct. See paragraph 1: "Technology conquers nature . . . to do so it must first conquer man . . . it demands a very high degree of control over the training, mobility, and skills of the work force."

30. Choice D is correct. See paragraph 6: ". . . the work force within technologically advanced organizations is asked to work not less hard but more so."

31. Choice E is correct. See paragraph 3: ". . . there are very profound social antagonisms or contradictions . . ." This article is one of skepticism. It frequently points out the contradictions, irrationality, and coercive tactics exhibited by advanced technological institutions.

32. Choice C is correct. See paragraph 6: "Salary and wage increases . . . lose their importance . . . once an ample supply of luxuries are assured."

33. Choice E is correct. We link "technical specialists" with "such retraining only for a managing elite." Therefore choice E is correct.

34. Choice E is correct. See paragraph 5: ". . . technological progress requires a continuous increase in the skill levels of its work force, levels which frequently embody a fairly rich scientific and technical training . . . those skills will be less and less fully used."

35. Choice B is correct. See paragraph 6: ". . . among young people one can already observe a radical weakening in the power of such incentives as money, status, and authority."

Explanatory Answers for Practice Test 1 (continued)

Section 4: Math Ability

As you read these solutions, you are advised to do two things if you answered the Math question incorrectly:

1. When a specific Strategy is referred to in the solution, study that strategy, which you will find in "Using Critical Thinking Skills in Math Questions" (beginning on page 174).

2. When the solution directs you to the "Math Refresher" (beginning on page 291)—for example, Math Refresher #305—study the 305th Math principle to get a clear idea of the Math operation that was necessary for you to know in order to answer the question correctly.

1. Choice A is correct.

Column A	Column B
The remainder when 14 is divided by 5	The remainder when 14 is divided by 3
$\frac{14}{5} = 2$ remainder 4	$\frac{14}{3} = 4$ remainder 2

(Math Refresher #101)

2. **Choice D is correct.**

$$\text{Given: } 4a > 3b \qquad \boxed{1}$$

(Use Strategy C: Use numerics if it appears that the answer can't be determined.)

Let $a = 1$ and $b = 1$ $\boxed{2}$
    Then $4a = 4(1) = 4$ and $3b = 3(1) = 3$
    and $\boxed{1}$ is satisfied.

Let $a = 2$ and $b = 1$ $\boxed{3}$
    Then $4a = 4(2) = 8$ and $3b = 3(1) = 3$
    and $\boxed{1}$ is satisfied.

From $\boxed{2}$ and $\boxed{3}$ we see that two different relationships are possible. Thus, the answer can't be determined from the given information.

(Math Refresher #431)

3. Choice C is correct.

$$\text{Given: John flips a quarter coin twice} \qquad \boxed{1}$$

Column A	Column B
The chances of John getting 2 tails	The chances of John getting no tails

(Use Strategy 17: Use the given information effectively.) Applying $\boxed{1}$, we get

$$\text{Chances of a tail} = \frac{1}{2} \qquad \boxed{2}$$

$$\text{Chances of no tail} = \frac{1}{2} \qquad \boxed{3}$$

Using $\boxed{2}$ and $\boxed{3}$, the columns become

Column A	Column B
$\left(\frac{1}{2}\right)\left(\frac{1}{2}\right)$	$\left(\frac{1}{2}\right)\left(\frac{1}{2}\right)$

(Logical Reasoning)

4. Choice B is correct. **(Use Strategy 2: Translate from words to algebra.)**

Let x = what Mary has obtained so far $\boxed{1}$
Then $x - 15$ = Mary's answer $\boxed{2}$
      $x + 20$ = Correct answer $\boxed{3}$

Column A	Column B
Mary's answer to the question	The correct answer to the question

Substituting ② and ③ into ④, the columns become

$x - 15$	$x + 20$

(Use Strategy A: Cancel equal things from both columns by subtracting.) Subtract x from both columns. We get

-15	$+20$

(Math Refresher #406)

5. Choice C is correct.

   Given: The regular price of a car is p dollars.

   (Use Strategy 2: Know how to find a percent less than a given amount.)

Column A	Column B
The price of the car after a 20 percent discount =	$0.80\,p$ dollars

$$p - \left(\frac{20}{100}\right)p =$$
$$p - .20p =$$

$0.80\,p$ dollars	$0.80\,p$ dollars

   (Math Refresher #114 and #119)

6. Choice B is correct.

   Given: $y^2 - 11y + 30 = 0$ ①

   (Use Strategy 17: Use the given information effectively.) Factoring ①, we have

   $$(y - 6)(y - 5) = 0$$
   $$y = 6 \text{ or } y = 5 \quad ②$$

Column A	Column B	
y	7	③

   Substituting each value from ② into ③, we have

5	7
or	
6	7

   In both cases, Column B is larger.

   (Math Refresher #409)

7. Choice C is correct. **(Use Strategy 2: Translate from words to algebra.)**

   Given: x = number of boys in high school A

   The number of girls = $4x - 8$ ①

Column A	Column B	
The number of girls in high school A	$4x - 8$	②

Substituting ① into ②, the columns become

$4x - 8$	$4x - 8$

(Math Refresher #406)

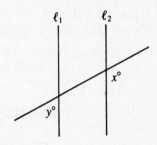

8. Choice D is correct.

   (Use Strategy C: Use numerical examples when it appears that a comparison cannot be determined.)

   We are given no information about the relationship between l_1, l_2 and the third line. l_1 may be parallel to l_2 or may not be.

   Choose x and y so that $x + y > 180$, and $x + y < 180$.

   If $x = 120$ and $y = 50$, then $x + y = 170$ ①
   If $x = 130$ and $y = 70$, then $x + y = 200$ ②

   Since two different results are possible, we cannot determine a specific relationship.

   (Math Refresher #504 and #501)

9. Choice D is correct.

   Given: a and b are positive   ①

   $b > a$ ②

   (Use Strategy A: Cancel expressions common to both columns by subtraction.)

   Cancel b^2 from both columns:

Column A	Column B
$\cancel{b^2} - a$	$\cancel{b^2} - a^2$

   (Use Strategy D: To make a comparison simpler, divide both columns by the same quantity, making sure that quantity is not negative or 0.)

   Divide by a:

Column A	Column B
$\dfrac{-a}{a}$	$\dfrac{-a^2}{a}$
-1	$-a$

(Use Strategy C: Use numbers in place of variables.)

Let $a = 1$: Column A = Column B
Now let $a = 2$: Column A > Column B
Two different results are possible, so Choice D is correct.

(Math Refresher #429 and #431)

10. Choice B is correct. **(Use Strategy 6: Know the properties of inequality relationships.)**

$$\text{Since } y < 0, (y)^5 < 0 \qquad \boxed{1}$$
$$(y)^2 > 0 \qquad \boxed{2}$$

Therefore, $\boxed{2}, > \boxed{1}$

(Math Refresher #428)

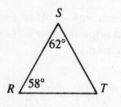

11. Choice B is correct.

Column A	Column B
Length ST	Length RT

(Use Strategy 18: Remember triangle facts.)
We know that in a triangle, the side opposite the larger angle is the larger side. Thus, $RT > ST$.

(Triangle inequalities)

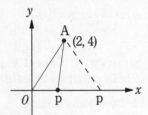

12. Choice D is correct.
See figure above. **(Use Strategy 14: Draw lines and label.)** For Column A, draw a line connecting the origin O with the point (2,4). For Column B, label "p" on x-axis. **(Use Strategy 18: Know about relations of sides and angles of triangles.)** I can draw $\angle$ ApO > $\angle$ AOp and so line AO > line Ap. I can also draw $\angle$ ApO < $\angle$ AOp, so line AO < line Ap. Thus a definite relation cannot be determined.

(Math Refresher #410)

13. Choice D is correct.

(Use Strategy 5: Average
$$= \frac{\text{Sum of values}}{\text{Total number of values}})$$

Since we know the definition of arithmetic mean, we are really trying to compare:

Column A	Column B
$\dfrac{m + n + p}{3}$	$\dfrac{m^3 + n^3 + p^3}{3}$

(Use Strategy C: Use numbers in place of variables when a comparison is difficult.)

Choose specific values of m, n, and p.

EXAMPLE 1

When $m = 1$, $n = 1$, and $p = 1$, the columns become

Column A	Column B
1	1

The two quantities are equal in this example.

EXAMPLE 2

When $m = 2$, $n = 2$, and $p = 2$, the columns become

Column A	Column B
4	8

The quantity in Column B is greater. Hence, the answer to this question depends on specific values of m, n, and p.

(Math Refresher #601, #431, and #429)

14. Choice D is correct.

(Use Strategy 11: Use new definitions carefully.)

(Use Strategy C: When a comparison of the two columns is difficult, use numbers instead of variables.)

Choose value for x and y.

Example 1: $x = 1$, $y = 2$

Thus, $\boxed{x} = 1$, $\boxed{y} = 2$

The columns become

Column A	Column B
2	2

Example 2: $x = \dfrac{3}{2}$, $y = 2$

Thus, $\boxed{x} = 1$, $\boxed{y} = 2$

The columns become

Column A	Column B
3	2

Since 2 different answers are possible, the answer cannot be determined.

(Math Refresher #431)

15. Choice B is correct.

(Use Strategy 17: Use the given information effectively.)

From the diagram, it is clear that the perimeter of $ABCDE$ < Circumference of the circle.　　　　　　　　　　1️⃣

Since the diameter of the circle = 2,

$$\text{its radius} = 1$$
$$\text{Circumference} = 2\pi r = 2(\pi)(1)$$
$$\text{Circumference} = 2\pi$$
$$\approx 2(3.14)$$
$$\approx 6.28 \qquad \boxed{2}$$

Clearly, Circumference < 7

(Use Strategy 6: Know how to manipulate inequalities.)

Combining 1️⃣ and 2️⃣, we have

$$\text{Perimeter } ABCD < \text{Circumference of circle} < 7$$
$$\text{Perimeter } ABCD < 7$$

(Math Refresher #310 and 419)

16. **7/24 or any number between 0.25 and .3333.**
Without a calculator:

Get a common denominator 12. Then write $\frac{1}{4} = \frac{3}{12}$ and $\frac{1}{3} = \frac{4}{12}$ to get a quantity *in between* $\frac{3}{12}$ and $\frac{4}{12}$.

Write $\frac{3}{12} = \frac{6}{24}$ and $\frac{4}{12} = \frac{8}{24}$

Thus $\frac{6}{24} < x < \frac{8}{24}$ and x can be $\frac{7}{24}$.

With a calculator:

Calculate $\frac{1}{4} = 0.25$; Calculate $\frac{1}{3} = 0.3333\ldots$.

"Grid" any number between 0.25 and 0.3333 like 0.26, 0.27 .... .332, .333.

(Math Refresher #419)

17. **12**
$$\text{Given: } 3x + y = 17 \qquad \boxed{1}$$
$$x + 3y = -1 \qquad \boxed{2}$$

(Use Strategy 13: Find unknowns by adding.)
Adding 1️⃣ and 2️⃣, we get

$$4x + 4y = 16 \qquad \boxed{3}$$

(Use Strategy 13: Find unknowns by division.) Dividing 3️⃣ by 4. We have

$$x + y = 4 \qquad \boxed{4}$$

(Use Strategy 13: Find unknowns by multiplying.) Multiply 4️⃣ by 3. We get

$$3x + 3y = 12$$

(Math Refresher #407)

18. **60**

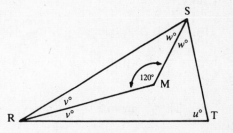

$$\text{Given: } \angle\ M = 120° \qquad \boxed{1}$$
$$\angle RST = 80° \qquad \boxed{2}$$

(Use Strategy 3: The whole equals the sum of its parts.) From the diagram we see that

$$\angle RST = w + w \qquad \boxed{3}$$

Substitute 2️⃣ into 3️⃣. We get
$$80° = w + w$$
$$80° = 2w$$
$$40° = w \qquad \boxed{4}$$

We know that in triangle RMS

$$v + w + 120° = 180° \qquad \boxed{5}$$

Substituting 4️⃣ into 5️⃣, we get

$$v + 40° + 120° = 180°$$
$$v + 160° = 180°$$
$$v = 20° \qquad \boxed{6}$$

From the diagram we see that

$$\angle SRT = v + v \qquad \boxed{7}$$

Substitute 6️⃣ into 7️⃣. We get

$$\angle SRT = 20° + 20°$$
$$\angle SRT = 40° \qquad \boxed{8}$$

We know that in triangle RST

$$\angle RST + \angle SRT + u = 180° \qquad \boxed{9}$$

Substitute $\boxed{2}$ and $\boxed{8}$ into $\boxed{9}$. We get

$$80° + \; 40° + u = 180°$$
$$120° + u \quad 180°$$
$$u = \; 60°$$

(Math Refresher #505)

19. **6 (Use Strategy 17: Use the given information effectively.)** If the tram carries its maximum of 4 people then

$$\dfrac{22 \text{ people}}{\dfrac{4 \text{ people}}{\text{trip}}} = 5\frac{1}{2} \text{ trips,}$$

(Use Strategy 16: The obvious may be tricky!)

There is no such thing as $\frac{1}{2}$ a trip. The $\frac{1}{2}$ arises because the last trip, the *6th* trip only, takes 2 people.

The $\frac{1}{2}$ represents $\dfrac{2 \text{ people}}{\dfrac{4 \text{ people}}{\text{trip}}} = \dfrac{1}{2}$

There are 5 trips at 4 people each = 20 people
$$\underline{\text{1 trip at 2 people} \qquad = \; \underline{2 \text{ people}}}$$
TOTAL = 6 trips $\quad$ totaling $\quad$ 22 people

(Logical Reasoning)

20. **24** *Method 1:* **(Use Strategy 4: Remember classic expressions.)**

$$(a + b)^2 = a^2 + 2ab + b^2 \qquad \boxed{1}$$
$$(a - b)^2 = a^2 - 2ab + b^2 \qquad \boxed{2}$$

(Use Strategy 11: Use new definitions carefully. These problems are generally easy.)

Using $\boxed{1}$ and $\boxed{2}$, we have

$$a \odot b = (a + b)^2 - (a - b^2)$$
$$= a^2 + 2ab + b^2 - (a^2 - 2ab + b^2)$$
$$= 4ab \qquad \boxed{3}$$

When, we use $\boxed{3}$, we get

$$\sqrt{18} \odot \sqrt{2} = 4(\sqrt{18})(\sqrt{2})$$
$$= 4\sqrt{36}$$
$$= 4(6)$$
$$= 24$$

Method 2: $a \odot b = (a + b)^2 - (a - b)^2$
$$\sqrt{18} \odot \sqrt{2}$$
$$= (\sqrt{18} + \sqrt{2})^2 - (\sqrt{18} - \sqrt{2})^2$$
$$= 18 + 2\sqrt{36} + 2 - (18 - 2\sqrt{36} + 2)$$
$$= 18 + 12 + 2 - 18 + 12 - 2$$
$$= 24$$

The calculations in Method 2 are much more complex!

(Math Refresher #409 and #431)

21. **25** If you have patience, it is not too hard to list all ordered pairs of integers (x, y) such that

$$x^2 + y^2 < 9$$

(Use Strategy 17: Use the given information effectively.)

Another way to do this problem is to note that $x^2 + y^2 = 9$ is the equation of a circle of radius 3 whose center is at $(0, 0)$.

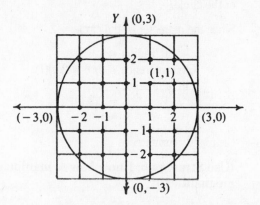

Thus, $x^2 + y^2 < 9$ is the region inside the circle. We want to find the number of ordered pairs of integers (x, y) inside the circle. As we can count from the picture above, there are 25 such ordered pairs.

(Math Refresher #410 and #431)

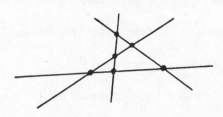

22. **6**

Method 1: The figure above shows 4 straight lines intersecting in 6 points. 6 is the maximum number of points of intersection of 4 straight lines.

Method 2: There is a formula for finding the maximum number of points of intersection of n straight line segments. It is $\dfrac{n(n - 1)}{2}$ $\qquad \boxed{1}$

Substituting 4 into $\boxed{1}$, we get

$$\frac{4(4-1)}{2} = \frac{4(3)}{2} =$$

$$\frac{12}{2} = 6$$

(Logical Reasoning)

23. **35**

    (Use Strategy 2: Translate from words to algebra.) The boy originally had enough money to buy 21 bars at 50¢ per bar. Thus, he had $21 \times 50 =$ 1,050 cents = \$10.50. Therefore,

    Number of 30¢ bars he bought

    $$= \frac{\text{Total amount he had}}{\text{Price of each bar}}$$

    $$= \frac{\$10.50}{\$\ .30}$$

    $$= 35 \text{ bars (Answer)}$$

    (Math Refresher #200 and #406)

24. **333**

    (Use Strategy 16: The obvious may be tricky!) From the problem, we see that

    $$d = 96,999;\ not\ 97,777$$

    Thus, $d - 96,666 = 333$

    (Logical Reasoning)

25. $\frac{1}{8}$ or **.125**

    (Use Strategy 2: Remember the definition of percent.) 25 percent of 2 is

    $$\frac{25}{100} \times 2$$

    Thus, 25 percent of 25 percent of 2 is

    $$\frac{25}{100} \times \frac{25}{100} \times 2 = \frac{1}{4} \times \frac{1}{4} \times 2$$

    $$= \frac{2}{16}$$

    $$= \frac{1}{8}$$

    (Math Refresher #114)

Explanatory Answers for Practice Test 1 (continued)

Section 5: Verbal Ability

As you read these Explanatory Answers, you are advised to refer to "Using Critical Thinking Skills in Verbal Questions" (beginning on page 236) whenever a specific Strategy is referred to in the answer. Of particular importance are the following Master Verbal Strategies:

Reading Comprehension Master Strategy 2—page 263

1. Choice A is correct. The main idea of the passage is expressed in lines 18–19: "Science seems to have come into existence merely for its bearings on practical life." This main idea is also expressed in other parts of the passage. For example—Lines 1–2: "Science, like everything else ... needs and desires." Also lines 15–16: "... the bulk of mankind ... advantages it brings with it." Finally, all through the last paragraph of the passage we learn how the Babylonians and the Egyptians reaped practical benefits with the help of science. Choices B, C, D, and E are true, but they are too confining to be considered the main idea of the passage. Therefore, these choices are incorrect.

2. Choice E is correct. See lines 8–14: "Science is valued ... most important consideration of all to scientific men." Choice A is incorrect. The passage does not indicate that this choice is true. Furthermore, others *before* the Babylonians and the Egyptians also used scientific methods. Choice B is incorrect. See lines 27–29: "The cultivation of crops ... made a calendar almost a necessity [for the Babylonians and Egyptians]." Choice C is incorrect. First see lines 20–23: "More than two thousand years before ... measuring space and time." Now see lines 32–34: "Twelve of these months ... putting in extra months." Choice D is incorrect. See lines 20–23 again.

3. Choice B is correct. See lines 8–14: "Science is valued ... provides the imagination ... most important consideration of all to scientific men." Choices A, C, D, and E are incorrect because the author does not imply in any way that scientists are sociable, practical, philosophical, or arrogant people.

4. Choice B is correct. The author is, in effect, saying that one must appreciate the forest as a whole—not merely certain individual trees. He therefore implies that we should not separate physics from the body of all creative work. See lines 55–56: "It is pointless ... all creative work ..." Choices A, C, D, and E are incorrect because they are not justified by the content of the passage.

5. The two labels (lines 48–49) obviously have negative implications about the value of physics and thus indicate that physics is uninteresting and pointless. Accordingly, Choice C is correct. It follows, then, that Choice B—which states that physics "is a cause for great excitement"—is incorrect. Choices A, D, and E are incorrect because none of these choices is stated or implied in the passage.

6. Choice A is correct. See lines 60–62: "Yet what little we do know ... grandeur and intricate beauty." Choices B, C, D, and E are incorrect because none of these choices is brought out in the passage.

7. Choice C is correct. See lines 51–54: "There is nothing . . . what we lack of the other." Also see lines 55–58: "It is pointless . . . all-knowing and infallible." None of the other choices is indicated in the passage. Accordingly, choices A, B, D, and E are incorrect.

8. Choice E is correct. See the very first sentence of the passage: "Let's be honest right at the start." This frankness on the part of the author pervades the entire passage. Choices A, B, C, and D are, therefore, incorrect.

9. Choice D is correct. You can see from lines 53–59 that "rudimentary" must be related to something fundamental or basic. In fact in lines 57–58, this rudimentary science met the practical needs of the population, so choices B, C, and E would have been ruled out anyway.

10. Choice D is correct. The practical use of science is discussed in lines 20–34 of Passage A but not in Passage B. Choice A is incorrect: Lines 44–51 imply the way laymen view physics. Choice B is incorrect: Specialization in science is mentioned in lines 44–47 of Passage B. Choice C is incorrect: Purity of physics is mentioned in line 57 of Passage B. Choice E is incorrect: Lines 51–54 address the arguments between humanists and scientists.

11. Choice A is correct. See lines 44–48 of Passage B: "boxes." Choices B, C, D, and E are incorrect: Critique is certainly used by both authors. The author in Passage A contrasts with respect to perceived values in lines 8–16. Historical referencing and examples to support a claim are used in Passage A in lines 20–34.

12. Choice E is correct. Choice A, agriculture, is mentioned in line 25. Choice B, astronomy, is mentioned in line 24. Choice C, art, is mentioned in line 43. Choice D, philosophy, is mentioned in line 57. However, Choice A, chemistry, is not directly mentioned.

13. Choice B is correct. Choice A can be immediately ruled out because it repeats the meaning of "grandeur" and would make it redundant (line 61). Since the author described physics as complex, "intricate" would be a good choice. Note that Choices D and E are incorrect because the author believes that although the outside world may view physics as uninteresting or pointless, it is not the real characteristic of physics. It would be unlikely that the noun "beauty" (line 62) would be described by a negative adjective or word (especially because it is also associated with the positive word "grandeur"). Thus it is unlikely that "intricate" is a negative word such as *devastating*, *uninteresting*, or *pointless*, ruling out Choices C, D, and E.

Explanatory Answers for Practice Test 1 (continued)

Section 6: Math Ability

As you read these solutions, you are advised to do two things if you answered the Math question incorrectly:

1. When a specific Strategy is referred to in the solution, study that strategy, which you will find in "Using Critical Thinking Skills in Math Questions" (beginning on page 174).

2. When the solution directs you to the "Math Refresher" (beginning on page 291)—for example, Math Refresher #305—study the 305 Math principle to get a clear idea of the Math operation that was necessary for you to know in order to answer the question correctly.

1. Choice D is correct.
Method 1: (Use Strategy 8: When all choices must be tested, start with Choice E.)

Since $\sqrt{x}$ is odd, then x is odd. $\boxed{1}$
Let us start with solution E.

Choice E: If x is odd (from $\boxed{1}$ above), then x^2 is odd.

Choice D: If $\sqrt{x}$ is odd, $2\sqrt{x}$ is *even*, and the solution if found.

(Use Strategy 7: Use numerics to help you get the answer.)

Method 2: Choose an odd number for $\sqrt{x}$—for example,
$$\sqrt{x} = 3$$
$$\text{Then } x = 9$$
$$\text{Choice E} \quad x^2 = 81 \text{ (odd)}$$
$$\text{Choice D} \quad 2\sqrt{x} = 2(3) = 6 \text{ (even)}$$

The answer is clearly Choice D.

(Math Refresher #430 and #431, and #603)

2. Choice E is correct. **(Use Strategy 8: When all choices must be tested, start with Choice E.)**
Since we must check all the choices, we should start

with Choice E. Clearly, if x is the point whose coordinates are (5,2), then $m \angle MXN = 90°$ and Choice E must be correct.

(Math Refresher #410)

3. Choice E is correct. **(Use Strategy 2: Translate from words to algebra.)** The sum of the degree measures of the 4 angles of any quadrilateral is always 360. Therefore,

$$w + x + y + z = 360° \quad \boxed{1}$$

$$\left(\text{Use Strategy 5: Average} = \frac{\text{Sum of values}}{\text{Total number of values}}\right)$$

If w is the average (arithmetic mean of x, y, and z, then

$$w = \frac{x + y + z}{3}$$

Multiplying both sides of the above equation by 3, we have

$$3w = x + y + z \quad \boxed{2}$$

Substituting equation $\boxed{2}$ into equation $\boxed{1}$, we get

$$w + 3w = 360°$$
or $\qquad 4w = 360°$
or $\qquad w = 90°$

From equation $\boxed{2}$, we conclude that
$$x + y + z = 3w = 3(90) = 270°$$

(Math Refresher #521, #601, and #406)

4. Choice B is correct. The circle graph tells you that 19% of this mixture is carbon. Since the total mixture weighs 24 pounds, 19% of that will be the amount of carbon in the mixture (in pounds). We would multiply 24 lbs × .19. But since we are looking for the *closest* number of pounds, make the problem simpler by multiplying 24 × .20 = 4.8.

(Math Refresher #705)

5. Choice B is correct. **(Use Strategy 2: Translate from words to algebra.)** Each complete revolution is one circumference.

one circumference = 120 feet

B completed 600 revolutions.

Total distance =
$\qquad$ (600 revolutions)(120 feet/revolution)
Total distance = 600 × 120 feet

(Use Strategy 9: Know the rate, time, and distance relationship.)

$$\text{Time for } B = \frac{\text{Total distance}}{\text{Rate}} =$$

$$\frac{600 \times 120 \text{ feet}}{8 \text{ feet/second}}$$

Use a calculator for the above or use Strategy 19: Factor and reduce.

$$\frac{600 \times \cancel{8} \times 15 \text{ feet}}{\cancel{8} \text{ feet/second}}$$

Time for B = 9,000 seconds

A traveled at 5 feet/second
A's total distance is
$\qquad$ 5 feet/second × 9,000 seconds
$\qquad\qquad$ = 45,000 feet

Dividing by the circumference of 120 feet, we have
$$\text{number of revolutions} = \frac{45,000 \text{ feet}}{120 \text{ feet/revolution}}$$

Use a calculator for the above or use Strategy 19: Factor and reduce.

$$\frac{3 \times 15 \times \cancel{10} \times 25 \times \cancel{4}}{\cancel{3} \times \cancel{4} \times \cancel{10}}$$

375 revolutions (*Answer*)
(Math Refresher #200, #201, and #202)

6. Choice D is correct. The key to this problem is to find the area of the shaded region in terms of known quantities. **(Use Strategy 3: The whole equals the sum of its parts.)** Area of shaded region and also the area of the rectangle

$\qquad$ = Area of triangle − Area of square
$\qquad$ = $x^2\sqrt{3} - x^2$
$\qquad$ = $x^2(\sqrt{3} - 1)$

We are given that an unknown rectangle
has width = x $\qquad\qquad\qquad\boxed{1}$
and area = $x^2(\sqrt{3} - 1)$ $\qquad\boxed{2}$

Since length × width = area,
length = area ÷ width $\qquad\qquad\boxed{3}$
Substituting $\boxed{1}$ and $\boxed{2}$ into $\boxed{3}$, we have

$$\text{length of rectangle} = \frac{x^2(\sqrt{3} - 1)}{x}$$

$$\text{length of rectangle} = x(\sqrt{3} - 1)$$

(Math Refresher #303, #304, and #306)

7. Choice A is correct.

(Use Strategy 5: Average
$$= \frac{\textbf{Sum of values}}{\textbf{Total number of values}}\bigg)$$

$$p = \frac{x + y}{2} \qquad\qquad\boxed{1}$$

$$q = \frac{y + z}{2} \qquad\qquad\boxed{2}$$

$$r = \frac{x + z}{2} \qquad\qquad\boxed{3}$$

(Use Strategy 13: Find unknown expressions by adding equations.) Adding $\boxed{1}$, $\boxed{2}$ and $\boxed{3}$ we get

$$p + q + r = \frac{x + y}{2} + \frac{y + z}{2} + \frac{x + z}{2}$$

$$= \frac{2x + 2y + 2z}{2}$$

$$p + q + r = x + y + z \qquad\boxed{4}$$

The average of x, y and $z = \dfrac{x + y + z}{3}$ $\quad\boxed{5}$
Substitute $\boxed{4}$ into $\boxed{5}$. We have

The average of x, y and $z = \dfrac{p + q + r}{3}$ (*Answer*)

(Math Refresher #601 and #109)

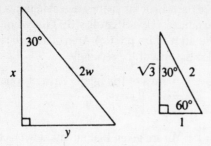

8. Choice A is correct. (**Use Strategy 18: Remember special right triangles.**) The triangle at left (given) is similar to the triangle at right, which is one of the standard triangles.

Corresponding sides of similar triangles are proportional. Thus,

$$\frac{2w}{2} = \frac{y}{1} \text{ and } \frac{2w}{2} = \frac{x}{\sqrt{3}}$$

or $\qquad y = w$ and $x = w\sqrt{3}$

Area of rectangle = 1/2 (base)(height)
$$= 1/2 \ (y)(x)$$
$$= 1/2 \ (w)(w\sqrt{3})$$

Area of triangle $= \dfrac{\sqrt{3}}{2} \ w^2 \qquad \boxed{1}$

Area of rectangle $= (3w)(w) = 3w^2 \qquad \boxed{2}$

Using $\boxed{1}$ and $\boxed{2}$, we have

$$\frac{\text{Area of rectangle}}{\text{Area of triangle}} = \frac{3w^2}{\dfrac{\sqrt{3}}{2}w^2}$$

$$= \frac{3}{\dfrac{\sqrt{3}}{2}} = 3 \times \frac{2}{\sqrt{3}}$$

$$= \frac{6}{\sqrt{3}} = \frac{6\sqrt{3}}{3} = 2\sqrt{3}$$

or $2\sqrt{3} : 1$ (*Answer*)

(**Math Refresher #510, #509, #306, and #304**)

9. Choice B is correct.
(**Use Strategy 2: Translate from words to algebra.**)

Let f = Number of freshmen
s = Number of seniors

We are given $f = 3s \qquad\qquad \boxed{1}$
1/4 of the freshmen $= \dfrac{1}{4}f \qquad \boxed{2}$

1/3 of the seniors $= \dfrac{1}{3}s \qquad\qquad \boxed{3}$

Total number of freshmen
and seniors $= f + s \qquad\qquad \boxed{4}$

(**Use Strategy 17: Use the given information effectively.**)

The desired fraction uses $\boxed{2}$, $\boxed{3}$ and $\boxed{4}$ as follows:

$$\frac{\dfrac{1}{4}f + \dfrac{1}{3}s}{f + s} \qquad\qquad \boxed{5}$$

Substituting $\boxed{1}$ in $\boxed{5}$, we get

$$\frac{\dfrac{1}{4}(3s) + \dfrac{1}{3}s}{3s + s} = \frac{\dfrac{3}{4}s + \dfrac{1}{3}s}{4s} \qquad \boxed{6}$$

Multiplying $\boxed{6}$, numerator and denominator, by 12 we get:

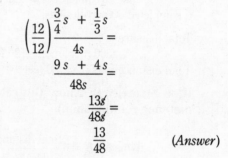

$$\frac{9s + 4s}{48s} =$$

$$\frac{13s}{48s} =$$

$$\frac{13}{48} \qquad\qquad (\textit{Answer})$$

(**Math Refresher #200, #402, and #108**)

10. Choice C is correct.
(**Use Strategy 2: Translate from words to algebra.**) Set up a Venn diagram:

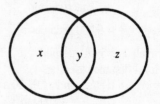

x = number of students with *only* a car
z = number of students with *only* a bicycle
y = number of students having a car and a bicycle

Total students = 100 $\qquad \boxed{1}$
We are given: $x + y = 30$ $\qquad \boxed{2}$
$z + y = 50$ $\qquad \boxed{3}$
$y = 20$ $\qquad \boxed{4}$

Substituting $\boxed{4}$ into $\boxed{2}$ and into $\boxed{3}$, we get

$x = 10, z = 30 \qquad\qquad \boxed{5}$

Using $\boxed{4}$ and $\boxed{5}$, we have:

The sum of $x + y + z =$
$$10 + 20 + 30 = 60 \qquad \boxed{6}$$

This is the number of students who have either a car, a bicycle, or both.

Using $\boxed{1}$ and $\boxed{6}$, we get $100 - 60 = 40$ as the number who have neither a car nor a bicycle nor both.

(Math Refresher #200 and #406)

Explanatory Answers for Practice Test 1 (continued)

Section 7: Math Ability

As you read these solutions, you are advised to do two things if you answered the Math question incorrectly:

1. When a specific Strategy is referred to in the solution, study that strategy, which you will find in "Using Critical Thinking Skills in Math Questions" (beginning on page 174).

2. When the solution directs you to the "Math Refresher" (beginning on page 291)—for example, Math Refresher #305—study the 305 Math principle to get a clear idea of the Math operation that was necessary for you to know in order to answer the question correctly.

1. Choice E is correct.

    (Use Strategy 2: Translate from words to algebra.)

    Let g = number of games the team played
    28 = number of games Bobby watched
    $\frac{2}{3}g$ = number of games Tommy watched

    We are given

    $$\frac{2}{3}\,g > 28 \qquad \boxed{1}$$

    Multiplying $\boxed{1}$ by $\frac{3}{2}$, we get

    $$\left(\frac{3}{2}\right)\frac{2}{3}\,g > 28\left(\frac{3}{2}\right)$$
    $$g > 42$$

    Only Choice E satisfies this relationship.
    (Math Refresher #200, #422, and #426)

2. Choice D is correct.

    Using the distributive property, we get $3x(4x + 2y)$
    $= 12x^2 + 6xy$

    (Math Refresher #409)

3. Choice D is correct.

    We are told that 1 decimeter = 100 millimeters

    (Use Strategy 17: Use the given information effectively.)

    Dividing each height from the table, we get:

    (A) $\frac{1700}{100} = 17$

    (B) $\frac{2450}{100} = 24.5$

    (C) $\frac{2735}{100} = 27.35$

    (D) $\frac{1928}{100} = 19.28$

    (E) $\frac{2130}{100} = 21.3$

    Note that choices B, C, and E are greater than 20.

    (Math Refresher #121 and Division)

4. Choice E is correct

    Given: $a - 3 = 7$ $\qquad \boxed{1}$

    (Use Strategy 13: Find unknowns by addition, subtraction, and multiplication.)

Fast Method: From $\boxed{1}$, we can subtract 7 from both sides, and then add 3 to both sides to get

$$a - 7 = 3 \qquad \boxed{2}$$

Multiplying $\boxed{2}$ by 2,

$$2a - 14 = 6 \qquad (Answer)$$

Slow Method: Solve $\boxed{1}$ to get

$$a = 10 \qquad \boxed{3}$$

Now substitute $\boxed{3}$:

$$2a - 14 = 2(10) - 14 = 6 \qquad (Answer)$$

(Math Refresher #406 and #431)

5.   Choice C is correct.

(Use Strategy 10: Know how to use units.)

We are given his rate is $\dfrac{90 \text{ laps}}{6 \text{ hours}}$

$$\frac{90 \text{ laps}}{6 \text{ hours}} \times \frac{1 \text{ hour}}{60 \text{ minutes}} =$$

(Use Strategy 19: Factor and reduce.)

$$\frac{\cancel{3} \times 3 \times \cancel{10} \text{ laps}}{\cancel{3} \times 2 \times 3 \times 2 \times \cancel{10} \text{ minutes}} =$$

$\dfrac{1}{4}$ lap per minute *(Answer)*

(Math Refresher #121)

6.   Choice D is correct.

(Use Strategy 17: Use the given information effectively.)

Change all fractions to decimal form:

$$\frac{7}{10} = .7$$

$$\frac{7}{100} = .07$$

$$\frac{7}{1000} = .077$$

Adding these we get .847   *(Answer)*

(Math Refresher #104)

7.   Choice A is correct.

Know the properties of parallel lines. If 2 parallel lines are crossed by a transversal, the pairs of corresponding angles are equal. Thus,

$$x = a \qquad \boxed{1}$$
From the diagram, $a + y = 180 \qquad \boxed{2}$

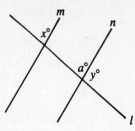

Substituting $\boxed{1}$ into $\boxed{2}$, we get

$$x + y = 180 \qquad (Answer)$$

(Math Refresher #504)

8.   Choice B is correct.

12 must be substituted for P in each of the five expressions and the results evaluated.

Item 1: $P = 12$ — 12
Item 2: $P \times 3 = 12 \times 3 =$ — 36
Item 3: $(P \times 3 \div 2 = (12 \times 3) \div 2 =$ — 18
Item 4: $[(P \times 3 \div 2] + 12 =$
$\quad\quad [(12 \times 3) \div 2] + 12 =$ — 30
Item 5: $[(P \times 3) \div 2] + 12 - 1 =$
$\quad\quad [(12 \times 3) \div 2] + 12 - 1 =$ — 29

Item 2 is greatest in value.

(Math Refresher #431)

9.   Choice E is correct.

Given: $\dfrac{3x}{4} = 9 \qquad \boxed{1}$

(Use Strategy 13: Find unknowns by multiplication.)

Multiplying $\boxed{1}$ by 4, we get

$$\cancel{4}\left(\frac{3x}{\cancel{4}}\right) = (9)4$$
$$3x = 36$$

Multiply $\boxed{2}$ by 2. We have
$$2(3x) = (36)2$$
$$6x = 72$$

(Math Refresher #406)

10.   Choice D is correct.

Given: 8 people divide a cash prize equally $\boxed{1}$

(Use Strategy 2: Translate from words to algebra.)

From $\boxed{1}$ we get:

Each person receives $\dfrac{1}{8}$ of the total prize $\boxed{2}$

2 people receive $\dfrac{2}{8} = \dfrac{1}{4}$ of the prize $\boxed{3}$

To change $\boxed{3}$ to a percent we multiply by 100.

$$100\left(\frac{1}{4}\right) = \frac{100}{4}$$
$$= 25\%$$

(Math Refresher #200 and #106)

11. Choice C is correct.

Given: $8r + 3s = 12$ $\boxed{1}$
        $7r + 2s = 9$ $\boxed{2}$

(Use Strategy 13: Find unknowns by subtracting.)

Subtracting $\boxed{2}$ from $\boxed{1}$, we get

$$r + s = 3 \qquad \boxed{3}$$

Multiplying $\boxed{3}$ by 5, we get

$$5\,(r + s) = (3)5$$
$$5\,(r + s) = 15$$

(Math Refresher #406 and #407)

12. Choice B is correct.

Given: Paul's average on 3 tests = 85 $\boxed{1}$
       Paul's average on first 2 tests = 85 $\boxed{2}$

(Use Strategy 5:

$$\textbf{Average} = \frac{\textbf{Sum of values}}{\textbf{Total number of values}}\Bigg)$$

We know Average $= \dfrac{\text{Sum of values}}{\text{Total number of values}}$ $\boxed{3}$

Let x be the first test score $\boxed{4}$
   y be the second test score $\boxed{5}$
   z be the third test score $\boxed{6}$

Substituting $\boxed{1}$, $\boxed{4}$, $\boxed{5}$ and $\boxed{6}$ into $\boxed{3}$, we have

$$85 = \frac{x + y + z}{3} \qquad \boxed{7}$$

(Use Strategy 13: Find unknowns by multiplication.)

Multiply $\boxed{7}$ by 3. We get

$$3(85) = \left(\frac{x + y + z}{3}\right)3 \qquad \boxed{8}$$
$$255 = x + y + z$$

Substituting $\boxed{2}$, $\boxed{4}$ and $\boxed{5}$ into $\boxed{3}$, we have

$$85 = \frac{x + y}{2} \qquad \boxed{9}$$

Multiply $\boxed{9}$ by 2, we get

$$2(85) = \left(\frac{x + y}{2}\right)2$$
$$170 = x + y \qquad \boxed{10}$$

Substituting $\boxed{10}$ into $\boxed{8}$, we get

$$225 = 170 + z$$
$$85 = z$$

(Math Refresher #601, #431, and #406)

13. Choice A is correct.
(Use Strategy 11: Use new definitions carefully.)

Given: $x \boxdot y = 3 + xy$ $\boxed{1}$
         $y \neq 0$ $\boxed{2}$
       $x \boxdot y = 3$ $\boxed{3}$

Substituting $\boxed{3}$ into $\boxed{1}$, we get

$$3 = 3 + xy$$
$$0 = xy \qquad \boxed{4}$$

Noting $\boxed{2}$, we divide $\boxed{4}$ by y

$$\frac{0}{y} = \frac{xy}{y}$$
$$0 = x$$

(Math Refresher #431 and #406)

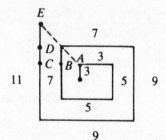

14. Choice C is correct.

From the diagram we find that

$$AB = 2 \qquad \boxed{1}$$
$$BC = 2 \qquad \boxed{2}$$
$$CD = 2 \qquad \boxed{3}$$
$$DE = 2 \qquad \boxed{4}$$

(Use Strategy 3: The whole equals the sum of its parts.)

We know $AB + BC = AC$ $\boxed{5}$

Substituting $\boxed{1}$ and $\boxed{2}$ into $\boxed{5}$, we get

$$2 + 2 = AC$$
$$4 = AC \quad \boxed{6}$$
We know $CD + DE = CE$ $\boxed{7}$

Substituting $\boxed{3}$ and $\boxed{4}$ into $\boxed{7}$, we get

$$2 + 2 = CE$$
$$4 = CE \qquad \boxed{8}$$

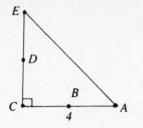

Filling ⑥ and ⑧ into the diagram and using the fact that all the segments drawn were perpendicular, we have △*ECA* is an isosceles right triangle.

(Use Strategy 18: Remember the isosceles right triangle.)

In the isosceles right triangle, the

$$\text{hypotenuse} = \text{leg}(\sqrt{2}) \qquad ⑨$$

Substituting ⑥ or ⑧ into ⑨, we get

$$EA = 4\sqrt{2}. \qquad ⑥$$

(Math Refresher #507 and #509)

15. Choice D is correct.

(Use Strategy 11: Use new definitions carefully.)

Two-digit numbers which have a units-digit = 0 that can be tripled in value when the tens-digit is tripled are the following:

Original number	Tripled tens digit number
10	30
20	60
30	90

The above numbers are the only numbers that result in a two-digit number as defined in the problem. Thus, 3 is the correct answer.

(Logical Reasoning)

16. Choice C is correct.

(Use Strategy 11: Use new definitions carefully.)

$$\text{By definition, } A = 12345 \qquad ①$$
$$B = 98765 \qquad ②$$

(Use Strategy 13: Find unknowns by subtracting.)

Subtracting ① from ②, we get

$$B - A = 98765 - 12345$$
$$B - A = 86420$$

(Logical Reasoning)

17. Choice D is correct.

Given:

Meteor 1 travels at 300 meters/second ①
Meteor 2 travels at 700 meters/second ②

Draw a diagram:

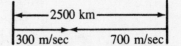

Let *t* be the time it takes meteors to meet. Call *x* the distance Meteor 1 travels. Then 2500 − *x* is the distance Meteor 2 travels.

(Use Strategy 9: Know Rate, Time, and Distance relationship.)

$$\text{Rate} \times \text{Time} = \text{Distance}$$
$$300 \text{ m/sec} \times t = x \qquad ③$$
$$700 \text{ m/sec} \times t = 2500 - x \qquad ④$$

(Use Strategy 13: Find unknowns by addition.)

Add ③ and ④

$$(300 \text{ m/sec})t + (700 \text{ m/sec})t = 2500 \text{ km}$$
$$(1000 \text{ m/sec})t = 2500 \text{ km} \qquad ⑤$$

(Use Strategy 10: Know how to use units.)

$$1 \text{ km} = 1000 \text{ m}$$

Substitute ⑥ in ⑤:

$$(1000 \text{ m/sec})t = 2500(1000)\text{m}$$

Divide ⑦ by 1000 m:

$$t/\text{sec} = 2500$$
$$t = 2500 \text{ sec}$$

(Math Refresher #121, #201, and #202)

18. Choice E is correct.

(Use Strategy 17: Use the given information effectively.)

$$x = \sqrt{\frac{1}{9} + \left(\frac{1}{3} + \frac{1}{9} + \frac{1}{27} + \frac{1}{81}\right)}$$

The common denominator for all the fractions is 81.

We have: $x = \sqrt{\dfrac{9}{81} + \dfrac{27}{81} + \dfrac{9}{81} + \dfrac{3}{81} + \dfrac{1}{81}}$

$= \sqrt{\dfrac{9 + 27 + 9 + 3 + 1}{81}}$

$= \sqrt{\dfrac{49}{81}}$

$= \dfrac{7}{9}$

(Math Refresher #110 and #430)

19. Choice A is correct.

    (Use Strategy 3: The whole equals the sum of its parts.)

    From the given diagram, it is clear that

    $$z + 2w = 180 \qquad \boxed{1}$$

    Since the sum of the measures of the angles of a triangle is 180, then

    $$x + y + z = 180 \qquad \boxed{2}$$

    (Use Strategy 13: Find unknowns by subtracting equations.)
    Subtracting $\boxed{2}$ from $\boxed{1}$,

    $$2w - (x + y) = 0$$
    or $\quad 2w = x + y \qquad \boxed{3}$

    Using $\boxed{3}$, we calculate the unknown expression,

    $$w + x + y = w + 2w$$
    $$= 3w$$

    (Math Refresher #501, #505, and #406)

20. Choice A is correct.

    (Use Strategy 11: Use new definitions carefully.)

    All choices must be evaluated using the definition.

    Choice A, 934432, would be assigned $6 + 3 + 4 = 13$ points, while the other choices all receive fewer than 13 points.

    (Logical Reasoning)

Number Pair	Number of Points
"33"	11
"34"	6
"43"	4
"44"	3

21. Choice D is correct.

    Given: A certain number has 13 points.

    (Use Strategy 11: Use new definitions carefully.)

    From the chart, the only ways to accumulate 13 points are:

    $$6 + 4 + 3 \qquad \boxed{1}$$
    $$3 + 3 + 3 + 4 \qquad \boxed{2}$$

    I. 33 is not in the number is always true.
    II. 34 and 43 are both in the number is *not* true in $\boxed{2}$
    III. 43 is in the number is always true.

    Thus, I and III are always true.

    (Logical Reasoning)

22. Choice E is correct.

    (Use Strategy 17: Use the given information effectively.)

    The center point inside a cube is the midpoint of an inner diagonal of the cube. Thus, the distance from any vertex to this center point is

    $\dfrac{1}{2}$ length of the inner diagonal.

    We know length of inner diagonal of a cube

    $$= \sqrt{(\text{edge})^2 + (\text{edge})^2 + (\text{edge})^2}$$
    inner diagonal $= \sqrt{3(\text{edge})^2}$
    inner diagonal $= \text{edge}\sqrt{3} \qquad \boxed{2}$
    Given: Volume = 8 cubic meters $\qquad \boxed{3}$
    We know volume of a cube $= (\text{edge})^3 \qquad \boxed{4}$
    Substituting $\boxed{3}$ into $\boxed{4}$, we get
    $$8 \text{ cubic meters} = (\text{edge})^3$$
    $$\sqrt[3]{8 \text{ cubic meters}} = \sqrt[3]{(\text{edge})^3}$$
    $$2 \text{ meters} = \text{edge} \qquad \boxed{5}$$

    Substituting $\boxed{5}$ into $\boxed{2}$, we get

    inner diagonal $= (2)\sqrt{3}$
    inner diagonal $= 2\sqrt{3}$ meters $\qquad \boxed{6}$

Using $\boxed{1}$ and $\boxed{6}$ we find

$$\text{distance we need} = \frac{1}{2}(\text{inner diagonal})$$

$$= \frac{1}{2}(2\sqrt{3}\text{ meters})$$

$$= \sqrt{3}\text{ meters}$$

$$\text{Distances we need} = \sqrt{3}\,m$$

(Math Refresher #313, #430, and #406)

23. Choice A is correct.

(Use Strategy 2: Translate from words to algebra.)

The ratio of Sue's age to Bob's age is 3 to 7, becomes

$$\frac{\text{Sue's age }(S)}{\text{Bob's age }(B)} = \frac{3}{7}$$

or $\qquad \dfrac{S}{B} = \dfrac{3}{7}$ $\qquad\boxed{1}$

The ratio of Sue's age to Joe's age is 4 to 9, becomes

$$\frac{S}{J} = \frac{4}{9} \qquad\boxed{2}$$

Cross multiplying $\boxed{1}$, we have $7S = 3B$

or $\qquad \dfrac{7S}{3} = B$ $\qquad\boxed{3}$

Cross multiplying $\boxed{2}$, we have $9S = 4J$

or $\qquad \dfrac{9S}{4} = J$ $\qquad\boxed{4}$

We need the ratio of Bob's age to Joe's age. $\qquad\boxed{5}$

Substituting $\boxed{3}$ and $\boxed{4}$ into $\boxed{5}$, we get

$$\frac{\text{Bob's age}}{\text{Joe's age}} = \frac{\dfrac{7S}{3}}{\dfrac{9S}{4}}$$

$$= \frac{7S}{3} \div \frac{9S}{4}$$

$$= \frac{7S}{3} \times \frac{4}{9S}$$

$$\frac{\text{Bob's age}}{\text{Joe's age}} = \frac{28}{27}$$

(Math Refresher #200, #120, and #112)

24. Choice C is correct.

(Use Strategy 2: Translate from words to algebra.)

Let $a = $ a positive integer
Then $a + 1, a + 2, a + 3, a + 4$, etc., are the next positive integers.

(Use Strategy 13: Find unknowns by addition.)

Add the first 2 positive integers. We get
Sum of first 2 positives integers =
$a + a + 1 = 2a + 1$ $\qquad\boxed{1}$

$\boxed{1}$ is not divisible by 2.

Now add the third positive integer, $a + 2$, to $\boxed{1}$. We get

Sum of first 3 positive integers =
$2a + 1 + a + 2 = 3a + 3$ $\qquad\boxed{2}$

$\boxed{2}$ is not divisible by 2.

Now add the fourth positive integer, $a + 3$, to $\boxed{2}$ We have

Sum of first 4 positive integers
$= 3a + 3 + a + 3$
$= 4a + 6$ $\qquad\boxed{3}$

Since $\boxed{3}$ can be written as $2(2a + 3)$, it is divisible by 2.

Thus, if r is a multiple of 4, the sum of r consecutive positive integers will be divisible by 2.

(Math Refresher #200 and #607)

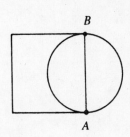

25. Choice B is correct.

(Use Strategy 17: Use the given information effectively.)

Given: Area of circle $= 9a^2\pi^2$ $\qquad\boxed{1}$
$\qquad$ Two sides of square are
$\qquad\qquad$ tangent to the circle $\qquad\boxed{2}$

We know that area of a circle $= \pi(\text{radius})^2$ $\qquad\boxed{3}$
Substituting $\boxed{1}$ into $\boxed{3}$, we have

$$9a^2\pi^2 = \pi(\text{radius})^2 \qquad\boxed{4}$$

(Use Strategy 13: Find unknowns by division.)

Divide $\boxed{4}$ by π. We get

$$\frac{9a^2\pi^2}{\pi} = \frac{\pi}{\pi}\,(\text{radius})^2$$

$$9a^2\pi = (\text{radius})^2$$

$$\sqrt{9a^2\pi} = \sqrt{(\text{radius})^2}$$

$$3a\sqrt{\pi} = \text{radius} \qquad \boxed{5}$$

Using $\boxed{2}$ we know that AB is a diameter of the circle $\qquad \boxed{6}$

We know diameter = 2(radius) $\qquad \boxed{7}$

Using $\boxed{5}$, $\boxed{6}$ and $\boxed{7}$ we get

$$AB = 2(3a\sqrt{\pi}) = 6a\sqrt{\pi} \qquad \boxed{8}$$

We know that Area of a square = (side)^2 $\qquad \boxed{9}$

Substituting $\boxed{8}$ into $\boxed{9}$, we have

$$\text{Area of square} = (6a\sqrt{\pi})^2$$
$$= 36a^2\pi$$

(Math Refresher #303, #310, #430, and #406)

What You Must Do Now to Raise Your SAT Score

1. Go back to the SAT Diagnostic Pre-Test you have just taken.
   a) Count the number of correct answers that you had for the Verbal part and for the Math part of the Pre-Test.
   b) Determine your Scaled Score for each part by referring to the Raw Score/Scaled Score Conversion Tables on page 90. These results will give you a good idea about whether or not you ought to study hard in order to achieve a certain score on the actual SAT.
   c) Using your Pre-Test correct answer count as a basis, indicate for yourself your areas of strength and weakness as revealed by the "Self-Appraisal Chart" on page 91.

2. Eliminate your weaknesses in each of the SAT test areas (as revealed in the "Self-Appraisal Chart") by taking the following Giant Steps toward SAT success:

Verbal Part

Giant Step 1

Take advantage of the Verbal Strategies that begin on page 236. Read again the Explanatory Answer for each of the Verbal questions that you got wrong. Refer to the Verbal Strategy that applies to each of your incorrect answers. Learn each of these Verbal Strategies thoroughly. These strategies are crucial if you want to raise your SAT Verbal score substantially.

Giant Step 2

You can improve your vocabulary by doing the following:

1) Study the SAT 3,400-Word List beginning on page 479.

2) Take the 100 SAT-type "tough word" Vocabulary Tests beginning on page 531.

3) Study "Word Building with Roots, Prefixes, and Suffixes," beginning on page 468.

4) Read as widely as possible—not only novels. Nonfiction is important too . . . and don't forget to read newspapers and magazines.

5) Listen to people who speak well. Tune in to worthwhile TV programs also.

6) Use the dictionary frequently and extensively—at home, on the bus, at work, etc.

7) Play word games—for example, crossword puzzles, anagrams, and Scrabble. Another game is to compose your own Antonym, Analogy, and Sentence Completion questions. Try them on your friends.

Math Part

Giant Step 3

Make good use of the Math Strategies that begin on page 174. Read again the solutions for each Math question that you answered incorrectly. Refer to the Math Strategy that applies to each of your incorrect answers. Learn each of these Math Strategies thoroughly. We repeat that these strategies are crucial if you want to raise your SAT Math score substantially.

Giant Step 4

You may want to take **The 101 Most Important Basic Skills Math Questions You Need to Know How to Solve** test on page 131 and follow the directions after the test for a basic math skills diagnosis.

For each Math question that you got wrong in the Pre-Test, note the reference to the Math Refresher section on page 150. This reference will explain clearly the mathematical principle involved in the solution of the question you answered incorrectly. Learn that particular mathematical principle thoroughly.

For Both the Math and Verbal Parts
Giant Step 5

You may want to take the **Strategy Diagnostic Test** on page 93 to assess whether you're using the best strategies for the questions.

3. After you have done some of the tasks you have been advised to do in the suggestions above, proceed to Practice Test 2, beginning on page 602. (We consider the Pre-Test that you have already taken as Practice Test 1.)

   After taking Practice Test 2, concentrate on the weaknesses that still remain.

4. Continue the foregoing procedures for Practice Tests 3, 4, and 5.

   If you do the job *right* and follow the steps listed above, you are likely to raise your SAT score on both the Verbal and the Math part of the test 50 points—maybe 100 points—and even more.

   I am the master of my fate;
   I am the captain of my soul.

   —From the poem "Invictus"
   by William Ernest Henley

How to Score the SAT I: Reasoning Test

Verbal

Count the number of correct and incorrect answers in verbal sections 1, 3, and 5. Enter these numbers on the worksheet. Multiply the number of incorrect answers by ¼. Subtract the result from the number of verbal questions answered correctly; record the result on the worksheet (A), keeping any fractions. Round A to the nearest whole number: ½ or more, round up; less than ½, round down. The number you get is your **total verbal raw score**. Enter this number on line B.

Mathematics

Count the number of correct and incorrect answers in math sections 2 and 6. Enter these numbers on the worksheet. Multiply the number of incorrect answers by ¼. Subtract the result from the number of questions answered correctly; record the result on the worksheet (subtotal A), keeping any fractions.

Count the number of correct and incorrect answers in math section 4, questions 1–15. **Note: Do not count any E responses to questions 1 through 15 as correct or incorrect. Because these four-choice questions have no E answer choices, E responses to these questions are treated as omits.** Enter these numbers on the worksheet. Multiply the number of incorrect answers by ⅓. Subtract the result from the number of questions answered correctly; record the result on the worksheet (subtotal B), keeping any fractions.

Count the number of correct answers in math section 4, questions 16–25. Enter the number on the worksheet (subtotal C).

Add subtotals A, B, and C to get D, keeping any fractions. Round D to the nearest whole number: ½ or more, round up; less than ½, round down. The number you get is your **total mathematics raw score**. Enter this number on line E.

Worksheet for Calculating Your Scores

Verbal

A Sections 1, 3, and 5 _____ − (¼ × _____) = _____
    no. correct   no. incorrect   A

B Total rounded verbal raw score
                                                          _____
                                                          B

Mathematics

A Sections 2 and 6 _____ −(¼ × _____) = _____
    no. correct   no. incorrect   subtotal A

B Section 4   _____ − (⅓ × _____) = _____
    Questions 1–15   no. correct   no. incorrect   subtotal B

C Section 4   _____   = _____
    Questions 16–25 no. correct   subtotal C

D Total unrounded math raw score (A + B + C)
                                                          _____
                                                          D

E Total rounded math raw score
                                                          _____
                                                          E

Use the table on page 90 to convert your raw scores to scaled scores. For example, if you are taking the SAT-I before April, 1995, you would find that a raw verbal score of 39 corresponds to a verbal scaled score of 450; a math raw score of 24 corresponds to a math scaled score of 430. If you are taking the SAT-I in April, 1995, or after, you will find that a raw verbal score of 39 corresponds to a verbal scaled score of 530; a math raw score of 24 corresponds to a math scaled score of 470.

Scores on the new SAT I range from 200 to 800.

Note: For these particular practice tests in this book, we have chosen Section 7 to be experimental and thus this section will not count toward your SAT-I score for the tests in this book.

Raw Score/Scaled Score Conversion Tables for the Practice Test You Have Just Taken

The College Board will send you your SAT I results about six weeks after you have taken the test. The report will include two separate scores—Verbal and Math. Each score consists of three digits, from 200 to 800. These scores are your so-called scaled scores, which constitute an important factor in a college's acceptance decision.

This Scaled Score is derived by a statistical process from the Raw Score. The Raw Score is the number of questions you answered correctly, with a penalty for each incorrectly answered question. For each incorrectly answered Verbal or Regular Math multiple-choice question, there is a deduction of ¼ of a question. For each incorrectly answered Quantitative Comparison Math question (which has 4 choices), there is a deduction of ⅓ of a question. A Scaled Score of 500 is equivalent to a 50th percentile ranking—that is, about half of those taking the test scored better than you, and half scored below you.

The following unofficial Raw Score/Scaled Score Tables will give you an idea of what your Scaled Score should be for the SAT Practice Test you have just taken.

SCORE CONVERSION TABLE

This table reflects score conversions for those taking the SAT-I after or in April, 1995 and before April, 1995. Make sure that you choose the appropriate conversion for the times that you are taking the SAT-I.

Raw Score	Verbal Scaled Score		Math Scaled Score		Raw Score	Verbal Scaled Score		Math Scaled Score	
	Before 4/95	In or after 4/95	Before 4/95	In or after 4/95		Before 4/95	In or after 4/95	Before 4/95	In or after 4/95
78	800	800			36	430	510	540	560
77	780	800			35	430	510	530	550
76	770	800			34	420	500	520	540
75	760	800			33	420	500	510	530
74	740	800			32	410	490	500	520
73	720	790			31	400	480	490	520
72	710	780			30	400	480	480	510
71	700	760			29	390	470	470	500
70	690	750			28	380	460	460	490
69	670	740			27	380	460	450	480
68	660	720			26	370	450	450	480
67	650	710			25	370	450	440	480
66	640	700			24	360	440	430	470
65	630	690			23	350	430	420	460
64	620	680			22	350	430	410	450
63	610	670			21	340	420	400	440
62	600	670			20	330	410	390	430
61	590	660			19	330	410	390	430
60	590	660	800	800	18	320	400	380	430
59	580	650	780	800	17	310	390	370	420
58	570	640	770	790	16	300	380	360	410
57	570	640	760	770	15	300	380	350	400
56	560	630	750	760	14	290	370	340	390
55	550	620	740	740	13	280	360	340	390
54	550	620	730	730	12	270	350	330	380
53	540	610	710	700	11	270	350	320	370
52	530	600	700	690	10	260	340	310	350
51	530	600	690	680	9	250	330	300	340
50	520	600	670	660	8	250	330	300	340
49	510	590	660	650	7	240	310	290	330
48	510	590	650	650	6	230	300	280	310
47	500	580	640	640	5	220	290	270	300
46	490	570	630	630	4	210	270	270	300
45	490	570	620	620	3	210	270	260	280
44	480	560	610	610	2	200	260	250	260
43	480	560	600	600	1	200	250	250	260
42	470	550	590	600	0	200	240	240	240
41	470	550	580	590	−1	200	230	230	220
40	460	540	570	580	−2	200	220	230	220
39	450	530	560	570	−3	200	210	220	210
38	450	530	550	560	−4	200	200	210	200
37	440	520	550	560	−5 and below	200	200	200	200

CHART FOR SELF-APPRAISAL BASED ON THE PRACTICE TEST YOU HAVE JUST TAKEN

The Self-Appraisal Chart below tells you quickly where your SAT strengths and weaknesses lie. Check or circle the appropriate box in accordance with the number of your correct answers for each area of the Practice Test you have just taken.

	Analogies	*Sentence Completions*	*Reading Comprehension*	*Math Questions**
EXCELLENT	16–19	16–19	34–40	50–60
GOOD	13–15	13–15	29–33	35–49
FAIR	9–12	9–12	20–28	27–34
POOR	5–8	5–8	13–19	16–26
VERY POOR	0–4	0–4	0–12	0–15

* Sections 2, 4, 6 only.

Note: In our tests, we have chosen to have Section 7 as the experimental section. We have also chosen it to be a math section since we felt that students may need more practice in the math area than in the verbal area. Note that on the actual SAT you will take, the order of the sections can vary and you will not know which one is experimental, so it is wise to answer all sections and not to leave any section out.

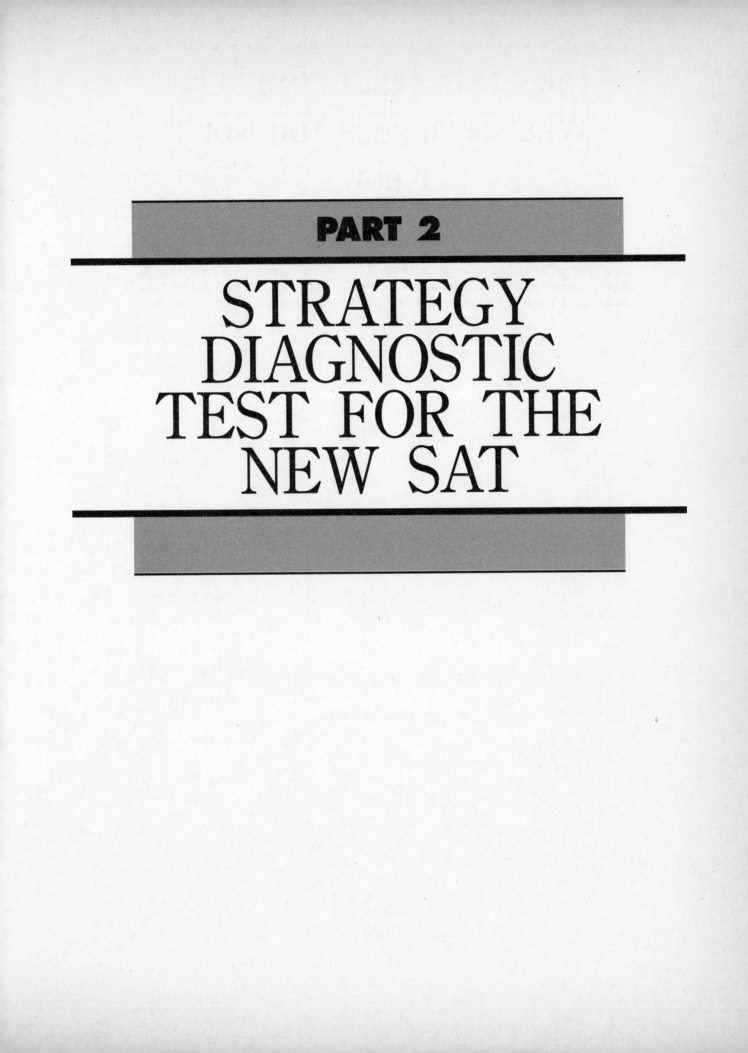

PART 2

STRATEGY DIAGNOSTIC TEST FOR THE NEW SAT

Take This Test to Find Out What Strategies You Don't Know

The purpose of this test is to find out *how* you approach SAT problems of different types and to reveal your understanding and command of the various strategies and Critical Thinking Skills. After checking your answers in the table at the end of the test, you will have a profile of your performance. You will know exactly what strategies you must master and where you may learn them.

Directions for Taking the Diagnostic Test

For each odd-numbered question (1, 3, 5, 7, etc.) choose the best answer. In the even-numbered questions (2, 4, 6, 8, etc.) you will be asked how you solved the preceding odd-numbered question. Make sure that you answer the even-numbered question carefully, as your answer will determine whether or not you used the right strategy. Be completely honest in your answers to the even-numbered questions, since you do want an accurate assessment in order to be helped.

EXAMPLE:

1. The value of $17 \times 98 + 17 \times 2 =$

    (A) 1,550   (B) 1,600   (C) 1,700   (D) 1,800
    (E) 1,850
    (The correct answer is Choice C.)

2. How did you get your answer?

    (A) I multiplied 17×98 and added that to 17×2.
    (B) I approximated and found the closest match in the choices.
    (C) I factored 17 to get $17(98 + 2)$.
    (D) I guessed.
    (E) By none of the above methods.

In question 2:

• If you chose A, you did the problem the long way unless you used a calculator.

• If you chose B, you probably approximated 98 by 100 and got 1,700, which matched choice C.

• If you chose C, you factored out the 17 to get $17(98 + 2) = 17(100) = 1,700$. This was the best strategy to use.

• If you chose D, you probably didn't know how to solve the problem and just guessed.

• If you chose E, you did not use any of the methods above but used your own different method.

Note: In the even-numbered questions, you may have used a different approach from what will be described in the answer to that question. It is, however, a good idea to see if the alternate approach is described, as you may want to use that approach for solving other questions. Now turn to the next page to take the test.

Strategy Diagnostic Test
Answer Sheet

SECTION 1
Verbal Ability

1 Ⓐ Ⓑ Ⓒ Ⓓ Ⓔ	16 Ⓐ Ⓑ Ⓒ Ⓓ Ⓔ	31 Ⓐ Ⓑ Ⓒ Ⓓ Ⓔ	46 Ⓐ Ⓑ Ⓒ Ⓓ Ⓔ	61 Ⓐ Ⓑ Ⓒ Ⓓ Ⓔ
2 Ⓐ Ⓑ Ⓒ Ⓓ Ⓔ	17 Ⓐ Ⓑ Ⓒ Ⓓ Ⓔ	32 Ⓐ Ⓑ Ⓒ Ⓓ Ⓔ	47 Ⓐ Ⓑ Ⓒ Ⓓ Ⓔ	62 Ⓐ Ⓑ Ⓒ Ⓓ Ⓔ
3 Ⓐ Ⓑ Ⓒ Ⓓ Ⓔ	18 Ⓐ Ⓑ Ⓒ Ⓓ Ⓔ	33 Ⓐ Ⓑ Ⓒ Ⓓ Ⓔ	48 Ⓐ Ⓑ Ⓒ Ⓓ Ⓔ	63 Ⓐ Ⓑ Ⓒ Ⓓ Ⓔ
4 Ⓐ Ⓑ Ⓒ Ⓓ Ⓔ	19 Ⓐ Ⓑ Ⓒ Ⓓ Ⓔ	34 Ⓐ Ⓑ Ⓒ Ⓓ Ⓔ	49 Ⓐ Ⓑ Ⓒ Ⓓ Ⓔ	64 Ⓐ Ⓑ Ⓒ Ⓓ Ⓔ
5 Ⓐ Ⓑ Ⓒ Ⓓ Ⓔ	20 Ⓐ Ⓑ Ⓒ Ⓓ Ⓔ	35 Ⓐ Ⓑ Ⓒ Ⓓ Ⓔ	50 Ⓐ Ⓑ Ⓒ Ⓓ Ⓔ	65 Ⓐ Ⓑ Ⓒ Ⓓ Ⓔ
6 Ⓐ Ⓑ Ⓒ Ⓓ Ⓔ	21 Ⓐ Ⓑ Ⓒ Ⓓ Ⓔ	36 Ⓐ Ⓑ Ⓒ Ⓓ Ⓔ	51 Ⓐ Ⓑ Ⓒ Ⓓ Ⓔ	66 Ⓐ Ⓑ Ⓒ Ⓓ Ⓔ
7 Ⓐ Ⓑ Ⓒ Ⓓ Ⓔ	22 Ⓐ Ⓑ Ⓒ Ⓓ Ⓔ	37 Ⓐ Ⓑ Ⓒ Ⓓ Ⓔ	52 Ⓐ Ⓑ Ⓒ Ⓓ Ⓔ	67 Ⓐ Ⓑ Ⓒ Ⓓ Ⓔ
8 Ⓐ Ⓑ Ⓒ Ⓓ Ⓔ	23 Ⓐ Ⓑ Ⓒ Ⓓ Ⓔ	38 Ⓐ Ⓑ Ⓒ Ⓓ Ⓔ	53 Ⓐ Ⓑ Ⓒ Ⓓ Ⓔ	68 Ⓐ Ⓑ Ⓒ Ⓓ Ⓔ
9 Ⓐ Ⓑ Ⓒ Ⓓ Ⓔ	24 Ⓐ Ⓑ Ⓒ Ⓓ Ⓔ	39 Ⓐ Ⓑ Ⓒ Ⓓ Ⓔ	54 Ⓐ Ⓑ Ⓒ Ⓓ Ⓔ	69 Ⓐ Ⓑ Ⓒ Ⓓ Ⓔ
10 Ⓐ Ⓑ Ⓒ Ⓓ Ⓔ	25 Ⓐ Ⓑ Ⓒ Ⓓ Ⓔ	40 Ⓐ Ⓑ Ⓒ Ⓓ Ⓔ	55 Ⓐ Ⓑ Ⓒ Ⓓ Ⓔ	70 Ⓐ Ⓑ Ⓒ Ⓓ Ⓔ
11 Ⓐ Ⓑ Ⓒ Ⓓ Ⓔ	26 Ⓐ Ⓑ Ⓒ Ⓓ Ⓔ	41 Ⓐ Ⓑ Ⓒ Ⓓ Ⓔ	56 Ⓐ Ⓑ Ⓒ Ⓓ Ⓔ	71 Ⓐ Ⓑ Ⓒ Ⓓ Ⓔ
12 Ⓐ Ⓑ Ⓒ Ⓓ Ⓔ	27 Ⓐ Ⓑ Ⓒ Ⓓ Ⓔ	42 Ⓐ Ⓑ Ⓒ Ⓓ Ⓔ	57 Ⓐ Ⓑ Ⓒ Ⓓ Ⓔ	72 Ⓐ Ⓑ Ⓒ Ⓓ Ⓔ
13 Ⓐ Ⓑ Ⓒ Ⓓ Ⓔ	28 Ⓐ Ⓑ Ⓒ Ⓓ Ⓔ	43 Ⓐ Ⓑ Ⓒ Ⓓ Ⓔ	58 Ⓐ Ⓑ Ⓒ Ⓓ Ⓔ	73 Ⓐ Ⓑ Ⓒ Ⓓ Ⓔ
14 Ⓐ Ⓑ Ⓒ Ⓓ Ⓔ	29 Ⓐ Ⓑ Ⓒ Ⓓ Ⓔ	44 Ⓐ Ⓑ Ⓒ Ⓓ Ⓔ	59 Ⓐ Ⓑ Ⓒ Ⓓ Ⓔ	74 Ⓐ Ⓑ Ⓒ Ⓓ Ⓔ
15 Ⓐ Ⓑ Ⓒ Ⓓ Ⓔ	30 Ⓐ Ⓑ Ⓒ Ⓓ Ⓔ	45 Ⓐ Ⓑ Ⓒ Ⓓ Ⓔ	60 Ⓐ Ⓑ Ⓒ Ⓓ Ⓔ	

SECTION 2
Math Ability

1 Ⓐ Ⓑ Ⓒ Ⓓ Ⓔ	14 Ⓐ Ⓑ Ⓒ Ⓓ Ⓔ	27 Ⓐ Ⓑ Ⓒ Ⓓ Ⓔ	39 Ⓐ Ⓑ Ⓒ Ⓓ Ⓔ	51 Ⓐ Ⓑ Ⓒ Ⓓ Ⓔ
2 Ⓐ Ⓑ Ⓒ Ⓓ Ⓔ	15 Ⓐ Ⓑ Ⓒ Ⓓ Ⓔ	28 Ⓐ Ⓑ Ⓒ Ⓓ Ⓔ	40 Ⓐ Ⓑ Ⓒ Ⓓ Ⓔ	52 Ⓐ Ⓑ Ⓒ Ⓓ Ⓔ
3 Ⓐ Ⓑ Ⓒ Ⓓ Ⓔ	16 Ⓐ Ⓑ Ⓒ Ⓓ Ⓔ	29 Ⓐ Ⓑ Ⓒ Ⓓ Ⓔ	41 Ⓐ Ⓑ Ⓒ Ⓓ Ⓔ	53 Ⓐ Ⓑ Ⓒ Ⓓ Ⓔ
4 Ⓐ Ⓑ Ⓒ Ⓓ Ⓔ	17 Ⓐ Ⓑ Ⓒ Ⓓ Ⓔ	30 Ⓐ Ⓑ Ⓒ Ⓓ Ⓔ	42 Ⓐ Ⓑ Ⓒ Ⓓ Ⓔ	54 Ⓐ Ⓑ Ⓒ Ⓓ Ⓔ
5 Ⓐ Ⓑ Ⓒ Ⓓ Ⓔ	18 Ⓐ Ⓑ Ⓒ Ⓓ Ⓔ	31 Ⓐ Ⓑ Ⓒ Ⓓ Ⓔ	43 Ⓐ Ⓑ Ⓒ Ⓓ Ⓔ	55 Ⓐ Ⓑ Ⓒ Ⓓ Ⓔ
6 Ⓐ Ⓑ Ⓒ Ⓓ Ⓔ	19 Ⓐ Ⓑ Ⓒ Ⓓ Ⓔ	32 Ⓐ Ⓑ Ⓒ Ⓓ Ⓔ	44 Ⓐ Ⓑ Ⓒ Ⓓ Ⓔ	56 Ⓐ Ⓑ Ⓒ Ⓓ Ⓔ
7 Ⓐ Ⓑ Ⓒ Ⓓ Ⓔ	20 Ⓐ Ⓑ Ⓒ Ⓓ Ⓔ	33 Ⓐ Ⓑ Ⓒ Ⓓ Ⓔ	45 Ⓐ Ⓑ Ⓒ Ⓓ Ⓔ	57 Ⓐ Ⓑ Ⓒ Ⓓ Ⓔ
8 Ⓐ Ⓑ Ⓒ Ⓓ Ⓔ	21 Ⓐ Ⓑ Ⓒ Ⓓ Ⓔ	34 Ⓐ Ⓑ Ⓒ Ⓓ Ⓔ	46 Ⓐ Ⓑ Ⓒ Ⓓ Ⓔ	58 Ⓐ Ⓑ Ⓒ Ⓓ Ⓔ
9 Ⓐ Ⓑ Ⓒ Ⓓ Ⓔ	22 Ⓐ Ⓑ Ⓒ Ⓓ Ⓔ	35 Ⓐ Ⓑ Ⓒ Ⓓ Ⓔ	47 Ⓐ Ⓑ Ⓒ Ⓓ Ⓔ	59 Ⓐ Ⓑ Ⓒ Ⓓ Ⓔ
10 Ⓐ Ⓑ Ⓒ Ⓓ Ⓔ	23 Ⓐ Ⓑ Ⓒ Ⓓ Ⓔ	36 Ⓐ Ⓑ Ⓒ Ⓓ Ⓔ	48 Ⓐ Ⓑ Ⓒ Ⓓ Ⓔ	60 Ⓐ Ⓑ Ⓒ Ⓓ Ⓔ
11 Ⓐ Ⓑ Ⓒ Ⓓ Ⓔ	24 Ⓐ Ⓑ Ⓒ Ⓓ Ⓔ	37 Ⓐ Ⓑ Ⓒ Ⓓ Ⓔ	49 Ⓐ Ⓑ Ⓒ Ⓓ Ⓔ	61 Ⓐ Ⓑ Ⓒ Ⓓ Ⓔ
12 Ⓐ Ⓑ Ⓒ Ⓓ Ⓔ	25 Ⓐ Ⓑ Ⓒ Ⓓ Ⓔ	38 Ⓐ Ⓑ Ⓒ Ⓓ Ⓔ	50 Ⓐ Ⓑ Ⓒ Ⓓ Ⓔ	62 Ⓐ Ⓑ Ⓒ Ⓓ Ⓔ
13 Ⓐ Ⓑ Ⓒ Ⓓ Ⓔ	26 Ⓐ Ⓑ Ⓒ Ⓓ Ⓔ			

Section 1: Verbal Ability

For each question in this section, choose the best answer and blacken the corresponding space on the answer sheet.

Each of the following questions consists of a related pair of words or phrases, followed by five lettered pairs of words or phrases. Select the lettered pair that *best* expresses a relationship similar to that expressed in the original pair.

EXAMPLE:

> YAWN : BOREDOM :: (A) dream : sleep
> (B) anger : madness (C) smile : amusement
> (D) face : expression (E) impatience : rebellion
>
> Ⓐ Ⓑ ● Ⓓ Ⓔ

1. THIEF : ROBBERY ::

   (A) burglar : diamonds
   (B) jail : crime
   (C) kidnapper : hostage
   (D) criminal : capture
   (E) counterfeiter : forgery

2. How did you get your answer?

   (A) I said that the first word in the choice is associated with THIEF and the second word in the choice is associated with ROBBERY.
   (B) I put the analogy into the form of a sentence. I said that THIEF commits a ROBBERY. Then I looked for a choice whose words fit the same sentence form.
   (C) I looked for the choice whose words were the most difficult to define, thinking that the test-maker would try to make the most difficult choice the correct one.
   (D) I guessed.
   (E) None of these.

3. MOTH : CLOTHING ::

   (A) sheep : wool
   (B) butterfly : wood
   (C) puncture : tire
   (D) tear : sweater
   (E) termite : house

4. How did you get your answer?

   (A) I thought that MOTH was associated with the first word in the correct choice and/or CLOTHING was associated with the second word in the choice.
   (B) I said that MOTH does something to CLOTHING and found that the same sentence relationship fit one of the choices, realizing that MOTH is a *living thing*.
   (C) I said that MOTH does something to CLOTHING and found that the same sentence relationship fit one of the choices but did *not* take into account that MOTH is a *living thing*.
   (D) I guessed.
   (E) None of these.

5. FARE : PASSENGER : :

(A) magazine : subscriber
(B) parking : ticket
(C) tuition : student
(D) bond : premium
(E) usury : interest

6. How did you get your answer?

(A) I put the analogy into the form of a sentence and then figured out which choice fit the same sentence form.
(B) I thought FARE and PASSENGER related to words or some choice dealing with subscribers or transportation.
(C) I related FARE to the first word in the choice and PASSENGER to the second word in the choice.
(D) I guessed.
(E) None of these.

7. BUILDING : CHURCH : :

(A) dance : ballet
(B) poetry : sonnet
(C) museum : relics
(D) song : hymn
(E) morality : ethics

8. How did you get your answer?

(A) I put the CAPITALIZED words in a sentence, then used the same sentence form with the choices.
(B) I associated the first CAPITALIZED word with the first word in the choice.
(C) I associated the second CAPITALIZED word with the second word in the choice.
(D) I did not know the relationship of the CAPITALIZED words but figured out what the analogy was from looking at the choices.
(E) I did not use any of the above methods.

9. SEQUESTER : ISOLATION : :

(A) debase : degradation
(B) stunt : growth
(C) vaccinate : disease
(D) warm : boil
(E) study : text

10. How did you get your answer?

(A) I did not know what one of the CAPITALIZED words meant but figured out the correct answer through the choices.
(B) I knew what the word SEQUESTER meant, and I put the words into a sentence.
(C) I tried to associate SEQUESTER with the first word in the choices and to associate ISOLATION with the second word in the choices.
(D) I guessed.
(E) None of these.

11. HAMLET : VILLAGE : :

(A) street : sidewalk
(B) highway : car
(C) building : skyscraper
(D) photograph : portrait
(E) cottage : house

12. How did you get your answer?

(A) I did not know what one of the CAPITALIZED words meant but figured out the correct answer through the choices.
(B) I knew what the word VILLAGE meant and I put the words into a sentence.
(C) I tried to associate HAMLET with the first word in the choices and to associate VILLAGE with the second word in the choices.
(D) I guessed.
(E) None of these.

13. HELMET : HEAD : :

(A) sword : warrior
(B) umbrella : clothing
(C) shoe : stocking
(D) watch : wrist
(E) thimble : finger

14. How did you get your answer?

(A) I said a HELMET was worn on the head and looked for a choice that showed something worn on a part of the body.
(B) I associated HELMET with the first word in the choices and HEAD with the second word in the choices.
(C) I put the CAPITALIZED words in a relationship in a sentence but noticed that HELMET was used to *protect* the HEAD.
(D) I guessed.
(E) None of these.

15. COLLAGE : ARTIST : :

    (A) opera : musician
    (B) novel : author
    (C) decision : umpire
    (D) interest : spectator
    (E) graduation : student

16. How did you get your answer?

    (A) I did not know what one of the CAPITALIZED words meant but figured out the correct answer through the choices.
    (B) I knew what the word COLLAGE meant and put the words into a sentence.
    (C) I tried to associated COLLAGE with the first word in the choices and to associate ARTIST with the second word in the choices.
    (D) I guessed.
    (E) None of these.

17. CHARLATAN : DECEIT : :

    (A) magician : trickery
    (B) dancer : ballet
    (C) customer : bargain
    (D) playwright : ticket
    (E) chemist : laboratory

18. How did you get your answer?

    (A) I did not know what one of the CAPITALIZED words meant but figured out the correct answer through the choices.
    (B) I knew what the word CHARLATAN meant and put the words into a sentence.
    (C) I tried to associate CHARLATAN with the first word in the choices and to associate DECEIT with the second word in the choices.
    (D) I guessed.
    (E) None of these.

Each of the following sentences has one or two blanks, each blank indicating that something has been omitted. Beneath the sentence are five lettered words or sets of words. Choose the word or set of words that *best* fits the meaning of the sentence as a whole.

EXAMPLE:

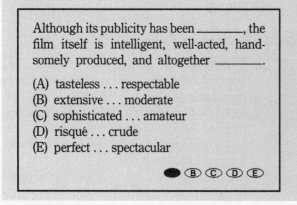

Although its publicity has been _____, the film itself is intelligent, well-acted, handsomely produced, and altogether _____.

(A) tasteless ... respectable
(B) extensive ... moderate
(C) sophisticated ... amateur
(D) risqué ... crude
(E) perfect ... spectacular

19. He believed that while there is serious unemployment in our auto industry, we should not _____ foreign cars.

    (A) build
    (B) repair
    (C) review
    (D) import
    (E) consolidate

20. How did you get your answer?

    (A) I tried the word from each choice in the blank and came up with the best answer.
    (B) I chose a word from the choices that "sounded good" but that I am really not sure is correct.
    (C) I tried to figure out, *before* looking at the choices, what word would fit into the blank. Then I matched that word with the choices.
    (D) I guessed.
    (E) None of these.

21. The salesmen in that clothing store are so _____ that it is impossible to even look at a garment without being _____ by their efforts to convince you to purchase.

    (A) offensive . . . considerate
    (B) persistent . . . irritated
    (C) extensive . . . induced
    (D) immune . . . aided
    (E) intriguing . . . evaluated

22. How did you get your answer?

    (A) I tried each choice (two words at a time) in the blanks to see which made for the best sentence.
    (B) I tried to see what words I could come up with for the blanks *before* looking at the choices.
    (C) I tried the first word from each of the choices in the first blank in the sentence to see which made the most sense. Then I eliminated the choices whose first words didn't make sense in the sentence. Finally, I tried both words in the remaining choices to further eliminate incorrect choices.
    (D) I guessed.
    (E) None of these.

23. Many buildings with historical significance are now being _____ instead of being torn down.

    (A) built
    (B) forgotten
    (C) destroyed
    (D) praised
    (E) repaired

24. How did you get your answer?

    (A) I tried each of the choices in the blank.
    (B) I tried to find my own word that would fit the blank *before* looking at the choices. Then I matched one of the choices with my word.
    (C) I looked for a word that meant the opposite of "being torn down."
    (D) I guessed.
    (E) None of these.

25. Being _____ person, he insisted at the conference that when he spoke he was not to be interrupted.

    (A) a successful
    (B) a delightful
    (C) a headstrong
    (D) an understanding
    (E) a solitary

26. How did you get your answer?

    (A) I tried all the choices in the sentence and selected the best one.
    (B) I realized, from the word *Being* and from the phrase after the comma, that there was a connection between the two parts of the sentence.
    (C) I looked for the most difficult-sounding word.
    (D) I guessed.
    (E) None of these.

27. In spite of the _____ of her presentation, many people were _____ with the speaker's concepts and ideas.

    (A) interest . . . enthralled
    (B) power . . . taken
    (C) intensity . . . shocked
    (D) greatness . . . gratified
    (E) strength . . . bored

28. How did you get your answer?

    (A) I tried both words from each choice in the blanks to see which choice made the sentence sound best.
    (B) I tried the first word from each choice in the first blank of the sentence to eliminate choices. Then I tried both words from the remaining choices to further eliminate choices.
    (C) I realized that the words *in spite of* would create an opposition or contrast between the two parts of the sentence and therefore looked for words in the choices that were opposites.
    (D) I guessed.
    (E) None of these.

29. Richard Wagner was frequently intolerant; moreover, his strange behavior caused most of his acquaintances to _____ the composer whenever possible.

    (A) contradict
    (B) interrogate
    (C) shun
    (D) revere
    (E) tolerate

30. How did you get your answer?

    (A) I tried all the choices in the blank and selected the best one.
    (B) I realized that the word *moreover* indicated support so I looked for a choice that would represent a *support* of what was in the first part of the sentence.
    (C) I tried to find my own word to fit the blank. Then I matched that word with a word in one of the choices.
    (D) I guessed.
    (E) None of these.

Each of the following questions consists of a word in capital letters, followed by five lettered words or phrases. Choose the word or phrase that is most nearly *opposite* in meaning to the word in capital letters. Since some of the questions require you to distinguish fine shades of meaning, consider all the choices before deciding which is best.

EXAMPLE:

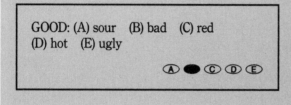

GOOD: (A) sour   (B) bad   (C) red
(D) hot   (E) ugly

Note: Although Antonyms is no longer a part of the new SAT, we are still testing vocabulary through antonyms on this particular test, since it is still important for you to develop vocabulary strategies for the Analogies, Sentence Completions, and Reading Comprehension parts of the new SAT.

31. TENACIOUS:

    (A) changing
    (B) stupid
    (C) unconscious
    (D) poor
    (E) antagonistic

32. How did you get your answer?

    (A) I knew the meaning of the word TENACIOUS.
    (B) I knew what the root TEN meant and looked for the opposite of that root.
    (C) I did not know what TENACIOUS meant but knew a word that sounded like TENACIOUS.
    (D) I guessed.
    (E) None of these.

33. PROFICIENT:

    (A) antiseptic
    (B) unwilling
    (C) inconsiderate
    (D) retarded
    (E) awkward

34. How did you get your answer?

    (A) I knew what the prefix PRO meant and used it to figure out the capitalized word, but I didn't use any root of PROFICIENT.
    (B) I used the meaning of the prefix PRO and the meaning of the root FIC to figure out the meaning of the word PROFICIENT.
    (C) I knew from memory what the word PROFICIENT meant.
    (D) I guessed.
    (E) None of these.

35. DELUDE:

    (A) include
    (B) guide
    (C) reply
    (D) upgrade
    (E) welcome

36. How did you get your answer?

    (A) I knew what the prefix DE meant and used it to figure out the meaning of the word DELUDE, but I didn't use any root of DELUDE.
    (B) I used the meaning of the prefix DE and the meaning of the root LUD to figure out the meaning of the word DELUDE.
    (C) I knew from memory what the word DELUDE meant.
    (D) I guessed.
    (E) None of these.

37. POTENT:
    (A) imposing
    (B) pertinent
    (C) feeble
    (D) comparable
    (E) frantic

38. How did you get your answer?

    (A) I knew what the CAPITALIZED word meant.
    (B) I knew a word or part of a word that sounded the same as POTENT or had a close association with the word POTENT.
    (C) I knew a prefix or root of the CAPITALIZED word, which gave me a clue to the meaning of the word.
    (D) I knew from a part of the CAPITALIZED word that the word had a negative or positive association. Thus, I selected a choice that was opposite in flavor (positive or negative).
    (E) None of these.

39. RECEDE:
    (A) accede
    (B) settle
    (C) surrender
    (D) advance
    (E) reform

40. How did you get your answer?

    (A) I found a word opposite in meaning to the word RECEDE, *without* looking at the choices. Then I matched my word with the choices.
    (B) I used prefixes and/or roots to get the meaning of the word RECEDE.
    (C) I looked at the choices to see which word was opposite to RECEDE. I *did not* try first to get my own word that was opposite to the meaning of RECEDE, as in Choice A.
    (D) I guessed.
    (E) None of these.

41. THERMAL:
    (A) improving
    (B) possible
    (C) beginning
    (D) reduced
    (E) frigid

42. How did you get your answer?

    (A) I knew what the CAPITALIZED word meant.
    (B) I knew a word or part of a word that sounded the same as THERMAL or had a close association with the word THERMAL.
    (C) I knew a prefix or root of the CAPITALIZED word, which gave me a clue to the meaning of the word.
    (D) I knew from a part of the CAPITALIZED word that the word had a negative or positive association. Thus, I selected a choice that was opposite in flavor (positive or negative).
    (E) None of these.

43. SLOTHFUL:
    (A) permanent
    (B) ambitious
    (C) average
    (D) truthful
    (E) plentiful

44. How did you get your answer?

    (A) I knew what the CAPITALIZED word meant.
    (B) I knew a word or part of a word that sounded the same as SLOTH or had a close association with the word SLOTH.
    (C) I knew a prefix or root of the CAPITALIZED word, which gave me a clue to the meaning of the word.
    (D) I knew from a part of the CAPITALIZED word that the word had a negative or positive association. Thus, I selected a choice that was opposite in flavor (positive or negative).
    (E) None of these.

45. MUNIFICENCE:

(A) disloyalty
(B) stinginess
(C) dispersion
(D) simplicity
(E) vehemence

46. How did you get your answer?

(A) I knew what the CAPITALIZED word meant.
(B) I knew a word or part of a word that sounded the same as MUNIFICENCE or had a close association with the word MUNIFICENCE.
(C) I knew a prefix or root of the CAPITALIZED word, which gave me a clue to the meaning of the word.
(D) I knew from a part of the CAPITALIZED word that the word had a negative or positive association. Thus, I selected a choice that was opposite in flavor (positive or negative).
(E) None of these.

47. FORTITUDE:

(A) timidity
(B) conservatism
(C) placidity
(D) laxness
(E) ambition

48. How did you get your answer?

(A) I knew what the CAPITALIZED word meant.
(B) I knew a word or part of a word that sounded the same as FORTITUDE or had a close association with the word FORTITUDE.
(C) I knew a prefix or root of the CAPITALIZED word, which gave me a clue to the meaning of the word.
(D) I knew from a part of the CAPITALIZED word that the word had a negative or positive association. Thus, I selected a choice that was opposite in flavor (positive or negative).
(E) None of these.

49. DETRIMENT:

(A) recurrence
(B) disclosure
(C) resemblance
(D) enhancement
(E) postponement

50. How did you get your answer?

(A) I knew what the CAPITALIZED word meant.
(B) I knew a word or part of a word that sounded the same as DETRIMENT or had a close association with the word DETRIMENT.
(C) I knew a prefix or root of the CAPITALIZED word, which gave me a clue to the meaning of the word.
(D) I knew from a part of the CAPITALIZED word that the word had a negative or positive association. Thus, I selected a choice that was opposite in flavor (positive or negative).
(E) None of these.

51. CIRCUMSPECT:

(A) suspicious
(B) overbearing
(C) listless
(D) determined
(E) careless

52. How did you get your answer?

(A) I knew what the CAPITALIZED word meant.
(B) I knew a word or part of a word that sounded the same as CIRCUMSPECT or had a close association with the word CIRCUMSPECT.
(C) I knew a prefix or root of the CAPITALIZED word, which gave me a clue to the meaning of the word.
(D) I knew from a part of the CAPITALIZED word that the word had a negative or positive association. Thus, I selected a choice that was opposite in flavor (positive or negative).
(E) None of these.

53. LUCID:

(A) underlying
(B) complex
(C) luxurious
(D) tight
(E) general

54. How did you get your answer?

(A) I knew what the CAPITALIZED word meant.
(B) I knew a word or part of a word that sounded the same as LUCID or had a close association with the word LUCID.
(C) I knew a prefix or root of the CAPITALIZED word, which gave me a clue to the meaning of the word.
(D) I knew from a part of the CAPITALIZED word that the word had a negative or positive association. Thus, I selected a choice that was opposite in flavor (positive or negative).
(E) None of these.

Each of the following passages is followed by questions based on its content. Answer all questions following a passage on the basis of what is *stated* or *implied* in that passage.

She walked along the river until a policeman stopped her. It was one o'clock, he said. Not the best time to be walking alone by the side of a half-frozen river. He smiled at her, then offered to walk her home. It was the first day of the new year,
5 1946, eight and a half months after the British tanks had rumbled into Bergen-Belsen.

That February, my mother turned twenty-six. It was difficult for strangers to believe that she had ever been a concentration camp inmate. Her face was smooth and round.
10 She wore lipstick and applied mascara to her large dark eyes. She dressed fashionably. But when she looked into the mirror in the mornings before leaving for work, my mother saw a shell, a mannequin who moved and spoke but who bore only a superficial resemblance to her real self. The people
15 closest to her had vanished. She had no proof that they were truly dead. No eyewitnesses had survived to vouch for her husband's death. There was no one living who had seen her parents die. The lack of confirmation haunted her. At night before she went to sleep and during the day as she stood
20 pinning dresses she wondered if, by some chance, her parents had gotten past the Germans or had crawled out of the mass grave into which they had been shot and were living, old and helpless, somewhere in Poland. What if only one of them had died? What if they had survived and had died of
25 cold or hunger after she had been liberated, while she was in Celle* dancing with British officers?

She did not talk to anyone about these things. No one, she thought, wanted to hear them. She woke up in the morning, went to work, bought groceries, went to the Jewish
30 Community Center and to the housing office like a robot.

* Celle is a small town in Germany.

55. The policeman stopped the author's mother from walking along the river because

(A) the river was dangerous
(B) it was the wrong time of day
(C) it was still wartime
(D) it was too cold
(E) she looked suspicious

56. Which part of the passage gives you the best clue for getting the right answer?

(A) Lines 1–2: "It was one o'clock, he said."
(B) Lines 1–3: "It was one o'clock, he said. Not the best time to be walking alone."
(C) Lines 1–4: "It was one o'clock, he said. Not the best time to be walking alone by the side of a half-frozen river."
(D) None of these.
(E) I don't know.

57. The author states that his mother thought about her parents when she

(A) walked along the river
(B) thought about death
(C) danced with the officers
(D) arose in the morning
(E) was at work

58. Which part of the passage gives you the best clue for getting the right answer?

(A) Lines 18–19: "At night before she went to sleep . . ."
(B) Lines 19–20: ". . . and during the day as she stood pinning dresses she wondered . . ."
(C) Lines 11–12: "But when she looked into the mirror in the mornings . . ."
(D) Lines 24–26: "What if they had survived and died of cold . . . while she was . . . dancing with British officers?"
(E) I don't know.

59. When the author mentions his mother's dancing with the British officers, he implies that his mother

(A) compared her dancing to the suffering of her parents
(B) had clearly put her troubles behind her
(C) felt it was her duty to dance with them
(D) felt guilty about dancing
(E) regained the self-confidence she once had

60. Which words expressed in the passage lead us to the right answer?

(A) Line 24: "had survived"
(B) Lines 24–25: "had died of cold or hunger"
(C) Line 21: "gotten past the Germans"
(D) Line 30: "like a robot"
(E) I don't know.

That one citizen is as good as another is a favorite American axiom, supposed to express the very essence of our Constitution and way of life. But just what do we mean when we utter that platitude? One surgeon is not as good as another.
5 One plumber is not as good as another. We soon become aware of this when we require the attention of either. Yet in political and economic matters we appear to have reached a point where knowledge and specialized training count for very little. A newspaper reporter is sent out on the street to
10 collect the views of various passers-by on such a question as "Should the United States defend El Salvador?" The answer

of the barfly who doesn't even know where the country is located, or that it is a country, is quoted in the next edition just as solemnly as that of the college teacher of history.
15 With the basic tenets of democracy—that all men are born free and equal and are entitled to life, liberty, and the pursuit of happiness—no decent American can possibly take issue. But that the opinion of one citizen on a technical subject is just as authoritative as that of another is manifestly absurd.
20 And to accept the opinions of all comers as having the same value is surely to encourage a cult of mediocrity.

61. Which phrase best expresses the main idea of this passage?

    (A) the myth of equality
    (B) a distinction about equality
    (C) the essence of the Constitution
    (D) a technical subject
    (E) knowledge and specialized training

62. Which is the best title for this passage?

    (A) "Equality—for Everyone, for Every Situation?"
    (B) "Dangers of Opinion and Knowledge"
    (C) "The American Syndrome"
    (D) "Freedom and Equality"
    (E) I don't know.

63. The author most probably included the example of the question on El Salvador (line 11) in order to

    (A) move the reader to rage
    (B) show that he is opposed to opinion sampling
    (C) show that he has thoroughly researched his project
    (D) explain the kind of opinion sampling he objects to
    (E) provide a humorous but temporary diversion from his main point

64. The distinction between a "barfly" and a college teacher (lines 12–14) is that

    (A) one is stupid, the other is not
    (B) one is learned, the other is not
    (C) one is anti-American, the other is not
    (D) one is pro–El Salvadoran, the other is not
    (E) I don't know.

65. The author would be most likely to agree that

    (A) some men are born to be masters; others are born to be servants
    (B) the Constitution has little relevance for today's world
    (C) one should never express an opinion on a specialized subject unless he is an expert in that subject
    (D) every opinion should be treated equally
    (E) all opinions should not be given equal weight

66. Which lines give the best clue to the answer to this question?

    (A) Lines 3–5
    (B) Lines 4–6
    (C) Lines 14–17
    (D) Lines 18–22
    (E) I don't know.

Mist continues to obscure the horizon, but above us the sky is suddenly awash with lavender light. At once the geese respond. Now, as well as their cries, a beating roar rolls across the water as if five thousand housewives have taken it
5 into their heads to shake out blankets all at one time. Ten thousand housewives. It keeps up—the invisible rhythmic beating of all those goose wings—for what seems a long time. Even Lonnie is held motionless with suspense.
    Then the geese begin to rise. One, two, three hundred—
10 then a thousand at a time—in long horizontal lines that unfurl like pennants across the sky. The horizon actually darkens as they pass. It goes on and on like that, flock after flock, for three or four minutes, each new contingent announcing its ascent with an accelerating roar of cries and
15 wingbeats. Then gradually the intervals between flights become longer. I think the spectacle is over, until yet another flock lifts up, following the others in a gradual turn toward the northeastern quadrant of the refuge.
    Finally the sun emerges from the mist; the mist itself
20 thins a little, uncovering the black line of willows on the other side of the wildlife preserve. I remember to close my mouth—which has been open for some time—and inadvertently shut two or three mosquitoes inside. Only a few straggling geese oar their way across the sun's red surface.
25 Lonnie wears an exasperated, proprietary expression, as if he had produced and directed the show himself and had just received a bad review. "It would have been better with more light," he says; "I can't always guarantee just when they'll start moving." I assure him I thought it was a fantastic sight.
30 "Well," he rumbles, "I guess it wasn't too bad."

67. In the descriptive phrase "shake out blankets all at one time" (line 5), the author is appealing chiefly to the reader's

    (A) background
    (B) sight
    (C) emotions
    (D) thoughts
    (E) hearing

68. Which words preceding the above "descriptive phrase" in the passage give us a clue to the correct answer?

    (A) "into their heads"
    (B) "lavender light"
    (C) "across the water"
    (D) "a beating roar"
    (E) I don't know.

69. The mood created by the author is one of

    (A) tranquility
    (B) excitement
    (C) sadness
    (D) bewilderment
    (E) unconcern

70. Which word in the passage is most closely associated with the correct answer?

    (A) mist
    (B) spectacle
    (C) geese
    (D) refuge
    (E) I don't know.

71. The main idea expressed by the author about the geese is that they

    (A) are spectacular to watch
    (B) are unpredictable
    (C) disturb the environment
    (D) produce a lot of noise
    (E) fly in large flocks

72. Which line(s) gives us a clue to the correct answer?

    (A) Line 1
    (B) Lines 16–17
    (C) Line 19
    (D) Line 30
    (E) I don't know.

73. Judging from the passage, the reader can conclude that

    (A) the speaker dislikes nature's inconveniences
    (B) the geese's timing is predictable
    (C) Lonnie has had the experience before
    (D) both observers are hunters
    (E) the author and Lonnie are the same person

74. Which gives us a clue to the right answer?

    (A) Lines 9–10
    (B) Line 19
    (C) Lines 21–22
    (D) Lines 28–29
    (E) I don't know.

Section 2: Math Ability

In this section solve each problem, using any available space on the page for scratchwork. Then decide which is the best of the choices given and blacken the corresponding space on the answer sheet.
The following information is for your reference in solving some of the problems.

Circle of radius r. Area $= \pi r^2$; Circumference $= 2\pi r$
The number of degrees of arc in a circle is 360.
The measure in degrees of a straight angle is 180.

Definitions of symbols:

$=$ is equal to	$\leqq$ is less than or equal to
$\neq$ is unequal to	$\geqq$ is greater than or equal to
$<$ is less than	$\parallel$ is parallel to
$>$ is greater than	$\perp$ is perpendicular to

Triangle: The sum of the measures in degrees of the angles of a triangle is 180.

If $\angle CDA$ is a right angle, then

(1) area of $\triangle ABC = \dfrac{AB \times CD}{2}$

(2) $AC^2 = AD^2 + DC^2$

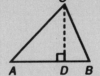

NOTE: Figures that accompany problems in this test are intended to provide information useful in solving the problems. They are drawn as accurately as possible EXCEPT when it is stated in a specific problem that its figure is not drawn to scale. All figures lie in a plane unless otherwise indicated. All numbers used are real numbers.

1. If $P \times \dfrac{11}{14} = \dfrac{11}{14} \times \dfrac{8}{9}$, then $P =$
    (A) $\dfrac{8}{9}$
    (B) $\dfrac{9}{8}$
    (C) 11
    (D) 14
    (E) 8

2. How did you get your answer?
    (A) I multiplied $\dfrac{11}{14}$ by $\dfrac{8}{9}$, *reducing first.*
    (B) I multiplied 11×8 and then divided the product by 14×9.
    (C) I cancelled $\dfrac{11}{14}$ from both sides of the equal sign.
    (D) I guessed.
    (E) None of these.

3. Sarah is twice as old as John. Six years ago, Sarah was 4 times as old as John was then. How old is John now?

   (A) 3
   (B) 18
   (C) 20
   (D) 9
   (E) Cannot be determined.

4. How did you get your answer?

   (A) I substituted *S* for *Sarah*, = for *is*, and *J* for *John* in the first sentence of the problem. Then I translated the second sentence into mathematical terms also.
   (B) I tried specific numbers for *Sarah* and/or *John*.
   (C) I racked my brains to figure out the ages but didn't write any equations down.
   (D) I guessed.
   (E) None of these.

5. 200 is what percent of 20?

   (A) ¹⁄₁₀
   (B) 10
   (C) 100
   (D) 1,000
   (E) 10,000

6. How did you get your answer?

   (A) I translated *is* to =, *what* to a variable, *of* to ×, etc. Then I was able to set up an equation.
   (B) I just divided the two numbers and multiplied by 100 to get the percent.
   (C) I tried to remember how to work with *is-of* problems, putting the *of* over *is* or the *is* over *of*.
   (D) I guessed.
   (E) None of these.

7. In this diagram, $\triangle XYZ$ has been inscribed in a circle. If the circle encloses an area of 64, and the area of $\triangle XYZ$ is 15, then what is the area of the shaded region?

   (A) 25
   (B) 36
   (C) 49
   (D) 79
   (E) Cannot be determined.

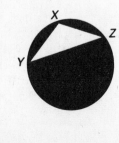

8. How did you get your answer?

   (A) I tried to calculate the area of the circle and the area of the triangle.
   (B) I used a special triangle or tried different triangles whose area was 15.
   (C) I subtracted 15 from 64.
   (D) I guessed.
   (E) None of these.

9. $66^2 + 2(34)(66) + 34^2 =$

   (A) 9,950
   (B) 9,860
   (C) 10,000
   (D) 4,730
   (E) 5,000

10. How did you get your answer?

    (A) I multiplied 66×66, $2 \times 34 \times 66$, and 34×34.
    (B) I approximated a solution.
    (C) I noticed that $66^2 + 2(34)(66) + 34^2$ had the form of $a^2 + 2ab + b^2$ and set the form equal to $(a + b)^2$.
    (D) I guessed.
    (E) None of these.

11. The average height of three students is 68 inches. If two of the students have heights of 70 inches and 72 inches respectively, then what is the height (in inches) of the third student?

    (A) 60
    (B) 62
    (C) 64
    (D) 65
    (E) 66

12. How did you get your answer?

    (A) I used the following equation:

    $$(68 + 2) + (68 + 4) + x = 68 + 68 + 68$$

    Then I got:
    $68 + 68 + (x + 6) = 68 + 68 + 68$, and crossed off the two 68's on both sides of the equation to come up with $x + 6 = 68$.
    (B) I was able to eliminate the incorrect choices without figuring out a complete solution.
    (C) I got the equation $\dfrac{(70 + 72 + x)}{3} = 68$, then solved for *x*.
    (D) I guessed.
    (E) None of these.

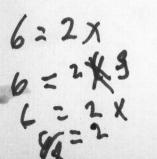

13. If $0 < x < 1$, then which of the following must be true?

    (A) I only
    (B) II only
    (C) I and II only
    (D) II and III only
    (E) I, II, and III

    I. $2x < 2$

    II. $x - 1 < 0$

    III. $x^2 < x$

14. How did you get your answer?

    (A) I plugged in only one number for x in I, II, and III.
    (B) I plugged in more than one number for x and tried I, II, and III using each set of numbers.
    (C) I used the fact that $0 < x$ and $x < 1$ and manipulated those inequalities in I, II, and III.
    (D) I guessed.
    (E) None of these.

15. The sum of the cubes of any two consecutive positive integers is always

    (A) an odd integer
    (B) an even integer
    (C) the cube of an integer
    (D) the square of an integer
    (E) the product of an integer and 3

16. How did you get your answer?

    (A) I translated the statement into the form $x^3 + (x + 1)^3 = $ _____ and tried to see what I would get.
    (B) I tried numbers like 1 and 2 for the consecutive integers. Then I calculated the sum of the cubes of those numbers. I was able to eliminate some choices and then tried some other numbers for the consecutive integers to eliminate more choices.
    (C) I said, of two consecutive positive integers, one is even and therefore its cube is even. The other integer is odd, therefore its cube is odd. An odd + an even is an odd.
    (D) I guessed.
    (E) None of these.

17. If p is a positive integer, which *could* be an odd integer?

    (A) $2p + 2$
    (B) $p^3 - p$
    (C) $p^2 + p$
    (D) $p^2 - p$
    (E) $7p - 3$

18. How did you get your answer?

    (A) I plugged in a number or numbers for p and started testing all the choices, *starting with Choice A*.
    (B) I plugged in a number or numbers for p in each of the choices, *starting with Choice E*.
    (C) I looked at Choice E first to see if $7p - 3$ had the form of an even or odd integer.
    (D) I guessed.
    (E) None of these.

19. In this figure, two points, B and C, are placed to the right of point A such that $4AB = 3AC$. The value of BC/AB

    (A) equals $\dfrac{1}{3}$
    (B) equals $\dfrac{2}{3}$
    (C) equals $\dfrac{3}{2}$
    (D) equals 3
    (E) cannot be determined

    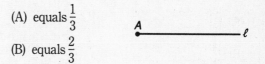

20. How did you get your answer?

    (A) I drew points B and C on the line and labeled AB as a and BC as b and then worked with a and b.
    (B) I substituted numbers for AB and AC.
    (C) I drew points B and C on the line and worked with equations involving BC and AB.
    (D) I guessed.
    (E) None of these.

21. A man rode a bicycle a straight distance at a speed of 10 miles per hour. He came back the same way, traveling the same distance at a speed of 20 miles per hour. What was the man's total number of miles for the trip back and forth if his total traveling time was one hour?

    (A) 15
    (B) $7\dfrac{1}{2}$
    (C) $6\dfrac{1}{3}$
    (D) $6\dfrac{2}{3}$
    (E) $13\dfrac{1}{3}$

22. How did you answer this question?

    (A) I used Rate × Time = Distance and plugged in my own numbers.
    (B) I averaged 10 and 20 and worked from there.
    (C) I called the times going back and forth by two different unknown variables but noted that the sum of these times was 1 hour.
    (D) I guessed.
    (E) None of these.

23. If the symbol ϕ is defined by the equation

    $$a\phi b = a - b - ab$$

    for all a and b, then $\left(-\dfrac{1}{3}\right)\phi(-3) =$

    (A) $\dfrac{5}{3}$
    (B) $\dfrac{11}{3}$
    (C) $-\dfrac{13}{3}$
    (D) -4
    (E) -5

24. How did you get your answer?

    (A) I played around with the numbers $-\dfrac{1}{3}$ and -3 to get my answer. I didn't use any substitution method.
    (B) I substituted in $a\phi b = a - b - ab$, $-\left(\dfrac{1}{3}\right)$ for a and -3 for b.
    (C) I worked backward.
    (D) I guessed.
    (E) None of these.

25. If $y^8 = 4$ and $y^7 = \dfrac{3}{x}$, what is the value of y in terms of x?

    (A) $\dfrac{4x}{3}$
    (B) $\dfrac{3x}{4}$
    (C) $\dfrac{4}{x}$
    (D) $\dfrac{x}{4}$
    (E) $\dfrac{12}{x}$

26. How did you get your answer?

    (A) I solved for the value of y from $y^8 = 4$. Then I substituted that value of y in $y^7 = \dfrac{3}{x}$.
    (B) I took the seventh root of y in the second equation.
    (C) I divided the first equation by the second equation to get y alone in terms of x.
    (D) I guessed.
    (E) None of these.

27. If $4x + 5y = 10$ and $x + 3y = 8$, then $\dfrac{5x + 8y}{3} =$

    (A) 18
    (B) 12
    (C) 9
    (D) 6
    (E) 15

28. How did you get your answer?

    (A) I solved both simultaneous equations for x and for y, then substituted the values of x and y into $\dfrac{(5x + 8y)}{3}$.
    (B) I tried numbers for x and for y that would satisfy the first two equations.
    (C) I added both equations to get $5x + 8y$. Then I divided my result by 3.
    (D) I guessed.
    (E) None of these.

29. The circle with center A and radius AB is inscribed in the square here. AB is extended to C. What is the ratio of AB to AC?

    (A) $\sqrt{2}$
    (B) $\dfrac{\sqrt{2}}{4}$
    (C) $\sqrt{2} - 1$
    (D) $\dfrac{\sqrt{2}}{2}$
    (E) None of these.

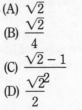 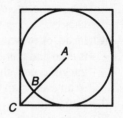

30. How did you get your answer?

(A) I approximated the solution. I looked to see what the ratio of AB to AC might be from the diagram. Then I looked through the choices to see which choice was reasonable or to eliminate incorrect choices.

(B) I saw a relationship between AB and AC but didn't draw any other lines.

(C) I dropped a perpendicular from A to one of the sides of the square, then worked with the isosceles right triangle. I also labeled lengths AB by a single letter, and BC by another single letter.

(D) I guessed.

(E) None of these.

---

31. In the accompanying figure, side BC of triangle ABC is extended to D. What is the value of a?

(A) 15
(B) 17
(C) 20
(D) 24
(E) 30

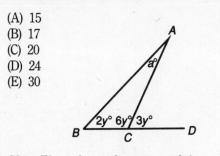

(Note: Figure is not drawn to scale.)

32. How did you get your answer?

(A) I *first* said that $2y + 6y + a = 180$.
(B) I *first* said that $6y + 3y = 180$, then solved for y.
(C) I *first* said $3y = 2y + a$.
(D) I guessed.
(E) None of these.

---

33. What is the perimeter of the accompanying figure if B and C are right angles?

(A) 14
(B) 16
(C) 18
(D) 20
(E) Cannot be determined.

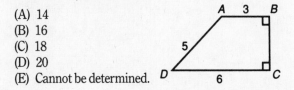

(Note: Figure is not drawn to scale.)

34. How did you get your answer?

(A) I tried to first find angles A and D.
(B) I drew a perpendicular from A to DC, and labeled BC as an unknown (x or y, etc.).
(C) I labeled BC as an unknown (x or y, etc.) but *did not* draw a perpendicular line from A to DC.
(D) I guessed.
(E) None of these.

---

35. Which of the angles below has a degree measure that can be determined?

(A) ∠ WOS
(B) ∠ SOU
(C) ∠ WOT
(D) ∠ ROV
(E) ∠ WOV

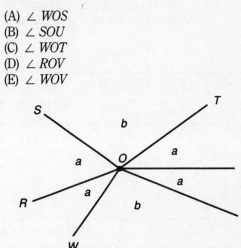

(Note: Figure is not drawn to scale.)

36. How did you get your answer?

(A) I first said that $4a + 2b = 360$, got $2a + b = 180$, then looked through the choices.
(B) I looked through the choices first.
(C) I knew that the sum of the angles added up to 360 degrees but didn't know where to go from there.
(D) I guessed.
(E) None of these.

The following questions each consist of two quantities, one in Column A and one in Column B. You are to compare the two quantities and on the answer sheet blacken space

A if the quantity in Column A is greater;
B if the quantity in Column B is greater;
C if the two quantities are equal;
D if the relationship cannot be determined from the information given.

Notes:
1. In certain questions, information concerning one or both of the quantities to be compared is centered above the two columns.
2. In a given question, a symbol that appears in both columns represents the same thing in Column A as it does in Column B.
3. Letters such as x, n, and k stand for real numbers.

EXAMPLES

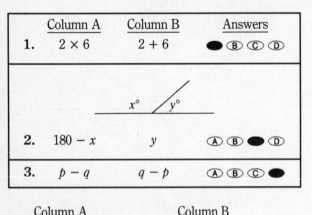

	Column A	Column B	Answers
1.	2×6	$2 + 6$	● Ⓑ Ⓒ Ⓓ
2.	$180 - x$	y	Ⓐ Ⓑ ● Ⓓ
3.	$p - q$	$q - p$	Ⓐ Ⓑ Ⓒ ●

Column A	Column B
37. $\dfrac{1}{2} + \dfrac{1}{6} + \dfrac{1}{17}$	$\dfrac{1}{17} + \dfrac{1}{2} + \dfrac{1}{7}$

38. How did you get your answer?

(A) I added the fractions in Column A and then added the fractions in Column B. Then I compared the results.

(B) I canceled the $\dfrac{1}{2}$ and the $\dfrac{1}{17}$ from both columns.

(C) I added the denominators.
(D) I guessed.
(E) None of these.

SUMMARY DIRECTIONS FOR COMPARISON QUESTIONS

Choose A if the quantity in Column A is greater;   Choose D if the relationship cannot be determined from the Choose B if the quantity in Column B is greater;   information given. Choose C if the two quantities are equal;

Column A	Column B
39. $24 \times 46 \times 35$	$46 \times 24 \times 36$

40. How did you get your answer?

   (A) I multiplied the numbers in Column A and multiplied the numbers in Column B. Then I compared results.

   (B) I approximated a solution for Column A and for Column B.

   (C) I canceled common quantities from both columns.

   (D) I guessed.

   (E) None of these.

Column A	Column B
	$b > 1$
	$a > 1$
	$a \neq b$
41. $\dfrac{a}{b}$	$\dfrac{b}{a}$

42. How did you get your answer?

   (A) I tried different numbers for the variables to get different comparisons, making sure that $b > 1$, $a > 1$, and $a \neq b$.

   (B) I thought that because variables and not actual numbers were given that the answer was indeterminable.

   (C) I tried different numbers for the variables, *not* making sure that $b > 1$, $a > 1$, or $a \neq b$.

   (D) I guessed.

   (E) None of these.

Column A	Column B
	$a > 0$
43. $\dfrac{1}{a}$	a

44. How did you get your answer?

   (A) I substituted different numbers for a, trying to get different comparisons.

   (B) I first found a number for a that would make the columns equal. Then I looked for a number for a that would make the columns unequal.

   (C) I thought because variables and not actual numbers were given in the columns that the answer was indeterminable.

   (D) I guessed.

   (E) None of these.

Column A	Column B
45. $\quad 1$	$\dfrac{\frac{7}{9}}{\frac{9}{7}}$

46. How did you get your answer?

   (A) I first divided $\dfrac{7}{9}$ by $\dfrac{9}{7}$ in Column B.

   (B) I saw that in Column B, $\dfrac{7}{9}$ was less than $\dfrac{9}{7}$, so I realized that Column B must be less than 1.

   (C) I multiplied both columns by $\dfrac{9}{7}$ to get rid of the denominator in Column B.

   (D) I guessed.

   (E) None of these.

Column A	Column B
	$ab \neq 0$
47. $\quad -a^2 b$	ab

48. How did you get your answer?

   (A) I substituted numbers for a and b to get different comparisons.

   (B) I divided both columns by b, then divided both by a.

   (C) I divided both columns by ab since $ab \neq 0$.

   (D) I guessed.

   (E) None of these.

SUMMARY DIRECTIONS FOR COMPARISON QUESTIONS

Choose A if the quantity in Column A is greater;
Choose B if the quantity in Column B is greater;
Choose C if the two quantities are equal;

Choose D if the relationship cannot be determined from the information given.

Column A	Column B

$$30 > ab > 5$$
a and b are whole numbers

49. $a + b$ $\qquad\qquad$ ab

50. How did you answer this question?

(A) I substituted whole numbers for a and b in the columns, making sure that $30 > ab > 5$. Then I substituted another set of whole numbers for a and for b in the columns, making sure again that $30 > ab > 5$.
(B) I thought because only variables were given that the answer was obvious.
(C) I tried different numbers for a and for b, *not* checking to see if $30 > ab > 5$.
(D) I guessed.
(E) None of these.

Column A	Column B

(Note: Figure is not drawn to scale.)

51. a $\qquad\qquad$ $8 - a$

52. How did you get your answer?

(A) I added a to both columns and then divided by 2.
(B) I let a be a number between 0 and 3, then substituted that number for the a in both columns.
(C) I determined that $8 - a > 5$ since $a < 3$. Then I said $8 - a > 5 > 3 > a$.
(D) I guessed.
(E) None of these.

Column A	Column B

$$m > n$$
$$n > p$$

53. m $\qquad\qquad$ p

54. How did you get your answer?

(A) I substituted numbers for m and for n.
(B) I substituted n for p in Column B and n for m in Column A.
(C) I saw a relation between m and p from the given, $m > n$ and $n > p$.
(D) I guessed.
(E) None of these.

Column A	Column B

$$-5 < x < +5$$

55. -6 $\qquad\qquad$ $-x$

56. How did you get your answer?

(A) I tried different values for x.
(B) I multiplied the number in each column by -1 to get 6 and x, respectively.
(C) I multiplied $-5 < x < +5$ by -1 to get $5 > -x > -5$ so that I could compare that with $-x$ and -6.
(D) I guessed.
(E) None of these.

Column A	Column B

57. $(a^3)^4$ $\qquad\qquad$ a^7

58. How did you answer this question?

(A) I said $(a^3)^4 = a^{12}$ and then set $a^{12} > a^7$.
(B) I said $(a^3)^4 = a^7$ and then set $a^7 = a^7$.
(C) I said $(a^3)^4 = a^{12}$ and then tried $a = 1$ or $a = 0$ as one number for a in the columns.
(D) I said $(a^3)^4 = a^{12}$ and then tried numbers *other than* $a = 0$ or $a = 1$.
(E) None of these.

Column A	Column B

$$a > 0$$

59. $\sqrt{a} + \sqrt{3}$ $\qquad\qquad$ $\sqrt{a + 3}$

SUMMARY DIRECTIONS FOR COMPARISON QUESTIONS

Choose A if the quantity in Column A is greater;
Choose B if the quantity in Column B is greater;
Choose C if the two quantities are equal;

Choose D if the relationship cannot be determined from the information given.

60. How did you get your answer?

(A) I plugged in only one number for *a*.
(B) I plugged in two or more numbers for *a*.
(C) I squared both columns, then canceled the *a* and the 3 from both columns.
(D) I guessed.
(E) None of these.

Column A	Column B
61. $\sqrt{17} - \sqrt{3}$	$\sqrt{14}$

62. How did you get your answer?

(A) I first squared both columns.
(B) I approximated a solution by approximating $\sqrt{17}$, $\sqrt{3}$, and $\sqrt{14}$.
(C) I added $\sqrt{3}$ to both columns, first. Then I squared both columns.
(D) I guessed.
(E) None of these.

This is the end of the Strategy Diagnostic Test for the SAT. You've answered the questions in both the Verbal and Math sections, and you've recorded how you arrived at each answer.

Now you're ready to find out how you did. Go right to the table that follows for answer checking, diagnosis, and prescription.

Remember, the questions are in pairs—the odd-numbered ones are the questions themselves, the even-numbered ones, the approach you used to solve the questions. If either or both of your answers—solution and/or approach—fail to correspond to the answers given in the table, you should study the strategy for that pair.

The table also gives the SAT score increase that's possible if you master that strategy. The approximate time it should take to answer a particular question is also supplied. By using the best strategies throughout the actual SAT, you should increase accuracy, make the best use of your time, and thus improve your score dramatically.

Note: If the even-numbered answer (for questions 2, 4, 6, etc.) does not match with your answer, you may want to look at the approach described in the answer as you may be able to use that approach with other questions.

STRATEGY DIAGNOSTIC TEST ANSWER AND DIAGNOSIS TABLE

Section 1 Verbal Ability

Question number	Answer	*If either or both of your answers do not match the answers to the left, then refer to this strategy:	Possible score increase if strategy is learned	Estimated time to solve each odd-numbered question (in seconds)
1	E	Analogy 1, p. 236	190	20
2	B			
3	E	Analogy 4, p. 240	40	30
4	B			
5	C	Analogy 1, p. 236	190	20
6	A			
7	D	Analogy 6, 3 p. 243, 239	20	30
8	A,C			
9	A	Analogy 6, p. 243	20	30
10	A			
11	E	Analogy 6, p. 243	20	20
12	A			
13	E	Analogy 4, p. 240	40	30
14	C			
15	B	Analogy 6, p. 243	20	30
16	A			
17	A	Analogy 6, p. 243	20	30
18	A			
19	D	Sentence Completion 1, p. 245	70	20
20	A			
21	B	Sentence Completion 2, p. 246	40	40
22	C			
23	E	Sentence Completion 3, p. 248	40	30
24	B			
25	C	Sentence Completion 4, p. 249	100	30
26	B			
27	E	Sentence Completion 4, p. 249	30	40
28	C			
29	C	Sentence Completion 4, p. 249	100	30
30	B			
31	A	Vocabulary 1, p. 275	60	20
32	B			
33	E	Vocabulary 1, p. 275	60	20
34	B			

STRATEGY DIAGNOSTIC TEST ANSWER AND
DIAGNOSIS TABLE (Continued)

Section 1 Verbal Ability

Question number	Answer	* If either or both of your answers do not match the answers to the left, then refer to this strategy:	Possible score increase if strategy is learned	Estimated time to solve each odd-numbered question (in seconds)
35	B	Vocabulary 2, p. 277	60	20
36	B			
37	C	Vocabulary 3, p. 279	30	20
38	B			
39	D	Vocabulary 1, p. 275	60	20
40	B			
41	E	Vocabulary 3, p. 279	30	20
42	B			
43	B	Vocabulary 3, p. 279	30	20
44	B			
45	C	Vocabulary 2, p. 277	30	20
46	B,C			
47	A	Vocabulary 3, p. 279	30	20
48	B			
49	B	Vocabulary 2, p. 277	30	20
50	B,C,D			
51	E	Vocabulary 1, p. 275	60	30
52	B			
53	B	Vocabulary 3, p. 279	30	20
54	B			
55	B	Reading Comprehension 1, 2, p. 260, 263	200	15
56	B			
57	E	Reading Comprehension 1, 2, p. 260, 263	200	20
58	B			
59	D	Reading Comprehension 1, 2, p. 260, 263	200	20
60	B			
61	B	Reading Comprehension 1, 2, p. 260, 263	200	20
62	B			
63	D	Reading Comprehension 1, 2, p. 260, 263	200	30
64	B			
65	E	Reading Comprehension 1, 2, p. 260, 263	200	30
66	D			
67	E	Reading Comprehension 1, 2, p. 260, 263	200	20
68	D			

STRATEGY DIAGNOSTIC TEST ANSWER AND DIAGNOSIS TABLE (Continued)

Section 1 Verbal Ability

Question number	Answer	*If either or both of your answers do not match the answers to the left, then refer to this strategy:	Possible score increase if strategy is learned	Estimated time to solve each odd-numbered question (in seconds)
69 70	B B	Reading Comprehension 1, 2, p. 260, 263	200	20
71 72	A B	Reading Comprehension 1, 2, p. 260, 263	200	20
73 74	C D	Reading Comprehension 1, 2, p. 260, 263	200	30

Section 2 Math Ability

Question number	Answer	Strategy	Possible score increase if strategy is learned	Estimated time to solve each odd-numbered question (in seconds)
1 2	A C	Math 1, p. 174	20	10
3 4	D A	Math 2, p. 176	50	40
5 6	D A	Math 2, p. 176	50	30
7 8	C C	Math 3, p. 180	10	20
9 10	C C	Math 4, p. 183	20	40
11 12	B C	Math 5, p. 185	20	40
13 14	E C	Math 6, p. 188	140	50
15 16	A B	Math 7, p. 191	30	40
17 18	E B or C	Math 8, p. 193	20	30
19 20	A A	Math 14, p. 205	40	40
21 22	E C	Math 9, p. 195	10	60
23 24	A B	Math 11, p. 199	30	50
25 26	A C	Math 12 or 13, p. 201, 203	30	30
27 28	D C	Math 13, p. 203	10	20

STRATEGY DIAGNOSTIC TEST ANSWER AND
DIAGNOSIS TABLE (Continued)

Section 1 Verbal Ability

Question number	Answer	* If either or both of your answers do not match the answers to the left, then refer to this strategy:	Possible score increase if strategy is learned	Estimated time to solve each odd-numbered question (in seconds)
29 30	D C	Math 14, 18, p. 205, 215	20	50
31 32	C B	Math 17, 18, p. 212, 215	140	40
33 34	C B	Math 14, 18, p. 205, 215	20	30
35 36	C A	Math 17, p. 212	140	40
37† 38†	A B	Math A, p. 221	20	10
39† 40†	B C	Math B, p. 223	20	10
41† 42†	D A	Math C, p. 224	20	30
43† 44†	D B	Math C, p. 224	10	20
45† 46†	A C	Math D, p. 227	20	10
47† 48†	D A	Math C, p. 224	10	20
49† 50†	D A	Math C, p. 224	20	30
51† 52†	B A	Math D, p. 227	10	20
53† 54†	A C	Math E, p. 232	20	10
55† 56†	B C	Math E, p. 232	20	20
57† 58†	D C	Math C, p. 224	10	20
59† 60†	A C	Math D, p. 227	10	20
61† 62†	B C	Math D, p. 227	10	30

* NOTE: The solution to the odd-numbered question appears in the strategy section listed.
† NOTE: If more than 15 of your answers to questions with an asterisk are incorrect, then review the introduction to the section of this book on quantitative comparison strategies (p. 220) before studying specific quantitative comparison strategies.

PART 3

THE 19 QUESTIONS THAT CAN DETERMINE TOP COLLEGE ELIGIBILITY

If You're in Top Shape,
Take This Test

Although it shouldn't take you more than 40 seconds to answer each verbal question and 1 minute to answer each math question, you may take this test untimed and still get a fairly accurate prediction.

Note: The PSAT score is approximately calculated by dividing the SAT score by 10 and is used for National Merit Scholarships.

The top schools require SAT scores in the 1200+ range. Following is a test that can determine if you have the goods—and it won't take you more than 18 minutes.

Verbal

Vocabulary

Note: Antonyms are not on the new SAT, but we have included the first two antonym questions because they test your vocabulary strategizing, which is necessary for the analogies, sentence completions, and reading parts of the test.

Find the opposite of:

1. OBSTREPEROUS:

    (A) quiet and docile
    (B) flat and solid
    (C) old and venerable
    (D) exotic and unfamiliar
    (E) loyal and honest

2. INEXTRICABLE:

    (A) reasonable
    (B) durable
    (C) separable
    (D) finite
    (E) appropriate

Analogies

Complete the analogy:

3. BUILDING : CHURCH ::

    (A) dance : ballet
    (B) poetry : sonnet
    (C) museum : relics
    (D) song : hymn
    (E) morality : ethics

4. SHARD : GLASS ::

    (A) wool : sheep
    (B) crumb : cookie
    (C) pound : weight
    (D) rung : ladder
    (E) slice : meat

Sentence Completions

Fill in the blank(s) with the appropriate choice:

5. The instructor displayed extreme stubbornness; although he _____ the logic of the student's argument, he _____ to acknowledge her conclusion as correct.

    (A) accepted . . . refused
    (B) concluded . . . consented
    (C) denounced . . . declined
    (D) asserted . . . acceded
    (E) rejected . . . preferred

Reading Comprehension

Read the following passage, then answer the questions:

1 Sometimes the meaning of glowing water is ominous. Off the Pacific Coast of North America, it may mean that the sea is filled with a minute plant that contains a poison of strange and terrible virulence. About four days after this minute
5 plant comes to dominate the coastal plankton, some of the fishes and shellfish in the vicinity become toxic.

6. Fish and shellfish become toxic when they

    (A)   swim in poisonous water
    (B)   feed on poisonous plants
    (C)   change their feeding habits
    (D)   give off a strange glow
    (E)   take strychnine into their systems

7. In the context of the passage, the word *virulence* in line 4 means

    (A)   strangeness
    (B)   interest
    (C)   calamity
    (D)   potency
    (E)   powerful odor

8. The paragraph preceding this one most probably discussed

    (A)   phenomena of the Pacific coastline
    (B)   poisons that affect man
    (C)   the culture of the early Indians
    (D)   characteristics of plankton
    (E)   phenomena of the sea

Regular Math

Answer the following questions:

1. If $y^8 = 4$ and $y^7 = \dfrac{3}{x}$, what is the value of y in terms of x?

   (A) $\dfrac{4x}{3}$

   (B) $\dfrac{3x}{4}$

   (C) $\dfrac{4}{x}$

   (D) $\dfrac{x}{4}$

   (E) $\dfrac{12}{x}$

2. If $y + 2q = 15$, $q + 2p = 5$, and $p + 2y = 7$, then $p + q + y =$

   (A) 6
   (B) 7
   (C) 8
   (D) 9
   (E) 10

3. Sarah is twice as old as John. Six years ago Sarah was 4 times as old as John was then. How old is John now?

   (A) 3
   (B) 18
   (C) 20
   (D) 9
   (E) Cannot be determined

4. $\dfrac{8^7 - 8^6}{7} =$

   (A) $\dfrac{1}{7}$

   (B) $\dfrac{8}{7}$

   (C) 8^5

   (D) $\dfrac{8^4}{7}$

   (E) 8^6

5. If $x + y = 7$ and $xy = 4$, then $x^2 + y^2 =$

   (A) 38
   (B) 39
   (C) 40
   (D) 41
   (E) 42

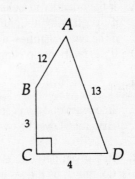

Note: Figure is not drawn to scale.

6. The area of the above figure $ABCD$

   (A) is 36
   (B) is 108
   (C) is 156
   (D) is 1872
   (E) Cannot be determined

7. On a street with 25 houses, 10 houses have *fewer than 6 rooms*, 10 houses have *more than 7 rooms*, and 4 houses have *more than 8 rooms*. What is the total number of houses on the street that are *either* 6-, 7-, or 8-room houses?

   (A) 5
   (B) 9
   (C) 11
   (D) 14
   (E) 15

Quantitative Comparison Math

Quantitative Comparison

The following questions each consist of two quantities, one in Column A and one in Column B. You are to compare the two quantities and on the answer sheet blacken space

A   if the quantity in Column A is greater;
B   if the quantity in Column B is greater;
C   if the two quantities are equal;
D   if the relationship cannot be determined from the information given.

Notes:

1. In certain questions, information concerning one or both of the quantities to be compared is centered above the two columns.

2. In a given question, a symbol that appears in both columns represents the same thing in Column A as it does in Column B.

3. Letters such as x, n, and k stand for real numbers.

SUMMARY DIRECTIONS FOR COMPARISON QUESTIONS

Choose A if the quantity in Column A is greater;
Choose B if the quantity in Column B is greater;
Choose C if the two quantities are equal;

Choose D if the relationship cannot be determined from the information given.

Column A	Column B

8. $h \times AB$ $AD \times CD$

Column A	Column B

Note: Figure is not drawn to scale.

9. $a^2 - c^2$ $d^2 - b^2$

Column A	Column B
10.	$\sqrt{29} - \sqrt{7}$	$\sqrt{35} - \sqrt{13}$

Column A	Column B

$a \neq b \neq 0;\ a + b > 0$

11. $\dfrac{2ab}{a + b}$ $\dfrac{a + b}{2}$

Answers

Verbal

1. A
2. C
3. D
4. B
5. A
6. B
7. D
8. E

Math

1. A
2. D
3. D
4. E
5. D
6. A
7. C
8. B
9. C
10. A
11. B

Scoring

Approximate SAT Score

Number Right

Verbal: 6 = 600
     7 = 700
     8 = 750+
     (*or* 6 or more over 600)

Math: 8 = 600
     9 = 650
   10 = 700
   11 = 750+
     (*or* 8 or more over 600)

Answers and Hints

VERBAL

1. A VOCABULARY STRATEGY 1, 2

   Strategy: Use Prefixes/Roots-Ob negative, get a feel for sound of word

2. C VOCABULARY STRATEGY 1, 3

   Strategy: Use Prefixes, Roots, In = not, Associate parts of word with other words-EXTRI -extract

3. D ANALOGY STRATEGY 4

   Strategy: Use sentence form, then modify sentence: Church is a type of Building—Church is a *religious* type of building—hymn is a religious type of song.

4. B ANALOGY STRATEGY 6

   Strategy: Suppose you don't know the meaning of SHARD. All first words in choices are nouns. So SHARD must be a *type* of glass, a *small piece* of glass, or a *piece of art made from* glass. These are the most common things to think about. Choice B is the only one that fits.

5. A SENTENCE COMPLETION STRATEGY 4

   Strategy: Watch for key words—*Although* signals contrast—the blanks should be opposites.

6. B READING COMPREHENSION STRATEGY 2

   Strategy: Underline important parts of passage.

7. D READING COMPREHENSION STRATEGY 1, Sentence Completion Strategy 1, 4

   Strategy: Look at grammar: adjectives modifying virulence.

8. E READING COMPREHENSION STRATEGY 1

   Strategy: Look at the phrase that introduces the passage.

MATH

1. A STRATEGY 12, 13

   Strategy: Simiplify by *dividing* equations.

2. D STRATEGY 13

   Strategy: Simplify by *adding* equations:

$$\begin{aligned} y + 2q &= 15 \\ q + 2p &= 5 \\ + \quad p + 2y &= 7 \\ \hline 3q + 3p + 3y &= 27 \end{aligned}$$

   Now *divide* by 3 to get

   $q + p + y = 9$

3. D STRATEGY 2

   Strategy: Translate verbal to math—know the translation rules

4. E STRATEGY 4, 12

   Strategy: Factor 8^6 to simplify

5. D STRATEGY 4

   Strategy: Square $x + y = 7$:

   $(x + y)^2 = x^2 + 2xy + y^2 = 49$ $\boxed{1}$

   Then subtract from Equation $\boxed{1}$,

   $2xy = 8$ to get
   $x^2 + y^2 = 41$

6. A STRATEGY 14

   Strategy: Draw *BD*, then find length *BD* to see that *ABD* is a right triangle.

7. C STRATEGY 17

   Strategy: Use an indirect method—find houses that have fewer than 6 rooms, more than 8 rooms.

8. B   STRATEGY B, 14

    Strategy: Label sides, then cancel quantities from Column A,B.

9. C   STRATEGY 17, 14, D

    Strategy: Find remaining angle, draw diagonal, then add quantities to both columns to simplify.

10. A   STRATEGY D

    Strategy: First add $\sqrt{7}$ and $\sqrt{13}$ to both columns; then square both columns.

11. B   STRATEGY D

    Strategy: Cross multiply, then subtract 4ab from both columns.

PART 4

THE 101 MOST IMPORTANT BASIC SKILLS MATH QUESTIONS YOU NEED TO KNOW HOW TO SOLVE

Take This Test to Determine Your Basic (as Contrasted with Strategy) Math Weaknesses (Diagnosis and Corrective Measures Follow Test)

101 Math Questions— Answer Sheet

A. Fractions

   1.
   2.
   3.
   4.
   5.

B. Even–Odd Relationships

   6.
   7.
   8.
   9.
  10.
  11.
  12.

C. Factors

  13.
  14.
  15.
  16.
  17.
  18.
  19.
  20.
  21.

D. Exponents

  22.
  23.
  24.
  25.
  26.
  27.
  28.
  29.
  30.
  31.
  32.

E. Percentages

  33.
  34.
  35.

F. Equations

  36.
  37.
  38.
  39.
  40.

G. Angles

  41.
  42.
  43.
  44.

H. Parallel Lines

45.
46.
47.
48.
49.
50.
51.

I. Triangles

52.
53.
54.
55.
56.
57.
58.
59.
60.
61.
62.
63.
64.
65.

J. Circles

66.
67.
68.
69.
70.

K. Other Figures

71.
72.
73.
74.
75.
76.
77.
78.
79.
80.

L. Number Lines

81.
82.

M. Coordinates

83.
84.
85.

N. Inequalities

86.
87.
88.
89.
90.
91.

O. Averages

92.
93.

P. Shortcuts

94.
95.
96.
97.
98.
99.
100.
101.

Following are the 101 most important basic skills math questions you should know how to solve. After you take the test, check to see whether your answers are the same as those described, and whether or not you answered the question in the way described. After a solution there is usually (where appropriate) a rule or generalization of the math concept just used in the solution to the particular problem. Make sure that you understand this generalization or rule, as it will apply to many other questions. Remember that these are the most important basic math questions you need to know how to solve. Make sure that you understand *all of them* before taking any standardized math test such as the SAT.

DO NOT GUESS AT ANY ANSWER! LEAVE ANSWER BLANK IF YOU DON'T KNOW HOW TO SOLVE.

A. Fractions

1. $\dfrac{\frac{a}{b}}{c} =$

    (A) $\dfrac{ab}{c}$

    (B) $\dfrac{ac}{b}$

    (C) $\dfrac{a}{bc}$

    (D) abc
    (E) none of these

2. $\dfrac{1}{\frac{1}{y}} =$

    (A) y
    (B) y^2
    (C) $\dfrac{1}{y}$

    (D) infinity
    (E) none of these

3. $\dfrac{a}{\frac{b}{c}} =$

    (A) $\dfrac{a}{bc}$

    (B) $\dfrac{ac}{b}$

    (C) $\dfrac{ab}{c}$

    (D) abc
    (E) none of these

4. $\dfrac{1}{\frac{x}{y}} =$

    (A) xy

    (B) $\dfrac{x}{y}$

    (C) $\dfrac{y}{x}$

    (D) $\left(\dfrac{x}{y}\right)^2$

    (E) none of these

5. $\dfrac{\frac{a}{b}}{\frac{b}{a}} =$

    (A) $\dfrac{b^2}{a^2}$

    (B) $\dfrac{a^2}{b^2}$

    (C) 1

    (D) $\dfrac{a}{b}$

    (E) none of these

B. Even–Odd Relations (Note: CBD = Cannot Be Determined)

6. ODD INTEGER $\times$ ODD INTEGER =

    (A) odd integer
    (B) even integer
    (C) no integer or cbd

7. ODD INTEGER + or − ODD INTEGER =

    (A) odd integer
    (B) even integer
    (C) no integer or cbd

8. EVEN INTEGER $\times$ EVEN INTEGER =

    (A) odd integer
    (B) even integer
    (C) no integer or cbd

9. EVEN INTEGER + or − EVEN INTEGER =

    (A) odd integer
    (B) even integer
    (C) no integer or cbd

10. (ODD INTEGER)$^{\text{ODD POWER}}$ =

    (A) odd integer
    (B) even integer
    (C) cbd

11. (EVEN INTEGER)$^{\text{EVEN POWER}}$ =

    (A) odd integer
    (B) even integer
    (C) cbd

12. (EVEN INTEGER)$^{\text{ODD POWER}}$ =

    (A) odd integer
    (B) even integer
    (C) cbd

C. Factors

13. $(x + 3)(x + 2) =$

    (A) $x^2 + 5x + 6$
    (B) $x^2 + 6x + 5$
    (C) $x^2 + x + 6$
    (D) $2x + 5$
    (E) none of these

14. $(x + 3)(x - 2) =$

    (A) $x^2 - x + 6$
    (B) $x^2 + x + 5$
    (C) $x^2 + x - 6$
    (D) $2x + 1$
    (E) none of these

15. $(x - 3)(y - 2) =$

    (A) $xy - 5y + 6$
    (B) $xy - 2x - 3y + 6$
    (C) $x + y + 6$
    (D) $xy - 3y + 2x + 6$
    (E) none of these

16. $(a + b)(b + c) =$

    (A) $ab + b^2 + bc$
    (B) $a + b^2 + c$
    (C) $a^2 + b^2 + ca$
    (D) $ab + b^2 + ac + bc$
    (E) none of these

17. $(a + b)(a - b) =$

    (A) $a^2 + 2ba - b^2$
    (B) $a^2 - 2ba - b^2$
    (C) $a^2 - b^2$
    (D) 0
    (E) none

18. $(a + b)^2 =$

    (A) $a^2 + 2ab + b^2$
    (B) $a^2 + b^2$
    (C) $a^2 + b^2 + ab$
    (D) $2a + 2b$
    (E) none

19. $-(a - b) =$

    (A) $a - b$
    (B) $-a - b$
    (C) $a + b$
    (D) $b - a$
    (E) none of these

20. $a(b + c) =$

    (A) $ab + ac$
    (B) $ab + c$
    (C) abc
    (D) $ab + bc$
    (E) none of these

21. $-a(b - c) =$

(A) $ab - ac$
(B) $-ab - ac$
(C) $ac - ab$
(D) $ab + ac$
(E) none of these

D. Exponents

22. $10^5 =$

(A) 1000
(B) 10,000
(C) 100,000
(D) 1,000,000
(E) none of these

23. $107076.5 = 1.070765 \times$

(A) 10^4
(B) 10^5
(C) 10^6
(D) 10^7
(E) none of these

24. $a^2 \times a^5 =$

(A) a^{10}
(B) a^7
(C) a^3
(D) $(2a)^{10}$
(E) none of these

25. $(ab)^7 =$

(A) ab^7
(B) $a^7 b$
(C) $a^7 b^7$
(D) $a^{14} b^{14}$
(E) none of these

26. $\left(\dfrac{a}{c}\right)^8 =$

(A) $\dfrac{a^8}{c^8}$

(B) $\dfrac{a^8}{c}$

(C) $\dfrac{a}{c^8}$

(D) $\dfrac{a^7}{c}$

(E) none of these

27. $a^4 \times b^4 =$

(A) $(ab)^4$
(B) $(ab)^8$
(C) $(ab)^{16}$
(D) $(ab)^{12}$
(E) none of these

28. $a^{-3} \times b^5 =$

(A) $\dfrac{b^5}{a^3}$

(B) $(ab)^2$

(C) $(ab)^{-15}$

(D) $\dfrac{a^3}{b^5}$

(E) none of these

29. $(a^3)^5 =$

(A) a^8
(B) a^2
(C) a^{15}
(D) a^{243}
(E) none of these

30. $2a^{-3} =$

(A) $\dfrac{2}{a^3}$

(B) $2a^3$

(C) $2\sqrt[3]{a}$

(D) a^{-6}

(E) none of these

31. $2a^m \times \dfrac{1}{3} a^{-n} =$

(A) $\dfrac{2}{3} a^{m+n}$

(B) $\dfrac{2}{3} \dfrac{a^m}{a^n}$

(C) $\dfrac{2}{3} a^{-mn}$

(D) $-\dfrac{2}{3} a^{mn}$

(E) none of these

32. $3^2 + 3^{-2} + 4^1 + 6^0 =$

(A) $8\dfrac{1}{9}$

(B) $12\dfrac{1}{9}$

(C) $13\dfrac{1}{9}$

(D) $14\dfrac{1}{9}$

(E) none of these

E. Percentages

33. 15% of 200 =

(A) 3
(B) 30
(C) 300
(D) 3,000
(E) none of these

34. What is 3% of 5?

(A) $\frac{5}{3}$%
(B) 15
(C) $\frac{3}{20}$
(D) $\frac{3}{5}$
(E) none of these

35. What percent of 3 is 6?

(A) 50
(B) 20
(C) 200
(D) ½
(E) none of these

F. Equations

36. If $y^2 = 16$, $y =$

(A) +4 only
(B) −4 only
(C) + or − 4
(D) + or − 8
(E) none of these

37. If $x - y = 10$, $y =$

(A) $x - 10$
(B) $10 + x$
(C) $10 - x$
(D) 10
(E) none of these

38. What is the value of x if $x + 4y = 7$ and $x - 4y = 8$?

(A) 15
(B) $\frac{15}{2}$
(C) 7
(D) $\frac{7}{2}$
(E) none of these

39. What is the value of x and y if $x - 2y = 2$ and $2x + y = 4$?

(A) $x = 2, y = 0$
(B) $x = 0, y = -2$
(C) $x = -1, y = 2$
(D) $x = 0, y = 2$
(E) none of these

40. If $\frac{x}{5} = \frac{7}{12}$, $x =$

(A) $\frac{35}{12}$
(B) $\frac{12}{35}$
(C) $\frac{7}{60}$
(D) $\frac{60}{7}$
(E) none of these

G. Angles (Vertical, Supplementary)

Questions 41–42 refer to the diagram below:

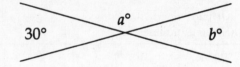

41. $a =$

(A) 30
(B) 150
(C) 45
(D) 90
(E) none of these

42. $b =$

(A) 30
(B) 150
(C) 45
(D) 90
(E) none of these

Question 43 refers to the diagram below:

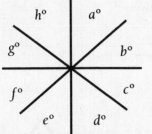

43. $a + b =$

(A) 155
(B) 165
(C) 180
(D) 145
(E) none of these

___

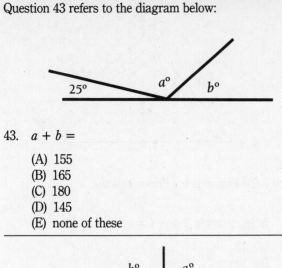

44. What is the value of $a + b + c + d + e + f + g + h$ in the diagram above?

(A) 180
(B) 240
(C) 360
(D) 540
(E) none of these

H. Angles (Parallel Lines)

Questions 45–51 refer to the diagram below:

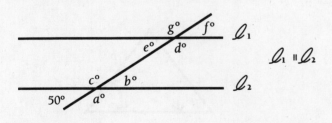

45. $a =$

(A) 50
(B) 130
(C) 100
(D) 40
(E) none of these

46. $b =$

(A) 50
(B) 130
(C) 100
(D) 40
(E) none of these

47. $c =$

(A) 50
(B) 130
(C) 100
(D) 40
(E) none of these

48. $d =$

(A) 50
(B) 130
(C) 100
(D) 40
(E) none of these

49. $e =$

(A) 50
(B) 130
(C) 100
(D) 40
(E) none of these

50. $f =$

(A) 50
(B) 130
(C) 100
(D) 40
(E) none of these

51. $g =$

(A) 50
(B) 130
(C) 100
(D) 40
(E) none of these

I. Triangles

52.

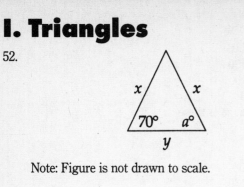

Note: Figure is not drawn to scale.

$a =$

(A) 70
(B) 40
(C) $\frac{xy}{70}$
(D) cannot be determined
(E) none of these

53.

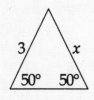

Note: Figure is not drawn to scale.

$x =$

(A) 3
(B) $\frac{50}{3}$
(C) $3\sqrt{2}$
(D) cannot be determined
(E) none of these

54.

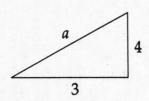

Note: Figure is not drawn to scale.

Which is a possible value for a?

(A) 1
(B) 6
(C) 10
(D) 7
(E) none of these

55.

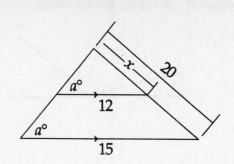

Note: Figure is not drawn to scale.

In the triangle above, $x =$

(A) 12
(B) 16
(C) 15
(D) 10
(E) none of these

56.

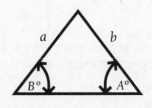

In the triangle above, if B>A, then

(A) $b = a$
(B) b>a
(C) b<a
(D) a relation between b and a cannot be determined
(E) none of these

57.

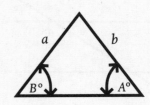

In the triangle above, if b<a, then

(A) B>A
(B) B = A
(C) B<A
(D) a relation between B and A cannot be determined
(E) none of these

58.

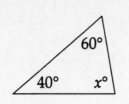

In the triangle above, $x =$

(A) 100
(B) 80
(C) 90
(D) 45
(E) none of these

59.

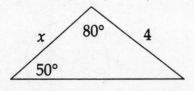

Note: Figure is not drawn to scale.

In the triangle above, $x =$

(A) $4\sqrt{2}$
(B) 8
(C) 4
(D) a number between 1 and 4
(E) none of these

60.

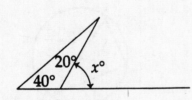

In the diagram above, $x =$

(A) 40
(B) 20
(C) 60
(D) 80
(E) none of these

61.

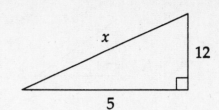

Note: Figure is not drawn to scale.

In the right triangle above as shown, $x =$

(A) 17
(B) 13
(C) 15
(D) $12\sqrt{2}$
(E) none of these

Questions 62–63 refer to the diagram below:

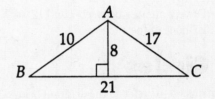

Note: Figure is not drawn to scale.

62. The perimeter of the triangle ABC is

(A) 16
(B) 48
(C) 168
(D) 84
(E) none of these

63. The area of triangle ABC is

(A) 170
(B) 85
(C) 168
(D) 84
(E) none of these

Questions 64–65 refer to the diagram below:

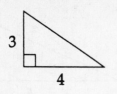

64. The area of the triangle is

   (A) 6
   (B) 7
   (C) 12
   (D) any number between 5 and 7
   (E) none of these

65. The perimeter of the triangle is

   (A) 7
   (B) 12
   (C) 15
   (D) any number between 7 and 12
   (E) none of these

J. Circles

Questions 66–67 refer to the diagram below:

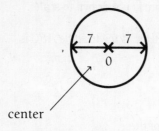

center

66. The area of the circle is

   (A) 49
   (B) 49π
   (C) 14π
   (D) 196π
   (E) none of these

67. The circumference of the circle is

   (A) 14π
   (B) 7π
   (C) 49π
   (D) 14
   (E) none of these

68.

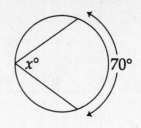

In the diagram above, $x =$

   (A) 70
   (B) 35
   (C) 90
   (D) a number that cannot be determined
   (E) none of these

69.

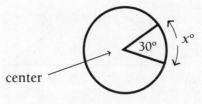

center

In the diagram above, $x =$

   (A) 30
   (B) 60
   (C) 90
   (D) a number that cannot be determined
   (E) none of these

70.

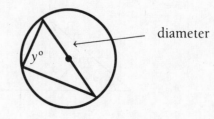

diameter

In the diagram above, $y =$

   (A) 145
   (B) 60
   (C) 90
   (D) a number that cannot be determined
   (E) none of these

K. Other Figures

Questions 71–72 refer to the diagram below:

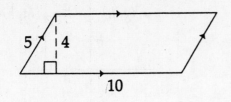

71. The area of the figure is

    (A) 15
    (B) 20
    (C) 40
    (D) 50
    (E) none of these

72. The perimeter of the figure is

    (A) 15
    (B) 30
    (C) 40
    (D) 50
    (E) none of these

Questions 73–75 refer to the figure below:

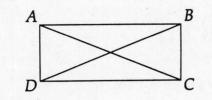

ABCD is a rectangle

73. What is *BC* if *AD* = 6?

    (A) 4
    (B) 6
    (C) 8
    (D) 10
    (E) 12

74. What is *DC* if *AB* = 8?

    (A) 4
    (B) 6
    (C) 8
    (D) 10
    (E) 12

75. What is *DB* if *AC* = 10?

    (A) 4
    (B) 6
    (C) 8
    (D) 10
    (E) 12

Questions 76–77 refer to the diagram below:

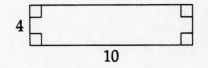

76. The area of the figure is

    (A) 14
    (B) 40
    (C) 80
    (D) 28
    (E) none of these

77. The perimeter of the figure is

    (A) 14
    (B) 28
    (C) 36
    (D) 40
    (E) none of these

Questions 78–79 refer to the figure below:

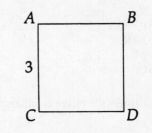

ABCD is a square; *AC* = 3

78. What is the area of the square?

    (A) 9
    (B) 12
    (C) 16
    (D) 20
    (E) none of these

79. What is the perimeter of the square?

    (A) 9
    (B) 12
    (C) 16
    (D) 20
    (E) none of these

80. The volume of the rectangular solid below is

    (A) 48
    (B) 64
    (C) 128
    (D) 72
    (E) none of these

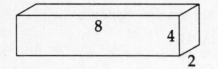

L. Number Lines

Questions 81–82 refer to the diagram below:

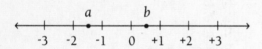

81. Which defines the range in values of b best?

    (A) $1>b>-2$
    (B) $2>b>0$
    (C) $1>b>0$
    (D) $3>b>-3$
    (E) $b>0$

82. Which defines the range in values of a best?

    (A) $a>-2$
    (B) $-1>a>-2$
    (C) $0>a>-2$
    (D) $-1>a$
    (E) $0>a>-3$

M. Coordinates

Questions 83–85 refer to the diagram below:

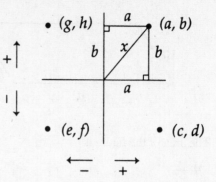

83. How many of the variables a,b,c,d,e,f,g,h are positive?

    (A) 1
    (B) 2
    (C) 3
    (D) 4
    (E) 5

84. How many of the variables a,b,c,d,e,f,g,h are negative?

    (A) 1
    (B) 2
    (C) 3
    (D) 4
    (E) 5

85. If $a = 3$, $b = 4$, what is x?

    (A) 3
    (B) 4
    (C) 5
    (D) 6
    (E) none of these

N. Inequalities

Note: Any variable can be positive or negative or 0.

86. If $x>y$, then $4x>4y$

    (A) always
    (B) sometimes
    (C) never

87. If $x + y > z$, then $y > z - x$

    (A) always
    (B) sometimes
    (C) never

88. If $-4 < -x$, then $+4 > +x$

    (A) always
    (B) sometimes
    (C) never

89. If $m > n$, where q is any number, then $qm > qn$

    (A) always
    (B) sometimes
    (C) never

90. If $x > y$ and $p > q$, then $x + p > y + q$

    (A) always
    (B) sometimes
    (C) never

91. If $x > y$ and $p > q$, then $xp > qy$

    (A) always
    (B) sometimes
    (C) never

O. Averages

92. What is the average of 30, 40, and 80?

    (A) 150
    (B) 75
    (C) 50
    (D) 45
    (E) none of these

93. What is the average speed in mph of a car traveling 40 miles for 4 hours?

    (A) 160
    (B) 10
    (C) 120
    (D) 30
    (E) none of these

P. Shortcuts

94. Which is greater? *Don't calculate a common denominator!*

    $$\frac{7}{16} \quad \text{or} \quad \frac{3}{7}$$

    (A) $\frac{7}{16}$

    (B) $\frac{3}{7}$

    (C) They are equal
    (D) A relationship cannot be determined

95. Add: $\frac{7}{12} + \frac{3}{5}$:

    (A) $1\frac{11}{60}$

    (B) $1\frac{13}{60}$

    (C) $1\frac{15}{60}$

    (D) $\frac{10}{17}$

    (E) none of these

96. Subtract: $\frac{7}{12} - \frac{3}{5}$:

    (A) $-\frac{1}{60}$

    (B) $-\frac{3}{60}$

    (C) $-1\frac{11}{60}$

    (D) $\frac{4}{7}$

    (E) none of these

97. $\frac{4}{250} =$

    (A) .016
    (B) .04
    (C) .004
    (D) .025
    (E) none of these

    Note: Do not divide 250 into 4 in the above question!

98. What is c if

$$200 = \frac{a + b + c}{2} \text{ and } 80 = \frac{a + b}{3}$$

    (A) 160
    (B) 140
    (C) 120
    (D) 100
    (E) none of these

99. What is the value of $95 \times 75 - 95 \times 74$? (*Don't multiply 95×75 or 95×74!*)

    (A) 65
    (B) 75
    (C) 85
    (D) 95
    (E) none of these

100. Find the value of

$$\frac{140 \times 15}{5 \times 7} \quad (\textit{Don't multiply } 140 \times 15!)$$

    (A) 20
    (B) 40
    (C) 60
    (D) 90
    (E) none of these

101. What is the value of $70 \times 21 \times 36 \times 4$?

    (A) 211,680
    (B) 211,681
    (C) 211,682
    (D) 211,683
    (E) 211,684
    (*Don't multiply!*)

101 Math Questions: Solutions, Generalizations, Rules

101 Math Questions: Answers

A. Fractions

1. B
2. A
3. A
4. C
5. B

B. Even-Odd Relationships

6. A
7. B
8. B
9. B
10. A
11. B
12. B

C. Factors

13. A
14. C
15. B
16. D
17. C
18. A
19. D
20. A
21. C

D. Exponents

22. C
23. B
24. B
25. C
26. A
27. A
28. A
29. C
30. A
31. B
32. D

E. Percentages

33. B
34. C
35. C

F. Equations

36. C
37. A
38. B
39. A
40. A

G. Angles

41. B
42. A
43. A
44. C

H. Parallel Lines

45. B
46. A
47. B
48. B
49. A
50. A
51. B

I. Triangles

52. A
53. A
54. B
55. B
56. B
57. C
58. B
59. C
60. C
61. B
62. B
63. D
64. A
65. B

J. Circles

66. B
67. A
68. B
69. A
70. C

K. Other Figures

71. C
72. B
73. B
74. C
75. D
76. B
77. B
78. A
79. B
80. B

L. Number Lines

81. C
82. B

M. Coordinates

83. D
84. D
85. C

N. Inequalities

86. A
87. A
88. A
89. B
90. A
91. B

O. Averages

92. C
93. B

P. Shortcuts

94. A
95. A
96. A
97. A
98. A
99. D
100. C
101. A

BASIC SKILL MATH DIAGNOSIS

Math Area	Total Questions	If you got any of the answers to the following questions wrong, study answers to those questions*	Page in text for review
A. Fractions	5	1–5	151
B. Integers	7	6–12	151
C. Factors	9	13–21	152
D. Exponents	11	22–32	152–153
E. Percentages	3	33–35	153
F. Equations	5	36–40	153–154
G. Angles	4	41–44	154
H. Angles (parallel lines)	7	45–51	154
I. Triangles	14	52–65	154–157
J. Circles	5	66–70	158
K. Other Figures	10	71–80	158–159
L. Number Lines	2	81–82	159
M. Coordinates	3	83–85	159
N. Inequalities	6	86–91	160
O. Averages	2	92–93	160
P. Shortcuts	8	94–101	160–161

* Answer sheet is on pages 148–149.

Solutions

A. Fractions

1. (B)

$$\frac{\dfrac{a}{b}}{c} = a \times \frac{c}{b} = \boxed{\frac{ac}{b}}$$

INVERT TO MULTIPLY

Alternate way:

$$\frac{\dfrac{a}{b}}{\dfrac{c}{c}} = \frac{a}{b} \times \frac{c}{c} = \frac{ac}{b \times c} = \boxed{\frac{ac}{b}}$$

2. (A)

$$\frac{1}{\dfrac{1}{y}} = 1 \times \frac{y}{1} = y$$

INVERT TO MULTIPLY

3. (A)

$$\frac{\dfrac{a}{b}}{c} = \frac{\dfrac{a}{b} \times b}{c \times b} = \frac{\dfrac{a}{b} \times b}{c \times b} = \boxed{\frac{a}{cb}}$$

4. (C)

$$\frac{1}{\dfrac{x}{y}} = 1 \times \frac{y}{x} = \boxed{\frac{y}{x}}$$

INVERT TO MULTIPLY

5. (B)

$$\frac{\dfrac{a}{b}}{\dfrac{b}{a}} = \frac{a}{b} \times \frac{a}{b} = \boxed{\frac{a^2}{b^2}}$$

INVERT TO MULTIPLY

Alternate way:

$$\frac{\dfrac{a}{b}}{\dfrac{b}{a}} = \frac{\dfrac{a}{b} \times a}{\dfrac{b}{a} \times a} = \frac{\dfrac{a^2}{b}}{\dfrac{b}{a}a} = \frac{\dfrac{a^2}{b}}{b}$$

$$= \frac{\dfrac{a^2}{b} \times b}{b \times b} = \boxed{\frac{a^2}{b^2}}$$

B. Even-Odd Relations

6. (A) ODD × ODD = $\boxed{\text{ODD}}$
   $3 \times 3 = 9; 5 \times 5 = 25$

7. (B) ODD + or − ODD = $\boxed{\text{EVEN}}$
   $5 + 3 = 8$
   $5 - 3 = 2$

8. (B) EVEN × EVEN = $\boxed{\text{EVEN}}$
   $2 \times 2 = 4; 4 \times 2 = 8$

9. (B) EVEN + or − EVEN = $\boxed{\text{EVEN}}$
   $6 + 2 = 8; 10 - 4 = 6$

10. (A) (ODD)^{ODD} = $\boxed{\text{ODD}}$
    $3^3 = 3 \times 3 \times 3 = 27$ (odd)
    $1^{27} = 1 = $ odd

11. (B) (EVEN)^{EVEN} = $\boxed{\text{EVEN}}$
    $2^2 = 4$(even); $4^2 = 16$ (even)

12. (B) (EVEN)^{ODD} = $\boxed{\text{EVEN}}$
    $2^3 = 2 \times 2 \times 2 = 8$ (even)
    $4^1 = 4$ (even)

C. Factors

13. (A) $(x + 3)(x + 2) = x^2 \ldots$

    $(x + 3)(x + 2) = x^2 + 3x + 2x \ldots$

    $(x + 3)(x + 2) = x^2 + 3x + 2x + 6$

    $(x + 3)(x + 2) = \boxed{x^2 + 5x + 6}$

14. (C) $(x + 3)(x - 2) = x^2 \ldots$

    $(x + 3)(x - 2) = x^2 - 2x + 3x \ldots$

    $(x + 3)(x - 2) = x^2 - 2x + 3x - 6$

    $(x + 3)(x - 2) = \boxed{x^2 + x - 6}$

15. (B) $(x - 3)(y - 2) = xy \ldots$

    $(x - 3)(y - 2) = xy - 2x - 3y \ldots$

    $(x - 3)(y - 2) = \boxed{xy - 2x - 3y + 6}$

16. (D) $(a + b)(b + c) = ab \ldots$

    $(a + b)(b + c) = ab + ac + b^2 \ldots$

    $(a + b)(b + c) = \boxed{ab + ac + b^2 + bc}$

17. (C) $(a + b)(a - b) =$

    $(a + b)(a - b) = a^2 \ldots$

    $(a + b)(a - b) = a^2 - ab + ba \ldots$

    $(a + b)(a - b) = a^2 - ab + ba - b^2$

    $(a + b)(a - b) = a^2 - \cancel{ab} + \cancel{ba} - b^2$

    $\boxed{(a + b)(a - b) = a^2 - b^2}$ MEMORIZE

18. (A) $(a + b)^2 = (a + b)(a + b)$

    $(a + b)(a + b) = a^2 \ldots$

    $(a + b)(a + b) = a^2 + ab + ba \ldots$

    $(a + b)(a + b) = a^2 + ab + ba + b^2$

    $\boxed{(a + b)^2 = a^2 + 2ab + b^2}$ MEMORIZE

19. (D) $-(a - b) = -a - (-b)$

    $-(a - b) = -a + b$

    $\boxed{-(a - b) = b - a}$ MEMORIZE

20. (A) $a(b + c) =$

    $a(b + c) = \boxed{ab + ac}$

21. (C) $-a(b - c) =$

    $-a(b - c) = -ab - a(-c)$

    $= -ab + ac = \boxed{ca - ab}$

D. Exponents (Solutions)

22. (C) $10^5 = 100000$

    5 zeroes

23. (B) $107076.5 = 1\,0\,7\,0\,7\,6.5$

    $5\;4\;3\;2\;1$

    $= 1.070765 \times \boxed{10^5}$

24. (B) ADD EXPONENTS

    $a^2 \times a^5 = \boxed{a^7}$ $a^m \times a^n = a^{m+n}$

25. (C) $(ab)^7 = \boxed{a^7 b^7}$
    $(ab)^m = a^m b^m$

26. (A)

    $\left(\dfrac{a}{c}\right)^8 = \boxed{\dfrac{a^8}{c^8}}$; $\left(\dfrac{a}{c}\right)^m = \dfrac{a^m}{c^m}$

27. (A) $a^4 \times b^4 = \boxed{(ab)^4}$; $a^m \times b^m = (ab)^m$

28. (A)

    $a^{-3} \times b^5 = \boxed{\dfrac{b^5}{a^3}}$

    $a^{-m} \times b^n = \dfrac{b^n}{a^m}$

29. (C) $(a^3)^5 = \boxed{a^{15}}$ $(a^m)^n = a^{mn}$

    MULTIPLY EXPONENTS

30. (A)

    $2a^{-3} = \boxed{\dfrac{2}{a^3}}$

    $ax^{-b} = \dfrac{a}{x^b}$

    Since $a^{-n} = \dfrac{1}{a^n}$

31. (B)
$$2a^m \times \frac{1}{3}a^{-n} = \frac{2}{3}a^m\,a^{-n}$$
$$= \frac{2}{3}a^{m-n} \text{ or } \boxed{\frac{2}{3}\frac{a^m}{a^n}}$$

32. (D) $3^2 = 3 \times 3 = 9$

$$3^{-2} = \frac{1}{3^2} = \frac{1}{9}$$

$4^1 = 4$

$6^0 = 1$ (any number to 0 power $= 1$)

$$3^2 + 3^{-2} + 4^1 + 6^0 = 9 + \frac{1}{9} + 4 + 1 = \boxed{14\frac{1}{9}}$$

E. Percentages

Questions 33–35

Translate is $\rightarrow =$
  of $\rightarrow \times$ (times)
  percent(%) $\rightarrow \dfrac{}{100}$
  what $\rightarrow x$ (or y, etc.)

33. (B)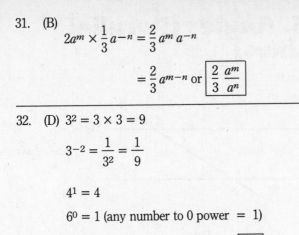
$$15\% \quad \text{of } 200 \;=$$
$$\downarrow \;\downarrow \quad\; \downarrow \;\;\downarrow \quad\; \downarrow$$
$$15\frac{}{100} \times 200 \;=$$
$$\frac{15}{100} \times 200 \;=$$
$$\frac{15}{100} \times 200 = \boxed{30}$$

34. (C) What is 3 % of 5 ?
$$\quad\;\; \downarrow \;\;\; \downarrow\downarrow\;\; \downarrow\;\; \downarrow\downarrow$$
$$\quad x \;\; = 3\frac{}{100} \times 5$$

$$x = \frac{3}{100} \times 5$$

$$x = \frac{15}{100} = \boxed{\frac{3}{20}}$$

35. (C) What percent of 3 is 6 ?
$$\quad\; \downarrow \qquad\; \downarrow \quad\; \downarrow\downarrow\downarrow$$
$$\quad x \qquad \frac{}{100} \;\times 3 = 6$$

$$\frac{x}{100} \times 3 = 6$$

$$\frac{3x}{100} = 6$$

$$3x = 600$$

$$x = \boxed{200}$$

F. Equations

36. (C)
$$y^2 = \qquad 16$$
$$\sqrt{y^2} = \pm\sqrt{16}$$
$$y = \boxed{\pm 4}$$

Note: y means the *positive* square root of y. That is, the positive number when multiplied by itself that will give you the value of y.

$$(\sqrt{y}) \times (\sqrt{y}) = y$$

37. (A) $x - y = 10$
Add y:
$x - y + y = 10 + y$
$x = 10 + y$
Subtract 10:
$x - 10 = 10 - 10 + y$
$\boxed{x - 10 = y}$

38. (B) Add equations:
$$x + 4y = 7$$
$$\underline{x - 4y = 8}$$
$$2x + 4y - 4y = 15$$
$$2x = 15$$
$$\boxed{x = \frac{15}{2}}$$

39. (A) $x - 2y = 2$ $\qquad\qquad$ $\boxed{1}$
$2x + y = 4$ $\qquad\qquad$ $\boxed{2}$
Multiply $\boxed{1}$ by 2:
$2(x - 2y) = 2(2)$
We get:
$2x - 4y = 4$

Subtract $\boxed{2}$ from $\boxed{3}$:
$$2x - 4y = 4 \qquad\qquad \boxed{3}$$
$$\underline{- (2x + \; y = 4)} \qquad \boxed{2}$$
$$0 \; - 5y = 0$$
$$\boxed{y = 0} \qquad\qquad\qquad \boxed{4}$$

Substitute: $\boxed{4}$ into either $\boxed{1}$ or $\boxed{2}$:
In $\boxed{1}$:
$$x - 2y = 2$$
$$x - 2(0) = 2$$
$$\boxed{x = 2}$$

40. (A) $\dfrac{x}{5} = \dfrac{7}{12}$

Cross-multiply x :

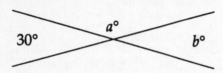

$12x = 35$

Divide by 12:

$$\dfrac{12x}{12} = \dfrac{35}{12}$$

$$\boxed{x = \dfrac{35}{12} = 2\dfrac{11}{12}}$$

G. Angles (Vertical and Supplementary)

This diagram refers to questions 41–42

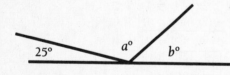

41. (B) $a°$ and 30° are supplementary angles (they add up to 180°).
So $a + 30 = 180$; $a = \boxed{150}$.

42. (A) $b°$ and 30° are *vertical* angles (vertical angles are equal).
So $b = \boxed{30}$

---

43. (A) This diagram refers to questions 43–44

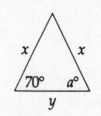

$a°$, $b°$ and 25° make up a *straight* angle which is 180°.
$a + b + 25 = 180$
$a + b = 180 - 25$
$a + b = \boxed{155}$

44. (C) The sum of the angles in the diagram is $\boxed{360°}$, the number of degrees around the circumference of a circle.

H. Angles (Parallel Lines)

Questions 45–51

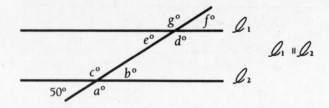

45. (B) $a + 50 = 180$
$a = \boxed{130}$

46. (A) $\boxed{b = 50}$ (vertical angles)

47. (B) $c = a$ (vertical angles)
$= \boxed{130}$

48. (B) $d = c$ (alternate interior angles are equal)
$= \boxed{130}$

49. (A) $e = b$ (alternate interior angles)
$= \boxed{50}$

50. (A) $f = e$ (vertical angles)
$= \boxed{50}$

51. (B) $g = d$ (vertical angles)
$= \boxed{130}$

I. Triangles

52. (A)

Note: Figure is not drawn to scale.

If two sides are equal, base angles are equal. Thus $a = \boxed{70°}$

53. (A)

Note: Figure is not drawn to scale.

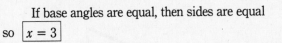

If base angles are equal, then sides are equal

so $\boxed{x = 3}$

54. (B)

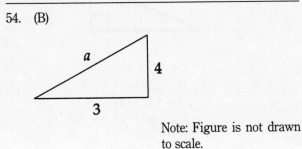

Note: Figure is not drawn to scale.

The sum of two sides must be *greater* than the third side. Try choices:

(A) $1 + 3 \not> 4$: (A) is not possible
(B) $3 + 4 > 6$; $6 + 3 > 4$, $4 + 6 > 3$ ... O.K.
(C) $3 + 4 \not> 10$. (C) is not possible
(D) $4 + 3 = 7$. (D) is not possible

55. (B) Using similar triangles, write a *proportion*.

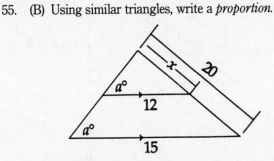

Note: Figure is not drawn to scale.

$$\frac{x}{20} = \frac{12}{15}$$

$$15x = 12 \times 20$$

$$x = \frac{12 \times 20}{15}$$

$$x = \frac{\overset{4}{\cancel{12}} \times \overset{4}{\cancel{20}}}{\underset{5}{\cancel{15}}} = \boxed{16}$$

In general:

$$\frac{m}{n} = \frac{q}{p} = \frac{r}{r + s}$$

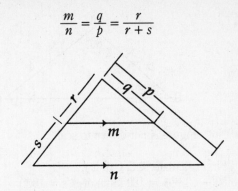

Note: Figure is not drawn to scale.

56. (B) The greater angle lies opposite the greater side and vice-versa

If $B > A$, $\boxed{b > a}$

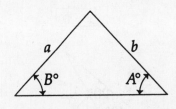

57. (C) The greater side lies opposite the greater angle and vice-versa.

If $b < a$ then $\boxed{B < A}$

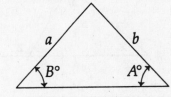
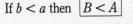

58. (B) Sum of angles of triangle $= 180°$.
So $40 + 60 + x = 180$
$$100 + x = 180$$

$$\boxed{x = 80}$$

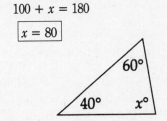

59. (C)

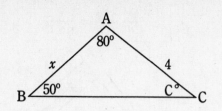

Note: Figure is not drawn to scale.

First calculate ∢ C. Call it y.
$80 + 50 + y = 180$ (Sum of ∢'s = 180°)
$y = 50$
Since ∢ $C = y = 50$ and ∢ $B = 50$, sides $AB = AC$.
$AB = \boxed{x = 4}$

60. (C) $x° = 20° + 40°$ (sum of *remote* interior angles = exterior angle).

$$\boxed{x = 60}$$

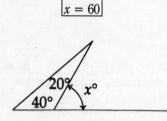

In general,

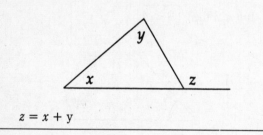

$$z = x + y$$

61. (B)

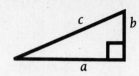

In right △, $a^2 + b^2 = c^2$
So for

$$5^2 + 12^2 = x^2$$
$$25 + 144 = x^2$$
$$169 = x^2$$
$$\sqrt{169} = x$$
$$\boxed{13} = x$$

Note: Specific right triangles you should memorize:
Use multiples to generate other triangles.
Example of multiple:

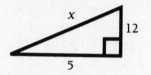

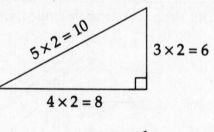

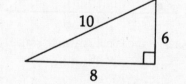

Memorize the following standard triangles:

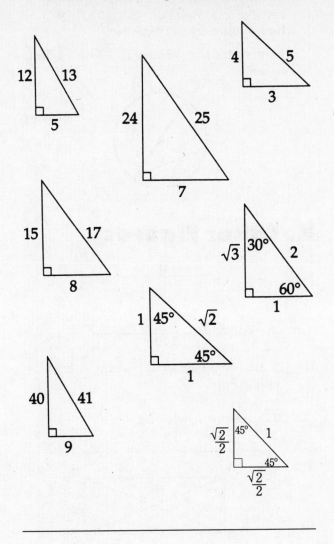

62. (B) Perimeter = sum of sides

$$10 + 17 + 21 = \boxed{48}$$

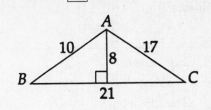

63. (D)

Area of $\triangle = \frac{1}{2}hb$

Area of $\triangle = \frac{1}{2}(8)(21) = \boxed{84}$

64. (A) Area of any triangle = ½ base × height

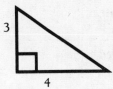

Here 4 is base and 3 is height. So area = ½ (4×3) = ½ (12) = $\boxed{6}$

65. (B)

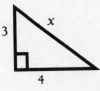

To find perimeter we need to find the sum of the sides. The sum of the sides is $3 + 4 + x$

We need to find x. From the solution in Question 61, we should realize that we have a 3-4-5 right triangle so $x = 5$. The perimeter is then $3 + 4 + 5 = \boxed{12}$.

Note that you could have found x by using the Pythagorean Theorem:

$3^2 + 4^2 = x^2$; $9 + 16 = x^2$; $25 = x^2$; $\sqrt{25} = x$; $5 = x$.

J. Circles

66. (B) Area = $\pi r^2 = \pi(7)^2$
$$= \boxed{49\pi}$$

---

67. (A) Circumference =
$2\pi r = 2\pi(7)$
$$= \boxed{14\pi}$$

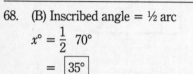

center

---

68. (B) Inscribed angle = ½ arc
$$x° = \frac{1}{2} \, 70°$$
$$= \boxed{35°}$$

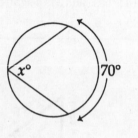

---

69. (A) Central angle = arc
$$\boxed{30°} = x°$$

Note: The *total* number of degrees around the circumference is 360°. So a central angle of 30° like the one above, cuts $\frac{30}{360} = \frac{1}{12}$ the circumference.

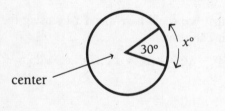

center

---

70. (C) The diameter cuts a 180° arc on circle so an inscribed angle $y = ½$ arc $= ½ (180°) = \boxed{90°}$. Here is a good thing to remember:

Any inscribed angle whose triangle base is a diameter is 90°.

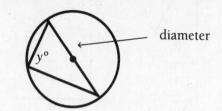

diameter

K. Other Figures

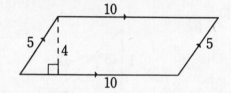

71. (C) Area of parallelogram = base × height = (10)(4) = $\boxed{40}$

72. (B) Perimeter = sum of sides =
5 + 5 + 10 + 10 = $\boxed{30}$

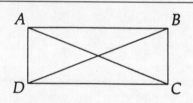

ABCD is a rectangle

---

73. (B) In a rectangle (as in a parallelogram) opposite sides are equal.
So $AD = BC = \boxed{6}$.

---

74. (C) In a rectangle (as in a parallelogram) opposite sides are equal.
So $DC = AB = \boxed{8}$.

---

75. (D) In a rectangle (but not in a parallelogram) the diagonals are equal.
So $DB = AC = \boxed{10}$.

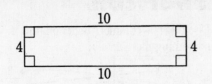

76. (B) Area of rectangle = length × width = 4 × 10 = 40 .

77. (B) Perimeter = sum of sides = 4 + 4 + 10 + 10 = 28 .

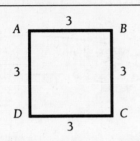

78. (A) Area of square with side x is x^2. (All sides of a square are equal.) So length = width. Since $x = 3$, $x^2 =$ 9 .

79. (B) Perimeter of square is the sum of all sides of square. Since all sides are equal, if one side is x, perimeter = $4x$.
$x = 3$, so $4x =$ 12 .

80. (B) VOLUME OF RECTANGULAR SOLID shown below = $a \times b \times c$

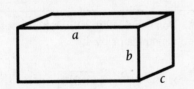

So for:

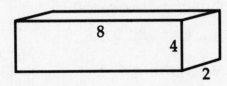

$a = 8$, $b = 4$, $c = 2$
and $a \times b \times c = 8 \times 4 \times 2 =$ 64 .

Note: VOLUME OF CUBE shown below = $a \times a \times a = a^3$

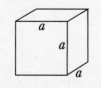

L. Number Lines

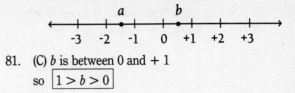

81. (C) b is between 0 and +1 so $1 > b > 0$

82. (B) a is between −2 and −1 so $-1 > a > -2$

M. Coordinates

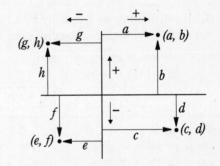

Horizontal right = +
Horizontal left = −
Vertical up = +
Vertical down = −

83. (D) a, b, c, h positive (4 letters)

84. (D) d, e, f, g negative (4 letters)

85. (C)

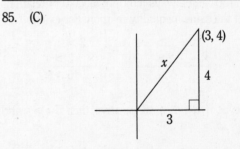

Remember 3-4-5 right triangle. $x = 5$
You can also use the Pythagorean Theorem:
$3^2 + 4^2 = x^2$; $9 + 16 = x^2$; $x^2 = 25$; $x = 5$

N. Inequalities

86. (A) You can multiply inequality by a positive number and retain the same inequality:

$x > y$

$\boxed{4x > 4y}$ $\quad$ $\boxed{\text{ALWAYS}}$

87. (A) You can subtract both sides of an inequality by the same number and retain the same inequality:

$$x + y > z$$
$$x + y - x > z - x$$

$\boxed{y > z - x}$ $\quad$ $\boxed{\text{ALWAYS}}$

88. (A) If you multiply an inequality by a minus sign, you *reverse* the original inequality sign:

$$-4 < -x$$
$$-(-4 < -x)$$

$\boxed{+4 > +x}$ $\quad$ $\boxed{\text{ALWAYS}}$

89. (B) If $m > n$,

$qm > qn$ if q is *positive*
$qm < qn$ if q is *negative*
$qm = qn$ if q is *zero*

So, $\boxed{qm > qn}$ $\quad$ $\boxed{\text{SOMETIMES}}$

90. (A) You can always add inequality relations:

$$\begin{array}{r} x > y \\ + p > q \\ \hline x + p > y + q \end{array}$$ $\quad$ $\boxed{\text{ALWAYS}}$

91. (B) You can't always multiply inequality relations to get the same inequality relation: For example:

$$\begin{array}{r} 3 > 2 \\ \times \; -2 > -3 \\ \hline -6 \not> -6 \end{array} \qquad \begin{array}{r} 3 > 2 \\ \times \; 2 > 1 \\ \hline 6 > 2 \end{array}$$

However, if x, y, p, q are positive, then if $x > y$ and $p > q$, $xp > yq$

O. Averages

92. (C) Average of $30 + 40 + 80 =$
$$\frac{30 + 40 + 80}{3} = \boxed{50}$$

Average of $x + y + z + t + \ldots =$
$$\frac{x + y + z + t + \ldots}{\text{number of terms}}$$

93. (B) Average speed $= \dfrac{\text{TOTAL DISTANCE}}{\text{TOTAL TIME}}$

Distance $= 40$ miles, Time $= 4$ hours

Average speed $= \dfrac{40 \text{ miles}}{4 \text{ hours}} = \boxed{10 \text{ miles per hour}}$

P. Shortcuts

94. Don't get a common denominator if you can do something more easily:

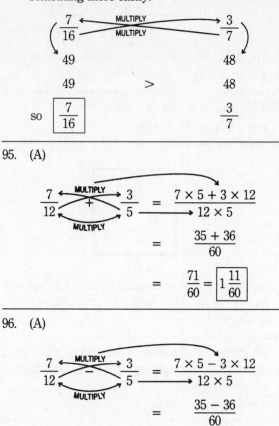

$$49 \qquad > \qquad 48$$

so $\boxed{\dfrac{7}{16}} \qquad\qquad \dfrac{3}{7}$

95. (A)

$$\dfrac{7}{12} \overset{\text{MULTIPLY}}{\underset{\text{MULTIPLY}}{+}} \dfrac{3}{5} = \dfrac{7 \times 5 + 3 \times 12}{12 \times 5}$$

$$= \dfrac{35 + 36}{60}$$

$$= \dfrac{71}{60} = \boxed{1\frac{11}{60}}$$

96. (A)

$$\dfrac{7}{12} \overset{\text{MULTIPLY}}{\underset{\text{MULTIPLY}}{-}} \dfrac{3}{5} = \dfrac{7 \times 5 - 3 \times 12}{12 \times 5}$$

$$= \dfrac{35 - 36}{60}$$

$$= \boxed{-\dfrac{1}{60}}$$

97. (A) Don't divide by 250! Multiply both numerator and denominator by 4:

$$\dfrac{4}{250} \times \dfrac{4}{4} = \dfrac{16}{1000} = \boxed{0.016}$$

98. (A) Get rid of denominators!

$$200 = \dfrac{a + b + c}{2} \qquad\qquad ①$$

Multiply ① by 2:

$$200 \times 2 = a + b + c \qquad ②$$
$$80 = \dfrac{a + b}{3} \qquad ③$$

Multiply ③ by 3:

$$80 \times 3 = a + b \qquad ④$$

Now subtract ④ from ②:

$$200 \times 2 - 80 \times 3 = a + b + c - (a + b)$$
$$= \cancel{a} + \cancel{b} + c - \cancel{a} - \cancel{b}$$
$$400 - 240 = c$$
$$\boxed{160} = c$$

99. (D) Don't multiply 95×75 or 95×74!

Factor <u>common</u> 95:

$$95 \times 75 - 95 \times 74 =$$
$$= 95(75 - 74)$$
$$= 95(1)$$
$$= \boxed{95}$$

100. (C) $\dfrac{140 \times 15}{5 \times 7}$

Don't multiply 140×15 if you can first *reduce*.

$$\frac{\overset{20}{\cancel{140}} \times 15}{5 \times \cancel{7}_{\,1}} = \frac{20 \times 15}{5}$$

Further reduce:

$$\frac{20 \times \overset{3}{\cancel{15}}}{\cancel{5}_{\,1}} = \boxed{60}$$

101. (A) You'd be crazy to multiply $70 \times 21 \times 36 \times 4$! You also cannot approximate because the choices are so close. So look at the product:

$$70 \times 21 \times 36 \times 4$$

Since 70 ends in "0," the product $70 \times 21 \times 36 \times 4$ must end in 0! The only choice that ends in 0 is Choice A: $\boxed{211680}$.

Using Critical Thinking
Skills to Score High on the

PART 5

STRATEGY SECTION

Using Critical Thinking Skills to Score High on the New SAT

5 General Strategies

General Strategies for Taking the SAT Examination

Before studying the 50 specific strategies for the Math and Verbal Questions, you will find it useful to review the following Five General Strategies for taking the SAT Examination.

Strategy 1:

DON'T RUSH INTO GETTING AN ANSWER WITHOUT THINK-ING. BE CAREFUL IF YOUR ANSWER COMES TOO EASILY, ESPECIALLY IF THE QUESTION IS TOWARD THE END OF THE SECTION.

Beware of Choice A If You Get the Answer Fast or Without Really Thinking

Everybody panics when they take an exam like the SAT. And what happens is that they rush into getting answers. That's OK, except that you have to think carefully. If a problem looks too easy, beware! And, especially beware of the Choice A answer. It's usually a "lure" choice for those who rush into getting an answer without critically thinking about it. Here's an example:

Below is a picture of a digital clock. The clock shows that the time is 6:06. Consider all the times on the clock where the hour digit is the same as the minute digit like in the clock shown below. Another such "double" time would be 8:08 or 9:09. What is the *smallest* time period between any two such doubles?

(A) 61 minutes
(B) 11 minutes
(C) 60 minutes
(D) 101 minutes
(E) 49 minutes

6:06

Did you subtract 8:08 from 7:07 and get 1 hour and 1 minute (61 minutes)? If you did you probably chose Choice A: the *lure choice*. Think—do you really believe

that the test maker would give you such an easy question? The fact that you figured it out so easily and saw that Choice A was your answer should make you think twice. The thing you have to realize is that there is another possibility: 12:12 to 1:01 gives 49 minutes, and so Choice E is correct.

So, in summary, if you get the answer fast and without doing much thinking, and it's a Choice A answer, think again. You may have fallen for the Choice A lure.

NOTE: Choice A is often a "lure choice" for those who quickly get an answer without doing any real thinking. However, you should certainly realize that Choice A answers can occur, especially if there is no "lure choice."

Strategy 2:

KNOW AND LEARN THE DIRECTIONS TO THE QUESTION TYPES BEFORE YOU TAKE THE ACTUAL TEST.

Never Spend Time Reading Directions During the Test or Doing Sample Questions That Don't Count

All SATs are standardized. For example, all the Analogy questions have the same directions from test to test as do the Sentence Completions, etc. So it's a good idea to learn these sets of directions and familiarize yourself with their types of questions early in the game before you take your actual SAT.

Here's an example of a set of SAT directions, together with an accompanying example for the Sentence Completion type of questions.

For each question in this section, select the best answer from among the choices given and fill in the corresponding oval on the answer sheet.

Directions

Each sentence below has one or two blanks, each blank indicating that something has been omitted. Beneath the sentence are five words or set of words labeled A through E. Choose the word or set of words that, when inserted in the sentence, *best* fits the meaning of the sentence as a whole.

Example:

Medieval kingdoms did not become constitutional republics overnight; on the contrary, the change was----.

(A) unpopular
(B) unexpected
(C) advantageous
(D) sufficient
(E) gradual

Ⓐ Ⓑ Ⓒ Ⓓ ⬤

If on your actual test you spend time reading these directions and/or answering the sample question, you will waste valuable time.

As you go through this book, you will become familiar with all the question types so that you won't have to read their directions on the actual test.

Strategy 3:

IT MAY BE WISER NOT TO LEAVE AN ANSWER BLANK

The Penalty for Guessing Is Much Smaller Than You Might Expect

On the SAT you lose a percentage of points if you guess and get the wrong answer. Of course, you should always try to eliminate choices. You'll find that, after going through this book, you'll have a better chance of eliminating wrong answers. However, if you cannot eliminate any choice in a question and have no idea of how to arrive at an answer, you might want to pick any answer and go on to the next question.

There are two reasons for this:
1. You don't want to risk mismarking a future answer by leaving a previous answer blank.
2. Even though there is a penalty for guessing, the penalty is much smaller than you might expect, and this way

you have at least a chance of getting the question right. Suppose, for example, that you have a five-choice question:

> From a probablistic point of view, it is very likely that you would get one question right and four wrong (you have a 1 in 5 chance of getting a five-choice question right) if you randomly guess at the answers. Since ¼ point is taken off for each wrong five-choice question, you've gotten $1 - ¼ \times 4 = 0$ points, because you've gotten 1 question right and 4 wrong. Thus you break even. So the moral is whether you randomly guess at questions you're not sure of at all or whether you leave those question answers blank, it doesn't make a difference in the long run!

Strategy 4:

WRITE AS MUCH AS YOU WANT IN YOUR TEST BOOKLET

Test Booklets Aren't Graded—So Use Them As You Would Scrap Paper

Many students are afraid to mark up their test booklets. But, the booklets are not graded! Make any marks you want. In fact, some of the strategies demand that you extend or draw lines in geometry questions or label diagrams, or circle incorrect answers, etc. That's why when I see computer programs that show only the questions on a screen and prevent the student from marking a diagram or circling an answer, I realize that such programs prevent the student from using many powerful strategies. *So write all you want on your test booklet—use your test paper as you would scrap paper.*

Strategy 5:

USE YOUR OWN CODING SYSTEM TO TELL YOU WHICH QUESTIONS TO RETURN TO

If You Have Extra Time After Completing a Test Section, You'll Know Exactly Which Questions Need More Attention

When you are sure that you have answered a question correctly, mark your question paper with ✓. For questions you are not sure of but for which you have eliminated some of the choices, use **?**. For questions that you're not sure of at all or for which you have not been able to eliminate any choices, use **??**. This will give you a bird's-eye view of what questions you should return to, if you have time left after completing a particular test section.

47 Easy-to-Learn Strategies

25 Math Strategies + 22 Verbal Strategies

Critical thinking is the ability to think clearly in order to solve problems and answer questions of all types—SAT questions, for example, both Math and Verbal!

Educators who are deeply involved in research on Critical Thinking Skills tell us that such skills are straightforward, practical, teachable, and learnable.

The 25 Math strategies and 22 Verbal strategies in this section are Critical Thinking Skills. These strategies have the potential to raise your SAT scores dramatically. A realistic estimate is anywhere from approximately 50 points to 300 points in each part of the test—Verbal and Math. Since each correct SAT question gives you an additional 10 points on the average, it is reasonable to assume that, if you can learn and then use these valuable SAT strategies, you can boost your SAT scores phenomenally!

BE SURE TO LEARN AND USE THE STRATEGIES THAT FOLLOW!

HOW TO LEARN THE STRATEGIES

1. For each strategy, look at the heading describing the strategy.

2. Try to answer the first example without looking at the EXPLANATORY ANSWER.

3. Then look at the EXPLANATORY ANSWER and if you got the right answer, see if the method described would enable you to solve the question in a better way with a faster approach.

4. Then try each of the next EXAMPLES without looking at the EXPLANATORY ANSWERS.

5. Use the same procedure as in (3) for each of the EXAMPLES.

The MATH STRATEGIES start on page 174, and the VERBAL STRATEGIES start on page 236. However, before you start the Math Strategies, it would be wise for you to look at the *Important Note on the Allowed Use of Calculators on the New SAT following. The Important Note on Math Questions on the new SAT, page 168. The New Grid Type Question on page 168 and Use of a Calculator in the Grid-Type Question on page 172.*

Important Note on the Allowed Use of Calculators on the New SAT

Although the use of calculators on the SAT I will be allowed, using a calculator may be sometimes more tedious, when in fact you can use another problem-solving method or short cut. So you must be selective on when and when not to use a calculator on the test.

Here's an example of when a calculator should *not* be used:

$$\frac{2}{5} \times \frac{5}{6} \times \frac{6}{7} \times \frac{7}{8} \times \frac{8}{9} \times \frac{9}{10} \times \frac{10}{11} =$$

(A) $\frac{9}{11}$ (B) $\frac{2}{11}$ (C) $\frac{11}{36}$ (D) $\frac{10}{21}$ (E) $\frac{244}{360}$

Here the use of a calculator may take some time. However, if you use the strategy of canceling numerators and denominators (Math Strategy 1 on pages 174–175) as shown:

Cancel numerators/denominators:

$$\frac{2}{\cancel{5}} \times \frac{\cancel{5}}{\cancel{6}} \times \frac{\cancel{6}}{\cancel{7}} \times \frac{\cancel{7}}{\cancel{8}} \times \frac{\cancel{8}}{\cancel{9}} \times \frac{\cancel{9}}{\cancel{10}} \times \frac{\cancel{10}}{11} = \frac{2}{11}$$

You can see that the answer comes easily as $\frac{2}{11}$.

Later I will show you an example in the new *grid-type* question where the use of a calculator will also take you a longer time to solve a problem than without the calculator. Here's an example where using a calculator may get you the solution *as fast as* using a strategy without the calculator:

25 percent of 16 is equivalent to ½ of what number?

(A) 2   (B) 4   (C) 8   (D) 16   (E) 32

Using a calculator, you'd use Math Strategy 2 (page 176) (translating *of* to *times* and *is* to *equals*) first calculating 25 percent of 16 to get **4**. Then you'd say 4 = half of what number and you'd find that number to be **8**.

Without using a calculator, you'd still use Math Strategy 2 (the translation strategy), but you could write 25 percent as ¼, so you'd figure out what ¼ × 16 was (**4**). Then you'd call the number you want to find x, and say 4 = ½(x). You'd find $x = $ **8**.

Note that both methods, with and without a calculator, are about equally efficient; however, the technique in the second method can be used for many more problems and hones more thinking skills.

Important Note on Math Questions on the New SAT

There are three types of math questions on the new SAT.

1. The Regular Math (total of 35 counted questions), which has five choices. The strategies for these start on page 174.

2. The Quantitative Comparison (total of 15 counted questions), which has four choices and is described on page 220. The strategies for the Quantitative Comparison questions start on page 221.

3. The newest addition, the "Grid Type" Math Question (total of 10 counted questions), are described below.

   Note: The grid-type questions can be solved using the Regular Math Strategies.

The New Grid-Type Math Question

There will be 10 questions on the SAT I where you will have to "grid" in your answer rather than choose from a set of five choices. Here are the directions to the "grid-type" question. Make sure that you understand these directions completely before you answer any of the grid-type questions.

Directions: Each of the remaining 10 questions (16–25) requires you to solve the problem and enter your answer by marking the ovals in the special grid, as shown in the examples below.

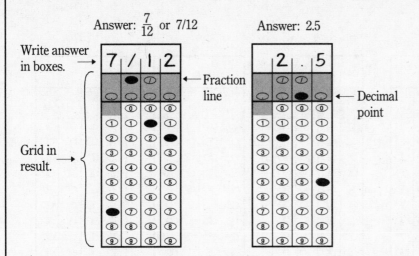

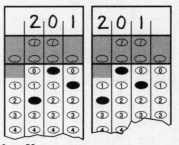

Write answer in boxes. →

Grid in result. →

← Fraction line

Answer: $\frac{7}{12}$ or 7/12

Answer: 2.5

← Decimal point

Answer: 201
Either position is correct.

Note: You may start your answers in any column, space permitting. Columns not needed should be left blank.

- Mark no more than one oval in any column.

- Because the answer sheet will be machine-scored, **you will receive credit only if the ovals are filled in correctly.**

- Although not required, it is suggested that you write your answer in the boxes at the top of the columns to help you fill in the ovals accurately.

- Some problems may have more than one correct answer. In such cases, grid only one answer.

- No question has a negative answer.

- **Mixed numbers** such as $2\frac{1}{2}$ must be gridded as 2.5 or 5/2. (If $\boxed{2\,1/2}$ is gridded, it will be interpreted as $\frac{21}{2}$, not $2\frac{1}{2}$.)

- Decimal Accuracy: If you obtain a decimal answer, **enter the most accurate value the grid will accommodate.** For example, if you obtain an answer such as 0.6666 ..., you should record the result as .666 or .667. **Less accurate values such as .66 or .67 are not acceptable.**

Acceptable ways to grid $\frac{2}{3}$ = .6666 ...

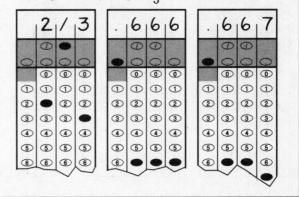

Practice with Grids

According to the directions on the previous page, grid the following values in the grids 1–15:

317 4.2 .5 $\frac{1}{12}$ 2474

$3\frac{1}{2}$ $\frac{57}{3}$ 0 .346 $4\frac{3}{4}$

39 1 $\frac{3}{8}$ 45.3 $8\frac{1}{7}$

Answers

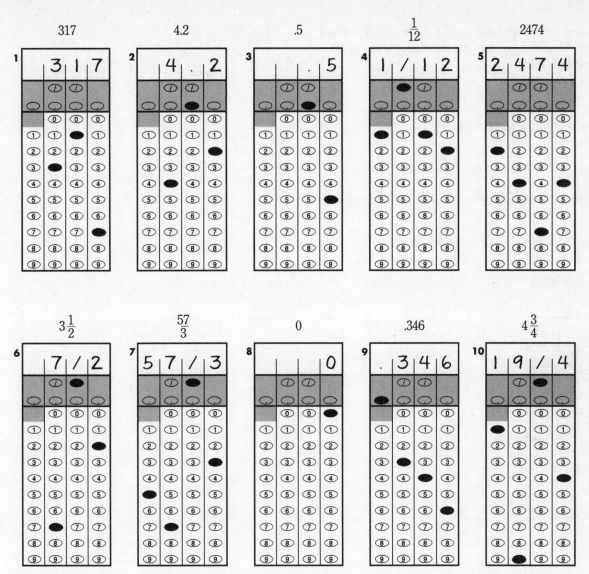

Use of a Calculator in the Grid-Type Question

In the following example, you can either use a calculator or not. However, the use of a calculator will require a different gridding.

EXAMPLE:

If $\dfrac{2}{7} < x < \dfrac{3}{7}$ find one value of x.

SOLUTION WITHOUT A CALCULATOR:

Get some value between $\dfrac{2}{7}$ and $\dfrac{3}{7}$. Write $\dfrac{2}{7} = \dfrac{4}{14}$ and $\dfrac{3}{7} = \dfrac{6}{14}$

So we have $\dfrac{4}{14} < x < \dfrac{6}{14}$ and x can be $\dfrac{5}{14}$

The grid will look like:

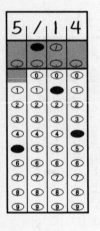

SOLUTION *WITH* A CALCULATOR:

Calculate on calculator:

$$\frac{3}{7} = .4285714\ldots$$

$$\frac{2}{7} = .2857142\ldots$$

So $.2857142 < x < .4285714$

You could have the grid as follows:

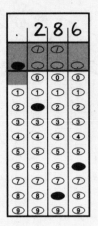 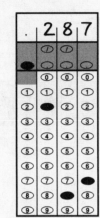

all the way to:

25 Math Strategies

Using Critical Thinking Skills in Math Questions*

MATH STRATEGY **1**

Cancel Quantities to Make the Problem Simpler

Cancel numbers or expressions that appear on both sides of an equation; cancel same numerators and denominators. But make sure that you don't divide by 0 in what you're doing! You will save precious time by using this strategy. You won't have to make any long calculations.

EXAMPLE 1

If $P \times \frac{11}{14} = \frac{11}{14} \times \frac{8}{9}$, then $P =$

(A) $\frac{8}{9}$

(B) $\frac{9}{8}$

(C) 11

(D) 14

(E) 8

Choice A is correct. Do not multiply $\frac{11}{14} \times \frac{8}{9}$!

Cancel the common $\frac{11}{14}$:

$$P \times \frac{\cancel{11}}{\cancel{14}} = \frac{\cancel{11}}{\cancel{14}} \times \frac{8}{9}$$

$P = \frac{8}{9}$ (*Answer*)

Note: You can cancel the $\frac{11}{14}$ because you are *dividing* both sides by the same nonzero number. Suppose you had a problem like the following:

If $R \times a = a \times \frac{4}{5}$ then $R =$

* Math Strategies 1–19 refer to Regular Math questions. Math Strategies A–F refer to Quantitative Comparison questions.

(A) $\frac{4}{5}$

(B) $\frac{5}{4}$

(C) 1

(D) $\frac{2}{3}$

(E) Cannot be determined

What do you think the answer is? It's not choice A! It is Choice E because you cannot cancel the "*a*" because *a* may be 0 and you cannot divide by 0. So if $a = 0$, R can be *any* number.

EXAMPLE 2

If $y + \frac{7}{13} + \frac{6}{19} = \frac{3}{5} + \frac{7}{13} + \frac{6}{19}$, then $y =$

(A) $\frac{6}{19}$

(B) $\frac{13}{32}$

(C) $\frac{7}{13}$

(D) $\frac{3}{5}$

(E) $\frac{211}{247}$

Choice D is correct. *Do not add the fractions!*

$\frac{3}{5} + \frac{7}{13} + \frac{6}{19}$! You will waste a lot of time! There is a much shorter way to do the problem. Cancel $\frac{7}{13} + \frac{6}{19}$ from both sides of the equation. Thus,

$$y + \frac{\cancel{7}}{\cancel{13}} + \frac{\cancel{6}}{\cancel{19}} = \frac{3}{5} + \frac{\cancel{7}}{\cancel{13}} + \frac{\cancel{6}}{\cancel{19}}$$

$$y = \frac{3}{5} \ (Answer)$$

EXAMPLE 3

$$\frac{2}{5} \times \frac{5}{6} \times \frac{6}{7} \times \frac{7}{8} \times \frac{8}{9} \times \frac{9}{10} \times \frac{10}{11} =$$

(A) $\frac{9}{11}$

(B) $\frac{2}{11}$

(C) $\frac{11}{36}$

(D) $\frac{10}{21}$

(E) $\frac{244}{360}$

Choice B is correct.

Cancel numerators/denominators:

$$\frac{2}{\cancel{5}} \times \frac{\cancel{5}}{\cancel{6}} \times \frac{\cancel{6}}{\cancel{7}} \times \frac{\cancel{7}}{\cancel{8}} \times \frac{\cancel{8}}{\cancel{9}} \times \frac{\cancel{9}}{\cancel{10}} \times \frac{\cancel{10}}{11} = \frac{2}{11}$$

EXAMPLE 4

If $a + b > a - b$, which must follow?

(A) $a < 0$
(B) $b < 0$
(C) $a > b$
(D) $b > a$
(E) $b > 0$

Choice E is correct.

$a + b > a - b$

Cancel common a's:

$$\cancel{a} + b > \cancel{a} - b$$
$$b > -b$$
$$\text{Add } b: \quad b + b > b - b$$
$$2b > 0$$
$$b > 0$$

EXAMPLE 5

If $7\frac{2}{9} = 6 + \frac{y}{27}, y =$

(A) 8
(B) 30
(C) 35
(D) 37
(E) 33

Choice E is correct.

Subtract 6 from both sides:

$$7\frac{2}{9} - 6 = 6 + \frac{y}{27} - 6$$

$$1\frac{2}{9} = \frac{y}{27}$$

$$\frac{11}{9} = \frac{y}{27}$$

$$\frac{33}{27} = \frac{y}{27}$$

$$y = 33$$

MATH STRATEGY 2

Translate English Words into Mathematical Expressions

Many of the SAT problems are word problems. Being able to translate word problems from English into mathematical expressions or equations will help you to score high on the test. The following table translates some commonly used words into their mathematical equivalents:

TRANSLATION TABLE

Words	Math Way to Say It
is, as was, has, cost	= (equals)
of	× (times)
percent	/100 (the percent number over 100)
x percent	$x/100$
which, what	x (or any other variable)
x and y	$x + y$
the sum of x and y	$x + y$
the difference between x and y	$x - y$
x more than y	$x + y$
x less than y	$y - x$
the product of x and y	xy
the square of x	x^2
x is greater than y	$x > y$ (or $y < x$)
x is less than y	$x < y$ (or $y > x$)
y years ago	$-y$
y years from now	$+y$
c times as old as John	$c \times$ (John's age)
x older than y	$x + y$
x younger than y	$y - x$
the increase from x to y	$y - x$
the decrease from x to y	$x - y$
the percent increase from x to y $(y>x)$	$\left(\dfrac{y-x}{x}\right)100$
the percent decrease from x to y $(y<x)$	$\left(\dfrac{x-y}{x}\right)100$
the percent of increase	$\left(\dfrac{\text{amount of increase}}{\text{original amount}}\right) \times 100$
the percent of decrease	$\left(\dfrac{\text{amount of decrease}}{\text{original amount}}\right) \times 100$
n percent greater than x	$x + \left(\dfrac{n}{100}\right)x$
n percent less than x	$x - \left(\dfrac{n}{100}\right)x$

By knowing this table, you will find word problems much easier to do.

EXAMPLE 1

Sarah is twice as old as John. Six years ago, Sarah was 4 times as old as John was then. How old is John now?

(A) 3
(B) 18
(C) 20
(D) 9
(E) impossible to determine

Choice D is correct. Translate:

$$\begin{array}{ccccc} \text{Sarah} & \text{is} & \text{twice} & \text{as old as} & \text{John.} \\ \downarrow & \downarrow & \downarrow & \downarrow & \downarrow \\ S & = & 2 & \times & J \end{array}$$

$$S = 2J \qquad \boxed{1}$$

$$\begin{array}{ccccc} \text{Six years ago} & \text{Sarah} & \text{was} & 4 & \text{times as old as} & \underbrace{\text{John was then}} \\ \downarrow & & \downarrow & \downarrow & \downarrow & \downarrow \\ -6 & & S & = & 4 & \times & (J-6) \end{array}$$

This becomes $S - 6 = 4(J - 6) \qquad \boxed{2}$

Substituting $\boxed{1}$ into $\boxed{2}$:

$$2J - 6 = 4(J - 6)$$
$$2J - 6 = 4J - 24$$
$$18 = 2J$$
$$9 = J \quad (Answer)$$

EXAMPLE 2

200 is what percent of 20?

(A) $\frac{1}{10}$
(B) 10
(C) 100
(D) 1000
(E) 10000

Choice D is correct. Translate:

$$\begin{array}{cccccc} 200 & \text{is} & \text{what} & \text{percent} & \text{of} & 20 \\ \downarrow & \downarrow & \downarrow & \downarrow & \downarrow & \downarrow \\ 200 & = & x & \frac{}{100} & \times & 20 \end{array}$$

$$200 = \frac{x}{100}(20)$$

Divide by 20: $10 = \frac{x}{100}$

Multiply by 100: $1000 = x$ (*Answer*)

EXAMPLE 3

If A is 250 percent of B, what percent of A is B?

(A) 125%
(B) $\frac{1}{250}$%
(C) 50%
(D) 40%
(E) 400%

Choice D is correct.

"If A is 250 percent of B" becomes

$$\begin{array}{cccccc} \downarrow\downarrow\downarrow & & \downarrow & & \downarrow\downarrow \\ A = 250 & & /100 & & \times B \end{array}$$

"What percent of A is B?" becomes

$$\begin{array}{ccccc} \downarrow & & \downarrow & \downarrow\downarrow\downarrow \\ x & & /100 & \times A = B \end{array}$$

Set up the equations:

$$A = \frac{250}{100}B \qquad \boxed{1}$$

$$\frac{x}{100}A = B \qquad \boxed{2}$$

Divide the equations, $\boxed{1}$ and $\boxed{2}$

$$\frac{A = \frac{250}{100}B}{\frac{x}{100}A = B}$$

We get:

$$\frac{1}{\frac{x}{100}} = \frac{250}{100}$$

Inverting, we get:

$$\frac{x}{100} = \frac{100}{250}$$

$$x = \frac{10,000}{250}$$

To simplify, multiply both numerator and denominator by 4:

$$x = \frac{10,000 \times 4}{250 \times 4} = 40$$

Alternate way:

Let B = 100 (choose any number for B)
We get (after translation)

$$A = \left(\frac{250}{100}\right) 100 \qquad \boxed{1}$$

$$\left(\frac{x}{100}\right) A = 100 \qquad \boxed{2}$$

From $\boxed{1}$,

$$A = 250 \qquad \boxed{3}$$

Substituting $\boxed{3}$ into $\boxed{2}$, we get

$$\left(\frac{x}{100}\right) 250 = 100 \qquad \boxed{4}$$

Multiplying both sides of $\boxed{4}$ by 100,

$$(x)(250) = (100)(100)$$

Dividing by 250:

$$x = \frac{100 \times 100}{250}$$

Simplify by multiplying numerator and denominator by 4:

$$x = \frac{100 \times 100 \times 4}{250 \times 4} = \frac{40000}{1000}$$
$$= 40$$

EXAMPLE 4

John is now m years old and Sally is 4 years older than John. Which represents Sally's age 6 years ago?

(A) $m + 10$
(B) $m - 10$
(C) $m - 2$
(D) $m - 4$
(E) $4m - 6$

Choice C is correct.

Translate:

John is now m years old
↓ ↓   ↓
J = m

Sally is 4 years older than John
↓ ↓ ↓   ↓   ↓
S = 4   + J

Sally's age 6 years ago =
   ↓   ↓
   S − 6   =

So we get: $J = m$
$$S = 4 + J$$

and find: $S - 6 = 4 + J - 6$

$$S - 6 = J - 2 \text{ (substituting } m \text{ for } J)$$

$$S - 6 = m - 2$$

EXAMPLE 5

Phil has three times as many records as Sam has. Even after Phil gives Sam 6 records, he still has 16 more records than Sam has. What was the original number of records that Phil had?

(A) 20
(B) 24
(C) 28
(D) 33
(E) 42

Choice E is correct.

Translate:

Phil has three times as many records as Sam has
↓ ↓ ↓ ↓   ↓
P = 3 × S

Even after Phil gives Sam 6 records, he still has 16
     ↓ ↓ ↓   ↓ ↓
     P − 6   = 16

more records than Sam has
  ↓   ↓
  + $S + 6$

Sam now has $S + 6$ records because Phil gave Sam 6 records. So we end up with the equations:

$$P = 3S$$

$$P - 6 = 16 + S + 6$$

Find P; get rid of S:

$$P = 3S; \qquad \frac{P}{3} = S$$

$$P - 6 = 16 + \frac{P}{3} + 6$$

$$P - 6 = \frac{48 + P + 18}{3}$$

$$3P - 18 = 48 + P + 18$$
$$2P = 84$$
$$P = 42$$

EXAMPLE 6

If q is 10% greater than p and r is 10% greater than y, qr is what percent greater than py?

(A) 20%
(B) 100%
(C) 1%
(D) 30%
(E) 21%

Choice E is correct.

Translate:

If q is 10% greater than p

$$q = \frac{10}{100}p + p$$

and r is 10% greater than y

$$r = \frac{10}{100}y + y$$

qr is what percent greater than py?

$$qr = \frac{x}{100}py + py$$

So we have three equations:

$$q = \frac{10}{100}p + p = \left(\frac{10}{100} + 1\right)p \quad \boxed{1}$$

$$r = \frac{10}{100}y + y = \left(\frac{10}{100} + 1\right)y \quad \boxed{2}$$

$$qr = \frac{x}{100}py + py = \left(\frac{x}{100} + 1\right)py \quad \boxed{3}$$

Multiply $\boxed{1}$ and $\boxed{2}$:

$$qr = \left(\frac{10}{100} + 1\right)^2 py \quad \boxed{4}$$

Now equate $\boxed{4}$ with $\boxed{3}$:

$$qr = \left(\frac{x}{100} + 1\right)py = \left(\frac{10}{100} + 1\right)^2 py$$

You can see that $\left(\frac{10}{100} + 1\right)^2 = \frac{x}{100} + 1$, canceling py.

So, $\left(\frac{10}{100} + 1\right)^2 = \frac{100}{10{,}000} + 1 + 2\left(\frac{10}{100}\right) = \frac{x}{100} + 1$

$$\frac{100}{10{,}000} + \frac{20}{100} = \frac{21}{100} = \frac{x}{100}$$
$$21 = x$$

The answer is $x = 21$

Alternate approach: Choose numbers for p and for y:

Let $p = 10$ and $y = 20$

Then, since q is 10% greater than p:

$q = $ 10% greater than 10

$$q = \left(\frac{10}{100}\right)10 + 10 = 11$$

Next, r is 10% greater than y:

$r = $ 10% greater than 20

Or, $r = \left(\frac{10}{100}\right)20 + 20 = 22$

Then:

$$qr = 11 \times 22$$
$$\text{and } py = 20 \times 10$$

So, to find what percent qr is greater than py, you would need to find:

$$\frac{qr - py}{py} \times 100 \text{ or}$$

$$\frac{11 \times 22 - 20 \times 10}{20 \times 10} \times 100$$

This is:

$$\frac{42}{200} \times 100 = 21$$

EXAMPLE 7

Sales of Item X
Jan–June, 1993

Month	Sales ($)
Jan	800
Feb	1,000
Mar	1,200
Apr	1,300
May	1,600
Jun	1,800

According to the above table, the percent increase in sales was greatest for which of the following periods?

(A) Jan–Feb
(B) Feb–Mar
(C) Mar–Apr
(D) Apr–May
(E) May–Jun

Choice A is correct.

The percent increase from Month A to Month B =

$$\frac{\text{Sales (Month B)} - \text{Sales (Month A)}}{\text{Sales (Month A)}} \times 100$$

Month	Sales ($)		% Increase in Sales
Jan	800	Jan–Feb	$\frac{1000 - 800}{800} \times 100 = \frac{200}{800} \times 100$
Feb	1000	Feb–Mar	$\frac{1200 - 1000}{1000} \times 100 = \frac{200}{1000} \times 100$
Mar	1200	Mar–Apr	$\frac{1300 - 1200}{1200} \times 100 = \frac{100}{1200} \times 100$
Apr	1300	Apr–May	$\frac{1600 - 1300}{1300} \times 100 = \frac{300}{1300} \times 100$
May	1600	May–Jun	$\frac{1800 - 1600}{1600} \times 100 = \frac{200}{1600} \times 100$
Jun	1800		

You can see that $\frac{200}{800} \times 100$ (Jan–Feb) is the greatest.

MATH STRATEGY **3**

Know How to Find Unknown Quantities (Areas, Lengths, Arc and Angle Measurements) From Known Quantities (the Whole Equals the Sum of Its Parts)

When Asked to Find a Particular Area or Length, Instead of Trying to Calculate It Directly, Find It by Subtracting Two Other Areas or Lengths—a Method Based on the Fact That the Whole Minus a Part Equals the Remaining Part

This strategy is very helpful in many types of geometry problems. A very important equation to remember is

The whole = the sum of its parts $\boxed{1}$

Equation $\boxed{1}$ is often disguised in many forms, as seen in the following examples:

EXAMPLE 1

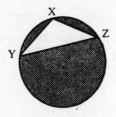

In the diagram above, ΔXYZ has been inscribed in a circle. If the circle encloses an area of 64, and the area of ΔXYZ is 15, then what is the area of the shaded region?

(A) 25
(B) 36
(C) 49
(D) 79
(E) It cannot be determined from the information given.

Choice C is correct. Use equation $\boxed{1}$. Here, the whole refers to the area within the circle, and the parts refer to the areas of the shaded region and the triangle. Thus,

Area within circle =
Area of shaded region +
Area of ΔXYZ

64 = Area of shaded region + 15

or Area of shaded region = 64 − 15 = 49
(*Answer*)

EXAMPLE 2

In the diagram below, $\overline{AE}$ is a straight line, and F is a point on $\overline{AE}$. Find an expression for $m \measuredangle$ DFE.

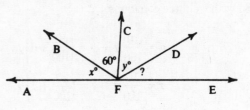

(A) $x + y - 60$
(B) $x + y + 60$
(C) $90 - x - y$
(D) $120 - x - y$
(E) $180 - x - y$

Choice D is correct. Use equation $\boxed{1}$. Here, the whole refers to the straight angle, $\measuredangle$AFE, and its parts refer to $\measuredangle$AFB, $\measuredangle$BFC, $\measuredangle$CFD, and $\measuredangle$DFE. Thus,

$$m\measuredangle\text{AFE} = m\measuredangle\text{AFB} + m\measuredangle\text{BFC} + m\measuredangle\text{CFD} + m\measuredangle\text{DFE}$$
$$180 = x + 60 + y + m\measuredangle\text{DFE}$$
or
$$m\measuredangle\text{DFE} = 180 - x - 60 - y$$
$$m\measuredangle\text{DFE} = 120 - x - y \text{ (Answer)}$$

EXAMPLE 3

In the diagram below, AB= m, BC = n, and AD = 10. Find an expression for CD.

(Note: Diagram represents a straight line.)

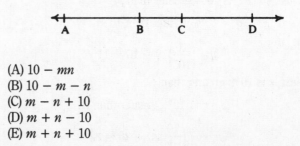

(A) $10 - mn$
(B) $10 - m - n$
(C) $m - n + 10$
(D) $m + n - 10$
(E) $m + n + 10$

Choice B is correct. Use equation $\boxed{1}$. Here, the whole refers to AD, and its parts refer to AB, BC, and CD. Thus,

$$AD = AB + BC + CD$$
$$10 = m + n + CD$$
$$\text{or} \quad CD = 10 - m - n \ (Answer)$$

EXAMPLE 4

The area of triangle $ACE = 64$. The sum of the areas of the shaded triangles ABF and FDE is 39. What is the side of square $BFDC$?

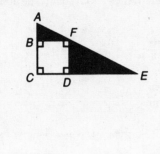

(A) 5
(B) 4
(C) $\sqrt{5}$
(D) $\sqrt{44}$
(E) Cannot be determined

EXPLANATORY ANSWER

Choice A is correct

Since we are dealing with areas, let's establish the area of the square $BFDC$, which will then enable us to get its side.

Now, the area of square $BFDC$ = area of triangle ACE − (area of triangles ABF + FDE)

Area of square $BFDC = 64 - 39$
$$= 25$$

Therefore, the side of square $BFDC = 5$.

EXAMPLE 5

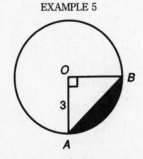

In the figure above, O is the center of the circle. Triangle AOB has side 3 and angle $AOB = 90°$. What is the area of the shaded region?

(A) $9\left(\dfrac{\pi}{4} - \dfrac{1}{2}\right)$

(B) $9\left(\dfrac{\pi}{2} - 1\right)$

(C) $9(\pi - 1)$

(D) $9\left(\dfrac{\pi}{4} - \dfrac{1}{4}\right)$

(E) Cannot be determined

EXPLANATORY ANSWER

Choice A is correct.

Subtract knowns from knowns:

Area of shaded region = area of quarter circle AOB − area of triangle AOB

Area of quarter circle $AOB = \dfrac{\pi(3)^2}{4}$

Area of triangle $AOB = \dfrac{3 \times 3}{2}$ (since $OB = 3$ and area of a triangle $= \dfrac{1}{2}$ base × height)

Thus, area of shaded region $= \dfrac{9\pi}{4} - \dfrac{9}{2} = 9\left(\dfrac{\pi}{4} - \dfrac{1}{2}\right)$

EXAMPLE 6

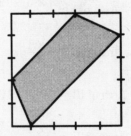

The sides in the square above are each divided into five equal segments. What is the value of

$$\frac{\text{Area of square}}{\text{Area of shaded region}}?$$

(A) $\dfrac{50}{29}$

(B) $\dfrac{50}{21}$

(C) $\dfrac{25}{4}$

(D) $\dfrac{29}{25}$

(E) None of these

EXPLANATORY ANSWER

Choice B is correct.

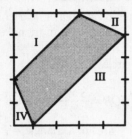

Subtract knowns from knowns:

Area of square = 5 × 5 = 25
Area of shaded region = area of square − area of I −
area of II − area of III − area of IV

$$\text{Area of I} = \frac{3 \times 3}{2} = \frac{9}{2}$$

$$\text{Area of II} = \frac{2 \times 1}{2} = 1$$

$$\text{Area of III} = \frac{4 \times 4}{2} = 8$$

$$\text{Area of IV} = \frac{2 \times 1}{2} = 1$$

$$\text{Area of shaded region} = 25 - \frac{9}{2} - 1 - 8 - 1 = \frac{21}{2}$$

$$\frac{\text{Area of square}}{\text{Area of shaded region}} = \frac{25}{\frac{21}{2}} = 25 \times \frac{2}{21} = \frac{50}{21}$$

EXAMPLE 7

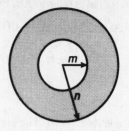

Two concentric circles are shown above with inner radius of m and outer radius of n. What is the area of the shaded region?

(A) $\pi(n - m)^2$
(B) $\pi(n^2 + m^2)$
(C) $\pi(n^2 - m^2)$
(D) $2\pi(n - m)$
(E) $2\pi(n + m)$

EXPLANATORY ANSWER

Choice C is correct.

Subtract knowns from knowns:

Area of shaded region = area of circle of radius n −
area of circle of radius m

Area of circle of radius $n = \pi n^2$
Area of circle of radius $m = \pi m^2$

$$\text{Area of shaded region} = \pi n^2 - \pi m^2$$
$$= \pi(n^2 - m^2)$$

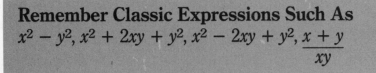

Remember Classic Expressions Such As
$$x^2 - y^2, x^2 + 2xy + y^2, x^2 - 2xy + y^2, \frac{x + y}{xy}$$

Memorize the following factorizations and expressions:

$x^2 - y^2 = (x + y)(x - y)$	Equation 1
$x^2 + 2xy + y^2 = (x + y)(x + y) = (x + y)^2$	Equation 2
$x^2 - 2xy + y^2 = (x - y)(x - y) = (x - y)^2$	Equation 3
$\frac{x + y}{xy} = \frac{1}{x} + \frac{1}{y} \qquad x, y \neq 0$	Equation 4
$\frac{x - y}{xy} = \frac{1}{y} - \frac{1}{x} \qquad x, y \neq 0$	Equation 4A
$xy + xz = x(y + z)$	Equation 5
$xy - xz = x(y - z)$	Equation 5A

Examples 1, 3, 4, and 9 can also be solved with the aid of a calculator and some with the aid of a calculator allowing for exponential calculations. However, to illustrate the effectiveness of Math Strategy 4, we did not use the calculator method of solution of these examples.

Use algebra to see patterns.

EXAMPLE 1

$$66^2 + 2(34)(66) + 34^2 =$$

(A) 9950
(B) 9860
(C) 10000
(D) 4730
(E) 5000

Choice C is correct. Notice that there is a 34 and 66 running through the left side of the equality. To see a pattern, *use algebra. Substitute a* for 66 and *b* for 34. You get:

$$66^2 + 2(34)(66) + 34^2 =$$
$$a^2 + 2(b)(a) \quad + b^2$$

But from Equation 2,

$$a^2 + 2ab + b^2 = \qquad \boxed{1}$$
$$(a + b)(a + b) =$$
$$(a + b)^2$$

Now substitute the numbers 34, and 66 *back into* $\boxed{1}$ to get:

$$66^2 + 2(34)(66) + 34^2 =$$
$$(66 + 34)(66 + 34) =$$
$$100 \times 100 =$$

$$10000 \qquad (Answer)$$

EXAMPLE 2

If $(x + y) = 9$ and $xy = 14$, find $\frac{1}{x} + \frac{1}{y}$.

(Note: $x, y > 0$)

(A) $\frac{1}{9}$ (B) $\frac{2}{7}$ (C) $\frac{9}{14}$ (D) 5 (E) 9

Choice C is correct. We are given:

$$(x + y) = 9 \qquad \boxed{1}$$
$$xy = 14 \qquad \boxed{2}$$
$$x, y > 0 \qquad \boxed{3}$$

I hope that you did not solve $\boxed{2}$ for x (or y), and then substitute it into $\boxed{1}$. If you did you obtained a quadratic equation.

Here is the FAST method. Use Equation 4:

$$\frac{1}{x} + \frac{1}{y} = \frac{x + y}{xy} \qquad \boxed{4}$$

From $\boxed{1}$ and $\boxed{2}$, we find that $\boxed{4}$ becomes

$$\frac{1}{x} + \frac{1}{y} = \frac{9}{14} \quad (Answer)$$

EXAMPLE 3

The value of $100 \times 100 - 99 \times 99 =$

(A) 1
(B) 2
(C) 99
(D) 199
(E) 299

Choice D is correct.
Write a for 100 and b for 99 to see a pattern:
$100 \times 100 - 99 \times 99$
$a \times a - b \times b = a^2 - b^2$ Use Equation 1:
Use the fact that $a^2 - b^2 = (a + b)(a - b)$ $\boxed{1}$
Put back 100 for a and 99 for b in $\boxed{1}$:
$a^2 - b^2 = 100^2 - 99^2 = (100 + 99)(100 - 99) = 199$

EXAMPLE 4

Use factoring to make problems simpler

$$\frac{8^7 - 8^6}{7} =$$

(A) $8/7$
(B) 8^7
(C) 8^6
(D) 8^5
(E) 8^4

Choice C is correct.
Factor: $8^7 - 8^6 = 8^6(8^1 - 1)$ (Equation 5A)
$\qquad\qquad\qquad = 8^6(8 - 1)$
$\qquad\qquad\qquad = 8^6(7)$

So $\dfrac{8^7 - 8^6}{7} = \dfrac{8^6\,(7)}{7} = \dfrac{8^6\,\cancel{(7)}}{\cancel{7}} = 8^6$

EXAMPLE 5

If $y + \dfrac{1}{y} = 9$, then $y^2 + \dfrac{1}{y^2} =$

(A) 76
(B) 77
(C) 78
(D) 79
(E) 81

Choice D is correct.

Square $\left(y + \dfrac{1}{y}\right)$

$\left(y + \dfrac{1}{y}\right)^2 = 81 = y^2 + \dfrac{1}{y^2} + 2$ (Equation 2)

$79 = y^2 + \dfrac{1}{y^2}$

EXAMPLE 6

If $a - b = 4$ and $a + b = 7$, then $a^2 - b^2 =$

(A) 11
(B) 5½
(C) 28
(D) 29
(E) 56

Choice C is correct.
Use $(a - b)(a + b) = a^2 - b^2$ (Equation 1)
$\qquad\qquad a - b = 4$
$\qquad\qquad a + b = 7$
$(a - b)(a + b) = 28 = a^2 - b^2$

EXAMPLE 7

What is the least possible value of $\dfrac{x + y}{xy}$ if
$2 \leqq x < y \leqq 11$ and x and y are integers?

(A) $\dfrac{22}{121}$

(B) $\dfrac{5}{6}$

(C) $\dfrac{21}{110}$

(D) $\dfrac{13}{22}$

(E) 1

Choice C is correct.

Use $\dfrac{x + y}{xy} = \dfrac{1}{x} + \dfrac{1}{y}$ (Equation 4)

$\dfrac{1}{x} + \dfrac{1}{y}$ is *least* when x is *greatest* and y is *greatest*.
Since it was given that x and y are integers and that $2 \leqq x < y \leqq 11$, the greatest value of x is 10 and the greatest value of y is 11.

So the *least* value of $\dfrac{1}{x} + \dfrac{1}{y} = \dfrac{x + y}{xy} =$

$$\frac{10 + 11}{10 \times 11} = \frac{21}{110}$$

EXAMPLE 8

If $(a + b)^2 = 20$ and $ab = -3$, then $a^2 + b^2 =$

(A) 14
(B) 20
(C) 26
(D) 32
(E) 38

Choice C is correct.

Use $(a + b)^2 = a^2 + 2ab + b^2 = 20$ (Use Equation 2)

$ab = -3$

So, $2ab = -6$

Substitute $2ab = -6$ in:

$a^2 + 2ab + b^2 = 20$

We get:

$$a^2 - 6 + b^2 = 20$$
$$a^2 + b^2 = 26$$

EXAMPLE 9

If $998 \times 1002 > 10^6 - x$, x could be

(A) 4 but not 3
(B) 4 but not 5
(C) 5 but not 4
(D) 3 but not 4
(E) 3, 4, or 5

Choice C is correct.

Use $(a + b)(a - b) = a^2 - b^2$ (Use Equation 1)

Write: $998 \times 1002 = (1000 - 2)(1000 + 2) > 10^6 - x$
$$= 1000^2 - 4 > 10^6 - x$$
$$= (10^3)^2 - 4 > 10^6 - x$$
$$= 10^6 - 4 > 10^6 - x$$

Multiply by -1; *reverse inequality sign*:

$$-1(-4 > -x)$$
$$+4 < +x$$

EXAMPLE 10

If $x^2 + y^2 = 2xy$ and $x > 0$ and $y > 0$, then

(A) $x = 0$ only
(B) $y = 0$ only
(C) $x = 1, y = 1$, only
(D) $x > y > 0$
(E) $x = y$

Choice E is correct. Simplify by subtracting to get form of Equation 3: $x^2 - 2xy + y^2 = (x - y)(x - y)$. That is, subtract $2xy$ from both sides of given problem equation to get $x^2 - 2xy + y^2 = 0$. Thus $(x - y)(x - y) = x^2 - 2xy + y^2 = 0$ so $x - y = 0$ and thus $x = y$.

MATH STRATEGY 5

Know How to Manipulate Averages

Almost all problems involving averages can be solved by remembering that

$$\text{Average} = \frac{\text{Sum of the individual quantities or measurements}}{\text{Number of quantities or measurements}}$$

(Note: Average is also called Arithmetic Mean.)

EXAMPLE 1

The average height of 3 students is 68 inches. If two of the students have heights of 70 inches and 72 inches respectively, then what is the height (in inches) of the third student?

(A) 60
(B) 62
(C) 64
(D) 65
(E) 66

Choice B is correct. Recall that

$$\text{Average} = \frac{\text{Sum of the individual measurements}}{\text{Number of measurements}}$$

Let x = height (in inches) of the third student. Thus,

$$68 = \frac{70 + 72 + x}{3}$$

Multiplying by 3,

$$204 = 70 + 72 + x$$
$$\text{or } 204 = 142 + x$$
$$\text{or } x = 62 \text{ inches } (\textit{Answer})$$

EXAMPLE 2

The average of 30 numbers is 65. If one of these numbers is 65, the sum of the remaining numbers is

(A) 65×64
(B) 30×64
(C) 29×30
(D) 29×64
(E) 29×65

Choice E is correct.

$$\text{Average} = \frac{\text{sum of numbers}}{30}$$

Call the numbers a, b, c, d, etc.

$$\text{So } 65 = \frac{a + b + c + d + \ldots}{30}$$

Now immediately, get rid of the fractional part: Multiply by 30 to get: $65 \times 30 = a + b + c + d + \ldots$.

Since we were told *one of the numbers is 65,* let $a = 65$:

$65 \times 30 = 65 + b + c + d + \ldots$.
So $65 \times 30 - 65 = \underbrace{b + c + d + \ldots}_{}$.

sum of remaining numbers

Factor:
$65 \times 30 - 65 = 65 (30 - 1) = $ sum of remaining numbers
$65 \times 29 = $ sum of remaining numbers

EXAMPLE 3

The average (arithmetic mean) of 28 numbers is 64. If one of the numbers is 64, the sum of the remaining numbers is equal to

(A) 63×64
(B) 28×63
(C) 27×28
(D) 27×63
(E) 27×64

Choice E is correct.

Average of 28 numbers is:

$$64 = \frac{a + b + c + \ldots}{28}$$

Now *get rid of fraction* by multiplying by 28:
$64 \times 28 = a + b + c + \ldots$.

It is stated that one of the numbers, let's say a, is 64.
So $64 \times 28 = 64 + b + c + \ldots$

The *sum of the remaining numbers* is

$$64 \times 28 - 64 = b + c + \ldots.$$
$$= 64(28 - 1)$$
$$= 64(27)$$

EXAMPLES 4–7

4. The average length of 6 objects is 25 cm. If five objects are each 20 cm in length, what is the length of the sixth object in cm?

   (A) 55
   (B) 50
   (C) 45
   (D) 40
   (E) 35

5. Scores on five tests range from 0 to 100 inclusive. If Don gets 70 on the first test, 76 on the second, and 75 on the third, what is the minimum score Don may get on the fourth test to average 80 on all five tests?

   (A) 76
   (B) 79
   (C) 99
   (D) 89
   (E) 82

6. 18 students attained an average score of 70 on a test and 12 students on the same test scored an average of 90. What is the average score for all 30 students on the test?

   (A) 80
   (B) 78
   (C) 85
   (D) 82
   (E) Cannot be determined

7. The average length of 10 objects is 25 inches. If the average length of 2 of these objects is 20 inches, what is the average length of the remaining 8 objects?

   (A) 22½ inches
   (B) 24 inches
   (C) 26¼ inches
   (D) 28 inches
   (E) Cannot be determined

EXPLANATORY ANSWERS FOR EXAMPLES 4–7

4. (B) *Use the formula:*

$$\text{Average} = \frac{\text{Sum of individual items}}{\text{Number of items}}$$

Now call the length of the sixth item, x. Then:

$$25 = \frac{20 + 20 + 20 + 20 + 20 + x}{6}$$

$$\text{or } 25 = \frac{20 \times 5 + x}{6}$$

Multiply by 6:

$$25 \times 6 = 20 \times 5 + x$$
$$150 = 100 + x$$
$$50 = x$$

5. (B) *Use the formula:*

$$\text{Average} = \frac{\text{Sum of scores on tests}}{\text{Number of tests}}$$

Lex x be the score on the fourth test and y be the score on the fifth test.

Then:

$$80 = \text{Average} = \frac{70 + 76 + 75 + x + y}{5}$$

The minimum score x Don can get is the *lowest* score he can get. The higher the score y is, the lower the score x can be. The greatest value of y can be 100. So:

$$80 = \frac{70 + 76 + 75 + x + 100}{5}$$

$$80 = \frac{321 + x}{5}$$

Multiply by 5:

$$400 = 321 + x$$
$$79 = x$$

6. (B) *Use the formula:*

$$\text{Average} = \frac{\text{Sum of scores}}{\text{Number of students}}$$

"18 students attained an average of 70 on a test" translates mathematically to:

$$70 = \frac{\text{Sum of scores of 18 students}}{18} \qquad \boxed{1}$$

"12 students on the same test scored an average of 90" translates to:

$$90 = \frac{\text{Sum of scores of other 12 students}}{12} \qquad \boxed{2}$$

Now what you are looking for is the *average score of all 30 students.* That is, you are looking for:

$$\text{Average of 30 students} = \frac{\text{Sum of scores of all 30 students}}{30} \qquad \boxed{3}$$

So, if you can find the *sum of scores of all 30 students,* you can find the required average.

Now, the sum of all 30 students = sum of scores of 18 students + sum of scores of other 12 students

And this can be gotten from $\boxed{1}$ and $\boxed{2}$:

From $\boxed{1}$: $70 \times 18 = $ sum of scores of 18 students

From $\boxed{2}$: $90 \times 12 = $ sum of scores of other 12 students

So adding:

$70 \times 18 + 90 \times 12 = $ sum of scores of 18 students + sum of scores of other 12 students = sum of scores of 30 students

Put all this in $\boxed{3}$:

$$\text{Average of 30 students} = \frac{70 \times 18 + 90 \times 12}{30}$$

$$= \frac{\cancel{70} \times 18 + \cancel{90} \times 12}{\cancel{30}}$$

$$= \frac{7 \times 18 + 9 \times 12}{3}$$

$$= \frac{7 \times \overset{6}{\cancel{18}} + \overset{3}{\cancel{9}} \times 12}{\cancel{3}}$$

$$= 42 + 36 = 78$$

7. (C) Denote the lengths of the objects by a, b, c, d, etc. Since the average length of 10 objects is given to be 25 inches, establish an equation for the average length:

$$\text{Average length} = 25 = \frac{\overset{\text{sum of 10 lengths}}{a + b + c + d + \cdots + j}}{\underset{\text{number of objects}}{10}} \qquad \boxed{1}$$

The question also says that the average length of 2 of these objects is 20. Let the lengths of two we choose be a and b. So,

lengths of 2 objects

$$\text{Average length of } a \text{ and } b = 20 = \frac{a + b}{2} \quad \boxed{2}$$

number of objects

Now we want to find the average length of the *remaining* objects. There are 8 remaining objects of lengths $c, d, e, \ldots j$. Call the average of these lengths x, which is what we want to find.

sum of lengths of remaining objects ($a + b$ are not present because only $c + d + \cdots + j$ remain)

$$\text{Average length} = x = \frac{c + d + e + \cdots + j}{8}$$

number of remaining objects

Use equations $\boxed{1}$ and $\boxed{2}$:

$$25 = \frac{a + b + c + \cdots + j}{10} \quad \boxed{1}$$

$$20 = \frac{a + b}{2} \quad \boxed{2}$$

Now, remember, we want to find the value of x:

$$x = \frac{c + d + e + \cdots + j}{8}$$

Multiply Equation $\boxed{1}$ by 10 to get rid of the denominator. We get:

$$25 \times 10 = 250 = a + b + c + \ldots + j$$

Now multiply Equation $\boxed{2}$ by 2 to get rid of the denominator:

$$20 \times 2 = 40 = a + b$$

Subtract these two new equations:

$$250 = a + b + c + \cdots + j$$
$$- [40 = a + b]$$

You get: $210 = \qquad c + d + \cdots + j$

Now you just have to divide by 8 to get:

$$\frac{210}{8} = \frac{c + d + \cdots + j}{8} = x$$

$$= 26\frac{1}{4}$$

MATH STRATEGY **6**

Know How to Manipulate Inequalities

Most problems involving inequalities can be solved by remembering one of the following statements.

If $x > y$, then $x + z > y + z$	Statement 1
If $x > y$ and $w > z$, then $x + w > y + z$	Statement 2
If $w > 0$ and $x > y$, then $wx > wy$	Statement 3
If $w < 0$ and $x > y$, then $wx < wy$	Statement 4
If $x > y$ and $y > z$, then $x > z$	Statement 5
$x > y$ is the same as $y < x$	Statement 6
$a < x < b$ is the same as both $a < x$ and $x < b$	Statement 7
If $x > y > 0$ and $w > z > 0$, then $xw > yz$	Statement 8

If $x > 0$ and $z = x + y$, then $z > y$ Statement 9

Note that Statement 1 and Statement 2 are also true if all the ">" signs are changed to "<" signs.

If $x < 0$ then $\begin{cases} x^n < 0 \text{ if } n \text{ is odd} & \text{Statement 10} \\ x^n < 0 \text{ if } n \text{ is even} & \text{Statement 11} \end{cases}$

If $xy > 0$, then $x > 0$ and $y > 0$ or $x < 0$ and $y < 0$ Statement 12

If $xy < 0$, then $x > 0$ and $y < 0$ or $x < 0$ and $y > 0$ Statement 13

EXAMPLE 1

If $0 < x < 1$, then which of the following must be true?

I. $2x < 2$
II. $x - 1 < 0$
III. $x^2 < x$

(A) I only
(B) II only
(C) I and II only
(D) II and III only
(E) I, II, and III

Choice E is correct. We are told that $0 < x < 1$. Using ⎡Statement 7⎤, we have

$$0 < x \qquad \boxed{1}$$
$$x < 1 \qquad \boxed{2}$$

For Item I, we multiply $\boxed{2}$ by 2.

See ⎡Statement 3⎤

$$2x < 2$$

Thus, Item I is true.
  For Item II, we add -1 to both sides of $\boxed{2}$.

See ⎡Statement 1⎤ to get

$$x - 1 < 0$$

Thus Item II is true.
  For Item III, we multiply $\boxed{2}$ by x.

See ⎡Statement 3⎤ to get

$$x^2 < x$$

Thus, Item III is true.
All items are true, so Choice E is correct.

EXAMPLE 2

Given that $\dfrac{a}{b}$ is less than 1, $a > 0$, $b > 0$. Which of the following must be greater than 1?

(A) $\dfrac{a}{2b}$

(B) $\dfrac{b}{2a}$

(C) $\dfrac{\sqrt{b}}{a}$

(D) $\dfrac{b}{a}$

(E) $\left(\dfrac{a}{b}\right)^2$

Choice D is correct.

$$\text{Given: } \frac{a}{b} < 1 \qquad \boxed{1}$$
$$a > 0 \qquad \boxed{2}$$
$$b > 0 \qquad \boxed{3}$$

See ⎡Statement 3⎤ : Multiply $\boxed{1}$ by b. We get

$$\not{b}\left(\frac{a}{\not{b}}\right) < b(1)$$
$$a < b \qquad \boxed{4}$$

Use ⎡Statement 3⎤ where $w = \dfrac{1}{a}$: Divide $\boxed{4}$ by a.
We get

$$\frac{a}{a} < \frac{b}{a}$$
$$1 < \frac{b}{a}$$

or

$$\frac{b}{a} > 1$$

EXAMPLE 3

Which combination of the following statements can be used to demonstrate that x is positive?

I. $x > y$
II. $1 < y$

(A) I alone but not II
(B) II alone but not I
(C) I and II taken together but neither taken alone
(D) Both I alone and II alone
(E) Neither I nor II nor both

Choice C is correct. We want to know which of the following

$$x > y \qquad \boxed{1}$$
$$1 < y \qquad \boxed{2}$$

is enough information to conclude that

$$x > 0 \qquad \boxed{3}$$

$\boxed{1}$ alone is not enough to determine $\boxed{3}$ because $0 > x > y$ could be true. (Note: x is greater than y, but they both could be negative.)

$\boxed{2}$ alone is not enough to determine $\boxed{3}$ because we don't know whether x is greater than, less than, or equal to y.

However, if we use $\boxed{1}$ and $\boxed{2}$ together, we can compare the two:

$$1 < y \text{ is the same as } y > 1$$

Therefore, $x > y$ with $y > 1$ yields: ⎡Statement 5⎤

$$x > 1 \qquad \boxed{4}$$

Since $1 > 0$ is always true, then from $\boxed{4}$

$$x > 0 \text{ is always true}$$

EXAMPLE 4

What are all values of x such that $(x - 7)(x + 3)$ is positive?

(A) $x > 7$
(B) $-7 < x < 3$
(C) $-3 < x < 7$
(D) $x > 7$ or $x < -3$
(E) $x > 3$ or $x < -7$

Choice D is correct.

$$(x - 7)(x + 3) > 0 \text{ when}$$
$$x - 7 > 0 \text{ and } x + 3 > 0 \quad \boxed{1}$$
$$\text{or} \quad x - 7 < 0 \text{ and } x + 3 < 0 \quad \boxed{2}$$

Statement 12

From $\boxed{1}$ we have $x > 7$ and $x > -3$ $\quad\boxed{3}$

when $x > 7$ $\quad\boxed{4}$
then $\boxed{3}$ and $\boxed{1}$ are always satisfied.

From $\boxed{2}$, we have $x < 7$ and $x < -3$ $\quad\boxed{5}$

when $x < -3$ $\quad\boxed{6}$
then $\boxed{5}$ and $\boxed{2}$ are always satisfied.

Thus, $\boxed{4}$ and $\boxed{6}$ together represent the entire solution.

EXAMPLE 5

If p and q are nonzero real numbers and if $p^2 + q^3 < 0$ and if $p^3 + q^5 > 0$, which of the following number lines shows the relative positions of p, q, and 0?

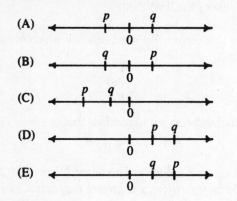

Choice B is correct.

Method 1: Given: $p^2 + q^3 < 0$ $\quad\boxed{1}$
$p^3 + q^5 > 0$ $\quad\boxed{2}$

Subtracting p^2 from $\boxed{1}$ and q^5 from $\boxed{2}$, we have

$$q^3 < -p^2 \quad\boxed{3}$$
$$p^3 > -q^5 \quad\boxed{4}$$

But $p^2 > 0$ so $-p^2 < 0$ $\quad\boxed{5}$

Using Statement 5, combining $\boxed{3}$ and $\boxed{5}$ we get

$$q^3 < -p^2 < 0 \quad\boxed{6}$$
and get $q^3 < 0$ $\quad\boxed{7}$

Thus, $q < 0$ $\quad\boxed{8}$
From $\boxed{8}$, we can say $q^5 < 0$ or $-q^5 > 0$ $\quad\boxed{9}$

Using Statement 5, combining $\boxed{4}$ and $\boxed{9}$,
$p^3 > -q^5 > 0$ and $p^3 > 0$. Thus $p > 0$ $\quad\boxed{10}$

Using $\boxed{8}$ and $\boxed{10}$, it is easily seen that Choice B is correct.

Method 2: **(Use Strategy 6: Know how to interpret inequalities.)**

Given: $p^2 + q^3 < 0$ $\quad\boxed{1}$
$p^3 + q^5 > 0$ $\quad\boxed{2}$

Since p^2 is always > 0, using this with $\boxed{1}$, we know that $q^3 < 0$ and, therefore, $q < 0$ $\quad\boxed{3}$

If $q^3 < 0$ then $q^5 < 0$. $\quad\boxed{4}$

Using $\boxed{4}$ and $\boxed{2}$ we know that
$p^3 > 0$, and therefore $p > 0$ $\quad\boxed{5}$

Using $\boxed{3}$ and $\boxed{5}$, only Choice B is correct.

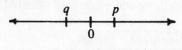

EXAMPLE 6

Janie is older than Tammy, but she is younger than Lori. Let j, t, and l be the ages in years of Janie, Tammy, and Lori, respectively. Which of the following is true?

(A) $j < t < l$
(B) $t < j < l$
(C) $t < l < j$
(D) $l < j < t$
(E) $l < t < j$

Choice B is correct. **(First, use Strategy 2: Translate from words to algebra.)** Janie is older than Tammy but she is younger than Lori, translates to:

Janie's age > Tammy's age $\quad\boxed{1}$
Janie's age < Lorie's age $\quad\boxed{2}$

Given: Janie's age $= j$ $\quad\boxed{3}$
Tammy's age $= t$ $\quad\boxed{4}$
Lori's age $= l$ $\quad\boxed{5}$

Substituting $\boxed{3}$, $\boxed{4}$ and $\boxed{5}$ into $\boxed{1}$ and $\boxed{2}$, we get
$$j > t \quad\boxed{6}$$
$$j < l \quad\boxed{7}$$

Use Statement 5. Reversing $\boxed{6}$, we get

$$t < j \quad\boxed{8}$$

Combining $\boxed{8}$ and $\boxed{7}$, we get
$$t < j < l$$

Use Specific Numerical Examples to Prove or Disprove Your Guess

When you do not want to do a lot of algebra, or when you are unable to prove what you think is the answer, you may want to substitute numbers.

EXAMPLE 1

The sum of the cubes of any two consecutive positive integers is always

(A) an odd integer
(B) an even integer
(C) the cube of an integer
(D) the square of an integer
(E) the product of an integer and 3

Choice A is correct. Try specific numbers. Call consecutive positive integers 1 and 2.

Sum of cubes:

$$1^3 + 2^3 = 1 + 8 = 9$$

You have now eliminated choices B and C. You are left with choices A, D, and E.

Now try two other consecutive integers: 2 and 3

$$2^3 + 3^3 = 8 + 27 = 35$$

Choice A is acceptable. Choice D is false. Choice E is false.

Thus, Choice A is the only choice remaining.

EXAMPLE 2

John is now m years old and Sally is 4 years older than John. Which represents Sally's age 6 years ago?

(A) $m + 10$
(B) $m - 10$
(C) $m - 2$
(D) $m - 4$
(E) $4m - 6$

Choice C is correct.

Try a specific number.

Let $m = 10$

John is 10 years old.
Sally is 4 years older than John, so Sally is 14 years old.
Sally's age 6 years ago was 8 years.

Now look for the choice that gives you 8 with $m = 10$.

(A) $m + 10 = 10 + 10 = 20$
(B) $m - 10 = 10 - 10 = 0$
(C) $m - 2 = 10 - 2 = 8$—that's the one

EXAMPLE 3

If $x \neq 0$, then $\dfrac{(-3x)^3}{-3x^3} =$

(A) -9
(B) -1
(C) 3
(D) 1
(E) 9

Choice E is correct.

Try a specific number.

Let $x = 1$. Then:

$$\frac{(-3x)^3}{-3x^3} = \frac{(-3(1))^3}{-3(1^3)} = \frac{(-3)^3}{-3} = 9$$

EXAMPLE 4

If $a = 4b$, then the average of a and b is

(A) $\dfrac{1}{2}b$

(B) $\dfrac{3}{2}b$

(C) $\dfrac{5}{2}b$

(D) $\dfrac{7}{2}b$

(E) $\dfrac{9}{2}b$

Choice C is correct.

Try a specific number.

Let $b = 1$. Then $a = 4b = 4$. So the average $=$

$$\frac{1+4}{2} = \frac{5}{2}$$

Look at choices where $b = 1$. The only choice that gives $\frac{5}{2}$ is Choice C.

EXAMPLE 5

The sum of three consecutive even integers is P. Find the sum of the next three consecutive *odd* integers that follow the greatest of the three even integers.

(A) $P + 9$
(B) $P + 15$
(C) $P + 12$
(D) $P + 20$
(E) None of these

Choice B is correct.

Try specific numbers.

Let the three consecutive even integers be 2, 4, 6.

$$\text{So, } 2 + 4 + 6 = P = 12$$

The next three consecutive odd integers that follow 6 are:

$$7, 9, 11$$

So the sum of

$$7 + 9 + 11 = 27$$

Now, where $P = 12$, look for a choice that gives you 27:

(A) $P + 9 = 12 + 9 = 21$—NO
(B) $P + 15 = 12 + 15 = 27$—YES

EXAMPLE 6

If $3 > a$, which of the following is *not* true?

(A) $3 - 3 > a - 3$
(B) $3 + 3 > a + 3$
(C) $3(3) > a(3)$
(D) $3 - 3 > 3 - a$
(E) $\frac{3}{3} > \frac{a}{3}$

Choice D is correct.

Try specific numbers.

Work backward from Choice E if you wish.

Let $a = 1$.

Choice E:

$$\frac{3}{3} > \frac{a}{3} = \frac{1}{3} \quad \text{TRUE STATEMENT}$$

Choice D:

$$3 - 3 > 3 - a = 3 - 1 \text{ or } 0 > 2 \quad \text{FALSE STATEMENT}$$

EXAMPLE 7

In the figure of intersecting lines above, which of the following is equal to $180 - a$?

(A) $a + d$
(B) $a + 2d$
(C) $c + b$
(D) $b + 2a$
(E) $c + d$

Choice A is correct.

Try a specific number.

Let $\boxed{a = 20°}$

Then $2a = 40°$

Be careful now—all of the other angles are now determined, so don't choose any more.

Because vertical angles are equal, $2a = b$, so

$$\boxed{b = 40°}$$

Now $c + b = 180°$, so $c + 40 = 180$ and

$$\boxed{c = 140°}$$

Thus, $\boxed{d = 140°}$ (vertical angles are equal)

Now look at the question:

$$180 - a = 180 - 20 = 160$$

Which is the correct choice?

(A) $a + d = 20 + 140 = 160$—that's the one!

When Each Choice Must Be Tested, Start with Choice E and Work Backward

If you must check each choice for the correct answer, start with Choice E and work backward. The reason for this is that the test maker of a question *in which each choice must be tested* often puts the correct answer as Choice D or E. In this way, the careless student must check all or most of the choices before finding the correct one. So if you're trying all the choices, start with the last choice, then the next to last choice, etc.

EXAMPLE 1

If p is a positive integer, which *could* be an odd integer?

(A) $2p + 2$
(B) $p^3 - p$
(C) $p^2 + p$
(D) $p^2 - p$
(E) $7p - 3$

Choice E is correct. Start with Choice E first since you have to *test* out the choices.

Method 1: Try a number for p. Let $p = 1$. Then (starting with choice E)

$7p - 3 = 7(1) - 3 = 4$. 4 is even, so try another number for p to see whether $7p - 3$ is odd. Let $p = 2$.

$7p - 3 = 7(2) - 3 = 11$. 11 is odd. Therefore, Choice E is correct.

Method 2: Look at Choice E. $7p$ could be even or odd, depending on what p is. If p is even, $7p$ is even. If p is odd, $7p$ is odd. Accordingly, $7p - 3$ is either even or odd. Thus, Choice E is correct.

Note: By using either Method 1 or Method 2, it is not necessary to test the other choices.

EXAMPLE 2

If $y = x^2 + 3$, then for which value of x is y divisible by 7?

(A) 3
(B) 4
(C) 7
(D) 8
(E) 5

Choice E is correct. Since you must check all of the choices, start with Choice E:

$$y = 5^2 + 3 = 25 + 3 = 28$$

28 is divisible by 4 (*Answer*)

If you had started with Choice A, you would have had to test four choices, instead of one choice before finding the correct answer.

EXAMPLE 3

Which fraction is greater than $\frac{1}{2}$?

(A) $\frac{4}{9}$

(B) $\frac{17}{35}$

(C) $\frac{6}{13}$

(D) $\frac{12}{25}$

(E) $\frac{8}{15}$

Choice E is correct.

<u>Look at Choice E first.</u>

$$\text{Is } \frac{1}{2} > \frac{8}{15}?$$

Use the cross multiplication method.

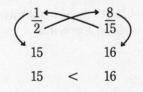

$$15 \quad \quad 16$$
$$15 \quad < \quad 16$$

So, $\frac{1}{2} < \frac{8}{15}$

You also could have looked at Choice E and said $\frac{8}{16} = \frac{1}{2}$ and realized that $\frac{8}{15} > \frac{1}{2}$ because $\frac{8}{15}$ has a smaller denominator than $\frac{8}{16}$.

EXAMPLE 4

If n is an even integer, which of the following is an odd integer?

(A) $n^2 - 2$
(B) $n - 4$
(C) $(n - 4)^2$
(D) n^3
(E) $n^2 - n - 1$

Choice E is correct.

Look at Choice E first.

$$n^2 - n - 1$$
$$\text{If } n \text{ is even}$$
$$n^2 \text{ is even}$$
$$n \text{ is even}$$
$$1 \text{ is odd}$$

So, $n^2 - n - 1 = \text{even} - \text{even} - \text{odd} = \text{odd}$.

EXAMPLE 5

Which of the following is an odd number?

(A) 7×22
(B) $59 - 15$
(C) $55 + 35$
(D) $75 \div 15$
(E) 4^7

Choice D is correct.

Look at Choice E first.

4^7 is even, since $4 \times 4 \times 4 \ldots$ is even

So now look at Choice D: $\dfrac{75}{15} = 5$, which is odd.

EXAMPLE 6

$$\begin{array}{r} 3 \ \# \ 2 \\ \times \quad 8 \\ \hline 28 \ \star \ 6 \end{array}$$

If # and $\star$ are different digits in the correctly calculated multiplication problem above, then # could be

(A) 2
(B) 3
(C) 4
(D) 7
(E) 6

Choice E is correct.

Try Choice E first.

$$\begin{array}{r} 3 \ \# \ 2 \\ \times \quad 8 \\ \hline 28 \ \star \ 6 \end{array} \qquad \begin{array}{r} 3 \ ⑥ \ 2 \\ \times \quad 8 \\ \hline 28 \ ⑨ \ 6 \end{array}$$

9 and 6 are different numbers, so Choice E is correct.

EXAMPLE 7

Which choice describes a pair of numbers that are *unequal*?

(A) $\dfrac{1}{6}, \dfrac{11}{66}$

(B) $3.4, \dfrac{34}{10}$

(C) $\dfrac{15}{75}, \dfrac{1}{5}$

(D) $\dfrac{3}{8}, 0.375$

(E) $\dfrac{86}{24}, \dfrac{42}{10}$

Choice E is correct.

Look at Choice E first.

$$\dfrac{86}{24} \qquad ? \qquad \dfrac{42}{10}$$

Cross multiply:

860 ends in 0 24×42 ends in 8

Thus, the numbers must be *different* and *unequal*.

EXAMPLE 8

$$\begin{array}{r} \star \ 3 \\ 4 \ \star \\ \star \ 1 \\ 6 \ \star \\ \star \ 3 \\ \hline 203 \end{array}$$

In the above addition problem, the symbol $\star$ describes a particular digit in each number. What must $\star$ be in order to make the answer correct?

(A) 7
(B) 6
(C) 5
(D) 4
(E) 3

Choice E is correct.

Try substituting the number in Choice E first for the $\star$.

$$\begin{array}{rr} \star \ 3 & 33 \\ 4 \ \star & 43 \\ \star \ 1 & 31 \\ 6 \ \star & 63 \\ \star \ 3 & 33 \\ \hline 203 & 203 \end{array}$$

Since you get 203 for the addition, Choice E is correct.

Know How to Solve Problems Using the Formula R × T = D

Almost every problem involving motion can be solved using the formula

R × T = D

or

rate × elapsed time = distance

EXAMPLE 1

The diagram below shows two paths: Path 1 is 10 miles long, and Path 2 is 12 miles long. If person X runs along Path 1 at 5 miles per hour and person Y runs along Path 2 at y miles per hour, and if it takes exactly the same amount of time for both runners to run their whole path, then what is the value of y?

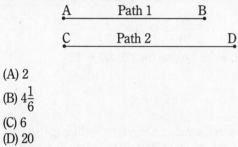

(A) 2

(B) $4\frac{1}{6}$

(C) 6

(D) 20

(E) 24

Choice C is correct. Let T = Time (in hours) for either runner to run the whole path.

Using R × T = D, for Person X, we have

(5mi./hr.)(T hours) = 10 miles

or   5T = 10 or

T = 2 $\boxed{1}$

For Person Y, we have

(y mi./hr.)(T hours) = 12 miles

or yT = 12

Using $\boxed{1}$ y(2) = 12 or y = 6

EXAMPLE 2

A car traveling at 50 miles per hour for two hours travels the same distance as a car traveling at 20 miles per hour for x hours. What is x?

(A) $\frac{4}{5}$

(B) $\frac{5}{4}$

(C) 5

(D) 2

(E) $\frac{1}{2}$

Choice C is correct.

Use $R \times T = D$. Call distance both cars travel, D (since distance is same for both cars).

So we get:

$$50 \times 2 = D \, (=100) \qquad \boxed{1}$$
$$20 \times x = D \, (=100) \qquad \boxed{2}$$

Solving $\boxed{2}$ you can see that $x = 5$.

EXAMPLE 3

John walks at a rate of 4 miles per hour. Sally walks at a rate of 5 miles per hour. If both John and Sally both start at the same starting point, how many miles is one person from the other after t hours of walking?

(A) $\frac{t}{2}$

(B) t

(C) $2t$

(D) $\frac{4}{5}t$

(E) $\frac{5}{4}t$

Choice B is correct.

Draw a diagram:

John (4 mph)

Sally (5 mph)

Let D_J be distance that John walks in t hours.
Let D_S be distance that Sally walks in t hours.
Then, using $R \times T = D$,

$$\text{for John: } 4 \times t = D_J$$
$$\text{for Sally: } 5 \times t = D_S$$

The distance between Sally and John after t hours of walking is:

$$D_S - D_J = 5t - 4t = t$$

EXAMPLE 4

A man rode a bicycle a straight distance at a speed of 10 miles per hour and came back the same distance at a speed of 20 miles per hour. What was the man's total number of miles for the trip back and forth, if his total traveling time was 1 hour?

(A) 15

(B) $7\frac{1}{2}$

(C) $6\frac{1}{3}$

(D) $6\frac{2}{3}$

(E) $13\frac{1}{3}$

Choice E is correct.

Always use $R \times T = D$ (Rate $\times$ Time = Distance) in problems like this. Call the first distance D and the time for the first part, T_1. Since he rode at 10 mph:

$$10 \times T_1 = D \qquad \boxed{1}$$

Now for the trip back. He rode at 20 mph. Call the time it took to go back, T_2. Since he came back the *same* distance, we can call that distance D also. So for the trip back using $R \times T = D$, we get:

$$20 \times T_2 = D \qquad \boxed{2}$$

Since it was given that the total traveling time was 1 hour, the total traveling time is:

$$T_1 + T_2 = 1$$

Now here's the trick: Let's make use of the fact that $T_1 + T_2 = 1$. Dividing Equation $\boxed{1}$ by 10 we get:

$$T_1 = \frac{D}{10}$$

Dividing Equation $\boxed{2}$ by 20 we get:

$$T_2 = \frac{D}{20}$$

Now add $T_1 + T_2$ and we get:

$$T_1 + T_2 = 1 = \frac{D}{10} + \frac{D}{20}$$

Factor D:

$$1 = D\left(\frac{1}{10} + \frac{1}{20}\right)$$

Add $\frac{1}{10} + \frac{1}{20}$. Remember the fast way of adding fractions?

$$\frac{1}{10} \underset{+}{\times} \frac{1}{20} = \frac{20 + 10}{20 \times 10} = \frac{30}{200}$$

So:

$$1 = (D)\frac{30}{200}$$

Multiply by 200 and divide by 30 and we get:

$$\frac{200}{30} = D; \; D = 6\frac{2}{3}$$

Don't forget, we're looking for $2D$: $2D = 13\frac{1}{3}$

EXAMPLE 5

What is the average rate of a bicycle traveling at 10 mph a distance of 5 miles and at 20 mph the same distance?

(A) 15 mph

(B) 20 mph

(C) $12\frac{1}{2}$ mph

(D) $13\frac{1}{3}$ mph

(E) 16 mph

Choice D is correct.

Ask yourself, what does *average rate* mean? It *does not* mean the average of the rates! If you thought it did, you would have selected Choice A as the answer (averaging 10 and 20 to get 15)—the "lure" choice.

Average is a word that *modifies* the word *rate* in this case. So you must define the word *rate* first, before you do anything with averaging. Since Rate $\times$ Time = Distance,

$$\text{Rate} = \frac{\text{Distance}}{\text{Time}}$$

Then *average* rate must be:

$$\text{Average rate} = \frac{\text{TOTAL distance}}{\text{TOTAL time}}$$

The *total distance* is the distance covered on the whole trip, which is $5 + 5 = 10$ miles.

The *total time* is the time traveled the first 5 miles at 10 mph added to the time the bicycle traveled the next 5 miles at 20 mph.

Let t_1 be the time bicycle traveled first 5 miles.

Let t_2 be the time bicycle traveled next 5 miles.

Then the *total time* $= t_1 + t_2$.

Since $R \times T = D$,

for the first 5 miles: $10 \times t_1 = 5$
for the next 5 miles: $20 \times t_2 = 5$

Finding t_1 : $t_1 = \dfrac{5}{10}$

Finding t_2 : $t_2 = \dfrac{5}{20}$

So, $t_1 + t_2 = \dfrac{5}{10} + \dfrac{5}{20}$

$\qquad = \dfrac{1}{2} + \dfrac{1}{4}$

$\qquad = \dfrac{4 + 2}{8}$ (remembering how to quickly add fractions)

$\qquad = \dfrac{6}{8} = \dfrac{3}{4}$

$$\text{Average rate} = \frac{\text{TOTAL DISTANCE}}{\text{TOTAL TIME}}$$

$$= \frac{5 + 5}{\dfrac{3}{4}}$$

$$= (5 + 5) \times \frac{4}{3}$$

$$= 10 \times \frac{4}{3} = \frac{40}{3} = 13\frac{1}{3} \text{ (Choice D)}$$

Here's a formula you can memorize:
If a vehicle travels a certain distance at a mph and travels the same distance at b mph, the *average rate* is

$$\frac{2ab}{a + b}$$

Try doing the problem using this formula:

$$\frac{2ab}{a + b} = \frac{2 \times (10) \times (20)}{10 + 20} = \frac{400}{30} = 13\frac{1}{3}$$

Caution: Use this formula only when you are looking for *average rate and when the distance is the same for both speeds.*

Know How to Use Units of Time, Distance, Area, or Volume to Find or Check Your Answer.

By knowing what the units in your answer must be, you will often have an easier time finding or checking your answer. A very helpful thing to do is to treat the units of time or space as variables (like "x" or "y"). Thus, you should substitute, multiply, or divide these units as if they were ordinary variables. The following examples illustrate this idea.

EXAMPLE 1

What is the distance in miles covered by a car that traveled at 50 miles per hour for 5 hours?

(A) 10
(B) 45
(C) 55
(D) 200
(E) 250

Choice E is correct. Although this is an easy "$R \times T = D$" problem, it illustrates this strategy very well.

Recall that

$$\text{rate} \times \text{time} = \text{distance}$$
$$(50 \text{ mi./hr.})(5 \text{ hours}) = \text{distance}$$

Notice that when I substituted into $R \times T = D$, *I kept the units of rate and time* (miles/hour and hours). Now I will *treat these units as if they were ordinary variables.* Thus,

$$\text{distance} = (50 \text{ mi./hr.})(5 \text{ hours})$$

I have canceled the variable "hour(s)" from the numerator and denominator of the right side of the equation. Hence,

$$\text{distance} = 250 \text{ miles}$$

The distance has units of "miles" as I would expect. In fact, if the units in my answer had been "miles/hour" or "hours," then I would have been in error.

Thus, *the general procedure* for problems using this strategy is:

Step 1. Keep the units given in the question.
Step 2. Treat the units as ordinary variables.
Step 3. Make sure the answer has units that you would expect.

EXAMPLE 2

How many inches is equivalent to 2 yards, 2 feet, and 7 inches?

(A) 11
(B) 37
(C) 55
(D) 81
(E) 103

Choice E is correct.
Remember that

$$1 \text{ yard} = 3 \text{ feet} \qquad \boxed{1}$$
$$1 \text{ foot} = 12 \text{ inches} \qquad \boxed{2}$$

Treat the units of length as variables! Divide $\boxed{1}$ by 1 yard, and $\boxed{2}$ by 1 foot, to get

$$1 = \frac{3 \text{ feet}}{1 \text{ yard}} \qquad \boxed{3}$$

$$1 = \frac{12 \text{ inches}}{1 \text{ foot}} \qquad \boxed{4}$$

We can multiply any expression by 1 and get the same value. Thus, 2 yards + 7 inches = (2 yards)(1)(1) + (2 feet)(1) + 7 inches.
Substituting $\boxed{3}$ and $\boxed{4}$ into $\boxed{5}$, 2 yards + 2 feet + 7 inches.

$$= 2 \text{ yards} \left(\frac{3 \text{ feet}}{\text{yard}}\right)\left(\frac{12 \text{ inches}}{\text{foot}}\right) + 2 \text{ feet}\left(\frac{12 \text{ inches}}{\text{foot}}\right) + 7 \text{ inches}$$
$$= 72 \text{ inches} + 24 \text{ inches} + 7 \text{ inches}$$
$$= 103 \text{ inches}$$

Notice that the answer is in "inches" as I expected. If the answer had come out in "yards" or "feet," then I would have been in error.

EXAMPLE 3

A car wash cleans x cars per hour, for y hours at z dollars per car. How much money in *cents* did the car wash receive?

(A) $\dfrac{xy}{100z}$

(B) $\dfrac{xyz}{100}$

(C) $100xyz$

(D) $\dfrac{100x}{yz}$

(E) $\dfrac{yz}{100x}$

Choice C is correct.

Use units: $\left(\dfrac{x \text{ cars}}{\text{hour}}\right)(y \text{ hours})\left(\dfrac{z \text{ dollars}}{\text{car}}\right) = xyz \text{ dollars} \quad \boxed{1}$

Multiply $\boxed{1}$ by 100. We get
$100\,xyz$ cents.

EXAMPLE 4

There are 3 feet in a yard and 12 inches in a foot. How many yards are there altogether in 1 yard, 1 foot, and 1 inch?

(A) $1\dfrac{1}{3}$

(B) $1\dfrac{13}{36}$

(C) $1\dfrac{11}{18}$

(D) $2\dfrac{5}{12}$

(E) $4\dfrac{1}{12}$

Choice B is correct. **Know how to work with units.**

$$\textit{Given}: 3 \text{ feet} = 1 \text{ yard}$$
$$12 \text{ inches} = 1 \text{ foot}$$

Thus,

$$1 \text{ yard} + 1 \text{ foot} + 1 \text{ inch} =$$
$$1 \text{ yard} + 1 \text{ foot}\left(\frac{1 \text{ yard}}{3 \text{ feet}}\right) +$$
$$1 \text{ inch}\left(\frac{1 \text{ foot}}{12 \text{ inches}}\right)\left(\frac{1 \text{ yard}}{3 \text{ feet}}\right) =$$
$$1 + \frac{1}{3} + \frac{1}{36} \text{ yards} \qquad =$$
$$1 + \frac{12}{36} + \frac{1}{36} \text{ yards} \qquad =$$
$$1\frac{13}{36} \text{ yards}$$

Use New Definitions and Functions Carefully

Some SAT questions use new symbols, functions, or definitions that were created in the question. At first glance, these questions may seem difficult because you are not familiar with the new symbol, function, or definition. *However, most of these questions can be solved through simple substitution or application of a simple definition.*

EXAMPLE 1

If the symbol ϕ is defined by the equation

$$a \phi b = a - b - ab$$

for all a and b, then $\left(-\dfrac{1}{3}\right) \phi (-3) =$

(A) $\dfrac{5}{3}$

(B) $\dfrac{11}{3}$

(C) $-\dfrac{13}{3}$

(D) -4

(E) -5

Choice A is correct. All that is required is substitution:

$$a \phi b = a - b - ab$$

$$\left(-\dfrac{1}{3}\right) \phi (-3)$$

Substitute $-\dfrac{1}{3}$ for a and

-3 for b in $a - b - ab$:

$$\left(-\dfrac{1}{3}\right) \phi (-3) = -\dfrac{1}{3} - (-3) - \left(-\dfrac{1}{3}\right)(-3)$$

$$= -\dfrac{1}{3} + 3 - 1$$

$$= 2 - \dfrac{1}{3}$$

$$= \dfrac{5}{3} \ (Answer)$$

EXAMPLE 2

Let $\boxed{x} = \begin{cases} \dfrac{5}{2}(x+1) & \text{if } x \text{ is an odd integer} \\[2mm] \dfrac{5}{2}x & \text{if } x \text{ is an even integer} \end{cases}$

Find $\boxed{2y}$, where y is an integer.

(A) $\dfrac{5}{2}y$ (B) $5y$ (C) $\dfrac{5}{2}y + 1$

(D) $5y + \dfrac{5}{2}$ (E) $5y + 5$

Choice B is correct. All we have to do is to substitute $2y$ into the definition of $\boxed{x}$. In order to know which definition of $\boxed{x}$ to use, we want to know if $2y$ is even. Since y is an integer, then $2y$ is an even integer. Thus,

$$\boxed{2y} = \dfrac{5}{2}(2y)$$

or

$$\boxed{2y} = 5y \ (Answer)$$

EXAMPLE 3

As in the previous example 1, ø is defined as
$$a \text{ ø } b = a - b - ab.$$
If $a \text{ ø } 3 = 6$, $a =$

(A) $\dfrac{9}{2}$

(B) $\dfrac{9}{4}$

(C) $-\dfrac{9}{4}$

(D) $-\dfrac{4}{9}$

(E) $-\dfrac{9}{2}$

Choice E is correct.

$$a \text{ ø } b = a - b - ab$$
$$a \text{ ø } 3 = 6$$

Substitute a for a, 3 for b:

$$a \text{ ø } 3 = a - 3 - a(3) = 6$$
$$= a - 3 - 3a = 6$$
$$= -2a - 3 = 6$$
$$2a = -9$$
$$a = -\frac{9}{2}$$

EXAMPLE 4

The symbol $\left(\,x\,\right)$ is defined as the greatest integer less than or equal to x.

$\left(-3.4\right) + \left(21\right) =$

(A) 16.6
(B) 18
(C) 17
(D) 16
(E) 17.6

Choice C is correct

$\left(-3.4\right)$ is defined as the *greatest integer less than or equal to* -3.4. This is -4, since $-4 < -3.4$.

$\left(21\right)$ is defined as the *greatest integer less than or equal to* 21. That is just 21, since $21 = 21$.
Thus, $-4 + 21 = 17$

EXAMPLE 5

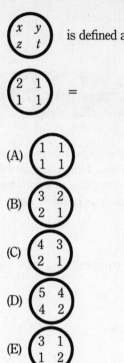

$\left(\begin{smallmatrix} x & y \\ z & t \end{smallmatrix}\right)$ is defined as $xz - yt$

$\left(\begin{smallmatrix} 2 & 1 \\ 1 & 1 \end{smallmatrix}\right) =$

(A) $\left(\begin{smallmatrix} 1 & 1 \\ 1 & 1 \end{smallmatrix}\right)$

(B) $\left(\begin{smallmatrix} 3 & 2 \\ 2 & 1 \end{smallmatrix}\right)$

(C) $\left(\begin{smallmatrix} 4 & 3 \\ 2 & 1 \end{smallmatrix}\right)$

(D) $\left(\begin{smallmatrix} 5 & 4 \\ 4 & 2 \end{smallmatrix}\right)$

(E) $\left(\begin{smallmatrix} 3 & 1 \\ 1 & 2 \end{smallmatrix}\right)$

Choice E is correct.

$\left(\begin{smallmatrix} x & y \\ z & t \end{smallmatrix}\right) = xz - yt;\quad \left(\begin{smallmatrix} 2 & 1 \\ 1 & 1 \end{smallmatrix}\right) = ?$

Substituting 2 for x, 1 for z, 1 for y, and 1 for t,

$\left(\begin{smallmatrix} 2 & 1 \\ 1 & 1 \end{smallmatrix}\right) = (2)(1) - (1)(1)$
$= 1$

Now work from Choice E:

(E) $\left(\begin{smallmatrix} 3 & 1 \\ 1 & 2 \end{smallmatrix}\right) = xz - yt = (3)(1) - (1)(2)$
$= 3 - 2 = 1$

EXAMPLE 6

If for all numbers a, b, c the operation • is defined as
$$a \bullet b = ab - a$$
then
$$a \bullet (b \bullet c) =$$

(A) $a(bc - b - 1)$
(B) $a(bc + b + 1)$
(C) $a(bc - c - b - 1)$
(D) $a(bc - b + 1)$
(E) $a(b - a + c)$

Choice A is correct.

$a \bullet b = ab - a$
$a \bullet (b \bullet c) = ?$

Find $(b \bullet c)$ first. <u>Use substitution:</u>

$$a \bullet b = ab - a$$
$$\uparrow \quad \uparrow$$
$$b \bullet c$$

Substitute b for a and c for b:

$$b \bullet c = b(c) - b$$

Now, $a \bullet (b \bullet c) = a \bullet (bc - b)$
Use definition $a \bullet b = ab - a$
Substitute a for a and $bc - b$ for b:

$$a \bullet b = ab - a$$
$$a \bullet (bc - b) = a(bc - b) - a$$
$$= abc - ab - a$$
$$= a(bc - b - 1)$$

MATH STRATEGY 12

Try Not to Make Tedious Calculations Since There Is Usually an Easier Way

In many of the examples given in these strategies, it has been explicitly stated that one should not calculate complicated quantities. In some of the examples, we have demonstrated a fast and a slow way of solving the same problem. On the actual exam, if you find that your solution to a problem involves a tedious and complicated method, then you are probably doing the problem in a long, hard way.* Almost always there will be an easier way.

Examples 3, 7, and 8 can also be solved with the aid of a calculator and some with the aid of a calculator allowing for exponential calculations. However, to illustrate the effectiveness of Math Strategy 12, we did not use the calculator method of solving these examples.

EXAMPLE 1

If $y^8 = 4$ and $y^7 = \dfrac{3}{x}$,

what is the value of y in terms of x?

(A) $\dfrac{4x}{3}$

(B) $\dfrac{3x}{4}$

(C) $\dfrac{4}{x}$

(D) $\dfrac{x}{4}$

(E) $\dfrac{12}{x}$

Choice A is correct.

Don't solve for the *value* of y first, by finding $y = 4$!

*Many times, you can DIVIDE, MULTIPLY, ADD, SUBTRACT or FACTOR to simplify.

Just divide the two equations:

(Step 1) $y^8 = 4$

(Step 2) $y^7 = \dfrac{3}{x}$

(Step 3) $\dfrac{y^8}{y^7} = \dfrac{4}{\dfrac{3}{x}}$

(Step 4) $y = 4 \times \dfrac{x}{3}$

(Step 5) $y = \dfrac{4x}{3}$ *(Answer)*

EXAMPLE 2

If $x = 1 + 2 + 2^2 + 2^3 + 2^4 + 2^5 + 2^6 + 2^7 + 2^8 + 2^9$ and $y = 1 + 2x$, then $y - x =$

(A) 2^7
(B) 2^8
(C) 2^9
(D) 2^{10}
(E) 2^{11}

Choice D is correct. I hope you did not calculate $1 + 2 + \ldots \ldots 2^9$. If you did, then you found that $x = 1,023$ and $y = 2,047$ and $y - x = 1,024$.

Here is the FAST method. Instead of making these tedious calculations, observe that since

$$x = 1 + 2 + 2^2 + 2^3 + 2^4 + 2^5 + 2^6$$
$$+ 2^7 + 2^8 + 2^9 \qquad \boxed{1}$$

then $2x = 2 + 2^2 + 2^3 + 2^4 + 2^5 + 2^6 + 2^7$
$$+ 2^8 + 2^9 + 2^{10} \qquad \boxed{2}$$

and $y = 1 + 2x = 1 + 2 + 2^2 + 2^3 + 2^4$
$$+ 2^5 + 2^6 + 2^7 + 2^8 + 2^9 + 2^{10} \qquad \boxed{3}$$

Thus, calculating $\boxed{3} - \boxed{1}$, we get

$$y - x = 1 + 2 + 2^2 + 2^3 + 2^4 + 2^5 + 2^6 + 2^7$$
$$+ 2^8 + 2^9 + 2^{10}$$
$$- \quad (1 + 2 + 2^2 + 2^3 + 2^4 + 2^5 + 2^6 + 2^7$$
$$+ 2^8 + 2^9)$$
$$= 2^{10} \ (Answer)$$

EXAMPLE 3

Use factoring to make problems simpler

$\sqrt{(88)^2 + (88)^2\,(3)} =$

(A) 88   (B) 176   (C) 348   (D) 350   (E) 352

Choice B is correct. Factor:

$$(88)^2 + (88)^2(3) = 88^2(1 + 3) = 88^2(4)$$

So: $\sqrt{(88)^2 + (88)^2\,(3)} = \sqrt{88^2(4)}$
$$= \sqrt{88^2} \times \sqrt{4}$$
$$= 88 \times 2$$
$$= 176$$

EXAMPLE 4

If $16r - 24q = 2$,   then $2r - 3q =$

(A) 4

(B) $\dfrac{1}{8}$

(C) $\dfrac{1}{4}$

(D) $\dfrac{1}{2}$

(E) 2

Choice C is correct.

Divide by 8:

$$\frac{16r - 24q}{8} = \frac{2}{8}$$
$$2r - 3q = \frac{1}{4}$$

EXAMPLE 5

If $(a^2 + a)^3 = (a + 1)^3 x$, where $a + 1 \neq 0$, then $x =$

(A) a
(B) a^2
(C) a^3
(D) $\dfrac{a + 1}{a}$
(E) $\dfrac{a}{a + 1}$

Choice C is correct.

Isolate x first:

$$x = \frac{(a^2 + a)^3}{(a + 1)^3}$$

Now use the fact that $\left(\dfrac{x^3}{y^3}\right) = \left(\dfrac{x}{y}\right)^3$

$$\frac{(a^2 + a)^3}{(a + 1)^3} = \left(\frac{a^2 + a}{a + 1}\right)^3$$

Now factor $a^2 + a = a(a + 1)$
So:

$$\left(\frac{a^2 + a}{a + 1}\right)^3 = \left[\frac{a(a + 1)}{a + 1}\right]^3$$
$$= \left[\frac{a(a + 1)}{a + 1}\right]^3$$
$$= a^3$$

EXAMPLE 6

If $\dfrac{p + 1}{r + 1} = 1$ and p, r are nonzero, and p is not equal to -1, and r is not equal to -1, then

(A) $2 > p/r > 1$ always
(B) $p/r < 1$ always
(C) $p/r = 1$ always
(D) p/r can be greater than 2
(E) $p/r = 2$ always

Choice C is correct.

Get rid of the fraction. Multiply both sides of the equation

$$\frac{p + 1}{r + 1} = 1 \text{ by } r + 1!$$

$$\left(\frac{p + 1}{r + 1}\right) r + 1 = r + 1$$
$$p + 1 = r + 1$$

Cancel the 1's:

$$p = r$$

So

$$\frac{p}{r} = 1$$

EXAMPLE 7

$$\frac{4}{250} =$$

(A) 0.16
(B) 0.016
(C) 0.0016
(D) 0.0125
(E) 0.025

Choice B is correct.

Don't divide 4 into 250! Multiply:

$$\frac{4}{250} \times \frac{4}{4} = \frac{16}{1000}$$

Now $\frac{16}{100} = .16$ so $\frac{16}{1000} = .016$

EXAMPLE 8

$$(3 \times 4^{14}) - 4^{13} =$$

(A) 4
(B) 12
(C) 2×4^{13}
(D) 3×4^{13}
(E) 11×4^{13}

Choice E is correct.

Factor 4^{13} from
$(3 \times 4^{14}) - 4^{13}$
We get $4^{13}[(3 \times 4^1) - 1]$
or $4^{13}[12 - 1] = 4^{13}[11]$.

You will see more of the technique of dividing, multiplying, adding, and subtracting in the next strategy, MATH STRATEGY 13.

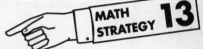

MATH STRATEGY **13**

Know How to Find Unknown Expressions by Adding, Subtracting, Multiplying, or Dividing Equations or Expressions

When you want to calculate composite quantities like $x + 3y$ or $m - n$, often you can do it by adding, subtracting, multiplying, or dividing the right equations or expressions.

EXAMPLE 1

If $4x + 5y = 10$ and $x + 3y = 8$,
then $\frac{5x + 8y}{3} =$

(A) 18
(B) 12
(C) 9
(D) 6
(E) 15

Choice D is correct. Don't solve for x, then for y.

Try to get the quantity $\frac{5x + 8y}{3}$ by adding or subtracting

the equations. In this case, <u>add</u> equations.

$$
\begin{array}{r}
4x + 5y = 10 \\
+\ \ x + 3y = \ 8 \\
\hline
5x + 8y = 18
\end{array}
$$

Now divide by 3:

$$\frac{5x + 8y}{3} = \frac{18}{3} = 6 \ (Answer)$$

EXAMPLE 2

If $25x + 8y = 149$ and $16x + 3y = 89$, then

$$\frac{9x + 5y}{5} =$$

(A) 12
(B) 15
(C) 30
(D) 45
(E) 60

Choice A is correct. We are told

$$
\begin{array}{r}
25x + 8y = 149 \ \boxed{1} \\
16x + 3y = \ \ 89 \ \boxed{2}
\end{array}
$$

The long way to do this problem is to solve $\boxed{1}$ and $\boxed{2}$
for x and y, and then substitute these values into $\frac{9x + 5y}{5}$

The fast way to do this problem is to <u>subtract</u> $\boxed{2}$ from $\boxed{1}$ and get

$$9x + 5y = 60 \ \boxed{3}$$

Now all we have to do is to divide $\boxed{3}$ by 5

$$\frac{9x + 5y}{5} = 12 \ (Answer)$$

EXAMPLE 3

If $21x + 39y = 18$, then $7x + 13y =$

(A) 3
(B) 6
(C) 7
(D) 9
(E) It cannot be determined from the information given.

Choice B is correct We are given

$$21x + 39y = 18 \quad \boxed{1}$$

Divide $\boxed{1}$ by 3

$$7x + 13y = 6 \; (Answer)$$

EXAMPLE 4

If $x + 2y = 4$, then $5x + 10y - 8 =$

(A) 10
(B) 12
(C) −10
(D) −12
(E) 0

Choice B is correct.

Multiply $x + 2y = 4$ by 5 to get:

$$5x + 10y = 20$$

Now subtract 8:

$$5x + 10y - 8 = 20 - 8$$
$$= 12$$

EXAMPLE 5

If $6x^5 = y^2$ and $x = \dfrac{1}{y}$, then $y =$

(A) x^6
(B) $\dfrac{x^5}{6}$
(C) $6x^6$
(D) $\dfrac{6x^5}{5}$
(E) $\dfrac{x^5}{5}$

Choice C is correct.

Multiply $6x^5 = y^2$ by $x = \dfrac{1}{y}$ to get:

$$6x^6 = y^2 \times \frac{1}{y} = y$$

EXAMPLE 6

If $x > 0, y > 0$ and $x^2 = 27$ and $y^2 = 3$, then $\dfrac{x^3}{y^3} =$

(A) 9
(B) 27
(C) 36
(D) 48
(E) 54

Choice B is correct

Divide: $\dfrac{x^2}{y^2} = \dfrac{27}{3} = 9$

Take square root: $\dfrac{x}{y} = 3$

So $\left(\dfrac{x}{y}\right)^3 = \dfrac{x^3}{y^3} = 3^3 = 27$

EXAMPLE 7

If $\dfrac{m}{n} = \dfrac{3}{8}$ and $\dfrac{m}{q} = \dfrac{4}{7}$, then $\dfrac{n}{q} =$

(A) $\dfrac{12}{15}$
(B) $\dfrac{12}{56}$
(C) $\dfrac{56}{12}$
(D) $\dfrac{32}{21}$
(E) $\dfrac{21}{32}$

Choice D is correct.

First get rid of fractions!

Cross multiply $\dfrac{m}{n} = \dfrac{3}{8}$ to get $\mathbf{8m = 3n}$ $\boxed{1}$.

Now cross multiply $\dfrac{m}{q} = \dfrac{4}{7}$ to get $\mathbf{7m = 4q}$ $\boxed{2}$.

Now divide equations $\boxed{1}$ and $\boxed{2}$:

$$\frac{8m}{7m} = \frac{3n}{4q} \quad \boxed{3}$$

The m's cancel and we get:

$$\frac{8}{7} = \frac{3n}{4q} \quad \boxed{4}$$

Multiply Equation 4 by 4 and divide by 3 to get

$$\frac{8 \times 4}{7 \times 3} = \frac{n}{q}$$

Thus

$$\frac{n}{q} = \frac{32}{21}$$

MATH STRATEGY 14

Draw or Extend Lines in a Diagram to Make a Problem Easier; Label Unknown Quantities

EXAMPLE 1

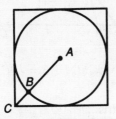

The circle with center A and radius AB is inscribed in the square to the left. AB is extended to C. What is the ratio of AB to AC?

(A) $\sqrt{2}$

(B) $\frac{\sqrt{2}}{4}$

(C) $\frac{\sqrt{2} - 1}{2}$

(D) $\frac{\sqrt{2}}{2}$

(E) none of these

Choice D is correct. Always draw or extend lines to get more information. Also label unknown lengths, angles, or arcs with letters.

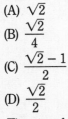

Label $AB = a$ and $BC = b$.
Draw perpendicular AD. Note it is just the radius, a. CD also $= a$.

We want to find $\frac{AB}{AC} = \frac{a}{a + b}$

Now $\triangle ADC$ is an isosceles right triangle so $AD = CD = a$.

By the Pythagorean Theorem,
$a^2 + a^2 = (a + b)^2$ where $a + b$ is hypotenuse of right triangle.

We get: $2a^2 = (a + b)^2$
Divide by $(a + b)^2$:

$$\frac{2a^2}{(a + b)^2} = 1$$

Divide by 2:

$$\frac{a^2}{(a + b)^2} = \frac{1}{2}$$

Take square roots of both sides:

$$\frac{a}{(a + b)} = \frac{1}{\sqrt{2}} =$$

$$= \frac{1}{\sqrt{2}}\left(\frac{\sqrt{2}}{\sqrt{2}}\right)$$

$$= \frac{\sqrt{2}}{2} \ (Answer)$$

EXAMPLE 2

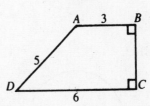

What is the perimeter of the above figure if B and C are right angles?

(A) 14
(B) 16
(C) 18
(D) 20
(E) It cannot be determined.

Choice C is correct.

Draw perpendicular AE. Label side $BC = h$. You can see that $AE = h$.

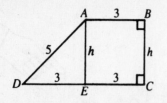

$ABCE$ is a rectangle, so $CE = 3$. This makes $ED = 3$ since the whole $DC = 6$.

Now use the Pythagorean Theorem for triangle AED:

$$h^2 + 3^2 = 5^2$$
$$h^2 = 5^2 - 3^2$$
$$h^2 = 25 - 9$$
$$h^2 = 16$$
$$h = 4$$

So the perimeter is $3 + h + 6 + 5 = 3 + 4 + 6 + 5 = 18$ (*Answer*)

EXAMPLE 3

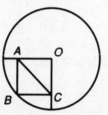

In the figure above, O is the center of a circle with a radius of 6, and $AOCB$ is a square. If point B is on the circumference of the circle, the length of $AC =$

(A) $6\sqrt{2}$
(B) $3\sqrt{2}$
(C) 3
(D) 6
(E) $6\sqrt{3}$

Choice D is correct.

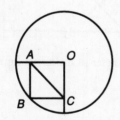

This is tricky if not impossible if you don't draw OB. So draw OB:

Since $AOCB$ is a square, $OB = AC$ and since $OB =$ radius $= 6$, $AC = 6$.

EXAMPLE 4

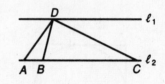

Lines ℓ_1 and ℓ_2 are parallel. $AB = \frac{1}{3}AC$.

$$\frac{\text{The area of triangle } ABD}{\text{The area of triangle } DBC} =$$

(A) $\frac{1}{3}$

(B) $\frac{1}{2}$

(C) $\frac{1}{4}$

(D) $\frac{3}{8}$

(E) Cannot be determined

Choice B is correct.

$AB = \frac{1}{3} AC$

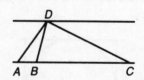

Ask yourself, what is the area of a triangle? It is ½ (height × base). So let's get the heights and the bases of the triangles ABD and DBC. First draw the altitude (call it h).

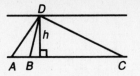

Now label $AB = \frac{1}{3}AC$ (given)

This makes $BC = \frac{2}{3}AC$, since $AB + BC = AC$

Thus the area of $\triangle ABD = \frac{1}{2}h(AB) = \frac{1}{2}h\left(\frac{1}{3}AC\right)$

Area of $\triangle DBC = \frac{1}{2}h(BC) = \frac{1}{2}h\left(\frac{2}{3}AC\right)$

$$\frac{\text{Area of } ABD}{\text{Area of } DBC} = \frac{\frac{1}{2}h\left(\frac{1}{3}AC\right)}{\frac{1}{2}h\left(\frac{2}{3}AC\right)}$$

$$= \frac{\frac{1}{3}}{\frac{2}{3}} = \frac{1}{3} \times \frac{3}{2} = \frac{1}{2}$$

EXAMPLE 5

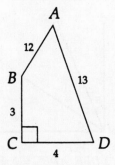

Note: Figure is not drawn to scale.

The area of the above figure ABCD

(A) is 36
(B) is 108
(C) is 156
(D) is 1,872
(E) Cannot be determined

Choice A is correct.

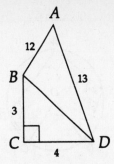

Draw BD. BCD is a 3-4-5 right triangle so BD = 5. Now remember that a 5-12-13 triangle is also a right triangle, so angle ABD is a right angle. The area of triangle BCD is $(3 \times 4)/2 = \mathbf{6}$ and the area of triangle BAD is $(5 \times 12)/2 = \mathbf{30}$, so the total area is **36.**

EXAMPLE 6

In the above figure, two points, B and C, are placed to the right of point A such that $4AB = 3AC$. The value of $\frac{BC}{AB}$

(A) equals $\frac{1}{3}$

(B) equals $\frac{2}{3}$

(C) equals $\frac{3}{2}$

(D) equals 3
(E) Cannot be determined

Choice A is correct.

Place B and C to the right of A:

Now label $AB = a$ and $BC = b$:

$$\frac{BC}{AB} = \frac{b}{a} \quad \left(\frac{b}{a} \text{ is what we want to find}\right)$$

We are given $4AB = 3AC$

So, $4a = 3(a + b)$
Expand: $4a = 3a + 3b$
Subtract $3a$: $a = 3b$

Divide by 3 and a: $\frac{1}{3} = \frac{b}{a}$

But remember $\frac{BC}{AB} = \frac{b}{a}$, so $\frac{BC}{AB} = \frac{1}{3}$

EXAMPLE 7

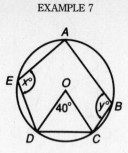

In the figure above, *ABCDE* is a pentagon inscribed in the circle with center at *O*. $\angle DOC = 40°$. What is the value of $x + y$?

(A) 80
(B) 180
(C) 100
(D) 200
(E) It cannot be determined

Choice D is correct.

Label degrees in each arc.

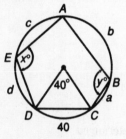

$\angle x$ is measured by ½ arc it cuts.

$$\text{So, } x = \frac{1}{2}(b + a + 40)$$

$$\text{Likewise, } y = \frac{1}{2}(c + d + 40)$$

You want to find $x + y$, so add:

$$x = \frac{1}{2}(b + a + 40)$$

$$y = \frac{1}{2}(c + d + 40)$$

$$\overline{}$$

$$x + y = \frac{1}{2}(b + a + 40 + c + d + 40)$$

But what is $a + b + c + d + 40$? It is the total number of degrees around the circumference, which is 360.

$$\text{So, } x + y = \frac{1}{2}(\underbrace{b + a + c + d + 40}_{} + 40)$$

$$= \frac{1}{2}(360 + 40)$$

$$= \frac{1}{2}(400) = 200$$

EXAMPLE 8

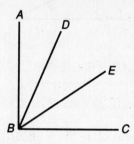

In the above figure, if $\angle ABE = 40°$, $\angle DBC = 60°$, and $\angle ABC = 90°$, what is the measure of $\angle DBE$?

(A) 10°
(B) 20°
(C) 40°
(D) 100°
(E) It cannot be determined

Choice A is correct.

Label angles first.

Now $\angle ABE = 40$, so $a + b = 40$
$\angle DBC = 60$, so $b + c = 60$
$\angle ABC = 90$, so $a + b + c = 90$

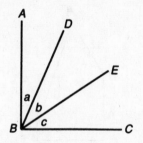

You want to find $\angle DBE$. $\angle DBE = b$ and you want to get the value of b from:

$$a + b = 40 \quad \boxed{1}$$
$$b + c = 60 \quad \boxed{2}$$
$$a + b + c = 90 \quad \boxed{3}$$

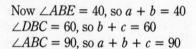

Add $\boxed{1}$ and $\boxed{2}$: $a + b = 40$
$ + b + c = 60$
$\overline{a + 2b + c = 100}$
Subtract $\boxed{3}$ $- (a + b + c = 90)$
$\overline{b = 10}$

EXAMPLE 9

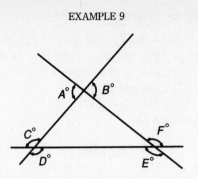

In the figure above, three lines intersect at the points shown. What is the value of $A + B + C + D + E + F$?

(A) 1080
(B) 720
(C) 540
(D) 360
(E) It cannot be determined

Choice B is correct.

(B) <u>Relabel,</u> using the fact that *vertical angles are equal.*

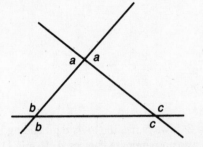

Now use the fact that a straight angle has 180° in it:

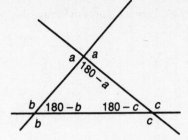

Now use the fact that the sum of the angles of a triangle = 180°:

$$180 - a + 180 - b + 180 - c = 180$$
$$540 - a - b - c = 180$$
$$540 - 180 = a + b + c$$
$$360 = a + b + c$$

Now remember what we are looking to find (the sum):

$$a + a + b + b + c + c = 2a + 2b + 2c$$

But this is just $2(a + b + c) = 2(360) = 720$

MATH STRATEGY **15**

Know How to Eliminate Certain Choices

Instead of working out a lot of algebra, you may be able to eliminate several of the choices at first glance. In this way you can save yourself a lot of work. The key is to remember to use pieces of the given information to eliminate several of the choices at once.

EXAMPLE 1

The sum of the digits of a three-digit number is 15. If this number is not divisible by 2 but is divisible by 5, which of the following is the number?

(A) 384
(B) 465
(C) 635
(D) 681
(E) 780

Choice B is correct. Use pieces of the given information to eliminate several of the choices.

Which numbers are divisible by 2? Choices A and E are divisible by 2 and, thus, can be eliminated. Of Choices B, C, and D, which are *not* divisible by 5? Choice D can be eliminated. We are left with Choices B and C.

Only Choice B (465) has the sum of its digits equal to 15. Thus, 465 is the only number that satisfies all the pieces of the given information.

If you learn to use this method well, you can save loads of time.

EXAMPLE 2

Which of the following numbers is divisible by 5 and 9, but not by 2?

(A) 625
(B) 639
(C) 650
(D) 655
(E) 675

Choice E is correct. Clearly, a number is divisible by 5 if, and only if, its last digit is either 0 or 5. A number is also divisible by 2 if, and only if, its last digit is divisible by 2. Certain choices are easily eliminated. Thus we can *eliminate* Choices B and C.

Method 1: To eliminate some more choices, remember that a number is divisible by 9 if, and only if, the sum of its digits is divisible by 9. Thus, Choice E is the only correct answer.

Method 2: If you did not know the test for divisibility by 9, divide the numbers in Choice A, D, and E by 9 to find the answer.

EXAMPLE 3

If the last digit and the first digit are interchanged in each of the numbers below, which will result in the number with the *largest* value?

(A) 2,534
(B) 4,235
(C) 5,243
(D) 4,352
(E) 2,345

Choice E is correct.

The number with the largest last digit will become the largest number after interchanging. ⬚1

Certain choices are easily eliminated.

Using ⬚1, we see that Choices B and E each end in 5. All others end in digits less than 5 and may be eliminated. Starting with Choice E (See Strategy 8).
Choice E, 2,345, becomes 5,342. ⬚2
Choice B, 4,235, becomes 5,234. ⬚3
⬚2 is larger than ⬚3.

EXAMPLE 4

Which of the following could be the value of 3^x where x is an integer?

(A) 339,066
(B) 376,853
(C) 411,282
(D) 422,928
(E) 531,441

Choice E is correct. Let's look at what 3^x looks like for integral values of x:

$3^1 = 3$
$3^2 = 9$
$3^3 = 27$
$3^4 = 81$
$3^5 = 243$
$3^6 = \ldots 9$
$3^7 = \ldots 7$
$3^8 = \ldots 1$

Note that 3^x always has the *units* digit ending in *3, 9, 7, or 1*. So we can eliminate choices A, C, and D since the units digits in those choices end in other numbers than 3, 9, 7, or 1. We are left with Choices B and E. The number in the correct choice must be exactly divisible by 3 since it is of the form 3^x ($= 3 \times 3 \times 3 \ldots$) where x is an integer. This is a good time to use your calculator. Divide the number in choice B by 3: You get 125617.66. That's *not* an integer. So the only remaining choice is Choice E.

MATH
STRATEGY **16**

Watch Out for Questions That Seem Very Easy but That Can Be Tricky—Beware of Choice A as a "Lure Choice"

When questions appear to be solved very easily, think again! Watch out especially for the "lure" Choice A.

EXAMPLE 1*

6:06

The diagram above shows a digital clock whose hour digit is the same as the minutes digit. Consider each time when the same number appears for both the hour and the minutes as a "double time" situation. What is the shortest elapsed time period between the appearance of one double time and an immediately succeeding double time?

(A) 61 minutes
(B) 11 minutes
(C) 60 minutes
(D) 101 minutes
(E) 49 minutes

Choice E is correct. Did you think that just by subtracting something like 8:08 from 9:09 you would get the answer (1 hour and 1 minute = 61 minutes)? That's Choice A, which is wrong. So beware, because your answer came too easily for a test like the SAT. You must realize that there is another possibility of double time occurrence—12:12 and 1:01, whose difference is 49 minutes. This is Choice E, the correct answer.

EXAMPLE 2

The letters d and m are integral digits in a certain number system. If $0 \leq d \leq m$, how many different, possible values are there for d?

(A) m
(B) $m - 1$
(C) $m - 2$
(D) $m + 1$
(E) $m + 2$

Choice D is correct. Did you think that the answer was m? Do not be careless! The list 1, 2, 3, ..., m contains m

*Note: This problem also appears in Strategy 1 of the 5 General Strategies on page 165.

elements. If 0 is included in the list, then there are $m + 1$ elements. Hence, if $0 \leq d \leq m$ where d is integral, then d can have $m + 1$ different values.

EXAMPLE 3

There are some flags hanging in a horizontal row. Starting at one end of the row, the U.S. flag is 25th. Starting at the other end of the row, the U.S. flag is 13th. How many flags are in the row?

(A) 36
(B) 37
(C) 38
(D) 39
(E) 40

Choice B is correct. **The obvious may be tricky!**

Method 1: Given:

| The U.S. flag is 25th from one end. | $\boxed{1}$ |
| The U.S. flag is 13th from the other end. | $\boxed{2}$ |

At first glance it may appear that adding $\boxed{1}$ and $\boxed{2}$, $25 + 13 = 38$, will be the correct answer. This is WRONG!

The U.S. flag is being counted twice: Once as the 25th and again as the 13th from the other end. The correct answer is

$$25 + 13 - 1 = 37.$$

Method 2:

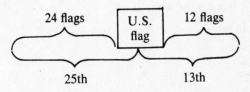

$24 + 12 + \text{U.S. flag} = 36 + \text{U.S. flag} = 37$

EXAMPLE 4

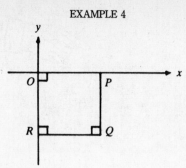

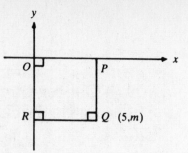

$OR = RQ$ in the figure above. If the coordinates of Q are $(5, m)$, find the value of m.

(A) -5
(B) $-\sqrt{5}$
(C) 0
(D) $\sqrt{5}$
(E) 5

Choice A is correct.

Given: $OR = RQ$ ☐1
Coordinates of $Q = (5, m)$ ☐2
From ☐2, we get $RQ = 5$ ☐3
Substitute ☐3 into ☐1. We get
$$OR = 5$$

The obvious may be tricky! Since Q is below the x-axis, its y-coordinate is negative. Thus $m = -5$.

MATH STRATEGY **17**

Use the Given Information Effectively (and Ignore Irrelevant Information)

You should always use first the piece of information that tells you the most, or gives you a useful idea, or that brings you closest to the answer.

EXAMPLE 1

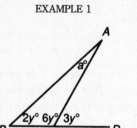

(*Note:* Figure is not drawn to scale.)

In the figure above, side BC of triangle ABC is extended to D. What is the value of a?

(A) 15
(B) 17
(C) 20
(D) 24
(E) 30

Choice C is correct.

Use the piece of information that will give you something definite. You might have first thought of using the fact that the sum of the angles of a triangle = 180°. However, that will give you

$$a + 2y + 6y = 180$$

That's not very useful. However, if you use the fact that the sum of the angles in a straight angle is 180 we get:

$$6y + 3y = 180$$
and we get $9y = 180$
$$y = 20.$$

Now we have gotten something useful. At this point, we can use the fact that the sum of the angles in a triangle is 180.

$$a + 2y + 6y = 180$$

Substituting 20 for y, we get

$$a + 2(20) + 6(20) = 180$$
$$a = 20 \quad (Answer)$$

EXAMPLE 2

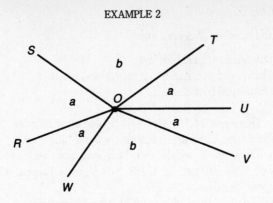

(*Note:* Figure is not drawn to scale.)

Which of the above angles has a degree measure that can be determined?

(A) ∠WOS
(B) ∠SOU
(C) ∠WOT
(D) ∠ROV
(E) ∠WOV

Choice C is correct.

Use information that will get you something useful.

$$4a + 2b = 360 \text{ (sum of all angles} = 360°)$$

Divide by 2 to simplify:

$$2a + b = 180$$

Now try all the choices. You could work backward from Choice E, but we'll start with Choice A:

(A) ∠WOS = $2a$—You know that $2a + b = 180$ but don't know the value of $2a$.
(B) ∠SOU = $b + a$—You know $2a + b = 180$ but don't know the value of $b + a$.
(C) ∠WOT = $b + 2a$—You know that $2a + b = 180$, so you know the value of $b + 2a$.

Choice C is correct.

EXAMPLE 3

If a ranges in value from 0.003 to 0.3 and b ranges in value from 3.0 to 300.0, then the minimum value of $\frac{a}{b}$ is

(A) 0.1
(B) 0.01
(C) 0.001
(D) 0.0001
(E) 0.00001

Choice E is correct.

Start by using the definition of *minimum* and *maximum*.

The minimum value of $\frac{a}{b}$ is when a is *minimum* and b is *maximum*.

The minimum value of $a = .003$
The maximum value of $b = 300$

So the minimum value of $\frac{a}{b} = \frac{.003}{300} = \frac{.001}{100} = .00001$

EXAMPLE 4

If $xry = 0$, $yst = 0$, and $rxt = 1$, then which must be 0?

(A) r
(B) s
(C) t
(D) x
(E) y

Choice E is correct.

Use information that will give you something to work with.

$rxt = 1$ tell you that $r \neq 0$, $x \neq 0$, and $t \neq 0$
So if $xry = 0$ then y must be 0.

EXAMPLE 5*

On a street with 25 houses, 10 houses have *fewer than 6 rooms*, 10 houses have *more than 7 rooms*, and 4 houses have *more than 8 rooms*. What is the total number of houses on the street that are either 6-, 7-, or 8-room houses?

(A) 5
(B) 9
(C) 11
(D) 14
(E) 15

Choice C is correct.

There are three possible situations:

(a) Houses that have *fewer than 6 rooms* (call the number a)
(b) Houses that have *6, 7, or 8 rooms* (call the number b)
(c) Houses that have *more than 8 rooms* (call the number c)

$a + b + c$ must total **25** (given). ☐1

a is **10** (given). ☐2

c is **4** (given). ☐3

Substituting ☐2 and ☐3 in ☐1 we get $10 + b + 4 = 25$.
b must therefore be **11**.

* This problem also appears in the 19 Questions That Can Determine Top College Eligibility, Part 3.

EXAMPLE 6

In a room, there are *5 blue-eyed blondes*. If altogether there are 14 *blondes* and 8 people with *blue eyes* in the room, how many people are there in the room?

(A) 11
(B) 17
(C) 22
(D) 25
(E) 27

Choice B is correct.

Method 1:

Draw two intersecting circles.

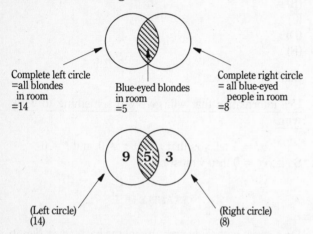

Complete left circle
=all blondes
in room
=14

Blue-eyed blondes
in room
=5

Complete right circle
= all blue-eyed
people in room
=8

(Left circle)
(14)

(Right circle)
(8)

Above, subtracting: all blondes (14) − blue-eyed blondes (5), we get **9**.
Above subtracting: all blue-eyed people (8) − blue-eyed blondes (5), we get **3**
So the number of people in room are 9 + 5 + 3 = 17.

Method 2:

Total number of people are:

(a) blondes *without* blue eyes
(b) blue-eyed people *who are not* blonde
(c) blue-eyed blondes

(a) There are 14 blondes and 5 blue-eyed blondes, so, subtracting, there are **9** blondes *without* blue eyes.
(b) There are 8 people with blue eyes and 5 blue-eyed blondes, so, subtracting, there are **3** blue-eyed people who are *not* blonde.
(c) The number of blue-eyed blondes is **5** (given).

Adding the number of people in a, b, and c, we get
9 + 3 + 5 = 17

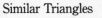

MATH STRATEGY **18**

Know and Use Facts About Triangles

By remembering these facts about triangles, you can often save yourself a lot of time and trouble.

I.

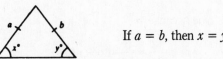

If $a = b$, then $x = y$

The base angles of an isosceles triangle are equal

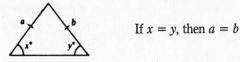

If $x = y$, then $a = b$

If the base angles of a triangle are equal, the triangle is isosceles

II.

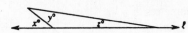

ℓ is a straight line.
Then, $x = y + z$

The measure of an exterior angle is equal to the sum of the measures of the remote interior angles

III.

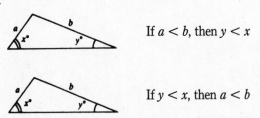

If $a < b$, then $y < x$

If $y < x$, then $a < b$

In a triangle, the greatest angle lies opposite the greatest side

IV. Similar Triangles

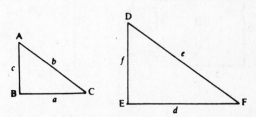

If $\triangle ABC \sim \triangle DEF$, then

$$m \angle A = m \angle D$$
$$m \angle B = m \angle E$$
$$m \angle C = m \angle F$$

and $\dfrac{a}{d} = \dfrac{b}{e} = \dfrac{c}{f}$

V.

$m \angle A + m \angle B + m \angle C = 180°$

The sum of the interior angles of a triangle is 180 degrees

VI.

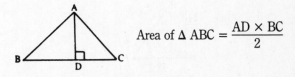

Area of $\triangle ABC = \dfrac{AD \times BC}{2}$

The area of a triangle is one-half the product of the altitude to a side and the side.
Note: If $m \angle A = 90°$,

Area is also $= \dfrac{AB \times AC}{2}$

VII.

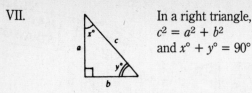

In a right triangle,
$c^2 = a^2 + b^2$
and $x° + y° = 90°$

VIII. Memorize the following standard triangles:

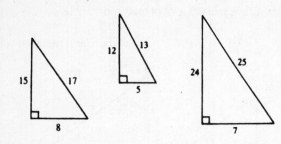

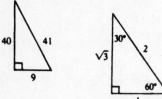

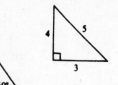

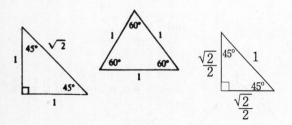

EXAMPLE 1

In the diagram below, what is the value of x?

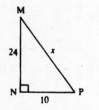

(A) 20
(B) 25
(C) 26
(D) 45
(E) 48

Choice C is correct.

Method 1: Use VII above. Then,

$$x^2 = 24^2 + 10^2$$
$$= 576 + 100$$
$$= 676$$

Thus, $x = 26$ (*Answer*)

Method 2: Look at VIII in left column. Notice that $\triangle MNP$ is similar to one of the standard triangles:

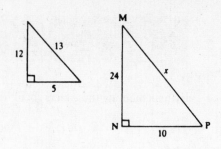

This is true because

$$\frac{12}{24} = \frac{5}{10} \text{ (Look at IV)}$$

Hence, $\frac{12}{24} = \frac{13}{x}$ or $x = 26$ (*Answer*)

EXAMPLE 2

If Masonville is 50 kilometers due north of Adamston and Elvira is 120 kilometers due east of Adamston, then the minimum distance between Masonville and Elvira is

(A) 125 kilometers
(B) 130 kilometers
(C) 145 kilometers
(D) 160 kilometers
(E) 170 kilometers

Choice B is correct. <u>Draw a diagram first.</u>

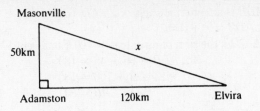

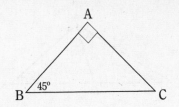

EXAMPLE 4

The given information translates into the diagram above. Note Statement VIII on p. 216. The triangle above is a multiple of the special 5, 12, 13 right triangle

$$50 = 10(5)$$
$$120 = 10(12)$$
$$\text{Thus, } x = 10(13) = 130 \text{km.}$$

(Note: The Pythagorean Theorem could also have been used: $50^2 + 120^2 = x^2$)

EXAMPLE 3

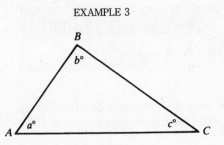

Note: Figure is not drawn to scale.

In triangle ABC, if $a > c$, which of the following is true?

(A) $BC = AC$
(B) $AB > BC$
(C) $AC > AB$
(D) $BC > AB$
(E) $BC > AC$

Choice D is correct. (Remember triangle inequality facts.) From basic geometry, Statement III, we know that, since $m \angle BAC > m \angle BCA$, then leg opposite $\angle$ BAC > leg opposite $\angle$ BCA or

$$BC > AB$$

(*Note:* Figure is not drawn to scale.)

The triangle above has side $BC = 10$ angle $B = 45°$ and angle $A = 90°$. The area of the triangle

(A) is 15
(B) is 20
(C) is 25
(D) is 30
(E) cannot be determined

Choice C is correct.

First find angle C using V.
$$90° + 45° + m \angle C = 180°$$
So $m \angle C = 45°$.
Using I, we find $AB = AC$
since $m \angle B = m \angle C = 45°$.
Since our right triangle ABC has $BC = 10$, using

VIII, (the right triangle $\frac{\sqrt{2}}{2}, \frac{\sqrt{2}}{2}, 1$) multiply by 10 to

get a right triangle:

$$\frac{10\sqrt{2}}{2}, \frac{10\sqrt{2}}{2}, 10.$$

Thus side $AB = \dfrac{10\sqrt{2}}{2} = 5\sqrt{2}$

side $AC = \dfrac{10\sqrt{2}}{2} = 5\sqrt{2}$

Now the area of triangle ABC, according to VI is

$$\frac{5\sqrt{2} \times 5\sqrt{2}}{2} = \frac{25 \times 2}{2} = 25.$$

EXAMPLE 5

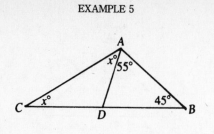

In the figure above what is the value of *x*?

(A) 30
(B) 40
(C) 50
(D) 80
(E) 100

Choice B is correct.

Remember triangle facts. Use Statement II.
$\angle ADB$ is an exterior angle of $\angle ACD$, so
$m\angle ADB = x + x = 2x$ ⬜1
In $\triangle ADB$, the sum of its angles = 180 (Statement V), so
$$m\angle ADB + 55 + 45 = 180$$
or
$$m\angle ADB + 100 = 180$$
or
$$m\angle ADB = 80 \qquad ⬜2$$

Equating ⬜1 and ⬜2 we have
$$2x = 80$$
$$x = 40 \qquad (Answer)$$

MATH STRATEGY 19

When Calculating Answers, Never Multiply and/or Do Long Division, If Reducing Can Be Done First

Note: On the new SAT I exam, because calculators are permitted, you may do the following problems with a calculator also. But it would be wise for you to see the other approach too—how the problem can be solved *without* the use of a calculator.

EXAMPLE 1

If $w = \dfrac{81 \times 150}{45 \times 40}$, then $w =$

(A) 3
(B) $6\dfrac{3}{4}$
(C) $7\dfrac{1}{4}$
(D) 9
(E) $20\dfrac{1}{4}$

Do not multiply in this case } 81×150 and 45×40 to get $\dfrac{12150}{1800}$

Factor first

$$\underset{45}{\underbrace{\overset{81}{\overbrace{9 \times 9}} \times \overset{150}{\overbrace{15 \times 10}}}}{9 \times 5 \times \underset{40}{\underbrace{4 \times 10}}}$$

Then cancel like factors in numerator and denominator

$$\frac{\cancel{9} \times 9 \times 15 \times \cancel{10}}{\cancel{9} \times 5 \times 4 \times \cancel{10}}$$

Reduce further $\quad \dfrac{9 \times \cancel{5} \times 3}{\cancel{5} \times 4}$

Then simplify

$$\frac{27}{4} = 6\frac{3}{4} \quad (Answer)$$

Thus, Choice B is correct.

EXAMPLE 2

$$\frac{4^2 + 4^2 + 4^2}{3^3 + 3^3 + 3^3} =$$

(A) $\dfrac{16}{27}$

(B) $\dfrac{8}{9}$

(C) $\dfrac{4}{3}$

(D) $\dfrac{64}{27}$

(E) $\dfrac{512}{81}$

Choice A is correct.

$$\frac{4^2 + 4^2 + 4^2}{3^3 + 3^3 + 3^3} =$$

Factor and reduce:

$$\frac{\cancel{3}(4^2)}{\cancel{3}(3^3)} =$$

$$\frac{16}{27}$$

EXAMPLE 3

If $6 \times 7 \times 8 \times 9 = \dfrac{12 \times 14 \times 18}{x}$, then $x =$

(A) $\dfrac{1}{2}$

(B) 1

(C) 4

(D) 8

(E) 12

Choice B is correct.

Given: $\quad 6 \times 7 \times 8 \times 9 = \dfrac{12 \times 14 \times 18}{x}$ $\boxed{1}$

$$\text{so that } x = \frac{12 \times 14 \times 18}{6 \times 7 \times 8 \times 9} \quad \boxed{2}$$

Do *not* multiply the numbers out in the numerator and denominator of $\boxed{2}$! It is too much work! Rewrite $\boxed{2}$.

Factor and reduce.

$x =$

$$\frac{12 \times 14 \times 18}{6 \times 7 \times 8 \times 9} = \frac{2 \times \cancel{6} \times 2 \times \cancel{7} \times 2 \times 9}{\cancel{6} \times \cancel{7} \times 8 \times \cancel{9}}$$

$$= \frac{2 \times 2 \times 2}{8} = \frac{8}{8} = 1 \qquad (Answer)$$

EXAMPLE 4

If $\dfrac{81 \times y}{27} = 21$, then $y =$

(A) $\dfrac{1}{21}$

(B) $\dfrac{1}{7}$

(C) 3

(D) 7

(E) 21

Choice D is correct.

$$\text{Given: } \frac{81 \times y}{27} = 21$$

Multiply both sides by 27 to get $81 \times y = 21 \times 27$

$$y = \frac{27 \times 21}{81}$$

Factor and reduce.

$$y = \frac{3 \cdot 7 \times 3 \cdot \cancel{9}}{9 \cdot \cancel{9}}$$

$$= \frac{\cancel{3} \cdot 7 \times \cancel{3}}{\cancel{3} \cdot \cancel{3}}$$

$$y = 7$$

EXAMPLE 5

Find the value of $\dfrac{y^2 - 7y + 10}{y - 2}$ rounded to the nearest whole number if $y = 8.000001$

(A) 2

(B) 3

(C) 5

(D) 6

(E) 16

Choice B is correct.

$$\text{Given: } \frac{y^2 - 7y + 10}{y - 2} \qquad \boxed{1}$$

Factor and reduce.

Factor the numerator of $\boxed{1}$. We get

$$\frac{(y - 5)\cancel{(y - 2)}}{\cancel{y - 2}} =$$
$$y - 5 \qquad \boxed{2}$$

Substitute 8.000001 in $\boxed{2}$. We have
$$8.000001 - 5 =$$
$$3.000001 \approx 3$$

Quantitative Comparison Strategies

Introduction

In the quantitative comparison question, you are presented with quantities under two columns. You have to determine whether the quantity under Column A is less than, greater than, or equal to the quantity in Column B. There is also a possibility that a definite comparison cannot be made. In very, very few cases will you ever have to calculate quantities. Since you just have to compare the relative values, you can usually manipulate the columns to get a simple comparison, as you will see.

Things You Must Know First!

1. MEMORIZE DIRECTIONS FOR QUANTITATIVE COMPARISON QUESTIONS. The following rewording of the standard directions given on the SAT tells you *precisely* how to choose an answer:

-   If Column A is *always greater* than Column B (or if Column B is always less than Column A), select CHOICE A.

-   If Column A is *always less* than Column B (or if Column B is always greater than Column A), select CHOICE B.

-   If Column A is *always equal* to Column B, select CHOICE C.

-   If there is no way to make any of the above definite comparisons, select CHOICE D. (In other words if a definite comparison or relationship cannot be made, select CHOICE D.)

Note that: If there is a quantity centered between the columns, you may use that information in the columns. A symbol such as x, a, etc., means the same thing in both columns. All variables like x, n, a, represent real numbers. MAKE SURE THAT YOU MEMORIZE THESE DIRECTIONS.

EXAMPLE:

Column A	Column B
1	$\frac{1}{2}$

In this example you would select Choice A since Column A > Column B.

2. WHEN THERE'S A QUANTITY BETWEEN THE COLUMNS USE THE *MIDDLE QUANTITY* IN BOTH COLUMNS.

EXAMPLE:

Column A		Column B
	$x = 2$	
x		$x + 1$

In this example, substitute 2 for x:

2	$(2 + 1)$

Column A < Column B so Choice B is correct.

3. YOU CAN ADD OR SUBTRACT THE SAME QUANTITY TO (OR FROM) BOTH COLUMNS AND STILL GET THE SAME COMPARISON.

EXAMPLE:

	Column A	Column B	
	$8 - 3$	7	(Column A < Column B)
Add 3 to both columns:	8	$7 + 3$	(Column A < Column B)

SUMMARY DIRECTIONS FOR COMPARISON QUESTIONS

Choose A if the quantity in Column A is greater; Choose B if the quantity in Column B is greater; Choose C if the two quantities are equal;   Choose D if the relationship cannot be determined from the information given.

4. YOU CAN MULTIPLY OR DIVIDE BOTH COLUMNS BY THE *SAME POSITIVE* NUMBER AND STILL <u>GET THE SAME COMPARISON.</u>

EXAMPLE:

Column A	Column B	
$\frac{7}{4}$	$\frac{9}{4}$	(Column A < Column B)

Multiply by 4:   7   9   (Column A < Column B)

5. REMEMBER THE FOLLOWING:

- Any variable like x, a, etc., can be *negative, positive,* or *0* unless otherwise specified.

- If you get different comparisons when you try numbers (for example, if you were to find that in one case Column A > Column B and in another Column A < Column B), then Choice D is correct.

- Never divide or multiply columns by a negative number or by 0. Also, never cancel negative numbers from both columns.

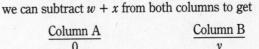
MATH STRATEGY A

Cancel Numbers or Expressions Common to Both Columns by an Addition or Subtraction

If the same expression or number appears in both columns, we can then subtract it from both columns.

Examples 1, 4, and 5 can also be solved with the aid of a calculator. However, to illustrate the effectiveness of Math Strategy A, we did not use the calculator method of solution of these examples.

EXAMPLE 1

Column A	Column B
$\frac{1}{2} + \frac{1}{6} + \frac{1}{17}$	$\frac{1}{17} + \frac{1}{2} + \frac{1}{7}$

Choice A is correct.
Don't add fractions in columns! Cancel common quantities:

Column A	Column B
$\cancel{\frac{1}{2}} + \frac{1}{6} + \cancel{\frac{1}{17}}$	$\cancel{\frac{1}{17}} + \cancel{\frac{1}{2}} + \frac{1}{7}$
$\frac{1}{6}$	$\frac{1}{7}$

Column A > Column B.

EXAMPLE 2

$y > 0$

Column A	Column B
$w + x$	$w + x + y$

Choice B is correct. Since $w + x$ appears in both columns, we can subtract $w + x$ from both columns to get

Column A	Column B
0	y

and from the given information we knew that $y > 0$.

EXAMPLE 3

Column A	Column B
	y is an integer
	$y < 0$
-1	$\frac{1}{y} - 1$

Choice A is correct.

SUMMARY DIRECTIONS FOR COMPARISON QUESTIONS

Choose A if the quantity in Column A is greater;
Choose B if the quantity in Column B is greater;
Choose C if the two quantities are equal;

Choose D if the relationship cannot be determined from the information given.

Column A	Column B
-1	$\frac{1}{y} - 1$

Cancel -1:
$$\begin{array}{cc} \cancel{-1} & \frac{1}{y} \cancel{-1} \\ \downarrow & \downarrow \\ 0 & \frac{1}{y} \end{array}$$

Since $y < 0$, $\frac{1}{y} < 0$, and Column A > Column B.

EXAMPLE 4

Column A	Column B
$5 - 0.005$	$5 - 0.0055$

Choice A is correct.

Column A	Column B
$5 - 0.005$	$5 - 0.0055$

Cancel 5:

$$\begin{array}{ccc} \cancel{5} - 0.005 & & \cancel{5} - 0.0055 \\ -\ 0.0050 & & -\ 0.0055 \\ -\ 0.0050 & > & -\ 0.0055 \end{array}$$

EXAMPLE 5

Column A	Column B
	$a \leq 15$
$7 + 3 + 15$	$7 + 3 + a$

Choice D is correct.

Column A	Column B
	$a \leq 15$
$7 + 3 + 15$	$7 + 3 + a$

Cancel $7 + 3$:

$$\begin{array}{cc} \cancel{7} + \cancel{3} + 15 & \cancel{7} + \cancel{3} + a \\ 15 & a \end{array}$$

Since $15 \geq a$ (given), you can't make a definite comparison.

EXAMPLE 6

Column A	Column B

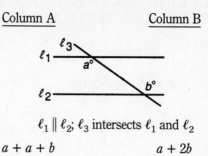

$\ell_1 \parallel \ell_2$; ℓ_3 intersects ℓ_1 and ℓ_2

$a + a + b$	$a + 2b$

Choice C is correct.

Column A	Column B
$a + a + b$	$a + 2b$

Subtract a, b from both columns:

$$\begin{array}{cc} \cancel{a} + a + \cancel{b} & \cancel{a} + 2b \\ -\ \cancel{a} - \cancel{b} & -\ \cancel{a} - b \\ \downarrow & \downarrow \\ a & b \end{array}$$

Now $a = b$ because if $\ell_1 \parallel \ell_2$, alternate interior angles a and b are equal.

MATH
STRATEGY **B**

Cancel Numbers or Expressions (Positive Quantities Only!!) Common to Both Columns by Multiplication or Division

If the same expression or number (positive quantities only which may be multiplied by other expressions) appears in both columns, we can then divide it from both columns. NEVER divide both columns by zero or a negative number.

Examples 1 and 3 can also be solved with the aid of a calculator. However, to illustrate the effectiveness of Math Strategy B, we did not use the calculator method of solution of these examples.

EXAMPLE 1

Column A	Column B
$24 \times 46 \times 35$	$46 \times 24 \times 36$

Column B is greater.
Don't multiply out! Cancel 24×46 from both columns (by dividing both columns by 24×46).

Column A	Column B
$\cancel{24} \times \cancel{46} \times 35$	$\cancel{46} \times \cancel{24} \times 36$

Column A < Column B.

EXAMPLE 2

$$m > 1$$
$$n > 0$$

Column A	Column B
mn	n

Choice A is correct. Since $n > 0$ and n appears in both columns, we can divide it from both columns to get

Column A	Column B
m	1

and we are given that $m > 1$.

EXAMPLE 3

Column A	Column B
$\dfrac{3}{14} \times \dfrac{5}{7} \times \dfrac{2}{3}$	$\dfrac{5}{7} \times \dfrac{3}{14} \times \dfrac{3}{4}$

Choice B is correct.

Column A	Column B
$\dfrac{3}{14} \times \dfrac{5}{7} \times \dfrac{2}{3}$	$\dfrac{5}{7} \times \dfrac{3}{14} \times \dfrac{3}{4}$

Cancel common fractions:

$\dfrac{\cancel{3}}{\cancel{14}} \times \dfrac{\cancel{5}}{\cancel{7}} \times \dfrac{2}{3}$		$\dfrac{\cancel{5}}{\cancel{7}} \times \dfrac{\cancel{3}}{\cancel{14}} \times \dfrac{3}{4}$
$\dfrac{2}{3}$		$\dfrac{3}{4}$
$\dfrac{2}{3}$	<	$\dfrac{3}{4}$

EXAMPLE 4

Column A Column B

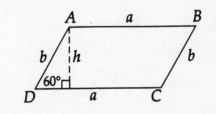

$ABCD$ is a parallelogram

$h \times AB$ $AD \times CD$

Choice B is correct.

SUMMARY DIRECTIONS FOR COMPARISON QUESTIONS

Choose A if the quantity in Column A is greater;
Choose B if the quantity in Column B is greater;
Choose C if the two quantities are equal;

Choose D if the relationship cannot be determined from the information given.

Label $AB = a$ and $AD = b$

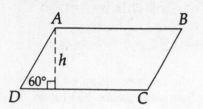

$AB = a$ $AD = b$ $CD = a$

	Column A	Column B
	$h \times AB$	$AD \times CD$
So	$h \times a$	$b \times a$

Cancel a:

h $\qquad\qquad$ b

Since b is the hypotenuse of the right triangle, it must be greater than h. So $h < b$.

MATH STRATEGY C

When a Comparison of the Two Columns Is Difficult, Use Numbers in Place of Variables

Sometimes by using numbers in place of variables, you can show that different comparisons exist, making choice D correct.

EXAMPLE 1

Column A	Column B
$b > 1$	
$a > 1$	
$a \neq b$	
$\dfrac{a}{b}$	$\dfrac{b}{a}$

Choice D is correct. Let us take numerical examples that satisfy $a, b > 1$

CASE 1

$a = 6, b = 3$ Then the columns become

Column A	Column B
$\dfrac{6}{3} = 3$	$\dfrac{3}{6} = \dfrac{1}{2}$

and the quantity in Column A is greater.

CASE 2

$a = 4, b = 12$

Then the columns become

Column A	Column B
$\dfrac{4}{12} = \dfrac{1}{3}$	$\dfrac{12}{4} = 3$

and the quantity in *Column B is greater.*

In one case, Column A > Column B. In the second case, Column B > Column A. Thus, a definite comparison *cannot* be made.

EXAMPLE 2

Column A	Column B
	$a > 0$
$\dfrac{1}{a}$	a

Choice D is correct.

Often you can find a number for the variable that makes the columns equal. Then all you have to find is another number that will make them unequal. In the above example, choose $a = 1$. This makes the columns equal. You can see that any other value of a, like $a = 100$, will make the columns unequal. Thus, a definite relation *cannot* be obtained.

EXAMPLE 3

Column A	Column B
	$30 > ab > 5$
	a and b are whole numbers
$a + b$	ab

Choice D is correct.

Try $a = 6$, $b = 4$. We get:

Column A		Column B
$6 + 4$		6×4
10		24
10	$<$	24

Try $a = 1$, $b = 6$. We get:

Column A		Column B
$1 + 6$		1×6
7		6
7	$>$	6

A definite comparison cannot be made.

EXAMPLES 4–6

Column A	Column B
4.	$a > b > 1$
	a and b are whole numbers
a^b	b^a

	Column A	Column B
5.		x is an integer
	x^{x+1}	$(x + 1)^x$

	Column A	Column B
6.		$ab \neq 0$
	$-a^2 b$	ab^2

EXPLANATORY ANSWERS FOR EXAMPLES 4–6

	Column A		Column B
4. (D)		$a > b > 1$	
	a^b		b^a
	Let $a = 3$, $b = 2$:		
	3^2		2^3
	9	$>$	8
	Let $a = 4$, $b > 2$:		
	4^2		2^4
	16	$=$	16

A definite comparison cannot be made.

	Column A		Column B
5. (D)		x in an integer	
	x^{x+1}		$(x + 1)^x$
	Try $x = 1$:		
	1^{1+1}		$(1 + 1)^1$
	1	$<$	2
	Try $x = 2$:		
	2^{2+1}		$(2 + 1)^2$
	8	$<$	9
	Make sure. Try $x = 3$:		
	3^{3+1}		$(3 + 1)^3$
	81	$>$	64

In one case Column A < Column B; in another case Column A > Column B. Thus, a definite comparison cannot be made.

	Column A		Column B
6. (D)		$ab \neq 0$	
	$-a^2 b$		ab^2

You can't cancel or divide by a or b because a or b *may be negative.* Try $a = 1$, $b = 1$. We get:

-1	$<$	1

Try $a = -1$, $b = 1$. We get:

-1	$=$	-1

A definite comparison cannot be made.

For examples 7–10, use the Gruber equal/not equal method to prove that Choice D is correct

If Possible, Find a Number (or Numbers) That Makes the Columns Equal and Another Number (or Numbers) That Makes Them Unequal to Ensure That Choice D Is the Right Answer

If you feel that a definite comparison cannot be made, try to find one particular number that when substituted for the variable in the columns will make the columns *equal*. All you then have to do to prove that Choice D is correct is find another number that will make the columns *unequal*.

EXAMPLE 7

Column A	Column B
	$x^2 = y^2$
x^2	xy

Choice D is correct.

SUMMARY DIRECTIONS FOR COMPARISON QUESTIONS

Choose A if the quantity in Column A is greater;
Choose B if the quantity in Column B is greater;
Choose C if the two quantities are equal;

Choose D if the relationship cannot be determined from the information given.

Column A	Column B

$$x^2 = y^2$$

| x^2 | xy |

You can't divide by x since x may be negative.
Try $x = 1, y = 1$:

| 1^2 | $(1)(1)$ |
| 1   = | 1 |

Now try $x = -1$ and $y = +1$:

$(-1)^2$	$(-1)(+1)$
↓	↓
$+1$ >	-1

Thus a definite comparison cannot be made.

EXAMPLE 8

Column A	Column B

$$0 > a$$

| $(a + 4)(a + 5)$ | $(a + 4)^2$ |

Choice D is correct.

Column A	Column B

$$0 > a$$

| $(a + 4)(a + 5)$ | $(a + 4)^2$ |

You may be tempted to cancel $(a + 4)$ from both columns. Because $(a + 4)$ *may be* negative you are not allowed to do this. If you did you'd get

Column A	Column B
$a + 5$	$a + 4$
5 >	4

and you would think Choice A correct, which is *wrong*! Here's the best way:

Let $a = -4$. That way the columns become equal (both equal to 0).
Now let $a = -1$:

$$(-1 + 4)(-1 + 5) \neq (-1 + 4)^2$$

Don't bother to calculate out because you can see that the columns aren't equal. Thus a definite comparison cannot be made.

EXAMPLE 9

Column A	Column B

$$x > 0, y > 0, z > 0$$

| $\dfrac{1}{x + y + z}$ | $x + y + z$ |

Choice D is correct.

Column A	Column B

$$x > 0, y > 0, z > 0$$

| $\dfrac{1}{x + y + z}$ | $x + y + z$ |

Let $x = y = z = \dfrac{1}{3}$ to get the columns *equal*.

Thus:

| $\dfrac{1}{\frac{1}{3} + \frac{1}{3} + \frac{1}{3}} = 1$ | 1 |

Any other numbers, such as $x = 2, y = 2, z = 2$, will make the columns *unequal*:

$$\frac{1}{2 + 2 + 2} \neq 2 + 2 + 2$$

Therefore, Choice D is correct.

EXAMPLE 10

Column A	Column B
$(a^3)^4$	a^7

Choice D is correct.

Column A	Column B
$(a^3)^4$	a^7

First calculate $(a^3)^4 = a^{12}$ (remember your basic math skills?) The columns become:

| a^{12} | a^7 |

Now try $a = 1$ to get the columns equal. If we then try $a = 2$, we can see that the columns are unequal. Thus a definite comparison cannot be made.

MATH STRATEGY D

To Make a Comparison Simpler—Especially of Fractions—Multiply, Divide, Add to, or Subtract from Both Columns by a Quantity (Never Multiply or Divide by Zero or by a Negative Number)

Examples 1, 3, 4, 12, 13, 16, and 18 can also be solved with the aid of a calculator and some with the aid of a calculator allowing for exponential calculations. However, to illustrate the effectiveness of Math Strategy D, we did not use the calculator method of solution of these examples.

EXAMPLE 1

Column A	Column B
1	$\dfrac{7}{9} \Big/ \dfrac{9}{7}$

Choice A is correct.

Don't divide 7/9 by 9/7. <u>Multiply</u> both columns by 9/7 to get rid of the complicated fraction in Column B:

Column A	Column B
$1 \times 9/7$	$\dfrac{7/9}{9/7} \times 9/7$
9/7	7/9

Column A > Column B.

EXAMPLE 2

Column A	Column B

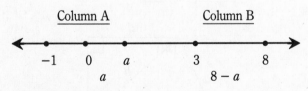

Choice B is correct.

Get rid of the minus sign by <u>adding</u> *a* to both columns:

Column A	Column B
$a + a$	$8 - a + a$
$2a$	8

Divide by 2: a 4

Now look at the diagram: $a < 3$, so $a < 4$.
Column A < Column B.

EXAMPLE 3

Column A	Column B
$\sqrt{19} - \sqrt{3}$	$\sqrt{16}$

Choice B is correct. First, get rid of the minus sign by adding $\sqrt{3}$ to both columns.

Column A	Column B
$\sqrt{19}$	$\sqrt{16} + \sqrt{3}$

Now *square* both columns:

Column A	Column B
$(\sqrt{19})^2$	$(\sqrt{16} + \sqrt{3})^2$
19	$16 + 3 + 2\sqrt{16}\,\sqrt{3}$
19	$19 + 2\sqrt{16}\,\sqrt{3}$

Cancel the 19's:

Column A	Column B
0	$2\sqrt{16}\,\sqrt{3}$

Column B > Column A

For Examples 4–7, try to get rid of minus signs by adding.

To Simplify a Problem, You Can Often Get Rid of Minus Signs Just by Adding the Same Quantity to Both Columns

You learned addition before you learned subtraction, and addition *is* more fundamental and basic than subtraction. Thus it would seem that it is easier and more natural to add whenever you can rather than to subtract. So try not to deal with minus signs or subtraction if the problem looks tedious—try to use addition.

SUMMARY DIRECTIONS FOR COMPARISON QUESTIONS

Choose A if the quantity in Column A is greater;
Choose B if the quantity in Column B is greater;
Choose C if the two quantities are equal;

Choose D if the relationship cannot be determined from the information given.

EXAMPLES 4–7

Column A	Column B

4. $\dfrac{7}{12} - \dfrac{1}{14}$ $\dfrac{6}{14}$

5. $0 > a > b$
     $-3b$ a

6. $b - a$ a -2 -1 0 $+1$ $+2$ b $a - b$

Column A	Column B

Note: Figure is not drawn to scale.

7. $a^2 - c^2$ $d^2 - b^2$

EXPLANATORY ANSWERS TO EXAMPLES 4–7

Column A	Column B

4. (A) $\dfrac{7}{12} - \dfrac{1}{14}$ $\dfrac{6}{14}$

Add $\dfrac{1}{14}$ to both columns to get rid of the minus sign:

$$\dfrac{7}{12} - \dfrac{\cancel{1}}{\cancel{14}} + \dfrac{\cancel{1}}{\cancel{14}} \qquad \dfrac{6}{14} + \dfrac{1}{14}$$

$$\dfrac{7}{12} \qquad\qquad \dfrac{7}{14}$$

$$\dfrac{7}{12} \quad > \quad \dfrac{7}{14}$$

Column A	Column B

5. (A) $0 > a > b$
     $-3b$ a

Add $3b$ to both columns:

$$-3b + 3b \qquad\qquad a + 3b$$
$$\downarrow \qquad\qquad\qquad \downarrow$$
$$0 \qquad\qquad\qquad a + 3b$$

Since $0 > a$ and $0 > b$, $a + 3b$ is *negative*. So Column A > Column B.

Column A   Column B

6. (A)

$b - a$ $a - b$

Add a to both columns; then add b to both columns to get rid of minus signs:

	Column A	Column B
	$b - a$	$a - b$
Add a:	$b - \cancel{a} + \cancel{a}$	$a - b + a$
	b	$2a - b$
Add b:	$b + b$	$2a - \cancel{b} + \cancel{b}$
	$2b$	$2a$
Divide by 2:	b	a
From diagram:	b $>$	a

7. (C)

Note: Figure is not drawn to scale.

Sum of internal angles of a quadrilateral is 360 degrees. Find remaining angle: $140 + 40 + 90 + x = 360$

$$x = 90$$

Now <u>draw line</u> and <u>label it</u> h.

Note: Figure is not drawn to scale.

By the Pythagorean Theorem,

$$a^2 + b^2 = h^2$$
$$d^2 + c^2 = h^2$$
$$\text{so } a^2 + b^2 = d^2 + c^2 \qquad \boxed{1}$$

Add c^2 and b^2 to both columns:

Column A	Column B
$a^2 - c^2$	$d^2 - b^2$
Add c^2: a^2	$d^2 - b^2 + c^2$
Add b^2: $a^2 + b^2$	$d^2 + c^2$

The columns are therefore equal because of $\boxed{1}$.

For Examples 8–14, multiply or divide to simplify the problem, but never multiply by 0 or by a negative number.

Often You Can Multiply or Divide Each Column by the Same Number to Simplify the Problem and Avoid Tedious Calculations

EXAMPLES 8–14

	Column A		Column B
8.		$a \neq 0$	
	0		$\dfrac{5}{a^2}$
9.		$a > 0$	
	$2a$		$\dfrac{a}{0.4}$
10.		$a > 0$	
	$\dfrac{1}{a}$		a
11.		$a > b > 0$	
	$\dfrac{a^2 + b^2}{a - b}$		$a - b$
12.	7×8^{12}		8×7^{12}
13.	35×65		34×66
14.		$a > b > 0$	
	$\dfrac{2ab}{a + b}$		$\dfrac{a + b}{2}$

EXPLANATORY ANSWERS FOR EXAMPLES 8–14

	Column A		Column B
8. (B)		$a \neq 0$	
	0		$\dfrac{5}{a^2}$

Since $a^2 > 0$ (even if a is negative, $a^2 > 0$) you can multiply by a^2:

Column A		Column B
0		$\dfrac{5}{a^2}$
$0 \times a^2$		$\dfrac{5}{a^2} \times a^2$
0		5
0	$<$	5

	Column A		Column B
9. (B)		$a > 0$	
	$2a$		$\dfrac{a}{0.4}$

Multiply by 0.4 to get rid of the denominator:

Column A		Column B
$(2a)(0.4)$		$\dfrac{a}{0.4} \, 0.4$
$\downarrow$		$\downarrow$
$0.8a$		a

Since $a > 0$, divide by a:

Column A		Column B
$\dfrac{0.8a}{a}$		$\dfrac{a}{a}$
$\downarrow$		$\downarrow$
0.8		1
0.8	$<$	1

	Column A		Column B
10. (D)		$a > 0$	
	$\dfrac{1}{a}$		a

Since $a > 0$, multiply both columns by a:

$a > 0$

Column A	Column B
$\dfrac{1}{a} \times a$	$a \times a$
1	a^2

Now you have to be careful: If $a > 1$, certainly $a^2 > 1$. But if a is a fraction such as $\dfrac{1}{4}$, then $a^2 = \dfrac{1}{16} < 1$, so a definite comparison cannot be made.

SUMMARY DIRECTIONS FOR COMPARISON QUESTIONS

Choose A if the quantity in Column A is greater;	Choose D if the relationship cannot be determined from the information given.
Choose B if the quantity in Column B is greater;	
Choose C if the two quantities are equal;	

Column A	Column B

11. (A) $a > b > 0$

$$\frac{a^2 + b^2}{a - b} \qquad\qquad a - b$$

Since $a > b$, $a - b > 0$,
So we can <u>multiply both columns by $a - b$</u>:

$$\frac{a^2 + b^2}{a - b} \times a - b \qquad\qquad (a - b)(a - b)$$

$$a^2 + b^2 \qquad\qquad a^2 - 2ab + b^2$$

Cancel
$a^2 + b^2$
from both columns

$$0 \qquad\qquad -2ab$$

Since $a > b > 0$, $2ab > 0$ and $-2ab < 0$. Thus Column A > Column B.

Column A	Column B

12. (A) 7×8^{12} 8×7^{12}

Use logic. It's obviously too hard to calculate 7×8^{12} and 8×7^{12}. So let's try to take advantage of the curious form of the numbers. <u>Divide</u> both columns by 7 and then divide by 8:

$$\frac{7 \times 8^{12}}{7} \qquad\qquad \frac{8 \times 7^{12}}{7}$$

$$8^{12} \qquad\qquad 8 \times 7^{11}$$

Now divide by 8:

$$\frac{8^{12}}{8} \qquad\qquad \frac{8 \times 7^{11}}{8}$$

$$8^{11} \qquad\qquad 7^{11}$$

Column A > Column B.

Column A	Column B
35×65	34×66

13. (A) You *do not* have to multiply 35×65 and 34×66! *Note the relationship of the numbers in the columns:* That is, between 35 and 34 and 65 and 66. Divide 34 into the quantities in both columns and divide 65 into the quantities in both columns. We get

Column A	Column B
$\dfrac{35 \times 65}{34 \times 65}$	$\dfrac{34 \times 66}{34 \times 65}$

Simplified, this becomes

Column A	Column B
$\dfrac{35}{34}$	$\dfrac{66}{65}$

Now $\frac{35}{34}$ is $1\frac{1}{34}$ and $\frac{66}{65}$ is $1\frac{1}{65}$. Since $\frac{1}{34} > \frac{1}{65}$ the quantity in Column A is greater than the quantity in Column B and Choice A is correct.

14. (B)   Column A   Column B

$$\frac{2ab}{a + b} \quad a > b > 0 \quad \frac{a + b}{2}$$

<u>Multiply</u> both columns by $a + b$ and by 2 to get rid of fractions:

Column A	Column B
$2(a + b) \; \dfrac{2ab}{a + b}$	$2(a + b) \; \dfrac{a + b}{2}$
$\downarrow$	$\downarrow$
$2(a + b) \; \dfrac{2ab}{a + b}$	$\dfrac{2(a + b)(a + b)}{2}$
$\downarrow$	$\downarrow$
$4ab$	$(a + b)(a + b)$
$\downarrow$	$\downarrow$
$4ab$	$a^2 + 2ab + b^2$
$\downarrow$	$\downarrow$

Subtract
$4ab$: $4ab - 4ab$ $a^2 + 2ab + b^2 - 4ab$

$\downarrow$	$\downarrow$
0	$a^2 - 2ab + b^2$
$\downarrow$	$\downarrow$
0	$(a - b)(a - b)$

Since $a > b > 0$, $(a - b)(a - b) > 0$
So Column B > Column A.

For Examples 15–18, square both columns to get rid of square roots.

In Comparing Square Roots, Instead of Calculating or Substituting Numbers You Can Usually Just Square the Square Roots to Get Rid of Square Root Signs

EXAMPLE 15

Column A		Column B
$\sqrt{a} + \sqrt{3}$	$a > 0$	$\sqrt{a + 3}$

Choice A is correct.

Square both columns:

Column A	Column B
$(\sqrt{a} + \sqrt{3})^2$	$(\sqrt{a + 3})^2$
↓	↓
$a + 3 + 2\sqrt{a}\sqrt{3}$	$a + 3$

Cancel $a + 3$:

$\cancel{a + 3} + 2\sqrt{a}\sqrt{3}$	$\cancel{a + 3}$
↓	
$2\sqrt{a}\sqrt{3}$	0
$2\sqrt{a}\sqrt{3} \quad > $	0

EXAMPLES 16–18

	Column A		Column B
16.	$\sqrt{19}$		$\sqrt{6} + \sqrt{13}$
17.	$\sqrt{x + y}$	$x > y > 0$	$\sqrt{x} + \sqrt{y}$
18.	$\sqrt{17} - \sqrt{3}$		$\sqrt{14}$

EXPLANATORY ANSWERS TO EXAMPLES 16–18

16. (B)

Column A	Column B
$\sqrt{19}$	$\sqrt{6} + \sqrt{13}$

Square both columns:

$\sqrt{19} \times \sqrt{19}$	$(\sqrt{6} + \sqrt{13})(\sqrt{6} + \sqrt{13})$
19	$6 + 13 + 2\sqrt{13}\sqrt{6}$

Cancel 19:

Column A		Column B
$0 \quad <$		$2\sqrt{13}\sqrt{6}$

17. (B)

Column A		Column B
$\sqrt{x + y}$	$x > y > 0$	$\sqrt{x} + \sqrt{y}$

Square both columns:

$(\sqrt{x + y})(\sqrt{x + y})$	$(\sqrt{x} + \sqrt{y})(\sqrt{x} + \sqrt{y})$
$x + y$	$x + y + 2\sqrt{x}\sqrt{y}$

Cancel *common* $x + y$ from both columns:

0	$2\sqrt{x}\sqrt{y}$

Column A < Column B.

18. (B)

Column A	Column B
$\sqrt{17} - \sqrt{3}$	$\sqrt{14}$

First, *add* $\sqrt{3}$ to both columns to get rid of $(-\sqrt{3})$ from Column A. (It is usually easier to work with $+$ than with $-$.)

$\sqrt{17} - \cancel{\sqrt{3}} + \cancel{\sqrt{3}}$	$\sqrt{14} + \sqrt{3}$

Now square both columns:

17	$(\sqrt{14} + \sqrt{3})^2$
17	$14 + 3 + 2\sqrt{14}\sqrt{3}$
$17 \quad <$	$17 + 2\sqrt{14}\sqrt{3}$

For Examples 19–22, make sure you don't divide by 0 or by a negative number.

When Canceling a Quantity from Both Columns, Make Sure You Are Not Actually Dividing by 0 or by a Negative Number.

EXAMPLE 19

Column A		Column B
	$0 > a$	
	$b > 2$	
$\dfrac{a}{b}$		ab

Choice A is correct.

Don't divide by a because $a < 0$. But you can multiply by b:

Column A	Column B
$\dfrac{a}{b} \times b$	$ab \times b$

Now since a is negative and $b > 2$, you can see that $a > ab^2$ and so Column A is greater than Column B.

EXAMPLES 20–22

	Column A		Column B
20.		$c > b > a$	
	bc		ab
21.		$0 > a > b$	
	ab		b
22.		$a < 1$	
	a^2		a

EXPLANATORY ANSWERS TO EXAMPLES 20–22

Column A	Column B
20. (D)	$c > b > a$
bc	ab

Don't cancel b since b may be negative.
Suppose $b = 0$. Then the columns are =
Suppose $b = 1$. Then Column A > Column B since $c > a$. Therefore, you cannot make a definite comparison.

Column A	Column B
21. (A)	$0 > a > b$
ab	b

Since $b < 0$, don't cancel b.
But think—if $0 > a$ and $0 > b$ then ab is *positive*.
So:

Column A		Column B
positive		negative
positive	>	negative

Column A	Column B
22. (D)	$a < 1$
a^2	a

We don't know if $a = 0$, so we can't divide by a to get a comparison. However, we know that a^2 (Column A) is always positive or zero. If a is negative, Column A > Column B. If $a = 0$, Column A = Column B. In one case, Column A > Column B, in another Column A = Column B. So a definite comparison cannot be made.

MATH STRATEGY E

Try to Get the Columns and the Given to Look Similar

The quantities to be compared in the columns and the information given may look different. Whenever it is possible, you should try to get the columns to look like what is given, or try to get the given to look like what is in the columns.

EXAMPLE 1

Column A	Column B
	$m > n$
	$n > p$
m	p

Choice A is correct. We want to compare m and p. However, the given information,

$$m > n \boxed{1}$$
$$n > p \boxed{2}$$

does not directly relate to m and p. So we should try to get the given information to look similar to what we want to compare. By comparing $\boxed{1}$ and $\boxed{2}$ we have

$$m > p$$

This is the piece of information we need in order to compare the two columns. Clearly, Choice A is correct.

EXAMPLE 2

Column A	Column B
	$-5 < x < +5$
-6	$-x$

Choice B is correct.
Try to get the given to look like what's in the columns. Multiply the given by -1. You get

$$-1(-5 < x < +5) \rightarrow +5 > -x > -5$$

remembering to reverse the inequality signs when multiplying by a negative number.

Now we found $-x > -5$. Now look at the columns:

If $-x > -5$, surely
$-x > -6$ and Column A < Column B.

EXAMPLES 3–8

Column A		Column B
3.	$-y = x$	
0		$x + y$

	Column A		Column B
4.		$66 < 6a < 140$	
	23.4		a

	Column A		Column B
5.		18% of $4x = 86$	
	43		18% of $2x$

	Column A		Column B
6.		$5x < 30 < 6x$	
	6		x

	Column A		Column B
7.		$a + b + c = 8$ $a - b + c = 4$	
	$2a + 2c$		13

	Column A		Column B
8.		$3 > 12a + 12$	
	0		a

EXPLANATORY ANSWERS TO EXAMPLES 3–8

	Column A		Column B
3. (C)		$-y = x$	
	0		$x + y$

Get the given to look like what's in the columns.
$-y = x$, so $x + y = 0$
Now you can see that Column A = Column B.

	Column A		Column B
4. (A)		$66 < 6a < 140$	
	23.4		a

Get the given to look like what's in the columns.
Divide the given by 6:

$$\frac{66}{6} < \frac{6a}{6} < \frac{140}{6}$$

$$11 < a < 23\frac{1}{3}$$

Now $23\frac{1}{3} > a$ and 23.4 (Column A) $> 23\frac{1}{3}$

So, $23.4 > 23\frac{1}{3} > a$ and $23.4 > a$

	Column A		Column B
5. (C)		18% of $4x = 86$	
	43		18% of $2x$

Get the given to look like what's in the columns.
Divide the given by 2:

$$\frac{18\% \text{ of } 4x}{2} = \frac{86}{2}$$

$$18\% \text{ of } 2x = 43$$

Column A = Column B.

	Column A		Column B
6. (A)		$5x < 30 < 6x$	
	6		x

Get the given to look like what's in the columns.
You want to get something like $x > 6$ or $6 > x$ from the given $5x < 30 < 6x$
So divide by 5:

$$\frac{5x}{5} < \frac{30}{5} < \frac{6x}{5}$$

$$x < 6 < \frac{6x}{5}$$

NOTE: If you had divided $5x < 30 < 6x$ by 6, you would have gotten:

$$\frac{5x}{6} < 5 < x$$

but that wouldn't have given you $x > 6$ or $6 > x$.

	Column A		Column B
7. (B)		$a + b + c = 8$ $a - b + c = 4$	
	$2a + 2c$		13

Relate the given to the columns:
Add:

$$a + b + c = 8$$
$$a - b + c = 4$$
$$\overline{2a + 2c = 12}$$

Substitute $2a + 2c = 12$ in Column A to get:

12		13
	$12 < 13$	

	Column A		Column B
8. (A)		$3 > 12a + 12$	
	0		a

Relate the given to the columns:
Divide the given by 12:

$$\frac{3}{12} > \frac{12a + 12}{12}$$

$$\frac{1}{4} > \frac{12a}{12} + \frac{12}{12}$$

$$\frac{1}{4} > a + 1$$

Subtract 1 to get a alone.

$$\frac{1}{4} - 1 > a$$

$$-\frac{3}{4} > a$$

Since $0 > -\frac{3}{4}$ and $-\frac{3}{4} > a$, then $0 > -\frac{3}{4} > a$ and $0 > a$.

SUMMARY DIRECTIONS FOR COMPARISON QUESTIONS

Choose A if the quantity in Column A is greater,
Choose B if the quantity in Column B is greater,
Choose C if the two quantities are equal;

Choose D if the relationship cannot be determined from the
information given.

MATH STRATEGY **F**

Use the Choice C Method When Straightforward Computations Must Be Made

This strategy should be used only if you must guess the answer or if you do not have the time to work out tedious arithmetic. When the answer to a problem requires only a straightforward computation and if there are very specific numbers (like 17 or 23) involved in the problem, Choice C is almost always correct. The reason is that the test maker has a logical reason to make Choice C the answer. We see this in the following problem.

EXAMPLE 1

Column A	Column B
$5x + 12 = 27$	
x	3

Choice C is correct. Look at all the specific numbers that are involved in this question: 5, 12, 27, and 3. These numbers were not accidentally chosen! The solution to this problem involves a straightforward calculation!

$$5x + 12 = 27 \;\boxed{1}$$
$$5x = 15$$
$$x = 3$$

Why did the test maker want Choice C as the answer? The reason is that if you could not solve $\boxed{1}$, then you guessed what x should be. You probably guessed that x is some number greater than 3 or less than 3. In addition, if you made a mistake solving $\boxed{1}$, then you obtained a value for x that was greater than 3 or less than 3. Either way, you wrote Choice A or B as your answer. You may even have written Choice D if you could not do the problem correctly. Thus, the test maker felt that only someone who really knew how to solve the problem would write Choice C. Let us look at another problem.

EXAMPLE 2

Column A	Column B
Last year, Jack had 60 marbles.	This year Jack has 75 marbles.
The percent increase in the number of marbles Jack had since last year.	25%

Choice C is correct. Look at all the specific numbers in this problem: 60, 75, and 25. These numbers were not accidentally chosen! The solution to this problem involves a straightforward computation:

The percent increase in the number of marbles Jack had since last year =

$$\frac{\text{Number of} \atop \text{marbles Jack} \atop \text{has now} - \text{Number of} \atop \text{marbles Jack} \atop \text{had last year}}{\text{Number of marbles} \atop \text{Jack had last year}} \times 100$$

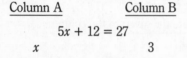

$$= \frac{75 - 60}{60} \times 100$$
$$= \frac{15}{60} \times 100$$
$$= 25\% \; (Answer)$$

Anyone who guessed the answer or who made a mistake in the above calculation probably wrote A, B, or D as the answer. Only someone who really solved the problem correctly was able to get the right answer, Choice C.

EXAMPLE 3

Column A	Column B
The length of the hypotenuse of a right triangle whose legs are 7 inches and 24 inches long.	The length of the hypotenuse of a right triangle whose legs are 15 inches and 20 inches long.

Choice C is correct. Look at all the specific numbers in this question: 7, 24, 15, and 20. These numbers were not accidentally chosen! The solution to this problem involves straightforward calculation!

$$(\text{hypotenuse})^2 = (\text{first leg})^2 + (\text{second leg})^2$$

Thus, for Column A,

$$(\text{hypotenuse})^2 = 7^2 + 24^2$$
$$= 49 + 576$$
$$= 625$$

hypotenuse in Column A = 25 [1]

For Column B

$$(\text{hypotenuse})^2 = 15^2 + 20^2$$
$$= 225 + 400$$
$$= 625$$

hypotenuse in Column B = 25 [2]

From [1] and [2] the answer is clear. Anyone who guessed the answer or who made a mistake in the above calculation probably wrote A, B, or D as the answer. Only someone who really solved the problem correctly was able to get the right answer.

22 Verbal Strategies

Using Critical Thinking Skills in Verbal Questions

6 Analogy Strategies

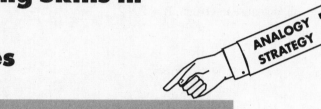

ANALOGY STRATEGY 1

Always Express an Analogy in Sentence Form*

Without looking at the answer choices, try to establish a meaningful relationship between the CAPITALIZED pair of words. When you do establish the relationship, *express it in sentence form.* Then use that same sentence form in the choices to get the correct answer.

* Strategy 1 is considered the Master Analogy Strategy because it can be used effectively in every Analogy question. However, it is important that you learn the other Analogy Strategies also since they can often be used to double-check your answers.

EXAMPLE 1

THIEF : ROBBERY ::

(A) burglar : diamonds
(B) jail : crime
(C) kidnapper : hostage
(D) criminal : capture
(E) counterfeiter : forgery

EXPLANATORY ANSWER

Put the capitalized words in the form of a sentence: THIEF *commits* a ROBBERY. Now put the choice words in the same sentence form: counterfeiter *commits* a forgery.

By using this analogy strategy you will not get "lured" into a wrong answer. In fact, you will immediately be able to eliminate all wrong choices by trying the sentence form with all the choices:

THIEF *commits* a ROBBERY

(A) burglar *commits* diamonds—NO!
(B) jail *commits* a crime—NO!
(C) kidnapper *commits* a hostage—NO!
(D) criminal *commits* capture—NO!
(E) counterfeiter *commits* a forgery—YES!

(Person to Action relationship)

EXAMPLE 2

CLOCK : TIME ::

(A) minute : hour
(B) dimension : space
(C) distance : meter
(D) thermometer : temperature
(E) gravity : weight

EXPLANATORY ANSWER

Choice D is correct. A CLOCK <u>is used to tell or determine the</u> TIME. A thermometer <u>is used to tell or determine the</u> temperature. The other choices do not lend themselves to this sentence relationship.

(Purpose relationship)

EXAMPLE 3

PIG : SNOUT ::

(A) elephant : trunk
(B) bill : bird
(C) hide : horse
(D) scorpion : sting
(E) lion : den

Choice A is correct. A pig's nose is called a snout. An elephant's "nose" is called a trunk.

(Association relationship)

EXAMPLE 4

PUNCTURE : TIRE : :

(A) pierce : ear
(B) retract : statement
(C) inflate : balloon
(D) catch : fish
(E) owe : favor

EXPLANATORY ANSWER

Choice A is correct. When a tire is punctured, it results in a hole in the tire. A pierced ear results in a hole in the ear.

(Result relationship)

EXAMPLE 5

ADVOCATE : CHANGE : :

(A) bypass : road
(B) endorse : candidate
(C) raze : building
(D) provoke : anger
(E) eradicate : mistake

EXPLANATORY ANSWER

Choice is B correct. To advocate a change is to encourage its acceptance. To endorse a candidate is to encourage his or her acceptance.

(Action to Object relationship)

EXAMPLE 6

FARE : PASSENGER : :

(A) magazine : subscriber
(B) parking : ticket
(C) tuition : student
(D) bond : premium
(E) usury : interest

EXPLANATORY ANSWER

Choice C is correct. A fare is paid by a passenger. Tuition is paid by a student.

(Purpose relationship)

ANALOGY STRATEGY 2

Know the Most Common Analogy Types

Be familiar with the various types of word-pair relationships. This familiarity will help you to detect relationships in analogy questions.

Following are analogy types most commonly used on the SAT.

Analogy Type	*Example*
PART : WHOLE	LEG : BODY
PURPOSE	SCISSORS : CUT
DEGREE	GRIN : LAUGH
OPPOSITES	COY : AGGRESSIVE
CHARACTERISTIC	SANDPAPER : ROUGH
CAUSE : EFFECT	PRACTICE : IMPROVEMENT
ASSOCIATION	COW : MILK
HABITAT	AIRPLANE : HANGAR
ACTION : SITUATION	RUN : MARATHON
ACTION : OBJECT	SHOOT : RIFLE
RESULT	TRIAL : JUDGMENT
PLACE : PERSON	SCHOOL : TEACHER
CLASSIFICATION (TYPE)	CHURCH : BUILDING

Note: Some Analogy types may be used in reverse. You may have WHOLE : PART, EFFECT : CAUSE, etc.

EXAMPLE 1

DRIZZLE : RAIN ::

(A) diamond : ruby
(B) novel : autobiography
(C) lightning : thunderstorm
(D) blizzard : avalanche
(E) surprise : shock

EXPLANATORY ANSWER

Choice E is correct. A DRIZZLE is a fine, gentle falling of water drops from the sky. RAIN has a greater intensity of such falling of water drops. You have here a relationship of Degree. A shock is an emotional disturbance and is more extreme than a surprise is. In other words, a person who is shocked is more violently upset than when merely surprised.

(Degree relationship)

EXAMPLE 2

SALUTATION : FAREWELL ::

(A) birth : death
(B) army : navy
(C) noon : midnight
(D) friendship : divorce
(E) plane : bus

EXPLANATORY ANSWER

Choice A is correct. We have here an Opposite analogy of a certain type—a *beginning-end* analogy. A SALUTATION may be the beginning of a letter—"Dear Sir," for example; or it could be a greeting such as "Hello." A FAREWELL expresses the end of something such as a visit. A farewell expression is "goodbye." It is obvious that *birth* and *death* represent a beginning and an end.

(Opposites relationship)

EXAMPLE 3

WRITE : PENCIL ::

(A) hammer : nail
(B) inflate : tire
(C) open : door
(D) fly : kite
(E) wash : hose

EXPLANATORY ANSWER

Choice E is correct. We WRITE with a PENCIL and we wash with a hose. The other choices are incorrect because one does *not* hammer *with* a nail, or inflate *with* a tire, or open *with* a door, or fly *with* a kite.

(Action to Object relationship)

EXAMPLE 4

TENSION : HEADACHE: :

(A) disposition : anger
(B) volt : electricity
(C) virus : malady
(D) tree : leaf
(E) mistake : correction

EXPLANATORY ANSWER

Choice C is correct. TENSION is likely to cause a HEADACHE, and a virus is likely to cause a malady or disease.

(Cause and Effect relationship)

EXAMPLE 5

STAPLE : SHEETS ::

(A) balance : scales
(B) nail : boards
(C) grind : kernels
(D) mold : clay
(E) type : memos

EXPLANATORY ANSWER

Choice B is correct. One *staples sheets* to hold them together. One *nails boards* to hold them together.

(Purpose relationship)

EXAMPLE 6

HUTCH : RABBIT ::

(A) barn : hay
(B) sty : pig
(C) dairy : cow
(D) refuge : wildlife
(E) field : corn

EXPLANATORY ANSWER

Choice B is correct. A *rabbit* is kept in a *hutch*. A *pig* is kept in a *sty*.

(Habitat relationship)

Check to See That the Capitalized Words and the Words of Your Choice Have the Same Sequence

Be sure that the one-two position of the capitalized words is the same as the one-two position of the words of the answer you have chosen. Beware of the choice that would be correct if the words of that choice were reversed.

EXAMPLE 1

ANGER : INSULT ::

(A) business : judgment
(B) admiration : happiness
(C) conduct : behavior
(D) appreciation : kindness
(E) willingness : refusal

EXPLANATORY ANSWER

Choice D is correct. We have here a Cause and Effect analogy. However, the effect word (ANGER) is presented first and the cause word (INSULT) is presented second. So we really have an Effect-Cause relationship here. Anger on the part of one person is likely the effect of an insult on the part of another person. Choice D (appreciation : kindness) has the same Effect-Cause relationship. Appreciation on the part of one person is likely the effect of kindness on the part of the other person. Note the position of the words in Choice B (admiration : happiness). It is true that happiness on the part of one person is likely caused by admiration on the part of another person. In order to follow through with the ANGER : INSULT position, we would have to change Choice B to happiness : admiration.

(Effect-Cause relationship)

EXAMPLE 2

HOSPITAL : NURSE ::

(A) college : professor
(B) theater : dramatist
(C) artist : studio
(D) drugs : pharmacist
(E) cathedral : architect

EXPLANATORY ANSWER

Choice A is correct. A hospital is a place where a nurse works. A college is a place where a professor works. Note the position of the words in Choice C—artist : studio. It is true that an artist works in a studio. In order to follow through with the HOSPITAL : NURSE position, we would have to change Choice C to studio : artist.

(Place-Worker relationship)

EXAMPLE 3

TEPID : HOT ::

(A) cool : frigid
(B) spotless : clean
(C) warm : comfortable
(D) humorous : mature
(E) curious : coy

EXPLANATORY ANSWER

Choice A is correct. The word "tepid" means moderately warm. When something is very, very warm, it is hot. The word "cool" means moderately cold. When something is very, very cold, it is frigid. We have here a Degree relationship. Note the position of the words in Choice (B) spotless : clean. "Spotless" means perfectly clean. We have here a Degree relationship also. But in order to follow through with the TEPID : HOT position of words, we would have to change Choice B to clean : spotless.

(Degree relationship)

EXAMPLE 4

SURFACE : SUBMERGE ::

(A) sail : navigate
(B) conceal : reveal
(C) mount : ascend
(D) sink : swim
(E) emerge : withdraw

EXPLANATORY ANSWER

Choice E is correct. To surface is the opposite of to submerge. To emerge is the opposite of to withdraw. The relationship is opposite in each case. In Choice B, conceal is the opposite of reveal, but the order of the words is a reverse of the order of the capitalized words and the Choice E words.

(Opposite relationship)

EXAMPLE 5

BARBER : SCISSORS ::

(A) nurse : patient
(B) plumber : sink
(C) gardener : weed
(D) chef : knife
(E) telescope : astronomer

EXPLANATORY ANSWER

Choice D is correct. A barber uses scissors to do his job. A chef uses a knife to do his job. We have here a Purpose relationship. Choice (E) telescope : astronomer does *not* have the proper word order necessary to be the correct answer. A telescope does not use an astronomer to do its job. If this choice were reversed to read astronomer : telescope, it would have the proper word order for the correct answer since an astronomer *does* use a telescope to do his job.

(Association and Purpose relationship)

EXAMPLE 6

RECESS : SCHOOL ::

(A) parole : convict
(B) session : government
(C) work : vacation
(D) intermission : theater
(E) convention : delegation

EXPLANATORY ANSWER

Choice D is correct. A recess is a break or pause in a school for relaxation. An intermission is a break or pause in a theater for relaxation. Choice (C), work : vacation, also indicates a break or pause at a place or in an activity. However, the two words of Choice C would have to be reversed to be considered as a correct choice. Therefore, Choice C, as it stands, is an incorrect choice.

(Purpose relationship)

ANALOGY STRATEGY **4**

Make Sure to Get the *Exact* Relationship of the Capitalized Words and Your Choice to Eliminate All Incorrect Choices

Two or more of the answer choices may, at first glance, show a relationship *similar* to the relationship of the capitalized pair of words. It is necessary to go back to the capitalized pair of words sometimes in order to establish an *exact or more specific* relationship. Then find the choice that has the two words with the *very same* relationship as that of the capitalized words.

EXAMPLE 1

MOTH : CLOTHING ::

(A) sheep : wool
(B) butterfly : wood
(C) puncture : tire
(D) tear : sweater
(E) termite : house

EXPLANATORY ANSWER

Choice E is correct. You may have thought that MOTH is related to *sheep* and that *wood* is related to CLOTHING. Or you may have thought that *butterfly* and MOTH are related. But if you use the sentence strategy, you'll never be lured into these relationships. Let's figure out a sen-

tence relating MOTH to CLOTHING: MOTH destroys CLOTHING. Now look at the choices:

(A) sheep *destroys* wool—NO
(B) butterfly *destroys* wood—NO
(C) puncture *destroys* a tire—YES
(D) tear *destroys* a sweater—YES
(E) termite *destroys* a house—YES

So which is it? Since you have found more than one possible answer, you have to modify your sentence and get a more *specific* one. Say MOTH is a *living thing* that destroys CLOTHING.

Now you can see that you can eliminate choices C and D:

(C) puncture is a *living thing*—NO
(D) tear is a *living thing*—NO
(E) termite is a *living thing*—YES!

(Cause and Effect relationship)

EXAMPLE 2

JUROR : JUDGE ::

(A) criminal : sentence
(B) doctor : cure
(C) umpire : strikeout
(D) decision : vacillate
(E) broom : sweep

EXPLANATORY ANSWER

Choice B is correct. You might have used a sentence like: "A JUROR listens to a JUDGE." Then you would have looked at the choices and said for (A) "criminal listens to a sentence—No! (B) "doctor listens to a cure"—No! (C) "umpire listens to a strikeout"—No! (D) "decision listens to vacillate"—No! and (E) "broom listens to sweep"—No! So what do you do? You have eliminated *all* the choices! Don't panic! Just modify your sentence. In this case you should think that JUDGE can be used as a *noun or* as a *verb*. You originally used it as a *noun* in your sentence. Now try using it as a *verb*. Say "A JUROR can be used to JUDGE." Now you can see that Choice B fits—"A doctor can be used to cure." Also Choice E fits: "A broom can be used to sweep." Again modify your sentence, still using JUDGE as a verb: "A JUROR is a person who can be used to JUDGE." Choice B: "A doctor is a person who can be used to cure." Choice E: "A broom is a person"—No! Choice B is the only choice remaining.

(Purpose relationship)

EXAMPLE 3

BUILDING : CHURCH ::

(A) dance : ballet
(B) poetry : sonnet
(C) museum : relics
(D) song : hymn
(E) morality : ethics

EXPLANATORY ANSWER

Choice D is correct. Use sentences: CHURCH is a *type* of BUILDING. The best choices are

(A) ... ballet is a *type* of dance
(B) ... sonnet is a *type* of poetry
(C) ... hymn is a *type* of song

Now *fine-tune* your sentence to eliminate wrong choices: CHURCH is a *religious type* of BUILDING. Only Choice D fits: **hymn** is a *religious type* of **song**.

(Classification)

EXAMPLE 4

HELMET : HEAD ::

(A) sword : warrior
(B) umbrella : clothing
(C) shoe : stocking
(D) watch : wrist
(E) thimble : finger

EXPLANATORY ANSWER

Choice E is correct. Try the sentence "HELMET is worn on the HEAD." Now look at the choices, using the same sentence form. The most likely choices are Choices D and E: (D) watch is worn on a wrist and (E) thimble is worn on a finger. So to come up with only one correct choice, modify your sentence. Say "HELMET is worn on the HEAD to protect the head." Now look at Choice D: watch is worn on the wrist to protect the wrist—No! Choice E: thimble is worn on the finger to protect the finger—Yes!

(Purpose relationship)

EXAMPLE 5

MUSIC : VIOLIN ::

(A) wood : hammer
(B) furniture : carpentry tools
(C) symphony : piano
(D) sound : cello
(E) notes : composer

EXPLANATORY ANSWER

Choice B is correct. You may have used the sentence "MUSIC is created with a VIOLIN." Then you would have found Choices B, D, and E correct: (B) furniture is created with carpentry tools, (D) sound is created with a cello, and (E) notes are created with a composer. What do you do? Just modify your sentence: "MUSIC is created with a VIOLIN by someone who knows only how to play the violin." Now look at the choices, using your new sentence: (B) furniture is created with carpentry tools by someone who knows only how to use carpentry tools—Yes! (D) sound is created with a cello by someone who knows only how to play the cello—No! (E) notes are created by a composer who knows only how to compose—No! So Choice B remains.

(Effect-Cause relationship)

EXAMPLE 6

SUSPECT : CONVICT ::

(A) agony : prolong
(B) president : impeach
(C) student : expel
(D) enemy : condemn
(E) slave : fetter

EXPLANATORY ANSWER

Choice C is correct. A suspect may be convicted if wrong-doing has been shown. A student may be expelled if wrongdoing has been shown. Choice C may seem correct but it is not. A president is impeached simply because he is accused. Wrongdoing has not been decided at the time of impeachment.

(Result relationship)

ANALOGY STRATEGY **5**

Be Aware That Certain Words May Have Two Different Meanings

Sometimes a word may have two different meanings. If you find it difficult to establish a relationship between the capitalized pair of words and a pair of words among the choices, study carefully the capitalized pair to get its *precise* relationship. With this in mind, try to get the same *precise* relationship while keeping in mind that certain words have more than one meaning.

EXAMPLE 1

STRIKE : PRODUCTION ::

(A) manufacture : merchandise
(B) injure : repair
(C) employ : inflation
(D) collide : car
(E) vaccinate : disease

EXPLANATORY ANSWER

Choice E is correct. In this question, STRIKE is a verb that means to stop work. Employees strike to stop production. A doctor vaccinates to prevent (or stop) a disease. We have here a Purpose analogy. The word "strike" can also mean to hit or collide with—but not in this question.

(Purpose relationship)

EXAMPLE 2

BULB : PLANT ::

(A) leaf : tree
(B) tadpole : frog
(C) biology : chemistry
(D) pupil : teacher
(E) switch : light

EXPLANATORY ANSWER

Choice B is correct. A bulb has the biological meaning of an underground stem or bud here—not the meaning of an object that you put into an electric lamp. A bulb, then, grows into a plant, and a tadpole grows into a frog. We have here a Degree of Development relationship—or a Part-Whole relationship (partially developed–wholly developed).

(Degree relationship and Part : Whole relationship)

EXAMPLE 3

PRESERVE : ANIMALS ::

(A) lighthouse : signals
(B) reservation : wigwams
(C) orphanage : institution
(D) vault : money
(E) penitentiary : warden

EXPLANATORY ANSWER

Choice D is correct. A preserve is a place that protects animals. A vault is a place that protects money. Note that the word "preserve" in this analogy is a noun. This word may also be used as a verb—but not in this analogy.

(Purpose relationship)

EXAMPLE 4

HECKLER : PERFORMER ::

(A) foghorn : boat
(B) audience : stage
(C) hunter : rifle
(D) tick : cat
(E) pest : nuisance

EXPLANATORY ANSWER

Choice D is correct. A heckler annoys a performer. A tick, which is a blood-sucking arachnid, annoys animals like cats and dogs. Note that the word "tick" has other meanings.

(Action to Object relationship)

EXAMPLE 5

MINT : MONEY ::

(A) pound : gold
(B) mail : stamp
(C) inform : notice
(D) obliterate : movement
(E) publish : literature

EXPLANATORY ANSWER

Choice E is correct. In this question the word MINT means to coin money—as when the government mints money by stamping metal. (The word "mint" may also refer to a special type of plant whose leaves are used for flavoring and in medicine—but not in this question.) Just as money is minted for general circulation to the public, literature is published for the public to read. We have here an Action to Object as well as a Purpose analogy.

(Purpose relationship)
(Action to Object relationship)

EXAMPLE 6

PRIDE : LIONS ::

(A) gaggle : geese
(B) nest : birds
(C) slyness : wolves
(D) hospital : nurses
(E) family : children

EXPLANATORY ANSWER

Choice A is correct. A pride of lions is a group of lions. A gaggle of geese is a group of geese. Note that the word "pride" also has the meaning of "self-respect"—but *not* in this analogy.

(Whole : Part relationship)

EXAMPLE 7

BOAT : SLIP ::

(A) skate : rink
(B) surfboard : wave
(C) train : schedule
(D) paddle : oar
(E) airplane : hangar

EXPLANATORY ANSWER

Choice E is correct. A slip is a place to keep a boat when it is not being used. A hangar is a place to keep an airplane when it is not being used. Note that the word "slip" is a *noun* in this analogy question because all of the other second-choice words are *nouns* in each of the choices. "Slip" thus cannot act as a verb meaning to slide suddenly and accidentally in this question.

(Purpose and Place relationship)

ANALOGY STRATEGY **6**

Use the Context Method for Unfamiliar Words

If you don't know the meaning of one of the *capitalized* words, try to find its meaning through the context of the choices.

EXAMPLE 1

CHARLATAN : DECEIT ::

(A) magician : trickery
(B) dancer : ballet
(C) customer : bargain
(D) playwright : ticket
(E) chemist : laboratory

EXPLANATORY ANSWER

Choice A is correct. Suppose that you don't know what the word CHARLATAN means. Look at the first word in each of the choices. They all refer to people, and the second word is something associated with these people. So you can say that CHARLATAN must be *some type of person who deceives* or who fools other people—or *who uses* DECEIT. The only choice that makes sense is Choice A: *a magician is a type of person who uses trickery.*

(Association relationship)

EXAMPLE 2

SEQUESTER : ISOLATION ::

(A) debase : degradation
(B) stunt : growth
(C) vaccinate : disease
(D) warm : boil
(E) study : text

EXPLANATORY ANSWER

Choice A is correct. Suppose you don't know the meaning of SEQUESTER. You see that the first word in each of the choices is a *verb*. In fact if just one of the first words in the choices (*like vaccinate—Choice C*) is a verb, then all of the first words in the choices must be verbs. So SEQUESTER therefore must also be a *verb* associated with ISOLATION. You might try: When you SEQUESTER (using SEQUESTER as a verb), you create or put in ISOLATION. Now try each of the choices using the same sentence:

(A) When you *debase*, you create *degradation*—not bad.
(B) When you *stunt*, you create *growth*—No!
(C) When you *vaccinate* you create *disease*—No!
(D) When you *warm*, you create a *boil*—No!
(E) When you *study*, you create *text*—No!

Thus Choice A is correct.

(Action to Situation relationship)

EXAMPLE 3

COLLAGE : ARTIST ::

(A) opera : musician
(B) novel : author
(C) decision : umpire
(D) interest : spectator
(E) graduation : student

EXPLANATORY ANSWER

Choice B is correct. Suppose that you don't know the meaning of COLLAGE. Look at the choices. The first word in each choice is a noun that is associated with a person (the second word). So you can safely say that COLLAGE is something associated with an ARTIST. You can then say that COLLAGE is probably a *painting or type of painting* done by an ARTIST. What else could really be associated with an ARTIST? Right? So Choice B looks best: A *novel* is done by an *author*. Note in Choice A: An opera is not created by a musician but by a composer.

(Association relationship)

EXAMPLE 4

HAMLET : VILLAGE ::

(A) street : sidewalk
(B) highway : car
(C) building : skyscraper
(D) photograph : portrait
(E) cottage : house

EXPLANATORY ANSWER

Choice E is correct. Because HAMLET is linked to VILLAGE we can assume that a HAMLET is a small, a large, a type of, or a part of a VILLAGE for starters. Let's look at the choices:

(A) A *street* is a small, a large, a type of, or a part of a *sidewalk*—No!
(B) A *highway* is a small, a large, a type of, or a part of a *car*—No!
(C) A *building* is a small, a large, a type of, or a part of a *skyscraper*—No!
   Note: **Analogy Strategy 3** here: the sequence is important, if it were (C) skyscraper : building, you could have said a *skyscraper* was a large *building*.
(D) A *photograph* is a small, a large, a type of, or part of a *portrait*—No!
(E) A *cottage* is a small *house*—YES!

(Degree relationship)

EXAMPLE 5

SHARD : GLASS ::

(A) wool : sheep
(B) crumb : cookie
(C) pound : weight
(D) rung : ladder
(E) slice : meat

EXPLANATORY ANSWER

Choice B is correct. Suppose you don't know the meaning of SHARD. All first words in choices are nouns. So SHARD must be a *type* of glass, a *small piece* of glass, or a *piece of art made from* glass. These are the most common things to think about. Choice B is the only one that fits.

(Part-whole relationship)

4 Sentence Completion Strategies

SENT. COMPL. STRATEGY 1

For a Sentence with Only One Blank, Fill the Blank with Each Choice to See the Best Fit*

Before you decide which is the best choice, fill the blank with each of the five answer choices to see which word will fit best into the sentence as a whole.

EXAMPLE 1

He believed that while there is serious unemployment in our auto industry, we should not _____ foreign cars.

(A) discuss
(B) regulate
(C) research
(D) import
(E) disallow

EXPLANATORY ANSWER

Choice D is correct. The word "import" means to bring in from another country or place. The sentence now makes good sense. The competition resulting from importation of foreign cars reduces the demand for American-made cars. This throws many American auto workers out of jobs.

EXAMPLE 2

His attempt to _____ his guilt was betrayed by the tremor of his hand as he picked up the paper.

(A) extenuate
(B) determine
(C) conceal
(D) intensify
(E) display

EXPLANATORY ANSWER

Choice C is correct. The word "conceal" means to keep secret or to hide. The sentence now makes good sense. The nervousness caused by his guilty conscience is shown by the shaking of his hand. He is thus prevented in his attempt to hide his guilt.

EXAMPLE 3

In large cities, the number of family-owned grocery stores has fallen so sharply that the opportunity to shop in such a place is _____ occasion.

(A) a celebrated
(B) an old
(C) a fanciful
(D) a rare
(E) an avid

EXPLANATORY ANSWER

Choice D is correct. A rare occasion is one that you seldom have the opportunity to participate in. Shopping in a family-owned grocery store in a large city today is, indeed, a rare occasion.

EXAMPLE 4

Legal _____ initiated by the government necessitate that manufacturers use _____ in choosing food additives.

(A) entanglements . . . knowledge
(B) devices . . . intensification
(C) talents . . . decretion
(D) proclivities . . . moderation
(E) restraints . . . caution

EXPLANATORY ANSWER

Choice E is correct. Although this is a two-blank question, we should use Sentence Completion Strategy 1. Try the words in each of the choices in the blanks in the sentence.

Another possibility is Choice A. But the point of the sentence evidently is that government prohibitions of certain food additives necessitate care by manufacturers in choosing food additives that are permitted. Thus Choice A is not as good as Choice E.

---

* Strategy 1 is considered the Master Strategy for *one-blank* Sentence Completion questions because it can be used effectively to answer every *one-blank* Sentence Completion question. However, it is important that you learn all of the other Sentence Completion Strategies because they can be used to double-check your answers.

EXAMPLE 5

It is unthinkable for a prestigious conductor to agree to include _____ musicians in his orchestra.

(A) capable
(B) seasoned
(C) mediocre
(D) recommended
(E) professional

EXPLANATORY ANSWER

Choice C is correct. The word "mediocre" (meaning average, ordinary) completes the sentence so that it makes good sense. The other choices do *not* do that.

EXAMPLE 6

A desire to be applauded by those in attendance, not his sensitivity to the plight of the underprivileged, was the reason for his _____ at the charity affair.

(A) shyness
(B) discomfort
(C) surprise
(D) arrogance
(E) generosity

EXPLANATORY ANSWER

Choice E is correct. No other choice makes sense in the sentence. It is clear that the person was primarily interested in being appreciated for his donation.

For a Sentence with Two Blanks Begin by Eliminating the Initial Words That Don't Make Sense in the Sentence*

This strategy consists of 2 steps.

Step 1. Find out which "first words" of the choices make sense in the first blank of the sentence. Don't consider the second word of each pair yet. *Eliminate those choices that contain "first words" that don't make sense in the sentence.*

Step 2. Now consider the *remaining* choices by filling in the pair of words for each choice.

EXAMPLE 1

The salesmen in that clothing store are so _____ that it is impossible to even look at a garment without being _____ by their efforts to convince you to purchase.

(A) offensive . . . considerate
(B) persistent . . . harassed
(C) extensive . . . induced
(D) immune . . . aided
(E) intriguing . . . evaluated

EXPLANATORY ANSWER

Choice B is correct.

STEP 1 [ELIMINATION]

We have eliminated Choice (C) extensive . . . induced because saying salesmen who are "extensive" does not make sense here. We have eliminated Choice (D) immune . . . aided because salesmen who are "immune" does not make sense here.

STEP 2 [REMAINING CHOICES]

This leaves us with these remaining choices to be considered. Choice (A) offensive . . . considerate. The sentence *does not* make sense. Choice (B) persistent . . . harassed. The sentence *does* make sense. Choice (E) intriguing . . . evaluated. The sentence *does not* make sense.

---

* Strategy 2 is considered the Master Strategy for *two-blank* Sentence Completion questions because it can be used effectively to answer every *two-blank* Sentence Completion question. However, it is important to learn all of the other Sentence Completion Strategies because they can be used to double-check your answers.

EXAMPLE 2

Television in our society is watched so _____ that intellectuals who detest the "tube" are _____.

(A) reluctantly . . . offended
(B) stealthily . . . ashamed
(C) frequently . . . revolted
(D) intensely . . . exultant
(E) noisily . . . amazed

EXPLANATORY ANSWER

Choice C is correct. We have eliminated Choice A because television is not watched reluctantly in our society. We have eliminated Choice B because television is not watched stealthily in our society. We have eliminated Choice E because it is not common for the viewer to watch television noisily. This leaves us with these remaining choices to be considered. Choice D—intensely . . . exultant. The sentence does *not* make sense. Choice C— frequently . . . revolted. The sentence *does* make sense.

EXAMPLE 3

In view of the company's _____ claims that its scalp treatment would grow hair on bald heads, the newspaper _____ its advertising.

(A) unproved . . . banned
(B) interesting . . . canceled
(C) unreasonable . . . welcomed
(D) innocent . . . settled
(E) immune . . . questioned

EXPLANATORY ANSWER

Choice A is correct. The first step is to examine the first words of each choice. We eliminate Choice (D) innocent . . . and Choice (E) immune . . . because "claims" are not innocent or immune. Now we go on to the remaining choices. When you fill in the two blanks of Choice B and of Choice C, the sentence does *not* make sense. So these two choices are also incorrect. Filling in the two blanks of Choice A makes the sentence meaningful.

EXAMPLE 4

The renowned behaviorist B. F. Skinner believes that those colleges set up to train teachers should _____ change their training philosophy, or else be

_____.

(A) inconsistently . . . supervised
(B) drastically . . . abolished
(C) haphazardly . . . refined
(D) secretly . . . dedicated
(E) doubtlessly . . . destroyed

EXPLANATORY ANSWER

Choice B is correct. We can first eliminate Choice (A) inconsistently, Choice (C) haphazardly, and Choice (D) secretly because these first blank words do *not* make sense in the sentence. This leaves us with Choice (B) drastically and Choice (E) doubtlessly. But Choice (E) doubtlessly . . . destroyed does *not* make sense. Choice (B) drastically . . . abolished *does* make sense.

EXAMPLE 5

The report indicates that the crime rate in the United States remains _____ and that one in every three households _____ some form of major crime in any year.

(A) incredible . . . visualizes
(B) astronomical . . . experiences
(C) simultaneous . . . welcomes
(D) unsuccessful . . . initiates
(E) constant . . . anticipates

EXPLANATORY ANSWER

Choice B is correct. Examine the first word of each choice. We eliminate Choice (C) simultaneous and Choice (D) unsuccessful because it does not make sense to say that the crime rate remains simultaneous or successful. Now we consider Choice (A), which does *not* make sense in the sentence; Choice B, *does* make sense; and Choice E does *not* make sense.

EXAMPLE 6

The discouragement and _____ that so often plague perfectionists can lead to decreases in _____ and production.

(A) pressure . . . creativity
(B) uplift . . . motivation
(C) enthusiasm . . . efficiency
(D) boredom . . . idleness
(E) involvement . . . laziness

EXPLANATORY ANSWER

Choice A is correct. Examine the first word of each choice. Choice (B) uplift and Choice (C) enthusiasm do not make sense because "uplift" and "enthusiasm" are not likely to plague any person. Now consider the other choices. Choice (D) boredom . . . idleness and Choice (E) involvement . . . laziness do *not* make sense in the sentence as a whole. Choice (A) pressure . . . creativity *does* make sense.

Try to Complete the Sentence in Your Own Words Before Looking at the Choices

This strategy often works well, especially with one-blank sentences. You may be able to fill in the blank with a word of your own that makes good sense. Then look at the answer choices to see whether any of the choices has the same meaning as your own word.

EXAMPLE 1

Many buildings with historical significance are now being _____ instead of being torn down.

(A) built
(B) forgotten
(C) destroyed
(D) praised
(E) repaired

EXPLANATORY ANSWER

Choice E is correct. The key words "instead of" constitute an *opposite indicator*. The words give us a good clue—we should fill the blank with an antonym (opposite) for "torn down." If you used the strategy of trying to complete the sentence *before* looking at the five choices, you might have come up with any of the following appropriate words:

remodeled
reconstructed
remade
renovated

These words all mean the same as the correct Choice E word, "repaired."

EXAMPLE 2

Wishing to _____ the upset passenger who found a nail in his steak, the flight attendant offered him a complimentary bottle of champagne.

(A) appease
(B) berate
(C) disregard
(D) reinstate
(E) acknowledge

EXPLANATORY ANSWER

Choice A is correct. Since the passenger was upset, the flight attendant wished to do something to make him feel better. If you used the strategy of trying to complete the sentence *before* looking at the five choices, you might have come up with the following words that would have the meaning of "to make someone feel better":

pacify
soothe
satisfy
conciliate
relieve

These words all mean the same as the Choice A word, "appease."

EXAMPLE 3

Just as the person who is kind brings happiness to others, so does he bring _____ to himself.

(A) wisdom
(B) guidance
(C) satisfaction
(D) stinginess
(E) insecurity

EXPLANATORY ANSWER

Choice C is correct. You must look for a word that balances with "happiness." Here are some of the words:

joy
goodness
satisfaction
enjoyment

All these words can be linked to Choice C.

EXAMPLE 4

Actors are sometimes very _____ since they must believe strongly in their own worth and talents.

(A) laconic
(B) unequivocal
(C) tedious
(D) egotistic
(E) reticent

EXPLANATORY ANSWER

Choice D is correct. "Since" signifies *result*. So the second clause of the sentence, starting with "since," really tells us that the missing word or words must be

boastful
very much interested in one's own self
egotistic
self-centered

Thus, Choice D is correct.

EXAMPLE 5

Hunger has reached epidemic proportions nationwide, leaving up to 20 million people _____ to illness and fear.

(A) agreeable
(B) vulnerable
(C) obvious
(D) acclimated
(E) sensitive

EXPLANATORY ANSWER

Choice B is correct. You might have come up with any of the following words:

susceptible (to)
open (to)
unprotected (from)

These words all mean about the same as the correct one, Choice B: "vulnerable."

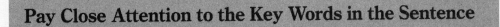

Pay Close Attention to the Key Words in the Sentence

A key word may indicate what is happening in the sentence. Here are some examples of key words and what these words may indicate.

Key Word	Indicating
although	
however	
in spite of	
rather than	OPPOSITION
nevertheless	
on the other hand	
but	

Key Word	Indicating
moreover	
besides	
additionally	SUPPORT
furthermore	
in fact	

Key Word	Indicating
therefore	
consequently	
accordingly	RESULT
because	
when	
so	

There are many other words—in addition to these—that can act as key words to help you considerably in getting the right answer. A key word frequently appears in the sentence. Watch for it!

EXAMPLE 1

Richard Wagner was frequently intolerant; moreover, his strange behavior caused most of his acquaintances to _____ the composer whenever possible.

(A) contradict
(B) interrogate
(C) shun
(D) revere
(E) tolerate

EXPLANATORY ANSWER

Choice C is correct. The word "moreover" is a *support indicator* in this sentence. As we try each choice word in the blank, we find that "shun" (avoid) is the only logical word that fits. You might have selected Choice A ("contradict"), but very few would seek to contradict Wagner because most of his acquaintances tried to avoid him.

EXAMPLE 2

The dinosaurs were feared by all other forms of life because they were much larger and stronger, but their bulkiness _____ their ability to adjust to new situations.

(A) improved
(B) welcomed
(C) explained
(D) interrupted
(E) limited

EXPLANATORY ANSWER

Choice E is correct. The word "but" is an *opposition indicator* in this sentence. As we try each choice word in the blank, we find that "limited" is the only word that fits. You might have chosen Choice D ("interrupted") because it does have some opposition sense. However, "their bulkiness" would not *interrupt* their ability to adjust. So Choice D is incorrect.

EXAMPLE 3

Until we are able to improve substantially the _____ status of the underprivileged in our country, a substantial _____ in our crime rate is remote.

(A) burdensome . . . harmony
(B) beneficial . . . gloom
(C) financial . . . reduction
(D) remarkable . . . puzzle
(E) questionable . . . disappointment

EXPLANATORY ANSWER

Choice C is correct. The word "Until" is a *result indicator*. As we try the first word of each choice in the first blank, we find that "burdensome," "financial," and "questionable" all make sense up until the second part of the sentence. We therefore eliminate Choices B and D. Now let us try both words in Choices A, C, and E. We then find that we can eliminate Choices A and E as not making sense in the entire sentence. This leaves us with the correct Choice C, which *does* bring out the result of what is stated in the first part of the sentence.

EXAMPLE 4

All of the efforts of the teachers will bring about no _____ changes in the scores of the students because the books and other _____ educational materials are not available.

(A) impartial . . . worthwhile
(B) unique . . . reflected
(C) spiritual . . . inspiring
(D) marked . . . necessary
(E) effective . . . interrupted

EXPLANATORY ANSWER

Choice D is correct. First see **Sentence Strategy 2.** Let us first eliminate Choices (A) impartial . . . and (C) spiritual . . . because we do not speak of "impartial" or "spiritual" changes. Now note that we have a *result* situation here as indicated by the presence of the conjunction "because" in the sentence. Choices B and E do not make sense because "unique" changes have nothing to do with "reflected" educational materials, and "effective" changes have nothing to do with "interrupted" educational materials. Choices B and E certainly do not meet the *result* requirement. Choice D is the only correct choice because it makes sense to say that there will be no "marked" changes in the scores because the books and other "necessary" educational materials are not available.

EXAMPLE 5

Being _____ person, he insisted at the conference that when he spoke he was not to be interrupted.

(A) a successful
(B) a delightful
(C) a headstrong
(D) an understanding
(E) a solitary

EXPLANATORY ANSWER

Choice C is correct. The main clause of the sentence—"he insisted ... not be interrupted"—*supports* the idea expressed in the first three words of the sentence. Accordingly, Choice C "headstrong" (meaning stubborn) is the only correct choice.

EXAMPLE 6

Although Grete Waitz is a celebrated female marathon runner, she is noted for her _____ .

(A) vigor
(B) indecision
(C) modesty
(D) speed
(E) endurance

EXPLANATORY ANSWER

Choice C is correct. The beginning word "Although" constitutes an *opposition indicator*. We can then expect the second part of the sentence to indicate an idea that is opposite to what is said in the first part of the sentence. Choice C "modesty" provides the word that gives us the closest to an opposite idea. Since Waitz is celebrated, we expect her to be immodest. The words in the other choices do *not* give us that opposite idea.

For two-blank sentences, look for contrasts or opposition in the two parts of the sentence—then look for opposite relationships in the choices.

EXAMPLE 7

In spite of the _____ of his presentation, many people were _____ with the speaker's concepts and ideas.

(A) interest ... enthralled
(B) power ... taken
(C) intensity ... shocked
(D) greatness ... gratified
(E) strength ... bored

EXPLANATORY ANSWER

Choice E is correct. The words *in spite of* at the beginning of the sentence tell you that the two blanks have an *opposite* flavor. Watch for opposites in the choices:

(A) interest ... enthralled—NOT OPPOSITE
(B) power ... taken—NOT OPPOSITE
(C) intensity ... shocked—NOT OPPOSITE
(D) greatness ... gratified—NOT OPPOSITE
(E) strength ... bored—OPPOSITE

Critical Reading Strategies

Introduction

Before getting into the detailed strategies, I want to say that the most important way to really understand what you're reading is to **get involved** with the passage—as if a friend of yours were reading the passage to you and you had to be interested so you wouldn't slight your friend. When you see the passage on paper it is also a good idea to **underline** important parts of the passage—which we'll also go over later in one of the strategies.

So many students ask, How do I answer reading comprehension questions? How do I read the passage effectively? Do I look at the questions before reading the passage? Do I underline things in the passage? Do I have to memorize details and dates? How do I get interested and involved in the passage?

All these are good questions. They will be answered carefully and in the right sequence.

What Reading Comprehension Questions Ask

First of all it is important to know that most reading comprehension questions ask about one of four things:

1. the MAIN IDEA of the passage
2. INFORMATION SPECIFICALLY MENTIONED in the passage
3. INFORMATION IMPLIED (not directly stated) in the passage
4. the TONE or MOOD of the passage

For example, following are some typical question stems. Each lets you immediately know which of the above four things is being asked about.

1. It can be inferred from the passage that . . . (IMPLIED INFORMATION)

2. According to the author . . . (MAIN IDEA)

3. The passage is primarily concerned with . . . (MAIN IDEA)

4. The author's statement that . . . (SPECIFIC INFORMATION)

5. Which of the following describes the mood of the passage? (TONE or MOOD)

6. The author implies that . . . (IMPLIED INFORMATION)

7. The use of paper is described in lines 14–16 . . . (SPECIFIC INFORMATION)

8. The main purpose of the passage . . . (MAIN IDEA)

9. The author's tone is best described as . . . (TONE OR MOOD)

10. One could easily see the author as . . . (IMPLIED INFORMATION)

Getting Involved with the Passage

Now, let's first put aside the burning question, Should I read the questions first, before reading the passage? The answer is NO! If you have in mind the four main question types given above, you will not likely be in for any big surprises. Many questions, when you get to them, will be reassuringly familiar in the way they're framed and in their intent. You can best answer them by reading the passage first, allowing yourself to become involved with it.

To give you an idea of what I mean, look over the following passage. When you have finished, I'll show you how you might read it so as to get involved with it and with the author's intent.

Introductory Passage 1

We should also know that "greed" has little to do with the environmental crisis. The two main causes are population pressures, especially the pressures of large metropolitan populations, and the desire—a highly commendable one—to bring a decent living at the lowest possible cost to the largest possible number of people.

The environmental crisis is the result of success—success in cutting down the mortality of infants (which has given us the population explosion), success in raising farm output sufficiently to prevent mass famine (which has given us contamination by pesticides and chemical fertilizers), success in getting the people out of the tenements of the 19th-century cities and into the greenery and privacy of the single-family home in the suburbs (which has given us urban sprawl and traffic jams.) The environmental crisis, in other words, is largely the result of doing too much of the right sort of thing.

To overcome the problems that success always creates, one must build on it. But where to start? Cleaning up the environment requires determined, sustained effort with clear targets and deadlines. It requires, above all, concentration of effort. Up to now we have tried to do a little bit of everything—and tried to do it in the headlines—when what we ought to do first is draw up a list of priorities.

Breakdown and Underlining of Passage

Before going over the passage with you, I want to suggest some underlining you might want to make and to show what different parts of the passage refer to.

We should also know that "greed" has little to do with the environmental crisis. The two main causes are <u>population pressures</u>, especially the pressures of large metropolitan populations, and the <u>desire</u>—a highly commendable one—<u>to bring a decent living at the lowest possible cost</u> to the largest possible number of people.

Sets stage.

<u>The environmental crisis is the result of success</u>—success in cutting down the mortality of infants (which has given us the population explosion), success in raising farm output sufficiently to prevent mass famine (which has given us contamination by pesticides and chemical fertilizers), success in getting the people out of the tenements of the 19th-century cities and into the greenery and privacy of the single-family home in the suburbs (which has given us urban sprawl and traffic jams). The environmental crisis, in other words, is largely the result of doing <u>too much of the right sort of thing</u>.

This should interest and surprise you.

Examples of success.

Summary of the success examples.

To overcome the problems that success always creates, <u>one must build on it</u>. But where to start? Cleaning up the environment requires determined, <u>sustained effort with clear targets and deadlines</u>. It requires above all, <u>concentration of effort</u>. Up to now we have tried to do a little bit of everything—and tried to do it in the headlines—when what we ought to do first is <u>draw up a list of priorities</u>.

Solutions.

Now I'll go over the passage with you, showing you what might go through your mind as you read. This will let you see how to get involved with the passage, and how this involvement facilitates answering the questions that follow the passage. In many cases, you'll actually be able to anticipate the questions. Of course, when you are preparing for the SAT, you'll have to develop this skill so that you do it rapidly and almost automatically.

Let's look at the first sentence:

We should also know that "greed" has little to do with the environmental crisis.

Immediately you should say to yourself, "So something else must be involved with the environmental crisis." Read on:

The two main causes are population pressures, especially the pressures of large metropolitan populations, and the desire—a highly commendable one—to bring a decent living at the lowest possible cost to the largest possible number of people.

Now you can say to yourself, "Oh, so population pressures and the desire to help the people in the community caused the environmental crisis." You should also get a feeling that the author is not really against these causes of the environmental crisis, and that he or she believes that the crisis is in part a side effect of worthwhile efforts and enterprises. Read on:

The environmental crisis is the result of success—success in cutting down the mortality of infants (which has given us the population explosion), success in raising farm output sufficiently to prevent mass famine (which has given us contamination by pesticides and chemical fertilizers), success in getting the people out of the tenements of the 19th-century city and into the greenery and privacy of the single-family home in the suburbs (which has given us urban sprawl and traffic jams).

Now you should say to yourself, "It seems that for every positive thing that the author mentions, there is a negative occurrence that leads to the environmental crisis."

Now read the last sentence of this paragraph:

The environmental crisis, in other words, is largely the result of doing too much of the right sort of thing.

Now you can say to yourself, "Gee, we wanted to do the right thing, but we created something bad. It looks like you can't have your cake and eat it, too!"

Now you should anticipate that in the next and final paragraph, the author will discuss what may be done to reduce the bad effects that come from the good. Look at the first sentence of the third paragraph:

To overcome the problem that success always creates, one must build on it.

Now you can say to yourself, "Well, how?" In fact, in the next sentence the author asks the very question you just asked: *But where to start?* Read on to find out the author's answer.

Cleaning up the environment requires determined, sustained effort with clear targets and deadlines. It requires, above all, concentration and effort.

So now you can say to yourself, "Oh, so that's what we need—definite goals, deadlines for reaching those goals, and genuine effort to achieve the goals."

The author then discusses what you may have already thought about:

Up to now we have tried to do a little bit of everything . . .

What the author is saying (and you should realize this) is that up to now, we haven't concentrated on one particular problem at a time. We used "buckshots instead of bullets." Read on:

—and tried to do it in the headlines—when what we ought to do first is to draw up a list of priorities.

So you can now see that, in the author's opinion, making a list of priorities and working on them one at a time, with a target in mind, may get us out of the environmental crisis and still preserve our quality of life.

How to Answer Reading Comprehension Questions Most Effectively

Before we start to answer the questions, let me tell you the best and most effective way of answering passage questions. You should read the question and proceed to look at the choices in the order of Choice A, Choice B, etc. If a choice (such as Choice A) doesn't give you the definite feeling that it is correct, don't try to analyze it further. Go on to Choice B. Again, if that choice (Choice B) doesn't make you feel that it's the right one, and you really have to think carefully about the choice, go on to Choice C. The first choice that you definitely feel is correct (let's say it's Choice C) is the one you should mark on your answer sheet. Don't bother going on to the rest of the choices. In other words, stop at the choice that you feel is obviously the right one.

Suppose you have gone through all five choices, and you don't know which one is correct, or you don't see any one that stands out as obviously being correct. Then quickly guess or leave the question blank if you wish and go on to the next question. You can go back after you have answered the other questions relating to the passage. But remember, when you return to the questions you weren't sure of, don't spend too much time on them. Try to forge ahead on the test.

Let's proceed to answer the questions now. Look at the first question:

1. This passage assumes the desirability of

   (A) using atomic energy to conserve fuel
   (B) living in comfortable family lifestyles
   (C) settling disputes peacefully
   (D) combating cancer and heart disease with energetic research
   (E) having greater government involvement in people's daily lives

Look at Choice A. That doesn't seem correct. Now look at Choice B. Do you remember that the author claimed that the environmental crisis is the result of the successful attempt to get people out of their tenements into a better environment? We can only feel that the author *assumes* this desirability of *living in comfortable family lifestyles* (Choice B) since the author uses the word *success* in describing the transition from living in tenements to living in single-family homes. Therefore, Choice B is correct. You don't need to analyze or even consider the other choices, since we have zeroed in on Choice B.

Let's look at Question 2:

2. According to this passage, one early step in any effort to improve the environment would be to

    (A) return to the exclusive use of natural fertilizers
    (B) put a high tax on profiteering industries
    (C) ban the use of automobiles in the cities
    (D) study successful efforts in other countries
    (E) set up a timetable for corrective actions

Again let's go through the choices in the order Choice A, Choice B, etc., until we come up with the right choice, Choices A, B, C, and D seem unlikely to be correct. So look at Choice E. We remember that the author said that we should establish clear targets and deadlines to improve the environment. That makes Choice E look like the correct answer.

Let's look at Question 3:

3. The passage indicates that the conditions which led to overcrowded roads also brought about

    (A) more attractive living conditions for many people
    (B) a healthier younger generation
    (C) greater occupational opportunities
    (D) the population explosion
    (E) greater concentration of population pressures

Here we would go back to the part of the passage that discussed overcrowded roads. This is where (second paragraph) the author says that urban sprawl and traffic jams are one result of success in getting people out of tenements to single-family homes. So you can see that Choice A is correct. Again, there is no need to consider other choices, since you should be fairly comfortable with Choice A.

Let's look at Question 4:

4. It could logically be assumed that the author of this passage would support legislation to

    (A) ban the use of all pesticides
    (B) prevent the use of automobiles in the cities
    (C) build additional conventional power plants immediately
    (D) organize an agency to coordinate efforts to cope with environmental problems
    (E) restrict the press coverage of protests led by environmental groups

This is the type of question that asks you to determine what the author would feel about something else, when you already know something about the author's sentiments on one particular subject.

Choices A, B, and C do not seem correct. But look at Choice D. The author said that the way to get out of the energy crisis is to set targets and deadlines in order to cope with specific problems. The author would therefore probably organize an agency to do this. Choice D is correct.

Let's look at another passage, and what I'm going to tell you is what would be going through my mind as I'm reading it. The more you can get involved with the passage in an "active" and not "passive" way, the faster you'll read it, and the more you'll get out of it.

Introductory Passage 2

Some scraps of evidence bear out those who hold a very high opinion of the average level of culture among the Athenians of the great age. The funeral speech of Pericles is the most famous indication from Athenian literature that its level was indeed high. Pericles was, however, a politician, and he may have been flattering his audience. We know that thousands of Athenians sat hour after hour in the theater listening to the plays of the great Greek dramatists. These plays, especially the tragedies, are at a very high intellectual level throughout. There are no letdowns, no concessions to the lowbrows or to the demands of "realism," such as the scene of the gravediggers in *Hamlet*. The music and dancing woven into these plays were almost certainly at an equally high level. Our opera—not Italian opera, not even Wagner, but the restrained, difficult opera of the 18th century—is probably the best modern parallel. The comparison is no doubt dangerous, but can you imagine almost the entire population of an American city (in suitable installments, of course) sitting through performances of Mozart's *Don Giovanni* or Gluck's *Orpheus*? Perhaps the Athenian masses went to these plays because of a lack of other amusements. They could at least understand something of what went on, since the subjects were part of their folklore. For the American people, the subjects of grand opera are not part of their folklore.

Let's start reading the passage:

Some scraps of evidence bear out those who hold a very high opinion of the average level of culture among the Athenians of the great age.

Now this tells you that the author is going to talk about the culture of the Athenians. Thus the stage is set. Go on reading now:

The funeral speech of Pericles is the most famous indication from Athenian literature that its level was indeed high.

At this point you should say to yourself: "That's interesting, and there was an example of the high level of culture."

Read on:

Pericles was, however, a politician, and he may have been flattering his audience.

Now you can say, "So that's why those people were so attentive in listening—they were being flattered."

Read on:

We know that thousands of Athenians sat hour after hour in the theater listening to the plays of the great Greek dramatists. These plays, especially the tragedies, are at a very high intellectual level throughout. There are no letdowns, no concessions to the low-brows or to the demands of "realism" . . .

At this point you should say to yourself, "That's strange—it could not have been just flattery that kept them listening hour after hour. How did they do it?" You can almost anticipate that the author will now give examples and contrast what he is saying to our plays and our audiences.

Read on:

The music and dancing woven into these plays were almost certainly at an equally high level. Our opera, not Italian opera . . . *is probably the best modern parallel. The comparison is no doubt dangerous, but can you imagine almost the entire population of an American city* . . . *sitting through performances of* . . .

Your feeling at this point should be, "No, I cannot imagine that. Why is that so?" So you should certainly be interested to find out.

Read on:

Perhaps the Athenian masses went to these plays because of a lack of other amusements. They could at least understand something of what went on, since the subjects were part of their folklore.

Now you can say, "So that's why those people were able to listen hour after hour—the material was all part of their folklore!"

Read on:

For the American people, the subjects . . . *are not part of their folklore.*

Now you can conclude, "So that's why the Americans cannot sit through these plays and perhaps cannot understand them—they were not part of their folklore!"

Here are the questions that follow the passage:

1. The author seems to question the sincerity of

   (A) politicians
   (B) playwrights
   (C) opera goers
   (D) "low brows"
   (E) gravediggers

2. The author implies that the average American

   (A) enjoys *Hamlet*
   (B) loves folklore
   (C) does not understand grand opera
   (D) seeks a high cultural level
   (E) lacks entertainment

3. The author's attitude toward Greek plays is one of

   (A) qualified approval
   (B) grudging admiration
   (C) studied indifference
   (D) partial hostility
   (E) great respect

4. The author suggest that Greek plays

   (A) made great demands upon their actors
   (B) flattered their audiences
   (C) were written for a limited audience
   (D) were dominated by music and dancing
   (E) stimulated their audiences

Let's try to answer them.

Question 1: Remember the statement about Pericles? This statement was almost unrelated to the passage since it was not discussed or referred to again. And here we have a question about it. Usually, if you see something that you think is irrelevant in a passage you may be pretty sure that a question will be based on that irrelevancy. It is apparent that the author seems to question the sincerity of politicians (*not* playwrights) since Pericles was a politician. Therefore Choice A is correct.

Question 2: We know that it was implied that the average American does not understand grand opera. Therefore Choice C is correct.

Question 3: From the passage, we see that the author is very positive about the Greek plays. Thus the author must have great respect for the plays. Note that the author may not have respect for Pericles, but Pericles was not a playwright; he was a politician. Therefore Choice E (not Choice A) is correct.

Question 4: It is certainly true that the author suggests that the Greek plays stimulated their audiences. They didn't necessarily flatter their audiences—there was only one indication of flattery, and that was by Pericles, who

was not a playwright, but a politician. Therefore Choice E (not Choice B) is correct.

Example of Underlinings

Some scraps of evidence bear out those who hold a very high ← *sets stage*
opinion of the average level of culture among the Athenians of
the great age. The funeral speech of Pericles is the most famous
indication from Athenian literature that its level was indeed
high. Pericles was, however, a politician, and he may have been ← *example*
flattering his audience. We know that thousands of Athenians
sat hour after hour in the theater listening to the plays of the ← *qualification*
great Greek dramatists. These plays, especially the tragedies,
are at a very high intellectual level throughout. There are no
letdowns, no concessions to the lowbrows or to the demands of
"realism," such as the scene of the gravediggers in HAMLET. ← *further*
The music and dancing woven into these plays were almost   *examples*
certainly at an equally high level. Our opera—not Italian opera, ↙
not even Wagner, but the restrained, difficult opera of the 18th
century—is probably the best modern parallel. The comparison ← *comparison*
is no doubt dangerous, but can you imagine almost the entire
population of an American city (in suitable installments, of
course) sitting through performances of Mozart's DON GIO-
VANNI or Gluck's ORPHEUS? Perhaps the Athenian masses
went to these plays because of a lack of other amusements.
They could at least understand something of what went on, ← *explanation*
since the subjects were part of their folklore. For the American   *of previous*
people, the subjects of grand opera are not part of their folklore.   *statements*

Now the whole purpose of analyzing this passage the way I did was to show you that if you get involved and interested in the passage, you will not only anticipate many of the questions, but when you answer them you can zero in on the right question choice without having to necessarily analyze or eliminate the wrong choices first. That's a great time save on a standardized test such as the SAT.

Now here's a short passage from which four questions were derived. Let's see if you can answer them after you've read the passage.

Introductory Passage 3*

Sometimes the meaning of glowing water is ominous. Off the Pacific Coast of North America, it may mean that the sea is filled with a minute plant that contains a poison of strange and terrible virulence. About four days after this
5 minute plant comes to dominate the coastal plankton, some of the fishes and shellfish in the vicinity become toxic. This is because in their normal feeding, they have strained the poisonous plankton out of the water.

* Note: This example also appears in Part 3, The 19 Questions That Can Determine Top College Eligibility.

1. Fish and shellfish become toxic when they

   (A) swim in poisonous water
   (B) feed on poisonous plants
   (C) change their feeding habits
   (D) give off a strange glow
   (E) take strychnine into their systems

2. One can most reasonably conclude that plankton are

   (A) minute organisms
   (B) mussels
   (C) poisonous fish
   (D) shellfish
   (E) fluids

3. In the context of the passage, the word "virulence" in line 4 means

   (A) strangeness
   (B) interest
   (C) calamity
   (D) potency
   (E) powerful odor

4. The paragraph preceding this one most probably discussed

(A) phenomena of the Pacific coastline
(B) poisons that affect man
(C) the culture of the early Indians
(D) characteristics of plankton
(E) phenomena of the sea

EXPLANATORY ANSWERS

1. Choice B is correct. See the second sentence: Fish become toxic when they feed on poisonous plants. Don't be fooled by using the first sentence, which seemingly leads to Choice A.

2. Choice A is correct. Since we are talking about *minute* plants (second sentence), it is reasonable to assume that plankton are *minute* organisms.

3. Choice D is correct. We understand that the poison is very strong and toxic. Thus it is "potent," virulent.

4. Choice E is correct. Since the second and not the first sentence was about the Pacific Coast, the paragraph preceding this one probably didn't discuss the phenomena of the Pacific coastline. It would have, if the first sentence—the sentence that links the ideas in the preceding paragraph—were about the Pacific coastline. Now, since we are talking about glowing water being ominous (first sentence), the paragraph preceding the passage is probably about the sea or the phenomena of the sea.

Summary

So in summary:

1. Make sure that you get involved with the passage. You may even want to select first the passage that interests you most. For example, if you're interested in science, you may want to choose the science passage first. Just make sure that you make some notation so that you don't mismark your answer sheet by putting the answers in the wrong answer boxes.
2. Pay attention to material that seems unrelated in the passage—there will probably be a question or two based on that material.
3. Pay attention to the mood created in the passage or the tone of the passage. Here again, especially if the mood is striking, there will probably be a question relating to mood.
4. Don't waste valuable time looking at the questions before reading the passage.
5. When attempting to answer the questions (after reading the passage) it is sometimes wise to try to figure out the answer before going through the choices. This will enable you to zero in on the correct answer without wasting time with all of the choices.
6. You may want to underline any information in the passages involving dates, specific names, etc., on your test to have as ready reference when you come to the questions.
7. Always try to see the overall attempt of the author of the passage or try to get the main gist of why the passage was being written. Try to get involved by asking yourself if you agree or disagree with the author, etc.

Next, the 9 Reading Comprehension Strategies

9 Reading Comprehension Strategies

This section of Reading Comprehension Strategies includes several passages. These passages, though somewhat shorter than the passages that appear on the actual SAT and in the 5 SAT Practice Tests in this book, illustrate the general nature of the "real" SAT reading passages.

Each of the 9 Reading Comprehension Strategies that follow is accompanied by at least two different passages followed by questions and explanatory answers in order to explain how the strategy is used.

READ. COMP. STRATEGY 1

As You Read Each Question, Determine the Type: Main Idea, Detecting Details, Inference, Tone/Mood

Here are the 4 major abilities tested in Reading Comprehension questions:

1. **Main Idea.** Selection of the main thought of a passage; ability to judge the general significance of a passage; ability to select the best title of a passage.

2. **Detecting Details.** Ability to understand the writer's explicit statements; to get the literal meaning of what is written; to identify details.

3. **Inferential Reasoning.** Ability to weave together the ideas of a passage and to see their relationships; to draw correct inferences; to go beyond literal interpretation to the implications of the statements.

4. **Tone/Mood.** Ability to determine from the passage the tone or mood that is dominant in the passage—humorous, serious, sad, mysterious, etc.

EXAMPLE 1

The fight crowd is a beast that lurks in the darkness behind the fringe of white light shed over the first six rows by the incandescents atop the ring, and is not to be trusted with pop bottles or other hardware.

5   People who go to prize fights are sadistic.

When two prominent pugilists are scheduled to pummel one another in public on a summer's evening, men and women file into the stadium in the guise of human beings, and thereafter become a part of a gray thing that squats in
10 the dark until, at the conclusion of the bloodletting, they may be seen leaving the arena in the same guise they wore when they entered.

As a rule, the mob that gathers to see men fight is unjust, vindictive, swept by intense, unreasoning hatreds,
15 proud of its swift recognition of what it believes to be sportsmanship. It is quick to greet the purely phony move of the boxer who extends his gloves to his rival, who has slipped or been pushed to the floor, and to reward this stimulating but still baloney gesture with a pattering of
20 hands which indicates the following: "You are a good sport. We recognize that you are a good sport, and we know a sporting gesture when we see one. Therefore we are all good sports, too. Hurrah for us!"

The same crowd doesn't see the same boxer stick his
25 thumb in his opponent's eye or try to cut him with the laces of his glove, butt him or dig him a low one when the referee

isn't in a position to see. It roots consistently for the smaller man, and never for a moment considers the desperate psychological dilemma of the larger of the two. It howls with
30 glee at a good finisher making his kill. The Roman hordes were more civilized. Their gladiators asked them whether the final blow should be administered or not. The main attraction at the modern prize fight is the spectacle of a man clubbing a helpless and vanquished opponent into complete
35 insensibility. The referee who stops a bout to save a slugged and punch-drunken man from the final ignominy is hissed by the assembled sportsmen.

QUESTIONS

1. The tone of the passage is chiefly

   (A) disgusted
   (B) jovial
   (C) matter-of-fact
   (D) satiric
   (E) devil-may-care

2. Which group of words from the passage best indicates the author's opinion?

   (A) "referee," "opponent," "finisher"
   (B) "gladiators," "slugged," "sporting gesture"
   (C) "stimulating," "hissing," "pattering"
   (D) "beast," "lurks," "gray thing"
   (E) "dilemma," "hordes," "spectacle"

3. Apparently, the author believes that boxing crowds find the referee both

   (A) gentlemanly and boring
   (B) entertaining and essential
   (C) blind and careless
   (D) humorous and threatening
   (E) necessary and bothersome

EXPLANATORY ANSWERS

1. Choice A is correct. The author is obviously much offended (disgusted) by the inhuman attitude of the crowd watching the boxing match. For example, see these lines:
   Line 1: "The crowd is a beast."
   Line 5: "People who go to prize fights are sadistic."
   Lines 13–14: ". . . the mob that gathers to see men fight is unjust, vindictive, swept by intense hatreds."
   Lines 30–31: "The Roman hordes were more civilized."

   To answer this question, you must be able to determine the tone that is dominant in the passage. Accordingly, this is a TONE/MOOD type of question.

2. Choice D is correct. The author's opinion is clearly one of disgust and discouragement because of the behavior of the fight crowd. Accordingly, you would expect the author to use words that were condemnatory, like "beast," and gloom-filled words like "lurks" and "gray thing." To answer this question, you must see relationships between words and feelings. So, we have here an INFERENTIAL REASONING question-type.

3. Choice E is correct. Lines 24–27 show that the referee is *necessary*: "The same crowd doesn't see the same boxer stick his thumb into his opponent's eye . . . when the referee isn't in a position to see." Lines 35–37 show that the referee is bothersome: "The referee who stops a bout . . . is hissed by the assembled sportsmen." To answer this question, the student must have the ability to understand the writer's specific statements. Accordingly, this is a DETECTING DETAILS type of question.

EXAMPLE 2*

Mist continues to obscure the horizon, but above us the sky is suddenly awash with lavender light. At once the geese respond. Now, as well as their cries, a beating roar rolls across the water as if five thousand housewives have taken it
5 into their heads to shake out blankets all at one time. Ten thousand housewives. It keeps up—the invisible rhythmic beating of all those goose wings—for what seems a long time. Even Lonnie is held motionless with suspense.
   Then the geese begin to rise. One, two, three hundred—
10 then a thousand at a time—in long horizontal lines that unfurl like pennants across the sky. The horizon actually darkens as they pass. It goes on and on like that, flock after flock, for three or four minutes, each new contingent announcing its ascent with an accelerating roar of cries and
15 wingbeats. Then gradually the intervals between flights become longer. I think the spectacle is over, until yet another flock lifts up, following the others in a gradual turn toward the northeastern quadrant of the refuge.
   Finally the sum emerges from the mist; the mist it-
20 self thins a little, uncovering the black line of willows on the other side of the wildlife preserve. I remember to close my mouth—which has been open for some time—and inadvertently shut two or three mosquitoes inside. Only a few straggling geese oar their way across the sun's red surface.
25 Lonnie wears an exasperated, proprietary expression, as if he had produced and directed the show himself and had just received a bad review. "It would have been better with more light," he says; "I can't always guarantee just when they'll start moving." I assure him I thought it was a fantastic sight.
30 "Well," he rumbles, "I guess it wasn't too bad."

* Note this example also appears in Part 2, Strategy Diagnostic Test for the new SAT.

QUESTIONS

1. In the descriptive phrase "shake out blankets all at one time" (line 5), the author is appealing chiefly to the reader's

   (A) background
   (B) sight
   (C) emotions
   (D) thoughts
   (E) hearing

2. The mood created by the author is one of

   (A) tranquility
   (B) excitement
   (C) sadness
   (D) bewilderment
   (E) unconcern

3. The main idea expressed by the author about the geese is that they

   (A) are spectacular to watch
   (B) are unpredictable
   (C) disturb the environment
   (D) produce a lot of noise
   (E) fly in large flocks

4. Judging from the passage, the reader can conclude that

   (A) the speaker dislikes nature's inconveniences
   (B) the geese's timing is predictable
   (C) Lonnie has had the experience before
   (D) both observers are hunters
   (E) the author and Lonnie are the same person

EXPLANATORY ANSWERS

1. Choice E is correct. See lines 3–5: "... a beating roar rolls across the water ... shake out blankets all at one time." The author, with these words, is no doubt appealing to the reader's hearing. To answer this question, the reader has to identify those words dealing with sound and noise. Therefore, we have here a DETECTING DETAILS type of question. It is also an INFERENTIAL REASONING question-type in that the "sound" words such as "beating" and "roar" lead the reader to infer that the author is appealing to the auditory (hearing) sense.

2. Choice B is correct. Excitement courses right through this passage. Here are examples:
   Lines 6–7: "... the invisible rhythmic beating of all those goose wings."
   Line 8: "Even Lonnie is held motionless with suspense."
   Lines 9–10: "Then the geese begin to rise ... a thousand at a time."
   Lines 12–15: "... flock after flock ... roar of cries and wingbeats."

   To answer this question, you must determine the dominant tone in this passage. Therefore, we have here a TONE/MOOD question-type.

3. Choice A is correct. The word "spectacular" means *dramatic, thrilling, impressive*. There is considerable action expressed throughout the passage. Sometimes there is a lull—then the action begins again. See lines 16–17: "I think the spectacle is over, until yet another flock lifts up, following the others." To answer this question, you must have the ability to judge the general significance of the passage. Accordingly, we have here a MAIN IDEA type of question.

4. Choice C is correct. See lines 25–29: "Lonnie wears an exasperated proprietary expression ... when they will start moving." To answer this question, you must be able to draw a correct inference. Therefore, we have here an INFERENTIAL REASONING type of question.

Underline the Key Parts of the Reading Passage*

The underlinings will help you to answer questions. Reason: Practically every question will ask you to detect

a) the main idea

or

b) information that is specifically mentioned in the passage

or

c) information that is implied (not directly stated) in the passage

or

d) the tone or mood of the passage

If you find out quickly what the question is aiming for, you will more easily arrive at the correct answer by referring to your underlinings in the passage.

EXAMPLE 1

That one citizen is as good as another is a favorite American axiom, supposed to express the very essence of our Constitution and way of life. But just what do we mean when we utter that platitude? One surgeon is not as good as another.
5 One plumber is not as good as another. We soon become aware of this when we require the attention of either. Yet in political and economic matters we appear to have reached a point where knowledge and specialized training count for very little. A newspaper reporter is sent out on the street to
10 collect the views of various passers-by on such a question as "Should the United States defend El Salvador?" The answer of the bar-fly who doesn't even know where the country is located, or that it is a country, is quoted in the next edition just as solemnly as that of the college teacher of history.
15 With the basic tenets of democracy—that all men are born free and equal and are entitled to life, liberty, and the pursuit of happiness—no decent American can possibly take issue. But that the opinion of one citizen on a technical subject is just as authoritative as that of another is manifestly absurd.
20 And to accept the opinions of all comers as having the same value is surely to encourage a cult of mediocrity.

QUESTIONS

1. Which phrase best expresses the main idea of this passage?

   (A) the myth of equality
   (B) a distinction about equality
   (C) the essence of the Constitution
   (D) a technical subject
   (E) knowledge and specialized training.

2. The author most probably included the example of the question on El Salvador (lines 11–13) in order to

   (A) move the reader to rage
   (B) show that he is opposed to opinion sampling
   (C) show that he has thoroughly researched his project
   (D) explain the kind of opinion sampling he objects to
   (E) provide a humorous but temporary diversion from his main point

3. The author would be most likely to agree that

   (A) some men are born to be masters; others are born to be servants
   (B) the Constitution has little relevance for today's world
   (C) one should never express an opinion on a specialized subject unless he is an expert in that subject
   (D) every opinion should be treated equally
   (E) all opinions should not be given equal weight

EXPLANATORY ANSWERS

1. Choice B is correct. See lines 1–6: "That one citizen ... attention of either." These lines indicate that there is quite a distinction about equality when we are dealing with all the American people.

2. Choice D is correct. See lines 9–14: "A newspaper reporter ... college teacher of history." These lines show that the author probably included the example of the question of El Salvador in order to explain the kind of opinion sampling he objects to.

* Strategy 2 is considered the Master Reading Comprehension Strategy because it can be used effectively in every Reading Comprehension question. However, it is important that you learn the other Reading Comprehension Strategies because they can often be used to double-check your answers.

3. Choice E is correct. See lines 18–21: "But that the opinion ... to encourage a cult of mediocrity." Accordingly, the author would be most likely to agree that all opinions should *not* be given equal weight.

EXAMPLE 2

She walked along the river until a policeman stopped her. It was one o'clock, he said. Not the best time to be walking alone by the side of a half-frozen river. He smiled at her, then offered to walk her home. It was the first day of the new year,
5 1946, eight and a half months after the British tanks had rumbled into Bergen-Belsen.
That February, my mother turned twenty-six. It was difficult for strangers to believe that she had ever been a concentration camp inmate. Her face was smooth and round.
10 She wore lipstick and applied mascara to her large dark eyes. She dressed fashionably. But when she looked into the mirror in the mornings before leaving for work, my mother saw a shell, a mannequin who moved and spoke but who bore only a superficial resemblance to her real self. The people
15 closest to her had vanished. She had no proof that they were truly dead. No eyewitnesses had survived to vouch for her husband's death. There was no one living who had seen her parents die. The lack of confirmation haunted her. At night before she went to sleep and during the day as she stood
20 pinning dresses she wondered if, by some chance, her parents had gotten past the Germans or had crawled out of the mass grave into which they had been shot and were living, old and helpless, somewhere in Poland. What if only one of them had died? What if they had survived and had died of
25 cold or hunger after she had been liberated, while she was in Celle* dancing with British officers?
She did not talk to anyone about these things. No one, she thought, wanted to hear them. She woke up in the mornings, went to work, bought groceries, went to the Jew-
30 ish Community Center and to the housing office like a robot.

* Celle is a small town in Germany.

QUESTIONS

1. The policeman stopped the author's mother from walking along the river because

    (A) the river was dangerous
    (B) it was the wrong time of day
    (C) it was still wartime
    (D) it was so cold
    (E) she looked suspicious

2. The author states that his mother thought about her parents when she

    (A) walked along the river
    (B) thought about death
    (C) danced with officers
    (D) arose in the morning
    (E) was at work

3. When the author mentions his mother's dancing with the British officers, he implies that his mother

    (A) compared her dancing to the suffering of her parents
    (B) had clearly put her troubles behind her
    (C) felt it was her duty to dance with them
    (D) felt guilty about dancing
    (E) regained the self-confidence she once had

EXPLANATORY ANSWERS

1. Choice B is correct. See lines 1–4: "She walked along ... offered to walk her home." The policeman's telling her that it was not the best time to be walking alone indicates clearly that "it was the wrong time of day."

2. Choice E is correct. Refer to lines 19–26: "... during the day ... dancing with the British officers."

3. Choice D is correct. See lines 24–26: "What if they had survived ... dancing with British officers?"

Look Back at the Passage When in Doubt

Sometimes while you are answering a question, you are not quite sure whether you have chosen the correct answer. Often, the underlinings that you have made in the reading passage will help you to determine whether a certain choice is the only correct choice.

EXAMPLE 1

Despite the many categories of the historian, there are only two ages of man. The first age, the age from the beginnings of recorded time to the present, is the age of the cave man. It is the age of war. It is today. The second age, still only a
5 prospect, is the age of civilized man. The test of civilized man will be represented by his ability to use his inventiveness for his own good by substituting world law for world anarchy. That second age is still within the reach of the individual in our time. It is not a part-time job, however. It
10 calls for total awareness, total commitment.

QUESTION

1. The author's attitude toward the possibility of man's reaching the age of civilization is one of

    (A) limited hope
    (B) complete despair
    (C) marked uncertainty
    (D) untempered complacency
    (E) extreme anger

EXPLANATORY ANSWER

1. Choice A is correct. An important idea that you might have underlined is expressed in lines 8–9: "That second age is still within the reach of the individual in our time."

EXAMPLE 2

All museum adepts are familiar with examples of *ostrakoi*, the oystershells used in balloting. As a matter of fact, these "oystershells" are usually shards of pottery, conveniently glazed to enable the voter to express his wishes in writing. In
5 the Agora, a great number of these have come to light, bearing the thrilling name, Themistocles. Into rival jars were dropped the ballots for or against his banishment. On account of the huge vote taken on that memorable date, it was to be expected that many ostrakoi would be found, but the
10 interest of this collection is that a number of these ballots are inscribed in an *identical* handwriting. There is nothing mysterious about it! The Boss was on the job, then as now. He prepared these ballots and voters cast them—no doubt for

the consideration of an obol or two. *The ballot box was*
15 *stuffed.*
    How is the glory of the American boss diminished! A vile imitation, he. His methods as old as Time!

QUESTION

1. The title that best expresses the ideas of this passage is

    (A) An Odd Method of Voting
    (B) Themistocles, an Early Dictator
    (C) Democracy in the Past
    (D) Political Trickery—Past and Present
    (E) The Diminishing American Politician

EXPLANATORY ANSWER

1. Choice D is correct. An important idea that you might have underlined is expressed in line 12: "The Boss was on the job, then as now."

EXAMPLE 3

But the weather predictions which an almanac always contains are, we believe, mostly wasted on the farmer. He can take a squint at the moon before turning in. He can "smell" snow or tell if the wind is shifting dangerously east. He can
5 register forebodingly an extra twinge in a rheumatic shoulder. With any of these to go by, he can be reasonably sure of tomorrow's weather. He can return the almanac to the nail behind the door and put a last stick of wood in the stove. For an almanac, a zero night or a morning's drifted road—none
10 of these has changed much since Poor Richard wrote his stuff and barns were built along the Delaware.

QUESTION

1. The author implies that, in predicting weather, there is considerable value in

    (A) reading the almanac
    (B) placing the last stick of wood in the stove
    (C) sleeping with one eye on the moon
    (D) keeping an almanac behind the door
    (E) noting rheumatic pains

EXPLANATORY ANSWER

1. Choice E is correct. Important ideas that you might have underlined are the following
    Lines 2–3: "He can take a squint at the moon."
    Line 3: "He can 'smell' snow . . ."

Lines 4–6: "He can register forebodingly an extra twinge in a rheumatic shoulder."
These underlinings will reveal that, in predicting weather, the quote in lines 4–6 gives you the correct answer.

READ. COMP. 4
STRATEGY

Before You Start Answering the Questions, Read the Passage *Carefully*.

A great advantage of careful reading of the passage is that you will, thereby, get a very good idea of what the passage is about. If a particular sentence is not clear to you as you read, then re-read that sentence to get a better idea of what the author is trying to say.

EXAMPLE 1

The American Revolution is the only one in modern history which, rather than devouring the intellectuals who prepared it, carried them to power. Most of the signatories of the Declaration of Independence were intellectuals. This tradi-
5 tion is ingrained in America, whose greatest statesmen have been intellectuals—Jefferson and Lincoln, for example. These statesmen performed their political function, but at the same time they felt a more universal responsibility, and they actively defined this responsibility. Thanks to them
10 there is in America a living school of political science. In fact, it is at the moment the only one perfectly adapted to the emergencies of the contemporary world, and one which can be victoriously opposed to communism. A European who follows American politics will be struck by the constant
15 reference in the press and from the platform to this political philosophy, to the historical events through which it was best expressed, to the great statesmen who were its best representatives.

[Underlining important ideas as you are reading this passage is strongly urged.]

QUESTIONS

1. The title that best expresses the ideas of this passage is

    (A) Fathers of the American Revolution
    (B) Jefferson and Lincoln—Ideal Statesmen
    (C) The Basis of American Political Philosophy
    (D) Democracy versus Communism
    (E) The Responsibilities of Statesmen

2. According to the passage, intellectuals who pave the way for revolutions are usually

    (A) honored
    (B) misunderstood
    (C) destroyed
    (D) forgotten
    (E) elected to office

3. Which statement is true according to the passage?

    (A) America is a land of intellectuals.
    (B) The signers of the Declaration of Independence were well educated.
    (C) Jefferson and Lincoln were revolutionaries
    (D) Adaptability is a characteristic of American political science.
    (E) Europeans are confused by American politics.

EXPLANATORY ANSWERS

1. Choice C is correct. Throughout this passage, the author speaks about the basis of American political philosophy. For example, see lines 4–10: "This tradition is ingrained in American . . . a living school of political science."

2. Choice C is correct. See lines 1–3: "The American Revolution is the only one . . . carried them to power." These lines may be interpreted to mean that intellectuals who pave the way for revolutions—other than the American Revolution—are usually destroyed.

3. Choice D is correct. The word "adaptability" means the ability to adapt—to adjust to a specified use or situation. Now see lines 10–13: "... there is in America ... opposed to communism."

EXAMPLE 2

The microscopic vegetables of the sea, of which the diatoms are most important, make the mineral wealth of the water available to the animals. Feeding directly on the diatoms and other groups of minute unicellular algae are the marine
5 protozoa, many crustaceans, the young of crabs, barnacles, sea worms, and fishes. Hordes of small carnivores, the first link in the chain of flesh eaters, move among these peaceful grazers. There are fierce little dragons half an inch long, the sharp-jawed arrowworms. There are gooseberrylike comb
10 jellies, armed with grasping tentacles, and there are the shrimplike euphausiids that strain food from the water with their bristly appendages. Since they drift where the currents carry them, with no power or will to oppose that of the sea, this strange community of creatures and the marine plants
15 that sustain them are called plankton, a word derived from the Greek, meaning wandering.

[Underling important ideas as you are reading this passage is strongly urged.]

QUESTIONS

1. According to the passage, diatoms are a kind of

   (A) mineral
   (B) alga
   (C) crustacean
   (D) protozoan
   (E) fish

2. Which characteristic of diatoms does the passage emphasize?

   (A) size
   (B) feeding habits
   (C) activeness
   (D) numerousness
   (E) cellular structure

EXPLANATORY ANSWERS

1. Choice B is correct. See lines 3–5: "Feeding directly on the diatoms ... minute unicellular algae are the marine protozoa...." These lines indicate that diatoms are a kind of alga.

2. Choice A is correct. See line 1–4: "The microscopic vegetables of the sea ... minute unicellular algae ..." In these lines, the words "microscopic" and "minute" emphasize the small size of the diatoms.

READ. COMP. STRATEGY 5

Get the Meanings of "Tough" Words by Using the Context Method

Suppose you don't know the meaning of a certain word in a passage. Then try to determine the meaning of that word from the context—that is, from the words that are close in position to that word whose meaning you don't know. Knowing the meanings of difficult words in the passage will help you to better understand the passage as a whole.

EXAMPLE 1

Like all insects, it wears its skeleton on the outside—a marvelous chemical compound called chitin which sheathes the whole of its body. This flexible armor is tremendously tough, light and shatterproof, and resistant to alkali and acid
5 compounds which would eat the clothing, flesh and bones of man. To it are attached muscles so arranged around catapult-like hind legs as to enable the hopper to hop, if so diminutive a term can describe so prodigious a leap as ten or twelve feet—about 150 times the length of the one-inch or so
10 long insect. The equivalent feat for a man would be a casual jump, from a standing position, over the Washington Monument.

QUESTIONS

1. The word "sheathes" (line 2) means

   (A) strips
   (B) provides
   (C) exposes
   (D) encases
   (E) excites

2. The word '"prodigious" (line 8) means

(A) productive
(B) frightening
(C) criminal
(D) enjoyable
(E) enormous

EXPLANATORY ANSWERS

1. Choice D is correct. The words in line 1: "it wears a skeleton on the outside" gives us the idea that "sheathes" probably means "covers" or "encases."

2. Choice E is correct. See the surrounding words in lines 7–10 "enable the hopper to hop . . . so prodigious a leap as ten or twelve feet—about 150 times the length of the one-inch or so long insect." We may easily imply that the word "prodigious" means "great in size"; "enormous."

EXAMPLE 2

Since the days when the thirteen colonies, each so jealous of its sovereignty, got together to fight the British soldiers, the American people have exhibited a tendency—a genius to maintain widely divergent viewpoints in normal times, but
5 to unite and agree in times of stress. One reason the federal system has survived is that it has demonstrated this same tendency. Most of the time the three coequal divisions of the general government tend to compete. In crises they tend to cooperate. And not only during war. A singular instance of
10 cooperation took place in the opening days of the first administration of Franklin D. Roosevelt, when the harmonious efforts of Executive and Legislature to arrest the havoc of depression brought to term *rubber-stamp Congress* into the headlines. One the other hand, when in 1937 Roosevelt at-
15 tempted to bend the judiciary to the will of the executive by "packing" the Supreme Court, Congress rebelled. This frequently proved flexibility—this capacity of both people and government to shift from competition to cooperation and back again as circumstances warrant—suggests that the
20 federal system will be found equal to the very real dangers of the present world situation.

QUESTIONS

1. The word "havoc" (line 12) means

(A) possession
(B) benefit
(C) destruction
(D) symptom
(E) enjoyment

2. The word "divergent" (line 4) means

(A) interesting
(B) discussed
(C) flexible
(D) differing
(E) appreciated

EXPLANATORY ANSWERS

1. Choice C is correct. The prepositional phrase "of depression," which modifies "havoc," should indicate that this word has an unfavorable meaning. The only choice that has an unfavorable meaning is Choice C—"destruction."

2. Choice D is correct. See lines 2–5: ". . . the American people . . . widely divergent viewpoints . . . but to unite and agree in times of stress." The word "but" in this sentence is an *opposite* indicator. We may, therefore, assume that a "divergent viewpoint" is a "differing" one from the idea expressed in the words "to unite and agree in times of stress."

Circle Transitional Words in the Passage

There are certain transitional words—also called "bridge" or "key" words—that will help you to discover logical connections in a reading passage. *Circling* these transitional words will help you to get a better understanding of the passage.

Here are examples of commonly used transitional words and what these words may indicate.

Transitional Word	Indicating
although however in spite of rather than nevertheless on the other hand but	OPPOSITION

Key Word	Indicating
moreover besides additionally furthermore in fact	SUPPORT

Key Word	Indicating
therefore consequently accordingly because when so	RESULT

EXAMPLE 1

Somewhere between 1860 and 1890, the dominant emphasis in American literature was radically changed. But it is obvious that this change was not necessarily a matter of conscious concern to all writers. In fact, many writers may seem
5 to have been actually unaware of the shifting emphasis. Moreover, it is not possible to trace the steady march of the realistic emphasis from its first feeble notes to its dominant trumpet-note of unquestioned leadership. The progress of realism is, to change the figure, rather that of a small stream,
10 receiving accessions from its tributaries at unequal points along its course, its progress now and then balked by the sand bars of opposition or the diffusing marshes of error and compromise. Again, it is apparent that any attempt to classify rigidly, as romanticists or realists, the writers of this
15 period is doomed to failure, since it is not by virtue of the writer's conscious espousal of the romantic or realistic creed that he does much of his best work, but by virtue of that writer's sincere surrender to the atmosphere of the subject.

QUESTIONS

1. The title that best expresses the ideas of this passage is

   (A) Classifying American Writers
   (B) Leaders in American Fiction
   (C) The Sincerity of Writers
   (D) The Values of Realism
   (E) The Rise of Realism

2. Which characteristic of writers does the author praise?

   (A) their ability to compromise
   (B) their allegiance to a "school"
   (C) their opposition to change
   (D) their awareness of literary trends
   (E) their intellectual honesty

EXPLANATORY ANSWERS

1. Choice E is correct. Note some of the transitional words that will help you to interpret the passage: "but" (line 2); "in fact" (line 4); "moreover" (line 6); "again" (line 13). A better understanding of the passage should indicate to you that the main idea (title)—"The Rise of Realism"—is emphasized throughout the passage.

2. Choice E is correct. See lines 15–18: "... since it is not by virtue of ... but by virtue of the writer's sincere ... of the subject." The transitional word "but" helps us to arrive at the correct answer, which is "their intellectual honesty."

EXAMPLE 2

A humorous remark or situation is, furthermore, always a pleasure. We can go back to it and laugh at it again and again. One does not tire of the *Pickwick Papers*, or of the humor of Mark Twain, any more than the child tires of a
5 nursery tale which he knows by heart. Humor is a feeling and feelings can be revived. But wit, being an intellectual and not an emotional impression, suffers by repetition. A witticism is really an item of knowledge. Wit, again, is distinctly a gregarious quality; whereas humor may abide in
10 the breast of a hermit. Those who live by themselves almost always have a dry humor. Wit is a city, humor a country, product. Wit is the accomplishment of persons who are busy with ideas; it is the fruit of intellectual cultivation and abounds in coffeehouses, in salons, and in literary clubs. But
15 humor is the gift of those who are concerned with persons rather than ideas, and it flourishes chiefly in the middle and lower classes.

QUESTION

1. It is probable that the paragraph preceding this one discussed the

   (A) *Pickwick Papers*
   (B) characteristics of literature
   (C) characteristics of human nature
   (D) characteristics of humor
   (E) nature of human feelings

EXPLANATORY ANSWER

1. Choice D is correct. See lines 1–2: "A humorous remark or situation is, furthermore, always a pleasure." The transitional word "furthermore" means "in addition." We may, therefore, assume that something dealing with humor has been discussed in the previous paragraph.

READ. COMP. **7**
STRATEGY

Don't Answer a Question on the Basis of Your Own Opinion

Answer each question on the basis of the information given or suggested in the passage itself. Your own views or judgments may sometimes conflict with what the author of the passage is expressing. Answer the question according to what the author believes.

EXAMPLE 1

The drama critic, on the other hand, has no such advantages. He cannot be selective; he must cover everything that is offered for public scrutiny in the principal playhouses of the city where he works. The column space that seemed, yester-
5 day, so pitifully inadequate to contain his comments on *Long Day's Journey Into Night* is roughly the same as that which yawns today for his verdict on some inane comedy that has chanced to find for itself a numskull backer with five hundred thousand dollars to lose. This state of affairs may help
10 to explain why the New York theater reviewers are so often, and so unjustly, stigmatized as baleful and destructive fiends. They spend most of their professional lives attempting to pronounce intelligent judgments on plays that have no aspiration to intelligence. It is hardly surprising that they
15 lash out occasionally; in fact, what amazes me about them is that they do not lash out more violently and more frequently. As Shaw said of his fellow-critics in the nineties, they are "a culpably indulgent body of men." Imagine the verbal excoriations that would be inflicted if Lionel Trilling, or someone
20 of comparable eminence, were called on to review five books a month of which three were novelettes composed of criminal confessions. The butchers of Broadway would seem lambs by comparison.

QUESTIONS

1. In writing this passage, the author's purpose seems to have been to

   (A) comment on the poor quality of our plays
   (B) show why book reviewing is easier than play reviewing
   (C) point up the opinions of Shaw
   (D) show new trends in literary criticism
   (E) defend the work of the play critic

2. The passage suggests that, as a play, *Long Day's Journey Into Night* was

   (A) inconsequential
   (B) worthwhile
   (C) poorly written
   (D) much too long
   (E) pleasant to view

EXPLANATORY ANSWERS

1. Choice E is correct. Throughout the passage, the author is defending the work of the play critic. See, for example, lines 9–14: "This state of affairs ... plays that have no aspiration to intelligence." Be sure that you do not answer a question on the basis of your own views. You yourself may believe that the plays presented on the stage today are of poor quality (Choice A) generally. The question, however, asks about the *author's opinion*—not yours.

2. Choice B is correct. See lines 4–9: "The column space ... dollars to lose." You yourself may believe that *Long Day's Journey Into Night* is a bad play. (Choice A or C or D.) But remember—the author's opinion, not yours, is asked for.

EXAMPLE 2

History has long made a point of the fact that the magnificent flowering of ancient civilization rested upon the institution of slavery, which released opportunity at the top of the art and literature which became the glory of antiquity. In a
5 way, the mechanization of the present-day world produces the condition of the ancient in that the enormous development of laborsaving devices and of contrivances which amplify the capacities of mankind affords the base for the leisure necessary to widespread cultural pursuits. Mechani-
10 zation is the present-day slave power, with the difference that in the mechanized society there is no group of the community which does not share in the benefits of its inventions.

QUESTION

1. The author's attitude toward mechanization is one of

(A) awe
(B) acceptance
(C) distrust
(D) fear
(E) devotion

EXPLANATORY ANSWER

1. Choice B is correct. Throughout the passage, the author's attitude toward mechanization is one of acceptance. Such acceptance on the part of the author is indicated particularly in lines 9–13: "Mechanization is ... the benefits of its inventions." You yourself may have a feeling of distrust (Choice C) or fear (Choice D) toward mechanization. But the author does not have such feelings.

READ. COMP. STRATEGY 8

After Reading the Passage, Read Each Question *Carefully*

Be sure that you read *with care* not only the stem (beginning) of a question, but also *each* of the five choices. Some students select a choice just because it is a true statement—or because it answers part of a question. This can get you into trouble.

EXAMPLE 1

The modern biographer's task becomes one of discovering the "dynamics" of the personality he is studying rather than allowing the reader to deduce that personality from documents. If he achieves a reasonable likeness, he need not fear
5 too much that the unearthing of still more material will alter the picture he has drawn; it should add dimension to it, but not change its lineaments appreciably. After all, he has had more than enough material to permit him to reach conclusions and to paint his portrait. With this abundance of
10 material he can select moments of high drama and find episodes to illustrate character and make for vividness. In any event, biographers, I think, must recognize that the writing of a life may not be as "scientific" or as "definitive" as we have pretended. Biography partakes of a large part of
15 the subjective side of man; and we must remember that those who walked abroad in our time may have one appearance for us—but will seem quite different to posterity.

QUESTION

1. According to the author, which is the real task of the modern biographer?

(A) interpreting the character revealed to him by study of the presently available data
(B) viewing the life of the subject in the biographer's own image
(C) leaving to the reader the task of interpreting the character from contradictory evidence
(D) collecting facts and setting them down in chronological order
(E) being willing to wait until all the facts on his subject have been uncovered

EXPLANATORY ANSWER

1. Choice A is correct. See lines 1–7: "The modern biographer's task ... but not change its lineaments appreciably." The word "dynamics" is used here to refer to the physical and moral forces which exerted influence on the main character of the biography. The lines quoted indicate that the author believes that the real task of the biographer is to study the *presently available data*. Choice D may also appear to be a correct choice since a biographer is likely to consider his job to be collecting facts and setting them down in chronological order. But the passage does not directly state that a biographer has such a procedure.

EXAMPLE 2

Although patience is the most important quality a treasure hunter can have, the trade demands a certain amount of courage too. I have my share of guts, but make no boast about ignoring the hazards of diving. As all good divers
5 know, the business of plunging into an alien world with an artificial air supply as your only link to the world above can be as dangerous as stepping into a den of lions. Most of the danger rests within the diver himself.

10 The devil-may-care diver who shows great bravado underwater is the worst risk of all. He may lose his bearings in the glimmering dim light which penetrates the sea and become separated from his diving companions. He may dive too deep, too long and suffer painful, sometimes fatal, bends.

QUESTION

1. According to the author, an underwater treasure hunter needs above all, to be

   (A) self-reliant
   (B) adventuresome
   (C) mentally alert
   (D) patient
   (E) physically fit

EXPLANATORY ANSWER

1. Choice D is correct. See lines 1–3: "Although patience is the most important ... courage too." Choice E ("physically fit") may also appear to be a correct choice since an underwater diver certainly has to be physically fit. Nevertheless, the passage nowhere states this directly.

READ. COMP. STRATEGY 9

Increase Your Vocabulary to Boost Your Reading Comprehension Score

1. You can increase your vocabulary tremendously by learning Latin and Greek roots, prefixes, and suffixes. Knowing the meanings of difficult words will thereby help you to understand a passage better.

   Sixty percent of all the words in our English language are derived from Latin and Greek. By learning certain Latin and Greek roots, prefixes, and suffixes, you will be able to understand the meanings of over 100,000 additional English words. See "Word Building with Roots, Prefixes, and Suffixes" beginning on page 468.

2. This book also includes "A 3,400 SAT Word List" beginning on page 479. This Word List will prove to be a powerful vocabulary builder for you.

   There are other steps—in addition to the two steps explained above—to increase your vocabulary. Here they are:

3. Take vocabulary tests like the 100 SAT-type "tough word" vocabulary tests beginning on page 531.
4. Read as widely as possible—novels, nonfiction, newspapers, magazines.
5. Listen to people who speak well. Many TV programs have very fine speakers. You can pick up many new words listening to such programs.
6. Get into the habit of using the dictionary often. Why not carry a pocket-size dictionary with you?
7. Play word games—crossword puzzles will really build up your vocabulary.

EXAMPLE 1

Acting, like much writing, is probably a compensation for
and release from the strain of some profound maladjustment
of the psyche. The actor lives most intensely by proxy. He
has to be somebody else to be himself. But it is all done
5 openly and for our delight. The dangerous man, the enemy
of nonattachment or any other wise way of life, is the born
actor who has never found his way into the Theater, who
never uses a stage door, who does not take a call and then
wipe the paint off his face. It is the intrusion of this tempera-
10 ment into political life, in which at this day it most em-
phatically does not belong, that works half the mischief in
the world. In every country you may see them rise, the actors
who will not use the Theater, and always they bring down
disaster from the angry gods who like to see mountebanks
15 in their proper place.

QUESTIONS

1. The meaning of "maladjustment" (line 2) is a

   (A) replacement of one thing for another
   (B) profitable experience in business
   (C) consideration for the feelings of others
   (D) disregard of advice offered by other
   (E) poor relationship with one's environment

2. The meaning of "psyche" (line 3) is

   (A) person
   (B) mind
   (C) personality
   (D) psychology
   (E) physique

3. The meaning of "intrusion" (line 9) is

   (A) entering without being welcome
   (B) acceptance after considering the facts
   (C) interest that has developed after a period of time
   (D) fear as the result of imagination
   (E) refusing to obey a command

4. The meaning of "mountebanks" (line 14) is

   (A) mountain climbers
   (B) cashiers
   (C) high peaks
   (D) fakers
   (E) mortals

EXPLANATORY ANSWERS

1. Choice E is correct. The prefix "mal" means bad.
   Obviously a maladjustment is a bad adjustment—
   that is, a poor relationship with one's environment.

2. Choice B is correct. The root "psyche" means the
   mind functioning as the center of thought, feeling,
   and behavior.

3. Choice A is correct. The prefix "in" means "into" in
   this case. The root "trud, trus" means "pushing
   into"—or entering without being welcome.

4. Choice D is correct. The root "mont" means "to
   climb." The root "banc" means a "bench." A mountebank means literally "one who climbs on a bench."
   The actual meaning of mountebank is a quack (faker)
   who sells useless medicines from a platform in a
   public place.

EXAMPLE 2

The American Museum of Natural History has long portrayed various aspects of man. Primitive cultures have been
shown through habitat groups and displays of man's tools,
utensils, and art. In more recent years, there has been a
5 tendency to delineate man's place in nature, displaying his
destructive and constructive activities on the earth he in-
habits. Now, for the first time, the Museum has taken man
apart, enlarged the delicate mechanisms that make him run,
and examined his as a biological phenomenon.
10   In the new Hall of the Biology of Man, Museum techni-
cians have created a series of displays that are instructive to
a degree never before achieved in an exhibit hall. Using new
techniques and new materials, they have been able to produce movement as well as form and color. It is a human
15 belief that beauty is only skin deep. But nature has proved to
be a master designer, not only in the matter of man's bilateral
symmetry but also in the marvelous packaging job that has
arranged all man's organs and systems within his skin-
covered case. When these are taken out of the case,
20 greatly enlarged and given color, they reveal form and design that give the lie to that old saw. Visitors will be surprised to discover that man's insides, too, are beautiful.

QUESTIONS

1. The meaning of "bilateral" (line 16) is

   (A) biological
   (B) two-sided
   (C) natural
   (D) harmonious
   (E) technical

2. The meaning of "symmetry" (line 17) is

   (A) simplicity
   (B) obstinacy
   (C) sincerity
   (D) appearance
   (E) proportion

EXPLANATORY ANSWERS

1. Choice B is correct. The prefix "bi" means "two." The root "latus" means "side." Therefore, "bilateral" means "two-sided."

2. Choice E is correct. The prefix "sym" means "together." The root "metr" means "measure." The word "symmetry," therefore, means "proportion," "harmonious relation of parts," "balance."

3 Vocabulary Strategies

Introduction

Although **antonyms** (opposites of words) are not on the new SAT, it is still important for you to know vocabulary and the strategies to figure out the meanings of words, since there are many questions involving difficult words in all the sections on the Verbal part of the SAT, that is the **Analogies, Sentence Completions, and Critical Reading Parts.**

VOCABULARY
STRATEGY **1**

Use Roots, Prefixes, and Suffixes to Get the Meanings of Words

You can increase your vocabulary tremendously by learning Latin and Greek roots, prefixes, and suffixes. Sixty percent of all the words in our English language are derived from Latin and Greek. By learning certain Latin and Greek roots, prefixes, and suffixes, you will be able to understand the meanings of more than 100,000 additional English words. See "Word Building with Roots, Prefixes, and Suffixes" beginning on page 468.

EXAMPLE 1

Opposite of PROFICIENT:

(A) antiseptic
(B) unwilling
(C) inconsiderate
(D) neglectful
(E) awkward

EXPLANATORY ANSWER

Choice E is correct. The prefix PRO means *forward, for the purpose of.* The root FIC means *to make* or *to do.* Therefore, PROFICIENT literally means *doing something in a forward way.* The definition of *proficient* is *skillful, adept, capable.* The antonym of *proficient* is, accordingly, *awkward; incapable.*

EXAMPLE 2

Opposite of DELUDE:

(A) include
(B) guide
(C) reply
(D) upgrade
(E) welcome

EXPLANATORY ANSWER

Choice B is correct. The prefix DE means *downward, against.* The root LUD means *to play* (a game). Therefore, DELUDE literally means *to play a game against.* The definition of *delude* is *to deceive, to mislead.* The antonym of *delude* is accordingly to guide.

EXAMPLE 3

Opposite of LAUDATORY:

(A) vacating
(B) satisfactory
(C) revoking
(D) faultfinding
(E) silent

EXPLANATORY ANSWER

Choice D is correct. The root LAUD means *praise*. The suffix ORY means a *tendency toward*. Therefore, LAUDATORY means having a *tendency toward praising someone*. The definition of *laudatory* is *praising*. The antonym of laudatory is, accordingly, *faultfinding*.

EXAMPLE 4

Opposite of SUBSTANTIATE:

(A) reveal
(B) intimidate
(C) disprove
(D) integrate
(E) assist

EXPLANATORY ANSWER

Choice C is correct. The prefix SUB means *under*. The root STA means *to stand*. The suffix ATE is a verb form indicating *the act of*. Therefore, SUBSTANTIATE literally means *to perform the act of standing under*. The definition of *substantiate* is *to support* with proof or evidence. The antonym is, accordingly, *disprove*.

EXAMPLE 5

Opposite of TENACIOUS:

(A) changing
(B) stupid
(C) unconscious
D) poor
(E) antagonistic

EXPLANATORY ANSWER

Choice A is correct.
(A) TEN = to hold; TENACIOUS = holding—OPPOSITE = *changing*

EXAMPLE 6

Opposite of RECEDE:

(A) accede
(B) settle
(C) surrender
(D) advance
(E) reform

EXPLANATORY ANSWER

Choice D is correct.
RE = back; CED = to go; RECEDE = to go back—OPPOSITE = *advance*

EXAMPLE 7

Opposite of CIRCUMSPECT:

(A) suspicious
(B) overbearing
(C) listless
(D) determined
(E) careless

EXPLANATORY ANSWER

Choice E is correct.
CIRCUM = around; SPECT = to look or see; CIRCUMSPECT = to look all around or make sure that you see everything, careful—OPPOSITE = *careless*

EXAMPLE 8

Opposite of MALEDICTION:

(A) sloppiness
(B) praise
(C) health
(D) religiousness
(E) proof

EXPLANATORY ANSWER

Choice B is correct.
MAL = bad; DICT = to speak; MALEDICTION = to speak badly about—OPPOSITE = *praise*

EXAMPLE 9

Opposite of PRECURSORY:

(A) succeeding
(B) flamboyant
(C) cautious
(D) simple
(E) cheap

Choice A is correct.
PRE = before; CURS = to run; PRECURSORY = run before—OPPOSITE = *succeeding*

EXAMPLE 10

Opposite of CIRCUMVENT:

(A) to go the straight route
(B) alleviate
(C) to prey on one's emotions
(D) scintillate
(E) perceive correctly

Choice A is correct.
CIRCUM = around (like a circle); VENT = to come; CIRCUMVENT = to come around—OPPOSITE = *to go the straight route*

VOCABULARY STRATEGY 2

Pay Attention to the Sound or Feeling of the Word— Whether Positive or Negative, Harsh or Mild, Big or Little, Etc.

If the word sounds harsh or terrible, such as "obstreperous," the meaning probably is something harsh or terrible. If you're looking for a word opposite in meaning to "obstreperous," look for a word or words that have a softer sound, such as "pleasantly quiet or docile." The sense of "obstreperous" can also seem to be negative—so if you're looking for a synonym, look for a negative word. If you're looking for an opposite (antonym) look for a positive word.

EXAMPLE 1

Opposite of BELLIGERENCY:

(A) pain
(B) silence
(C) homeliness
(D) elegance
(E) peace

Choice E is correct. The word BELLIGERENCY imparts a tone of forcefulness or confusion and means warlike. The opposite would be calmness or peacefulness. The closest choices are choice B or E, with E a little closer to the opposite in tone for the CAPITALIZED word. Of course, if you knew the root BELLI means "war," you could see the opposite as (E) peace.

EXAMPLE 2

Opposite of DEGRADE:

(A) startle
(B) elevate
(C) encircle
(D) replace
(E) assemble

Choice B is correct. Here you can think of the DE in DEGRADES as a prefix that is negative (bad) and means *down*, and in fact DEGRADE does mean to debase or lower. So you should look for an opposite that would be a word with a *positive* (good) meaning. The best word from the choices is (B) elevate.

EXAMPLE 3

Opposite of OBFUSCATION:

(A) illumination
(B) irritation
(C) conviction
(D) minor offense
(E) stable environment

Choice A is correct. The prefix OB is usually negative, as in obstacle or obliterate, and in fact OBFUSCATE means darken or obscure. So since we are looking for an opposite, you would look for a *positive* word. Choices A and E are positive, and you should go for the more positive of the two, which is Choice A.

EXAMPLE 4

Opposite of MUNIFICENCE:

(A) disloyalty
(B) stinginess
(C) dispersion
(D) simplicity
(E) vehemence

EXPLANATORY ANSWER

Choice B is correct because MUNIFICENCE means generosity. Many of the words ending in ENCE, like OPULENCE, EFFERVESCENCE, LUMINESCENCE, QUINTESSENCE, etc., represent or describe something big or bright. So the opposite of one of these words would denote something small or dark.

You can associate the prefix MUNI with MONEY, as in "municipal bonds," so the word MUNIFICENCE must deal with money and in a big way. The opposite deals with money in a small way. Choice B fits the bill.

EXAMPLE 5

Opposite of DETRIMENT:

(A) recurrence
(B) disclosure
(C) resemblance
(D) enhancement
(E) postponement

EXPLANATORY ANSWER

Choice D is correct. The prefix DE can also mean against and is negative, and DETRIMENT means something that causes damage or loss. So you should look for a positive word. The only one is *enhancement*.

EXAMPLE 6

Opposite of UNDERSTATE:

(A) embroider
(B) initiate
(C) distort
(D) pacify
(E) reiterate

EXPLANATORY ANSWER

Choice A is correct. UNDERSTATE means something said in a restrained or downplayed manner. You see "under" in UNDERSTATE so look for a choice that gives you the impression of something that is "over" as in "overstated." The only choice is (A) embroider, which means to embellish.

EXAMPLE 7

Opposite of DISHEARTEN:

(A) engage
(B) encourage
(C) predict
(D) dismember
(E) misinform

EXPLANATORY ANSWER

Choice B is correct. You see "HEART" in DISHEARTEN. The DIS is negative or means "not to," or "not to have heart," and dishearten does mean to discourage. So you want to look for a *positive* word. Choice (B) encourage fits the bill.

EXAMPLE 8

Opposite of FIREBRAND:

(A) an intellect
(B) one who is charitable
(C) ones who makes peace
(D) a philanthropist
(E) one who is dishonest

EXPLANATORY ANSWER

Choice C is correct. You see FIRE in FIREBRAND. So think of something fiery or dangerous. The opposite of FIREBRAND must be something that's calm or safe. The best choice is Choice C, whereas a FIREBRAND is someone who causes trouble.

VOCABULARY STRATEGY 3

Use Word Associations to Determine Word Meanings and Their Opposites

Looking at the root or part of any capitalized word may suggest an association with another word that looks similar and whose meaning you know. This new word's meaning may give you a clue as to the meaning of the original word or the opposite in meaning to the original word if you need an opposite. For example, *extricate* reminds us of the word "extract," the opposite of which is "to put together."

EXAMPLE 1

Opposite of THERMAL:

(A) improving
(B) possible
(C) beginning
(D) reduce
(E) frigid

EXPLANATORY ANSWER

Choice E is correct. Here you may associate the word THERMAL with THERMOMETER. A thermometer measures temperature, so it usually measures something that is warm or cold. Look for a choice that has something to do with temperature. Since THERMAL means caused by or producing heat, the only one is (E), frigid.

EXAMPLE 2

Opposite of STASIS:

(A) stoppage
(B) reduction
(C) depletion
(D) fluctuation
(E) completion

EXPLANATORY ANSWER

Choice D is correct. Think of STATIC or STATIONARY. The opposite would be moving or fluctuating since STASIS means stopping or retarding movement.

EXAMPLE 3

Opposite of APPEASE:

(A) criticize
(B) analyze
(C) correct
(D) incense
(E) develop

EXPLANATORY ANSWER

Choice D is correct. Appease means to placate. Think of PEACE in APPEASE. The opposite would be violent or incense.

EXAMPLE 4

Opposite of COMMISERATION:

(A) undeserved reward
(B) lack of sympathy
(C) unexpected success
(D) absence of talent
(E) inexplicable danger

EXPLANATORY ANSWER

Choice B is correct. Think of MISERY in the word COMMISERATION. Commiseration means the sharing of misery. Choice B is the only appropriate choice.

EXAMPLE 5

Opposite of JOCULAR:

(A) unintentional
(B) exotic
(C) muscular
(D) exaggerated
(E) serious

EXPLANATORY ANSWER

Choice E is correct. Think of JOKE in the word JOCU-LAR, which means given to joking. The opposite would be serious.

EXAMPLE 6

Opposite of ELONGATE:

(A) melt
(B) wind
(C) confuse
(D) smooth
(E) shorten

EXPLANATORY ANSWER

Choice E is correct. Think of the word LONG in ELON-GATE, which means to lengthen. The opposite would be short or shorten.

EXAMPLE 7

Opposite of SLOTHFUL:

(A) permanent
(B) ambitious
(C) average
(D) truthful
(E) plentiful

EXPLANATORY ANSWER

Choice B is correct. Think of SLOTH, a very, very slow animal. So SLOTHFUL, which means lazy or sluggish, must be slow and unambitious. The opposite would be ambitious.

EXAMPLE 8

Opposite of FORTITUDE:

(A) timidity
(B) conservatism
(C) placidity
(D) laxness
(E) ambition

EXPLANATORY ANSWER

Choice A is correct. FORTITUDE means strength in the face of adversity; you should think of FORT or FORTIFY as something strong. The opposite would be weak or timid.

EXAMPLE 9

Opposite of LUCID:

(A) underlying
(B) complex
(C) luxurious
(D) tight
(E) general

EXPLANATORY ANSWER

Choice B is correct. LUCID means easily understood or clear; you should think of LUCITE, a clear plastic. The opposite of clear is hard to see through or complex.

EXAMPLE 10

Opposite of POTENT:

(A) imposing
(B) pertinent
(C) feeble
(D) comparable
(E) frantic

EXPLANATORY ANSWER

Choice C is correct.
Think of the word *POTENT*IAL or *POWERFUL*. To have potential is to have the ability or power to be able to do something. So the opposite would be *feeble*. You could also have thought of POTENT as a POSITIVE word. The opposite would be a negative word. The only two choices that are negative are choices C and E.

PART 6

MINI–MATH REFRESHER

The Most Important Basic Math Rules and Concepts You Need to Know

Make sure that you understand each of the following math rules and concepts. It is a good idea to memorize them all. Refer to the section of the Math Refresher (Part 7 starting on page 291) shown in parentheses, *e.g.*, (409), for a complete explanation of each.

Algebra and Arithmetic

(409)
$$a(b + c) = ab + ac$$
Example:
$$5(4 + 5) = 5(4) + 5(5)$$
$$= 20 + 25$$
$$= 45$$

(409)
$$(a + b)^2 = a^2 + 2ab + b^2$$

(409)
$$(a - b)^2 = a^2 - 2ab + b^2$$

(409)
$$(a + b)(a - b) = a^2 - b^2$$

(409)
$$-(a - b) = b - a$$

(429)
$$a^0 = 1$$
$$10^0 = 1$$
$$10^1 = 10$$
$$10^2 = 100$$
$$10^3 = 1000, \text{ etc.}$$
Example:
$$8.6 \times 10^4 = 8.\underset{1\,2\,3\,4}{6\,0\,0\,0}.\,0$$

(409)
$$(a + b)(c + d) = ac + ad + bc + bd$$
Example:
$$(2 + 3)(4 - 6) = (2)(4) + (2)(-6)$$
$$+ (3)(4) + (3)(-6)$$
$$= 8 - 12 + 12 - 18$$
$$= -10$$

(429)
$$a^2 = (a)(a)$$
Example:
$$2^2 = (2)(2) = 4$$
$$a^3 = (a)(a)(a), \text{ etc.}$$

(429)
$$a^x a^y = a^{x+y}$$
Examples:
$$a^2 \times a^3 = a^5;$$
$$2^2 \times 2^3 = 2^5 = 32$$

(429)
$$(a^x)^y = a^{xy}$$
Examples:
$$(a^3)^5 = a^{15}; (2^3)^5 = 2^{15}$$

(429)
$$(ab)^x = a^x b^x$$
Examples:
$$(2 \times 3)^3 = 2^3 \times 3^3; (ab)^2 = a^2 b^2$$

(429)
$$\frac{a^x}{a^y} = a^{x-y}$$
Examples:
$$\frac{a^3}{a^2} = a^{3-2} = a;$$
$$\frac{2^3}{2^2} = 2^{3-2} = 2$$

(430)

If $y^2 = x$ then $y = \pm \sqrt{x}$

Example:
If $y^2 = 4$,
then $y = \pm \sqrt{4} = \pm 2$

$a^{-y} = \dfrac{1}{a^y}$

Example: $2^{-3} = \dfrac{1}{2^3} = \dfrac{1}{8}$

(429)

(107)

Percentage

$x\% = \dfrac{x}{100}$

Example:
$5\% = \dfrac{5}{100}$

Percentage Problems

(107)

Examples:
(1) What percent of 5 is 2?

$\dfrac{x}{100}$ $\times$ 5   =   2

or

$\left(\dfrac{x}{100}\right)(5) = 2$

$\dfrac{5x}{100} = 2$

$5x = 200$

$x = 40$

Answer $= 40\%$

RULE: "What" becomes x

"Percent" becomes $\dfrac{1}{100}$

"of" becomes $\times$ (times)
"is" becomes $=$ (equals)

(107)

(2) 6 is what percent of 24?

$6 = \dfrac{x}{100}$ $\times$ 24

$6 = \dfrac{24x}{100}$

$600 = 24x$

$100 = 4x$ (dividing both sides by 6)

$25 = x$

Answer $= 25\%$

Equations

(409)

> *Example:* $x^2 - 2x + 1 = 0$. Solve for x.
> 　Procedure:
> 　Factor: $(x - 1)(x - 1) = 0$
> $$x - 1 = 0$$
> $$x = 1$$

(407)

> *Example:* $x + y = 1$; $x - y = 2$. Solve for x and y.
> 　Procedure:
> 　Add equations:
>
> $$x + y = 1$$
> $$\underline{x - y = 2}$$
> $$2x + 0 = 3$$
>
> Therefore $2x = 3$ and $x = \dfrac{3}{2}$
>
> Substitute $x = \dfrac{3}{2}$ back into one of the equations:
>
> $$x + y = 1$$
> $$\frac{3}{2} + y = 1$$
> $$y = -\frac{1}{2}$$

Equalities

(402)

$$
\begin{array}{ll}
a + b = c & 3 + 4 = 7 \\
\underline{+\quad d = d} & \underline{+\quad 2 = 2} \\
a + b + d = c + d & 3 + 4 + 2 = 7 + 2
\end{array}
$$

Inequalities

(419–425)

$>$ means greater than, $<$ means less than, $\geqq$ means greater than or equal to, etc.

$$
\begin{array}{lll}
b > c & 4 > 3 & 4 > 3 \\
\underline{d > e} & \underline{7 > 6} & \underline{-6 > -7} \\
b + d > c + e & 11 > 9 & -2 > -4
\end{array}
$$

$$
\begin{array}{ll}
5 > 4 & -5 < -4 \\
(6)5 > 4(6) & -(-5) > -(-4) \quad \text{(reversing inequality)}
\end{array}
$$

Thus

$$
\begin{array}{ll}
30 > 24 & 5 > 4
\end{array}
$$

$$
\begin{array}{ll}
\text{If} \quad -2 < x < +2 & a > b > 0 \\
\text{then} +2 > -x > -2 & \text{Thus } a^2 > b^2
\end{array}
$$

Geometry

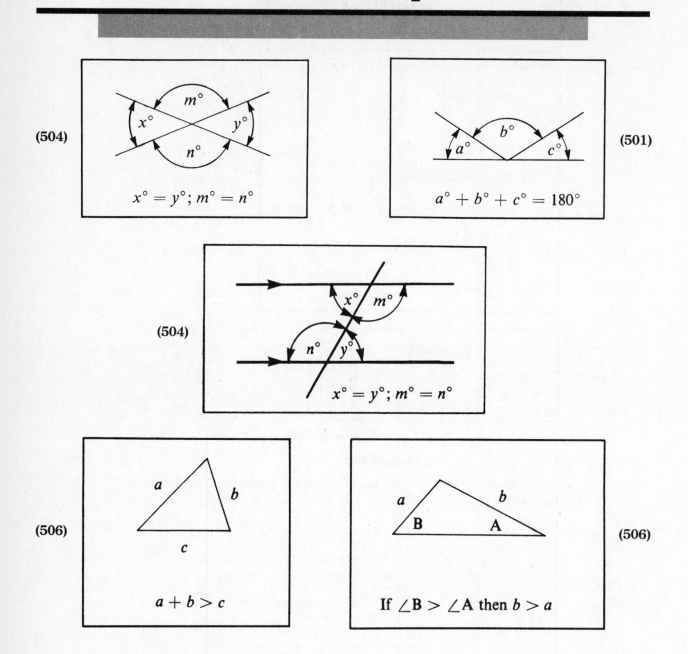

(504) $x° = y°;\ m° = n°$

(501) $a° + b° + c° = 180°$

(504) $x° = y°;\ m° = n°$

(506) $a + b > c$

(506)   If $\angle B > \angle A$ then $b > a$

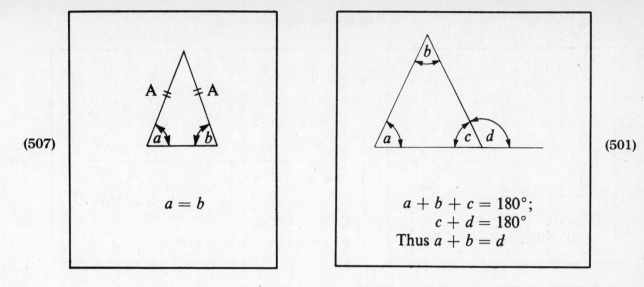

(507)

$a = b$

(501)

$a + b + c = 180°;$
$c + d = 180°$
Thus $a + b = d$

Areas & Perimeters

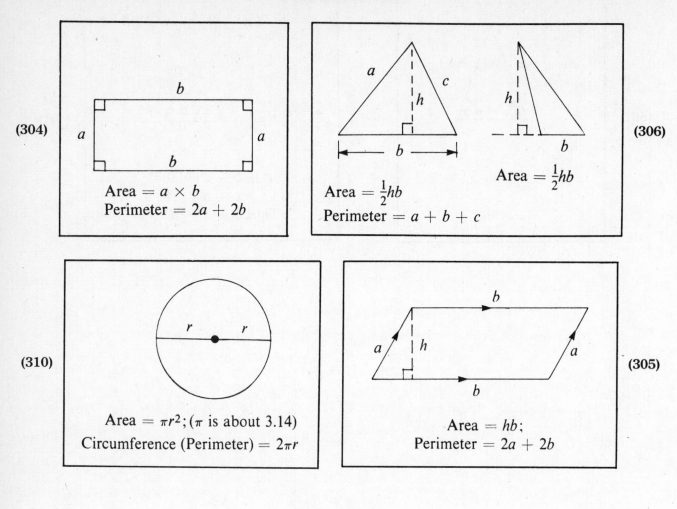

(304)

Area $= a \times b$
Perimeter $= 2a + 2b$

(306)

Area $= \frac{1}{2}hb$
Perimeter $= a + b + c$

Area $= \frac{1}{2}hb$

(310)

Area $= \pi r^2$; (π is about 3.14)
Circumference (Perimeter) $= 2\pi r$

(305)

Area $= hb$;
Perimeter $= 2a + 2b$

More on Circles

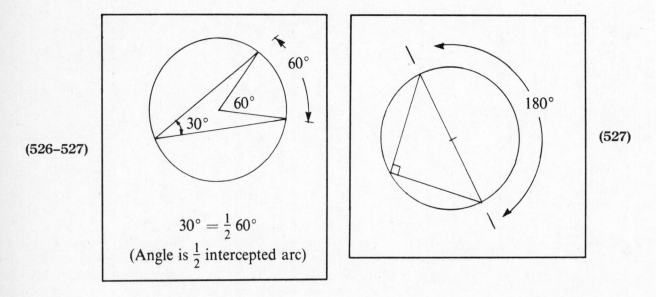

(526–527)

$30° = \frac{1}{2} 60°$
(Angle is $\frac{1}{2}$ intercepted arc)

(527)

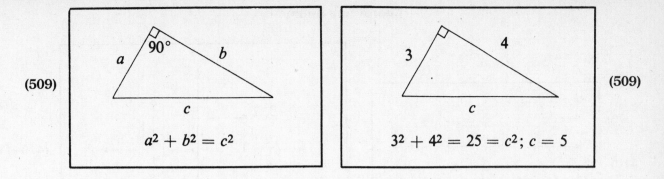

(509) (509)

$$a^2 + b^2 = c^2$$

$$3^2 + 4^2 = 25 = c^2; \; c = 5$$

Here are some right triangles whose relationship of sides you should memorize:

(509)

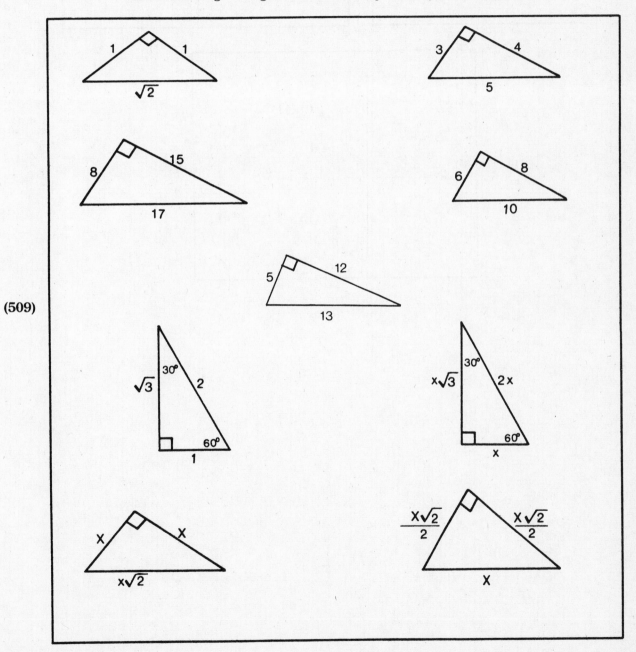

Coordinate Geometry

(410)

(410–411)

(411)

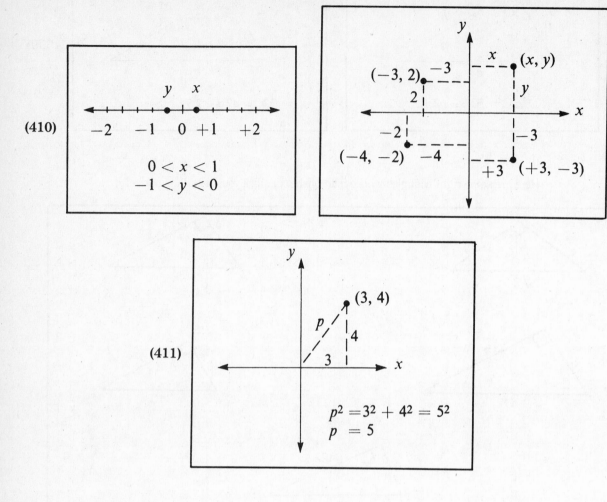

PART 7

COMPLETE
NEW SAT
MATH
REFRESHER

There are many new SAT exam-takers whose Math background is not quite up to par—probably because their basic Math skills are "rusty," or because they never did do well in their Math classes. For these Math-troubled students, this Math Refresher section will be "manna from heaven." The pages that follow constitute a complete basic Math course that will help students greatly in preparing for the Math part of the new SAT.

This Math Refresher offers the following:

1. a systematic review of every Math area covered by the questions in the Math part of the SAT

and

2. short review tests throughout the Refresher to check whether the student has grasped the math principles that he or she has just studied.

The review tests will also provide students with valuable reinforcement so that they will remember how to go about solving math problems they would otherwise have difficulty with on the actual SAT.

Each of the 7 "Sessions" in this Math Refresher has a review test ("Practice Test"). Every review test has 50 questions followed by 50 detailed solutions.* All of the solutions for the 7 review tests include a number (or numbers) in parentheses *after each solution*. The number refers to a specific instructional section where the rules and principles involved in the question are explained simply and clearly.

There is another very important purpose that this Math Refresher serves. You will find, after every solution in the Math sections of the 5 SAT Practice Tests in this book, a key to the mathematical principles of this Math Refresher. For example, a solution may direct you to Math Refresher 202, which deals with Distance and Time problems. If you happen to be weak in this mathematical operation, the 202 Math Refresher explanation will immediately clarify for you how to do Distance and Time problems. In other words, for those who are weak in any phase of Basic Math, this invaluable keying system will help you get the right answer to your SAT Math question—and thereby add approximately 10 points to your SAT score.

---

* Except for the 7th session.

Math Refresher*
Session 1

* Note: Many of the examples or methods can be done with a calcuator, but it is wise for you to know how to solve problems without a calculator.

293

Fractions, Decimals, Percentages, Deviations, Ratios and Proportions, Variations, and Comparison of Fractions

Fractions, Decimals, Percentages

These problems involve the ability to perform numerical operations quickly and correctly. It is essential that you learn the arithmetical procedures outlined in this section.

101. Four different ways to write "*a* divided by *b*" are $a \div b$, $\dfrac{a}{b}$, $a : b$, $b\,\overline{)a}$.

Example: 7 divided by 15 is $7 \div 15 = \dfrac{7}{15} = 7 : 15 = 15\,\overline{)7}$.

102. The numerator of a fraction is the upper number and the denominator is the lower number.

Example: In the fraction $\dfrac{8}{13}$, the numerator is 8 and the denominator is 13.

103. Moving a decimal point one place to the right multiplies the value of a number by 10, whereas moving the decimal point one place to the left divides a number by 10. Likewise, moving a decimal point two places to the right multiplies the value of a number by 100, whereas moving the decimal point two places to the left divides a number by 100.

Example: $24.35 \times 10 = 243.5$ (decimal point moved to *right*)
$24.35 \div 10 = 2.435$ (decimal point moved to *left*)

104. To change a fraction to a decimal, divide the numerator of the fraction by its denominator.

Example: Express $\dfrac{5}{6}$ as a decimal. We divide 5 by 6, obtaining 0.83.

$$\frac{5}{6} = 5 \div 6 = 0.833 \ldots$$

105. To convert a decimal to a fraction, delete the decimal point and divide by whatever unit of 10 the number of decimal places represents.

Example: Convert 0.83 to a fraction. First, delete the decimal point. Second, two decimal places represent hundredths, so divide 83 by 100: $\dfrac{83}{100}$.

$$0.83 = \frac{83}{100}$$

106. To change a fraction to a percent, find its decimal form, multiply by 100, and add a percent sign.

Example: Express $\frac{3}{8}$ as a percent. To convert $\frac{3}{8}$ to a decimal, divide 3 by 8, which gives us 0.375. Multiply 0.375 by 100 gives us 37.5%.

$$\frac{3}{8} = 3 \div 8 = .375$$
$$.375 \times 100 = 37.5\%$$

107. To change a percent to a fraction, drop the percent sign and divide the number by 100.

Example: Express 17% as a fraction. Dropping the % sign gives us 17, and dividing by 100 gives us $\frac{17}{100}$.

108. To *reduce* a fraction, divide the numerator and denominator by the largest number that divides them both evenly.

Example: Reduce $\frac{10}{15}$. Dividing both the numerator and denominator by 5 gives us $\frac{2}{3}$.

Example: Reduce $\frac{12}{36}$. The largest number that goes into both 12 and 36 is 12. Reducing the fraction, we have $\dfrac{\overset{1}{\cancel{12}}}{\underset{3}{\cancel{36}}} = \frac{1}{3}$.

Note: In both examples, the reduced fraction is exactly equal to the original fraction: $\frac{2}{3} = \frac{10}{15}$ and $\frac{12}{36} = \frac{1}{3}$.

109. To add fractions with like denominators, add the numerators of the fractions, keeping the same denominator.

Example: $\frac{1}{7} + \frac{2}{7} + \frac{3}{7} = \frac{6}{7}$.

110. To add fractions with different denominators, you must first change all of the fractions to *equivalent fractions* with the same denominators.

STEP 1. Find the *lowest (or least) common denominator,* the smallest number divisible by all of the denominators.

Example: If the fractions to be added are $\frac{1}{3}, \frac{1}{4}$, and $\frac{5}{6}$, then the lowest common denominator is 12, because 12 is the smallest number that is divisible by 3, 4, and 6.

STEP 2. Convert all of the fractions to *equivalent fractions,* each having the lowest common denominator as its denominator. To do this, multiply the numerator of each fraction by the number of times that its denominator goes into the lowest common denominator. The product of this multiplication will be the *new numerator.* The denominator of the equivalent fractions will be the lowest common denominator. (See Step 1 above.)

Example: The lowest common denominator of $\frac{1}{3}, \frac{1}{4}$, and $\frac{5}{6}$ is 12. Thus, $\frac{1}{3} = \frac{4}{12}$, because 12 divided by 3 is 4, and 4 times 1 = 4. $\frac{1}{4} = \frac{3}{12}$, because 12 divided by 4 is 3, and 3 times 1 = 3. $\frac{5}{6} = \frac{10}{12}$ because 12 divided by 6 is 2, and 2 times 5 = 10.

STEP 3. Now add all of the equivalent fractions by adding the numerators.

Example: $\frac{4}{12} + \frac{3}{12} + \frac{10}{12} = \frac{17}{12}$

STEP 4. Reduce the fraction if possible, as shown in Section 108.

Example: Add $\frac{4}{5}, \frac{2}{3}$ and $\frac{8}{15}$. The lowest common denominator is 15 because 15 is the smallest number that is divisible by 5, 3, and 15. Then, $\frac{4}{5}$ is equivalent to $\frac{12}{15}$; $\frac{2}{3}$ is equivalent to $\frac{10}{15}$; and $\frac{8}{15}$ remains as $\frac{8}{15}$. Adding these numbers gives us $\frac{12}{15} + \frac{10}{15} + \frac{8}{15} = \frac{30}{15}$. Both 30 and 15 are divisible by 15, giving us $\frac{2}{1}$, or 2.

111. To *multiply fractions*, follow this procedure:

STEP 1. To find the numerator of the product, multiply all the numerators of the fractions being multiplied.

STEP 2. To find the denominator of the answer, multiply all of the denominators of the fractions being multiplied.

STEP 3. Reduce the product.

Example: $\frac{5}{7} \times \frac{2}{15} = \frac{5 \times 2}{7 \times 15} = \frac{10}{105}$. Reduce by dividing both the numerator and denominator by 5, the common factor. $\frac{10}{105} = \frac{2}{21}$.

112. To *divide fractions*, follow this procedure:

STEP 1. Invert the divisor. That is, switch the positions of the numerator and denominator in the fraction you are dividing *by*.

STEP 2. Replace the division sign with a multiplication sign.

STEP 3. Carry out the multiplication indicated.

STEP 4. Reduce the product.

Example: Find $\frac{3}{4} \div \frac{7}{8}$. Inverting $\frac{7}{8}$, the divisor, gives us $\frac{8}{7}$. Replacing the division sign with a multiplication sign gives us $\frac{3}{4} \times \frac{8}{7}$. Carrying out the multiplication gives us $\frac{3}{4} \times \frac{8}{7} = \frac{24}{28}$. The fraction $\frac{24}{28}$ may then be reduced to $\frac{6}{7}$ by dividing both the numerator and the denominator by 4.

113. To multiply decimals, follow this procedure:

STEP 1. Disregard the decimal point. Multiply the factors (the numbers being multiplied) as if they were whole numbers.

STEP 2. In each factor, count the number of digits to the *right* of the decimal point. Find the total number of these digits in all the factors. In the product start at the right and count to the left this (total) number of places. Put the decimal point there.

Example: Multiply 3.8 × 4.01. First, multiply 38 and 401, getting 15,238. There is a total of 3 digits to the right of the decimal points in the factors. Thus, the decimal point in the product is placed 3 units to the left of the digit farthest to the right (8).

$$3.8 \times 4.01 = 15.238$$

Example: 0.025 × 3.6. First, multiply 25 × 36, getting 900. In the factors, there is a total of 4 digits to the right of the decimal points; therefore, in the product, we place the decimal point 4 units to the left of the digit farthest to the right in 900. However, there are only 3 digits in the product, so we add a 0 to the left of the 9, getting 0900. This makes it possible to place the decimal point correctly, thus: .0900. From this example, we can make up the rule that in the product we add as many zeros as are needed to provide the proper number of digits to the left of the digit farthest to the right.

114.   To find a percent of a given quantity:

STEP 1.   Replace the word "of" with a multiplication sign.

STEP 2.   Convert the percent to a decimal: drop the percent sign and divide the number by 100. This is done by moving the decimal point two places to the left, adding zeros where necessary.

Examples: $30\% = 0.30$. $2.1\% = 0.021$. $78\% = 0.78$.

STEP 3.   Multiply the given quantity by the decimal.

Example: Find 30% of 200.

30% of $200 = 30\% \times 200 = 0.30 \times 200 = 60.00$

Deviations

Estimation problems arise when dealing with approximations, that is, numbers that are not mathematically precise. The error, or *deviation*, in an approximation is a measure of the closeness of that approximation.

115.   *Absolute error*, or *absolute deviation*, is the difference between the estimated value and the real value (or between the approximate value and the exact value).

Example: If the actual value of a measurement is 60.2 and we estimate it as 60, then the absolute deviation (absolute error) is $60.2 - 60 = 0.2$.

116.   *Fractional error*, or *fractional deviation*, is the ratio of the absolute error to the exact value of the quantity being measured.

Example: If the exact value is 60.2 and the estimated value is 60, then the fractional error is

$$\frac{60.2 - 60}{60.2} = \frac{0.2}{60.2} = \frac{1}{301}$$

117.   *Percent error*, or *percent deviation*, is the fractional error expressed as a percent. (See Section 106 for the method of converting fractions to percents.)

118.   Many business problems, including the calculation of loss, profit, interest, and so forth, are treated as deviation problems. Generally, these problems concern the difference between the original value of a quantity and some new value after taxes, after interest, etc. The following chart shows the relationship between business and estimation problems.

Business Problems		*Estimation Problems*
original value	=	exact value
new value	=	approximate value
net profit net loss net interest	=	absolute error
fractional profit fractional loss fractional interest	=	fractional error
percent profit percent loss percent interest	=	percent error

Example: An item that originally cost $50 is resold for $56. Thus the *net profit* is $56 − $50 = $6. The *fractional profit* is $\dfrac{\$56 - \$50}{\$50} = \dfrac{\$6}{\$50} = \dfrac{3}{25}$. The *percent profit* is equal to the percent equivalent of $\dfrac{3}{25}$, which is 12%.

119. When there are two or more *consecutive changes in value*, remember that the new value of the first change becomes the original value of the second; consequently, successive fractional or percent changes may not be added directly.

Example: Suppose that a $100 item is reduced by 10% and then by 20%. The first reduction puts the price at $90 (10% of $100 = $10; $100 − $10 = $90). Then, reducing the $90 (the new original value) by 20% gives us $72 (20% of $90 = $18; $90 − $18 = $72). Therefore, it is *not* correct to simply add 10% and 20% and then take 30% of $100.

Ratios and Proportions

120. A proportion is an equation stating that two ratios are equal. For example, $3 : 2 = 9 : x$ and $7 : 4 = a : 15$ are proportions. To solve a proportion:

STEP 1. First change the ratios to fractions. To do this, remember that $a : b$ is the same as $\dfrac{a}{b}$, or 1 : 2 is equivalent to $\dfrac{1}{2}$, or $7 : 4 = a : 15$ is the same as $\dfrac{7}{4} = \dfrac{a}{15}$.

STEP 2. Now cross-multiply. That is, multiply the numerator of the first fraction by the denominator of the second fraction. Also multiply the denominator of the first fraction by the numerator of the second fraction. Set the first product equal to the second. This rule is sometimes stated as "The product of the means equals the product of the extremes."

Example: When cross-multiplying in the equation $\dfrac{3}{2} = \dfrac{9}{y}$, we get $3 \times y = 2 \times 9$, or $3y = 18$.

When we cross-multiply in the equation $\dfrac{a}{2} = \dfrac{4}{8}$, we get $8a = 8$.

STEP 3. Solve the resulting equation. This is done algebraically.

Example: Solve for a in the proportion $7 : a = 6 : 18$.

Change the ratios to the fractional relation $\dfrac{7}{a} = \dfrac{6}{18}$. Cross-multiply: $7 \times 18 = 6 \times a$, or $126 = 6a$.

Solving for a gives us $a = 21$.

121. In solving proportions that have units of measurement (feet, seconds, miles, etc.), each ratio must have the same units. For example, if we have the ratio 5 inches : 3 feet, we must convert the 3 feet to 36 inches and then set up the ratio 5 inches : 36 inches, or 5 : 36. We might wish to convert inches to feet. Noting that 1 inch $= \dfrac{1}{12}$ foot, we get 5 inches : 3 feet $= 5 \left(\dfrac{1}{12}\right)$ feet : 3 feet $= 5$ feet : 36 feet, or again, 5 : 36.

Example: On a blueprint, a rectangle measures 6 inches in width and 9 inches in length. If the actual width of the rectangle is 16 inches, how many feet are there in the length?

Solution: We set up the proportions, 6 inches : 9 inches = 16 inches : x feet. Since x feet is equal to $12x$ inches, we substitute this value in the proportion. Thus, 6 inches : 9 inches = 16 inches : $12x$ inches. Since all of the units are now the same, we may work with the numbers alone. In fractional terms we have $\dfrac{6}{9} = \dfrac{16}{12x}$. Cross-multiplication gives us $72x = 144$, and solving for x gives us $x = 2$. The rectangle is 2 feet long.

Variations

122. In a variation problem, you are given a relationship between certain variables. The problem is to determine the change in one variable when one or more of the other variables changes.

Example: In the formula $A = bh$, if b doubles and h triples, what happens to the value of A?

STEP 1. Express the new values of the variables in terms of their original values, *i.e.*, $b' = 2b$ and $h' = 3h$.

STEP 2. Substitute these values in the formula and solve for the desired variable: $A' = b'h' = (2b)(3h) = 6bh$.

STEP 3. Express this answer in terms of the original value of the variable, *i.e.*, since the new value of A is $6bh$, and the old value of A was bh, we can express this as $A_{\text{new}} = 6A_{\text{old}}$. The new value of the variable is expressed with a prime mark and the old value of the variable is left as it was. In this problem the new value of A would be expressed as A' and the old value as A. $A' = 6A$.

Example: If $V = e^3$ and e is doubled, what happens to the value of V?

Solution: Replace e with $2e$. The new value of V is $(2e)^3$. Since this is a new value, V becomes V'. Thus $V' = (2e)^3$, or $8e^3$. Remember, from the original statement of the problem, that $V = e^3$. Using this, we may substitute V for e^3 found in the equation $V' = 8e^3$. The new equation is $V' = 8V$. Therefore, the new value of V is 8 times the old value.

Comparison of Fractions

In fraction comparison problems, you are given two or more fractions and are asked to arrange them in increasing or decreasing order, or to select the larger or the smaller. The following rules and suggestions will be very helpful in determining which of two fractions is greater.

123. If fractions A and B have the same denominators, and A has a larger numerator, then fraction A is larger. (We are assuming here, and for the rest of this Refresher Session, that numerators and denominators are positive.)

Example: $\dfrac{56}{271}$ is greater than $\dfrac{53}{271}$ because the numerator of the first fraction is greater than the numerator of the second.

124. If fractions A and B have the same numerator, and A has a larger denominator, then fraction A is smaller.

Example: $\dfrac{37}{256}$ is smaller than $\dfrac{37}{254}$.

125. If fraction A has a larger numerator and a smaller denominator than fraction B, then fraction A is larger than B.

Example: $\dfrac{6}{11}$ is larger than $\dfrac{4}{13}$. (If this does not seem obvious, compare both fractions with $\dfrac{6}{13}$.)

126. Another method is to convert all of the fractions to equivalent fractions. To do this follow these steps:

STEP 1. First find the *lowest common denominator* of the fractions. This is the smallest number that is divisible by all of the denominators of the original fractions. See Section 108 for the method of finding lowest common denominators.

STEP 2. The fraction with the greatest numerator is the largest fraction.

127. Still another method is the *conversion to approximating decimals*.

Example: To compare $\frac{5}{9}$ and $\frac{7}{11}$, we might express both as decimals to a few places of accuracy: $\frac{5}{9}$ is approximately equal to 0.555, while $\frac{7}{11}$ is approximately equal to 0.636, so $\frac{7}{11}$ is obviously greater. To express a fraction as a decimal, divide the numerator by the denominator.

128. If all of the fractions being compared are very close in value to some easy-to-work-with number, such as $\frac{1}{2}$ or 5, you may subtract this number from each of the fractions without changing their order.

Example: To compare $\frac{151}{75}$ with $\frac{328}{163}$ we notice that both of these fractions are approximately equal to 2. If we subtract 2 (that is $\frac{150}{75}$ and $\frac{326}{163}$, respectively) from each, we get $\frac{1}{75}$ and $\frac{2}{163}$, respectively. Since $\frac{1}{75}$ (or $\frac{2}{150}$) exceeds $\frac{2}{163}$, we see that $\frac{151}{75}$ must also exceed $\frac{328}{163}$.

Solution: We notice that both these numbers are close to $\frac{1}{4}$:

An alternative method of comparing fractions is to change the fractions to their decimal equivalents and then compare the decimals. (See Section 104.) The student would weigh the relative amount of work and difficulty involved in each method when he faces each problem.

Quick Way of Comparing Fractions

Example: Which is greater, $\frac{3}{8}$ or $\frac{7}{18}$?

Procedure:

$$\frac{3}{8} \xleftarrow{\text{MULTIPLY}} \quad \xrightarrow{\text{MULTIPLY}} \frac{7}{18}$$

Multiply the 18 by the 3. We get 54. Put the 54 on the *left* side.

$$54$$

Now *multiply* the 8 by the 7. We get 56. Put the 56 on the *right* side:

$$54 \qquad\qquad\qquad 56$$

Since 56 > 54 and 56 is on the *right* side, the fraction $\frac{7}{18}$ (which was also originally on the *right* side) is *greater* than the fraction $\frac{3}{8}$ (which was originally on the *left* side).

Example: If $y > x$, which is greater, $\frac{1}{x}$ or $\frac{1}{y}$? (x and y are positive numbers).

Procedure:

$$\frac{1}{x} \xleftarrow{\text{MULTIPLY}} \quad \xrightarrow{\text{MULTIPLY}} \frac{1}{y}$$

Multiply y by 1. We get y. Put y on the left:

$$y$$

Multiply x by 1. We get x. Put x on the right side.

$$y \qquad\qquad x$$

Since $y > x$ (given), $\dfrac{1}{x}$ (which was originally on the left) is greater than $\dfrac{1}{y}$ (which was originally on the right).

Example: Which is greater?

$$\frac{7}{9} \qquad\qquad \text{or} \qquad\qquad \frac{3}{4}$$

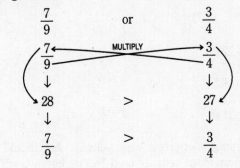

$$28 \qquad > \qquad 27$$

$$\frac{7}{9} \qquad > \qquad \frac{3}{4}$$

Practice Test 1

Fractions, Decimals, Percentages, Deviations, Ratios and Proportions, Variations, and Comparison of Fractions

Correct answers and solutions follow each test.

1. A B C D E

1. Which of the following answers is the sum of the following numbers:

$2\frac{1}{2}, \frac{21}{4}, 3.350, \frac{1}{8}$?

(A) 8.225
(B) 9.825
(C) 10.825
(D) 11.225
(E) 12.350

2. A B C D E

2. A chemist was preparing a solution that should have included 35 milligrams of a chemical. If she actually used 36.4 milligrams, what was her percentage error (to the nearest 0.01%)?

(A) 0.04%
(B) 0.05%
(C) 1.40%
(D) 3.85%
(E) 4.00%

3. A B C D E

3. A retailer buys a radio from the wholesaler for $75.00. He then marks up the price by $\frac{1}{3}$ and sells it at a discount of 20%. What was his profit on the radio (to the nearest cent)?

(A) $5.00
(B) $6.67
(C) $7.50
(D) $10.00
(E) $13.33

4. A B C D E

4. On a blueprint, $\frac{1}{4}$ inch represents 1 foot. If a window is supposed to be 56 inches wide, how wide would its representation on the blueprint be?

(A) $1\frac{1}{6}$ inches

(B) $4\frac{2}{3}$ inches

(C) $9\frac{1}{3}$ inches

(D) 14 inches

(E) $18\frac{2}{3}$ inches

5. A B C D E

5. If the radius of a circle is increased by 50%, what will be the percent increase in the circumference of the circle? (Circumference $= 2\pi r$)

(A) 25%
(B) 50%
(C) 100%
(D) 150%
(E) 225%

6. A B C D E

6. Which of the following fractions is the greatest?

(A) $\dfrac{403}{134}$

(B) $\dfrac{79}{26}$

(C) $\dfrac{527}{176}$

(D) $\dfrac{221}{73}$

(E) $\dfrac{99}{34}$

7. A B C D E

7. A store usually sells a certain item at a 40% profit. One week the store has a sale, during which the item is sold for 10% less than the usual price. During the sale, what is the percent profit the store makes on each of these items?

(A) 4%
(B) 14%
(C) 26%
(D) 30%
(E) 36%

8. A B C D E

8. What is 0.05 percent of 6.5?

(A) 0.00325
(B) 0.013
(C) 0.325
(D) 1.30
(E) 130.0

9. A B C D E

9. What is the value of $\dfrac{3\frac{1}{2} + 3\frac{1}{4} + 3\frac{1}{4} + 3\frac{1}{2}}{4\frac{1}{2}}$?

(A) $1\dfrac{1}{2}$

(B) $2\dfrac{1}{4}$

(C) 3

(D) $3\dfrac{1}{4}$

(E) $3\dfrac{3}{8}$

10. A B C D E

10. If 8 men can chop down 28 trees in one day, how many trees can 20 men chop down in one day?

(A) 28 trees
(B) 160 trees
(C) 70 trees
(D) 100 trees
(E) 80 trees

11. A B C D E   **11.** What is the product of the following fractions: $\dfrac{3}{100}, \dfrac{15}{49}, \dfrac{7}{9}$?

(A) $\dfrac{215}{44,100}$

(B) $\dfrac{1}{140}$

(C) $\dfrac{1}{196}$

(D) $\dfrac{25}{158}$

(E) $\dfrac{3}{427}$

12. A B C D E   **12.** In reading a thermometer, Mr. Downs mistakenly observed a temperature of 72° instead of 77°. What was his percentage error (to the nearest hundredth of a percent)?

(A) 6.49%
(B) 6.50%
(C) 6.64%
(D) 6.94%
(E) 6.95%

13. A B C D E   **13.** A businessman buys 1,440 dozen pens at $2.50 a dozen and then sells them at a price of 25¢ apiece. What is his total profit on the lot of pens?

(A) $60.00
(B) $72.00
(C) $720.00
(D) $874.00
(E) $8740.00

14. A B C D E   **14.** On a map, 1 inch represents 1,000 miles. If the area of a country is actually 16 million square miles, what is the area of the country's representation on the map?

(A) 4 square inches
(B) 16 square inches
(C) 4,000 square inches
(D) 16,000 square inches
(E) 4,000,000 square inches

15. A B C D E   **15.** The formula for the volume of a cone is $V = \dfrac{1}{3}\pi r^2 h$. If the radius ($r$) is doubled and the height (h) is divided by 3, what will be the ratio of the new volume to the original volume?

(A) 2 : 3
(B) 3 : 2
(C) 4 : 3
(D) 3 : 4
(E) none of these

16. $\begin{array}{ccccc} A & B & C & D & E \\ || & || & || & || & || \\ || & || & || & || & || \end{array}$ **16.** Which of the following fractions has the smallest value:

(A) $\dfrac{34.7}{163}$

(B) $\dfrac{125}{501}$

(C) $\dfrac{173}{700}$

(D) $\dfrac{10.9}{42.7}$

(E) $\dfrac{907}{3715}$

17. $\begin{array}{ccccc} A & B & C & D & E \\ || & || & || & || & || \\ || & || & || & || & || \end{array}$ **17.** Mr. Cutler usually makes a 45% profit on every radio he sells. During a sale, he reduces his margin of profit to 40%, while his sales increase by 10%. What is the ratio of his new total profit to the original profit?

(A) 1 : 1
(B) 9 : 8
(C) 9 : 10
(D) 11 : 10
(E) 44 : 45

18. $\begin{array}{ccccc} A & B & C & D & E \\ || & || & || & || & || \\ || & || & || & || & || \end{array}$ **18.** What is 1.3 percent of 0.26?

(A) 0.00338
(B) 0.00500
(C) 0.200
(D) 0.338
(E) 0.500

19. $\begin{array}{ccccc} A & B & C & D & E \\ || & || & || & || & || \\ || & || & || & || & || \end{array}$ **19.** What is the average of the following numbers: $3.2, \dfrac{47}{12}, \dfrac{10}{3}$?

(A) 3.55

(B) $\dfrac{10}{3}$

(C) $\dfrac{103}{30}$

(D) $\dfrac{209}{60}$

(E) $\dfrac{1254}{120}$

20. $\begin{array}{ccccc} A & B & C & D & E \\ || & || & || & || & || \\ || & || & || & || & || \end{array}$ **20.** If it takes 16 faucets 10 hours to fill 8 tubs, how long will it take 12 faucets to fill 9 tubs?

(A) 10 hours
(B) 12 hours
(C) 13 hours
(D) 14 hours
(E) 15 hours

21. A B C D E   **21.** If the 8% tax on a sale amounts to 96¢, what is the final price (tax included) of the item?

    (A) $1.20
    (B) $2.16
    (C) $6.36
    (D) $12.00
    (E) $12.96

22. A B C D E   **22.** In a certain class, 40% of the students are girls, and 20% of the girls wear glasses. What percent of the children in the class are girls who wear glasses?

    (A) 6%
    (B) 8%
    (C) 20%
    (D) 60%
    (E) 80%

23. A B C D E   **23.** What is 1.2% of 0.5?

    (A) 0.0006
    (B) 0.006
    (C) 0.06
    (D) 0.6
    (E) 6.0

24. A B C D E   **24.** Which of the following quantities is the largest?

    (A) $\dfrac{275}{369}$

    (B) $\dfrac{134}{179}$

    (C) $\dfrac{107}{144}$

    (D) $\dfrac{355}{476}$

    (E) $\dfrac{265}{352}$

25. A B C D E   **25.** If the length of a rectangle is increased by 120%, and its width is decreased by 20%, what happens to the area of the rectangle?

    (A) It decreases by 4%.
    (B) It remains the same.
    (C) It increases by 24%.
    (D) It increases by 76%.
    (E) It increases by 100%.

26. A B C D E   **26.** A merchant buys an old carpet for $25.00. He spends $15.00 to have it restored to good condition and then sells the rug for $50.00. What is the percent profit on his total investment?

    (A) 20%
    (B) 25%
    (C) 40%
    (D) 66⅔%
    (E) 100%

27. A B C D E

27. Of the following sets of fractions, which one is arranged in *decreasing* order?

(A) $\dfrac{5}{9}$, $\dfrac{7}{11}$, $\dfrac{3}{5}$, $\dfrac{2}{3}$, $\dfrac{10}{13}$

(B) $\dfrac{2}{3}$, $\dfrac{3}{5}$, $\dfrac{7}{11}$, $\dfrac{5}{9}$, $\dfrac{10}{13}$

(C) $\dfrac{3}{5}$, $\dfrac{5}{9}$, $\dfrac{7}{11}$, $\dfrac{10}{13}$, $\dfrac{2}{3}$

(D) $\dfrac{10}{13}$, $\dfrac{2}{3}$, $\dfrac{7}{11}$, $\dfrac{3}{5}$, $\dfrac{5}{9}$

(E) none of these

28. A B C D E

28. If the diameter of a circle doubles, the circumference of the larger circle is how many times the circumference of the original circle? (Circumference = πd)

(A) π

(B) 2π

(C) 1

(D) 2

(E) 4

29. A B C D E

29. The scale on a set of plans is 1 : 8. If a man reads a certain measurement on the plans as 5.6″, instead of 6.0″, what will be the resulting approximate percent error on the full-size model?

(A) 6.7%

(B) 7.1%

(C) 12.5%

(D) 53.6%

(E) 56.8%

30. A B C D E

30. A salesman bought 2 dozen television sets at $300 each. He sold two-thirds of them at a 25% profit but was forced to take a 30% loss on the rest. What was his total profit (or loss) on the television sets?

(A) a loss of $200

(B) a loss of $15

(C) no profit or loss

(D) a gain of $20

(E) a gain of $480

31. A B C D E

31. The sum of $\dfrac{1}{2}$, $\dfrac{1}{3}$, $\dfrac{1}{8}$, and $\dfrac{1}{15}$ is:

(A) $\dfrac{9}{8}$

(B) $\dfrac{16}{15}$

(C) $\dfrac{41}{40}$

(D) $\dfrac{65}{64}$

(E) $\dfrac{121}{120}$

32. A B C D E

32. What is $\frac{2}{3}$ % of 90?

(A) 0.006
(B) 0.06
(C) 0.6
(D) 6.0
(E) 60

33. A B C D E

33. A man borrows $360. If he pays it back in 12 monthly installments of $31.50, what is his interest rate?

(A) 1.5%
(B) 4.5%
(C) 10%
(D) 5%
(E) 7.5%

34. A B C D E

34. A merchant marks a certain lamp up 30% above original cost. Then he gives a customer a 15% discount. If the final selling price of the lamp was $86.19, what was the original cost?

(A) $66.30
(B) $73.26
(C) $78.00
(D) $99.12
(E) $101.40

35. A B C D E

35. In a certain recipe, $2\frac{1}{4}$ cups of flour are called for to make a cake that serves 6. If Mrs. Jenkins wants to use the same recipe to make a cake for 8, how many cups of flour must she use?

(A) $2\frac{1}{3}$ cups

(B) $2\frac{3}{4}$ cups

(C) 3 cups

(D) $3\frac{3}{8}$ cups

(E) 4 cups

36. A B C D E

36. If 10 men can survive for 24 days on 15 cans of rations, how many cans will be needed for 8 men to survive for 36 days?

(A) 15 cans
(B) 16 cans
(C) 17 cans
(D) 18 cans
(E) 19 cans

37. A B C D E

37. If, on a map, $\frac{1}{2}$ inch represents 1 mile, how long is a border whose representation is $1\frac{1}{15}$ feet long?

(A) $2\frac{1}{30}$ miles

(B) $5\frac{1}{15}$ miles

(C) $12\frac{4}{5}$ miles

(D) $25\frac{3}{5}$ miles

(E) $51\frac{1}{5}$ miles

38. A B C D E

38. In the formula $e = hf$, if e is doubled and f is halved, what happens to the value of h?

(A) h remains the same.
(B) h is doubled.
(C) h is divided by 4.
(D) h is multiplied by 4.
(E) h is halved.

39. A B C D E

39. Which of the following expresses the ratio of 3 inches to 2 yards?

(A) $3 : 2$
(B) $3 : 9$
(C) $3 : 12$
(D) $3 : 24$
(E) $3 : 72$

40. A B C D E

40. If it takes Mark twice as long to earn $6.00 as it takes Carl to earn $4.00, what is the ratio of Mark's pay per hour to Carl's pay per hour?

(A) $2 : 1$
(B) $3 : 1$
(C) $3 : 2$
(D) $3 : 4$
(E) $4 : 3$

41. A B C D E

41. What is the lowest common denominator of the following set of fractions: $\frac{1}{6}, \frac{13}{27}, \frac{4}{5}, \frac{3}{10}, \frac{2}{15}$?

(A) 27
(B) 54
(C) 135
(D) 270
(E) none of these

42. A B C D E

42. The average grade on a certain examination was 85. Ralph, on the same examination, scored 90. What was Ralph's *percent* deviation from the average score (to the nearest tenth of a percent)?

(A) 5.0%
(B) 5.4%
(C) 5.5%
(D) 5.8%
(E) 5.9%

43. A B C D E

43. Successive discounts of 20% and 12% are equivalent to a single discount of:

(A) 16.0%
(B) 29.6%
(C) 31.4%
(D) 32.0%
(E) 33.7%

44. A B C D E

44. On a blueprint of a park, 1 foot represents $\frac{1}{2}$ mile. If an error of $\frac{1}{2}$ inch is made in reading the blueprint, what will be the corresponding error on the actual park?

(A) 110 feet
(B) 220 feet
(C) 330 feet
(D) 440 feet
(E) none of these

45. A B C D E

45. If the two sides of a rectangle change in such a manner that the rectangle's area remains constant, and one side increases by 25%, what must happen to the other side?

(A) It decreases by 20%
(B) It decreases by 25%
(C) It decreases by $33\frac{1}{3}$%
(D) It decreases by 50%
(E) none of these

46. A B C D E

46. Which of the following fractions has the smallest value?

(A) $\frac{6043}{2071}$

(B) $\frac{4290}{1463}$

(C) $\frac{5107}{1772}$

(D) $\frac{8935}{2963}$

(E) $\frac{8016}{2631}$

47. A B C D E

47. A certain company increased its prices by 30% during 1992. Then, in 1993, it was forced to cut back its prices by 20%. What was the net change in price?

(A) A net decrease in prices of more than 10%
(B) A net decrease in prices of 10% or less
(C) No net change in prices
(D) A net increase in prices of 10% or less
(E) A net increase in prices of more than 10%

48. A B C D E

48. What is 0.04%, expressed as a fraction?

(A) $\dfrac{2}{5}$

(B) $\dfrac{1}{25}$

(C) $\dfrac{4}{25}$

(D) $\dfrac{1}{250}$

(E) $\dfrac{1}{2500}$

49. A B C D E

49. What is the value of the fraction

$$\dfrac{16 + 12 + 88 + 34 + 66 + 21 + 79 + 11 + 89}{25}?$$

(A) 15.04
(B) 15.44
(C) 16.24
(D) 16.64
(E) none of these

50. A B C D E

50. If coconuts are twice as expensive as bananas, and bananas are one-third as expensive as grapefruits, what is the ratio of the price of one coconut to one grapefruit?

(A) 2 : 3
(B) 3 : 2
(C) 6 : 1
(D) 1 : 6
(E) none of these

Answer Key for Practice Test 1

1. D	14. B	27. D	39. E
2. E	15. C	28. D	40. D
3. A	16. A	29. A	41. D
4. A	17. E	30. E	42. E
5. B	18. A	31. C	43. B
6. B	19. D	32. C	44. A
7. C	20. E	33. D	45. A
8. A	21. E	34. C	46. C
9. C	22. B	35. C	47. D
10. C	23. B	36. D	48. E
11. B	24. E	37. D	49. D
12. A	25. D	38. D	50. A
13. C	26. B		

Answers and Solutions for Practice Test 1

1. Choice D is correct. First, convert the fractions to decimals, as the final answer must be expressed in decimals: $2.500 + 5.250 + 3.350 + 0.125 = 11.225$. (104,109)

2. Choice E is correct. This is an estimation problem. Note that the correct value was 35, not 36.4. Thus the *real* value is 35 mg. and the *estimated* value is 36.4 mg. Thus, percent error is equal to $(36.4 − 35) ÷ 35$, or 0.04, expressed as a percent, which is 4%. (117)

3. Choice A is correct. This is a business problem. First, the retailer marks up the wholesale price by $\frac{1}{3}$, so the marked-up price equals $75 $(1 + \frac{1}{3})$, or $100; then it is reduced 20% from the $100 price, leaving a final price of $80. Thus, the net profit on the radio was $5.00. (118)

4. Choice A is correct. Here we have a proportion problem: length on blueprint : actual length $= \frac{1}{4}$ inch ; 1 foot. The second ratio is the same as 1 : 48 because 1 foot = 12 inches. In the problem the actual length is 56 inches, so that if the length on the blueprint equals x, we have the proportion $x : 56 = 1 : 48$; $\frac{x}{56} = \frac{1}{48}$. $48x = 56$; so $x = \frac{56}{48}$, or $1\frac{1}{6}$ inches. (120)

5. Choice B is correct. Since $C = 2\pi r$ (where r is the radius of the circle, and C is its circumference), the new value of r, r', is $(1.5) r$ since r is increased by 50%. Using this value of r', we get the new C, $C' = 2\pi r' = 2\pi (1.5) r = (1.5) 2\pi r$. Remembering that $C = 2\pi r$, we get that $C' = (1.5) C$. Since the new circumference is 1.5 times the original, there is an increase of 50%. (122)

6. Choice B is correct. In this numerical comparison problem, it is helpful to realize that all of these fractions are approximately equal to 3. If we subtract 3 from each of the fractions, we get $\frac{1}{134}, \frac{1}{26}$, $\frac{-1}{176}, \frac{2}{73}$, and $\frac{-3}{34}$, respectively. Clearly, the greatest of these is $\frac{1}{26}$ and is therefore the greatest of the five given fractions. Another method of solving this type of numerical comparison problem is to convert the fractions to decimals by dividing the numerator by the denominator. (127,128)

7. Choice C is correct. This is another business problem, this time asking for percentage profit. Let the original price be P. Then the marked-up price will be $1.4(P)$. Ten percent is taken off this price, to yield a final price of $(0.90) (1.40) (P)$, or $(1.26) (P)$. Thus, the fractional increase was 0.26, so the percent increase was 26%. (118)

8. Choice A is correct. Remember that the phrase "percent of" may be replaced by a multiplication sign. Thus, $0.05\% \times 6.5 = 0.0005 \times 6.5$, so the answer is 0.00325. (114)

9. Choice C is correct. First, add the fractions in the numerator to obtain $13\frac{1}{2}$. Then divide $13\frac{1}{2}$ by $4\frac{1}{2}$. If you cannot see immediately that the answer is 3, you can convert the halves to decimals and divide, or you can express the fractions in terms of their common denominator, thus: $13\frac{1}{2} = \frac{27}{2}$; $4\frac{1}{2} = \frac{9}{2}$; $\frac{27}{2} \div \frac{9}{2}$ $= \frac{27}{2} \times \frac{2}{9} = \frac{54}{18} = 3$. (110,112)

10. Choice C is correct. This is a proportion problem. If x is the number of men needed to chop down 20 trees, then we form the proportion: 8 men : 28 trees $=$ 20 men : x trees, or $\frac{8}{28} = \frac{20}{x}$. Solving for x, we get $x = \frac{(28)(20)}{8}$, or $x = 70$. (120)

11. Choice B is correct. $\frac{3}{100} \times \frac{15}{49} \times \frac{7}{9} = \frac{3 \times 15 \times 7}{100 \times 49 \times 9}$. Canceling 7 out of the numerator and denominator gives us $\frac{3 \times 15}{100 \times 7 \times 9}$. Canceling 5 out of the nu-

merator and denominator gives us $\dfrac{3 \times 3}{20 \times 7 \times 9}$.

Finally, canceling 9 out of both numerator and denominator gives us $\dfrac{1}{20 \times 7}$, or $\dfrac{1}{140}$. (111)

12. Choice A is correct. Percent error = (absolute error) ÷ (correct measurement) = $5 \div 77 = 0.0649$ (approximately) $\times 100 = 6.49\%$. (117)

13. Choice C is correct. Profit on each dozen pens = selling price − cost = 12(25¢) − $2.50 = $3.00 − $2.50 = 50¢, profit per dozen. Total profit = profit per dozen × number of dozens = 50¢ × 1440 = $720.00. (118)

14. Choice B is correct. If 1 inch represents 1,000 miles, then 1 square inch represents 1,000 miles squared, or 1,000,000 square miles. Thus, the area would be represented by 16 squares of this size, or 16 square inches. (120)

15. Choice C is correct. Let V' equal the new volume. Then if $r' = 2r$ is the new radius, and $h' = \dfrac{h}{3}$ is the new height, $V' = \dfrac{1}{3}\pi (r')^2 (h') = \dfrac{1}{3}\pi (2r)^2 \left(\dfrac{h}{3}\right) = \dfrac{4}{9}\pi r^2 h = \dfrac{4}{3}V$, so the ratio $V' : V$ is equal to 4 : 3. (122)

16. Choice A is correct. All of these fractions are approximately equal to $\dfrac{1}{4}$. Thus, by subtracting $\dfrac{1}{4}$ from each one we get remainders of, respectively, $\dfrac{-6.05}{163}$, $\dfrac{-0.25}{501}$, $\dfrac{-2}{700}$, $+\dfrac{0.225}{42.7}$, and $\dfrac{-21.75}{3715}$. The first of these is the smallest. That is because of all of the negative fractions, it has the largest value without its sign. Therefore, it is the most negative and, consequently, the smallest so that $\dfrac{34.7}{163}$ is the desired answer. (123–128)

17. Choice E is correct. Let N = the original cost of a radio. Then, original profit = $45\% \times N$. New profit = $40\% \times 110\%N = 44\% \times N$. Thus, the ratio of new profit to original profit is 44 : 45. (118)

18. Choice A is correct.
$1.3\% \times 0.26 = 0.013 \times 0.26 = 0.00338$. (114)

19. Choice D is correct. Average $= \dfrac{1}{3}\left(3.2 + \dfrac{47}{12} + \dfrac{10}{3}\right)$. The decimal $3.2 = \dfrac{320}{100} = \dfrac{16}{5}$, and the lowest common denominator of the three fractions is 60, then

$\dfrac{16}{5} = \dfrac{192}{60}, \dfrac{47}{12} = \dfrac{235}{60}$, and $\dfrac{10}{3} = \dfrac{200}{60}$. Then, $\dfrac{1}{3}\left(\dfrac{192}{60}\right.$ $+ \dfrac{235}{60} + \left.\dfrac{200}{60}\right) = \dfrac{1}{3}\left(\dfrac{627}{60}\right) = \dfrac{209}{60}$ (101, 105, 109)

20. Choice E is correct. If it takes 16 faucets 10 hours to fill 8 tubs, then it takes 1 faucet 160 hours to fill 8 tubs (16 faucets : 1 faucet = x hours : 10 hours; $\dfrac{16}{1} = \dfrac{x}{10}$; $x = 160$). If it takes 1 faucet 160 hours to fill 8 tubs, then (dividing by 8) it takes 1 faucet 20 hours to fill 1 tub. If it takes 1 faucet 20 hours to fill 1 tub, then it takes 1 faucet 180 hours (9×20 hours) to fill 9 tubs. If it takes 1 faucet 180 hours to fill 9 tubs, then it takes 12 faucets $\dfrac{180}{12}$ or 15 hours to fill 9 tubs. (120)

21. Choice E is correct. Let P be the original price. Then $0.08P = 96$¢, so that $8P = \$96$, or $P = \$12$. Adding the tax, which equals 96¢, we obtain our final price of $12.96. (118)

22. Choice B is correct. The number of girls who wear glasses is 20% of 40% of the children in the class. Thus, the indicated operation is multiplication; $20\% \times 40\% = 0.20 \times 0.40 = 0.08 = 8\%$. (114)

23. Choice B is correct. $1.2\% \times 0.5 = 0.012 \times 0.5 = 0.006$. (114)

24. Choice E is correct. Here, we can use $\dfrac{3}{4}$ as an approximate value for all the fractions, Subtracting $\dfrac{3}{4}$ from each, we get remainders of: $\dfrac{-1.75}{369}$, $\dfrac{-0.25}{179}$, $\dfrac{-1.00}{144}$, $\dfrac{-2.00}{476}$, and $\dfrac{+1.00}{352}$. Clearly, the last of these is the greatest (it is the only positive one), so $\dfrac{256}{352}$ is the fraction that is the largest. This problem may also be solved by converting the fractions to decimals. (104, 123, 127)

25. Choice D is correct. Area = length × width. The new area will be equal to the new length (2.20 times the old length) times the new width (0.80 times the old width), giving a product of 1.76 times the original area, an increase of 76%. (122)

26. Choice B is correct. Total cost to merchant = $25.00 + $15.00 = $40.00.

Profit = selling price − cost = $50 − $40 = $10. Percent profit = profit ÷ cost = $10 ÷ $40 = 25%. (118)

27. Choice D is correct. We can convert the fractions to decimals or to fractions with a lowest common denominator. Inspection will show that all sets of fractions contain the same members; therefore, if we convert one set to decimals or find the lowest common denominator for one set, we can use our results for all sets. Converting a fraction to a decimal involves only one operation, a single division, whereas converting to the lowest common denominator involves a multiplication, which must be followed by a division and a multiplication to change each fraction to one with the lowest common denominator. Thus, conversion to decimals is often the simpler method: $\frac{10}{13} = 0.769$; $\frac{2}{3} = 0.666$; $\frac{7}{11} = 0.636$; $\frac{3}{5} = 0.600$; $\frac{5}{9} = 0.555$.　　(104)

However, in this case there is an even simpler method. Convert two of the fractions to equivalent fractions: $\frac{3}{5} = \frac{6}{10}$ and $\frac{2}{3} = \frac{8}{12}$. We now have $\frac{5}{9}, \frac{6}{10}, \frac{7}{11}, \frac{8}{12}$, and $\frac{10}{13}$. Remember this rule: When the numerator and denominator of a fraction are both positive, adding 1 to both will bring the value of the fraction closer to 1. (For example, $\frac{3}{4} = \frac{2+1}{3+1}$, so $\frac{3}{4}$ is closer to 1 than $\frac{2}{3}$ and is therefore the greater fraction.) Thus we see that $\frac{5}{9}$ is less than $\frac{6}{10}$, which is less than $\frac{7}{11}$, which is less than $\frac{8}{12}$, which is less than $\frac{9}{13}$. $\frac{9}{13}$ is obviously less than $\frac{10}{13}$, so $\frac{10}{13}$ must be the greatest fraction. Thus, in decreasing order the fractions are $\frac{10}{13}, \frac{2}{3}, \frac{7}{11}, \frac{3}{5}$, and $\frac{5}{9}$. This method is a great time-saver once you become accustomed to it.

28. Choice D is correct. The formula governing this situation is $C = \pi d$, where C = circumference, and d = diameter. Thus, if the new diameter is $d' = 2d$, then the new circumference is $C' = \pi d' = 2\pi d = 2C$. Thus, the new, larger circle has a circumference of twice that of the original circle.　　(122)

29. Choice A is correct. The most important feature of this problem is recognizing that the scale does not affect percent (or fractional) error, since it simply results in multiplying the numerator and denominator of a fraction by the same factor. Thus, we need only calculate the original percent error. Although it would not be incorrect to calculate the

full-scale percent error, it would be time-consuming and might result in unnecessary errors.) Absolute error = 0.4″. Actual measurement = 6.0″. Therefore, percent error = (absolute error ÷ actual measurement) × 100% = $\frac{0.4}{6.0}$ × 100%, which equals 6.7% (approximately).　　(117)

30. Choice E is correct. Total cost = number of sets × cost of each = 24 × \$300 = \$7200.
Revenue = (number sold at 25% profit × price at 25% profit) + (number sold at 30% loss × price at 30% loss)
= (16 × \$375) + (8 × \$210) = \$6000 + \$1680 = \$7680.

Profit = revenue − cost = \$7680 − \$7200 = \$480.　　(118)

31. Choice C is correct. $\frac{1}{2} + \frac{1}{3} + \frac{1}{8} + \frac{1}{15} = \frac{60}{120} + \frac{40}{120} + \frac{15}{120} + \frac{8}{120} = \frac{123}{120} = \frac{41}{40}$.　　(110)

32. Choice C is correct. $\frac{2}{3}\% \times 90 = \frac{2}{300} \times 90 = \frac{180}{300} = \frac{6}{10} = 0.6$.　　(114)

33. Choice D is correct. If the man makes 12 payments of \$31.50, he pays back a total of \$378.00. Since the loan is for \$360.00, his net interest is \$18.00. Therefore, his rate of interest is $\frac{\$18.00}{\$360.00}$, which can be reduced to 0.05, or 5%.　　(118)

34. Choice C is correct. Final selling price = 85% × 130% × cost = $110\frac{1}{2}$ × cost. Thus, \$86.19 = 1.105C, where C = cost. C = \$86.19 ÷ 1.105 = \$78.00 (exactly).　　(118)

35. Choice C is correct. If x is the amount of flour needed for 8 people, then we can set up the proportion $2\frac{1}{4}$ cups : 6 people = x : 8 people. Solving for x gives us $x = \frac{8}{6} \times 2\frac{1}{4}$ or $\frac{8}{6} \times \frac{9}{4} = 3$.　　(120)

36. Choice D is correct. If 10 men can survive for 24 days on 15 cans, then 1 man can survive for 240 days on 15 cans. If 1 man can survive for 240 days on 15 cans, then 1 man can survive for $\frac{240}{15}$ or 16 days on 1 can. If 1 man can survive for 16 days on 1 can, then 8 men can survive for $\frac{16}{8}$ or 2 days on 1

can. If 8 men can survive for 2 days on 1 can, then for 36 days 8 men need $\frac{36}{2}$ or 18 cans to survive.

(120)

37. Choice D is correct. $1\frac{1}{15}$ feet $= 12\frac{4}{5}$ inches. Thus, we have the proportion: $\frac{1}{2}$ inch : 1 mile $= 12.8$ inches : x. Solving for x, we have $x = 25.6$ miles $= 25\frac{3}{5}$ miles. (120)

38. Choice D is correct. If $e = hf$, then $h = \frac{e}{f}$. If e is doubled and f is halved, then the new value of h, $h' = \left(\frac{2e}{\frac{1}{2}f}\right)$. Multiplying the numerator and denominator by 2 gives us $h' = \frac{4e}{f}$. Since $h = \frac{e}{f}$ and $h' = \frac{4e}{f}$ we see that $h' = 4h$. This is the same as saying that h is multiplied by 4. (122)

39. Choice E is correct. 3 inches : 2 yards = 3 inches : 72 inches = 3 : 72. (121)

40. Choice D is correct. If Carl and Mark work for the same length of time, then Carl will earn $8.00 for every $6.00 Mark earns (since in the time Mark can earn one $6.00 wage, Carl can earn *two* $4.00 wages). Thus, their hourly wage rates are in the ratio $6.00 (Mark) : $8.00 (Carl) = 3 : 4. (120)

41. Choice D is correct. The lowest common denominator is the smallest number that is divisible by all of the denominators. Thus we are looking for the smallest number that is divisible by 6, 27, 5, 10, and 15. The smallest number that is divisible by 6 and 27 is 54. The smallest number that is divisible by 54 and 5 is 270. Since 270 is divisible by 10 and 15 also, it is the lowest common denominator. (110, 126)

42. Choice E is correct.
Percent deviation $= \frac{\text{absolute deviation}}{\text{average score}} \times 100\%$.

Absolute deviation = Ralph's score − average score $= 90 - 85 = 5$.
Percent deviation $= \frac{5}{85} \times 100\% = 500\% \div 85 = 5.88\%$ (approximately).
5.88% is closer to 5.9% than to 5.8%, so 5.9% is correct. (117)

43. Choice B is correct. If we discount 20% and then 12%, we are, in effect, taking 88% of 80% of the original price. Since "of" represents multiplication, when we deal with percent we can multiply 88% × 80% = 70.4%. This is a deduction of 29.6% from the original price. (119, 114)

44. Choice A is correct.
This is a simple proportion: $\frac{1 \text{ foot}}{\frac{1}{2} \text{ mile}} = \frac{\frac{1}{2} \text{ inch}}{x}$. Our first step must be to convert all these measurements to one unit. The most logical unit is the one our answer will take—feet. Thus, $\frac{1 \text{ ft.}}{2640 \text{ ft.}} = \frac{\frac{1}{24} \text{ ft.}}{x}$. (1 mile equals 5,280 feet.) Solving for x, we find $x = \frac{2640}{24}$ feet $= 110$ feet. (120, 121)

45. Choice A is correct. Let the two original sides of the rectangle be a and b, and the new sides be a' and b'. We know that $a' = 1.25a = \frac{5a}{4}$, and that $ab = (a')(b') = \frac{5a(b')}{4}$. Therefore, $b' = \left(\frac{4}{5}\right)b$, a decrease of $\frac{1}{5}$, or 20%. (122)

46. Choice C is correct. The first thing to notice is that these fractions are all approximately equal to 3. Thus, it will aid our comparison if we subtract 3 from each of the numbers and compare the remainders instead. The five remainders are: $\frac{-170}{2071}$, $\frac{-99}{1463}$, $\frac{-209}{1772}$, $\frac{+46}{2963}$, and $\frac{+123}{2631}$, respectively. We must find the smallest of these remainders, which is obviously the third one (the fourth and fifth are positive, and the other two are greater than $\frac{-1}{10}$).
Thus, the third choice, $\frac{5107}{1772}$, is the smallest one. (123–128)

47. Choice D is correct. The new prices are 80% of 130% of the original prices; multiplying 80% by 130%, we obtain 104%, which is the new price as a percent of the original one. Thus, the increase was 4%. (118)

48. Choice E is correct. $0.04\% = \frac{0.04}{100} = \frac{4}{10,000} = \frac{1}{2500}$. (107)

49. Choice D is correct. Before adding you should examine the numbers to be added. They form pairs, like this: $16 + (12 + 88) + (34 + 66) + (21 + 79) + (11 + 89)$, which equals $16 + 100 + 100 + 100 + 100 = 416$. Dividing 416 by 25, we obtain $16\frac{16}{25}$, which equals 16.64. (112)

50. Choice A is correct. We can set up a proportion as follows:

$\frac{1 \text{ coconut}}{1 \text{ banana}} = \frac{2}{1}$, $\frac{1 \text{ banana}}{1 \text{ grapefruit}} = \frac{1}{3}$, so by multiplying the two equations together $\left(\frac{1 \text{ coconut}}{1 \text{ banana}} \times \frac{1 \text{ banana}}{1 \text{ grapefruit}} \text{ and } \frac{2}{1} \times \frac{1}{3}\right)$ and canceling the bananas and the 1's in the numerators and denominators, we get: $\frac{1 \text{ coconut}}{1 \text{ grapefruit}} = \frac{2}{3}$.

(120)

Math Refresher
Session 2

Rate Problems: Distance and Time, Work, Mixture, and Cost

Word Problem Set-up

200. Some problems require translation of words into algebraic expressions or equations. For example: 8 more than 7 times a number is 22. Find the number. Let n = the number. We have

$$7n + 8 = 22 \qquad 7n = 14 \qquad n = 2$$

Another example: There are 3 times as many boys as girls in a class. What is the ratio of boys to the total number of students? Let n = number of girls. Then

$$3n = \text{number of boys}$$
$$4n = \text{Total number of students}$$

$$\frac{\text{number of boys}}{\text{Total students}} = \frac{3n}{4n} = \frac{3}{4}$$

201. Rate problems concern a special type of relationship that is very common: rate × input = output. This results from the definition of rate as *the ratio between output and input*. In these problems, input may represent any type of "investment," but the most frequent quantities used as inputs are time, work, and money. Output is usually distance traveled, work done, or money spent.

Note that the word *per*, as used in rates, signifies a ratio. Thus a rate of 25 miles per hour signifies the ratio between an output of 25 miles and an input of 1 hour.

Frequently, the word *per* will be represented by the fraction sign, thus $\frac{25 \text{ miles}}{1 \text{ hour}}$.

> **Example:** Peter can walk a mile in 10 minutes. He can travel a mile on his bicycle in 2 minutes. How far away is his uncle's house if Peter can walk there and bicycle back in 1 hour exactly?

To solve a rate problem such as the one above, follow these steps:

STEP 1. Determine the names of the quantities that represent input, output, and rate in the problem you are doing. In the example, Peter's input is *time*, and his output is *distance*. His rate will be *distance per unit of time*, which is commonly called *speed*.

STEP 2. Write down the fundamental relationship in terms of the quantities mentioned, making each the heading of a column. In the example, set up the table like this:

$$\text{speed} \times \text{time} = \text{distance}$$

STEP 3. Directly below the name of each quantity, write the unit of measurement in terms of the answer you want. Your choice of unit should be the most convenient one, but remember, once you have chosen a unit, you must convert all quantities to that unit.

We must select a unit of time. Since a *minute* was the unit used in the problem, it is the most logical choice. Similarly, we will choose a *mile* for our unit of distance. *Speed* (which is the ratio of distance to time) will therefore be expressed in *miles per minute*, usually abbreviated as mi/min. Thus, our chart now looks like this:

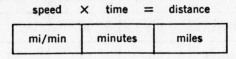

speed	× time =	distance
mi/min	minutes	miles

STEP 4. The problem will mention various situations in which some quantity of input is used to get a certain quantity of output. Represent each of these situations on a different line of the table, leaving blanks for unknown quantities.

In the sample problem, four situations are mentioned: Peter can walk a mile in 10 minutes; he can bicycle a mile in 2 minutes; he walks to his uncle's house; and he bicycles home. On the diagram, with the appropriate boxes filled, the problem will look like this:

	speed mi/min	× time = minutes	distance miles
1. walking		10	1
2. bicycling		2	1
3. walking			
4. bicycling			

STEP 5. From the chart and from the relationship at the top of the chart, quantities for filling some of the empty spaces may become obvious. Fill in these values directly.

In the example, on the first line of the chart, we see that the walking speed times 10 equals 1.

Thus, the walking *speed* is 0.1 mi/min (mi/min × 10 = 1 mi; mi/min = $\frac{1 \text{ mi}}{10 \text{ min}}$ = 0.1).

Similarly, on the second we see that the bicycle speed equals 0.5 mi/min. Furthermore, his walking speed shown on line 3 will be 0.1, the same speed as on line 1; and his bicycling speed shown on line 4 will equal the speed (0.05) shown on line 2. Adding this information to our table, we get:

	speed mi/min	× time = minutes	distance miles
1. walking	0.1	10	1
2. bicycling	0.5	2	1
3. walking	0.1		
4. bicycling	0.5		

STEP 6. Next, fill in the blanks with algebraic expressions to represent the quantities indicated, being careful to take advantage of simple relationships stated in the problem or appearing in the chart.

Continuing the example, we represent the time spent traveling shown on line 3 by x. According to the fundamental relationship, the distance traveled on this trip must be (0.1) x. Similarly, if y represents the time shown on line 4, the distance traveled is (0.5) y. Thus our chart now looks like this:

speed	×	time	=	distance

	mi/min	minutes	miles
1. walking	0.1	10	1
2. bicycling	0.5	2	1
3. walking	0.1	x	$(0.1)x$
4. bicycling	0.5	y	$(0.5)y$

STEP 7. Now, from the statement of the problem, you should be able to set up enough equations to solve for all the unknowns. In the example, there are two facts that we have not used yet. First, since Peter is going to his uncle's house and back, it is assumed that the distances covered on the two trips are equal. Thus we get the equation: $(0.1)x = (0.5)y$. We are told that the total time to and from his uncle's house is one hour. Since we are using minutes as our unit of time, we convert the one hour to 60 minutes. Thus we get the equation: $x + y = 60$. Solving these two equations ($0.1x = 0.5y$ and $x + y = 60$) algebraically, we find that $x = 50$ and $y = 10$. (See Section 407 for the solution of simultaneous equations.)

STEP 8. Now that you have all the information necessary, you can calculate the answer required. In the sample problem we are required to determine the distance to the uncle's house, which is $(0.1)x$ or $(0.5)y$. Using $x = 50$ or $y = 10$ gives us the distance as 5 miles.

Now that we have shown the fundamental steps in solving a rate problem, we shall discuss various types of rate problems.

Distance and Time

202. In *distance and time problems* the fundamental relationship that we use is *speed × time = distance*. Speed is the rate, time is the input, and distance is the output. The example in Section 201 was this type of problem.

> **Example:** In a sports-car race, David gives Kenny a head start of 10 miles. David's car goes 80 miles per hour and Kenny's car goes 60 miles per hour. How long should it take David to catch up to Kenny if they both leave their starting marks at the same time?

STEP 1. Here the fundamental quantities are *speed, time,* and *distance*.

STEP 2. The fundamental relationship is speed × time = distance. Write this at the top of the chart.

STEP 3. The unit for *distance* in this problem will be a *mile*. The unit for *speed* will be *miles per hour*. Since the speed is in miles per hour, our *time* will be in *hours*. Now our chart looks like this:

speed	×	time	=	distance

mi/hr	hours	miles

STEP 4. The problem offers us certain information that we can add to the chart. First we must make two horizontal rows, one for Kenny and one for David. We know that Kenny's speed is 60 miles per hour and that David's speed is 80 miles per hour.

STEP 5. In this case, none of the information in the chart can be used to calculate other information in the chart.

STEP 6. Now we must use algebraic expressions to represent the unknowns. We know that both Kenny and David travel for the same amount of time, but we do not know for how much time, so we will place an x in the space for each boy's time. Now from the relationship of speed × time = distance, we can calculate Kenny's distance as $60x$ and David's distance as $80x$. Now the chart looks like this:

speed	×	time	=	distance	
	mi/hr	**hours**		**miles**	
Kenny	60	x		$60x$	
David	80	x		$80x$	

STEP 7. From the statement of the problem we know that David gave Kenny a 10-mile head start. In other words, David's distance is 10 more miles than Kenny's distance. This can be stated algebraically as $60x + 10 = 80x$. That is, Kenny's distance + 10 miles = David's distance. Solving for x gives us $x = \dfrac{1}{2}$.

STEP 8. The question asks how much time is required for David to catch up to Kenny. If we look at the chart, we see that this time is x, and x has already been calculated as $\dfrac{1}{2}$ so the answer is $\dfrac{1}{2}$ hour.

Work

203. In *work problems* the input is time and output is the amount of work done. The rate is the work per unit of time.

Example: Jack can chop down 20 trees in 1 hour, whereas it takes Ted $1\dfrac{1}{2}$ hours to chop down 18 trees. If the two of them work together, how long will it take them to chop down 48 trees?

Solution: By the end of Step 5 your chart should look like this:

rate	×	time	=	work
	trees/hr.	**hours**		**trees**
1. Jack	20	1		20
2. Ted	12	$1\frac{1}{2}$		18
3. Jack	20			
4. Ted	12			

In Step 6, we represent the time that it takes Jack by x in line 3. Since we have the relationship that rate × time = work, we see that in line 3 the work is $20x$. Since the two boys work together (therefore, for the same amount of time), the time in line 4 must be x, and the work must be $12x$. Now, in Step 7, we see that the total work is 48 trees. From lines 3 and 4, then $20x + 12x = 48$. Solving for x gives us $x = 1\dfrac{1}{2}$. We are asked to find the number of hours needed by the boys to chop down the 48 trees together, and we see that this time is x, or $1\frac{1}{2}$ hours.

Mixture

204. In *mixture problems* you are given a percent or a fractional composition of a substance, and you are asked questions about the weights and compositions of the substances. The basic relationship here is that the percentage of a certain substance in a mixture × the amount of the mixture = the amount of substance.

Note that it is often better to change percents to decimals because it makes it easier to avoid errors.

Example: A chemist has two quarts of 25% acid solution and one quart of 40% acid solution. If he mixes these, what will be the concentration of the mixture?

Solution: Let x = concentration of the mixture. At the end of Step 6, our table will look like this:

	rate × $\dfrac{\text{qt (acid)}}{\text{qt (sol)}}$	amount of sol = qts (sol)	amount of acid = qts (acid)
25%, solution	0.25	2	0.50
40% solution	0.40	1	0.40
mixture	x	3	$3x$

We now have one additional bit of information: The amount of acid in the mixture must be equal to the total amount of acid in each of the two parts, so $3x = 0.50 + 0.40$. Therefore x is equal to 0.30, which is the same as a 30% concentration of the acid in the mixture.

Cost

205. In *cost problems* the rate is the *price per item*, the input is the *number of items*, and the output is the *value* of the items considered. When you are dealing with dollars and cents, you must be very careful to use the decimal point correctly.

Example: Jim has $3.00 in nickels and dimes in his pocket. If he has twice as many nickels as he has dimes, how many coins does he have altogether?

Solution: After Step 6, our chart should look like this (where c is the number of dimes Jim has):

	rate × cents/coin	number = coins	value = cents
nickels	5	$2c$	$10c$
dimes	10	c	$10c$

Now we recall the additional bit of information that the total value of the nickels and dimes is $3.00, or 300 cents. Thus, $5(2c) + 10c = 300$; $20c = 300$; so $c = 15$, the number of dimes. Jim has twice as many nickels, so $2c = 30$.

The total number of coins is $c + 2c = 3c = 45$.

The following table will serve as review for this Refresher Section.

TYPE OF PROBLEM	FUNDAMENTAL RELATIONSHIP
distance	speed $\times$ time = distance
work	rate $\times$ time = work done
mixture	concentration $\times$ amount of solution = amount of ingredient
cost	rate $\times$ number of items = value

Practice Test 2

Rate Problems: Distance and Time, Work, Mixture, and Cost

Correct answers and solutions follow each test.

1. A B C D E

1. A man rowed 3 miles upstream in 90 minutes. If the river flowed with a current of 2 miles per hour, how long did the man's return trip take?

   (A) 20 minutes
   (B) 30 minutes
   (C) 45 minutes
   (D) 60 minutes
   (E) 80 minutes

2. A B C D E

2. Charles can do a job in 1 hour, Bill can do the same job in 2 hours, and Bob can do the job in 3 hours. How long does it take them to do the job working together?

   (A) $\frac{6}{11}$ hours
   (B) $\frac{1}{2}$ hour
   (C) 6 hours
   (D) $\frac{1}{3}$ hours
   (E) $\frac{1}{6}$ hours

3. A B C D E

3. Mr. Smith had $2,000 to invest. He invested part of it at 5% per year and the remainder at 4% per year. After one year, his investment grew to $2,095. How much of the original investment was at the 5% rate?

   (A) $500
   (B) $750
   (C) $1,000
   (D) $1,250
   (E) $1,500

4. A B C D E

4. A man walks down the road for half an hour at an average speed of 3 miles per hour. He waits 10 minutes for a bus, which brings him back to his starting point at 3:15. If the man began his walk at 2:25 the same afternoon, what was the average speed of the bus?

   (A) 1.5 miles per hour
   (B) 3 miles per hour
   (C) 4.5 miles per hour
   (D) 6 miles per hour
   (E) 9 miles per hour

5. A B C D E

5. Faucet A lets water flow into a 5-gallon tub at a rate of 1.5 gallons per minute. Faucet B lets water flow into the same tub at a rate of 1.0 gallons per minute. Faucet A runs alone for 100 seconds; then the two of them together finish filling up the tub. How long does the whole operation take?

   (A) 120 seconds
   (B) 150 seconds
   (C) 160 seconds
   (D) 180 seconds
   (E) 190 seconds

6. A B C D E

6. Coffee A normally costs 75¢ per pound. It is mixed with Coffee B, which normally costs 80¢ per pound, to form a mixture that costs 78¢ per pound. If there are 10 pounds of the mix, how many pounds of Coffee A were used in the mix?

(A) 3
(B) 4
(C) 4.5
(D) 5
(E) 6

7. A B C D E

7. If a man can run p miles in x minutes, how long will it take him to run q miles at the same rate?

(A) $\dfrac{pq}{x}$ minutes

(B) $\dfrac{px}{q}$ minutes

(C) $\dfrac{q}{px}$ minutes

(D) $\dfrac{qx}{p}$ minutes

(E) $\dfrac{x}{pq}$ minutes

8. A B C D E

8. A train went 300 miles from City X to City Y at an average rate of 80 mph. At what speed did it travel on the way back if its average speed for the whole trip was 100 mph?

(A) 120 mph
(B) 125 mph
(C) $133\dfrac{1}{3}$ mph
(D) $137\dfrac{1}{2}$ mph
(E) 150 mph

9. A B C D E

9. A man spent exactly $2.50 on 3¢, 6¢, and 10¢ stamps. If he bought ten 3¢ stamps and twice as many 6¢ stamps as 10¢ stamps, how many 10¢ stamps did he buy?

(A) 5
(B) 10
(C) 12
(D) 15
(E) 20

10. A B C D E

10. If 6 workers can complete 9 identical jobs in 3 days, how long will it take 4 workers to complete 10 such jobs?

(A) 3 days
(B) 4 days
(C) 5 days
(D) 6 days
(E) more than 6 days

11. A B C D E

11. A barge travels twice as fast when it is empty as when it is full. If it travels 20 miles north with a cargo, spends 20 minutes unloading, and returns to its original port empty, taking 8 hours to complete the entire trip, what is the speed of the barge when it is empty?

(A) less than 3 mph
(B) less than 4 mph but not less than 3 mph
(C) less than 6 mph but not less than 4 mph
(D) less than 8 mph but not less than 6 mph
(E) 8 mph or more

12. A B C D E

12. Bill can hammer 20 nails in 6 minutes. Jeff can do the same job in only 5 minutes. How long will it take them to finish if Bill hammers the first 5 nails, then Jeff hammers for 3 minutes, then Bill finishes the job?

(A) 4.6 minutes
(B) 5.0 minutes
(C) 5.4 minutes
(D) 5.8 minutes
(E) 6.0 minutes

13. A B C D E

13. Jack has two quarts of a 30% acid solution and three pints of a 20% solution. If he mixes them, what will be the concentration (to the nearest percent) of the resulting solution?

(A) 22%
(B) 23%
(C) 24%
(D) 25%
(E) 26%

14. A B C D E

14. Robert has 12 coins totaling $1.45. None of his coins is larger than a quarter. Which of the following *cannot* be the number of quarters he has?

(A) 1
(B) 2
(C) 3
(D) 4
(E) 5

15. A B C D E

15. Jim's allowance is $1.20 per week. Stan's is 25¢ per day. How long will they have to save, if they save both their allowances together, before they can get a model car set that costs $23.60?

(A) 6 weeks
(B) 8 weeks
(C) 10 weeks
(D) 13 weeks
(E) 16 weeks

16. A B C D E

16. Chuck can earn money at the following schedule: $2.00 for the first hour, $2.50 an hour for the next two hours, and $3.00 an hour after that. He also has the opportunity of taking a different job that pays $2.75 an hour. He wants to work until he has earned $15.00. Which of the following is true?

(A) The first job will take him longer by 15 minutes or more.
(B) The first job will take him longer by less than 15 minutes.
(C) The two jobs will take the same length of time.
(D) The second job will take him longer by 30 minutes or more.
(E) The second job will take him longer by less than 10 minutes.

17. A B C D E

17. If Robert can seal 40 envelopes in one minute, and Paul can do the same job in 80 seconds, how many minutes (to the nearest minute) will it take the two of them, working together, to seal 350 envelopes?

(A) 4 minutes
(B) 5 minutes
(C) 6 minutes
(D) 7 minutes
(E) 8 minutes

18. A B C D E

18. Towns A and B are 400 miles apart. If a train leaves A in the direction of B at 50 miles per hour, how long will it take before that train meets another train, going from B to A, at a speed of 30 miles per hour?

(A) 4 hours
(B) $4\frac{1}{3}$ hours
(C) 5 hours
(D) $5\frac{2}{3}$ hours
(E) $6\frac{2}{3}$ hours

19. A B C D E

19. A tub is shaped like a rectangular solid, with internal measurements of 2 feet × 2 feet × 5 feet. If two faucets, each with an output of 2 cubic feet of water per minute, pour water into the tub simultaneously, how many minutes does it take to fill the tub completely?

(A) less than 3 minutes
(B) less than 4 minutes, but not less than 3
(C) less than 5 minutes, but not less than 4
(D) less than 6 minutes, but not less than 5
(E) 6 minutes or more

20. A B C D E

20. A 30% solution of barium chloride is mixed with 10 grams of water to form a 20% solution. How many grams of the original solution did we start with?

(A) 10
(B) 15
(C) 20
(D) 25
(E) 30

21. A B C D E

21. Mr. Adams had a coin collection including only nickels, dimes, and quarters. He had twice as many dimes as he had nickels, and half as many quarters as he had nickels. If the total face value of his collection was $300.00, how many quarters did the collection contain?

(A) 75
(B) 100
(C) 250
(D) 400
(E) 800

22. A B C D E

22. A storekeeper stocks a high-priced pen and a lower-priced model. If he sells the high-priced pens, which yield a profit of $1.20 per pen sold, he can sell 30 in a month. If he sells the lower-priced pens, making a profit of 15¢ per pen sold, he can sell 250 pens in a month. Which type of pen will yield more profit per month, and by how much?

(A) The cheaper pen will yield a greater profit, by $1.50.
(B) The more expensive pen will yield a greater profit, by $1.50.
(C) The cheaper pen will yield a greater profit, by 15¢.
(D) The more expensive pen will yield a greater profit, by 15¢.
(E) Both pens will yield exactly the same profit.

23. A B C D E

23. At a cost of $2.50 per square yard, what would be the price of carpeting a rectangular floor, 18′ × 24′?

(A) $120
(B) $360
(C) $750
(D) $1,000
(E) $1,080

24. A B C D E

24. Tom and Bill agreed to race across a 50-foot pool and back again. They started together, but Tom finished 10 feet ahead of Bill. If their rates were constant, and Tom finished the race in 27 seconds, how long did Bill take to finish it?

(A) 28 seconds
(B) 30 seconds
(C) $33\frac{1}{3}$ seconds
(D) 35 seconds
(E) 37 seconds

25. A B C D E

25. If four men need $24.00 worth of food for a three-day camping trip, how much will two men need for a two-week trip?

(A) $12.00
(B) $24.00
(C) $28.00
(D) $42.00
(E) $56.00

26. A B C D E

26. A man walks 15 blocks to work every morning at a rate of 2 miles per hour. If there are 20 blocks in a mile, how long does it take him to walk to work?

(A) $12\frac{1}{2}$ minutes

(B) 15 minutes
(C) $22\frac{1}{2}$ minutes

(D) $37\frac{1}{2}$ minutes

(E) 45 minutes

27.   A   B   C   D   E

27. A certain river has a current of 3 miles per hour. A boat takes twice as long to travel upstream between two points as it does to travel downstream between the same two points. What is the speed of the boat in still water?

(A) 3 miles per hour
(B) 6 miles per hour
(C) 9 miles per hour
(D) 12 miles per hour
(E) The speed cannot be determined from the given information.

28.   A   B   C   D   E

28. Stan can run 10 miles per hour, whereas Jack can run only 8 miles per hour. If they start at the same time from the same point and run in opposite directions, how far apart (to the nearest mile) will they be after 10 minutes?

(A) 1 mile
(B) 2 miles
(C) 3 miles
(D) 4 miles
(E) 5 miles

29.   A   B   C   D   E

29. Machine A can produce 40 bolts per minute, whereas Machine B can produce only 30 per minute. Machine A begins alone to make bolts, but it breaks down after $1\frac{1}{2}$ minutes, and Machine B must complete the job. If the job requires 300 bolts, how long does the whole operation take?

(A) $7\frac{1}{2}$ minutes

(B) 8 minutes
(C) $8\frac{1}{2}$ minutes

(D) 9 minutes
(E) $9\frac{1}{2}$ minutes

30.   A   B   C   D   E

30. Ten pints of 15% salt solution are mixed with 15 pints of 10% salt solution. What is the concentration of the resulting solution?

(A) 10%
(B) 12%
(C) 12.5%
(D) 13%
(E) 15%

31.   A   B   C   D   E

31. Jeff makes $5.00 every day, from which he must spend $3.00 for various expenses. Pete makes $10.00 a day but has to spend $7.00 each day for expenses. If the two of them save together, how long will it take before they can buy a $150 car?

(A) 10 days
(B) 15 days
(C) 30 days
(D) 50 days
(E) 75 days

32. A B C D E

32. Two cities are 800 miles apart. At 3:00 P.M., Plane A leaves one city, traveling toward the other city at a speed of 600 miles per hour. At 4:00 the same afternoon, Plane B leaves the first city, traveling in the same direction at a rate of 800 miles per hour. Which of the following answers represents the actual result?

(A) Plane A arrives first, by an hour or more.
(B) Plane A arrives first, by less than an hour.
(C) The two planes arrive at exactly the same time.
(D) Plan A arrives after Plane B, by less than an hour.
(E) Plane A arrives after Plane B, by an hour or more.

33. A B C D E

33. Peter has as many nickels as Charlie has dimes; Charlie has twice as many nickels as Peter has dimes. If together they have $2.50 in nickels and dimes, how many nickels does Peter have?

(A) 1 nickel
(B) 4 nickels
(C) 7 nickels
(D) 10 nickels
(E) The answer cannot be determined from the given information.

34. A B C D E

34. A man can travel 120 miles in either of two ways. He can travel at a constant rate of 40 miles per hour, or he can travel halfway at 50 miles per hour, then slow down to 30 miles per hour for the second 60 miles. Which way is faster, and by how much?

(A) The constant rate is faster by 10 minutes or more.
(B) The constant rate is faster by less than 10 minutes.
(C) The two ways take exactly the same time.
(D) The constant rate is slower by less than 10 minutes.
(E) The constant rate is slower by 10 minutes or more.

35. A B C D E

35. John walks 10 miles at an average rate of 2 miles per hour and returns on a bicycle at an average rate of 10 miles per hour. How long (to the nearest hour) does the entire trip take him?

(A) 3 hours
(B) 4 hours
(C) 5 hours
(D) 6 hours
(E) 7 hours

36. A B C D E

36. If a plane can travel P miles in Q hours, how long will it take to travel R miles?

(A) $\dfrac{PQ}{R}$ hours

(B) $\dfrac{P}{QR}$ hours

(C) $\dfrac{QR}{P}$ hours

(D) $\dfrac{Q}{PR}$ hours

(E) $\dfrac{PR}{Q}$ hours

37. A B C D E

37. A boy can swim 75 feet in 12 seconds. What is his rate to the nearest mile per hour?

(A) 1 mph
(B) 2 mph
(C) 3 mph
(D) 4 mph
(E) 5 mph

38. A B C D E

38. How many pounds of a $1.20-per-pound nut mixture must be mixed with two pounds of a 90¢-per-pound mixture to produce a mixture that sells for $1.00 per pound?

(A) 0.5
(B) 1.0
(C) 1.5
(D) 2.0
(E) 2.5

39. A B C D E

39. A broken clock is set correctly at 12:00 noon. However, it registers only 20 minutes for each hour. In how many hours will it again register the correct time?

(A) 12
(B) 18
(C) 24
(D) 30
(E) 36

40. A B C D E

40. If a man travels p hours at an average rate of q miles per hour, and then r hours at an average rate of s miles per hour, what is his overall average rate of speed?

(A) $\dfrac{pq + rs}{p + r}$

(B) $\dfrac{q + s}{2}$

(C) $\dfrac{q + s}{p + r}$

(D) $\dfrac{p}{q} + \dfrac{r}{s}$

(E) $\dfrac{p}{s} + \dfrac{r}{q}$

41. A B C D E

41. If Walt can paint 25 feet of fence in an hour, and Joe can paint 35 feet in an hour, how many minutes will it take them to paint a 150-foot fence, if they work together?

(A) 150
(B) 200
(C) 240
(D) 480
(E) 500

42. A B C D E

42. If a man travels for a half hour at a rate of 20 miles per hour, and for another half hour at a rate of 30 miles per hour, what is his average speed?

(A) 24 miles per hour
(B) 25 miles per hour
(C) 26 miles per hour
(D) 26.5 miles per hour
(E) The answer cannot be determined from the given information.

43.

A B C D E

43. New York is 3,000 miles from Los Angeles. Sol leaves New York aboard a plane heading toward Los Angeles at the same time that Robert leaves Los Angeles aboard a plane heading toward New York. If Sol is moving at 200 miles per hour and Robert is moving at 400 miles per hour, how soon will one plane pass the other?

(A) 2 hours
(B) $22\frac{1}{2}$ hours
(C) 5 hours
(D) 4 hours
(E) 12 hours

44.

A B C D E

44. A man exchanged a dollar bill for change and received 7 coins, none of which were half dollars. How many of these coins were dimes?

(A) 0
(B) 1
(C) 4
(D) 5
(E) The answer cannot be determined from the information given.

45.

A B C D E

45. A man adds two quarts of pure alcohol to a 30% solution of alcohol in water. If the new concentration is 40%, how many quarts of the original solution were there?

(A) 12
(B) 15
(C) 18
(D) 20
(E) 24

46.

A B C D E

46. A certain power company charges 8¢ per kilowatt-hour for the first 1000 kilowatt-hours, and 6¢ per kilowatt-hour after that. If a man uses a 900-watt toaster for 5 hours, a 100-watt lamp for 25 hours, and a 5-watt clock for 400 hours, how much is he charged for the power he uses? (1 kilowatt = 1,000 watts)

(A) 56¢
(B) 64¢
(C) 72¢
(D) $560.00
(E) $720.00

47.

A B C D E

47. At 30¢ per yard, what is the price of 96 inches of ribbon?

(A) 72¢
(B) 75¢
(C) 80¢
(D) 84¢
(E) 90¢

48.

A B C D E

48. A man travels for 6 hours at a rate of 50 miles per hour. His return trip takes him $7\frac{1}{2}$ hours. What is his average speed for the whole trip?

(A) 44.4 miles per hour
(B) 45.0 miles per hour
(C) 46.8 miles per hour
(D) 48.2 miles per hour
(E) 50.0 miles per hour

49. A B C D E

49. Stanley puts $100 in the bank for two years at 5% interest compounded annually. At the end of the two years, what was his balance?

(A) $100.00
(B) $105.00
(C) $105.25
(D) $110.00
(E) $110.25

50. A B C D E

50. A 12-gallon tub has a faucet that lets water in at a rate of 3 gallons per minute, and a drain that lets water out at a rate of 1.5 gallons per minute. If you start with 3 gallons of water in the tub, how long will it take to fill the tub completely?

(A) 3 minutes
(B) 4 minutes
(C) 6 minutes
(D) 7.5 minutes
(E) 8 minutes

Answer Key for Practice Test 2

1. B	14. A	27. C	39. B
2. A	15. B	28. C	40. A
3. E	16. B	29. E	41. A
4. E	17. B	30. B	42. B
5. C	18. C	31. C	43. C
6. B	19. D	32. B	44. E
7. D	20. C	33. E	45. A
8. C	21. D	34. A	46. C
9. B	22. A	35. D	47. C
10. C	23. A	36. C	48. A
11. D	24. B	37. D	49. E
12. C	25. E	38. B	50. C
13. E	26. C		

Answers and Solutions for Practice Test 2

1. **Choice B is correct.** The fundamental relationship here is: rate × time = distance. The easiest units to work with are miles per hour for the rate, hours for time, and miles for distance. Note that the word *per* indicates division because when calculating a rate, we *divide* the number of miles (distance units) by the number of hours (time units).

   We can set up our chart with the information given. We know that the upstream trip took $1\frac{1}{2}$ hours (90 minutes) and that the distance was 3 miles. Thus the upstream rate was 2 miles per hour. The downstream distance was also 3 miles, but we use t for the time, which is unknown. Thus the downstream rate was $\frac{3}{t}$. Our chart looks like this:

	rate	× time	= distance
	mi/hr	hours	miles
upstream	2	$1\frac{1}{2}$	3
downstream	$\frac{3}{t}$	t	3

   We use the rest of the information to solve for t. We know that the speed of the current is 2 miles per hour. We assume the boat to be in still water and assign it a speed, s; then the upstream (against the current) speed of the boat is $s - 2$ miles per hour. Since $s - 2 = 2$, $s = 4$.

Now the speed of the boat downstream (with the current) is $s + 2$, or 6 miles per hour. This is equal to $\frac{3}{t}$, and we get the equation $\frac{3}{t} = 6$, so $t = \frac{1}{2}$ hour. We must be careful with our units because the answer must be in minutes. We can convert $\frac{1}{2}$ hour to 30 minutes to get the final answer. (201, 202)

2. **Choice A is correct.**

	rate	× time	= work
	job/hr	hours	jobs
Charles	1	1	1
Bill	$\frac{1}{2}$	2	1
Bob	$\frac{1}{3}$	3	1
together	r	t	1

   Let r = rate together and t = time together.

   Now, $r = 1 + \frac{1}{2} + \frac{1}{3} = \frac{11}{6}$ because *whenever two or more people are working together, their joint rate is the sum of their individual rates.* This is not necessarily true of the time or the work done. In this case, we know that $r \times t = 1$ and $r = \frac{11}{6}$, so $t = \frac{6}{11}$. (201, 203)

3. **Choice E is correct.**

	rate	× principal	= interest
	$/$	$	$
5%	0.05	x	0.05x
4%	0.04	y	0.04y

   Let x = part of the \$2,000 invested at 5%. Let y = part of \$2,000 invested at 4%. We know that since the whole \$2,000 was invested, $x + y$ must equal \$2,000. Furthermore, we know that the sum of the interests on both investments equaled \$95, so $0.05x + 0.04x = 95$. Since we have to solve only for x, we can express this as $0.01x + 0.04x + 0.04y = 95$. Then we factor out 0.04. Thus $0.01x + 0.04(x + y) = 95$. Since we know that $x + y = 2,000$, we have $0.01x + 0.04(2,000) = 95$; $0.01x + 80 = 95$, and $x = 1,500$. Thus, \$1,500 was invested at 5%. (201,205)

4. Choice E is correct.

	rate	×	times	=	distance
	mi/min		min		miles
walk	$\frac{1}{20}$		30		a
wait	0		l		0
bus	r		t		a

Let a = distance the man walks. Since the man walks at 3 miles per hour, he walks at $\frac{3 \text{ mi}}{60 \text{ min}}$ or $\frac{1 \text{ mi}}{20 \text{ min}}$. From this we can find $a = \frac{1 \text{ mi}}{20 \text{ min}} \times 30 \text{ min} = 1\frac{1}{2}$ miles. The total time he spent was 50 minutes (the difference between 3:15 and 2:25), and $30 + 10 + t = 50$, so t must be equal to 10 minutes. This reduces our problem to the simple equation $10r = 1\frac{1}{2}$ (where r = rate of the bus), and, on solving, $r = 0.15$ miles per minute. But the required answer is in miles per hour. In one hour, or 60 minutes, the bus can travel 60 times as far as the 0.15 miles it travels in one minute, so that the bus travels $60 \times 0.15 = 9$ miles per hour.

(201, 202)

5. Choice C is correct.

	rate	×	time	=	water
	gal/min		min		gal
A only	1.5		$\frac{5}{3}$*		2.5
B only	1.0		0		0
A and B	2.5		t		x

*($\frac{5}{3}$ min = 100 sec)

Let t = time faucets A and B run together.

Let x = amount of water delivered when A and B run together.

We know that the total number of gallons is 5, and A alone delivers 2.5 gallons (1.5 gal/min × $\frac{5}{3}$ min = 2.5 gal), so x equals 2.5. This leads us to the simple equation $2.5t = 2.5$, so $t = 1$ minute, or 60 seconds. Thus, the whole operation takes $\frac{5}{3} + t$ minutes, or 100 + 60 seconds, totaling 160 seconds.

(201, 203)

6. Choice B is correct.

	rate	×	amount	=	cost
	¢/lb		lb		¢
Coffee A	75		x		$75x$
Coffee B	80		y		$80y$
mix	78		10		780

Let x = weight of Coffee A in the mix.

Let y = weight of Coffee B in the mix.

We know that the weight of the mix is equal to the sum of the weights of its components. Thus, $x + y = 10$. Similarly, the cost of the mix is equal to the sum of the costs of the components. Thus, $75x + 80y = 780$. Solving these two equations simultaneously gives us $x = 4$ and $y = 6$, so 4 pounds of Coffee A were used. (201, 204, 407)

7. Choice D is correct.

	rate	×	time	=	distance
	mi/min		min		miles
first run	r		x		p
second run	r		t		q

Let r = rate of the man.

Let t = time it takes him to run q miles.

From the first line, we know that $rx = p$, then $r = \frac{p}{x}$. Substituting this in the second line, we get $\left(\frac{p}{x}\right)t = q$, so $t = q\left(\frac{x}{p}\right)$, or $\frac{qx}{p}$ minutes. (201, 202)

8. Choice C is correct.

	rate	×	time	=	distance
	mi/hr		hrs		miles
X to Y	80		t		300
Y to X	r		s		300
whole trip	100		$s + t$		600

Let t = time from city X to city Y.

Let s = time from city Y to city X.

Let r = rate of the train from Y to X.

We know that $80t = 300$, so $t = \dfrac{300}{80}$, or $\dfrac{15}{4}$. Also, $100(s + t) = 600$, so $s + t = 6$. This and the last equation lead us to the conclusion that $s = 6 - \dfrac{15}{4}$, or $\dfrac{9}{4}$. Now, from the middle line, we have $r\left(\dfrac{9}{4}\right) = 300$, so $r = \dfrac{400}{3}$, or $133\dfrac{1}{3}$ miles per hour. (Note that the reason why we chose the equations in this particular order was that it is easiest to concentrate first on those with the most data already given.) (201, 202)

9. Choice B is correct.

	rate ×	number =	cost
	¢/stamp	stamps	¢
3¢ stamps	3	10	30
10¢ stamps	10	x	$10x$
6¢ stamps	6	$2x$	$12x$

Let x = the number of 10¢ stamps bought.

We know that the total cost is 250¢, so $30 + 10x + 12x = 250$. This is the same as $22x = 220$, so $x = 10$. Therefore, he bought ten 10¢ stamps. (201, 205)

10. Choice C is correct.

	rate ×	time =	work
	jb/day	days	jobs
6 workers	$6r$	3	9
4 workers	$4r$	t	10

Let r = rate of one worker.

Let t = time for 4 workers to do 10 jobs.

From the first line, we have $18r = 9$, so $r = \frac{1}{2}$. Substituting this in the second line, $4r = 2$, so $2t = 10$. Therefore, $t = 5$. The workers will take 5 days. (201, 203)

11. Choice D is correct.

	rate ×	time =	distance
	mi/hr	hrs	miles
north	r	$\dfrac{20}{r}$	20
unload	0	$\dfrac{1}{3}$	0
return	$2r$	$\dfrac{10}{r}$	20

Let r = loaded rate; then

$2r$ = empty rate

Total time $= \dfrac{20}{r} + \dfrac{1}{3} + \dfrac{10}{r} = 8$ hours.

Multiplying by $3r$ on both sides, we get $90 = 23r$, so $r = 90 \div 23$, or about 3.9 miles per hour. However, the problem asks for the speed *when empty*, which is $2r$, or 7.8. This is less than 8 mph, but not less than 6 mph. (201, 202)

12. Choice C is correct.

	rate ×	time =	work
	nl/min	min	nails
Bill	r	6	20
Jeff	s	5	20
Bill	r	$\dfrac{5}{r}$	5
Jeff	s	3	$3s$
Bill	r	$\dfrac{x}{r}$	x

r = Bill's rate

s = Jeff's rate

x = number of nails left after Jeff takes his turn.

$6r = 20$, so $r = 3\dfrac{1}{3}$

$5s = 20$, so $s = 4$

Total work $= 5 + 3s + x = 20 = 5 + 12 + x$, so $x = 3$. Thus $\dfrac{x}{r} = 0.9$

Total time $= \dfrac{5}{r} + 3 + \dfrac{x}{r} = 1.5 + 3 + 0.9 = 5.4$.

(201, 203)

13. Choice E is correct.

	% acid	pts	pts
old sol	30%	4	1.2
	20%	3	0.6
new sol	x%	7	1.8

concentration × volume = amount of acid

2 qts = 4 pts

Let x% = concentration of new solution.

4 pts of 30% + 3 pts of 20% = 7 pts of x%

1.2 pts + 0.6 pt = 1.8 pts

$(x\%)\,(7) = 1.8$, so $x = 180 \div 7 = 25.7$ (approximately), which is closest to 26%.   (201, 204)

14. Choice A is correct.

	¢/coin	coins	cents
pennies	1	p	p
nickels	5	n	$5n$
dimes	10	d	$10d$
quarters	25	q	$25q$

coin × number = total value

Let p = number of pennies

n = number of nickels

d = number of dimes

q = number of quarters

Total number of coins = $p + n + d + q = 12$

Total value = $p + 5n + 10d + 25q = 145$

Now, if $q = 1$, then $p + n + d = 11$, $p + 5n + 10d = 120$. But in this case, the greatest possible value of the other eleven coins would be the value of eleven dimes, or 110 cents, which falls short of the amount necessary to give a total of 145 cents for the twelve coins put together. Therefore, Robert cannot have only one quarter.   (201, 205)

15. Choice B is correct.

	¢/wk	weeks	cents
Jim	120	w	$120w$
Stan	175	w	$175w$
together	295	w	$295w$

rate × time = money

(25¢/day = $1.75/week)

Let w = the number of weeks they save.

Total money = $295w = 2,360$.

Therefore, $w = 2,360 \div 295 = 8$.

So, they must save for 8 weeks.   (201, 205)

16. Choice B is correct.

	¢/hr	hours	¢
first job	200	1	200
	250	2	500
	300	x	$300x$
second job	275	y	$275y$

rate × time = pay

Let x = hours at $3.00.

Let y = hours at $2.75.

Total pay first job = $200 + 500 + 300x = 1,500$, so $x = 2\frac{2}{3}$

Total time first job = $1 + 2 + 2\frac{2}{3} = 5\frac{2}{3}$

Total pay second job = $275y = 1500$, so $y = 5\frac{5}{11}$

Total time second job = $5\frac{5}{11}$.

$\frac{2}{3}$ hour = 40 minutes

$\frac{5}{11}$ hour = 27.2727 ... minutes (less than $\frac{2}{3}$ hour)

Thus, the first job will take him longer by less than 15 minutes.

17. Choice B is correct.

	rate ×	time =	work
	envelopes/min	min	envelopes
Robert	40	t	$40t$
Paul	30	t	$30t$
both	70	t	$70t$

Let t = time to seal 350 envelopes.

Paul's rate is 30 envelopes/minute, as shown by the proportion:

$$\text{rate} = \frac{40 \text{ envelopes}}{80 \text{ seconds}} = \frac{30 \text{ envelopes}}{60 \text{ seconds}}$$

Total work = $70t$ = 350, so t = 5 minutes.

(201, 203)

18. Choice C is correct.

	rate ×	time =	distance
	mi/hr	hr	miles
A to B	50	t	$50t$
B to A	30	t	$30t$

Let t = time to meet

Total distance traveled by two trains together equals $50t + 30t = 80t = 400$ miles, so t = 5 hrs.

(201, 202)

19. Choice D is correct.

	rate ×	time =	amount of water
	cu. ft/m	min	cu. ft.
2 faucets	4	t	20

Let t = time to fill the tub.

Volume of tub = $2' \times 2' \times 5'$ = 20 cu. ft.

Rate = 2 × rate of each faucet = 2 × 2 cu. ft./min. = 4 cu. ft./min.

Therefore, t = 5 minutes. (201, 203)

20. Choice C is correct.

	concentration ×	weight =	amount of barium chloride
	%	grams	grams
original	30%	x	$0.30x$
water	0%	10	0
new	20%	$10 + x$	$0.30x$

Let x = number of grams of original solution.

Total weight and amounts of barium chloride may be added by column.

$(20\%) \times (10 + x) = 0.30x$, so $10 + x = 1.50x$, $x = 20$. (201, 204)

21. Choice D is correct.

	coin ×	number =	value
	¢/coin	coins	cents
nickels	5	n	$5n$
dimes	10	$2n$	$20n$
quarters	25	$\dfrac{n}{2}$	$\dfrac{25n}{2}$

Let n = number of nickels.

Total value $= 5n + 20n + \dfrac{25n}{2} = \left(37\dfrac{1}{2}\right)n = 30{,}000$

Thus, $n = 30{,}000 \div 37\dfrac{1}{2} = 800$.

The number of quarters is then $\dfrac{n}{2} = \dfrac{800}{2} = 400$.

(201, 205)

22. Choice A is correct.

	rate ×	number =	profit
	¢/pen	pens	cents
high-price	120	30	3600
low-price	15	250	3750

Subtracting 3,600¢ from 3,750¢, we get 150¢.

Thus, the cheaper pen yields a profit of 150¢, or $1.50, more per month than the more expensive one. (201, 205)

23. Choice A is correct.

price ×	area =	cost
$/sq yd	sq yd	dollars
2.50	48	120

Area must be expressed in square yards; $18' = 6$ yds, and $24' = 8$ yds, so $18' \times 24' = 6$ yds $\times$ 8 yds $= 48$ sq yds. The cost would then be $\$2.50 \times 48 = \$120.00$. (201, 205)

24. Choice B is correct.

	rate ×	time =	distance
	ft/sec	sec	feet
Tom	r	27	100
Bill	s	27	90
Bill	s	t	100

Let r = Tom's rate.

Let s = Bill's rate.

Let t = Bill's time to finish the race.

$27r = 100$, so $r = \dfrac{100}{27}$;

$27s = 90$, so $s = \dfrac{90}{27} = \dfrac{10}{3}$;

$st = 100$, and $s = \dfrac{10}{3}$, so $\dfrac{10t}{3} = 100$, thus $t = 30$. (201, 202)

25. Choice E is correct. This is a rate problem in which the fundamental relationship is rate $\times$ time $\times$ number of men = cost. The rate is in dollars/man-days. Thus, our chart looks like this:

	rate ×	time ×	number =	cost
	$/man-days	days	men	$
1st trip	r	3	4	$12r$
2nd trip	r	14	2	$28r$

The cost of the first trip is $24, so $12r = 24$ and $r = 2$.

The cost of the second trip is $28r$, or $56. (201, 205)

26. Choice C is correct.

rate ×	time =	distance
blocks/min.	min	blocks
$\dfrac{2}{3}$	t	15

Let t = time to walk to work.

2 miles/hr = 2 (20 blocks)/(60 min) = $\dfrac{2}{3}$ blocks/minute

$t = 15 \div \dfrac{2}{3} = 22\dfrac{1}{2}$ minutes. (201, 202)

27. Choice C is correct.

	rate ×	time =	distance
	mi/hr	hrs	miles
down	$r + 3$	h	$h(r + 3)$
up	$r - 3$	$2h$	$2h(r - 3)$

Let h = time to travel downstream.

Let r = speed of the boat in still water.

Since the two trips cover the same distance, we can write the equation: $h(r + 3) = 2h(r - 3)$. Dividing by h, $r + 3 = 2r - 6$, so $r = 9$. (201, 202)

28. Choice C is correct. We could treat this as a regular distance problem and make up a table that would solve it, but there is an easier way here, if we consider the quantity representing the distance between the boys. This distance starts at zero and increases at the rate of 18 miles per hour. Thus, in 10 minutes, or $\dfrac{1}{6}$ hour, they will be 3 miles apart.

$(\dfrac{1}{6}$ hr $\times 18 \dfrac{\text{mi}}{\text{hr}} = 3$ mi$)$. (201, 202)

29. Choice E is correct.

	rate ×	time =	work
	bolts/min	min	bolts
A	40	$1\dfrac{1}{2}$	60
B	30	t	240

Let t = time B works.

Since A produces only 60 out of 300 that must be produced, B must produce 240; then, $30t = 240$, so $t = 8$.

Total time $= t + 1\dfrac{1}{2} = 8 + 1\dfrac{1}{2} = 9\dfrac{1}{2}$. (201, 203)

30. Choice B is correct.

concentration ×	volume =	amount of salt
%	pints	"pints" of salt*

	%	pints	"pints" of salt*
15%	15	10	1.5
10%	10	15	1.5
Total	x	25	3.0

* One "pint" of salt actually represents a weight of salt equal to the weight of one pint of water.

Let x = concentration of resulting solution.

$(x\%)(25) = 3.0$, so $x = 300 \div 25 = 12$. (201, 204)

31. Choice C is correct.

rate ×	time =	pay (net)
$/day	days	$

	$/day	days	$
Jeff	2	d	$2d$
Pete	3	d	$3d$
total	5	d	$5d$

(Net pay = pay − expenses.)

Let d = the number of days it takes to save.

Total net pay = $150.00, so $150 = 5d$, thus $d = 30$.

Do not make the mistake of using 5 and 10 as the rates! (201, 205)

32. Choice B is correct.

rate ×	time =	distance
mi/hr	hours	miles

	mi/hr	hours	miles
plane A	600	h	800
plane B	0	1	0
plane B	800	t	800

Let h = time for trip at 600 mph − waiting time before second flight.

Let t = time for trip at 800 mph.

Plane A: $600h = 800$, so $h = \dfrac{800}{600} = 1\dfrac{1}{3}$ hours =

1 hour, 20 minutes

Plane B: $800t = 800$, so $t = 1$

Total time for plane A = 1 hour, 20 minutes

Total time for plane B = 1 hour + 1 hour = 2 hours

Thus, plane A arrives before plane B by 40 minutes (less than an hour). (201, 202)

33. Choice E is correct.

coin ×	number =	value
¢/coin	coins	cents

	¢/coin	coins	cents
Peter	5	n	$5n$
Peter	10	d	$10d$
Charlie	5	$2d$	$10d$
Charlie	10	n	$10n$

Let n = number of Peter's nickels.

Let d = number of Peter's dimes.

Total value of coins = $5n + 10d + 10d + 10n = 15n + 20d$

Thus, $15n + 20d = 250$. This has many different solutions, each of which is possible (e.g., $n = 2$, $d = 11$, or $n = 6$, $d = 8$, etc.) (201, 205)

34. Choice A is correct.

rate ×	time =	distance
mi/hr	hours	miles

	mi/hr	hours	miles
constant rate	40	h	120
two rates	50	m	60
	30	n	60

Let h = time to travel 120 miles at the constant rate.

Let m = time to travel 60 miles at 50 mi/hr.

Let n = time to travel 60 miles at 30 mi/hr.

Forming the equations for h, m, and n, and solving, we get:

$$40h = 120; \quad h = \frac{120}{40}; \quad h = 3$$

$$50m = 60; \quad m = \frac{60}{50}; \quad m = 1.2$$

COMPLETE NEW SAT MATH REFRESHER • 341

$$30n = 60; n = \frac{60}{30}; n = 2$$

Total time with constant rate = h = 3 hours.

Total time with changing rate = $m + n$ = 3.2 hours.

Thus, the constant rate is faster by 0.2 hours, or 12 minutes. (201, 202)

35. Choice D is correct.

	rate	×	time	=	distance
	mi/hr		hours		miles
walking	2		h		10
bicycling	10		t		10

Let h = time to walk.

Let t = time to bicycle.

Forming equations: $2h = 10$, so $h = 5$; and $10t = 10$, so $t = 1$.

Total time = $h + t = 5 + 1 = 6$. (201, 202)

36. Choice C is correct.

	rate	×	time	=	distance
mi/hr		hours		miles	
x		Q		P	
x		y		R	

Let x = rate of traveling Q miles.

Let y = time to travel R miles.

$Qx = P$, so $x = \dfrac{P}{Q}$

$xy = \left(\dfrac{P}{Q}\right)y = R$, so $y = \dfrac{RQ}{P}$ hours = time to travel R miles. (201, 202)

37. Choice D is correct.

rate	×	time	=	distance
mi/hr		hours		miles
r		$\dfrac{1}{300}$		$\dfrac{75}{5280}$

Let r = rate of swimming.

$$75 \text{ feet} = 75\left(\frac{1}{5280}\text{ mile}\right) = \frac{75}{5280}\text{ mile}$$

$$12 \text{ seconds} = 12\left(\frac{1}{3600}\text{ hour}\right) = \frac{1}{300}\text{ hour}$$

$r = \dfrac{75}{5280} \div \dfrac{1}{300} = \dfrac{22500}{5280} = 4.3$ (approximately) = 4 mi/hr (approximately). (201, 202)

38. Choice B is correct.

	price	×	amount	=	value
	¢/lb		lbs.		cents
$1.20 nuts	120		x		$120x$
$0.90	90		2		180
mixture	100		$x + 2$		$180 + 120x$

Let x = pounds of $1.20 mixture.

Total value of mixture = $100(x + 2) = 180 + 120x$

$100x + 200 = 180 + 120x$, so $x = 1$ pound. (201, 204)

39. Choice B is correct.

rate	×	time	=	loss
hr/hr		hrs		hrs
$\dfrac{2}{3}$		t		12

(Loss is the amount by which the clock time differs from real time.)

Let t = hours to register the correct time.

If the clock registers only 20 minutes each hour, it loses 40 minutes, or $\dfrac{2}{3}$ hour each hour. The clock will register the correct time only if it has lost some multiple of 12 hours. The first time this can occur is after it has lost 12 hours. $\left(\dfrac{2}{3}\right)t = 12$, so $t = 18$ hours. (201)

40. Choice A is correct.

rate	×	time	=	distance
mi/hr		hrs		miles
q		p		pq
s		r		rs
total x		$p + r$		$pq + rs$

Let x = average speed.

We may add times of travel at the two rates, and also add the distances. Then, $x(p + r) = pq + rs$;

thus, $x = \dfrac{pq + rs}{p + r}$.   (201, 202)

41. Choice A is correct.

rate	×	time	=	work
	ft/hr		hrs		feet
Joe	35		x		$35x$
Walt	25		x		$25x$
Both	60		x		$60x$

Let x = the time the job takes.

Since they are working together, we add their rates and the amount of work they do. Thus, $60x = 150$, so $x = 2.5$ (hours) = 150 minutes.   (201, 203)

42. Choice B is correct.

rate	×	time	=	distance
	mi/hr		hrs		miles
first $\frac{1}{2}$ hour	20		$\frac{1}{2}$		10
second $\frac{1}{2}$ hour	30		$\frac{1}{2}$		15
total	x		1		25

Let x = average speed.

We add the times and distances; then, using the rate formula, $(x)(1) = 25$, so $x = 25$ mi/hr. (201, 202)

43. Choice C is correct.

rate	×	time	=	distance
	mi/hr		hours		miles
Sol	200		t		$200t$
Robert	400		t		$400t$

Let t = time from simultaneous departure to meeting.

Sol's time is equal to Robert's time because they leave at the same time and then they meet. Their combined distance is 3,000 miles, so $200t + 400t = 3,000$, or $t = 5$ hours.   (201, 202)

44. Choice E is correct.

coin	×	number	=	value
	¢/coin		coins		¢
pennies	1		p		p
nickels	5		n		$5n$
dimes	10		d		$10d$
quarters	25		q		$25q$

Let p = number of pennies.

Let n = number of nickels.

Let d = number of dimes.

Let q = number of quarters.

Adding the numbers of coins and their values, we get $p + n + d + q = 7$, and $p + 5n + 10d + 25q = 100$. These equations are satisfied by several values of p, n, d, and q. For example, $p = 0$, $n = 0$, $d = 5$, $q = 2$ satisfies the equation, as does $p = 0$, $n = 3$, $d = 1$, $q = 3$, and other combinations.

Thus, the number of dimes is not determined.
                    (201, 205)

45. Choice A is correct.

concentration × am't of solution = amount of alcohol			
	%	qts	qts
pure alcohol	100%	2	2
solution	30%	x	0.30x
mixture	40%	2 + x	2 + 0.30x

Let x = qts of original solution

Amounts of solution and of alcohol may be added.

(40%) (2 + x) = 2 + 0.30x; so 0.8 + 0.4x = 2.0 + 0.30x; thus, x = 12. (201, 204)

46. Choice C is correct.

rate × time = cost			
	¢/kwh	kwh	¢
first 1000 kwh	8¢	t	8t

(time expressed in kilowatt-hours, or kwh)

Let t = number of kwh.

This problem must be broken up into two different parts: (1) finding the total power or the total number of kilowatt-hours (kwh) used, and (2) calculating the charge for that amount. (1) Total power used, t = (900w) (5 hr) + (100w) (25 hr) + (5w) (400 hr) = (4,500 + 2,500 + 2,000) watt-hours = 9,000 watt-hours. One thousand watt-hours equals one kilowatt-hour. Thus, t = 9 kilowatt-hours, so that the charge is (8¢) (9) = 72¢. (201, 205)

47. Choice C is correct.

rate × amount = cost			
	¢/in	in	¢
1 yard	r	36	30
96 inches	r	96	96r

Let r = cost per inch of cloth.

From the table, r × 36 in = 30¢; $r = \dfrac{30¢}{36\text{ in}} = \dfrac{5¢}{6\text{ in}}$

Thus, $96r = 96\dfrac{5}{6} = 80¢$. (201, 205)

48. Choice A is correct.

rate × time = distance			
	mi/hr	hrs	miles
trip	50	6	300
return	r	$7\frac{1}{2}$	300
total	s	$13\frac{1}{2}$	600

Let r = rate for return.

Let s = average overall rate.

(13½) (s) = 600; thus, $s = 600 \div 13\frac{1}{2} = 44.4$ (approximately). (201, 202)

49. Choice E is correct.

rate × principal = interest			
	%/year	$	$/year
first year	5	100	5
second year	5	105	5.25

Interest first year equals rate × principal = 5% × $100 = $5.

New principal = $105.00.

Interest second year = rate × new principal = 5% × $105 = $5.25.

Final principal = $105.00 + $5.25 = $110.25. (201, 205)

50. Choice C is correct.

rate × time = amount			
	gal/min	min	gallons
in	3	x	3x
out	$1\frac{1}{2}$	x	$1\frac{1}{2}x$
net	$1\frac{1}{2}$	x	$1\frac{1}{2}x$

(Net = in − out.)

Let x = time to fill the tub completely.

Since only 9 gallons are needed (there are already 3 in the tub), we have $1\frac{1}{2}x$ = 9, so x = 6. (201)

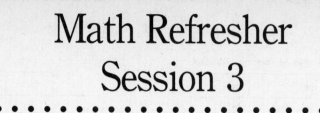

Math Refresher
Session 3

Area, Perimeter, and Volume Problems

301. *Formula Problems.* Here, you are given certain data about one or more geometric figures, and you are asked to supply some missing information. To solve this type of problem, follow this procedure:

STEP 1. If you are not given a diagram, draw your own; this may make the answer readily apparent or may suggest the best way to solve the problem. You should try to make your diagram as accurate as possible, but *do not waste time perfecting your diagram.*

STEP 2. Determine the formula that relates to the quantities involved in your problem. In many cases it will be helpful to set up tables containing the various data. (See Sections 303–316.)

STEP 3. Substitute the given information for the unknown quantities in your formulas to get the desired answer.

When doing volume, area, and perimeter problems, keep this hint in mind: Often the solutions to such problems can be expressed as the sum of the areas *or* volumes *or* perimeters of simpler figures. In such cases do not hesitate to break down your original figure into simpler parts.

In doing problems involving the following figures, these approximations and facts will be useful:

$\sqrt{2}$ is approximately 1.4. $\sin 45° = \dfrac{\sqrt{2}}{2}$ which is approximately 0.71.

$\sqrt{3}$ is approximately 1.7.

$\sqrt{10}$ is approximately 3.16. $\sin 60° = \dfrac{\sqrt{3}}{2}$ which is approximately 0.87.

π is approximately $\frac{22}{7}$ or 3.14.

$\sin 30° = \frac{1}{2}$

Example: The following figure contains a square, a right triangle, and a semicircle. If $ED = CD$ and the length of CD is 1 unit, find the area of the entire figure.

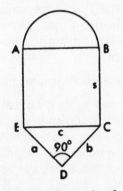

Solution: To calculate the area of the entire figure, we calculate the areas of the triangle, square, and semicircle and then add these together. In a right triangle, the area is

$\frac{1}{2}ab$ where a and b are the sides of the triangle. In this case we will call side ED, a and side CD, b. $ED = CD = 1$, so the area of the triangle is $\frac{1}{2}$ (1) (1), or $\frac{1}{2}$.

The area of a square is s^2, where s is a side. We see that the side EC of the square is the hypotenuse of the right triangle. We can calculate this length by using the formula $c^2 = a^2 + b^2$ where $a = b = 1$; then we can see that $c = \sqrt{2}$. Thus, in this case, $s = \sqrt{2}$ so the area of the square is $(\sqrt{2})^2 = 2$.

AB is the diameter of the semicircle, so $\frac{1}{2} AB$ is the radius. Since all sides of a square are equal, $AB = \sqrt{2}$, and the radius is $\frac{1}{2}\sqrt{2}$. Further, the area of a semicircle is $\frac{1}{2}\pi r^2$ where r is the radius, so the area of this semicircle is $\frac{1}{2}\pi(\frac{1}{2}\sqrt{2})^2 = \frac{1}{4}\pi$.

The total area of the whole figure is equal to the area of the triangle plus the area of the square plus the area of the semicircle $= \frac{1}{2} + 2 + \frac{1}{4}\pi = 2\frac{1}{2} + \frac{1}{4}\pi$.

The total area of the whole figure is equal to the area of the triangle plus the area of the square plus the area of the semicircle $= \frac{1}{2} + 2 + \frac{1}{4}\pi = 2\frac{1}{2} + \frac{1}{4}\pi$.

Example: If water flows into a rectangular tank with dimensions of 12 inches, 18 inches, and 30 inches at the rate of 0.25 cubic feet per minute, how long will it take to fill the tank?

Solution: This problem is really a combination of a rate problem and a volume problem. First we must calculate the volume, and then we must substitute in a rate equation to get our final answer. The formula for the volume of a rectangular solid is $V = lwh$ where l, w, and h are the length, width, and height, respectively. We must multiply the three dimensions of the tank to get the volume. However, if we look ahead to the second part of the problem, we see that we want the volume in cubic *feet;* therefore we convert 12 inches, 18 inches, and 30 inches to 1 foot, 1.5 feet, and 2.5 feet, respectively. Multiplying gives us a volume of 3.75 cubic feet. Now substituting in the equation: rate $\times$ time = volume, we get $0.25 \times$ time $= 3.75$; time $= \frac{3.75}{0.25}$; thus, the time is 15 minutes.

302. *Comparison problems.* Here you are asked to identify the largest, or smallest, of a group of figures, or to place them in ascending or descending order of size. The following procedure is the most efficient one:

STEP 1. Always diagram each figure before you come to any conclusions. Whenever possible, try to include two or more of the figures in the same diagram, so that their relative sizes are most readily apparent.

STEP 2. If you have not already determined the correct answer, then (and only then) determine the size of the figures (as you would have done in Section 301) and compare the results. (Note that even if Step 2 is necessary, Step 1 should eliminate most of the possible choices, leaving only a few formula calculations to be done.)

Example: Which of the following is the greatest in length?

(A) The perimeter of a square with a side of 4 inches.
(B) The perimeter of an isosceles right triangle whose equal sides are 8 inches each.
(C) The circumference of a circle with a diameter of 4 $\sqrt{2}$ inches.
(D) The perimeter of a pentagon whose sides are all equal to 3 inches.
(E) The perimeter of a semicircle with a radius of 5 inches.

Solution: Diagramming the five figures mentioned, we obtain the following illustration:

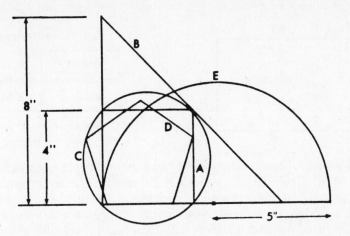

From the diagram, it is apparent that the square and the pentagon are both smaller than the circle. Further observation should show that the circle is smaller than the triangle. Thus we need only to see which is larger—the semicircle or the triangle. The perimeter of the semicircle is found by the formula: $P = 2r + \pi r$ (the sum of the diameter and the semicircular arc, where r, is the radius). Since r in this case is 5 inches, the perimeter is approximately $10 + (3.14)5$, or 25.7 inches. The formula for the perimeter of a triangle is the sum of the sides. In this case, two of the sides are 8 inches and the third side can be found by using the relationship $c^2 = a^2 + b^2$, where a and b are the sides of a right triangle, and c is the hypotenuse. Since in our problem $a = b = 8$ inches, $c = \sqrt{8^2 + 8^2} = \sqrt{128} = \sqrt{2(64)} = 8\sqrt{2}$, which is the third side of the triangle. The perimeter is $8 + 8 + 8\sqrt{2}$, which is $16 + 8\sqrt{2}$. This is approximately equal to $16 + 8(1.4)$ or 27.2, so the triangle is the largest of the figures.

FORMULAS USED IN AREA, PERIMETER, AND VOLUME PROBLEMS

It is important that you know as many of these formulas as possible. Problems using these formulas appear frequently on tests of all kinds. You should not need to refer to this table when you do problems. Learn these formulas before you go any further.

---

303. *Square.* The area of a square is the square of one of its sides. Thus, if A represents the area, and s represents the length of a side, $A = s^2$. The area of a square is also one-half of the square of its diagonal and may be written as $A = \frac{1}{2}d^2$, where d represents the length of a diagonal. The perimeter of a square is 4 times the length of one of its sides, or $4s$.

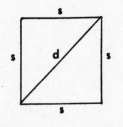

Square

quantity	formula
area	$A = s^2$ $A = \frac{1}{2}d^2$
perimeter	$P = 4s$

304. *Rectangle.* Let *a* and *b* represent the length of two adjacent sides of a rectangle, and let *A* represent the area. Then the area of a rectangle is the product of the two adjacent sides. $A = ab$. The perimeter, *P*, is the sum of twice one side and twice the adjacent side. $P = 2a + 2b$.

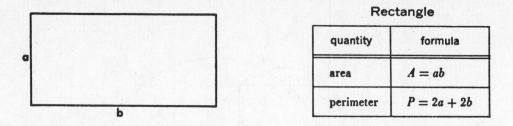

Rectangle

quantity	formula
area	$A = ab$
perimeter	$P = 2a + 2b$

305. *Parallelogram.* The area of a parallelogram is the product of a side and the altitude, *h*, to that side. $A = bh$ (in this case the altitude to side *b*). The area can also be expressed as the product of two adjacent sides and the sine of the included angle: $A = ab \sin c$, where *c* is the angle included between side *a* and side *b*. The perimeter is the sum of twice one side and twice the adjacent side. $P = 2a + 2b$. Let *a* and *b* represent the length of 2 adjacent sides of a parallelogram. Then, *c* is the included angle. But *A* represents its area, *P* its perimeter, and *h* the altitude to one of its sides.

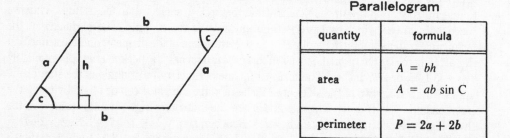

Parallelogram

quantity	formula
area	$A = bh$ $A = ab \sin C$
perimeter	$P = 2a + 2b$

306. *Triangle.* The area of any triangle is one-half of the product of any side and the altitude to that side. $A = \frac{1}{2}bh$, where *b* is a side, and *h* the altitude to that side. The area may be written also as one-half of the product of any two adjacent sides and the sine of the included angle. $A = \frac{1}{2}ab \sin C$, where *A* is the area, *a* and *b* are two adjacent sides, and *C* is the included angle. The perimeter of a triangle is the sum of the sides of the triangle. $P = a + b + c$, where *P* is the perimeter, and *c* is the third side.

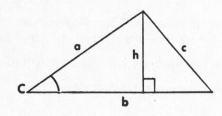

Triangle

quantity	formula
area	$A = \frac{1}{2}bh$ $A = \frac{1}{2}ab \sin C$
perimeter	$P = a + b + c$

307. *Right triangle.* The area of a right triangle is one-half of the product of the two sides adjacent to the right angle. $A = \frac{1}{2}ab$, where A is the area, and a and b are the adjacent sides. The perimeter is the sum of the sides. $P = a + b + c$, where c is the third side, or hypotenuse.

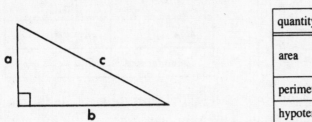

Right Triangle

quantity	formula
area	$A = \frac{1}{2}ab$
perimeter	$P = a + b + c$
hypotenuse	$c^2 = a^2 + b^2$

308. *Equilateral triangle.* The area of an equilateral triangle is one-fourth the product of a side squared and $\sqrt{3}$. $A = \frac{1}{4}s^2\sqrt{3}$, where A is the area, and s is one of the equal sides. The perimeter of an equilateral triangle is 3 times one side. $P = 3s$, where P is the perimeter.

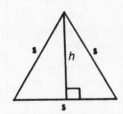

Equilateral Triangle

quantity	formula
area	$A = \frac{1}{4}s^2\sqrt{3}$
perimeter	$P = 3s$
altitude	$h = \frac{1}{2}s\sqrt{3}$

NOTE: The equilateral triangle and the right triangle are special cases of the triangle, and any law that applies to the triangle applies to both the right triangle and to the equilateral triangle.

309. *Trapezoid.* The area of a trapezoid is one-half of the product of the altitude and the sum of the bases. $A = \frac{1}{2}h(B + b)$, where A is the area, B and b are the bases, and h is their altitude. The perimeter is the sum of the 4 sides. $P = B + b + c + d$, where P is the perimeter, and c and d are the other 2 sides.

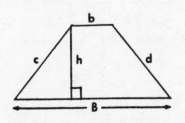

Trapezoid

quantity	formula
area	$A = \frac{1}{2}h(B + b)$
perimeter	$P = B + b + c + d$

310. *Circle.* The area of a circle is π (pi) times the square of the radius. $A = \pi r^2$, where A is the area, and r is the radius. The circumference is pi times the diameter or pi times twice the radius. $C = \pi d = 2\pi r$, where C is the circumference, d the diameter, and r the radius.

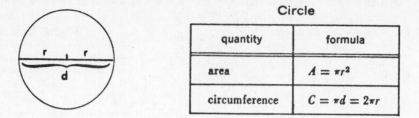

Circle

quantity	formula
area	$A = \pi r^2$
circumference	$C = \pi d = 2\pi r$

311. *Semicircle.* The area of a semicircle is one-half pi times the square of the radius. $A = \frac{1}{2}\pi r^2$, where A is the area and r is the radius. The length of the curved portion of the semicircle is one-half pi times the diameter or pi times the radius. $C = \frac{1}{2}\pi d = \pi r$, where C is the circumference, d is the diameter, and r is the radius. The perimeter of a semicircle is equal to the circumference plus the length of the diameter. $P = C + d = \frac{1}{2}\pi d + d$, where P is the perimeter.

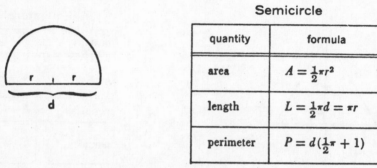

Semicircle

quantity	formula
area	$A = \frac{1}{2}\pi r^2$
length	$L = \frac{1}{2}\pi d = \pi r$
perimeter	$P = d(\frac{1}{2}\pi + 1)$

312. *Rectangular solid.* The volume of a rectangular solid is the product of the length, width, and height. $V = lwh$, where V is the volume, l is the length, w is the width, and h is the height. The volume is also the product of the area of one side and the altitude to that side. $V = Bh$, where B is the area of its base and h the altitude to that side. The surface area is the sum of the area of the six faces. $S = 2wh + 2hl + 2wl$, where S is the surface area.

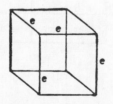

Rectangular Solid

quantity	formula
volume	$V = lwh$ $V = Bh$
surface area	$S = 2wh + 2hl + 2lw$

313. *Cube.* The volume of a cube is its edge cubed. $V = e^3$, where V is the volume and e is an edge. The surface area is the sum of the areas of the six faces. $S = 6e^2$, where S is the surface area.

Cube

quantity	formula
volume	$V = e^3$
surface area	$S = 6e^2$

314. *Cylinder.* The volume of a cylinder is the area of the base times the height. $V = Bh$, where V is the volume, B is the area of the base, and h is the height. Note that the area of the base is the area of the circle $= \pi r^2$, where r is the radius of a base. The surface area not including the bases is the circumference of the base times the height. $S_1 = Ch = 2\pi rh$, where S_1 is the surface area without the bases, C the circumference, and h the height. The area of the bases $= 2\pi r^2$. Thus, the area of the cylinder, including the bases, $S_2 = 2\pi rh + 2\pi r^2 = 2\pi r(h + r)$.

Cylinder

quantity	formula
volume	$V = Bh$ $V = \pi r^2 h$
surface area	$S_1 = 2\pi rh$ (without bases) $S_2 = 2\pi r\ (h + r)$ (with bases)

315. *Sphere.* The volume of a sphere is four-thirds π times the cube of the radius. $V = \dfrac{4}{3}\pi r^3$, where V is the volume and r is the radius. The surface area is 4π times the square of the radius. $S = 4\pi r^2$, where S is the surface area.

Sphere

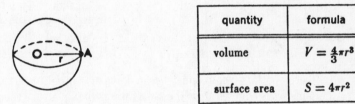

quantity	formula
volume	$V = \frac{4}{3}\pi r^3$
surface area	$S = 4\pi r^2$

316. *Hemisphere.* The volume of a hemisphere is two-thirds π times the cube of the radius. $V = \dfrac{2}{3}\pi r^3$ where V is the volume and r is the radius. The surface area not including the area of the base is 2π times the square of the radius. $S_1 = 2\pi r^2$, where S_1 is the surface area without the base. The total surface area, including the base, is equal to the surface area without the base plus the area of the base. $S_2 = 2\pi r^2 + \pi r^2 = 3\pi r^2$, where S_2 is the surface area including the base.

Hemisphere

quantity	formula
volume	$V = \frac{2}{3}\pi r^3$
surface area	$S_1 = 2\pi r^2$ (without bases) $S_2 = 3\pi r^2$ (with bases)

317. *Pythagorean Theorem.* The Pythagorean Theorem states a very important geometrical relationship. It states that in a right triangle, if c is the hypotenuse (side opposite the right angle), and a and b are sides adjacent to the right angle, then $c^2 = a^2 + b^2$.

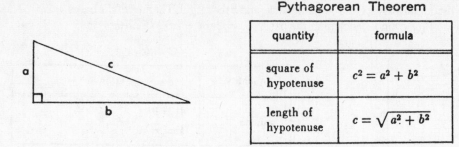

Pythagorean Theorem

quantity	formula
square of hypotenuse	$c^2 = a^2 + b^2$
length of hypotenuse	$c = \sqrt{a^2 + b^2}$

Examples of right triangles are triangles with sides of 3, 4, and 5 or 5, 12, and 13. Any multiples of these numbers also form right triangles—for example, 6, 8, and 10 or 30, 40, 50.

Using the Pythagorean Theorem to find the diagonal of a square we get $d^2 = s^2 + s^2$ or $d^2 = 2s^2$, where d is the diagonal and s is a side. Therefore, $d = s\sqrt{2}$, or the diagonal of a square is $\sqrt{2}$ times the side.

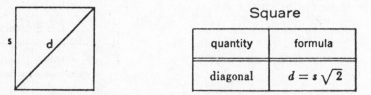

Square

quantity	formula
diagonal	$d = s\sqrt{2}$

318. Another important fact to remember in doing area problems is that areas of two similar (having the same shape) figures are in the same ratio as the squares of corresponding parts of the figures.

Example: Triangles P and Q are similar. Side p of triangle P is 2 inches, the area of triangle P is 3 square inches, and corresponding side q of triangle Q is 4 inches. What is the area of triangle Q?

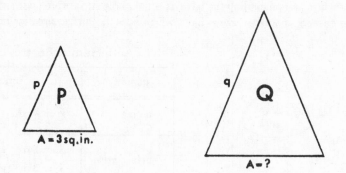

Solution: The square of side p is to the square of side q as the area of P is to the area of Q. If we call x the area of triangle Q, then we get the following relationship: The square of side p is to the square of side q as the area of P is to the area of Q, or

$$\frac{2^2}{4^2} = \frac{3}{x} \text{ or } \frac{4}{16} = \frac{3}{x}$$

Therefore, $x = 12$ square inches.

Practice Test 3

Area, Perimeter, and Volume Problems

Correct answers and solutions follow each test.

1. A B C D E

1. Which of the following figures has the largest area?

   (A) a square with a perimeter of 12 inches
   (B) a circle with a radius of 3 inches
   (C) a right triangle with sides of 3, 4, and 5 inches
   (D) a rectangle with a diagonal of 5 inches
   (E) a regular hexagon with a perimeter of 18 inches

2. A B C D E

2. If the area of the base of a rectangular solid is tripled, what is the percent increase in its volume?

   (A) 200%
   (B) 300%
   (C) 600%
   (D) 800%
   (E) 900%

3. A B C D E

3. How many yards of a carpeting that is 26 inches wide will be needed to cover a floor that is 12′ by 13′?

   (A) 22 yards
   (B) 24 yards
   (C) 27 yards
   (D) 36 yards
   (E) 46 yards

4. A B C D E

4. If water flows into a rectangular tank at the rate of 6 cubic feet per minute, how long will it take to fill the tank, which measures 18″ × 32″ × 27″?

   (A) less than one minute
   (B) less than two minutes, but not less than one minute
   (C) less than three minutes, but not less than two minutes
   (D) less than four minutes, but not less than three minutes
   (E) four minutes or more

5. A B C D E

5. The ratio of the area of a circle to the radius of the circle is

   (A) π
   (B) 2π
   (C) π^2
   (D) $4\pi^2$
   (E) not determinable

6. A B C D E

6. Which of the following figures has the smallest perimeter or circumference?

   (A) a circle with a diameter of 2 feet
   (B) a square with a diagonal of 2 feet
   (C) a rectangle with sides of 6″ and 4 feet
   (D) a pentagon with each side equal to 16 inches
   (E) a hexagon with each side equal to 14 inches

7. A B C D E

7. In the figure shown, *DE* is parallel to *BC*. If the area of triangle *ADE* is half that of trapezoid *DECB*, what is the ratio of *AE* to *AC*?

(A) $1:2$
(B) $1:\sqrt{2}$
(C) $1:3$
(D) $1:\sqrt{3}$
(E) $1:\sqrt{3}-1$

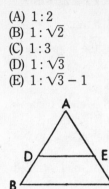

8. A B C D E

8. At a speed of 22 revolutions per minute, how long will it take a wheel of radius 10″, rolling on its edge, to travel 10 feet? (Assume π equals $\frac{22}{7}$, and express answer to nearest 0.1 second.)

(A) 0.2 seconds
(B) 0.4 seconds
(C) 5.2 seconds
(D) 6.3 seconds
(E) 7.4 seconds

9. A B C D E

9. If the diagonal of a square is 16″ long, what is the area of the square?

(A) 64 square inches
(B) $64\sqrt{2}$ square inches
(C) 128 square inches
(D) $128\sqrt{2}$ square inches
(E) 256 square inches

10. A B C D E

10. In the diagram shown, *ACDF* is a rectangle, and *GBHE* is a circle. If *CD* = 4 inches, and *AC* = 6 inches, what is the number of square inches in the shaded area?

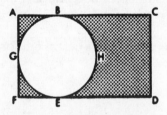

(A) $16 - 4\pi$ square inches
(B) $24 - 4\pi$ square inches
(C) $24 - 16\pi$ square inches
(D) $16 - 2\pi$ square inches
(E) $24 - 2\pi$ square inches

11.
A B C D E

11. What is the area of an equilateral triangle with a side of 1 inch?

(A) 1 square inch

(B) $\dfrac{\sqrt{3}}{2}$ square inch

(C) $\dfrac{1}{2}$ square inch

(D) $\dfrac{\sqrt{3}}{4}$ square inch

(E) $\dfrac{1}{3}$ square inch

12.
A B C D E

12. The measurements of a rectangle are 12 feet by 16 feet. What is the area of the smallest *circle* that can cover this rectangle entirely (so that no part of the rectangle is outside the circle)?

(A) 192 square feet
(B) 384 square feet
(C) 100π square feet
(D) 128π square feet
(E) 400π square feet

13.
A B C D E

13. A man wishes to cover his floor with tiles, each one measuring $\dfrac{3}{4}$ inch by 2 inches. If his room is a rectangle, measuring 12 feet by 18 feet, how many such tiles will he need?

(A) 144
(B) 1,152
(C) 1,728
(D) 9,216
(E) 20,736

14.
A B C D E

14. The volume of a sphere is equal to the volume of a cylinder. If the radius of the sphere is 4 miles and the radius of the cylinder is 8 miles, what is the height of the cylinder?

(A) 8 miles

(B) $\dfrac{4}{3}$ miles

(C) 4 miles

(D) $\dfrac{16}{3}$ miles

(E) 1 mile

15.
A B C D E

15. A wheel travels 33 yards in 15 revolutions. What is its diameter? (Assume $\pi = \dfrac{22}{7}$.)

(A) 0.35 feet
(B) 0.70 feet
(C) 1.05 feet
(D) 1.40 feet
(E) 2.10 feet

16. A B C D E

16. If a rectangle with a perimeter of 48 inches is equal in area to a right triangle with legs of 12 inches and 24 inches, what is the rectangle's diagonal?

(A) 12 inches
(B) $12\sqrt{2}$ inches
(C) $12\sqrt{3}$ inches
(D) 24 inches
(E) The answer cannot be determined from the given information

17. A B C D E

17. What is the approximate area that remains after a circle $3\frac{1}{2}''$ in diameter is cut from a square piece of cloth with a side of 8"? (Use $\pi = \frac{22}{7}$.)

(A) 25.5 square inches
(B) 54.4 square inches
(C) 56.8 square inches
(D) 142.1 square inches
(E) 284.2 square inches

18. A B C D E

18. A container is shaped like a rectangular solid with sides of 3 inches, 3 inches, and 11 inches. What is its approximate capacity, if 1 gallon equals 231 cubic inches?

(A) 14 ounces
(B) 27 ounces
(C) 55 ounces
(D) 110 ounces
(E) 219 ounces

19. A B C D E

19. The 20-inch-diameter wheels of one car travel at a rate of 24 revolutions per minute, while the 30-inch-diameter wheels of another car travel at a rate of 18 revolutions per minute. What is the ratio of the speed of the second car to that of the first?

(A) 1 : 1
(B) 3 : 2
(C) 4 : 3
(D) 6 : 5
(E) 9 : 8

20. A B C D E

20. A circular garden twenty feet in diameter is surrounded by a path three feet wide. What is the area of the path?

(A) 9π square feet
(B) 51π square feet
(C) 60π square feet
(D) 69π square feet
(E) 90π square feet

21. A B C D E

21. What is the area of a semicircle with a diameter of 16 inches?

(A) 32π square inches
(B) 64π square inches
(C) 128π square inches
(D) 256π square inches
(E) 512π square inches

22. A B C D E

22. If the edges of a cube add up to 4 feet in length, what is the volume of the cube?

(A) 64 cubic inches
(B) 125 cubic inches
(C) 216 cubic inches
(D) 512 cubic inches
(E) none of these

23. A B C D E

23. The inside of a trough is shaped like a rectangular solid, 25 feet long, 6 inches wide, and filled with water to a depth of 35 inches. If we wish to raise the depth of the water to 38 inches, how much water must be let into the tank?

(A) $\dfrac{25}{96}$ cubic foot

(B) $\dfrac{25}{8}$ cubic feet

(C) $\dfrac{75}{2}$ cubic foot

(D) 225 cubic feet
(E) 450 cubic feet

24. A B C D E

24. If one gallon of water equals 231 cubic inches, approximately how much water will fill a cylindrical vase 7 inches in diameter and 10 inches high? (Assume $\pi = \dfrac{22}{7}$.)

(A) 1.7 gallons
(B) 2.1 gallons
(C) 3.3 gallons
(D) 5.3 gallons
(E) 6.7 gallons

25. A B C D E

25. Tiles of linoleum, measuring 8 inches × 8 inches, cost 9¢ apiece. At this rate, what will it cost a man to cover a floor with these tiles, if his floor measures 10 feet by 16 feet?

(A) $22.50
(B) $25.00
(C) $28.00
(D) $32.40
(E) $36.00

26. A B C D E

26. Which of the following figures has the largest area?

(A) a 3 : 4 : 5 triangle with a hypotenuse of 25 inches
(B) a circle with a diameter of 20 inches
(C) a square with a 20-inch diagonal
(D) a regular hexagon with a side equal to 10 inches
(E) a rectangle with sides of 10 inches and 30 inches

27. A B C D E

27. If the radius of the base of a cylinder is tripled, and its height is divided by three, what is the ratio of the volume of the new cylinder to the volume of the original cylinder?

(A) 1 : 9
(B) 1 : 3
(C) 1 : 1
(D) 3 : 1
(E) 9 : 1

28. A B C D E

28. If one cubic foot of water equals 7.5 gallons, how long will it take for a faucet that flows at a rate of 10 gal/min to fill a cube 2 feet on each side (to the nearest minute)?

    (A) 4 minutes
    (B) 5 minutes
    (C) 6 minutes
    (D) 7 minutes
    (E) 8 minutes

29. A B C D E

29. The ratio of the area of a square to the *square of its diagonal* is which of the following?

    (A) $2:1$
    (B) $\sqrt{2}:1$
    (C) $1:1$
    (D) $1:\sqrt{2}$
    (E) $1:2$

30. A B C D E

30. If *ABCD* is a square, with side $AB = 4$ inches, and *AEB* and *CED* are semicircles, what is the area of the shaded portion of the diagram below?

    (A) $8 - \pi$ square inches
    (B) $8 - 2\pi$ square inches
    (C) $16 - 2\pi$ square inches
    (D) $16 - 4\pi$ square inches
    (E) $16 - 8\pi$ square inches

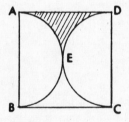

31. A B C D E

31. If the area of a circle is equal to the area of a rectangle, one of whose sides is equal to π, express the other side of the rectangle, *x*, in terms of the radius of the circle, *r*.

    (A) $x = r$
    (B) $x = \pi r$
    (C) $x = r^2$
    (D) $x = \sqrt{r}$
    (E) $x = \dfrac{1}{r}$

32. A B C D E

32. If the volume of a cube is 27 cubic meters, find the surface area of the cube.

    (A) 9 square meters
    (B) 18 square meters
    (C) 54 square meters
    (D) 3 square meters
    (E) 1 square meter

33. A B C D E

33. What is the area of a regular hexagon one of whose sides is 1 inch?

    (A) $\dfrac{3\sqrt{3}}{4}$

    (B) $\sqrt{3}$

    (C) $\dfrac{3\sqrt{3}}{2}$

    (D) 3

    (E) 6

34. A B C D E

34. What is the area of the triangle pictured below?

    (A) 18 square units
    (B) 32 square units
    (C) 24 square units
    (D) 12 square units
    (E) 124 square units

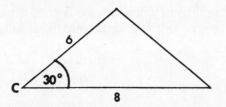

35. A B C D E

35. If a wheel travels 1 mile in 1 minute, at a rate of 600 revolutions per minute, what is the diameter of the wheel, in feet? (Use $\pi = \dfrac{22}{7}$.)

    (A) 2.2 feet
    (B) 2.4 feet
    (C) 2.6 feet
    (D) 2.8 feet
    (E) 3.0 feet

36. A B C D E

36. Which of the following figures has the largest perimeter?

    (A) a square with a diagonal of 5 feet
    (B) a rectangle with sides of 3 feet and 4 feet
    (C) an equilateral triangle with a side equal to 48 inches
    (D) a regular hexagon whose longest diagonal is 6 feet
    (E) a parallelogram with sides of 6 inches and 7 feet

37. A B C D E

37. A man has two containers: The first is a rectangular solid, measuring 3 inches × 4 inches × 10 inches; the second is a cylinder having a base with a radius of 2 inches and a height of 10 inches. If the first container is filled with water, and then this water is poured into the second container, which of the following occurs?

    (A) There is room for more water in the second container.
    (B) The second container is completely filled, without overflowing.
    (C) The second container overflows by less than 1 cubic inch.
    (D) The second container overflows by less than 2 (but not less than 1) cubic inches.
    (E) The second container overflows by 2 or more cubic inches.

38. A B C D E   **38.** If, in this diagram, A represents a square with a side of 4″, and B, C, D, and E are semicircles, what is the area of the entire figure?

(A) $16 + 4\pi$ square inches
(B) $16 + 8\pi$ square inches
(C) $16 + 16\pi$ square inches
(D) $16 + 32\pi$ square inches
(E) $16 + 64\pi$ square inches

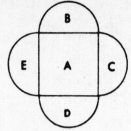

39. A B C D E   **39.** The area of a square is $81p^2$. What is the length of the square's diagonal?

(A) $9p$
(B) $9p\sqrt{2}$
(C) $18p$
(D) $9p^2$
(E) $18p^2$

40. A B C D E   **40.** The following diagram represents the floor of a room that is to be covered with carpeting at a price of $2.50 a square yard. What will be the cost of the carpeting?

(A) $70
(B) $125
(C) $480
(D) $630
(E) none of these

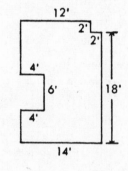

41. A B C D E   **41.** Which of the following has the largest perimeter?

(A) a square with a diagonal of 10 inches
(B) a 3-4-5 right triangle with a hypotenuse of 15 inches
(C) a pentagon, each of whose sides is 5 inches
(D) a right isosceles triangle with an area of 72 square inches
(E) a regular hexagon with a radius of 5 inches

42. A B C D E   **42.** If you double the area of the base of a rectangular solid, and also triple the solid's height, what is the ratio of the new volume to the old volume?

(A) $2:3$
(B) $3:2$
(C) $1:6$
(D) $6:1$
(E) none of these

43. A B C D E   **43.** A certain type of linoleum costs $1.50 per square yard. If a room measures 27 feet by 14 feet, what will be the cost of covering it with linoleum?

(A) $44.10
(B) $51.60
(C) $63.00
(D) $132.30
(E) $189.00

44. A B C D E

44. How many circles, each with a 4-inch radius, can be cut from a rectangular sheet of paper, measuring 16 inches × 24 inches?

(A) 6
(B) 7
(C) 8
(D) 12
(E) 24

45. A B C D E

45. The ratio of the area of an equilateral triangle, in square inches, to its perimeter, in inches, is

(A) 3 : 4
(B) 4 : 3
(C) $\sqrt{3}$: 4
(D) 4 : $\sqrt{3}$
(E) The answer cannot be determined from the given information

46. A B C D E

46. What is the volume of a cylinder whose radius is 4 inches, and whose height is 10 inches? (Assume that $\pi = 3.14$.)

(A) 125.6 cubic inches
(B) 134.4 cubic inches
(C) 144.0 cubic inches
(D) 201.2 cubic inches
(E) 502.4 cubic inches

47. A B C D E

47. The area of a square is $144s^2$. What is the square's diagonal?

(A) $12s$
(B) $12s\sqrt{2}$
(C) $24s$
(D) $144s$
(E) $144s^2$

48. A B C D E

48. A circular pool is ten feet in diameter and five feet deep. What is its volume, in cubic feet?

(A) 50 cubic feet
(B) 50π cubic feet
(C) 125π cubic feet
(D) 250π cubic feet
(E) 500π cubic feet

49. A B C D E

49. A certain type of carpeting is 30 inches wide. How many yards of this carpet will be needed to cover a floor that measures 20 feet by 24 feet?

(A) 48
(B) 64
(C) 144
(D) 192
(E) none of these

50. A B C D E

50. Two wheels have diameters of 12 inches and 18 inches, respectively. Both wheels roll along parallel straight lines at the same linear speed until the large wheel has revolved 72 times. At this point, how many times has the small wheel revolved?

(A) 32
(B) 48
(C) 72
(D) 108
(E) 162

Answer Key for Practice Test 3

1. B	14. B	27. D	39. B
2. A	15. E	28. C	40. A
3. B	16. B	29. E	41. D
4. B	17. B	30. B	42. D
5. E	18. C	31. C	43. C
6. B	19. E	32. C	44. A
7. D	20. D	33. C	45. E
8. C	21. A	34. D	46. E
9. C	22. A	35. D	47. B
10. B	23. B	36. D	48. C
11. D	24. A	37. A	49. B
12. C	25. D	38. B	50. D
13. E	26. B		

Answers and Solutions for Practice Test 3

1. Choice B is correct. This is a fairly difficult comparison problem, but the use of diagrams simplifies it considerably.

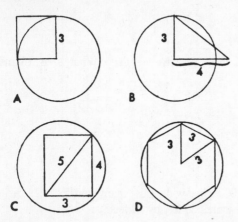

From diagram A it is apparent that the circle is larger than the square. Diagram B shows that the circle is larger than the right triangle. And, since a rectangle with a diagonal of 5 inches is made up of two right triangles, as shown in diagram C, the circle is larger than the rectangle. Finally, as shown in diagram D, the circle is larger than the hexagon. Thus, the circle is the largest of the five figures described. (302)

2. Choice A is correct. This is a formula problem: letting V_o represent the original volume, B_o represent the original area of the base, and h_o represent

the original height of the figure, we have the formula $V_o = h_o B_o$. The new volume, V is equal to $3h_o B_o$. Thus, the new volume is three times the original volume—an *increase* of 200%. (301)

3. Choice B is correct. Here, we must find the length of carpeting needed to cover an area of $12' \times 13'$, or 156 square feet. The formula needed is: $A = lw$, where l = length and w = width, both expressed in *feet*. Now, since we know that $A = 156$ square feet, and $w = 26$ inches, or $\frac{26}{12}$ feet, we can calculate l as $156 \div \left(\frac{26}{12}\right)$, or 72 feet. But since the answer must be expressed in yards, we express 72 feet as 24 yards. (304)

4. Choice B is correct. First we must calculate the volume of the tank in cubic feet. Converting the dimensions of the box to feet, we get $1\frac{1}{2}$ feet $\times$ $2\frac{2}{3}$ feet $\times$ $2\frac{1}{4}$ feet, so the total volume is $\frac{3}{2} \times \frac{8}{3} \times \frac{9}{4}$, or 9, cubic feet. Thus, at a rate of 6 cubic feet per minute, it would take $\frac{9}{6}$, or $1\frac{1}{2}$ minutes to fill the the tank. (312, 201)

5. Choice E is correct. Here, we use the formula $A = \pi r^2$, where A = area, and r = radius. Thus, the ratio of A to r is just $\frac{A}{r} = \pi r$. Since r is not a constant, the ratio cannot be determined. (310)

6. Choice B is correct. First, we diagram the circle and the square and see that the square has a smaller perimeter. Next, we notice that the circle, which has a larger circumference than the square, has circumference 2π, or about 6.3 feet. But the perimeters of the rectangle (9 feet), of the pentagon (5×16 inches = 80 inches = 6 feet, 8 inches), and of the hexagon (6×14 inches = 84 inches = 7 feet) are all greater than the circumference of the circle, and therefore also greater than the perimeter of the square. Thus, the square has the smallest perimeter. (302)

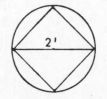

7. Choice D is correct. The formula involved here is $A_1 : A_2 = s_1{}^2 : s_2{}^2$, where A_1 represents the area of the triangle with one side of length s_1, and A_2

represents the area of the triangle corresponding to s_2. If we let s_1 represent AE, and s_2 represent AC, so that A_1 is the area of ADE and A_2 is the area of ABC, then we have the resulting formula $\dfrac{AE}{AC} = \dfrac{s_1}{s_2} = \sqrt{\dfrac{A_1}{A_2}}$. The area of the trapezoid $DEBC$ is twice the area of ADE, or $2A_1$, so the area of ABC is equal to the sum of the area of ADE and $DECB$, which equal A_1 and $2A_1$, respectively; thus, the area of ABC is $3A_1$. So, $A_1 : A_2 = 1 : 3$. Thus, $s_1 : s_2 = \sqrt{\dfrac{1}{3}} = 1 : \sqrt{3}$. (318)

8. Choice C is correct. Since the radius of the circle is 10 inches, its circumference is 2π (10 inches), or $2\left(\dfrac{22}{7}\right)$ (10 inches), which equals $\dfrac{440}{7}$ inches. This is the distance the wheel will travel in one revolution. To travel 10 feet, or 120 inches, it must travel $120 \div \dfrac{440}{7}$, or $\dfrac{21}{11}$ revolutions. At a speed of 22 revolutions per minute, or $\dfrac{11}{30}$ revolutions per second, it will take $\dfrac{21}{11} \div \dfrac{11}{30}$ or $\dfrac{630}{121}$ seconds. Carrying the division to the nearest tenth of a second, we get 5.2 seconds. (310)

9. Choice C is correct. If we let d represent the diagonal of a square, s represent the length of one side, and A represent its area, then we have two formulas: $d = s\sqrt{2}$, and $A = s^2$, relating the three quantities. However, from the first equation, we can see that $s^2 = \dfrac{d^2}{2}$, so we can derive a third formula, $A = \dfrac{d^2}{2}$, relating A and d. We are given that d equals $16''$, so we can calculate the value of A as $\dfrac{(16 \text{ inches})^2}{2}$, or 128 square inches. (303)

10. Choice B is correct. The area of the shaded figure is equal to the difference between the areas of the rectangle and the circle. The area of the rectangle is defined by the formula $A = bh$, where b and h are the two adjacent sides of the rectangle. In this case, A is equal to 4 inches $\times$ 6 inches, or 24 square inches. The area of the circle is defined by the formula $A = \pi r^2$, where r is the radius. Since BE equals the diameter of the circle and is equal to 4

inches, then the radius must be 2 inches. Thus, the area of the circle is $\pi(2 \text{ inches})^2$, or 4π square inches. Subtracting, we obtain the area of the shaded portion: $24 - 4\pi$ square inches. (304, 310)

11. Choice D is correct. We use the formula for the area of an equilateral triangle, $\dfrac{\sqrt{3}\,s^2}{4}$, where s is a side. If $s = 1$, then the area of the triangle is $\dfrac{\sqrt{3}}{4}$. (308)

12. Choice C is correct. An angle, which is inscribed in a circle, whose sides cut off an arc of 180° (that is, intersects the ends of a diameter) is a right angle. According to the Pythagorean Theorem, the diameter AC, being the hypotenuse of a triangle with sides of 12 feet and 16 feet, has a length of $\sqrt{12^2 + 16^2} = \sqrt{400} = 20$ feet. Therefore, if we call d the diameter, the area of the circle is $A = \pi\left(\dfrac{d}{2}\right)^2 = \pi\left(\dfrac{20}{2}\right)^2 = 100\pi$ square feet.

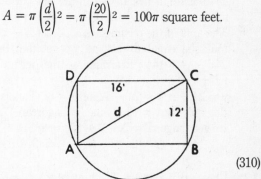

(310)

13. Choice E is correct. The area of the room = 12 feet $\times$ 18 feet = 216 square feet. The area of one tile = $\dfrac{3}{4}$ inches $\times$ 2 inches = $\dfrac{3}{2}$ square inches. The number of tiles = area of the room ÷ area of one tile = $\dfrac{216 \text{ square feet}}{\dfrac{3}{2} \text{ square inch}} = \dfrac{216 \times 144 \text{ square inches}}{\dfrac{3}{2} \text{ square inch}}$ = $216 \times \overset{48}{\cancel{144}} \times \dfrac{2}{\cancel{3}} = 20{,}736$ tiles. (304)

14. Choice B is correct. The volume of a sphere is found by using the formula $\dfrac{4}{3}\pi r^3$ where r is the radius. In this case, the radius is 4 miles, so the volume is $\dfrac{256}{3}\pi$ cubic miles. This is equal to the volume of a cylinder of radius 8 miles so $\dfrac{256}{3}\pi = \pi 8^2 h$, since the volume of a cylinder is $\pi r^2 h$, where h is the

height, and r is the radius of the base. Solving $\dfrac{256\pi}{3}$

$= \pi 8^2 h; \dfrac{\dfrac{256\pi}{3}}{\pi 64} = \dfrac{\overset{16}{\cancel{256}}}{3} \times \dfrac{1}{\cancel{\pi 64}} = \dfrac{16}{12} = \dfrac{4}{3}$ miles.

(314, 315)

15. Choice E is correct. 33 yards = 99 feet = 15 revolutions. Thus, 1 revolution = $\dfrac{99}{15}$ feet = $\dfrac{33}{5}$ feet = 6.6 feet. Since 1 revolution = the circumference of the wheel, the wheel's diameter = circumference ÷ π. 6.6 feet ÷ $\dfrac{22}{7}$ = 2.10 feet. (310)

16. Choice B is correct. The area of the right triangle is equal to $\dfrac{1}{2}ab$ where a and b are the legs of the triangle. In this case, the area is $\dfrac{1}{2} \times 12 \times 24$, or

144 square inches. If we call the sides of the rectangle x and y we get. $2x + 2y = 48$, or $y = 24 - x$. The area of the rectangle is xy, or $x(24 - x)$. This must be equal to 144, so we get the equation $24x - x^2 = 144$. Rearranging the terms gives us $x^2 - 24x + 144 = 0$, or $(x - 12)^2$. Since $y = 24 - x$, $y = 24 - 12$, or $y = 12$. This is satisfied only by $x = 12$. By the Pythagorean Theorem we get: diagonal = $\sqrt{12^2 + 12^2} = \sqrt{144 + 144} = \sqrt{2(144)} = 12\sqrt{2}$. (304, 306, 317)

17. Choice B is correct. The area of the square is 64 square inches, since $A = s^2$ where s is the length of a side, and A is the area. The area of the circle is $\pi \left(\dfrac{7}{4}\right)^2 = \dfrac{22}{7} \times \dfrac{49}{16} = \dfrac{77}{8} = 9.625$. Subtracting,

$64 - 9.625 = 54.375 = 54.4$ (approximately). (304, 310)

18. Choice C is correct. The capacity of the volume ($V = lwh$, where l, w, h, are the adjacent sides of the solid) of the container = (3 inches) (3 inches) (11 inches) = 99 cubic inches; since 1 gallon equals 231 cubic inches, 99 cubic inches equal $\dfrac{99}{231}$ gallons (the fraction reduces to $\dfrac{3}{7}$). One gallon equals 128 ounces (1 gallon = 4 quarts, 1 quart = 2 pints, 1 pint = 16 ounces), so the container holds $\dfrac{384}{7}$ ounces = 55 ounces (approximately). (312)

19. Choice E is correct. The speed of the first wheel is equal to its rate of revolution multiplied by its

circumference, which equals 24 × 20 inches × π = 480π inches per minute. The speed of the second is 18 × 30 inches × π = 540π inches per minute. Thus, their ratio is 540π : 480π = 9 : 8. (310)

20. Choice D is correct. The area of the path is equal to the area of the ring between two concentric circles of radii 10 feet and 13 feet. This area is obtained by subtracting the area of the smaller circle from the area of the larger circle. The area of the larger circle is equal to π × its radius squared = $\pi(13)^2$ feet^2 = 169π square feet. By the same process, the area of the smaller circle = 100π square feet. The area of the shaded part = 169π − 100π = 69π square feet. (310)

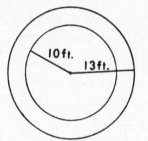

21. Choice A is correct. The diameter = 16 inches, so the radius = 8 inches. Thus, the area of the whole circle = $\pi(8 \text{ inches})^2 = 64\pi$ square inches. The area of the semicircle is one-half of the area of the whole circle, or 32π square inches. (311)

22. Choice A is correct. A cube has twelve equal edges, so the length of one side of the cube is $\dfrac{1}{12}$ of 4 feet, or 4 inches. Thus, its volume is 4 inches × 4 inches × 4 inches = 64 cubic inches. (313)

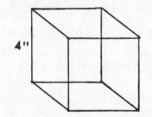

23. Choice B is correct. The additional water will take the shape of a rectangular solid measuring 25 feet × 6 inches × 3 inches (3″ = the added depth) = $25 \times \dfrac{1}{2} \times \dfrac{1}{4}$ cubic feet = $\dfrac{25}{8}$ cubic feet. (312)

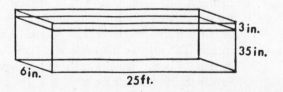

24. Choice A is correct. The volume of the cylinder $= \pi r^2 h = \left(\frac{22}{7}\right)\left(\frac{7}{2}\right)^2$ (10) cubic inches $= 385$ cubic inches. 231 cubic inches $= 1$ gallon, so 385 cubic inches $= \frac{385}{231}$ gallons $= \frac{5}{3}$ gallons $= 1.7$ gallons (approximately). (314)

25. Choice D is correct. The area of floor $= 10$ feet $\times 16$ feet $= 160$ square feet. Area of one tile $= 8$ inches $\times 8$ inches $= 64$ square inches $= \frac{64}{144}$ square feet $= \frac{4}{9}$ square feet. Thus, the number of tiles $=$ area of floor $\div$ area of tile $= 160 \div \frac{4}{9} = 360$. At 9¢ apiece, the tiles will cost $32.40. (304)

26. Choice B is correct. Looking at the following three diagrams, we can observe that the triangle, square, and hexagon are all smaller than the circle.

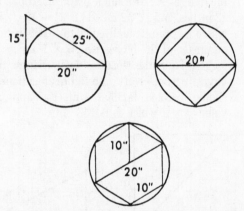

Comparing the areas of the circle and the rectangle, we notice that the area of the circle is $\pi(10 \text{ inches})^2 = 100\pi$ square inches, which is greater than (10 inches) (30 inches) $= 300$ square inches, the area of the rectangle. (π is approximately 3.14.) (302)

27. Choice D is correct. In a cylinder, $V = \pi r^2 h$, where r is the radius of the base, and h is the height. The new volume, $V' = \pi(3r)^2 \left(\frac{h}{3}\right) = 3\pi r^2 h = 2V$. Thus, the ratio of the new volume to the old volume is 3:1. (314)

28. Choice C is correct. A cube 2 feet on each side has a volume of $2 \times 2 \times 2 = 8$ cubic feet. Since 1 cubic foot equals 7.5 gallons, 8 cubic feet equals 60 gallons. If the faucet flows at the rate of 10 gallons/minute it will take 6 minutes to fill the cube. (313)

29. Choice E is correct. Let $s =$ the side of the square. Then, the area of the square is equal to s^2. The diagonal of the square is $s\sqrt{2}$, so the square of the diagonal is $2s^2$. Thus, the ratio of the area of the square to the square of the diagonal is $s^2 : 2s^2$ or $1 : 2$. (303)

30. Choice B is correct. The area of the square $ABCD$ is equal to 4 inches $\times$ 4 inches $= 16$ square inches. The two semicircles can be placed together diameter-to-diameter to form a circle with a radius of 2 inches, and thus, an area of 4π. Subtracting the area of the circle from the area of the square, we obtain the combined areas of AED and BEC. But, since the figure is symmetrical, AED and BEC must be equal, so the area of AED is one-half of this remainder, which equals $16 - 4\pi$, or $8 - 2\pi$ square inches. (303, 310)

31. Choice C is correct. The area of the circle is equal to πr^2, and the area of the rectangle is equal to πx. Since these areas are equal, $\pi r^2 = \pi x$, and $x = r^2$. (304, 310)

32. Choice C is correct. The volume of a cube is e^3 where e is the length of an edge. If the volume is 27 cubic meters, then $e^3 = 27$ and $e = 3$ meters. The surface area of a cube is $6e^2$, and if $e = 3$ meters, then the surface area is 54 square meters. (313)

33. Choice C is correct. The area of a regular hexagon, one of whose sides is 1 inch, is equal to the sum of the areas of 6 equilateral triangles, each with a side of 1 inch. The area of an equilateral triangle with a side of 1 inch is equal to $\frac{\sqrt{3}}{4}$ square inches. (The formula for the area of an equilateral triangle with a side of s is $A = s^2 \frac{\sqrt{3}}{4}$.) The sum of 6 such triangles is $\frac{6\sqrt{3}}{4}$, or $\frac{3\sqrt{3}}{2}$. (308)

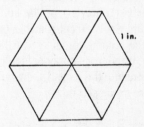

34. Choice D is correct. The area of a triangle can be expressed as $\frac{1}{2}ab \sin C$ where a and b are any two sides and C is the angle between them. In this case $a = 6$, $b = 8$, and $<C = 30°$. You should remember that the sine of 30° is $\frac{1}{2}$ so the area is $\frac{1}{2}(6)(8)\left(\frac{1}{2}\right) = 12$. (307)

35. Choice D is correct. Since the wheel takes 1 minute to make 600 revolutions and travels 1 mile in that time, we have the relation 1 mile = 5,280 feet = 600 revolutions. Thus, 1 revolution = $\frac{5,280}{600}$ feet = 8.8 feet = circumference = π(diameter) = $\left(\frac{22}{7}\right)$ (diameter). Therefore, the diameter = 8.8 feet $\div \left(\frac{22}{7}\right)$ = 2.8 feet. (310)

36. Choice D is correct. In this case, it is easiest to calculate the perimeters of the 5 figures. According to the Pythagorean Theorem, a square with a diagonal of 5 feet has a side of $\frac{5}{\sqrt{2}}$, which is equal to $\frac{5\sqrt{2}}{2}$. (This is found by multiplying the numerator and denominator of $\frac{5}{\sqrt{2}}$ by $\sqrt{2}$.) If each side of the square is $\frac{5\sqrt{2}}{2}$, then the perimeter is $\cancel{4} \times \frac{5\sqrt{2}}{\cancel{2}} = 10\sqrt{2}$ feet. A rectangle with sides of 3 feet and 4 feet has a perimeter of 2(3) + 2(4), or 14 feet. An equilateral triangle with a side of 48 inches, or 4 feet, has a perimeter of 12 feet. A regular hexagon whose longest diagonal is 6 feet has a side of 3 feet and, therefore, a perimeter of 18 feet. (See the diagram for Solution 33.) Finally, a parallelogram with sides of 6 inches, or $\frac{1}{2}$ foot, and 7 feet has a perimeter of 15 feet. Therefore, the hexagon has the largest perimeter. (302, 317)

37. Choice A is correct. The volume of the first container is equal to 3 inches × 4 inches × 10 inches, or 120 cubic inches. The volume of the second container, the cylinder, is equal to $\pi r^2 h = \pi(2$ inches$)^2$ (10 inches), or 40π cubic inches, which is greater than 120 cubic inches (π is greater than 3). So the second container can hold more than the first. If the first container is filled and the contents poured into the second, there will be room for more water in the second. (312, 314)

38. Choice B is correct. The area of the square is 16 square inches. The four semicircles can be added to form two circles, each of radius 2 inches, so the area of each circle is 4π square inches, and the two circles add up to 8π square inches. Thus, the total area is $16 + 8\pi$ square inches. (303, 311)

39. Choice B is correct. Since the area of the square is $81p^2$, one side of the square will equal $9p$. According to the Pythagorean Theorem, the diagonal will equal $\sqrt{81p^2 + 81p^2} = 9p\sqrt{2}$. (303, 317)

40. Choice A is correct. We can regard the area as a rectangle, 20 ft × 14 ft, with two rectangles, measuring 4 ft × 6 ft and 2 ft × 2 ft, cut out. Thus, the area is equal to 280 sq ft − 24 sq ft − 4 sq ft = 252 sq ft = $\frac{252}{9}$ sq yd = 28 sq yds. (Remember, 1 square yard equals 9 square feet.) At \$2.50 a square yard, 28 square yards will cost \$70. (304)

41. Choice D is correct. The perimeter of the square is equal to four times its side; since a side is $\frac{1}{\sqrt{2}}$, or $\frac{\sqrt{2}}{2}$ times the diagonal, the perimeter of the square in question is $4 \times 5\sqrt{2} = 20\sqrt{2}$, which is approximately equal to 28.28 inches. The perimeter of a right triangle with sides that are in a 3–4–5 ratio, i.e., 9 inches, 12 inches, and 15 inches is 9 + 12 + 15 = 36 inches. The perimeter of the pentagon is 5 × 5 inches, or 25 inches. The perimeter of the right isosceles triangle (with sides of 12 inches, 12 inches, and $12\sqrt{2}$ inches) is $24 + 12\sqrt{2}$ inches, which is approximately equal to 40.968 inches. The perimeter of the hexagon is 6 × 5 inches, or 30 inches. Thus, the isosceles right triangle has the largest perimeter of those figures mentioned. You should become familiar with the approximate value of $\sqrt{2}$, which is 1.414. (302)

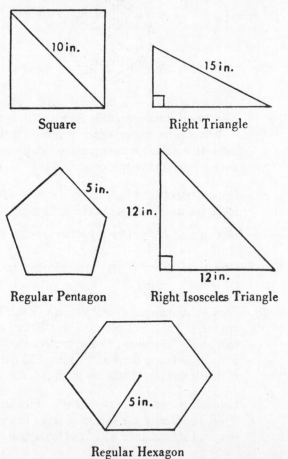

Square   Right Triangle

Regular Pentagon   Right Isosceles Triangle

Regular Hexagon

42. Choice D is correct. For rectangular solids, the following formula holds:

$V = Ah$, where A is the area of the base, and h is the height.

If we replace A by $2A$, and h by $3h$, we get $V' = (2A)(3h) = 6V$. Thus, $V' : V = 6 : 1$. (312)

43. Choice C is correct. The area of the room is 27 feet × 14 feet = 378 square feet. 9 square feet = 1 square yard, so the area of the room is 42 square yards. At $1.50 per square yard the linoleum to cover the floor will cost $63.00. (304)

44. Choice A is correct. A circle with a 4-inch radius has an 8-inch diameter, so there can be only 2 rows of 3 circles each, or 6 circles. (310)

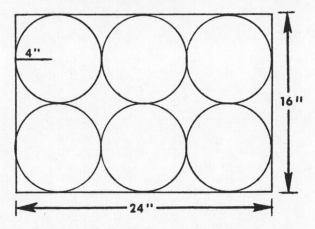

45. Choice E is correct. Let one side of the triangle be s. Then the area of the triangle is $\frac{s^2\sqrt{3}}{4}$. (Either memorize this formula or remember that it is derived by drawing an altitude to divide the triangle into two congruent 30° : 60° : 90° right triangles.) The perimeter of the equilateral triangle is $3s$, so the ratio of the area to the perimeter is $\frac{s^2\sqrt{3}}{4} : 3s$, or $s : 4\sqrt{3}$, which cannot be determined unless we know the value of s. (308)

46. Choice E is correct. The formula for volume of a cylinder is $V = r^2h$, where r is the radius of the base, and h is the height. Here, $r = 4$ inches, and $h = 10$ inches, while $\pi \approx 3.14$. (The symbol $\approx$ means "approximately equal to.") Thus $V \approx (4)^2(10)(3.14) = 160(3.14) = 502.4$ cubic inches. (314)

47. Choice B is correct. If the area of a square is $144s^2$, then one side will equal $12s$, so the diagonal will equal $12s\sqrt{2}$. (The Pythagorean Theorem may be used here to get $d = \sqrt{144s^2 + 144s^2}$, where d is the diagonal.) (303, 317)

48. Choice C is correct. The inside of the pool forms a cylinder of radius 5 feet, and height 5 feet. The volume is $\pi r^2 h$, or $\pi \times 5 \times 5 \times 5 = 125\pi$ cubic feet. (314)

49. Choice B is correct. The area of the floor is 20 feet × 24 feet = 480 square feet. 30 inches is equal to $2\frac{1}{2}$ feet, and we must find the length which, when multiplied by $2\frac{1}{2}$ feet, will yield 480 square feet.

This length is 192 feet, which equals 64 yards (3 feet = 1 yard). (304)

50. Choice D is correct. The circumference of the larger wheel is 18π inches ($C = \pi d$). After 72 revolutions, the larger wheel will have gone a distance of $72(18\pi)$ inches. Since the smaller wheel moves at the same linear speed, it will also have gone $72(18\pi)$ inches. The circumference of the smaller wheel is 12π inches, and if we call the number of revolutions that the smaller wheel makes, r, then we know that $12\pi r = 72(18\pi)$. Dividing both sides by 12π gives us $r = 6(18)$ or 108 revolutions. Note that in this problem we have used the relation, distance = rate × time, where the time for both wheels is a fixed quantity. (310)

Math Refresher
Session 4

Algebra Problems

Algebraic Properties

Algebra is the branch of mathematics that applies the laws of arithmetic to symbols that represent unknown quantities. The most commonly used symbols are the letters of the alphabet such as A, B, C, x, y, z, etc. These symbols can be added, subtracted, multiplied, and divided like numbers. For example, $3a + 2a = 5a$, $2x - x = x$, $3(5b) = 15b$, $\frac{6x}{3x} = 2$. These symbols can be raised to powers like a^3 or y^2. Remember that raising a number to a power means multiplying the number by itself a number of times. For example, $a^3 = a \cdot a \cdot a$. The power is 3 and a is multiplied by itself 3 times.

Generally, in algebra, a variable (an unknown represented by a symbol) appears in an *equation* (a statement that defines the relationship between certain quantities), and values of the variable that *satisfy* the equation must be found. For example, the equation $6a = 12$ is satisfied when the variable, a, is equal to 2. This section is a discussion on how to solve complicated algebraic equations and other related topics.

Fundamental Laws of Our Number System

Following is a list of laws that apply to all the numbers necessary to work with when doing arithmetic and algebra problems. Remember these laws and use them in doing problems.

401. If $x = y$ and $y = z$, then $x = z$. This is called *transitivity*. For example, if $a = 3$ and $b = 3$, then $a = b$.

402. If $x = y$, then $x + z = y + z$, and $x - z = y - z$. This means that the same quantity can be added to or subtracted from both sides of an equation. For example, if $a = b$, then add any number to both sides, say 3, and $a + 3 = b + 3$. Or if $a = b$, then $a - 3 = b - 3$.

403. If $x = y$, then $x \cdot z = y \cdot z$ and $x \div z = y \div z$, unless $z = 0$ (see Section 404). This means that both sides of an equation can be multiplied by the same number. For example, if $a = n$, then $5a = 5n$. It also means that both sides of an equation can be divided by the same nonzero number. If $a = b$, then $\frac{a}{3} = \frac{b}{3}$.

404. *Never divide by zero.* This is a very important fact that must be remembered. The quotient of *any* quantity (except zero) divided by zero is infinity.

405. $x + y = y + x$, and $x \cdot y = y \cdot x$. Therefore, $2 + 3 = 3 + 2$, and $2 \cdot 3 = 3 \cdot 2$. Remember that this does not work for division and subtraction. $3 \div 2$ does not equal $2 \div 3$; and $3 - 2$ does not equal $2 - 3$. The property described above is called *commutativity*.

Equations

406. *Linear equation in one unknown.* Equations with one variable are linear equations in one unknown. The variable is always in the first power, i.e., x or y or a, but never in a higher or fractional power, i.e., x^2, y^3, or $a^{1/2}$. Examples of linear equations in one unknown are $x + 5 = 7$, $3a - 2 = 7a + 1$, $2x - 7x = 8 + x$, $8 = -4y$, etc. To solve these equations, follow these steps:

STEP 1. Combine the terms on the left and right sides of the equality. That is, (1) add all of the numerical terms on each side, and (2) add all of the terms with variables on each side. For example, if you have $7 + 2x + 9 = 4x - 3 - 2x + 7 + 6x$, combining terms on the left gives you $16 + 2x$, because $7 + 9 = 16$, and $2x$ is the only variable term on that side. On the right we get $8x + 4$, since $4x - 2x + 6x = 8x$ and $-3 + 7 = 4$. Therefore the new equation is $16 + 2x = 8x + 4$.

STEP 2. Put all of the numerical terms on the right side of the equation and all of the variable terms on the left side. This is done by subtracting the numerical term on the left from both sides of the equation and by subtracting the variable term on the right side from both sides of the equation. In the example $16 + 2x = 8x + 4$, subtract 16 from both sides and obtain $2x = 8x - 12$; then subtracting $8x$ from both sides gives $-6x = -12$.

STEP 3. Divide both sides by the coefficient of the variable. In this case, where $-6x = -12$, dividing by -6 gives 2. This is the final solution to the problem.

> **Example:** Solve for a in the equation $7a + 4 - 2a = 18 + 17a + 10$.
>
> **Solution:** From Step 1, we combine terms on both sides to get $5a + 4 = 28 + 17a$. As in Step 2, we then subtract 4 and $17a$ from both sides to give $-12a = 24$. By Step 3, we then divide both sides of the equation by the coefficient of a, which is -12, to get $a = -2$.
>
> **Example:** Solve for x in $2x + 6 = 0$.
>
> **Solution:** Here Step 1 is eliminated because there are no terms to combine on either side. Step 2 requires that 6 be subtracted from both sides to get $2x = -6$. Then dividing by 2 gives $x = -3$.

407. *Simultaneous equations in two unknowns.* These are problems in which two equations, each with two unknowns, are given. These equations must be solved together (simultaneously) in order to arrive at the solution.

STEP 1. Rearrange each equation so that both are in the form that has the x term on the left side and the y term and the constant on the right side. In other words, put the equations in the form $Ax = By + C$ where A, B, and C are numerical constants. For example, if one of the equations is $9x - 10y + 30 = 11y + 3x - 6$, then subtract $-10y$ and 30 from both sides to get $9x = 21y + 3x - 36$. Subtracting $3x$ from both sides gives $6x = 21y - 36$, which is in the form of $Ax = By + C$.

The first equation should be in the form $Ax = By + C$ and the second equation should be in the form $Dx = Ey + F$ where A, B, C, D, E, and F are numerical constants.

STEP 2. Multiply the first equation by the coefficient of x in the second equation (D). Multiply the second equation by the coefficient of x in the first equation (A). Now the equations are in the form $ADx = BDy + CD$ and $ADx = AEy + AF$. For example, in the two equations $2x = 7y - 12$ and $3x = y + 1$, multiply the first by 3 and the second by 2 to get $6x = 21y - 36$ and $6x = 2y + 2$.

STEP 3. Equate the right sides of both equations. This can be done because both sides are equal to ADx. (See Section 401 on transitivity.) Thus, $BDy + CD = AEy + AF$. So $21y - 36$ and $2y + 2$ are both equal to $6x$ and are equal to each other: $21y - 36 = 2y + 2$.

STEP 4. Solve for y. This is done in the manner outlined in Section 406. In the equation $21y - 36 = 2y + 2$, $y = 2$. By this method $y = \dfrac{AF - CD}{BD - AE}$.

STEP 5. Substitute the value of y into either of the original equations and solve for x. In the general equations we would then have either $x = \dfrac{B}{A}\left[\dfrac{AF-CD}{BD-AE}\right] + \dfrac{C}{A}$, or $x = \dfrac{E}{D}\left[\dfrac{AF-CD}{BD-AE}\right] + \dfrac{E}{D}$.

In the example, if $y = 2$ is substituted into either $2x = 7y - 12$ or $3x = y + 1$, then $2x = 14 - 12$ or $3x = 3$ can be solved to get $x = 1$.

Example: Solve for a and b in the equation $3a + 4b = 24$ and $2a + b = 11$.

Solution: First note that it makes no difference in these two equations whether the variables are a and b instead of x and y. Subtract $4b$ from the first equation and b from the second equation to get the equations $3a = 24 - 4b$ and $2a = 11 - b$. Multiply the first by 2 and the second by 3. Thus, $6a = 48 - 8b$ and $6a = 33 - 3b$. Equate $48 - 8b$ and $33 - 3b$ to get $48 - 8b = 33 - 3b$. Solving for b in the usual manner gives us $b = 3$. Substituting the value of $b = 3$ into the equation $3a + 4b = 24$ obtains $3a + 12 = 24$. Solving for a gives $a = 4$. Thus the complete solution is $a = 4$ and $b = 3$.

408. *Quadratic Equations.* Quadratic equations are expressed in the form $ax^2 + bx + c = 0$; where a, b, and c are constant numbers (for example, $\frac{1}{2}$, 4, -2, etc.) and x is a variable. An equation of this form may be satisfied by two values of x, one value of x, or no values of x. Actually when there are no values of x that satisfy the equation, there are only *imaginary* solutions. These will not be dealt with. To determine the number of solutions, find the value of the expression $b^2 - 4ac$ where a, b, and c are the constant coefficients of the equation $ax^2 + bx + c = 0$.

If $b^2 - 4ac$ is *greater* than 0, there are two solutions.

If $b^2 - 4ac$ is *less* than 0, there are no solutions.

If $b^2 - 4ac$ is *equal* to 0, there is one solution.

If solutions exists, they can be found by using the formulas:

$$x = \frac{-b + \sqrt{b^2 - 4ac}}{2a} \text{ and } x = \frac{-b - \sqrt{b^2 - 4ac}}{2a}$$

Note that if $b^2 - 4ac = 0$, the two above solutions will be the same and there will be one solution.

Example: Determine the solutions, if they exist, to the equation $x^2 + 6x + 5 = 0$.

Solution: First, noting $a = 1$, $b = 6$, and $c = 5$, calculate $b^2 - 4ac$, or $6^2 - 4(1)(5)$. Thus, $b^2 - 4ac = 16$. Since this is greater than 0, there are two solutions. They are, from the formulas:

$$x = \frac{-6 + \sqrt{6^2 - 4 \cdot 1 \cdot 5}}{2 \cdot 1} \text{ and } x = \frac{-6 - \sqrt{6^2 - 4 \cdot 1 \cdot 5}}{2 \cdot 1}$$

Simplify these to:

$$x = \frac{-6 + \sqrt{16}}{2} \text{ and } x = \frac{-6 - \sqrt{16}}{2}$$

As $\sqrt{16} = 4$, $x = \dfrac{-6+4}{2} = \dfrac{-2}{2}$ and $x = \dfrac{-6-4}{2} = \dfrac{-10}{2}$. Thus, the two solutions are $x = -1$ and $x = -5$.

Another method of solving quadratic equations is to *factor* the $ax^2 + bx + c$ into two expressions. This will be explained in the next section.

409. *Factoring.* Factoring is breaking down an expression into two or more expressions, the product of which is the original expression. For example, 6 can be factored into 2 and 3 because

$2 \cdot 3 = 6$. Then, if $x^2 + bx + c$ is factorable, it will be factored into two expressions in the form $(x + d)$ and $(x + e)$. If the expression $(x + d)$ is multiplied by the expression $(x + e)$, their product is $x^2 + (d + e)x + de$. For example, $(x + 3) \cdot (x + 2)$ equals $x^2 + 5x + 6$. To factor an expression such as $x^2 + 6x + 8$, find a d and e such that $d + e = 6$ and $de = 8$. Of the various factors of 8, we find that $d = 4$ and $e = 2$. Thus $x^2 + 6x + 8$ can be factored into the expressions $(x + 4)$ and $(x + 2)$. Below are factored expressions.

$x^2 + 2x + 1 = (x + 1)(x + 1)$ $x^2 + 3x + 2 = (x + 2)(x + 1)$

$x^2 + 4x + 4 = (x + 2)(x + 2)$ $x^2 + 5x + 6 = (x + 3)(x + 2)$

$x^2 - 4x + 3 = (x - 3)(x - 1)$ $x^2 - 4x - 5 = (x - 5)(x + 1)$

$x^2 + 10x + 16 = (x + 8)(x + 2)$ $x^2 + 4x - 5 = (x + 5)(x - 1)$

$x^2 - 5x + 6 = (x - 2)(x - 3)$ $x^2 - x - 6 = (x - 3)(x + 2)$

An important rule to remember in factoring is that $a^2 - b^2 = (a + b)(a - b)$. For example, $x^2 - 9 = (x + 3)(x - 3)$. To apply factoring in solving quadratic equations, factor the quadratic expression into two terms and set each term equal to zero. Then, solve the two resulting equations.

Example: Solve $x^2 - x - 6 = 0$.

Solution: First factor the expression $x^2 - x - 6$ into $x - 3$ and $x + 2$. Setting each of these equal to 0 gives $x - 3 = 0$ and $x + 2 = 0$. Solving these equations gives us $x = 3$ and $x = -2$.

Algebra of Graphs

410. *Coordinate geometry.* These problems deal with the algebra of graphs. A graph consists of a set of points whose position is determined with respect to a set of axes usually labeled the X-axis and the Y-axis and divided into appropriate units. Locate a point on the graph with an "x coordinate" of a units and a "y coordinate" of b units. First move a units along the X axis (either to the left or right depending on whether a is positive or negative). Then move b units along the Y axis (either up or down depending on the sign of b). A point with an x coordinate of a, and a y coordinate of b, is represented by (a, b). The points $(2,3)$, $(-1,4)$, $(-2,-3)$, and $(4,-2)$ are shown on the following graph.

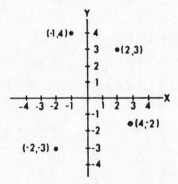

411. *Distance between two points.* If the coordinates of point A are (x_1, y_1) and the coordinates of point B are (x_2, y_2), then the distance on the graph between the two points is $d = \sqrt{(x_2 - x_1)^2 + (y_2 - y_1)^2}$.

Example: Find the distance between the point $(2,-3)$ and the point $(5,1)$.

Solution: In this case $x_1 = 2$, $x_2 = 5$, $y_1 = -3$, and $y_2 = 1$. Substituting into the above formula gives us

$$d = \sqrt{(5-2)^2 + [1-(-3)]^2} = \sqrt{3^2 + 4^2} = \sqrt{25} = 5$$

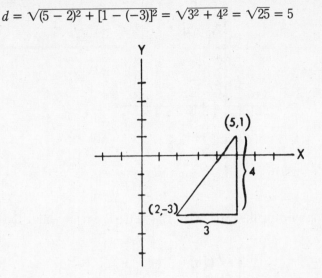

Note: This formula is a consequence of the Pythagorean Theorem. Pythagoras, an ancient Greek mathematician, discovered that the square of the length of the hypotenuse (longest side) of a right triangle is equal to the sum of the square of the lengths of the other two sides. See Sections 317 and 509.

412. *Midpoint of the line segment joining two points.* If the coordinates of the first point are (x_1, y_1) and the coordinates of the second point are (x_2, y_2), then the coordinates of the midpoint will be $\left(\dfrac{x_1 + x_2}{2}, \dfrac{y_1 + y_2}{2} \right)$. In other words, each coordinate of the midpoint is equal to the *average* of the corresponding coordinates of the endpoints.

Example: Find the midpoint of the segment connecting the points (2,4) and (6,2).

Solution: The average of 2 and 6 is 4 so the first coordinate is 4. The average of 4 and 2 is 3; thus the second coordinate is 3. The midpoint is (4,3). $\left[\dfrac{2+6}{2} = 4, \dfrac{4+2}{2} = 3 \right]$

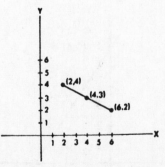

413. *Plotting the graph of a line.* An equation that can be put in the form of $y = mx + b$, where m and b are numerical constants can be represented as a line on a graph. This means that all of the points on the graph that the line passes through will satisfy the equation. Remember that each point has an x and a y value that can be substituted into the equation. To plot a line, follow the steps below:

STEP 1. Select two values of x and two values of y that will satisfy the equation. For example, in the equation $y = 2x + 4$, the point ($x = 1$, $y = 6$), will satisfy the equation as will the point ($x = -2$, $y = 0$). There are an infinite number of such points on a line.

STEP 2. Plot these two points on the graph. In this case, the two points are (1,6) and (−2,0). These points are represented below.

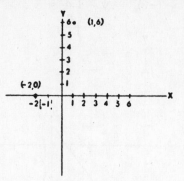

STEP 3. Draw a line connecting the two points. This is the line representing the equation.

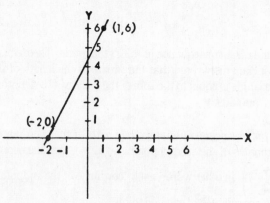

NOTE: A straight line is completely specified by two points.

Example: Graph the equation $2y + 3x = 12$.

Solution: Two points that satisfy this equation are (2,3) and (0,6). Plotting these points and drawing a line between them gives:

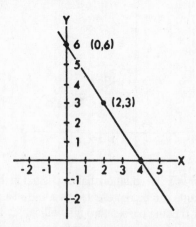

414. *Y-intercept.* The Y-intercept of a line is the point where the line crosses the Y-axis. At any point where a line crosses the Y-axis, $x = 0$. To find the Y-intercept of a line, simply substitute $x = 0$ into the equation of the line and solve for y.

Example: Find the Y-intercept of the equation $2x + 3y = 6$.

Solution: If $x = 0$ is substituted into the equation, it simplifies to $3y = 6$. Solving for y gives $y = 2$. Thus, 2 is the Y-intercept.

> **If an equation can be put into the form of $y = mx + b$, then b is the Y-intercept.**

415. *X-intercept.* The point where a line intersects the X-axis is called the X-intercept. At this point $y = 0$. To find the X-intercept of a line, substitute $y = 0$ into the equation and solve for x.

Example: Given the equation $2x + 3y = 6$, find the X-intercept.

Solution: Substitute $y = 0$ into the equation getting $2x = 6$. Solving for x, find $x = 3$. Thus the X-intercept is 3.

In the diagram below, the Y- and X-intercepts of the equation $2x + 3y = 6$ are illustrated.

Art 345 . . . gl

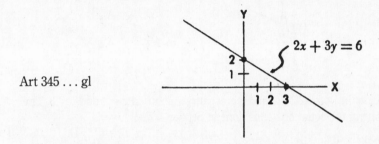

416. *Slope.* The slope of a line is the change in y caused by a 1 unit increase in x. If an equation is in the form of $y = mx + b$, then as x increases 1 unit, y will increase m units. Therefore the slope is m.

Example: Find the slope of the line $2x + 3y = 6$.

Solution: First put the equation into the form of $y = mx + b$. Subtract $2x$ from both sides and divide by 3. The equation becomes $y = -\dfrac{2}{3}x + 2$. Therefore the slope is $-\dfrac{2}{3}$.

The slope of the line joining two points, (x_1, y_1) and (x_2, y_2), is given by the expression $m_{12} = \dfrac{y_2 - y_1}{x_2 - x_1}$.

Example: Find the slope of the line joining the points $(3,2)$ and $(4,-1)$.

Solution: Substituting into the above formula gives us $m = \dfrac{-1 - 2}{4 - 3} = \dfrac{-3}{1} = -3$ where $x_1 = 3, x_2 = 4, y_1 = 2, y_2 = -1$.

417. *Graphing Simultaneous Equations.* Recall that simultaneous equations are a pair of equations in two unknowns. Each of these equations is graphed separately, and each is represented by a straight line. The solution of the simultaneous equations (i.e., the pair of values that satisfies *both* at the same time) is represented by the intersection of two lines. Now, for any pair of lines, there are three possible relationships:

1. The lines intersect at one and only one point; in this case, this point represents the unique solution to the pair of equations. This is most often the case. Such lines are called *consistent.*

2. The lines coincide exactly; this represents the case where the two equations are equivalent (just different forms of the same mathematical relation). Any point that satisfies *either* of the two equations automatically satisfies *both.*

3. The lines are parallel and never intersect. In this case the equations are called *inconsistent*, and they have *no* solution at all. Two lines that are parallel will have the same slope.

Example: Solve graphically the equations $4x - y = 5$ and $2x + 4y = 16$.

Solution: Plot the two lines represented by the two equations. (See Section 413.) The graph is shown below.

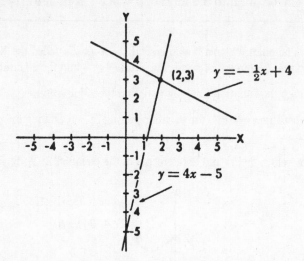

The two lines intersect in the point (2,3), which represents the solution $x = 2$ and $y = 3$. This can be checked by solving the equations as is done in Section 407.

Example: Solve $x + 2y = 6$ and $2x + 4y = 8$.

Solution: Find two points that satisfy each equation. Draw a line connecting these two points. The two graphs will look like this:

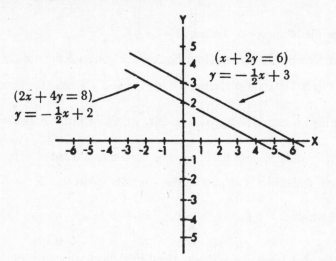

These lines will never intersect, and these equations are termed inconsistent. There is no solution.

Remember that two parallel lines have the same slope. This is an easy way to see whether two lines are consistent or inconsistent.

Example: Find the solution to $2x - 3y = 8$ and $4x = 6y + 16$.

Solution: On the graph these two lines are identical. This means that there are an infinite set of points that satisfy both equations.

Identical lines are products of each other and can be reduced to the same equation.

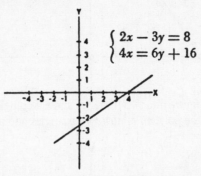

$$\begin{cases} 2x - 3y = 8 \\ 4x = 6y + 16 \end{cases}$$

418. *Areas of polygons.* Often, an elementary geometric figure is placed on a graph to calculate its area. This is usually simple for figures such as triangles, rectangles, squares, parallelograms, etc.

Example: Calculate the area of the triangle in the figure below.

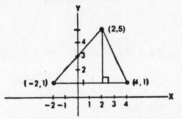

Solution: The area of a triangle is $\frac{1}{2}$ (base) (height). On the graph the length of the line joining $(-2,1)$ and $(4,1)$ is 6 units. The height, which goes from point $(5,2)$ to the base, has a length of 4 units. Therefore the area is $\frac{1}{2}$ (6) (4) = 12.

Example: Calculate the area of the square pictured below.

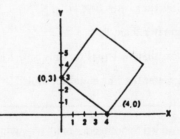

Solution: The area of a square is given by the square of the side. To find this area first find the length of one side. The length of a segment whose endpoints are (x_1, y_1) and (x_2, y_2) is given by the formula $\sqrt{(x_2 - x_1)^2 + (y_2 - y_1)^2}$. Substituting in $(0,3)$ and $(4,0)$ gives a length of 5 units. Thus the length of one side of the square is 5. Using the formula area = (side)^2 gives an area of 5^2 or 25 square units.

To find the area of more complicated polygons, divide the polygon into simple figures whose areas can be calculated. Add these areas to find the total area.

Example: Find the area of the figure below:

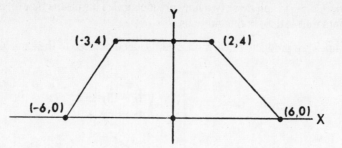

Solution: Divide the figure into two triangles and a rectangle by drawing vertical lines at $(-3,4)$ and $(2,4)$. Thus the polygon is now two triangles and a rectangle.

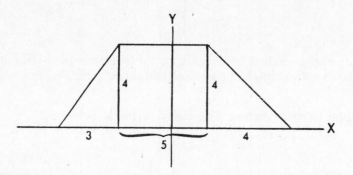

The height of the left triangle is 4 units, and the base is 3. Using $A = \frac{1}{2}bh$ gives the area as 6.

The height of the right triangle is 4 and the base is 4. The area is 8. The length of one side of the rectangle is 4, and the other side is 5. Using the formula, area = base • height, gives the area as 20. Thus the total area is $6 + 8 + 20 = 34$.

Inequalities

419. *Inequalities.* These problems deal with numbers that are less than, greater than, or equal to other numbers. The following laws apply to all inequalities:

$<$ means less than, thus $3 < 4$

$>$ means greater than, thus $5 > 2$

$\leq$ means less than or equal to, thus $3 \leq 4$ and $3 \leq 3$

$\geq$ means greater than or equal to, thus $5 \geq 2$ and $2 \geq 2$

420. If equal quantities are added to both sides of an inequality, the direction of the inequality does *not* change.

If $x < y$, then $x + z < y + z$ and $x - z < y - z$.

If $x > y$, then $x + z > y + z$ and $x - z > y - z$.

For example, given the inequality, $4 > 2$, with 1 added to or subtracted from both sides, the results, $5 > 3$ and $3 > 1$, have the same inequality sign as the original. If the problem is algebraic, i.e., $x + 3 < 6$, it is possible to subtract 3 from both sides to get this simple inequality $x < 3$.

421. Subtracting parts of an inequality from an equation *reverses* the order of the inequality.

If $x < y$, then $z - x > z - y$.
If $x > y$, then $z - x < z - y$.

For example, given that $3 < 5$, subtracting 3 from the left-hand and 5 from the right-hand sides of the equation $10 = 10$ results in $7 > 5$. Thus the direction of the inequality is reversed.

422. Multiplying or dividing an inequality by a number greater than zero does not change the order of the inequality.

If $x > y$, and $a > 0$, then $xa > ya$ and $\frac{x}{a} > \frac{y}{a}$.

If $x < y$, and $a > 0$, then $xa < ya$ and $\frac{x}{a} < \frac{y}{a}$.

For example, if $4 > 2$, multiplying both sides by any arbitrary number (for instance, 5) gives $20 > 10$, which is still true. Or, if algebraically $6h < 3$, dividing both sides by 6 gives $h < \frac{1}{2}$, which is true.

423. Multiplying or dividing an inequality by a number less than 0 reverses the order of the inequality.

If $x > y$, and $a < 0$, then $xa < ya$ and $\frac{x}{a} < \frac{y}{a}$.

If $x < y$, and $a < 0$, then $xa > ya$ and $\frac{x}{a} > \frac{y}{a}$.

If $-3 < 2$ is multiplied through by -2 it becomes $6 > -4$, and the order of the inequality is reversed.

> Note that negative numbers are always less than positive numbers. Note also that the greater the absolute value of a negative number, the smaller it actually is. Thus, $-10 < -9$, $-8 < -7$, etc.

424. The product of two numbers with like signs is positive.

If $x > 0$ and $y > 0$, then $xy > 0$.

If $x < 0$ and $y < 0$, then $xy > 0$.

For example, -3 times -2 is 6.

425. The product of two numbers with unlike signs is negative.

If $x < 0$ and $y > 0$, then $xy < 0$.

If $x > 0$ and $y < 0$, then $xy < 0$.

For example, -2 times 3 is -6. 8 times -1 is -8, etc.

426. *Linear inequalities in one unknown.* In these problems a first power variable is given in an inequality, and this variable must be solved for in terms of the inequality. Examples of linear inequalities in one unknown are: $2x + 7 > 4 + x$, $8y - 3 \le 2y$, etc.

STEP 1. By ordinary algebraic addition and subtraction (as if it were an equality) get all of the constant terms on one side of the inequality and all of the variable terms on the other side. In the inequality $2x + 4 < 8x + 16$ subtract 4 and $8x$ from both sides and get $-6x < 12$.

STEP 2. Divide both sides by the coefficient of the variable. Important: If the coefficient of the variable is negative, you must reverse the inequality sign. For example, in $-6x < 12$, dividing by -6 gives $x > 2$. (The inequality is reversed.) In $3x < 12$ dividing by 3 gives $x < 4$.

Example: Solve for y in the inequality $4y + 7 \geq 9 - 2y$.

Solution: Subtracting $-2y$ and 7 from both sides gives $6y \geq 2$. Dividing both sides by 6 gives $y \geq \dfrac{1}{3}$.

Example: Solve for a in the inequality $10 - 2a < 0$.

Solution: Subtracting 10 from both sides gives $-2a < -10$. Dividing both sides by -2 gives $a > \dfrac{-10}{-2}$ or $a > 5$. Note that the inequality sign has been reversed because of the division by a negative number.

427. *Simultaneous linear inequalities in two unknowns.* These are two inequalities, each one in two unknowns. The same two unknowns are to be solved for in each equation. This means the equations must be solved simultaneously.

STEP 1. Plot both inequalities on the same graph. Replace the inequality sign with an equality sign and plot the resulting line. The side of the line that makes the inequality true is then shaded in. For example, graph the inequality $(2x - y > 4)$. First replace the inequality sign getting $2x - y = 4$; then, plot the line. The X-intercept is 2. The Y-intercept is -4.

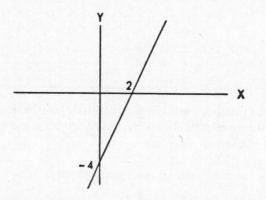

To decide which side of the line satisfies the inequality choose a convenient point on each side and determine which point satisfies the inequality. Shade in that side of the line. In this case, choose the point (0,0). With this point the equation becomes $2(0) - 0 > 4$ or $0 > 4$. This is not true. Thus, shade in the other side of the line.

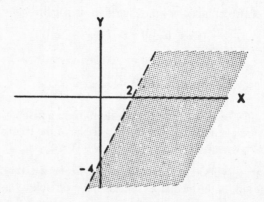

STEP 2. After both inequalities have been solved, the area that is common to both shaded portions is the solution to the problem.

Example: Solve $x + y > 2$ and $3x < 6$.

Solution: First graph $x + y > 2$ by plotting $x + y = 2$ and using the point $(4,0)$ to determine the region where the inequality is satisfied:

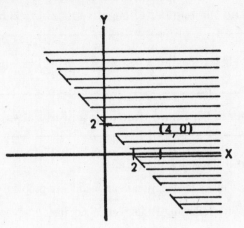

Graph the inequality $3x < 6$ on the same axes and get:

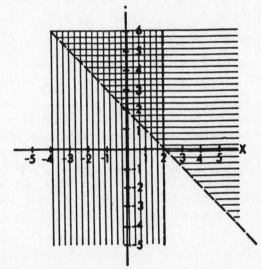

The solution is the double shaded area.

428. *Higher order inequalities in one unknown.* These are inequalities that deal with variables multiplied by themselves. For example, $x^2 + 3 \geq 0$, $(x - 1)(x + 2) < 4$ and $x^3 - 7x > 0$ are such inequalities. The basic rules to remember in doing such problems are:

---

1. **The product of any number of positive numbers is positive.**

For example, $2 \times 3 \times 4 \times 5 = 120$, which is positive, or $\frac{1}{2} \times \frac{1}{2} = \frac{1}{4}$, which is positive.

> **2. The product of an even number of negative numbers is positive.**

For example, $(-3)(-2) = 6$ or $(-3)(-1)(-9)(-2) = 54$, which is positive.

> **3. The product of an odd number of negative numbers is negative.**

For example, $(-1)(-2)(-3) = -6$ or $(-\frac{1}{2})(-2)(-3)(-6)(-1) = -18$.

> **4. Any number squared or raised to an even power is always positive or zero.**

For example, $x^2 \geq 0$ or $a^4 \geq 0$ for all x and for all a.

Often these basic rules will make the solution to an inequality problem obvious.

Example: Which of the following values can x^2 not have?

(A) 5   (B) −2   (C) 0   (D) 144   (E) 9

Solution: We know that $x^2 \geq 0$ for all x so x^2 cannot be negative. −2 is negative, so x^2 cannot equal −2.

The steps in solving a higher order inequality are:

STEP 1. Bring all of the terms to one side of the inequality, making the other side zero. For example, in the inequality $x^2 > 3x - 2$, subtract $3x - 2$ from both sides to get $x^2 - 3x + 2 > 0$.

STEP 2. Factor the resulting expression. To factor a quadratic expression means to write the original expression as the product of two terms in the 1st power, i.e., $x^2 = x \cdot x$. x is a factor of x^2. (See Section 409 for a detailed explanation of factoring.) The quadratic expression $x^2 - 3x + 2$ when factored is $(x - 2)(x - 1)$. Note that $x \cdot x = x^2$, $-2x - x = -3x$ and $(-1)(-2) = 2$. Most quadratic expressions can easily be factored by taking factors of the last term (in this case 2 and 1) and adding or subtracting them to x. Through trial and error the right combination is found. An important fact to remember when factoring is: $(a + b)(c + d) = ac + ad + bc + bd$. Example: $(x + 4)(x + 2) = x^2 + 4x + 2x + 8 = x^2 + 6x + 8$. Another is that $a^2 - b^2 = (a + b)(a - b)$. Example: $x^2 - 16 = (x + 4)(x - 4)$.

STEP 3. Investigate which terms are positive and which terms are negative. For example, in $(x - 3)(x + 2) > 0$, either $(x - 3)$ and $(x + 2)$ are both positive or $(x - 3)$ and $(x + 2)$ are both negative. If one were positive and the other were negative, the product would be negative and would not satisfy the inequality. If the factors are positive, then $x - 3 > 0$ and $x + 2 > 0$, which yields $x > 3$ and $x > -2$. For x to be greater than 3 and to be greater than −2, it must be greater than 3. If it is greater than 3 it is automatically greater than −2. Thus, with positive factors $x > 3$ is the answer. If the factors are negative, $x - 3 < 0$ and $x + 2 < 0$, or $x < -2$. For x to be less than 3 and less than −2 it must be less than −2. Thus, with negative factors $x < -2$ is the answer. As both answers are possible from the original equation, the solution to the original problem is $x > 3$ or $x < -2$.

Example: For which values of x is $x^2 + 5 < 6x$?

Solution: First subtract $6x$ from both sides to get $x^2 - 6x + 5 < 0$. The left side factors into $(x - 5)(x - 1) < 0$. Now for this to be true one factor must be positive and one must be negative, i.e., their product is less than zero. Thus, $x - 5 > 0$ and $x - 1 < 0$ or $x - 5 < 0$ and $x - 1 > 0$. If $x - 5 < 0$ and $x - 1 > 0$ then $x < 5$ and $x > 1$, or $1 < x < 5$. If $x - 5 > 0$ and $x - 1 < 0$ then $x > 5$ and $x < 1$, which is impossible because x cannot be less than 1 and greater than 5. Therefore, the solution is $1 < x < 5$.

Example: For what values of x is $x^2 < 4$?

Solution: Subtract 4 from both sides to get $x^2 - 4 < 0$. Remember that $a^2 - b^2 = (a + b)$ $(a - b)$; thus $x^2 - 4 = (x + 2)(x - 2)$. Hence, $(x + 2)(x - 2) < 0$. For this to be true $x + 2 > 0$ and $x - 2 < 0$ or $x + 2 < 0$ and $x - 2 > 0$. In the first case $x > -2$ and $x < +2$ or $-2 < x$ < 2. The second case is $x < -2$ and $x > +2$ is impossible because x cannot be less than -2 *and* greater than 2. Thus, the solution is $-2 < x < 2$.

Example 3: When is $(x^2 + 1)(x - 2)^2 (x - 3)$ greater than or equal to zero?

Solution: This can be written as $(x^2 + 1)(x - 2)^2 (x - 3) \geq 0$. This is already in factors. The individual terms must be investigated. $x^2 + 1$ is always positive because $x^2 \geq 0$ so $x^2 + 1$ must be greater than 0. $(x - 2)^2$ is a number squared so this is always greater than or equal to zero. Therefore, the product of the first two terms is positive or equal to zero for all values of x. The third term $x - 3$ is positive when $x > 3$, and negative when $x < 3$. For the entire expression to be positive, $x - 3$ must be positive, i.e., $x > 3$. For the expression to be equal to zero, $x - 3 = 0$, i.e., $x = 3$, or $(x - 2)^2 = 0$, i.e., $x = 2$. Thus, the entire expression is positive when $x > 3$ and zero when $x = 2$ or $x = 3$.

Exponents and Roots

429. *Exponents.* An exponent is an easy way to express repeated multiplication. For example, $5 \times 5 \times 5 \times 5 = 5^4$. The 4 is the exponent. In the expression $7^3 = 7 \times 7 \times 7$, 3 is the exponent. 7^3 means 7 is multiplied by itself three times. If the exponent is 0, the expression always has a value of 1. Thus, $6^0 = 15^0 = 1$, etc. If the exponent is 1, the value of the expression is the number base. Thus, $4^1 = 4$ and $9^1 = 9$.

In the problem $5^3 \times 5^4$, we can simplify by counting the factors of 5. Thus $5^3 \times 5^4 = 5^{3+4} = 5^7$. When we multiply and the base number is the same, we keep the base number and add the exponents. For example, $7^4 \times 7^8 = 7^{12}$.

For division, we keep the same base number and subtract exponents. Thus, $8^8 \div 8^2 = 8^{8-2} = 8^6$.

A negative exponent indicates the reciprocal of the expression with a positive exponent, thus $3^{-2} = \dfrac{1}{3^2}$.

430. *Roots.* The square root of a number is a number whose square is the original number. For example, $\sqrt{16} = 4$, since $4 \times 4 = 16$. (The $\sqrt{}$ symbol always means a positive number.)

To simplify a square root, we factor the number.

$$\sqrt{32} = \sqrt{16 \cdot 2} = \sqrt{16} \cdot \sqrt{2} = 4\sqrt{2}$$

$$\sqrt{72} = \sqrt{36 \cdot 2} = \sqrt{36} \cdot \sqrt{2} = 6\sqrt{2}$$

$$\sqrt{300} = \sqrt{25 \cdot 12} = \sqrt{25} \cdot \sqrt{12}$$

$$= 5 \cdot \sqrt{12}$$

$$= 5 \cdot \sqrt{4 \cdot 3}$$

$$= 5\sqrt{4} \ \sqrt{3}$$

$$= 5 \cdot 2\sqrt{3}$$

$$= 10\sqrt{3}$$

We can add expressions with the square roots only if the numbers inside the square root sign are the same. For example,

$$3\sqrt{7} + 2\sqrt{7} = 5\sqrt{7}$$

$$\sqrt{18} + \sqrt{2} = \sqrt{9 \cdot 2} + \sqrt{2} = \sqrt{9}\sqrt{2} + \sqrt{2} = 3\sqrt{2} + \sqrt{2} = \sqrt{2} = 4\sqrt{2}.$$

431. *Evaluation of expressions.* To evaluate an expression means to substitute a value in place of a letter. For example: Evaluate $3a^2 - c^3$; if $a = -2$, $c = -3$.

$$3a^2 - c^3 = 3(-2)^2 - (-3)^3 = 3(4) - (-27) = 12 + 27 = 39$$

Given: $a \triangledown b = ab + b^2$. Find: $-2 \triangledown 3$.

Using the definition, we get

$$
\begin{aligned}
-2 \triangledown 3 &= (-2)(3) + (3)^2 \\
&= -6 + 9 \\
-2 \triangledown 3 &= 3
\end{aligned}
$$

Practice Test 4

Algebra Problems

Correct answers and solutions follow each test.

1. A B C D E

1. For what values of x is the following equation satisfied: $3x + 9 = 21 + 7x$?

    (A) -3 only
    (B) 3 only
    (C) 3 or -3 only
    (D) no values
    (E) an infinite number of values

2. A B C D E

2. What values may z have if $2z + 4$ is greater than $z - 6$?

    (A) any values greater than -10
    (B) any values greater than -2
    (C) any values less than 2
    (D) any values less than 10
    (E) none of these

3. A B C D E

3. If $ax^2 + 2x - 3 = 0$ when $x = -3$, what value(s) can a have?

    (A) -3 only
    (B) -1 only
    (C) 1 only
    (D) -1 and 1 only
    (E) $-3, -1,$ and 1 only

4. A B C D E

4. If the coordinates of point P are (0,8), and the coordinates of point Q are (4,2), which of the following points represents the midpoint of PQ?

    (A) (0,2)
    (B) (2,4)
    (C) (2,5)
    (D) (4,8)
    (E) (4,10)

5. A B C D E

5. In the formula $V = \pi r^2 h$, what is the value of r, in terms of V and h?

    (A) $\dfrac{\sqrt{V}}{\pi h}$

    (B) $\pi \sqrt{\dfrac{V}{h}}$

    (C) $\sqrt{\pi V h}$

    (D) $\dfrac{\pi h}{\sqrt{V}}$

    (E) $\sqrt{\dfrac{V}{\pi h}}$

6. A B C D E

6. Solve the inequality $x^2 - 3x < 0$.

    (A) $x < -3$
    (B) $-3 < x < 0$
    (C) $x < 3$
    (D) $0 < x < 3$
    (E) $3 < x$

7. A B C D E

7. Which of the following lines is parallel to the line represented by $2y = 8x + 32$?

(A) $y = 8x + 32$
(B) $y = 8x + 16$
(C) $y = 16x + 32$
(D) $y = 4x + 32$
(E) $y = 2x + 16$

8. A B C D E

8. In the equation $4.04x + 1.01 = 9.09$, what value of x is necessary to make the equation true?

(A) -1.5
(B) 0
(C) 1
(D) 2
(E) 2.5

9. A B C D E

9. What values of x satisfy the equation $(x + 1)(x - 2) = 0$?

(A) 1 only
(B) -2 only
(C) 1 and -2 only
(D) -1 and 2 only
(E) any values between -1 and 2

10. A B C D E

10. What is the largest possible value of the following expression:

$$(x + 2)(3 - x)(2 + x)^2 (2x - 6)(2x + 4)?$$

(A) -576
(B) -24
(C) 0
(D) 12
(E) cannot be determined

11. A B C D E

11. For what value(s) of k is the following equation satisfied:

$$2k - 9 - k = 4k + 6 - 3k?$$

(A) -5 only
(B) 0 only
(C) $\dfrac{5}{2}$ only
(D) no values
(E) more than one value

12. A B C D E

12. In the equation $p = aq^2 + bq + c$, if $a = 1$, $b = -2$, and $c = 1$, which of the following expresses p in terms of q?

(A) $p = (q - 2)^2$
(B) $p = (q - 1)^2$
(C) $p = q^2$
(D) $p = (q + 1)^2$
(E) $p = (q + 2)^2$

13. A B C D E   **13.** If $A + B + C = 10$, $A + B = 7$, and $A - B = 5$, what is the value of C?

(A) 1
(B) 3
(C) 6
(D) 7
(E) The answer cannot be determined from the given information.

14. A B C D E   **14.** $5x + 15$ is greater than 20, which of the following best describes the possible values of x?

(A) x must be greater than 5
(B) x must be greater than 3
(C) x must be greater than 1
(D) x must be less than 5
(E) x must be less than 1

15. A B C D E   **15.** If $\dfrac{t^2 - 1}{t - 1} = 2$, then what value(s) may t have?

(A) 1 only
(B) -1 only
(C) 1 or -1
(D) no values
(E) an infinite number of values

16. A B C D E   **16.** If $4m = 9n$, what is the value of $7m$, in terms of n?

(A) $\dfrac{63n}{4}$

(B) $\dfrac{9n}{28}$

(C) $\dfrac{7n}{9}$

(D) $\dfrac{28n}{9}$

(E) $\dfrac{7n}{4}$

17. A B C D E   **17.** The coordinates of a triangle are (0,2), (2,4), and (1,6). What is the area of the triangle in square units (to the nearest unit)?

(A) 2 square units
(B) 3 square units
(C) 4 square units
(D) 5 square units
(E) 6 square units

18. A B C D E

18. In the formula $s = \frac{1}{2}gt^2$, what is the value of t, in terms of s and g?

(A) $\frac{2s}{g}$

(B) $2\sqrt{\frac{s}{g}}$

(C) $\frac{s}{2g}$

(D) $\sqrt{\frac{s}{2g}}$

(E) $\sqrt{\frac{2s}{g}}$

19. A B C D E

19. In the triangle ABC, angle A is a 30° angle, and angle B is obtuse. If x represents the number of degrees in angle C, which of the following best represents the possible values of x?

(A) $0 < x < 60$
(B) $0 < x < 150$
(C) $60 < x < 180$
(D) $120 < x < 180$
(E) $120 < x < 150$

20. A B C D E

20. Which of the following sets of coordinates does *not* represent the vertices of an isosceles triangle?

(A) (0,2), (0,−2), (2,0)
(B) (1,3), (1,5), (3,4)
(C) (1,3), (1,7), (4,5)
(D) (2,2), (2,0), (1,1)
(E) (2,3), (2,5), (3,3)

21. A B C D E

21. If $2 < a < 5$, and $6 > b > 3$, what are the possible values of $a + b$?

(A) $a + b$ must equal 8.
(B) $a + b$ must be between 2 and 6.
(C) $a + b$ must be between 3 and 5.
(D) $a + b$ must be between 5 and 8.
(E) $a + b$ must be between 5 and 11.

22. A B C D E

22. The area of a square will be doubled if:

(A) The length of the diagonal is divided by 2.
(B) The length of the diagonal is divided by $\sqrt{2}$.
(C) The length of the diagonal is multiplied by 2.
(D) The length of the diagonal is multiplied by $\sqrt{2}$.
(E) none of the above

23. A B C D E

23. Find the value of y that satisfies the equation $8.8y - 4 = 7.7y + 7$.

(A) 1.1
(B) 7.7
(C) 8.0
(D) 10.0
(E) 11.0

24. A B C D E

24. Which of the following is a factor of the expression $2x^2 + 1$?

(A) $x + 2$
(B) $x - 2$
(C) $x + \sqrt{2}$
(D) $x - \sqrt{2}$
(E) none of these

25. A B C D E

25. A businessman has ten employees; his salary is equal to six times the *average* of the employees' salaries. If the eleven of them received a total of $64,000 in one year, what was the businessman's salary that year?

(A) $4,000
(B) $6,000
(C) $24,000
(D) $40,000
(E) $44,000

26. A B C D E

26. If $6x + 3$ equals 15, what is the value of $12x - 3$?

(A) 21
(B) 24
(C) 28
(D) 33
(E) 36

27. A B C D E

27. If $2p + 7$ is greater than $3p - 5$, which of the following best describes the possible values of p?

(A) p must be greater than 2.
(B) p must be greater than 12.
(C) p must be less than 2.
(D) p must be less than 12.
(E) p must be greater than 2, but less than 12.

28. A B C D E

28. What is the value of q if $x^2 + qx + 1 = 0$, if $x = 1$?

(A) -2
(B) -1
(C) 0
(D) 1
(E) 2

29. A B C D E   **29.** What is the area (to the nearest unit) of the shaded figure in the diagram below, assuming that each of the squares has an area of 1?

         (A) 12
         (B) 13
         (C) 14
         (D) 15
         (E) 16

30. A B C D E   **30.** Which of the following statements is *false*?

         (A) Any two numbers, a and b, have a sum equal to $a + b$.
         (B) Any two numbers, a and b, have a product equal to $a \cdot b$.
         (C) Any two numbers, a and b, have a difference equal to $a - b$.
         (D) Any two numbers, a and b, have a quotient equal to $\dfrac{a}{b}$.
         (E) Any two numbers, a and b, have an average equal to $\dfrac{(a + b)}{2}$.

31. A B C D E   **31.** If $(x - 1)(x - 2)(x^2 - 4) = 0$, what are the possible values of x?

         (A) -2 only
         (B) $+2$ only
         (C) $-1, -2$, or -4 only
         (D) $+1, +2$, or $+4$ only
         (E) $+1, -2$, or $+2$ only

32. A B C D E   **32.** If $P + Q = R$, and $P + R = 2Q$, what is the ratio of P to R?

         (A) $1 : 1$
         (B) $1 : 2$
         (C) $2 : 1$
         (D) $1 : 3$
         (E) $3 : 1$

33. A B C D E   **33.** For what value(s) of r is $\dfrac{r^2 + 5r + 6}{r + 2}$ equal to 0?

         (A) -2 only
         (B) -3 only
         (C) $+3$ only
         (D) -2 or -3
         (E) $+2$ or $+3$

34. A B C D E   **34.** What is the value of $a^2b + 4ab^2 + 4b^3$, if $a = 15$ and $b = 5$?

         (A) 1625
         (B) 2125
         (C) 2425
         (D) 2725
         (E) 3125

35. A B C D E

35. If $m + 4n = 2n + 8m$, what is the ratio of n to m?

(A) $1 : 4$
(B) $1 : -4$
(C) $-4 : 1$
(D) $2 : 7$
(E) $7 : 2$

36. A B C D E

36. If the value of a lies between -5 and $+2$, and the value of b lies between -7 and $+1$, what are the possible values for the product, $a \cdot b$?

(A) between -14 and $+2$
(B) between -35 and $+2$
(C) between $+2$ and $+35$
(D) between -12 and $+3$
(E) between -14 and $+35$

37. A B C D E

37. What is the area, in square units, of a triangle whose vertices lie on points $(-5,1)$, $(-5,4)$, and $(2,4)$?

(A) 10.5 square units
(B) 12.5 square units
(C) 15.0 square units
(D) 20.0 square units
(E) 21.0 square units

38. A B C D E

38. If $A + B = 12$, and $B + C = 16$, what is the value of $A + C$?

(A) -4
(B) -28
(C) $+4$
(D) $+28$
(E) The answer cannot be determined from the given information.

39. A B C D E

39. What is the solution to the equation $x^2 + x + 1 = 0$?

(A) $-\dfrac{1}{2} + \dfrac{\sqrt{3}}{2}$ and $-\dfrac{1}{2} - \dfrac{\sqrt{3}}{2}$

(B) $-\dfrac{1}{2} + \dfrac{\sqrt{3}}{2}$ only

(C) $-\dfrac{1}{2} - \dfrac{\sqrt{3}}{2}$ only

(D) no real solutions

(E) 0

40. A B C D E

40. Which of the following equations will have a vertical line as its graph?

(A) $x + y = 1$
(B) $x - y = 1$
(C) $x = 1$
(D) $y = 1$
(E) $xy = 1$

41. A B C D E

41. For what values of x does $x^2 + 3x + 2$ equal zero?

(A) −1 only
(B) +2 only
(C) −1 or −2 only
(D) 1 or 2 only
(E) none of these

42. A B C D E

42. If $a + b$ equals 12, and $a - b$ equals 6, what is the value of b?

(A) 0
(B) 3
(C) 6
(D) 9
(E) The answer cannot be determined from the given information.

43. A B C D E

43. For what values of m is $m^2 + 4$ equal to $4m$?

(A) −2 only
(B) 0 only
(C) +2 only
(D) +4 only
(E) more than one value

44. A B C D E

44. If $x = 0$, and $y = 2$, and $x^2yz + 3xz^2 + y^2z + 3y + 4x = 0$, what is the value of z?

(A) $-\dfrac{4}{3}$

(B) $-\dfrac{3}{2}$

(C) $+\dfrac{3}{4}$

(D) $+\dfrac{4}{3}$

(E) The answer cannot be determined from the given information.

45. A B C D E

45. If $c + 4d = 3c - 2d$, what is the ratio of c to d?

(A) 1 : 3
(B) 1 : −3
(C) 3 : 1
(D) 2 : 3
(E) 2 : −3

46. A B C D E

46. If $3 < x < 7$, and $6 > x > 2$, which of the following best describes x?

(A) $2 < x < 6$
(B) $2 < x < 7$
(C) $3 < x < 6$
(D) $3 < x < 7$
(E) No value of x can satisfy both of these conditions.

47. A B C D E

47. What are the coordinates of the midpoint of the line segment whose endpoints are (4,9) and (5,15)?

(A) (4,5)
(B) (5,9)
(C) (4,15)
(D) (4.5,12)
(E) (9,24)

48. A B C D E

48. If $\dfrac{t^2 + 2t}{2t + 4} = \dfrac{t}{2}$, what does t equal?

(A) -2 only
(B) $+2$ only
(C) any value except $+2$
(D) any value except -2
(E) any value

49. A B C D E

49. If $x + y = 4$, and $x + z = 9$, what is the value of $(y - z)$?

(A) -5
(B) $+5$
(C) -13
(D) $+13$
(E) The answer cannot be determined from the given information.

50. A B C D E

50. Of the following statements, which are equivalent?

  I. $-3 < x < 3$
  II. $x^2 < 9$
  III. $\dfrac{1}{x} < \dfrac{1}{3}$

(A) I and II only
(B) I and III only
(C) II and III only
(D) I, II, and III
(E) none of the above

Answer Key for Practice Test 4

1. A	14. C	27. D	39. D
2. A	15. D	28. A	40. C
3. C	16. A	29. B	41. C
4. C	17. B	30. D	42. B
5. E	18. E	31. E	43. C
6. D	19. A	32. D	44. B
7. D	20. E	33. B	45. C
8. D	21. E	34. E	46. C
9. D	22. D	35. E	47. D
10. C	23. D	36. E	48. D
11. D	24. E	37. A	49. A
12. B	25. C	38. E	50. A
13. B	26. A		

Answers and Solutions for Practice Test 4

1. Choice A is correct. The original equation is $3x + 9 = 21 + 7x$. First subtract 9 and $7x$ from both sides to get: $-4x = 12$. Now divide both sides by the coefficient of x, -4, obtaining the solution, $x = -3$. (406)

2. Choice A is correct. Given $2z + 4 > x - 6$. Subtracting equal quantities from both sides of an inequality does not change the order of the inequality. Therefore, subtracting z and 4 from both sides gives a solution of $z > -10$. (419, 420)

3. Choice C is correct. Substitute -3 for x in the original equation to get the following:

$$a(-3)^2 + 2(-3) - 3 = 0$$
$$9a - 6 - 3 = 0$$
$$9a - 9 = 0$$
$$a = 1 \qquad (406)$$

4. Choice C is correct. To find the midpoint of the line segment connecting two points, find the point whose x-coordinate is the average of the two given x-coordinates, and whose y-coordinate is the average of the two given y-coordinates. The midpoint here will be $\left(\dfrac{0 + 4}{2}, \dfrac{8 + 2}{2} \right)$, or (2,5). (412)

5. Choice E is correct. Divide both sides of the equation by πh:

$$\frac{V}{\pi h} = r^2$$

Take the square root of both sides:

$$r \text{ equals } \sqrt{\frac{V}{\pi h}}. \qquad (408)$$

6. Choice D is correct. Factor the original expression into $x(x - 3) < 0$. In order for the product of two expressions to be less than 0 (negative), one must be positive and the other must be negative. Thus, $x < 0$ and $x - 3 > 0$; or $x > 0$ and $x - 3 < 0$. In the first case, $x < 0$ and $x > 3$. This is impossible because x cannot be less than 0 and greater than 3 at the same time. In the second case $x > 0$ and $x < 3$ which can be rewritten as $0 < x < 3$. (428)

7. Choice D is correct. Divide both sides of the equation $2y = 8x + 32$ by 2 to get $y = 4x + 16$. Now it is in the form of $y = mx + b$, where m is the slope of the line and b is the Y intercept. Thus the slope of the line is 4. Any line parallel to this line must have the same slope. The answer must have a slope of 4. This is the line $y = 4x + 32$. Note that all of the choices are already in the form of $y = mx + b$. (416)

8. Choice D is correct. Subtract 1.01 from both sides to give: $4.04x = 8.08$. Dividing both sides by 4.04 gives a solution of $x = 2$. (406)

9. Choice D is correct. If a product is equal to zero, then one of the factors must equal zero. If $(x + 1)(x - 2) = 0$, either $x + 1 = 0$, or $x - 2 = 0$. Solving these two equations, we see that either $x = -1$ or $x = 2$. (408, 409)

10. Choice C is correct. It is possible, but time-consuming, to examine the various ranges of x, but it will be quicker if you realize that the same factors appear, with numerical multiples, more than once in the expression. Properly factored, the expression becomes:

$$-4(x + 2)^4(3 - x)^2 = (x + 2)(2 + x)^2(2)(x + 2)(3 - x)(-2)(3 - x)$$

Since squares of real numbers can never be negative, the whole product has only one negative term and is therefore negative, except when one of the terms is zero, in which case the product is also zero. Thus, the product cannot be larger than zero for any x. (428)

11. Choice D is correct. Combine like terms on both sides of the given equations and obtain the equivalent form: $k - 9 = k + 6$. This is true for no values of k. If k is subtracted from both sides, -9 will equal 6, which is impossible. (406)

12. Choice B is correct. Substitute for the given values of a, b, and c and obtain $p = q^2 - 2q + 1$; or, rearranging terms, $p = (q - 1)^2$. (409)

13. Choice B is correct. $A + B + C = 10$. Also, $A + B = 7$. Substitute the value 7 for the quantity $(A + B)$ in the first equation and obtain the new equation: $7 + C = 10$ or $C = 3$. $A - B = 5$ could be used with the other two equations to find the values of A and B. (406)

14. Choice C is correct. If $5x + 15 > 20$, then subtract 15 from both sides to get $5x > 5$. Now divide both sides by 5. This does not change the order of the inequality because 5 is a positive number. The solution is $x > 1$. (419, 426)

15. Choice D is correct. Factor $(t^2 - 1)$ to obtain the product $(t + 1)(t - 1)$. For any value of t, except 1, the equation is equivalent to $(t + 1) = 2$, or $t = 1$. One is the only possible value of t. However this value is not possible as $t - 1$ would equal 0, and the quotient $\dfrac{t^2 - 1}{t - 1}$ would not be defined. (404, 409)

16. Choice A is correct. If $4m = 9n$, then $m = \dfrac{9n}{4}$. Multiplying both sides of the equation by 7, we obtain: $7m = \dfrac{63n}{4}$. (403)

17. Choice B is correct. As the diagram shows, the easiest way to calculate the area of this triangle is to start with the area of the enclosing rectangle and subtract the three shaded triangles.

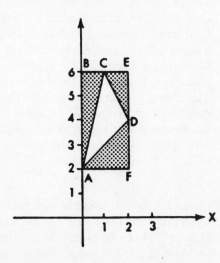

The area of the rectangle $ABEF = (2)(4) = 8$ square units.

The area of the triangle $ABC = \dfrac{1}{2}(1)(4) = 2$ square units.

The area of the triangle $CDE = \dfrac{1}{2}(1)(2) = 1$ square unit.

The area of the triangle $ADF = \dfrac{1}{2}(2)(2) = 2$ square units.

Thus the area of the triangle $ACD = 8 - 5 = 3$ square units. (418)

18. Choice E is correct. Since $s = \dfrac{1}{2}gt^2$, divide both sides of the equation by $\dfrac{1}{2}g$ to obtain the form, $\dfrac{2s}{g} = t^2$. Then, after taking the square roots, $t = \sqrt{\dfrac{2s}{g}}$. (403)

19. Choice A is correct. The sum of the three angles of a triangle must be 180°. Since angle A is 30°, and angle B is between 90° and 180° (it is obtuse), their sum is greater than 120° and less than 180° (the sum of all three angles is 180°). Their sum subtracted from the total of 180° gives a third angle greater than zero, but less than 60°. (419)

20. Choice E is correct. An isosceles triangle has two equal sides. To find the length of the sides, we use the distance formula, $\sqrt{(x_2 - x_1)^2 + (y_2 - y_1)^2}$. In the first case the lengths of the sides are 4, $2\sqrt{2}$ and $2\sqrt{2}$. Thus two sides have the same length, and it is an isosceles triangle. The only set of points that is not an isosceles triangle is the last one. (411)

21. Choice E is correct. The smallest possible value of a is 2, and the smallest possible value of b is 3, so the smallest possible value of $a + b$ must be $2 + 3 = 5$. Similarly, the largest values of a and b are 5 and 6, respectively, so the largest possible of $a + b$ is 11. Thus, the sum must be between 5 and 11. (419)

22. Choice D is correct. If the sides of the original square are each equal to s, then the area of the square is s^2, and the diagonal is $s\sqrt{2}$. Now, a new square, with an area of $2s^2$, must have a side of $s\sqrt{2}$. Thus, the diagonal is $2s$, which is $\sqrt{2}$ times the original length of the diagonal. (302, 303)

23. Choice D is correct. First place all of the variable terms on one side and all of the numerical terms on

the other side. Subtracting $7.7y$ and adding 4 to both sides of the equation gives $1.1y = 11$. Now divide both sides by 1.1 to solve for $y = 10$. (406)

24. Choice E is correct. To determine whether an expression is a factor of another expression, give the variable a specific value in both expressions. An expression divided by its factor will be a whole number. If we give x the value 0, then the expression $2x^2 + 1$ has the value of 1. $x + 2$ then has the value of 2. 1 is not divisible by 2, so the first choice is not a factor. The next choice has the value of -2, also not a factor of 1. Similarly $x + \sqrt{2}$ and $x - \sqrt{2}$ take on the values of $\sqrt{2}$ and $-\sqrt{2}$, respectively, when $x = 0$ and are not factors of $2x^2 + 1$. Therefore, the correct choice is (E). (409)

25. Choice C is correct. Let x equal the average salary of the employees. Then the employees receive a total of $10x$ dollars, and the businessman receives six times the average, or $6x$. Together, the eleven of them receive a total of $10x + 6x = 16x$, which equals $64,000. Thus, x equals $4,000, and the businessman's salary is $6x$, or $24,000. (406)

26. Choice A is correct. $6x + 3 = 15$, therefore $6x = 12$ and $x = 2$. Substituting $x = 2$ into the expression $12x - 3$, gives $24 - 3$ which equals 21. (406)

27. Choice D is correct. $2p + 7 > 3p - 5$. To both sides of the equation add 5 and subtract $2p$, obtaining $12 > p$. Thus, p is less than 12. (419, 426)

28. Choice A is correct. Substituting 1 for x in the given equation obtains $1 + q + 1 = 0$, or $q + 2 = 0$. This is solved only for $q = -2$. (406)

29. Choice B is correct.

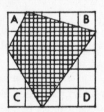

The area of the shaded figure can most easily be found by taking the area of the square surrounding it (25), and subtracting the areas of the four triangles marked A (1), B (2), C (3), and D (6), leaving an area of $25 - (1 + 2 + 3 + 6) = 13$ square units. (418)

30. Choice D is correct. If the number b is equal to zero, the quotient $\frac{a}{b}$ is not defined. For all other pairs, all five statements are true. (401–405)

31. Choice E is correct. If a product equals zero, one of the factors must be equal to zero also. Thus, either $x - 1 = 0$, or $x - 2 = 0$, or $x^2 - 4 = 0$. The possible solutions, therefore, are $x = 1$, $x = 2$, and $x = -2$. (408)

32. Choice D is correct. Solve the equation $P + Q = R$, for Q (the variable we wish to eliminate), to get $Q = R - P$. Substituting this for Q in the second equation yields $P + R = 2(R - P) = 2R - 2P$, or $3P = R$. Therefore, the ratio of P to R is $\frac{P}{R}$, or $\frac{1}{3}$. (406)

33. Choice B is correct. The fraction in question will equal zero if the numerator equals zero, and the denominator is nonzero. The expression $r^2 + 5r + 6$ can be factored into $(r + 2)(r + 3)$. As long as r is not equal to -2 the equation is defined, and $r + 2$ can be canceled in the original equation to yield $r + 3 = 0$, or $r = -3$. For r equals -2 the denominator is equal to zero, and the fraction in the original equation is not defined. (404, 409)

34. Choice E is correct. This problem can be shortened considerably by factoring the expression $a^2b + 4ab^2 + 4b^3$ into the product $(b)(a + 2b)^2$. Now, since $b = 5$, and $(a + 2b) = 25$, our product equals $5 \times 25 \times 25$, or 3,125. (409)

35. Choice E is correct. Subtract $m + 2n$ from both sides of the given equation and obtain the equivalent form, $2n = 7m$. Dividing this equation by $2m$ gives $\frac{n}{m} = \frac{7}{2}$, the ratio of n to m. (406)

36. Choice E is correct. The product will be positive in the case: a positive and b positive, or a negative and b negative; and negative in the case: a positive and b negative, or a negative and b positive. Thus, the positive products must be $(+2)(+1)$ and $(-5)(-7)$. The largest positive value is $+35$. Similarly, the negative products are $(-5)(+1)$ and $(+2)(-7)$; and the most negative value that can be obtained is -14. Thus, the product falls between -14 and $+35$. (419)

37. Choice A is correct. As can be seen from a diagram, this triangle must be a right triangle, since the line from $(-5,1)$ to $(-5,4)$ is vertical, and the line from $(-5,4)$ to $(2,4)$ is horizontal. The lengths of these two perpendicular sides are 3 and 7, respectively.

Since the area of a right triangle is half the product of the perpendicular sides, the area is equal to $\frac{1}{2} \times 3 \times 7$, or 10.5.   (410, 418)

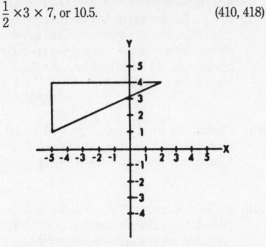

38. Choice E is correct. Solving the first equation for A gives $A = 12 - B$. Solving the second equation for C gives $C = 16 - B$. Thus, the sum $A + C$ is equal to $28 - 2B$. There is nothing to determine the value of B, so the sum of A and C is not determined from the information given.   (406)

39. Choice D is correct. The value of $b^2 - 4ac$ determines the nature of the roots. From the equation substitute $a = 1$, $b = 1$, and $c = 1$ into the expression. $b^2 - 4ac = 1 - 4 = -3$. As $b^2 - 4ac$ is negative, there are no real solutions to the equation.   (408)

40. Choice C is correct. If we graph the five choices we will get:

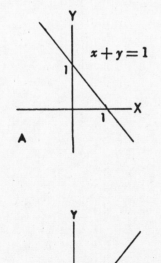

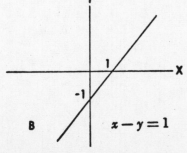

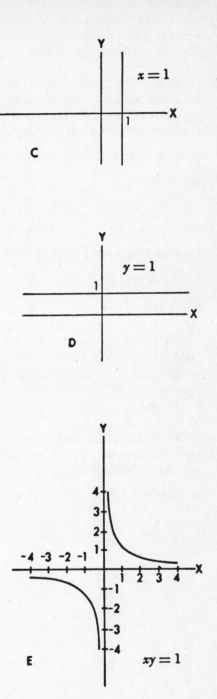

The only choice that is a vertical line is $x = 1$. (413)

41. Choice C is correct. The factors of $x^2 + 3x + 2$ are $(x + 1)$ and $(x + 2)$. Either $x + 1 = 0$, or $x + 2 = 0$. x may equal either -1 or -2.   (408)

42. Choice B is correct. $a + b = 12$ and $a - b = 6$. Rewrite these equations as $a = 12 - b$ and $a = 6 + b$. $12 - b$ and $6 + b$ are both equal to a. Or, $12 - b = 6 + b$. Thus, $6 = 2b$ and $b = 3$.   (407)

43. Choice C is correct. Let $m^2 + 4 = 4m$. Subtracting $4m$ from both sides yields $m^2 - 4m + 4 = 0$. Factor to get the following equation: $(m - 2)^2 = 0$. Thus, $m = 2$ is the only solution. (408)

44. Choice B is correct. Substitute for the given values of x and y, obtaining: $(0)^2(2)(z) + (3)(0)(z)^2 + (2)^2(z) + (3)(2) + (4)(0) = 0$. Perform the indicated multiplications, and combine terms. $0(z) + 0(z^2) + 4z + 6 + 0 = 4z + 6 = 0$. This equation has $z = -\dfrac{3}{2}$ as its only solution. (406)

45. Choice C is correct. $c + 4d = 3c - 2d$. Add $2d - c$ to each side and get $6d = 2c$. (Be especially careful about your signs here.) Dividing by $2d$: $\dfrac{c}{d} = \dfrac{6}{2} = \dfrac{3}{1}$. Thus, $c : d = 3 : 1$. (406)

46. Choice C is correct. x must be greater than 3, less than 7, greater than 2, and less than 6. These conditions can be reduced as follows: If x is less than 6 it is also less than 7. Similarly, x must be greater than 3, which automatically makes it greater than 2. Thus, x must be greater than 3 and less than 6. (419)

47. Choice D is correct. To obtain the coordinates of the midpoint of a line segment, average the corresponding coordinates of the endpoints. Thus, the midpoint will be $\left(\dfrac{4 + 5}{2}, \dfrac{9 + 15}{2}\right)$ or $(4.5, 12)$. (412)

48. Choice D is correct. If both sides of the equation are multiplied by $2t + 4$, we obtain: $t^2 + 2t = t^2 + 2t$, which is true for every value of t. However, when $t = -2$, the denominator of the fraction on the left side of the original equation is equal to zero. Since division by zero is not a permissible operation, this fraction will not be defined for $t = -2$. The equation cannot be satisfied for $t = -2$. (404, 406, 409)

49. Choice A is correct. If we subtract the second of our equations from the first, we will be left with the following: $(x + y) - (x + z) = 4 - 9$, or $y - z = -5$. (402)

50. Choice A is correct. If x^2 is less than 9, then x may take on any value greater than -3 and less than $+3$; other values will produce squares greater than or equal to 9. If $\dfrac{1}{x}$ is less than $\dfrac{1}{3}$, x is restricted to positive values greater than 3, and all negative values. For example, if $x = 1$, then conditions I and II are satisfied, but $\dfrac{1}{x}$ equals 1, which is greater than $\dfrac{1}{3}$. (419)

Math Refresher
Session 5

Geometry Problems

Basic Definitions

500. *Plane geometry* deals with points and lines. A point has no dimensions and is generally represented by a dot (.). A line has no thickness, but it does have length. Lines can be straight or curved, but here it will be assumed that a line is straight unless otherwise indicated. All lines have infinite length. Part of a line that has a finite length is called a line segment.

> Remember that the word *distance* always means the perpendicular distance. Thus, the distance between two lines pictured below is line **A** as this is the only perpendicular line. Also, the distance from a line to a point is the perpendicular from the point to the line. Thus, **AB** is the distance from the point **A** to the line segment **CBD**.

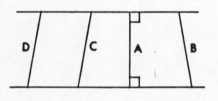 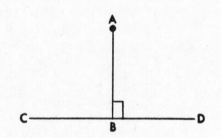

501. *Angles.* An angle is formed when two lines intersect at a point.

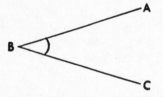

Angle *B*, angle *ABC*, ∠*B*, ∠*ABC* are all possible names for the angle shown.

The measure of the angle is given in degrees. If the sides of the angle form a straight line, then the angle is said to be a straight angle and has 180°. A circle has 360°, and a straight angle is a turning through a half circle. All other angles are either greater or less than 180°.

Angles are classified in different ways:
An *acute* angle has less than 90°.

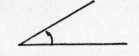

A *right* angle has exactly 90°.

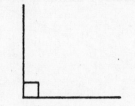

In the diagram, the small square in the corner of the angle indicates a right angle (90°).

An *obtuse* angle has between 90° and 180°.

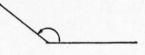

A *straight* angle has exactly 180°.

A *reflex* angle has between 180° and 360°.

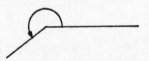

502. Two angles are *complementary* if their sum is 90°. For example, an angle of 30° and an angle of 60° are complementary. Two angles are *supplementary* if their sum is 180°. If one angle is 82°, then its supplement is 98°.

503. *Vertical angles.* These are pairs of opposite angles formed by the intersection of two straight lines. Vertical angles are always equal to each other.

   Example: In the diagram shown, angles *AEC* and *BED* are equal because they are vertical angles. For the same reason, angles *AED* and *BEC* are equal.

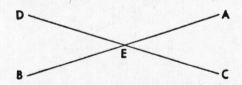

504. When two parallel lines are crossed by a third straight line (called a *transversal*), then all the acute angles formed are equal, and all of the obtuse angles are equal.

   Example: In the diagram below, angles 1, 4, 5, and 8 are all equal. Angles 2, 3, 6, and 7 are also equal.

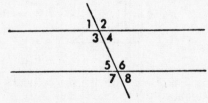

Triangles

505. *Triangles.* A triangle is a closed figure with three sides, each side being a line segment. The sum of the angles of a triangle is *always* 180°.

506. *Scalene triangles* are triangles with no two sides equal. Scalene triangles also have no two angles equal.

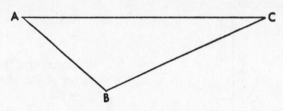

507. *Isosceles triangles* have two equal sides and two equal angles formed by the equal sides and the unequal side. See the figure below.

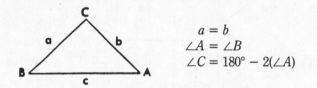

$$a = b$$
$$\angle A = \angle B$$
$$\angle C = 180° - 2(\angle A)$$

508. *Equilateral triangles* have all three sides and all three angles equal. Since the sum of the three angles of a triangle is 180°, each angle of an equilateral triangle is 60°.

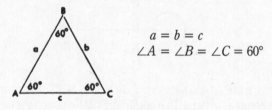

$$a = b = c$$
$$\angle A = \angle B = \angle C = 60°$$

509. A *right triangle* has one angle equal to a right angle (90°). The sum of the other two angles of a right triangle is, therefore, 90°. The most important relationship in a right triangle is the Pythagorean Theorem. It states that $c^2 = a^2 + b^2$ where c is the length of the side opposite the right angle and a and b are the lengths of the other two sides. Recall that this was discussed in Section 317.

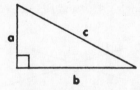

Example: If the two sides of a right triangle adjacent to the right angle are 3 inches and 4 inches respectively, find the length of the side opposite the right angle.

Solution:

Use the Pythagorean Theorem, $c^2 = a^2 + b^2$, where $a = 3$ and $b = 4$. Then, $c = 3^2 + 4^2$ or $c^2 = 9 + 16 = 25$. Thus $c = 5$.

Certain sets of numbers will always fit the formula $c^2 = a^2 + b^2$. These numbers can always represent the lengths of the sides of a right triangle. For example, a triangle whose sides are 3, 4, and 5 will always be a right triangle. Further examples are 5, 12, and 13; 8, 15, and 17. Any multiples of these numbers also satisfy the formula. For example, 6, 8, and 10; 9, 12, and 15; 10, 24, and 26; 24, 45, and 51, etc.

Properties of Triangles

510. Two triangles are said to be *similar* (having the same shape) if their corresponding angles are equal. The sides of similar triangles are in the same proportion. The two triangles below are similar because they have the same corresponding angles.

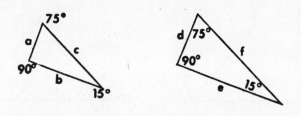

$$a : d = b : e = c : f$$

Example: Two triangles both have angles of 30°, 70° and 80°. If the sides of the triangles are as indicated below, find the length of side x.

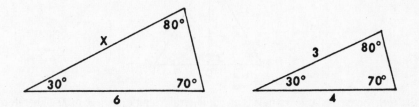

Solution: The two triangles are similar because they have the same corresponding angles. The corresponding sides of similar triangles are in proportion, so $x : 3 = 6 : 4$. This can be rewritten as $\frac{x}{3} = \frac{6}{4}$. Multiplying both sides by 3 gives $x = \frac{18}{4}$, or $x = 4\frac{1}{2}$.

511. Two triangles are *congruent* (*identical* in shape and size) if any one of the following conditions is met:

1. Each side of the first triangle equals the corresponding side of the second triangle.
2. Two sides of the first triangle equal the corresponding sides of the second triangle and their included angles are equal. The included angle is formed by the two sides of the triangle.
3. Two angles of the first triangle equal the corresponding angles of the second triangle, and any pair of corresponding sides are equal.

Example: Triangles *ABC* and *DEF* in the diagram below are congruent if any one of the following conditions can be met:

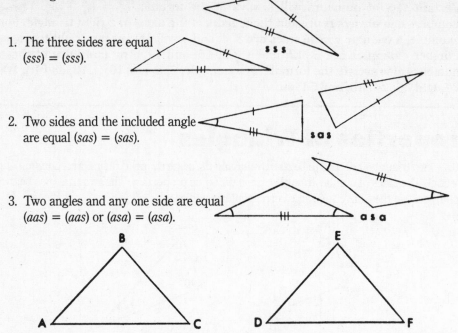

1. The three sides are equal
   (*sss*) = (*sss*).

2. Two sides and the included angle
   are equal (*sas*) = (*sas*).

3. Two angles and any one side are equal
   (*aas*) = (*aas*) or (*asa*) = (*asa*).

Example: In the equilateral triangle below, line *AD* is perpendicular (forms a right angle) to side *BC*. If the length of *BD* is 5 feet, what is the length of *DC*?

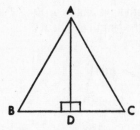

Solution: Since the large triangle is an equilateral triangle, each ∠ is 60°. Therefore ∠*B* is 60° and ∠*C* is 60°. Thus, ∠*B* = ∠*C*. *ADB* and *ADC* are both right angles and are equal. Two angles of each triangle are equal to the corresponding two angles of the other triangle. Side *AD* is shared by both triangles and side *AB* = side *AC*. Thus, according to condition 3 in Section 511, the two triangles are congruent. Then *BD* = *DC* and, since *BD* is 5 feet, *DC* is 5 feet.

512. The *medians* of a triangle are the lines drawn from each vertex to the midpoint of its opposite side. The medians of a triangle cross at a point that divides each median into two parts: one part of one third the length of the median and the other part of two thirds the length.

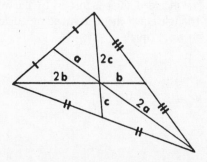

513. The *angle bisectors* of a triangle are the lines that divide each angle of the triangle into two equal parts. These lines meet in a point that is the center of a circle inscribed in the triangle.

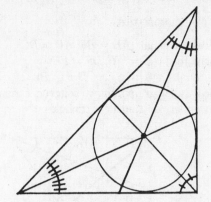

514. The *altitudes* of the triangle are lines drawn from the vertices perpendicular to the opposite sides. The lengths of these lines are useful in calculating the area of the triangle since the area of the triangle is $\frac{1}{2}$ (base) (height) and the height is identical to the altitude.

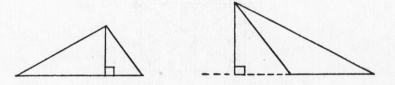

515. The *perpendicular bisectors* of the triangle are the lines that bisect and are perpendicular to each of the three sides. The point where these lines meet is the center of the circumscribed circle.

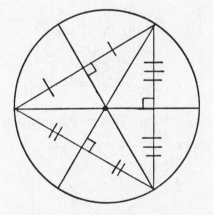

516. The sum of any two sides of a triangle is greater than the third side.

Example: If the three sides of a triangle are 4, 2, and x, then what is known about the value of x?

Solution: Since the sum of two sides of a triangle is always greater than the third side, then $4 + 2 > x$, $4 + x > 2$, and $2 + x > 4$. These three inequalities can be rewritten as $6 > x$, $x > -2$, and $x > 2$. For x to be greater than -2 and 2, it must be greater than 2. Thus, the values of x are $2 < x < 6$.

Four-Sided Figures

517. A *parallelogram* is a four-sided figure with each pair of opposite sides parallel.

A parallelogram has the following properties:

1. Each pair of opposite sides are equal. ($AD = BC$, $AB = DC$)
2. The diagonals bisect each other. ($AF = FC$, $DF = FB$)
3. The opposite angles are equal. ($\angle A = \angle C$, $\angle D = \angle B$)
4. One diagonal divides the parallelogram into two congruent triangles. Two diagonals divide the parallelogram into two pairs of congruent triangles.

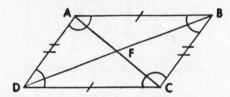

518. A *rectangle* is a parallelogram in which all the angles are right angles. Since a rectangle is a parallelogram, all of the laws that apply to a parallelogram apply to a rectangle. In addition, the diagonals of a rectangle are equal.

$AC = BD$

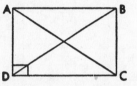

519. A *rhombus* is a parallelogram with four equal sides. Since a rhombus is a parallelogram, all of the laws that apply to a parallelogram apply to a rhombus. In addition, the diagonals of a rhombus are perpendicular to each other and bisect the vertex angles.

$\angle DAC = \angle BAC = \angle DCA = \angle BCA$
$\angle ADB = \angle CDB = \angle ABD = \angle CBD$
AC is perpendicular to DB

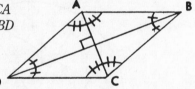

520. A *square* is a rectangular rhombus. Thus the square has the following properties:

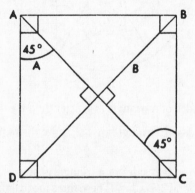

1. All four sides equal. ($AB = BC = CD = DA$)
2. Opposite pairs of sides are parallel. ($AD \parallel BC$, $AB \parallel DC$)
3. Diagonals are equal, are perpendicular to each other, and bisect each other. ($AC = BD$, $AC \perp BD$, $AE = EC = DE = EB$)

4. All the angles are right angles (90°). ($\angle A = \angle B = \angle C = \angle D = 90°$)
5. Diagonals intersect the vertices at 45°. ($\angle DAC = \angle BAC = 45°$, and similarly for the other 3 vertices)

Many-Sided Figures

521. A *polygon* is a closed plane figure whose sides are straight lines. The sum of the angles in any polygon is equal to $180(n-2)°$, where n is the number of sides. Thus, in a polygon of 3 sides (a triangle), the sum of the angles is $180(3-2)°$ or 180°.

522. A *regular polygon* is a polygon all of whose sides are equal and all of whose angles are equal. These polygons have special properties:

1. A regular polygon can be inscribed in a circle and can be circumscribed about another circle. For example, a hexagon is inscribed in a circle in the diagram below.

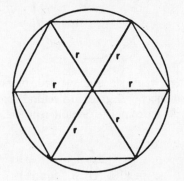

2. Each angle of a polygon is equal to the sum of the angles divided by the number of sides, $\dfrac{180(n-2)°}{n}$. Thus, a square, which is a regular polygon of 4 sides, has each angle equal to $\dfrac{180(4-2)°}{4}$ or 90°.

523. An important regular polygon is the *hexagon*. The diagonals of a regular hexagon divide it into 6 equilateral triangles, the sides of which are equal to the sides of the hexagon. If a hexagon is inscribed in a circle, the length of each side is equal to the length of the radius of the circle. (See diagram of hexagon.)

Circles

524. A *circle* (also see Section 310) is a set of points equidistant from a given point, the *center*. The distance from the center to the circle is the *radius*. Any line that connects two points on the circle is a *chord*. A chord through the center of the circle is a *diameter*. On the circle below O is the center, line segment OF is a radius, DOE is a diameter, and AC is a chord.

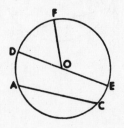

The length of the diameter of a circle is twice the length of the radius. The circumference (length of the curve) is 2π times the length of the radius. π is a constant approximately equal to $\frac{22}{7}$ or 3.14. The formula for the circumference of a circle is, $C = 2\pi r$ where C = circumference and r = radius.

525. A *tangent* to a circle is a line that is perpendicular to a radius and that passes through only one point of the circle. In the diagram AB is a tangent.

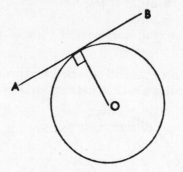

526. A *central angle* is an angle whose sides are two radii of the circle. The vertex of this angle is the center of the circle. The number of degrees in a central angle is equal to the amount of arc length that the radii intercept. As the complete circumference has 360°, any other arc lengths are less than 360°.

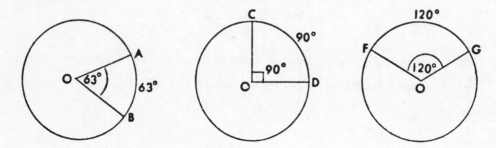

Angles AOB, COD, and FOG are all central angles.

527. An *inscribed angle* of a circle is an angle whose sides are two chords. The vertex of the angle lies on the circumference of the circle. The number of degrees in the inscribed angle is equal to one half the intercepted arc.

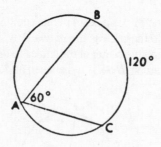

$\angle\ BAC$ is an inscribed angle.

528. An angle inscribed in a semicircle is always a right angle. $\angle ABC$ and $\angle ADC$ are inscribed in semicircles *AOCB* and *AOCD*, respectively, and are thus right angles. *Note:* A semicircle is one half of a circle.

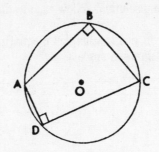

529. Two tangents to a circle from a point outside of the circle are always equal.

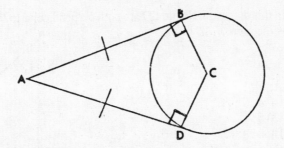

Tangents *AB* and *AD* are equal.

Practice Test 5

Geometry Problems

Correct answers and solutions follow each test.

1. A B C D E
   ⦀ ⦀ ⦀ ⦀ ⦀

1. In the following diagram, angle 1 is equal to 40°, and angle 2 is equal to 150°. What is the number of degrees in angle 3?

   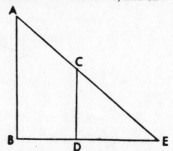

   (A) 70°
   (B) 90°
   (C) 110°
   (D) 190°
   (E) The answer cannot be determined from the given information.

2. A B C D E
   ⦀ ⦀ ⦀ ⦀ ⦀

2. In this diagram, *AB* and *CD* are both perpendicular to *BE*. If *EC* = 5, and *CD* = 4, what is the ratio of *AB* to *BE*?

   (A) 1 : 1
   (B) 4 : 3
   (C) 5 : 4
   (D) 5 : 3
   (E) none of these

3. A B C D E
   ⦀ ⦀ ⦀ ⦀ ⦀

3. In triangle *PQR*, *PR* = 7.0, and *PQ* = 4.5. Which of the following cannot possibly represent the length of *QR*?

   (A) 2.0
   (B) 3.0
   (C) 3.5
   (D) 4.5
   (E) 5.0

4. A B C D E
   ⦀ ⦀ ⦀ ⦀ ⦀

4. In this diagram, *AB* = *AC*, and *BD* = *CD*. Which of the following statements is true?

   (A) *BE* = *EC*
   (B) *AD* is perpendicular to *BC*.
   (C) Triangles *BDE* and *CDE* are congruent.
   (D) Angle *ABD* equals angle *ACD*.
   (E) All of these.

5. A B C D E
   ⦀ ⦀ ⦀ ⦀ ⦀

5. In the following diagram, if *BC* = *CD* = *BD* = 1, and angle *ADC* is a right angle, what is the perimeter of triangle *ABD*?

   (A) 3
   (B) $2 + \sqrt{2}$
   (C) $2 + \sqrt{3}$
   (D) $3 + \sqrt{3}$
   (E) 4

   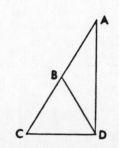

6. A B C D E

6. In this diagram, if *PQRS* is a parallelogram, which of the following can be deduced:

   I. $QT + PT = RT + ST$
   II. *QS* is perpendicular to *PR*
   III. The area of the shaded portion is exactly three times the area of triangle *QRT*.

   (A) I only
   (B) I and II only
   (C) II only
   (D) I and III only
   (E) I, II, and III

7. A B C D E

7. James lives on the corner of a rectangular field that measures 120 yards by 160 yards. If he wants to walk to the opposite corner, he can either travel along the perimeter of the field or cut directly across in a straight line. How many yards does he save by taking the direct route? (Express to the nearest ten yards.)

   (A) 40 yards
   (B) 60 yards
   (C) 80 yards
   (D) 100 yards
   (E) 110 yards

8. A B C D E

8. In a square, the perimeter is how many times the length of the diagonal?

   (A) $\dfrac{\sqrt{2}}{2}$
   (B) $\sqrt{2}$
   (C) 2
   (D) $2\sqrt{2}$
   (E) 4

9. A B C D E

9. How many degrees are there in the angle formed by two adjacent sides of a regular nonagon (nine-sided polygon)?

   (A) 40°
   (B) 70°
   (C) 105°
   (D) 120°
   (E) 140°

10. A B C D E

10. In the diagram below, $AB = CD$. From this we can deduce that:

    (A) *AB* is parallel to *CD*.
    (B) *AB* is perpendicular to *BD*.
    (C) $AC = BD$
    (D) Angle *ABD* equals angle *BDC*.
    (E) Triangle *ABD* is congruent to triangle *ACD*.

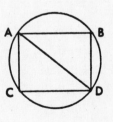

Note: Figure is not drawn to scale.

11.

11. If two lines, *AB* and *CD*, intersect at a point *E*, which of the following statements is *not* true?

(A) Angle *AEB* equals angle *CED*.
(B) Angles *AEC* and *BEC* are complementary.
(C) Angle *CED* is a straight angle.
(D) Angle *AEC* equals angle *BED*.
(E) Angle *BED* plus angle *AED* equals 180 degrees.

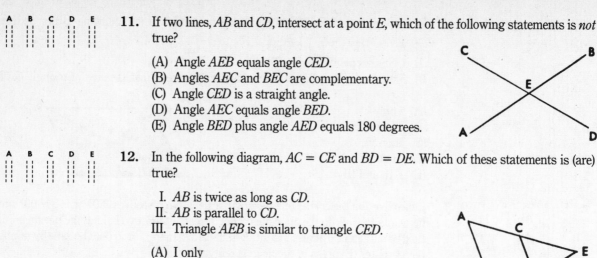

12. A B C D E

12. In the following diagram, *AC* = *CE* and *BD* = *DE*. Which of these statements is (are) true?

  I. *AB* is twice as long as *CD*.
 II. *AB* is parallel to *CD*.
III. Triangle *AEB* is similar to triangle *CED*.

(A) I only
(B) II and III, only
(C) I and III, only
(D) I, II, and III
(E) none of these

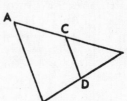

13. A B C D E

13. In triangle *ABC* angle *A* is obtuse, and angle *B* equals 30°. Which of the following statements *best* describes angle *C*?

(A) Angle C must be less than 60°.
(B) Angle C must be less than or equal to 60°.
(C) Angle C must be equal to 60°.
(D) Angle C must be greater than or equal to 60°.
(E) Angle C must be greater than 60°.

14. A B C D E

14. In this diagram, *ABCD* is a parallelogram, and *BFDE* is a square. If *AB* = 20 and *CF* = 16, what is the perimeter of the parallelogram *ABCD*?

(A) 72
(B) 78
(C) 86
(D) 92
(E) 96

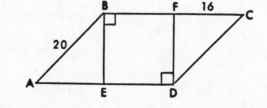

15. A B C D E

15. The hypotenuse of a right triangle is exactly twice as long as the shorter leg. What is the number of degrees in the smallest angle of the triangle?

(A) 30°
(B) 45°
(C) 60°
(D) 90°
(E) The answer cannot be determined from the given information.

16. A B C D E   **16.** The legs of an isosceles triangle are equal to 17 inches each. If the altitude to the base is 8 inches long, how long is the base of the triangle?

           (A) 15 inches
           (B) 20 inches
           (C) 24 inches
           (D) 25 inches
           (E) 30 inches

17. A B C D E   **17.** The perimeter of a right triangle is 18 inches. If the midpoints of the three sides are joined by line segments, they form another triangle. What is the perimeter of this new triangle?

           (A) 3 inches
           (B) 6 inches
           (C) 9 inches
           (D) 12 inches
           (E) The answer cannot be determined from the given information.

18. A B C D E   **18.** If the diagonals of a square divide it into four triangles, the triangles *cannot* be

           (A) right triangles
           (B) isosceles triangles
           (C) similar triangles
           (D) equilateral triangles
           (E) equal in area

19. A B C D E   **19.** In the diagram below, *ABCDEF* is a regular hexagon. How many degrees are there in angle *ADC*?

           (A) 45°
           (B) 60°
           (C) 75°
           (D) 90°
           (E) none of these

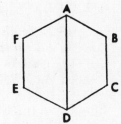

20. A B C D E   **20.** This diagram depicts a rectangle inscribed in a circle. If the measurements of the rectangle are 10″ × 14″, what is the area of the circle?

           (A) 74π
           (B) 92π
           (C) 144π
           (D) 196π
           (E) 296π

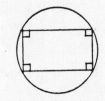

21. A B C D E   **21.** How many degrees are included between the hands of a clock at 5:00?

           (A) 50°
           (B) 60°
           (C) 75°
           (D) 120°
           (E) 150°

22. A B C D E

22. *ABCD* is a square. If the midpoints of the four sides are joined to form a new square, the perimeter of the old square is how many times the perimeter of the new square?

(A) 1
(B) $\sqrt{2}$
(C) 2
(D) $2\sqrt{2}$
(E) 4

23. A B C D E

23. Angles *A* and *B* of triangle *ABC* are both acute angles. Which of the following *best* describes angle *C*?

(A) Angle *C* is between 0° and 180°.
(B) Angle *C* is between 0° and 90°.
(C) Angle *C* is between 60° and 180°.
(D) Angle *C* is between 60° and 120°.
(E) Angle *C* is between 60° and 90°.

24. A B C D E

24. The angles of a quadrilateral are in the ratio 1 : 2 : 3 : 4. What is the number of degrees in the largest angle?

(A) 72
(B) 96
(C) 120
(D) 144
(E) 150

25. A B C D E

25. *ABCD* is a rectangle; the diagonals *AC* and *BD* intersect at *E*. Which of the following statements is *not necessarily true*?

(A) *AE = BE*
(B) Angle *AEB* equals angle *CED*.
(C) *AE* is perpendicular to *BD*.
(D) Triangles *AED* and *AEB* are equal in area.
(E) Angle *BAC* equals angle *BDC*.

26. A B C D E

26. City A is 200 miles from City B, and City B is 400 miles from City C. Which of the following best describes the distance between City A and City C? (Note: The cities A, B, C do *not* all lie on a straight line.)

(A) It must be greater than zero.
(B) It must be greater than 200 miles.
(C) It must be less than 600 miles and greater than zero.
(D) It must be less than 600 miles and greater than 200.
(E) It must be exactly 400 miles.

27. A B C D E

27. At 7:30, how many degrees are included between the hands of a clock?

(A) 15°
(B) 30°
(C) 45°
(D) 60°
(E) 75°

28. A B C D E

28. If a ship is sailing in a northerly direction and then turns to the right until it is sailing in a southwesterly direction, it has gone through a rotation of:

(A) 45°
(B) 90°
(C) 135°
(D) 180°
(E) 225°

29. A B C D E

29. x, y, and z are the angles of a triangle. If $x = 2y$, and $y = z + 30°$, how many degrees are there in angle x?

(A) 22.5°
(B) 37.5°
(C) 52.5°
(D) 90.0°
(E) 105.0°

30. A B C D E

30. In the diagram shown, AB is parallel to CD. Which of the following statements is *not necessarily true*?

(A) $\angle 1 + \angle 2 = 180°$
(B) $\angle 4 = \angle 7$
(C) $\angle 5 + \angle 8 + \angle 2 + \angle 4 = 360°$
(D) $\angle 2 + \angle 3 = 180°$
(E) $\angle 2 = \angle 6$

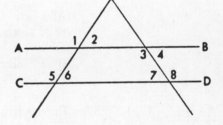

31. A B C D E

31. What is the ratio of the diagonal of a square to the hypotenuse of the isosceles right triangle having the same area?

(A) $1 : 2$
(B) $1 : \sqrt{2}$
(C) $1 : 1$
(D) $\sqrt{2} : 1$
(E) $2 : 1$

32. A B C D E

32. How many degrees are there between two adjacent sides of a regular ten-sided figure?

(A) 36°
(B) 72°
(C) 120°
(D) 144°
(E) 154°

33. A B C D E

33. Which of the following sets of numbers *cannot* represent the lengths of the sides of a right triangle?

(A) 5, 12, 13
(B) 4.2, 5.6, 7.0
(C) 9, 28, 35
(D) 16, 30, 34
(E) 7.5, 18, 19.5

34. A B C D E   **34.** How many degrees are there in the angle that is its own supplement?

(A) 30°
(B) 45°
(C) 60°
(D) 90°
(E) 180°

35. A B C D E   **35.** If a central angle of 45° intersects an arc 6 inches long on the circumference of a circle, what is the radius of the circle?

(A) $\frac{24}{\pi}$ inches

(B) $\frac{48}{\pi}$ inches

(C) 6π inches
(D) 24 inches
(E) 48 inches

36. A B C D E   **36.** What is the length of the line segment connecting the two most distant vertices of a 1-inch cube?

(A) 1 inch
(B) $\sqrt{2}$ inches
(C) $\sqrt{3}$ inches
(D) $\sqrt{5}$ inches
(E) $\sqrt{6}$ inches

37. A B C D E   **37.** Through how many degrees does the hour hand of a clock move in 70 minutes?

(A) 35°
(B) 60°
(C) 80°
(D) 90°
(E) 120°

38. A B C D E   **38.** In the diagram pictured below, BA is tangent to circle O at point A. CD is perpendicular to OA at C. Which of the following statements is (are) true?

    I. Triangles ODC and OBA are similar.
    II. $OA : DC = OB : AB$
    III. AB is twice as long as CD.

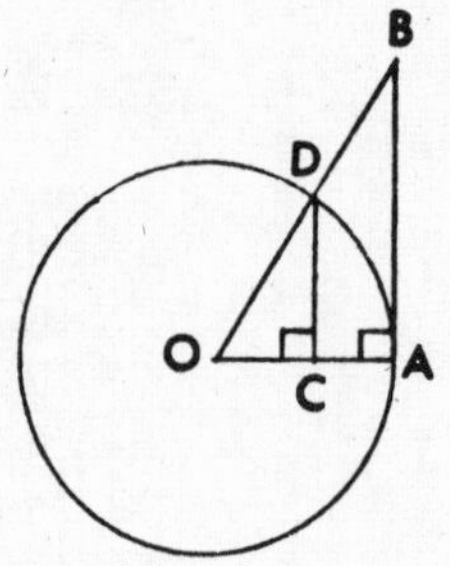

(A) I only
(B) III only
(C) I and II, only
(D) II and III, only
(E) none of the above combinations

39. A B C D E   **39.** The three angles of triangle ABC are in the ratio $1 : 2 : 6$. How many degrees are in the largest angle?

(A) 45°
(B) 90°
(C) 120°
(D) 135°
(E) 160°

40. A B C D E

40. In this diagram, $AB = AC$, angle $A = 40°$, and BD is perpendicular to AC at D. How many degrees are there in angle DBC?

(A) 20°
(B) 40°
(C) 50°
(D) 70°
(E) none of these

41. A B C D E

41. If the line AB intersects the line CD at point E, which of the following pairs of angles need *not* be equal?

(A) $\angle AEB$ and $\angle CED$
(B) $\angle AEC$ and $\angle BED$
(C) $\angle AED$ and $\angle CEA$
(D) $\angle BEC$ and $\angle DEA$
(E) $\angle DEC$ and $\angle BEA$

42. A B C D E

42. All right isosceles triangles must be

(A) similar
(B) congruent
(C) equilateral
(D) equal in area
(E) none of these

43. A B C D E

43. What is the area of a triangle whose sides are 10 inches, 13 inches, and 13 inches?

(A) 39 square inches
(B) 52 square inches
(C) 60 square inches
(D) 65 square inches
(E) The answer cannot be determined from the given information.

44. A B C D E

44. If each side of an equilateral triangle is 2 inches long, what is the triangle's altitude?

(A) 1 inch
(B) $\sqrt{2}$ inches
(C) $\sqrt{3}$ inches
(D) 2 inches
(E) $\sqrt{5}$ inches

45. A B C D E

45. In the parallelogram $ABCD$, diagonals AC and BD intersect at E. Which of the following must be true?

(A) $\angle AED = \angle BEC$
(B) $AE = EC$
(C) $\angle BDC = \angle DBA$
(D) Two of the above must be true.
(E) All three of the statements must be true.

46. A B C D E

46. If *ABCD* is a square, and diagonals *AC* and *BD* intersect at point *E*, how many isosceles right triangles are there in the figure?

(A) 4
(B) 5
(C) 6
(D) 7
(E) 8

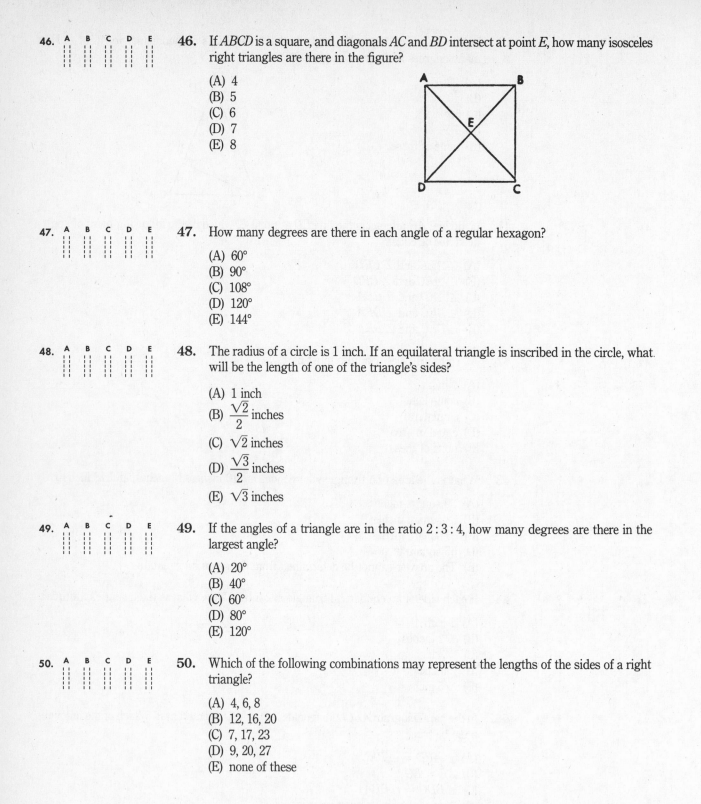

47. A B C D E

47. How many degrees are there in each angle of a regular hexagon?

(A) 60°
(B) 90°
(C) 108°
(D) 120°
(E) 144°

48. A B C D E

48. The radius of a circle is 1 inch. If an equilateral triangle is inscribed in the circle, what will be the length of one of the triangle's sides?

(A) 1 inch
(B) $\dfrac{\sqrt{2}}{2}$ inches
(C) $\sqrt{2}$ inches
(D) $\dfrac{\sqrt{3}}{2}$ inches
(E) $\sqrt{3}$ inches

49. A B C D E

49. If the angles of a triangle are in the ratio 2 : 3 : 4, how many degrees are there in the largest angle?

(A) 20°
(B) 40°
(C) 60°
(D) 80°
(E) 120°

50. A B C D E

50. Which of the following combinations may represent the lengths of the sides of a right triangle?

(A) 4, 6, 8
(B) 12, 16, 20
(C) 7, 17, 23
(D) 9, 20, 27
(E) none of these

Answer Key for Practice Test 5

1. C	14. E	27. C	39. C
2. B	15. A	28. E	40. A
3. A	16. E	29. E	41. C
4. E	17. C	30. D	42. A
5. C	18. D	31. B	43. C
6. D	19. B	32. D	44. C
7. C	20. A	33. C	45. E
8. D	21. E	34. D	46. E
9. E	22. B	35. A	47. D
10. D	23. A	36. C	48. E
11. B	24. D	37. A	49. D
12. D	25. C	38. C	50. B
13. A	26. D		

Answers and Solutions for Practice Test 5

1. Choice C is correct. In the problem it is given that $\angle 1 = 40°$ and $\angle 2 = 150°$. The diagram below makes it apparent that: (1) $\angle 1 = \angle 4$ and $\angle 3 = \angle 5$ (vertical angles); (2) $\angle 6 + \angle 2 = 180°$ (straight angle); (3) $\angle 4 + \angle 5 + \angle 6 = 180°$ (sum of angles in a triangle). To solve the problem, $\angle 3$ must be related through the above information to the known quantities in $\angle 1$ and $\angle 2$. Proceed as follows: $\angle 3 = \angle 5$, but $\angle 5 = 180° - \angle 4 - \angle 6$. $\angle 4 = \angle 1 = 40°$ and $\angle 6 = 180° - \angle 2 = 180° - 150° = 30°$. Therefore, $\angle 3 = 180° - 40° - 30° = 110°$.
(501, 503, 505)

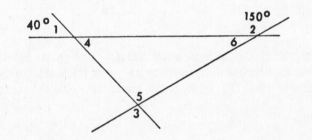

2. Choice B is correct. Since CD is perpendicular to DE, CDE is a right triangle, and using the Pythagorean Theorem yields $DE = 3$. Thus, the ratio of CD to DE is 4 : 3. But triangle ABE is similar to triangle CDE. Therefore, $AB : BE = CD : DE = 4 : 3$. (509, 510)

3. Choice A is correct. In a triangle, it is impossible for one side to be longer than the sum of the other two (a straight line is the shortest distance between two points). Thus 2.0, 4.5, and 7.0 cannot be three sides of a triangle. (516)

4. Choice E is correct. $AB = AC$, $BD = CD$, and AD equal to itself is sufficient information (three sides) to prove triangles ABD and ACD congruent. Also, since $AB = AC$, $AE = AE$, and $\angle BAE = \angle CAE$ (by the previous congruence), triangles ABE and ACE are congruent. Since $BD = CD$, $ED = ED$, and angle BDE equals angle CDE (by initial congruence), triangles BDE and CDE are congruent. Through congruence of triangle ABE and triangle ACE, angles BEA and CEA are equal, and their sum is a straight angle (180°). They must both be right angles. Thus, from the given information, we can deduce all the properties given as choices. (511)

5. Choice C is correct. The perimeter of triangle ABD is $AB + BD + AD$. The length of BD is 1. Since $BC = CD = BD$, triangle BCD is an equilateral triangle. Therefore, angle $C = 60°$ and angle $BDC = 60°$. Angle A + angle $C = 90°$ (the sum of two acute angles in a right

triangle is 90°) and angle BDC + angle BDA = 90° (these two angles form a right angle). Since angle C and angle BDC both equal 60°, angle A = angle BDA = 30°. Now two angles of triangle ADB are equal. Therefore, triangle ADB is an isosceles triangle with side BD = side AB. Since BD = 1, then AB = 1. AD is a leg of the right triangle, with side CD = 1 and hypotenuse AC = 2. ($AC = AB + BC = 1 + 1$.) Using the relationship $c^2 = a^2 + b^2$ gives us the length of AD as $\sqrt{3}$. Thus the perimeter is $1 + 1 + \sqrt{3}$ or $2 + \sqrt{3}$.

(505, 507, 509)

6. Choice D is correct. (I) must be true, since the diagonals of a parallelogram bisect each other, so $QT = ST$, and $PT = RT$. Thus, since the sums of equals are equal, $QT + PT = RT + ST$.

    (II) is not necessarily true and, in fact, can be true only if the parallelogram is also a rhombus (all four sides equal).

    (III) is true, since the four small triangles each have the same area. The shaded portion contains three such triangles. This can be seen by noting that the altitudes from point P to the bases of triangles PQT and PTS are identical. We have already seen from part (I) that these bases (QT and TS) are also equal. Therefore, only I and III can be deduced from the given information. (514, 517)

7. Choice C is is correct.

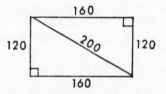

The diagonal path divides the rectangular field into two right triangles. The Pythagorean Theorem gives the length of the diagonal as 200 yards. If James takes the route around the perimeter, he will travel 120 + 160, or 280 yards. Thus, the shorter route saves him 80 yards. (509, 518)

8. Choice D is correct. Let one side of a square be s. Then the perimeter must be $4s$. The diagonal of a square with side s is equal to $s\sqrt{2}$. Dividing the perimeter by the diagonal produces $2\sqrt{2}$. The perimeter is $2\sqrt{2}$ times the diagonal. (509, 520)

9. Choice E is correct. The sum of the angles of any polygon is equal to 180° $(n - 2)$, where n is the number of sides. Thus the total number of degrees in a nonagon = 180°$(9 - 2)$ = 180° × 7 = 1260°. The number of degrees in each angle is $\dfrac{1260°}{n} = \dfrac{1260°}{9} = 140°$.

(521, 522)

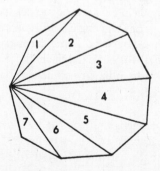

10. Choice D is correct. Since chord *AB* equals chord *CD*, it must be true that arc *AB* equals arc *CD*. By adding arc *AC* to arc *CD* and to arc *AB* it is apparent that arc *ACD* is equal to arc *CAB*. These arcs are intersected by inscribed angles *ABD* and *BDC*. Therefore, the two inscribed angles must be equal. If we redraw the figure as shown below, the falseness of statements (A), (B), (C), and (E) becomes readily apparent. (527)

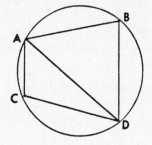

11. Choice B is correct. $\angle AEC + \angle BEC = \angle AEB$, a straight angle (180°). Thus, angles *AEC* and *BEC* are *supplementary*. (Complementary means that the two angles add up to a *right* angle, or 90°.) (501, 502)

12. Choice D is correct. Since *AC* = *CE* and *BD* = *DE*, triangles *AEB* and *CED* are similar, and *AE* is twice as long as *CE*, since by proportionality, *AB* : *CD* = *AE* : *CE* = 2 : 1. From the similarity it is found that angle *ABE* equals angle *CDE*, and, therefore, that *AB* is parallel to *CD*. Thus, all three statements are true. (504, 510)

13. Choice A is correct. Angle *A* must be greater than 90°; angle *B* equals 30°. Thus, the sum of angles *A* and *B* must be greater than 120°. Since the sum of the three angles *A*, *B*, and *C* must be 180°, angle *C* must be *less than* 60°. (It cannot equal 60°, because then angle *A* would be a right angle instead of an obtuse angle.) (501, 505)

14. Choice E is correct. *CDF* is a right triangle with one side of 16 and a hypotenuse of 20. Thus, the third side, *DF*, equals 12. Since *BFDE* is a square, *BF* and *ED* are also equal to 12. Thus, *BC* = 12 + 16 = 28, and *CD* = 20. *ABCD* is a parallelogram, so *AB* = *CD*, *AD* = *BC*. The perimeter is 28 + 20 + 28 + 20 = 96. (509, 517, 520)

15. Choice A is correct. Either recognize immediately that the sides of a 30° − 60° − 90° triangle are in the proportion $1 : \sqrt{3} : 2$, and the problem is solved, or construct an isosceles triangle by placing two of the right triangles so that the unknown sides touch (see diagram). This isosceles triangle is equilateral with angles of 60°. Therefore, the smallest angle in the right triangle is equal to angle *BAC*, or 30°. (509)

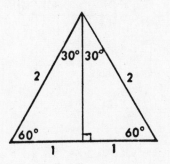

16. Choice E is correct. The altitude to the base of an isosceles triangle divides it into two congruent right triangles, each with one leg of 8 inches, and a hypotenuse of 17 inches. By the Pythagorean Theorem, the third side of each right triangle must be 15 inches long. The base of the isosceles triangle is the sum of two such sides, totaling 30 inches. (507, 509, 514)

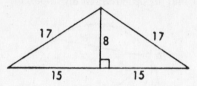

17. Choice C is correct. Call the triangle ABC, and the triangle of midpoints PQR, where P is the midpoint of BC, Q is the midpoint of AC, and R is the midpoint of AB. Then, PQ is equal to half the length of AB, $QR = \frac{1}{2}BC$, and $PR = \frac{1}{2}AC$. This has nothing to do with the fact that ABC is a right triangle. Thus, the perimeter of the small triangle is equal to $PQ + QR + PR = \frac{1}{2}(AB + BC + AC)$. The new perimeter is half the old perimeter, or 9 inches. (509, 510, 512)

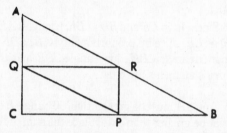

18. Choice D is correct. The diagonals of the square form four right triangles, each of which is isosceles because each has two 45° angles. The triangles are all identical in shape and size, so they all are similar and have the same area. The only choice left is equilateral, which cannot be true, since then the sum of the angles at the intersection of the diagonals must be 360°. The sum of four 60° angles would be only 240°. (520)

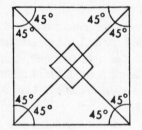

19. Choice B is correct. First, draw in the lines *CF* and *BE*. These intersect *AD* at its midpoint (also the midpoint of *CF* and *BE*) and divide the hexagon into six equilateral triangles. Since *ADC* is an angle of one of these equilateral triangles, it must be equal to 60°. (Another way to do this problem is to calculate the number of degrees in one angle of a regular hexagon and divide this by 2.)

(508, 523)

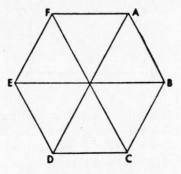

20. Choice A is correct. The diagonal of an inscribed rectangle is equal to the diameter of the circle. To find this length use the Pythagorean Theorem on one of the two triangles formed by two of the sides of the rectangle and the diagonal. Thus, the square of the diagonal is equal to $10^2 + 14^2 = 100 + 196 = 296$. The area of the circle is equal to π times the square of the radius. The square of the radius of the circle is one-fourth of the diameter squared (since $d = 2r$, $d^2 = 4r^2$) or 74. Thus, the area is 74π. (509, 518, 524)

21. Choice E is correct. Each number on a clock (or hour marking) represents an angle of 30°, as 360° divided by 12 is 30° (a convenient fact to remember for other clock problems). Since the hands of the clock are on the 12 and the 5, there are five hour units between the hands; $5 \times 30° = 150°$. (501, 526)

22. Choice B is correct.

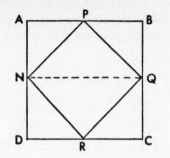

Let S represent the side of the large square. Then the perimeter is $4S$. Let s represent the side of the smaller square. Then the perimeter is $4s$. Line NQ is the diagonal of the smaller square, so the length of NQ is $\sqrt{2}s$. (The diagonal of a square is $\sqrt{2}$ times the side.) Now, NQ is equal to DC, or S, which is the side of the larger square. So now $S = \sqrt{2}s$. The perimeter of the large square equals $4S = 4\sqrt{2}s = \sqrt{2}(4s) = \sqrt{2} \times$ perimeter of the small square. (520)

23. Choice A is correct. Angles A and B are both greater than 0 degrees and less than 90 degrees, so their sum is between 0 degrees and 180 degrees. Then angle C must be between 0 and 180 degrees. (501, 505)

24. Choice D is correct. Let the four angles be x, $2x$, $3x$, and $4x$. The sum, $10x$, must equal $360°$. Thus, $x = 36°$, and the largest angle, $4x$, is $144°$. (505)

25. Choice C is correct. The diagonals of a rectangle are perpendicular only when the rectangle is a square. AE is part of the diagonal AC, so AE will not necessarily be perpendicular to BD. (518)

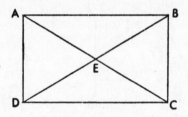

26. Choice D is correct.

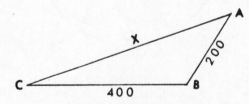

Draw the three cities as the vertices of a triangle. The length of side CB is 400 miles, the length of side AB is 200 miles, and x, the length of side AC, is unknown. The sum of any two sides of a triangle is greater than the third side, or in algebraic terms: $400 + 200 > x$, $400 + x > 200$ and $200 + x > 400$. These simplify to $600 > x$, $x > -200$, and $x > 200$. For x to be greater than 200 and -200, it must be greater than 200. Thus, the values of x are $200 < x < 600$. (506, 516)

27. Choice C is correct. At 7:30, the hour hand is *halfway between the 7 and the 8*, and the minute hand is on the 6. Thus, there are one and one-half "hour units," each equal to $30°$, so the whole angle is $45°$. (501, 526)

28. Choice E is correct. If a ship is facing north, a right turn of 90° will face it eastward. Another 90° turn will face it south, and an additional 45° turn will bring it to southwest. Thus, the total rotation is 90° + 90° + 45° = 225°. (501)

29. Choice E is correct. Since $y = z + 30°$ and $x = 2y$, then $x = 2(z + 30°) = 2z + 60°$. Thus, $x + y + z$ equals $(2z + 60°) + (z + 30°) + z = 4z + 90°$. This must equal 180° (the sum of the angles of a triangle). So $4z + 90° = 180°$, and the solution is $z = 22\frac{1}{2}°$; $x = 2z + 60° = 45° + 60° = 105°$. (505)

30. Choice D is correct. Since AB is parallel to CD, angle 2 = angle 6, and angle 3 + angle 7 = 180°. If angle 2 + angle 3 equals 180°, then angle 2 = angle 7 = angle 6. However, since there is no evidence that angles 6 and 7 are equal, angle 2 + angle 3 does not necessarily equal 180°. Therefore, the answer is (D). (504)

31. Choice B is correct. Call the side of the square, s. Then, the diagonal of the square is $\sqrt{2}s$ and the area is s^2. The area of an isosceles right triangle with leg r is $\frac{1}{2}r^2$. Now, the area of the triangle is equal to the area of the square so $s^2 = \frac{1}{2}r^2$. Solving for r gives $r = \sqrt{2}s$. The hypotenuse of the triangle is $\sqrt{r^2 + r^2}$. Substituting $r = \sqrt{2}s$, the hypotenuse is $\sqrt{2s^2 + 2s^2} = \sqrt{4s^2} = 2s$. Therefore, the ratio of the diagonal to the hypotenuse is $\sqrt{2}s : 2s$. Since $\sqrt{2}s : 2s$ is $\frac{\sqrt{2}s}{2s}$ or $\frac{\sqrt{2}}{2}$, multiply by $\frac{\sqrt{2}}{\sqrt{2}}$ which has a value of 1. Thus $\frac{\sqrt{2}}{2} \cdot \frac{\sqrt{2}}{\sqrt{2}} = \frac{2}{2\sqrt{2}} = \frac{1}{\sqrt{2}}$ or $1 : \sqrt{2}$, which is the final result. (507, 509, 520)

32. Choice D is correct. The formula for the number of degrees in the angles of a polygon is $180(n - 2)$, where n is the number of sides. For a ten-sided figure this is $10(180°) - 360° = (1800 - 360)° = 1440°$. Since the ten angles are equal, they must each equal 144°. (521, 522)

33. Choice C is correct. If three numbers represent the lengths of the sides of a right triangle, they must satisfy the Pythagorean Theorem: The squares of the smaller two must equal the square of the largest one. This condition is met in all the sets given except the set 9,28,35. There, $9^2 + 28^2 = 81 + 784 = 865$, but $35^2 = 1,225$. (509)

34. Choice D is correct. Let the angle be x. Since x is its own supplement, then $x + x = 180°$, or, since $2x = 180°$, $x = 90°$. (502)

35. Choice A is correct. The length of the arc intersected by a central angle of a circle is proportional to the number of degrees in the angle. Thus, if a 45° angle cuts off a 6-inch arc, a 360° angle intersects an arc eight times as long, or 48 inches. This is equal to the circle's circumference, or 2π times the radius. Thus, to obtain the radius, divide 48 inches by 2π. 48 inches $\div 2\pi = \frac{24}{\pi}$ inches. (524, 526)

36. Choice C is correct. Refer to the diagram pictured below. Calculate the distance from vertex 1 to vertex 2. This is simply the diagonal of a 1-inch square and equal to $\sqrt{2}$ inches. Now, vertices 1, 2, and 3 form a right triangle, with legs of 1 and $\sqrt{2}$. By the Pythagorean Theorem, the hypotenuse is $\sqrt{3}$. This is the distance from vertex 1 to vertex 3, the two most distant vertices. (509, 520)

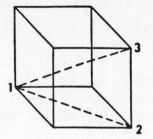

37. Choice A is correct. In one hour, the hour hand of a clock moves through an angle of 30° (one "hour unit"). 70 minutes equals $\frac{7}{6}$ hours, so during that time the hour hand will move through $\frac{7}{6} \times 30°$, or 35°. (501, 526)

38. Choice C is correct. In order to be similar, two triangles must have corresponding angles equal. This is true of triangles *ODC* and *OBA*, since angle *O* equals itself, and angles *OCD* and *OAB* are both right angles. (The third angles of these triangles must be equal, as the sum of the angles of a triangle is always 180°.) Since the triangles are similar, $OD : DC = OB : AB$. But, *OD* and *OA* are radii of the same circle and are equal. Therefore, substitute *OA* for *OD* in the above proportion. Hence, $OA : DC = OB : AB$. There is, however, no information given on the relative sizes of any of the line segments, so statement III may or may not be true. (509, 510, 524)

39. Choice C is correct. Let the three angles equal x, $2x$, and $6x$. Then, $x + 2x + 6x = 9x = 180°$. Therefore, $x = 20°$ and $6x = 120°$. (505)

40. Choice A is correct. Since $AB = AC$, angle *ABC* must equal angle *ACB*. (Base angles of an isosceles triangle are equal.) As the sum of angles *BAC*, *ABC*, and *ACB* is 180°, and angle *BAC* equals 40°, angle *ABC* and angle *ACB* must each equal 70°. Now, *DBC* is a right triangle, with angle *BDC* = 90° and angle *DCB* = 70°. (The three angles must add up to 180°.) Angle *DBC* must equal 20°. (507, 514)

41. Choice C is correct.

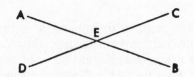

$\angle AEB$ and $\angle CED$ are both straight angles, and are equal; similarly, $\angle DEC$ and $\angle BEA$ are both straight angles. $\angle AEC$ and $\angle BED$ are vertical angles, as are $\angle BEC$ and $\angle DEA$, and are equal. $\angle AED$ and $\angle CEA$ are supplementary and need not be equal. (501, 502, 503)

42. Choice A is correct. All right isosceles triangles have angles of 45°, 45°, and 90°. Since all triangles with the same angles are similar, all right isosceles triangles are similar. (507, 509, 510)

43. Choice C is correct.

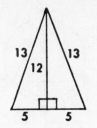

As the diagram shows, the altitude to the base of the isosceles triangle divides it into two congruent right triangles, each with 5–12–13 sides. Thus, the base is 10, height is 12 and the area is $\frac{1}{2}(10)(12) = 60$. (505, 507, 509)

44. Choice C is correct. The altitude to any side divides the triangle into two congruent 30°–60°–90° right triangles, each with a hypotenuse of 2 inches and a leg of 1 inch. The other leg equals the altitude. By the Pythagorean Theorem the altitude is equal to $\sqrt{3}$ inches. (The sides of a 30°–60°–90° right triangle are always in the proportion $1 : \sqrt{3} : 2$. (509, 514)

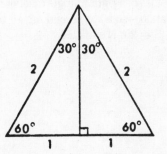

45. Choice E is correct.

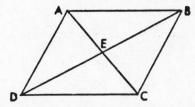

As the diagram illustrates, angles *AED* and *BEC* are vertical and, therefore, equal. *AE = EC*, because the diagonals of a parallelogram bisect each other. Angles *BDC* and *DBA* are equal because they are alternate interior angles of parallel lines (*AB* ∥ *CD*). (503, 517)

46. Choice E is correct. There are eight isosceles right triangles: *ABE, BCE, CDE, ADE, ABC, BCD, CDA,* and *ABD*. (520)

47. Choice D is correct. Recall that a regular hexagon may be broken up into six equilateral triangles.

Since the angles of each triangle are 60°, and two of these angles make up each angle of the hexagon, an angle of the hexagon must be 120°. (523)

48. Choice E is correct.

Since the radius equals 1″, *AD*, the diameter, must be 2″. Now, since *AD* is a diameter, *ACD* must be a right triangle, because an angle inscribed in a semicircle is a right angle. Thus, because ∠ *DAC* = 30°, it must be a 30°–60°–90° right triangle. The sides will be in the proportion 1 : √3 : 2. As *AD* : *AC* = 2 : √3, so *AC*, one of the sides of the equilateral triangle, must be √3 inches long. (508, 524)

49. Choice D is correct. Let the angles be $2x$, $3x$, $4x$. Their sum, $9x = 180°$ and $x = 20°$. Thus, the largest angle, $4x$, is 80°. (505)

50. Choice B is correct. The sides of a right triangle must obey the Pythagorean Theorem. The only group of choices that does so is the second: 12, 16, and 20 are in the 3 : 4 : 5 ratio, and the relationship $12^2 + 16^2 = 20^2$ is satisfied. (509)

Math Refresher Session 6

Miscellaneous Problems Including Averages, Series, Properties of Integers, Approximations, and Combinations and Probability

Averages, Medians, and Modes

601. *Averages.* The average of n numbers is merely their sum, divided by n.

Example: Find the average of: 20, 0, 80, and 12.

Solution: The average is the sum divided by the number of entries, or:

$$\frac{20 + 0 + 80 + 12}{4} = \frac{112}{4} = 28$$

A quick way of obtaining an average of a set of numbers that are close together is the following:

STEP 1. Choose any number that will approximately equal the average.

STEP 2. Subtract this approximate average from each of the numbers (this sum will give some positive and negative results). Add the results.

STEP 3. Divide this sum by the number of entries.

STEP 4. Add the result of Step 3 to the approximate average chosen in Step 1. This will be the true average.

Example: Find the average of 92, 93, 93, 96 and 97.

Solution: Choose 95 as an approximate average. Subtracting 95 from 92, 93, 93, 96, and 97 gives -3, -2, -2, 1, and 2. The sum is -4. Divide -4 by 5 (the number of entries) to obtain -0.8. Add -0.8 to the original approximation of 95 to get the true average, $95 - 0.8$ or 94.2

601a. *Median.* The median of a set of numbers is that number which is in the *middle* of all the numbers.

>**Example:** Find the median of 20, 0, 80, 12, and 30.

>*Solution:* Arrange the numbers in increasing order:

$$
\begin{array}{c}
0 \\
12 \\
20 \\
30 \\
80
\end{array}
$$

The *middle* number is 20, so 20 is the *median.*

>Note: If there is an *even* number of items, such as

$$
\begin{array}{c}
0 \\
12 \\
20 \\
24 \\
30 \\
80
\end{array}
$$

there is no *middle* number.

>So in this case we take the average of the two middle numbers, 20 and 24, to get 22, which is the *median.*

>If there are numbers like 20 and 22, the median would be 21 (just the average of 20 and 22).

601b. *Mode.* The mode of a set of numbers is the number that occurs most frequently.

If we have numbers 0, 12, 20, 30, and 80 there is *no* mode, since no one number appears with the greatest frequency. But consider this:

>**Example:** Find the mode of 0, 12, 12, 20, 30, 80.

>*Solution:* 12 appears most frequently, so it is the mode.

>**Example:** Find the mode of 0, 12, 12, 20, 30, 30, 80.

>*Solution:* Here *both* 12 and 30 are modes.

Series

602. *Number series or sequences* are progressions of numbers arranged according to some design. By recognizing the type of series from the first four terms, it is possible to know all the terms in the series. Following are given a few different types of number series that appear frequently.

1. *Arithmetic progressions* are very common. In an arithmetic progression, each term exceeds the previous one by some fixed number.

>**Example:** In the series 3, 5, 7, 9, . . . find the next term.

>*Solution:* Each term in the series is 2 more than the preceding one, so the next term is $9 + 2$ or 11.

If the difference in successive terms is negative, then the series decreases.

>**Example:** Find the next term: 100, 93, 86, 79 . . . .

>*Solution:* Each term is 7 less than the previous one, so the next term is 72.

2. *In a geometric progression* each term equals the previous term multiplied by a fixed number.

    Example: What is the term of the series 2, 6, 18, 54 . . . ?

    Solution: Each term is 3 times the previous term, so the fifth term is 3 times 54 or 162.

If the multiplying factor is negative, the series will alternate between positive and negative terms.

    Example: Find the next term of −2, 4, −8, 16 . . .

    Solution: Each term is −2 times the previous term, so the next term is −32.

    Example: Find the next term in the series 64, −32, 16, −8 . . .

    Solution: Each term is $-\frac{1}{2}$ times the previous term, so the next term is 4.

3. In *mixed step progression* the successive terms can be found by repeating a pattern of add 2, add 3, add 2, add 3; or a pattern of add 1, multiply by 5, add 1, multiply 5, etc. The series is the result of a combination of operations.

    Example: Find the next term in the series 1, 3, 9, 11, 33, 35 . . .

    Solution: The pattern of successive terms is add 2, multiply by 3, add 2, multiply by 3, etc. The next step is to multiply 35 by 3 to get 105.

    Example: Find the next term in the series 4, 16, 8, 32, 16 . . .

    Solution: Here, the pattern is to multiply by 4, divide by 2, multiply by 4, divide by 2, etc. Thus, the next term is 16 times 4 or 64.

4. If no obvious solution presents itself, it may be helpful to calculate the difference between each term and the preceding one. Then if it is possible to determine the next *increment* (the difference between successive terms), add it to the last term to obtain the term in question. Often the series of *increments* is a simpler series than the series of original terms.

    Example: Find the next term in the series 3, 9, 19, 33, 51 . . .

    Solution: Write out the series of increments: 6, 10, 14, 18 . . . (each term is the difference between two terms of the original series). This series is an arithmetic progression whose next term is 22. Adding 22 to the term 51 from the original series produces the next term, 73.

5. If none of the above methods is effective, the series may be a combination of two or three different series. In this case, make a series out of every other term or out of every third term and see whether these terms form a series that can be recognized.

    Example: Find the next term in the series 1, 4, 4, 8, 16, 12, 64, 16 . . .

    Solution: Divide this series into two series by taking out every other term, yielding: 1, 4, 16, 64 . . . and 4, 8, 12, 16 . . . These series are easy to recognize as a geometric and arithmetic series, but the first series has the needed term. The next term in this series is 4 times 64 or 256.

Properties of Integers

603. *Even-Odd.* These are problems that deal with even and odd numbers. An even number is divisible by 2, and an odd number is not divisible by 2. All even numbers end in the digits 0, 2, 4, 6, or 8; odd numbers end in the digits 1, 3, 5, 7, or 9. For example, the numbers 358, 90, 18, 9,874, and 46 are even numbers. The numbers 67, 871, 475, and 89 are odd numbers. It is important to remember the following facts:

604.   The sum of *two* even numbers is *even*, and the sum of *two odd* numbers is *even*, but the sum of an *odd* number *and* an *even* number is *odd*. For example, $4 + 8 = 12, 5 + 3 = 8$, and $7 + 2 = 9$.

605.   The product of *two odd* numbers is *odd,* but the product of an even number and *any other* number is an *even* number. For example, $3 \times 5 = 15$ (odd); $4 \times 5 = 20$ (even); $4 \times 6 = 24$ (even).

606.   Even numbers are expressed in the form *2k* where *k* may be any integer. Odd numbers are expressed in the form of *2k* + 1 or *2k* − 1 where *k* may be any integer. For example, if $k = 17$, then $2k = 34$ and $2k + 1 = 35$. If $k = 6$, then we have $2k = 12$ and $2k + 1 = 13$.

Example: If *m* is any integer, is the number $6m + 3$ an even or an odd number?

Solution: Rewrite the number $6m + 3$ as $2(3m + 1) + 1$. Since *m* is an arbitrary number, $3m + 1$ is an arbitrary number. Let $3m + 1$ be called *p*. Now, the number is in the form of an odd number, $2p + 1$. ($2k + 1$ is odd, where *k* is any number, so $2p + 1$ is also odd. In both cases, the *k* and the *p* are arbitrary.)

607.   *Divisibility.* If an integer *P* is divided by an integer *Q*, and an integer is obtained as the quotient, then *P* is said to be divisible by *Q*. In other words, if *P* can be expressed as an integral multiple of *Q*, then *P* is said to be divisible by *Q*. For example, dividing 51 by 17 gives 3, an integer. 51 is divisible by 17, or 51 equals 17 times 3. On the other hand, dividing 8 by 3 gives $2\frac{2}{3}$, which is not an integer. 8 is not divisible by 3, and there is no way to express 8 as an integral multiple of 3. There are various tests to see whether an integer is divisible by certain numbers. These tests are listed below:

1.   Any integer is divisible *by 2* if the last digit of the number is a 0, 2, 4, 6, or 8.

   Example: The numbers 98, 6,534, 70, and 32 are divisible by 2 because they end in 8, 4, 0, and 2, respectively.

2.   Any integer is divisible *by 3* if the sum of its digits is divisible by 3.

   Example: Is the number 34,237,023 divisible by 3?

   Solution: Add the digits of the number. $3 + 4 + 2 + 3 + 7 + 0 + 2 + 3 = 24$. Now, 24 is divisible by 3 ($24 \div 3 = 8$) so the number 34,237,023 is also divisible by 3.

3.   Any integer is divisible *by 4* if the last two digits of the number make a number that is divisible by 4.

   Example: Which of the following numbers is divisible by 4?
   3,456, 6,787,612, 67,408, 7,877, 345, 98.

   Solution: Look at the last two digits of the numbers, 56, 12, 08, 77, 45, 98. Only 56, 12, and 08 are divisible by 4, so only the numbers, 3,456, 6,787,612, and 67,408 are divisible by 4.

4.   An integer is divisible *by 5* if the last digit is either a 0 or a 5.

   Example: The numbers 780, 675, 9,000 and 15 are divisible by 5, while the numbers 786, 5,509, and 87 are not divisible by 5.

5.   Any integer is divisible *by 6* if it passes the divisibility tests for both 2 and 3.

   Example: Is the number 12,414 divisible by 6?

   Solution: Test whether 12,414 is divisible by 2 and 3. The last digit is a 4, so it is divisible by 2. Adding the digits yields $1 + 2 + 4 + 1 + 4 = 12$. 12 is divisible by 3 so the number 12,414 is divisible by 3. Since it is divisible by both 2 and 3, it is divisible by 6.

6. Any integer is divisible *by 8* if the last three digits are divisible by 8. (Since 1,000 is divisible by 8, you can ignore all multiples of 1,000.)

    Example: Is the number 342,169,424 divisible by 8?

    Solution: $424 \div 8 = 53$, so 342,169,424 is divisible by 8.

7. Any integer is divisible *by 9* if the sum of its digits is divisible by 9.

    Example: Is the number 243,091,863 divisible by 9?

    Solution: Adding the digits yields $2 + 4 + 3 + 0 + 9 + 1 + 8 + 6 + 3 = 36$. 36 is divisible by 9, so the number 243,091,863 is divisible by 9.

8. Any integer is divisible *by 10* if the last digit is a 0.

    Example: The numbers 60, 8,900, 5,640, and 34,000 are all divisible by 10 because the last digit in each is a 0.

Note that if a number *P* is divisible by a number *Q*, then *P* is also divisible by all the factors of *Q*. For example, 60 is divisible by 12, so 60 is also divisible by 2, 3, 4, and 6, which are all factors of 12.

---

608. *Prime numbers.* A prime number is one that is divisible only by 1 and itself. The first few prime numbers are 2, 3, 5, 7, 11, 13, 17, 19, 23, 29, 31, 37.... Note that the number 1 is not considered a prime number. To determine if a number is prime, follow these steps:

STEP 1: Determine a very rough approximate square root of the number. Remember that the square root of a number is that number which when multiplied by itself gives the original number. For example, the square root of 25 is 5 because $5 \times 5 = 25$.

STEP 2: Divide the number by all of the primes that are less than the approximate square root. If the number is not divisible by any of these primes, then it is prime. If it is divisible by one of the primes, then it is not prime.

   Example: Is the number 97 prime?

   Solution: An approximate square root of 97 is 10. All of the primes less than 10 are 2, 3, 5, and 7. Divide 97 by 2, 3, 5, and 7. No integer results, so 97 is prime.

   Example: Is the number 161 prime?

   Solution: An approximate square root of 161 is 13. The primes less than 13 are 2, 3, 5, 7, and 11. Divide 161 by 2, 3, 5, 7, and 11. 161 is divisible by 7 ($161 \div 7 = 23$), so 161 is not prime.

Approximations

609. *Rounding off.* A number expressed to a certain number of places is rounded off when it is approximated as a number with fewer places of accuracy. For example, the number 8.987 is expressed more accurately than the number rounded off to 8.99. To round off to *n* places, look at the digit that is to the right of the *n*th digit. (The *n*th digit is found by counting *n* places to the right of the decimal point.) If this digit is less than 5, eliminate all of the digits to the right of the *n*th digit. If the digit to the right of the *n*th digit is 5 or more, then add 1 to the *n*th digit and eliminate all of the digits to the right of the *n*th digit.

   Example: Round off 8.73 to the nearest tenth.

   Solution: The digit to the right of the 7 (.7 is seven tenths) is 3. Since this is less than 5, eliminate it, and the rounded off answer is 8.7

Example: Round off 986 to the nearest tens' place.

Solution: The number to the right of the tens' place is 6. Since this is 5 or more add 1 to the 8 and replace the 6 with a 0 to get 990.

610. *Approximating sums.* When adding a given set of numbers and when the answer must have a given number of places of accuracy, follow the steps below.

STEP 1: Round off each addend (number being added) to one more place than the number of places the answer is to have.

STEP 2: Add the rounded addends.

STEP 3: Round off the sum to the desired number of places of accuracy.

Example: What is the sum of 12.0775, 1.20163, and 121.303 correct to the nearest hundredth?

Solution: Round off the three numbers to the nearest thousandth (one more place than the accuracy of the sum): 12.078, 1.202, and 121.303. The sum of these is 134.583. Rounded off to the nearest hundredth, this is 134.58.

611. *Approximating products.* To multiply certain numbers and have an answer to the desired number of places of accuracy, follow the steps below.

STEP 1. Round off the numbers being multiplied to the number of places of accuracy desired in the answer.

STEP 2. Multiply the rounded off factors (numbers being multiplied).

STEP 3: Round off the product to the desired number of places.

Example: Find the product of 3,316 and 1,432 to three places.

Solution: First, round off 3,316 to 3 places, to obtain 3,320. Round off 1,432 to 3 places to give 1,430. The product of these two numbers is 4,747,600. Rounded off to 3 places this is 4,750,000.

612. *Approximating square roots.* The square root of a number is that number which, when multiplied by itself, gives the original number. For example, 6 is the square root of 36. Often on tests a number with different choices for the square root is given. Follow this procedure to determine which is the best choice.

STEP 1. Square all of the choices given.

STEP 2. Select the closest choice that is too large and the closest choice that is too small (assuming that no choice is the exact square root). Find the average of these two *choices* (not of their squares).

STEP 3: Square this average; if the square is greater than the original number, choose the lower of the two choices; if its square is lower than the original number, choose the higher.

Example: Which of the following is closest to the square root of 86: 9.0, 9.2, 9.4, 9.6, or 9.8?

Solution: The squares of the five numbers are: 81, 84.64, 88.36, 92.16, and 96.04, respectively. (Actually it was not necessary to calculate the last two, since they are greater than the third square, which is already greater than 86.) The two closest choices are 9.2 and 9.4; their average is 9.3. The square of 9.3 is 86.49. Therefore, 9.3 is greater than the square root of 86. So, the square root must be closer to 9.2 than to 9.4.

Combinations

613. Suppose that a job has 2 different parts. There are m different ways of doing the first part and there are n different ways of doing the second part. The problem is to find the number of ways of doing the entire job. For each way of doing the first part of the job, there are n ways of doing the second part. Since there are m ways of doing the first part, the total number of ways of doing the entire job is $m \times n$. The formula that can be used is

$$\text{Number of ways} = m \times n$$

For any problem that involves 2 actions or 2 objects, each with a number of choices, and asks for the number of combinations, the formula can be used. For example: A man wants a sandwich and a drink for lunch. If a restaurant has 4 choices of sandwiches and 3 choices of drinks, how many different ways can he order his lunch?

Since there are 4 choices of sandwiches and 3 choices of drinks, using the formula

$$\begin{aligned}\text{Number of ways} &= 4(3) \\ &= 12\end{aligned}$$

Therefore, the man can order his lunch 12 different ways.

If we have objects a, b, c, d, and want to arrange them two at a time—that is like ab, bc, cd, etc.—we have four combinations taken two at a time. This is denoted as $_4C_2$. The rule is that $_4C_2 = \dfrac{(4)\,(3)}{(2)\,(1)}$. In general, n combinations taken r at a time is represented by the formula:

$$_nC_r = \frac{(n)(n-1)(n-2)\ldots(n-r+1)}{(r)(r-1)(r-2)\ldots(1)}$$

$$\text{Examples: } _3C_2 = \frac{3 \times 2}{2 \times 1}; \, _8C_3 = \frac{8 \times 7 \times 6}{3 \times 2 \times 1}$$

Suppose there are two groups, each with a certain number of members. It is known that some members of one group also belong to the other group. The problem is to find how many members there are in the 2 groups altogether. To find the numbers of members altogether, use the following formula:

Total number of members = Number of members in group I
            + Number of members in group II
            = Number of members common to both groups

For example: In one class, 18 students received A's for English and 10 students received A's in math. If 5 students received A's in both English and math, how many students received at least one A?

In this case, let the students who received A's in English be in group I and let those who received A's in math be in group II.

Using the formula:

Number of students who received at least one A
    = Number in group I + Number in group II − Number in both
    = 18 + 10 − 5 = 23

Therefore, there are 23 students who received at least one A.

In combination problems such as these, the problems do not always ask for the total number. They may ask for any of the four numbers in the formula while the other three are given. In any case, to solve the problems, use the formula.

Probability

614. The probability that an event will occur equals the number of favorable ways divided by the total number of ways. If P is the probability, m is the number of favorable ways, and n is the total number of ways, then

$$P = \frac{m}{n}$$

For example: What is the probability that a head will turn up on a single throw of a penny?

The favorable number of ways is 1 (a head).

The total number of ways is 2 (a head and a tail). Thus, the probability is $\frac{1}{2}$.

If a and b are two mutually exclusive events, then the probability that a or b will occur is the sum of the individual probabilities.

Suppose P_a is the probability that an event a occurs. Suppose that P_b is the probability that the first event a occurs *and* the second event b occurs subsequently is $P_a \times P_b$.

The Absolute Value Sign

615. The symbol $|\ \ |$ denotes absolute value. The absolute value of a number is the numerical value of the number without the plus or minus sign in front of it. Thus all absolute values are positive. For example, $|+3|$ is 3, and $|-2|$ is 2. Here's another example:

If x is positive and y is negative $|x| + |y| = x - y$.

Functions

616. Suppose we have a function of x. This is denoted as $f(x)$ (or $g(y)$ or $h(z)$ etc.). As an example, if $f(x) = x$ then $f(3) = 3$.

In this example we substitute the value 3 wherever x appears in the function. Similarly $f(-2) = -2$. Consider another example: If $f(y) = y^2 - y$, then $f(2) = 2^2 - 2 = 2$. $f(-2) = (-2)^2 - (-2) = 6$. $f(z) = z^2 - z$. $f(2z) = (2z)^2 - (2z) = 4z^2 - 2z$.

Let us consider still another example: Let $f(x) = x + 2$ and $g(y) = 2^y$. What is $f[g(-2)]$? Now $g(-2) = 2^{-2} = \frac{1}{4}$. Thus $f[g(-2)] = f\left(\frac{1}{4}\right)$. Since $f(x) = x + 2, f\left(\frac{1}{4}\right) = \frac{1}{4} + 2 = 2\frac{1}{4}$.

Practice Test 6

Miscellaneous Problems Including Averages, Series, Properties of Integers, and Approximations

Correct answers and solutions follow each test.

1. A B C D E

1. If *n* is the first of five consecutive odd numbers, what is their average?

   (A) *n*
   (B) *n* + 1
   (C) *n* + 2
   (D) *n* + 3
   (E) *n* + 4

2. A B C D E

2. What is the average of the following numbers: 35.5, 32.5, 34.0, 35.0, 34.5?

   (A) 33.0
   (B) 33.8
   (C) 34.0
   (D) 34.3
   (E) 34.5

3. A B C D E

3. What is the next number in the following series: 1, 5, 9, 13, . . . ?

   (A) 11
   (B) 15
   (C) 17
   (D) 19
   (E) 21

4. A B C D E

4. Which of the following is the next number in the series: 3, 6, 4, 9, 5, 12, 6, . . . ?

   (A) 7
   (B) 9
   (C) 12
   (D) 15
   (E) 24

5. A B C D E

5. If *P* is an even number, and *Q* and *R* are both odd, which of the following *must* be true?

   (A) *P* • *Q* is an odd number
   (B) *Q* − *R* is an even number
   (C) *PQ* − *PR* is an odd number
   (D) *Q* + *R* cannot equal *P*
   (E) *P* + *Q* cannot equal *R*

6. A B C D E

6. If a number is divisible by 102, then it is also divisible by:

   (A) 23
   (B) 11
   (C) 103
   (D) 5
   (E) 2

7. A B C D E   **7.** Which of the following numbers is divisible by 36?

           (A) 35,924
           (B) 64,530
           (C) 74,098
           (D) 152,640
           (E) 192,042

8. A B C D E   **8.** How many prime numbers are there between 45 and 72?

           (A) 4
           (B) 5
           (C) 6
           (D) 7
           (E) 8

9. A B C D E   **9.** Which of the following represents the smallest possible value of $(M - \frac{1}{2})^2$, if M is an integer?

           (A) 0.00
           (B) 0.25
           (C) 0.50
           (D) 0.75
           (E) 1.00

10. A B C D E   **10.** Which of the following best approximates $\dfrac{7.40096 \times 10.0342}{.2001355}$?

           (A) 0.3700
           (B) 3.700
           (C) 37.00
           (D) 370.0
           (E) 3700

11. A B C D E   **11.** In a class with six boys and four girls, the students all took the same test. The boys' scores were 74, 82, 84, 84, 88, and 95 while the girls' scores were 80, 82, 86, and 86. Which of the following statements is true?

           (A) The boys' average was 0.1 higher than the average for the whole class.
           (B) The girls' average was 0.1 lower than the boys' average.
           (C) The class average was 1.0 higher than the boys' average.
           (D) The boys' average was 1.0 higher than the class average.
           (E) The girls' average was 1.0 lower than the boys' average.

12. A B C D E   **12.** If the following series continues to follow the same pattern, what will be the next number: 2, 6, 3, 9, 6, ... ?

           (A) 3
           (B) 6
           (C) 12
           (D) 14
           (E) 18

13. A B C D E

13. Which of the following numbers *must* be odd?

(A) The sum of an odd number and an odd number.
(B) The product of an odd number and an even number.
(C) The sum of an odd number and an even number.
(D) The product of two even numbers.
(E) The sum of two even numbers.

14. A B C D E

14. Which of the following numbers is the best approximation of the length of one side of a square with an area of 12 square inches?

(A) 3.2 inches
(B) 3.3 inches
(C) 3.4 inches
(D) 3.5 inches
(E) 3.6 inches

15. A B C D E

15. If n is an odd number, then which of the following *best* describes the number represented by $n^2 + 2n + 1$?

(A) It can be odd or even.
(B) It must be odd.
(C) It must be divisible by four.
(D) It must be divisible by six.
(E) The answer cannot be determined from the given information.

16. A B C D E

16. What is the next number in the series: 2, 5, 7, 8, . . . ?

(A) 8
(B) 9
(C) 10
(D) 11
(E) 12

17. A B C D E

17. What is the average of the following numbers: $3\frac{1}{2}, 4\frac{1}{4}, 2\frac{1}{4}, 3\frac{1}{4}, 4$?

(A) 3.25
(B) 3.35
(C) 3.45
(D) 3.50
(E) 3.60

18. A B C D E

18. Which of the following numbers is divisible by 24?

(A) 76,300
(B) 78,132
(C) 80,424
(D) 81,234
(E) 83,636

19. A B C D E

19. In order to graduate, a boy needs an average of 65 percent for his five major subjects. His first four grades were 55, 60, 65, and 65. What grade does he need in the fifth subject in order to graduate?

(A) 65
(B) 70
(C) 75
(D) 80
(E) 85

20. A B C D E

20. If t is any integer, which of the following represents an odd number?

(A) $2t$
(B) $2t + 3$
(C) $3t$
(D) $2t + 2$
(E) $t + 1$

21. A B C D E

21. If the average of five whole numbers is an even number, which of the following statements *is not true*?

(A) The sum of the five numbers must be divisible by 2.
(B) The sum of the five numbers must be divisible by 5.
(C) The sum of the five numbers must be divisible by 10.
(D) At least one of the five numbers must be even.
(E) All of the five numbers must be odd.

22. A B C D E

22. What is the product of 23 and 79 to one place of accuracy?

(A) 1,600
(B) 1,817
(C) 1,000
(D) 1,800
(E) 2,000

23. A B C D E

23. What is the next term in the series 1, 1, 2, 3, 5, 8, 13 . . . ?

(A) 18
(B) 21
(C) 13
(D) 9
(E) 20

24. A B C D E

24. What is the next number in the series 1, 4, 2, 8, 6, . . . ?

(A) 4
(B) 6
(C) 8
(D) 15
(E) 24

25. A B C D E

25. Which of the following is closest to the square root of $\frac{1}{2}$?

(A) 0.25
(B) 0.5
(C) 0.6
(D) 0.7
(E) 0.8

26. A B C D E

26. How many prime numbers are there between 56 and 100?

(A) 8
(B) 9
(C) 10
(D) 11
(E) none of the above

27. A B C D E

27. If you multiply one million, two hundred thousand, one hundred seventy-six by five hundred twenty thousand, two hundred four, and then divide the product by one billion, your result will be closest to:

(A) 0.6
(B) 6
(C) 600
(D) 6,000
(E) 6,000,000

28. A B C D E

28. The number 89.999 rounded off to the nearest tenth is equal to which of the following?

(A) 90.0
(B) 89.0
(C) 89.9
(D) 89.99
(E) 89.90

29. A B C D E

29. $a, b, c, d,$ and e are integers; M is their average; and S is their sum. What is the ratio of S to M?

(A) 1 : 5
(B) 5 : 1
(C) 1 : 1
(D) 2 : 1
(E) depends on the values of $a, b, c, d,$ and e

30. A B C D E

30. What is the next number in the series 1, 1, 2, 4, 5, 25, ... ?

(A) 8
(B) 12
(C) 15
(D) 24
(E) 26

31. A B C D E

31. The sum of five odd numbers is always:

(A) even
(B) divisible by three
(C) divisible by five
(D) a prime number
(E) none of the above

32. A B C D E

32. If E is an even number, and F is divisible by three, then what is the *largest* number by which E^2F^3 *must* be divisible?

(A) 6
(B) 12
(C) 54
(D) 108
(E) 144

33. A B C D E

33. If the average of five consecutive even numbers is 8, which of the following is the smallest of the five numbers?

(A) 4
(B) 5
(C) 6
(D) 8
(E) none of the above

34. A B C D E

34. What is the next number in the sequence 1, 4, 7, 10, . . . ?

(A) 13
(B) 14
(C) 15
(D) 16
(E) 18

35. A B C D E

35. If a number is divisible by 23, then it is also divisible by which of the following?

(A) 7
(B) 24
(C) 9
(D) 3
(E) none of these

36. A B C D E

36. What is the next term in the series 3, 6, 2, 7, 1, . . . ?

(A) 0
(B) 1
(C) 3
(D) 6
(E) 8

37. A B C D E

37. What is the average (to the nearest tenth) of the following numbers: 91.4, 91.5, 91.6, 91.7, 91.7, 92.0, 92.1, 92.3, 92.3, 92.4?

(A) 91.9
(B) 92.0
(C) 92.1
(D) 92.2
(E) 92.3

38. A B C D E

38. What is the next term in the following series: 8, 3, 10, 9, 12, 27, . . . ?

(A) 8
(B) 14
(C) 18
(D) 36
(E) 81

39. A B C D E

39. Which of the following numbers is divisible by 11?

(A) 30,217
(B) 44,221
(C) 59,403
(D) 60,411
(E) none of the above

40. What is the next number in the series 1, 4, 9, 16, ...?

(A) 22
(B) 23
(C) 24
(D) 34
(E) 25

41. Which of the following is the best approximation of the product (1.005) (20.0025) (0.0102)?

(A) 0.02
(B) 0.2
(C) 2.0
(D) 20
(E) 200

42. What is the next number in the series 5, 2, 4, 2, 3, 2, ...?

(A) 1
(B) 2
(C) 3
(D) 4
(E) 5

43. If *a*, *b*, and *c* are all divisible by 8, then their average must be

(A) divisible by 8
(B) divisible by 4
(C) divisible by 2
(D) an integer
(E) none of these

44. Which of the following numbers is divisible by 24?

(A) 13,944
(B) 15,746
(C) 15,966
(D) 16,012
(E) none of the above

45. Which of the following numbers is a prime?

(A) 147
(B) 149
(C) 153
(D) 155
(E) 161

46. What is the next number in the following series: 4, 8, 2, 4, 1, ...?

(A) 1
(B) 2
(C) 4
(D) 8
(E) 16

47. A B C D E   **47.** The sum of four consecutive odd integers must be:

   (A) even, but not necessarily divisible by 4
   (B) divisible by 4, but not necessarily by 8
   (C) divisible by 8, but not necessarily by 16
   (D) divisible by 16
   (E) none of the above

48. A B C D E   **48.** Which of the following is closest to the square root of $\frac{3}{5}$?

   (A) $\frac{1}{2}$

   (B) $\frac{2}{3}$

   (C) $\frac{3}{4}$

   (D) $\frac{4}{5}$

   (E) 1

49. A B C D E   **49.** What is the next term in the series: 9, 8, 6, 3, . . . ?

   (A) 0
   (B) −2
   (C) 1
   (D) −3
   (E) −1

50. A B C D E   **50.** The sum of an odd and an even number is

   (A) a perfect square
   (B) negative
   (C) even
   (D) odd
   (E) none of these

Answer Key for Practice Test 6

1. E	14. D	27. C	39. A
2. D	15. C	28. A	40. E
3. C	16. A	29. B	41. B
4. D	17. C	30. E	42. B
5. B	18. C	31. E	43. E
6. E	19. D	32. D	44. A
7. D	20. B	33. A	45. B
8. C	21. E	34. A	46. B
9. B	22. E	35. E	47. C
10. D	23. B	36. E	48. C
11. E	24. E	37. A	49. E
12. E	25. D	38. B	50. D
13. C	26. B		

Answers and Solutions for Practice Test 6

1. Choice E is correct. The five consecutive odd numbers must be n, $n + 2$, $n + 6$, and $n + 8$. Their average is equal to their sum, $5n + 20$, divided by the number of addends, 5, which yields $n + 4$ as the average. (601)

2. Choice D is correct. Choosing 34 as an approximate average results in the following addends: $+1.5$, -1.5, 0, $+1.0$, and $+0.5$. Their sum is $+1.5$. Now, divide by 5 to get $+0.3$ and add this to 34 to get 34.3. (To check this, add the five original numbers and divide by 5.) (601)

3. Choice C is correct. This is an arithmetic sequence: Each term is 4 more than the preceding one. The next term is $13 + 4$ or 17. (602)

4. Choice D is correct. This series can be divided into two parts: the even-numbered terms: 6, 9, 12, ... and the odd-numbered terms: 3, 4, 5, 6, ... (Even- and odd-numbered terms refers to the terms' *place* in the series and not if the term itself is even or odd.) The next term in the series is even-numbered, so it will be formed by adding 3 to the 12 (the last of the even-numbered terms) to get 15. (602)

5. Choice B is correct. Since Q is an odd number, it may be represented by $2m + 1$ where m is an integer. Similarly, call R, $2n + 1$ where n is an integer. Thus $Q - R$ is equal to $(2m + 1) - (2n + 1)$, $2m - 2n$, or $2(m - n)$. Now, since m and n are integers, $m - n$ will be some integer p. Thus $Q - R = 2p$. Any number in the form of $2p$, where p is any integer, is an even number. Therefore, $Q - R$ *must* be even. (A) and (C) are wrong, because an even number multiplied by an odd is always even. (D) and (E) are only true for specific values of P, Q, and R. (604)

6. Choice E is correct. If a number is divisible by 102 then it must be divisible by all of the factors of 102. The only choice that is a factor of 102 is 2. (607)

7. Choice D is correct. To be divisible by 36, a number must be divisible by both 4 and 9. Only (A) and (D) are divisible by 4. (Recall that only the last two digits must be examined.) Of these, only (D) is divisible by 9. (The sum of the digits of (A) is 23, which is not divisible by 9; the sum of the digits of (D) is 18.) (607)

8. Choice C is correct. The prime numbers between 45 and 72 are 47, 53, 59, 61, 67, and 71. All of the others have factors other than 1 and themselves. (608)

9. Choice B is correct. Since M must be an *integer*, the closest value it can have to $\frac{1}{2}$ is either 1 or 0. In either case, $(M - \frac{1}{2})^2$ is equal to $\frac{1}{4}$, or 0.25. (409)

10. Choice D is correct. Approximate to only one place (this is permissible, because the choices are so far apart; if they had been closer together, two or three places would have been used). After this approximation, the expression is: $\dfrac{7 \times 10}{0.2}$, which is equal to 350. This is closest to 370. (609)

11. Choice E is correct. The average for the boys alone was $\dfrac{74 + 82 + 84 + 84 + 88 + 95}{6}$, or $507 \div 6 = 84.5$. The girls' average was $\dfrac{80 + 82 + 86 + 86}{4}$, or $334 \div 4 = 83.5$, which is 1.0 below the boys' average. (601)

12. Choice E is correct. To generate this series start with 2; multiply by 3 to get 6; subtract 3 to get 3; multiply by 3; subtract 3; etc. Thus, the next term will be found by multiplying the previous term, 6, by 3 to get 18. (602)

13. Choice C is correct. The sum of an odd number and an even number can be expressed as $(2n + 1) + (2m)$, where n and m are integers. ($2n + 1$ must be odd, and $2m$ must be even.) Their sum is equal to $2n + 2m + 1$, or $2(m + n) + 1$. Since $(m + n)$ is an integer, the quantity $2(m + n) + 1$ *must* represent an odd integer. (604, 605)

14. Choice D is correct. The actual length of one of the sides would be the square root of 12. Square each of the five choices to find the square of 3.4 is 11.56, and the square of 3.5 is 12.25. The square root of 12 must lie between 3.4 and 3.5. Squaring 3.45 (halfway between the two choices) yields 11.9025, which is less than 12. Thus the square root of 12 must be greater than 3.45 and therefore closer to 3.5 than to 3.4. (612)

15. Choice C is correct. Factor $n^2 + 2n + 1$ to $(n + 1)(n + 1)$ or $(n + 1)^2$. Now, since n is an odd number, $n + 1$ must be even (the number after every odd number is even). Thus, representing $n + 1$ as $2k$ where k is an integer, ($2k$ is the standard representation for an even number) yields the expression: $(n + 1)^2 = (2k)^2$ or $4k^2$. Thus, $(n + 1)^2$ is a multiple of 4 and it must be divisible by 4. A number divisible by 4 must also be even, so (C) is the best choice. (604–607)

16. Choice A is correct. The differences between terms are as follows: 3, 2, and 1. Thus, the next term should be found by adding 0, leaving a result of 8. (602)

17. Choice C is correct. Convert to decimals. Then calculate the value of: $\dfrac{3.50 + 4.25 + 2.25 + 3.25 + 4.00}{5}$. This equals $17.25 \div 5$, or 3.45 (601)

18. Choice C is correct. If a number is divisible by 24, it must be divisible by 3 and 8. Of the five choices given, only choice (C) is divisible by 8. Add the digits in 80,424 to get 18. As this is divisible by 3, the number is divisible by 3. The number, therefore, is divisible by 24. (607)

19. Choice D is correct. If the boy is to average 65 for five subjects, the total of his five grades must be five times 65 or 325. The sum of the first four grades is $55 + 60 + 65 + 65$, or 245. Therefore, the fifth mark must be $325 - 245$, or 80. (601)

20. Choice B is correct. If t is any integer, then $2t$ is an even number. Adding 3 to an even number always produces an odd number. Thus, $2t + 3$ is always odd. (606)

21. Choice E is correct. Call the five numbers, a, b, c, d, and e. Then the average is $\dfrac{(a + b + c + d + e)}{5}$. Since this must be even, $\dfrac{(a + b + c + d + e)}{5} = 2k$, where k is an integer. Thus $a + b + c + d + e = 10k$. Therefore, the sum of the 5 numbers is divisible by 10, 2, and 5. Thus the first three choices are eliminated. If the five numbers were 1, 1, 1, 1,

and 6 then the average would be 2. Thus, the average is even, but not all of the numbers are even. Thus, choice (D) can be true. If all the numbers were odd the sum would have to be odd. This contradicts the statement that the average is even. Thus, choice (E) is the answer.

(601, 607)

22. Choice E is correct. First, round off 23 and 79 to one place of accuracy. The numbers become 20 and 80. The product of these two numbers is 1,600, which rounded off to one place is 2,000. (611)

23. Choice B is correct. Each term in this series is the sum of the two previous terms. Thus the next term is 8 + 13 or 21. (602)

24. Choice E is correct. This series can be generated by the following steps: multiply by 4; subtract 2; multiply by 4; subtract 2; etc. Since the term "6" was obtained by subtracting 2, multiply by 4 to obtain 4 × 6 = 24, the next term. (602)

25. Choice D is correct. 0.7 squared is 0.49. Squaring 0.8 yields 0.64. Thus, the square root of $\frac{1}{2}$ must lie between 0.7 and 0.8. Take the number halfway between these two, 0.75, and square it. This number, 0.5625, is more than $\frac{1}{2}$, so the square root must be closer to 0.7 than to 0.8. An easier way to do problems concerning the square roots of 2 and 3 and their multiples is to memorize the values of these two square roots. The square root of 2 is about 1.414 (remember fourteen-fourteen), and the square root of three is about 1.732 (remember that 1732 was the year of George Washington's birth). Apply these as follows: $\frac{1}{2} = \frac{1}{4} \times 2$.

Thus, $\sqrt{\frac{1}{2}} = \sqrt{\frac{1}{4}} \times \sqrt{2} = \frac{1}{2} \times 1.414 = 0.707$, which is very close to 0.7 (612)

26. Choice B is correct. The prime numbers can be found by taking all the odd numbers between 56 and 100 (the even ones cannot be primes) and eliminating all the ones divisible by 3, by 5, and by 7. If a number under 100 is divisible by none of these, it must be prime. Thus, the only primes between 56 and 100 are 59, 61, 67, 71, 73, 79, 83, 89, and 97. (608)

27. Choice C is correct. Since all the answer requires is an order-of-ten approximation, do not calculate the exact answer. Approximate the answer in the following manner: $\frac{1,000,000 \times 500,000}{1,000,000,000} = 500$. The only choice on the same order of magnitude is 600. (609)

28. Choice A is correct. To round off 89.999, look at the number in the hundredths' place. 9 is more than 5, so add 1 to the number in the tenths' place and eliminate all of the digits to the right. Thus, we get 90.0. (609)

29. Choice B is correct. The average of five numbers is found by dividing their sum by five. Thus, the sum is five times the average, so $S:M = 5:1$. (601)

30. Choice E is correct. The series can be generated by the following steps: To get the second term, square the first term; to get the third, add 1 to the second; to get the fourth, square the third; to get the fifth, add 1 to the fourth; etc. The pattern can be written as: square; add 1; repeat the cycle. Following this pattern, the seventh term is found by adding one to the sixth term. Thus, the seventh term is 1 + 25, or 26. (602)

31. Choice E is correct. None of the first four choices is necessarily true. The sum, 5 + 7 + 9 + 13 + 15 = 49, is not even, divisible by 3, divisible by 5, nor prime. (604, 607, 608)

32. Choice D is correct. Any even number can be written as $2m$ and any number divisible by 3 can be written as $3n$, where m and n are integers. Thus, E^2F^3 equals $(2m)^2 (3n)^3 = (4m^2)(27n^3) = 108 (m^2n^3)$, and 108 is the largest number by which E^2F^3 must be divisible. (607)

33. Choice A is correct. The five consecutive even numbers can be represented as n, $n + 2$, $n + 4$, $n + 6$, and $n + 8$. Taking the sum and dividing by five yields an average of $n + 4$. Thus, $n + 4 = 8$, the given average, and $n = 4$, the smallest number. (601)

34. Choice A is correct. To find the next number in this sequence add 3 to the previous number. This is an arithmetic progression. The next term is $10 + 3$, or 13. (602)

35. Choice E is correct. If a number is divisible by 23, then it is divisible by all of the factors of 23. But 23 is a prime with no factors except 1 and itself. Therefore, the correct choice is (E). (607)

36. Choice E is correct. The steps generating the successive terms in this series are (to the previous term): add 3; subtract 4; add 5; subtract 6; add 7; etc. The next term is $1 + 7 = 8$. (602)

37. Choice A is correct. To find the average, it is convenient to choose 92.0 as an approximate average and then find the average of the differences between the actual numbers and 92.0. Thus, add up: $(-0.6) + (-0.5) + (-0.4) + (-0.3) + (-0.3) + (0.0) + 0.1 + 0.3 + 0.3 + 0.4$, to -1.0; divide this by ten (the number of quantities to be averaged) to obtain -0.1. Finally, add this to the approximate average, 92.0, to obtain a final average of 91.9 (601)

38. Choice B is correct. This series is a combination of two sub-series: The odd-numbered terms, 3, 9, 27, etc., form a geometric series; the even-numbered terms, 8, 10, 12, 14, etc., form an arithmetic sequence. The next number in the sequence is from the arithmetic sequence and is 14. (Note that in the absence of any other indication, assume a series to be as simple as possible, i.e., arithmetic or geometric.) (602)

39. Choice A is correct. To determine if a number is divisible by 11, take each of the digits separately and, beginning with either end, subtract the second from the first, add the following digit, subtract the next one, add the one after that, etc. If this result is divisible by 11, the entire number is. Thus, because $3 - 0 + 2 - 1 + 7 = 11$, we know that 30,217 is divisible by 11. Using the same method, we find that the other four choices are not divisible by 11. (607)

40. Choice E is correct. This is the series of integers squared. $1^2, 2^2, 3^2, 4^2 \ldots$ the next term is 5^2 or 25. (602)

41. Choice B is correct. This is simply an order-of-ten approximation, so round off the numbers and work the following problem: $(1.0) (20.0) (0.01) = 0.20$. The actual answer is closest to 0.2. (611)

42. Choice B is correct. The even-numbered terms of this series form the sub-series: 2, 2, 2, $\ldots$ The odd-numbered terms form the arithmetic series: 5, 4, 3, 2, $\ldots$ The next term in the series is a 2. (602)

43. Choice E is correct. Represent the three numbers as $8p$ $8q$, and $8r$, respectively. Thus, their sum is $8p + 8q + 8r$, and their average is $\frac{(8p + 8q + 8r)}{3}$. This need not even be a whole number. For example, the average of 8, 16, and 32 is $\frac{56}{3}$, or $18\frac{2}{3}$. (601, 607)

44. Choice A is correct. To be divisible by 24, a number must be divisible by both 3 and 8. Only 13,944 and 15,966 are divisible by 3; of these, only 13,944 is divisible by 8 (13,944 = 24 × 581). (607)

45. Choice B is correct. The approximate square root of each of these numbers is 13. Merely divide each of these numbers by the primes up to 13, which are 2, 3, 5, 7, and 11. The only number not divisible by any of these primes is 149. (608, 612)

46. Choice B is correct. The sequence is formed by the following operations: Multiply by 2, divide by 4, multiply by 2, divide by 4, etc. Accordingly, the next number is 1×2, or 2. (602)

47. Choice C is correct. Call the first odd integer $2k + 1$. (This is the standard representation for a general odd integer.) Thus, the next 3 odd integers are $2k + 3$, $2k + 5$, and $2k + 7$. (Each one is 2 more than the previous one.) The sum of these integers is $(2k + 1) + (2k + 3) + (2k + 5) + (2k + 7) = 8k + 16$. This can be written as $8(k + 2)$, which is divisible by 8, but not necessarily by 16. (606, 607)

48. Choice C is correct. By squaring the five choices, it is evident that the two closest choices are: $\left(\dfrac{3}{4}\right)^2 = 0.5625$ and $\left(\dfrac{4}{5}\right)^2 = 0.64$. Squaring the number halfway between $\dfrac{3}{4}$ and $\dfrac{4}{5}$ gives $(0.775)^2 = 0.600625$. This is greater than $\dfrac{3}{5}$, so the square root of $\dfrac{3}{5}$ must be closer to $\dfrac{3}{4}$ than to $\dfrac{4}{5}$. (612)

49. Choice E is correct. The terms decrease by 1, then 2, then 3, so the next term is 4 less than 3, or −1. (602)

50. Choice D is correct. Let the even number be $2k$, where k is an integer, and let the odd number be $2m + 1$, where m is an integer. Thus, the sum is $2k + (2m + 1)$, $2k + 2m + 1$, or $2(k + m) + 1$. Now $k + m$ is an integer since k and m are integers. Call $k + m$ by another name, p. Thus, $2(k + m) + 1$ is $2p + 1$, which is the representation of an odd number. (604, 606)

Math Refresher
Session 7

Tables, Charts, and Graphs

Charts and Graphs

701. Graphs and charts show the relationship of numbers and quantities in visual form. By looking at a graph, you can see at a glance the relationship between two or more sets of information. If such information were presented in written form, it would be hard to read and understand.

Here are some things to remember when doing problems based on graphs or charts:

1. Understand what you are being asked to do before you begin figuring.

2. Check the dates and types of information required. Be sure that you are looking in the proper columns, and on the proper lines, for the information you need.

3. Check the units required. Be sure that your answer is in thousands, millions, or whatever the question calls for.

4. In computing averages, be sure that you add the figures you need and no others, and that you divide by the correct number of years or other units.

5. Be careful in computing problems asking for percentages.

   (a) Remember that to convert a decimal into a percent you must multiply it by 100. For example, 0.04 is 4%.
   (b) Be sure that you can distinguish between such quantities as 1% (1 percent) and .01% (one one-hundredth of 1 percent), whether in numerals or in words.
   (c) Remember that if quantity X is greater than quantity Y, and the question asks what percent quantity X is of quantity Y, the answer must be greater than 100 percent.

Tables and Charts

702. A table or chart shows data in the form of a box of numbers or chart of numbers. Each line describes how the numbers are connected.

Example:

Test Score	Number of Students
90	2
85	1
80	1
60	3

Example: How many students took the test?

Solution: To find out the number of students that took the test, just add up the numbers in the column marked "Number of Students." That is, add $2 + 1 + 1 + 3 = 7$.

Example: What was the difference in score between the highest and the lowest score?

Solution: First look at the highest score: 90. Then look at the lowest score: 60. Now calculate the difference: $90 - 60 = 30$.

Example: What was the median score?

Solution: The median score means the score that is in the *middle* of all the scores. That is, there are just as many scores above the median as below it. So in this example, the scores are 90, 90 (there are two 90's) 85, 80, and 60, 60, 60 (there are three 60's). So we have:

90
90
85
80
60
60
60

80 is right in the middle. That is, there are three scores above it and three scores below it. So 80 is the median.

Example: What was the mean score?

Solution: The mean score is defined as the *average* score. That is, it is the

$$\frac{\text{sum of the scores}}{\text{total number of scores}}$$

The sum of the scores is $90 + 90 + 85 + 80 + 60 + 60 + 60 = 525$. The total number of scores is $2 + 1 + 1 + 3 = 7$, so divide 7 into 525 to get the average: 75.

Graphs

703. To read a graph, you must know what *scale* the graph has been drawn to. Somewhere on the face of the graph will be an explanation of what each division of the graph means. Sometimes the divisions will be labeled. At other times, this information will be given in a small box called a *scale* or *legend*. For instance, a map, which is a specialized kind of graph, will always carry a scale or legend on its face telling you such information as $1'' = 100$ miles or $\frac{1''}{4} = 2$ miles.

Bar Graphs

704. The bar graph shows how the information is compared by using broad lines, called bars, of varying lengths. Sometimes single lines are used as well. Bar graphs are good for showing a quick comparison of the information involved, however, the bars are difficult to read accurately unless the end of the bar falls exactly on one of the divisions of the scale. If the end of the bar falls between divisions of the scale, it is not easy to arrive at the precise figure represented by the bar. In bar graphs, the bars can run either vertically or horizontally. The sample bar graph following is a horizontal graph.

EXPENDITURES PER PUPIL—1990

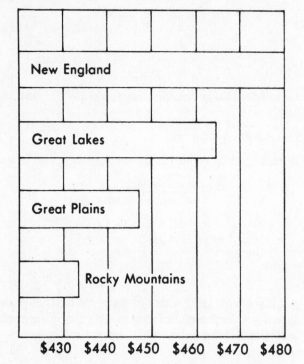

$430 $440 $450 $460 $470 $480

The individual bars in this kind of graph may carry a label within the bar, as in this example. The label may also appear alongside each bar. The scale used on the bars may appear along one axis, as in the example, or it may be noted somewhere on the face of the graph. Each numbered space on the x- (or horizontal) axis represents an expenditure of $10 per pupil. A wide variety of questions may be answered by a bar graph, such as:

(1) Which area of the country spends least per pupil? Rocky Mountains.
(2) How much does the New England area spend per pupil? $480.
(3) How much less does the Great Plains spend per pupil than the Great Lakes? $464 − 447 = $17/pupil.
(4) How much more does New England spend on a pupil than the Rocky Mountain area? $480 − 433 = $47/pupil.

Circle Graphs

705. A circle graph shows how an entire quantity has been divided or apportioned. The circle represents 100 percent of the quantity; the different parts into which the whole has been divided are shown by sections, or wedges, of the circle. Circle graphs are good for showing how money is distributed or collected, and for this reason they are widely used in financial graphing. The information is usually presented on the face of each section, telling you exactly what the section stands for and the value of that section in comparison to the other parts of the graph.

SOURCES OF INCOME—PUBLIC COLLEGES OF U.S.

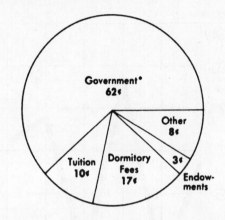

* Government refers to all levels of government—not exclusively the federal government.

The circle graph above indicates where the money originates that is used to maintain public colleges in the United States. The size of the sections tells you at a glance which source is most important (government) and which is least important (endowments). The sections total 100¢ or $1.00. This graph may be used to answer the following questions:

(1) What is the most important source of income to the public colleges? Government.
(2) What part of the revenue dollar comes from tuition? 10¢.
(3) Dormitory fees bring in how many times the money that endowments bring in? $5\frac{2}{3}$ times $\left(\frac{17}{3} = 5\frac{2}{3}\right)$.
(4) What is the least important source of revenue to public colleges? Endowments.

Line Graphs

706. Graphs that have information running both across (horizontally) and up and down (vertically) can be considered to be laid out on a grid having a y-axis and an x-axis. One of the two quantities being compared will be placed along the y-axis, and the other quantity will be placed along the x-axis. When we are asked to compare two values, we subtract the smaller from the larger.

SHARES OF STOCK SOLD
NEW YORK STOCK EXCHANGE DURING ONE SIX MONTH PERIOD

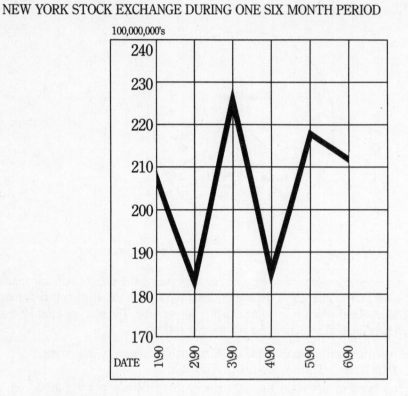

Our sample line graph represents the total shares of stock sold on the New York Stock Exchange between January and June. The months are placed along the x-axis, while the sales, in units of 100,000,000 shares, are placed along the y-axis.

(1) How many shares were sold in March? 225,000,000.
(2) What is the trend of stock sales between April and May? The volume of sales rose.
(3) Compare the share sales in January and February. 25,000,000 fewer shares were sold in February.
(4) During which months of the period was the increase in sales largest? February to March.

Practice Test 7

Tables, Charts, and Graphs Practice Tests

TABLE CHART TEST

Questions 1–5 are based on this Table Chart.

The following chart is a record of the performance of a baseball team for the first seven weeks of the season.

	Games Won	Games Lost	Total No. of Games Played
First Week	5	3	8
Second Week	4	4	16
Third Week	5	2	23
Fourth Week	6	3	32
Fifth Week	4	2	38
Sixth Week	3	3	44
Seventh Week	2	4	50

1. How many games did the team win during the first seven weeks?

   (A) 32
   (B) 29
   (C) 25
   (D) 21
   (E) 50

2. What percent of the games did the team win?

   (A) 75%
   (B) 60%
   (C) 58%
   (D) 29%
   (E) 80%

3. According to the chart, which week was the worst for the team?

   (A) second week
   (B) fourth week
   (C) fifth week
   (D) sixth week
   (E) seventh week

4. Which week was the best week for the team?

   (A) first week
   (B) third week
   (C) fourth week
   (D) fifth week
   (E) sixth week

5. If there are fifty more games to play in the season, how many more games must the team win to end up winning 70% of the games?

   (A) 39
   (B) 35
   (C) 41
   (D) 34
   (E) 32

Solutions

1. Choice B is correct. To find the total number of games won, add the number of games won for all the weeks, $5 + 4 + 5 + 6 + 4 + 3 + 2 = 29$.   (702)

2. Choice C is correct. The team won 29 out of 50 games or 58%.   (702)

3. Choice E is correct. The seventh week was the only week that the team lost more games than it won.   (702)

4. Choice B is correct. During the second week the team won 5 games and lost 2, or it won about 70% of the games that week. Compared with the winning percentages for other weeks, the third week's was the highest.   (702)

5. Choice C is correct. To win 70% of all the games, the team must win 70 out of 100. Since it won 29 games out of the first 50 games, it must win $70 - 29$ or 41 games out of the next 50 games.   (702)

PIE CHART TEST

Questions 1–5 are based on this Pie Chart.

POPULATION BY REGION, 1964

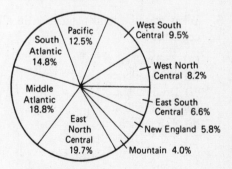

Total U.S. 191.3 million = 100%

1. Which region was the most populated region in 1964?

    (A) East North Central
    (B) Middle Atlantic
    (C) South Atlantic
    (D) Pacific
    (E) New England

2. What part of the entire population lived in the Mountain region?

    (A) $\frac{1}{10}$

    (B) $\frac{1}{30}$

    (C) $\frac{1}{50}$

    (D) $\frac{1}{25}$

    (E) $\frac{1}{8}$

3. What was the approximate population in the Pacific region?

    (A) 20 million
    (B) 24 million
    (C) 30 million
    (D) 28 million
    (E) 15 million

4. Approximately how many more people lived in the Middle Atlantic region than in the South Atlantic?

    (A) 4.0 million
    (B) 7.7 million
    (C) 5.2 million
    (D) 9.3 million
    (E) 8.5 million

5. What was the total population in all the regions combined?

    (A) 73.3 million
    (B) 100.0 million
    (C) 191.3 million
    (D) 126.8 million
    (E) 98.5 million

Solutions

1. Choice A is correct. East North Central with 19.7% of the total population had the largest population. (705)

2. Choice D is correct. The Mountain region had 4.0% of the population. 4.0% is $\frac{1}{25}$. (705)

3. Choice B is correct. Pacific had 12.5% of the population. 12.5% of 191.3 million is .125 × 191.3 or about 24 million. (705)

4. Choice B is correct. Middle Atlantic had 18.8% and South Atlantic had 14.8% of the population. So, Middle Atlantic had 4.0% more. 4.0% of 191.3 million is .04 × 191.3 or about 7.7 million. (705)

5. Choice C is correct. All the regions combined had 100% of the population or 191.3 million. (705)

LINE GRAPH TEST

Questions 1–5 are based on this Line Graph.

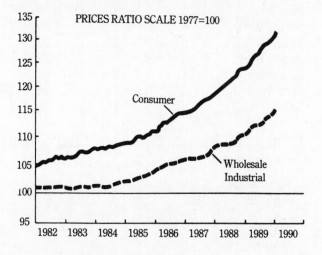

1. On the ratio scale what were consumer prices recorded as of the end of 1985?

    (A) 95
    (B) 100
    (C) 105
    (D) 110
    (E) 115

2. During what year did consumer prices rise fastest?

    (A) 1983
    (B) 1985
    (C) 1987
    (D) 1988
    (E) 1989

3. When wholesale and industrial prices were recorded as 110, consumer prices were recorded as

    (A) between 125 and 120
    (B) between 120 and 115
    (C) between 115 and 110
    (D) between 110 and 105
    (E) between 105 and 100

4. For the 8 years 1982–1989 inclusive, the average increase in consumer prices was

   (A) 1 point
   (B) 2 points
   (C) 3 points
   (D) 4 points
   (E) 5 points

5. The percentage increase in wholesale and industrial prices between the beginning of 1982 and the end of 1989 was

   (A) 1 percent
   (B) 5 percent
   (C) 10 percent
   (D) 15 percent
   (E) less than 1 percent

Solutions

1. Choice D is correct. Drawing a vertical line at the end of 1985, we reach the consumer price graph at about the 110 level. (706)

2. Choice E is correct. The slope of the consumer graph is clearly steepest in 1989. (706)

3. Choice A is correct. Wholesale and industrial prices were about 110 at the beginning of 1989, when consumer prices were between 120 and 125. (706)

4. Choice C is correct. At the beginning of 1982 consumer prices were about 105; at the end of 1989 they were about 130. The average increase is $\dfrac{130 - 105}{8}$

   $= \dfrac{25}{8}$ or about 3. (706)

5. Choice D is correct. At the beginning of 1982 wholesale prices were about 100; at the end of 1989 they were about 115. The percent increase is about $\dfrac{115 - 100}{100} \times 100\%$ or 15%. (706)

BAR GRAPH TEST

Questions 1–3 are based on this bar graph.

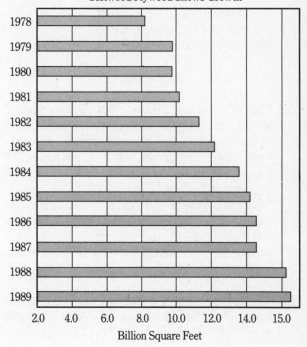

Softwood Plywood Shows Growth

1. What was the ratio of soft plywood produced in 1978 as compared with that produced in 1987?

   (A) 1 : 1
   (B) 2 : 3
   (C) 1 : 2
   (D) 3 : 4
   (E) 1 : 3

2. For the years 1978 through 1983, excluding 1982, how many billion square feet of plywood were produced altogether?

   (A) 23.2
   (B) 29.7
   (C) 34.1
   (D) 40.7
   (E) 50.5

3. Between which consecutive odd years and between which consecutive even years was the plywood production jump greatest?

    (A) 1985 and 1987; 1978 and 1980
    (B) 1983 and 1985; 1984 and 1986
    (C) 1979 and 1981; 1980 and 1982
    (D) 1981 and 1983; 1980 and 1982
    (E) 1983 and 1985; 1982 and 1984

Solutions

1. Choice C is correct. To answer this question, you will have to measure the bars accurately. In 1978, 6.2 billion square feet of plywood were produced. In 1987, 12.4 billion square feet were produced. The ratio of 6.2 : 12.4 is the same as 1 : 2.   (704)

2. Choice D is correct. All you have to do is to measure the bar for each year—of course, don't include the 1982 bar—and estimate the length of each bar. Then you add the five lengths. 1978 = 6.4; 1979 = 7.8; 1980 = 7.9; 1981 = 8.4; 1983 = 10.2. The total is 40.7. (704)

3. Choice E is correct. The jump from 1983 to 1985 was from 10.3 to 12.4 = 2.1 billion square feet. The jump from 1982 to 1984 was from 9.2 to 11.4 = 2.2 billion square feet. None of the other choices show such broad jumps.   (704)

CUMULATIVE GRAPH TEST

Questions 1–5 are based on this cumulative graph.

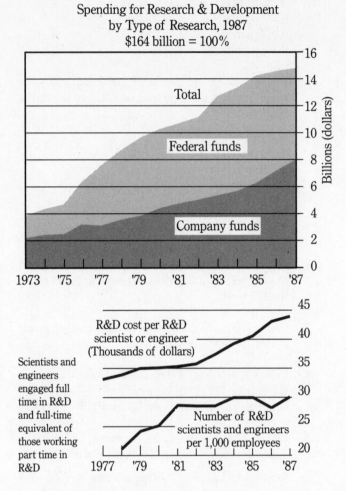

Spending for Research & Development by Type of Research, 1987
$164 billion = 100%

1. About how much in government funds was spent for research and development in 1987?

    (A) $16 billion
    (B) $8 billion
    (C) $12 billion
    (D) $24 billion
    (E) $4 billion

2. In 1987, about what percent of the total spending in research and development were company funds?

    (A) 40%
    (B) 25%
    (C) $33\frac{1}{3}$ %
    (D) 50%
    (E) 20%

3. What was the change in the relative number of research and development scientists and engineers with respect to all employees from 1984 to 1985?

    (A) 10%
    (B) 5%
    (C) 2%
    (D) 3%
    (E) 0%

4. What was the increase in company funds in research and development from 1973 to 1987?

    (A) $12 billion
    (B) $6 billion
    (C) $8 billion
    (D) $4 billion
    (E) $14 billion

5. What was the percent of increase of the company funds spent in research and development from 1973 to 1987?

    (A) 100%
    (B) 50%
    (C) 300%
    (D) 400%
    (E) 1000%

Solutions

1. Choice B is correct. Total spending was about $16 billion, and company spending was $8 billion. So, government spending was about $8 billion.   (706)

2. Choice D is correct. Company funds totaled $8 billion, and the total funds were $16 billion. So, company funds were $\frac{1}{2}$ of total funds or 50%.   (706)

3. Choice E is correct. The graph showing the relative employment of research and development scientists and engineers was horizontal between 1984 and 1985. This means no change.   (706)

4. Choice B is correct. Company funds totaled $8 billion in 1987 and $2 billion in 1973. The increase was $6 billion.   (706)

5. Choice C is correct. Company funds totaled $2 billion in 1973, and the increase from 1973 to 1987 was $6 billion or 300% of $2 billion.   (706)

Flash

Although the new SAT (SAT I) does not contain *antonyms*, it is very important that you know the meanings of difficult words since you will need to know them for the *Sentence Completion, Analogies*, and *Reading Comprehension* questions. In fact there are *more* questions involving hard vocabulary words in the analogies and sentence completions on the new SAT (SAT I) than there were on the old SAT.

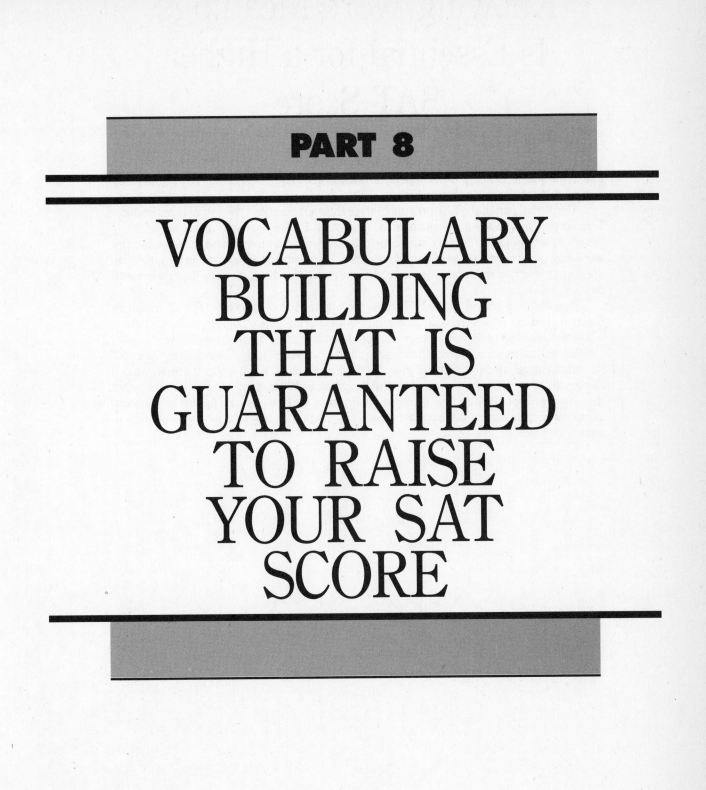

PART 8

VOCABULARY BUILDING THAT IS GUARANTEED TO RAISE YOUR SAT SCORE

Knowing Word Meanings Is Essential for a Higher SAT Score

Improving your vocabulary is essential if you want to get a high score on the Verbal part of the new SAT. We shall explain why this is so.

The Verbal part of the SAT consists of three different question-types: Analogies, Sentence Completions, and Reading Comprehension. Almost all SAT exam-takers come across many "tough" words in the Verbal part, whose meanings they do not know. These students, thereby, lose many, many points because if they do not know the meanings of the words in the questions, they aren't able to answer the questions confidently—and so, they are likely to answer incorrectly.

Every correct answer on the SAT gives you approximately 10 points. The 19 Analogies questions and the 19 Sentence Completion questions contain quite a number of "tough" words whose meanings you will have to know in order to answer these questions correctly.

We must also bring to your attention the fact that several "tough" words show up in the Reading Comprehension passages of every SAT exam. Knowing the meanings of these difficult words will, of course, help you to understand the passages better. It follows that knowing what the passages are all about will give you many more correct answers for the 40 Reading Comprehension questions that appear in the SAT—*and each correct answer nets you approximately 10 points.*

8 Steps to Word Power

1. Study vocabulary lists. You have in this book just the list you need for SAT preparation. The "SAT 3,400-Word List" begins on page 479.

2. Take vocabulary tests. "100 Tests to Strengthen Your Vocabulary" begins on page 531.

3. Learn those Latin and Greek roots, prefixes, and suffixes that make up many English words. It has been estimated that more than half of all English words come from Latin and Greek. "Word Building with Roots, Prefixes, and Suffixes" begins on page 468.

4. Have a college-level dictionary at home. Carry a pocket dictionary when you are moving about. Refer to a dictionary whenever you are not sure of the meaning of a word.

5. Read—read—read. By reading a great deal, you will encounter new and valuable words. You will learn the meanings of many of these words by context—that is, you will perceive a clear connection between a new word and the words that surround that word. In this way, you will learn the meaning of that new word.

6. Listen to what is worthwhile listening to. Listen to good radio and TV programs. Listen to people who speak well. Go to selected movies and plays. Just as you will increase your vocabulary by reading widely, you will increase your vocabulary by listening to English that is spoken well.

7. Play word games like crossword puzzles, anagrams, and Scrabble.

8. Make sure you learn the Vocabulary Strategies beginning on page 236.

No One Can Dispute This Fact!

You will pile up SAT points by taking advantage of the valuable Vocabulary Building study and practice materials that are offered to you in the following pages of this chapter.

You Don't Have to Learn the Meaning of Every Word In the SAT 3,400-Word List

Go as far into the alphabetized groups as time permits. Use the Vocabulary Learning Steps listed on page 479. If you cannot learn the meanings of all the words in the 3,400-Word List, don't fret. Whatever words you have added to your vocabulary *before* you take the actual test will raise your SAT Verbal score substantially.

IMPORTANT NOTE: If you cannot spend time in memorizing some of the words in the Gruber 3,400-Word List, I strongly suggest that you read through the Vocabulary Strategies in the Critical Thinking Strategies Section beginning on page 275.

The Prefix-Root-Suffix List That Gives You the Meanings of Over 150,000 Words

Word Building with Roots, Prefixes, and Suffixes

According to some linguistic studies, approximately 60 percent of our English words are derived from Latin and Greek. One reliable study has shown that a selected list of 20 prefixes and 14 root elements pertain to more than 100,000 words in an unabridged dictionary. The following entries of Latin and Greek roots, prefixes, and suffixes frequently show up in some of the words in all three SAT Verbal areas—Analogies, Sentence Completions, and Reading Comprehension. Learn these Latin and Greek word parts to increase your vocabulary immensely—and thus score well in the Verbal part of your SAT.

> The shortest and best way of learning a language is to know the
> roots of it; that is, those original primitive words from which
> other words are formed.
> —Lord Chesterfield

Lord Chesterfield is, in effect, saying that roots are used as important "building blocks" of many of our English words. As you study the following list of Latin and Greek roots, prefixes, and suffixes, have a dictionary by your side. Look up the meanings of the word examples that are given if you do not know their meanings.

Roots

> **A ROOT IS THE BASIC ELEMENT—FUNDAMENTAL OR ESSENTIAL PART—OF A WORD.**

ROOT	MEANING AND EXAMPLE*
ag, act	do, act; as *agent, counteract*
agr	field; as *agriculture, agoraphobia*
alt	high; as *altitude, altar*
alter	other; as *altercation, alternative*
am	friend, love; as *amity, amorous*
anim	year; as *annuity, annual*
anthrop	man; as *philanthropy, anthropoid*
aper	open; as *aperture, aperient*
apt	fit; as *adapt, aptitude*
aqu	water; as *aqueous, aquacade*
arch	rule, govern; as *anarchy, matriarch*
aster, astr	star; as *asteroid, disaster, astronomy*
aud	hear; as *audible, audition*
aur	gold; as *auriferous*
bas	low; as *debase, basement*
bell	war; as *bellicose, antebellum*
ben	good, well; as *benevolent, benefactor*
bibl	book; as *biblical, bibliography*
bio	life; as *biology, biopsy*
brev	short; as *brevity, abbreviation*
cad, cas, cid	fall; as *cadence, casualty, incident*
cand	white, shining; as *candid, candidate*
cap, capt	take, hold; as *capable, captive*
capit	head; as *capital, decapitate*
carn	flesh; as *carnal, carnivorous*
ced, cess	yield, go; as *cede, procession*
celer	swift; as *celerity, accelerate*
cent	hundred; as *century, centipede*
chrom	color; as *chromium, chromatic*
chron	time; as *chronology, chronic*
cid, cis	cut, kill; as *suicide, precision*
clin	lean, bend; as *inclination, recline*

ROOT	MEANING AND EXAMPLE
clud, clus	close, shut; as *conclude, recluse*
cogn	know; as *incognito, cognizant*
cord	heart; as *cordial, accord*
corp	body; as *corpulent, corpse*
cosm	world; as *cosmic, cosmopolitan*
cred	believe; as *incredible, credentials*
curr, curs	run; as *current, cursory*
dec	ten; as *decimal, decade*
dem	people; as *democracy, demographic*
derm	skin; as *epidermis, dermatologist*
di	day; as *diary, sundial*
dic, dict	speak, say; as *indicate, contradict*
dign	worthy; as *dignity, indignant*
domin	lord, master; as *dominate, indomitable*
dorm	sleep; as *dormant, dormitory*
duc, duct	lead; as *induce, ductile*
ego	I; as *egotism, egomaniac*
equ	equal; as *equity, equanimity*
fac, fact, fect, fic	make, do; as *facile, factory, infection, fiction*
fer	bear, carry; as *fertile, confer*
fid	faith, trust; as *confide, infidelity*
fin	end; as *infinite, final*
flect, flex	bend; as *reflect, flexible*
form	shape; as *conform, reformation*
fort	strong; as *fortitude, fortify*
frag, fract	break; as *fragile, fracture*
fug	flee; as *fugitive, refugee*
fus	pour; as *confuse, fusion*
gen	kind, race, birth; as *generate, generic, generation*
gest	carry, bring; as *congestion, gestation*
grad, gress	step, go; as *graduate, digress*

*Refer to dictionary for word meanings you don't know.

ROOT	MEANING AND EXAMPLE
graph	write; as *autograph, graphic*
grat	pleasing; as *gratitude, congratulate*
hydr	water; as *dehydrated, hydrant*
integr	entire, whole; as *integrate, integral*
ject	throw; as *inject, projection*
junct	join; as *conjunction, juncture*
lat	carry; as *translation, dilate*
leg, lig, lect	choose, gather; as *legible, eligible, collect*
liber	free; as *liberate, libertine*
loc	place; as *dislocate, local*
log	word, study; as *catalogue, psychology*
loqu, locut	speak, talk; as *loquacious, circumlocution*
luc, lum	light; as *translucent, illuminate*
magn	great; as *magnitude, magnificent*
man	hand; as *manufacture, manual*
mar	sea; as *marine, maritime*
mater	mother; as *maternal, matrimony*
mega	large; as *megaton, megaphone*
ment	mind; as *mentality, mentally*
merg	plunge, sink; as *submerge, merger*
meter	measure; as *chronometer, symmetry*
micro	small; as *microscope, microfilm*
migr	wander; as *migrate, immigration*
mir	look; as *admire, mirror*
mit, miss	send; as *admit, submission*
mon	advise, remind; as *admonish, monument*
mort	death; as *immortality, mortal*
mot, mov	move; as *motor, motility, movable*
mult	many; as *multitude, multifarious*
mut	change; as *mutation, transmute, immutable*
nat	born; as *natal, innate*
nav	ship; as *naval, navigate*
neg	deny; as *negate, renege*
nomen	name; as *nominee, nomenclature, cognomen*
nov	new; as *novelty, novice, innovation*
ocul	eye; as *oculist, binocular*

ROOT	MEANING AND EXAMPLE
oper	work; as *cooperation, operate*
pater, patri	father; as *paternal, patriot*
ped, pod	foot; as *impede, biped, tripod*
ped	child; as *pediatrics, pedagogue*
pel, puls	drive; as *compel, expulsion*
pend, pens	hang; as *pendant, pension*
pet	seek; as *impetus, petition*
petr	stone, rock; as *petrify*
phil	loving; as *philosophy*
phob	fear; as *claustrophobia*
phon	sound; as *phonic, phonetics*
plic	fold, bend; as *complicate, implicate*
pon, pos	place, put; as *component, compose*
port	carry, bring; as *porter, import*
pot	drink; as *potion, potable*
poten	powerful; as *potentate, impotent*
prehend, prehens	take, grasp; as *apprehend, comprehension*
prot	first; as *protagonist, prototype*
psych	mind; as *psychological, psychic*
quer, quir, quis, ques	ask, seek; as *query, inquiry, inquisition, quest*
reg, rig, rect	rule, govern; as *regent, rigid, corrective*
rid, ris	laugh; as *ridiculous, risible*
rupt	break; as *rupture, erupt, interruption*
sacr	holy; as *sacred, sacrificial*
sanct	holy; as *sanction, sanctify*
sci, scio	know; as *science, conscious, omniscient*
scop	watch; as *periscope, horoscope*
scrib, script	write; as *describe, prescription*
sec, sect	cut; as *secant, bisect*
sed, sid, sess	sit, seat; as *sedate, reside, session*
sent, sens	feel, think; as *sentiment, sensible*
sequ, secut	follow; as *sequel, consecutive*
serv	keep; as *reserve, conservation*
sist	place, stand; as *assist, resistance*

ROOT	MEANING AND EXAMPLE
solv, solu	loosen; as *dissolve, absolution*
somn	sleep; as *somnambulist, insomnia*
soph	wisdom; as *sophisticated, philosophy*
spec, spect, spic	look, appear; as *specimen, prospect, conspicuous*
spir	breathe; as *conspire, respiration*
stat, stab	stand; as *status, stability*
string, strict	bind; as *stringent, stricture*
stru, struct	build; as *construe, destructive*
sum, sumpt	take; as *assume, presumption*
tang, ting, tact, tig	touch; as *tangent, contingency, contact, contiguous*
teg, tect	cover; as *tegument, detect*
tele	distance; as *telescope, teletype*
tempor	time; as *temporary, extemporaneous*
ten, tain	hold, reach; as *tenant, tension, retain*
term	end; as *terminal, terminate*
ter, terr	land, earth; as *inter, terrace*
therm	heat; as *thermometer, thermos*

ROOT	MEANING AND EXAMPLE
tract	draw; as *attract, extract*
trit	rub; as *trite, attrition*
trud, trus	thrust; as *intrude, abstruse*
umbra	shade; as *umbrella, umbrage*
urb	city; as *suburb, urban*
vac	empty; as *vacate, evacuation*
vad, vas	go; as *evade, evasive*
val, vail	be strong; as *valid, prevail*
ven, vent	come; as *convene, prevention*
ver	true; as *veracity, aver*
verb	word; as *verbose, verbatim*
vert, vers	turn; as *convert, reverse*
vid, vis	see; as *evident, visible*
vinc, vict	conquer; as *invincible, evict*
viv, vit	live; as *vivacity, vital*
voc, vok	call; as in *vocation, revoke*
volv, volut	roll, turn; as in *involve, revolution*
tort, tors	twist; as *contort, torsion*

Prefixes

> **A PREFIX IS PART OF A WORD THAT MAY BE PLACED BEFORE THE BASIC ELEMENT (ROOT) OF A WORD.**

PREFIX	MEANING AND EXAMPLE
a, ab, abs	from, away; as *avert, abjure, absent*
ad	to; as *adhere*. By assimilation, *ad* takes the forms of **a, ac, af, al, an, ap, as, at**; as *aspire, accord, affect, allude, annex, appeal, assume, attract*
ambi, amphi	around, both; as *ambidextrous, amphibious*
ante, anti	before; as *antedate, anticipate*
anti	against; as *antidote, antislavery*
arch	first, chief; as *archangel, archenemy*
auto	self; as *autobiography, automatic*
ben	good, well; as *benediction, benefactor*
bi	two; as *bilateral, bisect*
circum	around; as *circumnavigate, circumvent*
com, con, col, cor, co	together; as *commit, concord, collect, correct, co-worker*

PREFIX	MEANING AND EXAMPLE
contra, contro, counter	against; as *contradict, controvert, counteract*
de	down, away from, about; as *descend, depart, describe*
demi	half; as *demigod, demitasse*
dia	across, through; as *diameter, diastole*
dis, di, dif	apart, not; as *dissension, division, diffident*
equi	equal; as *equinox, equivalent*
ex, e, ef	out of, from; as *extract, eject, efface*
extra	out of, beyond; as *extraordinary, extraterrestrial*
hyper	too much; as *hypercritical, hypersensitive*
hypo	too little, under; as *hypochondriac, hypodermic*

PREFIX	MEANING AND EXAMPLE
in, il, im, ir	into, in, on; as *invade, illustrate, immerse, irritate*
in, il, im, ir	not; as *indistinct, illegal, impossible, irresponsible*
inter, intro	between, among; as *interpose, introduce*
mal	bad; as *maltreat, malevolent*
mono	one, single; as *monotone, monorail*
neo	new; as *neoplasm, neophyte*
non	not; as *nonentity, nonconformist*
ob, of, op	against; as *obviate, offend, oppose*
omni	all; as *omniscient, omnipresent*
ortho	straight; as *orthodox, orthopedic*
pan	all; as *pantheism, Pan-American*
peri	around; as *perimeter, periscope*
poly	many; as *polygon, polygamy*
post	after; as *postpone, postmortem*

PREFIX	MEANING AND EXAMPLE
pro	forward, before; as *proceed, provide*
re	back, again; as *recur, recede*
retro	backward; as *retrogress, retrospect*
se	apart, away; as *seduce, sedition*
semi	half; as *semicircle, semiconscious*
sub	under; as *submarine, subversive*
super	above, beyond; as *superpose, supernatural*
syn, sym	with, at the same time; as *synonymous, sympathetic*
trans	across; as *transcontinental, transmit*
ultra	beyond; as *ultraliberal, ultramodern*
un	not; as *unaware, uninformed*
uni	one; as *unanimous, uniform*
vice	instead of; as *vice-chancellor, viceroy*

Suffixes

> **A SUFFIX IS PART OF A WORD THAT MAY FOLLOW THE BASIC ELEMENT (ROOT) OF A WORD.**

SUFFIX	MEANING AND EXAMPLE
able	able; as *pliable, returnable*
acious, cious	having the quality of; as *capacious, meretricious*
age	act, condition; as *courage, foliage*
al	belonging to; as *legal, regal*
ance, ence	state of; as *abundance, indulgence*
ate	one who; as *candidate, advocate*
ary, eer, er	one who, concerning; as *secretary, engineer, mariner*
cy	state, position of; as *adequacy, presidency*
dom	state of; as *freedom, serfdom*
ence	state of; as *presence, credence*
er, or	one who; as *player, actor*
escent	becoming; as *adolescent, putrescent*
fy	make; as *beautify, sanctify*
hood	state of; as *knighthood, childhood*
ic, id	of, like; as *bucolic, acrid*

SUFFIX	MEANING AND EXAMPLE
il, ile	capable of being; as *evil, servile*
ion	act of; as *desperation, perspiration*
ious	characterized by; as *spacious, illustrious*
ish	like; as *boyish, foolish*
ism	belief in or practice of; as *idealism, capitalism*
ist	one who practices or is devoted to; as *anarchist, harpist*
ive	relating to; as *abusive, plaintive*
mony	state of; as *harmony, matrimony*
ness	quality of; as *willingness, shrewdness*
or, er	one who; as *monitor, employer*
ory	a place for; as *factory, depository*
ous, ose	full of; as *ponderous, verbose*
ship	state of, skill; as *friendship, gamesmanship*
some	characteristic of; as *loathsome, fearsome*
tude	state of; as *lassitude, rectitude*
ward	in the direction of; as *windward, backward*
y	full of; as *unruly, showy*

A List of SAT Words Appearing More Than Once on Actual SAT Exams

We have made a computerized analysis of frequently occurring words on 47 complete recent SAT exams. (1,175 questions have been examined.) Following is a list of 132 SAT words appearing *more than once* on these 47 actual SAT exams.

The definitions of these words have not been included here because we want you to *refer to a dictionary* to learn the meanings of these words, which have been repeated in subsequent SAT question sections.

Note that after each word a numeral indicates the number of times that the word has appeared on the 47 actual SAT exams.

Also note that certain pairs of words have a left-side bracket. The bracket indicates that the words are very closely allied in meaning—so if you learn the meaning of one of the two words in the pair, you will easily arrive at the meaning of the other word of the pair.

Learn the meanings of these words, as they have a tendency to be repeated in questions of the SAT.

abolish 2
abridge 2
abstemious
[accent 1
[accented 1
accolade 2
acquiesce 2
affirmation 2
amass 2
[ambivalence 1
[ambivalent 1
ambulatory 2
ameliorate 2
amity 2
anchor 2
antediluvian 2
ascendancy 2
atrophy 2
[bane 1
[baneful 1
bizarre 2
blunder 2
bungle 2
burgeon 2
[capitulate 1
[capitulation 1
capricious 4
clemency 2

[coalesce 2
[coalescence 1
[cohere 1
[coherent 1
[compress 1
[compression 1
[confide 1
[confidential 1
confound 2
congeal 2
[contaminant 1
[contaminate 2
converge 2
convivial 2
copious 2
corroborate 2
corrugated 2
[corrupt 1
[corruption 1
cursory 2
[daunt 3
[dauntless 1
debilitate 2
deplete 2
discrepancy 3
disentangle 2
[disputatious 1
[dispute 2

[distend 1
[distention 1
drawback 2
efface 3
[effervesce 1
[effervescent 1
enhance 2
enigmatic 2
ephemeral 3
equilibrium 3
[euphonious 1
[euphony 1
evacuate 2
evanescent 2
[expedite 1
[expeditious 1
[expendable 1
[expenditures 1
exclude 2
facilitate 2
fallow 2
fertile 2
[flourish 3
[flower 1
fraudulent 3
[fruitful 1
[fruitless 1
garner 2

guile 2
hackneyed 2
hefty 2
hideous 2
hilarity 2
humane 2
[hypocrisy 1
[hypocritical 1
innocuous 2
irascible 2
jettison 2
kindle 2
[leniency 1
[lenient 1
[levity 1
[levitate 1
listless 2
maladroit 2
mitigate 2
mobile 2
munificent 2
munificence 1
myriad 2
nefarious 2
[obscure 1
[obscurity 1
[opaque 1
[opacity 1

parsimony 2
paucity 2
penury 2
[peripheral 2
[periphery 2
placate 2
[precise 1
[precision 1
premature 2
premeditated 2
prevalent 2
proclivity 2
[prodigal 1
[prodigious 2
[profuse 1
[profusion 2
[pulverize 1
[pulverized 1
rant 2
recalcitrant 2
recant 2
replete 2
rescind 2
reserve 2
ruffle 2
rupture 2
saccharine 2
salubrious 2

somber 4
[specify 1
[specificity 1
spurn 2
squander 2
stymie 2

subtle 2
summary 2
summon 3
sumptuous 2
[surreptitious 1
[surreptitiously 1

tantamount 2
[tenacious 1
[tenacity 1
[transience 1
[transient 1

turbulence 3
venturesome 3
viable 2
[vibrancy 1
[vibrant 1

vilification 2
[virulence 1
[virulent 1
whet 2
zany 2

The 291 Most Important SAT Words and Their Opposites

Following is a list of popular SAT words and their opposites. Note: These words fit into specific categories, and it may be a little easier memorizing the meaning of these important words knowing what category they fit into.

POSITIVE	NEGATIVE	POSITIVE	NEGATIVE
TO PRAISE	TO BELITTLE	TO CALM OR MAKE BETTER	TO MAKE WORSE OR RUFFLE
acclaim	admonish	abate	alienate
applaud	assail	accede	antagonize
commend	berate	accommodate	contradict
eulogize	calumniate	allay	dispute
exalt	castigate	ameliorate	fend off
extol	censure	appease	embitter
flatter	chastise	assuage	estrange
hail	chide	comply	incense
laud	decry	concede	infuriate
panegyrize	denigrate	conciliate	nettle
resound	denounce	gratify	oppugn
tout	disparage	mitigate	oppose
	excoriate	mollify	rebuff
	execrate	pacify	repel
	flay	palliate	repulse
	lambaste	placate	snub
	malign	propitiate	
	reprimand	quell	
	reproach	satiate	
	scold		
	upbraid		
	vilify		

POSITIVE	NEGATIVE	POSITIVE	NEGATIVE

PLEASANT

UNPLEASANT

YIELDING

NOT YIELDING

affable	callous	accommodating	adamant
amiable	cantankerous	amenable	determinate
agreeable	captious	compliant	immutable
captivating	churlish	deferential	indomitable
congenial	contentious	docile	inflexible
cordial	gruff	flexible	intractable
courteous	irascible	inclined	intransigent
decorous	ireful	hospitable	recalcitrant
engaging	obstinate	malleable	relentless
gracious	ornery	pliant	resolute
obliging	peevish	obliging	steadfast
sportive	perverse	submissive	tenacious
unblemished	petulant	subservient	
undefiled	querulous	tractable	
	testy		
	vexing		
	wayward		

GENEROUS

CHEAP

COURAGEOUS

TIMID

altruistic	frugal	audacious	diffident
beneficent	miserly	dauntless	indisposed
benevolent	niggardly	gallant	laconic
charitable	paltry	intrepid	reserved
effusive	parsimonious	stalwart	reticent
hospitable	penurious	undaunted	subdued
humanitarian	provident	valiant	timorous
magnanimous	skinflinty	valorous	
munificent	spartan		
philanthropic	tight-fisted		
	thrifty		

ABUNDANT OR RICH

SCARCE OR POOR

LIVELY

BLEAK

affluent	dearth	brisk	dejected
bounteous	deficit	dynamic	forlorn
copious	destitute	ebullient	lackluster
luxuriant	exiguous	exhilaration	lugubrious
multifarious	impecunious	exuberant	melancholy
multitudinous	impoverished	inspiring	muted
myriad	indigent	provocative	prostrate
opulent	insolvent	scintillating	somber
pecunious	meager	stimulating	tenebrous
plenteous	paltry	titillating	
plentiful	paucity		
plethoric	penurious		
profuse	scanty		
prosperous	scarcity		
superabundant	sparse		
teeming			
wealthy			

POSITIVE	NEGATIVE		
CAREFUL	CARELESS	HAUGHTY	HUMBLE
chary	culpable	affected	demure
circumspect	felonious	arrogant	diffident
conscientious	indifferent	aristocratic	indisposed
discreet	insouciant	audacious	introverted
exacting	lackadaisical	authoritarian	laconic
fastidious	lax	autocratic	plebian
gingerly	negligent	condescending	reluctant
heedful	perfunctory	disdainful	restrained
judicious	rash	egotistical	reticent
meticulous	remiss	flippant	subdued
provident	reprehensible	flagrant	subservient
prudent	temerarious	imperious	taciturn
punctilious		impertinent	timid
scrupulous		impudent	timorous
scrutiny		insolent	unassuming
wary		ostentatious	unpretentious
		pompous	unostentatious
		proud	
		supercilious	
		vainglorious	

Note: In many cases you can put a prefix "im" or "un" in front of the word and change its meaning to an opposite.

Example: Pecunious. Opposite: Impecunious.
Ostentatious. Opposite: Unostentatious.

Practice Questions

1. Example: Find OPPOSITE of EXTOL:

   (A) oppose (B) restrain (C) enter
   (D) deviate (E) denigrate

2. ALLAY (opposite):
   (A) incense (B) drive (C) berate
   (D) signify (E) determine

3. DECOROUS (opposite):

   (A) scanty (B) irascible (C) musty
   (D) pliant (E) rigid

4. AMENABLE (opposite):

   (A) tiresome (B) uncultured (C) intransigent
   (D) soothing (E) careless

5. MUNIFICENT (opposite):

   (A) simple (B) pallid (C) crafty
   (D) penurious (E) stable

6. PLETHORIC (opposite):

   (A) impecunious (B) slothful (C) indifferent
   (D) reticent (E) sly

7. METICULOUS (opposite):

   (A) timid (B) plenteous (C) peevish
   (D) intractible (E) perfunctory

8. IMPERIOUS (opposite):

   (A) unostentatious (B) lackadaisical
   (C) insolvent (D) churlish (E) immutable

9. TIMOROUS (opposite):

   (A) judicious (B) intrepid (C) multifarious
   (D) benevolent (E) tenebrous

10. LUGUBRIOUS (opposite):

    (A) flexible (B) unblemished (C) ebullient
    (D) concilatory (E) impertinent

Answers to Practice Questions

1. Choice E is correct. EXTOL fits into the category of TO PRAISE. Denigrate fits into the category TO BELITTLE—the opposite category.

2. Choice A is correct. ALLAY fits into the category of TO CALM. Incense fits into the opposite category—TO MAKE WORSE or TO RUFFLE.

3. Choice B is correct. DECOROUS fits into the category of PLEASANT. The opposite category is UNPLEASANT. Irascible fits into this category.

4. Choice C is correct. AMENABLE fits into the category of YIELDING. Intransigent fits into the opposite category—NOT YIELDING.

5. Choice D is correct. MUNIFICENT fits into the category of GENEROUS. Penurious fits into the category of CHEAP, the opposite category.

6. Choice A is correct. PLETHORIC fits into the category of ABUNDANT or RICH. Impecunious fits into the opposite category of SCARCE or POOR.

7. Choice E is correct. METICULOUS fits into the category of CAREFUL. Perfunctory fits into the category of CARELESS (or mechanical).

8. Choice A is correct. IMPERIOUS fits into the category of HAUGHTY (high-brow). Unostentatious fits into the category of HUMBLE, the opposite category.

9. Choice B is correct. TIMOROUS fits into the category of TIMID. Intrepid fits into the opposite category of COURAGEOUS.

10. Choice C is correct. LUGUBRIOUS fits into the category of BLEAK or dismal. Ebullient fits into the opposite category of LIVELY.

The Gruber SAT 3,400-Word List

Every new word that you learn in this SAT word-list can help you to add a possible 10 extra points to your SAT verbal score.

Vocabulary Learning Steps

1. Conceal each definition with a card as you go down the column.

2. *Jot down each word whose meaning you do not know.* Then prepare a flash card for each word you did not know.
   Write the synonym (similar meaning) on the back of the card.

3. Study the flash cards that you have made up.

4. After you have studied the DID-NOT-KNOW flash cards, give yourself a flash card test. Put aside the flash cards for the words you did know.

5. For each word you still do not know, write a sentence that includes the word you still have not learned well.

6. Now test yourself again on the DID-NOT-KNOW flash cards referred to in Step 5.
   Put aside your flash cards for the words you did know.

7. Study the new reduced pile of DID-NOT-KNOW flash cards.

8. Give yourself a flash card test on this new reduced DID-NOT-KNOW pile.

9. Keep reducing your DID-NOT-KNOW flash card pile until you have no DID-NOT-KNOW words.

IMPORTANT

Do not throw your flash cards away. Keep the cards for reinforcement testing in the future.

In past exams 70 to 80 percent of all test vocabulary words appeared on this list!

ABACK–AZURE

aback	(preceded by *taken*) surprised; startled	**abate**	to lessen; to decrease
abandon	to leave; to give up; to discontinue	**abdicate**	to yield; to give up
abase	to humiliate; to humble; to lower	**abduct**	to take away; to kidnap
abash	ashamed; embarrassed	**aberration**	abnormality; deviation

abet   to aid; to encourage

abeyance   a temporary postponement

abhor   to hate; to detest

abide (*two meanings*)   to remain; to put up with

abject   miserable; wretched

abjure   to give up (rights)

ablution   a washing; cleansing

abnegate   to deny; to reject

abolition   doing away with; putting an end to

abominate   to detest; to dislike strongly

aborigine   original inhabitant

abortive   unsuccessful

abound   to be large in number

aboveboard   honest; frank; open

abrade   to wear away

abridge   to shorten

abrogate   to abolish; to repeal

abscond   to leave secretly; to flee

absolve   to free from responsibility

abstemious   moderate or sparing in eating or drinking

abstinence   self-denial; resisting tempting foods

abstract (*two meanings*)   a summary (*noun*); to remove (*verb*)

abstruse   hard to understand

absurd   ridiculous; unreasonable

abut   to touch; to rest on or against

abysmal   wretched; extremely bad

abyss   a bottomless pit; anything infinite

academic (*two meanings*)   pertaining to school; theoretical or unrealistic

accede   to agree to

accelerate   to speed up; to move faster

accessible   easy to approach; open

access   approach; admittance

accessory   something additional

acclaim   to greet with approval

acclimate   to adapt; to get used to

acclivity   upward slope

accolade   honor; award; approval

accommodate   to make fit; to help

accomplice   a partner in crime

accord   agreement

accost   to approach and speak to

accoutrement   equipment; outfit

accredit   to approve; to certify

accretion   an increase; an addition

accrue   to gather; to accumulate

acerbic   sharp or bitter in smell or taste

Achilles' heel   a weakness

acknowledge   to admit; to confess

acme   highest point; peak

acoustics   branch of physics dealing with sound

acquiesce   to agree; to consent

acquit   to free of guilt; to clear

acrid   bitter to the taste or smell; sarcastic

acrimonious   harsh in speech or behavior

acronym   word formed from initials

acrophobia   fear of heights

actuate   to put into motion or action

acumen   mental keenness; shrewdness

acute   sharp; keen

ad infinitum   endlessly; forever

ad lib   to act or speak without preparation

adage   a familiar saying

adamant   stubborn; unyielding

adapt   to adjust; to change

addendum   something added as a supplement

addled   confused

adduce   to give an example in proving something

adept   highly skilled

adherent (*two meanings*)   sticking fast (*adjective*); a follower or a supporter (*noun*)

adipose   fatty

adjacent   near; close; adjoining

adjudicate   to judge

adjunct   a subordinate; an assistant

admonish   to warn

ado   fuss; trouble

adonis   a very handsome man

adorn   to dress up; to decorate

adroit   skillful; clever

adulation   excessive praise or flattery

adulterate   to make impure

advent   an arrival; a coming

adventitious   accidental; nonessential

adversary   enemy; opponent

adversity   a misfortune; distress

advocate   to recommend; to defend

aegis   a shield; protection; sponsorship

aesthetic   pertaining to beauty

affable   friendly; agreeable

affectation   a phony attitude; insincerity

affiliate   to associate or to unite with

affinity   attraction to

affirmation   a statement that something is true

affix   to attach

affliction   great suffering; hardship

affluence   wealth

affront   an insult

aftermath   outcome; result

agape   open-mouthed; surprised

agenda   a list or program of things to be done

aggrandize   to enlarge or to expand

aggravate   to worsen an already bad situation; to intensify

aggregate   to collect; to gather together

aghast   shocked; terrified

agile   able to move quickly

agitate   to upset; to stir up

agnostic   one who doubts the existence of God

agoraphobia   fear of open places

agrarian   pertaining to farmers and agriculture

ague   a fever; plague

alacrity   liveliness; willingness

albatross   (*two meanings*) a seabird; a constant burden

albeit   although

alchemy   chemistry of the Middle Ages

alias   an assumed name

alien   strange; foreign

alienate   to make others unfriendly to you

alimentary   furnishing food or nourishment

allay   to relieve or to calm

alleged   so-called; supposed

allegory   a symbolic work of literature

allegro   rapid; quick

alleviate   to lessen; to relieve

allocate   to set aside for a specific purpose

allude   to hint at; to refer to indirectly

alluring   tempting; fascinating; charming

alluvial   pertaining to a deposit of sand formed by flowing water

aloft   up in the air; high

aloof   reserved; cool; indifferent

alter   to change

altercation   an argument; a disagreement

altruism   unselfishness; concern for others

amalgamate   to combine; to unite; to blend

amass   to accumulate; to collect

amazon   a big, strong, masculine woman

ambidextrous   equally skillful with either hand

ambient   surround; on all sides

ambiguous   unclear; open to more than one interpretation

ambivalence   conflicting feelings toward something or someone

ambrosial   pleasing to the taste or smell

ambulatory   moving about; capable of walking

ambuscade   hidden or secret attack

ameliorate   to improve; to make better

amenable   agreeable; responsive

amend   to change; to alter

amenities   courtesies; social graces; pleasantries

amiable   friendly; pleasant

amicable   friendly; agreeable

amiss   wrong; faulty; improper

amity   friendship

amnesty   official pardon for an offense

amoral   lacking a sense of right and wrong

amorous   loving

amorphous   shapeless

amphibious   able to live on both land and water

ample   roomy; abundant

amplify   to make larger or greater

amulet   a charm worn to keep evil away

anachronism   something out of place or time

analgesic   drug that relieves pain

analogy   similarity or comparison

anarchy   absence of government

anathema   a curse; a person or thing to be avoided

ancillary   helping; subordinate

anecdote   a short, entertaining story

anent   regarding; concerning

anguish   great suffering or grief

anhydrous   without water

animadversion   criticism; comment that opposes

animate   to give life to

animosity   hatred; hostility

animus   hostile feeling

annals   historical records

anneal   to heat and then cool; to toughen

annihilate   to totally destroy

annuity   specified income payable at stated intervals

annul   to cancel; to do away with

anomalous   abnormal; inconsistent

anon   soon

anoxia   lack of oxygen

antecedent   that which goes before something else

antediluvian   very old-fashioned; primitive

anterior   located in front or forward

anteroom   a lobby or waiting room

anthem   song of praise

anthology   collection of literary works

anthropoid   resembling man

anthropomorphic   attributing human form to objects, gods, etc.

antic   playful or silly act; prank

anticlimax   something unimportant coming after something important

antidote   a remedy; a counteractive

antipathy   intense dislike

antipodes   opposite sides (of the earth)

antiquated   ancient; extremely old

antithesis   an exact opposite

apathy   indifference; lack of feeling

ape   (*two meanings*) a monkey (*noun*); to imitate or to mimic (*verb*)

aperture   an opening; a gap

apex   the highest point; summit

aphasia   loss of the ability to speak

aphorism   brief saying; proverb

apiary   place where bees are kept

aplomb   self-confidence; poise

apocryphal   doubtful; not authentic

apogee   farthest point away from the earth

apoplexy   sudden loss of consciousness; paralysis

apostate   one who gives up his beliefs

apothecary   druggist

apothegm   brief instructive saying

apotheosis   glorification of a person to the rank of God

appall   to frighten; to cause loss of courage

apparel   clothing; attire

apparition   a ghost

appease   to soothe; to satisfy

appellation   a name

append   to attach; to add

apposite   appropriate

apprehend   (*two meanings*) to seize; to understand

apprehensive   fearful; anxious

apprise   to inform

approbation   approval

appropriate   to take possession of (*verb*); suitable (*adjective*)

appurtenance   something added to another more important thing

apropos   relevant; appropriate; fitting

aptitude   ability

aquatic   pertaining to water

aquiline   like an eagle; curved or hooked

arable   good for farming

arbiter   a judge; an umpire

arbitrary   partial; biased

arbor   a shaded area

arcane   mysterious

archaic   out-dated; old-fashioned

archeology   study of remains of past cultures

archetype   original; first of its kind

archipelago   group of islands

archives   public records and documents

ardent   intensely enthusiastic

arduous   difficult; strenuous

aria   a solo in an opera

arid   dry

armistice   a truce; suspension of hostilities

aromatic   pleasant-smelling

arraign   to accuse

arrant   notorious; downright

array   an orderly arrangement

arrears   (preceded by *in*) in debt

arrogant   proud; haughty

arroyo   a deep ditch caused by running water

arson   illegal burning of property

artful   cunning; tricky; crafty

articulate   to speak clearly

artifact   a handmade object

artifice   trick; deception

artisan   one skilled in arts and crafts

ascendant   rising

ascertain   to find out; to determine

ascetic   one who denies his body pleasure and comfort

ascribe   to attribute; to credit as to a cause or source

aseptic   without bacteria

asinine   stupid; silly

askance   (preceded by *to look*) sidewise; suspiciously

askew   crooked; out of position

asperity   harshness; roughness

aspersion   a damaging remark

aspire   to desire; to have an ambition

assail   to attack; to assault

assay   to test; to try

assent   to agree; to accept

assess   to estimate the value of

assertive   confident; positive

assiduity   diligence; care

assimilate   to absorb

assuage   to calm; to make less severe

asteroid   a very small planet

astral   pertaining to the stars

astray   in the wrong direction

astringent   substance that contracts blood vessels or shrinks tissues

astute   shrewd; very smart

asunder   into separate parts

asylum   a safe place; a refuge

atavistic   going back to behavior found in a remote ancestor

atheist   one who denies God's existence

atlas   book of maps

atone   to make up for; to repent

atrocious   cruel; brutal

atrophy   to waste away; to become useless

attenuated   decreased; weakened

attest   to confirm; to declare to be correct

attribute   (*two meanings*) to credit or assign to (*verb*); a characteristic or trait (*noun*)

attrition   a wearing down or away; a decline

atypical   abnormal; not usual

au courant   up-to-date; fully informed

audacity   boldness; daring

audible   capable of being heard

audit   to examine accounts

augment   to increase; to make greater

augur   to predict

august   majestic; worthy of respect; impressive

aura   a radiance; a glow

aural   pertaining to the sense of hearing

auroral   rosy; pertaining to the dawn

auspices   approval; support

auspicious   favorable

austere   severe; stern; self-disciplined

authenticate   to confirm; to make acceptable

authoritative   dictatorial; having power

autocratic   despotic; unlimited in authority

automaton   self-operating machine; robot

autonomy   self-rule

autumnal   mature; declining

auxiliary   giving assistance; subordinate

avarice   greed

avenge   to get even; to take revenge

aver   to declare; to state firmly

averse   reluctant; not willing

aversion   intense dislike

avert   to prevent; to turn away

aviary   place where birds are kept

avid   enthusiastic

avocation   a hobby; not one's regular work

avoirdupois   heaviness; weight

avow   to declare openly

avuncular   like an uncle

awe   (*in awe of*) great admiration for or fear of

awry   twisted to one side; in the wrong direction

axiom   true statement; established principle

azure   blue

BACCHANALIAN–BUTTRESS

---

bacchanalian   wild with drunkenness

badger   to nag; to annoy

badinage   playful, teasing talk

baffle   to confuse; to bewilder

bagatelle   thing of little value; trifle

bait   (*two meanings*)   to entrap or to seduce (*verb*); a decoy (*noun*)

baleful   harmful; menacing; pernicious

balk   to stop short

balm   something that calms or soothes

balmy   (*two meanings*)   mild and refreshing; mentally unstable (*slang*)

banal   common; ordinary; trite

bandy   to exchange (*as words*)

bane   cause of ruin, harm, or distress

banter   teasing; good-natured joking

barb   a pointed part, as of an arrow or fishhook

barbarous   uncultured; crude

bard   a poet

bark   a boat or sailing vessel

baroque   overdecorated; showy

barrage   heavy attack

barrister   lawyer (*British*)

bask   to lie in or be exposed to warmth

bastion   a strong defense; a fort

bauble   showy but useless thing; trinket

bawdy   indecent; humorously obscene

bayou   marshy body of water

beacon   a light used for warning or guiding

beatitude   state of bliss

bedlam   (*two meanings*)   a madhouse; a noisy uproar

befuddle   to confuse; to perplex

beget   to produce

begrudge   to resent another's success or enjoyment

beguile   to deceive; to charm

behemoth   huge animal

beholden   obligate; indebted

belated   delayed or detained

beleaguer   to encircle (with an army); to annoy

belittle   to put down; to humiliate

belligerent   warlike; quarrelsome

bellow   to yell loudly

benediction   blessing

benefactor   one who helps or supports another

beneficiary   one who receives benefits or profits

benevolent   generous; kindly

benign   harmless; gentle

benignant   kindly; gentle

bequeath   to hand down; to pass on to

berate   to scold severely

bereave   to leave in a sad or lonely state; to deprive by force

berserk   frenzied; violently destructive

beseech   to beg; appeal to

beset   to attack

besiege   to overwhelm; to close in on

besmirch   to make dirty

bestial   savage; brutal

bestow   to give or present

bestride   to mount (a horse)

betrothed   engaged; pledged to marry

bevy   a large group

bewitch   to cast a spell on; to charm; to fascinate

bias   preference; prejudice

bibliophile   lover of books

bibulous   absorbent; fond of alcoholic beverages

bicker   to quarrel

bide   (*one's time*) to wait for a favorable opportunity

biennial   occurring every two years

bigot   a narrow-minded, prejudiced person

bilious   bad-tempered; cross

bilk   to cheat; to swindle

binge   a spree; wild party

biped   two-legged animal

bivouac   temporary shelter

bizarre   weird; strange

blanch   to whiten; to make pale

bland   mild; tasteless; dull

blandishment   flattery

blasé   bored with life; unexcited; indifferent

blasphemy   disrespect for holy places, people, or things; irreverence

blatant   annoyingly conspicuous; offensively noisy and loud

blazon   to display; to proclaim

bleak   unsheltered; gloomy

bleary   blurred; dimmed

blight   destruction; withering; disease

bliss   extreme happiness

blithe   carefree; light-hearted

bludgeon   a short, heavy club

blunt   (*two meanings*) abrupt in speech or manner; having a dull edge

blurt   (*out*) to utter suddenly or indiscreetly

bluster   to speak noisily; to boast

bode   to indicate in advance, as an omen does

bog   (*two meanings*) a swamp (*noun*); to sink or become stuck in (*verb*)

bogus   false; fake

bolster   to prop up; to support

bolt   to dash out suddenly; to discontinue support of

bombastic   using impressive but meaningless language

bon mot   witty remark

bona fide   genuine; in good faith

bondage   slavery

boon   a benefit; a blessing; a favor

boor   a rude or impolite person

booty   stolen money or goods

boreal   northern

borne   carried; put up with

botch   to mess up; to perform clumsily

bountiful   plentiful; abundant

bounty   reward; generosity

bourgeoisie   middle class

bovine   pertaining to cows or cattle

bowdlerize   to censor; to remove offensive passages of a play, novel, etc.

braggart   one who boasts

brandish   to shake or wave a weapon aggressively

brash   offensively bold; rude

bravado   a show of courage; false bravery

brawn   muscular strength

brazen   shameless or impudent

breach   a violation; a gap

breadth   width

brethren   brothers

brevity   briefness

brigand   a robber

brine   salt water

brisk   lively; quick

bristling   showing irritation

broach   to introduce (a subject)

brochure   a pamphlet

bronchial   pertaining to the windpipe

browbeat   to bully; to intimidate

bruit   to spread the news

brunt   shock, force, or impact, as of a blow

brusque   abrupt in manner, blunt; rough

buccaneer   a pirate

bucolic   pertaining to the countryside; rural

buffoon   clown or fool

bugbear   something causing fear

bulbous   swollen; shaped like a bulb

bulwark   a strong defense

bumptious   conceited; arrogant

bungle   to do things clumsily or badly

buoy   (*two meanings*) a floating object (*noun*); to encourage (*verb*)

buoyant   (*two meanings*)   able to float; lighthearted and lively

bureaucracy   system of government through departments

burgeon   to flourish; to grow rapidly

burlesque   a speech or action that treats a serious subject with ridicule

burly   muscular; husky

burnish   to polish

buttress   any prop or support

CABAL–CYNOSURE

cabal   a small, secret group

cache   a hiding place

cacophony   harsh or unpleasant sound

cadaverous   pale; ghastly; corpselike

cadence   rhythm; beat

caesura   pause

cajole   to coax; to persuade

calamitous   causing trouble or misery; disastrous

caliber   degree of worth

calligraphy   fancy handwriting

callous   unyielding; insensitive

callow   young and inexperienced

calumny   a false accusation; slander

camaraderie   loyalty; friendship

canard   a false story, report, or rumor

candor   honesty; openness; frankness

canine   pertaining to dogs

canny   shrewd

canon   rule; law; standard

cant   insincere statements usually made in a singsong tone

cantankerous   bad-tempered; quarrelsome

canter   smooth, easy pace; gallop

canvass   to make a survey

capacious   spacious; roomy

capitulate   to surrender

capricious   erratic; impulsive

captious   hard to please; faultfinding

captivate   to capture; to charm; to fascinate

carapace   shell; hard, protective covering

carcinogenic   causing cancer

cardinal   principal; chief

careen   to swerve; to dip to one side

caricature   an exaggerated portrayal

carnage   slaughter; massacre

carnal   sensual; sexual

carnivorous   flesh-eating

carouse   to engage in a noisy, drunken party

carp   (*two meanings*)   a type of fish (*noun*); to complain (*verb*)

carrion   decaying flesh

carte blanche   freedom to use one's own judgment

cartel   association of business firms

cartographer   mapmaker

cascade   a waterfall

caste   social class

castigate   to punish

casualty   (*two meanings*)   an accident; one who is hurt in an accident

cataclysm   a violent change

catacomb   underground burial place

catalyst   person or thing that speeds up a result

cataract   (*two meanings*)   large waterfall; abnormality of the eye

catastrophe   disaster; calamity

cathartic   cleansing

catholic   universal; wide-ranging

caucus   a private meeting

caustic   sarcastic; severely critical; corrosive

cauterize   to burn

cavalcade   a procession; a sequence of events

cavalier   a haughty and casually indifferent person

caveat   a warning

cavil   to quibble; to argue

cavort   to leap about; to frolic

celerity   speed; swiftness

celestial   heavenly

celibate   unmarried

censure   to criticize sharply

centrifugal   moving away from the center

cerebration   thinking; using one's brain

certitude   sureness; certainty

cessation   a stopping; a discontinuance

chafe   to irritate; to annoy

chaff   worthless matter

chagrin   embarrassment; complete loss of courage

chameleon   a lizard able to change its skin color; a changeable or fickle person

champ   (*verb*) to bite impatiently; to show impatience (*to champ at the bit*)

chaos   complete disorder

charisma   great appeal or attraction

charlatan   a fake; a quack

charnel   cemetery; tomb

chary   (*of*) careful; cautious

chasm   a wide gap

chaste   pure; virtuous

chastise   to punish; to purify

chattel   slave

chauvinism   fanatical devotion to one's country, sex, religion, etc.

cherub   angel; an innocent person

chic   stylish; fashionable

chicanery   trickery; deception

chide   to scold

chimerical   imaginary; fantastic; unreal

chirography   art of handwriting

chivalrous   courteous; courageous; loyal

choleric   easily angered

chronic   long-lasting

churlish   rude; ill-bred

cipher   person or thing of no value; zero

circuitous   roundabout; indirect

circumlocution   roundabout way of speaking

circumscribe   to encircle; to limit or confine

circumspect   cautious; careful

circumvent   to surround or entrap; to go around or bypass

citadel   a fortress

cite   to quote a passage, book, author, etc.; to refer to an example

civility   politeness

clairvoyant   having great insight; keenly perceptive

clamber   to climb with effort or difficulty

clamor   noise

clandestine   secretive; private

clangor   harsh ringing sound

clarify   to make clear

clarion   clear and shrill

claustrophobia   fear of enclosed spaces

cleave   (*two meanings*)   to split something apart; to stick or cling to something

cleft   split; divided

clemency   mercy; leniency

cliché   a trite or worn-out expression

clientele   customers

climax   highest point

clime   climate; region

clique   a small, exclusive group

cloistered   secluded; confined

clout   (*colloquial*) power; influence

cloven   divided; split

coadjutor   assistant; helper

coalesce   to blend; to merge; to fuse

coddle   to treat tenderly

coerce   to force

coffer   a strongbox

cog   a gear tooth; a minor part

cogent   convincing

cogitate   to think; to consider carefully

cognate   related; relevant

cognizant   aware

cognomen   family name; last name

coherent   logically connected; consistent

cohesive   tending to stick

cohort   colleague; associate; partner

coincide   to occur simultaneously

collaborate   to work together; to cooperate

collage   collection of various bits and pieces (*usually artistic*)

collate   to put together in order

collateral   security for payment of a loan

colloquial   informal

colloquy   conversation

collusion   conspiracy; agreement to commit a wrongful act

colossal   huge; enormous

combative   eager to fight; argumentative

combustible   capable of catching fire easily

comely   attractive

commemorative   honoring; remembering

commence   to begin

commendation   praise

commensurate   proportionate

commiserate   to express pity for

commodious   roomy; spacious

communal   shared; pertaining to a group of people

compact   (*two meanings*)   firmly packed (*adjective*); a treaty (*noun*)

compassion   pity; sympathy

compatible   agreeable; harmonious

compel   to force

compendium   brief summary

compensatory   paying back; making up for

complacent   self-satisfied

complement   (*note spelling*) to make whole; to complete

compliant   yielding; submissive

complicity   partnership in a wrongful act

components   ingredients; elements

composure   calmness of mind or manner

compulsory   required

compunction   uneasiness; remorse

compute   to calculate; to estimate

concave   hollow; curved inward

concede   to admit; to grant

concentrate   (*two meanings*) to think deeply; to increase in strength or degree

concentric   having a common center

conception   (*two meanings*) a beginning; original idea or plan

concession   allowance; the act of yielding

conciliate   to soothe the anger of; to win over

concise   brief and to the point

conclave   secret meeting

concoct   to invent; to devise

concomitant   accompanying; attending

concord   agreement; harmony

concourse   a crowd; a wide street

concur   to agree

condescend   to lower oneself to an inferior's level

condign   deserved; suitable

condiment   seasoning; spices

condolence   expression of sorrow

condone   to excuse; to overlook

conducive   tending to or leading to

conduit   pipe or tube through which fluid or electricity passes

confidant   a close, trusted friend

configuration   shape; arrangement

confiscate   to seize by way of penalty

conflagration   a large and destructive fire

confluent   merging; flowing together

conformity   agreement; doing the same as others

confounded   confused; amazed

congeal   to freeze solid; to thicken

congenial   friendly; agreeable

congenital   existing at birth

conglomerate   mass; cluster; corporation

congregate   to gather; to assemble

congruent   in agreement

coniferous   bearing cones (*pertaining to trees*)

conjecture   to guess

conjugal   pertaining to marriage

conjure   to call upon or to command a devil or spirit to practice magic; cast a spell on

connivance   pretend ignorance of another's wrongdoing; conspiracy

connoisseur   an expert

connote   to suggest or imply

connubial   pertaining to marriage

consanguinity   close relationship, usually by blood

consecrate   to make holy

consensus   general agreement, especially of opinion

console   (*two meanings*) a musical panel or unit (*noun*); to comfort (*verb*)

consolidate   to combine; to make or become solid

consonant   in agreement or harmony

consort   (*two meanings*) a husband or wife (*noun*); to associate or join (*verb*)

consternation   sudden confusion; panic

constituents   voters; supporters

constraints   restrictions; limits

constrict   to shrink; to bind

construe   to analyze; to interpret

consummate   to complete (*verb*); perfect (*adjective*)

contagious   likely to spread; infectious

contaminant   substance that pollutes or infects

contemn   to regard with scorn or contempt

contemporary happening in the same time period; current

contemptuous scornful

contentious ready to argue; quarrelsome

contest (*three meanings*) a competitive game (*noun*); to dispute (*verb*); to compete (*verb*)

contiguous nearby; neighboring

contingent possible

contort to twist; to distort

contraband smuggled or stolen goods

contrary opposite

contravene to go against; to oppose

contretemps an embarrassing occurrence

contrite sorrowful; penitent

controversial debatable; questionable

contumacious disobedient; obstinate

contumely rudeness

contusion a bruise

conundrum a riddle

convalesce to recover from an illness

convene to come together; to assemble

conventional ordinary; usual

converge to come together; to meet in a point or line

conversant being familiar with

converse (*two meanings*) to talk to someone (*verb*); the opposite (*noun*)

convex curving outward

conveyance a vehicle

convivial sociable; friendly

convoke to call together

convoluted twisted; coiled

cope (*with*) to deal with; to contend with

copious plentiful; abundant

coquetry flirtation

cordial friendly; courteous

cornucopia horn of plenty; abundance

corollary inference; deduction; consequence

corona crown; bright circle

corporeal pertaining to the body

corpulent fat; fleshy

corroborate to strengthen; to confirm

corrosive eating away, as an acid

corrugated wrinkled; ridged; furrowed

cortege funereal procession; group of followers

cosmic pertaining to the universe; vast

cosmopolitan worldly-wise; universal

coterie close circle of friends

countenance (*two meanings*) the face (*noun*); to permit, tolerate, or approve (*verb*)

countermand to cancel an order

counterpart duplicate; copy

coup a brilliant move; a successful and sudden attack

courier messenger

covenant an agreement; a contract

covert hidden; secretive

covet to desire

cower to tremble in fear

coy shy; modest

cozen to trick

crafty sly; tricky

crass stupid; unrefined

crave to desire strongly

craven cowardly

credence belief; trust

credible believable

credulity readiness to believe; gullibility

creed a religious belief

crescendo gradual increase in intensity or loudness

crestfallen dejected; humbled

crevice an opening; a crack

cringe to shrink back, as in fear

criterion measure of value; standard of judging

crone hag; withered old woman

crony close friend

crotchety grouchy; eccentric

crucial   extremely important; decisive

crucible   a severe test or trial

crux   the essential part

cryptic   mysterious; secretive

crystallize   to settle; to take on a definite form

cubicle   small compartment

cudgel   club; thick stick

cue   a hint; a signal

cuisine   style of cooking

culinary   pertaining to cooking

cull   to select; to pick

culminate   to result in; to reach the highest point

culpable   blameworthy

cumbersome   heavy; hard to handle because of size or weight

cumulative   collected; accumulated

cupidity   greed

curb   to control; to check

curry   to try to win favor by flattery

cursive   running or flowing

cursory   superficial; hasty

curtail   to cut short

cynic   one who is critical; a fault-finder

cynosure   center of attention

DAIS–DYSPHASIA

dais   platform; speaker's stand

dale   valley

dally   to waste time

dank   chilly and wet

dappled   spotted

dastardly   sneaking and cowardly; shameful

daub   to smear; to cover over with paint, etc.

daunt   to discourage

dawdle   to waste time; to idle

de facto   in fact; in reality

deadlock   a standstill; a tie

dearth   a scarcity or lack

debacle   a complete failure; total collapse

debase   to lower in rank; to humiliate

debauch   to corrupt

debilitate   to weaken

debonair   pleasant; courteous; charming

debris   fragments; litter; rubble

debut   first public appearance

decadence   moral deterioration

decant   to pour off (a liquid)

decapitate   to behead

decelerate   to slow down

deciduous   not permanent; passing

decipher   decode; figure out the meaning of

declaim   to speak dramatically

declivity   downward slope

decompose   to decay; to break up into parts

decorum   appropriate social behavior

decoy   a person or thing that entices or lures, as into danger

decrepit   broken down by age or disease

decry   to speak out against

deduce   to reason out; to infer

deem   to think; to believe; to judge

defalcate   to misuse funds; to embezzle

defamatory   damaging another's reputation with false remarks

default   to fail to pay a debt or to perform a task

defection   desertion

defer   to postpone; to put off

deference   respect

defile   to pollute; to corrupt

definitive   comprehensive; complete

deflect   to turn aside; to bend

defoliate   to strip of leaves

defray   to pay the cost of

deft   skillful

defunct   no longer in existence; extinct

degrade   to lower in degree or quality

deify   to idolize; to make god-like

deign   to lower oneself before an inferior

delectable   delicious; very pleasing

delete   to leave out; to cross out

deleterious   harmful

delineate   to describe; to depict

delirium   condition of mental disturbance; wild excitement

delude   to deceive; to mislead

deluge   a flood; a rush

delve   to search; to investigate

demagogue   a popular leader who appeals to the emotions

demean   to degrade; to lower

demeanor   behavior

demented   deranged; insane

demigod   a person who is partly a god and partly human

demise   death; ending

demography   study of population trends

demolish   to tear down

demoralize   to discourage; to cause to lose spirit

demur   to object; to take exception to

demure   shy

denigrate   to ruin the reputation of; to blacken

denizen   occupant; inhabitant; resident

denomination   the name or designation for a class of persons, such as a religious group

denouement   outcome; result

denounce   to publicly condemn

depict   to portray; to represent

depilate   to remove hair from

deplete   to use up gradually (resources, strength, etc.)

deplore   to regret

deploy   to place troops in position

depose   to remove from office

depraved   sinful; immoral

deprecate   to disapprove of

depreciate   to lessen in value

deranged   insane

derelict   (*three meanings*) abandoned (*adjective*); negligent (*adjective*); a vagrant or bum (*noun*)

deride   to ridicule

derision   ridicule

dermatology   study of skin diseases

derogatory   belittling

descry   to discover

desecrate   to damage a holy place

desiccate   to dry up; to wither

desist   to cease or stop

desolate   lonely; deserted

despicable   contemptible; hateful

despise   to scorn; to regard with disgust

despoil   to rob; to plunder

despondent   depressed; dejected

despot   a dictator

destitute   poor; lacking

desuetude   condition of disuse; extinction

desultory   wandering from subject to subject; rambling

détente   a lessening of tension or hostility

deter   to discourage; to hinder

detergent   a cleansing agent

detonate   explode

detoxify   remove the poison from

detract   to take away; to diminish

detriment   harm; damage

devastate   to destroy; to overwhelm

deviate   to turn aside; to digress

devious   sly; underhand

devoid   completely without

devotee   an enthusiastic follower

devout   religious; pious; sincere

dexterity   skill; cleverness

diabolical   devilish; cruel

diadem   crown

dialectic   logical discussion

diaphanous   transparent; very sheer and light

diatribe   bitter criticism

dichotomy   division into two parts

dicker   to bargain; to argue over prices

diction   style of speaking

dictum   a positive statement

didactic   instructive; inclined to lecture others too much

diffident   shy; modest

diffuse   to spread; to scatter

digress   to wander off the subject

dilapidated   broken down; falling apart

dilate   to expand; to become wider

dilatory   slow or late in doing things

dilemma   a troubling situation

dilettante   a dabbler in the fine arts; one who is not an expert

diligent   hard-working; industrious

diminutive   small

dint   powder; force

dipsomaniac   drunkard

dire   dreadful; causing disaster

dirge   a funeral song or hymn

disarray   disorder; confusion

disavow   to disown; to deny; to repudiate

disburse   to pay out

discern   to distinguish; to recognize; to perceive

disciple   a follower

disclaimer   denial; renunciation

disclose   to reveal; to make known

discomfiture   frustration; confusion

disconcert   to upset; to embarrass

disconsolate   without hope

discordant   disagreeing; harsh-sounding

discount   (*two meanings*) reduction (*noun*); to disregard (*verb*)

discountenance   to disapprove of

discourse   conversation; lecture

discredit   to disgrace; to cast doubt on

discreet   showing good judgment; cautious

discrepancy   inconsistency; difference

discrete   separate; not attached

discretion   good judgment

discrimination   (*two meanings*) prejudice; ability to distinguish

discursive   rambling; wandering

disdain   to scorn

disgruntled   unhappy; discontented

dishearten   to discourage; to depress

disheveled   untidy

disinter   to uncover; to dig up

disinterested   impartial; not prejudiced

dismal   gloomy; depressing

dismantle   to take apart

dismember   to cut or pull off limbs

disparage   to belittle; to put down

disparity   inequality; difference

dispassionate   calm; impartial

dispel   to drive away

disperse   to scatter

disputatious   fond of arguing

disreputable   having a bad reputation

dissection   cutting apart; analysis

dissemble   to conceal; to pretend

disseminate   to scatter; to spread

dissension   disagreement; opposition

dissertation   a written essay

dissident   disagreeing

dissimulate   to hide one's feelings

dissipate   to waste; to scatter

dissociate   to break ties with; to part company

dissolute   immoral; unrestrained

dissonant   out of harmony

dissuade   to advise or urge against

distend   to expand; to swell; to stretch out

distort   to twist out of shape

distraught   troubled

dither   (preceded by *in a*) nervously excited or confused

diurnal   daily

divergent   varying; different

divers   several

diverse   different

divest   to deprive

divination   the act of foretelling the future

divulge   to reveal; to make known

docile   obedient; submissive

doddering   shaky; senile

doff   to throw off or away

doggedly   stubbornly

dogmatic   having a definite opinion; authoritative

doldrums   low spirits

dole   to distribute; to give out sparingly

doleful   sorrowful

dolorous   mournful; sad

dolt   a dull, stupid person

domicile   home; residence

donnybrook   rough, rowdy fight

dormant   asleep; inactive

dorsal   pertaining to the back

dossier   a complete group of documents containing detailed information

dotage   feeblemindedness of old age

doughty   courageous; worthy

dour   gloomy

douse   to put out (a fire); to extinguish

dowdy   shabby; untidy

downtrodden   trampled on; suppressed

doyen   senior or eldest member

Draconian   severe; cruel

dregs   leftovers

drivel   childish nonsense; stupid talk

droll   amusing in an odd way

drone   (*three meanings*) a male bee (*noun*); an idle person (*noun*); to talk on and on monotonously (*verb*)

dross   waste matter

drudgery   hard, tiresome work

dual   consisting of two people, items, or parts

dubious   doubtful; questionable

ductile   capable of being molded or shaped

dudgeon   anger, resentment

dulcet   pleasing to the ear

dulcimer   a type of zither

dupe   to trick; to deceive

duplicity   deceit; double-dealing; dishonesty

duress   force

dutiful   obedient

dwindle   to shrink; to become smaller

dynamo   a powerful person

dyspepsia   poor digestion

dysphasia   difficulty in speaking

EARNEST–EXULT

earnest   sincere; serious

earthy   realistic; coarse

ebb   to slowly decrease

ebullient   enthusiastic

eccentric   odd; out of the ordinary

ecclesiastical   pertaining to the church

echelon   rank of authority; level of power

éclat   brilliance; fame

eclectic   selecting; choosing from various sources

eclipse   to overshadow; to outshine

ecology   study of the environment

ecstatic   extremely happy

edifice   structure; building

edify   to improve someone morally; to instruct

educe   to draw or bring out

eerie   weird; mysterious

efface   to erase; to wipe out

effectual   effective; adequate

effeminate   unmanly; womanly; soft and weak

effervescent   bubbly; spirited

effete   worn-out; barren

efficacy   power to produce an effect

effigy   a likeness; an image

efflorescent   blossoming; flowering

effluent   flowing out

effrontery   shameful boldness

effulgent   shining forth brilliantly; radiant

effusion   a pouring out; an uncontrolled display of emotion

egalitarian   pertaining to belief in the equality of all men

ego   a feeling of self-importance

egotism   selfishness; boasting about oneself

egregious   remarkably bad; outrageous

egress   exit (*noun and verb*)

ejaculation   an exclamation

eject   to throw out

elapse   to pass; to slip away

elated   overjoyed

electrify   to thrill

elegy   a sad or mournful poem

elicit   to draw forth; to cause to be revealed

elite   the choice or best of a group of persons

elixir   remedy

ellipsis   the omission in a sentence of a word or words

eloquent   convincing or forceful in speech

elucidate   to make clear

elude   to avoid; to escape notice

elusive   difficult to grasp

elysian   blissful; heavenly

emaciated   abnormally thin

emanate   to come forth; to send forth

emancipate   to set free

embark   (*on*) begin a journey or an endeavor

embellish   to decorate

embezzle   to steal

embroil   to involve in trouble; to complicate

embryonic   undeveloped; in an early stage

emendation   correction

emetic   causing vomiting

eminent   famous; renowned

emissary   one sent on a special mission

emit   to send out; to give forth

emollient   something that soothes or softens

emolument   profit; gain

empathy   understanding another's feelings

empirical   based on experience rather than theory

emulate   to imitate

emulous   jealous; envious

enamored   (*of*) in love with

enclave   a country, or part of a country, surrounded by another country

encomium   an expression of high praise

encompass   to include; to surround

encore   a repeat performance

encroach   (*upon*) to trespass; to intrude

encumbrance   hindrance; obstruction

encyclopedic   filled with knowledge; comprehensive

endearment   an expression of affection

endemic   confined to a particular country or area

energize   to rouse into activity

enervate   to weaken

enfranchise   to give the right to vote

engender   to promote

engrossed   completely absorbed in

engulf   to overwhelm

enhance   to increase in value or beauty; to improve

enigma   a puzzling situation; dilemma

enigmatic   mysterious; puzzling

enlighten   to inform; to reveal truths

enmity   hostility; hatred

ennui   boredom

enormity   an outrageous and immoral act

enrapture   to delight beyond measure

ensconce   to hide; to conceal; to settle comfortably

ensue   to follow; to result from

enthrall   to charm; to captivate

entice   to attract; to tempt

entity   independent being

entomology   study of insects

entourage   a group of personal attendants

entranced   filled with delight or wonder

entreaty   a request; a plea

entrenched   firmly established; dug in

entrepreneur   successful businessman; promoter

enunciate   to pronounce words clearly

environs   surroundings

envisage   to imagine; to form a mental picture

envoy   messenger; agent

eon   extremely long period of time

ephemeral   temporary; short-lived

epic   a long poem about heroic occurrences

epicure   one who seeks pleasure in fine foods

epigram   witty saying

epilogue   closing part of a speech or literary work

epiphany   appearance of a deity (god); revelation

epistle   a letter

epitaph   inscription on a tomb

epithet   a descriptive word or phrase

epitome   a typical example; a summary or condensed account

epoch   particular period of history

equanimity   calmness; evenness of temperament

equestrian   a horseback rider

equilibrium   balance; stability

equine   pertaining to horses

equinox   the time when day and night are of equal length

equipoise   balance

equitable   fair; just

equity   fairness; justice; impartiality

equivocal   doubtful; ambiguous

equivocate   to confuse by speaking in ambiguous terms

eradicate   to erase; to wipe out

ergo   therefore

erode   to wear away

erotic   pertaining to sexual love

err   to make a mistake

errant   wandering (*in search of adventure*); straying from what is right

erratic   irregular; abnormal

erroneous   mistaken; wrong

ersatz   artificial; inferior substitute

erstwhile   formerly; in the past

erudite scholarly; learned

escalate to increase; to grow rapidly; to intensify

escapade a reckless adventure

escarpment steep cliff

eschew to avoid; to keep away from

escrow (preceded by *in*) money deposited with a third person pending fulfillment of a condition

esoteric for a select few; not generally known

espionage spying

espouse to support (*a cause*)

essay (*verb*) to try; to attempt

estival pertaining to summer

estranged separated; alienated

ethereal spiritual; airy

ethnic pertaining to a particular race or culture

etymology the origin and development of words

eugenics science of improving the human race

eulogy praise for a dead person

euphemism substitution of a pleasant expression for an unpleasant one

euphonious having a pleasant sound; harmonious

euphoria a feeling of well-being

euthanasia mercy killing

evanescent temporary; fleeting

evasive not straightforward; tricky

eventuate to result; to happen finally

evict to expel; to throw out

evince to show clearly

evoke to call forth; to produce

evolve to develop gradually

exacerbate to aggravate; to make more violent

exact (*two meanings*) accurate (*adjective*); to demand or to require (*verb*)

exalt to raise in position; to praise

exasperate to irritate; to annoy extremely

excise (*two meanings*) a tax on liquor, tobacco, etc. (*noun*); to cut out or off (*verb*)

excoriate (*two meanings*) to scrape the skin off; to criticize sharply

excruciating unbearably painful

exculpate to free from blame; to vindicate

execrate to curse

exemplary worthy of imitation

exhilaration liveliness; high spirits

exhort to warn

exhume to bring out of the earth; to reveal

exigent urgent; critical

exiguous scanty; small in quantity

exodus a departure; a going out

exonerate to free from guilt or blame

exorbitant excessive; unreasonable

exorcise to drive out an evil spirit

exotic foreign; excitingly strange

expatiate to enlarge upon; to speak or write at length

expatriate a person who is banished from, or leaves, his native country

expectorate to spit out

expedient practical; advantageous

expedite to speed up; to make easy

expendable replaceable

expiate to atone for

explicate explain in detail; make clear

explicit clear; unambiguous; direct

exploit to use for one's own advantage

expound to explain; to interpret

expressly especially; particularly

expunge to erase

expurgate to remove offensive passages; to cleanse

extant still in existence

extemporaneous offhand; done without preparation

extenuating less serious

extinct no longer in existence

extirpate to destroy; to remove completely

extol to praise

extort to obtain by force

extradite	to give up a prisoner to another authority	**extrovert**	an outgoing person
extraneous	unrelated; not essential	**exuberant**	full of enthusiasm
extrapolate	to estimate; to infer	**exude**	to discharge; to ooze
extricate	to set free; to disentangle	**exult**	to rejoice
extrinsic	external; coming from outside		

FABRICATE–FUTILE

---

fabricate (*two meanings*) to construct; to lie

fabulous incredible; imaginative

facade outward appearance

facet aspect

facetious joking; sarcastic

facile easy; effortless

facilitate to make easy

facsimile an exact copy; a duplicate

faction a minority within a larger group

factious causing disagreement

factitious artificial

factotum an employee who can do all kinds of work

faculty power; ability; skill

fallacious misleading; deceptive

fallible capable of error

fallow inactive; unproductive

falter to stumble; to hesitate

fanatic a person with uncontrolled enthusiasm

fanciful unreal; imaginative; unpredictable

fanfare noisy or showy display

farcical absurd; ridiculous

fastidious hard to please

fatal causing death

fatalistic believing that all things in life are inevitable

fathom (*two meanings*) nautical measure of 6 feet in depth (*noun*); to comprehend (*verb*)

fatuous foolish

fauna animals of a certain area

fawn (*two meanings*) a young deer (*noun*); to act slavishly submissive (*verb*)

faze to disturb; to discourage

fealty loyalty; devotion

feasible capable of being accomplished; suitable

feat deed or accomplishment

febrile feverish

fecund fertile; productive

feign to pretend

feint a false show; a pretended blow

feisty quick-tempered or quarrelsome

felicity happiness

feline pertaining to cats

fell (*two meanings*) to knock down (*verb*); fierce or cruel (*adjective*)

felon a criminal

felonious treacherous; base; villainous

ferment a state of agitation or excitement

ferret (*two meanings*) a small animal of the weasel family (*noun*); to search or drive out (*verb*)

fervent eager; earnest

fervid very emotional

fester to rot

festive joyous; merry

fete to honor; to entertain

fetid foul-smelling

fetish object with magical power; object that receives respect or devotion

fetter to confine; to put into chains

fiasco a total disaster

fiat an official order

fickle changeable in affections; unfaithful

fictitious false; not genuine

fidelity   faithfulness

figment   something imagined

filch   to steal

filial   like a son or daughter

finale   the climax; end

finesse   diplomacy; tact

finicky   extremely particular; fussy

finite   limited; measurable

firebrand   one who stirs up a revolution

firmament   sky; heavens

fiscal   pertaining to finances

fissure   opening; groove; split

fitful   irregular; occurring in spurts

flabbergasted   astonished; made speechless

flaccid   flabby

flag   (*two meanings*)   a banner (*noun*); to droop or to slow down (*verb*)

flaggelate   to whip

flagrant   scandalous; shocking

flail   to strike freely and wildly

flair   a knack; a natural talent

flamboyant   showy; conspicuous

flaunt   to boast; to show off

flay   (*two meanings*)   to strip the skin off; to criticize sharply

fledgling   a young, inexperienced person

fleece   (*two meanings*)   wool of a lamb (*noun*); to swindle (*verb*)

flexible   bendable

flinch   to draw back; to cringe

flippant   treating serious matters lightly

flora   plant life of a certain area

florid   flowery; ornate

flotilla   small fleet of ships

flotsam   floating cargo or wreckage

flout   to mock; to ridicule

fluctuate   to move back and forth; to vary

fluent   flowing; able to speak and/or write easily and clearly

fluster   to upset; to confuse

fluvial   pertaining to a river

flux   state of continual change

foible   a weakness; minor fault

foil   (*two meanings*)   to prevent the success of a plan (*verb*); a person who, by contrast, makes another person seem better (*noun*)

foist   (*on*) to pass off merchandise which is inferior

folderol   nonsense

folly   a foolish action

foment   to stir up; to instigate

foolhardy   foolish; reckless

fop   an excessively vain man

foray   a sudden attack

forbearance   patience; restraint

forebear   ancestor

foreboding   a warning; an omen

foregone   long past

forensic   pertaining to a formal discussion or debate

forerunner   ancestor; predecessor

foreshadow   to hint

forestall   to prevent by action in advance; to anticipate

forfeit   to give up

forgo   to do without; to give up

formidable   dreadful; discouraging

forte   strong point

forthright   direct; frank

fortitude   strength; courage

fortnight   two weeks; fourteen days

fortuitous   lucky; by chance

foster   to nourish; to encourage

fracas   a loud quarrel

fractious   irritable; quarrelsome; stubborn

fracture   to break or to crack

frailty   a weakness; a defect

franchise   special right or privilege

fraternal   brotherly

fraudulent   dishonest; cheating

fraught   (*with*) filled

fray   (*two meanings*) a noisy quarrel (*noun*); to unravel or to come apart (*verb*)

frenetic   frantic; wild

frenzy   madness; fury

freshet   a fresh water stream

fretful   worried; irritated

friction   (*two meanings*) a rubbing together (*noun*); conflict or disagreement (*noun*)

frigid   extremely cold

frivolous   trivial; silly

frowzy   dirty; unkempt

frugal   economical; thrifty

fruition   fulfillment; realization

fruitless   barren; yielding no results

frustrate   to prevent; to discourage

fugacious   pertaining to the passing of time

fulminate   to explode; to denounce

fulsome   disgusting; sickening; repulsive

furor   rage; frenzy; fury

furtive   stealthy; secretive

fusion   a union; merging

futile   useless

GADFLY–GYRATE

---

gadfly   a person who annoys others

gaff   a hook

gainsay   to deny; to contradict

gait   manner of walking

gala   festive

galaxy   a group of stars; any large and brilliant assemblage of persons

gall   bitterness

gallant   polite; noble

galvanize   to stimulate; to startle into sudden activity

gambit   strategy; an opening one uses to advantage

gambol   to frolic; to romp about

gamut   the whole range or extent

gape   to stare with open mouth

garble   to distort

gargantuan   gigantic; huge

garish   tastelessly gaudy

garland   a wreath of flowers

garner   to gather; to acquire

garnish   to decorate; to trim

garrulous   talkative

gauche   awkward; tactless

gaudy   flashy; showy

gaunt   thin and bony; bleak and barren

gazebo   an open structure with an enjoyable view

gazette   newspaper

gelid   very cold; frozen

genealogy   family history

generate   to produce; to originate

generic   general; not specific; pertaining to a class

genesis   origin; beginning

genial   warm; friendly

genocide   killing of a race of people

genre   an art form or class

genteel   polite; refined

gentry   upper class people

genuflect   to kneel; to bend the knee

germane   relevant; fitting

gerontology   the study of older people and their problems

gesticulation   lively or excited gesture

ghastly   horrible; dreadful

ghoul   grave robber; ogre

gibberish   silly, unintelligible talk

gibbet   gallows from which criminals are hanged

give   to scoff; to ridicule

giddy   dizzy; flighty; whirling

gild   to cover with gold

gingerly   carefully; cautiously

gird   to encircle

gist   main point; essence

glazed   glassy; smooth; shiny

glean   to gather patiently and with great effort

glee   joy

glib   fluent; smooth

glissade   a skillful glide over snow or ice in descending a mountain

glitch   a malfunction; an error

gloaming   twilight; dusk

gloat   to look at or think about with great satisfaction

glower   to frown; to stare angrily at

glum   sad; gloomy

glutinous   gluey; sticky

glutton   one who eats or drinks too much

gnarled   knotty; twisted; roughened

gnome   a legendary dwarf-like creature

goad   to encourage; to spur on

gorge   (*two meanings*) a deep valley with steep sides (*noun*); to eat or to swallow greedily (*verb*)

gory   bloody

gossamer   light; flimsy; fine

Gothic   medieval; mysterious

gouge   (*two meanings*) to dig out; to swindle or overcharge

gourmand   a glutton; a person who eats excessively

gourmet   an expert of fine food and drink

gradient   a slope; a ramp

granary   a storehouse for grain

grandiloquent   pretentious; speaking in a pompous style

grandiose   impressive; showy

graphic   giving a clear and effective picture

grapple   to grip and hold; to struggle

grate   (*two meanings*) to grind to shreds; to irritate

gratify   to please; to satisfy

gratis   without payment; free

gratuitous   free of cost; unnecessary

grave   serious; somber

gregarious   sociable; friendly

grievous   causing grief or sorrow; distressing

grim   fierce; stern

grimace   a distorted face; an expression of disapproval

grime   dirt

gripe   complaint

grisly   horrible; gruesome; ghastly

grit   stubborn courage

gross   extreme; vulgar

grotesque   absurd; distorted

grotto   a cave

grovel   to lower oneself to please another

grudging   resentful; reluctant

grueling   exhausting

gruff   rough or harsh in manner

guile   deceit; trickery

guileless   sincere

guise   a false appearance

gull   to trick; to deceive

gullible   easily deceived; too trusting

gumption   courage and initiative

gustatory   pertaining to the sense of taste

gusto   hearty enjoyment

gusty   windy; stormy

guttural   pertaining to the throat

gyrate   to rotate; to spin

HABITAT–HYPOTHESIS

habitat   dwelling

hackneyed   trite; commonplace; overused

haggard   worn out from sleeplessness, grief, etc.

haggle   to bargain over a price

halcyon   calm

hale   healthy

hallmark   a symbol of high quality

hallow   to make holy; to bless

hallucination   illusion; a false notion

hamper   to hinder; to keep someone from acting freely

haphazard   dependent upon mere chance

hapless   unlucky

harangue   long speech

harass   to annoy; to bother

harbinger   an omen or sign

harbor   (*two meanings*) a body of water providing ships with protection from winds, waves, etc. (*noun*); to conceal or hide (*verb*)

hardy   courageous; sturdy

harlequin   a clown

harpy   a greedy, grasping person; a scolding, nagging, bad-tempered woman

harrowing   upsetting; distressing

harry   to worry; to torment

hart   a male deer

haughty   snobbish; arrogant

haunt   to appear as a spirit or ghost; to visit frequently; to disturb or distress

haven   a safe place

havoc   great destruction

hazard   risk; danger

headlong   recklessly; impulsively

headstrong   stubborn; willful

hearsay   rumor; gossip

hearth   fireplace

hector   to bully

hedonist   a pleasure-seeker

heedless   careless; unmindful

hefty   large and powerful; heavy

hegemony   leadership or strong influence

hegira   flight; escape

heinous   hateful; abominable

hemophilia   blood defect

herald   to announce; to usher in

herbivorous   feeding on vegetation

herculean   tremendous in size, strength, or difficulty

heresy   rejection of a religious belief

hermetic   airtight; tightly sealed

heterodox   departing from acceptable beliefs

heterogeneous   different; unlike; dissimilar

heyday   period of success

hiatus   pause or gap

hibernate   to be inactive, especially during the winter

hierarchy   a ranking, one above the other

hilarity   gaiety; joy

hircine   goat-like

hirsute   hairy; bearded

histrionic   theatrical; overly dramatic

hoard   to store away; to accumulate

hoary   white with age or frost

hoax   a practical joke

hobgoblin   a frightening apparition; something that causes fear

hodgepodge   mixture

hogwash   meaningless or insincere talk

hoi polloi   common people; the masses

holocaust   complete destruction

homage   respect; honor

homily   a sermon

homogeneous   composed of parts all of the same kind

homophonic   sounding alike

hone   to sharpen

hoodwink   to deceive

hoot   to shout in disapproval

horde   a crowd of people

horticulture   the science of gardening

hospice   shelter

hovel   a dirty, wretched living place

hover   to keep lingering about; to wait near at hand

hubris   excessive pride or self-confidence

hue   a color; a shade

humane   kind; compassionate

humbug   trick; hoax

humdrum   monotonous; routine

humid   moist

humility   lowliness; meekness

humus   black soil for fertilizing

hurtle   to dash; speed; run

husbandry   the science of raising crops; careful management

hybrid   mixed; assorted

hydrophobia   fear of water; rabies

hymeneal   pertaining to marriage

hyperbole   extreme exaggeration

hypercritical   overcritical; faultfinding

hypochondriac   a person with imaginary ailments

hypocrite   one who pretends to be someone or something he is not

hypothesis   an assumption; a theory

ICHTHYOLOGY–ITINERANT

---

ichthyology   study of fish

icon   a statue or idol

iconoclast   a rebel; one who breaks with tradition

idealist   one with very high standards

idiosyncrasy   a peculiar personality trait

idolatry   excessive or blind adoration; worship of idols

idyllic   charmingly simple or poetic

igneous   pertaining to fire

ignoble   dishonorable

ignominious   shameful; disgraceful

ignoramus   a stupid person

ilk   type; sort; kind

illicit   unlawful; illegal

illiterate   uneducated

illumine   to brighten; to inspire

illusion   fake impression

illustrious   distinguished; bright

imbibe   to drink; to absorb

imbroglio   a difficult or confusing situation

imbue   to fill completely; to penetrate

immaculate   spotless; pure

imminent   likely to happen; threatening

immolate   to kill someone as a sacrificial victim, usually by fire

immortal   not subject to death

immunity   freedom from disease

immutable   unchangeable

impair   to weaken; to cause to become worse

impale   to pierce with a sharp stake through the body

impalpable   vague; not understandable

impartial   without prejudice

impasse   a dead-end; a problem without a solution

impeach   to accuse

impeccable   flawless; without fault

impecunious   without money; penniless

impede   to hinder; to obstruct

impediment   a barrier; an obstruction

impel   push into motion; urge

impending   likely to happen soon

imperative   extremely necessary

imperious   domineering; haughty

impermeable   not permitting passage

impertinent   rude; disrespectful

imperturbable   steady; calm

impervious   not capable of being affected; hardened

impetuous   acting without thought; impulsive

impetus   a stimulus; a moving force

impinge   to strike; to collide; to encroach

impious   disrespectful toward God

implacable   unbending; inflexible; merciless

implausible   unbelievable

implement   (*two meanings*)   a tool (*noun*); to carry out or put into practice (*verb*)

implication   an indirect indication; a statement that suggests something

implicit   suggested, but not plainly expressed

imply   to suggest

import   (*two meanings*)   significance; meaning (*noun*); to bring in from a foreign country (*verb*)

importune   to persistently ask; to beg

impostor   a person who goes about under an assumed name or character

impotent   powerless; lacking strength

imprecation   a curse

impregnable   unconquerable

impromptu   without preparation; offhand

impropriety   pertaining to something that is not proper or suitable

improvident   wasteful

improvise   to do without preparation

impudent   disrespectful; shameless

impugn   to attack a person with words; to challenge a person in regard to motives

impunity   freedom from punishment

impute   to accuse a person of some wrongdoing; to attribute a fault or a crime to a person

inadvertent   unintentional

inalienable   not able to be transferred to another

inane   silly; meaningless

inanimate   lifeless; dull; dead

inarticulate   pertaining to speech that is not clear or understandable

incandescent   very bright; shining

incapacitated   disabled; unable to function

incarcerate   to imprison

incarnadine   blood-red; flesh-colored

incarnate   in human form

incendiary   causing fire; stirring up trouble

incense   to inflame; to enrage

incentive   something that incites to action

inception   beginning; start

incessant   continuous; without pause

inchoate   at an early stage; just beginning

incipient   beginning to exist or appear

incisive   sharp; keen

incite   to urge to action; to stir up

inclement   (*usually refers to weather*) harsh; unfavorable; severe

incognito   disguised

incoherent   rambling; not logically connected

incongruous   unsuited; inappropriate

inconsequential   unimportant

incontrovertible   certain; undeniable

incorrigible   bad beyond correction or reform

incredulous   skeptical; disbelieving

increment   an increase; a gain

incriminate   to charge with a crime; to connect or relate to a wrongdoing

incubus   nightmare

inculcate   (*in* or *upon*) to teach earnestly; to influence someone to accept an idea

incumbent   (*two meanings*)   resting or lying down (*adjective*); one who holds a political office (*noun*)

incur   to bring upon oneself; to run into some undesirable consequence

incursion   a raid; an invasion

indefatigable   incapable of being tired out

indelible   incapable of being erased

indemnify   to insure; to repay

indicative   signifying; implying

indict   to charge with a crime; to accuse of a wrong-doing

indigenous   native to a particular area; inborn

indigent   extremely poor

indignant   angry as a result of unjust treatment

indisputable   unquestionable; without doubt

indissoluble   permanent

indoctrinate   to teach someone principles or beliefs

indolent   lazy

indomitable   unconquerable; unyielding

indubitable   unquestionable; certain

induce   to cause; to bring about

indulgence   gentle treatment; tolerance

inebriated   drunk

ineffable   not able to be described; unspeakable

ineluctable   inevitable; inescapable

inept   unfit; bungling; inefficient

inert   without power to move; inactive

inevitable   unavoidable; sure to happen

inexorable   unyielding

infallible   certain; without mistakes

infamous   having an extremely bad reputation; detestable

infantile   childish; immature

infectious   passing on a disease with germs; likely to spread; contagious

infer   to conclude; to derive by reasoning

infernal   hellish; fiendish; diabolical

infidel   unbeliever

infinitesimal   exceedingly small; minute (pronounced *my-newt*)

infirmity   weakness; feebleness

inflated   puffed up; swollen

influx   a flowing in

infraction   the breaking of a law or rule

infringe   (*on* or *upon*) to break a law; to violate; to trespass

ingenious   clever

ingenuous   simple; innocent; naive

ingrate   ungrateful person

ingratiate   (*oneself*) to work one's way into another's favor

inherent   inborn

inhibition   restraint; reserve

inimical   harmful; unfriendly

inimitable   not able to be imitated or equaled

iniquity   wickedness

initiate   to begin

injunction   a command; an order

inkling   a hint

innate   inborn; existing from birth

innocuous   harmless

innovate   to introduce a new idea

innuendo   indirect remark; hint

inordinate   unusual; excessive

insatiable   unable to be satisfied

inscrutable   mysterious; difficult to understand

insidious   treacherous

insightful   having a penetrating understanding of things; mentally alert and sharp

insinuate   to hint; to suggest

insipid   tasteless; dull

insolent   boldly disrespectful

insolvent   bankrupt; unable to pay creditors

insomnia   sleeplessness

insouciant   carefree; happy-go-lucky

instigate   to provoke; to stir up

insubordinate   disobedient

insular   pertaining to an island; detached; isolated

insuperable   unconquerable

insurgence   rebellion; action against authority

insurrection   uprising; rebellion

intact   entire; left whole; sound

integral   essential; whole

integrate   unify; to bring together into a whole

integrity   honesty; sincerity

intellectual   intelligent; having mental capacity to a high degree

intelligentsia   highly educated, cultured people

inter   to bury

interdict   to prohibit; to ban

interim   meantime; period of time between

interlocutor   one who takes part in a conversion

interloper   an intruder

interlude   a period of time between two events

interminable   endless

intermittent   starting and stopping; periodic

interpolate   to insert between; to estimate

interpose   to place between

interregnum   pause; interval; any period during which a nation is without a permanent ruler

interrogate   to question

interstellar   between or among stars

intervene   to come between

intimate   (*two meanings*)   private or personal (*adjective*); to imply (*verb*)

intimidate   make afraid; threaten

intolerant   bigoted; narrow-minded

intractable   hard to manage

intransigent   stubborn; refusing to give in

intrepid   fearless; courageous

intricate   complex; hard to understand

intrinsic   essential; pertaining to a necessary part of something

introspective   looking into oneself

introvert   a person who is concerned with his own thoughts or feelings

intuitive   insightful; knowing by a hidden sense

inundate   to fill to overflowing; to flood

inured   (*to*) accustomed to

invalidate   deprive of legal value; to make null and void

invariably   constantly; uniformly; without changing

invective   strong verbal abuse

inveigh   (*against*) to make bitter verbal attack

inveigle   trick; lure; deceive

invert   to turn inside out or upside down

inveterate   firmly established; deep-rooted

invidious   causing resentment; offensive

invigorate   to fill with energy

invincible   not able to be defeated; unconquerable

invoke   to call upon

invulnerable   not able to be hurt; immune to attack

iota   a small quantity

irascible   easily angered

ire   anger; wrath

iridescent   displaying a wide range of colors like those of the rainbow

irksome   annoying; bothersome

ironic   contrary to what was expected

irrational   senseless; unreasonable

irreconcilable   unable to agree

irredeemable   hopeless; unable to be brought back

irremediable   unable to be corrected or cured

irreparable   beyond repair

irrepressible   unable to be controlled or restrained

irresolute   indecisive; doubtful; undecided

irreverent   disrespectful

irrevocable   final; unchangeable

itinerant   traveling from place to place

JADED–KNUCKLE

jaded   ired; worn out; dulled

jargon   vocabulary peculiar to a particular trade or group of people; meaningless talk; gibberish

jaundiced   (*two meanings*) pertaining to a yellowed skin; prejudiced

jaunt   short trip; excursion

jaunty   carefree; confident

jeer   to sneer; to mock

jeopardy   danger

jest   to joke; to make light of

jetsam   goods cast overboard to lighten a ship

jettison   to throw goods overboard

jilt   to reject; to cast off

jingoism   extreme patriotism

jinx   to bring bad luck to

jocose   joking; humorous

jocular   humorous

jostle   to bump; to push

jovial   jolly; good-natured

jubilation   celebration; rejoicing

judicious   wise; showing sound judgment

juggernaut   a terrible destructive force

jugular   pertaining to the throat or neck

juncture   a point of time; a crisis

junket   a pleasure trip; an excursion

junta   a small group ruling a country

jurisprudence   science of law

jut   to stick out; to project

juxtapose   to place side by side

kaleidoscopic   constantly changing

ken   range of knowledge

kindle   to set on fire; to excite

kindred   relative; family, tribe, or race

kinetic   pertaining to motion

kismet   destiny; fate

kleptomania   a compulsion to steal

knave   a tricky, deceitful person

knead   to work dough, clay, etc. into a uniform mixture

knell   the sound made by a bell rung slowly for a death or funeral

knoll   a small rounded hill

knuckle   (*under*) to yield; (*down*) to apply oneself vigorously

LABYRINTHINE–LUXURIANT

labyrinthine   complicated; intricate

lacerate   to tear (*flesh*) roughly; to mangle

lachrymose   tearful

lackadaisical   uninterested; listless

lackey   slavish follower

lackluster   lacking brilliance or liveliness; dull or vapid

laconic   using few words; concise

lactic   pertaining to milk

laden   burdened; loaded

laggard   a slow person; one who falls behind

laity   religious worshipers who are not clergy

lambent   softly bright or radiant; running or moving lightly over a surface

lament   to mourn

laminated   covered with thin sheets, often plastic

lampoon   a sharp, often harmful satire

languid   sluggish; drooping from weakness

languish   to become weak or feeble

lank   long and slender

lapidary   a dealer in precious stones

larceny   theft

largess   gifts that have been given generously

lascivious   lustful or lewd; inciting sexual desire

lassitude   a feeling of weakness and weariness

latent   present, but hidden

lateral   to the side; sideways

latitude   freedom; margin

laudable   praiseworthy

laureate   worthy of praise or honor

lave   to wash or bathe

lavish   very generous; extravagant

lax   careless or negligent

leeway   room for freedom of action; margin

legerdemain   sleight of hand; deception

lenient   mild; lax; permissive

leonine   lion-like; fierce; authoritative

lesion   an injury; a wound

lethal   deadly; fatal

lethargic   dull; slow-moving; sluggish

leviathan   anything vast or huge; a sea monster

levity   lightness of body or spirit; lack of seriousness

levy   to impose and collect taxes

lewd   pertaining to lust or sexual desire

lexicon   dictionary

liaison   a bond; a connection; an illicit relationship between a man and a woman

libation   a drink; a beverage

libel   a false statement in written form

liberal   giving freely; not strict

libertine   one who leads an immoral life

libretto   the words of an opera

licentious   lawless; immoral; lewd

liege   lord; master

lieu   (*in lieu of*) in place of; instead of

lilliputian   tiny; narrow-minded

limber   easily bent; flexible

limpid   clear, transparent

lineage   ancestry; descent

lineaments   facial features

linguistic   pertaining to language

lionize   to treat as a celebrity

liquidate   (*two meanings*)   to get rid of by killing; to wind up the affairs of a business

lissome   moving gracefully; agile or active

listless   feeling no interest in anything; indifferent

literal   exact; precise; word for word

lithe   graceful; flexible

litigation   lawsuit

livid   darkened or discolored; pale from anger or embarrassment

loath   reluctant; unwilling

loathe   to hate; to feel disgust for

locus   place

lode   a rich source of supply such as a mineral deposit

lofty   very high; formal; proud

logistics   military operations dealing with the supply and maintenance of equipment

loiter   to linger; to hang around

loll   to lean or lounge about; to droop

longevity   a long life

lope   to move along with a swinging walk

loquacious   talkative

lot   fate

lout   an awkward, stupid person

lowly   humble; ordinary

lucent   giving off light; shining

lucid   clear; easy to understand; rational or sane

lucrative   profitable; producing wealth or riches

ludicrous   ridiculous

lugubrious   sad; mournful

lull   to soothe or calm

luminous   bright

lunacy   insanity; madness

lunar   pertaining to the moon

lupine   wolflike; fierce

lurch	to move suddenly forward	**lush**	abundant; rich
lurid	shocking; glowing; sensational	**lustrous**	shining; bright
lurk	to lie concealed in waiting; to stay hidden	**luxuriant**	rich; extravagant

MACABRE–MYTHICAL

macabre   horrible; gruesome

Machiavellian   deceitful; tricky

machination   evil design

macroscopic   visible to the naked eye

maelstrom   whirlpool

magnanimous   generous

magnate   important person in any field

magnitude   size; extent

maim   to cripple; to deprive of the use of some part of the body

maladroit   clumsy; unskillful; awkward

malady   disease; illness

malaise   discomfort; uneasiness

malapropism   word humorously misused

malcontent   one who is dissatisfied

malediction   curse

malefactor   wrong-doer; villain

malevolent   showing ill will or hatred; very dangerous; harmful

malfeasance   wrongdoing

malicious   spiteful; vengeful

malign   to speak badly of

malignant   evil; deadly

malingerer   one who pretends to be sick to avoid work

malleable   capable of being changed; adaptable

malodorous   bad-smelling; stinking

mammoth   huge; enormous

manacle   handcuff; restraint

mandarin   influential person

mandate   an order; a command

mandatory   required; obligatory

mangle   to cut, slash, or crush so as to disfigure

mangy   shabby; filthy

manifest   evident; obvious

manifold   many; varied

manipulate   (*two meanings*) to handle or manage with skill; to influence a person in a bad way

manumit   to set free

maraud   to raid; to plunder

marital   pertaining to marriage

maritime   pertaining to the sea

marquee   a rooflike shelter, such as glass, projecting above an outer door

martial   warlike

martinet   a strict disciplinarian

martyr   one who suffers for a cause

marvel   to be amazed; to wonder

masochist   one who enjoys his own pain and suffering

massive   huge; bulky

masticate   to chew

maternal   motherly

matriarchy   a social organization in which the mother is the head of the family

matrix   a place of origin

maudlin   excessively sentimental

maul   to injure; to handle roughly

mausoleum   large tomb for many bodies

maverick   a rebel; a nonconformist

mawkish   sickeningly sweet; overly sentimental

maxim   a proverb or saying

meager   inadequate; of poor quality

mean   (*three meanings*) nasty or offensive (*adjective*); inferior or low (*adjective*); an average (*noun*)

meander   to wander aimlessly

meddlesome   interfering; curious

mediate   to settle a dispute; to act as a go-between

mediocre   ordinary; average; neither good nor bad

meditate   to think deeply; to ponder

medley   a mixture; a musical selection combining parts from various sources

megalomania   false impression of one's own greatness; tendency to exaggerate

melancholy   sad; depressed

melee   noisy fight

mellifluous   smoothly flowing; sweet-sounding

melodramatic   overly emotional

memento   remembrance; a souvenir

menace   a threat; a danger

ménage   household; domestic establishment

menagerie   collection of wide or strange animals

mendacious   lying; false

mendicant   a beggar

menial   low; degrading

mentor   adviser

mercantile   pertaining to merchants; commercial

mercenary   motivated only by a desire for money

mercurial   changeable; fickle; erratic

meretricious   gaudy; showy; attractive in a cheap, flashy way

mesa   a flat-topped elevation of land with steep rock walls

mesmerize   to hypnotize

metamorphosis   a change; a transformation

metaphor   comparison (without *like* or *as*)

metaphysics   pertaining to beyond what is natural

mete   (*out*) to distribute in portions

meteoric   momentarily dazzling; swift

meteorology   study of weather and climate

meticulous   excessively careful; finicky

metropolis   large city

mettle   courage; spirit

miasma   pollution; poisonous environment

microcosm   a miniature world

mien   manner; bearing

migratory   wandering; moving from place to place

milieu   environment; setting

militant   ready and willing to fight

millennium   a thousand years

mimic   to imitate

minion   a devoted follower; a highly regarded person

minuscule   very small

minute   (*two meanings*) sixtieth part of an hour (pronounced *min-ut*); very small and insignificant (pronounced *my-newt*)

minutiae   insignificant details; trivia

mirage   an apparition or illusion

mire   (*two meanings*) wet, swampy ground (*noun*); to involve in difficulties (*verb*)

mirth   joy; amusement; laughter

misanthrope   hater of mankind

misapprehension   a misunderstanding

miscegenation   mixture of races, especially through marriage

mischance   unlucky accident; bad luck

misconstrue   misinterpret; misjudge

miscreant   a vicious person; a villain

misdemeanor   a criminal offense less serious than a felony

misgiving   doubt; suspicion

misnomer   an error in listing the name of a person

misogamy   hatred of marriage

misogynist   woman-hater

missive   letter

mitigate   to make less severe; to become milder

mnemonic   pertaining to memory

mobile   movable; flexible

mock   to ridicule; to insult; to lower in esteem

modicum   a small amount

modish   fashionable; stylish

modulate   to soften; to tone down

mogul   powerful person

molest   to disturb; to bother

mollify   to pacify; to calm; to appease

molt   to shed, such as feathers and skin

molten   melted

momentous   very important

monarchy   government by one ruler

monastic   pertaining to a monk; self-denying

monetary   pertaining to money

monitor   one who watches or warns

monograph   a paper, book, etc. written about a single subject

monolithic   unyielding; unified

monologue   long speech by one person

monotheism   belief in one god

monumental   great; important

moot   doubtful; debatable

moratorium   delay; postponement

morbid   depressing; gruesome

mordant   sarcastic; biting

mores   customs; traditions; morals

moribund   dying

morose   gloomy; ill-humored

mortal   destined to die; causing death

mortify   to embarrass; to humiliate

motif   theme; central idea

motley   diverse; assorted; having different colors

mottled   spotted; blotched; streaked

mountebank   a phony; a fraud; a charlatan

muddle   to confuse; to mix up

mulct   to punish with a fine; to obtain money by extortion

mull   (*over*) to study or think about

multifarious   varied; having many parts

mundane   worldly

munificent   generous

murky   dark; unclear; gloomy

muse   to think deeply

muster   to gather together

musty   stale; moldy

mute   silent

mutilate   to disfigure; to cripple

mutinous   rebellious

muzzle   to restrain; to gag

myopic   near-sighted; having a limited point of view

myriad   infinitely vast in number

myrmidon   an unquestioning follower

mythical   imaginary; fictitious

NABOB–NUTRIMENT

---

nabob   a very wealthy or powerful person

nadir   lowest point

naive   simple; unsophisticated

narcissistic   conceited; vain

nascent   coming into being; being born

natation   the act or art of swimming

nativity   birth

naught   nothing

nautical   pertaining to ships, sailors, navigation

nebulous   hazy; vague; uncertain

necromancy   magic, especially that practiced by a witch

nefarious   wicked

negate   to deny; to make ineffective

negligent   careless

nemesis   something that a person cannot conquer or achieve

neologism   new use of a word

neophyte   a beginner; a novice

nepotism   favoritism shown toward relatives

nether   lower; under

nettle   to irritate; to annoy

neutralize   to make ineffective; to counteract

nexus   connection, tie, or link among the units of a group

nicety   delicacy; subtlety

niche   recess or hollow in a wall

niggardly   stingy; miserly

niggle   to spend excessive time on unimportant details

nihilism   total rejection of established laws

nimble   quick and light in motion

nirvana   place of great peace or happiness

nocturnal   pertaining to night

nodule   a small, rounded mass or lump

noisome   foul-smelling; harmful or injurious

nomadic   wandering; homeless

nomenclature   a set of names or terms

nominal   in name only; not in fact

non sequitur   something that does not logically follow

nonage   a period of immaturity

nonchalant   unconcerned; casual

noncommittal   having no definite point of view

nonentity   person or thing of little importance

nonpareil   unequaled; unrivaled

nonplus   to confuse; to perplex

nostalgia   homesickness; longing for the past

nostrum   quack medicine; supposed cure-all

notorious   having a bad reputation; infamous

novice   a beginner

noxious   harmful

nuance   delicate variation in meaning, tone, color, etc.

nub   a lump or small piece

nubile   suitable for marriage, in regard to age and physical development

nugatory   worthless; invalid

nullify   to make useless or ineffective

numismatist   coin collector

nuptial   pertaining to marriage

nurture   to feed; to sustain

nutriment   food; nourishment

OAF–OVOID

---

oaf   a dunce or blockhead

oasis   a place which offers a pleasant relief

obdurate   stubborn; hard-hearted

obeisance   a bow or similar gesture expressing deep respect

obese   very fat

obfuscate   to confuse; to bewilder; to perplex

oblation   an offering for religious or charitable purposes

obligatory   required; mandatory

oblique   slanted; indirect

obliterate   to erase; to do away with

oblivious   forgetful; unmindful

obloquy   strong disapproval; bad reputation resulting from public criticism

obnoxious   objectionable; offensive

obscurant   a person who tries to prevent the spread of knowledge

obscure   dim; not clear; not easily understood

obsequious   excessively submissive; overly attentive

obsequy   a funeral rite or ceremony

obsess   to control the thoughts or feelings of a person

obsolescent   going out of use; becoming extinct

obstinate   stubborn

obstreperous   boisterous; unruly

obtrude   to push something toward or upon a person

obtuse   slow to comprehend

obviate   to prevent

occidental   western; opposite of oriental

occlude   to close; to shut; to block out

occult   hidden; secret; mysterious

ocular   pertaining to sight

odious   disgusting; hateful

odoriferous   giving off a pleasant smell

odyssey   a long journey

offal   garbage; waste parts

officious   meddling; interfering

ogle   to look at with desire

ogre   monster; hideous being

olfactory   pertaining to smell

oligarchy   government in which power is in the hands of only a few individuals

Olympian   majestic

omen   an event which indicates the future

ominous   threatening; indicating evil or harm

omnifarious   of all kinds

omnipotent   all-powerful

omniscient   all-knowing

omnivorous   eating any kind of food; absorbing everything

onerous   burdensome; heavy

onslaught   a furious attack

onus   a burden; a responsibility

opaque   not transparent; not letting light pass through

opiate   narcotic; causing sleep or relief

opportunist   one who takes advantage of a situation

oppress   to rule harshly; tyrannize

opprobrious   shameful; disgraceful

opt   (*for*) to choose

optimist   one who sees the good side of things

optimum   the best; most favorable

opulent   rich; luxurious

oracular   mysterious; predicting

oration   a speech delivered on a special occasion

orbit   a curved path, such as a planet takes around the sun

ordain   to order; to establish; to arrange

ordeal   difficult or painful experience; a primitive form of trial

ordinance   law; regulation

organic   fundamental; essential

orient   (*two meanings*) an area of the Far East, such as Asia (*noun*); to adjust or adapt to (*verb*)

orifice   mouth; opening

ornate   showy; highly decorated

ornithology   study of birds

orthodox   accepting the usual or traditional beliefs

orthography   correct spelling

oscillate   to swing or move back and forth, like a pendulum

ossify   to change into bone; to become rigid

ostensible   apparent; conspicuous

ostentatious   showing off; boastful

ostracize   to banish; to exclude

oust   to drive out; to expel

outwit   to trick; to get the better of

overt   open; aboveboard; not hidden

ovine   of or like a sheep

ovoid   egg-shaped

PACIFY–PYRRHIC

pacify   to calm down

pact   an agreement

paean   song of praise or joy

palatable   pleasant to the taste

palatial   magnificent

paleontology   study of prehistoric life

pall   (*two meanings*) something that covers or conceals (*noun*); to become wearisome or unpleasant (*verb*)

palliate   to ease; to lessen

pallid   pale; dull

palpable   obvious; capable of being touched or felt

palpitate   to beat rapidly; to tremble

palsy   muscle paralysis

paltry   trivial; worthless

panacea   a cure-all; an answer for all problems

panache   self-confidence; a showy manner

pandemic   general; widespread

pandemonium   wild disorder; confusion

panegyric   an expression of praise

pang   a sharp pain

panoply   suit of armor; any protective covering

panorama   unlimited view; comprehensive survey

parable   a simple story giving a moral or religious lesson

paradigm   a model; an example

paradox   a statement that seems contradictory, but probably true

paragon   a model of excellence or perfection

parameter   boundary; limits

paramount   chief; supreme

paranoia   mental disorder characterized by a feeling of being persecuted

paraphernalia   personal belongings; equipment

paraphrase   to reword; to restate

parched   dried up; extremely thirsty

pariah   an outcast

parity   equality; similarity

parley   discussion; conference

parlous   dangerous

parochial   local; narrow; limited

parody   a work which imitates another in a ridiculous manner

paroxysm   a sudden outburst; a fit

parrot   to repeat or imitate without understanding

parry   to avoid something such as a thrust or blow

parsimonious   stingy; miserly

partisan   a strong supporter of a cause

passé   old fashioned; out-of-date

passive   submissive; unresisting

pastoral   pertaining to the country; rural

patent   (*two meanings*) a government protection for an inventor (*noun*); evident or obvious (*adjective*)

paternal   fatherly

pathogenic   causing disease

pathos   pity; deep feeling

patriarch   an early Biblical person regarded as one of the fathers of the human race

patrician   aristocratic

patrimony   inherited right; heritage

patronage   the control of power to make appointments to government jobs

patronize   (*two meanings*) to be a customer; to talk down to

paucity   scarcity; lack

peccadillo   a minor offense

pectoral   pertaining to the chest

peculate   to steal; to embezzle

pecuniary   pertaining to money

pedagogue   a schoolteacher

pedantic   tending to show off one's learning

pedestrian   (*two meanings*) one who walks (*noun*); ordinary or dull (*adjective*)

pedigree   a record of ancestors; a line of descent

peer   (*two meanings*)   an equal (*noun*); to look closely (*verb*)

peerless   without equal; unmatched

peevish   hard to please; irritable

pejorative   having a negative effect; insulting

pellucid   transparent; clear

pelt   (*two meanings*)   skin of a fur-bearing animal (*noun*); to throw things at (*verb*)

penal   pertaining to punishment

penchant   a strong liking for; an inclination

pendant   anything that hangs or is suspended

penitent   expressing sorrow for sin or wrongdoing

pensive   dreamily thoughtful

penury   extreme poverty

peon   common worker

perceive   to observe

perceptible   observable; recognizable

perdition   damnation; ruin; hell

peregrinate   to travel from place to place

peremptory   decisive; final; not open to debate

perennial   lasting for a long time; perpetual

perfidious   deceitful; treacherous; unfaithful

perforce   of necessity

perfunctory   done without care; routine

perigee   point nearest to the earth

perilous   dangerous; risky

periphery   outside boundary; unimportant aspects of a subject

periphrastic   said in a roundabout way

perjury   making a false statement while under oath

permeate   to spread throughout

pernicious   deadly; destructive

peroration   the concluding part of a speech

perpetrate   to do something evil; to be guilty of

perpetuate   to cause to continue

perplexity   confusion

perquisite   something additional to regular pay

persevere   to endure; to continue

personification   giving human qualities to a non-human being

perspicacity   keenness of judgment

perspicuity   clearness, as of a statement

pert   bold; saucy

pertinent   relevant; to the point

perturb   to unsettle; to disturb

peruse   to read carefully

pervade   to spread throughout; to pass through

perverse   contrary; cranky

pervert   to lead astray; to corrupt

pessimist   one who sees the worst in everything

petrify   to turn to rock; to paralyze with fear

petrology   study of rocks

petty   unimportant; minor

petulant   irritable; rude

phalanx   closely massed body of persons

phenomenon   extraordinary person, thing, or event

philander   to engage in various love affairs

philanthropy   a desire to help mankind; generosity

philately   stamp collecting

philippic   a bitter verbal attack

philistine   uncultured; common

phlegmatic   unemotional; cool; not easily excited

phobia   intense fear

phoenix   a bird which symbolizes immortality

picaresque   pertaining to an adventurous wanderer

piddling   trifling; petty

piecemeal   bit by bit; gradually

pied   many-colored; variegated

piety   reverence; devotion

pigment   dye; coloring matter

pilgrimage   a journey to a holy place

pillage   to rob by violence

pillory   to expose to public ridicule or abuse

pinnacle   peak; highest point

pious   religious

piquant   stimulating to the taste; exciting interest

pique   to irritate or annoy

piscine   of or like a fish

pitfall   unexpected difficulty; a trap

pithy   concise; to the point

pittance   small share or amount

pivotal   central; crucial

placard   small poster

placate   to soothe; to calm

placebo   harmless, phony medicine; something said or done to soothe

placid   calm

plagiarism   claiming another's work to be one's own

plague   (*two meanings*) a contagious disease (*noun*); to torment; to trouble (*verb*)

plaintive   sorrowful; sad

platitude   a dull or trite remark

platonic   spiritual; free from sensual desire

plaudit   applause; (in the plural) any expression of approval

plausible   apparently true, fair, or reasonable

plebeian   pertaining to a member of the lower classes

plenary   full; complete; absolute

plethora   abundance

pliant   easily bent; adaptable

plight   a sad or dangerous situation

ploy   a gimmick; a trick

pluck   (*two meanings*) to pull at (*verb*); courage (*noun*)

plumb   to test; to measure

plunder   to rob; to take by force

plutocracy   rule by the wealthy class

poach   to trespass

podium   a platform

poignant   keenly distressing; affecting the emotions

polarize   to separate into opposing groups

polemic   a controversy or argument

politic   diplomatic; shrewd

poltroon   a coward

polychromatic   many-colored

polyglot   speaking or writing several languages

polymorphic   having many forms

polytheism   belief in many gods

pomp   brilliant show or display

ponder   to think deeply; to consider carefully

ponderous   heavy; burdensome

porcine   of or like a pig

portable   capable of being carried

portal   door; gate; entrance

portentous   warning; foreshadowing

portly   stout; large

posterity   future generations

posthumous   occurring after death

postulate   to assume without proof; to take for granted

potable   drinkable

potent   powerful; strong

potentate   ruler; monarch

potential   capacity for being or becoming something

potion   a drink

potpourri   a mixture

pragmatic   practical

prate   to talk extensively and pointlessly; to babble

precarious   uncertain; dangerous; risky

precede   to be, come, or go before

precedent   an act that may be used as an example in the future

precept   a rule of conduct

precipice   cliff

precipitate   to bring about an action suddenly

precipitous   extremely steep

précis   brief summary

preclude   to prevent; to shut out

precocious   prematurely developed

precursor   a forerunner; predecessor

predatory   living by plunder, exploitation, etc.

predicate   to declare; to assert

predilection   a liking; preference; inclination

predispose   to make susceptible

preeminent   standing out above all others

preen   to dress oneself carefully or smartly

prehensile   adapted for seizing or grasping something

prelude   an introduction

premeditate   to plan beforehand

premier   first in importance or time

premise   statement from which a conclusion is drawn

premonition   forewarning; hunch

preponderance   superiority in quantity or power; dominance

preposterous   absurd; ridiculous

prerogative   privilege or right

presage   to indicate or warn in advance

prescience   knowledge of things before they happen

presentiment   anticipation, especially of something evil

prestige   influence; importance

presumptuous   boldly assuming

pretentious   showy; putting on airs

preternatural   abnormal; beyond what is natural

pretext   a false reason or motive; an excuse

prevail   to succeed; to gain the advantage

prevaricate   to lie

prim   formal; proper

primary   first; chief

primeval   of the earliest times or ages

primogeniture   state of being the first born

primordial   first; original

primp   to dress up in a fussy way

prismatic   many-colored

pristine   uncorrupted; in its original state

privation   loss or lack of something essential

privy   (*to*) having knowledge of something private or secret

probe   to investigate; to examine

probity   honesty; integrity

proclivity   inclination; tendency

procrastinate   to postpone; to delay

procreate   to beget or produce

procrustean   designed to get conformity at any cost

procure   to obtain; to secure

prod   to urge; to poke or jab

prodigal   wasteful

prodigious   enormous; vast

profane   showing disrespect for sacred things

profess   to acknowledge; to admit frankly

proffer   to offer

proficiency   skill; competency

profligate   shamelessly immoral; extremely wasteful

profound   very deep

profuse   abundant

progeny   descendants

prognosticate   to predict; to foretell

projectile   a bullet, shell, grenade, etc., for firing from a gun

proletarian   one who belongs to the working class

proliferate   to expand; to increase

prolific   productive; fertile

prolix   tediously long and wordy

prologue   introduction

promenade   a stroll or a walk; an area used for walking

promiscuous   sexually loose

promontory   piece of land that juts out

promulgate   to announce; to advocate

prone   reclining; lying flat; inclined

propagate   to spread; to multiply

propensity   inclination; tendency

prophetic   predicting

propinquity   nearness; closeness

propitious   favorable

proponent   a person who supports a cause or doctrine

propriety   conformity; appropriateness

prosaic   dull; commonplace; unimaginative

proscribe   to denounce; exile

proselyte   a person who has changed from one religion to another; a convert

prospectus   a report describing a forthcoming project

prostrate   lying flat; thrown or fallen to the ground

protagonist   main character

protean   changeable; variable

protégé   one who has been guided or instructed by another

protocol   the etiquette observed by diplomats

prototype   the original; first of its kind; a model

protract   to draw out; to prolong

protrude   to stick out; to project

proverbial   well-known

provident   having foresight

provincial   countrified; narrow; limited

provisional   temporary

proviso   a condition; a stipulation

provoke   to anger; to irritate; to annoy

prowess   skill; strength; daring

proximity   nearness in place or time

proxy   one who acts in place of another

prude   an overly proper person

prudence   caution; good judgment

prune   to cut off or lop off such as twigs, branches, or roots

prurient   lustful; obscene; lewd

pseudo   false; counterfeit

pseudonym   a fake or assumed name

psyche   the human soul or spirit

puerile   childish; immature

pugilist   a boxer

pugnacious   eager to fight; quarrelsome

puissant   powerful; strong

pulchritude   beauty

pulmonary   pertaining to the lungs

pulverize   crush or grind into powder; totally destroy

pummel   to beat or thrash with the fists

pun   the use of words alike in sound but different in meaning

punctilious   very exact; precise

pundit   a learned man; an expert or authority

pungent   having a sharp taste or smell; severely critical or sarcastic

punitive   pertaining to punishment

puny   weak; inferior

purge   to cleanse; to purify

puritanical   strict; rigid; harsh

purloin   to steal

purport   to claim to be

purvey   to furnish; to supply

pusillanimous   cowardly; fearful

putative   supposed; believed

putrefy   to rot; to decay

pyre   a funeral fire in which the corpse is burned

pyretic   pertaining to fever

pyromaniac   one who likes to start fires; arsonist

Pyrrhic victory   success gained at too high a cost

QUACK–QUOTIDIAN

quack   an untrained doctor; a pretender to any skill

quadruped   a four-footed animal

quaff   to gulp; to drink in large quantities

quagmire   a swamp; a difficult situation

quail   to lose courage; to shrink with fear

quaint   strange or unusual in a pleasing or amusing way

qualm   a feeling of uneasiness

quandary   a puzzling situation; a dilemma

quarry   an animal that is being hunted down

quash   to cancel; to set aside (as an indictment)

quasi   resembling; seeming

quaver   to tremble; to shake

quay   a wharf

queasy   uneasy; nauseated

quell   to subdue; to calm down

querulous   complaining

query   a question

quest   a search

queue   a line of people waiting their turn

quibble   petty objection or argument

quiddity   essential quality

quidnunc   a gossip or busybody

quiescent   at rest; motionless

quietus   finishing stroke; anything that ends an activity

quintessence   the pure and concentrated essence of something

quip   a witty or sarcastic remark

quirk   a peculiar characteristic of a person; a sudden twist or turn

quiver   to tremble; to shake

quixotic   extremely idealistic; romantic; not practical

quizzical   odd, questioning; puzzled

quotidian   daily

RABBLE–RUTHLESS

rabble   mob; disorderly crowd

rabid   intense; furious or raging; mad

rack   to torment; to torture

raconteur   storyteller

radical   extreme; complete; violent

rail   (*at* or *against*) to complain bitterly

raillery   good-humored ridicule

raiment   clothing; garments

rakish   carefree; lively

rambunctious   restless; hard to control

ramification   a result; a consequence; a branch

rampant   widespread; raging

ramshackle   shaky; ready to fall apart

rancid   having a bad taste or smell; stale; repulsive

rancor   bitter resentment; hatred

rankle   to cause irritation; to fester

rant   to speak in a loud or violent manner

rapacious   taking by force; greedy

rapport   a close relationship; harmony

rapt   completely absorbed in; overcome with joy, love, etc.

rarefy   to make less dense; to refine

rash   (*two meanings*)   a skin irritation (*noun*); reckless or daring (*adjective*)

raspy   harsh; grating

ratify   to officially approve of

ratiocinate   to reason

ration   a fixed portion; a share

rational   sensible; reasonable

rationalize   to make an excuse for

raucous   irritating or harsh in sound

ravage   to damage; ruin

ravenous   extremely hungry; greedy

raze   to destroy; to level to the ground

realm   kingdom; region

rebuff   to refuse; to snub

rebuke   to scold; to blame

rebuttal   contradiction; opposing argument

recalcitrant   disobedient; hard to manage

recant   to withdraw or disavow a statement or opinion

recapitulate   to summarize; repeat briefly

recede   to go or move back; to withdraw

recess   (*two meanings*) a cut or notch in something; a pause or rest

recidivist   a person who goes back to crime

recipient   one who receives

reciprocal   interchangeable; mutual

reciprocate   to give in return

recluse   hermit; one who shuts himself off from the world

recoil   to retreat; to draw back

reconcile   to bring into agreement or harmony

recondite   difficult to understand; profound

reconnoiter   to survey; to check out in advance

recount   to tell or relate, as a story

recreant   coward; traitor

recrimination   countercharge

rectify   to correct; to make right

rectitude   honesty; moral uprightness

recumbent   lying down; reclining

recuperate   to get well

recur   to happen again

redemption   deliverance from sin; a rescue

redolent   having a pleasant odor

redoubtable   formidable; commanding respect

redress   to set right; to remedy

redundant   repetitious; unnecessary

reek   to give off; emit

refractory   stubborn; hard to manage

refulgent   shining; glowing

refurbish   to make new; to freshen up

refute   to prove wrong, such as an opinion

regal   pertaining to a king; splendid

regale   to entertain

regenerate   to re-create; to reform morally; to replace a lost part of the body

regent   one who governs

regicide   the killing of a king

regime   a system of government

regimen   a regular system (of exercise, diet, etc.)

regressive   moving in a backward direction

regurgitate   to rush or surge back, as undigested food

rehabilitate   to restore to useful life

reimburse   to pay back

reiterate   to repeat

rejuvenate   to make young again

relegate   to banish; to assign to an inferior position

relentless   unyielding

relevant   significant; pertaining to the subject

relinquish   to give up; to let go

relish   to enjoy; to take delight in

remediable   capable of being corrected

remedial   intended to correct

reminisce   to remember

remiss   negligent

remission   a lessening; a forgiveness as of sins or offenses

remonstrate   to protest; to complain

remorse   regret for wrongdoing

remuneration   payment for a service

renaissance   rebirth; renewal; revival

renal   pertaining to the kidneys

rend   to split; to tear apart

rendezvous   a meeting; appointment

renegade   a deserter; a traitor

renege   to go back on one's word

renounce   to give up (a belief)

renovate   to make new; to repair

reparation   compensation; something done to make up for a wrong or injury done

repartee   a quick, wirty reply

repast   a meal

repellent   something that drives away or wards off (insects, etc.)

repercussion   reaction; aftereffect

repertoire   special skills or talents one possesses; collection

repine   to complain; to fret

replenish   to fill up again

replete   well-filled

repose   to rest; to sleep

reprehensible   deserving criticism or blame; shameful

repress   to control; to subdue

reprimand   to scold

reprisal   retaliation; revenge

reproach   to blame; to scold

reprobate   a wicked person

reproof   a rebuke

repudiate   to reject; to disown

repugnant   distasteful; disgusting

repulse   to drive back; to repel

reputed   supposed to be

requiem   funeral hymn; mass for the dead

requisite   required or necessary; indispensable

requite   to make a return or repayment

rescind   to cancel; to repeal

residue   that which remains

resilient   recovering quickly; elastic

resolute   very determined

resonance   fullness of sound

resourceful   able to deal effectively with problems

respite   a delay; rest

resplendent   shining brightly; dazzling

restitution   repayment; a giving back

restive   restless; uneasy; impatient

restrain   to hold back; to control

résumé   a summary

resurge   to rise again

resurrection   revival; rebirth

resuscitate   to revive from apparent death or from unconsciousness

retaliation   revenge; repayment for an evil act

retentive   having a good memory; remembering

reticent   silent or reserved in manner

retinue   body of attendants or followers

retort   a short, witty reply

retract   to take back (a statement); to withdraw

retrench   to cut down or reduce expenses

retribution   deserved punishment

retrieve   to get or bring back

retroactive   applying to a period before a certain law was passed

retrogressive   going backward; becoming worse

retrospect   (preceded by *in*) looking back on past events

revelation   something made known; a disclosure

revelry   noisy merrymaking

reverberate   to echo; to resound

revere   to honor; to respect

reverie   a daydream

revile   to abuse; to slander

rhetorical   concerned with mere style or effect

ribald   vulgar; indecent

rife   frequently occurring; widespread

rift   a break or split

righteous   behaving justly or morally

rigorous   strict

risible   laughable; funny

risqué   daring or indecent; not proper

rite   a religious ceremony; a solemn act

robust   strong; hearty

rogue   a dishonest person; a scoundrel

rollicking   jolly; carefree

roster   a list

rote   (preceded with *by*) from memory, without thought for meaning

rotund   round; fat

rout   overwhelming defeat

rudimentary   elementary; basic

rue   to regret; to be sorrowful

ruffian   hoodlum; lawless person

ruffle   (*two meanings*)   a wrinkle or a ripple (*noun*); to irritate or to annoy (*verb*)

ruminate   to consider carefully; to meditate on

rupture   to break apart; to burst

ruse   a skillful trick or deception

rustic   pertaining to the country

rustle   (*two meanings*)   to steal; to make a swishing sound

ruthless   cruel; merciless

SACCHARINE–SYNTHETIC

---

saccharine   overly sweet

sacrilege   the violation of anything sacred

sacrosanct   extremely holy

sadistic   deriving pleasure from inflicting pain on others

saga   a long story of adventure

sagacious   wise

sage   a wise person

salacious   obscene; lusty

salient   significant; conspicuous

saline   salty

sallow   sickly pale

salubrious   healthful

salutary   healthful; wholesome

salutatory   a welcoming address, as at a graduation

salvage   to rescue; to save from destruction

sanctimonious   hypocritical in regard to religious belief

sanction   to authorize; to give permission

sangfroid   calmness; composure

sanguinary   bloody

sanguine   cheerful; optimistic

sapient   wise

sardonic   mocking; scornful

sartorial   pertaining to clothes or tailoring

satiated   satisfied; filled up

satirical   sarcastic; ironic

saturate   to soak; to fill up

saturnine   gloomy; sluggish

saunter   to stroll; to walk leisurely

savant   a person of extensive learning

savoir faire   tact; knowledge of just what to do in any situation

savor   to enjoy, as by taste or smell

scant   inadequate in size or amount

scapegoat   one who takes the blame for others

scathing   extremely severe or harsh, such as a re- mark

schism   a split or break

scintilla   a tiny amount; a speck

scintillate   to sparkle; to twinkle

scion   an offspring; a descendant

scoff   to ridicule

scope   range; extent

scourge   a whip or a lash; a person or thing that punishes or destroys

scrupulous   honest; ethical; precise

scrutinize   to examine closely

scurrilous   coarsely abusive; vulgar

scurry   run about; to hurry

scuttle   to sink (a ship); to abandon

sear   to burn; to scorch

sebaceous   fatty

seclude   to keep apart; to isolate

secrete   to hide or conceal

secular   worldly; nonreligious

sedate   quiet; calm; serious

sedentary   sitting most of the time

sediment   material that settles on the bottom; residue

sedition   rebellion

sedulous   hard-working; industrious; diligent

seedy   run-down; shabby

seethe   to boil; to be violently agitated

seismic   pertaining to earthquakes

semblance   outward appearance

senile   pertaining to mental weakness due to old age

sensate   pertaining to feeling

sensual   pertaining to enjoyment of food and sex

sensuous   pertaining to enjoyment of art, music, etc.

sententious   concise; including proverbs and brief remarks

sentient   conscious; capable of feeling

sentinel   a guard

sepulcher   tomb; burial vault

sequel   an event or literary work that follows a previous one

sequester   to separate; to set aside

seraphic   angelic; pure

serendipity   a talent for making desirable discoveries by accident

serene   calm; peaceful

serpentine   winding

serrated   having tooth-like edges

servile   like a slave

servitude   slavery; bondage

sever   to cut in two; to separate

shackle   to keep prisoner; to restrain

sham   a pretense

shambles   a slaughterhouse; great disorder

shard   a fragment

sheepish   embarrassed; bashful

shibboleth   a slogan; a password

shiftless   lazy; inefficient

shoal   a shallow place in the water; a reef

shortcomings   defects; deficiencies

shrew   a nagging, bad-tempered woman

shroud   a cloth or sheet in which a corpse is wrapped for burial

sibilant   hissing

sibling   a brother or sister

simian   pertaining to an ape or monkey

simile   a comparison using *like* or *as*

simony   the sin of buying or selling church benefits

simper   to smile in a silly way

simulacrum   an image; a likeness

simulate   to pretend; to imitate

simultaneous   occurring at the same time

sinecure   job with no responsibility

sinewy   tough; firm; strong

singular   extraordinary; remarkable; exceptional

sinister   threatening evil; ominous

sinuous   curving; winding

siren   an attractive but dangerous woman

skeptic   one who doubts

skinflint   stingy person; miser

skittish   restless; excitable; nervous

skulduggery   trickery; deception

skulk   to sneak around; to lie in hiding

slacken   become loose; to relax

slake   to lessen (thirst, desire, anger, etc.) by satisfying; to quench

slander   to make a false statement against someone

slattern   an untidy woman

sleazy   cheap; flimsy

sleek   smooth and shiny

slither   to slide or glide

slothful   lazy

slough   (*off*) to discard; to shed

slovenly   untidy; dirty; careless

smirk   to smile in an affected or offensive way

smite   to strike forcefully

smolder   to burn without flame; to keep feelings concealed

smug   self-satisfied

snare   to trap

sneer   to look at with contempt; to scorn; to deride

snicker   to laugh in a half-suppressed way

snippet   a small fragment

snivel   to whine; to complain

sober   not drunk; serious

sobriquet   nickname; assumed name

sodden   soaked; damp

sojourn   a brief stay or visit

solace   comfort

solar   pertaining to the sun

solecism   ungrammatical usage; an error or inconsistency

solicit   to ask; to seek; to try to get an order in business

solicitude   concern; anxiety

soliloquy   act of talking to oneself

solipsistic   pertaining to the theory that only oneself exists or can be proved to exist

solitude   loneliness

solon   a wise man

solvent   (*two meanings*) having the ability to pay a debt (*adjective*); a substance that dissolves another (*noun*)

somber   dark; gloomy

somnambulate   walk in one's sleep

somniferous   causing sleep

somnolent   drowsy; sleepy

sonorous   producing a deep, rich sound

sophistry   a deceptive, tricky argument

sophomoric   immature; pretentious

soporific   causing sleep

sordid   dirty; filthy

sot   a drunkard

sobriquet   nickname; assumed name

sovereign   a monarch or other supreme ruler

spacious   roomy; convenient

Spartan   warlike; brave; disciplined

spasm   a sudden burst of energy

specious   not genuine; pleasing to the eye but deceptive

specter   a ghost; a phantom

speculate   (*two meanings*) to meditate; to participate in a risky business transaction

sphinx   person who is difficult to understand

splenetic   bad-tempered; irritable

sporadic   infrequent; irregular

spry   full of life; active

spume   foam

spurious   deceitful; counterfeit

spurn   to reject

squalid   filthy; dirty

staccato   made up of short, abrupt sounds

stagnant   not flowing; stale; sluggish

staid   sedate; settled

stalemate   a deadlock; a draw

stalwart   strong; sturdy

stamina   endurance; resistance to fatigue

stance   attitude; posture

stark   complete; harsh; severe

static   inactive; motionless

stationary   standing still; not moving

statute   law; rule

steadfast   firm in purpose; dependable; constant

stench   a foul smell

stentorian   very loud

stereotyped   not original; commonplace

sterling   of high quality; excellent

stigma   mark of disgrace

stilted   artificially formal

stint   to be sparing; to conserve

stipend   salary

stipulate   to specify; to arrange definitely

stoic   showing no emotion; indifferent to pleasure or pain

stolid   impassive; having little emotion

strait   a position of difficulty; a narrow passage of water

stratagem   a plan, scheme, or trick

strew   to spread about; to scatter

striated   striped; marked with lines

stricture   negative criticism; a restriction

strident   harsh sounding; loud and shrill

stringent   strict; tight

strut   to walk in a proud manner; to show off

stultify   make absurd or ridiculous; render worthless

stupefy   to stun; to amaze

stygian   dark; gloomy

stymie   to hinder; to block

suave   polished; sophisticated

sub rosa   secretly; confidentially

subaqueous   underwater

subjective   not objective; personal

subjugate   to conquer

sublimate   to make a person act noble or moral

sublime   majestic; elevated or lofty in thought

subliminal   subconscious; unaware

submissive   yielding; humbly obedient

subordinate   of lower rank

suborn   to hire for an unlawful act

subsequent   following; occurring later

subservient   submissive; helpful, in an inferior capacity

subside   to become quiet; to settle down

subsidiary   auxiliary; supplementary; serving to assist

substantiate   to prove; to confirm; to support

subterfuge   trickery; deceit

subterranean   underground

subversive   tending to overthrow or undermine

succinct   concise; brief and to the point

succor   assistance; help; relief

succulent   juicy

succumb   to yield; to give in

suffrage   the right to vote

sullen   gloomy; showing irritation

sully   to soil, stain, or tarnish

sultry   hot and moist

sumptuous   luxurious; lavish; extravagant

sundry   various; assorted

superannuated   retired because of old age

supercilious   proud; haughty

superficial   on the surface; shallow

superfluous   excessive; unnecessary

supernal   heavenly

supernumerary   extra; more than necessary

supersede   to take the place of

supervene   to take place or occur unexpectedly

supine   lying on the back

supplant   to replace

supple   flexible

suppliant   begging; asking humbly

supplicate   to pray humbly; to beg

surfeit   an excessive amount

surly   rude; bad-tempered

surmise   to guess

surmount   to go beyond; to overcome

surreptitious   acting in a sneaky way

surrogate   substitute

surveillance   supervision; close watch

sustenance   nourishment

susurration   whispering; murmuring

suture   to join together, as with stitches

svelte   slender; graceful

swarthy   dark-complexioned

swathe   to wrap closely or fully

sybarite   one who is fond of luxuries and pleasure

sycophant   a flatterer; a parasite

sylvan   wooded; pertaining to the forest

symbiosis   mutual dependence between two different organisms

symmetrical   balanced; well-proportioned

synchronize   to happen at the same time

synthesis   a combination; a fusion

synthetic   not genuine; artificial

TABLEAU–TYRO

---

tableau   dramatic scene or picture

taboo   forbidden; unacceptable

tabulation   a systematic listing by columns or rows

tacit   silent; not expressed

taciturn   speaking very little

tactics   plan; method; strategy

tactile   pertaining to sense of touch

taint   to infect; to harm a person's reputation

talisman   a good luck charm

tally   to count; to make a record of

tangent   touching

tangible   real; capable of being touched

tantalize   to tease or torment

tantamount   equivalent to

tarn   a small lake or pool

tarnish   to soil; to discolor; to stain

tarry   to linger; to delay

taunt   to ridicule; to tease

taurine   like a bull

taut   tight; tense

tawdry   cheap; showy; flashy

tawny   yellowish-brown

tedious   boring; monotonous

teeming   overfilled; pouring out

temerity   reckless boldness; rashness

temper   (*verb*) to moderate; to soften or tone down

temperate   not extreme; moderate

temporal   pertaining to time

temporize   to be indecisive; to be evasive; to delay an action

tenacious   holding on; persistent; stubborn

tendentious   biased; favoring a cause

tenet   a doctrine; a belief

tensile   capable of being stretched; elastic

tentative   for the time being; experimental

tenuous   slender; flimsy; without substance

tenure   the holding or possessing of anything

tepid   lukewarm

terminate   to put an end to; to conclude

terminus   a boundary; a limit

terpsichorean   pertaining to dancing

terrestrial   earthly; living on land

terse   brief; to the point

testy   irritable

thanatology   the study of death and dying

theocracy   government by religious leaders

therapeutic   pertaining to the treatment and curing of disease

thermal   pertaining to heat

thesaurus   a book of synonyms and antonyms; a dictionary

thespian   an actor

thrall   a slave

threnody   a funeral song

throes   a violent struggle; pains (*of childbirth*); agony (*of death*)

throng   a crowd

thwart   to prevent or hinder

timorous   fearful; cowardly

tinge   a faint color; a trace

tirade   a long angry speech; an outburst of bitter denunciation

titanic   huge

titillate   to tickle; to excite agreeably

titter   to laugh in a self-conscious or nervous way

token   (*two meanings*) sign or symbol (*noun*); slight or unimportant (*adjective*)

tome   large, heavy book

toothsome   tasty

topple   to overturn; to fall over

torpid   inactive; sluggish

torsion   twisting; bending

torso   the human body excluding the head and limbs

tortuous   twisting; winding

torturous   causing extreme pain

touchstone   standard; a test or criterion for quality

toxic   poisonous; harmful

tractable   easy to manage

traduce   to speak badly of; to slander

trait   a characteristic; a quality

tranquil   calm; peaceful

transcend   to go beyond; to overcome

transcendental   supernatural; going beyond ordinary experience or belief

trangression   violation of a rule or law

transient   temporary; passing

transitory   lasting a short time; brief

translucent   letting light pass through

transmute   to change from one form to another; to transform

transparent   easily seen through; clear

transpire   to be revealed or become known; to occur

trappings   articles of dress; equipment

trauma   a shock; an aftereffect

travail   very hard work; intense pain

travesty   an absurd or inadequate imitation

treacherous   dangerous; deceptive; disloyal

treatise   a book or writing about some particular subject

treble   three times as much

tremulous   trembling; quivering

trenchant   keen or incisive; vigorous; effective

trepidation   fear; alarm

trespass   to invade; to enter wrongfully

tribulation   trouble

tributary   a stream flowing into a river

tribute   a gift; an acknowledgment to show admiration

trinity   group of three

trite   worn out; stale; commonplace

trivia   matters or things that are very unimportant; trivialities

truckle   (*to*) to submit; to yield

truculent   savage; brutal; cruel

truism   a self-evident, obvious truth

truncate   to shorten; to cut off

truncheon   a club

tryst   a secret meeting

tumid   swollen; bulging

tumult   great noise and confusion

turbid   muddy; unclear

turbulence   wild disorder; violent motion

turgid   swollen

turmoil   confusion

turpitude   baseness; shameful behavior

tussle   a struggle; a fight

tutelage   instruction

twain   two

tycoon   a wealthy businessman

tyro   a beginner

UBIQUITOUS–UXURIOUS

ubiquitous   present everywhere

ulcerous   infected

ulterior   lying beyond; hidden

ultimatum   a final demand or proposal

umbrage   a feeling of resentment

unanimity   agreement; oneness

unassailable   unable to be attacked

uncanny   weird; strange

unconscionable   unreasonable; excessive

uncouth   crude; clumsy

unctuous   oily; excessively polite

undue   inappropriate; unreasonable

undulate   to move or sway in wavelike motion

unequivocal   clear; definite

unerring   accurate; not going astray or missing the mark

unfledged   not feathered; immature

unilateral   one-sided

unimpeachable   above suspicion; unquestionable

uninhibited   free; not restricted

unique   being the only one of its kind

unison   harmony; agreement

universal   broad; general; effective everywhere or in all cases

unkempt   untidy; sloppy

unmindful   unaware

unmitigated   absolute; not lessened

unobtrusive   inconspicuous; not noticeable

unruly   not manageable; disorderly

unsavory   unpleasant to taste or smell

unscathed   unharmed; uninjured

unseemly   not in good taste

untenable   unable to be defended or upheld

unwieldy   hard to manage because of size or weight

unwitting   unintentional; unaware

upbraid   to scold; to find fault with

uproarious   loud; outrageously funny

urbane   refined; suave; citified

urchin   a mischievous child

ursine   like a bear

usurp   to seize illegally

usury   excessive amount of money charged as interest

utilitarian   useful; practical

utopian   perfect; ideal

uxorious   overly fond of one's wife

VACILLATE–VULPINE

vacillate   to sway back and forth; to hesitate in making a decision

vagabond   a wanderer

vagary   an odd notion; an unpredictable action

vagrant   a homeless person; a wanderer

vain   conceited; excessively proud about one's appearance

vainglorious   boastfully proud

valedictory   saying farewell

valiant   courageous; brave

valid   true; logical; sound

validate   to approve; to confirm

valor   courage; bravery

vanguard   the front part

vanity   excessive pride; conceit

vanquish   to defeat

vapid   uninteresting; tasteless; tedious

variegated   having different colors; diversified

vaunt   to brag or boast

veer   to change direction

vegetate   lead a dull, inactive life

vehement   forceful; furious

velocity   speed

venal   corrupt; able to be bribed

vendetta   bitter quarrel or feud

veneer   an outward show that misrepresents

venerable   worthy of respect

venerate   to regard with respect

venial   excusable; minor

venomous   poisonous; spiteful; malicious

vent   to give release to; to be relieved of a feeling

venturesome   daring; adventurous; risky

veracious   truthful; honest

verbatim   word for word

verbiage   overabundance of words

verbose   wordy

verdant   green; flourishing

verisimilitude   the appearance of truth

veritable   true; actual; genuine

verity   truth

vernacular   native language; informal speech

vernal   pertaining to spring

versatile   good at many things; serving many purposes

vertex   top; highest point

vertiginous   whirling; dizzy; unstable

verve   energy; enthusiasm

vestige   a trace; visible evidence of something that is no longer present

veteran   an experienced person

vex   to irritate; to annoy

viable   capable of living; workable; practicable

viaduct   a bridge

viands   various foods

vicarious   taking the place of another person or thing; substituted

viceroy   a representative; a deputy appointed by a sovereign to rule a province

vicissitudes   unpredictable changes; ups and downs

victimize   to make a victim of; to swindle or cheat

victuals   food

vie   to compete

vigilant   watchful

vignette   a short literary sketch; a decorative design

vilify   to speak evil of; to defame

vindicate   to clear of guilt or blame

vindictive   spiteful; seeking revenge

vintage   representative of the best (*especially of wines*)

viper   a poisonous snake; a malignant or spiteful person

virago   a loud, bad-tempered woman; a shrew

virile   masculine; manly

virtuoso   an expert; a skilled person

virulent   deadly; poisonous; harmful

visage   the face; appearance

visceral   pertaining to instinctive rather than intellectual motivation

viscous   sticky

vista   a distant view

vitiate   to weaken; to impair

vitreous   of or like glass

vitriolic   biting; sharp; bitter

vituperate   to scold; to criticize

vivify   to give life to; to enliven

vixen   female fox; ill-tempered woman

vociferous   loud; shouting

vogue   fashion; style

volant   capable of flying

volatile   unstable; explosive

volition   free will

voluble   talkative; fluent

voluminous   large; copious

voluptuous   sensual; shapely**

voracious   extremely hungry; greedy

votary   loyal follower

vouchsafe   to grant; to allow or permit

vulgar   showing poor taste or manners

vulnerable   defenseless; open to attack

vulpine   like a fox; clever

WAIF–ZEST

---

waif   a homeless person

waive   to give up (a right)

wallow   to indulge oneself; to roll around in

wan   pale; weak; tired

wane   to gradually decrease in size or intensity

wangle   to manipulate; to obtain by scheming or by underhand methods

wanton   reckless; immoral

warble   to sing melodiously

warp   to bend out of shape; to pervert

wary   cautious; watchful

wastrel   a spendthrift; one who wastes

waver   to sway; to be uncertain

wax   to grow in size or intensity

weighty   of utmost importance

wend   to direct one's way

wheedle   to coax or to persuade

whet   to stimulate; to make sharp

whimsical   unpredictable; changeable

wield   to handle (*a tool*); to exercise control (*over others*)

willful   contrary; stubborn

wily   tricky; sly

wince   to shrink, as in pain, fear, etc.; to flinch

windfall   unexpected good fortune

winsome   pleasing; charming

withal   in spite of all; nevertheless

wizened   withered; shriveled

woe   sorrow; grief

wolfish   ferocious

wont   (*to*) accustomed (*adjective*)

workaday   everyday; ordinary

wraith   a ghost; an apparition

wrangle   to quarrel

wrath   anger; rage

wrench   to twist; to pull

wrest   to take away by force

wroth   angry

wrought   produced or shaped

wry   produced by distorting the face (*a wry grin*); ironic (*wry humor*)

xenophobia   fear of foreigners or strangers

xyloid   pertaining to wood

yen   an intense desire; a longing

yoke   to join together; to link

zany   comical; clownishly crazy

zeal   great enthusiasm

zealot   a fanatic

zenith   the highest point

zephyr   a gentle, mild breeze

zest   hearty enjoyment

100 Tests to Strengthen Your Vocabulary

This vocabulary section consists of 100 vocabulary tests. Each test consists of 10 multiple-choice questions, including SAT-type words. Practically all the words whose meanings you are tested on in these 100 tests are among the 3,400 words in the SAT Word List beginning on page 479.

These 100 vocabulary tests provide you with an opportunity to make sure that you really know the meanings of the hundreds of words you are being tested on. Several of these words are likely to appear on your actual SAT exam.

We suggest that you use the following procedure while you are taking these 100 tests:

1. Take Vocabulary Test 1.

2. Turn to the Answer Keys beginning on page 595.

3. For each word that you got wrong, jot down the word on a "Special List" of your own.

4. Make up a sentence using each word that you got wrong on Vocabulary Test 1.

5. Repeat the above procedure for Vocabulary Tests 2, 3, 4—right on through Vocabulary Test 100.

6. When you have finished taking the 100 Vocabulary Tests, go back to your "Special List." See whether you really know the meanings of these words by having someone else test you on them. For those words you still have trouble with, look up their meanings in a dictionary. Compose three sentences including each of these "troublemakers."

Gentle reminder: Knowing the meanings of many of the words in these 100 tests is likely to raise your score substantially in the Verbal sections—Analogies, Sentence Completions, and Reading Comprehension.

DIRECTIONS FOR THE 100 VOCABULARY TESTS

Each vocabulary question consists of a word in capital letters, followed by five lettered words or phrases. Choose the word or phrase that is most nearly the *same* in meaning as the word in capital letters. Since some of the questions require you to distinguish fine shades of meaning, consider all choices before deciding which is best.

Vocabulary Test 1

1. FILCH
   (A) hide
   (B) swindle
   (C) drop
   (D) steal
   (E) covet

2. URBANE
   (A) crowded
   (B) polished
   (C) rural
   (D) friendly
   (E) prominent

3. DECANT
   (A) bisect
   (B) speak wildly
   (C) bequeath
   (D) pour off
   (E) abuse verbally

4. ANTITHESIS
   (A) contrast
   (B) conclusion
   (C) resemblance
   (D) examination
   (E) dislike

5. HERETICAL
   (A) heathenish
   (B) impractical
   (C) quaint
   (D) rash
   (E) unorthodox

6. COALESCE
   (A) associate
   (B) combine
   (C) contact
   (D) conspire
   (E) cover

7. CHARLATAN
   (A) clown
   (B) philanthropist
   (C) jester
   (D) dressmaker
   (E) quack

8. GAUCHE
   (A) clumsy
   (B) stupid
   (C) feebleminded
   (D) impudent
   (E) foreign

9. REDUNDANT
   (A) necessary
   (B) plentiful
   (C) sufficient
   (D) diminishing
   (E) superfluous

10. ATROPHY
    (A) lose leaves
    (B) soften
    (C) waste away
    (D) grow
    (E) spread

Vocabulary Test 2

1. RESILIENCE
   (A) submission
   (B) elasticity
   (C) vigor
   (D) determination
   (E) recovery

2. ANALOGY
   (A) similarity
   (B) transposition
   (C) variety
   (D) distinction
   (E) appropriateness

3. FACETIOUS
   (A) obscene
   (B) shrewd
   (C) impolite
   (D) complimentary
   (E) witty

4. DIATRIBE
   (A) debate
   (B) monologue
   (C) oration
   (D) tirade
   (E) conversation

5. MALEDICTION
   (A) curse
   (B) mispronunciation
   (C) grammatical error
   (D) tactless remark
   (E) epitaph

6. AGGREGATE
   (A) result
   (B) difference
   (C) quotient
   (D) product
   (E) sum

7. APLOMB
    (A) caution
    (B) timidity
    (C) self-assurance
    (D) shortsightedness
    (E) self-restraint

8. THERAPEUTIC
    (A) curative
    (B) restful
    (C) warm
    (D) stimulating
    (E) professional

9. TRANSMUTE
    (A) remove
    (B) change
    (C) duplicate
    (D) carry
    (E) explain

10. ATTRITION
    (A) annihilation
    (B) encirclement
    (C) counterattack
    (D) appeasement
    (E) wearing down

Vocabulary Test 3

1. TRUNCATE
    (A) divide equally
    (B) end swiftly
    (C) cut off
    (D) act cruelly
    (E) cancel

2. OSCILLATE
    (A) confuse
    (B) kiss
    (C) turn
    (D) vibrate
    (E) whirl

3. INOCULATE
    (A) make harmless
    (B) infect
    (C) cure
    (D) overcome
    (E) darken

4. PERUSAL
    (A) approval
    (B) estimate
    (C) reading
    (D) translation
    (E) computation

5. QUERULOUS
    (A) peculiar
    (B) fretful
    (C) inquisitive
    (D) shivering
    (E) annoying

6. AUTONOMY
    (A) tyranny
    (B) independence
    (C) plebiscite
    (D) minority
    (E) dictatorship

7. MACHINATIONS
    (A) inventions
    (B) ideas
    (C) mysteries
    (D) plots
    (E) alliances

8. SCHISM
    (A) government
    (B) religion
    (C) division
    (D) combination
    (E) coalition

9. PUSILLANIMOUS
    (A) cowardly
    (B) extraordinary
    (C) ailing
    (D) evil-intentioned
    (E) excitable

10. TERMINOLOGY
    (A) technicality
    (B) finality
    (C) formality
    (D) explanation
    (E) nomenclature

Vocabulary Test 4

1. STIPEND
    (A) increment
    (B) bonus
    (C) commission
    (D) gift
    (E) salary

2. LITIGATION
    (A) publication
    (B) argument
    (C) endeavor
    (D) lawsuit
    (E) ceremony

3. FIASCO
   (A) disappointment
   (B) turning point
   (C) loss
   (D) celebration
   (E) complete failure

4. VAGARY
   (A) caprice
   (B) confusion
   (C) extravagance
   (D) loss of memory
   (E) shiftlessness

5. GRAPHIC
   (A) serious
   (B) concise
   (C) short
   (D) detailed
   (E) vivid

6. CONNOTATION
   (A) implication
   (B) footnote
   (C) derivation
   (D) comment
   (E) definition

7. TORTUOUS
   (A) crooked
   (B) difficult
   (C) painful
   (D) impassable
   (E) slow

8. FULMINATING
   (A) throbbing
   (B) pointed
   (C) wavelike
   (D) thundering
   (E) bubbling

9. CIRCUMVENT
   (A) freshen
   (B) change
   (C) control
   (D) harass
   (E) frustrate

10. CARTEL
   (A) rationing plan
   (B) world government
   (C) industrial pool
   (D) skilled craft
   (E) instrument of credit

Vocabulary Test 5

1. PROLIFIC
   (A) meager
   (B) obedient
   (C) fertile
   (D) hardy
   (E) scanty

2. ASSUAGE
   (A) create
   (B) ease
   (C) enlarge
   (D) prohibit
   (E) rub out

3. DECORUM
   (A) wit
   (B) charm
   (C) adornment
   (D) seemliness
   (E) charity

4. PHLEGMATIC
   (A) tolerant
   (B) careless
   (C) sensitive
   (D) stolid
   (E) sick

5. INTREPID
   (A) quick-witted
   (B) brutal
   (C) fearless
   (D) torrid
   (E) hearty

6. ACTUATE
   (A) frighten
   (B) direct
   (C) isolate
   (D) dismay
   (E) impel

7. MOUNTEBANK
   (A) trickster
   (B) courier
   (C) scholar
   (D) cashier
   (E) pawnbroker

8. LACONIC
   (A) terse
   (B) informal
   (C) convincing
   (D) interesting
   (E) tedious

9. BOORISH
(A) sporting
(B) tiresome
(C) argumentative
(D) monotonous
(E) rude

10. ERUDITE
(A) modest
(B) egotistical
(C) learned
(D) needless
(E) experienced

Vocabulary Test 6

1. ACRIMONIOUS
(A) repulsive
(B) enchanting
(C) stinging
(D) snobbish
(E) disgusting

2. EMBRYONIC
(A) hereditary
(B) arrested
(C) developed
(D) functioning
(E) rudimentary

3. INEXORABLE
(A) unfavorable
(B) permanent
(C) crude
(D) relentless
(E) incomplete

4. PROTRACTED
(A) boring
(B) condensed
(C) prolonged
(D) comprehensive
(E) measured

5. OBSEQUIOUS
(A) courteous
(B) fawning
(C) respectful
(D) overbearing
(E) inexperienced

6. LOQUACIOUS
(A) queer
(B) logical
(C) gracious
(D) rural
(E) voluble

7. PUGNACIOUS
(A) bold
(B) combative
(C) brawny
(D) pug-nosed
(E) valiant

8. ASTRINGENT
(A) bossy
(B) musty
(C) flexible
(D) corrosive
(E) contracting

9. ESCARPMENT
(A) threat
(B) limbo
(C) cliff
(D) behemoth
(E) blight

10. AMENITIES
(A) prayers
(B) ceremonies
(C) pageantries
(D) pleasantries
(E) social functions

Vocabulary Test 7

1. DEPLORE
(A) condone
(B) forget
(C) forgive
(D) deny
(E) regret

2. BANAL
(A) commonplace
(B) flippant
(C) pathetic
(D) new
(E) unexpected

3. ABACUS
(A) casserole
(B) blackboard
(C) slide rule
(D) adding device
(E) long spear

4. SEISMISM
(A) inundation
(B) tide
(C) volcano
(D) earthquake
(E) tornado

5. AMELIORATE
(A) favor
(B) improve
(C) interfere
(D) learn
(E) straddle

6. CHARY
(A) burned
(B) careful
(C) comfortable
(D) fascinating
(E) gay

7. CORPULENT
(A) dead
(B) fat
(C) full
(D) organized
(E) similar

8. ENIGMA
(A) ambition
(B) foreigner
(C) instrument
(D) officer
(E) riddle

9. INEPT
(A) awkward
(B) intelligent
(C) ticklish
(D) tawdry
(E) uninteresting

10. INVETERATE
(A) evil
(B) habitual
(C) inconsiderate
(D) reformed
(E) unintentional

Vocabulary Test 8

1. OBEISANCE
(A) salary
(B) justification
(C) conduct
(D) deference
(E) forethought

2. PEDANTIC
(A) stilted
(B) odd
(C) footworn
(D) selfish
(E) sincere

3. PETULANT
(A) lazy
(B) loving
(C) patient
(D) peevish
(E) wary

4. PROCLIVITY
(A) backwardness
(B) edict
(C) rainfall
(D) slope
(E) tendency

5. TRENCHANT
(A) keen
(B) good
(C) edible
(D) light
(E) subterranean

6. VAPID
(A) carefree
(B) crazy
(C) insipid
(D) spotty
(E) speedy

7. PROGNOSTICATE
(A) forecast
(B) ravish
(C) salute
(D) scoff
(E) succeed

8. PROPRIETY
(A) advancement
(B) atonement
(C) fitness
(D) sobriety
(E) use

9. PULCHRITUDE
(A) beauty
(B) character
(C) generosity
(D) intelligence
(E) wickedness

10. SCRUPULOUS
(A) drunken
(B) ill
(C) masterful
(D) exact
(E) stony

Vocabulary Test 9

1. INVARIABLE
   (A) diverse
   (B) eternal
   (C) fleeting
   (D) inescapable
   (E) uniform

2. VORACIOUS
   (A) excitable
   (B) honest
   (C) greedy
   (D) inclusive
   (E) circular

3. CONCENTRATE
   (A) agitate
   (B) protest
   (C) debate
   (D) harden
   (E) consolidate

4. PLAGIARIZE
   (A) annoy
   (B) borrow
   (C) steal ideas
   (D) imitate poorly
   (E) impede

5. CORTEGE
   (A) advisers
   (B) official papers
   (C) slaves
   (D) retinue
   (E) personal effects

6. ANTIPATHY
   (A) sympathy
   (B) detachment
   (C) aversion
   (D) amazement
   (E) opposition

7. DEMUR
   (A) object
   (B) agree
   (C) murmur
   (D) discard
   (E) consider

8. PARAGON
   (A) dummy
   (B) lover
   (C) image
   (D) model
   (E) favorite

9. FINITE
   (A) impure
   (B) firm
   (C) minute
   (D) limited
   (E) unbounded

10. ANARCHY
    (A) laissez-faire
    (B) motor-mindedness
    (C) pacifism
    (D) lawless confusion
    (E) self-sufficiency

Vocabulary Test 10

1. DISCRIMINATION
   (A) acquittal
   (B) insight
   (C) caution
   (D) indescretion
   (E) distortion

2. INVECTIVE
   (A) richness
   (B) goal
   (C) solemn oath
   (D) praise
   (E) verbal abuse

3. ADROIT
   (A) hostile
   (B) serene
   (C) pompous
   (D) skillful
   (E) allergic

4. DISTRESS
   (A) injury
   (B) contortion
   (C) suffering
   (D) convulsion
   (E) aggravation

5. DILETTANTE
   (A) epicure
   (B) dabbler
   (C) procrastinator
   (D) literary genius
   (E) playboy

6. PROVISIONAL
   (A) military
   (B) tentative
   (C) absentee
   (D) democratic
   (E) appointed

7. CONDIMENT
   (A) ledger
   (B) ore
   (C) telegraph device
   (D) musical instrument
   (E) spice

8. RECALCITRANT
   (A) insincere
   (B) obstinate
   (C) crafty
   (D) conservative
   (E) reconcilable

9. BON MOT
   (A) witticism
   (B) pun
   (C) praise
   (D) last word
   (E) exact meaning

10. ACCOUTREMENTS
    (A) sealed orders
    (B) equipment
    (C) cartons
    (D) correspondence
    (E) financial records

Vocabulary Test 11

1. HYPOTHESIS
   (A) assumption
   (B) proof
   (C) estimate
   (D) random guess
   (E) established truth

2. ALACRITY
   (A) slowness
   (B) indecision
   (C) caution
   (D) promptness
   (E) fearlessness

3. JETTISON
   (A) throw overboard
   (B) dismantle
   (C) scuttle
   (D) unload cargo
   (E) camouflage

4. VACILLATE
   (A) glitter
   (B) swerve
   (C) surrender
   (D) soften
   (E) waver

5. ASTUTE
   (A) shrewd
   (B) futile
   (C) potent
   (D) provocative
   (E) ruthless

6. PROVISO
   (A) final treaty
   (B) condition
   (C) demand
   (D) official document
   (E) proclamation

7. MACABRE
   (A) gruesome
   (B) meager
   (C) sordid
   (D) fantastic
   (E) cringing

8. AUGMENT
   (A) curtail
   (B) change
   (C) restore
   (D) conceal
   (E) increase

9. INTEGRAL
   (A) useful
   (B) powerful
   (C) essential
   (D) mathematical
   (E) indestructible

10. IMPUNITY
    (A) shamelessness
    (B) power of action
    (C) self-reliance
    (D) haughtiness
    (E) exemption from punishment

Vocabulary Test 12

1. LATENT
   (A) inherent
   (B) lazy
   (C) dormant
   (D) crushed
   (E) anticipated

2. OBDURATE
   (A) patient
   (B) stupid
   (C) rude
   (D) stubborn
   (E) tolerant

Vocabulary Test 13

3. BELLICOSE
   (A) boastful
   (B) warlike
   (C) sluggish
   (D) fantastic
   (E) oriental

4. ARROYO
   (A) cliff
   (B) plain
   (C) ranch
   (D) gully
   (E) cactus

5. AUGUR
   (A) enrage
   (B) foretell
   (C) suggest
   (D) evaluate
   (E) minimize

6. CONTRITE
   (A) infectious
   (B) worried
   (C) penitent
   (D) sympathetic
   (E) tolerant

7. PETULANT
   (A) silly
   (B) gay
   (C) sarcastic
   (D) officious
   (E) quarrelsome

8. PAEAN
   (A) prize
   (B) song of praise
   (C) decoration
   (D) certificate
   (E) story of heroism

9. EXOTIC
   (A) romantic
   (B) exciting
   (C) wealthy
   (D) strange
   (E) tropical

10. ARCHIPELAGO
    (A) slender isthmus
    (B) long, narrow land mass
    (C) string of lakes
    (D) high, flat plain
    (E) group of small islands

1. PREVARICATE
   (A) hesitate
   (B) lie
   (C) protest
   (D) ramble
   (E) remain silent

2. INCREDULOUS
   (A) argumentative
   (B) imaginative
   (C) indifferent
   (D) irreligious
   (E) skeptical

3. PLACATE
   (A) amuse
   (B) appease
   (C) embroil
   (D) pity
   (E) reject

4. COGNIZANT
   (A) afraid
   (B) aware
   (C) capable
   (D) ignorant
   (E) optimistic

5. DISSONANCE
   (A) disapproval
   (B) disaster
   (C) discord
   (D) disparity
   (E) dissimilarity

6. IMMINENT
   (A) declining
   (B) distinguished
   (C) impending
   (D) terrifying
   (E) unlikely

7. TORSION
   (A) bending
   (B) compressing
   (C) sliding
   (D) stretching
   (E) twisting

8. ACCRUED
   (A) added
   (B) incidental
   (C) miscellaneous
   (D) special
   (E) unearned

9. EFFRONTERY
    (A) bad taste
    (B) conceit
    (C) dishonesty
    (D) impudence
    (E) snobbishness

10. ACQUIESCENCE
    (A) advice
    (B) advocacy
    (C) compliance
    (D) friendliness
    (E) opposition

Vocabulary Test 14

1. RETICENT
    (A) fidgety
    (B) repetitious
    (C) reserved
    (D) restful
    (E) truthful

2. STIPULATE
    (A) bargain
    (B) instigate
    (C) prefer
    (D) request
    (E) specify

3. PSEUDO
    (A) deep
    (B) obvious
    (C) pretended
    (D) provoking
    (E) spiritual

4. FLOTSAM
    (A) dark sand
    (B) fleet
    (C) life preserver
    (D) shoreline
    (E) wreckage

5. AWRY
    (A) askew
    (B) deplorable
    (C) odd
    (D) simple
    (E) striking

6. NEFARIOUS
    (A) clever
    (B) necessary
    (C) negligent
    (D) short-sighted
    (E) wicked

7. GLIB
    (A) cheerful
    (B) delightful
    (C) dull
    (D) fluent
    (E) gloomy

8. PAUCITY
    (A) abundance
    (B) ease
    (C) hardship
    (D) lack
    (E) stoppage

9. LUCRATIVE
    (A) debasing
    (B) fortunate
    (C) influential
    (D) monetary
    (E) profitable

10. INDUBITABLE
    (A) doubtful
    (B) fraudulent
    (C) honorable
    (D) safe
    (E) undeniable

Vocabulary Test 15

1. CONNIVANCE
    (A) approval
    (B) collusion
    (C) conflict
    (D) permission
    (E) theft

2. SAVANT
    (A) diplomat
    (B) inventor
    (C) learned man
    (D) thrifty person
    (E) wiseacre

3. INCIPIENT
    (A) beginning
    (B) dangerous
    (C) hasty
    (D) secret
    (E) widespread

4. VIRILE
    (A) honest
    (B) loyal
    (C) manly
    (D) pugnacious
    (E) virtuous

5. ASSIDUOUS
   (A) courteous
   (B) diligent
   (C) discouraged
   (D) frank
   (E) slow

6. CATACLYSM
   (A) blunder
   (B) superstition
   (C) treachery
   (D) triumph
   (E) upheaval

7. AUSPICIOUS
   (A) condemnatory
   (B) conspicuous
   (C) favorable
   (D) questionable
   (E) spicy

8. SATIRE
   (A) conversation
   (B) criticism
   (C) gossip
   (D) irony
   (E) jesting

9. VERNACULAR
   (A) common speech
   (B) correct usage
   (C) long words
   (D) oratory
   (E) poetic style

10. EMOLUMENT
    (A) captial
    (B) compensation
    (C) liabilities
    (D) loss
    (E) output

Vocabulary Test 16

1. TURGID
   (A) dusty
   (B) muddy
   (C) rolling
   (D) swollen
   (E) tense

2. EXPUNGE
   (A) clarify
   (B) copy
   (C) delete
   (D) investigate
   (E) underline

3. ETHNOLOGY
   (A) causation
   (B) morals
   (C) social psychology
   (D) study of races
   (E) word analysis

4. DEDUCE
   (A) diminish
   (B) infer
   (C) outline
   (D) persuade
   (E) subtract

5. PANORAMIC
   (A) brilliant
   (B) comprehensive
   (C) pretty
   (D) fluorescent
   (E) unique

6. IGNOMINY
   (A) disgrace
   (B) isolation
   (C) misfortune
   (D) sorrow
   (E) stupidity

7. RELEVANT
   (A) ingenious
   (B) inspiring
   (C) obvious
   (D) pertinent
   (E) tentative

8. GAMUT
   (A) game
   (B) range
   (C) risk
   (D) organization
   (E) plan

9. APPOSITE
   (A) appropriate
   (B) contrary
   (C) different
   (D) spontaneous
   (E) tricky

10. AMBULATORY
    (A) able to walk
    (B) confined to bed
    (C) injured
    (D) quarantined
    (E) suffering from disease

Vocabulary Test 17

1. DISPARAGE
   (A) belittle
   (B) upgrade
   (C) erase
   (D) reform
   (E) scatter

2. LIMPID
   (A) calm
   (B) clear
   (C) crippled
   (D) delightful
   (E) opaque

3. DERISIVE
   (A) dividing
   (B) furnishing
   (C) reflecting
   (D) expressing ridicule
   (E) suggesting

4. DEBILITATE
   (A) encourage
   (B) insinuate
   (C) prepare
   (D) turn away
   (E) weaken

5. OPULENT
   (A) fearful
   (B) free
   (C) oversized
   (D) trustful
   (E) wealthy

6. BLANDISHMENT
   (A) dislike
   (B) flattery
   (C) ostentation
   (D) praise
   (E) rejection

7. CRYPTIC
   (A) appealing
   (B) arched
   (C) deathly
   (D) hidden
   (E) intricate

8. RAUCOUS
   (A) harsh
   (B) loud
   (C) querulous
   (D) rational
   (E) violent

9. AVIDITY
   (A) friendliness
   (B) greediness
   (C) resentment
   (D) speed
   (E) thirst

10. EPITOME
    (A) conclusion
    (B) effort
    (C) letter
    (D) summary
    (E) summit

Vocabulary Test 18

1. HIATUS
   (A) branch
   (B) disease
   (C) gaiety
   (D) insect
   (E) break

2. PLENARY
   (A) easy
   (B) empty
   (C) full
   (D) rewarding
   (E) untrustworthy

3. CAPRICIOUS
   (A) active
   (B) fickle
   (C) opposed
   (D) sheeplike
   (E) slippery

4. SPECIOUS
   (A) frank
   (B) particular
   (C) deceptive
   (D) suspicious
   (E) vigorous

5. EXTIRPATE
   (A) besmirch
   (B) clean
   (C) eradicate
   (D) favor
   (E) subdivide

6. EQUIVOCAL
   (A) doubtful
   (B) medium
   (C) monotonous
   (D) musical
   (E) well-balanced

7. RECOMPENSE
   (A) approval
   (B) blessing
   (C) gift
   (D) prayer
   (E) reward

8. BEATIFIC
   (A) giving bliss
   (B) eager
   (C) hesitant
   (D) lovely
   (E) sad

9. SANGUINE
   (A) limp
   (B) mechanical
   (C) muddy
   (D) red
   (E) stealthy

10. SURCEASE
    (A) end
    (B) hope
    (C) resignation
    (D) sleep
    (E) sweetness

Vocabulary Test 19

1. SENTIENT
   (A) very emotional
   (B) capable of feeling
   (C) hostile
   (D) sympathetic
   (E) wise

2. OBVIATE
   (A) grasp
   (B) reform
   (C) simplify
   (D) smooth
   (E) make unnecessary

3. PERUSE
   (A) endure
   (B) perpetuate
   (C) read
   (D) undertake
   (E) urge

4. RANCOR
   (A) dignity
   (B) fierceness
   (C) odor
   (D) spite
   (E) suspicion

5. TRUNCHEON
   (A) baton
   (B) canopy
   (C) dish
   (D) gun
   (E) rejected food

6. SEBACEOUS
   (A) fatty
   (B) fluid
   (C) porous
   (D) transparent
   (E) watery

7. DILATORY
   (A) hairy
   (B) happy-go-lucky
   (C) ruined
   (D) tardy
   (E) well-to-do

8. EBULLITION
   (A) bathing
   (B) boiling
   (C) refilling
   (D) retiring
   (E) returning

9. RELEGATE
   (A) banish
   (B) deprive
   (C) designate
   (D) report
   (E) request

10. RECONDITE
    (A) brittle
    (B) concealed
    (C) explored
    (D) exposed
    (E) uninformed

Vocabulary Test 20

1. REDOLENT
   (A) odorous
   (B) quick
   (C) refined
   (D) repulsive
   (E) supple

2. DISSIMULATE
   (A) confound
   (B) pretend
   (C) question
   (D) separate
   (E) strain

3. SUBLIME
(A) below par
(B) highly praised
(C) extreme
(D) noble
(E) settled

4. VIXEN
(A) fever
(B) quarrelsome woman
(C) sea bird
(D) sedative
(E) squirrel

5. SEDULOUS
(A) deceptive
(B) diligent
(C) grassy
(D) hateful
(E) sweet

6. VITIATE
(A) contaminate
(B) flavor
(C) freshen
(D) illuminate
(E) refer

7. CURVET
(A) come around
(B) follow
(C) leap
(D) restrain
(E) warp

8. ADVENTITIOUS
(A) accidental
(B) courageous
(C) favorable
(D) risk taking
(E) expected

9. ANIMUS
(A) animosity
(B) breath
(C) faith
(D) light
(E) poison

10. DESCRIED
(A) hailed
(B) rebuffed
(C) recalled
(D) regretted
(E) sighted

Vocabulary Test 21

1. ADULATION
(A) approach
(B) echo
(C) flattery
(D) gift
(E) imitation

2. SUBSEQUENTLY
(A) continually
(B) factually
(C) farther
(D) incidentally
(E) later

3. EXPURGATE
(A) amplify
(B) emphasize
(C) offend
(D) purify
(E) renew

4. LIAISON
(A) derivative
(B) liability
(C) link
(D) malice
(E) officer

5. SEDENTARY
(A) careful
(B) inactive
(C) notched
(D) pleasant
(E) uneventful

6. LASSITUDE
(A) childishness
(B) energy
(C) ignorance
(D) languor
(E) seriousness

7. ALTRUISTICALLY
(A) egotistically
(B) harmfully
(C) harshly
(D) highly
(E) unselfishly

8. PERFIDIOUS
(A) ambiguous
(B) flawless
(C) perforated
(D) treacherous
(E) trusting

9. CONSUMMATE
   (A) achieve
   (B) devour
   (C) effuse
   (D) ignite
   (E) take

10. MUNIFICENTLY
    (A) acutely
    (B) awkwardly
    (C) cruelly
    (D) generously
    (E) militarily

Vocabulary Test 22

1. LUGUBRIOUS
   (A) calm
   (B) doleful
   (C) tepid
   (D) wan
   (E) warm

2. DISCONSOLATE
   (A) desolate
   (B) emotional
   (C) incorrigible
   (D) gloomy
   (E) sad

3. COTERIE
   (A) clique
   (B) cure-all
   (C) expert judge
   (D) forerunner
   (E) society girl

4. CONDUIT
   (A) doorway
   (B) electric generator
   (C) power
   (D) screen
   (E) tube

5. SHIBBOLETH
   (A) a friend in need
   (B) lonely home
   (C) personal complaint
   (D) reason for action
   (E) watchword

6. EVANESCENT
   (A) colorful
   (B) consecrated
   (C) converted
   (D) empty
   (E) vanishing

7. PARSIMONIOUS
   (A) cautious
   (B) ecclesiastical
   (C) luxurious
   (D) stingy
   (E) unique

8. MACHIAVELLIAN
   (A) cunning
   (B) humble
   (C) kingly
   (D) machine-like
   (E) saintly

9. COMPENDIUM
   (A) amplification
   (B) appendix
   (C) expansion
   (D) paraphrase
   (E) summary

10. MEGALOMANIA
    (A) desire for beauty
    (B) mania for sympathy
    (C) miserliness
    (D) passion for grandeur
    (E) pity for the poor

Vocabulary Test 23

1. TORPOR
   (A) cyclone
   (B) frenzy
   (C) sluggishness
   (D) strain
   (E) twisting

2. ESOTERIC
   (A) clear
   (B) external
   (C) popular
   (D) secret
   (E) uncertain

3. SUPERCILIOUSLY
   (A) critically
   (B) disdainfully
   (C) hypersensitively
   (D) naïvely
   (E) softly

4. ABSTEMIOUS
   (A) blatant
   (B) exhilarating
   (C) greedy
   (D) temperate
   (E) wasteful

5. KEN
   (A) acceptance
   (B) belief
   (C) dune
   (D) knowledge
   (E) woody glen

6. GERMANE
   (A) diseased
   (B) foreign
   (C) infected
   (D) pertinent
   (E) polished

7. VITUPERATION
   (A) abuse
   (B) appendectomy
   (C) complication
   (D) rejuvenation
   (E) repeal

8. CHIMERICAL
   (A) clever
   (B) imaginary
   (C) experimental
   (D) foreign
   (E) provisional

9. DULCIMER
   (A) dolly
   (B) doublet
   (C) duenna
   (D) gadget
   (E) musical instrument

10. SARTORIAL
    (A) disheveled
    (B) frozen
    (C) satirical
    (D) tailored
    (E) warm

Vocabulary Test 24

1. VERTIGO
   (A) curiosity
   (B) dizziness
   (C) enlivenment
   (D) greenness
   (E) invigoration

2. DEBACLE
   (A) ceremony
   (B) collapse
   (C) dance
   (D) deficit
   (E) dispute

3. CONDIGN
   (A) deserved
   (B) hidden
   (C) perplexed
   (D) pretended
   (E) unworthy

4. EPHEMERALLY
   (A) enduringly
   (B) lightly
   (C) openly
   (D) suspiciously
   (E) transiently

5. HISTRIONIC
   (A) authentic
   (B) hysterical
   (C) reportorial
   (D) sibilant
   (E) theatrical

6. URBANITY
   (A) aggressiveness
   (B) mercenary
   (C) municipality
   (D) rustic
   (E) suavity

7. TRUCULENT
   (A) rambling
   (B) relenting
   (C) savage
   (D) tranquil
   (E) weary

8. INVEIGH
   (A) allure
   (B) entice
   (C) guide cautiously
   (D) originate
   (E) speak bitterly

9. DESULTORY
   (A) delaying
   (B) disconnected
   (C) flagrant
   (D) insulting
   (E) irritating

10. INGENUOUS
    (A) clever
    (B) naïve
    (C) ignorant
    (D) native
    (D) unkind

Vocabulary Test 25

1. CUMULATIVE
   (A) additive
   (B) clumsy
   (C) cumbersome
   (D) incorrect
   (E) secretive

2. EPIGRAM
   (A) chemical term
   (B) exclamation
   (C) outer skin
   (D) pithy saying
   (E) tombstone

3. GESTICULATE
   (A) dance
   (B) digest easily
   (C) ridicule
   (D) travel
   (E) use gestures

4. BEGUILE
   (A) benefit
   (B) bind
   (C) deceive
   (D) envy
   (E) petition

5. AVID
   (A) eager
   (B) glowing
   (C) indifferent
   (D) lax
   (E) potent

6. LABYRINTH
   (A) laboratory
   (B) maze
   (C) path
   (D) portal
   (E) room

7. REGURGITATE
   (A) make new investments
   (B) obliterate
   (C) restore to solvency
   (D) slacken
   (E) surge back

8. PODIUM
   (A) chemical element
   (B) dais
   (C) foot specialist
   (D) magistrate
   (E) Roman infantryman

9. BEREFT
   (A) annoyed
   (B) awarded
   (C) deprived
   (D) enraged
   (E) insane

10. ELUCIDATE
    (A) condense
    (B) escape
    (C) evade
    (D) explain
    (E) shine through

Vocabulary Test 26

1. EMOLLIENT
   (A) comical
   (B) despicable
   (C) enthusiastic
   (D) raucous
   (E) soothing

2. NOSTALGIC
   (A) expressive
   (B) forgetful
   (C) homesick
   (D) inconstant
   (E) seasick

3. EXPIATE
   (A) atone for
   (B) die
   (C) hasten
   (D) imitate
   (E) make holy

4. PARADOX
   (A) accepted opinion
   (B) axiom
   (C) contradiction
   (D) enigma
   (E) pattern

5. ARCHETYPE
   (A) bowman
   (B) original model
   (C) public records
   (D) roguishness
   (E) star

6. MUNDANE
   (A) deformed
   (B) free
   (C) rough-shelled
   (D) tearful
   (E) worldly

7. PALLIATIVE
   (A) boring
   (B) callous
   (C) permanent
   (D) softening
   (E) unyielding

8. FOMENT
   (A) curb
   (B) explode
   (C) exclude
   (D) turn into wine
   (E) instigate

9. PREDACIOUS
   (A) beautiful
   (B) incongruous
   (C) peaceful
   (D) preying
   (E) valuable

10. RESILIENT
    (A) thrifty
    (B) elastic
    (C) timid
    (D) fragile
    (E) unsociable

Vocabulary Test 27

1. BLATANT
   (A) clamorous
   (B) conceited
   (C) prudish
   (D) reticent
   (E) unsuited

2. ADVERSITY
   (A) advertising
   (B) counsel
   (C) criticism
   (D) misfortune
   (E) proficiency

3. CADAVEROUS
   (A) cheerful
   (B) contemptible
   (C) ghastly
   (D) hungry
   (E) ill-bred

4. WRAITH
   (A) anger
   (B) apparition
   (C) figurine
   (D) mannequin
   (E) model

5. PERSPICACITY
   (A) clearness
   (B) dullness
   (C) keenness
   (D) vastness
   (E) wideness

6. EXTRANEOUS
   (A) derived
   (B) foreign
   (C) unsuitable
   (D) visible
   (E) wasteful

7. PAROXYSM
   (A) catastrophe
   (B) sudden outburst
   (C) illusion
   (D) lack of harmony
   (E) loss of all bodily movement

8. SAPIENT
   (A) discerning
   (B) foolish
   (C) mocking
   (D) soapy
   (E) youthful

9. FLACCID
   (A) flabby
   (B) golden
   (C) hard
   (D) strong
   (E) wiry

10. IMPECUNIOUS
    (A) frugal
    (B) guiltless
    (C) miserly
    (D) monied
    (E) poor

Vocabulary Test 28

1. ABDUCT
   (A) ruin
   (B) aid
   (C) fight
   (D) abolish
   (E) kidnap

2. DEMERIT
   (A) outcome
   (B) fault
   (C) prize
   (D) notice
   (E) belief

3. MUTINOUS
   (A) silent
   (B) oceangoing
   (C) rebellious
   (D) miserable
   (E) deaf

4. NEGLIGENT
   (A) lax
   (B) desperate
   (C) cowardly
   (D) ambitious
   (E) informal

5. CONTEST
   (A) disturb
   (B) dispute
   (C) detain
   (D) distrust
   (E) contain

6. QUERY
   (A) wait
   (B) lose
   (C) show
   (D) ask
   (E) demand

7. INSIDIOUS
   (A) treacherous
   (B) excitable
   (C) internal
   (D) distracting
   (E) secretive

8. PALPITATE
   (A) mash
   (B) stifle
   (C) creak
   (D) pace
   (E) throb

9. ANIMOSITY
   (A) hatred
   (B) interest
   (C) silliness
   (D) amusement
   (E) power

10. EGOTISM
    (A) sociability
    (B) aggressiveness
    (C) self-confidence
    (D) conceit
    (E) willingness

Vocabulary Test 29

1. CALLIGRAPHY
   (A) weaving
   (B) handwriting
   (C) drafting
   (D) mapmaking
   (E) graph making

2. SYNCHRONIZE
   (A) happen at the same time
   (B) follow immediately in time
   (C) alternate between events
   (D) postpone to a future time
   (E) have difficulty in hearing

3. SEMBLANCE
   (A) surface
   (B) diplomacy
   (C) replacement
   (D) appearance
   (E) confidence

4. WISTFUL
   (A) winding
   (B) mutual
   (C) exciting
   (D) rugged
   (E) yearning

5. CURTAIL
   (A) threaten
   (B) strengthen
   (C) lessen
   (D) hasten
   (E) collide

6. NOXIOUS
   (A) spicy
   (B) smelly
   (C) foreign
   (D) noisy
   (E) harmful

7. PAUCITY
   (A) fatigue
   (B) scarcity
   (C) nonsense
   (D) waste
   (E) motion

8. JEOPARDIZE
   (A) soothe
   (B) cleanse
   (C) enjoy
   (D) reward
   (E) endanger

9. INTREPID
   (A) exhausted
   (B) moderate
   (C) anxious
   (D) youthful
   (E) fearless

10. TREACHEROUS
   (A) ignorant
   (B) envious
   (C) disloyal
   (D) cowardly
   (E) inconsiderate

Vocabulary Test 30

1. UNSAVORY
   (A) unfriendly
   (B) joyless
   (C) tactless
   (D) colorless
   (E) tasteless

2. HEARSAY
   (A) testimony
   (B) argument
   (C) rumor
   (D) accusation
   (E) similarity

3. HAMPER
   (A) restrain
   (B) pack
   (C) clarify
   (D) grip
   (E) err

4. BEDLAM
   (A) inadequacy
   (B) confusion
   (C) translation
   (D) courtesy
   (E) curiosity

5. INFALLIBLE
   (A) negative
   (B) unfair
   (C) essential
   (D) certain
   (E) weary

6. CONTEND
   (A) solve
   (B) observe
   (C) outwit
   (D) encourage
   (E) compete

7. AMOROUS
   (A) shapeless
   (B) helpful
   (C) familiar
   (D) loving
   (E) solemn

8. ALLEVIATE
   (A) reject
   (B) ease
   (C) imitate
   (D) consent
   (E) elevate

9. NEOPHYTE
   (A) participant
   (B) officer
   (C) beginner
   (D) winner
   (E) quarrel

10. SOLACE
   (A) comfort
   (B) weariness
   (C) direction
   (D) complaint
   (E) respect

Vocabulary Test 31

1. ULTIMATUM
   (A) shrewd plan
   (B) final terms
   (C) first defeat
   (D) dominant leader
   (E) electric motor

2. GIRD
   (A) surround
   (B) appeal
   (C) request
   (D) break
   (E) glance

3. WANGLE
   (A) moan
   (B) mutilate
   (C) exasperate
   (D) manipulate
   (E) triumph

4. PROCUREMENT
   (A) acquisition
   (B) resolution
   (C) healing
   (D) importance
   (E) miracle

5. CULMINATION
   (A) rebellion
   (B) lighting system
   (C) climax
   (D) destruction
   (E) mystery

6. INSUPERABLE
   (A) incomprehensible
   (B) elaborate
   (C) unusual
   (D) indigestible
   (E) unconquerable

7. CLICHÉ
   (A) summary argument
   (B) new information
   (C) new hat
   (D) trite phrase
   (E) lock device

8. CONCESSION
   (A) nourishment
   (B) plea
   (C) restoration
   (D) similarity
   (E) acknowledgment

9. INSIPID
   (A) disrespectful
   (B) uninteresting
   (C) persistent
   (D) whole
   (E) stimulating

10. REPRISAL
    (A) retaliation
    (B) drawing
    (C) capture
    (D) release
    (E) suspicion

Vocabulary Test 32

1. DUBIOUS
   (A) economical
   (B) well-groomed
   (C) boring
   (D) discouraged
   (E) uncertain

2. ATROCIOUS
   (A) brutal
   (B) innocent
   (C) shrunken
   (D) yellowish
   (E) unsound

3. PRESTIGE
   (A) speed
   (B) influence
   (C) omen
   (D) pride
   (E) excuse

4. VINDICATE
   (A) outrage
   (B) waver
   (C) enliven
   (D) justify
   (E) fuse

5. EXUDE
   (A) accuse
   (B) discharge
   (C) inflect
   (D) appropriate
   (E) distress

6. FACTION
   (A) clique
   (B) judgment
   (C) truth
   (D) type of architecture
   (E) health

7. INCLEMENT
   (A) merciful
   (B) sloping
   (C) harsh
   (D) disastrous
   (E) personal

8. SPURIOUS
   (A) concise
   (B) false
   (C) obstinate
   (D) sarcastic
   (E) severe

9. SUBSERVIENT
   (A) existing
   (B) obsequious
   (C) related
   (D) underlying
   (E) useful

10. IMPORTUNE
    (A) aggrandize
    (B) carry
    (C) exaggerate
    (D) prolong
    (E) urge

Vocabulary Test 33

1. CONTROVERSIAL
   (A) faultfinding
   (B) pleasant
   (C) debatable
   (D) ugly
   (E) talkative

2. GHASTLY
   (A) hasty
   (B) furious
   (C) breathless
   (D) deathlike
   (E) spiritual

3. BELLIGERENT
   (A) worldly
   (B) warlike
   (C) loudmouthed
   (D) furious
   (E) artistic

4. PROFICIENCY
   (A) wisdom
   (B) oversupply
   (C) expertness
   (D) advancement
   (E) sincerity

5. COMPASSION
   (A) rage
   (B) strength of character
   (C) forcefulness
   (D) sympathy
   (E) uniformity

6. DISSENSION
   (A) treatise
   (B) pretense
   (C) fear
   (D) lineage
   (E) discord

7. INTIMATE
   (A) charm
   (B) hint
   (C) disguise
   (D) frighten
   (E) hum

8. BERATE
   (A) classify
   (B) scold
   (C) underestimate
   (D) take one's time
   (E) evaluate

9. DEARTH
   (A) scarcity
   (B) width
   (C) affection
   (D) wealth
   (E) warmth

10. MEDITATE
    (A) rest
    (B) stare
    (C) doze
    (D) make peace
    (E) reflect

Vocabulary Test 34

1. STAGNANT
   (A) inactive
   (B) alert
   (C) selfish
   (D) difficult
   (E) scornful

2. MANDATORY
   (A) insane
   (B) obligatory
   (C) evident
   (D) strategic
   (E) unequaled

3. INFERNAL
   (A) immodest
   (B) incomplete
   (C) domestic
   (D) second-rate
   (E) fiendish

4. EXONERATE
   (A) free from blame
   (B) warn
   (C) drive out
   (D) overcharge
   (E) plead

5. ARBITER
   (A) friend
   (B) judge
   (C) drug
   (D) tree surgeon
   (E) truant

6. ENMITY
   (A) boredom
   (B) puzzle
   (C) offensive language
   (D) ill will
   (E) entanglement

7. DISCRIMINATE
   (A) fail
   (B) delay
   (C) accuse
   (D) distinguish
   (E) reject

8. DERISION
   (A) disgust
   (B) ridicule
   (C) fear
   (D) anger
   (E) heredity

9. EXULTANT
   (A) essential
   (B) elated
   (C) praiseworthy
   (D) plentiful
   (E) high-priced

10. OSTENSIBLE
    (A) vibrating
    (B) odd
    (C) apparent
    (D) standard
    (E) ornate

Vocabulary Test 35

1. ABHOR
   (A) hate
   (B) admire
   (C) taste
   (D) skip
   (E) resign

2. DUTIFUL
   (A) lasting
   (B) sluggish
   (C) required
   (D) soothing
   (E) obedient

3. ZEALOT
   (A) breeze
   (B) enthusiast
   (C) vault
   (D) wild animal
   (E) musical instrument

4. MAGNANIMOUS
   (A) high-minded
   (B) faithful
   (C) concerned
   (D) individual
   (E) small

5. CITE
   (A) protest
   (B) depart
   (C) quote
   (D) agitate
   (E) perform

6. OBLIVION
   (A) hindrance
   (B) accident
   (C) courtesy
   (D) forgetfulness
   (E) old age

7. CARDINAL
   (A) independent
   (B) well-organized
   (C) subordinate
   (D) dignified
   (E) chief

8. DEPLETE
   (A) restrain
   (B) corrupt
   (C) despair
   (D) exhaust
   (E) spread out

9. SUPERSEDE
   (A) retire
   (B) replace
   (C) overflow
   (D) bless
   (E) oversee

10. SPORADIC
    (A) bad-tempered
    (B) infrequent
    (C) radical
    (D) reckless
    (E) humble

Vocabulary Test 36

1. NEUTRALIZE
   (A) entangle
   (B) strengthen
   (C) counteract
   (D) combat
   (E) converse

2. INSINUATE
   (A) destroy
   (B) hint
   (C) do wrong
   (D) accuse
   (E) release

3. DIMINUTIVE
   (A) proud
   (B) slow
   (C) small
   (D) watery
   (E) puzzling

4. PLIGHT
   (A) departure
   (B) weight
   (C) conspiracy
   (D) predicament
   (E) stamp

5. ILLICIT
   (A) unlawful
   (B) overpowering
   (C) ill-advised
   (D) small-scale
   (E) unreadable

6. BENIGN
   (A) contagious
   (B) fatal
   (C) ignorant
   (D) kindly
   (E) decorative

7. REVERIE
   (A) abusive language
   (B) love song
   (C) backward step
   (D) daydream
   (E) holy man

8. APPREHENSIVE
   (A) quiet
   (B) firm
   (C) curious
   (D) sincere
   (E) fearful

9. RECOIL
   (A) shrink
   (B) attract
   (C) electrify
   (D) adjust
   (E) enroll

10. GUISE
    (A) trickery
    (B) request
    (C) innocence
    (D) misdeed
    (E) appearance

Vocabulary Test 37

1. ACQUIT
   (A) increase
   (B) harden
   (C) clear
   (D) sharpen
   (E) sentence

2. DEXTERITY
   (A) conceit
   (B) skill
   (C) insistence
   (D) embarrassment
   (E) guidance

3. ASSIMILATE
   (A) absorb
   (B) imitate
   (C) maintain
   (D) outrun
   (E) curb

4. DESPONDENCY
   (A) relief
   (B) gratitude
   (C) dejection
   (D) hatred
   (E) poverty

5. BUOYANT
   (A) conceited
   (B) cautioning
   (C) youthful
   (D) musical
   (E) cheerful

6. CULINARY
   (A) having to do with cooking
   (B) pertaining to dressmaking
   (C) fond of eating
   (D) loving money
   (E) tending to be secretive

7. CAPRICE
   (A) wisdom
   (B) ornament
   (C) pillar
   (D) whim
   (E) energy

8. DETERRENT
   (A) restraining
   (B) cleansing
   (C) deciding
   (D) concluding
   (E) crumbling

9. PUGNACIOUS
   (A) sticky
   (B) cowardly
   (C) precise
   (D) vigorous
   (E) quarrelsome

10. ABSCOND
    (A) detest
    (B) reduce
    (C) swallow up
    (D) dismiss
    (E) flee

Vocabulary Test 38

1. BOUNTY
   (A) limit
   (B) boastfulness
   (C) cheerfulness
   (D) reward
   (E) punishment

2. NOVICE
   (A) storyteller
   (B) iceberg
   (C) adolescent
   (D) mythical creature
   (E) beginner

3. BOLSTER
   (A) contradict
   (B) insist
   (C) defy
   (D) sleep
   (E) prop

4. MOBILE
   (A) changeable
   (B) scornful
   (C) mechanical
   (D) stylish
   (E) solid

5. CREDULITY
   (A) prize
   (B) feebleness
   (C) balance
   (D) laziness
   (E) belief

6. DOLDRUMS
   (A) charity
   (B) curing agents
   (C) contagious disease
   (D) low spirits
   (E) places of safety

7. LOATH
   (A) idle
   (B) worried
   (C) unwilling
   (D) ready
   (E) sad

8. INVENTIVE
   (A) aimless
   (B) clever
   (C) moist
   (D) false
   (E) nearby

9. LITHE
   (A) tough
   (B) obstinate
   (C) flexible
   (D) damp
   (E) gay

10. VACILLATE
    (A) waver
    (B) defeat
    (C) favor
    (D) endanger
    (E) humiliate

Vocabulary Test 39

1. OBNOXIOUS
   (A) dreamy
   (B) visible
   (C) angry
   (D) daring
   (E) objectionable

2. VERBATIM
   (A) word for word
   (B) at will
   (C) without fail
   (D) in secret
   (E) in summary

3. ENTICE
   (A) inform
   (B) observe
   (C) permit
   (D) attract
   (E) disobey

4. ACCLAIM
   (A) discharge
   (B) excel
   (C) applaud
   (D) divide
   (E) speed

5. TURBULENCE
(A) treachery
(B) commotion
(C) fear
(D) triumph
(E) overflow

6. DEFER
(A) discourage
(B) postpone
(C) empty
(D) minimize
(E) estimate

7. ADAGE
(A) proverb
(B) supplement
(C) tool
(D) youth
(E) hardness

8. ENSUE
(A) compel
(B) remain
(C) absorb
(D) plead
(E) follow

9. ZENITH
(A) lowest point
(B) compass
(C) summit
(D) middle
(E) wind direction

10. HYPOTHETICAL
(A) magical
(B) visual
(C) two-faced
(D) theoretical
(E) excitable

Vocabulary Test 40

1. IMPROMPTU
(A) offhand
(B) laughable
(C) fascinating
(D) rehearsed
(E) deceptive

2. CHIVALROUS
(A) crude
(B) military
(C) handsome
(D) foreign
(E) courteous

3. HAVOC
(A) festival
(B) disease
(C) ruin
(D) sea battle
(E) luggage

4. REJUVENATE
(A) reply
(B) renew
(C) age
(D) judge
(E) reconsider

5. STILTED
(A) stiffly formal
(B) talking much
(C) secretive
(D) fashionable
(E) senseless

6. SOLILOQUY
(A) figure of speech
(B) historical incident
(C) monologue
(D) isolated position
(E) contradiction

7. AFFABLE
(A) monotonous
(B) affected
(C) wealthy
(D) sociable
(E) selfish

8. NEBULOUS
(A) subdued
(B) eternal
(C) dewy
(D) cloudy
(E) careless

9. STEREOTYPED
(A) lacking originality
(B) illuminating
(C) pictorial
(D) free from disease
(E) sparkling

10. STUPEFY
(A) lie
(B) talk nonsense
(C) bend
(D) make dull
(E) overeat

Vocabulary Test 41

1. SUPERFICIAL
   (A) shallow
   (B) unusually fine
   (C) proud
   (D) aged
   (E) spiritual

2. DISPARAGE
   (A) separate
   (B) compare
   (C) refuse
   (D) belittle
   (E) imitate

3. PROTAGONIST
   (A) prophet
   (B) explorer
   (C) talented child
   (D) convert
   (E) leading character

4. LUDICROUS
   (A) profitable
   (B) excessive
   (C) disordered
   (D) ridiculous
   (E) undesirable

5. INTREPID
   (A) moist
   (B) tolerant
   (C) fearless
   (D) rude
   (E) gay

6. SAGE
   (A) wise man
   (B) tropical tree
   (C) tale
   (D) era
   (E) fool

7. ADMONISH
   (A) polish
   (B) escape
   (C) worship
   (D) distribute
   (E) caution

8. BESET
   (A) plead
   (B) perplex
   (C) pertain to
   (D) deny
   (E) deprive of

9. FIGMENT
   (A) ornamental openwork
   (B) perfume
   (C) undeveloped fruit
   (D) statuette
   (E) invention

10. GLIB
    (A) dull
    (B) thin
    (C) weak
    (D) fluent
    (E) sharp

Vocabulary Test 42

1. FORTITUDE
   (A) wealth
   (B) courage
   (C) honesty
   (D) loudness
   (E) luck

2. ABOLITION
   (A) retirement
   (B) disgust
   (C) enslavement
   (D) unrestricted power
   (E) complete destruction

3. EPITOME
   (A) pool
   (B) summary
   (C) formula
   (D) monster
   (E) song

4. MAIM
   (A) heal
   (B) disable
   (C) outwit
   (D) murder
   (E) bury

5. CRESTFALLEN
   (A) haughty
   (B) dejected
   (C) fatigued
   (D) disfigured
   (E) impolite

6. CUISINE
   (A) headdress
   (B) game of chance
   (C) leisurely voyage
   (D) artistry
   (E) style of cooking

7. CENSURE
   (A) erase
   (B) build up
   (C) criticize adversely
   (D) charm
   (E) help

8. DEVIATE
   (A) destroy
   (B) lower in value
   (C) invent
   (D) stray
   (E) depress

9. SWARTHY
   (A) dark-complexioned
   (B) slender
   (C) grass-covered
   (D) springy
   (E) rotating

10. MERCENARY
    (A) poisonous
    (B) unworthy
    (C) serving only for pay
    (D) luring by false charms
    (E) showing pity

Vocabulary Test 43

1. ACUTE
   (A) keen
   (B) bitter
   (C) brisk
   (D) genuine
   (E) certain

2. CLIENTELE
   (A) legal body
   (B) customers
   (C) board of directors
   (D) servants
   (E) tenants

3. SUCCUMB
   (A) follow
   (B) help
   (C) respond
   (D) yield
   (E) overthrow

4. SLOTH
   (A) selfishness
   (B) hatred
   (C) laziness
   (D) misery
   (E) slipperiness

5. INFRINGE
   (A) enrage
   (B) expand
   (C) disappoint
   (D) weaken
   (E) trespass

6. UNCANNY
   (A) ill-humored
   (B) immature
   (C) weird
   (D) unrestrained
   (E) insincere

7. SUBMISSIVE
   (A) unintelligent
   (B) underhanded
   (C) destructive
   (D) enthusiastic
   (E) meek

8. PEER
   (A) ancestor
   (B) teacher
   (C) judge
   (D) equal
   (E) assistant

9. EULOGIZE
   (A) kill
   (B) apologize
   (C) glorify
   (D) soften
   (E) imitate

10. INNOVATION
    (A) change
    (B) prayer
    (C) hint
    (D) restraint
    (E) inquiry

Vocabulary Test 44

1. EXHILARATION
   (A) animation
   (B) withdrawal
   (C) payment
   (D) suffocation
   (E) despair

2. RASPING
   (A) irritating
   (B) scolding
   (C) fastening
   (D) sighing
   (E) plundering

3. PROPONENT
   - (A) spendthrift
   - (B) rival
   - (C) distributor
   - (D) advocate
   - (E) neighbor

4. REDUNDANT
   - (A) flooded
   - (B) dreadful
   - (C) aromatic
   - (D) excessive
   - (E) reclining

5. BEGRUDGING
   - (A) humid
   - (B) envious
   - (C) living in seclusion
   - (D) involving a choice
   - (E) aimless

6. EMPATHIZE
   - (A) cheapen
   - (B) underestimate
   - (C) charm
   - (D) sympathize
   - (E) forgive

7. PRUDENT
   - (A) lighthearted
   - (B) eager
   - (C) cautious
   - (D) insincere
   - (E) fast-moving

8. OMNIVOROUS
   - (A) devouring everything
   - (B) many-sided
   - (C) powerful
   - (D) living on plants
   - (E) all-knowing

9. APPEND
   - (A) rely
   - (B) recognize
   - (C) arrest
   - (D) divide
   - (E) attach

10. STRATAGEM
    - (A) sneak attack
    - (B) military command
    - (C) thin layer
    - (D) deceptive device
    - (E) narrow passage

Vocabulary Test 45

1. COLLABORATE
   - (A) condense
   - (B) converse
   - (C) arrange in order
   - (D) provide proof
   - (E) act jointly

(2. FUTILITY
   - (A) uselessness
   - (B) timelessness
   - (C) stinginess
   - (D) happiness
   - (E) indistinctness

3. INTACT
   - (A) blunt
   - (B) fashionable
   - (C) hidden
   - (D) uninjured
   - (E) attentive

4. FERVOR
   - (A) originality
   - (B) justice
   - (C) zeal
   - (D) productivity
   - (E) corruption

5. UNERRING
   - (A) modest
   - (B) illogical
   - (C) ghostly
   - (D) matchless
   - (E) unfailing

6. REFUTE
   - (A) polish
   - (B) disprove
   - (C) throw away
   - (D) break up
   - (E) shut out

7. CONSENSUS
   - (A) steadfastness of purpose
   - (B) general agreement
   - (C) lack of harmony
   - (D) informal vote
   - (E) impressive amount

8. COMPLIANT
   - (A) tangled
   - (B) grumbling
   - (C) self-satisfied
   - (D) treacherous
   - (E) submissive

9. ACCESS
(A) agreement
(B) rapidity
(C) welcome
(D) approach
(E) surplus

10. PRUDENT
(A) wise
(B) overcritical
(C) famous
(D) dull
(E) early

Vocabulary Test 46

1. APPEASE
(A) attack
(B) soothe
(C) pray for
(D) estimate
(E) confess

2. RUTHLESS
(A) senseless
(B) sinful
(C) ruddy
(D) pitiless
(E) degrading

3. MUSTER
(A) rebel
(B) mask
(C) gather
(D) dampen
(E) grumble

4. EXECRATE
(A) embarrass
(B) desert
(C) omit
(D) curse
(E) resign

5. KNOLL
(A) elf
(B) mound
(C) bell
(D) development
(E) technique

6. IRATE
(A) evil
(B) wandering
(C) repetitious
(D) colorful
(E) angry

7. GRIMACE
(A) peril
(B) subtle suggestion
(C) signal
(D) wry face
(E) impurity

8. ACME
(A) layer
(B) summit
(C) edge
(D) pit
(E) interval

9. COVENANT
(A) solemn agreement
(B) formal invitation
(C) religious ceremony
(D) general pardon
(E) hiding place

10. APPALL
(A) honor
(B) decorate
(C) calm
(D) bore
(E) dismay

Vocabulary Test 47

1. INCUR
(A) take to heart
(B) anticipate
(C) bring down on oneself
(D) impress by repetition
(E) attack

2. CAUSTIC
(A) solemn
(B) puzzling
(C) biting
(D) influential
(E) attentive

3. DILATE
(A) retard
(B) fade
(C) wander
(D) expand
(E) startle

4. APATHY
(A) fixed dislike
(B) skill
(C) sorrow
(D) lack of feeling
(E) discontent

5. ELICIT
   (A) draw forth
   (B) cross out
   (C) run away
   (D) lengthen
   (E) revise

6. JUDICIOUS
   (A) wise
   (B) dignified
   (C) light-hearted
   (D) confused
   (E) respectful

7. UNSCATHED
   (A) unashamed
   (B) uninjured
   (C) unskilled
   (D) unsuccessful
   (E) unconscious

8. CHIDE
   (A) misbehave
   (B) cool
   (C) select
   (D) conceal
   (E) scold

9. CHARLATAN
   (A) scholar
   (B) acrobat
   (C) quack
   (D) faithful servant
   (E) fast talker

10. DISBURSE
    (A) remove forcibly
    (B) twist
    (C) amuse
    (D) vary slightly
    (E) pay out

Vocabulary Test 48

1. PARAMOUNT
   (A) equal
   (B) supreme
   (C) well-known
   (D) difficult
   (E) ready

2. BROCHURE
   (A) heavy shoe
   (B) weapon
   (C) pamphlet
   (D) trite remark
   (E) ornament

3. FIDELITY
   (A) happiness
   (B) bravery
   (C) prosperity
   (D) hardness
   (E) loyalty

4. DIFFUSE
   (A) explain
   (B) scatter
   (C) differ
   (D) congeal
   (E) dart

5. AGGRESSIVE
   (A) disgusting
   (B) impulsive
   (C) short-sighted
   (D) coarse-grained
   (E) self-assertive

6. AMASS
   (A) accumulate
   (B) encourage
   (C) comprehend
   (D) blend
   (E) astonish

7. DIABOLIC
   (A) puzzling
   (B) uneducated
   (C) ornamental
   (D) fiendish
   (E) spinning

8. FORBEARANCE
   (A) rejection
   (B) forgetfulness
   (C) sensitivity
   (D) patience
   (E) expectation

9. TAINT
   (A) snarl
   (B) infect
   (C) unite
   (D) annoy
   (E) list

10. DISGRUNTLED
    (A) untidy
    (B) rambling
    (C) disabled
    (D) cheating
    (E) displeased

Vocabulary Test 49

1. PLACID
   (A) apparent
   (B) peaceful
   (C) wicked
   (D) unusual
   (E) absent-minded

2. EVASIVE
   (A) emotional
   (B) effective
   (C) destructive
   (D) empty
   (E) shifty

3. CHAOS
   (A) complete disorder
   (B) deep gorge
   (C) challenge
   (D) sudden attack
   (E) rejoicing

4. DESPICABLE
   (A) insulting
   (B) ungrateful
   (C) contemptible
   (D) unbearable
   (E) jealous

5. DERIDE
   (A) question
   (B) ignore
   (C) mock
   (D) unseat
   (E) produce

6. ELUDE
   (A) gladden
   (B) fascinate
   (C) mention
   (D) escape
   (E) ignore

7. MUTABLE
   (A) colorless
   (B) harmful
   (C) uniform
   (D) changeable
   (E) invisible

8. INDICATIVE
   (A) suggestive
   (B) curious
   (C) active
   (D) angry
   (E) certain

9. LEVITY
   (A) cleanness
   (B) tastiness
   (C) deadliness
   (D) sluggishness
   (E) lightness

10. EXCRUCIATING
    (A) disciplinary
    (B) screaming
    (C) torturing
    (D) offensive
    (E) outpouring

Vocabulary Test 50

1. PRECEPT
   (A) rule
   (B) disguise
   (C) refinement
   (D) hasty decision
   (E) delaying action

2. HOMOGENEOUS
   (A) numerous
   (B) healthful
   (C) similar
   (D) assorted
   (E) educational

3. ARCHIVES
   (A) public records
   (B) models
   (C) supporting columns
   (D) tombs
   (E) large ships

4. INFAMY
   (A) anger
   (B) truth
   (C) disgrace
   (D) weakness
   (E) excitement

5. IMPINGE
   (A) swear
   (B) involve
   (C) erase
   (D) encroach
   (E) beg

6. DEPOSE
   (A) lay bare
   (B) deprive of office
   (C) empty
   (D) behead
   (E) blemish

7. OSTENTATIOUS
   (A) unruly
   (B) showy
   (C) varied
   (D) scandalous
   (E) probable

8. CONCLAVE
   (A) private meeting
   (B) covered passage
   (C) solemn vow
   (D) curved surface
   (E) ornamental vase

9. FRAY
   (A) combat
   (B) trickery
   (C) unreality
   (D) madness
   (E) freedom

10. OBSESS
    (A) fatten
    (B) beset
    (C) make dull
    (D) exaggerate
    (E) interfere

Vocabulary Test 51

1. CHAFE
   (A) pretend
   (B) joke
   (C) drink deeply
   (D) irritate
   (E) lose courage

2. MISCONSTRUE
   (A) hate
   (B) destroy
   (C) misbehave
   (D) misinterpret
   (E) misplace

3. PHILANTHROPIST
   (A) student of language
   (B) collector of stamps
   (C) lover of mankind
   (D) seeker of truth
   (E) enemy of culture

4. CASTE
   (A) feudal system
   (B) division of society
   (C) political theory
   (D) method of punishment
   (E) monetary system

5. CHASTEN
   (A) punish
   (B) engrave
   (C) attract
   (D) trick
   (E) laugh at

6. CONDUCIVE
   (A) pardonable
   (B) identical
   (C) incidental
   (D) helpful
   (E) exceptional

7. SUBORDINATE
   (A) hostile
   (B) inferior
   (C) separate
   (D) earlier
   (E) adaptable

8. SUPERFLUOUS
   (A) inexact
   (B) excessive
   (C) insincere
   (D) excellent
   (E) unreal

9. WIELD
   (A) protect
   (B) handle
   (C) postpone
   (D) resign
   (E) unite

10. GARISH
    (A) showy
    (B) talkative
    (C) sleepy
    (D) thin
    (E) vine-covered

Vocabulary Test 52

1. MEANDER
   (A) grumble
   (B) wander aimlessly
   (C) come between
   (D) weigh carefully
   (E) sing

2. DESTITUTION
   (A) trickery
   (B) fate
   (C) lack of practice
   (D) recovery
   (E) extreme poverty

3. MALIGN
   (A) slander
   (B) prophesy
   (C) entreat
   (D) approve
   (E) praise

4. IMPOTENT
   (A) unwise
   (B) lacking strength
   (C) free of sin
   (D) without shame
   (E) commanding

5. SNIVEL
   (A) crawl
   (B) cut short
   (C) whine
   (D) doze
   (E) giggle

6. SOJOURN
   (A) court order
   (B) nickname
   (C) temporary stay
   (D) slip of the tongue
   (E) makeshift

7. PLATITUDE
   (A) home remedy
   (B) trite remark
   (C) balance wheel
   (D) rare animal
   (E) protective film

8. CONCORD
   (A) brevity
   (B) blame
   (C) kindness
   (D) worry
   (E) agreement

9. ABOMINABLE
   (A) hateful
   (B) ridiculous
   (C) untamed
   (D) mysterious
   (E) boastful

10. QUALM
    (A) sudden misgiving
    (B) irritation
    (C) cooling drink
    (D) deceit
    (E) attention to detail

Vocabulary Test 53

1. EQUITABLE
   (A) charitable
   (B) even-tempered
   (C) two-faced
   (D) undecided
   (E) just

2. AFFRONT
   (A) quarrel
   (B) fright
   (C) denial
   (D) boast
   (E) insult

3. EPOCH
   (A) heroic deed
   (B) legend
   (C) witty saying
   (D) period of time
   (E) summary

4. RETRIBUTION
   (A) donation
   (B) jealousy
   (C) intense emotion
   (D) slow withdrawal
   (E) punishment

5. ABASE
   (A) forgive
   (B) degrade
   (C) attach
   (D) take leave
   (E) cut off

6. CAREEN
   (A) celebrate
   (B) mourn
   (C) ridicule
   (D) lurch
   (E) beckon

7. CONVIVIAL
   (A) formal
   (B) gay
   (C) rotating
   (D) well-informed
   (E) insulting

8. RAMPANT
   (A) playful
   (B) crumbling
   (C) roundabout
   (D) unchecked
   (E) defensive

9. DOCILE
(A) delicate
(B) positive
(C) dreary
(D) obedient
(E) melodious

10. VESTIGE
(A) bone
(B) test
(C) entrance
(D) cloak
(E) trace

Vocabulary Test 54

1. IMPEDIMENT
(A) foundation
(B) conceit
(C) hindrance
(D) luggage
(E) instrument

2. ADHERE
(A) pursue
(B) control
(C) arrive
(D) cling
(E) attend

3. COMPOSURE
(A) sensitiveness
(B) weariness
(C) stylishness
(D) hopefulness
(E) calmness

4. PROVOCATION
(A) sacred vow
(B) formal announcement
(C) cause of irritation
(D) careful management
(E) expression of disgust

5. SAVORY
(A) thrifty
(B) wise
(C) appetizing
(D) warm
(E) uncivilized

6. CANDID
(A) hidden
(B) shining
(C) straightforward
(D) critical
(E) warmhearted

7. ECLIPSE
(A) stretch
(B) obscure
(C) glow
(D) overlook
(E) insert

8. CORRELATE
(A) punish
(B) wrinkle
(C) conspire openly
(D) give additional proof
(E) connect systematically

9. INFIRMITY
(A) disgrace
(B) unhappiness
(C) rigidity
(D) hesitation
(E) weakness

10. PALPITATE
(A) faint
(B) harden
(C) throb
(D) soothe
(E) taste

Vocabulary Test 55

1. DEBRIS
(A) sadness
(B) decay
(C) ruins
(D) landslide
(E) hindrance

2. CONSOLIDATE
(A) show pity
(B) strengthen
(C) restrain
(D) infect
(E) use up

3. STAMINA
(A) flatness
(B) clearness
(C) hesitation
(D) vigor
(E) reliability

4. FACET
(A) phase
(B) humor
(C) story
(D) discharge
(E) assistance

5. INANIMATE
   (A) emotional
   (B) thoughtless
   (C) lifeless
   (D) inexact
   (E) silly

6. CALLOUS
   (A) frantic
   (B) misinformed
   (C) youthful
   (D) impolite
   (E) unfeeling

7. ENHANCE
   (A) sympathize
   (B) act out
   (C) weaken
   (D) make greater
   (E) fascinate

8. DISREPUTABLE
   (A) impolite
   (B) bewildered
   (C) debatable
   (D) unavailable
   (E) shameful

9. SEDATE
   (A) sober
   (B) seated
   (C) buried
   (D) drugged
   (E) timid

10. LUCRATIVE
    (A) lazy
    (B) coarse
    (C) profitable
    (D) brilliant
    (E) amusing

Vocabulary Test 56

1. IMPRUDENT
   (A) reckless
   (B) unexcitable
   (C) poor
   (D) domineering
   (E) powerless

2. DISSENSION
   (A) friction
   (B) analysis
   (C) swelling
   (D) injury
   (E) slyness

3. DISCONCERT
   (A) separate
   (B) cripple
   (C) lessen
   (D) upset
   (E) dismiss

4. RUDIMENTARY
   (A) discourteous
   (B) brutal
   (C) displeasing
   (D) elementary
   (E) embarrassing

5. AUTONOMOUS
   (A) self-governing
   (B) self-important
   (C) self-educated
   (D) self-explanatory
   (E) self-conscious

6. ASCERTAIN
   (A) hold fast
   (B) long for
   (C) declare
   (D) find out
   (E) avoid

7. LITERAL
   (A) flowery
   (B) matter-of-fact
   (C) sidewise
   (D) well-educated
   (E) firsthand

8. OSCILLATE
   (A) please
   (B) swing
   (C) purify
   (D) saturate
   (E) harden

9. CONCISE
   (A) accurate
   (B) brief
   (C) sudden
   (D) similar
   (E) painful

10. CONSTERNATION
    (A) restraint
    (B) close attention
    (C) dismay
    (D) self-importance
    (E) acknowledgment

Vocabulary Test 57

1. COLOSSAL
   - (A) ancient
   - (B) influential
   - (C) destructive
   - (D) dramatic
   - (E) huge

2. EVICT
   - (A) summon
   - (B) excite
   - (C) force out
   - (D) prove
   - (E) draw off

3. MISCHANCE
   - (A) omission
   - (B) ill luck
   - (C) feeling of doubt
   - (D) unlawful act
   - (E) distrust

4. FELON
   - (A) criminal
   - (B) fugitive
   - (C) traitor
   - (D) coward
   - (E) loafer

5. CENSURE
   - (A) empty
   - (B) criticize
   - (C) spread out
   - (D) take an oath
   - (E) omit

6. IMPLICIT
   - (A) unquestioning
   - (B) rude
   - (C) relentless
   - (D) sinful
   - (E) daring

7. SLOVENLY
   - (A) sleepy
   - (B) tricky
   - (C) untidy
   - (D) moody
   - (E) cowardly

8. EXTRANEOUS
   - (A) familiar
   - (B) unprepared
   - (C) foreign
   - (D) proper
   - (E) utmost

9. IMPASSE
   - (A) command
   - (B) stubbornness
   - (C) crisis
   - (D) deadlock
   - (E) failure

10. ABSOLVE
    - (A) forgive
    - (B) reduce
    - (C) mix
    - (D) deprive
    - (E) detect

Vocabulary Test 58

1. CUMBERSOME
   - (A) habitual
   - (B) clumsy
   - (C) hasty
   - (D) blameworthy
   - (E) uneducated

2. CAPTIVATE
   - (A) charm
   - (B) dictate terms
   - (C) overturn
   - (D) find fault
   - (E) hesitate

3. ZEALOUS
   - (A) serious
   - (B) speedy
   - (C) flawless
   - (D) necessary
   - (E) enthusiastic

4. AROMATIC
   - (A) shining
   - (B) precise
   - (C) ancient
   - (D) fragrant
   - (E) dry

5. RETROSPECT
   - (A) careful inspection
   - (B) reversal of form
   - (C) review of the past
   - (D) respect for authority
   - (E) special attention

6. WHET
   - (A) bleach
   - (B) exhaust
   - (C) harden
   - (D) stimulate
   - (E) question

7. CONTUSION
   (A) puzzle
   (B) shrinkage
   (C) bruise
   (D) uncleanness
   (E) fraud

8. COMPATIBLE
   (A) eloquent
   (B) adequate
   (C) overfed
   (D) comfortable
   (E) harmonious

9. CALLOUS
   (A) secretive
   (B) unruly
   (C) gloomy
   (D) unfeeling
   (E) hotheaded

10. REPUDIATE
    (A) reject
    (B) revalue
    (C) repay
    (D) forget
    (E) forgive

Vocabulary Test 59

1. PROLETARIAT
   (A) revolutionists
   (B) intellectuals
   (C) slaves
   (D) laboring classes
   (E) landowners

2. REQUISITE
   (A) desirable
   (B) ridiculous
   (C) liberal
   (D) necessary
   (E) majestic

3. TENACIOUS
   (A) violent
   (B) given to arguing
   (C) slender
   (D) holding fast
   (E) menacing

4. SCINTILLATE
   (A) whirl
   (B) wander
   (C) scorch
   (D) sharpen
   (E) sparkle

5. PROPRIETY
   (A) success
   (B) cleverness
   (C) nearness
   (D) security
   (E) suitability

6. UNWITTING
   (A) undignified
   (B) unintentional
   (C) slack
   (D) obstinate
   (E) unaccustomed

7. ATTRIBUTE
   (A) quality
   (B) tax
   (C) desire
   (D) law
   (E) final sum

8. SCRUPULOUS
   (A) scornful
   (B) clean
   (C) frightening
   (D) doubting
   (E) conscientious

9. USURP
   (A) lend money
   (B) replace
   (C) murder
   (D) surrender
   (E) seize by force

10. CESSATION
    (A) witnessing
    (B) stopping
    (C) strain
    (D) leave-taking
    (E) unwillingness

Vocabulary Test 60

1. RESOLUTE
   (A) determined
   (B) vibrating
   (C) irresistible
   (D) elastic
   (E) demanding

2. CRYSTALLIZE
   (A) glitter
   (B) give definite form to
   (C) chill
   (D) sweeten
   (E) polish vigorously

Vocabulary Test 61

3. REGIME
   (A) ruler
   (B) military unit
   (C) form of government
   (D) contagion
   (E) guardian

4. LACERATED
   (A) unconscious
   (B) stitched
   (C) slender
   (D) raveled
   (E) mangled

5. AMISS
   (A) friendly
   (B) faulty
   (C) tardy
   (D) central
   (E) purposeless

6. INDOLENCE
   (A) poverty
   (B) laziness
   (C) danger
   (D) truth
   (E) attention

7. PRECARIOUS
   (A) trustful
   (B) early
   (C) previous
   (D) cautious
   (E) uncertain

8. CONNOISSEUR
   (A) investigator
   (B) government official
   (C) pretender
   (D) critical judge
   (E) portrait artist

9. HILARITY
   (A) wittiness
   (B) disobedience
   (C) mirth
   (D) heedlessness
   (E) contentment

10. EMIT
    (A) overlook
    (B) adorn
    (C) discharge
    (D) encourage
    (E) stress

1. DYNAMIC
   (A) specialized
   (B) active
   (C) fragile
   (D) magical
   (E) comparative

2. ACHILLES' HEEL
   (A) source of strength
   (B) critical test
   (C) hereditary curse
   (D) vulnerable point
   (E) base conduct

3. AD LIB
   (A) cheerfully
   (B) freely
   (C) carefully
   (D) literally
   (E) wisely

4. DECRY
   (A) baffle
   (B) weep
   (C) trap
   (D) belittle
   (E) imagine

5. RAVAGE
   (A) ruin
   (B) tangle
   (C) delight
   (D) scold
   (E) crave

6. RENDEZVOUS
   (A) surrender
   (B) appointment
   (C) souvenir
   (D) hiding place
   (E) mutual exchange

7. SKULK
   (A) trail
   (B) shadow
   (C) ambush
   (D) lurk
   (E) race

8. PLETHORA
   (A) formal farewell
   (B) exclusive group
   (C) abundance
   (D) conclusive argument
   (E) good taste

9. NUPTIAL
 (A) moonlike
 (B) blunted
 (C) ritualistic
 (D) matrimonial
 (E) blessed

10. BALKED
 (A) swindled
 (B) thwarted
 (C) enlarged
 (D) waved
 (E) punished

Vocabulary Test 62

1. AD INFINITUM
 (A) to a limit
 (B) from eternity
 (C) occasionally
 (D) endlessly
 (E) periodically

2. EXTRICATE
 (A) disentangle
 (B) die out
 (C) praise
 (D) purify
 (E) argue with

3. SQUALID
 (A) dirty
 (B) unresponsive
 (C) wasteful
 (D) stormy
 (E) congested

4. COERCE
 (A) coincide
 (B) strengthen
 (C) accompany
 (D) compel
 (E) seek out

5. INTER
 (A) bury
 (B) stab
 (C) change
 (D) make peace
 (E) emphasize

6. CRESCENDO
 (A) increasing volume
 (B) decreasing tempo
 (C) abrupt ending
 (D) discordant note
 (E) musical composition

7. INDISCREET
 (A) unpopular
 (B) embarrassing
 (C) disloyal
 (D) unwise
 (E) greatly upset

8. UNWIELDY
 (A) stubborn
 (B) unhealthy
 (C) monotonous
 (D) shameful
 (E) clumsy

9. ENVISAGE
 (A) plot
 (B) conceal
 (C) wrinkle
 (D) contemplate
 (E) sneer

10. INTERIM
 (A) go-between
 (B) meantime
 (C) mixture
 (D) hereafter
 (E) period of rest

Vocabulary Test 63

1. DISHEARTEN
 (A) shame
 (B) discourage
 (C) astound
 (D) disown
 (E) cripple

2. COMPONENT
 (A) memorial
 (B) pledge
 (C) convenience
 (D) ingredient
 (E) similarity

3. LURK
 (A) stagger
 (B) tempt
 (C) sneak
 (D) grin
 (E) rob

4. GRUDGING
 (A) impolite
 (B) dirty
 (C) hoarse
 (D) alarming
 (E) unwilling

5. SEMBLANCE
   (A) likeness
   (B) noise
   (C) foundation
   (D) glance
   (E) error

6. NETTLE
   (A) irritate
   (B) catch
   (C) accuse
   (D) make ill
   (E) fade away

7. TREMULOUS
   (A) slow
   (B) high-pitched
   (C) huge
   (D) shaking
   (E) spirited

8. TERSE
   (A) delicate
   (B) nervous
   (C) mild
   (D) numb
   (E) concise

9. AFFINITY
   (A) solemn declaration
   (B) indefinite amount
   (C) natural attraction
   (D) pain
   (E) wealth

10. VOLATILE
    (A) disobedient
    (B) changeable
    (C) forceful
    (D) willing
    (E) luxurious

Vocabulary Test 64

1. HOMAGE
   (A) welcome
   (B) honor
   (C) cosiness
   (D) criticism
   (E) regret

2. DISPERSE
   (A) restore
   (B) spread
   (C) grumble
   (D) soak
   (E) spend

3. RATIONAL
   (A) resentful
   (B) overjoyed
   (C) sensible
   (D) reckless
   (E) apologetic

4. RECLUSE
   (A) schemer
   (B) criminal
   (C) miser
   (D) adventurer
   (E) hermit

5. COMPLACENCY
   (A) tenderness
   (B) admiration
   (C) dependence
   (D) unity
   (E) self-satisfaction

6. MENACE
   (A) kill
   (B) threaten
   (C) waste
   (D) indicate
   (E) tease

7. DUPE
   (A) combine
   (B) reproduce
   (C) fool
   (D) grab
   (E) follow

8. ABATE
   (A) surprise
   (B) desert
   (C) decrease
   (D) humiliate
   (E) pay for

9. CONGENITAL
   (A) existing at birth
   (B) displaying weakness
   (C) related by marriage
   (D) overcrowded
   (E) unintelligent

10. INSURGENT
    (A) impractical
    (B) unbearable
    (C) over-hanging
    (D) rebellious
    (E) patriotic

Vocabulary Test 65

1. CONJECTURE
   (A) work
   (B) joke
   (C) initiate
   (D) add
   (E) guess

2. DAIS
   (A) platform
   (B) easy chair
   (C) waiting room
   (D) ornamental pin
   (E) figurehead

3. IMPETUS
   (A) deadlock
   (B) collision
   (C) warning
   (D) wickedness
   (E) stimulus

4. INTROSPECTIVE
   (A) lacking strength
   (B) practicing self-examination
   (C) highly critical
   (D) intrusive
   (E) lacking confidence

5. DEIFY
   (A) describe
   (B) disobey
   (C) make presentable
   (D) worship as a god
   (E) challenge

6. AGGREGATION
   (A) method
   (B) irritation
   (C) prize
   (D) collection
   (E) blessing

7. EXALTED
   (A) honored
   (B) underhanded
   (C) funny
   (D) conceited
   (E) secondary

8. POTENTATE
   (A) slave
   (B) soldier
   (C) adviser
   (D) informer
   (E) ruler

9. INTIMIDATE
   (A) frighten
   (B) suggest
   (C) dare
   (D) border upon
   (E) befriend

10. SARDONIC
    (A) decorative
    (B) polished
    (C) strange
    (D) fashionable
    (E) sarcastic

Vocabulary Test 66

1. ELECTRIFY
   (A) punish
   (B) improve
   (C) thrill
   (D) explain
   (E) investigate

2. DISCRETION
   (A) special privilege
   (B) individual judgment
   (C) unfair treatment
   (D) disagreement
   (E) embarrassment

3. GRAPPLE
   (A) dive
   (B) wrestle
   (C) handle
   (D) fit together
   (E) fondle

4. LAUDABLE
   (A) brave
   (B) comical
   (C) peaceful
   (D) praiseworthy
   (E) conspicuous

5. LONGEVITY
   (A) wisdom
   (B) length of life
   (C) society
   (D) system of measure
   (E) loudness

6. BLANCH
   (A) destroy
   (B) drink
   (C) whiten
   (D) feel
   (E) mend

7. SHREW
   (A) moneylender
   (B) fortuneteller
   (C) chronic invalid
   (D) unruly child
   (E) scolding woman

8. STALWART
   (A) diseased
   (B) feeble
   (C) needy
   (D) sturdy
   (E) truthful

9. APOGEE
   (A) rate of ascent
   (B) force of gravity
   (C) measuring device
   (D) expression of regret
   (E) highest point

10. BANTER
   (A) tease playfully
   (B) strut boldly
   (C) ruin
   (D) bend slightly
   (E) relieve

Vocabulary Test 67

1. REPRESS
   (A) sharpen
   (B) restrain
   (C) repeat
   (D) disgust
   (E) grieve

2. BREACH
   (A) obstruction
   (B) violation
   (C) anticipation
   (D) accusation
   (E) decoration

3. DILIGENT
   (A) hesitant
   (B) prosperous
   (C) offensive
   (D) industrious
   (E) straightforward

4. CONCOCT
   (A) devise
   (B) link together
   (C) harmonize
   (D) meet privately
   (E) sweeten

5. FLAMBOYANT
   (A) scandalous
   (B) showy
   (C) nonsensical
   (D) manly
   (E) temporary

6. ECCENTRICITY
   (A) overabundance
   (B) self-consciousness
   (C) adaptability
   (D) publicity
   (E) oddity

7. VINDICTIVE
   (A) gloomy
   (B) cowardly
   (C) vengeful
   (D) cheerful
   (E) boastful

8. GRAPHIC
   (A) vivid
   (B) harsh-sounding
   (C) free from error
   (D) dignified
   (E) pliable

9. PLACARD
   (A) poster
   (B) souvenir
   (C) soothing medicine
   (D) exact reproduction
   (E) contemptuous remark

10. PUTREFY
   (A) scour
   (B) paralyze
   (C) rot
   (D) neglect
   (E) argue

Vocabulary Test 68

1. GRANDIOSE
   (A) selfish
   (B) thankful
   (C) quarrelsome
   (D) elderly
   (E) impressive

2. INCONGRUOUS
   (A) indistinct
   (B) unsuitable
   (C) unimportant
   (D) illegal
   (E) inconvenient

3. PRONE
   (A) disposed
   (B) speechless
   (C) tardy
   (D) two-edged
   (E) quick

4. EMISSARY
   (A) rival
   (B) secret agent
   (C) master of ceremonies
   (D) refugee
   (E) clergyman

5. INVALIDATE
   (A) turn inward
   (B) deprive of force
   (C) mistrust
   (D) support with facts
   (E) neglect

6. CLEMENCY
   (A) purity
   (B) timidity
   (C) courage
   (D) simplicity
   (E) mildness

7. UNSCATHED
   (A) uninterested
   (B) unsettled
   (C) unspoken
   (D) unharmed
   (E) unknown

8. RELINQUISH
   (A) shrink from
   (B) take pity on
   (C) yield
   (D) lessen
   (E) recall

9. ALLAY
   (A) offend
   (B) suffer
   (C) resemble
   (D) assign
   (E) calm

10. ANIMOSITY
    (A) liveliness
    (B) worry
    (C) ill will
    (D) regret
    (E) sarcasm

Vocabulary Test 69

1. SOLICIT
   (A) request
   (B) worry
   (C) command
   (D) deny
   (E) depend

2. PERTURB
   (A) pierce
   (B) filter
   (C) calculate
   (D) agitate
   (E) disregard

3. JAUNTY
   (A) bored
   (B) envious
   (C) quarrelsome
   (D) chatty
   (E) lively

4. DRIVEL
   (A) shrill laughter
   (B) foolish talk
   (C) untidy dress
   (D) waste matter
   (E) quaint humor

5. FRUGAL
   (A) sickly
   (B) sparing
   (C) slow
   (D) chilled
   (E) frightened

6. IOTA
   (A) first step
   (B) sacred picture
   (C) ornamental scroll
   (D) crystalline substance
   (E) very small quantity

7. POACH
   (A) squander
   (B) trespass
   (C) outwit
   (D) bully
   (E) borrow

8. DEFECTION
   (A) delay
   (B) slander
   (C) respect
   (D) desertion
   (E) exemption

9. MASTICATE
(A) chew
(B) slaughter
(C) ripen
(D) enroll
(E) tangle

10. ANALOGY
(A) imitation
(B) research
(C) calendar
(D) similarity
(E) disagreement

Vocabulary Test 70

1. DILEMMA
(A) punishment
(B) division in ranks
(C) ability to detect
(D) perplexing choice
(E) word with two meanings

2. CELESTIAL
(A) musical
(B) heavenly
(C) stately
(D) unmarried
(E) aged

3. MILITANT
(A) political
(B) mighty
(C) aggressive
(D) peaceable
(E) illegal

4. EMINENT
(A) noted
(B) moral
(C) future
(D) low
(E) unwise

5. PERCEIVE
(A) resolve
(B) observe
(C) organize
(D) stick in
(E) copy down

6. IDIOSYNCRASY
(A) stupidity
(B) virtue
(C) personal peculiarity
(D) foreign dialect
(E) similarity

7. EDIFICE
(A) tool
(B) large building
(C) garden
(D) mushroom
(E) set of books

8. SEEDY
(A) dishonest
(B) helpless
(C) vague
(D) nervous
(E) shabby

9. SUPPLANT
(A) spend
(B) unite
(C) recall
(D) replace
(E) purpose

10. DESIST
(A) loiter
(B) stand
(C) hurry
(D) stumble
(E) stop

Vocabulary Test 71

1. GIRD
(A) stare
(B) thresh
(C) encircle
(D) complain
(E) perforate

2. BIZARRE
(A) charitable
(B) joyous
(C) flattering
(D) insane
(E) fantastic

3. PERENNIAL
(A) superior
(B) unceasing
(C) notable
(D) short-lived
(E) authoritative

4. PROGENITOR
(A) genius
(B) wastrel
(C) forefather
(D) magician
(E) publisher

5. EMBELLISH
   (A) organize
   (B) involve
   (C) rob
   (D) beautify
   (E) correct

6. IMPLEMENT
   (A) carry out
   (B) fall apart
   (C) give freely
   (D) object strongly
   (E) praise highly

7. INSUBORDINATE
   (A) unreal
   (B) disobedient
   (C) inferior
   (D) unfaithful
   (E) unnecessary

8. ITINERANT
   (A) small
   (B) intensive
   (C) repetitive
   (D) wandering
   (E) begging

9. ADVERSITY
   (A) misfortune
   (B) surprise
   (C) economy
   (D) publicity
   (E) warning

10. DISSIPATE
    (A) explain
    (B) puzzle
    (C) rearrange
    (D) envy
    (E) waste

Vocabulary Test 72

1. VALOR
   (A) courage
   (B) honesty
   (C) beauty
   (D) alertness
   (E) modesty

2. DISSUADE
   (A) offend
   (B) lessen
   (C) advise against
   (D) spread out
   (E) separate

3. ERRATIC
   (A) unpredictable
   (B) upright
   (C) well-informed
   (D) self-centered
   (E) artificial

4. COVET
   (A) take for granted
   (B) keep secret
   (C) disbelieve
   (D) steal
   (E) long for

5. VERBOSE
   (A) forbidden
   (B) expanding
   (C) talented
   (D) wordy
   (E) opinionated

6. FLIPPANT
   (A) fishlike
   (B) anxious
   (C) frivolous
   (D) savage
   (E) shy

7. ACCLAMATION
   (A) seasoning
   (B) applause
   (C) slope
   (D) harmony
   (E) collection

8. INCITE
   (A) include
   (B) destroy
   (C) withdraw
   (D) arouse
   (E) perceive

9. FINESSE
   (A) end
   (B) skill
   (C) habit
   (D) expense
   (E) vanity

10. TANTALIZE
    (A) prevent
    (B) protect
    (C) rob
    (D) predict
    (E) torment

Vocabulary Test 73

1. INSOMNIA
   (A) boredom
   (B) loss of memory
   (C) seasickness
   (D) sleeplessness
   (E) lonesomeness

2. FEASIBLE
   (A) enjoyable
   (B) juicy
   (C) regrettable
   (D) responsible
   (E) possible

3. BLURT
   (A) brag
   (B) utter impulsively
   (C) challenge
   (D) shout angrily
   (E) weep noisily

4. ALIENATE
   (A) advise
   (B) entertain
   (C) forgive
   (D) sympathize with
   (E) make unfriendly

5. STARK
   (A) barely
   (B) offensively
   (C) uselessly
   (D) completely
   (E) artistically

6. NONCHALANCE
   (A) refinement
   (B) foresight
   (C) air of indifference
   (D) lack of knowledge
   (E) lack of common sense

7. GRIT
   (A) honesty
   (B) reverence
   (C) trustworthiness
   (D) cheerfulness
   (E) bravery

8. MEDIATE
   (A) make changes
   (B) argue earnestly
   (C) consider carefully
   (D) propose hesitantly
   (E) reconcile differences

9. DE FACTO
   (A) commercial
   (B) economic
   (C) in reality
   (D) unnecessary
   (E) the following

10. IRREVOCABLE
    (A) unreliable
    (B) disrespectful
    (C) unforgivable
    (D) unalterable
    (E) heartless

Vocabulary Test 74

1. ABYSMAL
   (A) bottomless
   (B) ill
   (C) forgetful
   (D) unoccupied
   (E) slight

2. PREROGATIVE
   (A) forewarning
   (B) formal investigation
   (C) privilege
   (D) reputation
   (E) opening speech

3. ILLUSTRIOUS
   (A) believable
   (B) unrewarding
   (C) cynical
   (D) decorative
   (E) famous

4. INTERMINABLE
   (A) scanty
   (B) secret
   (C) open-faced
   (D) endless
   (E) stationary

5. FRANCHISE
   (A) secrecy
   (B) right to vote
   (C) imprisonment
   (D) free-for-all
   (E) avoidable tragedy

6. LINEAGE
   (A) brilliance
   (B) ancestry
   (C) narrowness
   (D) straightness
   (E) ceremony

7. RECIPROCATE
   (A) reconsider
   (B) refresh
   (C) repay
   (D) recall
   (E) reclaim

8. REBUFF
   (A) send back
   (B) make over
   (C) snub
   (D) defend
   (E) remind

9. CLANDESTINE
   (A) unfriendly
   (B) fateful
   (C) unified
   (D) secret
   (E) argumentative

10. LETHARGY
    (A) unnatural drowsiness
    (B) excessive caution
    (C) lack of consideration
    (D) vice
    (E) foolishness

Vocabulary Test 75

1. ACCREDITED
   (A) obligated
   (B) approved
   (C) discharged
   (D) quickened
   (E) confessed

2. ADHERENT
   (A) clergyman
   (B) critic
   (C) executive
   (D) supporter
   (E) journalist

3. WHEEDLE
   (A) mourn
   (B) coax
   (C) revolve
   (D) hesitate
   (E) entertain

4. CIRCUITOUS
   (A) electrical
   (B) watery
   (C) roundabout
   (D) forbidding
   (E) tender

5. DESPOT
   (A) murderer
   (B) impostor
   (C) invader
   (D) avenger
   (E) tyrant

6. DETER
   (A) hinder
   (B) mistake
   (C) neglect
   (D) injure
   (E) restore

7. UTILITARIAN
   (A) practical
   (B) widespread
   (C) inexpensive
   (D) praiseworthy
   (E) fortunate

8. INCREDULITY
   (A) forgetfulness
   (B) faithlessness
   (C) immaturity
   (D) disbelief
   (E) unreality

9. INTERDICT
   (A) lessen
   (B) separate
   (C) fatigue
   (D) permit
   (E) forbid

10. TIMOROUS
    (A) necessary
    (B) expected
    (C) afraid
    (D) wild
    (E) brief

Vocabulary Test 76

1. BRAWN
   (A) boldness
   (B) muscular strength
   (C) rustiness
   (D) unruliness
   (E) protective covering

2. STALEMATE
   (A) athletic contest
   (B) complete defeat
   (C) deadlock
   (D) storm
   (E) refusal to fight

3. KINDLE
   - (A) relate
   - (B) pass on
   - (C) pretend
   - (D) arouse
   - (E) punish

4. POMP
   - (A) splendor
   - (B) illness
   - (C) hopefulness
   - (D) apple
   - (E) posture

5. TINGE
   - (A) mold
   - (B) draw forth
   - (C) color slightly
   - (D) sketch
   - (E) create

6. RECOIL
   - (A) steer
   - (B) link up
   - (C) put down
   - (D) scrape
   - (E) shrink back

7. QUASH
   - (A) creep
   - (B) mix thoroughly
   - (C) repeat
   - (D) suppress completely
   - (E) falsify

8. PALTRY
   - (A) trivial
   - (B) sacred
   - (C) metallic
   - (D) careless
   - (E) positive

9. IMPETUOUS
   - (A) controlled
   - (B) hasty
   - (C) vigorous
   - (D) defamatory
   - (E) vehement

10. HARANGUE
   - (A) unintelligible prose
   - (B) ranting speech
   - (C) poetic imagery
   - (D) anonymous letter
   - (E) heavy overcoat

Vocabulary Test 77

1. APROPOS
   - (A) witty
   - (B) forceful
   - (C) nearly correct
   - (D) richly decorated
   - (E) to the point

2. INIMICAL
   - (A) speechless
   - (B) unfriendly
   - (C) unnecessarily rude
   - (D) poor
   - (E) hopelessly sad

3. SORDID
   - (A) biting
   - (B) filthy
   - (C) mysterious
   - (D) griefstricken
   - (E) sickly

4. CATACLYSM
   - (A) severe criticism
   - (B) gorge
   - (C) launching device
   - (D) unconsciousness
   - (E) violent upheaval

5. FETTERED
   - (A) stricken
   - (B) scolded
   - (C) commanded
   - (D) confined
   - (E) loosened

6. VERACITY
   - (A) endurance
   - (B) selfishness
   - (C) truthfulness
   - (D) courtesy
   - (E) thoughtfulness

7. REPLETE
   - (A) filled
   - (B) tarnished
   - (C) golden
   - (D) economical
   - (E) wrecked

8. TREED
   - (A) met
   - (B) cornered
   - (C) followed
   - (D) searched
   - (E) scented

9. DERISIVE
   - (A) hereditary
   - (B) rebellious
   - (C) fragmentary
   - (D) scornful
   - (E) determined

10. TEMPER
    - (A) decorate
    - (B) annoy
    - (C) blame
    - (D) postpone
    - (E) moderate

Vocabulary Test 78

1. RESIDUE
   - (A) dwelling
   - (B) remainder
   - (C) debt
   - (D) sample
   - (E) storehouse

2. BUNGLE
   - (A) complain
   - (B) approach
   - (C) live in
   - (D) handle badly
   - (E) talk boastfully

3. ADVOCATE
   - (A) flatter
   - (B) caution
   - (C) recommend
   - (D) take an oath
   - (E) charge

4. CALAMITOUS
   - (A) disastrous
   - (B) inexperienced
   - (C) hard-hearted
   - (D) scheming
   - (E) slanderous

5. JILT
   - (A) fill in
   - (B) cast aside
   - (C) move about
   - (D) pick up
   - (E) help forward

6. FUTILE
   - (A) violent
   - (B) one-sided
   - (C) weary
   - (D) stingy
   - (E) useless

7. INCESSANT
   - (A) even
   - (B) illegal
   - (C) dirty
   - (D) continuous
   - (E) loud

8. PRATTLE
   - (A) sell
   - (B) storm
   - (C) babble
   - (D) explain
   - (E) keep

9. PERVERSE
   - (A) contrary
   - (B) rhythmic
   - (C) imaginary
   - (D) alert
   - (E) rich

10. QUARRY
    - (A) dispute
    - (B) prey
    - (C) initial
    - (D) request
    - (E) output

Vocabulary Test 79

1. PATERNAL
   - (A) generous
   - (B) aged
   - (C) fatherly
   - (D) thrifty
   - (E) narrowminded

2. CALIBER
   - (A) gaiety
   - (B) quality
   - (C) hope
   - (D) similarity
   - (E) politeness

3. PARADOX
   - (A) virtuous man
   - (B) equal rights
   - (C) seeming contradiction
   - (D) complicated design
   - (E) geometric figure

4. DISPEL
   - (A) punish
   - (B) excite
   - (C) pay out
   - (D) drive away
   - (E) misunderstand

5. VERBATIM
   (A) out loud
   (B) word for word
   (C) in set phrases
   (D) elegantly expressed
   (E) using too many words

6. GRUELING
   (A) exhausting
   (B) surprising
   (C) insulting
   (D) embarrassing
   (E) boring

7. CREDIBILITY
   (A) freedom from prejudice
   (B) religious doctrine
   (C) capacity for belief
   (D) questioning attitude
   (E) good judgment

8. APPROPRIATE
   (A) betray
   (B) compliment
   (C) take possession of
   (D) give thanks
   (E) draw near to

9. EXONERATE
   (A) overcharge
   (B) lengthen
   (C) leave out
   (D) free from blame
   (E) serve as a model

10. BLAND
    (A) flattering
    (B) foolish
    (C) successful
    (D) soothing
    (E) sharp

Vocabulary Test 80

1. EFFIGY
   (A) representation
   (B) shadow
   (C) parade
   (D) ancestor
   (E) present

2. ZEST
   (A) operation
   (B) mood
   (C) great dismay
   (D) keen enjoyment
   (E) false alarm

3. ASTUTE
   (A) shrewd
   (B) inflammable
   (C) defiant
   (D) out of tune
   (E) bitter

4. DISCREPANCY
   (A) variance
   (B) disbelief
   (C) feebleness
   (D) insult
   (E) forcefulness

5. COPIOUS
   (A) copyrighted
   (B) tricky
   (C) abundant
   (D) complete
   (E) sincere

6. ADVENT
   (A) approval
   (B) opportunity
   (C) welcome
   (D) recommendation
   (E) arrival

7. IMMINENT
   (A) about to occur
   (B) never-ending
   (C) up-to-date
   (D) inconvenient
   (E) youthful

8. RANKLE
   (A) spread around
   (B) seize quickly
   (C) crease
   (D) search
   (E) irritate deeply

9. INJUNCTION
   (A) exclamation
   (B) rebellion
   (C) directive
   (D) crisis
   (E) illegality

10. DEFT
    (A) critical
    (B) conceited
    (C) lighthearted
    (D) skillful
    (E) tactful

Vocabulary Test 81

1. HEEDLESS
   (A) unfortunate
   (B) expensive
   (C) careless
   (D) happy
   (E) weatherbeaten

2. IMPEDIMENT
   (A) obstacle
   (B) base
   (C) spice
   (D) mechanism
   (E) footstool

3. QUAVER
   (A) launch
   (B) quicken
   (C) sharpen
   (D) tremble
   (E) forget

4. SHACKLE
   (A) hide
   (B) glide
   (C) anger
   (D) quiet
   (E) hamper

5. LOWLY
   (A) idle
   (B) silent
   (C) humble
   (D) sorrowful
   (E) solitary

6. CUBICLE
   (A) wedge
   (B) puzzle
   (C) tiny amount
   (D) unit of measure
   (E) small compartment

7. ARRAIGN
   (A) debate
   (B) accuse
   (C) excite
   (D) cancel
   (E) protect

8. OBLIVIOUS
   (A) unwanted
   (B) disorderly
   (C) unaware
   (D) sickly
   (E) evident

9. PROFOUND
   (A) plentiful
   (B) beneficial
   (C) lengthy
   (D) religious
   (E) deep

10. WAN
    (A) pale
    (B) humorous
    (C) pleasing
    (D) watchful
    (E) lovesick

Vocabulary Test 82

1. HAUNT
   (A) contain
   (B) give up
   (C) expect
   (D) stay around
   (E) extend greatly

2. UNMINDFUL
   (A) unaware
   (B) illogical
   (C) unaccustomed
   (D) unchanging
   (E) inefficient

3. EMANCIPATE
   (A) change
   (B) overjoy
   (C) bring forward
   (D) raise up
   (E) set free

4. LOLL
   (A) find
   (B) respect
   (C) lounge
   (D) steal
   (E) trap

5. SUBSEQUENT
   (A) later
   (B) lower
   (C) thick
   (D) secret
   (E) light

6. CRUCIAL
   (A) reverent
   (B) decisive
   (C) tiresome
   (D) dangerous
   (E) rude

7. REBUKE
(A) prove
(B) dislike
(C) overwork
(D) swallow
(E) criticize

8. CLOISTERED
(A) uneasy
(B) agreeable
(C) sincere
(D) regretful
(E) confined

9. DRONE
(A) beggar
(B) nightmare
(C) queen bee
(D) humming sound
(E) delaying action

10. PEDESTRIAN
(A) clumsy
(B) senseless
(C) curious
(D) learned
(E) commonplace

Vocabulary Test 83

1. DAWDLE
(A) hang loosely
(B) waste time
(C) fondle
(D) splash
(E) paint

2. ANGUISH
(A) torment
(B) boredom
(C) resentment
(D) stubbornness
(E) clumsiness

3. IMPARTIAL
(A) unlawful
(B) incomplete
(C) unprejudiced
(D) unfaithful
(E) unimportant

4. FORESTALL
(A) press
(B) preserve
(C) prevent
(D) boil
(E) restore

5. EFFONTERY
(A) boldness
(B) agitation
(C) brilliance
(D) toil
(E) talkativeness

6. EMBROIL
(A) explain
(B) entangle
(C) swindle
(D) greet
(E) imitate

7. INCANDESCENT
(A) insincere
(B) melodious
(C) electrical
(D) magical
(E) glowing

8. STENTORIAN
(A) extremely careful
(B) little known
(C) hardly capable
(D) rarely reliable
(E) very loud

9. RENEGADE
(A) retired soldier
(B) public speaker
(C) complainer
(D) traitor
(E) comedian

10. INTERMITTENT
(A) emphatic
(B) stormy
(C) hopeless
(D) innermost
(E) periodic

Vocabulary Test 84

1. INTERLOPER
(A) thief
(B) intruder
(C) translator
(D) inquirer
(E) representative

2. SCATHING
(A) bitterly severe
(B) hastily spoken
(C) unnecessary
(D) ill-advised
(E) easily misunderstood

3. ACRID
   (A) abnormal
   (B) gifted
   (C) insincere
   (D) drying
   (E) irritating

4. TALISMAN
   (A) peddler
   (B) mechanic
   (C) charm
   (D) juryman
   (E) metal key

5. DISPATCH
   (A) stir up
   (B) leave out
   (C) glorify
   (D) persuade
   (E) send away

6. BOOTY
   (A) navy
   (B) arson
   (C) police
   (D) voyage
   (E) spoils

7. DEMURE
   (A) unforgiving
   (B) out-of-date
   (C) modest
   (D) uncooperative
   (E) overemotional

8. CRUX
   (A) great disappointment
   (B) supporting argument
   (C) debatable issue
   (D) critical point
   (E) criminal act

9. AGGRANDIZE
   (A) enlarge
   (B) condense
   (C) astonish
   (D) interpret
   (E) attack

10. SUMPTUOUS
    (A) dictatorial
    (B) topmost
    (C) radiant
    (D) luxurious
    (E) additional

Vocabulary Test 85

1. VERSATILE
   (A) lonesome
   (B) backward
   (C) talkative
   (D) brave
   (E) all-around

2. FORTHRIGHT
   (A) frank
   (B) joyful
   (C) imaginary
   (D) conscious
   (E) preferred

3. TUSSLE
   (A) meet
   (B) struggle
   (C) confuse
   (D) murmur
   (E) practice

4. CLARITY
   (A) loudness
   (B) certainty
   (C) clearness
   (D) glamour
   (E) tenderness

5. ASSESSMENT
   (A) appraisal
   (B) revision
   (C) property
   (D) illness
   (E) warning

6. CLIQUE
   (A) social outcast
   (B) ringing sound
   (C) headdress
   (D) exclusive group
   (E) tangled web

7. NEGATE
   (A) polish to a bright shine
   (B) find quickly
   (C) make ineffective
   (D) file a protest
   (E) take into consideration

8. IMPEL
   (A) accuse
   (B) force
   (C) encourage
   (D) prevent
   (E) pierce

9. CONSTRAINTS
   (A) group processes
   (B) new laws
   (C) doctrines
   (D) current news
   (E) limits

10. ORTHODOX
    (A) accepted
    (B) flawless
    (C) contradictory
    (D) dignified
    (E) extraordinary

Vocabulary Test 86

1. COUNTERPART
   (A) hindrance
   (B) peace offering
   (C) password
   (D) balance of power
   (E) duplicate

2. LOW-KEY
   (A) official
   (B) secret
   (C) restrained
   (D) unheard of
   (E) complicated

3. STIPULATION
   (A) imitation
   (B) signal
   (C) excitement
   (D) agreement
   (E) decoration

4. ANTITHESIS
   (A) fixed dislike
   (B) musical response
   (C) lack of feeling
   (D) direct opposite
   (E) prior knowledge

5. TRANSITORY
   (A) short-lived
   (B) delayed
   (C) idle
   (D) unexpected
   (E) clear

6. ENTRENCHED
   (A) filled up
   (B) bordered by
   (C) followed by
   (D) kept down
   (E) dug in

7. LOT
   (A) name
   (B) right
   (C) folly
   (D) fate
   (E) oath

8. APPREHENSION
   (A) gratitude
   (B) requirement
   (C) apology
   (D) dread
   (E) punishment

9. AMENABLE
   (A) religious
   (B) masculine
   (C) proud
   (D) brave
   (E) agreeable

10. AFFLUENT
    (A) neutral
    (B) sentimental
    (C) wealthy
    (D) handsome
    (E) evil

Vocabulary Test 87

1. VELOCITY
   (A) willingness
   (B) swiftness
   (C) truthfulness
   (D) smoothness
   (E) skillfulness

2. ENVOY
   (A) messenger
   (B) assistant
   (C) planner
   (D) expert
   (E) leader

3. AUXILIARY
   (A) reliable
   (B) mechanical
   (C) sociable
   (D) supporting
   (E) protective

4. PINNACLE
   (A) topmost point
   (B) feather
   (C) fastener
   (D) card game
   (E) small boat

5. BOORISH
   (A) shy
   (B) rude
   (C) thieving
   (D) cunning
   (E) foreign

6. ENCOMPASS
   (A) include
   (B) measure
   (C) attempt
   (D) direct
   (E) border on

7. LURCH
   (A) trap
   (B) brake
   (C) stagger
   (D) waste time
   (E) laugh noisily

8. EFFACE
   (A) rub out
   (B) paint red
   (C) build upon
   (D) stay in front
   (E) bring about

9. ABOUND
   (A) do good
   (B) store up
   (C) run away
   (D) stand firm
   (E) be plentiful

10. THWART
    (A) avoid
    (B) accuse
    (C) suffer
    (D) block
    (E) serve

Vocabulary Test 88

1. PRUNE
   (A) cut off
   (B) expect
   (C) put away
   (D) lay waste
   (E) remind

2. AMIABLE
   (A) active
   (B) good-natured
   (C) religious
   (D) changeable
   (E) absentminded

3. IMPROVISE
   (A) object loudly
   (B) predict
   (C) refuse support
   (D) prepare offhand
   (E) translate

4. CONNIVE
   (A) cooperate secretly
   (B) enter quickly
   (C) pause slightly
   (D) push unexpectedly
   (E) need greatly

5. GAIT
   (A) turning over and over
   (B) passing in review
   (C) manner of walking
   (D) fundamental attitude
   (E) crowd of spectators

6. BOTCH
   (A) weep
   (B) rebel
   (C) resent
   (D) blunder
   (E) complain

7. DEVOID OF
   (A) accompanied by
   (B) in the care of
   (C) without
   (D) behind
   (E) despite

8. PANG
   (A) feeling of indifference
   (B) sense of duty
   (C) fatal disease
   (D) universal remedy
   (E) spasm of pain

9. TEDIUM
   (A) bad temper
   (B) boredom
   (C) warmth
   (D) abundance
   (E) musical form

10. INTIMATE
    (A) hospitable
    (B) well-behaved
    (C) familiar
    (D) plainly seen
    (E) forgiving

Vocabulary Test 89

1. DELVE
   (A) hope for
   (B) believe in
   (C) set upon
   (D) take into account
   (E) dig into

2. SHROUDED
   (A) found
   (B) torn
   (C) stoned
   (D) wrapped
   (E) rewarded

3. EXPLOIT
   (A) annoy
   (B) join
   (C) use
   (D) mix up
   (E) set free

4. RUT
   (A) fixed practice
   (B) honest labor
   (C) useless regret
   (D) happy home
   (E) vain hope

5. CONSTITUENTS
   (A) tradesmen
   (B) students
   (C) voters
   (D) judges
   (E) ministers

6. REPREHENSIBLE
   (A) distracting
   (B) blameworthy
   (C) glowing
   (D) frightening
   (E) truthful

7. HAZARD
   (A) confuse
   (B) avoid
   (C) resign
   (D) chance
   (E) overlook

8. ROBUST
   (A) bragging
   (B) huge
   (C) sincere
   (D) upright
   (E) sturdy

9. PIECEMEAL
   (A) on the spur of the moment
   (B) bit by bit
   (C) over and over
   (D) as a matter of course
   (E) from first to last

10. INSCRUTABLE
    (A) disorderly
    (B) shallow
    (C) unwritten
    (D) painful
    (E) mysterious

Vocabulary Test 90

1. NEEDLE
   (A) join
   (B) prod
   (C) discuss
   (D) give
   (E) command

2. TENTATIVE
   (A) forgotten
   (B) fabricated
   (C) sunny
   (D) temporary
   (E) absentee

3. HUMDRUM
   (A) false
   (B) ugly
   (C) uninteresting
   (D) mournful
   (E) disappointing

4. RATIFY
   (A) create
   (B) revive
   (C) deny
   (D) confirm
   (E) displease

5. HORDE
   (A) crowd
   (B) framework
   (C) nonbeliever
   (D) choir
   (E) warrior

6. RELENTLESS
   (A) unwise
   (B) fearless
   (C) straightforward
   (D) unappetizing
   (E) unyielding

7. MUDDLE
   (A) saucy remark
   (B) confused mess
   (C) delaying tactics
   (D) simple truth
   (E) great outcry

8. ADULTERATE
   (A) grow up
   (B) push ahead
   (C) make impure
   (D) send away
   (E) die off

9. CONCEDE
   (A) gain
   (B) join
   (C) force
   (D) struggle
   (E) admit

10. PLIGHT
    (A) final decision
    (B) spy system
    (C) plant disease
    (D) bad situation
    (E) listening post

Vocabulary Test 91

1. BURLY
   (A) useless
   (B) wild
   (C) strong
   (D) easy
   (E) medical

2. DEBASE
   (A) call to mind
   (B) send from home
   (C) rely upon
   (D) take part in
   (E) reduce the value of

3. STANCE
   (A) performance
   (B) defense
   (C) length
   (D) posture
   (E) concentration

4. EXACT
   (A) fall
   (B) appeal
   (C) strain
   (D) loosen
   (E) demand

5. DANK
   (A) moist
   (B) unhealthy
   (C) smoky
   (D) frozen
   (E) cloudy

6. EXPRESSLY
   (A) definitely
   (B) regularly
   (C) quickly
   (D) safely
   (E) loudly

7. DISCOUNT
   (A) discover
   (B) disgrace
   (C) disregard
   (D) dislike
   (E) display

8. TOKEN
   (A) timely
   (B) minimal
   (C) stiff
   (D) imaginary
   (E) enforced

9. DECADENCE
   (A) false reasoning
   (B) hasty retreat
   (C) self-assurance
   (D) period of decline
   (E) fraud

10. ALACRITY
    (A) eagerness
    (B) joy
    (C) criticism
    (D) milkiness
    (E) fullness

Vocabulary Test 92

1. CLAMOR
   (A) magic spell
   (B) loose garment
   (C) poisoned arrow
   (D) loud noise
   (E) deep-sea fisherman

2. CONVENTIONAL
   (A) inexperienced
   (B) close
   (C) foolish
   (D) kindly
   (E) usual

3. INDISPUTABLE
   (A) unjust
   (B) undeniable
   (C) indelicate
   (D) indescribable
   (E) unconcerned

4. PUNY
   (A) weak
   (B) humorous
   (C) quarrelsome
   (D) studious
   (E) innocent

5. FACILITATE
   (A) make angry
   (B) copy
   (C) make easier
   (D) joke about
   (E) decorate

6. REPULSE
   (A) force
   (B) disown
   (C) restore
   (D) repel
   (E) indicate

7. CHARISMA
   (A) happy feeling
   (B) quality of leadership
   (C) Greek letter
   (D) deep hole
   (E) contrary view

8. RIGOR
   (A) padding
   (B) mold
   (C) liner
   (D) building
   (E) strictness

9. NOXIOUS
   (A) harmful
   (B) lively
   (C) uncertain
   (D) unprepared
   (E) calming

10. ENLIGHTEN
   (A) please
   (B) put away
   (C) instruct
   (D) reduce
   (E) criticize

Vocabulary Test 93

1. INTANGIBLE
   (A) incomplete
   (B) individual
   (C) vagie
   (D) uninjured
   (E) careless

2. COMPLIANT
   (A) yielding
   (B) standing
   (C) admiring
   (D) trusting
   (E) grabbing

3. ERADICATE
   (A) exclaim
   (B) heat up
   (C) break out
   (D) plant
   (E) eliminate

4. ABYSS
   (A) great ignorance
   (B) evil man
   (C) bottomless pit
   (D) wide sea
   (E) religious sign

5. CRITERION
   (A) standard
   (B) award
   (C) achievement
   (D) objection
   (E) claim

6. IRREVERENT
   (A) illogical
   (B) unimportant
   (C) violent
   (D) disrespectful
   (E) unafraid

7. SALLOW
   (A) temporary
   (B) animal-like
   (C) stupid
   (D) clean
   (E) yellowish

8. RENOUNCE
   (A) proclaim
   (B) approve
   (C) give up
   (D) guarantee
   (E) speak plainly

9. ASSIMILATE
   (A) pretend
   (B) absorb
   (C) poke
   (D) copy
   (E) expect

10. EXHORT
    (A) annoy
    (B) deduct
    (C) enlarge quickly
    (D) urge strongly
    (E) stick out

Vocabulary Test 94

1. JEST
   (A) spout
   (B) trot
   (C) joke
   (D) judge
   (E) leap

2. MOLEST
   (A) disturb
   (B) reduce
   (C) submit
   (D) delight
   (E) urge

3. TURMOIL
   (A) conclusion
   (B) reversal
   (C) meanness
   (D) confusion
   (E) mistake

4. ORDINANCE
   (A) trial
   (B) law
   (C) right
   (D) fault
   (E) property

5. LATERAL
   (A) financial
   (B) lingering
   (C) of the past
   (D) from the beginning
   (E) to the side

6. PIGMENT
   (A) light
   (B) pillar
   (C) dye
   (D) weed
   (E) book

7. CONCEPT
   (A) desire
   (B) thought
   (C) solution
   (D) method
   (E) experiment

8. ORNATE
   (A) elaborate
   (B) original
   (C) systematic
   (D) unbecoming
   (E) obsolete

9. BEGRUDGE
   (A) roar mightily
   (B) walk swiftly
   (C) give reluctantly
   (D) await eagerly
   (E) seek desperately

10. REPOSE
    (A) task
    (B) calm
    (C) strain
    (D) fact
    (E) surprise

Vocabulary Test 95

1. BOLSTER
   (A) reinforce
   (B) thicken
   (C) uncover
   (D) quote
   (E) bother

2. INFRINGEMENT
   (A) old age
   (B) added benefit
   (C) protection
   (D) violation
   (E) fireproofing

3. AGILE
   (A) colored
   (B) healthy
   (C) dull
   (D) false
   (E) nimble

4. DIVERSIFY
   (A) fix
   (B) vary
   (C) correct
   (D) relieve
   (E) explain

5. RUSTLE
   (A) steal
   (B) instruct
   (C) strive
   (D) bend
   (E) tax

6. HAPLESS
   (A) optimistic
   (B) uncounted
   (C) unfortunate
   (D) simple
   (E) unyielding

7. UNPRETENTIOUS
   (A) loyal
   (B) virtuous
   (C) modest
   (D) fair
   (E) extravagant

8. BUOY
   (A) wet
   (B) dry up
   (C) rescue
   (D) sustain
   (E) direct

9. PARAGON
   (A) weak pun
   (B) even distribution
   (C) geometric figure
   (D) moralistic story
   (E) model of excellence

10. INDIGENOUS
    (A) confused
    (B) native
    (C) poor
    (D) unconcerned
    (E) wrathful

Vocabulary Test 96

1. PROLOGUE
   (A) stairway
   (B) introduction
   (C) conversation
   (D) reading
   (E) extension

2. ACKNOWLEDGE
   (A) propose
   (B) strangle
   (C) convict
   (D) advance
   (E) admit

3. INDICTMENT
   (A) accusation
   (B) publisher
   (C) announcer
   (D) conviction
   (E) trial

4. LACKLUSTER
   (A) sparkling
   (B) tender
   (C) misty
   (D) uninspired
   (E) disobedient

5. CONDOMINIUM
   (A) new type of metal
   (B) noisy celebration
   (C) individually owned apartment
   (D) important decision
   (E) group meeting

6. INCUMBENT
   (A) office holder
   (B) lawyer
   (C) politician
   (D) green vegetable
   (E) sacred honor

7. POLARIZATION
   (A) performance in cold weather
   (B) point of view
   (C) change in opinion
   (D) division into opposites
   (E) cultural bias

8. GENESIS
   (A) wisdom
   (B) origin
   (C) classification
   (D) humor
   (E) night

9. DIMINUTION
   (A) devotion
   (B) difference
   (C) difficulty
   (D) decision
   (E) decrease

10. WARY
    (A) sorrowful
    (B) lazy
    (C) unfriendly
    (D) cautious
    (E) hopeful

Vocabulary Test 97

1. SLEEK
   - (A) smooth
   - (B) moldy
   - (C) loose
   - (D) small
   - (E) delicate

2. SUCCULENT
   - (A) literal
   - (B) tardy
   - (C) yielding
   - (D) sportsmanlike
   - (E) juicy

3. LACERATED
   - (A) bright
   - (B) gaunt
   - (C) punishable
   - (D) torn
   - (E) tied

4. SUBSIDE
   - (A) pay in full
   - (B) become quiet
   - (C) return soon
   - (D) rush around
   - (E) send forth

5. ACQUITTAL
   - (A) setting free
   - (B) agreeing with
   - (C) holding forth
   - (D) getting up steam
   - (E) appealing to higher authority

6. APPREHEND
   - (A) inform
   - (B) resound
   - (C) frighten
   - (D) squeeze
   - (E) seize

7. IMPERATIVE
   - (A) unbiased
   - (B) obscure
   - (C) repetitious
   - (D) compulsory
   - (E) unworthy

8. SUBSTANTIATE
   - (A) verify
   - (B) replace
   - (C) influence
   - (D) condemn
   - (E) accept

9. RANCID
   - (A) illegal
   - (B) rotten
   - (C) ashen
   - (D) flimsy
   - (E) mean

10. OUST
    - (A) nag
    - (B) evict
    - (C) excel
    - (D) defy
    - (E) emerge

Vocabulary Test 98

1. TOPPLE
   - (A) drink
   - (B) choose
   - (C) stray
   - (D) stumble
   - (E) overturn

2. PREVAIL
   - (A) preview
   - (B) question
   - (C) relax
   - (D) triumph
   - (E) restore

3. CREDENCE
   - (A) cowardice
   - (B) size
   - (C) belief
   - (D) variety
   - (E) nobility

4. DIVULGE
   - (A) send
   - (B) shrink
   - (C) despair
   - (D) separate
   - (E) reveal

5. MISGIVINGS
   - (A) cheap gifts
   - (B) feelings of doubt
   - (C) added treats
   - (D) false promises
   - (E) slips of the tongue

6. ACCLAIM
   - (A) find
   - (B) restore
   - (C) praise
   - (D) judge
   - (E) demand

7. HALLOWED
   (A) sacred
   (B) noisy
   (C) deep
   (D) permitted
   (E) costumed

8. GUISE
   (A) ability
   (B) direction
   (C) guilt
   (D) appearance
   (E) mistake

9. TUMULT
   (A) vacation
   (B) reversal
   (C) swelling
   (D) suffering
   (E) commotion

10. REMINISCENT
    (A) amazed by
    (B) obligated to
    (C) suggestive of
    (D) under the control of
    (E) careless with

Vocabulary Test 99

1. REMIT
   (A) promise
   (B) injure
   (C) send
   (D) profit
   (E) menace

2. PANDEMONIUM
   (A) wild uproar
   (B) diseased state
   (C) contempt
   (D) luxury
   (E) gloom

3. EJECT
   (A) expose
   (B) exceed
   (C) extend
   (D) expel
   (E) excite

4. TALLY
   (A) load
   (B) record
   (C) hunt
   (D) play
   (E) move

5. DEVASTATE
   (A) cough
   (B) ruin
   (C) chop
   (D) point
   (E) swell

6. MAUL
   (A) trap
   (B) cuddle
   (C) carve
   (D) throw
   (E) beat

7. ANIMATION
   (A) liveliness
   (B) automation
   (C) carelessness
   (D) dispute
   (E) exchange

8. SMOLDER
   (A) show suppressed anger
   (B) grow up quickly
   (C) find easily
   (D) report back
   (E) become weary

9. PROTRUDE
   (A) make a fool of
   (B) fall into
   (C) put down
   (D) thrust out
   (E) steer clear of

10. BENEVOLENT
    (A) profitable
    (B) sociable
    (C) wealthy
    (D) receptive
    (E) charitable

Vocabulary Test 100

1. UNOBSTRUSIVE
   (A) annoying
   (B) unquestionable
   (C) inconspicuous
   (D) united
   (E) healthy

2. SCRUTINY
   (A) signal
   (B) plot
   (C) delay
   (D) investigation
   (E) announcement

3. HEINOUS
   (A) evil
   (B) permanent
   (C) unreasonable
   (D) open
   (E) timid

4. GARRULOUS
   (A) confused
   (B) eager
   (C) panting
   (D) talkative
   (E) informal

5. CONVERSE
   (A) junction
   (B) poetry
   (C) ancestor
   (D) follower
   (E) opposite

6. MALEFACTOR
   (A) fugitive
   (B) joker
   (C) showoff
   (D) evildoer
   (E) daydreamer

7. MARTIAL
   (A) heavenly
   (B) keen
   (C) warlike
   (D) tremendous
   (E) masculine

8. RETORT
   (A) answer
   (B) jot
   (C) retire
   (D) recall
   (E) decay

9. VIGILANCE
   (A) lawlessness
   (B) funeral
   (C) watchfulness
   (D) processional
   (E) strength

10. LESION
    (A) dream
    (B) group
    (C) justice
    (D) style
    (E) injury

Answers to Vocabulary Tests

Test 1	Test 5	Test 9	Test 13	Test 17	Test 21	Test 25	Test 29
1. D	1. C	1. E	1. B	1. A	1. C	1. A	1. B
2. B	2. B	2. C	2. E	2. B	2. E	2. D	2. A
3. D	3. D	3. E	3. B	3. D	3. D	3. E	3. D
4. A	4. D	4. C	4. B	4. E	4. C	4. C	4. E
5. E	5. C	5. D	5. C	5. E	5. B	5. A	5. C
6. B	6. E	6. C	6. C	6. B	6. D	6. B	6. E
7. E	7. A	7. A	7. E	7. D	7. E	7. E	7. B
8. A	8. A	8. D	8. A	8. A	8. D	8. B	8. E
9. E	9. E	9. D	9. D	9. B	9. A	9. C	9. E
10. C	10. C	10. D	10. C	10. D	10. D	10. D	10. C

Test 2	Test 6	Test 10	Test 14	Test 18	Test 22	Test 26	Test 30
1. B	1. C	1. B	1. C	1. E	1. B	1. E	1. E
2. A	2. E	2. E	2. E	2. C	2. D	2. C	2. C
3. E	3. D	3. D	3. C	3. B	3. A	3. A	3. A
4. D	4. C	4. C	4. E	4. C	4. E	4. C	4. B
5. A	5. B	5. B	5. A	5. C	5. E	5. B	5. D
6. E	6. E	6. B	6. E	6. A	6. E	6. E	6. E
7. C	7. B	7. E	7. D	7. E	7. D	7. D	7. D
8. A	8. E	8. B	8. D	8. A	8. A	8. E	8. B
9. B	9. C	9. A	9. E	9. D	9. E	9. D	9. C
10. E	10. D	10. B	10. E	10. A	10. D	10. B	10. A

Test 3	Test 7	Test 11	Test 15	Test 19	Test 23	Test 27	Test 31
1. C	1. E	1. A	1. B	1. B	1. C	1. A	1. B
2. D	2. A	2. D	2. C	2. E	2. D	2. D	2. A
3. B	3. D	3. A	3. A	3. C	3. B	3. C	3. D
4. C	4. D	4. E	4. C	4. D	4. D	4. B	4. A
5. B	5. B	5. A	5. B	5. A	5. D	5. C	5. C
6. B	6. B	6. B	6. E	6. A	6. D	6. B	6. E
7. D	7. B	7. A	7. C	7. D	7. A	7. B	7. D
8. C	8. E	8. E	8. D	8. E	8. B	8. A	8. E
9. A	9. A	9. C	9. A	9. A	9. E	9. A	9. B
10. E	10. B	10. E	10. B	10. B	10. D	10. E	10. A

Test 4	Test 8	Test 12	Test 16	Test 20	Test 24	Test 28	Test 32
1. E	1. D	1. C	1. D	1. A	1. B	1. E	1. E
2. D	2. A	2. D	2. C	2. B	2. B	2. B	2. A
3. E	3. D	3. B	3. D	3. D	3. A	3. C	3. B
4. A	4. E	4. D	4. B	4. B	4. E	4. A	4. D
5. E	5. A	5. B	5. B	5. B	5. E	5. B	5. B
6. A	6. C	6. C	6. A	6. A	6. E	6. D	6. A
7. A	7. A	7. E	7. D	7. C	7. C	7. A	7. C
8. D	8. C	8. B	8. B	8. A	8. E	8. E	8. B
9. E	9. A	9. D	9. A	9. A	9. B	9. A	9. B
10. C	10. D	10. E	10. A	10. E	10. B	10. D	10. E

Test 33	Test 37	Test 41	Test 45	Test 49	Test 53	Test 57	Test 61
1. C	1. C	1. A	1. E	1. B	1. E	1. E	1. B
2. D	2. B	2. D	2. A	2. E	2. E	2. C	2. D
3. B	3. A	3. E	3. D	3. A	3. D	3. B	3. B
4. C	4. C	4. D	4. C	4. C	4. E	4. A	4. D
5. D	5. E	5. C	5. E	5. C	5. B	5. B	5. A
6. E	6. A	6. A	6. B	6. D	6. C	6. A	6. B
7. B	7. D	7. E	7. B	7. D	7. B	7. C	7. D
8. B	8. A	8. B	8. E	8. A	8. D	8. C	8. C
9. A	9. E	9. E	9. D	9. E	9. D	9. D	9. D
10. E	10. E	10. D	10. A	10. C	10. E	10. A	10. B

Test 34	Test 38	Test 42	Test 46	Test 50	Test 54	Test 58	Test 62
1. A	1. D	1. B	1. B	1. A	1. C	1. B	1. D
2. B	2. E	2. E	2. D	2. C	2. D	2. A	2. A
3. E	3. E	3. B	3. C	3. A	3. E	3. E	3. A
4. A	4. A	4. B	4. D	4. C	4. C	4. D	4. D
5. B	5. E	5. B	5. B	5. D	5. C	5. C	5. A
6. D	6. D	6. E	6. E	6. B	6. C	6. D	6. A
7. D	7. C	7. C	7. D	7. B	7. B	7. C	7. D
8. B	8. B	8. D	8. B	8. A	8. E	8. E	8. E
9. B	9. C	9. A	9. A	9. A	9. E	9. D	9. D
10. C	10. A	10. C	10. E	10. B	10. C	10. A	10. B

Test 35	Test 39	Test 43	Test 47	Test 51	Test 55	Test 59	Test 63
1. A	1. E	1. A	1. C	1. D	1. C	1. D	1. B
2. E	2. A	2. B	2. C	2. D	2. B	2. D	2. D
3. B	3. D	3. D	3. D	3. C	3. D	3. D	3. C
4. A	4. C	4. C	4. D	4. B	4. A	4. E	4. E
5. C	5. B	5. E	5. A	5. A	5. C	5. E	5. A
6. D	6. B	6. C	6. A	6. D	6. E	6. B	6. A
7. E	7. A	7. E	7. B	7. B	7. D	7. A	7. D
8. D	8. E	8. D	8. E	8. B	8. E	8. E	8. E
9. B	9. C	9. C	9. C	9. B	9. A	9. E	9. C
10. B	10. D	10. A	10. E	10. A	10. C	10. B	10. B

Test 36	Test 40	Test 44	Test 48	Test 52	Test 56	Test 60	Test 64
1. C	1. A	1. A	1. B	1. B	1. A	1. A	1. B
2. B	2. E	2. A	2. C	2. E	2. A	2. B	2. B
3. C	3. C	3. D	3. E	3. A	3. D	3. C	3. C
4. D	4. B	4. D	4. B	4. B	4. D	4. E	4. E
5. A	5. A	5. B	5. E	5. C	5. A	5. B	5. E
6. D	6. C	6. D	6. A	6. C	6. D	6. B	6. B
7. D	7. D	7. C	7. D	7. B	7. B	7. E	7. C
8. E	8. D	8. A	8. D	8. E	8. B	8. D	8. C
9. A	9. A	9. E	9. B	9. A	9. B	9. C	9. A
10. E	10. D	10. D	10. E	10. A	10. C	10. C	10. D

Test 65	Test 69	Test 73	Test 77	Test 81	Test 85	Test 89	Test 93	Test 97
1. E	1. A	1. D	1. E	1. C	1. E	1. E	1. C	1. A
2. A	2. D	2. E	2. E	2. A	2. A	2. D	2. A	2. E
3. E	3. E	3. B	3. B	3. D	3. B	3. C	3. E	3. D
4. B	4. B	4. E	4. E	4. E	4. C	4. A	4. C	4. B
5. D	5. B	5. D	5. D	5. C	5. A	5. C	5. A	5. A
6. D	6. E	6. C	6. C	6. E	6. D	6. B	6. D	6. E
7. A	7. B	7. E	7. A	7. B	7. C	7. D	7. E	7. D
8. E	8. D	8. E	8. B	8. C	8. B	8. E	8. C	8. A
9. A	9. A	9. C	9. D	9. E	9. E	9. B	9. B	9. B
10. E	10. D	10. D	10. E	10. A	10. A	10. E	10. D	10. B

Test 66	Test 70	Test 74	Test 78	Test 82	Test 86	Test 90	Test 94	Test 98
1. C	1. D	1. A	1. B	1. D	1. E	1. B	1. C	1. E
2. B	2. B	2. C	2. D	2. A	2. C	2. D	2. A	2. D
3. B	3. C	3. E	3. C	3. E	3. D	3. C	3. D	3. C
4. D	4. A	4. D	4. A	4. C	4. D	4. D	4. B	4. A
5. B	5. B	5. B	5. B	5. A	5. A	5. A	5. E	5. B
6. C	6. C	6. B	6. E	6. B	6. E	6. E	6. C	6. C
7. E	7. B	7. C	7. D	7. E	7. D	7. B	7. B	7. A
8. D	8. E	8. C	8. C	8. E	8. D	8. C	8. A	8. D
9. E	9. D	9. D	9. A	9. D	9. E	9. E	9. C	9. E
10. A	10. E	10. A	10. B	10. E	10. C	10. D	10. B	10. C

Test 67	Test 71	Test 75	Test 79	Test 83	Test 87	Test 91	Test 95	Test 99
1. B	1. C	1. B	1. C	1. B	1. B	1. C	1. A	1. C
2. B	2. E	2. D	2. B	2. A	2. A	2. E	2. D	2. A
3. D	3. B	3. B	3. C	3. C	3. D	3. D	3. E	3. D
4. A	4. C	4. C	4. D	4. C	4. A	4. E	4. B	4. B
5. B	5. D	5. E	5. B	5. A	5. B	5. A	5. A	5. B
6. E	6. A	6. A	6. A	6. B	6. A	6. A	6. C	6. E
7. C	7. B	7. A	7. C	7. E	7. C	7. C	7. C	7. A
8. A	8. D	8. D	8. C	8. E	8. A	8. B	8. D	8. A
9. A	9. A	9. E	9. D	9. D	9. E	9. D	9. E	9. D
10. C	10. E	10. C	10. D	10. E	10. D	10. A	10. B	10. E

Test 68	Test 72	Test 76	Test 80	Test 84	Test 88	Test 92	Test 96	Test 100
1. E	1. A	1. B	1. A	1. B	1. A	1. D	1. B	1. C
2. B	2. C	2. C	2. D	2. A	2. B	2. E	2. E	2. D
3. A	3. A	3. D	3. A	3. E	3. D	3. B	3. A	3. A
4. B	4. E	4. A	4. A	4. C	4. A	4. A	4. D	4. D
5. B	5. D	5. C	5. C	5. E	5. C	5. C	5. C	5. E
6. E	6. C	6. E	6. E	6. E	6. D	6. D	6. A	6. D
7. D	7. B	7. D	7. A	7. C	7. C	7. B	7. D	7. C
8. C	8. D	8. A	8. E	8. D	8. E	8. E	8. B	8. A
9. E	9. B	9. E	9. C	9. A	9. B	9. A	9. E	9. C
10. C	10. E	10. B	10. D	10. D	10. C	10. C	10. D	10. E

PART 9

FOUR MORE SAT PRACTICE TESTS

Four Important Reasons for Taking These Practice Tests

Each of the 4 Practice SATs in the final part of this book is modeled very closely after the actual New SAT. You will find that each of these Practice Tests has

a) the same level of difficulty as the actual New SAT

and

b) the same question formats that the actual New SAT questions have.

Accordingly, *taking each of the following tests is like taking the actual New SAT.* There are four important reasons for taking each of these Practice SATs:

1. To find out in which areas of the SAT you are still weak.

2. To know just where to concentrate your efforts to eliminate these weaknesses.

3. To reinforce the Critical Thinking Skills—25 Math Strategies and 22 Verbal Strategies—that you learned in Part 5 of this book, "Using Critical Thinking Skills to Score High on the SAT." As we advised you, at the beginning of Part 5, diligent study of these strategies will result in a sharp rise in your SAT Math and Verbal scores.

4. To strengthen your Basic Math skills that might still be a bit rusty. We hope that Part 7, "SAT Math Refresher," helped you substantially to scrape off some of this rust.

These four reasons for taking the four Practice Tests in this section of the book tie up closely with a very important educational principle:

WE LEARN BY DOING!

10 Tips for Taking the Practice Tests

1. Observe the time limits exactly as given.

2. Allow no interruptions.

3. Permit no talking by anyone in the "test area."

4. Use the Answer Sheets provided at the beginning of each Practice Test. Don't make extra marks. Two answers for one question constitute an omitted question.

5. Use scratch paper to figure things out. (On your actual SAT, you are permitted to use the testbook for scratchwork.)

6. Omit a question when you start "struggling" with it. Go back to that question later if you have time to do so.

7. Don't get upset if you can't answer several of the questions. You can still get a high score on the test. Even if only 40 to 60 percent of the questions you answer are correct, you will get an average or above-average score.

8. You get the same credit for answering an easy question correctly as you do for answering a tough question correctly.

9. It is advisable to guess if you are sure that at least one of the question choices are wrong. If you are not sure whether one or more of the answer choices is wrong, statistically it will not make a difference to your total score if you guess or leave the answer blank.

10. *Your SAT score increases by approximately 10 points for every answer you get correct.*

SAT Practice Test 2*

* The Diagnostic SAT Pre-Test at the beginning of this book is considered Practice Test 1.

602

Answer Sheet—Practice Test 2

Make each mark a dark mark that completely fills the oval and is as dark as all your other marks. If you erase, do so completely. Incomplete erasures may be read as intended responses.

Use a No. 2 pencil only. Be sure each mark is dark and completely fills the oval. Completely erase any errors or stray marks.

Start with number 1 for each new section. If a section has fewer questions than answer spaces, leave the extra answer spaces blank.

SECTION 1

1 Ⓐ Ⓑ Ⓒ Ⓓ Ⓔ	11 Ⓐ Ⓑ Ⓒ Ⓓ Ⓔ	21 Ⓐ Ⓑ Ⓒ Ⓓ Ⓔ	31 Ⓐ Ⓑ Ⓒ Ⓓ Ⓔ
2 Ⓐ Ⓑ Ⓒ Ⓓ Ⓔ	12 Ⓐ Ⓑ Ⓒ Ⓓ Ⓔ	22 Ⓐ Ⓑ Ⓒ Ⓓ Ⓔ	32 Ⓐ Ⓑ Ⓒ Ⓓ Ⓔ
3 Ⓐ Ⓑ Ⓒ Ⓓ Ⓔ	13 Ⓐ Ⓑ Ⓒ Ⓓ Ⓔ	23 Ⓐ Ⓑ Ⓒ Ⓓ Ⓔ	33 Ⓐ Ⓑ Ⓒ Ⓓ Ⓔ
4 Ⓐ Ⓑ Ⓒ Ⓓ Ⓔ	14 Ⓐ Ⓑ Ⓒ Ⓓ Ⓔ	24 Ⓐ Ⓑ Ⓒ Ⓓ Ⓔ	34 Ⓐ Ⓑ Ⓒ Ⓓ Ⓔ
5 Ⓐ Ⓑ Ⓒ Ⓓ Ⓔ	15 Ⓐ Ⓑ Ⓒ Ⓓ Ⓔ	25 Ⓐ Ⓑ Ⓒ Ⓓ Ⓔ	35 Ⓐ Ⓑ Ⓒ Ⓓ Ⓔ
6 Ⓐ Ⓑ Ⓒ Ⓓ Ⓔ	16 Ⓐ Ⓑ Ⓒ Ⓓ Ⓔ	26 Ⓐ Ⓑ Ⓒ Ⓓ Ⓔ	36 Ⓐ Ⓑ Ⓒ Ⓓ Ⓔ
7 Ⓐ Ⓑ Ⓒ Ⓓ Ⓔ	17 Ⓐ Ⓑ Ⓒ Ⓓ Ⓔ	27 Ⓐ Ⓑ Ⓒ Ⓓ Ⓔ	37 Ⓐ Ⓑ Ⓒ Ⓓ Ⓔ
8 Ⓐ Ⓑ Ⓒ Ⓓ Ⓔ	18 Ⓐ Ⓑ Ⓒ Ⓓ Ⓔ	28 Ⓐ Ⓑ Ⓒ Ⓓ Ⓔ	38 Ⓐ Ⓑ Ⓒ Ⓓ Ⓔ
9 Ⓐ Ⓑ Ⓒ Ⓓ Ⓔ	19 Ⓐ Ⓑ Ⓒ Ⓓ Ⓔ	29 Ⓐ Ⓑ Ⓒ Ⓓ Ⓔ	39 Ⓐ Ⓑ Ⓒ Ⓓ Ⓔ
10 Ⓐ Ⓑ Ⓒ Ⓓ Ⓔ	20 Ⓐ Ⓑ Ⓒ Ⓓ Ⓔ	30 Ⓐ Ⓑ Ⓒ Ⓓ Ⓔ	40 Ⓐ Ⓑ Ⓒ Ⓓ Ⓔ

SECTION 2

1 Ⓐ Ⓑ Ⓒ Ⓓ Ⓔ	11 Ⓐ Ⓑ Ⓒ Ⓓ Ⓔ	21 Ⓐ Ⓑ Ⓒ Ⓓ Ⓔ	31 Ⓐ Ⓑ Ⓒ Ⓓ Ⓔ
2 Ⓐ Ⓑ Ⓒ Ⓓ Ⓔ	12 Ⓐ Ⓑ Ⓒ Ⓓ Ⓔ	22 Ⓐ Ⓑ Ⓒ Ⓓ Ⓔ	32 Ⓐ Ⓑ Ⓒ Ⓓ Ⓔ
3 Ⓐ Ⓑ Ⓒ Ⓓ Ⓔ	13 Ⓐ Ⓑ Ⓒ Ⓓ Ⓔ	23 Ⓐ Ⓑ Ⓒ Ⓓ Ⓔ	33 Ⓐ Ⓑ Ⓒ Ⓓ Ⓔ
4 Ⓐ Ⓑ Ⓒ Ⓓ Ⓔ	14 Ⓐ Ⓑ Ⓒ Ⓓ Ⓔ	24 Ⓐ Ⓑ Ⓒ Ⓓ Ⓔ	34 Ⓐ Ⓑ Ⓒ Ⓓ Ⓔ
5 Ⓐ Ⓑ Ⓒ Ⓓ Ⓔ	15 Ⓐ Ⓑ Ⓒ Ⓓ Ⓔ	25 Ⓐ Ⓑ Ⓒ Ⓓ Ⓔ	35 Ⓐ Ⓑ Ⓒ Ⓓ Ⓔ
6 Ⓐ Ⓑ Ⓒ Ⓓ Ⓔ	16 Ⓐ Ⓑ Ⓒ Ⓓ Ⓔ	26 Ⓐ Ⓑ Ⓒ Ⓓ Ⓔ	36 Ⓐ Ⓑ Ⓒ Ⓓ Ⓔ
7 Ⓐ Ⓑ Ⓒ Ⓓ Ⓔ	17 Ⓐ Ⓑ Ⓒ Ⓓ Ⓔ	27 Ⓐ Ⓑ Ⓒ Ⓓ Ⓔ	37 Ⓐ Ⓑ Ⓒ Ⓓ Ⓔ
8 Ⓐ Ⓑ Ⓒ Ⓓ Ⓔ	18 Ⓐ Ⓑ Ⓒ Ⓓ Ⓔ	28 Ⓐ Ⓑ Ⓒ Ⓓ Ⓔ	38 Ⓐ Ⓑ Ⓒ Ⓓ Ⓔ
9 Ⓐ Ⓑ Ⓒ Ⓓ Ⓔ	19 Ⓐ Ⓑ Ⓒ Ⓓ Ⓔ	29 Ⓐ Ⓑ Ⓒ Ⓓ Ⓔ	39 Ⓐ Ⓑ Ⓒ Ⓓ Ⓔ
10 Ⓐ Ⓑ Ⓒ Ⓓ Ⓔ	20 Ⓐ Ⓑ Ⓒ Ⓓ Ⓔ	30 Ⓐ Ⓑ Ⓒ Ⓓ Ⓔ	40 Ⓐ Ⓑ Ⓒ Ⓓ Ⓔ

Use a No. 2 pencil only. Be sure each mark is dark and completely fills the oval. Completely erase any errors or stray marks.

Start with number 1 for each new section. If a section has fewer questions than answer spaces, leave the extra answer spaces blank.

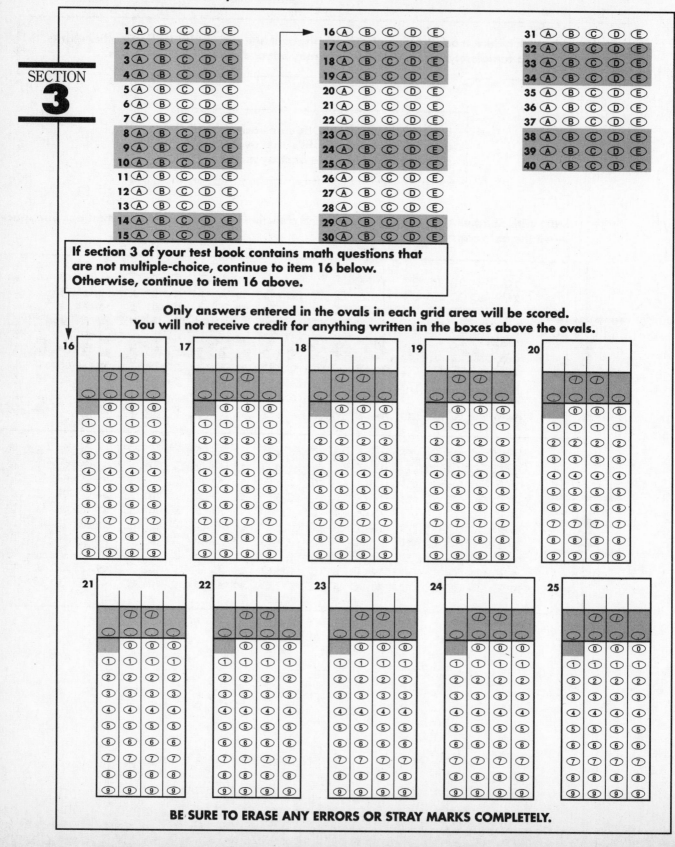

SECTION
3

If section 3 of your test book contains math questions that are not multiple-choice, continue to item 16 below. Otherwise, continue to item 16 above.

Only answers entered in the ovals in each grid area will be scored. You will not receive credit for anything written in the boxes above the ovals.

BE SURE TO ERASE ANY ERRORS OR STRAY MARKS COMPLETELY.

Use a No. 2 pencil only. Be sure each mark is dark and completely fills the oval. Completely erase any errors or stray marks.

Start with number 1 for each new section. If a section has fewer questions than answer spaces, leave the extra answer spaces blank.

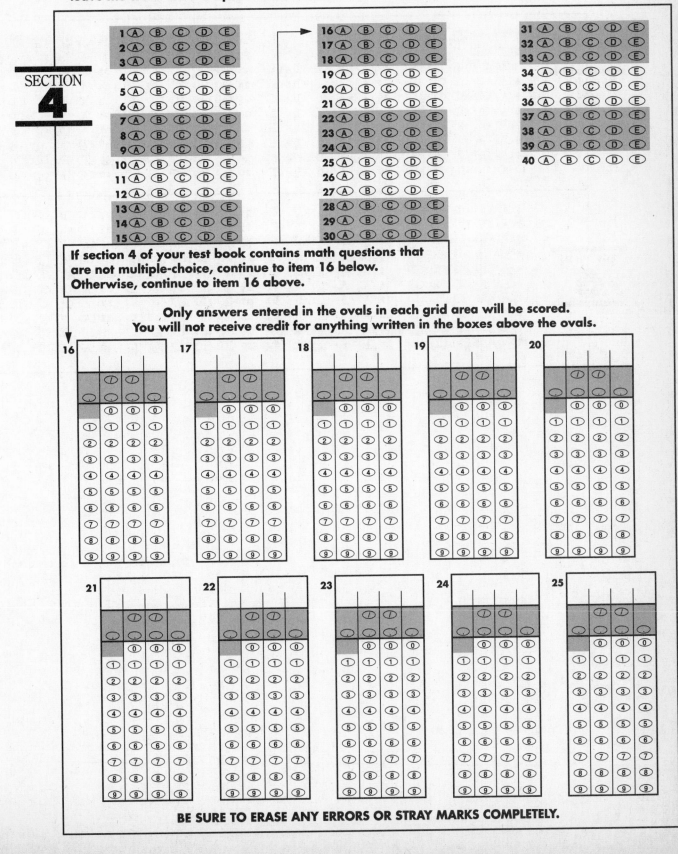

If section 4 of your test book contains math questions that are not multiple-choice, continue to item 16 below. Otherwise, continue to item 16 above.

Only answers entered in the ovals in each grid area will be scored. You will not receive credit for anything written in the boxes above the ovals.

BE SURE TO ERASE ANY ERRORS OR STRAY MARKS COMPLETELY.

Use a No. 2 pencil only. Be sure each mark is dark and completely fills the oval. Completely erase any errors or stray marks.

Start with number 1 for each new section. If a section has fewer questions than answer spaces, leave the extra answer spaces blank.

SECTION 5

1 Ⓐ Ⓑ Ⓒ Ⓓ Ⓔ   11 Ⓐ Ⓑ Ⓒ Ⓓ Ⓔ   21 Ⓐ Ⓑ Ⓒ Ⓓ Ⓔ   31 Ⓐ Ⓑ Ⓒ Ⓓ Ⓔ
2 Ⓐ Ⓑ Ⓒ Ⓓ Ⓔ   12 Ⓐ Ⓑ Ⓒ Ⓓ Ⓔ   22 Ⓐ Ⓑ Ⓒ Ⓓ Ⓔ   32 Ⓐ Ⓑ Ⓒ Ⓓ Ⓔ
3 Ⓐ Ⓑ Ⓒ Ⓓ Ⓔ   13 Ⓐ Ⓑ Ⓒ Ⓓ Ⓔ   23 Ⓐ Ⓑ Ⓒ Ⓓ Ⓔ   33 Ⓐ Ⓑ Ⓒ Ⓓ Ⓔ
4 Ⓐ Ⓑ Ⓒ Ⓓ Ⓔ   14 Ⓐ Ⓑ Ⓒ Ⓓ Ⓔ   24 Ⓐ Ⓑ Ⓒ Ⓓ Ⓔ   34 Ⓐ Ⓑ Ⓒ Ⓓ Ⓔ
5 Ⓐ Ⓑ Ⓒ Ⓓ Ⓔ   15 Ⓐ Ⓑ Ⓒ Ⓓ Ⓔ   25 Ⓐ Ⓑ Ⓒ Ⓓ Ⓔ   35 Ⓐ Ⓑ Ⓒ Ⓓ Ⓔ
6 Ⓐ Ⓑ Ⓒ Ⓓ Ⓔ   16 Ⓐ Ⓑ Ⓒ Ⓓ Ⓔ   26 Ⓐ Ⓑ Ⓒ Ⓓ Ⓔ   36 Ⓐ Ⓑ Ⓒ Ⓓ Ⓔ
7 Ⓐ Ⓑ Ⓒ Ⓓ Ⓔ   17 Ⓐ Ⓑ Ⓒ Ⓓ Ⓔ   27 Ⓐ Ⓑ Ⓒ Ⓓ Ⓔ   37 Ⓐ Ⓑ Ⓒ Ⓓ Ⓔ
8 Ⓐ Ⓑ Ⓒ Ⓓ Ⓔ   18 Ⓐ Ⓑ Ⓒ Ⓓ Ⓔ   28 Ⓐ Ⓑ Ⓒ Ⓓ Ⓔ   38 Ⓐ Ⓑ Ⓒ Ⓓ Ⓔ
9 Ⓐ Ⓑ Ⓒ Ⓓ Ⓔ   19 Ⓐ Ⓑ Ⓒ Ⓓ Ⓔ   29 Ⓐ Ⓑ Ⓒ Ⓓ Ⓔ   39 Ⓐ Ⓑ Ⓒ Ⓓ Ⓔ
10 Ⓐ Ⓑ Ⓒ Ⓓ Ⓔ   20 Ⓐ Ⓑ Ⓒ Ⓓ Ⓔ   30 Ⓐ Ⓑ Ⓒ Ⓓ Ⓔ   40 Ⓐ Ⓑ Ⓒ Ⓓ Ⓔ

SECTION 6

1 Ⓐ Ⓑ Ⓒ Ⓓ Ⓔ   11 Ⓐ Ⓑ Ⓒ Ⓓ Ⓔ   21 Ⓐ Ⓑ Ⓒ Ⓓ Ⓔ   31 Ⓐ Ⓑ Ⓒ Ⓓ Ⓔ
2 Ⓐ Ⓑ Ⓒ Ⓓ Ⓔ   12 Ⓐ Ⓑ Ⓒ Ⓓ Ⓔ   22 Ⓐ Ⓑ Ⓒ Ⓓ Ⓔ   32 Ⓐ Ⓑ Ⓒ Ⓓ Ⓔ
3 Ⓐ Ⓑ Ⓒ Ⓓ Ⓔ   13 Ⓐ Ⓑ Ⓒ Ⓓ Ⓔ   23 Ⓐ Ⓑ Ⓒ Ⓓ Ⓔ   33 Ⓐ Ⓑ Ⓒ Ⓓ Ⓔ
4 Ⓐ Ⓑ Ⓒ Ⓓ Ⓔ   14 Ⓐ Ⓑ Ⓒ Ⓓ Ⓔ   24 Ⓐ Ⓑ Ⓒ Ⓓ Ⓔ   34 Ⓐ Ⓑ Ⓒ Ⓓ Ⓔ
5 Ⓐ Ⓑ Ⓒ Ⓓ Ⓔ   15 Ⓐ Ⓑ Ⓒ Ⓓ Ⓔ   25 Ⓐ Ⓑ Ⓒ Ⓓ Ⓔ   35 Ⓐ Ⓑ Ⓒ Ⓓ Ⓔ
6 Ⓐ Ⓑ Ⓒ Ⓓ Ⓔ   16 Ⓐ Ⓑ Ⓒ Ⓓ Ⓔ   26 Ⓐ Ⓑ Ⓒ Ⓓ Ⓔ   36 Ⓐ Ⓑ Ⓒ Ⓓ Ⓔ
7 Ⓐ Ⓑ Ⓒ Ⓓ Ⓔ   17 Ⓐ Ⓑ Ⓒ Ⓓ Ⓔ   27 Ⓐ Ⓑ Ⓒ Ⓓ Ⓔ   37 Ⓐ Ⓑ Ⓒ Ⓓ Ⓔ
8 Ⓐ Ⓑ Ⓒ Ⓓ Ⓔ   18 Ⓐ Ⓑ Ⓒ Ⓓ Ⓔ   28 Ⓐ Ⓑ Ⓒ Ⓓ Ⓔ   38 Ⓐ Ⓑ Ⓒ Ⓓ Ⓔ
9 Ⓐ Ⓑ Ⓒ Ⓓ Ⓔ   19 Ⓐ Ⓑ Ⓒ Ⓓ Ⓔ   29 Ⓐ Ⓑ Ⓒ Ⓓ Ⓔ   39 Ⓐ Ⓑ Ⓒ Ⓓ Ⓔ
10 Ⓐ Ⓑ Ⓒ Ⓓ Ⓔ   20 Ⓐ Ⓑ Ⓒ Ⓓ Ⓔ   30 Ⓐ Ⓑ Ⓒ Ⓓ Ⓔ   40 Ⓐ Ⓑ Ⓒ Ⓓ Ⓔ

Use a No. 2 pencil only. Be sure each mark is dark and completely fills the oval. Completely erase any errors or stray marks.

Start with number 1 for each new section. If a section has fewer questions than answer spaces, leave the extra answer spaces blank.

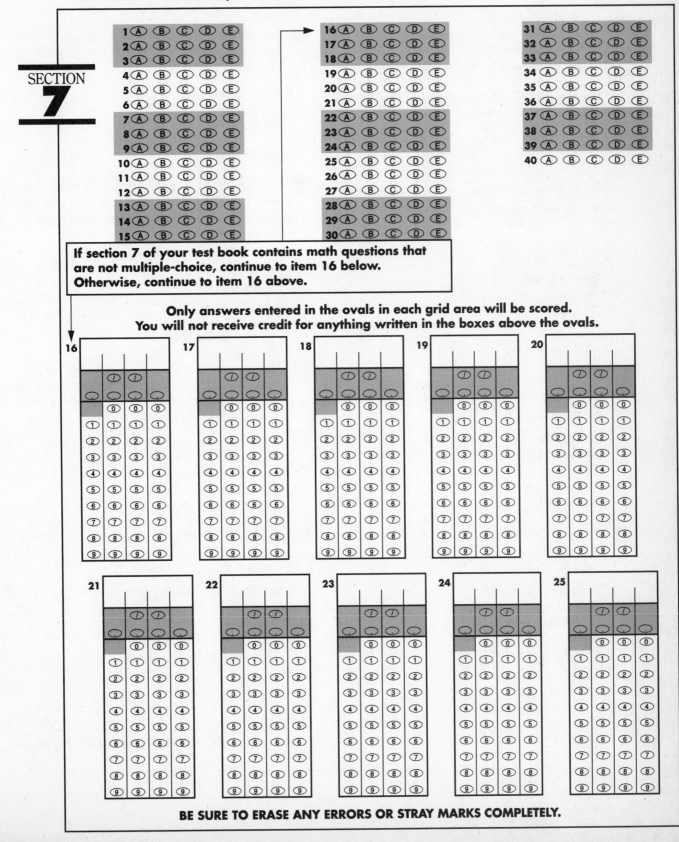

If section 7 of your test book contains math questions that are not multiple-choice, continue to item 16 below. Otherwise, continue to item 16 above.

Only answers entered in the ovals in each grid area will be scored. You will not receive credit for anything written in the boxes above the ovals.

BE SURE TO ERASE ANY ERRORS OR STRAY MARKS COMPLETELY.

Time: 30 Minutes   For each question in this section, select the best answer from among the choices given and fill in
 30 Questions   the corresponding oval on the answer sheet.

Each of the following sentences has one or two blanks, each blank indicating that something has been omitted. Beneath the sentence are five lettered words or sets of words labeled A through E. Choose the word or set of words that, when inserted in the sentence, *best* fits the meaning of the sentence as a whole.

Example:

Medieval kingdoms did not become constitutional republics overnight; on the contrary, the change was—.

(A) unpopular
(B) unexpected
(C) advantageous
(D) sufficient
(E) gradual

Ⓐ Ⓑ Ⓒ Ⓓ ●

1 Though he was a highly skilled computer programmer, he had little or no _____ in designing educational software.

(A) emotion
(B) opportunity
(C) exposure
(D) competition
(E) creativity

2 He is one of the most _____ professors that I have ever had, with a _____ knowledge of his subject and a thoroughness in his teaching.

(A) capable . . . limited
(B) tantamount . . . tremendous
(C) collegiate . . . remarkable
(D) scholarly . . . profound
(E) active . . . carefree

3 Because the people of India were _____ under British rule, many went over to the Japanese side during World War II.

(A) employed
(B) deported
(C) educated
(D) abused
(E) satisfied

4 The author told the publisher that the royalty payment specified in the contract was _____ because the research costs, including traveling for writing the book, were far more than the royalties projected for a year.

(A) rational
(B) precarious
(C) payable
(D) insufficient
(E) incomprehensible

5 Maggie was quite _____ about having her husband remove his shoes before he stepped into the living room; yet the rest of the apartment was very _____ whenever I visited them.

(A) indifferent . . . comfortable
(B) perplexed . . . weird
(C) firm . . . disorderly
(D) considerate . . . modern
(E) humorous . . . attractive

6 Those who were invited to Peter's party had to come dressed in _____ clothes, thus convincing all the guests of his _____ inclination.

(A) sonorous . . . imaginative
(B) tawdry . . . humble
(C) raucous . . . peaceloving
(D) tattered . . . nightmarish
(E) old-fashioned . . . nostalgic

GO ON TO THE NEXT PAGE

7 Her devotion to music _____ his own interest in an art he had once loved as a child.

(A) belied
(B) revived
(C) defiled
(D) reviled
(E) exiled

8 President Anwar el-Sadat of Egypt, disregarding _____ criticism in the Arab world and in his own government, _____ accepted Prime Minister Menachem Begin's invitation to visit Israel in order to address the Israeli Knesset.

(A) categorical . . . previously
(B) blemished . . . stiffly
(C) charismatic . . . meticulously
(D) acrimonious . . . formally
(E) malignant . . . plaintively

9 The foreman's leniency, especially in being over-friendly, had its _____, one of which was _____ workmanship.

(A) compensations . . . unacceptable
(B) innuendoes . . . superior
(C) drawbacks . . . shoddy
(D) frequencies . . . attractive
(E) cancellations . . . mediocre

GO ON TO THE NEXT PAGE

Each of the following questions consists of a related pair of words or phrases, followed by five pairs of words or phrases labeled A through E. Select the pair that *best* expresses a relationship similar to that expressed in the original pair.

Example:

CRUMB : BREAD ::
(A) ounce : unit
(B) splinter : wood
(C) water : bucket
(D) twine : rope
(E) cream : butter

Ⓐ ⬤ Ⓒ Ⓓ Ⓔ

10 AGENDA : CONFERENCE ::

(A) teacher : class
(B) agency : assignment
(C) map : trip
(D) man : woman
(E) executive : employee

11 EROSION : RAVINE ::

(A) sand : pearl
(B) derrick : equipment
(C) swelling : protrusion
(D) drilling : hole
(E) mountain : peak

12 TURTLE : REPTILE ::

(A) oak : tree
(B) leaf : branch
(C) trout : fish
(D) snake : rattle
(E) oyster : clam

13 QUIVER : ARROW ::

(A) trigger : gun
(B) purse : money
(C) pea : pod
(D) sheath : sword
(E) cabinet : cupboard

14 DISINTERESTED : BIASED ::

(A) pious : gullible
(B) affluent : impecunious
(C) ruthless : vicious
(D) haughty : careless
(E) quixotic : daring

15 ACCOLADE : HERO ::

(A) blame : culprit
(B) laughter : actor
(C) disgust : bully
(D) gratitude : ingrate
(E) anger : monster

GO ON TO THE NEXT PAGE

Each of the following passages is followed by questions based on its content. Answer the questions following each passage on the basis of what is *stated* or *implied* in that passage and in any introductory material that may be provided.

Questions 16–21 are based on the following passage.

The following passage describes the development of tumors, differentiating between the process of formation of malignant and benign ones.

Neoplasia, or the development of tumors, is the abnormal biological process in which some intrinsic cellular change within a group of normal cells produces a group of cells which no longer respond to the mechanisms which regulate
5 normal cells. As a result, this group of cells increases in number but fails to achieve the specialized characteristics associated with normal cells. The degree to which neoplastic cells resemble their normal counterpart cells, both in appearance and behavior, allows us to classify tumors as either
10 benign or malignant. Benign tumors look and behave like their normal tissue of origin, are usually slow-growing, are rarely fatal and remain localized. Malignant tumors, on the other hand, look very little like their tissue of origin and behave in such a manner that the animal which bears the
15 tumor frequently succumbs.

The characteristic which most strikingly separates malignant tumors from benign tumors is the ability of malignant cells to become widely disseminated and to establish secondary sites of tumor far distant from the original tumor.
20 This process of widespread dissemination, which is called metastasis, is not well understood; however, some of the features of the process have been ascertained. Before metastasis can occur, the malignant cells must invade the surrounding normal tissue. Initial attempts to invade are
25 inhibited by the normal tissue. With time, the neoplastic cells undergo changes which allow them to overcome this inhibition, and tumor cells leave the primary mass of tumor. The entire process of inhibition by normal tissue and the eventual breakdown of inhibition is undoubtedly complex.
30 Malignant cells are characteristically less adhesive, one to another, than are normal cells. The outer membrane of the malignant cells contains less calcium than the membrane of normal cells. The malignant cell also acquires a greater negative electrical charge. After malignant cells have in-
35 vaded the surrounding normal tissue, they ultimately enter the bloodstream where most of the cells die. Those cells which survive will form a metastasis at a distant site only if they can adhere to the wall of a small blood vessel. The factors which govern this adherence include the size of the
40 malignant cell or a clump of these cells, the diameter of the blood vessel and the stickiness of the blood vessel wall. Stickiness of the blood vessel wall is at least partially due to the status of bloodclotting components in the blood. In addition to these mechanical considerations, some patterns of
45 metastasis are explicable only on the basis of a receptive chemical environment or "soil" in which the malignant cell can grow. Finally, although a number of the characteristics of malignant neoplastic cells have been elucidated as described above, it still must be stated that many aspects of
50 their behavior remain a mystery.

16 The main topic of this passage is

(A) the meaning of neoplasia
(B) the inhibition of tumor metastasis by normal tissue
(C) the transformation of benign tumors into malignant tumors
(D) the manner in which malignant tumors behave in the body
(E) the fate of malignant cells after they enter the bloodstream

17 Before malignant cells can be disseminated to widespread parts of the body, they must first

(A) acquire new outer membrane characteristics
(B) inhibit the lethal effects of components of the blood
(C) penetrate the surrounding normal tissue
(D) locate the proper chemical environment in which to grow
(E) achieve sufficient size to become lodged in a blood vessel

18 According to the passage, the property of a malignant cell that most greatly enhances its metastatic potential is

(A) its ability to choose the proper "soil"
(B) its ability to invade the surrounding tissue
(C) the amount of calcium in the outer membrane of the cell
(D) the extent of deviation from the appearance of a normal cell
(E) its ability to attach itself to the wall of a small blood vessel

GO ON TO THE NEXT PAGE

19 It can be concluded from the passage that

(A) benign tumors usually progress to malignant tumors

(B) malignant cells reach distant tissues by routes yet to be ascertained

(C) if the wall of a blood vessel is "sticky," a tumor metastasis has a better chance to develop

(D) the outer membrane of malignant cells is the same as that of normal cells

(E) the pattern of metastasis of a particular tumor is predictable with considerable accuracy

20 According to this passage, characteristics that distinguish malignant neoplastic cells from normal cells include all of the following *except*

(A) their growth rate

(B) their physical appearance

(C) their outer membrane characteristics

(D) their normal tissue of origin

(E) their ability to invade surrounding tissue and metastasize

21 The word "explicable" in line 45 means

(A) withdrawn

(B) with exception

(C) created

(D) explainable

(E) malignant

GO ON TO THE NEXT PAGE

Questions 22–30 are based on the following passage.

The following passage is about the old Middle West and its influence on modern society.

The old Middle West is gone. However, it still lives in song and story. Give most children the choice of visiting Valley Forge or Dodge City . . . Dodge City wins. It is more glamorous in their imagination than Valley Forge.

5   The old Middle West developed a strong, compassionate people out of the hardships and suffering of the destructive blizzards of earlier generations—"northers" that swept over it with white clouds of blinding snow and ice—and southern winds that brought the black blizzards of dust
10 storms.

The Middle West is realistic about the nation's domestic and international affairs. It views both with intense interest and anxiety, for it knows that—although stubborn resistance to change can lead to catastrophe—change often
15 does have unforeseen ramifications.

This caution is still—especially on political major questions—present in the modern Middle West and is its particular contribution to our national relationships.

I think the Middle West's strength is in its customary
20 cautious approach to the day of reckoning in our complex industrial structure and what should be put forward for its solution. That solution will take time, for slapdash approaches never work.

It took thirty years for our great country to recover
25 from the upheaval of the Civil War. It took thirty years for our country to discard the Democrat policy that the way to settle economic troubles was with fiat money. It made inflation the prime issue in 1936. It still is.

Our era has seen some fifty years of war and interna-
30 tional tension piled on top of World War I, and enormous industrial development.

The new West is more worldly minded than the old Middle West was, and, in general, is a balance between the East Coast—with alignment toward Europe and the Atlan-
35 tic countries—and the West Coast—with its interests in Asian affairs.

There is still a noticeable difference between the atmosphere in the Middle West and that of the Eastern states. It is more free and easy. There are not as many old families with
40 local supremacy. The East's "money power"—as the old Middle West called it—is now the "Establishment."

The parallel factor is the desire on the part of many heads of families in many lines of activity to change from the tensions and insecurity of life in the big cities to the pleasure
45 and comfort that come from the security of living in smaller towns. In the Middle West, it has increasingly taken the form of people remaining in the smaller cities and giving them new life and intelligence. This has strengthened smaller communities and offset the flow of Middle Westerners to the

50 big cities. There are, however, signs that cities in general are no longer content to be corrupt. There is pragmatic awakening that can mean a new leadership—with a growing understanding of their problems and responsibilities. This newly awakened urban leadership, joining the Midwest and small
55 city leadership in the quest for stability, may just possibly be the salvation of the big cities.

That is a reversal of the trend that started some years ago that seemed to threaten the stagnation of the Middle West by the tide of migration to the big metropolitan areas.

60   The Jews are almost the only people in America today—or, in the world, for that matter—that, during Passover, recall to the memory of the present generation their tremendous racial achievements, their leadership and their heroes of long ago.

65   On the other hand, the freedom of communications—the easy movement of Americans around their great country—and the ease of changing occupations are remarkable in the United States. All contribute to breaking down ethnic and religious group prejudices.

70   Possibly one reason we have so much difficulty in resolving our problems of a complex society is that we have tended to lose not only a sense of national identity, but a sense of pride in and a strong feeling for the special qualities of our local area.

75   What Americans must find is a way to square their diversification, and the freedom upon which it is based, with the older sense of identity and of stability. Perhaps the contemporary Middle West offers the answer in its freer acceptance of people as they are, and as they are capable of
80 becoming—a surviving characteristic of mutual helpfulness, willingness to accept change—not for change's sake, but on its merits.

22   The author would agree that the "Old Middle West" remains

(A)   intact in only a few areas
(B)   only in tales that are told
(C)   unchanged in many small towns
(D)   in spirit but is lost in practice
(E)   a reality only to children who view it on television

23 The author feels that the strength of the Middle West lies in its

(A) tolerance of differences of opinion
(B) worldliness
(C) cautiousness
(D) free and easy atmosphere
(E) ability to recover from strife

24 A current trend that the author finds encouraging is

(A) a gradual reduction in inflation
(B) the increasing complexity of the national industrial structure
(C) realism in domestic and international affairs
(D) people staying in the smaller towns and cities
(E) a growing sense of national identity

25 The character of the old Middle West was formed by

I. weather hardships
II. the Gold Rush of 1849
III. the Civil War

(A) I only
(B) II only
(C) III only
(D) I and II only
(E) I and III only

26 The word "pragmatic" in line 51 means

(A) lethargic
(B) anticipatory
(C) flippant
(D) practical
(E) governmental

27 The author feels that we have had trouble in solving the problems of a complex society because

(A) of fiat money
(B) city governments are corrupt
(C) our cities are too large to be managed
(D) we have lost our attachment to local areas
(E) of the breakdown of ethnic and religious groups

28 It can be inferred that the author is

(A) a wealthy Middle West businessman
(B) a radical reformer
(C) a former political candidate
(D) a Middle West farmer
(E) a suburbanite

29 The word "diversification" in line 76 most likely refers to

(A) jobs
(B) income
(C) social stature
(D) intelligence
(E) race of religion

30 The author states that the following have been factors leading to the breakdown of ethnic and religious prejudices:

I. Ease of communications
II. Increased education at school and on the job
III. Ease of changing occupations

(A) I only
(B) II only
(C) III only
(D) I and II only
(E) I and III only

IF YOU FINISH BEFORE TIME IS CALLED, YOU MAY CHECK YOUR WORK ON THIS SECTION ONLY. DO NOT TURN TO ANY OTHER SECTION IN THE TEST.

614

Time: 30 Minutes   In this section solve each problem, using any available space on the page for scratchwork.
25 Questions   Then decide which is the best of the choices given and fill in the corresponding oval on the answer sheet.

Notes:

1. The use of a calculator is permitted. All numbers used are real numbers.
2. Figures that accompany problems in this test are intended to provide information useful in solving the problems. They are drawn as accurately as possible EXCEPT when it is stated in a specific problem that the figure is not drawn to scale. All figures lie in a plane unless otherwise indicated.

Reference Information

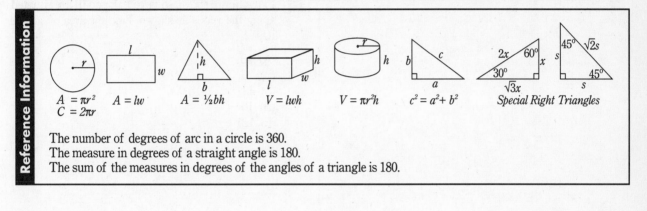

$A = \pi r^2$ $A = lw$ $A = \frac{1}{2}bh$ $V = lwh$ $V = \pi r^2 h$ $c^2 = a^2 + b^2$ *Special Right Triangles*
$C = 2\pi r$

The number of degrees of arc in a circle is 360.
The measure in degrees of a straight angle is 180.
The sum of the measures in degrees of the angles of a triangle is 180.

---

1 Given that $500w = 3 \times 700$, find the value of w.

(A) $\frac{5}{21}$

(B) 2

(C) $\frac{11}{5}$

(D) $\frac{21}{5}$

(E) 7

2 If $\frac{3 + y}{y} = 7$, then $y =$

(A) 4
(B) 3
(C) 2
(D) 1
(E) $\frac{1}{2}$

GO ON TO THE NEXT PAGE

3 The positive integer x is a multiple of 9 and also a multiple of 12. The smallest possible value of x is

(A) 3
(B) 12
(C) 21
(D) 36
(E) 72

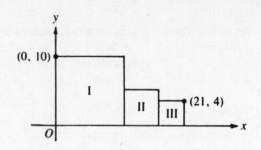

Note: Figure is not drawn to scale.

5 In the figure above, squares I, II, and III are situated along the x-axis as shown. Find the area of square II.

(A) 16
(B) 25
(C) 49
(D) 100
(E) 121

4 Find $(r - s)(t - s) + (s - r)(s - t)$ for all numbers r, s, and t.

(A) 0
(B) 2
(C) $2rt$
(D) $2(s - r)(t - s)$
(E) $2(r - s)(t - s)$

6 A certain cup holds 100 grams of butter. If a cake requires 75 grams of butter and a pie requires 225 grams of butter, then 4 cups of butter is *not* enough for any of the following *except*

(A) 6 cakes
(B) 2 pies
(C) 3 cakes and 1 pie
(D) 2 cakes and 2 pies
(E) 2 cakes and 1 pie

GO ON TO THE NEXT PAGE

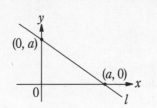

Note: Figure is not drawn to scale.

7 Which of the following is true about line ℓ above?

  I.   the slope is -1
  II. the distance of point $(0,a)$ to point $(a,0)$ is equal to $a\sqrt{2}$
  III. the acute angle that the line ℓ makes with the x-axis is $45°$

(A) I only
(B) II only
(C) III only
(D) II and III only
(E) I, II, and III

8 If 3 is added to a number and this sum is divided by 4, the result is 6. What is the number?

(A) 5
(B) 7
(C) 12
(D) 21
(E) 27

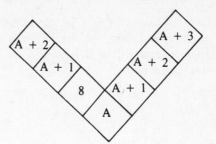

9 If the sum of the four terms in each of the diagonal rows is the same, then A =

(A) 4
(B) 5
(C) 6
(D) 7
(E) 8

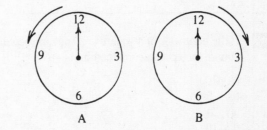

A   B

10 The two dials shown above operate simultaneously in the following manner: The hand in A turns *counterclockwise* while the hand in B turns *clockwise*. The hand of A moves to 9 at exactly the same moment that the hand of B moves to 3. Then the hand of A moves to 6 at exactly the same moment that the hand of B moves to 6, and so on. If each hand starts at 12, where will each hand be at the end of 17 moves?

(A) Both at 12
(B) Both at 9
(C) A at 3 and B at 12
(D) A at 3 and B at 9
(E) A at 9 and B at 3

GO ON TO THE NEXT PAGE

11 Given that $w = 7r + 6r + 5r + 4r + 3r$, which of the terms listed below may be added to w so that the resulting sum will be divisible by 7 for every positive integer r?

(A) $7r$
(B) $6r$
(C) $5r$
(D) $4r$
(E) $3r$

13 Given that $80 + a = -32 + b$, find the value of $b - a$.

(A) -112
(B) -48
(C) 2.5
(D) 48
(E) 112

12 If the perimeter of a square is 20 meters, how many square meters are contained in its area?

(A) 100
(B) 25
(C) 20
(D) 10
(E) 5

14 If x is a positive integer, which of the following must be an even integer?

(A) $x + 2$
(B) $2x + 1$
(C) $3x + 1$
(D) $x^2 + x + 1$
(E) $x^2 + x + 2$

GO ON TO THE NEXT PAGE

15 Given that $\frac{3}{4} < x < \frac{4}{5}$, which of the following is a possible value of x?

(A) $\frac{7}{16}$

(B) $\frac{13}{20}$

(C) $\frac{31}{40}$

(D) $\frac{16}{20}$

(E) $\frac{6}{7}$

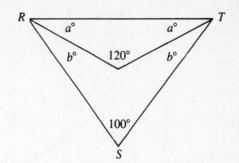

Note: Figure is not drawn to scale.

17 Given $\triangle RST$ above, what is the value of b?

(A) 50
(B) 40
(C) 30
(D) 20
(E) 10

16 A painter earns $10 an hour for all hours spent on a job. For a certain job, he worked from 7:00 A.M. until 5:00 P.M. on Monday, Tuesday, and Thursday and from 1:00 P.M. until 7:00 P.M. on Wednesday, Friday, and Saturday. How much did he earn for the entire job?

(A) $420
(B) $450
(C) $480
(D) $510
(E) $540

GO ON TO THE NEXT PAGE

Questions 18–19

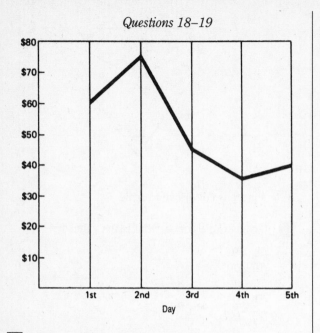

18 John works for 5 days. His daily earnings are displayed on the above graph. What is John's average daily wage during the 5 days?

(A) $75
(B) $35
(C) $50
(D) $51
(E) $39

19 If John earned $35 on the sixth day, what would be the difference between the median and the mode of the wages during the six days?

(A) 5.5
(B) 6.5
(C) 7.5
(D) 8.5
(E) 9.5

20 If $\textcircled{a}\textcircled{b} = \dfrac{a+1}{b-1}$ where a and b are positive integers and $b > 1$, which of the following is largest?

(A) $\textcircled{2}\textcircled{3}$
(B) $\textcircled{3}\textcircled{3}$
(C) $\textcircled{3}\textcircled{5}$
(D) $\textcircled{4}\textcircled{5}$
(E) $\textcircled{5}\textcircled{3}$

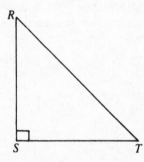

21 In $\triangle RST$ above, RS and ST have lengths equal to the same integer. All of the following could be the area of triangle RST except

(A) $\dfrac{1}{2}$

(B) 2

(C) $4\dfrac{1}{2}$

(D) $12\dfrac{1}{2}$

(E) 20

620

GO ON TO THE NEXT PAGE

22 A rectangular solid has dimensions of 2 feet × 2 feet × 1 foot. If it is sliced in small cubes, each of edge .1 foot, what is the maximum number of such cubes that can be formed?

(A) 40
(B) 500
(C) 1,000
(D) 2,000
(E) 4,000

Note: Figure is not drawn to scale.

24 In the figure above, *AC* is a straight line segment. Line segments are drawn from *B* to *D, E, F, G, H, I, J,* and *K,* respectively. Which of the following angles has a degree measure that can be found?

(A) ∠*FBG*
(B) ∠*EBG*
(C) ∠*DBG*
(D) ∠*GBI*
(E) ∠*GBJ*

23 A circle is inscribed in a square. If the perimeter of the square is 40, what is the area of the circle?

(A) 100π
(B) 50π
(C) 40π
(D) 25π
(E) 5π

25 If $ax = r$ and $by = r - 1$, then which of the following is a correct expression for *x*?

(A) $\dfrac{by + 1}{a}$

(B) $\dfrac{by - 1}{a}$

(C) $\dfrac{by + r}{a}$

(D) $by + ar$

(E) $ab + ry$

IF YOU FINISH BEFORE TIME IS CALLED, YOU MAY CHECK YOUR WORK ON THIS SECTION ONLY. DO NOT TURN TO ANY OTHER SECTION IN THE TEST.

Time: 30 Minutes   For each question in this section, choose the best answer from among the choices given and fill
35 Questions   in the corresponding oval on the answer sheet.

Each of the following sentences has one or two blanks, each blank indicating that something has been omitted. Beneath the sentence are five words or sets of words labeled A through E. Choose the word or set of words that, when inserted in the sentence, *best* fits the meaning of the sentence as a whole.

Example:

Medieval kingdoms did not become constitutional republics overnight; on the contrary, the change was—.

(A) unpopular
(B) unexpected
(C) advantageous
(D) sufficient
(E) gradual

Ⓐ Ⓑ ⒸⒹ ●

1 Although the physical setup of the high school's lunchroom seems rundown in many respects, it was enlarged and _____ quite recently.

(A) visited
(B) examined
(C) occupied
(D) renovated
(E) criticized

2 The activities that interested Jack were those that provided him with _____ pleasure, like dancing, feasting, and partying.

(A) questionable
(B) distant
(C) immediate
(D) limited
(E) delayed

3 His current inability to complete his assignments in a timely and efficient manner has resulted in a feeling of _____ even in his most _____ backers.

(A) urgency . . . lackadaisical
(B) flexibility . . . hostile
(C) expectancy . . . cautious
(D) dizziness . . . visible
(E) disappointment . . . fervent

4 The two performers taking the parts of shy, romantic teenagers were quite _____ in their roles even though they were actually man and wife.

(A) convincing
(B) flippant
(C) amateurish
(D) comfortable
(E) boring

5 He was _____ about a rise in the value of the stocks he had recently purchased and was eager to make a change in his investment portfolio.

(A) fearful
(B) unconcerned
(C) hesitant
(D) amused
(E) dubious

6 Nature's brute strength is never more _____ than during a major earthquake, when the earth shifts with a sickening sway.

(A) frightening
(B) effective
(C) replaceable
(D) placating
(E) complete

GO ON TO THE NEXT PAGE

7 Instead of providing available funds to education and thus _____ the incidence of crime, the mayor is _____ the funds to the building of more prisons.

(A) disdain . . . denying
(B) revoke . . . assigning
(C) abolish . . . confining
(D) reduce . . . diverting
(E) nourish . . . planning

8 The dancer excelled neither in grace nor technique, but the _____ musical accompaniment gives the performance a(n) _____ of excellence.

(A) gradual . . . sensation
(B) soothing . . . mandate
(C) well-rehearsed . . . diction
(D) superb . . . aura
(E) chronic . . . effervescence

9 Her fine reputation as a celebrated actress was _____ by her appearance in a TV soap opera.

(A) enhanced
(B) blemished
(C) appreciated
(D) concluded
(E) intensified

10 The dictator's slow, easy manner and his air of gentility _____ his firm intention to ensure no opposition to his planned _____ policies.

(A) revealed . . . eager
(B) accepted . . . professional
(C) belied . . . drastic
(D) disregarded . . . inane
(E) animated . . . crude

GO ON TO THE NEXT PAGE

Each of the following questions consists of a related pair of words or phrases, followed by five pairs of words or phrases labeled A through E. Select the pair that *best* expresses a relationship similar to that expressed in the original pair.

Example:

CRUMB : BREAD ::
(A) ounce : unit
(B) splinter : wood
(C) water : bucket
(D) twine : rope
(E) cream : butter

11 PEEL : ORANGE ::

(A) fur : coat
(B) cover : page
(C) petal : stem
(D) rind : melon
(E) crest : wave

12 TERMITE : WOOD ::

(A) mold : bread
(B) pearl : oyster
(C) weevil : cotton
(D) wasp : nest
(E) barnacle : ship

13 TEST : KEY ::

(A) weight : scale
(B) puzzle : solution
(C) anagram : word
(D) guide : tour
(E) lock : door

14 GORGE : NIBBLE ::

(A) laugh : guffaw
(B) quaff : sip
(C) hurry : amble
(D) scrutinize : examine
(E) spend : counterfeit

15 TIDAL WAVE : FLOOD ::

(A) earthquake : tremors
(B) avalanche : snow
(C) gale : wind
(D) sunspot : activity
(E) lava : eruption

16 BLEAT : SHEEP ::

(A) shear : lamb
(B) flight : plane
(C) honk : goose
(D) laughter : comedy
(E) sting : bee

17 LOBSTER : SHELL ::

(A) cattle : herb
(B) kangaroo : pouch
(C) mammal : whale
(D) insect : wing
(E) wool : sheep

18 AUTHENTICITY : COUNTERFEIT ::

(A) argument : contradictory
(B) reliability : erratic
(C) anticipation : solemn
(D) reserve : reticent
(E) mobility : energetic

19 GUILE : INGENUOUS ::

(A) appetite : voracious
(B) chivalry : natural
(C) prudence : demanding
(D) courage : timorous
(E) nobility : charming

20 ZEBRA : STRIATED ::

(A) penguin : flightless
(B) cat : domesticated
(C) sluggard : indolent
(D) monkey : imitative
(E) leopard : mottled

GO ON TO THE NEXT PAGE

21 DEFOLIATE : TREE : :

(A) molt : snake
(B) blossom : flower
(C) melt : glacier
(D) amputate : limb
(E) criticize : idea

 22 EMULATE : MODEL : :

(A) paraphrase : sentence
(B) provide : alibi
(C) testify : judge
(D) worship : icon
(E) smile : joke

23 PROTEAN : IMMUTABLE : :

(A) noxious : harmful
(B) prodigal : reckless
(C) perfidious : treacherous
(D) acquired : innate
(E) antiquated : archaic

GO ON TO THE NEXT PAGE

Questions 24–36 are based on the following passages. These two passages are followed by questions based on their content and on the relationship between the two passages. Answer the questions on the basis of what is *stated* or *implied* in the passages and in any introductory material that may be provided.

The following two passages describe two views of the make-up and character of an artist.

Passage A

The special quality which makes an artist of any worth might be defined, indeed, as an extraordinary capacity for irritation, a pathological sensitiveness to environmental pricks and stings. He differs from the rest of us mainly
5 because he reacts sharply and in an uncommon manner to phenomena which leave the rest of us unmoved, or, at most, merely annoy us vaguely. He is, in brief, a more delicate fellow than we are, and hence less fitted to prosper and enjoy himself under the conditions of life which he and we must
10 face alike. Therefore, he takes to artistic endeavor, which is at once a criticism of life and an attempt to escape from life.

So much for the theory of it. The more the facts are studied, the more they bear it out. In those fields of art, at all events, which concern themselves with ideas as well as with
15 sensations it is almost impossible to find any trace of an artist who was not actively hostile to his environment, and thus an indifferent patriot. From Dante to Tolstoy and from Shakespeare to Mark Twain the story is ever the same. Names suggest themselves instantly: Goethe, Heine, Shelley,
20 Byron, Thackeray, Balzac, Rabelais, Cervantes, Swift, Dostoevsky, Carlyle, Molière, Pope—all bitter critics of their time and nation, most of them piously hated by the contemporary 100 percenters, some of them actually fugitives from rage and reprisal.
25 Dante put all of the patriotic Italians of his day into Hell, and showed them boiling, roasting and writhing on hooks. Cervantes drew such a devastating picture of the Spain that he lived in that it ruined the Spaniards. Shakespeare made his heroes foreigners and his clowns English-
30 men. Goethe was in favor of Napoleon. Rabelais, a citizen of Christendom rather than of France, raised a cackle against it that Christendom is still trying in vain to suppress. Swift, having finished the Irish and then the English, proceeded to finish the whole human race. The exceptions are few and far
35 between, and not many of them will bear examination. So far as I know, the only eminent writer in English history who was also a 100% Englishman, absolutely beyond suspicion, was Samuel Johnson. But was Johnson actually an artist? If he was, then a kazoo-player is a musician. He employed the
40 materials of one of the arts, to wit, words, but his use of them was mechanical, not artistic. If Johnson were alive today, he would be a United States Senator, or a university president. He left such wounds upon English prose that it was a century recovering from them.

Passage B

45 For the ease and pleasure of treading the old road, accepting the fashions, the education, the religion of society, he takes the cross of making his own, and, of course, the self-accusation, the faint heart, the frequent uncertainty and loss of time, which are the nettles and tangling vines in the way
50 of the self-relying and self-directed, and the state of virtual hostility in which he seems to stand to society, and especially to educated society. For all this loss and scorn, what offset? The artist is to find consolation in exercising the highest functions of human nature. The artist is one who
55 raises himself from private consideration and breathes and lives on public and illustrious thoughts. The artist is the world's eye. He is the world's heart. He is to resist the vulgar prosperity that retrogrades ever to barbarism, by preserving and communicating heroic sentiments, noble biographies,
60 melodious verse, and the conclusions of history. Whatsoever oracles the human heart, in all emergencies, in all solemn hours, has uttered as its commentary on the world of actions—these he shall receive and impart. And whatsoever new verdict Reason from her inviolable seat pronounces on
65 the passing men and women and events of today—this he shall hear and promulgate.

These being his functions, it becomes the artist to feel all confidence in himself, and to defer never to the popular cry. He and he only knows the world. The world of any
70 moment is the merest appearance. Some great decorum, some fetish of a government, some ephemeral trade, or war, or man, is cried up by half mankind and cried down by the other half, as if all depended on this particular up or down. The odds are that the whole question is not worth the
75 poorest thought which the scholar has lost in listening to the controversy. Let her not quit her belief that a popgun is a popgun, though the ancient and honorable of the earth affirm it to be the crack of doom. In silence, in steadiness, in severe abstraction, let him hold by himself; add observation
80 to observation, patient of neglect, patient of reproach, and bide his own time—happy enough if he can satisfy himself alone that this day he has seen something truly. Success treads on every right step. For the instinct is sure, that prompts him to tell his brother what he thinks. The artist then

GO ON TO THE NEXT PAGE

85 learns that in going down into the secrets of his own mind he has descended into the secrets of all minds. He learns that the artist who has mastered any law in his private thoughts is master to that extent of all translated. The poet, in utter solitude remembering his spontaneous thoughts and record-

90 ing them, is found to have recorded that which men in crowded cities find true for them also. The orator distrusts at first the fitness of his frank confessions, his want of knowledge of the persons he addresses, until he finds that he is the complement of his hearers—that they drink his words be-

95 cause he fulfills for them their own nature; the deeper he dives into his privatest, secretest presentiment, to his wonder he finds this is the most acceptable, most public, and universally true. The people delight in it; the better part of every man feels. This is my music; this is myself.

24 Which of the following quotations is related most closely to the principal idea of Passage A?

(A) "All nature is but art unknown to thee,
      All chance, direction which thou canst not see."
(B) "When to her share some human errors fall,
      Look on her face and you'll forget them all."
(C) "All human things are subject to decay,
      "And, when fate summons, monarchs must obey."
(D) "A little learning is a dangerous thing;
      "Drink deep or taste not the Pierian spring."
(E) "Great wits are sure to madness near allied,
      And thin partitions do their bounds divide."

25 The author of Passage A seems to regard the artist as

(A) the best representative of his time
(B) an unnecessary threat to the social order
(C) one who creates out of discontent
(D) one who truly knows how to enjoy life
(E) one who is touched with genius

26 It can be inferred that the author of Passage A believes that United States Senators and university presidents

(A) must be treated with respect because of their position
(B) are to be held in low esteem
(C) are generally appreciative of the great literary classics
(D) have native writing ability
(E) have the qualities of the artist

27 All of the following ideas about artists are mentioned in Passage A *except* that

(A) they are irritated by their surroundings
(B) they are escapists from reality
(C) they are lovers of beauty
(D) they are hated by their contemporaries
(E) they are critical of their times

28 Which of the following best describes Passage A's author's attitude toward artists?

(A) sharply critical
(B) sincerely sympathetic
(C) deeply resentful
(D) mildly annoyed
(E) completely delighted

29 It is a frequent criticism of the artist that he lives by himself, in an "ivory tower," remote from the problems and business of the world. Which of these below constitutes the best refutation by the writer of Passage B to the criticism here noted?

(A) The world's concerns being ephemeral, the artist does well to renounce them and the world.
(B) The artist lives in the past to interpret the present.
(C) The artist at his truest is the spokesman of the people.
(D) The artist is not concerned with the world's doings because he is not selfish and therefore not engrossed in matters of importance to himself and neighbors.
(E) The artist's academic researches of today are the businessman's practical products of tomorrow.

30 The artist's road is rough, according to Passage B. Which of these is the artist's greatest difficulty?

(A) The artist must renounce religion.
(B) The artist must pioneer new approaches.
(C) The artist must express scorn for and hostility to society.
(D) The artist is uncertain of his course.
(E) There is a pleasure in the main-traveled roads in education, religion, and all social fashions.

GO ON TO THE NEXT PAGE

31 When the writer of Passage B speaks of the "world's eye" and the "world's heart" he means

(A) the same thing
(B) culture and conscience
(C) culture and wisdom
(D) a scanning of all the world's geography and a deep sympathy for every living thing
(E) mind and love

32 By the phrase "nettles and tangling vines" (line 49) the author probably refers to

(A) "self-accusation" and "loss of time"
(B) "faint heart" and "self-accusation"
(C) "the slings and arrows of outrageous fortune"
(D) a general term for the difficulties of a scholar's life
(E) "self-accusation" and "uncertainty"

33 The various ideas in Passage B are best summarized in which of these groups?
  I. truth versus society
     the artist and books
     the world and the artist
  II. the ease of living traditionally
     the glory of an artist's life
     true knowledge versus trivia
  III. the hardships of the scholar
     the artist's functions
     the artist's justifications for disregarding the world's business

(A) I and III together
(B) I only
(C) III only
(D) I, II, and III together
(E) I and II together

34 "seems to stand" (line 51) means

(A) is
(B) ends probably in becoming
(C) gives the false impression of being
(D) is seen to be
(E) the quicksands of time

35 The difference between the description of the artist in Passage A as compared with the artist in Passage B is that

(A) one is loyal to his fellow men and women whereas the other is opposed to his or her environment
(B) one is sensitive to his or her environment whereas the other is apathetic
(C) one has political aspirations; the other does not
(D) one has deep knowledge; the other has superficial knowledge
(E) one could be proficient in a field other than art; the other could create only in his or her present field

36 Which of the following describes statements that refer to the *same* one artist (either the one in Passage A *or* the one in Passage B)?

  I. This artist's thoughts are also the spectator's thoughts.
     This artist lives modestly and not luxuriously.
  II. This artist admires foreigners over his own countrymen.
     This artist reacts to many things that most people would be neutral to.
  III. This artist is happy to be at his best.
     This artist accepts society.

(A) I only
(B) II only
(C) III only
(D) I and III only
(E) I, II, and III

Time: 30 Minutes — This section consists of two types of questions. Each type has its own directions. You may use
25 Questions — any available space for scratchwork.

Notes:

1. The use of a calculator is permitted. All numbers are real numbers.
2. Figures that accompany problems in this test are intended to provide information useful in solving the problems. They are drawn as accurately as possible EXCEPT when it is stated in a specific problem that the figure is not drawn to scale. All figures lie in a plane unless otherwise indicated.

Reference Information

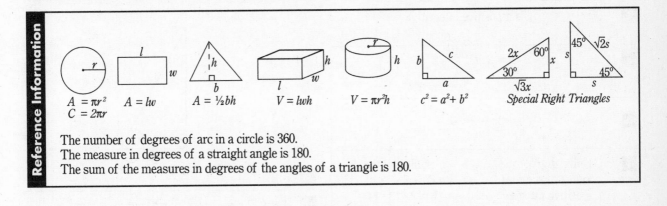

$A = \pi r^2$ $A = lw$ $A = \frac{1}{2}bh$ $V = lwh$ $V = \pi r^2 h$ $c^2 = a^2 + b^2$ *Special Right Triangles*
$C = 2\pi r$

The number of degrees of arc in a circle is 360.
The measure in degrees of a straight angle is 180.
The sum of the measures in degrees of the angles of a triangle is 180.

Directions for Quantitative Comparison Questions

Questions 1–15 each consist of two quantities in boxes, one in Column A and one in Column B. You are to compare the two quantities and on the answer sheet fill in oval

A if the quantity in Column A is greater;
B if the quantity in Column B is greater;
C if the two quantities are equal;
D if the relationship cannot be determined from the information given.

AN E RESPONSE WILL NOT BE SCORED.

Notes:

1. In some questions, information is given about one or both of the quantities to be compared. In such cases, the given information is centered above the two columns and is not boxed.
2. In a given question, a symbol that appears in both columns represents the same thing in Column A as it does in Column B.
3. Letters such as x, n, and k stand for real numbers.

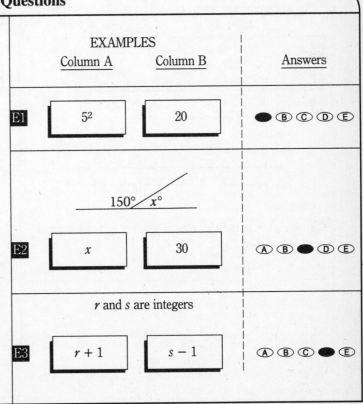

GO ON TO THE NEXT PAGE

SUMMARY DIRECTIONS FOR COMPARISON QUESTIONS

<u>Answer:</u> A   if the quantity in Column A is greater;
B   if the quantity in Column B is greater;
C   if the two quantities are equal;
D   if the relationship cannot be determined from the information given.

An E response will not be scored.

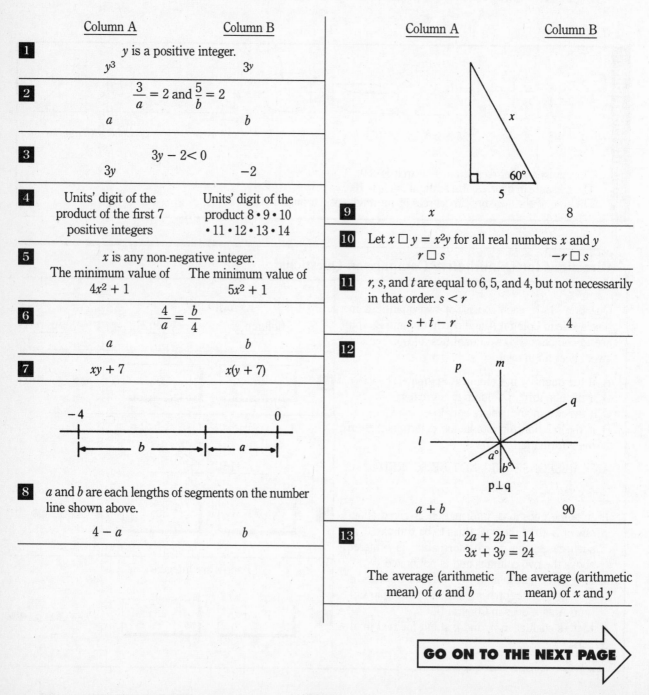

Column A	Column B

1 y is a positive integer.

y^3 $3y$

2 $\dfrac{3}{a} = 2$ and $\dfrac{5}{b} = 2$

a b

3 $3y - 2 < 0$

$3y$ -2

4 Units' digit of the product of the first 7 positive integers   Units' digit of the product $8 \cdot 9 \cdot 10 \cdot 11 \cdot 12 \cdot 13 \cdot 14$

5 x is any non-negative integer.
The minimum value of $4x^2 + 1$ The minimum value of $5x^2 + 1$

6 $\dfrac{4}{a} = \dfrac{b}{4}$

a b

7 $xy + 7$ $x(y + 7)$

8 a and b are each lengths of segments on the number line shown above.

$4 - a$ b

9 x 8

10 Let $x \,\square\, y = x^2 y$ for all real numbers x and y

$r \,\square\, s$ $-r \,\square\, s$

11 r, s, and t are equal to 6, 5, and 4, but not necessarily in that order. $s < r$

$s + t - r$ 4

12

$p \perp q$

$a + b$ 90

13 $2a + 2b = 14$
$3x + 3y = 24$

The average (arithmetic mean) of a and b The average (arithmetic mean) of x and y

GO ON TO THE NEXT PAGE

Column A   Column B

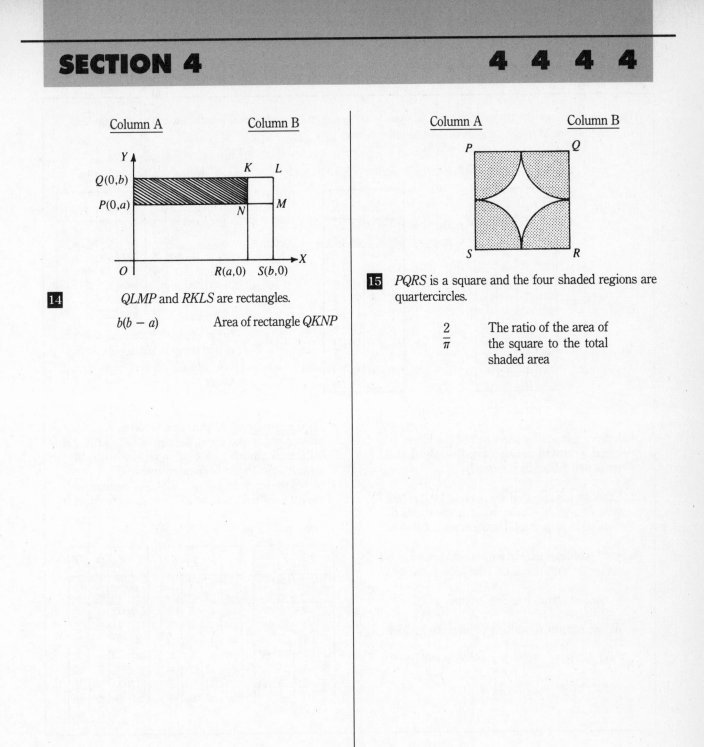

14

QLMP and *RKLS* are rectangles.

$b(b - a)$ Area of rectangle *QKNP*

Column A   Column B

15   *PQRS* is a square and the four shaded regions are quartercircles.

$\dfrac{2}{\pi}$ The ratio of the area of the square to the total shaded area

GO ON TO THE NEXT PAGE

Directions: Each of the 10 questions requires you to solve the problem and enter your answer by marking the ovals in the special grid, as shown in the examples below.

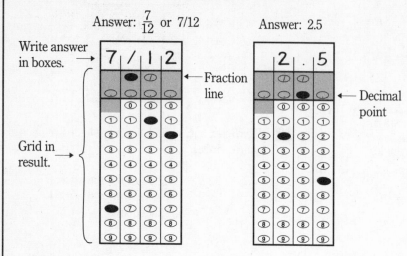

Answer: $\frac{7}{12}$ or 7/12

Answer: 2.5

Answer: 201
Either position is correct.

Write answer in boxes. → ← Fraction line

← Decimal point

Grid in result. →

Note: You may start your answers in any column, space permitting. Columns not needed should be left blank.

- Mark no more than one oval in any column.

- Because the answer sheet will be machine-scored, **you will receive credit only if the ovals are filled in correctly.**

- Although not required, it is suggested that you write your answer in the boxes at the top of the columns to help you fill in the ovals accurately.

- Some problems may have more than one correct answer. In such cases, grid only one answer.

- No question has a negative answer.

- **Mixed numbers** such as $2\frac{1}{2}$ must be gridded as 2.5 or 5/2. (If 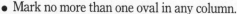 is gridded, it will be interpreted as $\frac{21}{2}$, not $2\frac{1}{2}$.)

- Decimal Accuracy: If you obtain a decimal answer, **enter the most accurate value the grid will accommodate.** For example, if you obtain an answer such as 0.6666 ... , you should record the result as .666 or .667. **Less accurate results such as .66 or .67 are not acceptable.**

Acceptable ways to grid $\frac{2}{3}$ = .6666 ...

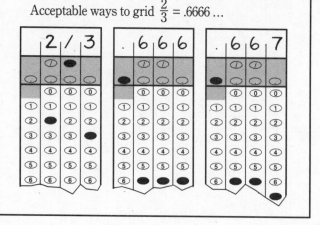

16 Given $r = a + b$ and $s = b - a$. When $a = 5$ and $b = 4$, find the value of $r - s$.

17 A bag contains exactly 4 blue marbles, 7 green marbles, and 8 yellow marbles. Fred draws marbles at random from the bag without replacement, one by one. If he does not look at the marbles he draws out, how many marbles will he have to draw out before he knows for sure that on his *next* draw he will have 1 marble for every color?

18 If 12 is the average (arithmetic mean) of 5 different integers, each integer > 0, then what is the greatest that any one of the integers could be?

19 A classroom has 12 seated students, 5 students at the board, and 7 empty seats. If 3 students leave the room, 2 enter, and all sit down, how many empty seats will there be?

20 How many different *pairs* of parallel edges are there on a rectangular solid?

21 If the sum of $2r$ and $2r + 3$ is less than 11, find a possible value of r?

22 Given the sum of two angles of a quadrilateral is 90°, find the average (arithmetic mean) of the measures of the other two angles. (Disregard the angle sign when gridding in your answer.)

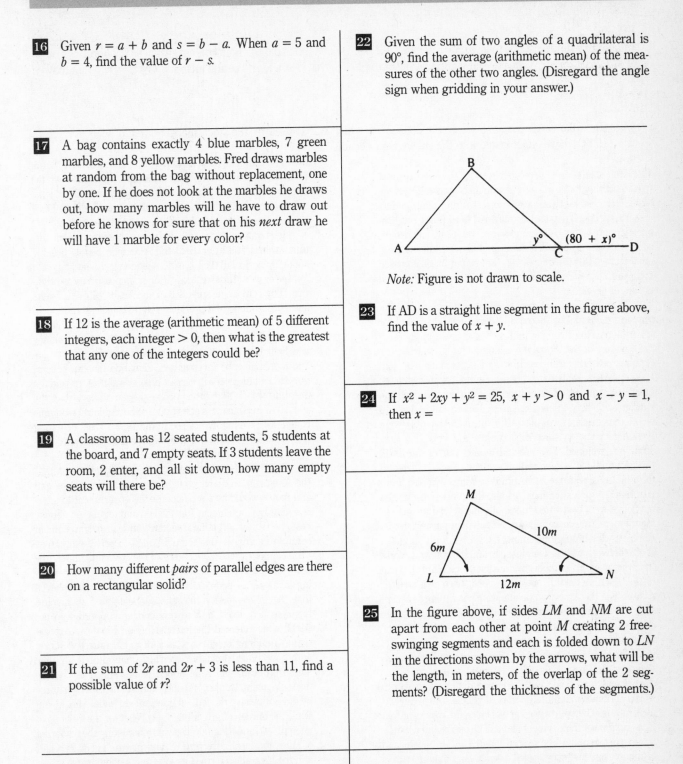

Note: Figure is not drawn to scale.

23 If AD is a straight line segment in the figure above, find the value of $x + y$.

24 If $x^2 + 2xy + y^2 = 25$, $x + y > 0$ and $x - y = 1$, then $x =$

25 In the figure above, if sides *LM* and *NM* are cut apart from each other at point *M* creating 2 free-swinging segments and each is folded down to *LN* in the directions shown by the arrows, what will be the length, in meters, of the overlap of the 2 segments? (Disregard the thickness of the segments.)

IF YOU FINISH BEFORE TIME IS CALLED, YOU MAY CHECK YOUR WORK ON THIS SECTION ONLY. DO NOT TURN TO ANY OTHER SECTION IN THE TEST.

Time: 15 Minutes
12 Questions

The following passage is followed by questions based on its content. Answer the questions on the basis of what is *stated* or *implied* in that passage and in any introductory material that may be provided.

The following passage is about the depression which was caused by the stock market crash of 1929, whose effect lasted into the subsequent decade.

The American people were dismayed by the sudden proof that something had gone wrong with their economic system, that it lacked stability and was subject to crises of unpredictable magnitude. They had encountered hard times and tem-
5 porary depressions before, and such reverses had tended for over a century to broaden out and to become international misfortunes. But the depression that began in 1929 proved so severe, so general, and so difficult to arrest, that it caused a "loss of nerve."
10   Students of economics pointed out that periods of inflation and deflation, of "boom and bust," had alternated for generations. Any strong stimulus such as a war might force the economy of the Western world into high gear; when the fighting ceased, reconstruction and a "backlog" of con-
15 sumers' orders unfilled in wartime might for a time keep the machines running at full speed; but within a decade the market was likely to become satiated and a fall in demand would then cause a recession. Adjustment and recovery were certain to come in time, and come the sooner if a new
20 stimulus developed. The threat of another war, or war itself, that put millions of men in uniform and created a demand for munitions, was one such stimulus. War provided a limitless market for expendable goods, the type of goods the machines were best fitted to supply, and solved unemploy-
25 ment by creating more military and civilian jobs. Such reasoning as this brought no comfort, however, for it implied a choice between war and depression, and the cure was worse than the disease. "Is modern industry a sick giant that can rouse itself only to kill?" one critic asked. There was no clear
30 answer. But the American people were not willing to accept such a grim diagnosis and insisted that there must be some method of coordinating a supply and demand within the framework of a peacetime economy.
    The problem appeared to be as much psychological as
35 economic. In prosperous times business expanded, prices rose, wages increased, and the expectation that the boom would continue indefinitely tempted people to live beyond their means. They purchased goods on credit, confident that they could meet the payments later. The increasing prosper-
40 ity, in part genuine but overstimulated by optimism and artificial elements, encouraged farmers and manufacturers to overproduce until the supply exceeded the capacity of the market to absorb it. Then when business confidence began to falter, and stock quotations began to drop, panic set in.
45 Speculators who saw their "paper profits" vanishing began to unload their securities with a disastrous effect on prices. Dealers with overloaded shelves slashed their prices to keep

their goods moving, and canceled outstanding orders. Manufacturers, seeing orders shrink, reduced output. All down the
50 line the contraction of business left employees without jobs, and lacking wages they could not meet their debts. Once started, this spiral of deflation seemed to have no limit.
    It is natural for people to blame others when misfortune strikes, and after 1929 the American people became
55 suddenly critical of their business leaders, who had failed to foresee or avert the swift transition from prosperity to privation. The conviction spread that the heads of great banks and corporations, the promoters and financiers and stockbrokers, had misled the public. Demands raised earlier in
60 American history were revived, demands for "cheap" money with which to pay off debts, demands that the great trusts and monopolies be investigated, demands that the federal government intervene to correct business abuses and aid the destitute. More and more people began to feel that the
65 system of free business enterprise, of unregulated economic competition, so highly praised in the 1920's, must be wrong if it could lead to crises that brought such widespread misery and unemployment.
    But President Hoover was firm in his conviction that
70 the American economic system was fundamentally sound and that it would be a mistake for the government to interfere unduly. Government supervision and regulation of business, he felt, would stifle freedom and lead to government control of activities that should be left to private initiative.
75 "You cannot extend the mastery of the government over the daily life of a people," he warned, "without somewhere making it master of people's souls and thoughts." He believed that the government's role should be limited to helping business help itself, and to this end he supported an act
80 (1932) which created the Reconstruction Finance Corporation to aid ailing businesses, as well as hard-pressed states, with government loans. Hoover also inaugurated a public works program which he hoped would effectively relieve unemployment. But beyond such indirect measures as these
85 he did not believe the federal government should go. Meanwhile the burden of providing direct relief for the millions of unemployed and their families was exhausting the resources of state and local governments and private agencies—and still the breadlines formed as jobs and savings went.

GO ON TO THE NEXT PAGE

1 According to the passage, President Hoover

(A) urged more and more government regulation
(B) did little or nothing to aid ailing business
(C) made efforts to relieve unemployment
(D) had sincere doubts about the soundness of the American economic system
(E) expressed the belief that we should convert gradually to a socialistic form of government

2 The author indicates that recovery from a recession most likely comes about

(A) during wartime
(B) during peacetime
(C) by decreasing manufacturing
(D) by lowering wages
(E) by raising the interest rate

3 Which of the following was *not* a cause of the 1929 Depression?

(A) too much buying on credit
(B) rising prices
(C) overproduction of goods
(D) lack of economic stability
(E) political unrest throughout the world

4 According to the passage, when the stock quotations began to drop,

(A) manufacturers immediately increased output
(B) unemployment decreased
(C) there was a reduction of business
(D) dealers increased their prices
(E) speculators held on to their securities

5 As used in lines 56–57 the word "privation" means

(A) solitude
(B) lack of basic necessities
(C) strictness
(D) a smooth transition
(E) a reduction in the usual business sales rate

6 The word "inaugurated" in line 82 means

(A) stifled
(B) amalgamated
(C) began
(D) commemorated
(E) oversaw

7 According to the passage, the Reconstruction Finance Corporation

(A) remodeled old private and government buildings
(B) served as a price-regulating organization
(C) helped the unemployed to find jobs during the Depression
(D) gave government loans to certain businesses
(E) supported the unemployed by public relief programs

8 Which statement would the author *not* agree to?

(A) There will continue to be economic crises.
(B) The end of the spiral of deflation was usually in sight.
(C) War tends to reduce unemployment.
(D) War is not the answer to avoiding economic depression.
(E) The depression of 1929 had psychological roots.

9 As seen from the passage, as a result of the Depression

(A) the value of the free enterprise system was questioned
(B) more people demanded that the government stay out of business
(C) people put more trust in business leaders
(D) a third of the population was unemployed
(E) the government was forced to increase taxes

10 The author would agree that war is economically advantageous in that

(A) it implies a choice between war and depression
(B) it increases unemployment
(C) the market becomes satiated
(D) it solves bouts of inflation
(E) it increases aggregate demand

11 After 1929, the following demands were raised *except*

(A) abolition of the great financial cartels
(B) cheap money
(C) investigation of trusts and monopolies
(D) intervention of the federal government to correct business abuses
(E) intervention of the federal government to aid the poor

GO ON TO THE NEXT PAGE

12 As seen by the passage, the contraction of business in 1929 led to

(A) war fever
(B) increased unemployment
(C) payment of debts
(D) demand exceeding supply
(E) skyrocketing prices

Time: 15 Minutes
10 Questions

In this section solve each problem, using any available space on the page for scratchwork. Then decide which is the best of the choices given and fill in the corresponding oval on the answer sheet.

Notes:

1. The use of a calculator is permitted. All numbers used are real numbers.
2. Figures that accompany problems in this test are intended to provide information useful in solving the problems. They are drawn as accurately as possible EXCEPT when it is stated in a specific problem that the figure is not drawn to scale. All figures lie in a plane unless otherwise indicated.

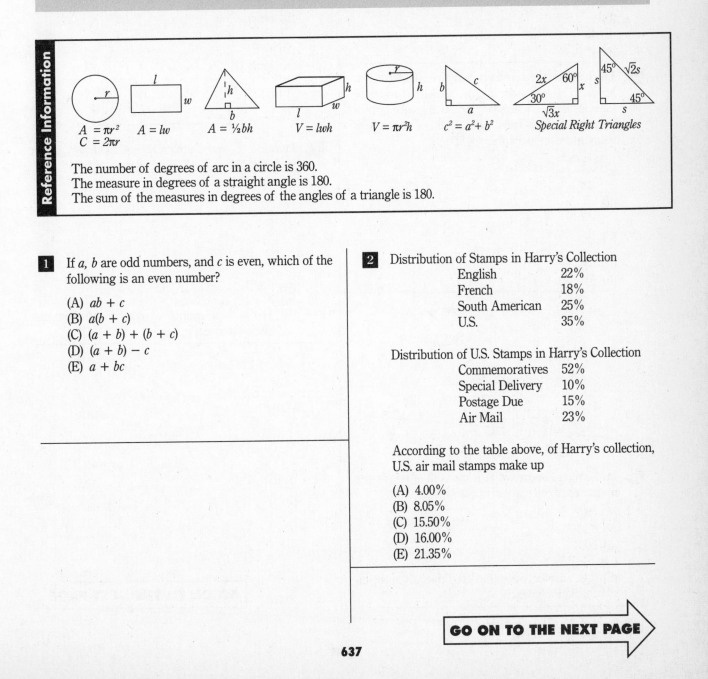

Reference Information

$A = \pi r^2$
$C = 2\pi r$

$A = lw$

$A = \frac{1}{2}bh$

$V = lwh$

$V = \pi r^2 h$

$c^2 = a^2 + b^2$

Special Right Triangles

The number of degrees of arc in a circle is 360.
The measure in degrees of a straight angle is 180.
The sum of the measures in degrees of the angles of a triangle is 180.

1 If *a, b* are odd numbers, and *c* is even, which of the following is an even number?

(A) $ab + c$
(B) $a(b + c)$
(C) $(a + b) + (b + c)$
(D) $(a + b) - c$
(E) $a + bc$

2 Distribution of Stamps in Harry's Collection

English	22%
French	18%
South American	25%
U.S.	35%

Distribution of U.S. Stamps in Harry's Collection

Commemoratives	52%
Special Delivery	10%
Postage Due	15%
Air Mail	23%

According to the table above, of Harry's collection, U.S. air mail stamps make up

(A) 4.00%
(B) 8.05%
(C) 15.50%
(D) 16.00%
(E) 21.35%

GO ON TO THE NEXT PAGE

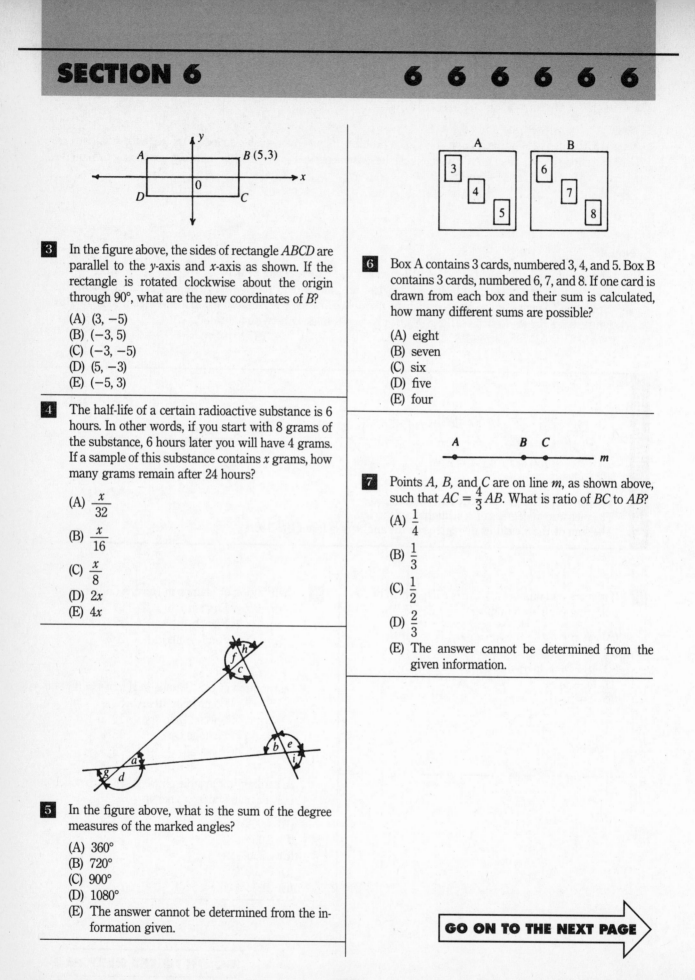

3 In the figure above, the sides of rectangle *ABCD* are parallel to the *y*-axis and *x*-axis as shown. If the rectangle is rotated clockwise about the origin through 90°, what are the new coordinates of *B*?

(A) $(3, -5)$
(B) $(-3, 5)$
(C) $(-3, -5)$
(D) $(5, -3)$
(E) $(-5, 3)$

4 The half-life of a certain radioactive substance is 6 hours. In other words, if you start with 8 grams of the substance, 6 hours later you will have 4 grams. If a sample of this substance contains *x* grams, how many grams remain after 24 hours?

(A) $\dfrac{x}{32}$

(B) $\dfrac{x}{16}$

(C) $\dfrac{x}{8}$

(D) $2x$

(E) $4x$

5 In the figure above, what is the sum of the degree measures of the marked angles?

(A) 360°
(B) 720°
(C) 900°
(D) 1080°
(E) The answer cannot be determined from the information given.

6 Box A contains 3 cards, numbered 3, 4, and 5. Box B contains 3 cards, numbered 6, 7, and 8. If one card is drawn from each box and their sum is calculated, how many different sums are possible?

(A) eight
(B) seven
(C) six
(D) five
(E) four

7 Points *A, B,* and *C* are on line *m*, as shown above, such that $AC = \frac{4}{3} AB$. What is ratio of *BC* to *AB*?

(A) $\dfrac{1}{4}$

(B) $\dfrac{1}{3}$

(C) $\dfrac{1}{2}$

(D) $\dfrac{2}{3}$

(E) The answer cannot be determined from the given information.

GO ON TO THE NEXT PAGE

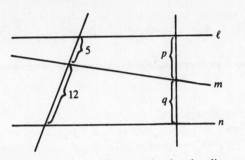

8 Lines ℓ and n are parallel to each other, but line m is parallel to neither of the other two. Find $\dfrac{p}{q}$ if $p + q = 13$.

(A) $\dfrac{13}{5}$

(B) $\dfrac{12}{5}$

(C) $\dfrac{7}{6}$

(D) $\dfrac{1}{5}$

(E) The answer cannot be determined from the information given.

9 Ross wants to make up 3 letter combinations. He wants each combination to have exactly 3 of the following letters: *A, B, C,* and *D.* No letter can be used more than once. For example, "*AAB*" is not acceptable. What is the maximum number of such triplets that Ross can make up? (The order of the letters must be considered. Example: "*ABC*" and "*CBA*" are acceptable triplets.)

(A) 6
(B) 9
(C) 24
(D) 27
(E) 64

10 If $x + y + z = 3(a + b)$, which of the following is the average (arithmetic mean) of $x, y, z, a,$ and b in terms of a and b?

(A) $\dfrac{a + b}{5}$

(B) $\dfrac{4(a + b)}{15}$

(C) $\dfrac{a + b}{2}$

(D) $\dfrac{4(a + b)}{5}$

(E) $a + b$

IF YOU FINISH BEFORE TIME IS CALLED, YOU MAY CHECK YOUR WORK ON THIS SECTION ONLY. DO NOT TURN TO ANY OTHER SECTION IN THE TEST.

STOP

Time: 30 Minutes   This section consists of two types of questions. Each type has its own directions. You may use
25 Questions   any available space for scratchwork.

Notes:

1. The use of a calculator is permitted. All numbers used are real numbers.
2. Figures that accompany problems in this test are intended to provide information useful in solving the problems. They are drawn as accurately as possible EXCEPT when it is stated in a specific problem that the figure is not drawn to scale. All figures lie in a plane unless otherwise indicated.

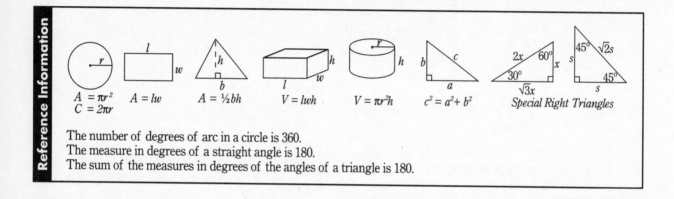

Reference Information

$A = \pi r^2$
$C = 2\pi r$

$A = lw$

$A = \frac{1}{2}bh$

$V = lwh$

$V = \pi r^2 h$

$c^2 = a^2 + b^2$

Special Right Triangles

The number of degrees of arc in a circle is 360.
The measure in degrees of a straight angle is 180.
The sum of the measures in degrees of the angles of a triangle is 180.

Directions for Quantitative Comparison Questions

Questions 1–15 each consist of two quantities in boxes, one in Column A and one in Column B. You are to compare the two quantities and on the answer sheet fill in oval

A if the quantity in Column A is greater;
B if the quantity in Column B is greater;
C if the two quantities are equal;
D if the relationship cannot be determined from the information given.

AN E RESPONSE WILL NOT BE SCORED.

Notes:

1. In some questions, information is given about one or both of the quantities to be compared. In such cases, the given information is centered above the two columns and is not boxed.
2. In a given question, a symbol that appears in both columns represents the same thing in Column A as it does in Column B.
3. Letters such as x, n, and k stand for real numbers.

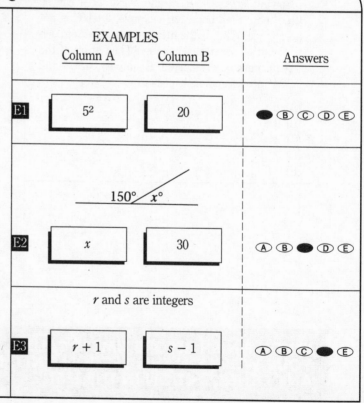

EXAMPLES

Column A   Column B   Answers

E1 5^2 20   ● Ⓑ Ⓒ Ⓓ Ⓔ

150° $x°$

E2 x 30   Ⓐ Ⓑ ● Ⓓ Ⓔ

r and s are integers

E3 $r + 1$ $s - 1$ Ⓐ Ⓑ Ⓒ ● Ⓔ

GO ON TO THE NEXT PAGE

SUMMARY DIRECTIONS FOR COMPARISON QUESTIONS

Answer: A if the quantity in Column A is greater;
B if the quantity in Column B is greater;
C if the two quantities are equal;
D if the relationship cannot be determined from the information given.
An E response will not be scored.

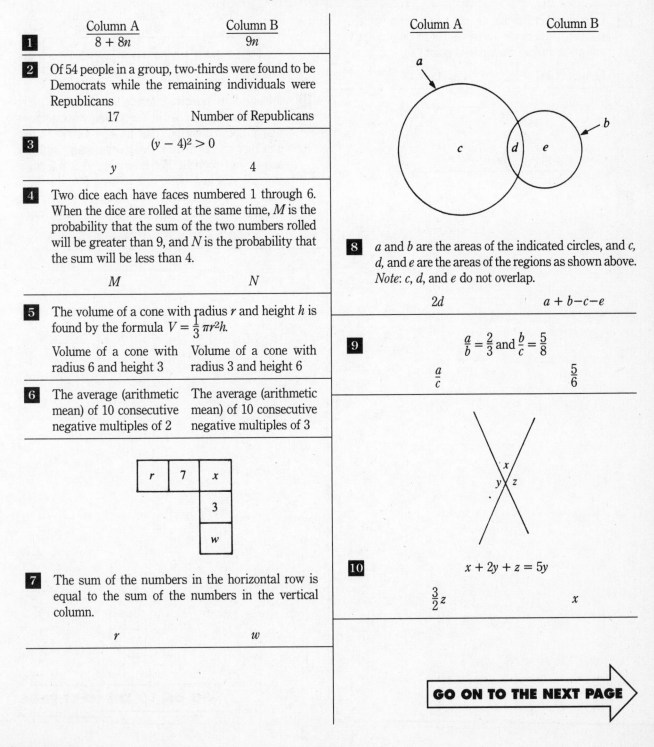

Column A	Column B
1 $8 + 8n$	$9n$

2 Of 54 people in a group, two-thirds were found to be Democrats while the remaining individuals were Republicans

17	Number of Republicans

3 $(y - 4)^2 > 0$

y	4

4 Two dice each have faces numbered 1 through 6. When the dice are rolled at the same time, M is the probability that the sum of the two numbers rolled will be greater than 9, and N is the probability that the sum will be less than 4.

M	N

5 The volume of a cone with radius r and height h is found by the formula $V = \frac{1}{3}\pi r^2 h$.

Volume of a cone with radius 6 and height 3	Volume of a cone with radius 3 and height 6

6 The average (arithmetic mean) of 10 consecutive negative multiples of 2 | The average (arithmetic mean) of 10 consecutive negative multiples of 3

7 The sum of the numbers in the horizontal row is equal to the sum of the numbers in the vertical column.

r	w

8 a and b are the areas of the indicated circles, and c, d, and e are the areas of the regions as shown above. *Note*: c, d, and e do not overlap.

$2d$	$a + b - c - e$

9 $\frac{a}{b} = \frac{2}{3}$ and $\frac{b}{c} = \frac{5}{8}$

$\frac{a}{c}$	$\frac{5}{6}$

10 $x + 2y + z = 5y$

$\frac{3}{2}z$	x

GO ON TO THE NEXT PAGE ⟩

Column A	Column B

11 An athlete pedals his bicycle 48 miles in $1\frac{1}{2}$ hours.

The average speed that the athlete pedaled at (in miles per hour)	36 miles per hour

12 Line segment EF has its end points on a circle. A radius of the circle intersects EF at only point G, and the center of the circle is point D.

Length of EG	Length of GF

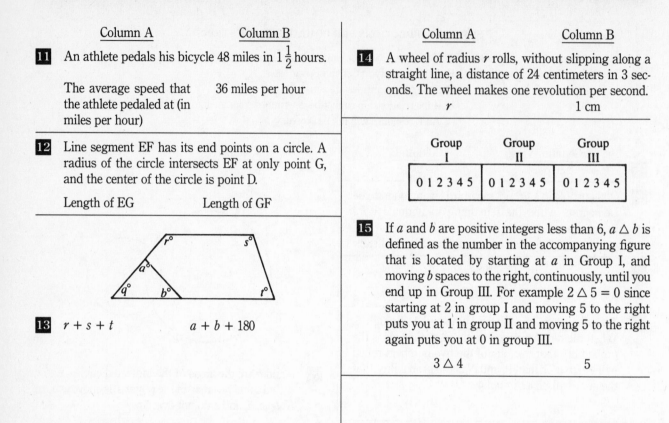

13 $r + s + t$	$a + b + 180$

Column A	Column B

14 A wheel of radius r rolls, without slipping along a straight line, a distance of 24 centimeters in 3 seconds. The wheel makes one revolution per second.

r	1 cm

Group I	Group II	Group III
0 1 2 3 4 5	0 1 2 3 4 5	0 1 2 3 4 5

15 If a and b are positive integers less than 6, $a \triangle b$ is defined as the number in the accompanying figure that is located by starting at a in Group I, and moving b spaces to the right, continuously, until you end up in Group III. For example $2 \triangle 5 = 0$ since starting at 2 in group I and moving 5 to the right puts you at 1 in group II and moving 5 to the right again puts you at 0 in group III.

$3 \triangle 4$	5

GO ON TO THE NEXT PAGE

Directions: Each of the 10 questions in this part requires you to solve the problem and enter your answer by marking the ovals in the special grid, as shown in the examples below.

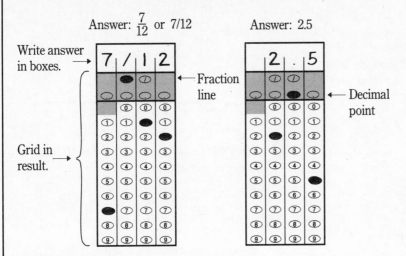

Answer: $\frac{7}{12}$ or 7/12

Write answer in boxes.

Fraction line

Grid in result.

Answer: 2.5

Decimal point

Answer: 201
Either position is correct.

Note: You may start your answers in any column, space permitting. Columns not needed should be left blank.

• Mark no more than one oval in any column.

• Because the answer sheet will be machine-scored, **you will receive credit only if the ovals are filled in correctly.**

• Although not required, it is suggested that you write your answer in the boxes at the top of the columns to help you fill in the ovals accurately.

• Some problems may have more than one correct answer. In such cases, grid only one answer.

• No question has a negative answer.

• **Mixed numbers** such as $2\frac{1}{2}$ must be gridded as 2.5 or 5/2. (If [2 1 / 2] is gridded, it will be interpreted as $\frac{21}{2}$, not $2\frac{1}{2}$.)

• Decimal Accuracy: If you obtain a decimal answer, **enter the most accurate value the grid will accommodate.** For example, if you obtain an answer such as 0.6666 ..., you should record the result as .666 or .667. **Less accurate results such as .66 or .67 are not acceptable.**

Acceptable ways to grid $\frac{2}{3}$ = .6666 ...

---

16 If $\frac{5}{8}$ of a number is 3 less than $\frac{3}{4}$ of the number, what is the number?

17 Let 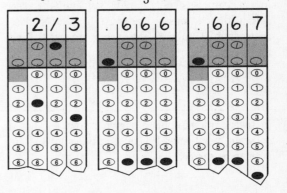 represent the greatest even integer less than n that divides n, for any positive integer n.

For example, [24] = 12. Find the value of [20]

GO ON TO THE NEXT PAGE

18 If $m = 94$ and $n = 6$, then find the value of $23m + 23n$.

19 A horizontal line has a length of 100 yards. A vertical line is drawn at one of its ends. If lines are drawn every ten yards thereafter, until the other end is reached, how many vertical lines are finally drawn?

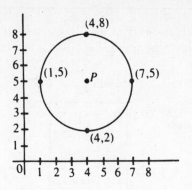

20 In the circle above with center O, diameter AC, and $AB = BC$, find the value of $x + y$.

21 In a certain class containing 60 students, the average (arithmetic mean) age is 20. In another class containing 20 students, the average age is 40. Find the average age of all 80 students.

22 In the addition problem shown below, if □ is a constant, what must □ equal in order for the answer to be correct?

$$
\begin{array}{r}
\square\,1 \\
6\,\square \\
\square\,9 \\
\hline
15\,\square
\end{array}
$$

23 Given the circle, above, with center P, what is the length of its radius?

24 A lawn covers 108.6 square feet. Russ mowed all of the lawn in three evenings. He mowed $\frac{2}{9}$ of the lawn during the first evening. He mowed twice that amount on the second evening. On the third and final evening he mowed the remaining lawn. How many square feet were mowed the third evening?

25 If 9 people are standing in a straight line, what is the *smallest* number of people who must move so that all 9 will be standing on the circumference of a circle?

IF YOU FINISH BEFORE TIME IS CALLED, YOU MAY CHECK YOUR WORK ON THIS SECTION ONLY. DO NOT TURN TO ANY OTHER SECTION IN THE TEST.

How Did You Do on This Test?

Step 1.   Go to the Answer Key on page 646.

Step 2.   For your "raw score," calculate it using the directions on page 87.

Step 3.   Get your "scaled score" for the test by referring to the Raw Score/Scaled Score Conversion Tables on page 90.

THERE'S ALWAYS ROOM FOR IMPROVEMENT!

Answer Key for Practice Test 2

Section 1—Verbal

1. E	8. D	15. A	22. B	29. E
2. D	9. C	16. D	23. C	30. E
3. D	10. C	17. C	24. D	
4. D	11. D	18. E	25. A	
5. C	12. C	19. C	26. D	
6. E	13. D	20. D	27. D	
7. B	14. B	21. D	28. C	

Section 2—Math

1. D	5. C	9. B	13. E	17. E	21. E	25. A
2. E	6. E	10. E	14. E	18. D	22. E	
3. D	7. E	11. E	15. C	19. C	23. D	
4. E	8. D	12. B	16. C	20. E	24. C	

Section 3—Verbal

1. D	7. D	13. B	19. D	25. C	31. C
2. C	8. D	14. B	20. E	26. B	32. E
3. E	9. B	15. A	21. A	27. C	33. C
4. A	10. C	16. C	22. D	28. B	34. C
5. E	11. D	17. B	23. D	29. C	35. A
6. A	12. C	18. B	24. E	30. B	36. E

Section 4—Math

1. D	6. D	11. D	16. 10	21. Any number, r, where $0 < r < 2$
2. B	7. D	12. C	17. 15	22. 135
3. D	8. C	13. B	18. 50	23. 100
4. C	9. A	14. A	19. 3	24. 3
5. C	10. C	15. B	20. 18	25. 4

Section 5—Verbal

1. C	4. C	7. D	10. E
2. A	5. B	8. B	11. A
3. E	6. C	9. A	12. B

Section 6—Math

1. D	6. D
2. B	7. B
3. A	8. E
4. B	9. C
5. B	10. D

Section 7—Math

1. D	6. D	11. B	16. 24	21. 25
2. B	7. B	12. D	17. 10	22. 4
3. D	8. C	13. C	18. 2300	23. 3
4. A	9. B	14. A	19. 11	24. 36.2
5. A	10. B	15. B	20. 125	25. 7

Explanatory Answers for Practice Test 2

Section 1: Verbal Ability

As you read these Explanatory Answers, refer to "Using Critical Thinking Skills in Verbal Questions" (beginning on page 236) whenever a specific Strategy is referred to in the answer. Of particular importance are the following Master Verbal Strategies:

Sentence Completion Master Strategy 1—page 245.
Sentence Completion Master Strategy 2—page 246.
Analogies Master Strategy 1—page 236.
Reading Comprehension Master Strategy 2—page 263.

1. Choice E is correct. See **Sentence Completion Strategy 4.** The first word, "Though," is an *opposition indicator.* The beginning of the sentence speaks positively about the computer programmer. We must find a word that gives us a negative idea about him. Choice (E), creativity, is the appropriate word. The other choices are incorrect because their words are not appropriate to give us that opposite feeling.

2. Choice D is correct. See **Sentence Completion Strategy 2.** Examine the first word of each choice. Choice (B) tantamount (meaning equivalent to) ... and Choice (C) collegiate ... do *not* make sense because we do not speak of a tantamount professor or a collegiate professor. Now consider the other choices. Choice (D) scholarly ... profound is the only choice which has a word pair that makes sentence sense.

3. Choice D is correct. See **Sentence Completion Strategy 1.** The beginning word "Because" is a *result indicator.* We may expect, then, a reason in the first part of the sentence for the Indian people to escape from British rule and join the Japanese. The word "abused" (Choice D) provides the reason. The words in the other choices do not make sense in the sentence.

4. Choice D is correct. See **Sentence Completion Strategy 1.** The author is obviously not satisfied with the royalty payment specified, as the sentence refers to the high research costs necessary for writing the book. Accordingly, Choices A, B, C, and E are incorrect.

5. Choice C is correct. See **Sentence Completion Strategy 2.** The first step is to examine the first words of each choice. We eliminate Choice (B), perplexed, and Choice (D), considerate, because the first part of the sentence makes no sense with these choices. Now we go to the remaining choices. Choice A and Choice E do *not* make sense in the sentence and are therefore incorrect. Choice C *does* make sense in the sentence.

6. Choice E is correct. See **Sentence Completion Strategy 2.** The first step is to examine the first words of each choice. We eliminate Choice A and Choice C because there are no such things as "sonorous clothes" or "raucous clothes." Now we go to the remaining choices. Choice (B) tawdry ... humble and Choice (D) tattered ... nightmarish do *not* make sense in the sentence. Choice (E) old-fashioned ... nostalgic *does* make sense in the sentence.

7. Choice B is correct. See **Sentence Completion Strategy 1.** Try each choice: Her devotion of music *brought back* or *reawakened* his former interest in it.

8. Choice D is correct. See **Sentence Completion Strategy 2.** Look at the first word of each choice.

The first words in Choices C and E do not quite sound right in the sentence. So eliminate Choices C and E. Now try both words in each of the remaining choices in the sentence. You can see that Choice D fits best: Sadat disregarded sharp or bitter criticism—that is, *acrimonious* criticism. He accepted Israel's invitation in accordance with conventional requirements—that is, *formally.*

9. Choice C is correct. See **Sentence Completion Strategy 2.** The first step is to examine the first words of each choice. We eliminate Choice (B), innuendoes, Choice (D), frequencies, and Choice (E), cancellations, because the foreman's leniency did not have innuendoes or frequencies or cancellations. Now we go to the remaining choices. Choice (A) compensations . . . unacceptable does *not* make sense in the sentence. Choice (C) drawbacks . . . shoddy makes the sentence meaningful.

10. Choice C is correct. An agenda is a guide or outline of things to be discussed at a conference. A map is a guide or representation to help a person find his way on a trip.
(Purpose relationship)

11. Choice D is correct. Erosion means wearing away. Erosion by something like water can cause a deep, narrow passage in the earth's surface. This passage or opening is called a ravine. Drilling causes an opening (in the form of a hole) if it is done in a substance like wood.
(Cause and Effect relationship)

12. Choice C is correct. A turtle is part of the reptile family. A trout is part of the fish family. This is a Part: Whole analogy type. You might have chosen A which is also a Part: Whole analogy. However, reptiles and fish are associated with the "animal kingdom" while oak and tree are associated with the "vegetable kingdom." Therefore, Choice A is incorrect. Also see **Analogy Strategy 4.**
(Part-Whole relationship)

13. Choice D is correct. A quiver is a case for holding or carrying an arrow. A sheath is a case for holding or carrying a sword. This is a PURPOSE analogy. Choice (B) purse : money is also a purpose analogy. However this choice is incorrect because this choice has a neutral or peaceful implication. The capitalized words and Choice D both have a battle or attack implication. See **Analogy Strategy 4.**
(Purpose relationship)

14. Choice B is correct. A person who is disinterested is *not* biased. A person who is affluent is *not* impecunious.
(Opposite relationship)

15. Choice A is correct. A hero gets approval or an award for his honorable action. A culprit gets blame or a punishment for his dishonorable action.
(Cause and Effect relationship)

Note: If you don't know the meaning of the word "accolade," you can use **Analogy Strategy 6**, the Context Method for Unfamiliar Words. You can see from the choices that the first word in each choice represents something that you *do* to the party in the second word in the choice. Thus you can logically assume that, in the analogy, ACCOLADE must be something you do or give to a HERO. I would assume that ACCOLADE must be something positive that you give to a hero, like a reward or prize. Now look for a choice that fits this sentence. Choice A fits: *Blame* is what you give to a *culprit.*

16. Choice D is correct. Beginning with lines 12–13 ("Malignant tumors on the other hand . . .") the passage is primarily concerned with the manner in which malignant tumors behave in the body. Choice A is incorrect because the definition of neoplasia is confined only to the first sentence: "Neoplasia . . . normal cells." Choice B is incorrect because the inhibition of tumor metastasis is discussed only in lines 22–29. Choice C does not occur and is not discussed in the passage. Therefore, Choice C is incorrect. Choice E is not discussed until lines 34–36. "After malignant cells . . . most of the cells die." Therefore, Choice E is not correct.

17. Choice C is correct. See lines 22–24: "Before metastasis can occur . . . surrounding normal tissue." Choice A is incorrect because the passage does not indicate that malignant cells shed their original membrane in order to acquire a new membrane. The passage simply states in lines 31–33: "The outer membrane . . . of normal cells." Choice B is incorrect because the passage nowhere states that malignant cells inhibit the lethal effects of the components of the blood." Choices D and E are incorrect because the passage does not indicate in any way what these two choices state.

18. Choice E is correct. See lines 36–38: "Those cells which survive . . . small blood vessel." Although the passage does refer to Choices A, B, C, and D, none of these choices represents a characteristic of a malignant cell that most greatly enhances its metastatic potential. Therefore, these four choices are all incorrect.

19. Choice C is correct. See lines 36–41: "Those cells which survive ... stickiness of the blood vessel wall." Choice A is incorrect because the passage does not indicate that benign tumors become malignant tumors. Choice B is incorrect. See lines 20–22: "This process ... have been ascertained." Choice D is incorrect. See lines 31–33: "The outer membrane ... of normal cells." Choice E is incorrect. See lines 49–50: "... it still must be stated ... a mystery."

20. Choice D is correct. First see lines 10–11: "Benign tumors ... tissue of origin." Now see lines 12–13: "Malignant tumors ... tissue of origin." Choice A is incorrect. See lines 10–11: "Benign tumors ... are usually slow growing." We infer, therefore, that malignant cells are fast growing. Choice B is incorrect. See lines 12–13: "Malignant tumors ... tissue of origin ..." Choice C is incorrect. See lines 31–33: "The outer membrane ... of normal cells." Choice E is incorrect. See lines 16–19: "The characteristic ... the original tumor."

21. Choice D is correct. From the context of the rest of the sentence, it can be seen that the word "explicable" means "explainable."

22. Choice B is correct. See line 1: "The old Middle West is gone. However, it still lives in song and story." Choices A, C, D, and E are incorrect because the passage makes no reference to what these choices state.

23. Choice C is correct. See lines 19–20: "I think the Middle West's strength is in its customary cautious approach ..." Choice D (line 39) is incorrect because it is not cited as the strength of the Middle West. Choices A, B, and E may be true, but they are not indicated in the passage.

24. Choice D is correct. See lines 46–49: "In the Middle West it has ... taken the form of people remaining in the smaller cities and giving them new life and intelligence. This has strengthened smaller communities ..." Choices A, B, C, and E are incorrect because the passage does not indicate these choices as current trends.

25. Choice A is correct. See lines 5–10: "The old Middle West developed ... out of destructive blizzards ... and ... dust storms." Therefore, Item I is true. Items II and III cannot be accepted because the passage says nothing about the Gold Rush of 1849 and the Civil War as factors in the formation of the Middle West. Accordingly, Choices B, C, D, and E are incorrect.

26. Choice D is correct. From the context of the sentence—"... with the growing understanding of their problems and responsibilities"—the best meaning of "pragmatic" would be "practical."

27. Choice D is correct. See the next-to-last paragraph: "... so much difficulty in resolving our problems of a complex society is that we have tended to lose ... a strong feeling for the special qualities of our local area."

28. Choice C is correct. See paragraph 6: "It made inflation the prime issue in 1936 ..." Also see paragraph 4: "especially on political major questions" and the flavor and content of the rest of the passage.

29. Choice E is correct. Given the context of the sentence with the ideas expressed throughout the passage, "diversification" refers to race or religion.

30. Choice E is correct. See the second-from-last paragraph: "... freedom of communications ... and the ease of changing occupations ... contribute to breaking down ethnic and religious group prejudices."

Explanatory Answers for Practice Test 2 (continued)

Section 2: Math Ability

As you read these solutions, do two things if you answered the Math question incorrectly:

1. When a specific Strategy is referred to in the solution, study that strategy, which you will find in "Using Critical Thinking Skills in Math Questions" (beginning on page 174).

2. When the solution directs you to the "Math Refresher" (beginning on page 291)—for example, Math Refresher #305—study the 305 Math principle to get a clear idea of the Math operation that was necessary for you to know in order to answer the question correctly.

1. Choice D is correct.

Given that $500w = 3 \times 700$ $\boxed{1}$

(Use Strategy 13: Find an unknown by dividing.)

Divide $\boxed{1}$ by 500, giving

$$\frac{\cancel{500}w}{\cancel{500}} = \frac{3 \times 700}{500}$$

(Use Strategy 19: Factor and reduce first. Then multiply.)

$$w = \frac{3 \times 7 \times \cancel{100}}{5 \times \cancel{100}}$$
$$w = \frac{21}{5}$$

(Math Refresher #406)

2. Choice E is correct.

$$\text{Given: } \frac{3 + y}{y} = 7 \qquad \boxed{1}$$

(Use Strategy 13: Find an unknown by multiplying.)

Multiply $\boxed{1}$ by y, to get

$$y\left(\frac{3 + y}{\cancel{y}}\right) = (7)y$$

$$3 + y = 7y$$
$$3 = 6y$$
$$\frac{3}{6} = y$$
$$\frac{1}{2} = y$$

(Math Refresher #406)

3. Choice D is correct. **(Use Strategy 2: Translate from words to algebra.)**

x is a multiple of 9, gives

$x \, \varepsilon \, \{9, 18, 27, 36, 45, 54, \ldots \ldots\}$ $\boxed{1}$

x is a multiple of 12, gives

$x \, \varepsilon \, \{12, 24, 36, 48, 60, 72, \ldots \ldots\}$ $\boxed{2}$

The smallest value that appears in both sets $\boxed{1}$ and $\boxed{2}$ is 36.

(Logical Reasoning)

4. Choice E is correct.

Method 1:

$$\text{Given: } (r-s)(t-s)$$
$$+ \quad (s-r)(s-t) \qquad \boxed{1}$$

(Use Strategy 17: Use the given information effectively.)

Recognizing that $(s-r) = -1(r-s)$ $\boxed{2}$
$(s-t) = -1(t-s)$ $\boxed{3}$

Substituting $\boxed{2}$ and $\boxed{3}$ into $\boxed{1}$, we get
$(r-s)(t-s) + [-1(r-s)][-1(t-s)] =$
$(r-s)(t-s) + (r-s)(t-s) =$
$2(r-s)(t-s)$

Method 2:

Given: $(r-s)(t-s) + (s-r)(s-t)$ $\boxed{1}$

Multiply both pairs of quantities from $\boxed{1}$, giving

$$rt - rs - st + s^2 + s^2 - st - rs + rt =$$
$$2rt - 2rs - 2st + 2s^2 =$$
$$2(rt - rs - st + s^2) =$$
$$2[r(t-s) - s(t-s)] =$$
$$2(r-s)(t-s)$$

(Math Refresher #409)

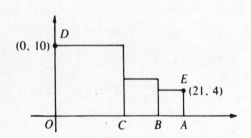

5. Choice C is correct.

We want to find the area of the middle square, which is $(CB)^2$. **(Use Strategy 3: The whole equals the sum of its parts.)**

$$OA = OC + CB + BA \qquad \boxed{1}$$

From the diagram, we get

$$OA = 21 \qquad \boxed{2}$$
$$AE = 4 \qquad \boxed{3}$$
$$OD = 10 \qquad \boxed{4}$$

Since each figure is a square, we get

$$BA = AE \qquad \boxed{5}$$
$$OC = OD \qquad \boxed{6}$$

Substituting $\boxed{5}$ into $\boxed{3}$, we get

$$AE = BA = 4 \qquad \boxed{7}$$

Substituting $\boxed{6}$ into $\boxed{4}$, we get

$$OD = OC = 10 \qquad \boxed{8}$$

Substituting $\boxed{2}$, $\boxed{7}$ and $\boxed{8}$ into $\boxed{1}$, we get

$$21 = 10 + CB + 4$$
$$21 = 14 + CB$$
$$7 = CB \qquad \boxed{9}$$

Area of square II = $(CB)^2$
Area of square II = 7^2 (From $\boxed{9}$)
Area of square II = 49

(Math Refresher #410 and #303)

6. Choice E is correct.

Given:
$$1 \text{ cup } = 100 \text{ grams} \qquad \boxed{1}$$
$$1 \text{ cake } = 75 \text{ grams} \qquad \boxed{2}$$
$$1 \text{ pie } = 225 \text{ grams} \qquad \boxed{3}$$

Using $\boxed{1}$, we get

$$4 \text{ cups } = 4 \ (100 \text{ grams})$$
$$4 \text{ cups } = 400 \text{ grams} \qquad \boxed{4}$$

(Using Strategy 8: When all choices must be tested, start with E and work backward.)

2 cakes and 1 pie is Choice E. $\boxed{5}$
Substituting $\boxed{2}$ and $\boxed{3}$ in $\boxed{5}$, we get

$$2(75 \text{ grams}) + 225 \text{ grams} =$$
$$150 \text{ grams} + 225 \text{ grams} =$$
$$375 \text{ grams} \qquad \boxed{6}$$

Since $\boxed{6}$ is less than $\boxed{4}$, there *is enough* in 4 cups. So Choice E is correct.

(Math Refresher #121 and #431)

7. Choice E is correct.
I: Slope is defined as $\dfrac{y_2 - y_1}{x_2 - x_1}$ where (x_1, y_1) and (x_2, y_2) are points on the line. Thus
Here $0 = x_1, a = y_1, a = x_2,$ and $0 = y_2$
Thus $\dfrac{y_2 - y_1}{x_2 - x_1} = \dfrac{o - a}{a - o} = -1$: I is therefore true.
II: The triangle created above is an isosceles right triangle with sides $a, a, a\sqrt{2}$. Thus II is true.
III: In an isosceles right triangle, the interior angles of the triangle are 90–45–45 degrees. Thus III is true.

(Math Refresher #416, #411, #509)

8. Choice D is correct. **(Use Strategy 2: Translate from words to algebra.)**

Let n = the number.
Then $\dfrac{n+3}{4} = 6$

Multiplying both sides by 4, we have

$$4\left(\frac{n+3}{4}\right) = (6)4$$

$$n + 3 = 24$$
$$n = 21$$

(Math Refresher #200)

9. Choice B is correct. **(Use Strategy 2: Translate from words to algebra.)** We are told:

$$A + 8 + A + 1 + A + 2$$
$$= A + A + 1 + A + 2 + A + 3 \qquad \boxed{1}$$

(Use Strategy 1: Cancel expressions that appear on both sides of an equation.)

Each side contains an A, $A + 1$, and $A + 2$. Canceling each of these from each side, we get
$\cancel{A} + 8 + \cancel{A+1} + \cancel{A+2} = \cancel{A} + \cancel{A+1} + \cancel{A+2} + A + 3$.

Thus, $8 = A + 3$
$$5 = A$$

(Math Refresher #406)

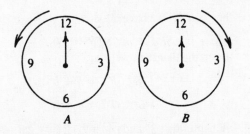

A   B

10. Choice E is correct. **(Use Strategy 11: New definitions lead to easy questions.)**

By the definition of a move, every 4 moves brings each hand back to 12.

Thus, after 4, 8, 12, and 16 moves, respectively, each hand is at 12.

Hand A, moving counterclockwise, moves to *9* on its 17th move.

Hand B, moving clockwise, moves to *3* on its 17th move.

(Logical Reasoning)

11. Choice E is correct. **(Use Strategy 17: Use the given information effectively.)**

$$\text{Given: } w = 7r + 6r + 5r + 4r + 3r$$
$$\text{Then, } w = 25r \qquad \boxed{1}$$

We are told we must add something to w so that the resulting sum will be divisible by 7 for every positive integer r.

Check the choices. **(Use Strategy 8: Start with Choice E.)** Add $3r$ to $\boxed{1}$

$$25r + 3r = 28r = 7(4r)$$

will always be divisible by 7. Thus, Choice E is correct.

(Math Refresher #431)

12. Choice B is correct. **(Use Strategy 2: Translate from words to algebra)**

Perimeter of a square = 4 × side. $\boxed{1}$
We are given that Perimeter = 20 meters $\boxed{2}$

Substituting $\boxed{2}$ into $\boxed{1}$, we get

20 meters = 4 × side.
5 meters = side $\boxed{3}$
Area of a square = (side)^2 $\boxed{4}$

Substituting $\boxed{3}$ into $\boxed{4}$, we get

Area of square = (5 meter)^2
Area of square = 25 square meters

(Math Refresher #303)

13. Choice E is correct. **(Use Strategy 17: Use the given information effectively.)**

Given: $80 + a = -32 + b$

Subtract a from both sides, getting

$$\begin{array}{r} 80 + a = -32 + b \\ \underline{-a \qquad -a} \\ 80 \quad = -32 + b - a \end{array}$$

Add 32 to both sides, giving

$$\begin{array}{r} 80 = -32 + b - a \\ \underline{+32 \quad +32} \\ 112 = \qquad b - a \end{array}$$

(Math Refresher #406)

14. Choice E is correct. **(Use Strategy 8: When all choices must be tested, start with E and work backward.)**

Choice E is $x^2 + x + 2$

(Use Strategy 7: Use specific number examples.)

Let $x = 3$ (an odd positive integer)

Then $x^2 + x + 2 =$
$3^2 + 3 + 2 =$
$9 + 3 + 2 =$
$14 \quad =$ (an even result)

Now let $x = 2$ (an even positive integer)

Then $x^2 + x + 2 =$
$$2^2 + 2 + 2 =$$
$$4 + 2 + 2 =$$
$$8 \quad = \text{(an even result)}$$

Whether x is odd or even, Choice E is even.

(Math Refresher #431)

15. Choice C is correct. **(Use Strategy 17: Use the given information effectively.)**

Given: $\dfrac{3}{4} < x < \dfrac{4}{5}$

Change both fractions to fractions with the same denominator. Thus,

$$\dfrac{3}{4} < x < \dfrac{4}{5}$$

becomes
$$\dfrac{15}{20} < x < \dfrac{16}{20}$$

(Use Strategy 15: Certain choices may be easily eliminated.)

Choice B $= \dfrac{13}{20}$ can be instantly eliminated.

Choice D $= \dfrac{16}{20}$ can be instantly eliminated.

Change both fractions to 40^{ths} to compare Choice C. Thus,

$$\dfrac{30}{40} < x < \dfrac{32}{40}$$

Choice C $= \dfrac{31}{40}$ is a possible value of x.

(Math Refresher #108 and #419)

16. Choice C is correct. **(Use Strategy 2: Translate from words to algebra.)**

The number of hours from 7:00 A.M. to 5:00 P.M. is 10.

The number of hours from 1:00 P.M. to 7:00 P.M. is 6.

He worked 10 hours for 3 days and 6 hours for 3 days. Thus,

Total Hours = 3(10) + 3(6)
$$= 30 + 18$$
Total hours = 48 $\boxed{1}$
Total Earnings = Hours worked ×
Hourly rate $\boxed{2}$
Given: He earns \$10 per hour $\boxed{3}$

Substituting $\boxed{1}$ and $\boxed{3}$ into $\boxed{2}$, we get

Total Earnings = 48 × \$10
Total Earnings = \$480

(Math Refresher #200 and #406)

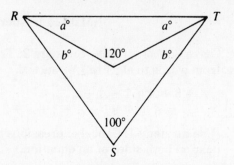

17. Choice E is correct. **(Use Strategy 3: The whole equals the sum of its parts.)**

The sum of the angles in a $\triangle = 180$. For the small triangle we have

$$120 + a + a = 180$$
$$120 + 2a = 180$$
$$2a = 60$$
$$a = 30 \qquad \boxed{1}$$

For $\triangle RST$, we have

$$100 + m\angle SRT + m\angle STR = 180 \qquad \boxed{2}$$
From the diagram, we get

$$m\angle SRT = a + b \qquad \boxed{3}$$
$$m\angle STR = a + b \qquad \boxed{4}$$

Substituting $\boxed{3}$ and $\boxed{4}$ into $\boxed{2}$, we get

$$100 + a + b + a + b = 180$$
$$100 + 2a + 2b = 180$$
$$2a + 2b = 80 \qquad \boxed{5}$$

Substituting $\boxed{1}$ into $\boxed{5}$, we get

$$2(30) + 2b = 80$$
$$60 + 2b = 80$$
$$2b = 20$$
$$b = 10$$

(Math Refreshers #505 and #406)

Questions 18–19

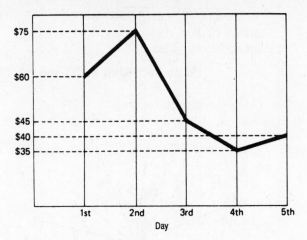

Day

18. Choice D is correct. The point at which the curve of the graph intersects the line representing the various days is the point that indicates the wage for that day. By dropping a perpendicular from that point to the wage line, you can determine the wage for that day. Using this method, one can determine that John earned $60, $75, $45, $35, and $40 during the 5 days. The average of these numbers is the average daily wage.

$$
\begin{array}{r}
\$\ 60 \\
\$\ 75 \\
\$\ 45 \\
\$\ 35 \\
\$\ 40 \\
\hline
\$255
\end{array}
\qquad
\begin{array}{r}
\$\ 51 \\
5\overline{)\$255}
\end{array}
$$

(Math Refresher #601, #706)

19. Choice C is correct. In ascending order, the wages for the six days are:

$$
\begin{array}{c}
35 \\
35 \\
40 \\
45 \\
60 \\
75
\end{array}
$$

The median is the middle number. But wait! There is no middle number. So we average the two middle numbers, 40 and 45, to get 42.5.

The mode is the number appearing most frequently, that is, 35. So $42.5 - 35 = 7.5$.

(Math Refresher #601a, #601b)

20. Choice E is correct. **(Use Strategy 11: Use new definitions carefully.) (Use Strategy 8: When all choices must be tested, start with E and work backward.)**

Given: $\textcircled{a}\textcircled{b} = \dfrac{a+1}{b-1}$

Choice E: $\textcircled{5}\textcircled{3} = \dfrac{5+1}{3-1} = \dfrac{6}{2} = 3$

Choice E is the only choice with $a > b$.

Therefore, it must be the largest.
The remaining choices are shown below.

Choice D: $\textcircled{4}\textcircled{5} = \dfrac{4+1}{5-1} = \dfrac{5}{4} = 1\dfrac{1}{4}$

Choice C: $\textcircled{3}\textcircled{5} = \dfrac{3+1}{5-1} = \dfrac{4}{4} = 1$

Choice B: $\textcircled{3}\textcircled{3} = \dfrac{3+1}{3-1} = \dfrac{4}{2} = 2$

Choice A: $\textcircled{2}\textcircled{3} = \dfrac{2+1}{3-1} = \dfrac{3}{2} = 1\dfrac{1}{2}$

(Math Refresher #431)

21. Choice E is correct. **(Use Strategy 17: Use the given information effectively.)**

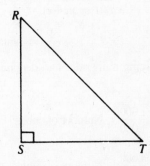

We know that Area of $\Delta = \dfrac{1}{2} \times$ base $\times$ height $\boxed{1}$

We are given that $RS = ST =$ an integer $\boxed{2}$
Substituting $\boxed{2}$ into $\boxed{1}$, we get

Area $\Delta RST = \dfrac{1}{2} \times$ (An integer) $=$ (same integer)

Area $\Delta RST = \dfrac{1}{2} \times$ (An integer)² $\boxed{3}$

Multiplying $\boxed{3}$ by 2, we have

2(Area ΔRST) $=$ (An integer)² $\boxed{4}$

(Use Strategy 8: When all choices must be tested, start with E and work backward.)

Substituting Choice E, 20, into $\boxed{4}$, we get

2(20) $=$ (An integer)²
40 $=$ (An integer)² $\boxed{5}$
$\boxed{5}$ is *not* possible, since
40 isn't the square of an integer.

(Math Refresher #366, #406, and #431)

22. Choice E is correct. (**Use Strategy 17: Use the given information effectively.**)

Volume of rectangler solid = $l \times w \times h$ $\boxed{1}$

Substituting the given dimensions into $\boxed{1}$, we get

Volume of solid = 2 feet × 2 feet × 1 foot

Volume of solid = 4 cubic feet $\boxed{2}$

Volume of cube = (edge)³ $\boxed{3}$

Substituting edge = .1 foot into $\boxed{3}$, we get

Volume of cube = (.1 foot)³

Volume of cube = .001 cubic feet $\boxed{4}$

(**Use Strategy 3: The whole equals the sum of its parts.**) Since the volume of the rectangular solid must equal the sum of the small cubes, we need to know

$$\frac{\text{Volume of rectangular solid}}{\text{Volume of cube}} = \text{Number of cubes} \boxed{5}$$

Substituting $\boxed{2}$ and $\boxed{4}$ into $\boxed{5}$, we get

$$\frac{\text{Volume of rectangular solid}}{\text{Volume of cube}} = \text{Number of cubes}$$

$$\frac{4 \text{ cubic feet}}{.001 \text{ cubic feet}} = \text{Number of cubes}$$

$$\frac{4}{.001} = \text{Number of cubes}$$

Multiplying numerator and denominator by 1,000, we get

$$\frac{4}{.001} \times \frac{1,000}{1,000} = \text{Number of cubes}$$

$$\frac{4,000}{1} = \text{Number of cubes}$$

$$4,000 = \text{Number of cubes}$$

(**Math Refresher #312 and #313**)

23. Choice D is correct. (**Use Strategy 2: Translate from words to algebra.**) (**Use Strategy 17: Use the given information effectively.**)

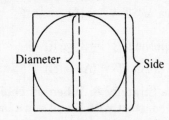

Diameter   Side

Given the perimeter of the square = 40

Thus, 4(side) = 40

side = 10 $\boxed{1}$

A side of the square = length of diameter of circle.

Thus, diameter = 10 from $\boxed{1}$

Since diameter = 2 (radius)

10 = 2 (radius)

5 = radius $\boxed{2}$

Area of a circle = πr^2 $\boxed{3}$

Substituting $\boxed{2}$ into $\boxed{3}$, we have

Area of circle = πr^2

Area of circle = 25π

(**Math Refresher #303 and #310**)

24. Choice C is correct.

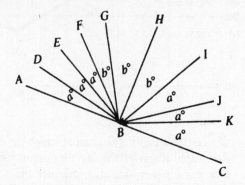

(**Use Strategy 3: The whole equals the sum of its parts.**) The whole straight angle ABC is equal to the sum of the individual angles.

Thus, $m \angle ABC = a + a + a + b + b +$

$b + a + a + a$ $\boxed{1}$

$m \angle ABC = 6a + 3b$

We know $m \angle ABC = 180°$ $\boxed{2}$

Substituting $\boxed{2}$ into $\boxed{1}$, we get

$180° = 6a + 3b$ $\boxed{3}$

(**Use Strategy 13: Find an unknown expression by dividing.**) Dividing both sides of $\boxed{3}$ by 3, we have

$60° = 2a + b$ $\boxed{4}$

Choice C, $m \angle DBG = 2a + b$, so its measure can be determined. It is 60° (from $\boxed{4}$).

(**Math Refresher #501 and #406**)

25. Choice A is correct. (**Use Strategy 17: Use the given information effectively.**)

Given: $ax = r$ $\boxed{1}$

$by = r - 1$ $\boxed{2}$

The quick method is to substitute $\boxed{1}$ into $\boxed{2}$, giving

$by = ax - 1$

$by + 1 = ax$

$$\frac{by + 1}{a} = x$$

(**Math Refresher #431 and #406**)

Explanatory Answers for Practice Test 2 (continued)

Section 3: Verbal Ability

As you read these Explanatory Answers, refer to "Using Critical Thinking Skills in Verbal Questions" (beginning on page 236) whenever a specific Strategy is referred to in the answer. Of particular importance are the following Master Verbal Strategies:

Sentence Completion Master Strategy 1—page 245.
Sentence Completion Master Strategy 2—page 246.
Analogies Master Strategy 1—page 236.
Reading Comprehension Master Strategy 2—page 263.

1. Choice D is correct. See **Sentence Completion Strategy 4.** The word "Although" at the beginning of the sentence is an opposition indicator. As a contrast to the rundown condition of the school, the word "renovated" is the acceptable choice.

2. Choice C is correct. The word "immediate" is the only one that makes sense in the blank. See **Sentence Completion Strategy 1.**

3. Choice E is correct. See **Sentence Completion Strategy 2.** The first words of Choice B (flexibility) and Choice D (dizziness) do not make sense in the first part of the sentence. Therefore, we eliminate these two choices. When we try the two words in each of the remaining choices, only Choice E (disappointment . . . fervent) makes good sense in the sentence as a whole.

4. Choice A is correct. See **Sentence Completion Strategy 4.** The opposition indicator "even though" should lead us to the correct Choice A with the fill-in word "convincing."

5. Choice E is correct. The fact that the investor was eager to make an investment change points to his being "dubious" about his current investment—the stocks he had recently purchased. See **Sentence Completion Strategy 1.**

6. Choice A is correct. See **Sentence Completion Strategy 4.** The word "when" is a support indicator in this sentence. As we try each choice, we find that "frightening" is the only word that fits in this

sentence. The fact that "the earth shifts with a sickening sway" reinforces the initial idea that "nature's brute strength is never more frightening."

7. Choice D is correct. See **Sentence Completion Strategy 2.** Consider the first word of each choice. We can thus eliminate Choice A disdain because one doesn't "disdain" the incidence of crime, and we can eliminate Choice B revoke because one doesn't "revoke" the incidence of crime. Now consider the other three choices. Choice D with its two fill-in words "reduce" and "diverting" is the only choice that makes sense in the sentence.

8. Choice D is correct. See **Sentence Completion Strategy 2.** Consider the first word of each choice. We can first eliminate Choice A gradual because "gradual" musical accompaniment does not make sense, and we can eliminate Choice E chronic because the "chronic" musical accompaniment does not make sense. Now consider the other three choices. Choice D with its two fill-in words "superb" and "aura" is the only choice that makes sense in the sentence.

9. Choice B is correct. See **Sentence Completion Strategy 4.** The first part of the sentence about her fine reputation as a celebrated actress is obviously in opposition to her appearance in a TV soap opera. Accordingly, the word "blemish" is the only possible choice.

10. Choice C is correct. See **Sentence Completion Strategy 2.** First, let us examine the first words in

each choice. We eliminate Choice B because one's manner does not "accept" his intention. We eliminate Choice D because one's manner does not "disregard" his intention. We eliminate Choice E because one's manner does not "animate" his intention. This leaves us with Choice A (revealed . . . eager), which does *not* make good sense, and Choice C (belied . . . drastic), which *does* make good sense.

11. Choice D is correct. The peel is the outer covering of an orange. The rind is the outer covering of a melon. Also see **Analogy Strategy 5.** The word "peel" may be a noun or a verb. It is a noun in this analogy.

(Part-Whole relationship)

12. Choice C is correct. A termite is an insect that feeds on wood in a destructive way. A weevil is a beetle (also an insect) that feeds on cotton in a destructive way. Note that, in Choice A, mold is a fungus growth that is destructive to bread. However, mold is not an insect. So Choice A is incorrect. See **Analogy Strategy 4**

(Action to Object relationship)

13. Choice B is correct. A key provides the answers to a test. A solution provides the answers to a puzzle. Note that "key" has a special meaning here as something that provides answers. See **Analogy Strategy 5.**

(Purpose relationship)

14. Choice B is correct. To gorge means to eat greedily; to nibble means to eat slightly—that is, in small pieces. To quaff is to drink heartily; to sip is to drink bit by bit. We have here a degree relationship. Choice A laugh : guffaw would be correct if the two words were reversed. See **Analogy Strategy 3.**

(Degree relationship)

15. Choice A is correct. A tidal wave may cause a flood. An earthquake may cause tremors.

(Cause and Effect relationship)

16. Choice C is correct. The cry of a sheep is a bleat. The cry of a goose is a honk.

(Association relationship)

17. Choice B is correct. A lobster has a shell. A kangaroo has a pouch. Choice D insect : wing is wrong because not all insects have wings. See **Analogy Strategy 4.** Choice E wool : sheep would be correct if the words were reversed. See **Analogy Strategy 3.**

(Whole-Part relationship)

18. Choice B is correct. Something that is counterfeit does not have authenticity. Someone who is erratic does not have reliability.

(Association relationship)

19. Choice D is correct. A person who has guile is *not* ingenuous. A person who has courage is *not* timorous.

(Opposite relationship)

20. Choice E is correct. A zebra's body is striated (marked with stripes). A leopard's body is mottled (spotted). We have here a characteristic relationship. Choices A, B, C, and D also have characteristic relationships. However, these four choices do not deal with a color pattern on the body. Accordingly, these four choices are incorrect. See **Analogy Strategy 4.**

(Characteristic relationship)

Note: If you don't know the meaning of the word "striated" you can use **Analogy Strategy 6,** The Context Method for Unfamiliar Words. You can see that the first word in every answer choice refers to an animal. Striated does not give you the feeling that it is a personality trait but rather a marking, so that you would say a *zebra* is *striated* (marked) as a *leopard* is *mottled*.

21. Choice A is correct. A tree defoliates (loses leaves, which are replaced by other leaves). A snake molts (loses its skin, which is replaced by other skin).

(Action to Object relationship)

22. Choice D is correct. Many people emulate (imitate) a model. Many people worship an icon (a picture or an image). The word "model" in this analogy means a standard or an example for imitation. The word has other meanings—for example, a person who poses for an artist or photographer—but not in this analogy. See **Analogy Strategy 5.**

(Action to Object relationship)

23. Choice D is correct. Protean means changeable, and immutable means unchangeable. Something that is acquired is gotten after one is born, and something that is innate is gotten (by way of genes) before one is born.

(Opposite and Association relationship)

24. Choice E is correct. The author is stressing the point that the true artist—the person with rare creative ability and keen perception, or high intelligence—fails to communicate well with those about him— "differs from the rest of us" (line 4). He is likely to be

considered a "nut" by many whom he comes in contact with. "Great wits" in the Choice E quotation refers to the true artist. The quotation states, in effect, that there is a thin line between the true artist and the "nut." Choices A, B, C, and D are incorrect because they have little, if anything, to do with the main idea of the passage.

[Note: Choices C and E were composed by John Dryden (1631–1700), and Choices A, B, and D by Alexander Pope (1688–1744).]

25. Choice C is correct. See lines 8–10. The artist creates because he is "less fitted to prosper and enjoy himself under the conditions of life which he and we must face alike." Choices A and E are incorrect. Although they may be true, they are never mentioned in the passage. Choice B is incorrect because, although the artist may be a threat to the social order, he is by no means an unnecessary one. The author, throughout the passage, is siding with the artist against the social order. Choice D is incorrect. See lines 10–11: "Therefore he takes ... attempt to escape from life." A person who is attempting to escape from life hardly knows how to enjoy life.

26. Choice B is correct. The author ridicules Samuel Johnson, saying that that he is as much a true artist as a kazoo player is a musician. He then says that if Johnson were alive today, he would be a Senator or a university president. The author thus implies that these positions do not merit high respect. Choice A is the opposite of Choice B. Therefore, Choice A is incorrect. Choice C is incorrect because, although the statement may be true, the author neither states nor implies that senators and university presidents are generally appreciative of the great literary classics. Choice D is incorrect. The fact that the author lumps Johnson, senators, and university presidents together as non-artistic people indicates that senators and university presidents do not have native writing ability. Choice E is incorrect for this reason: The author believes that Johnson lacked the qualities of an artist. Johnson, if alive today, would be a Senator or a university president. We may conclude, then, that Senators and university presidents lack the qualities of an artist.

27. Choice C is correct. Although a love of beauty is a quality we usually associate with artists, that idea about artists is never mentioned in the passage. All of the other characteristics are expressly mentioned in the first two paragraphs of the passage.

28. Choice B is correct. The author's sincere sympathy is shown toward artists in lines 17–24: "From Dante to Tolstoy ... actually fugitives from range and reprisal." There is no evidence in the passage to indicate that the author's attitude toward artists is Choice A, C, D, or E. Therefore, these choices are incorrect.

29. Choice C is correct. See the sentence in the second paragraph of Passage B: "He and only he knows the world."

30. Choice B is correct. See the first paragraph in Passage B.

31. Choice C is correct. From the context in Passage B, we see that "world's eye" and "world's heart" refer to culture and wisdom, respectively.

32. Choice E is correct. See the first sentence in Passage B: "... the self-accusation, the faint heart, the frequent uncertainty and loss of time, which are the nettles and tangling vines...." Here "nettles and tangling vines" refers to "self-accusation" and "uncertainty."

33. Choice C is correct. See Passage B: The most appropriate groups are the hardships of the scholar, the scholar's functions, and the scholar's justifications for disregarding the world's business, as can be seen from the structure and content of the passage.

34. Choice C is correct. Given the context of the rest of the sentence, the author uses the phrase "seems to stand" as "giving the false impression of being."

35. Choice A is correct. See lines 91–98 and 54–56 in Passage B and lines 13–17 and 25–34 in Passage A.

36. Choice E is correct. The statements in I can be seen to be associated with the artist in Passage B from lines 85–86 and 57–58 respectively. The statements in II can be seen to be associated with the artist in Passage A from lines 27–33 and 5, respectively. The statements in III can be seen to be associated with the artist in Passage B from lines 53–54 and 45–52 respectively.

Explanatory Answers for Practice Test 2 (continued)

Section 4: Math Ability

As you read these solutions, do two things if you answered the Math question incorrectly:

1. When a specific Strategy is referred to in the solution, study that strategy, which you will find in "Using Critical Thinking Skills in Math Questions" (beginning on page 174).

2. When the solution directs you to the "Math Refresher" (beginning on page 291)—for example, Math Refresher #305—study the 305 Math principle to get a clear idea of the Math operation that was necessary for you to know in order to answer the question correctly.

1. Choice D is correct. **(Use Strategy C: Use numerical examples when it appears that a comparison cannot be determined.)**

Let $y = 1$, then
$$y^3 = 1^3 = 1 \qquad 3y = 3^1 = 3$$
$$1 < 3$$
Let $y = 3$, then
$$y^3 = 3^3 = 27 \qquad 3y = 3^3 = 27$$
$$27 = 27$$

There are two different possibilities, so you cannot determine which is the correct answer.

(Math Refresher #431)

2. Choice B is correct.

Given: $\dfrac{3}{a} = 2$ $\boxed{1}$

$\dfrac{5}{b} = 2$ $\boxed{2}$

(Use Strategy 13: Find an unknown by multiplication.)

Multiplying $\boxed{1}$ by a, we get
$$a\left(\frac{3}{a}\right) = a(2)$$
$$3 = 2a$$
$$\frac{3}{2} = a \qquad \boxed{3}$$

Multiplying $\boxed{2}$ by b, we get
$$b\left(\frac{5}{b}\right) = b(2)$$
$$5 = 2b$$
$$\frac{5}{2} = b \qquad \boxed{4}$$

Comparing $\boxed{3}$ and $\boxed{4}$ we get $b > a$

(Math Refresher #406)

3. Choice D is correct. **(Use Strategy 6: Know how to work with inequalities.)**

Given: $3y - 2 < 0$ $\boxed{1}$
Add 2 to both sides of $\boxed{1}$. We get $3y < 2$ $\boxed{2}$

Now look at the two columns.
(Use Strategy C: Use number examples when it appears that a comparison cannot be determined.)

$3y$ could $= 1$ $\boxed{3}$
This satisfies $\boxed{2}$
$3y$ could $= -3$ $\boxed{4}$
This satisfies $\boxed{2}$
From $\boxed{3}$, $1 > -2$ $\boxed{5}$
From $\boxed{4}$, $-3 < -2$ $\boxed{6}$

Since there are 2 possible relations, we cannot determine a definite relationship for the columns.

(Math Refresher #419 and #431)

4. Choice C is correct.

Column A	Column B
Translates to the units' digit of $1 \cdot 2 \cdot 3 \cdot 4 \cdot 5 \cdot 6 \cdot 7$	The units' digit of $8 \cdot 9 \cdot 10 \cdot 11 \cdot 12 \cdot 13 \cdot 14$

(Use Strategy 17: Use the given information effectively.)

Seeing in Column A that $4 \cdot 5 = 20$, we know that any product of integers with 20 will have a units' digit of 0. $\boxed{1}$

Seeing in Column B that 10 is one of the factors, we know that any product of integers with 10 will have a units' digit of 0. $\boxed{2}$

Since $\boxed{1}$ and $\boxed{2}$, we know that Choice C is correct.

(Use Strategy 12: Do not make tedious calculations. No tedious calculations were necessary!)

(Math Refresher #200)

5. Choice C is correct.

Given: x is any non-negative integer, gives

$$x \; \varepsilon \; \{0,1,2,3,4,5,6, \ldots \ldots\}$$

Use Strategy C: Use number examples when it appears that a comparison cannot be determined.)

Column A	Column B
The minimum value of $4x^2 + 1$	The minimum value of $5x^2 + 1$

Let $x = 0$, we have

$4(0)^2 + 1$	$5(0)^2 + 1$
$0 + 1$	$0 + 1$
$1 \qquad = $	1

(Math Refresher #431)

6. Choice D is correct.

Given: $\dfrac{4}{a} = \dfrac{b}{4}$

Multiplying means and extremes (cross-multiplying), we get

$ab = 16$ $\boxed{1}$

(Use Strategy C: Use numerical examples when it appears that a comparison cannot be determined.)

If $a = 16$ and $b = 1$, then $ab = 16$ as in $\boxed{1}$

If $b = 16$ and $a = 1$, then $ab = 16$ as in $\boxed{1}$

$a > b$ or $b > a$

Since there are two possible answers, we cannot determine which is the correct answer.

(Math Refresher #120 and #431)

7. Choice D is correct.

	Column A	Column B
Given:	$xy + 7$	$x(y + 7)$
	Distribute in Column B, to get	
	$xy + 7$	$xy + 7x$

(Use Strategy A: Cancel equal quantities from both sides by subtracting.)

Subtract xy from both sides.
We then have

         7 $7x$

(Use Strategy C: Use number examples when it appears that a comparison cannot be determined.)

$7x$ in Column B depends on the specific value of x, which we don't know.

If $x = 0$, then $7x = 0$ and Column A > Column B
If $x = 1$, then $7x = 7$ and Column A = Column B

Thus, we cannot determine which is the correct answer.

(Math Refresher #431)

8. Choice C is correct.

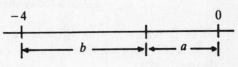

(Math Refresher #431)

Column A	Column B
$4 - a$	b

(Use Strategy D: Make comparison simpler by adding.) Add a to both columns:

Column A	Column B
$4 - a + a$	$b + a$
4	$b + a$

(Use Strategy 3: The whole equals the sum of its parts.) From the numberline we see that $b + a = 4$. (The distance from 0 to -4 is 4 units.)

(Math Refresher #410)

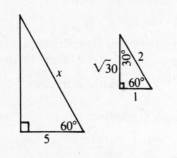

9. Choice A is correct. **(Use Strategy 18: Remember special right triangles.)**

The given triangle, at the left, is similar to the standard 30–60–90 triangle, at right. Thus, corresponding sides are in proportion.

$$\frac{x}{2} = \frac{5}{1}$$
$$x = 2 \times 5$$
$$x = 10$$

Clearly, 10 is greater than 8.

(Math Refresher #509 and #510)

10. Choice is correct. **(Use Strategy 11: Use new definitions carefully.)**

Column A	Column B
$r \square s$	$-r \square s$

By the given definition, we have

$$r \square s = r^2y \qquad -r \square s = (-r)^2y$$
$$= r^2y$$

The columns are equal.

(Math Refresher #431)

11. Choice D is correct. **(Use Strategy C: Use numerics if it appears that the answer can't be determined.)**

Column A	Column B
$s + t - r$	4	☐1

Given: $s < r$ and r, s, and t are equal to 6, 5, and 4, but not necessarily in that order. ☐2

Let $s = 4$, $r = 5$, and $t = 6$. The columns become

$4 + 6 - 5 =$	
5	4	☐3

Let $s = 4$, $r = 6$, $t = 5$. The columns become

$4 + 5 - 6 =$	
3	4	☐4

From ☐3 and ☐4 we see that two different relationships are possible. Thus, the answer can't be determined from the given information.

(Math Refresher #431)

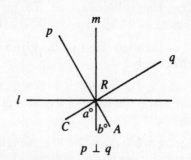

$p \perp q$

12. Choice C is correct.

Given: $p \perp q$ ☐1

From ☐1 we know that $\angle ARC = 90$ ☐2
(Use Strategy 3: The whole equals the sum of its parts.)
From the diagram we see that

$$\angle ARC = a + b \qquad ☐3$$

Substituting ☐3 and ☐2, the columns become

Column A	Column B
$a + b$	
90	90

(Math Refresher #501 and #511)

13. Choice B is correct. **(Use Strategy 13: Find unknowns by division.)**

We are given:

$2a + 2b = 14$	$3x + 3y = 24$
$2(a + b) = 14$	$3(x + y) = 24$
Dividing by 2, we get	Dividing by 3, we get
$a + b = 7$	$x + y = 8$ ☐1

Column A | Column B
The average of | The average of
a and b | x and y

$\left(\text{Use Strategy 5: Average} = \dfrac{\text{Sum of values}}{\text{Total number of values}} \right)$

By definition of average, the columns become

$$\dfrac{a+b}{2} \qquad\qquad \dfrac{x+y}{2} \qquad \boxed{2}$$

Substituting $\boxed{1}$ into $\boxed{2}$, we get

$$\dfrac{7}{2} \qquad\qquad\qquad \dfrac{8}{2}$$

$$3\tfrac{1}{2} < 4$$

(Math Refresher #601 and #406)

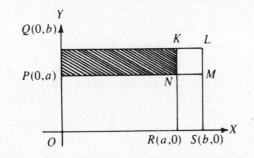

14. Choice A is correct. From the accompanying diagram, we see that

$$QP = b - a \qquad \boxed{1}$$
$$QK = a \qquad \boxed{2}$$
$$b > a \qquad \boxed{3}$$

Area of rectangle $= l \times w \qquad \boxed{4}$
Substituting $\boxed{1}$ and $\boxed{2}$ into $\boxed{4}$, we get
area of rectangle $QKNP = a(b-a) \qquad \boxed{5}$

Column A | Column B
Given: $b(b-a)$ | $a(b-a)$
 | :From $\boxed{5}$

(Use Strategy B: Cancel positive quantities from both sides by dividing.)

From $\boxed{3}$ we have that $b-a>0$ or $b-a$ is positive

Thus, we can divide both columns by $b-a$, giving

$$\dfrac{b\,\cancel{(b-a)}}{\cancel{b-a}} \qquad\qquad \dfrac{a\,\cancel{(b-a)}}{\cancel{b-a}}$$

$$b \qquad\qquad\qquad a$$

From $\boxed{3}$ we know that $b > a$
Thus, Column A > Column B

(Math Refresher #410 and #304)

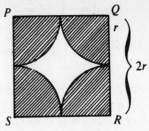

15. Choice B is correct. Since the diagram shows 4 quartercircles, the radius of each quartercircle is r, and each side of the square has length $2r$. We know that

$$\text{Area of circle} = \pi\,(\text{radius})^2$$
$$\text{Area of quartercircle} = \frac{1}{4}\,\pi\,(\text{radius})^2$$

(Use Strategy 3: The whole equals the sum of its parts.)

Area of shaded region = the sum of the areas
of the four quartercircles

$$= 4\left(\frac{1}{4}\right)\pi r^2$$
$$= \pi r^2$$
Area of square $= (\text{side})^2$
$$= (2r)^2$$
$$= 4r^2$$

Thus, ratio of the area of
the square to that of the $\quad = \dfrac{4r^2}{\pi r^2} = \dfrac{4}{\pi}$
shaded region

$$\text{and } \frac{4}{\pi} > \frac{2}{\pi}$$

(Math Refresher #310 and #303)

16. **10**

$$\text{Given: } r = a + b \qquad \boxed{1}$$
$$s = b - a \qquad \boxed{2}$$

(Use Strategy 13: Find unknowns by subtracting.)
Subtract $\boxed{2}$ from $\boxed{1}$. We get

$$r - s = a + b - (b - a)$$
$$= a + b - b + a$$
$$r - s = 2a \qquad \boxed{3}$$

Given: $a = 5$, $b = 4 \qquad \boxed{4}$

Substitute $\boxed{4}$ into $\boxed{3}$. We have

$$r - s = 2a$$
$$= 2(5)$$
$$r - s = 10$$

(Math Refresher #407)

17. **15** **(Use Strategy 17: Use the given information effectively.)**

Given a bag with 4 blue, 7 green, and 8 yellow marbles.

Fred could draw 15 marbles and have only green and yellow marbles (8 + 7). On his next pick, however, he would be sure of having one of each color.

(Use Strategy 16: The obvious may be tricky!)

It is his sixteenth draw that gets Fred one of each color, but the question asks how many Fred would have drawn, so that on his *next* draw he will have 1 marble of every color.

He will have *15*. The sixteenth is the next draw, but not the answer to the question.

The correct answer is 15.

(Logical Reasoning)

18. **50** $\Big($**Use Strategy 5: Remember**

$$\text{average} = \frac{\text{Sum of Values}}{\text{Total Number of Values}}\Big)$$

We are told that the average of 5 different integers is 12. Thus,

$$\frac{x + y + z + w + v}{5} = 12 \qquad \boxed{1}$$

Multiplying $\boxed{1}$ by 5, we get

$$\not{5}\left(\frac{x + y + z + w + v}{\not{5}}\right) = 5(12)$$

$$x + y + z + w + v = 60 \qquad \boxed{2}$$

(Use Strategy 17: Use the given information effectively.)

For one of the integers to be the greatest, the other 4 must be as small as possible. Thus,

let $x = 1$ $\boxed{3}$
let $y = 2$ $\boxed{4}$
let $z = 3$ $\boxed{5}$
let $w = 4$ $\boxed{6}$

The 4 smallest possible different integers > 0.

Substituting $\boxed{3}$, $\boxed{4}$, $\boxed{5}$ and $\boxed{6}$ into $\boxed{2}$ we get

$$1 + 2 + 3 + 4 + v = 60$$
$$10 + v = 60$$
$$v = 50$$

Thus, the greatest possible value for any of the integers is 50.

(Math Refresher #601 and #406)

19. **3** **(Use Strategy 2: Translate from words to algebra.)**

Given: 12 seated students, 5 students at board

This translates to 12 + 5 = 17 students in all. $\boxed{1}$

Given: 12 seated students, 7 empty seats

This translates to 12 + 7 = 19 seats in all. $\boxed{2}$

Subtracting $\boxed{1}$ from $\boxed{2}$ gives

19 − 17 = 2 vacant seats when all are seated $\boxed{3}$

Given: 3 leave and 2 enter

This translates to −3 + 2
            = −1, or a net loss of 1 student. $\boxed{4}$

Combining $\boxed{4}$ and $\boxed{3}$, we have
2 + 1 = 3 vacant seats.

(Math Refresher #200 and Logical Reasoning)

20. **18** **(Use Strategy 14: Draw lines to help solve the problem.)**

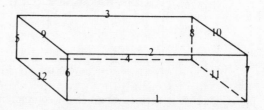

Above is a rectangular solid with each of its edges numbered 1 through 12, respectively. There are 3 groups of 4 parallel edges each.

1, 2, 3, and 4 are parallel.
5, 6, 7, and 8 are parallel.
9, 10, 11, and 12 are parallel.

For each group, there are 6 different pairs of edges. Thus, 3 × 6 = 18 different pairs of edges in all. Below is a listing of all the pairs:

1–2	2–3	5–6	6–7
1–3	2–4	5–7	6–8
1–4	3–4	5–8	7–8

9–10	10–11
9–11	10–12
9–12	11–12

(Math Refresher #312)

21. 1.999, 1.998 . . . .001, or any number

$0 < r < 2$, like $\frac{1}{2}$, $\frac{1}{4}$, etc. (Use Strategy 2:

Translate from words to algebra.)

$$2r + 2r + 3 < 11$$
$$4r + 3 < 11$$
$$4r < 8$$
$$r < 2 \qquad \boxed{1}$$

(Math Refresher #422)

22. **135 (Use Strategy 3: The whole equals the sum of its parts.)**

The sum of the four angles in a quadrilateral = 360° $\qquad \boxed{1}$
Given: the sum of two angles = 90° $\qquad \boxed{2}$
Let a and b represent the two remaining angles. $\qquad \boxed{3}$
Substituting $\boxed{2}$ and $\boxed{3}$ into $\boxed{1}$, we get

$$90° + a + b = 360°$$
$$a + b = 270° \qquad \boxed{4}$$

$\left(\text{Use Strategy 5: Average} = \dfrac{\text{Sum of values}}{\text{Total number of values}}\right)$

Average of a and $b = \dfrac{a + b}{2}$ $\qquad \boxed{5}$

Applying $\boxed{5}$ to $\boxed{4}$, we get

$$\frac{a + b}{2} = \frac{270°}{2}$$

Average of $a + b = 135°$

(Math Refresher #521)

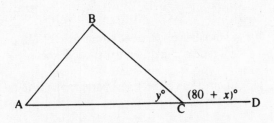

23. **100 (Use Strategy 3: The whole equals the sum of its parts.)**

$$m\angle ACB + m\angle BCD = m\angle ACD \qquad \boxed{1}$$

We are given that AD is a straight line segment. We know that

$$m\angle ACD = 180 \qquad \boxed{2}$$
$$Given: \quad m\angle ACD = y \qquad \boxed{3}$$
$$m\angle BCD = 80 + x \qquad \boxed{4}$$

We substitute $\boxed{2}$, $\boxed{3}$ and $\boxed{4}$ into $\boxed{1}$

Thus, $y + 80 + x = 180$
Subtract 80: $y + x = 100$

(Math Refresher #501 and #406)

24. **3 (Use Strategy 4: Remember classic expressions.)**

$$x^2 + 2xy + y^2 = (x + y)^2 \qquad \boxed{1}$$
$$Given: \ x^2 + 2xy + y^2 = 25 \qquad \boxed{2}$$

Substitute $\boxed{1}$ into $\boxed{2}$, giving

$$(x + y)^2 = 25$$
$$x + y = \pm 5 \qquad \boxed{3}$$
$$Given: \ x + y > 0 \qquad \boxed{4}$$

Using $\boxed{3}$ and $\boxed{4}$ together, we conclude that

$$x + y = +5 \qquad \boxed{5}$$
$$Given: \ x - y = 1 \qquad \boxed{6}$$

(Use Strategy 13: Find an unknown by adding equations.)

Adding $\boxed{5}$ and $\boxed{6}$, we have

$$2x = 6$$
$$x = 3$$

(Math Refresher #409 and #407)

25. 4 **(Use Strategy 17: Use the given information effectively.)**

Remembering that the sum of 2 sides of a triangle is greater than the third side, we know that

$$LM + MN > LN$$
or $\qquad 6 + 10 > 12$
$$16 > 12$$

The difference between 16 and 12: $16 - 12 = 4$ is the amount of overlap.

Method 2: **(Use Strategy 14: Draw lines when appropriate.)**

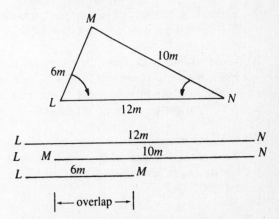

In the figure above, the segments have been redrawn so that the result can be easily discovered.

In $\boxed{2}$, the distance $LM = 12m - 10m = 2m$ $\quad \boxed{4}$

Subtracting $\boxed{4}$ from the distance LM in $\boxed{3}$, we get $6m - 2m = 4m$ overlap.

(Math Refresher #419)

Explanatory Answers for Practice Test 2 (continued)

Section 5: Verbal Ability

As you read these Explanatory Answers, refer to "Using Critical Thinking Skills in Verbal Questions" (beginning on page 236), whenever a specific Strategy is referred to in the answer. Of particular importance is the following Master Verbal Strategy:

Reading Comprehension Master Strategy 2—page 263

1. Choice C is correct. See paragraph 5, lines 82–84: "Hoover also inaugurated ... relieve unemployment."

2. Choice A is correct. See paragraph 2, lines 20–22: "The threat of another war ... was one such stimulus."

3. Choice E is correct. According to the passage, political unrest was the result—not the cause—of the 1929 Depression.

4. Choice C is correct. See paragraph 3, lines 49–51: "All down the line ... not meet their debts."

5. Choice B is correct. From the context of the sentence, we see that we should look for a word or phrase opposite in meaning or in contrast to the word "prosperity." Choice B is perfect.

6. Choice C is correct. Given the context of the rest of the sentence, "inaugurated" must have to do with having begun something. Therefore, Choice C is correct.

7. Choice D is correct. See paragraph 5, lines 80–82: "... Reconstruction Finance Corporation ... with government loans."

8. Choice B is correct. See paragraph 3, last sentence: "Once started, this spiral of deflation seemed to have no limit."

9. Choice A is correct. See paragraph 4, lines 64–68: "More and more ... spread misery and unemployment."

10. Choice E is correct. See paragraph 2: "War provided a limitless market for expendable goods."

11. Choice A is correct. See paragraph 4: All are mentioned except A.

12. Choice B is correct. See paragraph 3: "... the contraction of business left employees without jobs ..."

Explanatory Answers for Practice Test 2 (continued)

Section 6: Math Ability

As you read these solutions, do two things if you answered the Math question incorrectly:

1. When a specific Strategy is referred to in the solution, study that strategy, which you will find in "Using Critical Thinking Skills in Math Questions" (beginning on page 174).

2. When the solution directs you to the "Math Refresher" (beginning on page 291)—for example, Math Refresher #305—study the 305 Math principle to get a clear idea of the Math operation that was necessary for you to know in order to answer the question correctly.

---

1. Choice D is correct.
   Method 1: Remember that
   1. The sum of two odd numbers is even.
   2. The sum, difference, and product of two even numbers is even.
   3. The product of two odd numbers is odd.

   Given: a is odd, b is odd, c is even. Therefore, $a + b$ is even.

   $$(a + b) - c \text{ is even.}$$

   Method 2: Choose a numerical example.
   (Use Strategy 7: Use number examples.)
   Let $a = 3$, $b = 5$, and $c = 4$
   (Use Strategy 8: When all choices must be tested, start with Choice E and work backward.)
   Then Choice E $(a + bc) = 23$
   Therefore, Choice E is odd.
   Choice D $(a + b) - c = 4$
   Therefore, Choice D is even.

   (Math Refresher #603, #604, #605, and #431)

2. Choice B is correct. **(Use Strategy 2: Translate Verbal to Math.)** 35% of all of Harry's stamps are American, and 23% of these are air mail. 23% of 35% equals

   $$\frac{23}{100} \times \frac{35}{100} = \frac{805}{10,000} = \frac{8.05}{100}$$

   which equals 8.05%.

   (Math Refresher #702)

3. Choice A is correct. Before the rotation, we have

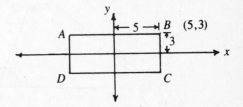

After the rotation, we have

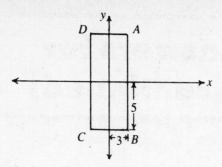

Note that the new y-coordinate of B is negative because B is below the x-axis. Since B is the right of the y-axis, its x-coordinate is positive. By looking at the second diagram, we see that the coordinates of B are

$$(3, -5)$$

(Math Refresher #410 and Logical Reasoning)

4.   Choice B is correct. **(Use Strategy 11: Use new definitions carefully.)**

After 6 hours $\dfrac{x}{2}$ grams remain.

After 12 hours, $\dfrac{1}{2}\left(\dfrac{x}{2}\right)$ grams remain.

After 18 hours, $\dfrac{1}{2}\left(\dfrac{1}{2}\right)\left(\dfrac{x}{2}\right)$ grams remain.

After 24 hours, $\dfrac{1}{2}\left(\dfrac{1}{2}\right)\left(\dfrac{1}{2}\right)\left(\dfrac{x}{2}\right) = \dfrac{x}{16}$ grams remain.

(Math Refresher #431)

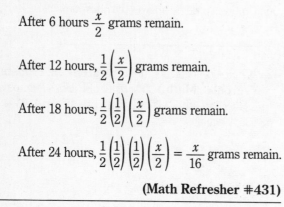

5.   Choice B is correct. From the diagram, we get

$$a + d = 180 \qquad \boxed{1}$$
$$b + e = 180 \qquad \boxed{2}$$
$$c + f = 180 \qquad \boxed{3}$$

(Use Strategy 13: Find unknowns by adding of equations.)

Adding $\boxed{1} + \boxed{2} + \boxed{3}$, we get

$$a + b + c + d + e + f = 540 \qquad \boxed{4}$$

(Use Strategy 3: The whole equals the sum of its parts.)

The sum of the angles of a $\triangle = 180$

Thus, $a + b + c = 180 \qquad \boxed{5}$

From the diagram (vertical angles), we have

$$a = g, b = i, c = h \qquad \boxed{6}$$

Substituting $\boxed{6}$ into $\boxed{5}$, we get

$$g + i + h = 180 \qquad \boxed{7}$$

Adding $\boxed{4} + \boxed{7}$, we get

$$a + b + c + d + f + g + i + h = 720$$

(Math Refresher #501, #505, and #406)

6.   Choice D is correct. **(Use Strategy 11: Use new definitions carefully.)** The smallest sum occurs when we choose 3 from A and 6 from B.

Therefore, the minimum sum $= 3 + 6 = 9$

The largest sum occurs when we choose 5 from A and 8 from B.

Therefore, the maximum sum $= 5 + 8 = 13$

All numbers from 9 to 13 inclusive can be sums.

Thus, there are 5 different sums possible.

(Math Refresher #431 and Logical Reasoning)

7.   Choice B is correct.

$$\text{Given: } AC = \frac{4}{3}(AB) \qquad \boxed{1}$$

(Use Strategy 13: Find unknowns by multiplication.)

Multiply $\boxed{1}$ by 3. We get

$$3(AC) = 4(AB) \qquad \boxed{2}$$

(Use Strategy 3: The whole equals the sum of its parts.)

From the diagram, we see that

$$AC = AB + BC \qquad \boxed{3}$$

Substituting $\boxed{3}$ into $\boxed{2}$, we have

$$3(AB + BC) = 4(AB)$$
$$3AB + 3BC = 4AB$$
$$3BC = 1AB \qquad \boxed{4}$$

(Use Strategy 13: Find unknowns by division.)

Dividing $\boxed{4}$ by $3AB$, we get

$$\frac{3BC}{3AB} = \frac{1\cancel{AB}}{3\cancel{AB}}$$

$$\frac{BC}{AB} = \frac{1}{3}$$

(Math Refresher #406 and #403)

8. Choice E is correct. Since we know only that $\overleftrightarrow{m}$ is not parallel to either $\overleftrightarrow{\ell}$ or $\overleftrightarrow{n}$, both of the following situations could be true. **(Use Strategy 17: Use the given information effectively.)**

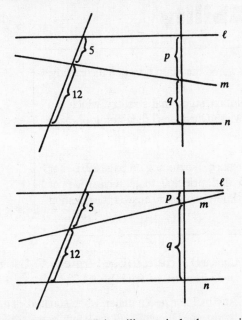

(Note: $p + q = 13$ is still true in both cases in the drawings above.) Clearly, the value of $\frac{p}{q}$ is different for each case. Hence, $\frac{p}{q}$ cannot be determined unless we know more about $\overleftrightarrow{m}$.

(Logical Reasoning)

9. Choice C is correct. There are 4 choices for the first letter of the 3 letter combinations. Since each letter cannot be used more than once in a combination, there are only 3 choices for the second letter and only 2 choices for the third letter. Thus, the maximum number of 3 letter combinations that Ross can make up is

$$= 4 \cdot 3 \cdot 2$$
$$= 24$$

(Logical Reasoning)

10. Choice D is correct.

$\left(\text{Use Strategy 5:}\right.$

$$\text{Average} = \frac{\text{Sum of values}}{\text{Total number of values}}\Big)$$

We want to find

$$\frac{x + y + z + a + b}{5} \qquad \boxed{1}$$

We are given

$$x + y + z = 3(a + b) \qquad \boxed{2}$$

By substituting $\boxed{2}$ into $\boxed{1}$, the unknown expression becomes

$$\frac{3(a + b) + a + \text{b}}{5}$$

$$= \frac{3a + 3b + a + b}{5}$$

$$= \frac{4a + 4b}{5}$$

$$= \frac{4(a + b)}{5}$$

(Math Refresher #601 and #431)

Explanatory Answers for Practice Test 2 (continued)

Section 7: Math Ability

As you read these solutions, do two things if you answered the Math question incorrectly:

1. When a specific Strategy is referred to in the solution, study that strategy, which you will find in "Using Critical Thinking Skills in Math Questions" (beginning on page 174).

2. When the solution directs you to the "Math Refresher" (beginning on page 291)—for example, Math Refresher #305—study the 305 Math principle to get a clear idea of the Math operation that was necessary for you to know in order to answer the question correctly.

1. Choice D is correct. **(Use Strategy C: Use numbers instead of variables.)**

   Try $n = 1$: Column A = 16, Column B = 9
   Try $n = 10$: Column A = 88, Column B = 90

   Depending on whether $n < 8$, $n = 8$, or $n > 8$, $8 + 8n$ will be greater than, equal to, or less than $9n$, respectively. Thus, the relationship cannot be determined.

   (Main Refresher #431)

2. Choice B is correct. **(Use Strategy 2: Translate from words to algebra.)**

   Given: $\frac{2}{3} \times 54$ = number of Democrats

   $$\frac{2}{\cancel{3}} \times \frac{18 \times \cancel{3}}{1} =$$

   36 = number of Democrats

   Thus, $54 - 36 = 18$ Republicans
   $18 > 17$

   (Math Refresher #200)

3. Choice D is correct. **(Use Strategy C: Use numbers instead of variables.)**

   Any real nonzero number, when squared, is greater than zero. Therefore, all we know from

   $$(y - 4)^2 > 0$$

   is that $y \neq 4$, else $(y - 4)^2 = 0$.

   However, we do not know whether y is less than or greater than 4.

   (Math Refreshers #419 and #431)

4. Choice A is correct. **(Use Strategy 17: Use given information effectively.)**

   The dice are numbered 1 through 6. Therefore, the sum of the two dice can be 2 through 12, or a total of 11 possible sums. $\boxed{1}$

   Given: M is the probability that the sum of the dice will be greater than 9. N is the probability that the sum of the dice will be less than 4.

   $$M = \frac{\text{number of possibilities under 9}}{\text{total possibilities}} \quad \boxed{2}$$

   $$N = \frac{\text{number of possibilities under 4}}{\text{total possibilities}} \quad \boxed{3}$$

There are 3 possibilities over 9 (10, 11, and 12.) ☐4

There are 2 possibilities under 4 (2 and 3). ☐5

Substituting ☐1, ☐4, and ☐5 into ☐2 and ☐3, we have

$$M = \frac{3}{11} > N = \frac{2}{11}$$

(Math Refresher #419 and #614)

5. Choice A is correct.

Column A	Column B
$r = 6$	$r = 3$
$h = 3$	$h = 6$

Do not be intimidated by the complex formula. Merely substitute the given into the formula for the volume of a cone.

$$V = \frac{1}{3}\pi(6)^2(3) \qquad V = \frac{1}{3}\pi(3)^2(6)$$

(Use Strategy A: Cancel numbers common to both columns.)

$$V = \frac{\cancel{1}}{\cancel{3}}\pi(36)(3) \qquad V = \frac{\cancel{1}}{\cancel{3}}\pi(9)(6)$$

$$V = 108 \qquad\qquad V = 54$$

(Math Refresher #200, #429, and #431)

6. Choice D is correct.

Do not attempt to substitute numbers into both columns. The answer depends on how large the multiples of 2 are for Column A and how large the multiples of 3 are for Column B. Since this information is not given, we cannot compare the two columns.

(Math Refresher #200 and Logical Reasoning)

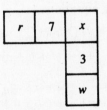

7. Choice B is correct. **(Use Strategy 2: Translate from words to algebra.)**

We are given:

$$r + 7 + x = w + 3 + x \qquad \boxed{1}$$

(Use Strategy 1: Cancel expressions from both sides of an equation.)

Subtracting x from both sides ☐1, we get

$$r + 7 = w + 3 \qquad \boxed{2}$$

Subtracting 7 from both sides of ☐2, we get

$$r = w - 4$$

This translates to r is 4 less than w, so

$$r < w$$

(Math Refresher #200 and #406)

8. Choice C is correct. **(Use Strategy 3: The whole equals the sum of its parts.)**

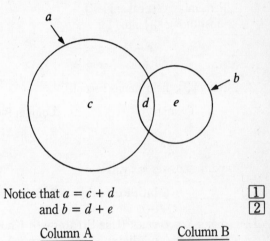

Notice that $a = c + d$ ☐1
and $b = d + e$ ☐2

Column A	Column B
$2d$	$a + b - c - e$ ☐3

Substitute ☐1 and ☐2 into ☐3:

$2d$	$\cancel{c} + d + d + \cancel{e} - \cancel{c} - \cancel{e}$
$2d$	$2d$

(Logical Reasoning and Substitution)

9. Choice B is correct. **(Use Strategy E: Try to get the columns and the given to look similar.)**

We need to find $\frac{a}{c}$

Given: $\qquad \dfrac{a}{b} = \dfrac{2}{3} \qquad \boxed{1}$

$\qquad\qquad\quad \dfrac{b}{c} = \dfrac{5}{8} \qquad \boxed{2}$

(Use Strategy 13: Find unknowns by multiplying equations.) Multiply ☐1 by ☐2:

$$\frac{a}{\not b} \cdot \frac{\not b}{c} = \frac{\not 2}{3} \cdot \frac{5}{\not 84}$$

$$\frac{a}{c} = \frac{5}{12}$$

$$\frac{5}{12} < \frac{5}{6}$$

(Math Refresher #101, #111, and #419)

10. Choice B is correct.

Given: $x + 2y + z = 5y$ ☐1

From the diagram and basic geometry,

$$y = z$$ ☐2

(Remember vertical angles?)
Substituting ☐2 into ☐1,

$$x + 2z + z = 5z$$
$$\text{or} \quad x = 2z$$ ☐3

Using ☐3, the columns become

Column A	Column B
$\frac{3}{2}z$	$2z$

and the answer is clear.

(Math Refresher #503 and #406)

11. Choice B is correct. **(Use Strategy 9: Know the rate, time, and distance relationship.)**

Remember the formula:

Average speed

$$= \frac{\text{total distance traveled}}{\text{total time elapsed}}$$

$$= \frac{48 \text{ miles}}{1\frac{1}{2} \text{ hours}}$$

$$= \frac{48}{\frac{3}{2}} = 48 \times \frac{2}{3} = 16 \times 3 \times \frac{2}{3}$$

$$= 32 \text{ miles per hour}$$

(Math Refresher #201 and #202)

12. Choice D is correct. **(Use Strategy 14: Draw a diagram to make a problem easier.)**

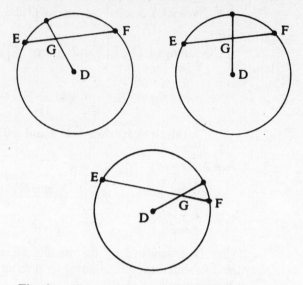

The three diagrams illustrate how EG may not be compared definitely with GF because of the infinite ways in which we can construct the diagram.

(Math Refresher #200 and #524)

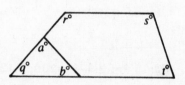

13. Choice C is correct. **(Use Strategy 3: The whole equals the sum of its parts.)**

The sum of the angles of a triangle = 180

So, $a + b + q = 180$ ☐1

We know that the sum of the angles of a quadrilateral = 360.

Therefore, $q + r + s + t = 360$ ☐2

(Use Strategy 13: Find unknowns by subtracting equations.)

Subtracting ☐1 from ☐2, we get

$$q + r + s + t - (a + b + q)$$
$$= 360 - 180$$
$$q + r + s + t - a - b - q = 180$$
$$r + s + t - a - b = 180$$ ☐3

(Use Strategy 13: Find unknowns by addition.)

Adding $a + b$ to both sides of $\boxed{3}$, we get

$$r + s + t = a + b + 180$$

and the answer is clear.

(Math Refresher #505 and #406)

14. Choice A is correct. **(Use Strategy 9: Know the rate, time, and distance relationship.)**

We are given that the wheel goes 24 cm in 3 sec.

Using Rate $= \dfrac{\text{Distance}}{\text{Time}}$, we have

$$\text{Rate} = \dfrac{24 \text{ cm}}{3 \text{ sec}} = 8 \text{ cm/sec} \qquad \boxed{1}$$

(Use Strategy 10: Know how to use units.)

We are told that the wheel makes one revolution per second.

One revolution
= the circumference of the wheel $\qquad \boxed{2}$
= $2\pi r$ cm

From $\boxed{1}$ we know 8 cm are covered in one second.

So, $\boxed{1} = \boxed{2}$. Thus,

$$8 \text{ cm} = 2\pi r \text{ cm}$$

Dividing both sides by 2π, we have

$$\frac{8 \text{ cm/sec}}{2\pi \text{ cm}} = \frac{2\pi r \text{ cm}}{2\pi \text{ cm}}$$

$$\frac{4}{\pi} = r$$

$$\frac{4}{3.14} \approx r$$

$$1.2 \approx r$$

$$r > 1$$

(Math Refresher #201, #202, and #310)

15. Choice B is correct. **(Use Strategy 11: Use new definitions carefully.)**

GROUP I	GROUP II	GROUP III
0 1 2 3 4 5	0 1 2 3 4 5	0 1 2 3 4 5

$\boxed{1}$ $\qquad$ $\boxed{2}$ $\qquad$ $\boxed{3}$

$3 \triangle 4$, using the definition, start at 3 in group I and move 4 to the right, ending up at 1 in group II. $\qquad \boxed{1}$

Move 4 to the right again. We end up at 5 in group III. $\qquad \boxed{2}$

Move 4 to the right again. We end up at 3 in group III. $\qquad \boxed{3}$

Column A	Column B
3	5

(Logical Reasoning)

16. **24 (Use Strategy 2: Translate from words to algebra.)**

Let $n = $ the number
We are given:

$$\frac{5}{8} n = \frac{3}{4} n - 3 \qquad \boxed{1}$$

(Use Strategy 13: Find unknowns by multiplication.) Multiply $\boxed{1}$ by 8. We get

$$8\left(\frac{5}{8}n\right) = 8\left(\frac{3}{4}n - 3\right)$$

$$5n = \frac{24}{4}n - 24$$

$$5n = 6n - 24$$

$$24 = n \qquad (Answer)$$

(Math Refresher #200 and #406)

17. **10 (Use Strategy 11: Use new definitions carefully.)**

By definition $\quad \boxed{20 \rangle} = 10$

(Math Refresher #603 and #607)

18. **2300 (Use Strategy 12: Try not to make tedious calculations.)**

$$23m + 23n = 23(m + n)$$
$$= 23(94 + 6)$$
$$= 23(100)$$
$$= 2300$$

Multiplying 23(94) and 23(6) and adding would be time consuming and therefore tedious.

(Math Refresher #431)

19. **11** Since lines are drawn every 10 yards after the first one, $\frac{100}{10}$ lines or 10 additional lines are drawn.

(Use Strategy 2: Translate from words to algebra.) The total number of lines on the field = the original line + the number of additional lines

$$= 1 + 10 = 11$$

(Math Refresher #200 and Logical Reasoning)

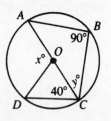

20. **125 (Use Strategy 18: Remember the isosceles triangle.)** Since $AB = BC$ in $\triangle ABC$, it is isosceles, and the opposite angles are equal. So

$$m \angle A = \angle y. \qquad \boxed{1}$$

(Use Strategy 3: The whole equals the sum of its parts.) The sum of the angles in a triangle is 180°, so

$$m \angle A + y + 90 = 180°$$

Subtracting 90 from both sides gives

$$m \angle A + y = 90 \qquad \boxed{2}$$

From $\boxed{1}$, the angles are =, so substituting y for $\angle A$ in $\boxed{2}$ gives

$$y + y = 90$$

$$\frac{2y}{2} = \frac{90}{2}$$

$$y = 45° \qquad \boxed{3}$$

Since OD and OC are radii of the circle, they are equal. $\triangle DOC$ is isosceles and $\angle D = \angle OCD$ (see $\boxed{1}$ above).

$$\text{Thus, } \angle D = 40° \qquad \boxed{4}$$

(Use Strategy 3: The whole equals the sum of its parts.) The sum of angles of

$$\triangle DOC = 180°$$

Therefore, $\angle D + \angle OCD + \angle DOC + 180 \qquad \boxed{5}$
Substituting from $\boxed{4}$ and the given into $\boxed{5}$, we have

$$40 + 40 + \angle DOC = 180$$
$$\angle DOC = 100 \qquad \boxed{6}$$

Since AC is a diameter, it is a straight line segment and $\angle AOC$ is a straight angle.

Thus, $\angle AOC = 180 \qquad \boxed{7}$

(Use Strategy 3: The whole equals the sum of its parts.)

$$\angle AOC = \angle AOD + \angle DOC \qquad \boxed{8}$$

Substituting $\boxed{6}$ and $\boxed{7}$ into $\boxed{8}$, we get

$$180 = \angle AOD + 100$$
$$80 = \angle AOD \qquad \boxed{9}$$

We need $x + y$, so substituting $\boxed{9}$ and $\boxed{3}$ here gives

$$80 + 45 = 125$$

(Math Refresher #507, #505, and #406)

21. **25**

$$\left(\text{Use Strategy 5:} \right.$$

$$\left. \textbf{Average} = \frac{\textbf{sum of values}}{\textbf{total number of values}} \right)$$

Average age of students in a class

$$= \frac{\text{sum of the ages of students in the class}}{\text{number of students in the class}} \qquad \boxed{1}$$

Thus,
Average age of all 80 students

$$= \frac{\text{sum of the ages of the 80 students}}{80} \qquad \boxed{2}$$

Using $\boxed{1}$, we know that

$$20 = \frac{\text{sum of the ages of the 60 students}}{60}$$

and $40 = \frac{\text{sum of the ages of the 20 students}}{20}$

Thus,
sum of the ages of the 60 students

$$= (60)(20) = 1200$$

and the sum of the ages of the 20 students

$$= (40)(20) = 800$$

Hence, the sum of the ages of the 80 students

= sum of the ages of the 60 students
+ sum of the ages of the 20 students
$$= 1,200 + 800 = 2,000 \qquad \boxed{3}$$

Substituting $\boxed{3}$ into $\boxed{2}$, we get

$$\frac{2,000}{80} = 25$$

Average age of all 80 students = 25 (*Answer*)

(Math Refresher #601 and #406)

22. **4** By trial and error, it can be seen that 4 is the answer.

(Math Refresher #431)

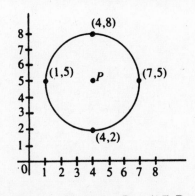

23. **3** The coordinates of the center *P* are (4,5). By definition, the length of a radius is the distance from the center to any point on the circle. Therefore,

radius = distance from (7,5) to (4,5) =
$$= 7 - 4$$
radius = 3

(Math Refresher #410 and #524)

24. **36.2 (Use Strategy 2: Translate from words to algebra.)**

Fraction mowed during evening 1 $= \dfrac{2}{9}$ $\qquad \boxed{1}$

Fraction mowed during evening 2 $= 2\left(\dfrac{2}{9}\right) = \dfrac{4}{9}$ $\quad \boxed{2}$

Adding $\boxed{1}$ and $\boxed{2}$, we get

Total fraction mowed during first two evenings $= \dfrac{2}{9} + \dfrac{4}{9}$

$$= \dfrac{6}{9}$$

Total fraction mowed during first two evenings $= \dfrac{2}{3}$

(Use Strategy 3: The whole equals the sum of its parts.)

Amount left for evening 3 =

1 whole lawn $- \dfrac{2}{3}$ already mowed $\qquad \boxed{3}$

Amount left for evening 3 $= \dfrac{1}{3}$ $\qquad \boxed{4}$

Given: Lawn area = 108.6 square feet

Multiplying $\boxed{3}$ by $\boxed{4}$, we get

Amount left for evening 3 $= \dfrac{1}{3} \times 108.6$ square feet

Amount left for evening 3 = 36.2 square feet

(Math Refresher #200 and #109)

25. **7** A line and a circle in the same plane can intersect either in no points, in one point (as a tangent), or in two points.

So any two people can remain representing the intersection of the straight line between them and the circumference of the circle. All others must move. Therefore, $9 - 2 = 7$ must move.

(Logical Reasoning)

SAT Practice Test 3

Answer Sheet—Practice Test 3

Make each mark a dark mark that completely fills the oval and is as dark as all your other marks. If you erase, do so completely. Incomplete erasures may be read as intended responses.

Use a No. 2 pencil only. Be sure each mark is dark and completely fills the intended oval. Completely erase any errors or stray marks.

Start with number 1 for each new section. If a section has fewer questions than answer spaces, leave the extra answer spaces blank.

SECTION 1

1 Ⓐ Ⓑ Ⓒ Ⓓ Ⓔ	11 Ⓐ Ⓑ Ⓒ Ⓓ Ⓔ	21 Ⓐ Ⓑ Ⓒ Ⓓ Ⓔ	31 Ⓐ Ⓑ Ⓒ Ⓓ Ⓔ
2 Ⓐ Ⓑ Ⓒ Ⓓ Ⓔ	12 Ⓐ Ⓑ Ⓒ Ⓓ Ⓔ	22 Ⓐ Ⓑ Ⓒ Ⓓ Ⓔ	32 Ⓐ Ⓑ Ⓒ Ⓓ Ⓔ
3 Ⓐ Ⓑ Ⓒ Ⓓ Ⓔ	13 Ⓐ Ⓑ Ⓒ Ⓓ Ⓔ	23 Ⓐ Ⓑ Ⓒ Ⓓ Ⓔ	33 Ⓐ Ⓑ Ⓒ Ⓓ Ⓔ
4 Ⓐ Ⓑ Ⓒ Ⓓ Ⓔ	14 Ⓐ Ⓑ Ⓒ Ⓓ Ⓔ	24 Ⓐ Ⓑ Ⓒ Ⓓ Ⓔ	34 Ⓐ Ⓑ Ⓒ Ⓓ Ⓔ
5 Ⓐ Ⓑ Ⓒ Ⓓ Ⓔ	15 Ⓐ Ⓑ Ⓒ Ⓓ Ⓔ	25 Ⓐ Ⓑ Ⓒ Ⓓ Ⓔ	35 Ⓐ Ⓑ Ⓒ Ⓓ Ⓔ
6 Ⓐ Ⓑ Ⓒ Ⓓ Ⓔ	16 Ⓐ Ⓑ Ⓒ Ⓓ Ⓔ	26 Ⓐ Ⓑ Ⓒ Ⓓ Ⓔ	36 Ⓐ Ⓑ Ⓒ Ⓓ Ⓔ
7 Ⓐ Ⓑ Ⓒ Ⓓ Ⓔ	17 Ⓐ Ⓑ Ⓒ Ⓓ Ⓔ	27 Ⓐ Ⓑ Ⓒ Ⓓ Ⓔ	37 Ⓐ Ⓑ Ⓒ Ⓓ Ⓔ
8 Ⓐ Ⓑ Ⓒ Ⓓ Ⓔ	18 Ⓐ Ⓑ Ⓒ Ⓓ Ⓔ	28 Ⓐ Ⓑ Ⓒ Ⓓ Ⓔ	38 Ⓐ Ⓑ Ⓒ Ⓓ Ⓔ
9 Ⓐ Ⓑ Ⓒ Ⓓ Ⓔ	19 Ⓐ Ⓑ Ⓒ Ⓓ Ⓔ	29 Ⓐ Ⓑ Ⓒ Ⓓ Ⓔ	39 Ⓐ Ⓑ Ⓒ Ⓓ Ⓔ
10 Ⓐ Ⓑ Ⓒ Ⓓ Ⓔ	20 Ⓐ Ⓑ Ⓒ Ⓓ Ⓔ	30 Ⓐ Ⓑ Ⓒ Ⓓ Ⓔ	40 Ⓐ Ⓑ Ⓒ Ⓓ Ⓔ

SECTION 2

1 Ⓐ Ⓑ Ⓒ Ⓓ Ⓔ	11 Ⓐ Ⓑ Ⓒ Ⓓ Ⓔ	21 Ⓐ Ⓑ Ⓒ Ⓓ Ⓔ	31 Ⓐ Ⓑ Ⓒ Ⓓ Ⓔ
2 Ⓐ Ⓑ Ⓒ Ⓓ Ⓔ	12 Ⓐ Ⓑ Ⓒ Ⓓ Ⓔ	22 Ⓐ Ⓑ Ⓒ Ⓓ Ⓔ	32 Ⓐ Ⓑ Ⓒ Ⓓ Ⓔ
3 Ⓐ Ⓑ Ⓒ Ⓓ Ⓔ	13 Ⓐ Ⓑ Ⓒ Ⓓ Ⓔ	23 Ⓐ Ⓑ Ⓒ Ⓓ Ⓔ	33 Ⓐ Ⓑ Ⓒ Ⓓ Ⓔ
4 Ⓐ Ⓑ Ⓒ Ⓓ Ⓔ	14 Ⓐ Ⓑ Ⓒ Ⓓ Ⓔ	24 Ⓐ Ⓑ Ⓒ Ⓓ Ⓔ	34 Ⓐ Ⓑ Ⓒ Ⓓ Ⓔ
5 Ⓐ Ⓑ Ⓒ Ⓓ Ⓔ	15 Ⓐ Ⓑ Ⓒ Ⓓ Ⓔ	25 Ⓐ Ⓑ Ⓒ Ⓓ Ⓔ	35 Ⓐ Ⓑ Ⓒ Ⓓ Ⓔ
6 Ⓐ Ⓑ Ⓒ Ⓓ Ⓔ	16 Ⓐ Ⓑ Ⓒ Ⓓ Ⓔ	26 Ⓐ Ⓑ Ⓒ Ⓓ Ⓔ	36 Ⓐ Ⓑ Ⓒ Ⓓ Ⓔ
7 Ⓐ Ⓑ Ⓒ Ⓓ Ⓔ	17 Ⓐ Ⓑ Ⓒ Ⓓ Ⓔ	27 Ⓐ Ⓑ Ⓒ Ⓓ Ⓔ	37 Ⓐ Ⓑ Ⓒ Ⓓ Ⓔ
8 Ⓐ Ⓑ Ⓒ Ⓓ Ⓔ	18 Ⓐ Ⓑ Ⓒ Ⓓ Ⓔ	28 Ⓐ Ⓑ Ⓒ Ⓓ Ⓔ	38 Ⓐ Ⓑ Ⓒ Ⓓ Ⓔ
9 Ⓐ Ⓑ Ⓒ Ⓓ Ⓔ	19 Ⓐ Ⓑ Ⓒ Ⓓ Ⓔ	29 Ⓐ Ⓑ Ⓒ Ⓓ Ⓔ	39 Ⓐ Ⓑ Ⓒ Ⓓ Ⓔ
10 Ⓐ Ⓑ Ⓒ Ⓓ Ⓔ	20 Ⓐ Ⓑ Ⓒ Ⓓ Ⓔ	30 Ⓐ Ⓑ Ⓒ Ⓓ Ⓔ	40 Ⓐ Ⓑ Ⓒ Ⓓ Ⓔ

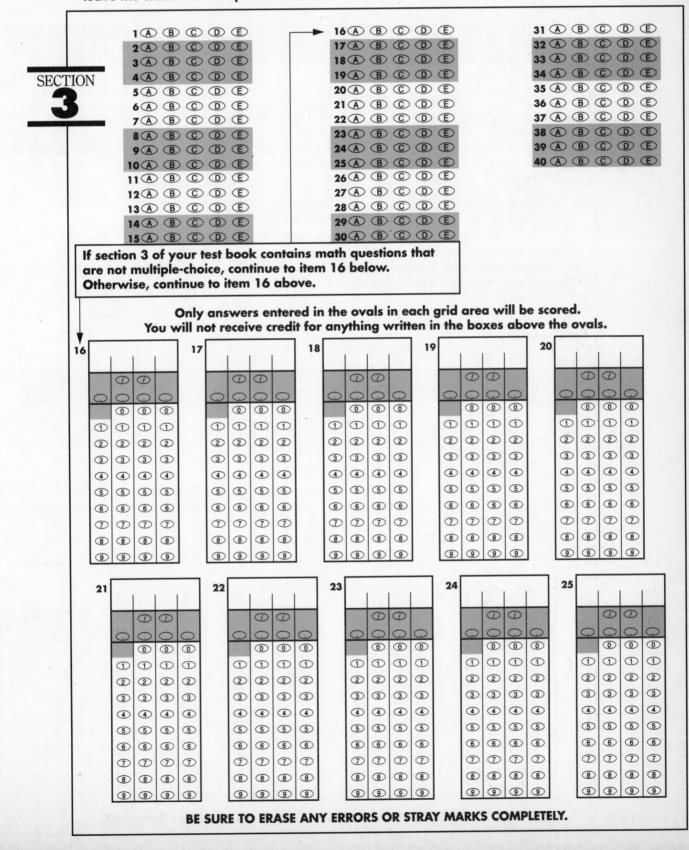

Use a No. 2 pencil only. Be sure each mark is dark and completely fills the intended oval. Completely erase any errors or stray marks.

Start with number 1 for each new section. If a section has fewer questions than answer spaces, leave the extra answer spaces blank.

SECTION
4

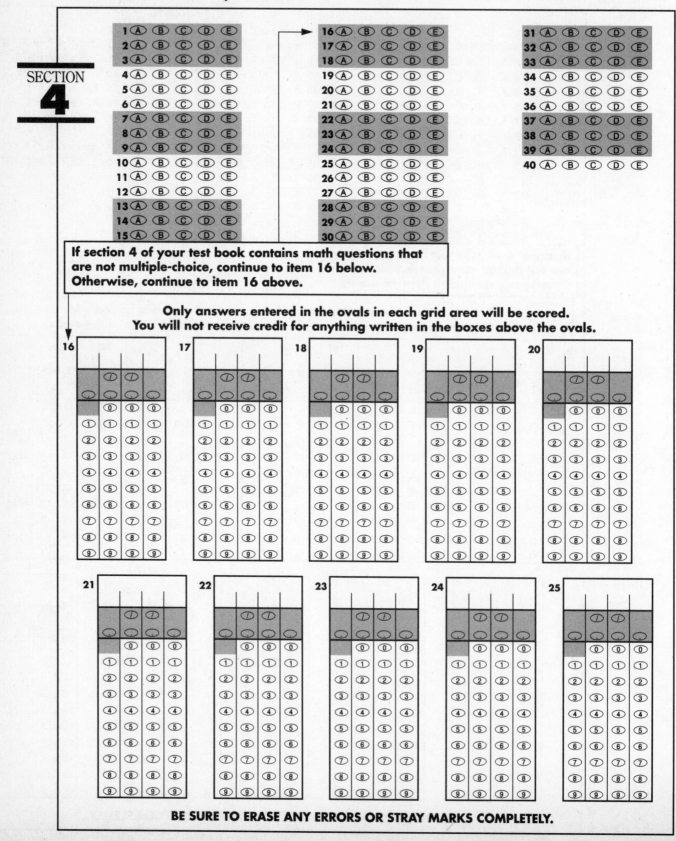

If section 4 of your test book contains math questions that are not multiple-choice, continue to item 16 below. Otherwise, continue to item 16 above.

Only answers entered in the ovals in each grid area will be scored. You will not receive credit for anything written in the boxes above the ovals.

BE SURE TO ERASE ANY ERRORS OR STRAY MARKS COMPLETELY.

Use a No. 2 pencil only. Be sure each mark is
dark and completely fills the intended oval.
Completely erase any errors or stray marks.

Start with number 1 for each new section. If a section has fewer questions than answer spaces,
leave the extra answer spaces blank.

SECTION 5

1 Ⓐ Ⓑ Ⓒ Ⓓ Ⓔ   11 Ⓐ Ⓑ Ⓒ Ⓓ Ⓔ   21 Ⓐ Ⓑ Ⓒ Ⓓ Ⓔ   31 Ⓐ Ⓑ Ⓒ Ⓓ Ⓔ
2 Ⓐ Ⓑ Ⓒ Ⓓ Ⓔ   12 Ⓐ Ⓑ Ⓒ Ⓓ Ⓔ   22 Ⓐ Ⓑ Ⓒ Ⓓ Ⓔ   32 Ⓐ Ⓑ Ⓒ Ⓓ Ⓔ
3 Ⓐ Ⓑ Ⓒ Ⓓ Ⓔ   13 Ⓐ Ⓑ Ⓒ Ⓓ Ⓔ   23 Ⓐ Ⓑ Ⓒ Ⓓ Ⓔ   33 Ⓐ Ⓑ Ⓒ Ⓓ Ⓔ
4 Ⓐ Ⓑ Ⓒ Ⓓ Ⓔ   14 Ⓐ Ⓑ Ⓒ Ⓓ Ⓔ   24 Ⓐ Ⓑ Ⓒ Ⓓ Ⓔ   34 Ⓐ Ⓑ Ⓒ Ⓓ Ⓔ
5 Ⓐ Ⓑ Ⓒ Ⓓ Ⓔ   15 Ⓐ Ⓑ Ⓒ Ⓓ Ⓔ   25 Ⓐ Ⓑ Ⓒ Ⓓ Ⓔ   35 Ⓐ Ⓑ Ⓒ Ⓓ Ⓔ
6 Ⓐ Ⓑ Ⓒ Ⓓ Ⓔ   16 Ⓐ Ⓑ Ⓒ Ⓓ Ⓔ   26 Ⓐ Ⓑ Ⓒ Ⓓ Ⓔ   36 Ⓐ Ⓑ Ⓒ Ⓓ Ⓔ
7 Ⓐ Ⓑ Ⓒ Ⓓ Ⓔ   17 Ⓐ Ⓑ Ⓒ Ⓓ Ⓔ   27 Ⓐ Ⓑ Ⓒ Ⓓ Ⓔ   37 Ⓐ Ⓑ Ⓒ Ⓓ Ⓔ
8 Ⓐ Ⓑ Ⓒ Ⓓ Ⓔ   18 Ⓐ Ⓑ Ⓒ Ⓓ Ⓔ   28 Ⓐ Ⓑ Ⓒ Ⓓ Ⓔ   38 Ⓐ Ⓑ Ⓒ Ⓓ Ⓔ
9 Ⓐ Ⓑ Ⓒ Ⓓ Ⓔ   19 Ⓐ Ⓑ Ⓒ Ⓓ Ⓔ   29 Ⓐ Ⓑ Ⓒ Ⓓ Ⓔ   39 Ⓐ Ⓑ Ⓒ Ⓓ Ⓔ
10 Ⓐ Ⓑ Ⓒ Ⓓ Ⓔ   20 Ⓐ Ⓑ Ⓒ Ⓓ Ⓔ   30 Ⓐ Ⓑ Ⓒ Ⓓ Ⓔ   40 Ⓐ Ⓑ Ⓒ Ⓓ Ⓔ

SECTION 6

1 Ⓐ Ⓑ Ⓒ Ⓓ Ⓔ   11 Ⓐ Ⓑ Ⓒ Ⓓ Ⓔ   21 Ⓐ Ⓑ Ⓒ Ⓓ Ⓔ   31 Ⓐ Ⓑ Ⓒ Ⓓ Ⓔ
2 Ⓐ Ⓑ Ⓒ Ⓓ Ⓔ   12 Ⓐ Ⓑ Ⓒ Ⓓ Ⓔ   22 Ⓐ Ⓑ Ⓒ Ⓓ Ⓔ   32 Ⓐ Ⓑ Ⓒ Ⓓ Ⓔ
3 Ⓐ Ⓑ Ⓒ Ⓓ Ⓔ   13 Ⓐ Ⓑ Ⓒ Ⓓ Ⓔ   23 Ⓐ Ⓑ Ⓒ Ⓓ Ⓔ   33 Ⓐ Ⓑ Ⓒ Ⓓ Ⓔ
4 Ⓐ Ⓑ Ⓒ Ⓓ Ⓔ   14 Ⓐ Ⓑ Ⓒ Ⓓ Ⓔ   24 Ⓐ Ⓑ Ⓒ Ⓓ Ⓔ   34 Ⓐ Ⓑ Ⓒ Ⓓ Ⓔ
5 Ⓐ Ⓑ Ⓒ Ⓓ Ⓔ   15 Ⓐ Ⓑ Ⓒ Ⓓ Ⓔ   25 Ⓐ Ⓑ Ⓒ Ⓓ Ⓔ   35 Ⓐ Ⓑ Ⓒ Ⓓ Ⓔ
6 Ⓐ Ⓑ Ⓒ Ⓓ Ⓔ   16 Ⓐ Ⓑ Ⓒ Ⓓ Ⓔ   26 Ⓐ Ⓑ Ⓒ Ⓓ Ⓔ   36 Ⓐ Ⓑ Ⓒ Ⓓ Ⓔ
7 Ⓐ Ⓑ Ⓒ Ⓓ Ⓔ   17 Ⓐ Ⓑ Ⓒ Ⓓ Ⓔ   27 Ⓐ Ⓑ Ⓒ Ⓓ Ⓔ   37 Ⓐ Ⓑ Ⓒ Ⓓ Ⓔ
8 Ⓐ Ⓑ Ⓒ Ⓓ Ⓔ   18 Ⓐ Ⓑ Ⓒ Ⓓ Ⓔ   28 Ⓐ Ⓑ Ⓒ Ⓓ Ⓔ   38 Ⓐ Ⓑ Ⓒ Ⓓ Ⓔ
9 Ⓐ Ⓑ Ⓒ Ⓓ Ⓔ   19 Ⓐ Ⓑ Ⓒ Ⓓ Ⓔ   29 Ⓐ Ⓑ Ⓒ Ⓓ Ⓔ   39 Ⓐ Ⓑ Ⓒ Ⓓ Ⓔ
10 Ⓐ Ⓑ Ⓒ Ⓓ Ⓔ   20 Ⓐ Ⓑ Ⓒ Ⓓ Ⓔ   30 Ⓐ Ⓑ Ⓒ Ⓓ Ⓔ   40 Ⓐ Ⓑ Ⓒ Ⓓ Ⓔ

Use a No. 2 pencil only. Be sure each mark is dark and completely fills the intended oval. Completely erase any errors or stray marks.

Start with number 1 for each new section. If a section has fewer questions than answer spaces, leave the extra answer spaces blank.

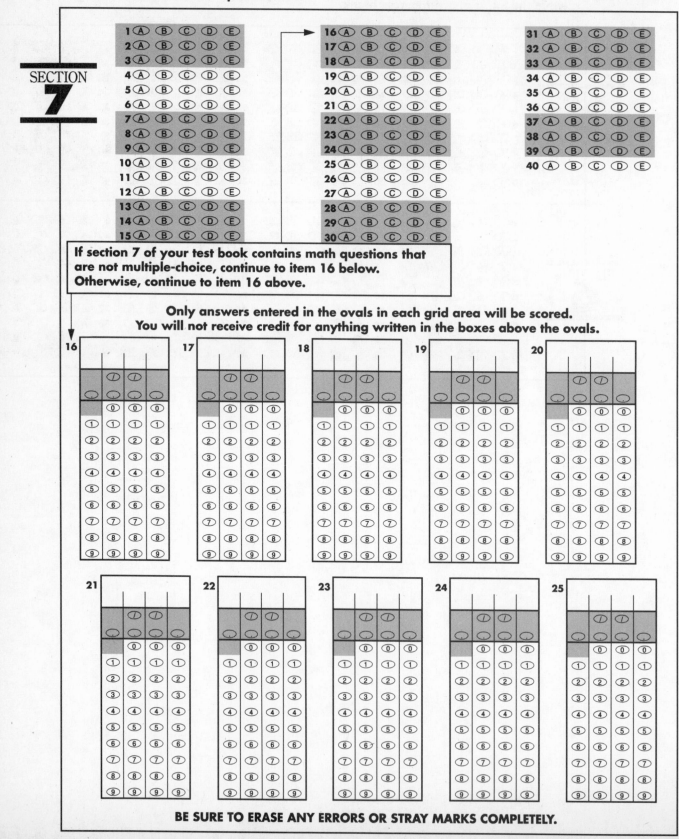

SECTION 7

If section 7 of your test book contains math questions that are not multiple-choice, continue to item 16 below.
Otherwise, continue to item 16 above.

Only answers entered in the ovals in each grid area will be scored.
You will not receive credit for anything written in the boxes above the ovals.

BE SURE TO ERASE ANY ERRORS OR STRAY MARKS COMPLETELY.

Time: 30 Minutes   For each question in this section, choose the best answer from among the choices given and
30 Questions   fill in the corresponding oval on the answer sheet.

Each of the following sentences has one or two blanks, each blank indicating that something has been omitted. Beneath the sentence are five lettered words or sets of words labeled A through E. Choose the word or set of words that, when inserted in the sentence, *best* fits the meaning of the sentence as a whole.

Example:

Medieval kingdoms did not become constitutional republics overnight; on the contrary, the change was _____.

(A) unpopular
(B) unexpected
(C) advantageous
(D) sufficient
(E) gradual

Ⓐ Ⓑ Ⓒ Ⓓ ●

1   As a general dealing with subordinates, he was like two sides of a coin: _____ yet known for his severity, _____ yet a man of few words.

(A) agreeable . . . talkative
(B) brilliant . . . handsome
(C) fair . . . outgoing
(D) understanding . . . candid
(E) harsh . . . pleasant

2   The profession of a major league baseball player involves more than _____ in these times when astronomical salaries and _____ contract bargaining are commonplace.

(A) skill . . . astute
(B) agitation . . . traditional
(C) practice . . . minimal
(D) enthusiasm . . . whimsical
(E) intellect . . . mystical

3   Internal dissension in this congressional committee can _____ affirmative action for months and increase the chances of racial _____.

(A) encourage . . . regard
(B) complicate . . . agreement
(C) induce . . . movement
(D) apply . . . validity
(E) delay . . . upheaval

4   Although there was considerable _____ among the members of the panel as to the qualities essential for a champion, Sugar Ray Robinson was _____ voted the greatest fighter of all time.

(A) suspicion . . . quietly
(B) disagreement . . . overwhelmingly
(C) discussion . . . incidentally
(D) sacrifice . . . happily
(E) research . . . irrelevantly

5   The police commissioner insisted on severity in dealing with the demonstrators rather than the _____ approach that his advisers suggested.

(A) arrogant
(B) defeatist
(C) violent
(D) conciliatory
(E) retaliatory

6   Feeling no particular affection for either of his two acquaintances, he was able to judge their dispute very _____.

(A) impartially
(B) accurately
(C) immaculately
(D) heatedly
(E) judiciously

GO ON TO THE NEXT PAGE

7 His choice for the new judge won the immediate _____ of city officials, even though some of them had _____ about him.

(A) acclaim . . . reservations
(B) disdain . . . information
(C) apprehension . . . dilemmas
(D) vituperation . . . repercussions
(E) enmity . . . preconceptions

8 There are some individuals who thrive on action and, accordingly, cannot tolerate a _____ life style.

(A) passive
(B) chaotic
(C) brazen
(D) grandiose
(E) vibrant

9 The girl's extreme state of _____ aroused in him a feeling of pity.

(A) disapproval
(B) exultation
(C) enthusiasm
(D) degradation
(E) jubilation

GO ON TO THE NEXT PAGE

Each of the following questions consists of a related pair of words or phrases, followed by five pairs of words or phrases labeled A through E. Select the pair that *best* expresses a relationship similar to that expressed in the original pair.

Example:

CRUMB : BREAD : :
(A) ounce : unit
(B) splinter : wood
(C) water : bucket
(D) twine : rope
(E) cream : butter

Ⓐ ● Ⓒ Ⓓ Ⓔ

10 CLIP : HAIR : :

(A) raze : building
(B) dress : dummy
(C) cross : river
(D) photograph : scene
(E) hew : bough

11 CLIENT : ATTORNEY : :

(A) teacher : principal
(B) prisoner : policeman
(C) patient : doctor
(D) shopkeeper : customer
(E) audience : actor

12 CANCEL : SUBSCRIPTION : :

(A) nullify : contract
(B) reprimand : child
(C) ignore : summons
(D) renew : prescription
(E) challenge : adversary

13 HUB : WHEEL : :

(A) spoke : bicycle
(B) link : chain
(C) bullseye : target
(D) earth : universe
(E) noon : morning

14 GENEALOGY : FAMILY : :

(A) pseudonym : author
(B) etymology : word
(C) password : entry
(D) royalty : king
(E) boundary : limit

15 CRASS : REFINEMENT : :

(A) frivolous : continuity
(B) fallow : emphasis
(C) indifferent : pretense
(D) orthodox : conviction
(E) craven : bravery

GO ON TO THE NEXT PAGE

Each of the following passages is followed by questions based on its content. Answer the questions following each passage on the basis of what is *stated* or *implied* in that passage and in any introductory material that may be provided.

Questions 16–21 are based on the following passage.

The following passage is about the literature of the African-American culture and its impact on society.

The literature of an oppressed people is the conscience of man, and nowhere is this seen with more intense clarity than in the literature of African-Americans. An essential element of African-American literature is that the literature as a
5 whole—not the work of occasional authors—is a movement against concrete wickedness. In African-American literature, accordingly, there is a grief rarely to be found elsewhere in American literature, and frequently a rage rarely to be found in American letters: a rage different in quality, pro-
10 founder, more towering, more intense—the rage of the oppressed. Whenever an African-American artist picks up pen or horn, his target is likely to be American racism, his subject the suffering of his people, and the core element his own grief and the grief of his people. Almost all of African-
15 American literature carries the burden of this protest.

The cry for freedom and the protest against injustice indicate a desire for the birth of the New Man, a testament to the New Unknown World to be discovered, to be created by man. African-American literature is, as a body, a declaration
20 that despite the perversion and cruelty that cling like swamproots to the flesh of man's feet, man has options for freedom, for cleanliness, for wholeness, for human harmony, for goodness: for a human world. Like the spirituals that are a part of it, African-American literature is a passionate
25 assertion that man will win freedom. Thus, African-American literature rejects despair and cynicism; it is a literature of realistic hope and life-affirmation. This is not to say that no African-American literary work reflects cynicism or despair, but rather that the basic theme of African-
30 American literature is that man's goodness will prevail.

African-American literature is a statement against death, a statement as to what life should be: life should be vivacious, exuberant, wholesomely uninhibited, sensual, sensuous, constructively antirespectable, life should abound
35 and flourish and laugh, life should be passionately lived and man should be loving: life should be not a sedate waltz or foxtrot but a vigorous breakdance; thus, when the African-American writer criticizes America for its cruelty, the criticism implies that America is drawn to death and repelled by
40 what should be the human style of life, the human way of living.

Black literature in America is, then, a setting-forth of man's identity and destiny; an investigation of man's iniquity and a statement of belief in his potential godliness; a

45 prodding of man toward exploring and finding deep joy in his humanity.

16 The author states or implies that

(A) a separate-but-equal doctrine is the answer to American racism
(B) African-American literature is superior to American literature
(C) hopelessness and lack of trust are the keynotes of African-American literature
(D) standing up for one's rights and protesting about unfairness are vital
(E) traditional forms of American-type dancing should be engaged in

17 When the author, in referring to African-American literature, states that "life should be ... constructively antirespectable" (lines 32–34), it can be inferred that people ought to

(A) do their own thing provided what they do is worthwhile
(B) show disrespect for others when they have the desire to do so
(C) be passionate in public whenever the urge is there
(D) shun a person because he is of another race or color
(E) be enraged if their ancestors have been unjustly treated

18 With reference to the passage, which of the following statements is true about African-American literature?

I. It expresses the need for nonviolent opposition to antiracism.
II. It urges a person to have respect for himself and for others.
III. It voices the need for an active, productive, and satisfying life.

(A) I only
(B) II only
(C) I and III only
(D) II and III only
(E) I, II, and III

GO ON TO THE NEXT PAGE

19 The tone of the passage is one of

(A) anger and vindictiveness
(B) hope and affirmation
(C) forgiveness and charity
(D) doubt and despair
(E) grief and cruelty

20 Which of the following constitute(s) the author's view of a "human world?"

I. harmony
II. cleanliness
III. wholeness

(A) I only
(B) I and II only
(C) II and III only
(D) I and III only
(E) I, II, and III

21 The word "iniquity" (lines 43–44) means

(A) potential
(B) creation
(C) wickedness
(D) cleverness
(E) greatness

GO ON TO THE NEXT PAGE

Questions 22–30 are based on the following passage.

The following passage is based on B. F. Skinner's book *About Behaviorism* and discusses the pros and cons of Skinner's work on behaviorism and the various points made by Skinner.

In his compact and modestly titled book *About Behaviorism*, Dr. B. F. Skinner, the noted behavioral psychologist, lists the 20 most salient objections to "behaviorism or the science of behavior," and he has gone on to answer them both implic-
5 itly and explicitly. He has answers and explanations for everyone.

For instance, to those who object "that behaviorists deny the existence of feelings, sensations, ideas, and other features of mental life," Dr. Skinner concedes that "a good
10 deal of clarification" is in order. What such people are really decrying is "methodological behaviorism," an earlier stage of the science whose goal was precisely to close off mentalistic explanations of behavior, if only to counteract the 2,500-year-old influence of mentalism. But Dr. Skinner is a "radical
15 behaviorist." "Radical behaviorism . . . takes a different line. It does not deny the possibility of self-observation or self-knowledge or its possible usefulness. . . . It restores introspection. . . ."

For instance, to those who object that behaviorism
20 "neglects innate endowment and argues that all behavior is acquired during the lifetime of the individual," Dr. Skinner expresses puzzlement. Granted, "A few behaviorists . . . have minimized if not denied a genetic contribution, and in their enthusiasm for what may be done through the environment,
25 others have no doubt acted as if a genetic endowment were unimportant, but few would contend that behavior is 'endlessly malleable.' " And Dr. Skinner himself, sounding as often as not like some latter-day Social Darwinist, gives as much weight to the "contingencies of survival" in the evolu-
30 tion of the human species as to the "contingencies of reinforcement" in the lifetime of the individual.

For instance, to those who claim that behaviorism "cannot explain creative achievements—in art, for example, or in music, literature, science, or mathematics"—Dr. Skinner
35 provides an intriguing ellipsis. "Contingencies of reinforcement also resemble contingencies of survival in the production of novelty. . . . In both natural selection and operant conditioning the appearance of 'mutations' is crucial. Until recently, species evolved because of random changes in
40 genes or chromosomes, but the geneticist may arrange conditions under which mutations are particularly likely to occur. We can also discover some of the sources of new forms of behavior which undergo selection by prevailing contingencies or reinforcement, and fortunately the creative
45 artist or thinker has other ways of introducing novelties."

And so go Dr. Skinner's answers to the 20 questions he poses—questions that range all the way from asking if behaviorism fails "to account for cognitive processes" to
50 wondering if behaviorism "is indifferent to the warmth and richness of human life, and . . . is incompatible with the . . . enjoyment of art, music, and literature and with love for one's fellow men."

But will it wash? Will it serve to silence those critics who have characterized B. F. Skinner variously as a mad,
55 manipulative doctor, as a naive 19th-century positivist, as an unscientific technician, and as an arrogant social engineer? There is no gainsaying that *About Behaviorism* is an unusually compact summary of both the history and "the philosophy of the science of human behavior" (as Dr. Skinner insists
60 on defining behaviorism). It is a veritable artwork of organization. And anyone who reads it will never again be able to think of behaviorism as a simplistic philosophy that reduces human beings to black boxes responding robotlike to external stimuli.

65 Still, there are certain quandaries that *About Behaviorism* does not quite dispel. For one thing, though Dr. Skinner makes countless references to the advances in experiments with human beings that behaviorism has made since it first began running rats through mazes many decades ago, he
70 fails to provide a single illustration of these advances. And though it may be true, as Dr. Skinner argues, that one can extrapolate from pigeons to people, it would be reassuring to be shown precisely how.

More important, he has not satisfactorily rebutted the
75 basic criticism that behaviorism "is scientistic rather than scientific. It merely emulates the sciences." A true science doesn't predict what it will accomplish when it is firmly established as a science, not even when it is posing as "the philosophy of that science." A true science simply advances
80 rules for testing hypotheses.

But Dr. Skinner predicts that behaviorism will produce the means to save human society from impending disaster. Two key concepts that keep accreting to that prediction are "manipulation" and "control." And so, while he reassures us
85 quite persuasively that his science would practice those concepts benignly, one can't shake off the suspicion that he was advancing a science just in order to save society by means of "manipulation" and "control." And that is not so reassuring.

GO ON TO THE NEXT PAGE

22 According to the passage, Skinner would be most likely to agree that

(A) studies of animal behavior are applicable to human behavior
(B) introspection should be used widely to analyze conscious experience
(C) behaviorism is basically scientist
(D) behavioristic principles and techniques will be of no use in preventing widespread disaster
(E) an individual can form an infinite number of sentences that he has never heard spoken

23 The reader may infer that

(A) Skinner's philosophy is completely democratic in its methodology
(B) behaviorism, in its early form, and mentalism were essentially the same
(C) the book *About Behaviorism* is difficult to understand because it is not well structured
(D) methodological behaviorism preceded both mentalism and radical behaviorism
(E) the author of the article has found glaring weaknesses in Skinner's defense of behaviorism

24 When Skinner speaks of "contingencies of survival" (line 29) and "contingencies of reinforcement" (lines 30–31), the word "contingency" most accurately means

(A) frequency of occurrence
(B) something incidental
(C) a quota
(D) dependence on chance
(E) one of an assemblage

25 The author of the article says that Skinner sounds "like some latter-day Social Darwinist" (line 28) most probably because Skinner

(A) is a radical behaviorist who has differed from methodological behaviorists
(B) has predicted that human society faces disaster
(C) has been characterized as a 19th-century positivist
(D) has studied animal behavior as applicable to human behavior
(E) believes that the geneticist may arrange conditions for mutations to occur

26 It can be inferred from the passage that "extrapolate" (line 72) means

(A) to gather unknown information by extending known information
(B) to determine how one organism may be used to advantage by another organism
(C) to insert or introduce between other things or parts
(D) to change the form or the behavior of one thing to match the form or behavior of another thing
(E) to transfer an organ of a living thing into another living thing

27 One *cannot* conclude from the passage that

(A) Skinner is a radical behaviorist but not a methodological behaviorist
(B) *About Behavior* does not show how behaviorists have improved in experimentation with human beings
(C) only human beings are used in experiments conducted by behaviorists
(D) methodological behaviorism rejects the introspective approach
(E) the book being discussed is to the point and well organized

28 In Skinner's statement that "few would contend that behavior is 'endlessly malleable'" (lines 26–27), he means that

(A) genetic influences are of primary importance in shaping human behavior
(B) environmental influences may be frequently supplemented by genetic influences
(C) self-examination is the most effective way of improving a behavior pattern
(D) the learning process continues throughout life
(E) psychologists will never come to a common conclusion about the best procedure for studying and improving human behavior

GO ON TO THE NEXT PAGE

29 According to the author, which of the following is true concerning *scientistic* and *scientific* disciplines?

I. The scientific one develops the rules for testing the theory; the scientistic one does not.
II. There is no element of prediction in scientistic disciplines.
III. Science never assumes a philosophical nature.

(A) I only
(B) I and III only
(C) I and II only
(D) II and III only
(E) I, II, and III

30 The word "veritable" (line 60) means

(A) abundant
(B) careful
(C) political
(D) true
(E) believable

IF YOU FINISH BEFORE TIME IS CALLED, YOU MAY CHECK YOUR WORK ON THIS SECTION ONLY. DO NOT TURN TO ANY OTHER SECTION IN THE TEST.

Time: 30 Minutes
25 Questions

In this section solve each problem, using any available space on the page for scratchwork. Then decide which is the best of the choices given and fill in the corresponding oval on the answer sheet.

Notes:

1. The use of a calculator is permitted. All numbers used are real numbers.

2. Figures that accompany problems in this test are intended to provide information useful in solving the problems. They are drawn as accurately as possible EXCEPT when it is stated in a specific problem that the figure is not drawn to scale. All figures lie in a plane unless otherwise indicated.

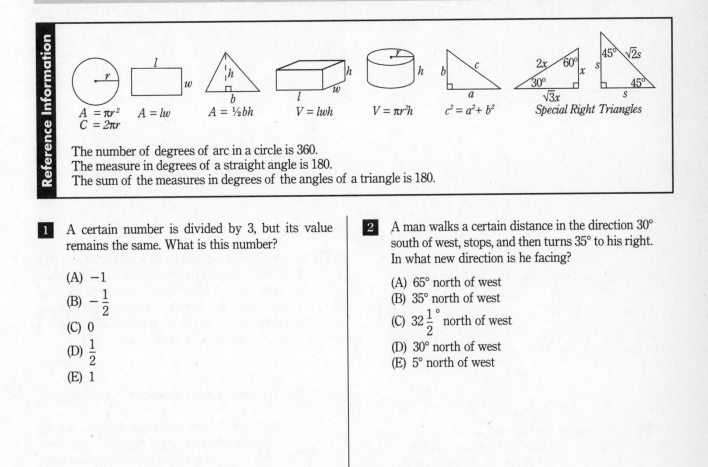

$A = \pi r^2$ $A = lw$ $A = \frac{1}{2}bh$ $V = lwh$ $V = \pi r^2 h$ $c^2 = a^2 + b^2$ *Special Right Triangles*
$C = 2\pi r$

The number of degrees of arc in a circle is 360.
The measure in degrees of a straight angle is 180.
The sum of the measures in degrees of the angles of a triangle is 180.

1 A certain number is divided by 3, but its value remains the same. What is this number?

(A) −1

(B) −$\frac{1}{2}$

(C) 0

(D) $\frac{1}{2}$

(E) 1

2 A man walks a certain distance in the direction 30° south of west, stops, and then turns 35° to his right. In what new direction is he facing?

(A) 65° north of west
(B) 35° north of west
(C) $32\frac{1}{2}$° north of west
(D) 30° north of west
(E) 5° north of west

3 What is the value of $\frac{1}{5}K$ if $\frac{9}{5}K = 18$?

(A) $\frac{1}{9}$

(B) $\frac{1}{5}$

(C) 2

(D) 5

(E) 10

5 Let x, y, and z be negative numbers such that $x < y < z$. Which expression is the smallest?

(A) $(z)(z)$
(B) $(y)(z)$
(C) $(x)(z)$
(D) $(y)(x)$
(E) $(x)(x)$

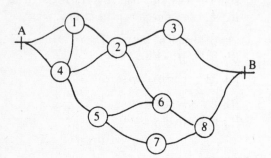

4 The figure above is a piece of fish net. Any path to get from point A to point B goes through points 1, 2, 3, 4, 5, 6, 7, and 8 as shown. Which of the following statements must be true about an ant crawling on the net from Point A to Point B?

(A) If it goes through 2, it must go through 7.
(B) If it goes through 3, it must go through 1.
(C) Its route must go through either 2 or 7.
(D) If it goes through 4, it must go through 3 or 5.
(E) If it goes through 8, it must go through 2 or 5.

6 A sequence of integers is defined as follows: The first term is 2, and every additional term is obtained by subtracting 2 from the previous term and tripling the resulting difference. For example, the second term would be 0. Which of the following is a true statement about this sequence?

(A) The terms behave as follows: even, even, odd, odd, even, even, odd, odd, . . .
(B) The terms behave as follows: even, odd, even, odd, even, odd, . . .
(C) The terms behave as follows: even, even, even, odd, odd, odd, even, even, even, . . .
(D) All of the terms, except for the first one, are odd.
(E) All of the terms are even.

GO ON TO THE NEXT PAGE

7 From the equations $7a = 4$ and $7a + 4b = 12$, one can conclude that b is

(A) -1
(B) 0
(C) 1
(D) 2
(E) any integer

9 How many integers x satisfy $-\dfrac{1}{2} < \dfrac{x}{3} < -\dfrac{1}{4}$

(A) none
(B) one
(C) two
(D) three
(E) infinitely many

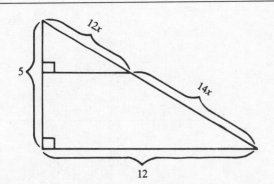

8 If the segments shown in the diagram have the indicated lengths, find the value of x.

(A) 13
(B) 12
(C) 5
(D) 2
(E) $\dfrac{1}{2}$

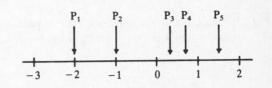

10 For the five numbers marked above by arrows, the best approximation to their product is

(A) $\dfrac{1}{3}$
(B) $\dfrac{2}{3}$
(C) $\dfrac{3}{2}$
(D) 3
(E) -3

GO ON TO THE NEXT PAGE

11 If K is the sum of three consecutive even integers and y is the sum of the greatest three consecutive *odd* integers that precede the least of the three even integers, express y in terms of K.

(A) $y = K - 5$
(B) $y = K - 10$
(C) $y = K - 15$
(D) $y = K - 20$
(E) The answer cannot be determined from the information given.

12 If John buys a 2-lb. apple pie with ingredients distributed as shown, how much of his pie is water?

(A) $\frac{1}{4}$ lb.

(B) $\frac{1}{2}$ lb.

(C) $\frac{3}{4}$ lb.

(D) 1 lb.

(E) $1\frac{1}{4}$ lb.

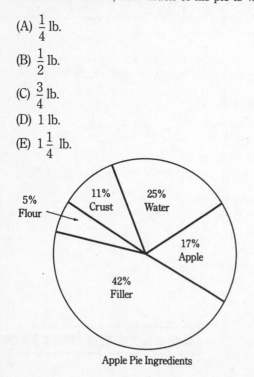

Apple Pie Ingredients

13 If r and s are negative numbers, then all of the following must be positive *except*

(A) $\dfrac{r}{s}$

(B) rs

(C) $(rs)^2$

(D) $r + s$

(E) $-r - s$

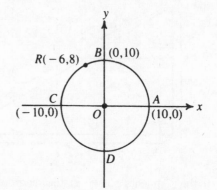

14 In the figure above, S is a point (not shown) such that segment RS divides the area of circle O into two equal parts. What are the coordinates of S?

(A) $(6, -8)$
(B) $(6, 8)$
(C) $(8, -6)$
(D) $(-6, -8)$
(E) $(8, 6)$

GO ON TO THE NEXT PAGE

694

	First Place (6 points)	Second place (4 points)	Third Place (2 points)
Game 1			
Game 2		Bob	
Game 3			Bob

15 The figure above is a partially filled-in score card for a video game contest. Alan, Bob, and Carl each played in all of the three games. There were no ties. What is the *minimum* possible score for Carl in this tournament?

(A) 2
(B) 6
(C) 8
(D) 12
(E) The answer cannot be determined from the information given.

17 Which of the rectangles below has a length of $\frac{4}{3}$, if each has an area of 4?

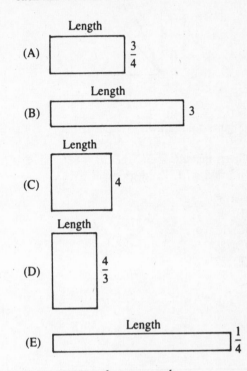

(A) Length 3/4

(B) Length 3

(C) Length 4

(D) Length $\frac{4}{3}$

(E) Length 1/4

Note: Figures are not drawn to scale.

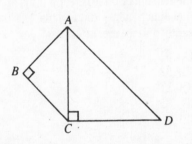

16 In the figure above, $AB = BC$ and $AC = CD$. How many of the angles have a measure of 45 degrees?

(A) none
(B) two
(C) three
(D) four
(E) five

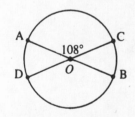

18 O is the center of a circle of diameter 20 and $\angle AOC = 108°$. Find the sum of the lengths of minor arcs $\overarc{AC}$ and $\overarc{DB}$.

(A) 5π
(B) 8π
(C) 10π
(D) 12π
(E) 15π

GO ON TO THE NEXT PAGE

695

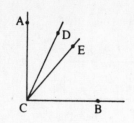

Note: Figure is not drawn to scale.

19 Given that $AC \perp BC$, $\angle DCB = 62°$ and $\angle ACE = 37°$, find $\angle DCE$ in degrees.

(A) 5°
(B) 9°
(C) 13°
(D) 25°
(E) 27°

20 $2 \times 10^{-5} \times 8 \times 10^2 \times 5 \times 10^2 =$

(A) .00008
(B) .008
(C) .08
(D) 8
(E) 800

21 Over the first few weeks of the baseball season, the league's five leading pitchers had the following won–lost records. (All games ended in a win or loss for that pitcher.)

	Won	Lost
Pitcher A	4	2
Pitcher B	3	2
Pitcher C	4	1
Pitcher D	2	2
Pitcher E	3	1

At the time these statistics were compiled, which pitcher was leading the league in winning percentage? (That is, which pitcher had won the greatest percentage of his games?)

(A) Pitcher A
(B) Pitcher B
(C) Pitcher C
(D) Pitcher D
(E) Pitcher E

22 Johnny spent $\frac{2}{5}$ of his allowance on candy and $\frac{5}{6}$ of the remainder on ice cream. If his allowance is $30, how much money did he have left after buying the candy and ice cream?

(A) $1
(B) $2
(C) $3
(D) $5
(E) $10

GO ON TO THE NEXT PAGE

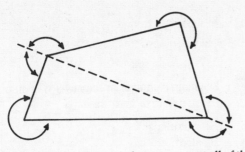

23 The arrows in the diagram above represent all of the exterior angles of the figure. The sum of the degree measures of these angles is

(A) 720
(B) 1,080
(C) 1,440
(D) 1,800
(E) The answer cannot be determined from the information given.

25 27 equal cubes, each with a side of length r, are arranged so as to form a single larger cube with a volume of 81. If the larger cube has a side of length s, then r divided by s equals

(A) $\frac{1}{3}$

(B) $\frac{1}{\sqrt{3}}$

(C) $\frac{1}{2}$

(D) $\frac{1}{8}$

(E) $\frac{1}{27}$

24 In the watch shown above, the normal numbers 1, 2, 3, ..., 12 have been replaced by the letters A, B, C, ..., L. In terms of these letters, a correct reading of the time shown would be

(A) I minutes after L
(B) 3E minutes before A
(C) 5C minutes after L
(D) I minutes before A
(E) None of the above

IF YOU FINISH BEFORE TIME IS CALLED, YOU MAY CHECK YOUR WORK ON THIS SECTION ONLY. DO NOT TURN TO ANY OTHER SECTION IN THE TEST.

Time: 30 Minutes   For each question in this section, choose the best answer from among the choices given and
35 Questions   fill in the corresponding oval on the answer sheet.

Each of the following sentences has one or two blanks, each blank indicating that something has been omitted. Beneath the sentence are five words or sets of words labeled A through E. Choose the word or set of words that, when inserted in the sentence, *best* fits the meaning of the sentence as a whole.

Example:

Medieval kingdoms did not become constitutional republics overnight; on the contrary, the change was—.

(A) unpopular
(B) unexpected
(C) advantageous
(D) sufficient
(E) gradual

Ⓐ Ⓑ Ⓒ Ⓓ ●

1 Although our team was aware that the Raiders' attack power was _____ as compared with that of our players, we were stupid to be so _____.

(A) calculated . . . alert
(B) sluggish . . . easygoing
(C) acceptable . . . serious
(D) determined . . . detailed
(E) premeditated . . . willing

2 The _____ prime minister caused the downfall of the once _____ country.

(A) heroic . . . important
(B) respected . . . rich
(C) incompetent . . . powerful
(D) vacillating . . . confidential
(E) insightful . . . unconquerable

3 The main character in the novel was dignified and _____, a man of great reserve.

(A) garrulous
(B) aloof
(C) boring
(D) hypocritical
(E) interesting

4 The nonsmoker's blood contains _____ amounts of carbon monoxide; on the other hand, the smoker's blood contains _____ amounts.

(A) frequent . . . extensive
(B) heavy . . . adequate
(C) minute . . . excessive
(D) definite . . . puzzling
(E) bland . . . moderate

5 As a truly objective person, Mr. Jones allows neither _____ attempts to please him nor open _____ on the part of his students to influence his marks.

(A) unearned . . . respect
(B) condescending . . . humor
(C) sincere . . . reliance
(D) backward . . . offense
(E) hypocritical . . . defiance

6 Because the subject matter was so technical, the instructor made every effort to use _____ terms to describe it.

(A) candid
(B) simplified
(C) discreet
(D) specialized
(E) involved

GO ON TO THE NEXT PAGE

7 Violent crime has become so ____ in our cities that hardly a day goes by when we are not made aware of some ____ act on our local news broadcasts.

(A) scarce . . . momentous
(B) pervasive . . . benign
(C) conclusive . . . serious
(D) common . . . heinous
(E) ridiculous . . . unacceptable

8 Although they are ____ by intense police patrols, burglars ____ to prowl the subways.

(A) incited . . . decline
(B) enlivened . . . attempt
(C) hindered . . . cease
(D) persuaded . . . refuse
(E) impeded . . . continue

9 Britain's seizure of American ships and ____ our sailors to serve in the British Navy were two major causes of the War of 1812.

(A) compelling
(B) recruiting
(C) bribing
(D) enlisting
(E) deriding

10 Since he had not worked very hard on his project, the student was quite ____ upon learning that he had won the contest.

(A) composed
(B) apathetic
(C) rebuffed
(D) dismayed
(E) enraptured

GO ON TO THE NEXT PAGE

Each of the following questions consists of a related pair of words or phrases, followed by five pairs of words or phrases labeled A through E. Select the pair that *best* expresses a relationship similar to that expressed in the original pair.

Example:

CRUMB : BREAD : :
(A) ounce : unit
(B) splinter : wood
(C) water : bucket
(D) twine : rope
(E) cream : butter

Ⓐ ● Ⓒ Ⓓ Ⓔ

11 HORSE : COLT : :

(A) bird : eaglet
(B) child : adult
(C) seed : fruit
(D) pig : sow
(E) sheep : lamb

12 WALK : STUMBLE : :

(A) trot : race
(B) look : ogle
(C) hear : ignore
(D) build : destroy
(E) speak : stammer

13 RUN : BASEBALL : :

(A) goal : soccer
(B) education : school
(C) puck : hockey
(D) down : football
(E) award : actress

14 SHARPEN : PENCIL : :

(A) hone : blade
(B) ice : cake
(C) wrap : package
(D) polish : furniture
(E) stretch : canvas

15 BACKLOG : MERCHANDISE : :

(A) jam : traffic
(B) intermission : play
(C) deficit : money
(D) bonus : worker
(E) prey : hunter

16 ORCHESTRA : MUSICIAN : :

(A) museum : statue
(B) school : desk
(C) team : owner
(D) army : soldier
(E) novel : author

17 SAND : DUNE : :

(A) rain : sleet
(B) beach : strand
(C) snow : bank
(D) sun : mist
(E) drift : ocean

18 EMBARRASS : HUMILIATE : :

(A) labor : succeed
(B) argue : bicker
(C) reduce : enlarge
(D) spank : whip
(E) pilfer : steal

19 CANDID : FURTIVE : :

(A) miserly : scanty
(B) transparent : opaque
(C) romantic : idealistic
(D) amicable : unfriendly
(E) closed : ajar

20 SPEAKER : DAIS : :

(A) policeman : car
(B) actor : stage
(C) physician : medicine
(D) owner : property
(E) salesman : briefcase

GO ON TO THE NEXT PAGE

21 IMITATION : INDIVIDUALITY : :

(A) veneration : deference
(B) determination : success
(C) recklessness : courage
(D) vanity : conformity
(E) debauchery : morality

22 ODORIFEROUS : SMELL : :

(A) rancid : taste
(B) myopic : vision
(C) euphonious : sound
(D) decrepit : age
(E) disoriented : thought

23 BLAND : PIQUANT : :

(A) pacific : grateful
(B) terse : serious
(C) slavish : servile
(D) naive : genuine
(E) inane : relevant

GO ON TO THE NEXT PAGE

The following passage is followed by questions based on its content. Answer the questions on the basis of what is *stated* or *implied* in that passage and in any introductory material that may be provided.

Questions 24–35 are based on the following passage.

The passage describes the author's attitude toward transportation.

Many people who are willing to concede that the railroad must be brought back to life are chiefly thinking of bringing this about on the very terms that have robbed us of a balanced transportation network—that is, by treating
5 speed as the only important factor, forgetting reliability, comfort and safety, and seeking some mechanical dodge for increasing the speed and automation of surface vehicles.

My desk is littered with such technocratic fantasies, hopefully offered as "solutions." They range from old-
10 fashioned monorails and jet-propelled hovercraft (now extinct) to a more scientific mode of propulsion at 2,000 miles an hour, from completely automated highway travel in private cars to automated vehicles a Government department is now toying with for "facilitating" urban traffic.

15 What is the function of transportation? What place does locomotion occupy in the whole spectrum of human needs? Perhaps the first step in developing an adequate transportation policy would be to clear our minds of technocratic cant. Those who believe that transportation is the
20 chief end of life should be put in orbit at a safe lunar distance from the earth.

The prime purpose of passenger transportation is not to increase the amount of physical movement but to increase the possibilities for human association, cooperation, per-
25 sonal intercourse, and choice.

A balanced transportation system, accordingly, calls for a balance of resources and facilities and opportunities in every other part of the economy. Neither speed nor mass demand offers a criterion of social efficiency. Hence such
30 limited technocratic proposals as that for high-speed trains between already overcrowded and overextended urban centers would only add to the present lack of functional balance and purposeful organization viewed in terms of human need. Variety of choices, facilities and destinations, not
35 speed alone, is the mark of an organic transportation system. And, incidentally, this is an important factor of safety when any part of the system breaks down. Even confirmed air travelers appreciate the railroad in foul weather.

If we took human needs seriously in recasting the
40 whole transportation system, we should begin with the human body and make the fullest use of pedestrian movement, not only for health but for efficiency in moving large crowds over short distances. The current introduction of shopping malls, free from wheeled traffic, is both a far simpler
45 and far better *technical* solution than the many costly proposals for introducing moving sidewalks or other rigidly automated modes of locomotion. At every stage we should provide for the right type of locomotion, at the right speed, within the right radius, to meet human needs. Neither
50 maximum speed nor maximum traffic nor maximum distance has by itself any human significance.

With the over-exploitation of the particular car comes an increased demand for engineering equipment, to roll ever wider carpets of concrete over the bulldozed landscape and
55 to endow the petroleum magnates of some places with fabulous capacities for personal luxury and political corruption. Finally, the purpose of this system, abetted by similar concentration on planes and rockets, is to keep an increasing volume of motorists and tourists in motion, at the highest
60 possible speed, in a sufficiently comatose state not to mind the fact that their distant destination has become the exact counterpart of the very place they have left. The end product everywhere is environmental desolation.

If this is the best our technological civilization can do to
65 satisfy genuine human needs and nurture man's further development, it's plainly time to close up shop. If indeed we go farther and faster along this route, there is plenty of evidence to show that the shop will close up without our help. Behind our power blackouts, our polluted environ-
70 ments, our transportation breakdowns, our nuclear threats, is a failure of mind. Technocratic anesthesia has put us to sleep. Results that were predictable—and predicted!— three-quarters of a century ago without awakening any response still find us unready to cope with them—or even to
75 admit their existence.

24 The author criticizes most railroad advocates because their emphasis is primarily on

(A) monetary costs
(B) speed
(C) traffic flow
(D) reliability
(E) pollution

GO ON TO THE NEXT PAGE

25 The author states that the purpose(s) of transportation is (are)

   I. to move people from place to place efficiently
   II. to increase social contact
   III. to open up opportunities

(A) I only
(B) II only
(C) III only
(D) I and II only
(E) I, II, and III

26 A solution advocated by the author for transporting masses of people over short distances involves

(A) jet-propelled hovercraft
(B) automated vehicles
(C) conveyor belts
(D) moving sidewalks
(E) pedestrian malls

27 Excessive reliance on the automobile, according to the author, is associated with

(A) the enrichment of the oil industry
(B) monopoly power
(C) our transportation breakdown
(D) inefficiency in transportation
(E) a policy of comfort and convenience at all costs

28 It can be inferred that the author would oppose

(A) a balanced transportation system
(B) shopping malls
(C) an expansion of the interstate highway system
(D) less emphasis on technological solutions
(E) sacrificing speed for comfort

29 The author predicts that if we continue our present transportation policy

(A) we will succumb to a technocratic dictatorship
(B) our society may die
(C) we will attain a balanced transportation system
(D) rockets and planes will predominate
(E) human needs will be surrendered

30 The word "radius" in line 49 refers to

(A) the distance from the center of a train wheel to the circumference
(B) the distance of places
(C) the latitude in connection with human needs
(D) the traffic in connection with travel
(E) the time it takes to go from one place to another

31 The author believes that "technocratic" thinking is not consistent with

(A) technological advances
(B) the labor relations groups
(C) faster-moving vehicles
(D) human interests
(E) the scientific mode

32 According to the article, the fulfillment of human needs will require

(A) far greater use of walking
(B) more resources devoted to transportation
(C) abandoning the profit system
(D) a better legislative policy
(E) automated travel

33 The author believes that the nation has placed too great an emphasis on all of the following *except*

(A) speed
(B) traffic flow
(C) diversity
(D) maximizing distance
(E) technological needs

34 It may be inferred that the author is a(n)

(A) highway engineer
(B) historian
(C) railroad industry spokesman
(D) lawyer
(E) oil baron

GO ON TO THE NEXT PAGE

35 It is stated in the article that safety in transportation is aided by the existence of

(A) remote air-to-ground control for airplanes
(B) technological sophistication
(C) a variety of transport modes
(D) fail-safe systems
(E) a combination of surface and subsurface systems

IF YOU FINISH BEFORE TIME IS CALLED, YOU MAY CHECK YOUR WORK ON THIS SECTION ONLY. DO NOT TURN TO ANY OTHER SECTION IN THE TEST.

STOP

Time: 30 Minutes   This section consists of two types of questions. Each type has its own directions. You may use
25 Questions   any available space for scratchwork.

Notes:

1. The use of a calculator is permitted. All numbers used are real numbers.

2. Figures that accompany problems in this test are intended to provide information useful in solving the problems. They are drawn as accurately as possible EXCEPT when it is stated in a specific problem that the figure is not drawn to scale. All figures lie in a plane unless otherwise indicated.

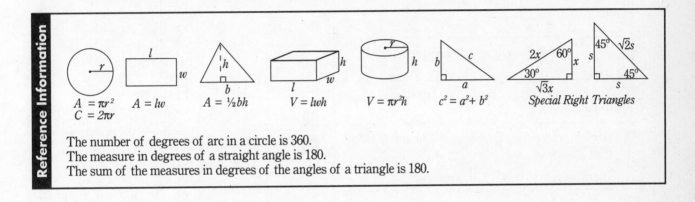

Reference Information

$A = \pi r^2$ $A = lw$ $A = \frac{1}{2}bh$ $V = lwh$ $V = \pi r^2 h$ $c^2 = a^2 + b^2$ *Special Right Triangles*
$C = 2\pi r$

The number of degrees of arc in a circle is 360.
The measure in degrees of a straight angle is 180.
The sum of the measures in degrees of the angles of a triangle is 180.

Directions for Quantitative Comparison Questions

Questions 1–15 each consist of two quantities in boxes, one in Column A and one in Column B. You are to compare the two quantities and on the answer sheet fill in oval

A if the quantity in Column A is greater;
B if the quantity in Column B is greater;
C if the two quantities are equal;
D if the relationship cannot be determined from the information given.

AN E RESPONSE WILL NOT BE SCORED.

Notes:

1. In some questions, information is given about one or both of the quantities to be compared. In such cases, the given information is centered above the two columns and is not boxed.
2. In a given question, a symbol that appears in both columns represents the same thing in Column A as it does in Column B.
3. Letters such as x, n, and k stand for real numbers.

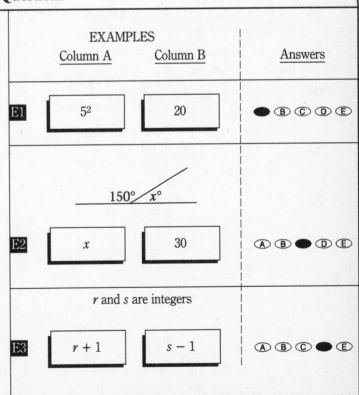

EXAMPLES

Column A   Column B   Answers

E1 5^2 20   ● Ⓑ Ⓒ Ⓓ Ⓔ

150° $x°$

E2 x 30   Ⓐ Ⓑ ● Ⓓ Ⓔ

r and s are integers

E3 $r + 1$ $s - 1$ Ⓐ Ⓑ Ⓒ ● Ⓔ

GO ON TO THE NEXT PAGE

SUMMARY DIRECTIONS FOR COMPARISON QUESTION

Answer: A if the quantity in Column A is greater;
B if the quantity in Column B is greater;
C if the two quantities are equal;
D if the relationship cannot be determined from the information given.
An E response will not be scored.

Column A	Column B

1

$$\frac{a}{18} = \frac{2}{9}$$

$$\frac{b}{28} = \frac{1}{7}$$

a	b

2 r is an even integer and $5 < r < 8$

$r + 1$	7

3   The number of hours in w days v hours

4   Darrin is older than Stephanie and Jimmy is older than Stephanie.

Darrin's age   Jimmy's age

5 $m - n > p - q$

n	p

6   On a certain test, 9 students received a 95 and one student received less than a 95.

average (arithmetic mean) of test scores	95

7 $\frac{2}{3} + \frac{r}{s} = \frac{5}{3}$

r	s

8 $x > 0 > y$

$y - x$	$x - y$

9 $w \leqq 60$
          $x \leqq 60$

80	$w + x$

Column A	Column B

Note: Figure is not drawn to scale.

10 a b

11

Note: Figure is not drawn to scale.
Line $\ell \parallel$ Line m. Line segments AC and EC intersect Line ℓ at B and D, respectively.

The length of BC	The length of DC

12   Slope of line represented by equation $3 + y = 2x$ Slope of line represented by equation $4x - 2y + 8 = 0$

13   Let $⊙y$ denote the decimal part of y. For example $⊙7.3 = .3$ and $⊙8 = 0$.
          x and y are positive numbers

$⊙x + ⊙y$	2

GO ON TO THE NEXT PAGE

706

Column A	Column B

14

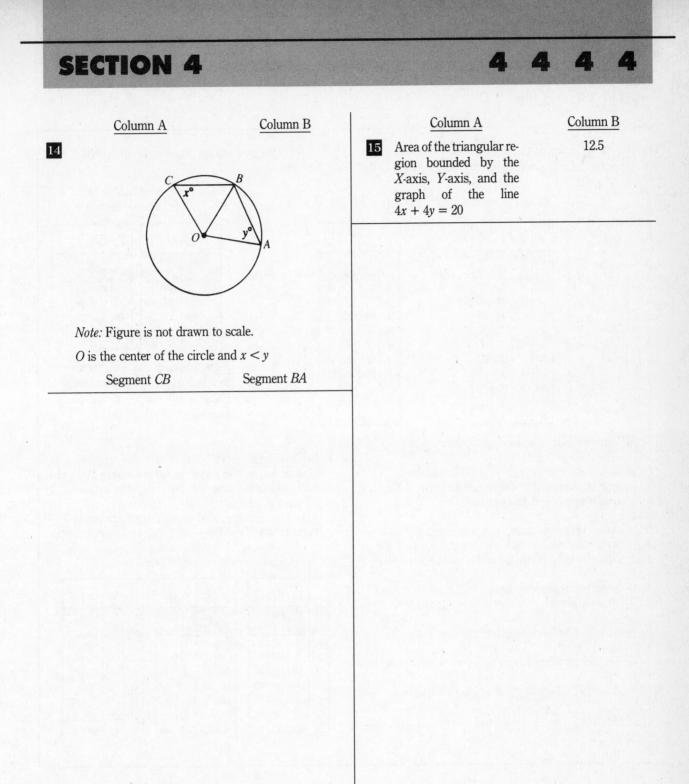

Note: Figure is not drawn to scale.

O is the center of the circle and $x < y$

Segment CB	Segment BA

Column A	Column B
15 Area of the triangular region bounded by the X-axis, Y-axis, and the graph of the line $4x + 4y = 20$	12.5

Directions: Each of the 10 questions in this part requires you to solve the problem and enter your answer by marking the ovals in the special grid, as shown in the examples below.

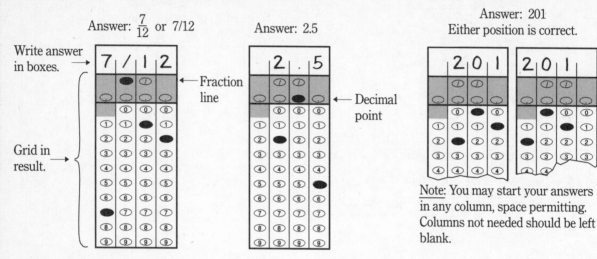

Answer: $\frac{7}{12}$ or 7/12

Answer: 2.5

Answer: 201
Either position is correct.

Write answer in boxes. → | Fraction line

Grid in result. →

← Decimal point

Note: You may start your answers in any column, space permitting. Columns not needed should be left blank.

- Mark no more than one oval in any column.

- Because the answer sheet will be machine-scored, **you will receive credit only if the ovals are filled in correctly.**

- Although not required, it is suggested that you write your answer in the boxes at the top of the columns to help you fill in the ovals accurately.

- Some problems may have more than one correct answer. In such cases, grid only one answer.

- No question has a negative answer.

- **Mixed numbers** such as $2\frac{1}{2}$ must be gridded as 2.5 or 5/2. (If ⬚ is gridded, it will be interpreted as $\frac{21}{2}$, not $2\frac{1}{2}$.)

- Decimal Accuracy: If you obtain a decimal answer, **enter the most accurate value the grid will accommodate.** For example, if you obtain an answer such as 0.6666 ..., you should record the result as .666 or .667. **Less accurate results such as .66 or .67 are not acceptable.**

Acceptable ways to grid $\frac{2}{3}$ = .6666 ...

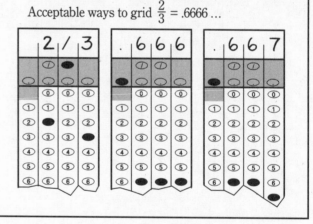

---

16 Susan has 3 times as many jellybeans as Mary, and Rose has 18 times as many jellybeans as Mary. What is the ratio

$$\frac{\text{Rose's jellybeans}}{\text{Susan's jellybeans}} ?$$

17 If two cubes have edges of 1 and 2, what is the sum of their volumes?

GO ON TO THE NEXT PAGE

18. If the numerical value of the binomial coefficient $\left(\dfrac{n}{2}\right)$ is given by the formula $\dfrac{n(n-1)}{2}$, then what is the numerical value of $\left(\dfrac{15}{2}\right)$?

19. The letters r and s represent numbers satisfying $r^2 = 9$ and $s^2 = 25$. What is the difference between the greatest possible values of $s - r$ and $r - s$?

20. According to the graph, what percent of the people in the group had brown eyes?

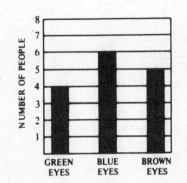

21. In the multiplication problem above, L, M, and N each represent one of the digits 0 through 9. If the problem is computed correctly, find N.

$$\begin{array}{r} N\,5 \\ \underline{L\,M} \\ 3\,8\,5 \\ 3\,8\,5 \\ \hline 4{,}2\,3\,5 \end{array}$$

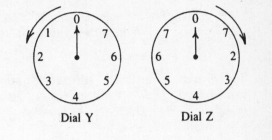

Dial Y   Dial Z

22. In the figure above, the hand of dial Z moves in a clockwise direction. When its hand makes one complete revolution, it causes the hand of dial Y to move 1 number in the counterclockwise direction. How many complete revolutions of the hand of dial Z are needed to move the hand of dial Y 3 complete revolutions?

23. To make enough paste to hang 6 rolls of wallpaper, a $\dfrac{1}{4}$-pound package of powder is mixed with $2\dfrac{1}{2}$ quarts of water. How many pounds of powder are needed to make enough of the same mixture of paste to hang 21 rolls of paper?

24. On a mathematics test, the average score for a certain class was 90. If 40 percent of the class scored 100 and 10 percent scored 80, what was the average score for the remainder of the class?

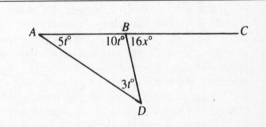

25. In the figure above, ABC is a line segment. What is the value of x?

IF YOU FINISH BEFORE TIME IS CALLED, YOU MAY CHECK YOUR WORK ON THIS SECTION ONLY. DO NOT TURN TO ANY OTHER SECTION IN THE TEST.

709

Time: 15 Minutes   For each question in this section, choose the best answer from among the choices given and fill
13 Questions   in the corresponding oval on the answer sheet.

The two passages that follow are followed by questions based on their content and on the relationship between the two passages. Answer the questions on the basis of what is *stated* or *implied* in the passages and in any introductory material that may be provided.

Questions 1–13 are based on the following passages.

The following two passages describe different time periods. Passage A discusses the medieval time period; Passage B describes the present and speculates on the future.

Passage A

To the world when it was half a thousand years younger, the outlines of all things seemed more clearly marked than to us. The contrast between suffering and joy, between adversity and happiness, appeared more striking. All experience had
5 yet to the minds of men the directness and absoluteness of the pleasure and pain of child-life. Every event, every action, was still embodied in expressive and solemn forms, which raised them to the dignity of a ritual.

Misfortunes and poverty were more afflicting than at
10 present; it was more difficult to guard against them, and to find solace. Illness and health presented a more striking contrast; the cold and darkness of winter were more real evils. Honors and riches were relished with greater avidity and contrasted more vividly with surrounding misery. We,
15 at the present day, can hardly understand the keenness with which a fur coat, a good fire on the hearth, a soft bed, a glass of wine, were formerly enjoyed.

Then, again, all things in life were of a proud or cruel publicity. Lepers sounded their rattles and went about in
20 processions, beggars exhibited their deformity and their misery in churches. Every order and estate, every rank and profession, was distinguished by its costume. The great lords never moved about without a glorious display of arms and liveries, exciting fear and envy. Executions and other
25 public acts of justice, hawking, marriages and funerals, were all announced by cries and processions, songs and music. The lover wore the colors of his lady; companions the emblem of their brotherhood; parties and servants the badges of their lords. Between town and country, too, the contrast
30 was very marked. A medieval town did not lose itself in extensive suburbs of factories and villas; girded by its walls, it stood forth as a compact whole, bristling with innumerable turrets. However tall and threatening the houses of noblemen or merchants might be, in the aspect of the town,
35 the lofty mass of the churches always remained dominant.

The contrast between silence and sound, darkness and light, like that between summer and winter, was more strongly marked than it is in our lives. The modern town hardly knows silence or darkness in their purity, nor the
40 effect of a solitary light or a single distant cry.

All things presenting themselves to the mind in violent contrasts and impressive forms lent a tone of excitement and passion to everyday life and tended to produce that perpetual oscillation between despair and distracted joy, between
45 cruelty and pious tenderness which characterize life in the Middle Ages.

Passage B

In 1575—over 400 years ago!—the French scholar Louis Le Roy published a learned book in which he voiced despair over the upheavals caused by the social and technological
50 innovations of his time, what we now call the Renaissance. "All is pell-mell, confounded, nothing goes as it should." We, also, feel that our times are out of joint; we even have reason to believe that our descendants will be worse off than we are.

The earth will soon be overcrowded and its resources
55 exhausted. Pollution will ruin the environment, upset the climate, damage human health. The gap in living standards between the rich and the poor will widen and lead the angry, hungry people of the world to acts of desperation including the use of nuclear weapons as blackmail. Such are the inevi-
60 table consequences of population and technological growth *if* present trends continue. But what a big *if* this is!

The future is never a projection of the past. Animals probably have no chance to escape from the tyranny of biological evolution, but human beings are blessed with the
65 freedom of social evolution. For us, trend is not destiny. The escape from existing trends is now facilitated by the fact that societies anticipate future dangers and take preventive steps against expected upheavals.

Despite the widespread belief that the world has be-
70 come too complex for comprehension by the human brain, modern societies have often responded effectively to critical situations.

The decrease in birth rates, the partial banning of pesticides, the rethinking of technologies for the production
75 and use of energy are but a few examples illustrating a sudden reversal of trends caused not by political upsets or scientific breakthroughs, but by public awareness of consequences.

GO ON TO THE NEXT PAGE

Even more striking are the situations in which social
80 attitudes concerning future difficulties undergo rapid
changes before the problems have come to pass—witness
the heated controversies about the ethics of behavior control
and of genetic engineering even though there is as yet no
proof that effective methods can be developed to manipulate
85 behavior and genes on a population scale.

One of the characteristics of our times is thus the
rapidity with which steps can be taken to change the orien-
tation of certain trends and even to reverse them. Such
changes usually emerge from grassroot movements rather
90 than from official directives.

1 Conditions like those described in Passage A would
most likely have occurred about

(A) A.D. 55
(B) A.D. 755
(C) A.D. 1055
(D) A.D. 1455
(E) A.D. 1755

2 The phrase "with greater avidity" in line 13 is best
interpreted to mean with greater

(A) desire
(B) sadness
(C) terror
(D) silence
(E) disappointment

3 In Passage A, all of the following are stated or
implied about towns in the Middle Ages *except*

(A) Towns had no suburbs.
(B) Towns were always quite noisy.
(C) Towns served as places of defense.
(D) Towns always had large churches.
(E) Merchants lived in the towns.

4 The author's main purpose in Passage A is to

(A) describe the miseries of the period
(B) show how life was centered on the town
(C) emphasize the violent course of life at the time
(D) point out how the upper classes mistreated the
lower classes
(E) indicate how religious people were in those
days

5 According to Passage A, people at that time, as
compared with people today, were

(A) worse off
(B) better off
(C) less intelligent
(D) more subdued
(E) more sensitive to certain events

6 In the first paragraph of Passage B, the mood expressed is one of

(A) blatant despair
(B) guarded optimism
(C) poignant nostalgia
(D) muted pessimism
(E) unbridled idealism

7 According to Passage B, if present trends continue,
which one of the following situations will *not* occur?

(A) New sources of energy from vast coal deposits
will be substituted for the soon-to-be-exhausted
resources of oil and natural gas.
(B) The rich will become richer and the poor will
become poorer.
(C) An overpopulated earth will be unable to sustain its inhabitants.
(D) Nuclear weapons will play a more prominent
role in dealings among peoples.
(E) The ravages of pollution will render the earth
and its atmosphere a menace to mankind.

8 Which of the following is the best illustration of the
meaning of "trend is not destiny" in line 65?

(A) Urban agglomerations are in a state of crisis.
(B) Human beings are blessed with the freedom of
social evolution.
(C) The world has become too complex for comprehension by the human brain.
(D) Critical processes can overshoot and cause
catastrophes.
(E) The earth will soon be overcrowded and its
resources exhausted.

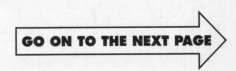

GO ON TO THE NEXT PAGE

9 According to Passage B, evidences of the insight of the public into the dangers that surround us can be found in all of the following *except*

    (A) an increase in the military budget by the president

    (B) a declining birth rate

    (C) picketing against expansion of nuclear plants

    (D) opposition to the use of pesticides

    (E) public meetings to complain about dumping chemicals

10 The author's attitude in Passage B is one of

    (A) willing resignation

    (B) definite optimism

    (C) thinly veiled cynicism

    (D) carefree abandon

    (E) angry impatience

11 If there is a continuity in history, which of the following situations in Passage A is thought to lead to violence in the future of Passage B?

    (A) the overcrowding of the population

    (B) the executions in public

    (C) the contrast between the social classes

    (D) the contrast between illness and health

    (E) the contrast between religion and politics

12 One can conclude from reading both passages that the difference between the people in Passage A and the people in Passage B is that

    (A) the people in Passage B act on their awareness in contrast to the people in Passage A.

    (B) the people in Passage B are more intense and colorful than the people in Passage A.

    (C) there was no controversy between sociology and science in the society in Passage B in contrast to the society mentioned in Passage A.

    (D) the people in Passage A are far more religious.

    (E) sociological changes were faster and more abrupt with the people of Passage A.

13 From a reading of both passages, one may conclude that

    (A) people in both passages are equally subservient to authority.

    (B) the future is a mirror to the past.

    (C) the topic of biological evolution is of great importance to the scientists of both periods.

    (D) the evolution of science has created great differences in the social classes.

    (E) the people in Passage A are more involved in everyday living, whereas the people in Passage B are usually seeking change.

IF YOU FINISH BEFORE TIME IS CALLED, YOU MAY CHECK YOUR WORK ON THIS SECTION ONLY. DO NOT TURN TO ANY OTHER SECTION IN THE TEST.

STOP

Time: 15 Minutes   In this section solve each problem, using any available space on the page for scratchwork.
10 Questions   Then decide which is the best of the choices given and fill in the corresponding oval on the answer sheet.

Notes:

1. The use of a calculator is permitted. All numbers used are real numbers.

2. Figures that accompany problems in this test are intended to provide information useful in solving the problems. They are drawn as accurately as possible EXCEPT when it is stated in a specific problem that the figure is not drawn to scale. All figures lie in a plane unless otherwise indicated.

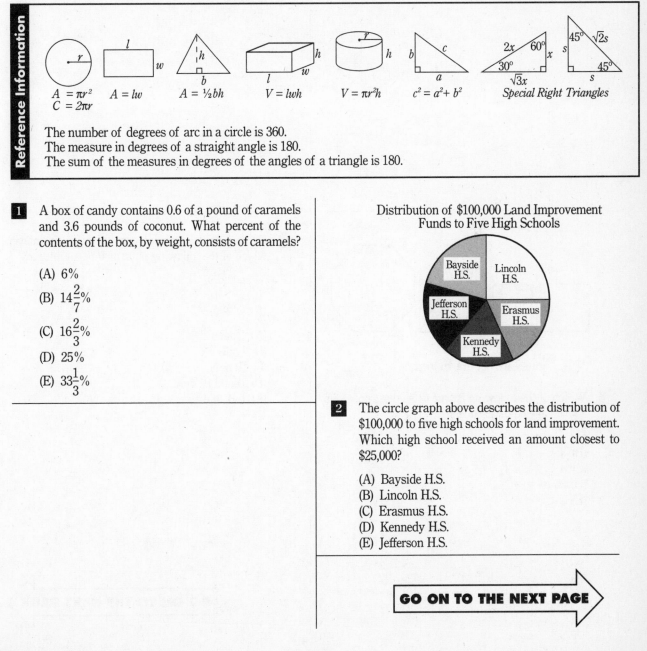

Reference Information

$A = \pi r^2$ $A = lw$ $A = \frac{1}{2}bh$ $V = lwh$ $V = \pi r^2 h$ $c^2 = a^2 + b^2$ *Special Right Triangles*
$C = 2\pi r$

The number of degrees of arc in a circle is 360.
The measure in degrees of a straight angle is 180.
The sum of the measures in degrees of the angles of a triangle is 180.

1   A box of candy contains 0.6 of a pound of caramels and 3.6 pounds of coconut. What percent of the contents of the box, by weight, consists of caramels?

(A) 6%

(B) $14\frac{2}{7}\%$

(C) $16\frac{2}{3}\%$

(D) 25%

(E) $33\frac{1}{3}\%$

Distribution of $100,000 Land Improvement
Funds to Five High Schools

Bayside H.S.   Lincoln H.S.   Jefferson H.S.   Erasmus H.S.   Kennedy H.S.

2   The circle graph above describes the distribution of $100,000 to five high schools for land improvement. Which high school received an amount closest to $25,000?

(A) Bayside H.S.
(B) Lincoln H.S.
(C) Erasmus H.S.
(D) Kennedy H.S.
(E) Jefferson H.S.

GO ON TO THE NEXT PAGE

3 If $y = r - 6$ and $z = r + 5$, which of the following is an expression representing r in terms of y and z?

(A) $\dfrac{y + z + 1}{2}$

(B) $\dfrac{y + z - 1}{2}$

(C) $y + z - 1$

(D) $y + z$

(E) $y + z + 1$

Town A   Town B   Town C

5 A car travels from Town A to Town B in 3 hours. It travels from Town B to Town C in 5 hours. If the distance AB is equal to the distance BC, what is the ratio of the car's average speed between A and B to its average speed for the whole distance AC?

(A) $5 : 3$

(B) $4 : 3$

(C) $1 : 1$

(D) $1 : 3$

(E) $1 : 5$

Note: Figures are not drawn to scale.

4 Which of the following is true if the three polygons above have equal perimeters?

(A) $b < a < c$

(B) $a < c < b$

(C) $a < b < c$

(D) $c < b < a$

(E) $c < a < b$

6 Given that ax is an integer and bx is an integer, which of the following must also be an integer?

  I. a and b

  II. x

  III. $(a + b)x$

(A) None

(B) I only

(C) III only

(D) II and III only

(E) I, II, and III

GO ON TO THE NEXT PAGE

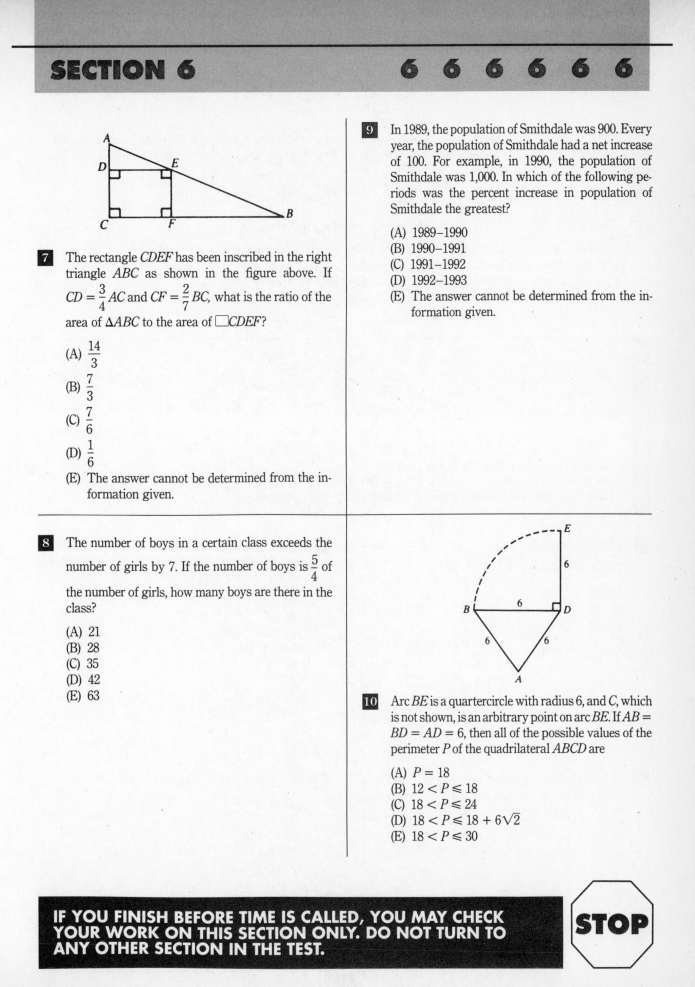

7 The rectangle *CDEF* has been inscribed in the right triangle *ABC* as shown in the figure above. If $CD = \frac{3}{4} AC$ and $CF = \frac{2}{7} BC$, what is the ratio of the area of $\triangle ABC$ to the area of $\square CDEF$?

(A) $\frac{14}{3}$

(B) $\frac{7}{3}$

(C) $\frac{7}{6}$

(D) $\frac{1}{6}$

(E) The answer cannot be determined from the information given.

8 The number of boys in a certain class exceeds the number of girls by 7. If the number of boys is $\frac{5}{4}$ of the number of girls, how many boys are there in the class?

(A) 21
(B) 28
(C) 35
(D) 42
(E) 63

9 In 1989, the population of Smithdale was 900. Every year, the population of Smithdale had a net increase of 100. For example, in 1990, the population of Smithdale was 1,000. In which of the following periods was the percent increase in population of Smithdale the greatest?

(A) 1989–1990
(B) 1990–1991
(C) 1991–1992
(D) 1992–1993
(E) The answer cannot be determined from the information given.

10 Arc *BE* is a quartercircle with radius 6, and *C*, which is not shown, is an arbitrary point on arc *BE*. If $AB = BD = AD = 6$, then all of the possible values of the perimeter *P* of the quadrilateral *ABCD* are

(A) $P = 18$
(B) $12 < P \leq 18$
(C) $18 < P \leq 24$
(D) $18 < P \leq 18 + 6\sqrt{2}$
(E) $18 < P \leq 30$

Time: 30 Minutes   In this section solve each problem, using any available space on the page for scratchwork.
25 Questions   Then decide which is the best of the choices given and fill in the corresponding oval on the answer sheet.

Notes:

1. The use of a calculator is permitted. All numbers used are real numbers.

2. Figures that accompany problems in this test are intended to provide information useful in solving the problems. They are drawn as accurately as possible EXCEPT when it is stated in a specific problem that the figure is not drawn to scale. All figures lie in a plane unless otherwise indicated.

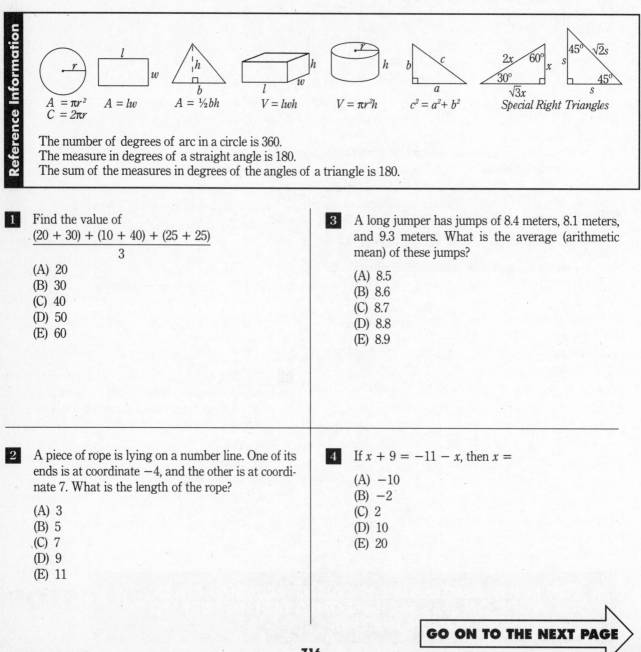

Reference Information

$A = \pi r^2$
$C = 2\pi r$

$A = lw$

$A = \frac{1}{2}bh$

$V = lwh$

$V = \pi r^2 h$

$c^2 = a^2 + b^2$

Special Right Triangles

The number of degrees of arc in a circle is 360.
The measure in degrees of a straight angle is 180.
The sum of the measures in degrees of the angles of a triangle is 180.

---

1 Find the value of

$$\frac{(20 + 30) + (10 + 40) + (25 + 25)}{3}$$

(A) 20
(B) 30
(C) 40
(D) 50
(E) 60

3 A long jumper has jumps of 8.4 meters, 8.1 meters, and 9.3 meters. What is the average (arithmetic mean) of these jumps?

(A) 8.5
(B) 8.6
(C) 8.7
(D) 8.8
(E) 8.9

2 A piece of rope is lying on a number line. One of its ends is at coordinate −4, and the other is at coordinate 7. What is the length of the rope?

(A) 3
(B) 5
(C) 7
(D) 9
(E) 11

4 If $x + 9 = -11 - x$, then $x =$

(A) −10
(B) −2
(C) 2
(D) 10
(E) 20

GO ON TO THE NEXT PAGE

5 If $3y = 12$ and $\dfrac{10}{x} = 5$, then

$$\frac{y + 11}{x + 15} =$$

(A) $\dfrac{7}{10}$

(B) $\dfrac{3}{4}$

(C) $\dfrac{15}{17}$

(D) 1

(E) $\dfrac{17}{15}$

7 If $(x + 6)^2 = 12x + 72$, then $x =$

(A) 0
(B) ± 1
(C) ± 3
(D) ± 6
(E) ± 12

6 Johnny deposited $50 in a savings bank at the beginning of the year. Johnny's money earns him interest at the rate of 8 percent of the amount deposited, for each year that Johnny leaves his money in the bank. If Johnny leaves his $50 in the bank for exactly one year and then decides to withdraw all of his money, how much money (including interest) can he withdraw? (The interest is not compounded.)

(A) $50.04
(B) $50.08
(C) $54.00
(D) $54.08
(E) $58.00

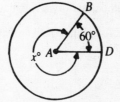

Note: Figure is not drawn to scale.

8 In the circle above, A is the center of the circle. Find the value of $x - 60$.

(A) 60
(B) 120
(C) 240
(D) 300
(E) 360

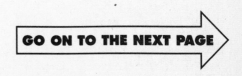

GO ON TO THE NEXT PAGE

9 To the nearest hundred, how many minutes are there in a week?

(A) 1,000
(B) 1,100
(C) 10,000
(D) 10,100
(E) 11,000

11 200 pieces of candy have been randomly put into five jars. The number of pieces of candy in three of the five jars is shown in the figure above. What is the maximum possible value of x? (x is the number of pieces of candy in the fourth jar.)

(A) 69
(B) 75
(C) 102
(D) 144
(E) 200

10 If ∇x is defined by the equation $\nabla x = \dfrac{x^3}{4}$ for real numbers x, which of the following equals 16?

(A) $\nabla 2$

(B) $\nabla 4$

(C) $\nabla 8$

(D) $\nabla 16$

(E) $\nabla 64$

12 There are 16 pages in a book. Last night, Ron read $\dfrac{1}{4}$ of the book. This morning, Ron read $\dfrac{1}{4}$ of the remaining pages. How many pages does Ron still have left to read?

(A) 7
(B) 8
(C) 9
(D) 10
(E) 11

GO ON TO THE NEXT PAGE

13 A sphere is inscribed in a cube whose volume is 64. What is the diameter of the sphere?

(A) 2
(B) $2\sqrt{2}$
(C) 8
(D) $4\sqrt{2}$
(E) 4

15 If $\dfrac{m}{n} = \dfrac{x}{m}$, then $x =$

(A) $\dfrac{m^2}{n}$
(B) $\dfrac{m}{n}$
(C) $\dfrac{n}{m^2}$
(D) $\dfrac{1}{n}$
(E) n

14 The ratio of girls to boys in a class is 8 : 7. The number of students in the class could be any of the following *except*

(A) 15
(B) 45
(C) 50
(D) 60
(E) 90

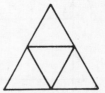

16 The above figure is an equilateral triangle divided into four congruent, smaller, equilateral triangles. If the perimeter of a smaller triangle is 1, then the perimeter of the whole large triangle is

(A) 2
(B) 4
(C) 6
(D) 8
(E) 16

GO ON TO THE NEXT PAGE

17 A different candle was lit at noon each day between December 9 and December 21, inclusive. How many candles were lit during this period?

(A) 10
(B) 11
(C) 12
(D) 13
(E) 14

19 The difference between the sum of two numbers and the difference of the two numbers is 6. Find the larger of the two numbers if their product is 15.

(A) 3
(B) 5
(C) 17
(D) 20
(E) 23

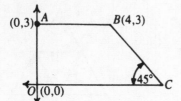

18 What is the area of quadrilateral *ABCO* in the figure above?

(A) 10.5
(B) 14.5
(C) 16.5
(D) 21.0
(E) The answer cannot be determined from the information given.

20 If $\dfrac{1}{a} + \dfrac{1}{b} = 10$, what is the value of $a + b$?

(A) $\dfrac{1}{10}$
(B) $\dfrac{2}{5}$
(C) 1
(D) 10
(E) The answer cannot be determined from the information given.

GO ON TO THE NEXT PAGE

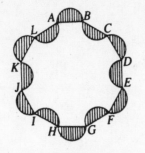

21 In the figure above, *ABCDEFGHIJKL* is a regular dodecagon (a regular twelve-sided polygon). The curved path is made up of 12 semicircles, each of whose diameters is a side of the dodecagon. If the perimeter of the dodecagon is 24, find the area of the shaded region.

(A) 6π

(B) 12π

(C) 24π

(D) 36π

(E) 48π

22 If $x > 0$ and $y > 0$ and $x^9 = 4$ and $x^7 = \dfrac{9}{y^2}$, which of the following is an expression for the value of x in terms of y?

(A) $\dfrac{4}{9}y$

(B) $\dfrac{2}{3}y$

(C) $\dfrac{3}{2}y^2$

(D) $6y$

(E) $36y^2$

23 Bobby had b marbles and Charlie had c marbles. After Bobby gave 6 marbles to Charlie, Bobby still had 18 more marbles than Charlie. Find $c - b$.

(A) 30

(B) 12

(C) 3

(D) -12

(E) -30

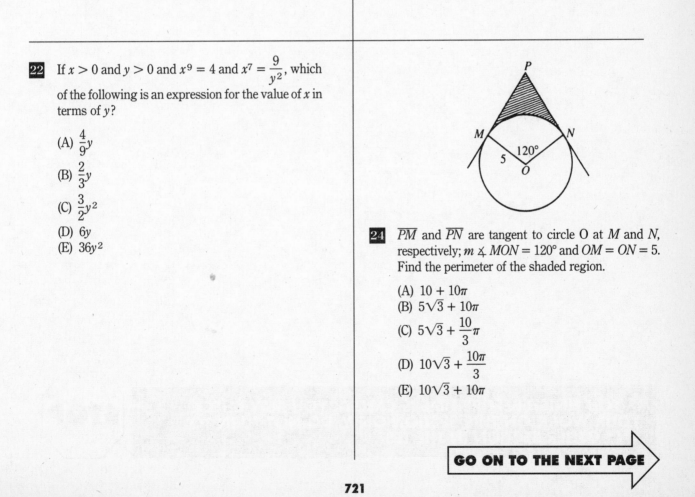

24 $\overline{PM}$ and $\overline{PN}$ are tangent to circle O at M and N, respectively; $m \angle MON = 120°$ and $OM = ON = 5$. Find the perimeter of the shaded region.

(A) $10 + 10\pi$

(B) $5\sqrt{3} + 10\pi$

(C) $5\sqrt{3} + \dfrac{10}{3}\pi$

(D) $10\sqrt{3} + \dfrac{10\pi}{3}$

(E) $10\sqrt{3} + 10\pi$

GO ON TO THE NEXT PAGE

25 When Stanley received $10x$ tapes, he then had $5y + 1$ times as many tapes as he had originally. In terms of x and y, how many tapes did Stanley have originally?

(A) $10x(5y + 1)$

(B) $\dfrac{5y + 1}{10x}$

(C) $\dfrac{2x}{y}$

(D) $\dfrac{10}{5y + 1}$

(E) None of the above

IF YOU FINISH BEFORE TIME IS CALLED, YOU MAY CHECK YOUR WORK ON THIS SECTION ONLY. DO NOT TURN TO ANY OTHER SECTION IN THE TEST.

STOP

How Did You Do on This Test?

Step 1. Go to the Answer Key on page 724.

Step 2. For your "raw score," calculate it using the directions on page 87.

Step 3. Get your "scaled score" for the test by referring to the Raw Score/Scaled Score Conversion Tables on page 90.

THERE'S ALWAYS ROOM FOR IMPROVEMENT!

Answer Key for Practice Test 3

Section 1—Verbal

1. C	8. A	15. E	22. A	29. A
2. A	9. D	16. D	23. E	30. D
3. E	10. E	17. A	24. D	
4. B	11. C	18. D	25. D	
5. D	12. A	19. B	26. A	
6. A	13. C	20. E	27. C	
7. A	14. B	21. C	28. B	

Section 2—Math

1. C	5. A	9. B	13. D	17. B	21. C	25. A
2. E	6. E	10. B	14. A	18. D	22. C	
3. C	7. D	11. C	15. C	19. B	23. B	
4. E	8. E	12. B	16. D	20. D	24. B	

Section 3—Verbal

1. B	7. D	13. A	19. D	25. D	31. D
2. C	8. E	14. A	20. B	26. E	32. A
3. B	9. A	15. A	21. E	27. A	33. C
4. C	10. E	16. D	22. C	28. C	34. B
5. E	11. E	17. C	23. E	29. B	35. C
6. B	12. E	18. D	24. B	30. B	

Section 4—Math

1. C	6. B	11. D	16. $6/1$, 6, or $12/2$, etc.	21. 5
2. C	7. C	12. C	17. 9	22. 24
3. D	8. B	13. B	18. 105	23. $7/8$ or .875
4. D	9. D	14. A	19. 0	24. 84
5. D	10. A	15. C	20. 33.3	25. 5

Section 5—Verbal

1. D	5. E	9. A	13. E
2. A	6. D	10. B	
3. B	7. A	11. C	
4. C	8. B	12. A	

Section 6—Math

1. B   6. C
2. B   7. B
3. A   8. C
4. E   9. A
5. B   10. D

Section 7—Math

1. D   6. C   11. B   16. A   21. A
2. E   7. D   12. C   17. D   22. B
3. B   8. C   13. E   18. C   23. E
4. A   9. D   14. C   19. B   24. D
5. C   10. B   15. A   20. E   25. C

Explanatory Answers for Practice Test 3

Section 1: Verbal Ability

As you read these Explanatory Answers, refer to "Using Critical Thinking Skills in Verbal Questions" (beginning on page 236), whenever a specific Strategy is referred to in the answer. Of particular importance are the following Master Verbal Strategies:

Sentence Completion Master Strategy 1—page 245.
Sentence Completion Master Strategy 2—page 246.
Analogies Master Strategy 1—page 236.
Reading Comprehension Master Strategy 2—page 263.

1. Choice C is correct. See **Sentence Completion Strategy 4.** Since the general "was like two sides of a coin," we have an opposition indicator to guide us. It is not ordinary for a man who is fair to be a man of severity. Nor is it ordinary for a man who is outgoing to be a man of few words.

2. Choice A is correct. See **Sentence Completion Strategy 2.**

   STEP 1 [ELIMINATION]
   We have eliminated Choices B and E because "agitation" and "intellect" do not make sense in the first blank.
   STEP 2 [REMAINING CHOICES]
   This leaves us with the remaining choices to be considered. The sentence *does not* make sense with the second word "minimal" of Choice C and the second word "whimsical" of Choice D. The sentence *does* make sense with the words "skill" and "astute" (meaning "cunning") of Choice A.

3. Choice E is correct. See **Sentence Completion Strategy 4.** "Internal dissension" is likely to have a negative effect on "affirmative action." We, accordingly, have an opposition indicator. Therefore, we eliminate Choice (A) encourage, Choice (C) induce, and Choice (D) apply. This leaves us with Choice (B) complicate and Choice (E) delay. Choice (B) complicate ... agreement *does not* make sense. Choice (E) delay ... upheaval *does* make sense.

4. Choice B is correct. See **Sentence Completion Strategy 2.** We can first eliminate Choice (A) suspicion ... and Choice (D) sacrifice ... because these first blank words do not make sense in the sentence. This leaves us with Choice (B) disagreement, Choice (C) discussion, and Choice (E) research. However, Choice (C) discussion ... incidentally and Choice (E) research ... irrelevantly *do not* make sense. Choice (B) disagreement ... overwhelmingly *does* make sense.

5. Choice D is correct. See **Sentence Completion Strategies 3 and 4.** The key words "rather than" tell us that a word *opposite* to "severity" is needed to fill the blank space. If you used the strategy of trying to complete the sentence *before* looking at the five choices, you might have chosen for your blank fill-in one of these appropriate words: easy, friendly, diplomatic, pleasing, soothing. Each of these words has a meaning much like that of the word "conciliatory." The words of the other four choices are *not* appropriate in the sentence. Therefore, these choices are incorrect.

6. Choice A is correct. See **Sentence Completion Strategy 1.** Try each choice. He would be able to be impartial, or unbiased, only as a result of not being emotionally attached to either acquaintance; he would not necessarily be able to be accurate (Choice B) or judicious (Choice E).

7. Choice A is correct. See **Sentence Completion Strategy 4.** This sentence calls for two words of contrasting nature, as shown by the words "even though." The only pair that has this contrast in meaning is Choice A.

8. Choice A is correct. The word "passive" means submissive, not participating, accepting without objection. See **Sentence Completion Strategy 1.** A person who loves action certainly cannot tolerate a passive life style. Choice B, C, D, and E are incorrect because an action-loving person may, indeed, tolerate a chaotic or brazen or grandiose or vibrant life style.

9. Choice D is correct. The word "degradation" means deterioration, a lowering of position. The sight of a person in such a state would generally bring about a feeling of pity. Choices A, B, C, and E do *not* make good sense in the sentence. Therefore, these choices are incorrect. See **Sentence Completion Strategy 1.**

10. Choice E is correct. Someone who clips hair from someone else's head or hews a bough from a tree is severing or separating a part from the whole in each case. This is an ACTION to OBJECT relationship. Choices A, B, C, and D are also action to object relationships, but they do not involve a part from the whole separation. Accordingly, these four choices are incorrect. See **Analogy Strategy 4.**

(Action to Object relationship)

11. Choice C is the answer. A client seeks the services of an attorney. A patient seeks the services of a doctor.

(Person-to-Person Association relationship)

12. Choice A is correct. One cancels (stops) a subscription, and one nullifies (stops) a contract.

(Action to Object relationship)

13. Choice C is correct. The hub is the central part of a wheel. The bullseye is the central part of a target.

(Part-Whole and Place relationship)

14. Choice B is correct. The genealogy of a family is the study of its history and origin. The etymology of a word is the study of its history and origin.

(Action-Object and Association relationship)

Note: If you don't know the meaning of a word, you can use **Analogy Strategy 6**, The Context Method for Unfamiliar Words. "Logy" means "the study of,"

so "genealogy" must mean the study of something. Since the word is linked to "family" is must mean the study of the family. The only choice that fits is B. *Etymology* is the study of *words*.

15. Choice E is correct. Someone who is crass lacks refinement. Someone who is craven lacks bravery. We have here an opposite relationship. Note Choice (A) frivolous : continuity. Someone who is frivolous does lack the ability to finish a job. However, we would not say that such a person lacks continuity. Therefore, Choice A is incorrect. See **Analogy Strategy 4.**

(Opposite relationship)

16. Choice D is correct. See lines 16–17: "The cry for freedom . . . the birth of the New Man." Choice A is incorrect. Although the author may agree to what the choice says, he does not actually state or imply such. Choice B is incorrect because nowhere in the passage is Choice B stated or implied. Choice C is incorrect. See lines 25—27: "African-American literature rejects the despair and cynicism; it is a literature of realistic hope and life-affirmation." Choice E is incorrect. See lines 36–37: ". . . life should not be a sedate waltz or foxtrot . . ."

17. Choice A is correct. See lines 32–36: ". . . life should be vivacious, exuberant, wholesomely uninhibited . . . and man should be loving." Choice B is incorrect because nowhere does the passage indicate that Choice B is true. Choice C is incorrect. Although lines 35–36 state that "life should be passionately lived and man should be loving," these lines do not mean that people should demonstrate their passions in public whenever the urge is there. Choice D is incorrect. Nowhere does the passage recommend Choice D. Choice E is incorrect. Although lines 6–11 state "In African-American literature . . . the rage of the oppressed," the passage does not state or imply that the ancestors of those who have been oppressed should be enraged.

18. Choice D is correct. Let us consider each item. Item I is incorrect because the passage nowhere expresses the need for *nonviolent* opposition to racism. Item II is correct. See lines 42–46: "Black literature in America [African-American literature] is . . . finding deep joy in humanity." Item III is correct. See lines 31–36: "African-American literature is a statement . . . and man should be loving." Accordingly, only Choices II and III are correct. Therefore, Choice D is correct, and Choices A, B, C, and E are incorrect.

19. Choice B is correct. See lines 23–27: "Like the spirituals . . . realistic hope and life-affirmation." Choice A is incorrect. See lines 6–15: "In African-American

literature ... the burden of protest." Although an indication of anger is present in the passage, it is not dominant. Moreover, nowhere in the passage is there evidence of vindictiveness. Choice C is incorrect because forgiveness and charity are not referred to in the passage. Choice D is incorrect. See lines 23–30: "Like the spirituals ... goodness will prevail." Choice E is incorrect. Although the passage refers to *grief* in line 14 and also *cruelty* in line 38, grief and cruelty do not represent the tone of the passage.

20. Choice E is correct. See lines 20–23: "... for a human world."

21. Choice C is correct. It can be seen from the context of the sentence that the word "iniquity" must mean something bad (the word is preceded by "investigation" and is in contrast to "an investigation ... potential godliness," which appears in the same sentence).

22. Choice A is correct. See lines 71–72: "... as Dr. Skinner argues, that one can extrapolate from pigeons to people ..." Choice B is incorrect because, though Skinner agrees that introspection may be of some use (lines 14–18), nowhere does the article indicate that he suggests wide use of the introspective method. Choice C is incorrect since Skinner, so the author says (lines 74–76), "has not satisfactorily rebutted ... rather than scientific." Choice D is incorrect because lines 81–82 state that "... Skinner predicts ... impending disaster." Choice E is incorrect because there is nothing in the passage to indicate this statement. Incidentally, this point of view (Choice E) is held by Noam Chomsky of linguistics fame.

23. Choice A is incorrect. See lines 83–89 to the end of the passage: "Two key concepts ... not so reassuring." Choice B is incorrect. See lines 11–14: "... an earlier stage of ... influence of mentalism." Choice C is incorrect. See lines 60–64: "It is a veritable ... to external stimuli." Choice D is incorrect since mentalism evolved before methodological and radical behaviorism. See lines 10—17: "What such people ... its possible usefulness." Choice E is correct. The passage, from line 63 to the end, brings out weaknesses in Skinner's presentation.

24. Choice D is correct. Skinner, in lines 26–27, says "... few would contend that behavior is 'endlessly malleable.'" Also, see lines 35–42: "Contingencies of reinforcement ... likely to occur." In effect, Skinner is saying that behavior cannot always, by plan or design, be altered or influenced; behavior must depend, to some extent, on the element of chance.

25. Choice D is correct. Skinner is known for his experiments with pigeons. Also, rats have been used frequently by behaviorists in experimentation. See lines 65–73. In addition, see lines 37–38: "In both natural ... is crucial." The other choices are not relevant to Darwin or his work.

26. Choice A is correct. From the context in the rest of the sentence where "extrapolate" appears, choice A fits best. Note, the word "extrapolate" is derived from the Latin "extra" (outside) and "polire" (to polish).

27. Choice A is incorrect because Choice A is true according to lines 14–15. Choice B is incorrect because Choice B is true according to lines 65–70. Choice C is correct because Choice C is *not* true according to lines 68–72. Choice D is incorrect because Choice D is true according to lines 10–18. Choice E is incorrect because Choice E is true according to lines 57–61.

28. Choice A is incorrect. See lines 19–22: "... to those who object ... Skinner expresses puzzlement." Choice B is correct because Skinner, a radical behaviorist, though believing that environmental influences are highly important in shaping human behavior, nevertheless states in lines 35–38: "Contingencies of reinforcement ... is crucial." Operant conditioning is, according to behaviorists, a vital aspect of learning. Choice C is incorrect. Although Skinner accepts introspection (lines 16–18) as part of his system, nowhere does he place primary importance on introspection. Choice D is incorrect. Though Skinner may agree with this choice, nowhere in the passage does he state or imply this opinion. Choice E is incorrect. The word "malleable" means capable of being shaped or formed—from the Latin "malleare," meaning "to hammer." The quote in the stem of the question says, in effect, that few people would say that behavior can always be shaped.

29. Choice A is correct. I is correct; see the eighth paragraph, last sentence. II is incorrect; don't be fooled by what is in the third sentence of the eighth paragraph. It does not refer to *scientistic* areas. III is incorrect; see the third sentence in the eighth paragraph.

30. Choice D is correct. Given the context of the sentence and the sentences preceding and succeeding it, "veritable" means "true." One may also note the "ver" in "veritable" and may associate that with the word "verify," which also means true. This is the association strategy, which can be used to figure out clues to meanings of words.

Explanatory Answers for Practice Test 3 (continued)

Section 2: Math Ability

As you read these solutions, do two things if you answered the Math question incorrectly:

1. When a specific Strategy is referred to in the solution, study that strategy, which you will find in "Using Critical Thinking Skills in Math Questions" (beginning on page 174).

2. When the solution directs you to the "Math Refresher" (beginning on page 291)—for example, Math Refresher #305—study the 305 Math principle to get a clear idea of the Math operation that was necessary for you to know in order to answer the question correctly.

1. Choice C is correct. **(Use Strategy 2: Translate from words to algebra.)** Let n = the number. We are told

$$\frac{n}{3} = n \qquad \boxed{1}$$

Subtracting $\frac{n}{3}$ from both sides of $\boxed{1}$,

$$n - \frac{n}{3} = 0 \qquad \boxed{2}$$

Multiplying $\boxed{2}$ by 3 we get

$$3\left(n - \frac{n}{3}\right) = 0$$
$$3n - n = 0$$
$$2n = 0$$
$$n = 0$$

(Math Refresher #200 and #406)

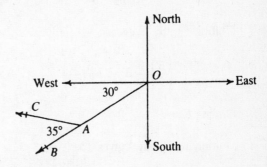

2. Choice E is correct.

Originally, the man is facing in the direction of OA.

After he turns, he is facing in the direction of $\overrightarrow{AC}$, where $m \measuredangle CAB = 35$. We want to find out the direction of $\overrightarrow{AC}$ with respect to the North–South–East–West axes. In other words, when we redraw the above diagram with $\overleftrightarrow{l} \parallel W\text{-}E$ axis, and $\overleftrightarrow{m} \parallel N\text{-}S$ axis, then $\overrightarrow{AC}$ is $x°$ north of west. $\boxed{1}$

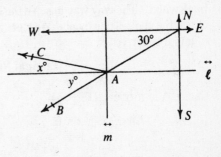

730 • **FOUR MORE PRACTICE SCHOLASTIC ASSESSMENT TESTS**

Since $m \measuredangle CAB = 35$, then

$$x + y = 35 \qquad \boxed{2}$$

Since $\overleftrightarrow{l} \parallel W\text{-}E$ axis, then

$$y = 30° \qquad \boxed{3}$$

Subtracting $\boxed{3}$ from $\boxed{2}$,

$$x = 5° \qquad \boxed{4}$$

Thus, using $\boxed{4}$ and $\boxed{1}$, $\overrightarrow{AC}$ is 5° north of west.

(Math Refresher #504 and #501)

3. Choice C is correct.

$$\text{Short Method: Given } \frac{9}{5}K = 18 \qquad \boxed{1}$$

(Use Strategy 13: Find unknowns by division.)

Dividing $\boxed{1}$ by 9, we have

$$\left(\frac{1}{\cancel{9}}\right)\frac{\cancel{9}}{5}K = \cancel{18}^{\,2}\left(\frac{1}{\cancel{9}}\right)$$

$$\frac{1}{5}K = 2 \text{ (Answer)}$$

Long Method: Given $\frac{9}{5}K = 18 \qquad \boxed{1}$

Multiply $\boxed{1}$ by $\frac{5}{9}$, getting

$$\left(\frac{\cancel{5}}{\cancel{9}}\right)\frac{\cancel{9}}{\cancel{5}}K = \cancel{18}^{\,2}\left(\frac{5}{\cancel{9}}\right)$$

Finding $K = 10 \qquad \boxed{2}$

Multiplying $\boxed{2}$ by $\frac{1}{5}$ gives

$$\frac{1}{5}K = \cancel{10}^{\,2}\left(\frac{1}{\cancel{5}}\right)$$

$$\frac{1}{5}K = 2 \text{ (Answer)}$$

(Math Refresher #406)

4. Choice E is correct. **(Use Strategy 8: When all choices must be tested, start with E and work backward.)** The only way to solve this question is to test the choices one by one. We start with Choice E, and it is correct.

(Logical Reasoning)

5. Choice A is correct.

$$\text{Given: } x, y, z < 0 \qquad \boxed{1}$$
$$x < y \qquad \boxed{2}$$
$$y < z \qquad \boxed{3}$$

(Use Strategy 6: Know how to manipulate inequalities.)

Method 1: When you multiply an inequality by a negative number, you must reverse the inequality. For example, multiplying $\boxed{2}$ and $\boxed{3}$ by x, we get

$$x^2 > xy \qquad \boxed{4}$$
$$xy > xz \qquad \boxed{5}$$

multiplying $\boxed{2}$ and $\boxed{3}$ by z, we get

$$xz > yz \qquad \boxed{6}$$
$$yz > z^2 \qquad \boxed{7}$$

Comparing $\boxed{4}$, $\boxed{5}$, $\boxed{6}$, and $\boxed{7}$, we have

$$x^2 > xy > xz > yz > z^2$$

Thus, Choice A is correct.

(Use Strategy 7: Use numerics to help.)

Method 2: Choose specific numeric values for x, y, z satisfying $\boxed{1}$, $\boxed{2}$, and $\boxed{3}$.

For example, let $x = -3, y = -2, z = -1$
The choices become

(A) 1
(B) 2
(C) 3
(D) 6
(E) 9

Choice A is correct.

(Math Refresher #419, #423, and #431)

6. Choice E is the correct answer. **Use Strategy 11: Use new definitions carefully. These problems are generally easy.)** The first few terms of the sequence are found as follows:

Given: Term 1 = 2

$$\begin{aligned} \text{By definition, Term 2} &= (\text{Term 1} - 2)3 \\ &= (2 - 2)3 \\ &= (0)3 \\ \text{Term 2} &= 0 \\ \text{Term 3} &= (\text{Term 2} - 2)3 \\ &= (0 - 2)3 \\ &= (-2)3 \\ &= -6 \\ \text{Term 4} &= (\text{Term 3} - 2)3 \\ &= (-6 - 2)3 \\ &= (-8)3 \\ &= -24 \end{aligned}$$

and so on.

2, 0, −6, −24 are all even, so Choices A, B, C, and D can be eliminated.

(Math Refresher #431)

7. Choice D is correct. **(Use Strategy 17: Use the given information effectively.)**
    Given:

    $$7a = 4 \qquad \boxed{1}$$
    $$7a + 4b = 12 \qquad \boxed{2}$$

    Substituting $\boxed{1}$ into $\boxed{2}$,

    $$4 + 4b = 12$$
    or $\qquad 4b = 8$
    or $\qquad b = 2$

    (Math Refresher #460)

8. Choice E is correct.

    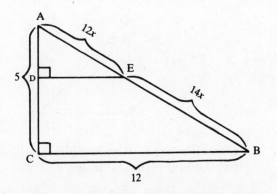

    Method 1: **(Use Strategy 18: Remember right triangle facts.)** Triangle B C A is a right triangle, so we can use the Pythagorean Theorem:

    $$(AB)^2 = (AC)^2 + (BC)^2$$
    $$(12x + 14x)^2 = 5^2 + 12^2$$
    $$(26x)^2 = 25 + 144$$
    $$676x^2 = 169$$

    $$x^2 = \frac{169}{676}$$

    (Use Strategy 19: Factor and reduce.)

    $$x^2 = \frac{13 \times 13}{13 \times 13 \times 4} = \frac{1}{4}$$

    $$x = \frac{1}{2}$$

    Method 2: **(Use Strategy 18: Remember special right triangles.)** Triangle B C A is a right triangle with legs 5 and 12. 5, 12, 13 is a special right triangle. Thus, AB must = 13

    Therefore $12x + 14x = 13$
    $$26x = 13$$

    $$x = \frac{13}{26}$$

    $$x = \frac{1}{2}$$

    (Math Refresher #509 and #406)

9. Choice B is correct. **(Use Strategy 6: Know how to manipulate inequalities.)**

    Multiply string of inequalities

    $-\dfrac{1}{2} < \dfrac{x}{3} < -\dfrac{1}{4}$, by 3 to get x alone:

    $$3\left[-\frac{1}{2} < \frac{x}{3} < -\frac{1}{4} \right] =$$

    $$-\frac{3}{2} < x < -\frac{3}{4} \qquad \boxed{1}$$

    Only one integer, $x = -1$, will satisfy $\boxed{1}$

10. Choice B is correct. **(Use Strategy 17: Use the given information effectively.)** By looking at the diagram, we have

    $$P_1 = -2$$
    $$P_2 = -1$$

    We can approximate the other numbers by looking at their positions on the number line:

    $$P_3 \approx \frac{1}{3}$$

    $$P_4 \approx \frac{2}{3}$$

    $$P_5 \approx \frac{3}{2}$$

    Thus,

    $$P_1 P_2 P_3 P_4 P_5 \approx (-2)(-1)\left(\frac{1}{3}\right)\left(\frac{2}{3}\right)\left(\frac{3}{2}\right)$$

    $$P_1 P_2 P_3 P_4 P_5 \approx \frac{2}{3}$$

    (Math Refresher #410)

11. Choice C is correct. **(Use Strategy 2: Translate from words to algebra.)** Let the 3 consecutive even integers be

    $$x, x + 2, x + 4 \qquad \boxed{1}$$

    where x is even. We are told that
    $$x + x + 2 + x + 4 = K$$
    or $\qquad 3x + 6 = K \qquad \boxed{2}$

From $\boxed{1}$, we know that

$$x - 5, x - 3, x - 1$$

must be the 3 consecutive odd integers immediately preceding x. We are told that

$$x - 5 + x - 3 + x - 1 = y$$
$$\text{or} \qquad 3x - 9 = y \qquad \boxed{3}$$

(Use Strategy 13: Find unknown expressions by subtraction.) Subtracting $\boxed{3}$ from $\boxed{2}$,

$$15 = K - y$$
$$\text{or} \quad y = K - 15$$

(Math Refresher #200 and #406)

12. Choice B is correct. **(Use Strategy 2: Translate from words to math.)** From the diagram we can see that 25% is water, so 0.25×2 lb. $= \frac{1}{2}$ lb. is water.

(Math Refresher #705)

13. Choice D is correct.

Method 1: By inspection, Choice D is the sum of two negatives which must be negative.

Method 2: **(Use Strategy 7: Try numerics to help find the answer.)**

Let $r = -1, s = -2$

(Use Strategy 8: When all choices must be tested, start with E and work backward.)

Choice E is $-r - s = -(-1) - (-2)$
$$= 1 + 2$$
$$= 3$$

Choice D is $r + s = -1 + (-2) = -3$
Thus D is negative and the answer.

(Math Refresher #431)

14. Choice A is correct. **(Use Strategy 17: Use the given information effectively.)** A segment that divides the area of a circle into two equal parts must be a diameter. Thus, segment RS must go through point O.

Since ROS is a diameter, then $RO = OS$, each segment being a radius.

Since R is the 2nd quadrant, S must be in the 4th quadrant.

The coordinates of S must each be the negative of the coordinates of R.

Thus, $S = (-1(-6), -1(8))$
$$S = (6, -8)$$

(Math Refresher #524 and #410)

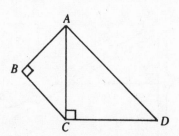

	First Place (6 points)	Second place (4 points)	Third Place (2 points)
Game 1			
Game 2		Bob	
Game 3			Bob

15. Choice C is correct.

(Use Strategy 17: Use the given information effectively.) Carl can attain the *minimum* possible score by placing third in Game 1 and Game 2 and second in Game 3.

From the chart he would have 2, 2, and 4 points for each of these finishes.
Thus, minimum score $= 2 + 2 + 4$
minimum score $= 8$ points

(Logical Reasoning)

16. Choice D is correct. **(Use Strategy 18: Remember the isosceles right triangle.)**

$$\text{Given: } AB = BC \qquad \boxed{1}$$
$$AC = CD \qquad \boxed{2}$$

From $\boxed{1}$ we get that $\triangle ABC$ is an isosceles right triangle. Therefore, $\angle BAC$ and $\angle BCA$ are each 45-degree angles.

From $\boxed{2}$ we get that $\triangle ACD$ is an isosceles right triangle. Therefore, $\angle CAD$ and $\angle CDA$ are each 45-degree angles.

Thus, there are four 45-degree angles.

(Math Refresher #505 and #509)

17. Choice B is correct. **(Use Strategy 2: Translate from words to algebra.)**

We know that:

$$\text{Area of rectangle} = \text{length} \times \text{width} \qquad \boxed{1}$$
$$\text{We are given: Area} = 4 \qquad \boxed{2}$$
$$\text{length} = \frac{4}{3} \qquad \boxed{3}$$

Substituting $\boxed{2}$ and $\boxed{3}$ into $\boxed{1}$, we get

$$4 = \frac{4}{3} \times \text{width} \qquad \boxed{4}$$

(Use Strategy 13: Find unknowns by multiplication.)

Multiply $\boxed{4}$ by $\frac{3}{4}$. We get

$$\frac{3}{4}\,(\cancel{4}) = \frac{\cancel{3}}{\cancel{4}}\left(\frac{\cancel{4}}{\cancel{3}} \times \text{width}\right)$$

$$3 = \text{width}$$

(Math Refresher #304 and #406)

18. Choice D is correct.

    Since vertical angles are equal, then

    $$m \angle AOC = m \angle DOB = 108 \qquad \boxed{1}$$

    Thus, from $\boxed{1}$, we get length of

    minor $\overset{\frown}{AC}$ = length of minor $\overset{\frown}{DB}$ $\qquad \boxed{2}$

    From geometry we know

    length of minor $\overset{\frown}{AC} = \dfrac{108}{360} \times$ circumference of circle

    $$= \frac{108}{360} \times \pi(\text{diameter})$$

    $$= \frac{108}{360} \times \pi(20)$$

    (Use Strategy 19: Factor and reduce.)

    length of minor $\overset{\frown}{AC} = \dfrac{\cancel{18} \times 6}{\cancel{18} \times \cancel{20}} \times \pi(\cancel{20})$

    length of minor $\overset{\frown}{AC} = 6\pi$ $\qquad \boxed{3}$

    Length $\overset{\frown}{AC}$ + Length $\overset{\frown}{DB}$ can be found using $\boxed{2}$ and $\boxed{3}$

    Length $\overset{\frown}{AC}$ + Length $\overset{\frown}{DB} = 6\pi + 6\pi$

    Length $\overset{\frown}{AC}$ + Length $\overset{\frown}{DB} = 12\pi$

    (Math Refresher #503 and #310)

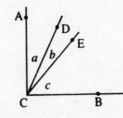

19. Choice B is correct.

    Label angles as above with a, b, c.

    You are given that

$$a + b + c = 90 \qquad \boxed{1}$$
$$b + c = 62 \qquad \boxed{3}$$
$$a + b = 37 \qquad \boxed{3}$$

You want to find $\angle DCE = b$

(Use Strategy 13: Find unknown expressions by adding or subtracting.)

First add $\boxed{2}$ and $\boxed{3}$:
We get:

$$a + 2b + c = 62 + 37 = 99 \qquad \boxed{4}$$

Now subtract $\boxed{1}$ from $\boxed{4}$:

$$\begin{array}{r} a + 2b + c = 99 \\ \underline{a + b + c = 90} \\ b = 9 \end{array}$$

(Math Refresher #509 and Angle Addition)

20. Choice D is correct.

    (Use Strategy 17: Use the given information effectively.)

    $$2 \times 10^{-5} \times 8 \times 10^2 \times 5 \times 10^2$$
    $$= 2 \times 8 \times 5 \times 10^{-5} \times 10^2 \times 10^2$$
    $$= 8 \times 10^0$$
    $$= 8 \times 1$$
    $$= 8$$

    (Math Refresher #429)

21. Choice C is correct.

    (Use Strategy 2: Remember how to calculate percent.)

    Winning percentage $= \dfrac{\text{\# of games won}}{\text{Total \# of games played}} \times 100$

    For example,

    Winning % for pitcher A

    $$= \frac{4}{4 + 2} \times 100 = \frac{4}{6} \times 100$$

    $$= \frac{\cancel{2} \times 2}{\cancel{2} \times 3} \times 100$$

    $$= \frac{200}{3} = 66\frac{2}{3}\%$$

    For each pitcher, we have

Pitcher	Winning Percentage
A	$66\frac{2}{3}\%$
B	60%
C	80%
D	50%
E	75%

Pitcher C has the highest winning percentage.

(Math Refresher #106)

22. Choice C is correct.

(Use Strategy 2: Translate from words to algebra.)

$$\text{Allowance} = \$30$$

$$\text{Amount spent on candy} = \frac{2}{5} \times \$30 = \$12$$

Amount left after
Johnny bought candy $= \$30 - \$12 = \$18$

$$\text{Amount spent on ice cream} = \frac{5}{6} \times \$18 = \$15$$

Amount left after buying
candy and ice cream $= \$18 - \$15$
$$= \$3$$

(Math Refresher #200)

23. Choice B is correct.

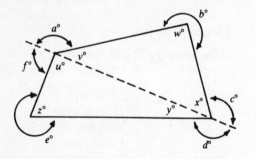

With the diagram labeled as above, we want to find

$$a + b + c + d + e + f \qquad \boxed{1}$$

(Use Strategy 3: The whole equals the sum of its parts.) Looking at the diagram, we see

$$a + f + u + v = 360$$
$$b + w = 360 \qquad \boxed{3}$$
$$c + d + x + y = 360 \qquad \boxed{4}$$
$$e + z = 360 \qquad \boxed{5}$$

(Use Strategy 13: Find unknown quantities by addition.) Adding equations $\boxed{2}$ through $\boxed{5}$,

$$a + b + c + d + e + f$$
$$+ u + v + w + x + y + z$$
$$= 1440 \qquad \boxed{6}$$

Since the sum of the measures of the angles of a triangle is 180, then

$$v + w + x = 180 \qquad \boxed{7}$$

$$u + y + z = 180 \qquad \boxed{8}$$

Substituting $\boxed{7}$ and $\boxed{8}$ into $\boxed{6}$

$$a + b + c + d + e + f + 180 + 180 = 1440$$
$$\text{or } a + b + c + d + e + f = 1080$$

(Math Refresher #526, #505, and #406)

24. Choice B is correct. **(Use Strategy 11: Use new definitions carefully.)**

Given: $\quad$ A, B, C, ..., L = $\qquad \boxed{1}$
1, 2, 3, ... 12 (respectively)

The time on the watch is 15 minutes before 1. $\boxed{2}$

From $\boxed{1}$, we know that

$$E = 5 \text{ and } A = 1 \qquad \boxed{3}$$

Substituting $\boxed{3}$ into $\boxed{2}$, we have

3E minutes before A.

(Math Refresher #431)

25. Choice A is correct.

$$\text{Volume of cube} = (\text{side})^3$$

Thus, Volume of each small cube $= r^3 \qquad \boxed{1}$
Volume of larger cube $= s^3 \qquad \boxed{2}$

and Sum of the volumes of the
27 cubes $= 27r^3 \qquad \boxed{3}$

(Use Strategy 3: The whole equals the sum of its parts.) We are told that the sum of the Volumes of the 27 cubes = the Volume of the larger cube

$$= 81 \qquad \boxed{4}$$

From $\boxed{2}$, $\boxed{3}$, and $\boxed{4}$ together, we have

$$27r^3 = 81 \qquad \boxed{5}$$
$$s^3 = 81 \qquad \boxed{6}$$

(Use Strategy 13: Find unknown expressions by division.) Dividing $\boxed{5}$ by $\boxed{6}$, we get

$$27\frac{r^3}{s^3} = 1 \qquad \boxed{7}$$

Multiplying $\boxed{7}$ by $\frac{1}{27}$, we get

$$\frac{r^3}{s^3} = \frac{1}{27}$$

$$\text{or } \frac{r}{s} = \frac{1}{3}$$

(Math Refresher #313 and #406)

Explanatory Answers for Practice Test 3 (continued)

Section 3: Verbal Ability

As you read these Explanatory Answers, refer to "Using Critical Thinking Skills in Verbal Questions" (beginning on page 236) whenever a specific Strategy is referred to in the answer. Of particular importance are the following Master Verbal Strategies:

Sentence Completion Master Strategy 1—page 245.
Sentence Completion Master Strategy 2—page 246.
Analogies Master Strategy 1—page 236.
Reading Comprehension Master Strategy 2—page 263.

1. Choice B is correct. See **Sentence Completion Strategy 4.** The key word "although" in this sentence indicates that there is opposition or difference between the first part of the sentence and the last part. Since our team knew that the opponents (the Raiders) were "sluggish," we were stupid—we should have pushed hard instead of being so "easygoing." The other four choices are incorrect because their word pairs do not make sense in the sentence.

2. Choice C is correct. See **Sentence Completion Strategy 2.**

   ### STEP 1
   We first examine the first word of each choice. We then eliminate Choice (A) heroic, Choice (B) respected, and Choice (E) insightful because a prime minister with any of these positive qualities would hardly be expected to cause a downfall of his country. So Choices A, B, and E are incorrect.

   ### STEP 2
   We now consider the remaining choices. Choice (D) vacillating ... confidential does not make sense in the sentence because we cannot refer to a country as confidential. Therefore, Choice D is also incorrect. Choice (C) incompetent ... powerful makes sense and *is* the correct choice.

3. Choice B is correct. See **Sentence Completion Strategy 1.** The word "aloof" means withdrawn, distant, uninvolved. A character who is dignified and who is a man of reserve is likely to be aloof.

4. Choice C is correct. See **Sentence Completion Strategy 2.**

   ### STEP 1
   Let us first examine the first words of each choice. We can then eliminate Choice (A) frequent, Choice (B) heavy, and Choice (E) bland because saying that blood contains frequent or heavy or bland amounts does not make sense. So Choices A, B, and E are incorrect.

   ### STEP 2
   We now consider the remaining choices. Choice (D) definite ... puzzling does *not* make sense because blood does not contain puzzling amounts. Therefore, Choice D is also incorrect. Choice (C) minute (pronounced "mine-yute"—meaning exceptionally small) ... excessive makes sense and *is* the correct choice.

5. Choice E is correct. See **Sentence Completion Strategy 2.**

STEP 1

Let us first examine the first word of each choice. We can then eliminate Choice (A) unearned and Choice (D) backward because saying unearned attempts to please or backward attempts to please *does not* make sense. So Choices A and D are incorrect.

STEP 2

Let us now consider the remaining choices. The second words of Choice (B) . . . humor and Choice (C) . . . reliance *do not* make sense in the sentence. Choice (E) hypocritical . . . defiance makes sense and is the correct choice.

6. Choice B is correct. See **Sentence Completion Strategy 3.** If you used this strategy of trying to complete the sentence *before* looking at the five choices, you might have come up with any of the following words:

> simple   ordinary
> understandable   common
> easy-to-understand

These words all mean about the same as the correct Choice B simplified. Therefore, Choices A, C, D, and E are incorrect.

7. Choice D is correct. See **Sentence Completion Strategy 2.** We first examine the first words of each choice. We can then eliminate Choice C conclusive . . . and Choice E ridiculous . . . because violent crime does not become conclusive or ridiculous. Now we go on to the three remaining choices. When you fill in the two blanks of Choice A and of Choice B, the sentence does not make sense. So these two choices are also incorrect. Filling in the two blanks of Choice D makes the sentence acceptable.

8. Choice E is correct. See **Sentence Completion Strategy 4.** We have an opposition indicator here with the first word "Although." We can now assume that the opening clause of the sentence—"Although . . . patrols"— will contradict the thought expressed in the rest of the sentence. Choice E impeded . . . continue fills in the blanks so that the sentence makes sense. The other choices are incorrect because their word-pairs do not make sense.

9. Choice A is correct. See **Sentence Completion Strategy 3.** This strategy suggests that you try to complete the sentence *before* looking at the five choices. Doing this, you might have come up with any of the following words that indicate an additional type of force or injury besides "seizure":

> coercing   forcing   pressuring

These words all come close to the meaning of the correct Choice A compelling. Therefore, Choices B, C, D, and E are incorrect.

10. Choice E is correct. See **Sentence Completion Strategy 4.** We have an opposition indicator here—the student's not working hard and his winning the contest. We, therefore, look for a definitely positive word as our choice to contrast with the negative thought embodied in his not working hard. That positive word is "enraptured" (Choice E), which means delighted beyond measure. Accordingly Choices A, B, C, and D are incorrect.

11. Choice E is correct. A colt is a young horse. A lamb is a young sheep. Choice A bird : eaglet is incorrect because *not* all young birds are eaglets. See **Analogy Strategy 4.** Choice B child : adult would be correct if the words were reversed. See **Analogy Strategy 3.**

(Part-Whole relationship)

12. Choice E is correct. To stumble is to walk defectively. To stammer is to speak defectively. Note that in Choice B, ogle is to look in a certain manner—but not defectively. So Choice B is incorrect.

(Action-Result relationship)

13. Choice A is correct. In baseball, a player scores a run. In soccer, a player scores a goal. The scores are made in order to win the game. You will note that in Choice D down : football, a player *makes* (not *scores*) a down. So Choice D is incorrect. See **Analogy Strategy 4.**

(Purpose relationship)

14. Choice A is correct. One sharpens a pencil for better use of the pencil. One hones a blade for better use of the blade. Note, however, that the better use comes about by *taking away* part of the pencil and the blade. Choice (C) wrap : package, Choice (D) polish : furniture, and Choice (E) stretch : canvas also involve a better use. However, nothing is taken away from the package, the furniture, or the canvas in bringing about a better use of these items. See **Analogy Strategy 4.**

(Action to Object Relationship)

15. Choice A is correct. A backlog holds up the flow of merchandise. A jam holds up the flow of traffic. We have here a cause-and-effect relationship. Choice B intermission : play also indicates cause and effect, but it does not have the *negative* quality of the cause-and-effect-relationship of the pair of capitalized words and the Choice A words. So Choice B is incorrect. See **Analogy Strategy 4.**

(Cause-and-Effect relationship)

16. Choice D is correct. A musician is an individual member of an orchestra. A soldier is an individual member of an army. We have here a Whole-Part relationship. Note that Choice A museum : statue and Choice B school : desk, are also whole-part relationships, but these two choices involve inanimate objects whereas a musician and a soldier are human beings. See **Analogy Strategy 4.**

(Whole-Part relationship)

17. Choice C is correct. Sand, as a result of the wind, may form a dune. Snow, as a result of the wind, may form a bank.

(Action to Object and Part-Whole relationship)

18. Choice D is correct. To embarrass is to cause a person to feel ill at ease; to humiliate is to humble or disgrace a person. To spank is a light form of punishment; to whip is a severe form of punishment. We have in this analogy a matter of degree. Also see **Analogy Strategy 4.**

(Degree relationship)

19. Choice D is correct. A person who is candid is *not* furtive. A person who is amicable is *not* unfriendly. We have an opposite relationship here. Choice B transparent : opaque and Choice E closed : ajar also express an opposite relationship. However, these two choices are incorrect because they do *not* refer to people. The capitalized words and the words of Choice D *do* refer to people. See **Analogy Strategy 4.**

(Opposite relationship)

20. Choice B is correct. A speaker uses a dais—which is on a higher level—so that he may be seen by the audience. An actor uses a stage—which is on a higher level—so that he may be seen by the audience.

(Purpose relationship)

21. Choice E is correct. A person who is characterized by imitation shows *no* individuality. A person who is characterized by debauchery shows *no* morality.

(Association relationship and Opposite relationship)

22. Choice C is correct. "Odoriferous" refers to a pleasant smell. "Euphonious" refers to a pleasant sound. Note that "odoriferous" and "euphonious" have positive connotations. Choices A, B, D, and E are incorrect because they have negative connotations. See **Analogy Strategy 4.**

(Association and Result relationship)

23. Choice E is correct. Something that is bland is *not* piquant. Something that is inane is *not* relevant.

(Opposite relationship)

24. Choice B is correct. See the first paragraph: "Many people who are willing to concede that the railroad must be brought back to life are chiefly thinking of bringing this about . . . by treating speed as the only important factor . . ."

25. Choice D is correct. See the fourth paragraph: "The prime purpose of passenger transportation is not to increase the amount of physical movement but to increase the possibilities for human association cooperation, personal intercourse and choice."

26. Choice E is correct. See paragraph 6: ". . . The current introduction of shopping malls . . . is a . . . far better *technical* solution than the many costly proposals for introducing moving sidewalks or other rigidly automated modes of locomotion."

27. Choice A is correct. See the next-to-last paragraph: "With the over-exploitation of the particular car comes an increased demand . . . to endow the petroleum magnates . . . with fabulous capacities for personal luxury . . ."

28. Choice C is correct. See the next-to-last paragraph: "With the over-exploitation of the particular car comes an increased demand . . . to roll ever wider carpets of concrete over the bulldozed landscape . . ."

29. Choice B is correct. See the last paragraph: ". . . If indeed we go farther and faster along this route, there is plenty of evidence to show that the shop will close up without our help."

30. Choice B is correct. From the context of the paragraph we are talking about distances. Don't get lured into Choice C because you read about "human needs" in the paragraph or Choice D just because you see "traffic" mentioned.

31. Choice D is correct. From lines 28–32 and other sections of the passage, we can see that the author believes that "technocratic" thinking neither addresses nor is concerned with real human needs.

32. Choice A is correct. See paragraph 6: "If we took human needs seriously . . . we should make the fullest use of pedestrian movement . . ."

33. Choice C is correct. See paragraph 5: ". . . Variety of choices, facilities and destinations, not speed alone, is the mark of an organic transportation system."

34. Choice B is correct. Judging from the time-perspective of the author, and the more general nature of the article, Choice B would be the best answer.

35. Choice C is correct. See paragraph 5: "... And [variety] is an important factor of safety when any part of the system breaks down."

Explanatory Answers for Practice Test 3 (continued)

Section 4: Math Ability

As you read these solutions, do two things if you answered the Math question incorrectly:

1. When a specific Strategy is referred to in the solution, study that strategy, which you will find in "Using Critical Thinking Skills in Math Questions" (beginning on page 174).

2. When the solution directs you to the "Math Refresher" (beginning on page 291)—for example, Math Refresher #305—study the 305 Math principle to get a clear idea of the Math operation that was necessary for you to know in order to answer the question correctly.

1. Choice C is correct.

Given: $\dfrac{a}{18} = \dfrac{2}{9}$ $\boxed{1}$

$\dfrac{b}{28} = \dfrac{1}{7}$ $\boxed{2}$

(Use Strategy 13: Find unknowns by multiplication.) Multiply $\boxed{1}$ by 18. We get

$$18\left(\dfrac{a}{18}\right) = 18\left(\dfrac{2}{9}\right)$$

$$a = 4$$

Multiply $\boxed{2}$ by 28. We get

$$28\left(\dfrac{b}{28}\right) = 28\left(\dfrac{1}{7}\right)$$

$$b = 4$$

(Math Refresher #406)

2. Choice C is correct.

Given: r is an even integer $\boxed{1}$
$5 < r < 8$ $\boxed{2}$

(Use Strategy 6: Know how to manipulate inequalities.) Using $\boxed{1}$ and $\boxed{2}$ together, the only even integer value of r between 5 and 8 is $r = 6$ $\boxed{3}$

Column A	Column B	
$r + 1$	7	$\boxed{4}$

Substituting $\boxed{3}$ into $\boxed{4}$, the columns become

$$6 + 1 = 7 \qquad\qquad 7$$

(Math Refresher #603 and #419)

3. Choice D is correct.

Column A	Column B
The number of hours in w days	v hours

(Use Strategy C: Use numerics if it appears that the answer cannot be determined.) Let $w = 1$ and $v = 30$. The columns become

The number of hours in 1 day = 24 hours	30 hours

Column B is larger.

Now, let $w = 1$ and $v = 1$, the columns become

The number of hours in 1 day = 24 hours	1 hour

Column A is larger.

Since two different answers are possible, the answer cannot be determined from the information given.

(Math Refresher #431)

4. Choice D is correct.

Given: Darrin is older than Stephanie. 1
          Jimmy is older than Stephanie. 2

(Use Strategy C: Use numerics if it appears that a unique comparison cannot be made.)

Let Darrin = 15, Jimmy = 13, Stephanie = 10 Darrin's age is greater than Jimmy's age.

Now, let Darrin = 15, Jimmy = 17, Stephanie = 10 Darrin's age is less than Jimmy's age.

Since two different results are possible, the answer cannot be determined.

(Math Refresher #431 and Logical Reasoning)

5. Choice D is correct. **(Use Strategy C: When a comparison is difficult, use numbers instead of variables.)**

Given: $m - n > p - q$ 1

Choose specific values of m, n, p, q that satisfy 1.

EXAMPLE 1

$m = 0, n = -1, p = 0, q = 0$

The columns become

Column A	Column B
-1	0

and the quantity in Column B is greater.

EXAMPLE 2

$m = 3, n = 0, p = 0, q = 1$

The columns become

Column A	Column B
0	0

and the two quantities are equal. Thus, the answer depends on specific values of $m, n, p,$ and q.

(Math Refresher #431)

6. Choice B is correct.

$\left(\text{Use Strategy 5: Average} = \right.$

$\left. \dfrac{\text{Sum of values}}{\text{Total number of values}} \right)$

If all 10 students received a 95, then the average would be 95. Since one student received a grade less than 95, the average of the ten test scores is less than 95.

Column A	Column B
Some number less than 95	95

So the answer is clear.

(Math Refresher #601)

7. Choice C is correct. **(Use Strategy 17: Use the given information effectively.)**

Given: $\dfrac{2}{3} + \dfrac{r}{s} = \dfrac{5}{3}$ 1

Subtract $\dfrac{2}{3}$ from both sides of 1, giving

$$\dfrac{r}{s} + \dfrac{3}{3}$$

$$\dfrac{r}{s} = 1$$

Thus, $r = s$.

(Math Refresher #406)

8. Choice B is correct. **(Use Strategy D: Add a quantity to both columns to get rid of minus signs.)**

	Column A	Column B
	$x > 0 > y$	
	$y - x$	$x - y$
Add x:	$y - x + x$	$x - y + x$
	y	$2x - y$
Add y:	$y + y$	$2x - y + y$
	$2y$	$2x$
Divide by 2:	y	x

Since $x > 0 > y$, $x > y$

(Math Refresher #421)

9. Choice D is correct.

Given: $w \leq 60$
            $x \leq 60$

(Use Strategy C: Use numerical examples when it appears that a comparison cannot be determined.)

First: Let $w = 50$
              $x = 50$

Then $w + x = 100$ 1
which is > 80

Second: $w = 30$
              $x = 20$

Then $w + x = 50$ 2
which is < 80

From $\boxed{1}$ and $\boxed{2}$ we see that two different comparisons are possible. Therefore, we cannot determine a unique comparison.

(Math Refresher #122)

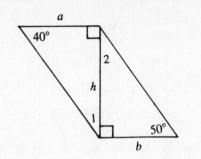

10. Choice A is correct.

(Use Strategy 18: Remember right triangle facts.)

In a right triangle, the sum of the 2 acute $\angle$ s is 90°

$$\boxed{1}$$

In the left hand triangle, using $\boxed{1}$, we have

$$40 + \angle 1 = 90$$
$$\angle 1 = 50 \qquad \boxed{2}$$

In the righthand triangle, using $\boxed{2}$, we have

$$50 + \angle 2 = 90$$
$$\angle 2 = 40 \qquad \boxed{3}$$

From $\boxed{1}$, $\boxed{2}$ and $\boxed{3}$ we see that each triangle has a 40°, 50°, and 90° angle.

METHOD 1

(Use Strategy 14: Label unknown quantities.) Label diagonal "h" as shown. In the left-hand triangle, $a > h$ because side a lies opposite the larger angle of 50° whereas side h lies opposite the smaller angle of 40°. In the right-hand triangle, $h > b$ because side h lies opposite the larger angle 50° and side b lies opposite the smaller angle of 40°. So we get $a > h$ and $h > b$, which means $a > b$. **(See Strategy 6, Statement 5: How to Manipulate Inequalities.)**

(Math Refresher #509)

METHOD 2

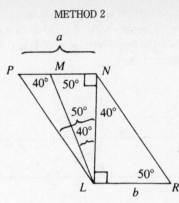

(Use Strategy 14: Draw lines to make the problem easier.) Draw LM, making a 50° angle with a.

$$\triangle MNL \cong \triangle RLN \text{ by Angle–Side–Angle}$$
$$\text{Therefore, } MN \cong LR$$
$$MN = b \qquad \boxed{4}$$

From the diagram, we know that

$$PN = a \qquad \boxed{5}$$

It is obvious that $PN > MN$. $\qquad \boxed{6}$

Substituting $\boxed{4}$ and $\boxed{5}$ into $\boxed{6}$, we get
$$a > b$$

(Math Refresher #501 and #511)

11. Choice D is correct.

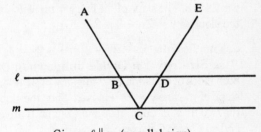

Given: $\ell \parallel m$ (parallel sign)

No information is supplied regarding the angle that AC or EC makes with *m*. **(Use Strategy 14: Draw lines to help solve the problem.)** Redraw AC at a different angle

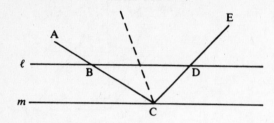

In the above diagram BC > CD $\boxed{1}$
Redraw EC at a different angle

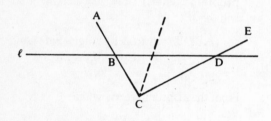

In the above diagram CD > BC $\boxed{2}$

Since two different results are possible, a comparison can't be determined from the information given.

(Math Refresher #504)

12. Choice C is correct. Column A: Write $3 + y = 2x$ as $y = 2x - 3$. The slope of the line $y = mx + b$ is *m*. So the slope of $y = 2x - 3$ is **2**.

Column B: Write $4x - 2y + 8 = 0$ as $2y = 4x + 8$. **(Use Strategy 13: Divide unknowns):** Divide both sides of equation by 2 to get: $y = 2x + 4$. The slope of the line $y = 2x + 4$ is **2**. Thus the slopes of the two lines in Column A and Column B are equal and so Choice C is correct.

(Math Refresher #416)

13. Choice B is correct. **(Use Strategy 11: Use new definitions carefully.)** Since $\bigcirc{y}$ denotes the decimal part of *y*, it follows that

$$\bigcirc{y} < 1 \qquad \boxed{1}$$
$$\bigcirc{x} < 1 \qquad \boxed{2}$$

(Use Strategy 6: Know how to manipulate inequalities.) Adding $\boxed{1}$ and $\boxed{2}$ above, we have

$$\bigcirc{x} + \bigcirc{y} < 2$$

Therefore, Choice B is greater.

(Math Refresher #420 and Logical Reasoning)

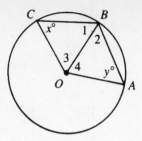

14. Choice A is correct.

Given: *O* is the center of the circle $\boxed{1}$
$$x < y \qquad \boxed{2}$$

From $\boxed{1}$ we know that *OC, OB,* and *OA* are radii and $OC = OB = OA$. $\boxed{3}$

(Use Strategy 18: Remember the isosceles triangle.)

From $\boxed{3}$ we know:

In $\triangle COB$, $\angle 1 = x°$ $\boxed{4}$
In $\triangle BOA$, $\angle 2 = y°$ $\boxed{5}$

(Use Strategy 3: The whole equals the sum of its parts.)

We know that the sum of angles of a triangle = 180°. $\boxed{6}$

Using $\boxed{6}$ in $\triangle COB$, we get

$$\angle 1 + x° + \angle 3 = 180° \qquad \boxed{7}$$

Substituting $\boxed{4}$ into $\boxed{7}$, we get

$$x° + x° + \angle 3 = 180°$$
$$2x° + \angle 3 = 180°$$
$$\angle 3 = 180° - 2x° \qquad \boxed{8}$$

Using $\boxed{6}$ in $\triangle BOA$, we get

$$\angle 2 + y° + \angle 4 = 180° \qquad \boxed{9}$$

Substituting $\boxed{5}$ into $\boxed{9}$, we get

$$y° + y° + \angle 4 = 180°$$
$$2y° + \angle 4 = 180°$$
$$\angle 4 = 180° - 2y° \qquad \boxed{10}$$

Multiply $\boxed{2}$ by 2. We get $2x < 2y$ $\boxed{11}$

(Use Strategy 6: Know how to manipulate inequalities.)

From $\boxed{11}$, we know that

$$180 - 2x > 180 - 2y \qquad \boxed{12}$$

Substituting $\boxed{8}$ and $\boxed{10}$ into $\boxed{12}$, we get
$$\angle 3 > \angle 4 \qquad \boxed{13}$$

Using $\boxed{1}$ and $\boxed{13}$, we know that
Segment *CB* > Segment *BA*

(Math Refresher #524, #507, #505, and #420)

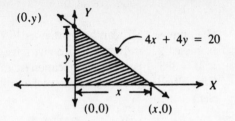

15. Choice C is correct.

The triangular region has been drawn above. Clearly, as labeled in the diagram, the area of the triangular region A is

$$A = \frac{1}{2}xy \qquad \boxed{1}$$

where x and y are the X-intercept and Y-intercept, respectively. To find the X-intercept, let $y = 0$, and solve for x in the equation of the line in the drawing.

$$\begin{aligned} 4x + 4y &= 20 \\ 4x + 4(0) &= 20 \\ 4x &= 20 \\ x &= 5 \end{aligned} \qquad \boxed{2}$$

To find the Y-intercept, let $x = 0$, and solve for y in the equation of the line in the drawing.

$$\begin{aligned} 4x + 4y &= 20 \\ 4(0) + 4y &= 20 \\ 4y &= 20 \\ y &= 5 \end{aligned} \qquad \boxed{3}$$

Substituting $\boxed{2}$ and $\boxed{3}$ into $\boxed{1}$,

$$A = \frac{1}{2}(5)(5) = 12.5$$

Thus, the columns become

Column A	Column B
12.5	12.5

and the quantities are equal.

(Math Refresher #306, #307, #406, and #410)

16. $\dfrac{6}{1}$ **or 6 or** $\dfrac{12}{2}$

(Use Strategy 2: Translate from words to algebra.)

Let M = number of Mary's jellybeans $\boxed{1}$
Let S = number of Susan's jellybeans $\boxed{2}$
And R = number of Rose's jellybeans $\boxed{3}$

We are looking for $\dfrac{\text{Rose's jellybeans}}{\text{Susan's jellybeans}}$ $\boxed{4}$

According to the given, S = 3M $\boxed{5}$
Also given, R = 18M $\boxed{6}$

Dividing $\boxed{6}$ by $\boxed{5}$, we get

$$\frac{R}{S} = \frac{6}{1}$$

(Math Refresher #200 and #120)

17. **9**

Volume of cube = (side)^3

Thus, the volume of a cube whose edge has length of $1 = 1^3 = 1$.
The volume of a cube whose edge has the length of $2 = 2^3 = 8$. Thus the sum of the volumes of the two cubes = $8 + 1 = 9$.

(Math Refresher #313)

18. **105**

(Use Strategy 11: Use new definitions carefully. These problems are generally easy.)

$$\text{Given: } \left(\frac{n}{2}\right) = \frac{n(n-1)}{2}$$

$$\begin{aligned} \text{Thus } \left(\frac{15}{2}\right) &= \frac{15(15-1)}{2} \\ &= \frac{15(14)}{2} \\ &= 105 \end{aligned}$$

(Math Refresher #431)

19. **0**

Given: $\qquad\quad r^2 = 9 \qquad \boxed{1}$
$\qquad\qquad\quad\; s^2 = 25 \qquad \boxed{2}$

(Use Strategy 17: Use the given information effectively.) From $\boxed{1}$ and $\boxed{2}$, we have

$$r = 3 \text{ or } -3 \qquad \boxed{3}$$
$$s = 5 \text{ or } -5 \qquad \boxed{4}$$

The greatest possible value of $s - r$ occurs when s is a maximum and r is a minimum or

$$5 - (-3) = 8 \qquad \boxed{5}$$

The greatest possible value of $r - s$ occurs when r is a maximum and s is a minimum or

$$3 - (-5) = 8 \qquad \boxed{6}$$

The answer to this question is the difference between $\boxed{5}$ and $\boxed{6}$:

$$8 - 8 = 0$$

(Math Refresher #430 and Logical Reasoning)

20. $33\dfrac{1}{3}$, **which translates to 33.3 in "grid" form.**

(Use Strategy 2: Translate from words to algebra.) According to the graph, 4 people had green eyes, 6 people had blue eyes, and 5 had brown eyes, so there were 15 people in the group. The percentage, x, can be found by setting up the ratio $\dfrac{x}{100} =$

$\dfrac{5}{15} = \dfrac{1}{3}$, or $x = 33\dfrac{1}{3}$. $33\dfrac{1}{3}$ % had brown eyes.

(Math Refresher #704)

21. **5**

$$
\begin{array}{r}
N5 \\
LM \\
\hline
385 \\
385 \\
\hline
4235
\end{array}
$$

(Use Strategy 17: Use the given information effectively.) From the given problem we see that

$$N5 \times M = 385$$

Use Strategy 7: Use numerical examples:

Try $N = 1$

$$15 \times M = 385$$

M must be greater than 10, which is incorrect.

Try $N = 2$

$$25 \times M = 385$$

M must be greater than 10, which is incorrect.

Try $N = 3$

$$35 \times M = 385$$

M must be greater than 10, which is incorrect.

Try $N = 4$

$$45 \times M = 385$$

M is not an integer.

Try $N = 5$

$$55 \times M = 385. \text{ Thus, } M = 7$$

Therefore, L can be equal to 7 to give:

$$
\begin{array}{r}
55 \\
\times\ 77 \\
\hline
385 \\
+\ 385 \\
\hline
4235
\end{array}
$$

(Logical Reasoning)

The number "$N5$" can be written as $10N + 5$. For example, "25" $= 10 \times 2 + 5$. So we have $(10N + 5) \times M = 385$ ☐1 in the multiplication example given. **(Use Strategy 12: *Factor* to make problem simpler.)**

$$10N + 5 = 5(2N + 1)$$

So from ☐1 , $5(2N + 1) \times M = 385$

Now divide by 5:

$$(2N + 1)\, M = 77$$

Because the only two integers that can give us 77 when multiplied are 11 and 7, or 77 and 1, and because N and M are integers, each must be less than 10, $2N + 1 = 11$, $M = 7$.

If $2N + 1 = 11$, then $N = 5$.

22. **24**

(Use Strategy 11: Use new definitions carefully.)

By definition, the hand of dial Y moves one number for each complete revolution of the hand of dial Z.

☐1

The hand of Dial Y must move 8 numbers to complete one of its own revolutions. Therefore, it must move 24 numbers to complete 3 of its revolutions.

From ☐1 above, 24 numbers on dial Y correspond to 24 complete revolutions on dial Z.

(Logical Reasoning)

23. $\dfrac{7}{8}$ **or .875**

(Use Strategy 17: Use the given information effectively.)

Given: 6 rolls uses $\dfrac{1}{4}$ pound of powder ☐1

6 rolls uses $2\dfrac{1}{2}$ quarts of water ☐2

Number ☐2 is not necessary to solve the problem!

We need to know how much powder is needed for the same mixture for 21 rolls. Let $x =$ number of pounds for 21 rolls. We set up a proportion:

$$\frac{6 \text{ rolls}}{\frac{1}{4} \text{ pound}} = \frac{21 \text{ rolls}}{x}$$

(Use Strategy 10: Know how to use units.)

$$(6 \text{ rolls})x = (21 \text{ rolls}) \times \left(\frac{1}{4} \text{ pound}\right)$$

$$6x = 21 \times \frac{1}{4} \text{ pound} \qquad \boxed{3}$$

(Use Strategy 13: Find unknowns by multiplication.) Multiply $\boxed{3}$ by $\frac{1}{6}$. We get

$$\frac{1}{6}\left(6x\right) = \frac{1}{6}\left(21 \times \frac{1}{4} \text{ pound}\right)$$

$$x = \frac{1}{6} \times 21 \times \frac{1}{4} \text{ pound}$$

$$x = \frac{21}{24} \text{ pound}$$

$$x = \frac{7}{8} \text{ of a pound}$$

(Math Refresher #200, #120, and #406)

24. **84**

$$\left(\begin{array}{c} \text{Use Strategy 5:} \\ \text{Average} = \dfrac{\textbf{Sum of the values}}{\textbf{Total number of values}} \end{array}\right)$$

Let x = Total number of students $\qquad \boxed{1}$
Then $\qquad \boxed{2}$
$.40x$ = Number of students scoring 100 $\quad \boxed{3}$
$.10x$ = Number of students scoring 80 $\quad \boxed{4}$
y = Average score of remaining students

We know the whole class is 100%. $\qquad \boxed{5}$

From $\boxed{2}$ and $\boxed{3}$ we know: 40% + 10% = 50% have been accounted for. $\qquad \boxed{6}$

(Use Strategy 3: The whole equals the sum of its parts.)

Subtracting $\boxed{6}$ from $\boxed{5}$, we get remaining students represent 50% of the class. $\qquad \boxed{7}$
Using $\boxed{7}$ and $\boxed{1}$, we get
Number of remaining students = $.5x$ $\qquad \boxed{8}$

We know

$$\text{Average} = \frac{\text{Sum of the values}}{\text{Total number of values}} \qquad \boxed{9}$$

Given: Average = 90 $\qquad \boxed{10}$

Substituting $\boxed{1}$, $\boxed{2}$, $\boxed{3}$, $\boxed{4}$, $\boxed{8}$, and $\boxed{10}$ into $\boxed{9}$, we get

$$90 = \frac{.40x(100) + .10x(80) + .5x(y)}{x} \qquad \boxed{11}$$

Multiply $\boxed{11}$ by x. We get

$$90x = 40x + 8x + .5xy$$
$$90x = 48x + .5xy$$
$$42x = .5xy$$
$$42 = .5y$$
$$84 = y$$

(Math Refresher #601, #114 and #406)

25. **5** **(Use Strategy 3: The whole equals the sum of its parts.)** The sum of the angles in a triangle = 180°.

Therefore $3t° + 5t° + 10t° = 180$
$$18t = 180$$
$$t = 10 \qquad \boxed{1}$$

Since ABC is a line segment, straight angle $ABC = 180°$ $\qquad \boxed{2}$

(Use Strategy 3: The whole equals the sum of its parts.)

$$\angle ABC = \angle ABD + \angle DBC \qquad \boxed{3}$$

Substituting the given and $\boxed{2}$ in $\boxed{3}$ gives

$$180 = 10t + 16x \qquad \boxed{4}$$

Substituting $\boxed{1}$ in $\boxed{4}$, we have

$$180 = 10(10) + 16x$$
$$180 = 100 + 16x$$
$$80 = 16x$$
$$5 = x$$

(Math Refresher #505, #406, and #501)

Explanatory Answers for Practice Test 3 (continued)

Section 5: Verbal Ability

> As you read these Explanatory Answers, refer to "Using Critical Thinking Skills in Verbal Questions" (beginning on page 236) whenever a specific Strategy is referred to in the answer. Of particular importance is the following Master Verbal Strategy:
>
> Reading Comprehension Master Strategy 2—page 263.

1. Choice D is correct. Line 1 ("To the world when it was half a thousand years younger . . .") indicates that the author is describing the world roughly 500 hundred years ago. Choice D—A.D. 1455—is therefore the closest date. Although Choice C is also in the Middle Ages, it is almost a thousand years ago. So it is an incorrect choice. Choices A, B, and E are obviously incorrect choices.

2. Choice A is correct. We can see that "with greater avidity" is an adverbial phrase telling the reader how "honors and riches" were enjoyed and desired. See lines 14–17: "We, at the present day . . . formerly enjoyed." The reader thus learns that even simple pleasures such as a glass of wine were more keenly enjoyed then. Choices B, C, D, and E are incorrect because the passage does *not* state or imply that "with greater avidity" means "with greater sadness *or* terror *or* silence *or* disappointment."

3. Choice B is not true—therefore it is the correct choice. See lines 36–38: "The contrast between silence and sound . . . than it is in our lives." The next sentence states that the modern town hardly knows silence. These two sentences together imply that the typical town of the Middle Ages did have periods of silence.

   Choice A is true—therefore an incorrect choice. See lines 30–31: "A medieval town . . . in extensive suburbs of factories and villas."

   Choice C is true—therefore an incorrect choice. See lines 32–33: ". . . it [a medieval town] stood forth . . . with innumerable turrets."

   Choice D is true—therefore an incorrect choice. See line 35: ". . . the lofty mass of the churches always remained dominant."

   Choice E is true—therefore an incorrect choice. See lines 33–34: "However tall . . . in the aspect of the town."

4. Choice C is correct. Throughout Passage A, the author is indicating the strong, rough, uncontrolled forces that pervaded the period. See, for example, the following references. Lines 9–10: "Misfortunes and poverty were more afflicting than at present." Lines 18–19: "Then, again, all things in life . . . cruel publicity." Lines 24–26: "Executions . . . songs and music." Therefore, Choice C is correct. Choice A is incorrect because the passage speaks of joys as well as miseries. See lines 14–17: "We, at the present day . . . formerly enjoyed." Choice B is incorrect for this reason: Although the author contrasts town and country, he gives no indication as to which was dominant in that society. Therefore, Choice B is incorrect. Choice D is incorrect. The author contrasts how it felt to be rich or poor, but he does not indicate that the rich mistreated the poor. Choice E is incorrect because the pious nature of the people in the Middle Ages is only one of the many elements discussed in the passage.

5. Choice E is correct. See lines 4–6: "All experience . . . pain of child-life." Throughout the passage, this theme is illustrated with specific examples. Choices A and B are incorrect because they are one-sided. In the passage, many conditions that may make the Middle Ages seem worse than today are matched with conditions that may make the Middle Ages seem better than today. Choice C is incorrect because nowhere in the passage is intelligence mentioned or implied. Choice D is incorrect because the third paragraph indicates that, far from being subdued, people went about their lives with a great deal of show and pageantry.

6. Choice A is incorrect because the author stops short of outright despair in the last sentence of the first paragraph by tempering the outbursts of the Renaissance scholar with the milder "our times are out of joint." Choices B and E are incorrect because there is no positive feeling expressed in the first paragraph. Choice C is incorrect because there is no feeling of attraction toward an earlier age. Choice D is correct because the negative feeling is not quite full-bodied.

7. Choice A is correct. There is no mention of energy sources at any point in the selection. Therefore this answer is correct. Choices B, C, D, and E are mentioned in paragraph 2.

8. The positive outlook of the words "trend is not destiny" is best exemplified by Choice B, which implies that man can improve his situation. The other statements are negative or pessimistic pronouncements.

9. Choice A is correct. The author cites Choices B, C, D, and E in paragraph 5 as examples of renewed public awareness. The reference to the president's increase in the military budget does not indicate evidence of the public's insight regarding a danger.

10. Choice A and C are incorrect because the author is consistently expressing optimism in man's ability to learn from past mistakes. Choice B is the correct answer. Accordingly, Choice D contradicts the realistic tone of the essay. Choice E is not at all characteristic of the writer's attitude.

11. Choice C is correct. See lines 13–14 and lines 56–59. Note that the author of Passage B states that *if* present trends continue, the gap in living standards between the rich and the poor will lead to acts of desperation, including the use of nuclear weapons.

12. Choice A is correct. See lines 73–78. Note that Choice B is incorrect; see lines 41–46 and the descriptions in the rest of Passage A. Choice C is incorrect; see lines 82–84. Choice E is incorrect; see lines 86–88.

13. Choice E is correct. See lines 73–90 and lines 41–46 and throughout Passage A. Note that Choice A is incorrect; see lines 88–90.

Explanatory Answers for Practice Test 3 (continued)

Section 6: Math Ability

As you read these solutions, do two things if you answered the Math question incorrectly:

1. When a specific Strategy is referred to in the solution, study that strategy, which you will find in "Using Critical Thinking Skills in Math Questions" (beginning on page 174).

2. When the solution directs you to the "Math Refresher" (beginning on page 291)—for example, Math Refresher #305—study the 305 math principle to get a clear idea of the Math operation that was necessary for you to know in order to answer the question correctly.

1. Choice B is correct. **(Use Strategy 2: Know the definition of percent.)**

$$\text{Percent of Caramels} =$$

$$\frac{\text{Weight of Caramels}}{\text{Total Weight}} \times 100 \qquad \boxed{1}$$

Given: $\qquad\qquad\qquad\qquad\qquad \boxed{2}$
Weight of Caramels = 0.6 pound $\quad \boxed{3}$
Weight of Coconuts = 3.6 pounds

Adding $\boxed{2}$ and $\boxed{3}$, we get

Total Weight = 0.6 pounds + 3.6 pounds
Total Weight = 4.2 pounds $\qquad \boxed{4}$

Substituting $\boxed{2}$ and $\boxed{4}$ into $\boxed{1}$, we have

$$\text{Percent of Caramels} = \frac{0.6 \ \text{pounds}}{4.2 \ \text{pounds}} \times 100$$

$$= \frac{.6}{4.2} \times 100$$

$$= \frac{6}{42} \times 100$$

$$= \frac{600}{42} = \frac{300}{21} =$$

$$\text{Percent of Caramels} = 14\frac{2}{7}$$

(Math Refresher #106 and #107)

2. Choice B is correct. Notice that $25,000 is one-fourth of $100,000 (the total funds).

That is, $\dfrac{25,000}{100,000} = \dfrac{1}{4}$.

So look for the piece or part of the circle that is closest to $\dfrac{1}{4}$ of the whole circle. $\dfrac{1}{4}$ of the whole circle (360°) is 90°. Lincoln H.S. represents about $\dfrac{1}{4}$ of the whole circle or 90°.

(Math Refresher #705)

3. Choice A is correct.

Given: $\quad y = r - 6 \qquad\qquad \boxed{1}$
$\qquad\qquad z = r + 5 \qquad\qquad \boxed{2}$

(Use Strategy 13: Find unknown expressions by addition of equations.)

Adding $\boxed{1}$ and $\boxed{2}$, we get

$$y + z = 2r - 1$$
$$y + z + 1 = 2r$$
$$\frac{y + z + 1}{2} = r$$

(Math Refresher #407)

4. Choice E is correct. **(Use Strategy 2: Translate from words to algebra.)**

Given: The 3 polygons have equal perimeters, gives us

$$6a = 3b \qquad \boxed{1}$$
$$8c = 6a \qquad \boxed{2}$$

Dividing $\boxed{1}$ by 6, we get

$$a = \frac{3}{6}b = \frac{1}{2}b \qquad \boxed{3}$$

Thus, $a < b$

Dividing $\boxed{2}$ by 8, we get

$$c = \frac{6}{8}a = \frac{3}{4}a \qquad \boxed{4}$$

Thus, $c < a$

(Use Strategy 6: Know how to use inequalities.)

Using the Transitive Property of Inequality with $\boxed{3}$ and $\boxed{4}$, we have $c < a < b$.

(Math Refresher #304, #306, and #406)

5. Choice B is correct. **(Use Strategy 9: Know the formula for rate, time, and distance.)**

$$\text{Rate} \times \text{Time} = \text{Distance} \qquad \boxed{1}$$

Given: Time from A to B = 3 hours $\boxed{2}$
Time from B to C = 5 hours $\boxed{3}$
Distance from A to B =
Distance from B to C $\boxed{4}$

Using $\boxed{4}$, let Distance from A to B =
Distance from B to C = D $\boxed{5}$

Substituting $\boxed{2}$ and $\boxed{5}$ into $\boxed{1}$, we get

$$\text{Rate}_{AB} \times 3 = D$$
$$\text{Rate}_{AB} = \frac{D}{3} \qquad \boxed{6}$$

Substituting $\boxed{3}$ and $\boxed{5}$ into $\boxed{1}$, we get

$$\text{Rate}_{BC} \times 5 = D$$
$$\text{Rate}_{BC} = \frac{D}{5} \qquad \boxed{7}$$

From $\boxed{5}$ we get whole distance from A to C = $2D$ $\boxed{8}$

From $\boxed{2}$ and $\boxed{3}$ we get time for whole trip
$= 3 + 5 = 8$ $\boxed{9}$

Substituting $\boxed{8}$ and $\boxed{9}$ into $\boxed{1}$, we get

$$\text{Rate}_{AC} \times 8 = 2D$$
$$\text{Rate}_{AC} = \frac{2D}{8}$$
$$\text{Rate}_{AC} = \frac{D}{4} \qquad \boxed{10}$$

We are asked to find the ratio

$$\frac{\text{Average Speed from } A \text{ to } B}{\text{Average Speed from } A \text{ to } C} \qquad \boxed{11}$$

Substituting $\boxed{6}$ and $\boxed{10}$ into $\boxed{11}$, we have

$$\frac{\text{Average Speed from } A \text{ to } B}{\text{Average Speed from } A \text{ to } C} =$$

$$\frac{\dfrac{D}{3}}{\dfrac{D}{4}} =$$

$$\frac{D}{3} \div \frac{D}{4} =$$

$$\frac{\cancel{D}}{3} \times \frac{4}{\cancel{D}} =$$

$$\frac{4}{3} = 4 : 3$$

(Math Refresher #201, #202, and #120)

6. Choice C is correct. **(Use Strategy 7: Use number examples.)**

$$\text{If } a = \frac{2}{3}, b = \frac{4}{3}, \text{ and } x = \frac{3}{2} \qquad \boxed{1}$$

Then, substituting from $\boxed{1}$, we get

$$ax = \frac{2}{3}\left(\frac{3}{2}\right) \qquad\qquad bx = \frac{4}{3}\left(\frac{3}{2}\right) = \frac{4}{2}$$

$$ax = 1 \qquad\qquad\qquad bx = 2$$

Neither a nor b nor x are integers, but both ax and bx are integers.

Thus, Choices B, D, and E are eliminated.

(Use Strategy 13: Find unknown expressions by addition of equations.)

Adding ax to bx, we get
$$ax + bx =$$
$$(a + b)x \qquad \boxed{2}$$

Since ax and bx are integers, $\boxed{2}$ is an integer. Thus, Choice C is correct.

(Math Refresher #431)

7. Choice B is correct. **(Use Strategy 17: Use the given information effectively.)** We are given

$$CD = \frac{3}{4} AC \qquad \boxed{1}$$

$$CF = \frac{2}{7} BC \qquad \boxed{2}$$

We want to find

$$\frac{\text{Area of } \triangle ABC}{\text{Area of Rectangle } CDEF}$$

We know that the Area of rectangle $CDEF$
$$= (CD)(CF) \qquad \boxed{3}$$
and Area of $\triangle ABC$
$$= \frac{1}{2} (AC)(BC) \qquad \boxed{4}$$

Substituting $\boxed{1}$ and $\boxed{2}$ into $\boxed{3}$,
Area of rectangle $CDEF$

$$= \left(\frac{3}{4} AC\right)\left(\frac{2}{7} BC\right) = \frac{3}{14} (AC)(BC) \qquad \boxed{5}$$

Substituting $\boxed{4}$ and $\boxed{5}$ into the unknown expression,

$$\frac{\text{Area of } \triangle ABC}{\text{Area of rectangle } CDEF} =$$

$$\frac{\frac{1}{2} (AC)(BC)}{\frac{3}{14} (AC)(BC)}$$

$$= \frac{1}{2} \times \frac{14}{3} = \frac{14}{6} = \frac{7}{3} \, (Answer)$$

(Math Refresher #304, #306, #431, and #120)

8. Choice C is correct. **(Use Strategy 2: Translate from words to algebra.)**

Let b = number of boys
  g = number of girls

We are given

$$b = g + 7 \qquad \boxed{1}$$

$$b = \frac{5}{4} g \qquad \boxed{2}$$

(Use Strategy 13: Find unknowns by multiplication.) Multiplying $\boxed{2}$ by $\frac{4}{5}$,

$$\frac{4}{5} b = g \qquad \boxed{3}$$

Substituting $\boxed{3}$ into $\boxed{1}$,

$$b = \frac{4}{5} b + 7$$
$$\qquad \boxed{4}$$

Multiplying $\boxed{4}$ by 5,

$$5b = 4b + 35$$
or $\qquad b = 35$

(Math Refresher #200 and #406)

9. Choice A is correct. **(Use Strategy 2: Translate words to algebra to find percent increase.)**

$$\text{Percent increase} = \frac{\text{Amount of increase}}{\text{Original amount}} \quad \boxed{1}$$

Amount of increase is given as 100 per year $\boxed{2}$

Substituting $\boxed{2}$ into $\boxed{1}$, we get

$$\% \text{ increase} = \frac{100}{\text{Original amount}} \qquad \boxed{3}$$

(Use Strategy 12: Try not to make tedious calculations.) The greatest % increase will occur when the original amount is least.

Since the population is increasing by 100 every year, it is least at the beginning, in 1989.

Thus $\boxed{3}$ will be greatest from 1989–1990.

(Math Refresher #114 and #118)

10. Choice D is correct.

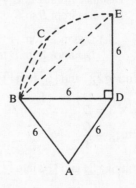

(Use Strategy 14: Draw lines where appropriate.)

Given: $\qquad AB = BD = AD = 6 \qquad \boxed{1}$

C can be any point on arc $\overset{\frown}{BE}$, not just where it appears in the drawing above. For any point C on arc $\overset{\frown}{BE}$

$$CD = 6 \qquad \boxed{2}$$
because CD = radius of the arc.

(Use Strategy 3: The whole equals the sum of its parts.) We want to find P = perimeter of

$$ABCD = AB + BC + CD + AD \qquad \boxed{3}$$

Substituting $\boxed{2}$ and $\boxed{1}$ into $\boxed{3}$,

$$P = 18 + BC \qquad \boxed{4}$$

We cannot find BC, but we can find the highest and lowest possible values for BC. Clearly, since BC is a side of an quadrilateral,

$$BC > 0 \qquad \boxed{5}$$

By looking at the diagram, we see that the highest possible value of BC occurs when C coincides with E.

$$BC \le BE \qquad \boxed{6}$$

must be true. BE can easily be found. $\triangle EDB$ is similar to one of the standard triangles discussed before. **(Use Strategy 18: Remember special right triangles.)**

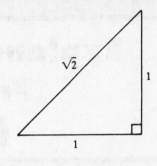

Corresponding sides of similar triangles are proportional, so that

$$\frac{\sqrt{2}}{1} = \frac{BE}{6}$$

or

$$BE = 6\sqrt{2} \qquad \boxed{7}$$

Substituting $\boxed{7}$ into $\boxed{6}$,

$$BC \le 6\sqrt{2} \qquad \boxed{8}$$

Comparing $\boxed{4}$ and $\boxed{8}$,

$$P = 18 + BC \le 18 + 6\sqrt{2} \qquad \boxed{9}$$

Comparing $\boxed{4}$ and $\boxed{5}$,

$$P = 18 + BC > 18 \qquad \boxed{10}$$

From $\boxed{9}$ and $\boxed{10}$ together,

$$18 < P \le 18 + 6\sqrt{2}$$

(Math Refresher #431, #507, #509, and #510)

Explanatory Answers for Practice Test 3 (continued)

Section 7: Math Ability

As you read these solutions, do two things if you answered the Math question incorrectly:

1. When a specific Strategy is referred to in the solution, study that strategy, which you will find in "Using Critical Thinking Skills in Math Questions" (beginning on page 174).

2. When the solution directs you to the "Math Refresher" (beginning on page 291)—for example, Math Refresher #305—study the 305 Math principle to get a clear idea of the Math operation that was necessary for you to know in order to answer the question correctly.

1. Choice D is correct. **(Use Strategy 17: Use the given information effectively.)**

   The most straightforward way to do this problem is to do the calculation. A second way, which may be faster, is to note that

   $$(20 + 30) = (10 + 40) = (25 + 25) = 50.$$

   Thus,

   $$\frac{(20 + 30) + (10 + 40) + (25 + 25)}{3}$$

   $$= \frac{3(50)}{3} = 50$$

   (Math Refresher #431)

2. Choice E is correct.

   The distance between points on a number line is found by:

   $$|a - b| = |-4 - (7)| =$$
   $$|-4 - 7| = |-11| = 11$$

   (Math Refresher #431)

3. Choice B is correct.

   $$\left(\text{Use Strategy 5: Average} \right.$$

   $$\left. = \frac{\textbf{Total of values}}{\textbf{Total number of values}} \right)$$

   The average is found by $\dfrac{8.4 + 8.1 + 9.3}{3} =$

   $$\frac{25.8}{3} =$$

   $$8.6$$

   (Math Refresher #601)

4. Choice A is correct.

   Given: $\qquad x + 9 = -11 - x \qquad \boxed{1}$

   Adding $x - 9$ to both sides of $\boxed{1}$,

   $$2x = -20$$
   $$\text{or } x = -10$$

   (Math Refresher #406)

5. Choice C is correct.

   Given: $3y = 12$ and $\dfrac{10}{x} = 5$ $\boxed{1}$

   Solving $\boxed{1}$ for x and y:

       $y = 4$ and $x = 2$ $\boxed{2}$

   Substitute equations $\boxed{2}$ into unknown expression.

   $$\frac{y + 11}{x + 15} = \frac{4 + 11}{2 + 15}$$

   $$= \frac{15}{17}$$

   (Math Refresher #406 and #431)

6. Choice C is correct. **(Use Strategy 10: Know how to use units.)**

   Interest = rate × time × amount deposited

   $$= \frac{8\%}{\text{year}} \times 1 \text{ year} \times \$50$$

   $$= .08 \times 1 \times \$50$$

   $$= \$4$$

   (Use Strategy 3: The whole equals the sum of its parts.)

   Total amount = Deposit + Interest
   $$= \$50 + \$4$$
   $$= \$54$$

   (Math Refresher #113, #114, and #121)

7. Choice D is correct.

   Given: $(x + 6)^2 = 12x + 72$ $\boxed{1}$

   (Use Strategy 17: Use the given information effectively.)

   Complete the squaring operation on the left side of the equation:

   $$(x + 6)^2 = x^2 + 12x + 36$$

   Continue the equation with $\boxed{1}$

   $$x^2 + 12x + 36 = 12x + 72 \quad \boxed{2}$$

   (Use Strategy 1: Cancel numbers and expressions that appear on both sides of an equation.)

   We get $x^2 + 36 = 72$
   therefore, $x^2 = 36$
               $x = \pm6$

   (Math Refresher #409)

8. Choice C is correct. **(Use Strategy 3: The whole equals the sum of its parts.)**

   From the diagram, we see that

   $$x + 60 = 360 \quad \boxed{1}$$

   Subtracting 60 from both sides of $\boxed{1}$, we get

   $$x = 300 \quad \boxed{2}$$

   Subtracting 60 from both sides of $\boxed{1}$, we get

   $$x - 60 = 240$$

   (Math Refresher #526 and #406)

9. Choice D is correct. **(Use Strategy 10: Know how to use units.)**

   Since 60 min = 1 hour, 24 hours = 1 day, and 7 days = 1 week, we have

   $$\left(\frac{60 \text{ min}}{\text{hour}}\right)\left(\frac{24 \text{ hours}}{\text{day}}\right)\left(\frac{7 \text{ days}}{\text{week}}\right) = 10{,}080$$

   or 1 week = 10,080 minutes. To the nearest hundred, 1 week ≈ 10,100 minutes.

   (Math Refresher #121)

10. Choice B is correct. **(Use Strategy 11: Use new definitions carefully.)**

    Method 1:   By definition $\nabla\!\!\!\!\!x = \dfrac{x^3}{4}$

    We are looking for
    $$\frac{x^3}{4} = 16 \quad \boxed{1}$$

    (Use Strategy 13: Find unknowns by multiplication.)

    Multiply $\boxed{1}$ by 4, we have

    $$x^3 = 64$$
    $$x = 4$$

    Method 2: Calculate each of the choices, A through E, until you find the one whose value is 16.

    (Math Refresher #429 and #431)

11. Choice B is correct. **(Use Strategy 2: Translate from words to algebra.)**

    We are given:

         $42 + 27 + 56 + x + y = 200$
    or $125 + x + y = 200$
    or $x + y = 75$
    or $x = 75 - y$ $\boxed{1}$

    (Use Strategy 17: Use the given information effectively.)

From $\boxed{1}$, it is clear that x is a maximum when y is a minimum. Since y is the number of pieces of candy in a jar, its minimum value is

$$y = 0 \qquad \boxed{2}$$

Substituting $\boxed{2}$ into $\boxed{1}$,

$$x = 75$$

(Math Refresher #200, #426, and #431)

12. Choice C is correct. **(Use Strategy 2: Translate from words to algebra.)**

Number of pages Ron read last night

$$= \frac{1}{4} \times 16 = 4$$

(Use Strategy 3: The whole equals the sum of its parts.)

Number of pages remaining immediately after Ron finished reading last night $= 16 - 4 = 12$

Number of pages read this morning $= \frac{1}{4} \times 12 = 3$

Pages still not read
= Remaining pages − pages read this morning
= 12 − 3
Pages still not read = 9

(Math Refresher #200 and Logical Reasoning)

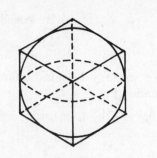

13. Choice E is correct. **(Use Strategy 17: Use the given information effectively.)**

Clearly, we can see from the picture above that the diameter of the sphere has the same length as a side of the cube. We know

$$\text{Volume of cube} = (\text{length of side})^3 \qquad \boxed{1}$$

We are given

$$\text{Volume of cube} = 64 \qquad \boxed{2}$$

Substituting $\boxed{2}$ into $\boxed{1}$, $64 = (\text{length of side})^3$

Thus,
length of side $= 4 =$ diameter of sphere

(Math Refresher #313 and #315)

14. Choice C is correct. **(Use Strategy 2: Translate from words to algebra.)**

$$\text{Let } 8n = \text{number of boys} \qquad \boxed{1}$$

$$7n = \text{number of girls} \qquad \boxed{2}$$

The ratio of $\dfrac{\text{boys}}{\text{girls}} = \dfrac{8n}{7n} = \dfrac{8}{7}$ and the given condition

is satisfied.

(Use Strategy 3: The whole equals the sum of its parts.)

Total number of students = Boys plus Girls $\boxed{3}$

Substitute $\boxed{1}$ and $\boxed{2}$ into $\boxed{3}$, we get

Total number of students $= 8n + 7n = 15n \qquad \boxed{4}$

$\boxed{4}$ is a multiple of 15

Choices A, B, D, and E are multiples of 15:

Ⓐ $15 = 15 \times 1$
Ⓑ $45 = 15 \times 3$
Ⓓ $60 = 15 \times 4$
Ⓔ $90 = 15 \times 6$

Only Choice C , 50, is *not* a multiple of 15.

(Math Refresher #200 and #431)

15. Choice A is correct.

Given: $\qquad \dfrac{m}{n} = \dfrac{x}{m} \qquad \boxed{1}$

(Use Strategy 13: Find unknowns by multiplication.)

Multiplying $\boxed{1}$ by m, we have

$$m\left(\frac{m}{n}\right) = \left(\frac{x}{\cancel{m}}\right)\cancel{m}$$

$$\frac{m^2}{n} = x$$

(Math Refresher #406)

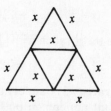

16. Choice A is correct. **(Use Strategy 2: Translate from words to algebra.)**

Let $x =$ side of smaller triangles
Thus, $3x =$ perimeter of each smaller triangle
$6x =$ perimeter of largest triangle

We are told

$$3x = 1$$

$$x = \frac{1}{3}$$ ☐1

(Use Strategy 13: Find unknowns by multiplication.)

Multiply ☐1 by 6, we get

$$6x = 2 = \text{perimeter of largest triangle}$$

(Math Refresher #200 and #306)

17.   Choice D is correct. **(Use Strategy 16: Watch out for questions that can be tricky.)**

Number of candles lit = Number of days between December 9 and 21, *inclusive* = 13

Not $21 - 9 = 12$

(Logical Reasoning)

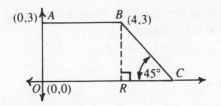

18.   Choice C is correct.

Method 1: **(Use Strategy 17: Use the given information effectively.)**

The above figure has AB parallel to the x-axis. (Both A and B have y-coordinate of 3.) Thus, the figure is a trapezoid.

Its height (OA) is 3   ☐1
Its top base is 4   ☐2

(Use Strategy 14: Draw lines when appropriate.)

Draw BR perpendicular to the x-axis.
$BR = OA = 3$ and $AB = OR = 4$

(Use Strategy 18: Remember isosceles triangle facts.)

Triangle BRC is an isosceles right triangle.
Thus, $RB = RC = 3$

The bottom base of the trapezoid   ☐3
$= OC = OR + RC = 4 + 3 = 7$ ☐4

The area of a trapezoid

$$= \frac{1}{2} h \,(\text{base 1} + \text{base 2})$$

Substituting ☐1, ☐2, and ☐3 into ☐4, we have

Area of trapezoid $= \frac{1}{2}(3)(4 + 7) = \frac{1}{2}(3)(11)$

$$= 16.5$$

Method 2: **(Use Strategy 14: Draw lines when appropriate.)**

Draw BR perpendicular to the x-axis.

$ABRO$ is a rectangle and BRC is an isosceles triangle.

Area $ABRO$ = (base) × (height)
$= 4 \times 3$
$= 12$ ☐1

Area $BRC = \frac{1}{2} \times (\text{base}) \times \text{height}$

$$= \frac{1}{2} \times 3 \times 3$$

$$= 4.5$$ ☐2

(Use Strategy 3: The whole equals the sum of its parts.)

Total Area of figure $ABCO$
$= \text{Area of } ABRO = \text{Area of } BRC$
$= 12 + 4.5$
$= 16.5$

(Math Refresher #410, #304, #306, #309, and #431)

19.   Choice B is correct. **(Use Strategy 2: Translate from words to algebra.)**

Let $x + y$ = sum of the 2 numbers   ☐1
$x - y$ = difference of the 2 numbers   ☐2
xy = product of the 2 numbers   ☐3

We are told that the difference between their sum and their difference is 6.   ☐4

Substituting ☐1 and ☐2 into ☐4, we have

$$x + y - (x - y) = 6$$
$$x + y - x + y = 6$$
$$2y = 6$$
$$y = 3$$ ☐5

Substituting ☐5 into ☐3, we get

$$x(3) = 15$$
$$x = 5$$

Clearly, 5 is the larger number.

(Math Refresher #200 and #406)

20. Choice E is correct.
Given:

$$\frac{1}{a} + \frac{1}{b} = 10 \qquad \boxed{1}$$

Method 1: You should suspect that $a + b$ does not have a unique value because $\boxed{1}$ is one equation in two variables, and thus a and b are not uniquely determined. To prove that $a + b$ is not uniquely determined, you can use the next method.

(Use Strategy 7: Use numerics to help find the answer.)

Method 2: Choose values of a and b

Satisfying $\boxed{1}$, and calculate $a + b$.

EXAMPLE 1

$$a = \frac{1}{4} \qquad b = \frac{1}{6}$$

$$a + b = \frac{5}{12}$$

EXAMPLE 2

$$a = -1 \qquad b = \frac{1}{11}$$

$$a + b = \frac{-10}{11}$$

Thus, $a + b$ has at least two different values.

(Math Refresher #431 and #110)

21. Choice A is correct. **(Use Strategy 3: The whole equals the sum of its parts.)**

The area between the curved path and the dodecagon is simply the sum of the areas of the 12 semicircles.

Since $\qquad$ area of circle $= \pi r^2$

then $\qquad$ area of semicircle $= \frac{1}{2}\pi r^2$

where r is radius of circle.

Thus, area of shaded region $= 12\left(\frac{1}{2}\pi r^2\right)$

$$= 6\pi r^2 \qquad \boxed{1}$$

We are told diameter of semicircle = side of dodecagon. $\qquad \boxed{2}$

Since each side of a regular dodecagon has the same length, then

length of a side of dodecagon =

$$\frac{\text{perimeter of dodecagon}}{12} =$$

$$\frac{24}{12} = 2$$

From $\boxed{2}$, we know that

diameter of semicircle = 2

Thus, radius of semicircle = 1 $\qquad \boxed{3}$

Substituting $\boxed{3}$ into $\boxed{1}$,

area of shaded region $= 6\pi$

(Math Refresher #310, #311, and #522)

22. Choice B is correct.
Given: $\qquad x^9 = 4 \qquad \boxed{1}$

$$x^7 = \frac{9}{y^2} \qquad \boxed{2}$$

$$x > 0 \text{ and } y > 0$$

(Use Strategy 13: Find unknown by division of equations.)

Divide $\boxed{1}$ by $\boxed{2}$. We get

$$\frac{x^9}{x^7} = \frac{4}{\frac{9}{y^2}}$$

$$x^2 = 4 \times \frac{y^2}{9}$$

$$x^2 = \frac{4}{9}y^2$$

$$\sqrt{x^2} = \sqrt{\frac{4}{9}y^2}$$

$$x = \frac{2}{3}y$$

(Note: This is the only solution because $x > 0$ and $y > 0$.)

(Math Refresher #431 and #430)

23. Choice E is correct. **(Use Strategy 2: Translate from words to algebra.)** From what we are told in the problem, notice that

$b - 6 =$ the number of Bobby's marbles after Bobby gave 6 away

$c + 6 =$ the number of Charlie's marbles after Bobby gave 6 away

We are told

$$b - 6 = c + 6 + 18$$
$$\text{or } b - 6 = c + 24 \qquad \boxed{1}$$

(Use Strategy 13: Find unknowns by adding equations or expressions.) Adding $-b - 24$ to both sides of $\boxed{1}$, we get

$$c - b = -30$$

(Math Refresher #200 and #406)

24. Choice D is correct. **(Use Strategy 3: The whole equals the sum of its parts.)** The perimeter of the shaded region

$$= PM + PN + \text{length of } \overset{\frown}{MN} \qquad \boxed{1}$$

From basic geometry, we know that

$$PM = PN \qquad m \sphericalangle PMO = 90 \qquad \boxed{2}$$

and that $\overleftrightarrow{OP}$ bisects $\sphericalangle MON$. **(Use Strategy 14: Draw additional lines.)** Thus, we can redraw the diagram. **(Use Strategy 18: Remember standard right triangles.)**

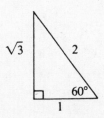

$\triangle PMO$ is similar to one of the standard triangles previously discussed.

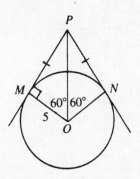

Corresponding sides of similar triangles are *in proportion*, so that

$$\frac{\sqrt{3}}{1} = \frac{PM}{5}$$

$$\text{or } PM = 5\sqrt{3} = PN \qquad \boxed{3}$$

It is always true that length of $\overset{\frown}{MN}$

$$= \frac{m \sphericalangle MON}{360} \times \text{circumference of the circle}$$

$$= \frac{m \sphericalangle MON}{360} \times 2\pi(5)$$

$$= \frac{120}{360} \times 2\pi(5)$$

(Use Strategy 19: Factor and reduce.)

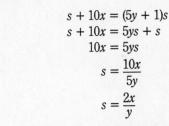

$$= \frac{12 \times \cancel{10}}{36 \times \cancel{10}} \times 2\pi(5)$$

$$= \frac{\cancel{12}}{\cancel{12} \times 3} \times 2\pi(5)$$

$$= \frac{10\pi}{3} \qquad \boxed{4}$$

Substituting $\boxed{4}$ and $\boxed{3}$ into $\boxed{1}$, we get the perimeter of shaded region $= 10\sqrt{3} + \dfrac{10\pi}{3}$

(Math Refresher #310, #509, #510, and #529)

25. Choice C is correct. **(Use Strategy 2: Translate from words to algebra.)** Let $s =$ the number of tapes Stanley originally had.

Thus, $s + 10x =$ the number of tapes Stanley had after receiving $10x$ tapes

We are told

$$s + 10x = (5y + 1)s$$
$$\text{or} \quad s + 10x = 5ys + s$$
$$\text{or} \quad 10x = 5ys$$
$$\text{or} \quad s = \frac{10x}{5y}$$
$$s = \frac{2x}{y}$$

(Math Refresher #200)

SAT Practice Test 4

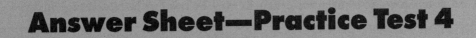

Answer Sheet—Practice Test 4

Make each mark a dark mark that completely fills the oval and is as dark as all your other marks. If you erase, do so completely. Incomplete erasures may be read as intended responses.

Use a No. 2 pencil only. Be sure each mark is dark and completely fills the intended oval. Completely erase any errors or stray marks.

Start with number 1 for each new section. If a section has fewer questions than answer spaces, leave the extra answer spaces blank.

SECTION 1

1 Ⓐ Ⓑ Ⓒ Ⓓ Ⓔ   11 Ⓐ Ⓑ Ⓒ Ⓓ Ⓔ   21 Ⓐ Ⓑ Ⓒ Ⓓ Ⓔ   31 Ⓐ Ⓑ Ⓒ Ⓓ Ⓔ
2 Ⓐ Ⓑ Ⓒ Ⓓ Ⓔ   12 Ⓐ Ⓑ Ⓒ Ⓓ Ⓔ   22 Ⓐ Ⓑ Ⓒ Ⓓ Ⓔ   32 Ⓐ Ⓑ Ⓒ Ⓓ Ⓔ
3 Ⓐ Ⓑ Ⓒ Ⓓ Ⓔ   13 Ⓐ Ⓑ Ⓒ Ⓓ Ⓔ   23 Ⓐ Ⓑ Ⓒ Ⓓ Ⓔ   33 Ⓐ Ⓑ Ⓒ Ⓓ Ⓔ
4 Ⓐ Ⓑ Ⓒ Ⓓ Ⓔ   14 Ⓐ Ⓑ Ⓒ Ⓓ Ⓔ   24 Ⓐ Ⓑ Ⓒ Ⓓ Ⓔ   34 Ⓐ Ⓑ Ⓒ Ⓓ Ⓔ
5 Ⓐ Ⓑ Ⓒ Ⓓ Ⓔ   15 Ⓐ Ⓑ Ⓒ Ⓓ Ⓔ   25 Ⓐ Ⓑ Ⓒ Ⓓ Ⓔ   35 Ⓐ Ⓑ Ⓒ Ⓓ Ⓔ
6 Ⓐ Ⓑ Ⓒ Ⓓ Ⓔ   16 Ⓐ Ⓑ Ⓒ Ⓓ Ⓔ   26 Ⓐ Ⓑ Ⓒ Ⓓ Ⓔ   36 Ⓐ Ⓑ Ⓒ Ⓓ Ⓔ
7 Ⓐ Ⓑ Ⓒ Ⓓ Ⓔ   17 Ⓐ Ⓑ Ⓒ Ⓓ Ⓔ   27 Ⓐ Ⓑ Ⓒ Ⓓ Ⓔ   37 Ⓐ Ⓑ Ⓒ Ⓓ Ⓔ
8 Ⓐ Ⓑ Ⓒ Ⓓ Ⓔ   18 Ⓐ Ⓑ Ⓒ Ⓓ Ⓔ   28 Ⓐ Ⓑ Ⓒ Ⓓ Ⓔ   38 Ⓐ Ⓑ Ⓒ Ⓓ Ⓔ
9 Ⓐ Ⓑ Ⓒ Ⓓ Ⓔ   19 Ⓐ Ⓑ Ⓒ Ⓓ Ⓔ   29 Ⓐ Ⓑ Ⓒ Ⓓ Ⓔ   39 Ⓐ Ⓑ Ⓒ Ⓓ Ⓔ
10 Ⓐ Ⓑ Ⓒ Ⓓ Ⓔ   20 Ⓐ Ⓑ Ⓒ Ⓓ Ⓔ   30 Ⓐ Ⓑ Ⓒ Ⓓ Ⓔ   40 Ⓐ Ⓑ Ⓒ Ⓓ Ⓔ

SECTION 2

1 Ⓐ Ⓑ Ⓒ Ⓓ Ⓔ   11 Ⓐ Ⓑ Ⓒ Ⓓ Ⓔ   21 Ⓐ Ⓑ Ⓒ Ⓓ Ⓔ   31 Ⓐ Ⓑ Ⓒ Ⓓ Ⓔ
2 Ⓐ Ⓑ Ⓒ Ⓓ Ⓔ   12 Ⓐ Ⓑ Ⓒ Ⓓ Ⓔ   22 Ⓐ Ⓑ Ⓒ Ⓓ Ⓔ   32 Ⓐ Ⓑ Ⓒ Ⓓ Ⓔ
3 Ⓐ Ⓑ Ⓒ Ⓓ Ⓔ   13 Ⓐ Ⓑ Ⓒ Ⓓ Ⓔ   23 Ⓐ Ⓑ Ⓒ Ⓓ Ⓔ   33 Ⓐ Ⓑ Ⓒ Ⓓ Ⓔ
4 Ⓐ Ⓑ Ⓒ Ⓓ Ⓔ   14 Ⓐ Ⓑ Ⓒ Ⓓ Ⓔ   24 Ⓐ Ⓑ Ⓒ Ⓓ Ⓔ   34 Ⓐ Ⓑ Ⓒ Ⓓ Ⓔ
5 Ⓐ Ⓑ Ⓒ Ⓓ Ⓔ   15 Ⓐ Ⓑ Ⓒ Ⓓ Ⓔ   25 Ⓐ Ⓑ Ⓒ Ⓓ Ⓔ   35 Ⓐ Ⓑ Ⓒ Ⓓ Ⓔ
6 Ⓐ Ⓑ Ⓒ Ⓓ Ⓔ   16 Ⓐ Ⓑ Ⓒ Ⓓ Ⓔ   26 Ⓐ Ⓑ Ⓒ Ⓓ Ⓔ   36 Ⓐ Ⓑ Ⓒ Ⓓ Ⓔ
7 Ⓐ Ⓑ Ⓒ Ⓓ Ⓔ   17 Ⓐ Ⓑ Ⓒ Ⓓ Ⓔ   27 Ⓐ Ⓑ Ⓒ Ⓓ Ⓔ   37 Ⓐ Ⓑ Ⓒ Ⓓ Ⓔ
8 Ⓐ Ⓑ Ⓒ Ⓓ Ⓔ   18 Ⓐ Ⓑ Ⓒ Ⓓ Ⓔ   28 Ⓐ Ⓑ Ⓒ Ⓓ Ⓔ   38 Ⓐ Ⓑ Ⓒ Ⓓ Ⓔ
9 Ⓐ Ⓑ Ⓒ Ⓓ Ⓔ   19 Ⓐ Ⓑ Ⓒ Ⓓ Ⓔ   29 Ⓐ Ⓑ Ⓒ Ⓓ Ⓔ   39 Ⓐ Ⓑ Ⓒ Ⓓ Ⓔ
10 Ⓐ Ⓑ Ⓒ Ⓓ Ⓔ   20 Ⓐ Ⓑ Ⓒ Ⓓ Ⓔ   30 Ⓐ Ⓑ Ⓒ Ⓓ Ⓔ   40 Ⓐ Ⓑ Ⓒ Ⓓ Ⓔ

Use a No. 2 pencil only. Be sure each mark is dark and completely fills the intended oval. Completely erase any errors or stray marks.

Start with number 1 for each new section. If a section has fewer questions than answer spaces, leave the extra answer spaces blank.

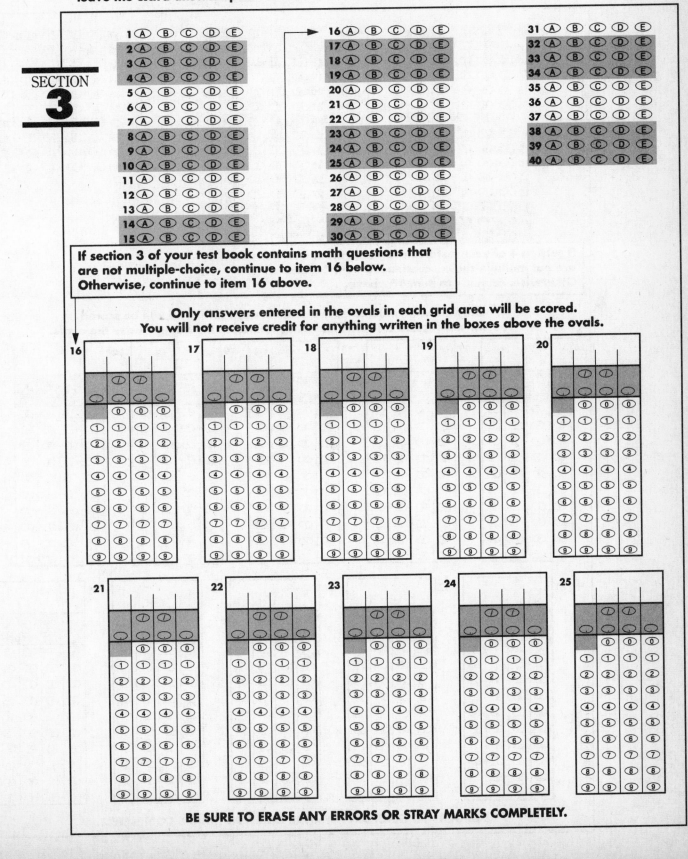

If section 3 of your test book contains math questions that are not multiple-choice, continue to item 16 below. Otherwise, continue to item 16 above.

Only answers entered in the ovals in each grid area will be scored. You will not receive credit for anything written in the boxes above the ovals.

BE SURE TO ERASE ANY ERRORS OR STRAY MARKS COMPLETELY.

Use a No. 2 pencil only. Be sure each mark is dark and completely fills the intended oval. Completely erase any errors or stray marks.

Start with number 1 for each new section. If a section has fewer questions than answer spaces, leave the extra answer spaces blank.

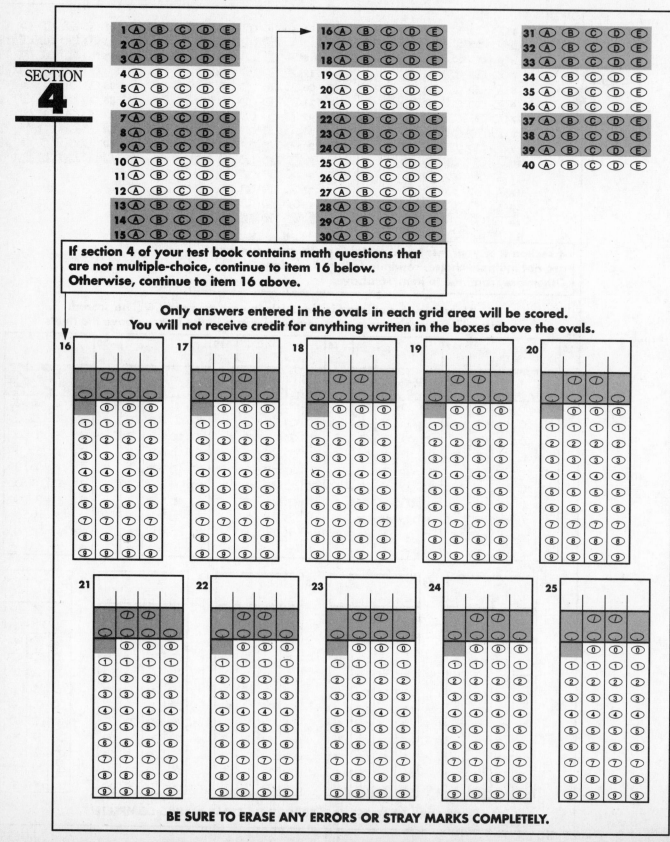

SECTION 4

If section 4 of your test book contains math questions that are not multiple-choice, continue to item 16 below. Otherwise, continue to item 16 above.

Only answers entered in the ovals in each grid area will be scored. You will not receive credit for anything written in the boxes above the ovals.

BE SURE TO ERASE ANY ERRORS OR STRAY MARKS COMPLETELY.

Use a No. 2 pencil only. Be sure each mark is dark and completely fills the intended oval. Completely erase any errors or stray marks.

Start with number 1 for each new section. If a section has fewer questions than answer spaces, leave the extra answer spaces blank.

SECTION 5

1 Ⓐ Ⓑ Ⓒ Ⓓ Ⓔ	11 Ⓐ Ⓑ Ⓒ Ⓓ Ⓔ	21 Ⓐ Ⓑ Ⓒ Ⓓ Ⓔ	31 Ⓐ Ⓑ Ⓒ Ⓓ Ⓔ
2 Ⓐ Ⓑ Ⓒ Ⓓ Ⓔ	12 Ⓐ Ⓑ Ⓒ Ⓓ Ⓔ	22 Ⓐ Ⓑ Ⓒ Ⓓ Ⓔ	32 Ⓐ Ⓑ Ⓒ Ⓓ Ⓔ
3 Ⓐ Ⓑ Ⓒ Ⓓ Ⓔ	13 Ⓐ Ⓑ Ⓒ Ⓓ Ⓔ	23 Ⓐ Ⓑ Ⓒ Ⓓ Ⓔ	33 Ⓐ Ⓑ Ⓒ Ⓓ Ⓔ
4 Ⓐ Ⓑ Ⓒ Ⓓ Ⓔ	14 Ⓐ Ⓑ Ⓒ Ⓓ Ⓔ	24 Ⓐ Ⓑ Ⓒ Ⓓ Ⓔ	34 Ⓐ Ⓑ Ⓒ Ⓓ Ⓔ
5 Ⓐ Ⓑ Ⓒ Ⓓ Ⓔ	15 Ⓐ Ⓑ Ⓒ Ⓓ Ⓔ	25 Ⓐ Ⓑ Ⓒ Ⓓ Ⓔ	35 Ⓐ Ⓑ Ⓒ Ⓓ Ⓔ
6 Ⓐ Ⓑ Ⓒ Ⓓ Ⓔ	16 Ⓐ Ⓑ Ⓒ Ⓓ Ⓔ	26 Ⓐ Ⓑ Ⓒ Ⓓ Ⓔ	36 Ⓐ Ⓑ Ⓒ Ⓓ Ⓔ
7 Ⓐ Ⓑ Ⓒ Ⓓ Ⓔ	17 Ⓐ Ⓑ Ⓒ Ⓓ Ⓔ	27 Ⓐ Ⓑ Ⓒ Ⓓ Ⓔ	37 Ⓐ Ⓑ Ⓒ Ⓓ Ⓔ
8 Ⓐ Ⓑ Ⓒ Ⓓ Ⓔ	18 Ⓐ Ⓑ Ⓒ Ⓓ Ⓔ	28 Ⓐ Ⓑ Ⓒ Ⓓ Ⓔ	38 Ⓐ Ⓑ Ⓒ Ⓓ Ⓔ
9 Ⓐ Ⓑ Ⓒ Ⓓ Ⓔ	19 Ⓐ Ⓑ Ⓒ Ⓓ Ⓔ	29 Ⓐ Ⓑ Ⓒ Ⓓ Ⓔ	39 Ⓐ Ⓑ Ⓒ Ⓓ Ⓔ
10 Ⓐ Ⓑ Ⓒ Ⓓ Ⓔ	20 Ⓐ Ⓑ Ⓒ Ⓓ Ⓔ	30 Ⓐ Ⓑ Ⓒ Ⓓ Ⓔ	40 Ⓐ Ⓑ Ⓒ Ⓓ Ⓔ

SECTION 6

1 Ⓐ Ⓑ Ⓒ Ⓓ Ⓔ	11 Ⓐ Ⓑ Ⓒ Ⓓ Ⓔ	21 Ⓐ Ⓑ Ⓒ Ⓓ Ⓔ	31 Ⓐ Ⓑ Ⓒ Ⓓ Ⓔ
2 Ⓐ Ⓑ Ⓒ Ⓓ Ⓔ	12 Ⓐ Ⓑ Ⓒ Ⓓ Ⓔ	22 Ⓐ Ⓑ Ⓒ Ⓓ Ⓔ	32 Ⓐ Ⓑ Ⓒ Ⓓ Ⓔ
3 Ⓐ Ⓑ Ⓒ Ⓓ Ⓔ	13 Ⓐ Ⓑ Ⓒ Ⓓ Ⓔ	23 Ⓐ Ⓑ Ⓒ Ⓓ Ⓔ	33 Ⓐ Ⓑ Ⓒ Ⓓ Ⓔ
4 Ⓐ Ⓑ Ⓒ Ⓓ Ⓔ	14 Ⓐ Ⓑ Ⓒ Ⓓ Ⓔ	24 Ⓐ Ⓑ Ⓒ Ⓓ Ⓔ	34 Ⓐ Ⓑ Ⓒ Ⓓ Ⓔ
5 Ⓐ Ⓑ Ⓒ Ⓓ Ⓔ	15 Ⓐ Ⓑ Ⓒ Ⓓ Ⓔ	25 Ⓐ Ⓑ Ⓒ Ⓓ Ⓔ	35 Ⓐ Ⓑ Ⓒ Ⓓ Ⓔ
6 Ⓐ Ⓑ Ⓒ Ⓓ Ⓔ	16 Ⓐ Ⓑ Ⓒ Ⓓ Ⓔ	26 Ⓐ Ⓑ Ⓒ Ⓓ Ⓔ	36 Ⓐ Ⓑ Ⓒ Ⓓ Ⓔ
7 Ⓐ Ⓑ Ⓒ Ⓓ Ⓔ	17 Ⓐ Ⓑ Ⓒ Ⓓ Ⓔ	27 Ⓐ Ⓑ Ⓒ Ⓓ Ⓔ	37 Ⓐ Ⓑ Ⓒ Ⓓ Ⓔ
8 Ⓐ Ⓑ Ⓒ Ⓓ Ⓔ	18 Ⓐ Ⓑ Ⓒ Ⓓ Ⓔ	28 Ⓐ Ⓑ Ⓒ Ⓓ Ⓔ	38 Ⓐ Ⓑ Ⓒ Ⓓ Ⓔ
9 Ⓐ Ⓑ Ⓒ Ⓓ Ⓔ	19 Ⓐ Ⓑ Ⓒ Ⓓ Ⓔ	29 Ⓐ Ⓑ Ⓒ Ⓓ Ⓔ	39 Ⓐ Ⓑ Ⓒ Ⓓ Ⓔ
10 Ⓐ Ⓑ Ⓒ Ⓓ Ⓔ	20 Ⓐ Ⓑ Ⓒ Ⓓ Ⓔ	30 Ⓐ Ⓑ Ⓒ Ⓓ Ⓔ	40 Ⓐ Ⓑ Ⓒ Ⓓ Ⓔ

Use a No. 2 pencil only. Be sure each mark is dark and completely fills the intended oval. Completely erase any errors or stray marks.

Start with number 1 for each new section. If a section has fewer questions than answer spaces, leave the extra answer spaces blank.

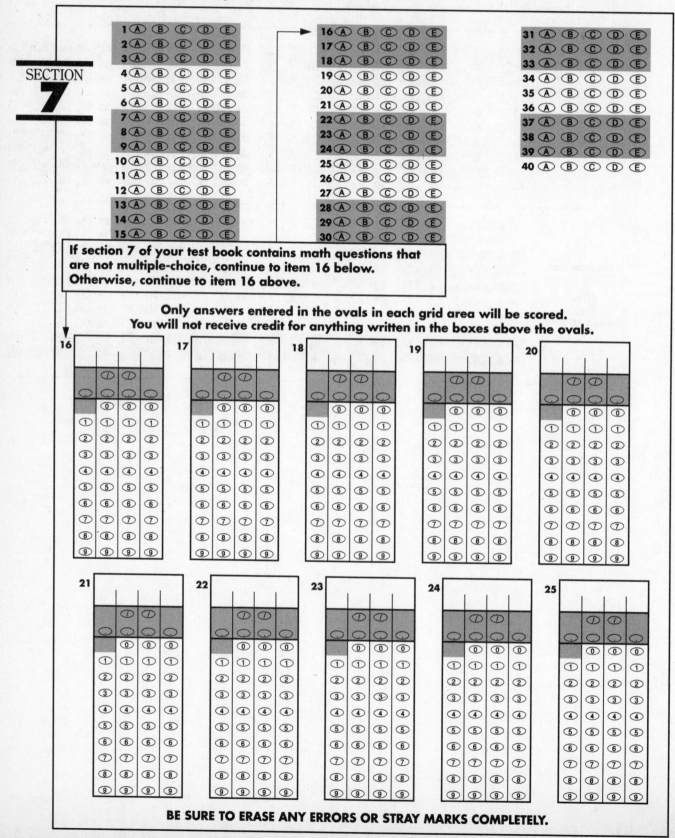

SECTION 7

If section 7 of your test book contains math questions that are not multiple-choice, continue to item 16 below. Otherwise, continue to item 16 above.

Only answers entered in the ovals in each grid area will be scored. You will not receive credit for anything written in the boxes above the ovals.

BE SURE TO ERASE ANY ERRORS OR STRAY MARKS COMPLETELY.

Time: 30 Minutes
30 Questions

For each question in this section, choose the best answer from among the choices given and fill in the corresponding oval on the answer sheet.

Each of the following sentences has one or two blanks, each blank indicating that something has been omitted. Beneath the sentence are five lettered words or sets of words labeled A through E. Choose the word or set of words that, when inserted in the sentence, *best* fits the meaning of the sentence as a whole.

Example:

Medieval kingdoms did not become constitutional republics overnight; on the contrary, the change was ---.

(A) unpopular
(B) unexpected
(C) advantageous
(D) sufficient
(E) gradual

Ⓐ Ⓑ Ⓒ Ⓓ ●

1 In a rising tide of _____ in public education, Miss Anderson was an example of an informed and _____ teacher—a blessing to children and an asset to the nation.

(A) compromise . . . inept
(B) pacifism . . . inspiring
(C) ambiguity . . . average
(D) mediocrity . . . dedicated
(E) oblivion . . . typical

2 It is _____ that primitive man considered eclipses to be _____.

(A) foretold . . . spectacular
(B) impossible . . . ominous
(C) understandable . . . magical
(D) true . . . rational
(E) glaring . . . desirable

3 By _____ the conversation, the girl had once again proved that she had overcome her shyness.

(A) appreciating
(B) recognizing
(C) hearing
(D) initiating
(E) considering

4 Only an authority in that area would be able to _____ such highly _____ subject matter included in the book.

(A) understand . . . general
(B) confuse . . . simple
(C) read . . . useless
(D) comprehend . . . complex
(E) misconstrue . . . sophisticated

5 The professor displayed extreme stubbornness; not only did he _____ the logic of the student's argument, but he _____ to acknowledge that the textbook conclusion was correct.

(A) amplify . . . hesitated
(B) reject . . . refused
(C) clarify . . . consented
(D) justify . . . expected
(E) ridicule . . . proposed

6 The _____ of the explorers was reflected in their refusal to give up.

(A) tenacity
(B) degradation
(C) greed
(D) harassment
(E) sociability

GO ON TO THE NEXT PAGE

7 Ironically, the protest held in order to strengthen the labor movement served to _____ it.

(A) justify
(B) coddle
(C) weaken
(D) invigorate
(E) appease

8 Governor Edwards combined _____ politics with administrative skills to dominate the state; in addition to these assets, he was also _____.

(A) corrupt ... glum
(B) inept ... civil
(C) incriminating ... sincere
(D) astute ... dapper
(E) trivial ... lavish

9 In spite of David's tremendous intelligence, he was frequently _____ when confronted with practical matters.

(A) coherent
(B) baffled
(C) cautious
(D) philosophical
(E) pensive

GO ON TO THE NEXT PAGE

Each of the following questions consists of a related pair of words or phrases, followed by five pairs of words or phrases labeled A through E. Select the pair that *best* expresses a relationship similar to that expressed in the original pair.

Example:

CRUMB : BREAD : :
(A) ounce : unit
(B) splinter : wood
(C) water : bucket
(D) twine : rope
(E) cream : butter

Ⓐ ● Ⓒ Ⓓ Ⓔ

10 MISNOMER : NAME : :

(A) malapropism : word
(B) faith : heresy
(C) rationalization : excuse
(D) autocracy : crime
(E) hypocrisy : follower

11 EMANCIPATE : SLAVERY : :

(A) erase : document
(B) inveigle : agreement
(C) exonerate : blame
(D) ratify : contract
(E) supplant : favor

12 CAST : ACTOR : :

(A) integrity : barrister
(B) molecule : space
(C) corporation : firm
(D) harem : sheik
(E) clientele : customer

13 ETERNAL : DURATION : :

(A) temporary : time
(B) weak : control
(C) harmonious : music
(D) dry : water
(E) omnipotent : power

14 SUBMISSIVE : DEFIANCE : :

(A) agile : alertness
(B) courageous : fear
(C) doubtful : indecision
(D) confident : poise
(E) violent : rebellion

15 PROFLIGATE : MORAL : :

(A) crook : fearful
(B) carpenter : patient
(C) lawyer : placid
(D) miser : generous
(E) profiteer : understanding

GO ON TO THE NEXT PAGE

767

Each of the following passages is followed by questions based on its content. Answer the questions following each passage on the basis of what is *stated* or *implied* in that passage and in any introductory material that may be provided.

Questions 16–21 are based on the following passage.

The following passage deals with adjustment to one's surroundings and the terms and theory associated with such adjustment.

As in the case of so many words used by the biologist and physiologist, the word acclimatization is hard to define. With increase in knowledge and understanding, meanings of words change. Originally the term acclimatization was
5 taken to mean only the ability of human beings or animals or plants to accustom themselves to new and strange climatic conditions, primarily altered temperature. A person or a wolf moves to a hot climate and is uncomfortable there, but after a time is better able to withstand the heat. But aside
10 from temperature, there are other aspects of climate. A person or an animal may become adjusted to living at higher altitudes than those it was originally accustomed to. At really high altitudes, such as aviators may be exposed to, the low atmospheric pressure becomes a factor of primary im-
15 portance. In changing to a new environment, a person may, therefore, meet new conditions of temperature or pressure, and in addition may have to contend with different chemical surroundings. On high mountains, the amount of oxygen in the atmosphere may be relatively small; in crowded cities, a
20 person may become exposed to relatively high concentrations of carbon dioxide or even carbon monoxide, and in various areas may be exposed to conditions in which the water content of the atmosphere is extremely high or extremely low. Thus in the case of humans, animals, and even
25 plants, the concept of acclimatization includes the phenomena of increased toleration of high or low temperature, of altered pressure, and of changes in the chemical environment.
Let us define acclimatization, therefore, as the process
30 in which an organism or a part of an organism becomes inured to an environment which is normally unsuitable to it or lethal for it. By and large, acclimatization is a relatively slow process. The term should not be taken to include relatively rapid adjustments such as our sense organs are con-
35 stantly making. This type of adjustment is commonly referred to by physiologists as "adaptation." Thus our touch sense soon becomes accustomed to the pressure of our clothes and we do not feel them; we soon fail to hear the ticking of a clock; obnoxious orders after a time fail to make
40 much impression on us, and our eyes in strong light rapidly become insensitive.
The fundamental fact about acclimatization is that all animals and plants have some capacity to adjust themselves to changes in their environment. This is one of the most
45 remarkable characteristics of living organisms, a characteristic for which it is extremely difficult to find explanations.

16 According to the reading selection, all animals and plants

(A) have an ability for acclimatization.
(B) can adjust to only one change in the environment at a time.
(C) are successful in adjusting themselves to changes in their environments.
(D) can adjust to natural changes in the environment but not to artificially induced changes.
(E) that have once acclimatized themselves to an environmental change can acclimatize themselves more rapidly to subsequent changes.

17 It can be inferred from the reading selection that

(A) every change in the environment requires acclimatization by living things.
(B) plants and animals are more alike than they are different.
(C) biologist and physiologists study essentially the same things.
(D) the explanation of acclimatization is specific to each plant and animal.
(E) as science develops, the connotation of terms may change.

18 According to the reading selection, acclimatization

(A) is similar to adaptation.
(B) is more important today than it formerly was.
(C) involves positive as well as negative adjustment.
(D) may be involved with a part of an organism but not with the whole organism.
(E) is more difficult to explain with the more complex present-day environment than formerly.

GO ON TO THE NEXT PAGE

19 By inference from the reading selection, which one of the following would *not* require the process of acclimatization?

(A) an ocean fish placed in a lake
(B) a skin diver making a deep dive
(C) an airplane pilot making a high-altitude flight
(D) a person going from daylight into a darkened room
(E) a businessman moving from Denver, Colorado, to New Orleans, Louisiana

20 The word "inured" in line 31 most likely means

(A) exposed
(B) accustomed
(C) attracted
(D) associated
(E) in love with

21 According to the passage, a major distinction between acclimatization and adaptation is that acclimatization

(A) is more important than adaptation.
(B) is relatively slow and adaptation is relatively rapid.
(C) applies to adjustments while adaptation does not apply to adjustments.
(D) applies to terrestrial animals and adaptation to aquatic animals.
(E) is applicable to all animals and plants and adaptation only to higher animals and man.

GO ON TO THE NEXT PAGE

Questions 22–30 are based on the following passage.

The following passage is about the Chinese Empire, the forces that kept the Empire together, its culture, and its philosophy.

First of all, it is important to note that the old China was an empire rather than a state. To the Chinese and their rulers, the word China did not exist and to them it would have been meaningless. They sometimes used a term which
5 we translate "the Middle Kingdom." To them there could be only one legitimate ruler for all civilized mankind. All others were rightly subordinate to him and should acknowledge his suzerainty. From this standpoint, there could not, as in Europe, be diplomatic relations between equal states, each of
10 them sovereign. When, in the nineteenth century, Europeans insisted upon intercourse with China on the basis of equality, the Chinese were at first amused and then scandalized and indignant. Centuries of training had bred in them the conviction that all other rulers should be tributary to the Son of
15 Heaven.

The tie which bound this world-embracing empire together, so the Chinese were taught to believe, was as much cultural as political. As there could be only one legitimate ruler to whom all mankind must be subject, so there could be
20 only one culture that fully deserved to be called civilized. Other cultures might have worth, but ultimately they were more or less barbarous. There could be only one civilization, and that was the civilization of the Middle Kingdom. Beginning with the Han, the ideal of civilization was held to
25 be Confucian. The Confucian interpretation of civilization was adopted and inculcated as the norm. Others might be tolerated, but if they seriously threatened the Confucian institutions and foundations of society they were to be curbed and, perhaps, exterminated as a threat to the highest
30 values.

Since the bond of the Empire was cultural and since the Empire should include all civilized mankind, racial distinctions were not so marked as in most other parts of the world. The Chinese did not have so strong a sense of being of
35 different blood from non-Chinese as twentieth-century conceptions of race and nation later led them to develop. They were proud of being "the sons of Han" or "the men of T'ang," but if a people fully adopted Chinese culture no great distinction was perceived between them and those who earlier had
40 been governed by that culture.

This helps to account for the comparative contentment of Chinese under alien rulers. If, as was usually the case, these invading conquerors adopted the culture of their subjects and governed through the accustomed machinery and
45 by traditional Confucian principles, they were accepted as legitimate Emperors. Few of the non-Chinese dynasties completely made this identification. This probably in part accounts for such restiveness as the Chinese showed under their rule. For instance, so long as they were dominant, the

50 Manchus, while they accepted much of the Chinese culture and prided themselves on being experts in it and posed as its patrons, never completely abandoned their distinctive ancestral ways.

The fact that the tie was cultural rather than racial
55 helps to account for the remarkable homogeneity of the Chinese. Many different ethnic strains have gone to make up the people whom we call the Chinese. Presumably in the Chou and probably, earlier, in the Shang, the bearers of Chinese culture were not a single race. As Chinese culture
60 moved southward it encountered differing cultures and, almost certainly, divergent stocks. The many invaders from the north and west brought in more variety. In contrast with India, where caste and religion have tended to keep apart the racial strata, in China assimilation made great progress.
65 That assimilation has not been complete. Today the discerning observer can notice differences even among those who are Chinese in language and customs, and in many parts of China Proper there are groups who preserve not only their racial but also their linguistic and cultural identity. Still,
70 nowhere else on the globe is there so numerous a people who are so nearly homogeneous as are the Chinese.

This homogeneity is due not merely to a common cultural tie, but also to the particular kind of culture which constitutes that tie. Something in the Chinese tradition rec-
75 ognized as civilized those who conformed to certain ethical standards and social customs. It was the fitting into Confucian patterns of conduct and of family and community life rather than blood kinship or ancestry which labeled one as civilized and as Chinese.

22 The force that kept the Chinese empire together was largely

(A) religious
(B) military
(C) economic
(D) a fear of invasion from the north and west
(E) the combination of a political and a cultural bond

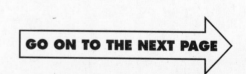

GO ON TO THE NEXT PAGE

23 The reason China resisted having diplomatic relations with European nations was that

(A) for centuries the Chinese had believed that their nation must be supreme among all other countries
(B) the Chinese saw nothing of value in European culture
(C) China was afraid of European military power
(D) such relations were against the teachings of the Son of Heaven
(E) the danger of disease was ever present when foreigners arrived

24 Confucianism stresses, above all,

(A) image worship
(B) recognition of moral values
(C) division of church and state
(D) acceptance of foreigners
(E) separation of social classes

25 Han and T'ang were Chinese

(A) philosophers
(B) holidays
(C) dynasties
(D) generals
(E) religions

26 If the unifying force in the Chinese empire had been racial, it is likely that

(A) China would have never become great
(B) China would be engaged in constant warfare
(C) China would have become a highly industrialized nation
(D) there would have been increasing discontent under foreign rulers
(E) China would have greatly expanded its influence

27 A problem of contemporary India that does not trouble China is

(A) overpopulation
(B) the persistence of the caste system
(C) a lack of modern industrial development
(D) a scarcity of universities
(E) a low standard of living

28 The Manchus encountered some dissatisfaction within the empire because

(A) of their tyrannical rule
(B) they retained some of their original cultural practices
(C) they were of a distinctly foreign race
(D) of the heavy taxes they levied
(E) they rejected totally Chinese culture

29 The Chinese are basically a homogeneous people because

(A) different races were able to assimilate to a great degree
(B) there has always been only one race in China
(C) the other races came to look like the Chinese because of geographical factors
(D) all other races were forcibly kept out of China
(E) of their antipathy toward intermarriage

30 The word "restiveness" in line 48 means

(A) authority
(B) happiness
(C) impatience
(D) hyperactivity
(E) quietude

IF YOU FINISH BEFORE TIME IS CALLED, YOU MAY CHECK YOUR WORK ON THIS SECTION ONLY. DO NOT TURN TO ANY OTHER SECTION IN THE TEST.

STOP

Time: 30 Minutes
25 Questions

In this section solve each problem, using any available space on this page for scratch-work. Then decide which is the best of the choices given and fill in the corresponding oval on the answer sheet.

Notes:

1. The use of a calculator is permitted. All numbers used are real numbers.

2. Figures that accompany problems in this test are intended to provide information useful in solving the problems. They are drawn as accurately as possible EXCEPT when it is stated in a specific problem that the figure is not drawn to scale. All figures lie in a plane unless otherwise indicated.

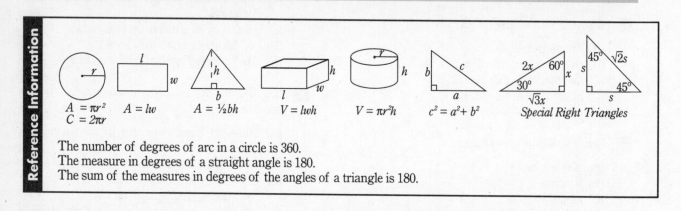

Reference Information

$A = \pi r^2$ $A = lw$ $A = \frac{1}{2}bh$ $V = lwh$ $V = \pi r^2 h$ $c^2 = a^2 + b^2$ *Special Right Triangles*
$C = 2\pi r$

The number of degrees of arc in a circle is 360.
The measure in degrees of a straight angle is 180.
The sum of the measures in degrees of the angles of a triangle is 180.

---

1 What is another expression for 8 less than the quotient of x and 3?

(A) $\dfrac{x-8}{3}$

(B) $\dfrac{x}{3} - 8$

(C) $8 - 3x$

(D) $3x - 8$

(E) $3(8-x)$

2 Each of Phil's buckets has a capacity of 11 gallons. Each of Mark's buckets can hold 8 gallons. How much more water, in gallons, can 7 of Phil's buckets hold than 7 of Mark's buckets?

(A) 3
(B) 7
(C) 21
(D) 24
(E) 56

GO ON TO THE NEXT PAGE

3 Which of the following is *not* equal to a whole number?

(A) $\dfrac{66 - 36}{3}$

(B) $\dfrac{66 + 36}{6}$

(C) $\dfrac{66 + 36}{12}$

(D) $\dfrac{66 - 36}{15}$

(E) $\dfrac{66 + 36}{17}$

5 Given $\dfrac{4^3 + 4^3 + 4^3 + 4^3}{4^y} = 4$, find y.

(A) 3
(B) 4
(C) 8
(D) 12
(E) 64

4 Dick has $15.25 and spent $7.50 at the sporting goods store. How much money does he have left?

(A) $0.25
(B) $1.75
(C) $6.75
(D) $7.75
(E) $8.25

6 The ratio of $3\frac{1}{3}$ hours to 11 hours is equal to

(A) $\dfrac{3}{110}$

(B) $\dfrac{3}{13}$

(C) $\dfrac{3}{11}$

(D) $\dfrac{10}{33}$

(E) $\dfrac{10}{13}$

GO ON TO THE NEXT PAGE

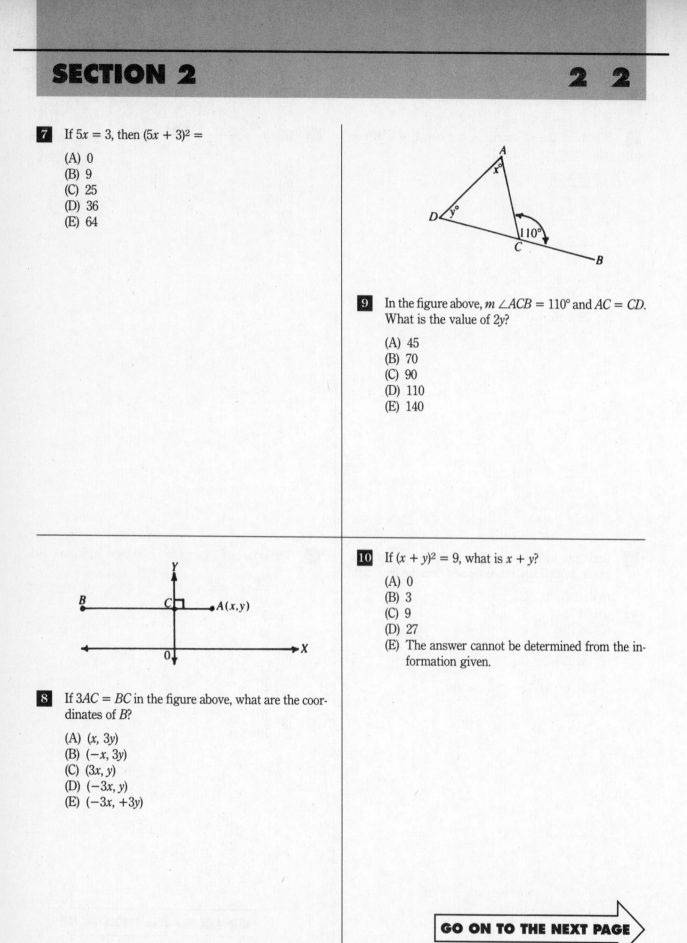

7 If $5x = 3$, then $(5x + 3)^2 =$

(A) 0
(B) 9
(C) 25
(D) 36
(E) 64

9 In the figure above, $m \angle ACB = 110°$ and $AC = CD$. What is the value of $2y$?

(A) 45
(B) 70
(C) 90
(D) 110
(E) 140

10 If $(x + y)^2 = 9$, what is $x + y$?

(A) 0
(B) 3
(C) 9
(D) 27
(E) The answer cannot be determined from the information given.

8 If $3AC = BC$ in the figure above, what are the coordinates of B?

(A) $(x, 3y)$
(B) $(-x, 3y)$
(C) $(3x, y)$
(D) $(-3x, y)$
(E) $(-3x, +3y)$

GO ON TO THE NEXT PAGE

11 The average (arithmetic mean) of five numbers is 34. If three of the numbers are 28, 30, and 32, what is the sum of the other two?

(A) 40
(B) 50
(C) 60
(D) 70
(E) 80

13 For any positive integer, x, $\odot = \dfrac{x^2}{3}$ and $\boxed{x} = \dfrac{9}{x}$.

What is an expression for $\odot \times \boxed{x}$?

(A) $3x$
(B) x
(C) 1
(D) $\dfrac{x^3}{64}$
(E) $27x^3$

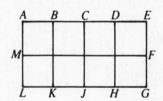

12 In the figure above, rectangle *AEGL* has been divided into 8 congruent squares. If the perimeter of one of these squares is 16, what is the value of *AE* + *MF* + *LG* + *AL* + *BK* + *CJ* + *DH* + *EG*?

(A) 32
(B) 44
(C) 88
(D) 128
(E) 176

14 If each of the 3 distinct points, *A*, *B*, and *C* are the same distance from point *D*, which of the following could be true?

   I. *A*, *B*, *C*, and *D* are the four vertices of a square.
  II. *A*, *B*, *C*, and *D* lie on the circumference of a circle.
 III. *A*, *B*, and *C*, lie on the circumference of the circle whose center is *D*.

(A) I only
(B) II only
(C) III only
(D) II and III only
(E) I, II, and III

775

15 If $x + by = 3x + y = 5$ and $y = 2$, then $b =$

(A) 0
(B) 1
(C) 2
(D) 3
(E) 4

16 There are 2 boys and 3 girls in the class. The ratio of boys to girls in the class is equal to all of the following *except*

(A) 4:6
(B) 9:12
(C) 6:9
(D) 12:18
(E) 18:27

17 At a certain small town, p gallons of gasoline are needed per month for each car in town. At this rate, if there are r cars in town, how long, in months, will q gallons last?

(A) $\frac{pq}{r}$

(B) $\frac{qr}{p}$

(C) $\frac{r}{pq}$

(D) $\frac{q}{pr}$

(E) pqr

18 What fraction of 1 week is 24 min?

(A) $\frac{1}{60}$

(B) $\frac{1}{168}$

(C) $\frac{1}{420}$

(D) $\frac{1}{1440}$

(E) $\frac{1}{10080}$

GO ON TO THE NEXT PAGE

Questions 19–20

The next two questions refer to the following definition:

The *l*-length of the segment from point A to point B is $B - A$.

19 What is the *l*-length from -3 to 3?

(A) -6
(B) -3
(C) 0
(D) 3
(E) 6

21 If the sum of 5 consecutive positive integers is w, in terms of w, which of the following represents the sum of the next 5 consecutive positive integers?

(A) $w + 5$
(B) $5w + 5$
(C) $5w + 25$
(D) $w + 25$
(E) $w^2 + 25$

$$R \quad S \quad T \quad U \quad V$$
$$-4$$

20 Of all segments beginning at -4 and ending at one of the integers indicated above on the number line, which segment has the *least l*-length?

(A) R
(B) S
(C) T
(D) U
(E) V

22 If the area of the square is twice the area of the triangle and $bc = 100$, then find a^2.

(A) 400
(B) 200
(C) 100
(D) 50
(E) 25

GO ON TO THE NEXT PAGE

777

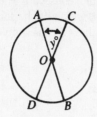

23 In the figure above, $\overline{AB}$ and $\overline{CD}$ are diameters of the circle whose center is O. If the radius of the circle is 2 inches and the sum of the lengths of arcs $\overset{\frown}{AD}$ and $\overset{\frown}{BC}$ is 3π inches, then $y =$

(A) 45
(B) 90
(C) 120
(D) 135
(E) 180

24 Five years ago, Ross was N times as old as Amanda was. If Amanda is now 19 years old, how old is Ross now in terms of N?

(A) $14N - 5$
(B) $14N + 5$
(C) $19N + 5$
(D) $15N + 5$
(E) $19N - 5$

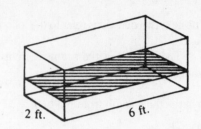

2 ft.   6 ft.

25 The figure above shows water in a tank whose base is 2 feet by 6 feet. If a rectangular solid whose dimensions are 1 foot by 1 foot by 2 feet is totally immersed in the water, how many *inches* will the water rise?

(A) $\frac{1}{6}$
(B) 1
(C) 2
(D) 3
(E) 12

IF YOU FINISH BEFORE TIME IS CALLED, YOU MAY CHECK YOUR WORK ON THIS SECTION ONLY. DO NOT TURN TO ANY OTHER SECTION IN THE TEST.

STOP

Time: 30 Minutes   For each question in this section, choose the best answer from among the choices given and
35 Questions   fill in the corresponding oval on the answer sheet.

Each of the following sentences has one or two blanks, each blank indicating that something has been omitted. Beneath the sentence are five words or sets of words labeled A through E. Choose the word or set of words that, when inserted in the sentence, *best* fits the meaning of the sentence as a whole.

Example:

Medieval kingdoms did not become constitutional republics overnight, on the contrary, the change was ---.

(A) unpopular
(B) unexpected
(C) advantageous
(D) sufficient
(E) gradual

Ⓐ Ⓑ Ⓒ Ⓓ ●

1   After four years of _____ curbs designed to protect the American auto industry, the president cleared the way for Japan to _____ more cars to the United States.

(A) profitable . . . drive
(B) flexible . . . produce
(C) motor . . . direct
(D) import . . . ship
(E) reciprocal . . . sell

2   Illegally parked vehicles block hydrants and crosswalks, _____ the flow of traffic when double-parked, and _____ the law.

(A) stem . . . enforce
(B) expedite . . . violate
(C) reduce . . . resist
(D) drench . . . challenge
(E) impede . . . flout

3   The photographs of Ethiopia's starving children demonstrate the _____ of drought, poor land use, and overpopulation.

(A) consequences
(B) prejudices
(C) inequities
(D) indications
(E) mortalities

4   There had been a yearning for an end to _____ with the Soviet Union, but little evidence had existed that nuclear-arms agreements had contributed to our _____ .

(A) treaties . . . silence
(B) advantages . . . relations
(C) differences . . . amity
(D) tensions . . . security
(E) commerce . . . decision

5   With the film rental business _____ , the video cassette recorder is changing the way millions of Americans use their _____ time.

(A) advertising . . . canceled
(B) suffering . . . valuable
(C) stabilizing . . . extra
(D) recording . . . unused
(E) booming . . . leisure

6   The union struck shortly after midnight after its negotiating committee _____ a company offer of a 20% raise.

(A) applauded
(B) rejected
(C) considered
(D) postponed
(E) accepted

779

7 The fact that the _____ of confrontation is no longer as popular as it once was _____ progress in race relations.

(A) practice . . . inculcates
(B) reticence . . . indicates
(C) glimmer . . . foreshadows
(D) insidiousness . . . reiterates
(E) technique . . . presages

8 The _____ of scarcity amidst plenty characterizes even a rich country in a time of inflation.

(A) coherence
(B) tedium
(C) facet
(D) sequence
(E) paradox

9 The scientist averred that a nuclear war could _____ enough smoke and dust to blot out the sun and freeze the earth.

(A) pervert
(B) extinguish
(C) generate
(D) evaluate
(E) perpetrate

10 Until his death he remained _____ in the belief that the world was conspiring against him.

(A) ignominious
(B) taciturn
(C) tantamount
(D) obdurate
(E) spurious

GO ON TO THE NEXT PAGE

Each of the following questions consists of a related pair of words or phrases, followed by five pairs of words or phrases labeled A through E. Select the pair that *best* expresses a relationship similar to that expressed in the original pair.

Example:

CRUMB : BREAD : :

(A) ounce : unit
(B) splinter : wood
(C) water : bucket
(D) twine : rope
(E) cream : butter

Ⓐ ● Ⓒ Ⓓ Ⓔ

11 SEW : TEAR : :

(A) settle : dispute
(B) caulk : leak
(C) alleviate : pain
(D) open : door
(E) research : dictionary

12 INFINITE : END : :

(A) spontaneous : occur
(B) isolated : envision
(C) buoyant : sink
(D) parallel : align
(E) condoned : excuse

13 COERCE : COAX : :

(A) avenge : reform
(B) suggest : demand
(C) declaim : argue
(D) diminish : expunge
(E) shove : nudge

14 REJUVENATE : YOUTH : :

(A) recuperate : disease
(B) reelect : president
(C) reiterate : item
(D) review : play
(E) reimburse : money

15 SNEER : CONTEMPT : :

(A) stalk : prey
(B) applaud : approval
(C) cringe : fear
(D) cough : throat
(E) grimace : pain

16 PLAYWRIGHT : SCRIPT : :

(A) composer : score
(B) physician : diagnosis
(C) verse : poet
(D) king : parliament
(E) daydreamer : fantasy

17 WANE : SIZE : :

(A) contort : shape
(B) abet : crime
(C) decelerate : speed
(D) exacerbate : annoyance
(E) amass : wealth

18 AMPLIFY : SOUND : :

(A) overthrow : dictator
(B) enlarge : photograph
(C) remediate : reader
(D) reflect : image
(E) alleviate : pain

19 UNPRETENTIOUS : OSTENTATION : :

(A) puerile : fact
(B) inconsequential : importance
(C) conventional : routine
(D) priceless : value
(E) lenient : humility

20 ENIGMATIC : CLEAR : :

(A) copious : scarce
(B) academic : masterful
(C) lucrative : monetary
(D) slanderous : illegal
(E) adroit : effective

GO ON TO THE NEXT PAGE

21 EMBARKATION : JOURNEY : :

(A) inception : project
(B) self-reliance : rebellion
(C) sanction : permission
(D) skepticism : failure
(E) suspicion : perjury

22 EPICURE : PLEASURE : :

(A) student : classes
(B) hermit : society
(C) critic : acceptance
(D) miser : wealth
(E) guardian : child

23 TOUCH : INTANGIBLE : :

(A) question : unreliable
(B) learn : ignorant
(C) convict : innocent
(D) fix : irreparable
(E) examine : vague

GO ON TO THE NEXT PAGE

The following two passages are followed by questions based on their content and on the relationship between the two passages. Answer the questions on the basis of what is *stated* or *implied* in the passages and in any introductory material that may be provided.

Questions 24—35 are based on the following passages

The following passages represent two different views of living—the views of living in the country and of living in the city.

Passage A

The snow falls gently on our quiet meadow sloping down to Penobscot Bay, with spruce trees back against the gray of the water. A raven croaks from a nearby treetop. Two gulls sail over the house and squawk unintelligibly together. The
5 only other sounds are the wood fire snapping, the kettle steaming on the stove and Pusso purring.

There is no phone to ring, no radio to turn on, no television to watch. We need don no city disguise and ride subways, catch trains, attend cocktail parties or dinners. We
10 can choose and make our own music, reread our favorite books, wear our old clothes, eat when and what we like from a well-stocked root cellar, or happily abstain from food, if we wish, the whole day. There is wood to cut, snow to shovel, mail to answer, but all in our own good time. No one is
15 pushing, no one shoving, no one ordering about. There is no job to lose; we make our own jobs. Free men? Almost.

A neighbor may amble in on snowshoes and bring us word of his horse's health or wife's pregnancy. Over a glass of cider we may talk of snowmobile incursions or hunters'
20 depredations. He may bring us a huge cabbage he has grown and we send him back with a bottle of our rosehips juice and a knitted doll for his little daughter. In our chat beside the fire we will probably not touch on the outside world, though we are not unaware of what stirs the nation.

25 The newspaper, reaching us by mail, brings us echoes of an inconsequential election between two shadow-boxing candidates for an office no one should covet. We read that two high officials, the Episcopal Bishop of New York and the chief of the Soviet delegation to the United Nations, have
30 separately been held up in daylight and robbed by armed men in Central Park. We learn that invaders are entering classrooms in Manhattan's public schools and at knife or gunpoint relieving teachers of their cash and trinkets before their open-mouthed pupils.

35 We thank our lucky stars that we live out in the wilderness, that we are not on congested streets and highways or clustered in high-rise city rookeries, with jangling noise and turmoil all about, that we are not in smog, that we can drink clean clear water, not fluoridized or chlorinated, from our
40 bubbling spring, that our homegrown food is not stale, preserved or embalmed and bought from the supermarket.

We are thankful for what the wilderness makes possible. Peace, progress, prosperity? We prefer peace, quiet, and frugality.

Passage B

45 You look out the window of your one-bedroom apartment and see swarms of people in the streets as if the day never ends. You live with the interminable sounds of the cars, trucks and repair services and hassles encountered. But there is an excitement that makes you alive. You can leave
50 your apartment at three in the morning and go to a coffee shop which remains open. You can lose your identity and forget about your problems by mingling during the day with the thousands of people roaming the streets. You may be walking right next to a famous celebrity or a lowly degener-
55 ate. But it doesn't matter. It is the excitement that counts, the fact that you can call anybody anytime by phone, get up-to-the-minute news through radio or TV. You can choose from hundreds of international restaurants, and although the food may not be home-grown, you certainly have the exciting
60 ambience of a packed restaurant with constant movement. You can choose from the best of hospitals and doctors, although it may take you some time to get an appointment with a doctor or get to the hospital because of traffic. But the noise, the inconveniences, the muggings, all this goes with
65 the territory—with the excitement. You can always escape to the country by train, car, bus, or even plane if you need to. However, city living is certainly not for everyone. And your ability to live or even survive in a city depends on your temperament, your principles, your occupation and your
70 interests. But for many, the tradeoff for a vibrant life, a pulse which never ends, and access to almost every cultural event almost at any time is certainly a lure to live in the city environment.

24 The general feeling running through Passage A is one of

(A) guarded resentment
(B) tolerable boredom
(C) restless indecision
(D) peaceful satisfaction
(E) marked indifference

GO ON TO THE NEXT PAGE

25 Which of the following is the most appropriate title for Passage A?

(A) Winter in the Country
(B) The Frills Aren't Needed
(C) Peace, Progress, and Prosperity
(D) Life Goes On
(E) A Lack of Conveniences

26 The author's reference to "an inconsequential election between two shadow-boxing candidates" (lines 26–27) indicates that the author

(A) has no faith in politicians
(B) is opposed to professional prizefighting
(C) does not believe in having any elections
(D) prefers that people govern themselves
(E) is of the opinion that all elections are fixed

27 The author of Passage A states or implies that

(A) there is no work to be done
(B) he is a completely free man
(C) his wife is pregnant
(D) he reads no newspapers
(E) he has a farm

28 Of the states below the location of the author's home in Passage A is most likely in the state of

(A) Arizona
(B) Florida
(C) Maine
(D) Louisiana
(E) Georgia

29 It can be inferred from Passage B that the author believes that in the city

(A) many people live in one-bedroom apartments
(B) when eating out, you'll never get home-grown food
(C) you can meet rich and poor at the most expensive restaurants
(D) losing one's identity is considered a "plus"
(E) friendliness is a "way of life"

30 The word "interminable" in line 47 means

(A) loud
(B) harsh
(C) ongoing
(D) bright
(E) close

31 The passages differ in that

(A) in Passage B, there is more of a tendency to qualify the good with the bad
(B) in Passage A there are no hospitals in the village whereas there are many in Passage B
(C) the author of Passage A believes that everyone should live in the country whereas in Passage B the author believes that everyone would do well in the city
(D) in Passage A there are no post offices to deliver mail
(E) in Passage A the author never reads newspapers whereas the author in Passage B is interested in up-to-the-minute news

32 Which is more likely to be surprising to the respective author?

(A) Passage A author: reading a headline in a newspaper: "Scientists Find Cancer Cure"
(B) Passage B author: speaking with a famous movie celebrity in the street
(C) Passage B author: finding a movie at two in the morning
(D) Passage A author: seeing some people skip a few meals
(E) Passage B author: hearing someone complain about city living

33 The word "frugality" in line 44 means

(A) progress
(B) stinginess
(C) wastefulness
(D) poverty
(E) quiet

34 The word "don" in line 8 is related to

(A) motion
(B) purchasing goods
(C) clothing
(D) eating
(E) fishing

GO ON TO THE NEXT PAGE

784

35 We can infer from the authors of each passage that

(A) the author of Passage A believes most news is bad whereas the author of Passage B believes most news is good

(B) the author of Passage A believes politics and elections are useless whereas the author in Passage B believes they are necessary

(C) the author of Passage A believes that city schools are dangerous and prefers not to have his or her children attend them whereas the author of Passage B may agree but accepts the situation

(D) the author of Passage A believes only the parks in the cities are safe whereas the author of Passage B believes that crime "goes with the territory"

(E) one author likes home-grown food, whereas the other does not

Time: 30 Minutes   This section contains two types of questions. You have 30 minutes to complete both
25 Questions   types. You may use any available space for scratchwork.

Notes:

1. The use of a calculator is permitted. All numbers used are real numbers.

2. Figures that accompany problems in this test are intended to provide information useful in solving the
    problems. They are drawn as accurately as possible EXCEPT when it is stated in a specific problem that the
    figure is not drawn to scale. All figures lie in a plane unless otherwise indicated.

Reference Information

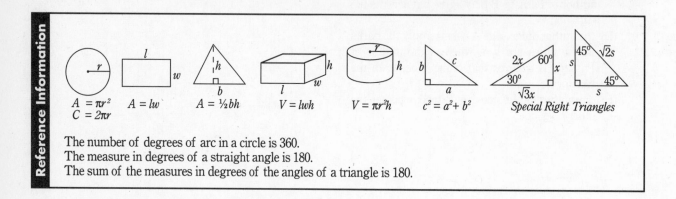

$A = \pi r^2$ $A = lw$ $A = \frac{1}{2}bh$ $V = lwh$ $V = \pi r^2 h$ $c^2 = a^2 + b^2$ *Special Right Triangles*
$C = 2\pi r$

The number of degrees of arc in a circle is 360.
The measure in degrees of a straight angle is 180.
The sum of the measures in degrees of the angles of a triangle is 180.

Directions for Quantitative Comparison Questions

Questions 1–15 each consist of two quantities in boxes, one in Column A and one in Column B. You are to compare the two quantities and on the answer sheet fill in oval

A if the quantity in Column A is greater;
B if the quantity in Column B is greater;
C if the two quantities are equal;
D if the relationship cannot be determined from the information given.

AN E RESPONSE WILL NOT BE SCORED.

Notes:

1. In some questions, information is given about one or both of the quantities to be compared. In such cases, the given information is centered above the two columns and is not boxed.
2. In a given question, a symbol that appears in both columns represents the same thing in Column A as it does in Column B.
3. Letters such as *x*, *n*, and *k* stand for real numbers.

EXAMPLES		
Column A	Column B	Answers

E1 | 5^2 | 20 | ●ⒷⒸⒹⒺ

150° *x*°

E2 | *x* | 30 | ⒶⒷ●ⒹⒺ

r and *s* are integers

E3 | $r + 1$ | $s - 1$ | ⒶⒷⒸ●Ⓔ

GO ON TO THE NEXT PAGE

SUMMARY DIRECTIONS FOR COMPARISON QUESTIONS

<u>Answer:</u>
A if the quantity in Column A is greater;
B if the quantity in Column B is greater;
C if the two quantities are equal;
D if the relationship cannot be determined from the information given.

AN E RESPONSE WILL NOT BE SCORED.

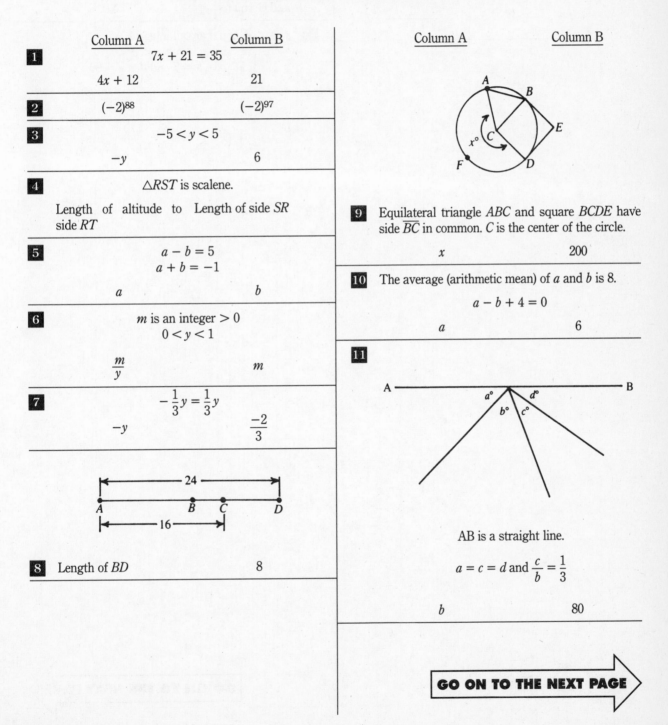

	Column A	Column B
1	$7x + 21 = 35$	
	$4x + 12$	21
2	$(-2)^{88}$	$(-2)^{97}$
3	$-5 < y < 5$	
	$-y$	6
4	$\triangle RST$ is scalene.	
	Length of altitude to side RT	Length of side SR
5	$a - b = 5$ $a + b = -1$	
	a	b
6	m is an integer > 0 $0 < y < 1$	
	$\dfrac{m}{y}$	m
7	$-\dfrac{1}{3}y = \dfrac{1}{3}y$	
	$-y$	$\dfrac{-2}{3}$

8   Length of BD 8

Column A   Column B

9 Equilateral triangle ABC and square $BCDE$ have side $\overline{BC}$ in common. C is the center of the circle.

x 200

10 The average (arithmetic mean) of a and b is 8.

$a - b + 4 = 0$

a 6

11

AB is a straight line.

$a = c = d$ and $\dfrac{c}{b} = \dfrac{1}{3}$

b 80

GO ON TO THE NEXT PAGE

787

	Column A	Column B

12 □ is one of the operations $+$, $-$, $\times$, or $\div$
□ satisfies $x \square (-x) = 0$ for all x

Column A	Column B
$x \square y$	$y \square x$

13

$$r, s, \text{ and } t > 0$$

Column A	Column B
$t + s + r$	$\dfrac{1}{t + s + r}$

14 For a class of 100 students, exactly 80 percent take calculus, exactly 60 percent take physics, and exactly 50 percent take German.

Column A	Column B
The number of students who take both physics and German.	50

15 a, b, c, d, and d are all integers > 0.

$$a < b < c < d < e$$
$$a \times b = 7 \text{ and } d \times e = 90$$

Column A	Column B
c	8

GO ON TO THE NEXT PAGE

Directions: Each of the 10 questions in this part requires you to solve the problem and enter your answer by marking the ovals in the special grid, as shown in the examples below.

Answer: $\frac{7}{12}$ or 7/12

Answer: 2.5

Answer: 201
Either position is correct.

Write answer in boxes.

Fraction line

Decimal point

Grid in result.

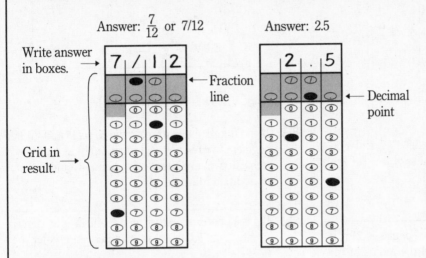

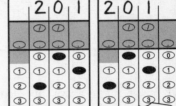

Note: You may start your answers in any column, space permitting. Columns not needed should be left blank.

- Mark no more than one oval in any column.

- Because the answer sheet will be machine-scored, **you will receive credit only if the ovals are filled in correctly.**

- Although not required, it is suggested that you write your answer in the boxes at the top of the columns to help you fill in the ovals accurately.

- Some problems may have more than one correct answer. In such cases, grid only one answer.

- No question has a negative answer.

- **Mixed numbers** such as $2\frac{1}{2}$ must be gridded as 2.5 or 5/2. (If ⬚ is gridded, it will be interpreted as $\frac{21}{2}$, not $2\frac{1}{2}$.)

- Decimal Accuracy: If you obtain a decimal answer, **enter the most accurate value the grid will accommodate.** For example, if you obtain an answer such as 0.6666…, you should record the result as .666 or .667. **Less accurate results such as .66 or .67 are not acceptable.**

Acceptable ways to grid $\frac{2}{3}$ = .6666…

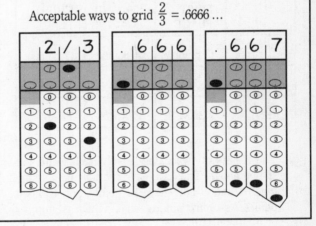

16 If $ab = 40$, $\frac{a}{b} = \frac{5}{2}$, and a and b are positive numbers, find the value of a.

17 Stephanie earned \$$x$ while working 10 hours. Evelyn earned \$$y$ while working 20 hours. If they both earn the same hourly wage and $x + y = 60$, how many dollars did Stephanie earn?

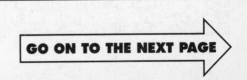

GO ON TO THE NEXT PAGE

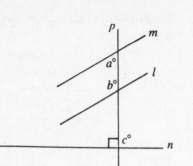

18 In the figure above, m is parallel to l and p is perpendicular to n. Find the value of $a + b + c$.

19 The difference of the areas of two circles is 21π. If their radii are $r + 3$ and r, find the radius of the *larger* circle.

	FIRST PLACE	SECOND PLACE	THIRD PLACE
	(8 points)	(4 points)	(2 points)
EVENT ①	TEAM A	TEAM B	TEAM C
EVENT ②	TEAM B	TEAM A	TEAM C

20 The results of two games involving 3 teams are shown above. Thus, we have the following standings: A and B both have 12 points, and C has 4 points. Assuming no ties, what is the least number of additional games that Team C will have to play in order to have the highest total score?

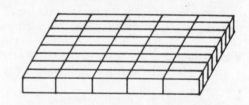

Note: Figure is not drawn to scale.

21 If the figure above were drawn to scale and all line segments were extended indefinitely in *both directions*, how many intersection points would there be in addition to N and M?

22 If a is 10 percent greater than b, and ac is 32 percent greater than bd, then c is what percent greater than d?

23 Since one gross = 12 dozen, what fraction of a gross of eggs is 3 eggs?

24 This figure above represents a layer of bricks, where each brick has a volume of 40 cubic inches. If all bricks are stacked in layers as shown, and the final pile of bricks occupies 8,000 cubic inches, how many layers are there in the final pile of bricks?

25 Let x be the smallest possible 3-digit number greater than or equal to 100 in which no digit is repeated. If y is the largest positive 3-digit number that can be made using all of the digits of x, which is the value of $y - x$?

IF YOU FINISH BEFORE TIME IS CALLED, YOU MAY CHECK YOUR WORK ON THIS SECTION ONLY. DO NOT TURN TO ANY OTHER SECTION IN THE TEST.

STOP

The passage below is followed by questions based on its content. Answer the questions on the basis of what is *stated* or *implied* in the passage and in any introductory material that may be provided.

Questions 1–13 are based on the following passage.

This passage describes the relationship between age and income throughout various periods of American history and the effects this trend will have on the various population groups in the future.

The relationship between age and income is only casually appreciated by recent theories on the purported redistribution of income. It is known, of course, that the average person's income begins to decline after he is fifty-five years

5 of age, and that it declines sharply after sixty-five. For example as early as in 1957, 58 percent of the spending units headed by persons sixty-five years and older earned less than $2,000. The relationship between old age and low income has often been considered a reflection of sociologi-

10 cal rather than economic factors—and therefore not to be included in any study of the economy. Actually, the character of the relationship is too integrated to be dissected. However, its significance is mounting with the increase in the number of older persons. The lowest-income groups

15 include a heavy concentration of older persons—in 1957, one-third of all spending units in the $0–$2,000 class were headed by persons sixty-five years and older; in 1948, it was 28 percent.

But in economic planning and social policy, it must be
20 remembered that, with the same income, the sixty-five-or-more spending unit will not spend less or need less than the younger spending unit, even though the pressure to save is greater than on the young. The functional ethos of our economy dictates that the comparatively unproductive old-

25 age population should consume in accordance with their output rather than their requirements. Most social scientists have accepted these values; they have assumed that the minimum economic needs of the aged should be lower than those of the younger family. But it is precisely at

30 retirement that personal requirements and the new demands of leisure call for an even larger income if this period is to be something more enjoyable than a wait for death.

The relationship between age and income is seen most clearly in the unionized blue-collar worker. Except for lay-
35 offs, which his seniority minimizes, and wage increments for higher productivity, awarded in many industries, his

income range is determined by his occupation. But within that income range, the deciding factor is the man's age. After forty-five, the average worker who loses his job has
40 more difficulty in finding a new one. Despite his seniority, the older worker is likely to be downgraded to a lower-paying job when he can no longer maintain the pace set by younger men. This is especially true of unskilled and semi-skilled workers.

45   The early and lower income period of a person's working life, during which he acquires his basic vocational skills, is most pronounced for the skilled, managerial, or professional worker. Then, between the ages of twenty-five and fifty, the average worker receives his peak earnings.

50 Meanwhile, his family expenses rise, there are children to support and basic household durables to obtain. Although his family's income may rise substantially until he is somewhere between thirty-five and forty-five, per capita consumption may drop at the same time. For the growing,

55 working-class family, limited in income by the very nature of the breadwinner's occupation, the economic consequences of this parallel rise in age, income, and obligations are especially pressing. Many in the low-income classes are just as vulnerable to poverty during middle age, when they

60 have a substantially larger income, as in old age. As family obligations finally do begin declining, so does income. Consequently, most members of these classes never have an adequate income.

Thus we see that, for a time, increasing age means
65 increasing income, and therefore a probable boost in income-tenth position. Although there are no extensive data in the matter, it can be confidently asserted that the higher income-tenths have a much greater representation of spending units headed by persons aged thirty-five to fifty-

70 five than do the lower income-tenths. This is demonstrably the case among the richest 5 percent of the consumer units. The real question is: To what extent does distribution of income-tenths within a certain age group deviate from distribution of income-tenths generally? Although information

75 is not as complete as might be desired, there is more than enough to make contingent generalizations. Detailed data

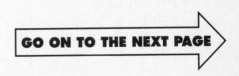

791

exist on income distribution by tenths and by age for 1935–36 and 1948, and on income-size distribution by age for the postwar years. They disclose sharp income inequal-
80 ities within every age group (although more moderate in the eighteen-to-twenty-five category)—inequalities that closely parallel the overall national income pattern. The implication is clear: A spending unit's income-tenth position *within his age category* varies much less, if at all, and is
85 determined primarily by his occupation.

In other words, in America, the legendary land of economic opportunity where any man can work his way to the top, there is only slight income mobility outside the natural age cycle of rising, then falling income. Since most
90 of the sixty-five-and-over age group falls into the low-income brackets and constitutes the largest segment of the $0–$2,000 income class, it is of obvious importance in analyzing future poverty in the United States to examine the growth trends of his group. The sixty-five-and-over
95 population composed 4.0 percent of the total population in 1900, 5.3 percent in 1930, 8.4 percent in 1955, and will reach an estimated 10.8 percent in 2000. Between 1900 and 2000, the total national population is expected to increase 276 percent, but those from ages forty-five through sixty-
100 four are expected to increase 416 percent, and those sixty-five and over are expected to increase 672 percent. Between 1990 and 2000, the population aged eighteen to twenty-five is also expected to grow far more rapidly than the middle-aged population. With the more rapid expansion of these
105 two low-income groups, the young and the old, in the years immediately ahead, an increase in the extent of poverty is probable.

1 According to the passage, most social scientists erroneously assume that

(A) personal expenses increase with the age of the spending unit
(B) the needs of the younger spending unit are greater than those of the aged
(C) the relationship between old age and low income is an economic and not a sociological problem
(D) members of the old-age population should consume in accordance with their requirements
(E) leisure living requires increased income

2 The word "appreciated" in line 2 most nearly means

(A) had artistic interest
(B) increased in value
(C) had curiosity
(D) had gratitude
(E) understood

3 It can be inferred that in the 35–55 age category

(A) income-tenth positions vary greatly
(B) income-tenth positions vary very little
(C) earning potential does not resemble the overall national income pattern
(D) occupations have little bearing on the income-tenth position
(E) there is great mobility between income-tenth positions

4 The author believes which of the following?

I. The aged will continue to increase as a percentage of the total population.
II. Income inequalities decrease with increasing age.
III. Managerial and professional workers have greater income mobility than blue-collar workers.

(A) I only
(B) II only
(C) III only
(D) I and II only
(E) I and III only

5 In the passage the term "functional ethos" in line 23 means

(A) national group
(B) ethnic influence
(C) prevailing ideology
(D) biased opinion
(E) practical ethics

6 The article states that the old-age population

(A) has increased because of longer life expectancy
(B) exceeds all but the 18–25 age group in growth rate
(C) is well represented among the higher income-tenths
(D) is increasing as a percentage of the low income-tenths
(E) has its greatest numbers among the middle income group

7 According to the author, aside from the natural age cycle, economic opportunity in America is greatly limited by

   I. occupation
   II. income inequality within every group
   III. class

(A) I only
(B) II only
(C) III only
(D) I and III only
(E) I and II only

8 The word "ethos" in line 23 most nearly means

(A) the character of a group of people
(B) economic–sociological ramifications
(C) the productivity of all age groups
(D) the management of large corporations
(E) the social scientists who deal with the economy

9 According to the passage, the older, unionized blue-collar workers are

(A) assured constant salary until retirement
(B) given preference over new workers because of seniority
(C) likely to receive downgraded salary
(D) more susceptible to layoff after 40
(E) encouraged to move to slower-paced but equal-paying jobs

10 The article states that the average worker finds that

(A) as family obligations begin escalating, income begins to decline
(B) he reaches economic stability at middle age because of the parallel rise in age, obligations, and income
(C) he earns least while he is acquiring vocational skills
(D) he reaches peak earning power between the ages of 40 and 65
(E) his wage gains coincide with the decline of family needs

11 The article states that within higher income-tenths

(A) 5% of the spending units are in the 35–55 age group
(B) the income-tenth increases occur only in the 35–55 age group
(C) members of the 35–55 age group have a greater representation than they do with the lower-income tenths
(D) the retirement age is approximately 10 years younger than that of the general population
(E) income variables show a higher correlation than those determined by occupation

12 It can be inferred that one could most accurately predict a person's income from

(A) his age
(B) his natural age cycle
(C) his occupation
(D) his occupation and age
(E) his seniority position

13 Which lines in the passage illustrate the author's sarcasm?

(A) lines 19–23
(B) lines 45–48
(C) lines 64–66
(D) lines 86–89
(E) lines 104–107

IF YOU FINISH BEFORE TIME IS CALLED, YOU MAY CHECK YOUR WORK ON THIS SECTION ONLY. DO NOT TURN TO ANY OTHER SECTION IN THE TEST.

Time: 15 Minutes   In this section solve each problem, using any available space on the page for scratchwork.
10 Questions   Then decide which is the best of the choices given and fill in the corresponding oval on the answer sheet.

Notes:

1. The use of a calculator is permitted. All numbers are real numbers.

2. Figures that accompany problems in this test are intended to provide information useful in solving the problems. They are drawn as accurately as possible EXCEPT when it is stated in a specific problem that the figure is not drawn to scale. All figures lie in a plane unless otherwise indicated.

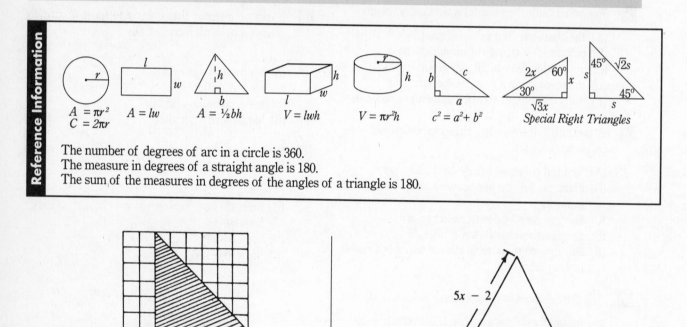

Reference Information

$A = \pi r^2$
$C = 2\pi r$

$A = lw$

$A = \frac{1}{2}bh$

$V = lwh$

$V = \pi r^2h$

$c^2 = a^2 + b^2$

Special Right Triangles

The number of degrees of arc in a circle is 360.
The measure in degrees of a straight angle is 180.
The sum of the measures in degrees of the angles of a triangle is 180.

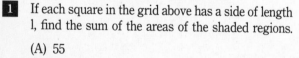

1 If each square in the grid above has a side of length 1, find the sum of the areas of the shaded regions.

(A) 55
(B) 46
(C) 37
(D) 30
(E) 24

2 The figure above is an equilateral triangle. What is its perimeter?

(A) $\frac{1}{4}$

(B) $\frac{1}{2}$

(C) $1\frac{1}{2}$

(D) $3\frac{1}{2}$

(E) The answer cannot be determined from the information given.

794

GO ON TO THE NEXT PAGE

3 If w waves pass through a certain point in s seconds, how many waves would pass through that point in t seconds?

(A) wst

(B) $\dfrac{t}{s}$

(C) $\dfrac{ws}{t}$

(D) $\dfrac{ts}{w}$

(E) $\dfrac{tw}{s}$

5 A box contains exactly 24 coins—nickels, dimes, and quarters. The probability of selecting a nickel by reaching into the box without looking is $\dfrac{3}{8}$. The probability of selecting a dime by reaching into the box without looking is $\dfrac{1}{8}$. How many quarters are in the box?

(A) 6
(B) 8
(C) 12
(D) 14
(E) 16

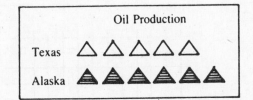

4 In the chart above, the amount represented by each shaded triangle is three times that represented by each unshaded triangle. What fraction of the total production represented by the chart was produced in Alaska?

(A) $\dfrac{6}{11}$

(B) $\dfrac{18}{5}$

(C) $\dfrac{18}{23}$

(D) $\dfrac{12}{17}$

(E) $\dfrac{23}{17}$

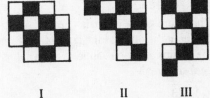

6 Which of the following designs *can* be formed by combining rectangles with size and shading the same as that shown above if overlap is not permitted?

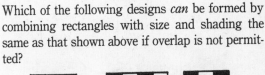

I   II   III

(A) I only
(B) II only
(C) III only
(D) I and II only
(E) II and III only

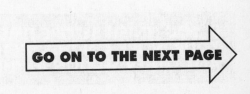

GO ON TO THE NEXT PAGE

7 Given that $r \neq 0$ and $r = 5w = 7a$, find the value of $r - w$ in terms of a.

(A) $\dfrac{1a}{7}$

(B) $\dfrac{7a}{5}$

(C) $3a$

(D) $\dfrac{28a}{5}$

(E) $28a$

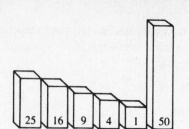

| 25 | 16 | 9 | 4 | 1 | 50 |

9 Six containers, whose capacities in cubic centimeters are shown, appear in the figure above. The 25-cubic centimeter container is filled with flour, and the rest are empty. The contents of the 25-cubic centimeter container are used to fill the 16-cubic centimeter container, and the excess is dumped into the 50-cubic centimeter container. Then the 16-cubic centimeter container is used to fill the 9-cubic centimeter container, and the excess is dumped into the 50-cubic centimeter container. The process is repeated until all containers, except the 1-cubic centimeter and the 50-cubic centimeter containers, are empty. What percent of the 50-cubic centimeter container is *empty*?

(A) 24%
(B) 48%
(C) 50%
(D) 52%
(E) 76%

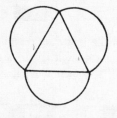

8 The figure above consists of equal semicircles each touching the other at the ends of their diameters. If the radius of each circle is 2, what is the *total enclosed* area?

(A) $\dfrac{\sqrt{3}}{4} + \pi$

(B) $\sqrt{3} + 2\pi$

(C) $4\sqrt{3} + 6\pi$

(D) 6π

(E) $\dfrac{\sqrt{2}}{4} + 4\pi$

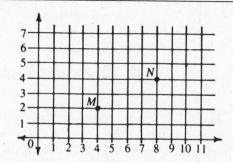

10 Which of the following points, when plotted on the grid above, will be three times as far from $M(4,2)$ as from $N(8,4)$?

(A) $(2,1)$
(B) $(4,4)$
(C) $(6,3)$
(D) $(7,1)$
(E) $(10,5)$

Time: 30 Minutes   This section contains two types of questions. You have 30 minutes to complete both types.
25 Questions   You may use any available space for scratchwork.

Notes:

1. The use of a calculator is permitted. All numbers are real numbers.

2. Figures that accompany problems in this test are intended to provide information useful in solving the problems. They are drawn as accurately as possible EXCEPT when it is stated in a specific problem that the figure is not drawn to scale. All figures lie in a plane unless otherwise indicated.

Reference Information

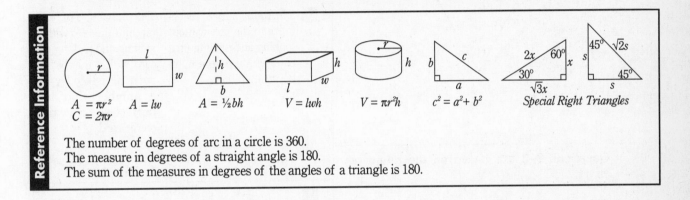

$A = \pi r^2$
$C = 2\pi r$

$A = lw$

$A = \frac{1}{2}bh$

$V = lwh$

$V = \pi r^2 h$

$c^2 = a^2 + b^2$

Special Right Triangles

The number of degrees of arc in a circle is 360.
The measure in degrees of a straight angle is 180.
The sum of the measures in degrees of the angles of a triangle is 180.

Directions for Quantitative Comparison Questions

Questions 1–15 each consist of two quantities in boxes, one in Column A and one in Column B. You are to compare the two quantities and on the answer sheet fill in oval

A if the quantity in Column A is greater;
B if the quantity in Column B is greater;
C if the two quantities are equal;
D if the relationship cannot be determined from the information given.

AN E RESPONSE WILL NOT BE SCORED.

Notes:

1. In some questions, information is given about one or both of the quantities to be compared. In such cases, the given information is centered above the two columns and is not boxed.
2. In a given question, a symbol that appears in both columns represents the same thing in Column A as it does in Column B.
3. Letters such as x, n, and k stand for real numbers.

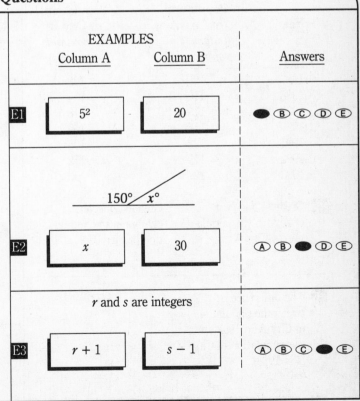

EXAMPLES

Column A	Column B	Answers
E1 5^2	20	● Ⓑ Ⓒ Ⓓ Ⓔ
E2 x	30	Ⓐ Ⓑ ● Ⓓ Ⓔ
E3 $r + 1$	$s - 1$	Ⓐ Ⓑ Ⓒ ● Ⓔ

$150°$ $x°$

r and *s* are integers

GO ON TO THE NEXT PAGE

SUMMARY DIRECTIONS FOR COMPARISON QUESTIONS

Answer: A if the quantity in Column A is greater;
B if the quantity in Column B is greater;
C if the two quantities are equal;
D if the relationships cannot be determined from the information given.

AN E RESPONSE WILL NOT BE SCORED.

	Column A	Column B

1

$$7$$

$$p \qquad p$$

$$60°$$

| 21 | | $3p$ |

Questions 2–3 are based on the following chart.

Population of City A and City B from 1987 to 1993

Year	Population of City A (*in thousands of persons*)	Population of City B (*in thousands of persons*)
1987	106	128
1988	110	124
1989	113	118
1990	115	109
1991	122	108
1992	119	112
1993	127	105

2 | Greatest one-year change in the population of City A | | Greatest one-year change in the population of City B |

3 | The difference between the population of City A in 1992 and the population of City B in 1988 | | 5,000 |

There are 10 cards in a box each marked with different numbers from 11 to 20 inclusive.

4 | The probability of reaching into the box without looking and picking up a card with a **prime** number written on it. | | The probability of reaching into the box without looking and picking up a card with a number **exactly divisible by 3** or **a number that is a perfect square** written on the card. |

5 | 25% of 90 | | $\frac{1}{2}$ of 45 |

6

$$x \neq 0$$

| x | | x^{-1} |

7 | Average (arithmetic mean) of 3, 7, 11, 15, and x | | Average (arithmetic mean) of 2, 6, 12, 16, and x |

8

$$1{,}000 \text{ grams} = 1 \text{ kilogram}$$

| Number of kilograms equal to 100,000 grams | | 100 |

GO ON TO THE NEXT PAGE →

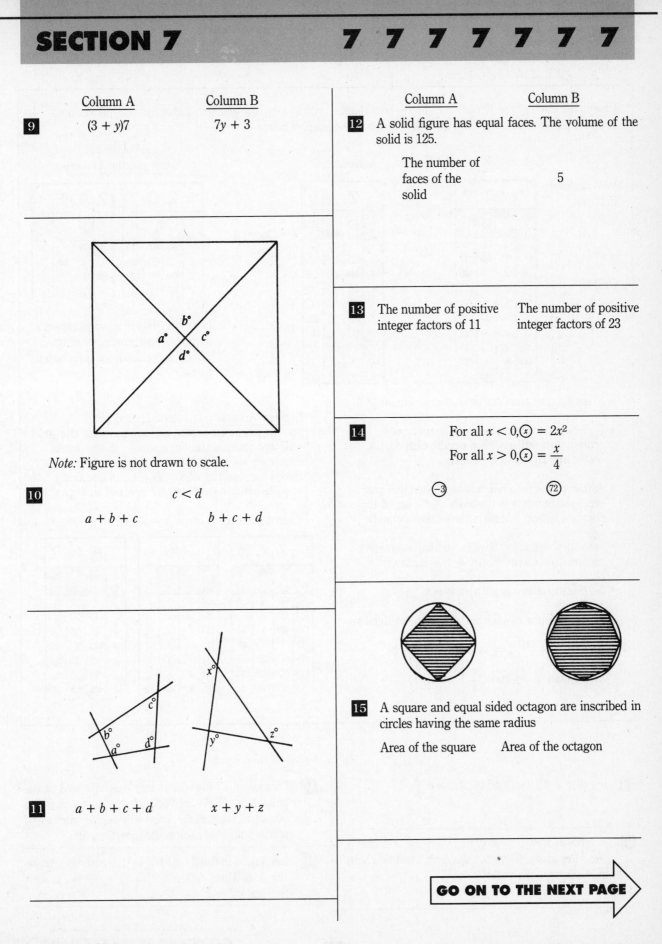

	Column A	Column B
9	$(3 + y)7$	$7y + 3$

Note: Figure is not drawn to scale.

10

$$c < d$$

$a + b + c$	$b + c + d$

11 $a + b + c + d$ $x + y + z$

	Column A	Column B
12	A solid figure has equal faces. The volume of the solid is 125.	
	The number of faces of the solid	5

13 The number of positive integer factors of 11   The number of positive integer factors of 23

14

For all $x < 0, \widehat{x} = 2x^2$

For all $x > 0, \widehat{x} = \dfrac{x}{4}$

$\widehat{-3}$ $\widehat{72}$

15 A square and equal sided octagon are inscribed in circles having the same radius

Area of the square   Area of the octagon

GO ON TO THE NEXT PAGE ▷

Directions: Each of the 10 questions in this part requires you to solve the problem and enter your answer by marking the ovals in the special grid, as shown in the examples below.

Answer: $\frac{7}{12}$ or 7/12

Answer: 2.5

Answer: 201
Either position is correct.

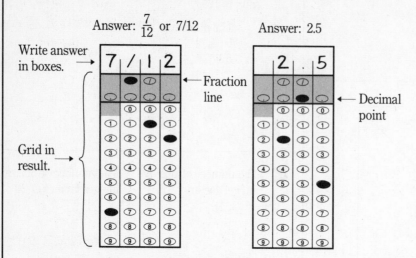

Write answer in boxes. →

← Fraction line

← Decimal point

Grid in result. →

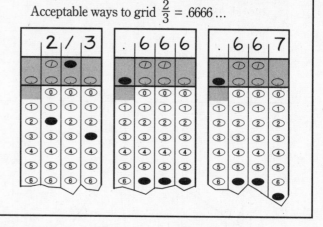

Note: You may start your answers in any column, space permitting. Columns not needed should be left blank.

- Mark no more than one oval in any column.

- Because the answer sheet will be machine-scored, **you will receive credit only if the ovals are filled in correctly.**

- Although not required, it is suggested that you write your answer in the boxes at the top of the columns to help you fill in the ovals accurately.

- Some problems may have more than one correct answer. In such cases, grid only one answer.

- No question has a negative answer.

- **Mixed numbers** such as $2\frac{1}{2}$ must be gridded as 2.5 or 5/2. (If is gridded, it will be interpreted as $\frac{21}{2}$, not $2\frac{1}{2}$.)

- Decimal Accuracy: If you obtain a decimal answer, **enter the most accurate value the grid will accommodate.** For example, if you obtain an answer such as 0.6666 … , you should record the result as .666 or .667. **Less accurate results such as .66 or .67 are not acceptable.**

Acceptable ways to grid $\frac{2}{3}$ = .6666 …

---

16 If $\frac{5}{8}$ of x is 40, then find the value of $\frac{3}{8}$ of x

17 A piece of wire is bent to form a circle of radius 3 feet. How many pieces of wire, each 2 feet long, can be made from the wire?

18 Dick spent $7 in order to buy baseballs and tennis balls. If baseballs are 70¢ each and tennis balls are 60¢ each, what is the greatest possible number of tennis balls that Dick could have bought?

19 Let $f(x)$ be defined for all x by the equation $f(x) = 12x + 8$. Thus, $f(2) = 32$. If $f(x) \div f(0) = 2x$, then find the value of x

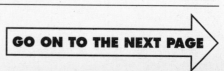

GO ON TO THE NEXT PAGE

ABA   BBB   CBA   BBA
ACC   CBC   CCC   ACA
BAC   ABC   BCA   CAB
CBB   BCA   AAB   ACC

20 In the triple arrangement of letters above, a triple has a value of 1 if exactly 2 of the letters in the triple are the same. Any other combination has a value of 0. The value of the entire arrangement is the sum of the values of each of the triples. What is the value of the above arrangement?

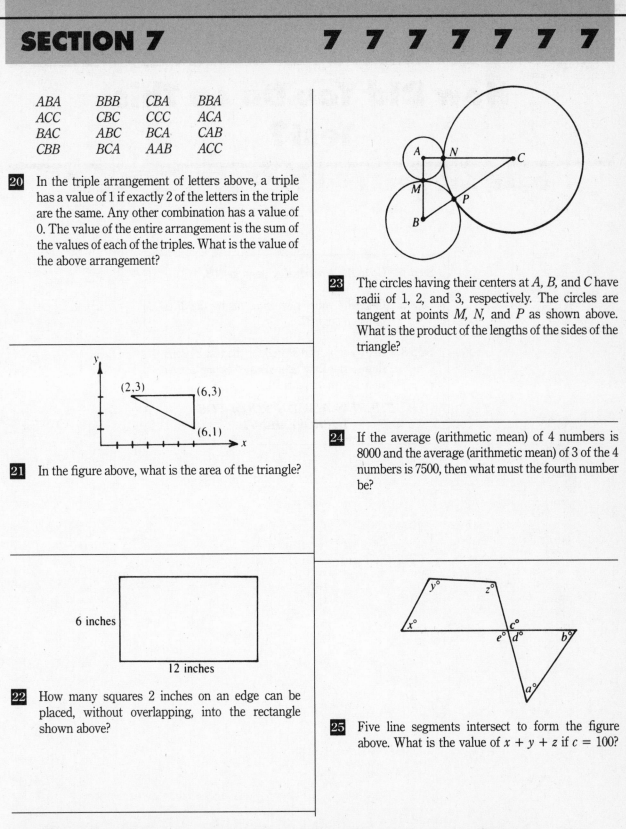

21 In the figure above, what is the area of the triangle?

22 How many squares 2 inches on an edge can be placed, without overlapping, into the rectangle shown above?

23 The circles having their centers at A, B, and C have radii of 1, 2, and 3, respectively. The circles are tangent at points M, N, and P as shown above. What is the product of the lengths of the sides of the triangle?

24 If the average (arithmetic mean) of 4 numbers is 8000 and the average (arithmetic mean) of 3 of the 4 numbers is 7500, then what must the fourth number be?

25 Five line segments intersect to form the figure above. What is the value of $x + y + z$ if $c = 100$?

IF YOU FINISH BEFORE TIME IS CALLED, YOU MAY CHECK YOUR WORK ON THIS SECTION ONLY. DO NOT TURN TO ANY OTHER SECTION IN THE TEST.

STOP

How Did You Do on This Test?

Step 1. Go to the Answer Key on page 803.

Step 2. Calculate your "raw score" using the directions on page 87.

Step 3. Get your "scaled score" for the test by referring to the Raw Score/Scaled Score Conversion Tables on page 90.

THERE'S ALWAYS ROOM FOR IMPROVEMENT!

Answer Key for Practice Test 4

Section 1—Verbal

1.	D	8.	D	15.	D	22.	E	29.	A
2.	C	9.	B	16.	A	23.	A	30.	C
3.	D	10.	A	17.	E	24.	B		
4.	D	11.	C	18.	A	25.	C		
5.	B	12.	E	19.	D	26.	D		
6.	A	13.	E	20.	B	27.	B		
7.	C	14.	B	21.	B	28.	B		

Section 2—Math

1.	B	5.	A	9.	D	13.	A	17.	D	21.	D	25. C
2.	C	6.	D	10.	E	14.	C	18.	C	22.	C	
3.	C	7.	D	11.	E	15.	C	19.	E	23.	A	
4.	D	8.	D	12.	C	16.	B	20.	A	24.	B	

Section 3—Verbal

1.	D	7.	E	13.	E	19.	B	25.	B	31.	A
2.	E	8.	E	14.	E	20.	A	26.	A	32.	A
3.	A	9.	C	15.	E	21.	A	27.	E	33.	B
4.	D	10.	D	16.	A	22.	D	28.	C	34.	C
5.	E	11.	B	17.	C	23.	D	29.	D	35.	C
6.	B	12.	C	18.	B	24.	D	30.	C		

Section 4—Math

1.	B	6.	A	11.	A	16.	10	21.	2
2.	A	7.	A	12.	C	17.	20	22.	20
3.	B	8.	A	13.	D	18.	270	23.	$\frac{1}{48}$
4.	B	9.	A	14.	D	19.	5	24.	5
5.	A	10.	C	15.	C	20.	2	25.	108

Section 5—Verbal

1.	B	5.	C	9.	C	13.	D
2.	E	6.	D	10.	C		
3.	A	7.	D	11.	C		
4.	E	8.	A	12.	C		

Section 6—Math

1.	C	6.	C
2.	C	7.	D
3.	E	8.	C
4.	C	9.	D
5.	C	10.	E

Section 7—Math

1.	C	6.	D	11.	C	16.	24	21.	4
2.	B	7.	C	12.	D	17.	9	22.	18
3.	C	8.	C	13.	C	18.	7	23.	60
4.	C	9.	A	14.	C	19.	2	24.	9,500
5.	C	10.	B	15.	B	20.	8	25.	280

Explanatory Answers for Practice Test 4

Section 1: Verbal Ability

As you read these Explanatory Answers, refer to "Using Critical Thinking Skills in Verbal Questions" (beginning on page 236) whenever a specific Strategy is referred to in the answer. Of particular importance are the following Master Verbal Strategies:

Sentence Completion Master Strategy 1—page 245.
Sentence Completion Master Strategy 2—page 246.
Analogies Master Strategy 1—page 236.
Reading Comprehension Master Strategy 2—page 263.

1. Choice D is correct. See **Sentence Completion Strategy 2**. Examine the first word of each choice. Choice (B) pacifism and Choice (E) oblivion are incorrect choices because a rising tide of pacifism or oblivion in public education does *not* make good sense. Now consider the other choices. Choice (A) compromise . . . inept and Choice (C) ambiguity . . . average do *not* make good sense in the sentence. Choice (D) mediocrity . . . dedicated *does* make good sense.

2. Choice C is correct. See **Sentence Completion Strategy 2**. First we eliminate Choice (A) foretold, Choice (B) impossible, and Choice (E) glaring. Reason: These choices do not make sense in the sentence up to the word "eclipses." We further eliminate Choice (D) true . . . rational, because it does not make sense for anyone to consider an eclipse rational. Only Choice (C) understandable . . . magical makes sense.

3. Choice D is correct. The fact that the girl had become more self-confident indicates that she would be more active in participating in a conversation. If you used **Sentence Completion Strategy 3**—trying to complete the sentence *before* looking at the five choices—you might have come up with any of the following appropriate words:

   starting   beginning
   launching   originating

   The other choices are, therefore, incorrect.

4. Choice D is correct. See **Sentence Completion Strategy 2**.

   STEP 1

   Let us first examine the first words of each choice. We can then eliminate Choice (B) confuse and Choice (E) misconstrue because it does *not* make sense to say that an authority would be able to "confuse" or "misconstrue" something in a book. So Choices B and E are incorrect.

   STEP 2

   Let us now consider the remaining choices. Choice (A) understand . . . simple and Choice (C) read . . . useless do *not* make sense in the sentence. Therefore, these choices are incorrect. Choice (D) comprehend . . . complex *does* make sense.

5. Choice B is correct. See **Sentence Completion Strategy 4**. The words "not only" constitute a Support indicator. The second part of the sentence is, therefore, expected to reinforce the first part of the sentence. Choice (B) reject . . . refused supplies the two words that provide a sentence that makes sense. Choices A, C, D, and E are incorrect because their word pairs do not produce sentences that make sense.

6. Choice A is correct. See **Sentence Completion Strategy 3**. If you used this strategy of trying to complete the sentence *before* looking at the five choices, you might have come up with any of the following appropriate words:

persistence   perseverance
steadfastness   indefatigability

These words all mean the same as Choice (A) tenacity. Accordingly, Choices B, C, D, and E are incorrect.

7. Choice C is correct. See **Sentence Completion Strategy 4**. The adverb "ironically" means in a manner so that the opposite of what is expected takes place. So we have an Opposition indicator here. Choice (C) weaken is, of course, the opposite of strengthen. Accordingly, Choices A, B, D, and E are incorrect.

8. Choice D is correct. See **Sentence Completion Strategy 4**. The words "in addition to" constitute a Support indicator. We can then expect an additional favorable word to complete the sentence. That word is dapper (Choice D), meaning "neatly dressed." Choices A, B, C, and E are incorrect because they do not make good sense in the sentence.

9. Choice B is correct. See **Sentence Completion Strategy 4**. The words "in spite of" constitute an Opposition indicator. We can then expect an opposing idea to complete the sentence. The word "baffled" means "puzzled" or "unable to comprehend." Choice (B) baffled gives us the word that brings out the opposition thought we expect in the sentence. Choices A, C, D, and E do not give us a sentence that makes sense.

10. Choice A is correct. A misnomer is an error in naming a person or thing. A malapropism is an error in the use of a word.

(Action to Object and Opposite relationship)

11. Choice C is correct. One who is emancipated is freed from slavery. One who is exonerated is freed from blame.

(Result relationship)

12. Choice E is correct. All the actors together make up the cast for a play. All the customers together make up the clientele for a business.

(Whole-Part relationship)

13. Choice E is correct. Something that is eternal has endless duration. Something or someone omnipotent has full or endless power.

(Degree relationship)

14. Choice B is correct. A person who is submissive is not likely to show defiance. A person who is courageous is not likely to show fear. We have here an Opposite relationship in a negative way. Choice D may seem correct because a person who is confident is likely to have poise. However, this relationship is not expressed in a negative way, so Choice D is incorrect.

(Opposite relationship)

15. Choice D is correct. A profligate is recklessly wasteful, wildly extravagant, and inclined to vice. Accordingly, a profligate is *not* a moral person. A miser is obviously *not* a generous person.

(Association relationship)

Note: If you don't know the meaning of the word "profligate," you can use **Analogy Strategy 6**, The Context Method for Unfamiliar Words.

Note also that the *first words* in each of the choices are *nouns and people*. Thus "profligate," the first word in the stem of the analogy, must be a person. Since "profligate" is linked to "moral," the only thing that would make sense is to say a PROFLIGATE is MORAL (or not MORAL). The only choice that fits the sentence and makes sense is D: A *miser* is not *generous*.

16. Choice A is correct. See lines 42–44: "The fundamental fact . . . in their environment." Choices B, D, and E are incorrect because the passage does not indicate that these statements are true. Choice C is incorrect because it is only partially true. The passage does not state that *all* animals and plants are successful in adjusting themselves to changes in their environments.

17. Choice E is correct. See lines 4–7: "Originally the term acclimatization . . . altered temperature." Also see lines 9–12: "But aside from temperature . . . originally accustomed to." Choices A, B, C, and D are incorrect because one *cannot* infer from the passage what any of these choices state.

18. Choice A is correct. Acclimatization and adaptation are both forms of adjustment. Accordingly, these two processes are similar. The difference between the two terms, however, is brought out in lines 32—36: "By and large . . . as adaptation." Choice D is incorrect because the passage does not indicate what is expressed in Choice D. See lines 29–32: "Let us define acclimatization . . . lethal for it." Choices B, C, and E are incorrect because the passage does not indicate that any of these choices are true.

19. Choice D is correct. A person going from daylight into a darkened room is an example of adaptation—not acclimatization. See lines 32–36: "By and large ... as 'adaptation.'" Choices A, B, C, and E all require the process of acclimatization. Therefore, they are incorrect choices. An ocean fish placed in a lake (Choice A) is a chemical change. Choices B, C, and E are all pressure changes. Acclimatization, by definition, deals with chemical and pressure changes.

20. Choice B is correct. Given the context in the sentence, Choice B is the best.

21. Choice B is correct. See lines 33–36: "The term [acclimatization] should not be taken ... as 'adaptation.'" Choices A, D, and E are incorrect because the passage does not indicate that these choices are true. Choice C is partially correct in that acclimatization does apply to adjustments, but the choice is incorrect because adaptation also applies to adjustments. See lines 35–36: "This type of adjustment ... as 'adaptation.'"

22. Choice E is correct. See paragraph 2 (beginning): "The tie which bound this world-embracing empire together ... was as much cultural as political."

23. Choice A is correct. See paragraph 1 (end): "Centuries of training had bred in them the conviction that all other rulers should be tributary to the Son of Heaven."

24. Choice B is correct. See the last paragraph about the close relationship between "ethical standards" and "Confucian patterns."

25. Choice C is correct. The reader should infer from paragraphs 3 and 4 that Han and T'ang were dynasties—just as there was a Manchu dynasty.

26. Choice D is correct. The passage points out that since more emphasis was placed on being members of the same culture, rather than on being members of the same race, there was a "comparative contentment of Chinese under alien rulers" (paragraph 4: beginning).

27. Choice B is correct. See paragraph 5 (middle): "In contrast with India, where caste and religion have tended to keep apart the racial strata, in China assimilation made great progress."

28. Choice B is correct. Paragraph 4 (end) points out that the Manchus never gave up some of their ancestral ways, and this disturbed segments of the population.

29. Choice A is correct. The passage states that assimilation made great progress in China. (See the answer to question 27.)

30. Choice C is correct. From the context of the sentence and the sentence before and after it, it can be seen that "restiveness" must mean impatience or restlessness.

Explanatory Answers for Practice Test 4 (continued)

Section 2: Math Ability

As you read these solutions, do two things if you answered the Math question incorrectly:

1. When a specific Strategy is referred to in the solution, study that strategy, which you will find in "Using Critical Thinking Skills in Math Questions" (beginning on page 174).

2. When the solution directs you to the "Math Refresher" (beginning on page 291)—for example, Math Refresher #305—study the 305 Math principles to get a clear idea of the Math operation that was necessary for you to know in order to answer the question correctly.

1. Choice B is correct. **(Use Strategy 2: Translate from words to algebra.)**

The quotient of x and 3

$$\frac{x}{3}$$

$\left.\begin{array}{l}\frac{x}{3} - 8\end{array}\right\}$ = 8 less than the quotient

and is the required answer.

(Math Refresher #200)

2. Choice C is correct. **(Use Strategy 2: Translate from words to algebra.)**

7 of Phil's buckets − 7 of Mark's buckets =
7 × 11 gallons − 7 × 8 gallons =
77 gallons − 56 gallons =
21 gallons

(Math Refresher #200)

3. Choice C is correct.

Method 1: Do the calculation of each of the answers until you find a solution which is not a whole number.

Method 2: Rewrite each choice as follows:

(A) $\frac{66}{3} - \frac{36}{3} = 22 - 12 = 10$

(B) $\frac{66}{6} + \frac{36}{6} = 11 + 6 = 17$

(C) $\frac{66}{12} + \frac{36}{12} = \frac{11}{2} + 3 = 5\frac{1}{2} + 3 = 8\frac{1}{2}$

Therefore, Choice C is correct.

(Math Refresher #431)

4. Choice D is correct. **(Use Strategy 3: The whole equals the sum of its parts.)**

Amount left = Original amount − Amount spent
= $15.25 − $7.50
= $ 7.75

(Subtracting Decimals)

5. Choice A is correct. **(Use Strategy 17: Use the given information effectively.)**

Given: $\dfrac{4^3 + 4^3 + 4^3 + 4^3}{4^y} = 4$

$$\dfrac{4(4^3)}{4^y} = 4$$

$$\dfrac{4^4}{4^y} = 4$$

$$4^{4-y} = 4^1 \qquad \boxed{1}$$

In $\boxed{1}$ each expression has base 4. Since the expressions are equal, the exponents must also be equal. Thus,

$$4 - y = 1$$
$$-y = -3$$
$$y = 3$$

(Math Refresher #429 and #406)

6. Choice D is correct. **(Use Strategy 2: Translate from words to algebra.)**

The ratio of $3\dfrac{1}{3}$ hours to 11 hours =

$$\dfrac{3\dfrac{1}{3} \text{ hours}}{11 \text{ hours}} \quad =$$

$$\dfrac{\dfrac{10}{3}}{11} \qquad \boxed{1}$$

(Use Strategy 13: Find unknowns by multiplication.)

Multiply $\boxed{1}$ by $\left(\dfrac{3}{3}\right)$, we get

$$\left(\dfrac{3}{3}\right)\dfrac{\dfrac{10}{3}}{11} =$$

$$\dfrac{10}{33}$$

Note: For those who prefer to use a calculator: This example may be difficult to solve on a calculator if you represent $3\dfrac{1}{3}$ by 3.3333 and then divide by 11, when you try to match your answer with one of the choices.

(Math Refresher #112)

7. Choice D is correct.

Given:

$$5x = 3 \qquad \boxed{1}$$

(Use Strategy 12: Try not to make tedious calculations.)

Method 1: Add 3 to both sides of $\boxed{1}$

$$5x + 3 = 6 \qquad \boxed{2}$$

(Use Strategy 13: Find unknown expressions by multiplication.)

Square both sides of $\boxed{2}$

$$(5x + 3)^2 = 36 \qquad \boxed{3}$$

This method involves simpler arithmetic (no fractions) than the next method.

Method 2: This method is a bit slower. Solve $\boxed{1}$ for x to get

$$x = \dfrac{3}{5} \qquad \boxed{4}$$

Using $\boxed{4}$, calculate the unknown expression.

$$(5x + 3)^2 =$$

$$\left[5\left(\dfrac{3}{5}\right) + 3\right]^2 =$$

$$(3 + 3)^2 =$$
$$6^2 = 36$$

(Math Refresher #406 and #431)

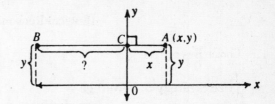

8. Choice D is correct.

As shown in the diagram above, the y-coordinates of A and B must be the same because they both lie along the same horizontal line. Since B lies to the left of the y-axis, its x-coordinate must be negative. Since $3AC = BC$, then the x-coordinate of B is

$$-3x$$

and we already know that the y-coordinate is y.

Thus, $(-3x, y)$ is the answer.

(Math Refresher #410)

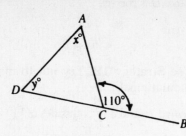

9. Choice D is correct. **(Use Strategy 18: Remember isosceles triangle facts.)**

    Since $AC = CD$, we know that

    $$x = y \qquad \boxed{1}$$

    We also know that

    $$m \angle ACB = m \angle D + m \angle A \qquad \boxed{2}$$

    Substituting the given into $\boxed{2}$, we have

    $$110 = y + x \qquad \boxed{3}$$

    Substituting $\boxed{1}$ into $\boxed{3}$, we get

    $$110 = y + y$$
    $$110 = 2y$$

    (Math Refresher #507 and #406)

10. Choice E is correct. **(Use Strategy 16: The obvious may be tricky!)**

    Given: $\qquad (x + y)^2 = 9$
    So that $\qquad x + y = 3 \text{ or} - 3$

    From the information given, we cannot determine whether $x + y$ equals 3 or $- 3$.

    (Logical Reasoning)

11. Choice E is correct.

    $$\left(\begin{array}{l} \textbf{Use Strategy 5:} \quad \textbf{Average =} \\ \qquad \dfrac{\textbf{sum of values}}{\textbf{total number of values}} \end{array} \right)$$

    Let x, y = two unknown numbers.

    Thus, $\dfrac{28 + 30 + 32 + x + y}{5} = 34 \qquad \boxed{1}$

    Multiplying $\boxed{1}$ by 5,

    $$28 + 30 + 32 + x + y = 170$$
    $$\text{or} \qquad 90 + x + y = 170$$
    $$\text{or} \qquad x + y = 80$$

    (Math Refresher #601 and #406)

12. Choice C is correct. **(Use Strategy 2: Translate from words to algebra.)**

    Let x = side of one of the eight squares.

    Thus, we are given

    $$4x = 16$$
    $$\text{or} \quad x = 4 \qquad \boxed{1}$$

    From what we are told in the problem, we conclude that

    $$AE = MF = LG = 4x \qquad \boxed{2}$$
    and $\qquad AL = BK = CJ = DH = EG = 2x \quad \boxed{3}$

    (Use Strategy 3: The whole equals the sum of its parts.)

    Thus,

    $AE + MF + LG + AL + BK + CJ + DH + EG =$
    $4x + 4x + 4x + 2x + 2x + 2x + 2x + 2x =$
    $22x = 88$

    using $\boxed{1}$, $\boxed{2}$, and $\boxed{3}$.

    (Math Refresher #200, #303, and #304)

13. Choice A is correct. **(Use Strategy 11: Use new definitions carefully.)**

    Given: $\qquad \textcircled{x} = \dfrac{x^2}{3}$ and $\boxed{x} = \dfrac{9}{x}$

    Thus, $\qquad \textcircled{x} \times \boxed{x} = \dfrac{x^2}{3} \times \dfrac{9}{x} = 3x$

    (Math Refresher #431)

14. Choice C is correct. **(Use Strategy 17: Use the given information effectively.)**

    For I, we have:

    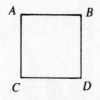

    Clearly $DB > DA$. So I could not be true.

    Clearly D can be the same distance from 2 points (A and B), but not from 3, so II does not apply.

    Only Choice C, III only, is now possible.

Choice III is demonstrated below, although it was not necessary for us to examine it.

By definition, all points on the circle are the same distance from the center. So $DA = DB = DC$.

(Math Refresher #303 and #310)

15. Choice C is correct. **(Use Strategy 17: Use the given information effectively.)**

    Given:
    $$x + by = 5 \quad \boxed{1}$$
    $$3x + y = 5 \quad \boxed{2}$$
    $$y = 2 \quad \boxed{3}$$

    We want to find b.

    Substituting $\boxed{3}$ into $\boxed{2}$, we get

    $$3x + 2 = 5$$
    $$\text{or} \quad x = 1 \quad \boxed{4}$$

    Substituting $\boxed{3}$ and $\boxed{4}$ into $\boxed{1}$, we have

    $$1 + 2b = 5$$
    $$\text{or} \quad 2b = 4$$
    $$\text{or} \quad b = 2$$

    (Math Refresher #406 and #431)

16. Choice B is correct.

    The ratio of boys to girls in the class is 2:3. Choice C is the answer because $9:12 = 3:4$, which does not equal 2:3.

    (Math Refresher #108)

17. Choice D is correct. **(Use Strategy 10: Know how to use units.)**

    $$\left(\frac{p \text{ gallons}}{\text{car}}\right) \times (r \text{ cars}) = pr \text{ gallons for each month}$$

    $$\frac{q \text{ gallons}}{\dfrac{pr \text{ gallons}}{\text{month}}} = \frac{q}{pr} \text{ months}$$

    (Math Refresher #121)

18. Choice C is correct. **(Use Strategy 10: Know how to use units.)**

    Since 7 days = 1 week, 24 hours = 1 day, and 60 minutes = 1 hour, then

1 week = (1 week)$\left(\dfrac{7 \text{ days}}{\text{week}}\right)\left(\dfrac{24 \text{ hours}}{\text{day}}\right)\left(\dfrac{60 \text{ minutes}}{\text{hour}}\right)$

$$= (7)(24)(60) \text{ minutes}$$

Thus,

$$\frac{24 \text{ minutes}}{1 \text{ week}} = \frac{24 \text{ minutes}}{(7)(24)(60) \text{ minutes}} = \frac{1}{420}$$

(Math Refresher #121)

19. Choice E is correct. **(Use Strategy 11: Use new definitions carefully.)**

    By definition, the l-length from -3 to 3 =

    $$3 - (-3) =$$
    $$3 + 3 =$$
    $$6$$

    (Math Refresher #431)

20. Choice A is correct.

    By definition, the l-length from -4 to each of the other points follow:

    $$R - (-4) = R + 4 \quad \boxed{1}$$
    $$S - (-4) = S + 4 \quad \boxed{2}$$
    $$T - (-4) = T + 4 \quad \boxed{3}$$
    $$U - (-4) = U + 4 \quad \boxed{4}$$
    $$V - (-4) = V + 4 \quad \boxed{5}$$

    From their position on the number line we know that:

    $$R < S < T < U < V \quad \boxed{6}$$

    (Use Strategy 6: Know how to manipulate inequalities.)

    Adding 4 to each term of $\boxed{6}$, we get

    $$R + 4 < S + 4 < T + 4 < U + 4 < V + 4 \quad \boxed{7}$$

    It is obvious from $\boxed{7}$ that $R + 4$ is smallest.

    Thus, $\boxed{1}$ above, point R, has the least l-length from -4.

    (Logical Reasoning)

21. Choice D is correct. **(Use Strategy 2: Translate from words to algebra.)**

    Let x, $x + 1$, $x + 2$, $x + 3$, $x + 4$ represent the 5 consecutive integers.

Then, $x + x + 1 + x + 2 + x + 3 + x + 4 = w$

$$5x + 10 = w \qquad \boxed{1}$$

The next 5 consecutive positive integers will be:

$x + 5, x + 6, x + 7, x + 8, x + 9$

Their sum will be:

$x + 5 + x + 6 + x + 7 + x + 8 + x + 9 =$

$$5x + 35 \qquad \boxed{2}$$

We can write $\boxed{2}$ as $5x + 35$

$$= 5x + 10 + 25 \qquad \boxed{3}$$

Substituting $\boxed{1}$ into $\boxed{3}$, we get

$$5x + 10 + 25 = w + 25$$

(Math Refresher #200 and #406)

22. Choice C is correct. **(Use Strategy 2: Translate from words to algebra.)**

We are told that area of the square is twice area of triangle. This translates to:

$$a^2 = 2\!\left(\frac{1}{\cancel{2}} \times b \times c\right)$$

$$a^2 = bc \qquad \boxed{1}$$
We are given that $bc = 100 \qquad \boxed{2}$

Substituting $\boxed{2}$ into $\boxed{1}$, we get

$$a^2 = 100$$

(Math Refresher #200, #303, and #306)

23. Choice A is correct.

Given
that the radius of the circle $= 2$, we have
Circumference $= 2\,\pi(\text{radius}) = 2\pi(2)$
$$= 4\pi \text{ inches} \qquad \boxed{1}$$

We are given that $\overarc{AD} + \overarc{BC} = 3\pi$ inches $\qquad \boxed{2}$

(Use Strategy 3: The whole equals the sum of its parts.)

We know that $\overarc{AD} + \overarc{BC} + \overarc{AC} + \overarc{DB} =$ circumference of circle $\qquad \boxed{3}$

Substituting $\boxed{1}$ and $\boxed{2}$ into $\boxed{3}$, we have

$$3\pi \text{ inches} + \overarc{AC} + \overarc{DB} = 4\pi \text{ inches}$$
$$\overarc{AC} + \overarc{DB} = \pi \text{ inches} \qquad \boxed{4}$$

We know that the measure of an arc can be found by:

$$\text{measure of arc} = \left(\frac{\text{length of arc}}{\text{circumference}}\right) \times 360 \qquad \boxed{5}$$
$$\text{of circle}$$

Substituting $\boxed{1}$ and $\boxed{4}$ into $\boxed{5}$, we get

measure of $AC + DB$

$$= \left(\frac{\pi \text{ inches}}{4\pi \text{ inches}}\right) \times 360 \times \frac{\cancel{4} \times 90}{\cancel{4}} = 90 \qquad \boxed{6}$$

(Use Strategy 19: Factor and reduce.)

From the diagram $m\,\angle AOC = m\,\angle DOB = y$

Therefore, $m\,\overarc{AC} = m\,\overarc{DB} = y \qquad \boxed{7}$

Substituting $\boxed{7}$ into $\boxed{6}$, we get

$$y + y = 90 \quad \text{or} \quad 2y = 90$$
$$\text{or} \quad y = 45$$

(Math Refresher #310 and #524)

24. Choice B is correct. **(Use Strategy 2: Translate from words to algebra.)**

Let $r =$ Ross's age now.
$19 =$ Amanda's age now.
Thus, $r - 5 =$ Ross's age five years ago. $\qquad \boxed{1}$
$19 - 5 = 14 =$ Amanda's age five years ago. $\qquad \boxed{2}$

We are given: Five years ago, Ross was N times as old as Amanda was.

Substituting $\boxed{1}$ and $\boxed{2}$ into $\boxed{3}$, we have

$$r - 5 = N(14)$$
$$r = 14N + 5$$

25. Choice C is correct.

The volume of the rectangular solid to be immersed is:

$$V = (1 \text{ ft})(1 \text{ ft})(2 \text{ ft}) = 2 \text{ cu. ft} \qquad \boxed{1}$$

When the solid is immersed, the volume of the displaced water will be:

$$(2 \text{ ft.})(6 \text{ ft.})(x \text{ ft.}) = 12x \text{ cu. ft.} \qquad \boxed{2}$$

where x represents the height of the displaced water. $\boxed{1}$ and $\boxed{2}$ must be equal. So

$$2 \text{ cu. ft.} = 12x \text{ cu. ft.}$$

$$\frac{1}{6} \text{ ft.} = x$$

(Use Strategy 10: Know how to use units.)

$$\left(\frac{1}{6} \text{ ft}\right)\left(\frac{12 \text{ inches}}{\text{foot}}\right) =$$

$$\frac{12}{6} = 2 \text{ inches that the displaced water will rise.}$$

(Math Refresher #312 and #121)

Explanatory Answers for Practice Test 4 (continued)

Section 3: Verbal Ability

As you read these Explanatory Answers, refer to "Using Critical Thinking Skills in Verbal Questions" (beginning on page 236) whenever a specific Strategy is referred to in the answer. Of particular importance are the following Master Verbal Strategies:

Sentence Complete Master Strategy 1—page 245.
Sentence Completion Master Strategy 2—page 246.
Analogies Master Strategy 1—page 236.
Reading Comprehension Master Strategy 2—page 263.

1. Choice D is correct. See **Sentence Completion Strategy 2**. Examine the first word of each choice. We eliminate Choice (C) motor and Choice (E) reciprocal because motor curbs and reciprocal curbs do not make good sense in the opening clause of the sentence. Now we consider Choice (A) profitable . . . drive, which does not make sentence sense; Choice (B) flexible . . . produce, which also does *not* make sentence sense; and Choice (D) export . . . ship, which *does* make sentence sense.

2. Choice E is correct. See **Sentence Completion Strategy 2**. Examine the first words of each choice. We eliminate Choice (B) expedite (meaning "to speed up") and Choice (D) drench (which means "to wet through and through") because the parked vehicles do not expedite or drench the flow of traffic. Now we consider Choices A, C, and E. The only word pair that makes good sentence sense is Choice (E) impede . . . flout. The word "impede" means "to block up or obstruct," and the word "flout" means "scoff at or show contempt for."

3. Choice A is correct. See **Sentence Completion Strategy 1**. Photographs of starving children demonstrate something. The logical choice among all the choices constitutes the results of consequences

of drought, poor land, and overpopulation. The other choices are incorrect because they do not make sense in the sentence.

4. Choice D is correct. See **Sentence Completion Strategy 2**. Examine the first words of each choice. We can eliminate Choice (B) advantages . . . because it doesn't make sense in the sentence. The first words of the other four choices *do* make sense, so let us proceed to fill the two spaces for each of these remaining choices. Only Choice (D) tension . . . security makes good sentence sense.

5. Choice E is correct. See **Sentence Completion Strategy 2**. Examine the first words of each choice. We eliminate Choice (D) recording because the film rental business is not recording. Now we consider the four remaining word pairs. The only choice that makes sense in the sentence is Choice (E) booming . . . leisure.

6. Choice B is correct. If you used **Sentence Completion Strategy 3**, you might have come up with any of the following words:

    refused   repudiated   shunned

    These words all mean about the same as the correct Choice (B) rejected.

7. Choice E is correct. See **Sentence Completion Strategy 2**. Look at the first word of each choice. The first words in Choices B, C, and D do not sound right when inserted in the first blank of the sentence. Thus we can eliminate Choices B, C, and D. Now try both words in the remaining Choices, A and E. Choice E is the only one that works.

8. Choice E is correct. See **Sentence Completion Strategy 1**. Try each choice. The *apparent contradiction* of scarcity amidst plenty characterizes even a rich country in a time of inflation.

9. Choice C is correct. See **Sentence Completion Strategy 1**. The word "generate" (meaning "to produce") completes the sentence so that it makes good sense. The other choices don't do that.

10. Choice D is correct. See **Sentence Completion Strategy 1**. Try each choice. The sentence implies that he retained the belief until his death; hence he was *stubborn* or unchanging in his belief.

11. Choice B is correct. One sews in order to fix a tear. One caulks in order to fix a leak (in a boat). Note that "tear" as it is spelled has another meaning—a "drop"—but not in this analogy. See **Analogy Strategy 5**.

   (Purpose relationship)

12. Choice C is correct. That which is infinite does not end. That which is buoyant does not sink.

   (Opposite relationship)

13. Choice E is correct. To coerce is to coax forcefully. To shove is to nudge forcefully. We have here a degree relationship. Choice (C) declaim : argue also has a degree relationship, but the two words would have to be reversed for the choice to be correct. See **Analogy Strategy 3**.

   (Degree relationship)

14. Choice E is correct. To rejuvenate is to give back youth. To reimburse is to give back money.

   (Result relationship)

15. Choice E is correct. One sneers in order to express contempt. One grimaces in order to express pain. We have here a Purpose relationship. Choices B and C are also Purpose relationships, but they do not have the facial quality that the capitalized words and the Choice E words have. Therefore, Choice B and C are incorrect. See **Analogy Strategy 4**.

   (Purpose relationship)

16. Choice A is correct. A playwright writes a script for a play. A composer writes a score for a musical performance. In Choice (C) verse : poet, there is also an Action to Object relationship since a poet does write verses in creating poetry. However, the words in Choice C would have to be reversed in order to make Choice C correct. See **Analogy Strategy 3**.

   (Action to Object relationship)

17. Choice C is correct. To wane is to decrease in size. To decelerate is to decrease in speed.

   (Result relationship)

18. Choice B is correct. One amplifies sound to make it more noticeable. One enlarges a picture to make it more noticeable.

   (Action to Object and Purpose relationship)

19. Choice B is correct. Something that is unpretentious lacks ostentation. Something that is inconsequential lacks importance.

   (Characteristic and opposite relationship)

20. Choice A is correct. Something that is enigmatic is not clear. Something that is copious is not scarce.

   (Opposite relationship)

21. Choice A is correct. An embarkation is the beginning of a journey. An inception is the beginning of a project.

   (Part-Whole relationship)

22. Choice D is correct. An epicure is a person whose main goal is pleasure. A miser is a person whose main goal is wealth.

   (Purpose relationship)

   Note: If you don't know the meaning of the word "epicure," you can use **Analogy Strategy 6**, The Context Method for Unfamiliar Words. All the first words in the choices are nouns and people. So we can assume that an epicure (the first word in the stem of the analogy) is a person. Since "epicure" is linked to "pleasure," you can use a sentence like "An epicure is a person who seeks pleasure." You can see that the only choice that makes sense using the sentence is D: A *miser* is a person who seeks *wealth*.

23. Choice D is correct. You can't touch something that is intangible. You can't fix something that is irreparable. Consider Choice (C) convict : innocent. It is possible that a court *can* convict someone who is innocent. Therefore Choice C is incorrect. See **Analogy Strategy 4**.

   (Result and Opposite relationship)

Note: If you don't know the meaning of the word "intangible," you can use **Analogy Strategy 6,** The context Method for Unfamiliar Words. It appears that since "intangible" is linked to "touch," "intangible" (because of the "in," which in this case means "not") must be something that you *cannot* touch. So use the sentence "You cannot touch something that is intangible." Choice D fits best: You cannot *fix* something that is *irreparable.*

24. Choice D is correct. The author is definitely satisfied and happy with the simple life he and his partner are leading. See lines such as the following: "We thank our lucky stars that we live out in the wilderness" (lines 35–36). "We are thankful for what the wilderness makes possible" (lines 42–43). Choices A, B, C, and E are incorrect because the author gives no indication that the lifestyle, as he describes it, is marked by resentment, boredom, indecision, or indifference.

25. Choice B is correct. Throughout the passage, the author is showing that frills are not necessary for a happy life. Example: "There is no phone to ring, no radio to turn on, no television to watch" (lines 7–8). Choices A and D are incorrect because they are much too general. Choice C is an inappropriate title because progress and prosperity are not of interest to the author. Choice E is an inappropriate title because the author is not concerned about conveniences such as a phone, radio, or television. He has what he needs—"peace, quiet, and frugality" (lines 43–44).

26. Choice A is correct. The author indicates that the typical election is inconsequential—that is, unproductive, of no use. One may conclude, then, that the author has no faith in the typical candidates who run for office. Choices B, C, D, and E are incorrect because the author does not express these sentiments in the passage—although he may agree with those choices.

27. Choice E is correct. The author must have a farm because he says: ". . . our homegrown food is not stale, preserved or embalmed and bought from the supermarket" (lines 40–41). Choice A is incorrect because the author states: "There is wood to cut, snow to shovel . . ." (line 13). Choice B is incorrect. See lines 14–16: "No one is pushing, no one is shoving . . . we make our own jobs. Free men? Almost." Therefore, the author is not *completely* a free man. Choice C is incorrect because it is his neighbor's wife who may be pregnant (line 18). Choice D is incorrect.

See line 25: "The newspaper reaching us by mail . . ."

28. Choice C is correct. Maine is the only one of the five states listed that would likely have snow (line 1) and spruce (evergreen) trees (line 2). Therefore, Choices A, B, D, and E are incorrect.

29. Choice D is correct. Choice A is incorrect. From line 45 you cannot conclude that the author believes that even though he or she lives in a one-bedroom apartment much of the population in the city lives in one-bedroom apartments. Choice B is incorrect. Although the author says in line 59 that food may not be home-grown, the author doesn't say that you'll never get home-grown food. Choice C is incorrect. Although the author states that you may bump into rich and poor on a street, the author doesn't claim that both eat at the most expensive restaurants. Choice D is correct. In lines 51–52 the author links losing one's identity with forgetting about problems. Thus it can be assumed that losing one's identity is a "plus." Choice E is incorrect. There is no reference to friendliness as a way of life.

30. Choice C is correct. The word "interminable" (line 47) refers to *sounds of cars, trucks, repair, services,* and *hassles encountered.* Thus the word cannot be "loud" (Choice A), "bright" (Choice D), "harsh" (Choice B), or "close" (Choice E). It makes sense that *interminable* relates to *time* (Choice C). Note that "term" has to do with a specific length of time, and the prefix "in" here means "not," so *interminable* must mean "not having a specific term or length of time," that is, *ongoing.*

31. Choice A is correct. Note that in Passage B, the author mentions in many instances the good with the bad: "Excitement, hassles, services, traffic," and so on.

32. Choice A is correct. The author of Passage A seems to feel (lines 25–34) that all or most news is bad, so the author would be surprised at seeing a headline as described in Choice A. Choice B is incorrect. The author of Passage B (line 54) may bump into a celebrity in the street and indeed talk with the celebrity. Choice C is incorrect. The author believes that he or she can go to a coffee shop at three in the morning, so a movie is also probably open at two in the morning. Choice D is incorrect. See line 12. Choice E is incorrect. The author of Passage B acknowledges that certain types of people may not enjoy living in the city (lines 67–70), and the author admits that there are negative aspects about city living.

33. Choice B is correct. Note the comparison in lines 43–44. "Peace, progress, prosperity? ... We prefer peace, quiet, and frugality." Thus "frugality" must relate to "prosperity" with a somewhat *opposite* meaning and obviously not have too negative a connotation since the author is striving for this. The only word that makes sense is "stinginess."

34. Choice C is correct. In lines 8–9 the author links "don" with "city disguise, cocktail parties, dinners." It is logical to assume that "don" relates to "clothing."

35. Choice C is correct. See lines 31–34. Choice A is incorrect: Although the author of Passage A may believe that most news is bad, there is no reference to the author of Passage B believing that most news is good. Choice B is incorrect: Although it is true that the author of Passage A may believe that most elections are useless, there is no reference to the author of Passage B believing that they are necessary. Choice D is incorrect: We cannot infer that the author of Passage A believes that the parks in cities are safe (see lines 27–31 about Central Park). The author of Passage B may agree that crime "goes with the territory." However, Choice D in its entirety is incorrect. Choice E is incorrect. We cannot assume that one author does not like home-grown food (even though for example, the author of Passage B may not get to eat it).

Explanatory Answers for Practice Test 4 (continued)

Section 4: Math Ability

As you read these solutions, do two things if you answered the Math question incorrectly:

1. When a specific Strategy is referred to in the solution, study that strategy, which you will find in "Using Critical Thinking Skills in Math Questions" (beginning on page 174).

2. When the solution directs you to the "Math Refresher" (beginning on page 291)—for example, Math Refresher #305—study the 305 Math principles to get a clear idea of the Math operation that was necessary for you to know in order to answer the question correctly.

1. Choice B is correct. **(Use Strategy 13: Find unknowns by multiplication.)**

Method 1: $7x + 21 = 35$ $\quad$ $\boxed{1}$

Multiplying $\boxed{1}$ by $\frac{4}{7}$,

$$4x + 12 = 20$$

Thus, the columns become

Column A	Column B
20	21

and the answer is clear.

Method 2:

Given: $7x + 21 = 35$

Solve to get x:

$$7x = 14$$
$$x = 2 \quad \boxed{1}$$

Substitute $\boxed{1}$ into $4x + 12$

$$4(2) + 12 = 8 + 12$$
$$= 20$$

Clearly $20 < 21$.

(Math Refresher #406 and #431)

2. Choice A is correct.

Method 1: $(-2)^{88}$ is a positive number [a negative number raised to an even power is always positive]
$(-2)^{97}$ is a negative number [a negative number raised to an odd power is always negative]
Any positive is larger than any negative. Thus, $(-2)^{88}$ is larger than $(-2)^{97}$

Method 2: $(-2)^{97} = (-2)^{88}(-2)^9$
Thus, the columns become

Column A	Column B
$(-2)^{88}$	$(-2)^{88}(-2)^9$

(Use Strategy B: Cancel equal, positive things from both sides by division.)

Dividing both columns by $(-2)^{88}$, we get

Column A	Column B
1	$(-2)^9 =$ negative

Thus, Column A is larger.

(Math Refresher #428 and #429)

3. Choice B is correct. **(Use Strategy 6: Know how to manipulate inequalities.)**

We are told

$$-5 < y \qquad \boxed{1}$$
$$y < 5 \qquad \boxed{2}$$

Multiplying $\boxed{1}$ by -1,

$$5 > -y \qquad \boxed{3}$$

It is always true that $6 > 5$ $\qquad \boxed{4}$

Comparing $\boxed{3}$ and $\boxed{4}$, we have

$$6 > -y$$

(Math Refresher #423)

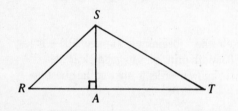

4. Choice B is correct. **(Use Strategy 18: Remember triangle facts.)**

SA is the altitude to side RT.
By definition, $SA \perp RT$.

The shortest distance from a point to a line is the length of $\perp$ segment from the point to the line. Thus, SA is the shortest distance from S to RT. Thus,

$$SA < SR$$

(Math Refresher #514)

5. Choice A is correct.

Given: $a - b = 5$ $\qquad \boxed{1}$
$\qquad\quad a + b = -1$ $\qquad \boxed{2}$

(Use Strategy 17: Use the given information effectively.)

Fast Method: Add b to both sides of $\boxed{1}$,

$$a = b + 5 \qquad \boxed{3}$$

From $\boxed{3}$, we can say right away that

$$a > b$$

Slow Method: Substitute $\boxed{3}$ into $\boxed{2}$,

$$b + 5 + b = -1$$
or $\qquad 2b + 5 = -1$
or $\qquad\quad 2b = -6$
or $\qquad\qquad b = -3 \qquad \boxed{4}$

Substituting $\boxed{4}$ into $\boxed{3}$,

$$a = 2 \qquad \boxed{5}$$

Comparing $\boxed{4}$ and $\boxed{5}$, we see that

$$a > b$$

(Math Refresher #406 and #407)

6. Choice A is correct.

Method 1

Given: m is an integer > 0 $\qquad \boxed{1}$
$\qquad\quad 0 < y < 1$ $\qquad \boxed{2}$

Column A	Column B
$\dfrac{m}{y}$	m

(Use Strategy 6: Know how to manipulate inequalities.) From $\boxed{2}$, since $y < 1$, we know that

$$\frac{1}{y} > 1 \qquad \boxed{3}$$

(Use Strategy 13: Find unknowns by multiplication.) (Use Strategy E: Try to get the columns and given to look similar.) Multiply $\boxed{3}$ by m, remembering, from $\boxed{1}$, that $m > 0$. We get

$$m\left(\frac{1}{y}\right) > (1)m$$

$$\frac{m}{y} > m$$

Method 2

$$m > 0$$
$$0 < y < 1$$

Column A	Column B
$\dfrac{m}{y}$	m

(Use Strategy B: Cancel numbers by division.) Cancel m, and we get

Column A	Column B
$\dfrac{1}{y}$	1

(Use Strategy D: Multiply both columns by y.) We get

Column A	Column B
1	y

From the given, $y < 1$. Therefore, Column A > Column B.

(Math Refresher #419 and #422)

7. Choice A is correct.

Given: $\qquad -\dfrac{1}{3}y = \dfrac{1}{3}y$ $\qquad$ $\boxed{1}$

(Use Strategy 13: Find unknowns by multiplication.) Multiply $\boxed{1}$ by 3. We get

$$3\left(-\dfrac{1}{3}y\right) = \left(\dfrac{1}{3}y\right)3$$
$$-y = y$$
$$0 = 2y$$
$$0 = y \qquad \boxed{2}$$

Column A	Column B
$-y$	$\dfrac{-2}{3}$

Substituting $\boxed{2}$ in $\boxed{3}$, the columns become

$-(0)$	$-\dfrac{2}{3}$

(Math Refresher #406)

8. Choice A is correct. **(Use Strategy 3: Know how to find unknown quantities from known quantities.)**

From the diagram,

$$AC + CD = AD \qquad \boxed{1}$$
$$\text{Given:} \quad AC = 16, AD = 24 \qquad \boxed{2}$$

Substituting $\boxed{2}$ into $\boxed{1}$, we have

$$16 + CD = 24$$
$$CD = 8 \qquad \boxed{3}$$

From the diagram, $BD > CD$ $\qquad \boxed{4}$

Substituting $\boxed{3}$ into $\boxed{4}$, we get

$$BD > 8$$

(Math Refresher #431 and Logical Reasoning)

9. Choice A is correct. **(Use Strategy 3: The whole equals the sum of its parts.)** Each angle in an equilateral triangle has a measure of 60°. Each one in a square has a measure of 90°. Thus, $m < ACD = 60 + 90 = 150$.
Hence, $x = 360 - 150 = 210$ and $210 > 200$.

(Math Refresher #508, #520, and #526)

10. Choice C is correct.

Given:
The average (arithmetic mean) of a and b is 8. $\boxed{1}$
$a - b + 4 = 0$ $\qquad \boxed{2}$

Column A	Column B
a	6

$\left(\text{Use Strategy 5:} \quad \text{Average} = \dfrac{\text{Sum of values}}{\text{Total number of values}}\right)$

From $\boxed{1}$, we get

$$\dfrac{a + b}{2} = 8 \qquad \boxed{3}$$

Multiply $\boxed{3}$ by 2. We get

$$2\left(\dfrac{a + b}{2}\right) = (8)2$$

$$a + b = 16 \qquad \boxed{4}$$

From $\boxed{2}$, $a - b + 4 = 0$, we get
$$a - b = -4 \qquad \boxed{5}$$

(Use Strategy 13: Find unknowns by addition.)

Adding $\boxed{4}$ and $\boxed{5}$, we have

$$2a = 12$$
$$a = 6 \qquad \boxed{6}$$

Using $\boxed{6}$, the columns become

Column A	Column B
$a = 6$	6

(Math Refresher #601, #406, and #407)

11. Choice A is correct.

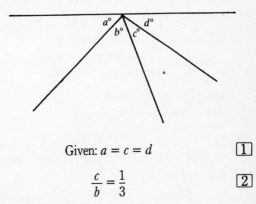

Given: $a = c = d$ $\qquad \boxed{1}$

$$\dfrac{c}{b} = \dfrac{1}{3} \qquad \boxed{2}$$

(Use Strategy 13: Find unknowns by multiplication.) Multiply $\boxed{2}$ by b. We get

$$\cancel{b}\left(\frac{c}{\cancel{b}}\right) = b\left(\frac{1}{3}\right)$$

$$c = \frac{b}{3} \qquad \boxed{3}$$

Substituting $\boxed{3}$ into $\boxed{1}$, we have

$$a = \frac{b}{3}, \quad d = \frac{b}{3} \qquad \boxed{4}$$

(Use Strategy 3: The whole equals the sum of its parts.) From the diagram we see that

$$a + b + c + d = 180° \qquad \boxed{5}$$

Substituting $\boxed{3}$ and $\boxed{4}$ into $\boxed{5}$, we get

$$\frac{b}{3} + b + \frac{b}{3} + \frac{b}{3} = 180° \qquad \boxed{6}$$

(Use Strategy 13: Find unknowns by multiplication.) Multiply $\boxed{6}$ by 3. We get

$$b + 3b + b + b = 540°$$
$$6b = 540°$$
$$b = 90° \qquad \boxed{7}$$

Column A	Column B
b	80

Substituting $\boxed{7}$ into $\boxed{8}$, the columns become

90	80

(Math Refresher #111, #406, and #501)

12. Choice C is correct. **(Use Strategy 11: Use new definitions carefully.)**

Given: $\quad x \,\square\, (-x) = 0 \qquad$ for all $x \qquad \boxed{1}$

where $\square$ is one of $+$, $-$, $\times$, or $\div$
Clearly, $\square$ cannot be $-$, $\times$, or $\div$ because

$$x - (-x) = 2x \neq 0$$
$$x \times (-x) = -x^2 \neq 0$$
$$x \div (-x) = -1 \neq 0$$

and $\boxed{1}$ is not satisfied.
But notice that

$$x + (-x) = 0$$

so that $\square$ is the same as $+$, thus, we want to compare

Column A	Column B
$x + y$	$y + x$

and the two quantities are equal.

(Math Refresher #431)

13. Choice D is correct.

Given: r, s, and $t > 0$

Column A	Column B
$r + s + t$	$\dfrac{1}{r + s + t}$

(Use Strategy C: Try numerics if it appears that the answer cannot be determined.)

Let $r = \dfrac{1}{4}$, $s = \dfrac{1}{4}$, $t = \dfrac{1}{4}$. The columns become

$$\frac{1}{4} + \frac{1}{4} + \frac{1}{4} = \qquad \frac{1}{\frac{1}{4} + \frac{1}{4} + \frac{1}{4}} = \frac{1}{\frac{3}{4}} =$$

$$\frac{3}{4} \quad < \quad \frac{4}{3}$$

Now let $r = 1$, $s = 2$, $t = 3$. The columns become

$$1 + 2 + 3 = \qquad \frac{1}{1 + 2 + 3} =$$

$$6 \quad > \quad \frac{1}{6}$$

Since two different relationships are possible, the answer cannot be determined from the information given.

(Math Refresher #109, #431, and #419)

14. Choice D is correct.

Given:
Total students = 100	$\boxed{1}$
Exactly 80% take calculus	$\boxed{2}$
Exactly 60% take physics	$\boxed{3}$
Exactly 50% take German	$\boxed{4}$

(Use Strategy 2: Translate from words to algebra.)

From $\boxed{3}$, we get

$$\text{Number of students taking physics} = .60 \times 100$$
$$= 60 \qquad \boxed{5}$$

From $\boxed{4}$, we get

$$\text{Number of students taking German} = .50 \times 100$$
$$= 50 \qquad \boxed{6}$$

(Use Strategy C: Try numerics if it appears that the answer cannot be determined.)

All 50 students taking German could also be taking physics.

Only 49 students taking German could also be taking physics.

Since there are two possible values for Column A—one equal to Column B and one less than Column B—the answer cannot be determined from the information given.

(Math Refresher #114)

15. Choice C is correct.

Given: a , b , c , d , and e are all integers > 0 . $\boxed{1}$
$a < b < c < d < e$ $\boxed{2}$
$a \times b = 7$ $\boxed{3}$
$d \times e = 90$ $\boxed{4}$

(Use Strategy 17: Use the given information effectively.)

From $\boxed{1}$, $\boxed{2}$ and $\boxed{3}$, we get
$$a = 1 \text{ and } b = 7 \qquad \boxed{5}$$

Using $\boxed{5}$, $\boxed{1}$, $\boxed{2}$ and $\boxed{4}$, we get
$$d = 9 \text{ and } e = 10 \qquad \boxed{6}$$

Using $\boxed{1}$, $\boxed{2}$, $\boxed{5}$ and $\boxed{6}$, we get
$$c = 8 \qquad \boxed{7}$$

Using $\boxed{7}$, the columns become

Column A	Column B
$c = 8$	8

(Math Refresher #419 and Logical Reasoning)

16. **10**

Given: $\qquad\qquad ab = 40 \qquad\qquad \boxed{1}$

$$\frac{a}{b} = \frac{5}{2} \qquad\qquad \boxed{2}$$

(Use Strategy 13: Find unknowns by multiplication.)

Multiplying $\boxed{2}$ by $2b$, we get
$$2b\left(\frac{a}{b}\right) = \left(\frac{5}{2}\right)2b$$

$$2a = 5b$$

$$\frac{2a}{5} = b \qquad\qquad \boxed{3}$$

Substitute $\boxed{3}$ into $\boxed{1}$. We have
$$ab = 40$$

$$a\left(\frac{2a}{5}\right) = 40$$

$$\frac{2a^2}{5} = 40 \qquad\qquad \boxed{4}$$

Multiplying $\boxed{1}$ by $\frac{5}{2}$, we get

$$\frac{5}{2}\left(\frac{2a^2}{5}\right) = (40)\frac{5}{2}$$

$$a^2 = 100$$
$$\sqrt{a^2} = \sqrt{100}$$
$$a = \pm\, 10$$

Since we were given that a is positive, we have $a = 10$.

(Math Refresher #406, #429, and #430)

17. **20**

Use Strategy 2: Translate from words to algebra.)

Given: Stephanie's earnings = \$ x $\boxed{1}$
Stephanie's time $\quad$ = 10 hours $\boxed{2}$
Evelyn's earnings $\quad$ = \$ y $\boxed{3}$
Evelyn's time $\qquad$ = 20 hours $\boxed{4}$
$x + y \qquad\quad$ = 60 $\boxed{5}$

We know that hourly wage $\quad = \dfrac{\text{Total Earnings}}{\text{Total Hours}}$

$\boxed{6}$

Substituting $\boxed{1}$ and $\boxed{2}$ into $\boxed{6}$, we get

Stephanie's hourly wage $= \dfrac{\$ x}{10 \text{ hours}}$ $\boxed{7}$

Substituting $\boxed{3}$ and $\boxed{4}$ into $\boxed{6}$, we get

Evelyn's hourly wage $= \dfrac{\$ y}{20 \text{ hours}}$ $\boxed{8}$

We are told that they have the same hourly wage. Using $\boxed{7}$ and $\boxed{8}$, we have

$$\frac{\$x}{10 \text{ hours}} = \frac{\$y}{20 \text{ hours}}$$

$$\frac{x}{10} = \frac{y}{20} \qquad \boxed{9}$$

$$\overset{2}{\cancel{20}}\left(\frac{x}{\cancel{10}}\right) = \left(\frac{y}{\cancel{20}}\right)\cancel{20}$$

$$2x = y \qquad \boxed{10}$$

Substituting $\boxed{10}$ into $\boxed{5}$, we get

$$x + 2x = 60$$
$$3x = 60$$
$$x = 20$$

(Math Refresher #200, #201, and #406)

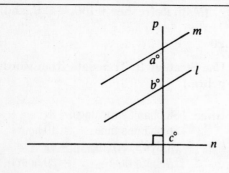

18. **270**

Given: $m \parallel l$ $\boxed{1}$
       $p \perp n$ $\boxed{2}$

From $\boxed{1}$ we get that $a + b = 180$, $\boxed{3}$
because when 2 lines are parallel, the interior angles on the same side of the transversal are supplementary.

From $\boxed{2}$ we get that $c = 90$ $\boxed{4}$
because perpendicular lines form right angles.

(Use Strategy 13: Find unknowns by addition.)

Add $\boxed{3}$ and $\boxed{4}$. We have

$$a + b + c = 180 + 90$$
$$= 270$$

(Math Refresher #504, #501, and #511)

19. **5**

We know Area of circle = $\pi(\text{radius})^2$ $\boxed{1}$

Given: radius of larger circle = $r + 3$ $\boxed{2}$
          radius of small circle = r $\boxed{3}$

Substitute $\boxed{2}$ into $\boxed{1}$. We have

$$\text{Area of larger circle} = \pi(r + 3)^2 \qquad \boxed{4}$$

(Use Strategy 4: Remember classic expressions.)

$$(r + 3)^2 = r^2 + 6r + 9 \qquad \boxed{5}$$

Substitute $\boxed{5}$ into $\boxed{4}$. We have

$$\text{Area of larger circle} = \pi(r^2 + 6r + 9) \qquad \boxed{6}$$

Substituting $\boxed{3}$ into $\boxed{1}$, we get

$$\text{Area of small circle} = \pi r^2 \qquad \boxed{7}$$

(Use Strategy 13: Find unknowns by subtraction.)

Subtract $\boxed{7}$ from $\boxed{6}$. We have

Difference of areas
$$= \pi(r^2 + 6r + 9) - \pi r^2 \qquad \boxed{8}$$

Given: Difference of areas = 21π $\boxed{9}$

Substitute $\boxed{9}$ into $\boxed{8}$. We have

$$21\pi = \pi(r^2 + 6r + 9) - \pi r^2 \qquad \boxed{10}$$

(Use Strategy 13: Find unknowns by division.)

$$\frac{21\cancel{\pi}}{\cancel{\pi}} = \frac{\cancel{\pi}(r^2 + 6r + 9)}{\cancel{\pi}} - \frac{\cancel{\pi}r^2}{\cancel{\pi}}$$
$$21 = \cancel{r^2} + 6r + 9 - \cancel{r^2}$$
$$21 = 6r + 9$$
$$12 = 6r$$
$$2 = r \qquad \boxed{11}$$

Substitute $\boxed{11}$ into $\boxed{2}$. We get

$$\text{radius of larger circle} = 2 + 3$$
$$= 5$$

(Math Refresher #409, #310, and #406)

20. **2**

(Use Strategy 17: Use the given information effectively.)

The most favorable conditions for Team C would be the following:

EVENT	FIRST PLACE (8 points)	SECOND PLACE (4 points)	THIRD PLACE (2 points)
3	Team C	Team A	Team B
4	Team C	Team B	Team A

Thus, Team C has a total of $4 + 8 + 8 = 20$ points after 2 more games. Team A has $12 + 4 + 2 = 18$

points. Team B has $12 + 2 + 4 = 18$ points. Thus, Team C will have to play at least 2 more games.

(Logical Reasoning)

21. **2**

(Use Strategy 17: Use the given information effectively.)

Since $x = 15$, then

$$m \angle LMN = 90$$
$$m \angle JNK = 75$$
$$m \angle KNM = 15$$
$$m \angle JNM = 90$$

Thus, the figure, with dashed line extensions, follows:

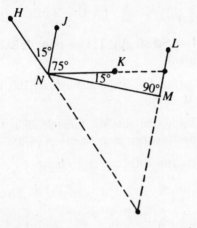

Clearly $\overleftrightarrow{JN} \parallel \overleftrightarrow{ML}$ and $\overleftrightarrow{JN}$ will not intersect $\overleftrightarrow{ML}$. $\overleftrightarrow{NK}$ and $\overleftrightarrow{NH}$ will each intersect $\overleftrightarrow{ML}$ exactly once. Thus, there will be exactly 2 more additional points of intersection.

(Math Refresher #504 and Logical Reasoning)

22. **20**

(Use Strategy 2: Translate from words to algebra.)

We are told that

$$a = b + \frac{10}{100}b = \frac{11}{10}b \qquad \boxed{1}$$

$$ac = bd + \frac{32}{100}bd = \frac{33}{25}bd \qquad \boxed{2}$$

(Use Strategy 13: Find unknowns by division.)

We divide $\boxed{2}$ by a

$$c = \frac{33}{25}\left(\frac{b}{a}\right)d \qquad \boxed{3}$$

(Use Strategy 13: Find unknowns by multiplication.)

Multiply $\boxed{1}$ by $\frac{1}{b}$, giving

$$\frac{a}{b} = \frac{11}{10}$$

or

$$\frac{b}{a} = \frac{10}{11} \qquad \boxed{4}$$

Substituting $\boxed{4}$ into $\boxed{3}$, we get

$$c = \frac{6}{5}d$$

or

$$c = d + \frac{1}{5}d$$

or

$$c = d + \frac{20}{100}d$$

Thus, c is 20 percent greater than d.

(Math Refresher #200, #406, and #431)

Alternate method:

Use Strategy 7. Use numerics. Let $b = 100$, $d = 10$. **Then use Strategy 2: Translate words to algebra.**

Then $a = \frac{10}{100}(100) + 100 = 110$

$ac = \frac{32}{100}bd + bd = \frac{32}{100}(100)d + 100d$

$110c = 32d + 100d = 132d \qquad \boxed{1}$

$c = \frac{x}{100}d + d = \frac{xd + 100d}{100} = \frac{(x + 100)d}{100} \quad \boxed{2}$

Divide $\boxed{1}$ by 110:

$$c = \frac{132}{110}d \qquad \boxed{3}$$

Compare $\boxed{3}$ with $\boxed{2}$:

$$\frac{132}{110} = \frac{x + 100}{100}$$

$$\frac{13200}{110} = x + 100$$

$$120 = x + 100$$

$$20 = x$$

23. $\dfrac{1}{48}$

(Use Strategy 2: Translate from words to algebra.)

Given: We know that

$$1 \text{ gross} = 12 \text{ dozen}$$
$$1 \text{ dozen} = 12 \text{ (eggs)}$$

Thus,

$$1 \text{ gross of eggs} = (12 \text{ dozens})(12 \text{ eggs/dozen})$$
$$= 144 \text{ eggs}$$

3 eggs, expressed as a fraction of a gross, $= \dfrac{3}{144}$

$$= \dfrac{1}{48}$$

(Math Refresher #200 and #121)

24. **5**

We are given that

Volume of 1 brick = 40 cubic inches $\boxed{1}$

Volume of the final pile
of bricks = 8000 cubic inches $\boxed{2}$

(Use Strategy 3: The whole equals the sum of its parts.) Logically, we know the number of layers in the final pile of bricks

$$= \dfrac{\text{Volume of the final pile of bricks}}{\text{Volume of each layer of bricks}} \quad \boxed{3}$$

From the diagram in the question, we see that

1 layer of bricks = 40 bricks $\boxed{4}$

Thus, by using $\boxed{1}$ and $\boxed{4}$, we know that the volume of each layer of bricks

= volume of 1 brick
   × number of bricks in 1 layer
= 40 cubic inches × 40
= 1600 cubic inches $\boxed{5}$

Substituting $\boxed{2}$ and $\boxed{5}$ into $\boxed{3}$, the number of layers in the final pile of bricks

$$= \dfrac{8000 \text{ cubic inches}}{1600 \text{ cubic inches}}$$

(Use Strategy 19: Factor and reduce.)

$$= \dfrac{8 \times 1000}{16 \times 100}$$

$$= \dfrac{8 \times 10 \times 100}{8 \times 2 \times 100}$$

$$= \dfrac{10}{2} = 5$$

(Math Refresher #200 and #601)

25. **108**

(Use Strategy 11: Use new definitions carefully.)

The first few 3-digit numbers are 100, 101, 102, 103, 104, etc.

Clearly, the smallest possible 3-digit number in which no digit is repeated is $x = 102$.

From the definition of y, y must be $y = 210$.

Thus, $y - x =$

$$210 - 102 =$$

$$108$$

(Logical Reasoning)

Explanatory Answers for Practice Test 4 (continued)

Section 5: Verbal Ability

As you read these Explanatory Answers, refer to "Using Critical Thinking Skills in Verbal Questions" (beginning on page 236) whenever a specific Strategy is referred to in the answer. Of particular importance is the following Master Verbal Strategy:

Reading Comprehension Master Strategy 2—page 263.

1. Choice B is correct. See paragraph 2: "Most social scientists ... have assumed that the minimum economic needs of the aged should be lower than those of the younger family."

2. Choice E is correct. Given the context of the sentence and the next sentence, Choice E is the best.

3. Choice A is correct. See paragraph 5: "[The data] disclose sharp income inequalities within every age group ..."

4. Choice E is correct. For I, see paragraph 6: "Those sixty-five and over are expected to increase 672 percent." For III, see paragraph 4: "For the growing working-class family, limited in income by the very nature of the breadwinner's occupation ..."

5. Choice C is correct. See paragraph 2: The sentence after the "functional ethos" sentence refers to "these values."

6. Choice D is correct. See paragraph 6: "With the more rapid expansion of these two low-income groups, the young and the old ..."

7. Choice D is correct. For I, see paragraph 5: "A spending unit's income-tenth position *within his age category* varies much less, if at all, and is determined

primarily by his occupation." For III, see paragraph 4: "For the growing working-class family, limited in income by the very nature of the breadwinner's occupation ..."

8. Choice A is correct. From the context of the sentence, it can be seen that Choice A is the best.

9. Choice C is correct. See paragraph 3: "Despite his seniority, the older worker is likely to be downgraded to a lower-paying job ..."

10. Choice C is correct. See paragraph 4: "The early and lower income period of a person's working life, during which he acquires his basic vocational skills..."

11. Choice C is correct. See paragraph 5: "... the higher income-tenths have a much greater representation of spending headed by persons aged thirty-five to fifty-five than do the lower income-tenths."

12. Choice C is correct. See paragraph 5: "A spending unit's income-tenth position is ... determined primarily by his occupation."

13. Choice D is correct. The phrase "the legendary land of economic opportunity where any man can work his way to the top" (lines 86–88), in contrast to what the author really believes, represents *sarcasm.*

Explanatory Answers for Practice Test 4 (continued)

Section 6: Math Ability

As you read these solutions, do two things if you answered the Math question incorrectly:

1. When a specific Strategy is referred to in the solution, study that strategy, which you will find in "Using Critical Thinking Skills in Math Questions" (beginning on page 174).

2. When the solution directs you to the "Math Refresher" (beginning on page 291)—for example, Math Refresher #305—study the 305 Math principles to get a clear idea of the Math operation that was necessary for you to know in order to answer the question correctly.

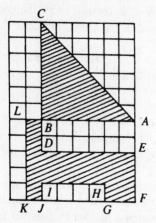

1. Choice C is correct.

Given: length of side of square = 1. $\boxed{1}$

Using $\boxed{1}$, we get $AB = 6$, $BC = 6$ $\boxed{2}$

We know that the Area of Triangle = $\frac{1}{2}$ (base)(height) $\boxed{3}$

Substituting $\boxed{2}$ into $\boxed{3}$, we get

Area of Shaded Triangle $ABC = \frac{1}{2}$ (6)(6)

$= 18$ $\boxed{4}$

We know that Area of square = (side)² $\boxed{5}$

Substituting $\boxed{1}$ into $\boxed{5}$, we have

Area of each square = (1)² = 1 $\boxed{6}$

Counting the number of squares in the other shaded figure ($BDEFGHIJKL$), we find 19. $\boxed{7}$

Multiplying $\boxed{6}$ by $\boxed{7}$, we have

Area of $BDEFGHIJKL = 19 \times 1 = 19$ $\boxed{8}$

(Use Strategy 3: The whole equals the sum of its parts.)

We know: Total Shaded Area

$= $ Area of $ABC +$
Area of $BDEFGHIJKL$ $\boxed{9}$

Substituting $\boxed{4}$ and $\boxed{8}$ into $\boxed{9}$, we get

Total Shaded Area = 18 + 19

$= 37$

(Math Refresher #303 and #307)

2. Choice C is correct. **(Use Strategy 17: Use the given information effectively.)**

Since the triangle is equilateral, all of its sides are equal. Thus,

$$5x - 2 = x$$
$$4x = 2$$
$$x = \frac{1}{2}$$

$$\text{Perimeter} = \text{Sum of 3 sides} = \frac{1}{2} + \frac{1}{2} + \frac{1}{2}$$
$$= 1\frac{1}{2}$$

(Math Refresher #508 and #406)

3. Choice E is correct. **(Use Strategy 10: Know how to use units of time, distance, area.)**

The number of waves that pass through a certain point in t seconds

$$= \frac{w \text{ waves}}{s \text{ seconds}} \, (t \text{ seconds})$$

$$= \frac{wt}{s} \text{ waves}$$

(Math Refresher #121)

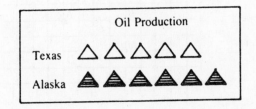

4. Choice C is correct. **(Use Strategy 2: Translate from words to algebra.)**

We are told ▲ = 3△

(Use Strategy 17: Use the given information effectively.)

$$\text{Texas total} = 5$$
$$\text{Alaska total} = 3(6) = 18$$

(Use Strategy 3: Know how to find unknown quantities from known quantities.)

$$\frac{\text{Alaska production}}{\text{Total production}} = \frac{18}{5 + 18} =$$

$$\frac{18}{23} = \text{required ratio}$$

(Math Refresher #200 and 431)

5. Choice C is correct. Probability is defined as

$$\frac{\text{number of favorable ways (coins)}}{\text{total number of ways (coins)}} = \frac{F}{N}.$$

If the probability of selecting a nickel is $\frac{3}{8}$, then for nickels, $\frac{F}{N} = \frac{3}{8}$. But N [the total number of ways (or coins)] is 24.

So $\frac{F}{N} = \frac{3}{8} = \frac{F}{24}$; F = 9 (nickels)

The probability of selecting a dime is $\frac{1}{8}$, so for a dime, $\frac{F}{N} = \frac{1}{8} = \frac{F}{24}$; F = 3 (dimes)

Since there are 24 coins and there are 9 nickels and 3 dimes, $24 - 3 - 9 = 12$ quarters. **(Use Strategy 3: Subtract whole from parts.)**

(Math Refresher #614)

6. Choice C is correct. **(Use Strategy 17: Use the given information effectively.)**

Given: ▯◼ ◻1◻

In order for a given figure to have been formed from ◻1◻, it must have the same number of shaded and unshaded squares.

Choice I has 8 unshaded and 6 shaded squares. Thus, it could *not* be formed from ◻1◻.

Choice II has 5 unshaded and 6 shaded squares. Thus, it could *not* be formed from ◻1◻.

Looking at Choices A through E, we see that the correct choice must be Choice C: III only.

(Logical Reasoning)

7. Choice D is correct.

$$\text{Given:} \quad r = 7a \qquad \boxed{1}$$
$$5w = 7a \qquad \boxed{2}$$
$$\text{From } \boxed{2} \text{ we get } w = \frac{7a}{5} \qquad \boxed{3}$$

(Use Strategy 13: Find unknowns by subtracting.)

Subtract $\boxed{3}$ from $\boxed{1}$. We get

$$r - w = 7a - \frac{7a}{5}$$

$$= \frac{35a}{5} - \frac{7a}{5}$$

$$r - w = \frac{28a}{5}$$

(Math Refresher #406)

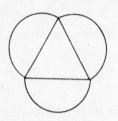

8. Choice C is correct. **(Use Strategy 3: The whole equals the sum of its parts.)**

Total area = Area of triangle + 3(area of semicircle) $\boxed{1}$

Given: Radius of each semicircle = 2 $\boxed{2}$
From $\boxed{2}$ we know each diameter = 4
Thus, the triangle has three equal sides of length 4
and is equilateral. $\boxed{3}$

We know: Area of equilateral triangle = $\dfrac{S^2\sqrt{3}}{4}$ $\boxed{4}$

Area of semicircle = $\dfrac{\pi r^2}{2}$ $\boxed{5}$

Substituting $\boxed{4}$ and $\boxed{5}$ into $\boxed{1}$, we get

Total area = $\dfrac{S^2\sqrt{3}}{4} + 3\left(\dfrac{\pi r^2}{2}\right)$ $\boxed{6}$

Substituting $\boxed{2}$ and $\boxed{3}$ into $\boxed{6}$, we get

Total area = $\dfrac{4^2\sqrt{3}}{4} + 3\left(\dfrac{\pi(2)^2}{2}\right)$

$= \dfrac{16\sqrt{3}}{4} + 3\left(\dfrac{4\pi}{2}\right)$

Total area = $4\sqrt{3} + 6\pi$

(Math Refresher #308, #310, and #311)

9. Choice D is correct. The procedure, as described, can be summarized in the following table:

Given Container	–	Receiving Container	=	Excess to 50 cc Container
25cc	–	16cc	=	9cc
16cc	–	9cc	=	7cc
9cc	–	4cc	=	5cc
4cc	–	1cc	=	3cc
			Total =	24cc

(Use Strategy 2: Remember the definition of percent.)

Thus, $\dfrac{24\text{cc}}{50\text{cc}} \times 100 = 48\%$ of the 50cc container is full.

(Use Strategy 3: The whole equals the sum of its parts.)

So, $100\% - 48\% = 52\%$ of the 50cc container is empty.

(Math Refresher #107 and Logical Reasoning)

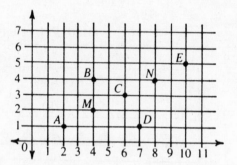

10. Choice E is correct. **(Use Strategy 8: When all choices must be tested, start with E and work backward.)**

In the diagram above, we have plotted each of the points given in the choices. From the diagram, it is clear that

$$MC = CN = NE$$

Thus, since $ME = MC + CN + NE$, then
$3NE = ME$

as required, so that point E is the answer.

(Math Refresher #410)

Explanatory Answers for Practice Test 4 (continued)

Section 7: Math Ability

As you read these solutions, do two things if you answered the Math question incorrectly:

1. When a specific Strategy is referred to in the solution, study that strategy, which you will find in "Using Critical Thinking Skills in Math Questions" (beginning on page 174).

2. When the solution directs you to the "Math Refresher" (beginning on page 291)—for example, Math Refresher #305—study the 305 Math principles to get a clear idea of the Math operation that was necessary for you to know in order to answer the question correctly.

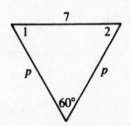

1. Choice C is correct. **(Use Strategy 18: Know equilateral and isosceles triangles.)**

   Since the triangle has 2 equal sides, the angles opposite these sides are equal. Thus,

   $$\angle 1 = \angle 2 \qquad \boxed{1}$$

   (Use Strategy 3: The whole equals the sum of its parts.)

   We know that the sum of the angles of a triangle = 180°

   Thus, $\angle 1 + \angle 2 + 60° = 180°$ $\qquad \boxed{2}$

Substituting $\boxed{1}$ into $\boxed{2}$, we get

$$\angle 1 + \angle 1 + 60° = 180°$$
$$2(\angle 1) + 60 = 180°$$
$$2(\angle 1) = 120°$$
$$\angle 1 = 60° \qquad \boxed{3}$$

Substituting $\boxed{3}$ into $\boxed{1}$, we have

$$\angle 1 = \angle 2 = 60°$$

Thus, all three angles each = 60°, and the triangle is equilateral.
Therefore all three sides are equal. $\qquad \boxed{4}$

From $\boxed{4}$ and the diagram, we get $p = 7$. $\qquad \boxed{5}$

Column A	Column B	
21	3p	$\boxed{6}$

Substituting $\boxed{5}$ into $\boxed{6}$, we get

21	$3p =$
	$3(7) =$
21	21

(Math Refresher #507, #508, and #505)

2. Choice B is correct. **(Use Strategy 2: Translate verbal into math.)** The greatest one-year change in City A's population is 8,000. This occurred in 1992–93, when the population went from 119,000 to 127,000. The greatest one-year change in City B's population came in 1989–90, when the population went from 118,000 to 109,000. This was a change of 9,000.

(Math Refresher #702)

3. Choice C is correct. **(Use Strategy 2: Translate verbal into math.)** The population of City A in 1992 was 119,000. The population of City B in 1988 was 124,000. Thus, the difference is 5,000.

(Math Refresher #702)

4. Choice C is correct. The numbers in the box are 11, 12, 13, 14, 15, 16, 17, 18, 19, 20. The prime numbers from these are 11, 13, 17, 19. The probability of picking a card with a prime number is defined as the favorable number of ways divided by the total number of ways. The favorable number is 4 since there are four prime numbers. The total number of ways is 10 since there are 10 total numbers to choose from (from 11 through 20). So the probability of getting a prime number is $\frac{4}{10}$. Column A is $\frac{4}{10}$. Now for Column B: The numbers from 11 through 20 that are exactly divisible by 3 are 12, 15, 18. The number that is a perfect square is 16 since $4 \times 4 = 16$. Thus there are a total of 4 numbers that are exactly divisible by 3 or a perfect square. The probability of getting a card with one of these numbers is $\frac{4}{10}$. The columns are therefore equal.

(Math Refresher #608 and #614)

5. Choice C is correct. **(Use Strategy 12: Try not to make tedious calculations since there is usually an easier way.)**

Column A	Column B
25% of 90	$\frac{1}{2}$ of 45
$\frac{1}{4} \times 90$	$\frac{1}{2} \times 45$
$\frac{90}{4}$	$\frac{45}{2}$
$\frac{45}{2}$	

Thus, Choice C is correct because the two quantities are equal.

(Math Refresher #107, #108, and #111)

6. Choice D is correct. **(Use Strategy C: Try numerics if it appears that a definite relationship of the columns can't be determined.)**

Choose numeric values of x.

EXAMPLE 1

$$x = 1$$

The columns then become

Column A	Column B
1	1

and the two quantities are equal.

EXAMPLE 2

$$x = 2$$

The columns then become

Column A	Column B
2	$\frac{1}{2}$

and the quantity in Column A is greater. Thus, a definite comparison cannot be made.

(Math Refresher #431)

7. Choice C is correct.
Method 1:

Use Strategy 5: Average = $\frac{\text{Sum of values}}{\text{Total number of values}}$

Column A	Column B
Average =	Average =
$\frac{3+7+11+15+x}{5}$	$\frac{2+6+12+16+x}{5}$
$= \frac{36+x}{5}$	$= \frac{36+x}{5}$

Method 2: If you have no idea:
(Use Strategy F: For straightforward calculations, use the Choice C method.)

(Math Refresher #601)

8. Choice C is correct.

Let K = number of kilograms equal to 100,000 grams. $\boxed{1}$

Given: 1,000 grams = 1 kilogram $\boxed{2}$

Set up a proportion using $\boxed{1}$ and $\boxed{2}$:

$$\frac{1 \text{ kilogram}}{1,000 \text{ grams}} = \frac{\text{K kilograms}}{100,000 \text{ grams}} \qquad \boxed{3}$$

(Use Strategy 13: Find unknowns by multiplication.) Multiply $\boxed{3}$ by 100,000 grams and simplify:

$$\text{K kilograms} = \frac{(1 \text{ kilogram})\;\overset{100}{\cancel{(100{,}000 \text{ grams})}}}{\cancel{1000} \text{ grams}}$$

$$\text{K} = 100$$
$$\text{Column B} = 100$$

(Math Refresher #120)

9. Choice A is correct. **(Use Strategy A: Cancel numbers common to both columns by subtraction.)**

Column A		Column B
$(3 + y)7$		$7y + 3$
$21 + \cancel{7y}$		$\cancel{7y} + 3$
21	>	3

(Math Refresher #419 and #420)

10. Choice B is correct.

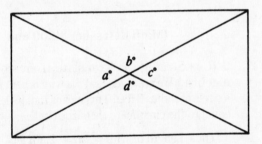

The figure above illustrates one way that c could be less than d, as given. **(Use Strategy 17: Use given information effectively.)**

$a = c$ ($a°$ and $c°$ are vertical angles) $\qquad \boxed{1}$
$b = d$ ($b°$ and $d°$ are vertical angles) $\qquad \boxed{2}$

Column A	Column B
$a + b + c$	$b + c + d$

Change all variables to either c or d by substituting $\boxed{1}$ and $\boxed{2}$ in $\boxed{3}$:

$$c + d + c \qquad\qquad d + c + d$$

(Use Strategy A: Cancel expressions common to both columns.) Cancel c and d from Column A and Column B:

$\cancel{c} + \cancel{d} + c$		$d + \cancel{c} + \cancel{d}$
c	<	d
		(from the given)

(Math Refresher #419, #501, and #503)

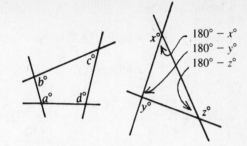

11. Choice C is correct. **(Use Strategy 3: The whole equals the sum of its parts.)**

$$a + b + c + d = 360$$

(the sum of the internal angles in a quadrilateral = 360) $\qquad \boxed{1}$

(Use Strategy 18: Know and use facts about triangles.) The sum of the internal angles of a triangle is 180°. So, $180 - x + 180 - y + 180 - z = 180$.

$$540 - x - y - z = 180$$
$$x + y + z = 360$$

(the sum of the external angles of a triangle = 360) $\qquad \boxed{2}$

Since $\boxed{1} = \boxed{2}$, Choice C is correct.

(Math Refresher #521)

12. Choice D is correct.

Given: A solid figure has equal faces. The volume of the solid is 125.

Column A	Column B
The number of faces of the solid	5

(Use Strategy 17: Use the given information effectively.) Equal faces and a volume of 125 are not enough information to determine the number of faces!

(Logical Reasoning)

13. Choice C is correct. **(Use Strategy 17: Use the given information effectively.)**

Since both 11 and 23 are prime, they each have only 2 positive integer factors: 1 and themselves.

(Math Refresher #608)

14. Choice C is correct.

Given: For all $x < 0$, $\bigcirc{x} = 2x^2$ $\boxed{1}$

           For all $x > 0$, $\bigcirc{x} = \dfrac{x}{4}$ $\boxed{2}$

Column A	Column B
$\bigcirc{-3}$	$\bigcirc{72}$

(**Use Strategy 11: Use new definitions carefully.**) Using $\boxed{1}$, Column A becomes

$\bigcirc{-3} = 2(-3)^2 =$
$\qquad 2(9) =$
$\qquad 18$ $\boxed{4}$

Using $\boxed{2}$, Column B becomes

$\bigcirc{72} = \dfrac{72}{4} =$
$\qquad 18$ $\boxed{5}$

From $\boxed{4}$ and $\boxed{5}$, we see that the columns are equal.

(Math Refresher #431 and #429)

15. Choice B is correct. (**Use Strategy 12: Try not to make tedious calculations.**) Whatever you do, do not calculate the areas of the polygons (in terms of, say, the radius of the circle). That would be very time consuming. In this problem it is much faster to use logic. (**Use Strategy 14: Draw lines when appropriate.**) Since the circles in both cases have the same radius, we can superimpose the two pictures.

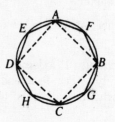

Clearly, the square (*ABCD*) is completely covered by the octagon (*AFBGCHDE*). The octagon has the greater area.

(Logical Reasoning)

16. **24 (Use Strategy 2: Translate from words to algebra.)**

Given: $\dfrac{5}{8}$ of x is 40

$\qquad\quad \downarrow \ \downarrow \ \downarrow \ \downarrow \ \downarrow$

$\qquad\quad \dfrac{5}{8} \times x = 40$ $\boxed{1}$

(Use Strategy 13: Find unknowns by multiplication.)

Fast Method: Multiply $\boxed{1}$ by $\dfrac{3}{5}$ to get

$$\frac{3}{5}\left(\frac{5}{8}x\right) = \frac{3}{5}(40)$$

$$\frac{3}{8}x = \frac{3}{5} \times 5 \times 8$$

$$\frac{3}{8}x = 24$$

Slow Method: Solve $\boxed{1}$ for x by multiplying $\boxed{1}$ by $\dfrac{8}{5}$:

$$x = 64 \qquad \boxed{2}$$

Now substitute $\boxed{2}$ into the unknown expression:

$$\frac{3}{8}x = \frac{3}{8}(64)$$

$$= \frac{3}{8} \times 8 \times 8$$

$$= 24$$

(Math Refresher #200 and #406)

17. **9 (Use Strategy 2: Translate from words to algebra.)** We are given that the wire is bent to form a circle of radius 3 feet. This means that its length is equal to the circumference of the circle.

Thus, Length of wire $= 2\pi r = 2\pi(3)$ feet
$\qquad\qquad\qquad\quad = 6\pi$ feet
$\qquad\qquad\qquad\quad \approx 6(3.14)$ feet
Length of wire ≈ 18.84 feet $\boxed{1}$

(Use Strategy 3: Know how to find unknown quantities.)

$$\frac{\text{Number of pieces}}{\text{2 feet long}} = \frac{\text{Total length}}{\text{2 feet}} \qquad \boxed{2}$$

Substituting $\boxed{1}$ into $\boxed{2}$, we have

$$\frac{\text{Number of pieces}}{\text{2 feet long}} \approx \frac{18.84 \text{ feet}}{2 \text{ feet}}$$

$$\approx 9.42$$
$$= 9 \text{ complete pieces}$$

(Math Refresher #310)

18. **7 (Use Strategy 2: Translate from words to algebra.)**

Let b = number of baseballs that Dick bought
t = number of tennis balls that Dick bought
$.70b$ = amount spent on baseballs
$.60t$ = amount spent on tennis balls

Thus, we are told

$$.70b + .60t = 7.00 \qquad \boxed{1}$$

Multiply $\boxed{1}$ by 10,

$$7b + 6t = 70 \qquad \boxed{2}$$

Solve $\boxed{2}$ for t,

$$t = \frac{70 - 7b}{6} \qquad \boxed{3}$$

(Use Strategy 17: Use the given information effectively.) From $\boxed{3}$, we see that the maximum value of t occurs at the minimum value of b. Since b and t are numbers of balls, b and t must be non-negative integers. Thus, the minimum value of b is 0. When $b = 0$, $t = \frac{70}{6}$, which is not intregral. For t to be an integer, $\boxed{3}$ tells us that $(10 - b)$ is a multiple of 6. The smallest value of b that makes $(10 - b)$ a multiple of 6 is $b = 4$. Thus, $t = 7$ is the maximum value of t, and 7 is the answer.

(Math Refresher #200, #406, and #431 and Logical Reasoning)

19. **2 (Use Strategy 11: Use new definitions carefully.)**

Given:

$$f(x) = 12x + 8 \qquad \boxed{1}$$
$$\text{and } f(x) \div f(0) = 2x \qquad \boxed{2}$$

Calculate $f(0)$:

$$f(0) = 12\,(0) + 8 = 8 \qquad \boxed{3}$$

Substitute $\boxed{1}$ and $\boxed{3}$ into $\boxed{2}$:

$$\frac{12x + 8}{8} = 2x \qquad \boxed{4}$$

Multiply both sides by $\boxed{4}$ by 8:

$$12x + 8 = 16x$$
or $\qquad 8 = 4x$
or $\qquad x = 2$

(Math Refresher #431 and #406)

20. **8 (Use Strategy 11: Use new definitions carefully.)**

In the given letter columns, only 8 triples have the property that exactly 2 of the letters in the triple are the same. Thus, 8 triples have a value of 1, and all the other triples have a value of 0. Hence, the value of the entire group of letter columns is 8.

(Logical Reasoning)

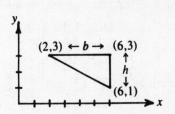

21. **4 (Use Strategy 17: Use the given information effectively.)**

It is clear from the diagram above that the triangle is a right triangle whose area is

$$A = \frac{1}{2}\,bh \qquad \boxed{1}$$

From the given coordinates, we can also say that

$$b = 6 - 2 = 4 \qquad \boxed{2}$$
$$h = 3 - 1 = 2 \qquad \boxed{3}$$

Substituting $\boxed{2}$ and $\boxed{3}$ into $\boxed{1}$,

$$A = \frac{1}{2}\,(4)(2)$$

$$A = 4$$

(Math Refresher #306 and #410)

22. **18 (Use Strategy 17: Use the given information effectively.)**

The area of a rectangle is length × width. The number of squares that can be packed into the rectangle

$$= \frac{\text{Area of entire rectangle}}{\text{Area of each square}}$$

$$= \frac{6 \times 12}{2 \times 2}$$

$$= \frac{72}{4}$$

$$= \frac{\cancel{4} \times 18}{\cancel{4}}$$

$$= 18$$

(Math Refresher #304 and #431)

23. **60** Since we are given the radii of the circles, we have

$$AN = AM = 1 \qquad \boxed{1}$$
$$BM = BP = 2 \qquad \boxed{2}$$
$$CN = CP = 3 \qquad \boxed{3}$$

We want to find

$$(AB)(BC)(AC) \qquad \boxed{4}$$

(Use Strategy 3: The whole equals the sum of its parts.) From the diagram, we see that

$$AB = AM + BM \qquad \boxed{5}$$
$$BC = BP + CP \qquad \boxed{6}$$
$$AC = AN + CN \qquad \boxed{7}$$

Substituting $\boxed{1}$, $\boxed{2}$, $\boxed{3}$ into $\boxed{5}$, $\boxed{6}$, $\boxed{7}$, we have

$$AB = 3$$
$$BC = 5$$
$$AC = 4$$

Thus,

$$(AB)(BC)(AC) = (3)(5)(4)$$
$$= 60$$

(Math Refresher #524)

24. **9,500**

$$\left(\text{Use Strategy 5:} \right.$$
$$\left. \text{Average} = \frac{\textbf{Sum of values}}{\textbf{Total number of values}} \right)$$

We are given:

$$\frac{x + y + z + w}{4} = 8,000 \qquad \boxed{1}$$

(Use Strategy 13: Find unknowns by multiplication.) Multiplying $\boxed{1}$ by 4, we get

$$x + y + z + w = 32,000 \qquad \boxed{2}$$

We are given any 3 have an average of 7,500, so using x, y and z as the 3, we get

$$\frac{x + y + z}{3} = 7,500 \qquad \boxed{3}$$

Multiplying $\boxed{3}$ by 3, we get

$$x + y + z = 22,500 \qquad \boxed{4}$$

Substituting $\boxed{4}$ into $\boxed{2}$, we get

$$22,500 + w = 32,000$$
or $\qquad w = 9,500$

(Math Refresher #601 and #406)

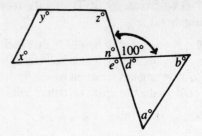

25. **280**

(Use Strategy 17: Use the given information effectively.)

From the diagram, $n = d$ (vertical angles) $\qquad \boxed{1}$
We know $x + y + z + n = 360$ $\qquad \boxed{2}$
Substituting $\boxed{1}$ into $\boxed{2}$, we get

$$x + y + z + d = 360 \qquad \boxed{3}$$

Subtracting d from $\boxed{3}$, we have

$$x + y + z = 360 - d \qquad \boxed{4}$$

We know that $100 + d = 180$ from the diagram

So, $d = 180 - 100 = 80$ $\qquad \boxed{5}$

Substituting $\boxed{5}$ into $\boxed{4}$, we get

$$x + y + z = 360 - 80$$
$$x + y + z = 280$$

(Math Refresher #521, #503, and #406)

SAT Practice Test 5

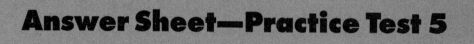

Answer Sheet—Practice Test 5

Make each mark a dark mark that completely fills the oval and is as dark as all your other marks. If you erase, do so completely. Incomplete erasures may be read as intended responses.

Use a No. 2 pencil only. Be sure each mark is dark and completely fills the intended oval. Completely erase any errors or stray marks.

Start with number 1 for each new section. If a section has fewer questions than answer spaces, leave the extra answer spaces blank.

SECTION 1

1 Ⓐ Ⓑ Ⓒ Ⓓ Ⓔ	11 Ⓐ Ⓑ Ⓒ Ⓓ Ⓔ	21 Ⓐ Ⓑ Ⓒ Ⓓ Ⓔ	31 Ⓐ Ⓑ Ⓒ Ⓓ Ⓔ
2 Ⓐ Ⓑ Ⓒ Ⓓ Ⓔ	12 Ⓐ Ⓑ Ⓒ Ⓓ Ⓔ	22 Ⓐ Ⓑ Ⓒ Ⓓ Ⓔ	32 Ⓐ Ⓑ Ⓒ Ⓓ Ⓔ
3 Ⓐ Ⓑ Ⓒ Ⓓ Ⓔ	13 Ⓐ Ⓑ Ⓒ Ⓓ Ⓔ	23 Ⓐ Ⓑ Ⓒ Ⓓ Ⓔ	33 Ⓐ Ⓑ Ⓒ Ⓓ Ⓔ
4 Ⓐ Ⓑ Ⓒ Ⓓ Ⓔ	14 Ⓐ Ⓑ Ⓒ Ⓓ Ⓔ	24 Ⓐ Ⓑ Ⓒ Ⓓ Ⓔ	34 Ⓐ Ⓑ Ⓒ Ⓓ Ⓔ
5 Ⓐ Ⓑ Ⓒ Ⓓ Ⓔ	15 Ⓐ Ⓑ Ⓒ Ⓓ Ⓔ	25 Ⓐ Ⓑ Ⓒ Ⓓ Ⓔ	35 Ⓐ Ⓑ Ⓒ Ⓓ Ⓔ
6 Ⓐ Ⓑ Ⓒ Ⓓ Ⓔ	16 Ⓐ Ⓑ Ⓒ Ⓓ Ⓔ	26 Ⓐ Ⓑ Ⓒ Ⓓ Ⓔ	36 Ⓐ Ⓑ Ⓒ Ⓓ Ⓔ
7 Ⓐ Ⓑ Ⓒ Ⓓ Ⓔ	17 Ⓐ Ⓑ Ⓒ Ⓓ Ⓔ	27 Ⓐ Ⓑ Ⓒ Ⓓ Ⓔ	37 Ⓐ Ⓑ Ⓒ Ⓓ Ⓔ
8 Ⓐ Ⓑ Ⓒ Ⓓ Ⓔ	18 Ⓐ Ⓑ Ⓒ Ⓓ Ⓔ	28 Ⓐ Ⓑ Ⓒ Ⓓ Ⓔ	38 Ⓐ Ⓑ Ⓒ Ⓓ Ⓔ
9 Ⓐ Ⓑ Ⓒ Ⓓ Ⓔ	19 Ⓐ Ⓑ Ⓒ Ⓓ Ⓔ	29 Ⓐ Ⓑ Ⓒ Ⓓ Ⓔ	39 Ⓐ Ⓑ Ⓒ Ⓓ Ⓔ
10 Ⓐ Ⓑ Ⓒ Ⓓ Ⓔ	20 Ⓐ Ⓑ Ⓒ Ⓓ Ⓔ	30 Ⓐ Ⓑ Ⓒ Ⓓ Ⓔ	40 Ⓐ Ⓑ Ⓒ Ⓓ Ⓔ

SECTION 2

1 Ⓐ Ⓑ Ⓒ Ⓓ Ⓔ	11 Ⓐ Ⓑ Ⓒ Ⓓ Ⓔ	21 Ⓐ Ⓑ Ⓒ Ⓓ Ⓔ	31 Ⓐ Ⓑ Ⓒ Ⓓ Ⓔ
2 Ⓐ Ⓑ Ⓒ Ⓓ Ⓔ	12 Ⓐ Ⓑ Ⓒ Ⓓ Ⓔ	22 Ⓐ Ⓑ Ⓒ Ⓓ Ⓔ	32 Ⓐ Ⓑ Ⓒ Ⓓ Ⓔ
3 Ⓐ Ⓑ Ⓒ Ⓓ Ⓔ	13 Ⓐ Ⓑ Ⓒ Ⓓ Ⓔ	23 Ⓐ Ⓑ Ⓒ Ⓓ Ⓔ	33 Ⓐ Ⓑ Ⓒ Ⓓ Ⓔ
4 Ⓐ Ⓑ Ⓒ Ⓓ Ⓔ	14 Ⓐ Ⓑ Ⓒ Ⓓ Ⓔ	24 Ⓐ Ⓑ Ⓒ Ⓓ Ⓔ	34 Ⓐ Ⓑ Ⓒ Ⓓ Ⓔ
5 Ⓐ Ⓑ Ⓒ Ⓓ Ⓔ	15 Ⓐ Ⓑ Ⓒ Ⓓ Ⓔ	25 Ⓐ Ⓑ Ⓒ Ⓓ Ⓔ	35 Ⓐ Ⓑ Ⓒ Ⓓ Ⓔ
6 Ⓐ Ⓑ Ⓒ Ⓓ Ⓔ	16 Ⓐ Ⓑ Ⓒ Ⓓ Ⓔ	26 Ⓐ Ⓑ Ⓒ Ⓓ Ⓔ	36 Ⓐ Ⓑ Ⓒ Ⓓ Ⓔ
7 Ⓐ Ⓑ Ⓒ Ⓓ Ⓔ	17 Ⓐ Ⓑ Ⓒ Ⓓ Ⓔ	27 Ⓐ Ⓑ Ⓒ Ⓓ Ⓔ	37 Ⓐ Ⓑ Ⓒ Ⓓ Ⓔ
8 Ⓐ Ⓑ Ⓒ Ⓓ Ⓔ	18 Ⓐ Ⓑ Ⓒ Ⓓ Ⓔ	28 Ⓐ Ⓑ Ⓒ Ⓓ Ⓔ	38 Ⓐ Ⓑ Ⓒ Ⓓ Ⓔ
9 Ⓐ Ⓑ Ⓒ Ⓓ Ⓔ	19 Ⓐ Ⓑ Ⓒ Ⓓ Ⓔ	29 Ⓐ Ⓑ Ⓒ Ⓓ Ⓔ	39 Ⓐ Ⓑ Ⓒ Ⓓ Ⓔ
10 Ⓐ Ⓑ Ⓒ Ⓓ Ⓔ	20 Ⓐ Ⓑ Ⓒ Ⓓ Ⓔ	30 Ⓐ Ⓑ Ⓒ Ⓓ Ⓔ	40 Ⓐ Ⓑ Ⓒ Ⓓ Ⓔ

Use a No. 2 pencil only. Be sure each mark is dark and completely fills the intended oval. Completely erase any errors or stray marks.

Start with number 1 for each new section. If a section has fewer questions than answer spaces, leave the extra answer spaces blank.

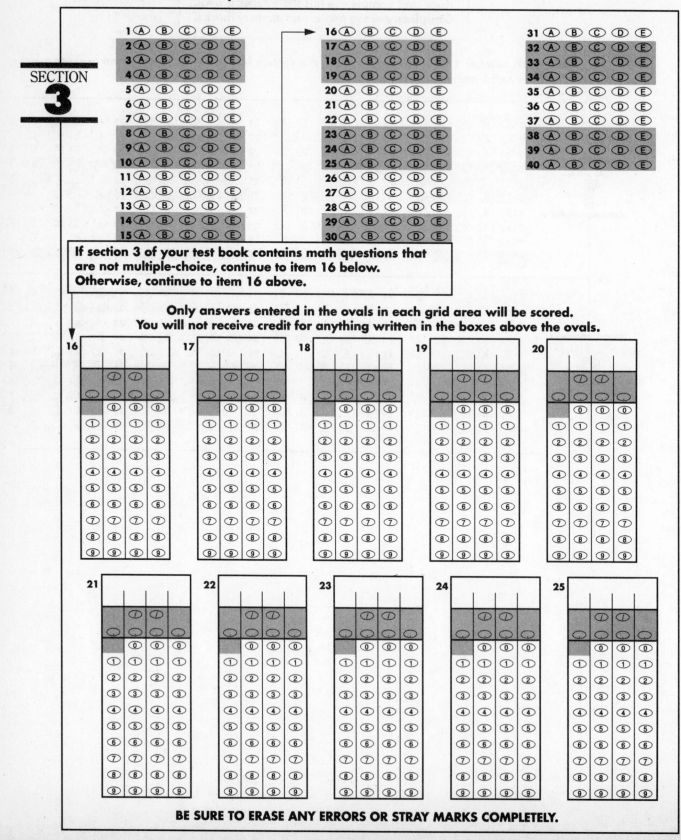

If section 3 of your test book contains math questions that are not multiple-choice, continue to item 16 below. Otherwise, continue to item 16 above.

Only answers entered in the ovals in each grid area will be scored. You will not receive credit for anything written in the boxes above the ovals.

BE SURE TO ERASE ANY ERRORS OR STRAY MARKS COMPLETELY.

Use a No. 2 pencil only. Be sure each mark is dark and completely fills the intended oval. Completely erase any errors or stray marks.

Start with number 1 for each new section. If a section has fewer questions than answer spaces, leave the extra answer spaces blank.

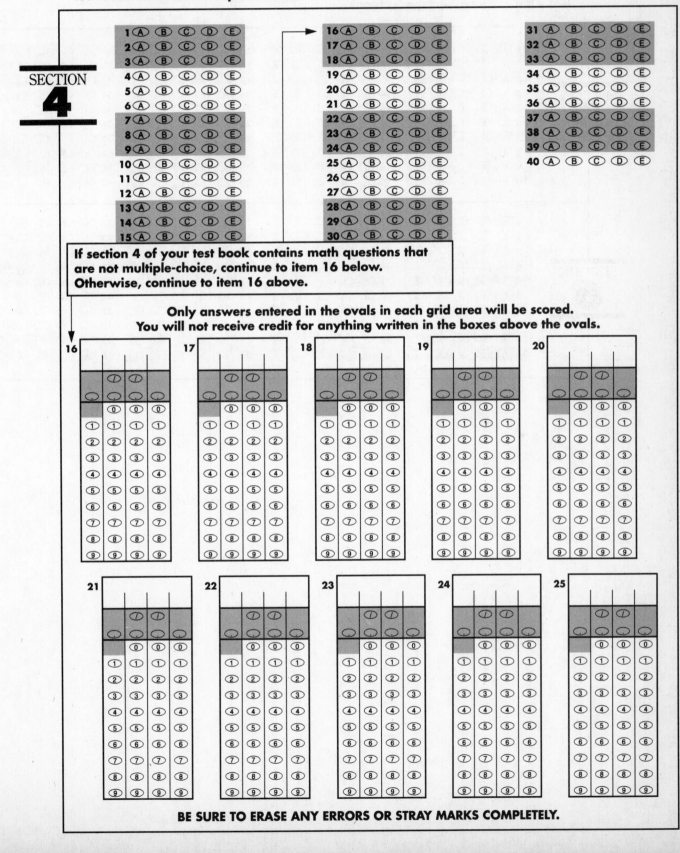

If section 4 of your test book contains math questions that are not multiple-choice, continue to item 16 below. Otherwise, continue to item 16 above.

Only answers entered in the ovals in each grid area will be scored. You will not receive credit for anything written in the boxes above the ovals.

BE SURE TO ERASE ANY ERRORS OR STRAY MARKS COMPLETELY.

Use a No. 2 pencil only. Be sure each mark is dark and completely fills the intended oval. Completely erase any errors or stray marks.

Start with number 1 for each new section. If a section has fewer questions than answer spaces, leave the extra answer spaces blank.

SECTION 5

1 Ⓐ Ⓑ Ⓒ Ⓓ Ⓔ	11 Ⓐ Ⓑ Ⓒ Ⓓ Ⓔ	21 Ⓐ Ⓑ Ⓒ Ⓓ Ⓔ	31 Ⓐ Ⓑ Ⓒ Ⓓ Ⓔ
2 Ⓐ Ⓑ Ⓒ Ⓓ Ⓔ	12 Ⓐ Ⓑ Ⓒ Ⓓ Ⓔ	22 Ⓐ Ⓑ Ⓒ Ⓓ Ⓔ	32 Ⓐ Ⓑ Ⓒ Ⓓ Ⓔ
3 Ⓐ Ⓑ Ⓒ Ⓓ Ⓔ	13 Ⓐ Ⓑ Ⓒ Ⓓ Ⓔ	23 Ⓐ Ⓑ Ⓒ Ⓓ Ⓔ	33 Ⓐ Ⓑ Ⓒ Ⓓ Ⓔ
4 Ⓐ Ⓑ Ⓒ Ⓓ Ⓔ	14 Ⓐ Ⓑ Ⓒ Ⓓ Ⓔ	24 Ⓐ Ⓑ Ⓒ Ⓓ Ⓔ	34 Ⓐ Ⓑ Ⓒ Ⓓ Ⓔ
5 Ⓐ Ⓑ Ⓒ Ⓓ Ⓔ	15 Ⓐ Ⓑ Ⓒ Ⓓ Ⓔ	25 Ⓐ Ⓑ Ⓒ Ⓓ Ⓔ	35 Ⓐ Ⓑ Ⓒ Ⓓ Ⓔ
6 Ⓐ Ⓑ Ⓒ Ⓓ Ⓔ	16 Ⓐ Ⓑ Ⓒ Ⓓ Ⓔ	26 Ⓐ Ⓑ Ⓒ Ⓓ Ⓔ	36 Ⓐ Ⓑ Ⓒ Ⓓ Ⓔ
7 Ⓐ Ⓑ Ⓒ Ⓓ Ⓔ	17 Ⓐ Ⓑ Ⓒ Ⓓ Ⓔ	27 Ⓐ Ⓑ Ⓒ Ⓓ Ⓔ	37 Ⓐ Ⓑ Ⓒ Ⓓ Ⓔ
8 Ⓐ Ⓑ Ⓒ Ⓓ Ⓔ	18 Ⓐ Ⓑ Ⓒ Ⓓ Ⓔ	28 Ⓐ Ⓑ Ⓒ Ⓓ Ⓔ	38 Ⓐ Ⓑ Ⓒ Ⓓ Ⓔ
9 Ⓐ Ⓑ Ⓒ Ⓓ Ⓔ	19 Ⓐ Ⓑ Ⓒ Ⓓ Ⓔ	29 Ⓐ Ⓑ Ⓒ Ⓓ Ⓔ	39 Ⓐ Ⓑ Ⓒ Ⓓ Ⓔ
10 Ⓐ Ⓑ Ⓒ Ⓓ Ⓔ	20 Ⓐ Ⓑ Ⓒ Ⓓ Ⓔ	30 Ⓐ Ⓑ Ⓒ Ⓓ Ⓔ	40 Ⓐ Ⓑ Ⓒ Ⓓ Ⓔ

SECTION 6

1 Ⓐ Ⓑ Ⓒ Ⓓ Ⓔ	11 Ⓐ Ⓑ Ⓒ Ⓓ Ⓔ	21 Ⓐ Ⓑ Ⓒ Ⓓ Ⓔ	31 Ⓐ Ⓑ Ⓒ Ⓓ Ⓔ
2 Ⓐ Ⓑ Ⓒ Ⓓ Ⓔ	12 Ⓐ Ⓑ Ⓒ Ⓓ Ⓔ	22 Ⓐ Ⓑ Ⓒ Ⓓ Ⓔ	32 Ⓐ Ⓑ Ⓒ Ⓓ Ⓔ
3 Ⓐ Ⓑ Ⓒ Ⓓ Ⓔ	13 Ⓐ Ⓑ Ⓒ Ⓓ Ⓔ	23 Ⓐ Ⓑ Ⓒ Ⓓ Ⓔ	33 Ⓐ Ⓑ Ⓒ Ⓓ Ⓔ
4 Ⓐ Ⓑ Ⓒ Ⓓ Ⓔ	14 Ⓐ Ⓑ Ⓒ Ⓓ Ⓔ	24 Ⓐ Ⓑ Ⓒ Ⓓ Ⓔ	34 Ⓐ Ⓑ Ⓒ Ⓓ Ⓔ
5 Ⓐ Ⓑ Ⓒ Ⓓ Ⓔ	15 Ⓐ Ⓑ Ⓒ Ⓓ Ⓔ	25 Ⓐ Ⓑ Ⓒ Ⓓ Ⓔ	35 Ⓐ Ⓑ Ⓒ Ⓓ Ⓔ
6 Ⓐ Ⓑ Ⓒ Ⓓ Ⓔ	16 Ⓐ Ⓑ Ⓒ Ⓓ Ⓔ	26 Ⓐ Ⓑ Ⓒ Ⓓ Ⓔ	36 Ⓐ Ⓑ Ⓒ Ⓓ Ⓔ
7 Ⓐ Ⓑ Ⓒ Ⓓ Ⓔ	17 Ⓐ Ⓑ Ⓒ Ⓓ Ⓔ	27 Ⓐ Ⓑ Ⓒ Ⓓ Ⓔ	37 Ⓐ Ⓑ Ⓒ Ⓓ Ⓔ
8 Ⓐ Ⓑ Ⓒ Ⓓ Ⓔ	18 Ⓐ Ⓑ Ⓒ Ⓓ Ⓔ	28 Ⓐ Ⓑ Ⓒ Ⓓ Ⓔ	38 Ⓐ Ⓑ Ⓒ Ⓓ Ⓔ
9 Ⓐ Ⓑ Ⓒ Ⓓ Ⓔ	19 Ⓐ Ⓑ Ⓒ Ⓓ Ⓔ	29 Ⓐ Ⓑ Ⓒ Ⓓ Ⓔ	39 Ⓐ Ⓑ Ⓒ Ⓓ Ⓔ
10 Ⓐ Ⓑ Ⓒ Ⓓ Ⓔ	20 Ⓐ Ⓑ Ⓒ Ⓓ Ⓔ	30 Ⓐ Ⓑ Ⓒ Ⓓ Ⓔ	40 Ⓐ Ⓑ Ⓒ Ⓓ Ⓔ

Use a No. 2 pencil only. Be sure each mark is dark and completely fills the intended oval. Completely erase any errors or stray marks.

Start with number 1 for each new section. If a section has fewer questions than answer spaces, leave the extra answer spaces blank.

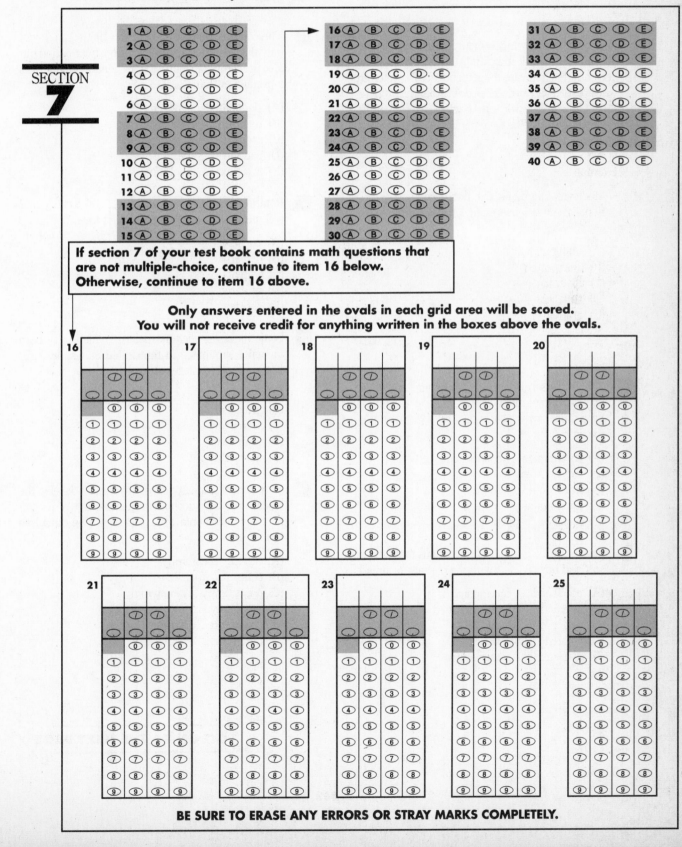

SECTION
7

If section 7 of your test book contains math questions that are not multiple-choice, continue to item 16 below.
Otherwise, continue to item 16 above.

Only answers entered in the ovals in each grid area will be scored.
You will not receive credit for anything written in the boxes above the ovals.

BE SURE TO ERASE ANY ERRORS OR STRAY MARKS COMPLETELY.

Time: 30 Minutes
30 Questions

For each question in this section, choose the best answer from among the choices given and fill in the corresponding oval on the answer sheet.

Each of the following sentences has one or two blanks, each blank indicating that something has been omitted. Beneath the sentence are five lettered words or sets of words labeled A through E. Choose the word or set of words that, when inserted in the sentence, *best* fits the meaning of the sentence as a whole.

Example:

Medieval kingdoms did not become constitutional republics overnight; on the contrary, the change was---.

(A) unpopular
(B) unexpected
(C) advantageous
(D) sufficient
(E) gradual

Ⓐ Ⓑ Ⓒ Ⓓ ●

1 Athens was ruled not by kings and emperors as was common among other _____ at the time, but by a citizenry, which _____ fully in the affairs of the city.

(A) committees . . . cooperated
(B) tribes . . . engaged
(C) cities . . . revolutionized
(D) populations . . . applied
(E) societies . . . participated

2 Fossils are _____ in rock formations that were once soft and have _____ with the passage of time.

(A) abolished . . . corresponded
(B) interactive . . . communicated
(C) preserved . . . hardened
(D) created . . . revived
(E) discounted . . . deteriorated

3 The social-cultural trends of the 1960s _____ not only the relative affluence of the postwar period but also the coming to maturity of a generation that was a product of that _____ .

(A) dominated . . . movement
(B) reflected . . . prosperity
(C) accentuated . . . depression
(D) cautioned . . . decade
(E) accepted . . . revolution

4 Rotation of crops helps to _____ soil fertility and soil usefulness for a long period of time.

(A) conserve
(B) disperse
(C) employ
(D) research
(E) shorten

5 Some illnesses, such as malaria, which have been virtually eliminated in the United States, are still _____ in many places abroad.

(A) discussed
(B) prevalent
(C) scarce
(D) unknown
(E) hospitalized

6 With lack of _____ , almost anyone can develop the disease we call alcoholism, just as any of us can contract pneumonia by _____ exposing ourselves to its causes.

(A) advice . . . carefully
(B) control . . . foolishly
(C) opportunity . . . knowingly
(D) sympathy . . . fortunately
(E) conscience . . . happily

GO ON TO THE NEXT PAGE

7 Use of air conditioners and other electrical apparatus had to be _____ that summer because of the _____ of the generating system.

(A) postulated . . . reaction
(B) curtailed . . . inefficiency
(C) implemented . . . residuals
(D) augmented . . . responsiveness
(E) manipulated . . . intensity

8 The Bavarians consider beer their national beverage, yet at the same time they do not view it as a drink but rather as _____ bread—a staple food.

(A) fresh
(B) liquid
(C) stale
(D) bitter
(E) costly

9 The Forest Service warned that the spring forest fire season was in full swing and urged that _____ caution be exercised in wooded areas.

(A) moderate
(B) scant
(C) customary
(D) extreme
(E) reasonable

Each of the following questions consists of a related pair of words or phrases, followed by five pairs of words or phrases labeled A through E. Select the pair that *best* expresses a relationship similar to that expressed in the original pair.

Example:

CRUMB : BREAD : :

(A) ounce : unit
(B) splinter : wood
(C) water : bucket
(D) twine : rope
(E) cream : butter

(A) ● (C) (D) (E)

10 APIARY : BEE : :

(A) mountain : skier
(B) airport : flight
(C) schedule : event
(D) theater : ticket
(E) stable : horse

11 FOREMAN : JURY :

(A) doctor : nurse
(B) fish : school
(C) policemen : law
(D) captain : team
(E) dancer : chorus

12 ADDENDUM : BOOK : :

(A) finale : music
(B) letter : envelope
(C) epilogue : play
(D) telegram : communication
(E) salad : appetizer

13 CATCHER : MASK : :

(A) artist : palette
(B) owner : insurance
(C) butcher : apron
(D) prisoner : sentence
(E) driver : visor

14 CONTRITE : CAREFREE : :

(A) commonplace : obvious
(B) accidental : injurious
(C) descriptive : informational
(D) contrary : doubtful
(E) dignified : informal

15 TAUNT : VILIFY : :

(A) favor : assist
(B) promote : discourage
(C) chuckle : guffaw
(D) remark : imply
(E) flaunt : display

Each of the following passages below is followed by questions based on its content. Answer the questions following each passage on the basis of what is *stated* or *implied* in that passage and in any introductory material that may be provided.

Questions 16–21 are based on the following passage.

The following passage is excerpted from the Brahmin's life, Siddhartha.

Siddhartha was now pleased with himself. He could have dwelt for a long time yet in that soft, well-upholstered hell, if this had not happened, this moment of complete hopelessness and despair and the tense moment when he
5 was ready to commit suicide. Was it not his Self, his small, fearful and proud Self, with which he had wrestled for many years, which had always conquered him again and again, which robbed him of happiness and filled him with fear?

Siddhartha now realized why he had struggled in vain
10 with this Self when he was a Brahmin and an ascetic. Too much knowledge had hindered him; too many holy verses, too many sacrificial rites, too much mortification of the flesh, too much doing and striving. He had been full of arrogance; he had always been the cleverest, the most eager—always a
15 step ahead of the others, always the learned and intellectual one, always the priest or the sage. His Self had crawled into his priesthood, into this arrogance, into this intellectuality. It sat there tightly and grew, while he thought he was destroying it by fasting and penitence. Now he understood it and
20 realized that the inward voice had been right, that no teacher could have brought him salvation. That was why he had to go into the world, to lose himself in power, women and money; that was why he had to be a merchant, a dice player, a drinker and a man of property, until the priest and Samana
25 in him were dead. That was why he had to undergo those horrible years, suffer nausea, learn the lesson of the madness of an empty, futile life till the end, till he reached bitter despair, so that Siddhartha the pleasure-monger and Siddhartha the man of property could die. He had died and a
30 new Siddhartha had awakened from his sleep. He also would grow old and die. Siddhartha was transitory, all forms were transitory, but today he was young, he was a child—the new Siddhartha—and he was very happy.

These thoughts passed through his mind. Smiling, he
35 listened thankfully to a humming bee. Happily he looked into the flowing river. Never had a river attracted him as much as this one. Never had he found the voice and appearance of flowing water so beautiful. It seemed to him as if the river had something special to tell him, something which he
40 did not know, something which still awaited him. The new Siddhartha felt a deep love for this flowing water and decided that he would not leave it again so quickly.

16 The "soft, well-upholstered hell" (lines 2–3) is a reference by the speaker to

(A) an attractive yet uncomfortable dwelling where he resided

(B) his lifestyle, which made him an unhappy person

(C) a place to which he went when he wished to be completely by himself

(D) his abode in a previous life not referred to in the passage

(E) a figment of his imagination that used to haunt him

17 Which of the following best describes the relation between the second and third paragraphs?

(A) Paragraph 3 shows how much happier one can be by living alone than in living with others, as brought out in paragraph 2.

(B) Paragraph 3 discusses the advantages of a simple life as opposed to the more complicated lifestyle discussed in paragraph 2.

(C) Paragraph 3 contrasts the life of a person without wealth and a formal religion with a person who has wealth and a formal religion, as in paragraph 2.

(D) Paragraph 3 demonstrates the happiness that can come as a result of giving up the power and the worldly pleasures referred to in paragraph 2.

(E) Paragraph 3 generalizes about the specific points made in paragraph 2.

18 Which of the following questions does the passage answer?

(A) What is the meaning of a Brahmin?

(B) Why did Siddhartha decide to commit suicide?

(C) Where did Siddhartha own property?

(D) For how many years was Siddhartha a member of the priesthood?

(E) Where did Siddhartha go to school?

GO ON TO THE NEXT PAGE

19 The word "transitory" in line 31 most likely means

(A) quick on one's feet
(B) invisible
(C) short-lived
(D) going from one place to another
(E) frozen

20 Which statement best expresses the main idea of this passage?

(A) Arrogance constitutes a great hindrance for one who seeks to lead a peaceful life.
(B) One has to discipline himself so that he will refrain from seeking pleasures that will prove harmful later.
(C) The quest for knowledge is commendable provided that search has its limitations.
(D) There is a voice within a person that can advise him how to attain contentment.
(E) Peace and quiet are more important than wealth and power in bringing happiness.

21 What is the meaning of "Self" as it is referred to in the passage?

(A) one's love of nature
(B) one's own lifestyle
(C) one's inner voice
(D) one's remembrances
(E) one's own interests

Questions 22–30 are based on the following passage.

The following passage explores how brilliant people think, how they may come up with their theories, and what motivates their thinking and creativity.

The discoveries made by scientific geniuses, from Archimedes through Einstein, have repeatedly revolutionized both our world and the way we see it. Yet no one really knows how the mind of a genius works. Most people think
5 that a very high IQ sets the great scientist apart. They assume that flashes of profound insight like Einstein's are the product of mental processes, so arcane, that they must be inaccessible to more ordinary minds.

But a growing number of researchers in psychology,
10 psychiatry, and the history of science are investigating the way geniuses think. The researchers are beginning to give us tantalizing glimpses of the mental universe that can produce the discoveries of an Einstein, an Edison, a DaVinci—or any Nobel prizewinner.
15 Surprisingly, most researchers agree that the important variable in genius is not the IQ but creativity. Testers start with 135 as the beginning of the "genius" category, but the researchers seem to feel that, while an IQ above a certain point—about 120—is very helpful for a scientist, having
20 an IQ that goes much higher is not crucial for producing a work of genius. All human beings has at least four types of intelligence. The great scientist possesses the ability to move back and forth among them—the logical-mathematical, the spatial which includes visual perception,
25 the linguistic, and the bodily-kinesthetic.

Some corroboration of these categories comes from the reports of scientists who describe thought processes centered around images, sensations, or words. Einstein reported a special "feeling at the tips of the fingers" that told him
30 which path to take through a problem. The idea for a self-starting electric motor came to Nikola Tesla one evening as he was reciting a poem by Goethe and watching a sunset. Suddenly he imagined a magnetic field rapidly rotating inside a circle of electro-magnets.
35 Some IQ tests predict fairly accurately how well a person will do in school and how quickly he or she will master knowledge, but genius involves more than knowledge. The genius has the capacity to leap significantly beyond his present knowledge and produces something new.
40 To do this, he sees the relationship between facts or pieces of information in a new or unusual way.

The scientist solves a problem by shifting from one intelligence to another, although the logical-mathematical intelligence is dominant. Creative individuals seem to be
45 marked by a special fluidity of mind. They may be able to think of a problem verbally, logically, and also spatially.

Paradoxically, fluid thinking may be connected to another generally agreed upon trait of the scientific genius—persistence, or unusually strong motivation to work on a
50 problem. Persistence kept Einstein looking for the solution to the question of the relationship between the law of gravity and his special theory of relativity. Yet surely creative fluidity enabled him to come up with a whole new field that included both special relativity and gravitation.
55 Many scientists have the ability to stick with a problem even when they appear not to be working on it. Werner Heisenberg discovered quantum mechanics one night during a vacation he had taken to recuperate from the mental jumble he had fallen into trying to solve the atomic-spectra
60 problem.

22 Which statement is true, according to the passage?

(A) The law of gravity followed the publication of Einstein's theory of relativity.
(B) Nikola Tesla learned about magnets from his research of the works of Goethe.
(C) Archimedes and Einstein lived in the same century.
(D) Most scientists have IQ scores above 120.
(E) We ought to refer to intelligences rather than to intelligence.

23 The author believes that, among the four intelligences he cites, the most important one is

(A) spatial
(B) bodily-kinesthetic
(C) linguistic
(D) logical-mathematical
(E) not singled out

24 The author focuses on the circumstances surrounding the work of great scientists in order to show that

(A) scientific geniuses are usually eccentric in their behavior
(B) the various types of intelligence have come into play during their work
(C) scientists often give the impression that they are relaxing when they are really working on a problem
(D) scientists must be happy to do their best work
(E) great scientific discoveries are almost always accidental

847

25 The passage can best be described as

(A) a comparison of how the average individual and the great scientist think

(B) an account of the unexpected things that led to great discoveries by scientists

(C) an explanation of the way scientific geniuses really think

(D) a criticism of intelligence tests as they are given today

(E) a lesson clarifying scientific concepts such as quantum mechanics and relativity

26 The paragraph suggest that a college football star who is majoring in literature is quite likely to have which intelligences to a high degree?

    I. logical-mathematical
    II. spatial
    III. linguistic
    IV. bodily-kinesthetic

(A) I only

(B) II only

(C) III only

(D) I, II, and III only

(E) II, III, and IV only

27 Which statement would the author most likely *not* agree with?

(A) Most people believe that IQ is what makes the brilliant scientist.

(B) Some scientists may come up with a solution to a problem when they are working on something else.

(C) Creativity is much more important than basic intelligence in scientific discovery.

(D) Scientists and artists may think alike in their creative mode.

(E) Scientists usually get the answer to a problem fairly quickly, and if they get stuck they usually go on to another problem.

28 "Fluidity" as described in line 52 can best be defined as

(A) persistence when faced with a problem

(B) having a flighty attitude in dealing with scientific problems

(C) being able to move from one scientific area to another

(D) having an open mind in dealing with scientific phenomena

(E) being able to generate enormous excitement in the scientist's work

29 The word "paradoxically" in line 47 means

(A) ironically

(B) seemingly contradictory

(C) in a manner of speaking

(D) experimentally

(E) conditionally

30 The author's attitude toward scientists in this passage can be seen as one of

(A) objective intrigue

(B) grudging admiration

(C) subtle jealousy

(D) growing impatience

(E) boundless enthusiasm

IF YOU FINISH BEFORE TIME IS CALLED, YOU MAY CHECK YOUR WORK ON THIS SECTION ONLY. DO NOT TURN TO ANY OTHER SECTION IN THE TEST.

STOP

Time: 30 Minutes
25 Questions

In this section solve each problem, using any available space on the page for scratch-work. Then decide which is the best of the choices given and fill in the corresponding oval on the answer sheet.

Notes:

1. The use of a calculator is permitted. All numbers are real numbers.

2. Figures that accompany problems in this test are intended to provide information useful in solving the problems. They are drawn as accurately as possible EXCEPT when it is stated in a specific problem that the figure is not drawn to scale. All figures lie in a plane unless otherwise indicated.

Reference Information

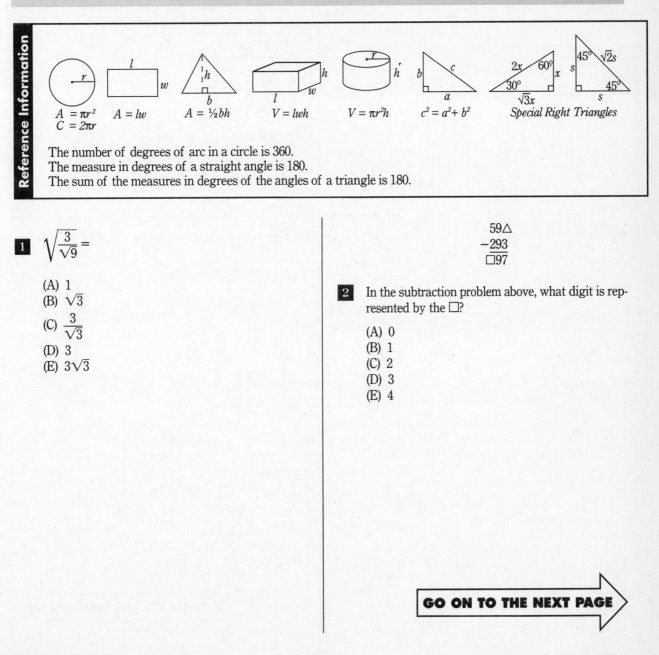

$A = \pi r^2$ $A = lw$ $A = \frac{1}{2}bh$ $V = lwh$ $V = \pi r^2 h$ $c^2 = a^2 + b^2$ *Special Right Triangles*
$C = 2\pi r$

The number of degrees of arc in a circle is 360.
The measure in degrees of a straight angle is 180.
The sum of the measures in degrees of the angles of a triangle is 180.

1 $\sqrt{\dfrac{3}{\sqrt{9}}} =$

(A) 1
(B) $\sqrt{3}$
(C) $\dfrac{3}{\sqrt{3}}$
(D) 3
(E) $3\sqrt{3}$

$$59\triangle$$
$$-293$$
$$\overline{\square 97}$$

2 In the subtraction problem above, what digit is represented by the $\square$?

(A) 0
(B) 1
(C) 2
(D) 3
(E) 4

GO ON TO THE NEXT PAGE

3 How many integers are between, but not including 1 and 1,000?

(A) 990
(B) 998
(C) 999
(D) 1,000
(E) 1,001

Number of pounds of force	Height object is raised
3	6 feet
6	12 feet
9	18 feet

5 In a certain pulley system, the height an object is raised is equal to a constant c times the number of pounds of force exerted. The table above shows some pounds of force and the corresponding height raised. If a particular object is raised 15 feet, how many pounds of force were exerted?

(A) $3\frac{3}{4}$
(B) 7
(C) $7\frac{1}{2}$
(D) 8
(E) 11

4 If $\dfrac{a - b}{b} = \dfrac{1}{2}$, find $\dfrac{a}{b}$.

(A) $\dfrac{9}{2}$
(B) $\dfrac{7}{2}$
(C) $\dfrac{5}{2}$
(D) $\dfrac{1}{2}$
(E) $\dfrac{3}{2}$

6 If $a = 1$, $b = -2$ and $c = -2$, find the value of

$$\dfrac{b^2 c}{(a - c)^2}$$

(A) $-\dfrac{8}{9}$
(B) $-\dfrac{2}{3}$
(C) $\dfrac{8}{9}$
(D) 8
(E) 9

GO ON TO THE NEXT PAGE

7 If $\frac{y}{3}$, $\frac{y}{4}$ and $\frac{y}{7}$ represent integers, then y could be

(A) 42
(B) 56
(C) 70
(D) 84
(E) 126

9 If $y = 28j$, where j is any integer, then $\frac{y}{2}$ will always be

(A) even
(B) odd
(C) positive
(D) negative
(E) less than $\frac{y}{3}$

P

$\uparrow\uparrow\uparrow\uparrow\uparrow\uparrow\uparrow\uparrow\uparrow\uparrow\uparrow\uparrow$

8 The above line is marked with 12 points. The distance between any 2 adjacent point is 3 units. Find the total number of points that are more than 19 units away from point P.

(A) 2
(B) 3
(C) 4
(D) 5
(E) 6

10 Given $(a + 2, a - 2) = [a]$ for all integers a, $(6, 2) =$

(A) [3]
(B) [4]
(C) [5]
(D) [6]
(E) [8]

GO ON TO THE NEXT PAGE

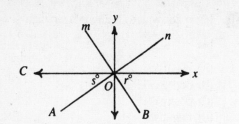

Note: Figure is not drawn to scale.

11 If $m \perp n$ in the figure above and COx is a straight line, find the value of $r + s$.

(A) 180
(B) 135
(C) 110
(D) 90
(E) The answer cannot be determined from the information given.

13 One out of 4 students at Ridge High School studies German. If there are 2,800 students at the school, how many students do *not* study German?

(A) 2,500
(B) 2,100
(C) 1,800
(D) 1,000
(E) 700

12 Points A and B have coordinates as shown in the figure above. Find the combined area of the two shaded rectangles.

(A) 20
(B) 26
(C) 32
(D) 35
(E) 87

14 The cost of a drive-in movie is $\$y$ per vehicle. A group of friends in a van shared the admission cost by paying \$0.40 each. If 6 more friends had gone along, everyone would have paid only \$0.25 each. What is the value of $\$y$?

(A) \$4
(B) \$6
(C) \$8
(D) \$10
(E) \$12

GO ON TO THE NEXT PAGE

15 8(679) + 679 =

(A) 5(679) + 3(679)
(B) 6(679) + 2(679)
(C) 5(679) + 6(679)
(D) 7(679) + 4(679)
(E) 6(679) + 3(679)

17 A certain store is selling an $80 radio for $64. If a different radio had a list price of $200 and was discounted at $1\frac{1}{2}$ times the percent discount on the $80 model, what would its selling price be?

(A) $90
(B) $105
(C) $120
(D) $140
(E) $160

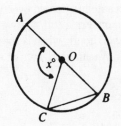

16 If AB is a diameter of circle O in the figure above, and CB = OB, then $\frac{x}{6}$ =

(A) 60
(B) 30
(C) 20
(D) 10
(E) 5

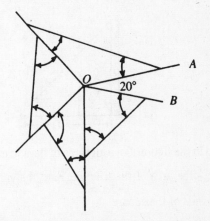

18 If ∠AOB = 20° in the figure above and O is a common vertex of the four triangles, find the sum of the measures of the marked angles in the triangles.

(A) 380
(B) 560
(C) 740
(D) 760
(E) 920

GO ON TO THE NEXT PAGE

19 If $3a + 4b = 4a - 4b = 21$, find the value of a.

(A) 3
(B) 6
(C) 21
(D) 42
(E) The answer cannot be determined from the information given.

21 A certain printer can print at the rate of 80 characters per second, and there is an average (arithmetic mean) of 2,400 characters per page. If the printer continued to print at this rate, how many *minutes* would it take to print an *M*-page report?

(A) $\dfrac{M}{30}$

(B) $\dfrac{M}{60}$

(C) $\dfrac{M}{2}$

(D) $\dfrac{2}{M}$

(E) $\dfrac{60}{M}$

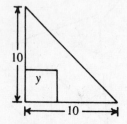

20 In the figure above, the area of the square is equal to $\dfrac{1}{5}$ the area of the triangle. Find the value of y, the side of the square.

(A) 2
(B) 4
(C) 5
(D) $2\sqrt{5}$
(E) $\sqrt{10}$

22 A certain satellite passed over Washington, D.C., at midnight on Friday. If the satellite completes an orbit every 5 hours, when is the next day that it will pass over Washington, D.C., at midnight?

(A) Monday
(B) Wednesday
(C) Friday
(D) Saturday
(E) Sunday

GO ON TO THE NEXT PAGE

23 The price of a car is reduced by 30 percent. The resulting price is reduced 40 percent. The two reductions are equal to one reduction of

(A) 28%
(B) 42%
(C) 50%
(D) 58%
(E) 70%

25 In the figure above, the circle is inscribed in the equilateral triangle. If the diameter of the circle is 2, what is the sum of the shaded area?

(A) $3\sqrt{3} - \pi$

(B) $3\sqrt{3} - 4\pi$

(C) $3\sqrt{3} - \dfrac{3\pi}{2}$

(D) $6\sqrt{3} - \dfrac{3\pi}{2}$

(E) $108 - \pi$

24 Find the difference between $\dfrac{2}{3}$ and the repeating decimal 0.393939 . . .

(A) $\dfrac{2}{11}$

(B) $\dfrac{3}{11}$

(C) $\dfrac{5}{9}$

(D) $\dfrac{7}{9}$

(E) $\dfrac{12}{13}$

IF YOU FINISH BEFORE TIME IS CALLED, YOU MAY CHECK YOUR WORK ON THIS SECTION ONLY. DO NOT TURN TO ANY OTHER SECTION IN THE TEST.

Time: 30 Minutes   For each question in this section, choose the best answer from among the choices given and
35 Questions   fill in the corresponding oval on the answer sheet.

Each of the following sentences has one or two blanks, each blank indicating that something has been omitted. Beneath the sentence are five words or sets of words labeled A through E. Choose the word or set of words that, when inserted in the sentence, *best* fits the meaning of the sentence as a whole.

Example:

Medieval kingdoms did not become constitutional republics overnight; on the contrary, the change was---.

(A) unpopular
(B) unexpected
(C) advantageous
(D) sufficient
(E) gradual

(A) (B) (C) (D) ●

1 The Classical age of Greek art ended with the defeat of Athens by Sparta; the _____ effect of the long war was the weakening and _____ of the Greek spirit.

(A) cumulative . . . corrosion
(B) immediate . . . storing
(C) imagined . . . cooperation
(D) delayed . . . rebuilding
(E) intuitive . . . cancelation

2 Mary, bored by even the briefest periods of idleness, was _____ switching from one activity to another.

(A) hesitantly
(B) lazily
(C) slowly
(D) surprisingly
(E) continually

3 The bee _____ the nectar from the different flowers and then _____ the liquid into honey.

(A) consumes . . . conforms
(B) observes . . . pours
(C) rejects . . . solidifies
(D) crushes . . . injects
(E) extracts . . . converts

4 Joining _____ momentum for reform in intercollegiate sports, university presidents have called for swift steps to correct imbalances between classwork and _____ .

(A) a maximum . . . studies
(B) a rational . . . awards
(C) an increasing . . . athletics
(D) an exceptional . . . professors
(E) a futile . . . contests

5 The plan turned out to be _____ because it would have required more financial backing than was available.

(A) intractable
(B) chaotic
(C) irreversible
(D) untenable
(E) superfluous

6 Thinking nothing can be done, many victims of arthritis ignore or delay _____ countermeasures, thus aggravating the problem.

(A) tardy
(B) injurious
(C) characteristic
(D) weird
(E) effective

GO ON TO THE NEXT PAGE

7 A strange and _____ fate seemed to keep him helpless and unhappy, despite occasional interludes of _____ .

(A) malevolent . . . conflict
(B) bizarre . . . disenchantment
(C) virulent . . . tension
(D) ineluctable . . . serenity
(E) intriguing . . . inactivity

8 Samuel Clemens chose the _____ Mark Twain as a result of his knowledge of riverboat piloting.

(A) protagonist
(B) pseudonym
(C) mountebank
(D) hallucination
(E) misanthrope

9 For years a vocalist of spirituals, Marian Anderson was finally recognized as _____ singer when the Metropolitan Opera House engaged her.

(A) a versatile
(B) an unusual
(C) an attractive
(D) a cooperative
(E) a mediocre

10 Leonardo da Vinci _____ the law of gravity two centuries before Newton and also made the first complete _____ charts of the human body.

(A) examined . . . colorful
(B) anticipated . . . anatomical
(C) avoided . . . meaningful
(D) realized . . . explanatory
(E) suspected . . . mural

GO ON TO THE NEXT PAGE

Each of the following examples consists of a related pair of words or phrases, followed by five pairs of words or phrases labeled A through E. Select the pair that *best* expresses a relationship similar to that expressed in the original pair.

Example:

CRUMB : BREAD : :

(A) ounce : unit
(B) splinter : wood
(C) water : bucket
(D) twine : rope
(E) cream : butter

Ⓐ ● Ⓒ Ⓓ Ⓔ

11 RUN : STOCKING : :

(A) pattern : flaw
(B) painting : image
(C) blemish : skin
(D) thread : fabric
(E) race : finish

12 PORTHOLE : SHIP : :

(A) stem : flower
(B) pupil : eye
(C) blister : skin
(D) score : music
(E) antenna : insect

13 PROCRASTINATOR : DELAY : :

(A) flatterer : undermine
(B) genius : creativity
(C) tyrant : influence
(D) general : salute
(E) historian : prediction

14 WATERTIGHT : MOISTURE : :

(A) hermetic : air
(B) claustrophobic : closeness
(C) combatant : strife
(D) somnolent : boredom
(E) ocean : shore

15 DRIZZLE : CLOUDBURST : :

(A) grass : dew
(B) wind : air
(C) shore : waves
(D) flurry : blizzard
(E) dune : sand

16 SEAMSTRESS : PATTERN : :

(A) teacher : classroom
(B) architect : blueprint
(C) army : maneuver
(D) novelist : typewriter
(E) cook : recipe

17 LOOT : BOOTY : :

(A) shout : attention
(B) travel : map
(C) rob : bank
(D) lace : shoe
(E) suckle : milk

18 PICK : BANJO : :

(A) string : violin
(B) compose : album
(C) strum : guitar
(D) pound : piano
(E) play : organ

GO ON TO THE NEXT PAGE

19 ARCHIPELAGO : ISLANDS : :

(A) universe : stars
(B) chorus : voices
(C) chaos : rules
(D) ocean : ships
(E) conspiracy : allies

20 NUGATORY : WORTH : :

(A) resonant : sound
(B) garbled : speech
(C) desultory : continuity
(D) circumspect : validity
(E) malleable : substance

21 ENERVATE : STRENGTH : :

(A) encourage : motivation
(B) conserve : excitement
(C) persecute : indulgence
(D) abase : destruction
(E) incarcerate : freedom

22 LICENTIOUS : MORALITY : :

(A) ludicrous : wittiness
(B) pugnacious : amiability
(C) stolid : ridicule
(D) nebulous : favoritism
(E) indelible : error

23 GLANCE : CURSORY : :

(A) scurry : relaxed
(B) delve : thorough
(C) insinuate : damaging
(D) mandate : conforming
(E) waive : restrictive

GO ON TO THE NEXT PAGE

The following passage is followed by questions based on its content. Answer the questions on the basis of what is *stated* or *implied* in that passage and in any introductory material that may be provided.

Questions 24–35 are based on the following passage.

The following passage deals with the importance of castles in medieval Europe and how they affected the society at that time.

Medieval Europe abounded in castles. Germany alone had ten thousand and more, most of them now vanished; all that a summer journey in the Rhineland and the south-west now can show are a handful of ruins and a few nineteenth
5 century restorations. Nevertheless, anyone journeying from Spain to the Dvina, from Calabria to Wales, will find castles rearing up again and again to dominate the open landscape. There they still stand, in desolate and uninhabited districts where the only visible forms of life are herdsmen and their
10 flocks, with hawks circling the battlements, far from the traffic and comfortably distant even from the nearest small town: these were the strongholds of the European aristocracy.

The weight of aristocratic dominance was felt in Eu-
15 rope until well after the French Revolution; political and social structure, the Church, the general tenor of thought and feeling were all influenced by it. Over the centuries, consciously or unconsciously, the other classes of this older European society—the clergy, the bourgeoisie and the
20 "common people"—adopted many of the outward characteristics of the aristocracy, who became their model, their standard, their ideal. Aristocratic values and ambitions were adopted alongside aristocratic manners and fashions of dress. Yet the aristocracy were the object of much conten-
25 tious criticism and complaint; from the thirteenth century onwards their military value and their political importance were both called in question. Nevertheless, their opponents continued to be their principal imitators. In the eleventh and twelfth centuries, the reforming Papacy and its clerical
30 supporters, although opposed to the excessively aristocratic control of the Church (as is shown by the Investiture Contest) nevertheless themselves first adopted and then strengthened the forms of this control. Noblemen who became bishops or who founded new Orders helped to im-
35 plant aristocratic principles and forms of government deep within the structure and spiritual life of the Church. Again, in the twelfth and thirteenth centuries the urban bourgeoisie, made prosperous and even rich by trade and industry, were rising to political power as the servants and legal
40 proteges of monarchy. These "patricians" were critical of the aristocracy and hostile towards it. Yet they also imitated the aristocracy, and tried to gain admittance to the closed circle and to achieve equality of status. Even the unarmed peasantry, who usually had to suffer more from

45 the unrelieved weight of aristocratic dominance, long remained tenaciously loyal to their lords, held to their allegiance by that combination of love and fear, *amor et timor*, which was so characteristic of the medieval relationship between lord and servant, between God and man.

50 The castles and strongholds of the aristocracy remind us of the reality of their power and superiority. Through the long warring centuries when men went defenceless and insecure, the "house," the lord's fortified dwelling, promised protection, security and peace to all whom it sheltered.
55 From the ninth to the eleventh centuries, if not later, Europe was in many ways all too open. Attack came from the sea, in the Mediterranean from Saracens and Vikings, the latter usually in their swift, dragon-prowed, easily manoeuvered longboats, manned by some sixteen pairs of oarsmen and
60 with a full complement of perhaps sixty men. There were periods when the British Isles and the French coasts were being raided every year by Vikings and in the heart of the continent marauding Magyar armies met invading bands of Saracens. The name of Pontresina, near St. Moritz in
65 Switzerland, is a memento of the stormy tenth century; it means *pons Saracenorum*, the "fortified Saracen bridge," the place where plundering expeditions halted on their way up from the Mediterranean.

It was recognized in theory that the Church and the
70 monarchy were the principal powers and that they were bound by the nature of their office to ensure peace and security and to do justice; but at this period they were too weak, too torn by internal conflicts to fulfill their obligations. Thus more and more power passed into the hands of
75 warriors invested by the monarchy and the Church with lands and rights of jurisdiction, who in return undertook to support their overlords and to protect the unarmed peasantry.

Their first concern, however, was self-protection. It is
80 almost impossible for us to realize how primitive the great majority of these early medieval "castles" really were. Until about 1150 the fortified houses of the Anglo-Norman nobility were simple dwellings surrounded by a mound of earth and a wooden stockade. These were the motte and
85 bailey castles: the motte was the mound and its stockade, the bailey an open court lying below and also stockaded. Both were protected, where possible, by yet another ditch filled with water, the moat. In the middle of the motte there was a wooden tower, the keep or *donjon*, which only be-
90 came a genuine stronghold at a later date and in places where stone was readily available. The stone castles of the French and German nobility usually had only a single communal room in which all activities took place.

In such straitened surroundings, where warmth, light
95 and comfort were lacking, there was no way of creating an
air of privacy. It is easy enough to understand why the life
of the landed nobility was often so unrestrained, so filled
with harshness, cruelty and brutality, even in later, more
"chivalrous" periods. The barons' daily life was bare and
100 uneventful, punctuated by war, hunting (a rehearsal for
war), and feasting. Boys were trained to fight from the age
of seven or eight, and their education in arms continued
until they were twenty-one, although in some cases they
started to fight as early as fifteen. The peasants of the
105 surrounding countryside, bound to their lords by a great
variety of ties, produced the sparse fare which was all that
the undeveloped agriculture of the early medieval period
could sustain. Hunting was a constant necessity, to make
up for the lack of butcher's meat, and in England and
110 Germany in the eleventh and twelfth centuries even the
kings had to progress from one crown estate to another,
from one bishop's palace to the next, to maintain themselves and their retinue.

24 According to the passage, class conflict in the Middle Ages was kept in check by

(A) the fact that most people belonged to the same
class
(B) tyrannical suppressions of rebellions by powerful monarchs
(C) the religious teachings of the church
(D) the fact that all other classes admired and at-
tempted to emulate the aristocracy
(E) the fear that a relatively minor conflict would
lead to a general revolution

25 According to the author, the urban bourgeoisie was
hostile to the aristocracy because

(A) the bourgeoisie was prevented by the aristocracy from seeking an alliance with the kings
(B) aristocrats often confiscated the wealth of the
bourgeoisie
(C) the bourgeoisie saw the aristocracy as their ri-
vals
(D) the aristocrats often deliberately antagonized
the bourgeoisie
(E) the bourgeoisie felt that the aristocracy was
immoral

26 According to the passage, castles were originally
built

(A) as status symbols
(B) as strongholds against invaders
(C) as simple places to live in
(D) as luxurious chateaux
(E) as recreation centers for the townspeople

27 One of the groups that invaded central Europe during the Middle Ages from the ninth century on was
the

(A) Magyars
(B) Franks
(C) Angles
(D) Celts
(E) Welsh

28 It can be seen from the passage that the aristocracy
was originally

(A) the great landowners
(B) members of the clergy
(C) the king's warriors
(D) merchants who became wealthy
(E) slaves who had rebelled

29 The reform popes eventually produced an aristocratic church because

(A) they depended on the aristocracy for money
(B) they themselves were more interested in money
than in religion
(C) they were defeated by aristocrats
(D) many aristocrats entered the structure of the
church and impressed their values on it
(E) the aristocrats were far more religious than
other segments of the population

30 The word "contentious" in lines 24–25 is best interpreted to mean

(A) careful
(B) solid
(C) controversial
(D) grandiose
(E) annoying

GO ON TO THE NEXT PAGE

31 According to the passage, hunting served the dual purpose of

(A) preparing for war and engaging in sport
(B) preparing for war and getting meat
(C) learning how to ride and learning how to shoot
(D) testing horses and men
(E) getting furs and ridding the land of excess animals

32 The phrase "amor et timor" in line 47 is used to describe

(A) the rivalry between the bourgeoisie and the aristocracy
(B) the Church's view of man and his relationship to God
(C) the peasant's loyalty to the aristocracy
(D) the adaptation of aristocratic manners and dress
(E) the payment of food in exchange for protection

33 The passage indicates that protection of the peasantry was implemented by

(A) the king's warriors
(B) the Magyar mercenaries
(C) the replacement of wood towers by stone donjons
(D) the princes of the Church
(E) the ruling monarchy

34 According to the passage, the effectiveness of the Church and king was diminished by

(A) the ambition of the military
(B) conflicts and weaknesses within the Church and Royal house
(C) peasant dissatisfaction
(D) the inherent flaws of feudalism
(E) economic instability

35 "Retinue," the last word in the passage, refers to

(A) food
(B) all material goods
(C) money
(D) attendants
(E) family

Time: 30 Minutes   This section contains two types of questions. You have 30 minutes to complete both types. You
25 Questions   may use any available space for scratchwork.

Notes:

1. The use of a calculator is permitted. All numbers are real numbers.

2. Figures that accompany problems in this test are intended to provide information useful in solving the problems. They are drawn as accurately as possible EXCEPT when it is stated in a specific problem that the figure is not drawn to scale. All figures lie in a plane unless otherwise indicated.

Reference Information

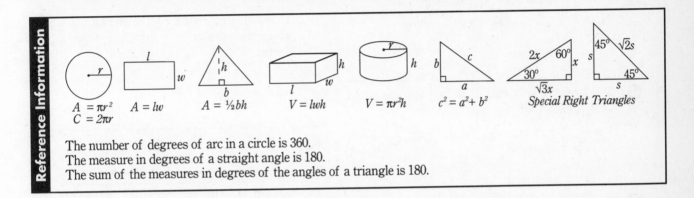

$A = \pi r^2$ $A = lw$ $A = \frac{1}{2}bh$ $V = lwh$ $V = \pi r^2 h$ $c^2 = a^2 + b^2$ *Special Right Triangles*
$C = 2\pi r$

The number of degrees of arc in a circle is 360.
The measure in degrees of a straight angle is 180.
The sum of the measures in degrees of the angles of a triangle is 180.

Directions for Quantitative Comparison Questions

Questions 1–15 each consist of two quantities in boxes, one in Column A and one in Column B. You are to compare the two quantities and on the answer sheet fill in oval

A if the quantity in Column A is greater;
B if the quantity in Column B is greater;
C if the two quantities are equal;
D if the relationship cannot be determined from the information given.

AN E RESPONSE WILL NOT BE SCORED.

Notes:

1. In some questions, information is given about one or both of the quantities to be compared. In such cases, the given information is centered above the two columns and is not boxed.
2. In a given question, a symbol that appears in both columns represents the same thing in Column A as it does in Column B.
3. Letters such as *x*, *n*, and *k* stand for real numbers.

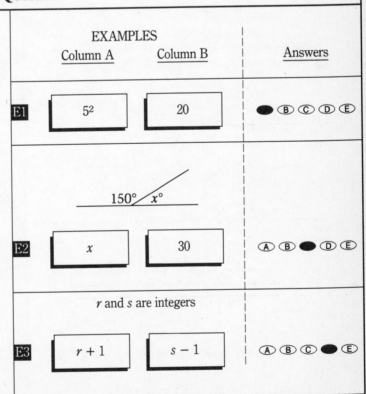

GO ON TO THE NEXT PAGE

SECTION 4

SUMMARY DIRECTIONS FOR COMPARISON QUESTIONS

Answer: A if the quantity in Column A is greater;
B if the quantity in Column B is greater;
C if the two quantities are equal;
D if the relationship cannot be determined from the information given.

AN E RESPONSE WILL NOT BE SCORED.

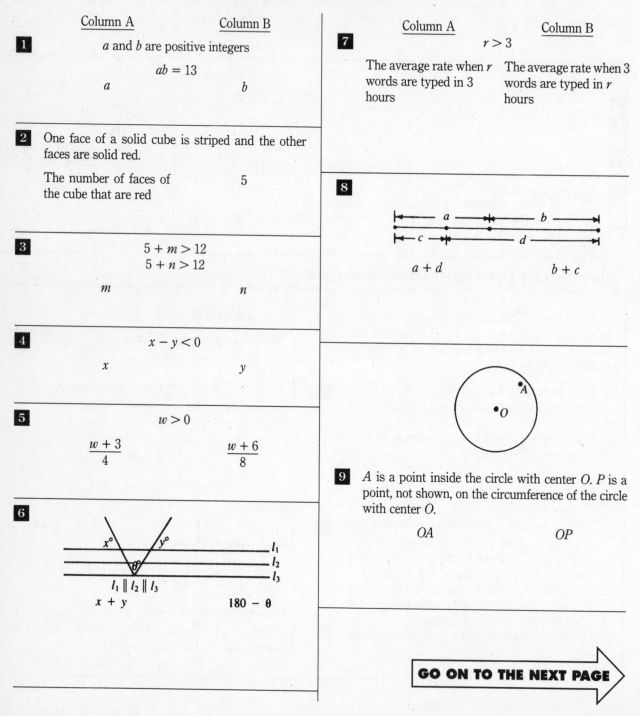

	Column A	Column B
1	*a* and *b* are positive integers	
	$ab = 13$	
	a	b

2 One face of a solid cube is striped and the other faces are solid red.

	The number of faces of the cube that are red	5

3
$$5 + m > 12$$
$$5 + n > 12$$

m	n

4
$$x - y < 0$$

x	y

5
$$w > 0$$

$\dfrac{w + 3}{4}$	$\dfrac{w + 6}{8}$

6

$l_1 \parallel l_2 \parallel l_3$

$x + y$	$180 - \theta$

	Column A	Column B
7	$r > 3$	
	The average rate when r words are typed in 3 hours	The average rate when 3 words are typed in r hours

8

$a + d$	$b + c$

9 A is a point inside the circle with center O. P is a point, not shown, on the circumference of the circle with center O.

OA	OP

GO ON TO THE NEXT PAGE

864

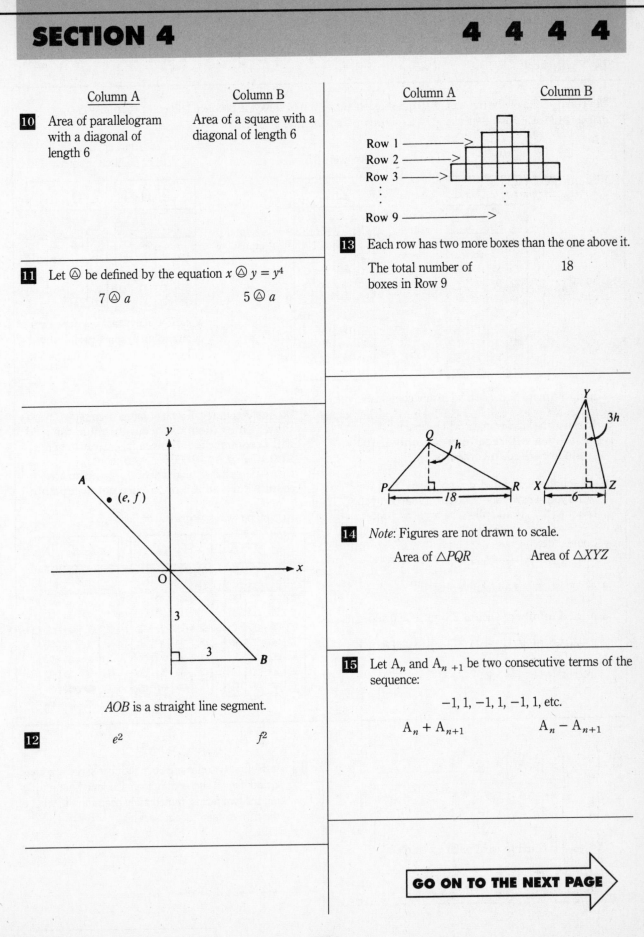

Column A | Column B

10 Area of parallelogram with a diagonal of length 6

Area of a square with a diagonal of length 6

11 Let ⬠ be defined by the equation $x \oslash y = y^4$

$7 \oslash a$

$5 \oslash a$

Column A | Column B

Row 1 ———→
Row 2 ———→
Row 3 ——→
⋮
Row 9 ————————→

13 Each row has two more boxes than the one above it.

The total number of boxes in Row 9

18

AOB is a straight line segment.

12

e^2

f^2

14 *Note*: Figures are not drawn to scale.

Area of $\triangle PQR$

Area of $\triangle XYZ$

15 Let A_n and A_{n+1} be two consecutive terms of the sequence:

$$-1, 1, -1, 1, -1, 1, \text{etc.}$$

$A_n + A_{n+1}$

$A_n - A_{n+1}$

GO ON TO THE NEXT PAGE

SECTION 4

<u>Directions:</u> Each of the remaining 10 questions requires you to solve the problem and enter your answer by marking the ovals in the special grid, as shown in the examples below.

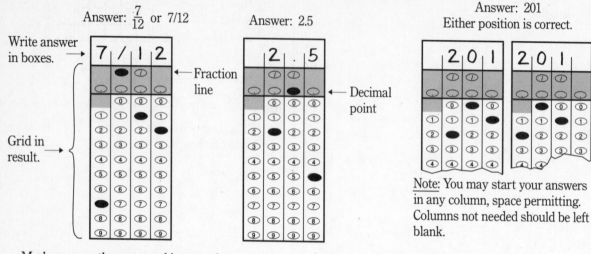

Answer: $\frac{7}{12}$ or 7/12

Answer: 2.5

Answer: 201
Either position is correct.

Write answer in boxes. →

← Fraction line

← Decimal point

Grid in result.

<u>Note:</u> You may start your answers in any column, space permitting. Columns not needed should be left blank.

- Mark no more than one oval in any column.

- Because the answer sheet will be machine-scored, **you will receive credit only if the ovals are filled in correctly.**

- Although not required, it is suggested that you write your answer in the boxes at the top of the columns to help you fill in the ovals accurately.

- Some problems may have more than one correct answer. In such cases, grid only one answer.

- No question has a negative answer.

- **Mixed numbers** such as $2\frac{1}{2}$ must be gridded as 2.5 or 5/2. (If $\boxed{2\,|\,1\,/\,2}$ is gridded, it will be interpreted as $\frac{21}{2}$, not $2\frac{1}{2}$.)

- <u>Decimal Accuracy:</u> If you obtain a decimal answer, **enter the most accurate value the grid will accommodate.** For example, if you obtain an answer such as 0.6666..., you should record the result as .666 or .667. **Less accurate results such as .66 or .67 are not acceptable.**

Acceptable ways to grid $\frac{2}{3}$ = .6666 ...

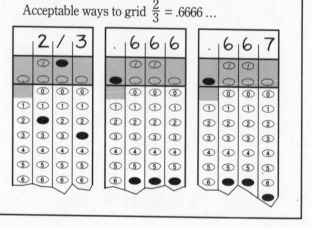

16 $\left(\frac{1}{2} - \frac{1}{3}\right) + \left(\frac{1}{3} - \frac{1}{4}\right) + \left(\frac{1}{4} - \frac{1}{5}\right) +$

$\left(\frac{1}{5} - \frac{1}{6}\right) + \left(\frac{1}{6} - \frac{1}{7}\right) + \left(\frac{1}{7} - \frac{1}{8}\right) +$

$\left(\frac{1}{8} - \frac{1}{9}\right)$ is equal to what value?

17 If the first two elements of a number series are 1 and 2, and if each succeeding term is found by multiplying the two terms immediately preceding it, what is the fifth element of the series?

866

GO ON TO THE NEXT PAGE ⟩

18 If p is $\frac{3}{5}$ of m and if q is $\frac{9}{10}$ of m, then, when $q \neq 0$, the ratio $\frac{p}{q}$ is equal to what value?

19 If the average (arithmetic mean) of 40, 40, 40, and z is 45, then find the value of z.

20 In the figure above, the perimeter of the equilateral triangle is 39 and the area of the rectangle is 65. What is the perimeter of the rectangle?

Game		Darrin	Tom
1		69	43
2		59	60
3		72	55
4		70	68
5		78	73
Totals		348	299

21 Darrin and Tom played five games of darts. The table above lists the scores for each of the games. By how many points was Tom behind Darrin at the end of the first four games?

22 A box contains 17 slips of paper. Each is labeled with a different integer from 1 to 17 inclusive. If 5 even-numbered slips of paper are removed, what fraction of the remaining slips of paper are even numbered?

Note: Figure is not drawn to scale.

23 In $\triangle RST$ above $UV \parallel RT$. Find b.

24 Rose has earned \$44 in 8 days. If she continues to earn at the same daily rate, in how many *more* days will her total earnings be \$99?

25 The areas of triangles I, II, III, IV, V, VI, VII, VIII, IX, X, XI, XII are the same. If the region outlined by the heavy line has area = 256 and the area of square $ABCD$ is 128, determine the shaded area.

IF YOU FINISH BEFORE TIME IS CALLED, YOU MAY CHECK YOUR WORK ON THIS SECTION ONLY. DO NOT TURN TO ANY OTHER SECTION IN THE TEST.

867

Time: 15 Minutes   For each question in this section, choose the best answer from among the choices given and
13 Questions   fill in the corresponding oval on the answer sheet.

The two passages that follow are followed by questions based on their content and on the relationship between the two passages. Answer the questions on the basis of what is *stated* or *implied* in the passages and in any introductory material that may be provided.

Questions 1–13 are based on the following passages.

The following two passages are about violence. The first discusses televised violence; the second attempts to address the history of violence in general.

Passage A

Violence is alive and well on television. Yet there appears to be a difference in the quality, variety and pervasiveness of today's televised violence. Some observers believe that, as a result of more than three decades of television,
5 viewers have developed a kind of immunity to the horror of violence. By the age of 16, for example, the average young person will have seen some 18,000 murders on television. One extension of this phenomenon may be an appetite for more varied kinds of violence. On the basis of the amount of
10 exposure, certain things that initially would have been beyond the pale have become more readily accepted.

Violence on TV has been more prevalent than in recent years, in large measure because there are fewer situation comedies and more action series. But also because some 25
15 million of the nation's 85 million homes with television now receive one of the pay cable services which routinely show uncut feature films containing graphic violence as early as 8 in the evening.

The evidence is becoming overwhelming that just as
20 witnessing violence in the home may contribute to children learning and acting out violent behavior, violence on TV and in the movies may lead to the same result. Studies have shown that a steady diet of watching graphic violence or sexually violent films such as those shown on cable TV has
25 caused some men to be more willing to accept violence against women such as rape and wife-beating. Not only actual violence, but the kind of violence coming through the television screen is causing concern. One of the principal developments is the increasing sophistication of the weap-
30 onry. The simple gunfight of the past has been augmented by high-tech crimes like terrorist bombings. A gunfighter shooting down a sheriff is one thing. When you have terrorist bombs, the potential is there for hundreds to die. Programs in the past used the occasional machine gun, but such
35 weapons as the M-60 machine gun and Uzi semi-automatic have become commonplace today on network shows.

Many people are no longer concerned about televised violence because they feel it is the way of the world. It is high time that broadcasters provide public messages on TV
40 screens that would warn viewers about the potentially harmful effects of viewing televised violence.

Passage B

We have always been a lawless and a violent people. Thus, our almost unbroken record of violence against the Indians and all others who got in our way—the Spaniards in
45 the Floridas, the Mexicans in Texas; the violence of the vigilantes on a hundred frontiers; the pervasive violence of slavery (a "perpetual exercise," Jefferson called it, "of the most boisterous passions"); the lawlessness of the Ku Klux Klan during Reconstruction and after; and of scores of race
50 riots from those of New Orleans in the 1960s to those of Chicago in 1919. Yet, all this violence, shocking as it doubtless was, no more threatened the fabric of our society or the integrity of the Union than did the lawlessness of Prohibition back in the Twenties. The explanation for this is to be
55 found in the embarrassing fact that most of it was official, quasi-official, or countenanced by public opinion: exterminating the Indian; flogging the slave; lynching the outlaw; exploiting women and children in textile mills and sweatshops; hiring Pinkertons to shoot down strikers;
60 condemning immigrants to fetid ghettos; punishing [Blacks] who tried to exercise their civil or political rights. Most of this was socially acceptable—or at least not wholly unacceptable—just as so much of our current violence is socially acceptable: the many thousands of automobile
65 deaths every year; the mortality rate for black babies twice that for white; the deaths from cancer induced by cigarettes or by air pollution; the sadism of our penal system and the horrors of our prisons; the violence of some police against the so-called "dangerous classes of society."
70 What we have now is the emergence of violence that is not acceptable either to the Establishment, which is frightened and alarmed, or to the victims of the Establishment, who are no longer submissive and who are numerous and powerful. This is now familiar "crime in the streets," or it is
75 the revolt of the young against the economy, the politics, and the wars of the established order, or it is the convulsive reaction of the blacks to a century of injustice. But now, too, official violence is no longer acceptable to its victims—or to their ever more numerous sympathizers: the violence of

GO ON TO THE NEXT PAGE

80 great corporations and of government itself against the natural resources of the nation; the long drawn-out violence of the white majority against Blacks and other minorities; the violence of the police and the National Guard against the young; the massive violence of the military against the
85 peoples of other countries. These acts can no longer be absorbed by large segments of our society. It is this new polarization that threatens the body politic and the social fabric much as religious dissent threatened them in the Europe of the sixteenth and seventeenth centuries.

1 The title that best summarizes the content of Passage A is

   (A) TV's Role in the Rising Crime Rate
   (B) Violence on TV—Past and Present
   (C) TV Won't Let Up on Violence
   (D) Violence Raises the TV Ratings
   (E) Violence Galore on Cable TV

2 Which of the following types of TV programs would the author of Passage A be *least* likely to approve of?

   (A) A cowboy Western called "Have Gun, Will Travel"
   (B) A talk show dealing with teenage pregnancy caused by a rape
   (C) A documentary dealing with Vietnam veterans suffering from the after-effects of herbicide spraying during the war
   (D) A movie showing a bomb exploding in a bus carrying civilians on their way to work
   (E) A soap opera in which a jealous husband is shown murdering his wife's lover, then his own wife

3 According to Passage A,

   (A) television programs are much different today from what they were a generation ago
   (B) a very large percentage of the viewers are presently worried about the showing of violence on television
   (C) situation comedy programs are more popular on TV now than ever before
   (D) broadcasting stations are considering notifying viewers about possible dangers of watching programs that include violence
   (E) violence on the television screen is more extreme than it was about 20 years ago

4 As an illustration of current "socially acceptable" violence the author of Passage B would probably include

   (A) National Guard violence at Kent, Ohio, during the Vietnam War
   (B) the Vietnam War
   (C) the cruelties of our prison system
   (D) the policy behavior in Chicago at the 1968 Democratic Convention
   (E) "crime in the streets"

5 It can be inferred that the author's definition of violence (Passage B)

   (A) includes the social infliction of harm
   (B) is limited to nongovernmental acts of force
   (C) is confined to governmental acts of illegal force
   (D) is synonymous with illegal conduct by either government or citizen
   (E) is shared by the FBI

6 The author of Passage B describes current violence as

   I. acceptable neither to the authorities nor to the victims
   II. carried out primarily by corporations
   III. increasingly of a vigilante nature

   (A) I only
   (B) II only
   (C) III only
   (D) I and II only
   (E) II and III only

7 The author of Passage B mentions all of the following forms of violence in the nineteenth century *except*

   (A) the activities of the Klan during Reconstruction
   (B) wiping out the Indians
   (C) the New York City draft riots of the 1860s
   (D) the Annexation of Texas and Florida
   (E) the practice of slavery

GO ON TO THE NEXT PAGE

8 Which action or activity would the author of Passage B be most likely to disapprove of?

(A) trying to prevent a mugging
(B) reading a science fiction story
(C) watching a rock music TV performance
(D) attending a Super Bowl football game
(E) participating in a country square dance

9 The word "pervasiveness" in lines 2–3 of Passage A (also note "pervasive" in line 46 of Passage B) means

(A) variety
(B) televised
(C) seeping through
(D) quality
(E) terribleness

10 Which of the following according to the author of Passage A is a contributing factor to the marked increase of violent deaths?

I. cable television
II. present feature films
III. technology

(A) I only
(B) II only
(C) II and III only
(D) I and II only
(E) I, II, and III

11 The author of Passage B would probably argue with the author of Passage A in the resolution of violence (lines 37–41) that

(A) if violence were curtailed on television, it would pop up elsewhere.
(B) television does not show a significant amount of violence to warrant warnings against such programs.
(C) television can also influence the public toward non-violence.
(D) there are more dangers to television than the portrayal of violence.
(E) violence is inbred in television.

12 From the passages, which can we assume to be *false*?

(A) Unlike the author of Passage A, the author of Passage B believes that society is disgusted with violence.
(B) The author of Passage A believes that sophisticated weaponry causes increased violence, whereas the author of Passage B believes that violence is inherent in society.
(C) The type of violence discussed by the author of Passage B is much more encompassing than the type of violence discussed by the author of Passage A.
(D) Both authors propose a direct resolution for at least a start to the end of violence.
(E) Both authors believe either that violence is a part of daily living or at least that many feel that violence is a part of daily living.

13 The word "polarization" in line 87 means

(A) electrical tendencies
(B) governments in different parts of the world
(C) completely opposing viewpoints
(D) extreme religious differences
(E) cold climatic conditions

IF YOU FINISH BEFORE TIME IS CALLED, YOU MAY CHECK YOUR WORK ON THIS SECTION ONLY. DO NOT TURN TO ANY OTHER SECTION IN THE TEST.

STOP

Time: 15 Minutes
10 Questions

In this section solve each problem, using any available space on the page for scratch-work. Then decide which is the best of the choices given and fill in the corresponding oval on the answer sheet.

Notes:

1. The use of a calculator is permitted. All numbers used are real numbers.

2. Figures that accompany problems in this test are intended to provide information useful in solving the problems. They are drawn as accurately as possible EXCEPT when it is stated in a specific problem that the figure is not drawn to scale. All figures lie in a plane unless otherwise indicated.

Reference Information

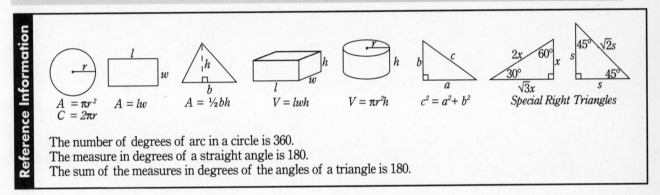

$A = \pi r^2$
$C = 2\pi r$

$A = lw$

$A = \frac{1}{2}bh$

$V = lwh$

$V = \pi r^2 h$

$c^2 = a^2 + b^2$

Special Right Triangles

The number of degrees of arc in a circle is 360.
The measure in degrees of a straight angle is 180.
The sum of the measures in degrees of the angles of a triangle is 180.

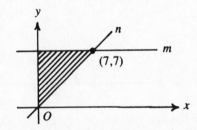

1 In the figure above, *m* is parallel to the *x*-axis. All of the following points lie in the shaded area EXCEPT

(A) (4,3)
(B) (1,2)
(C) (5,6)
(D) (4,5)
(E) (2,5)

2 At Lincoln County High School, 36 students are taking either calculus or physics or both, and 10 students are taking both calculus and physics. If there are 31 students in the calculus class, how many students are in the physics class?

(A) 14
(B) 15
(C) 16
(D) 17
(E) 18

GO ON TO THE NEXT PAGE

3 Johnny buys a frying pan and two coffee mugs for $27. Joanna buys the same-priced frying pan and one of the same-priced coffee mugs for $23. How much does one of those frying pans cost?

(A) $4
(B) $7
(C) $19
(D) $20
(E) $21

5 If 9 and 12 each divide Q without remainder, which of of the following must Q divide without remainder?

(A) 1
(B) 3
(C) 36
(D) 72
(E) The answer cannot be determined from the given information.

4 A rectangular floor 8 feet long and 6 feet wide is to be completely covered with tiles. Each tile is a square with a perimeter of 2 feet. What is the least number of such tiles necessary to cover the floor?

(A) 7
(B) 12
(C) 24
(D) 48
(E) 192

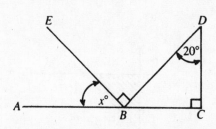

6 In the figure above, $DC \perp AC$, $EB \perp DB$, and AC is a line segment. What is the value of x?

(A) 15
(B) 20
(C) 30
(D) 80
(E) 160

GO ON TO THE NEXT PAGE

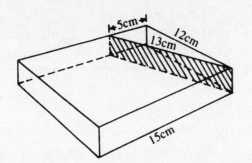

7 The rectangular box above has a rectangular dividing wall inside, as shown. The dividing wall has an area of 39 cm². What is the volume of the larger compartment?

(A) 90 cm³
(B) 180 cm³
(C) 360 cm³
(D) 450 cm³
(E) 540 cm³

8 Given three segments of length x, $11 - x$, and $x - 4$, respectively. Which of the following indicates the set of all numbers x such that the 3 segments could be the lengths of the sides of a triangle?

(A) $x > 4$
(B) $x < 11$
(C) $0 < x < 7$
(D) $5 < x < 15$
(E) $5 < x < 7$

9 $\dfrac{1}{11^{20}} - \dfrac{1}{11^{21}} =$

(A) $\dfrac{1}{11}$

(B) $\dfrac{10}{11^{21}}$

(C) $\dfrac{1}{11^{21}}$

(D) $-\dfrac{10}{11^{21}}$

(E) $-\dfrac{1}{11}$

10 Given three integers a, b and 4. If their average (arithmetic mean) is 6, which of the following could *not* be the value of the product ab?

(A) 13
(B) 14
(C) 40
(D) 48
(E) 49

IF YOU FINISH BEFORE TIME IS CALLED, YOU MAY CHECK YOUR WORK ON THIS SECTION ONLY. DO NOT TURN TO ANY OTHER SECTION IN THE TEST.

STOP

Time—30 Minutes
25 Questions

In this section solve each problem, using any available space on the page for scratch-work. Then decide which is the best of the choices given and fill in the corresponding oval on the answer sheet.

Notes:

1. The use of a calculator is permitted. All numbers used are real numbers.

2. Figures that accompany problems in this test are intended to provide information useful in solving the problems. They are drawn as accurately as possible EXCEPT when it is stated in a specific problem that the figure is drawn to scale. All figures lie in a plane unless otherwise indicated.

Reference Information

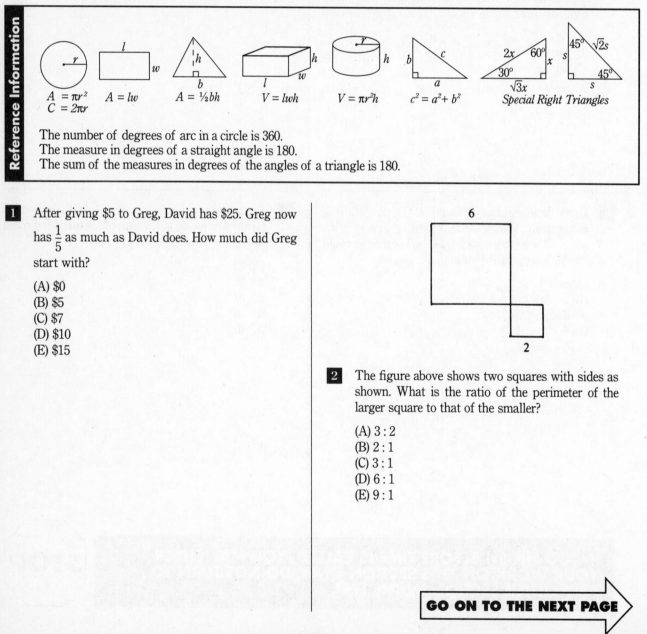

$A = \pi r^2$
$C = 2\pi r$

$A = lw$

$A = \frac{1}{2}bh$

$V = lwh$

$V = \pi r^2 h$

$c^2 = a^2 + b^2$

Special Right Triangles

The number of degrees of arc in a circle is 360.
The measure in degrees of a straight angle is 180.
The sum of the measures in degrees of the angles of a triangle is 180.

---

1 After giving $5 to Greg, David has $25. Greg now has $\frac{1}{5}$ as much as David does. How much did Greg start with?

(A) $0
(B) $5
(C) $7
(D) $10
(E) $15

2 The figure above shows two squares with sides as shown. What is the ratio of the perimeter of the larger square to that of the smaller?

(A) 3 : 2
(B) 2 : 1
(C) 3 : 1
(D) 6 : 1
(E) 9 : 1

GO ON TO THE NEXT PAGE

3 A car travels 1,056 feet in 12 seconds. In feet per second, what is the average speed of the car?

(A) 98.0
(B) 78.8
(C) 85.8
(D) 84.0
(E) 88.0

5 If $mn \neq 0$, then $\dfrac{1}{n^2}\left(\dfrac{m^5\,n^3}{m^3}\right)^2 =$

(A) mn^4
(B) m^4n^2
(C) m^4n^3
(D) m^4n^4
(E) m^4n^5

4 If $2z + 1 + 2 + 2z + 3 + 2z = 3 + 1 + 2$, then $z + 4 =$

(A) 1
(B) 4
(C) 5
(D) 6
(E) 10

6 $2(w)(x)(-y) - 2(-w)(-x)(y) =$

(A) 0
(B) $-4wxy$
(C) $4wxy$
(D) $-4w^2x^2y^2$
(E) $2w^2x^2y^2$

GO ON TO THE NEXT PAGE

7 What is an expression for 5 times the sum of the square of x and the square of y?

(A) $5(x^2 + y^2)$
(B) $5x^2 + y^2$
(C) $5(x + y)^2$
(D) $5x^2 + y$
(E) $5(2x + 2y)$

9 Under the given conditions, all of the following could be values of Z EXCEPT

(A) 1
(B) 2
(C) 3
(D) 4
(E) 5

Questions 8–9 refer to the figure above, where W, X, Y, and Z are four distinct digits from 0 to 9, inclusive, and $W + X + Y = 5Z$.

8 In the figure above, what is the value of Z?

(A) 3
(B) 5
(C) 8
(D) 10
(E) 15

10 If p and q are positive integers, x and y are negative integers, and if $p > q$ and $x > y$, which of the following must be less than zero?

  I. $q - p$
  II. qy
  III. $p + x$

(A) I only
(B) III only
(C) I and II only
(D) II and III only
(E) I, II, and III

GO ON TO THE NEXT PAGE

11 If N is a positive integer, which of the following does *not* have to be a divisor of the sum of N, $6N$, and $9N$?

(A) 1
(B) 2
(C) 4
(D) 9
(E) 16

12 If $x = 3a - 18$ and $5y = 3a + 7$, then find $5y - x$.

(A) -11
(B) 11
(C) 18
(D) 25
(E) $6a - 11$

13 If $p + pq$ is 4 times $p - pq$, which of the following has exactly one value? ($pq \neq 0$)

(A) p
(B) q
(C) pq
(D) $p + pq$
(E) $p - pq$

14 If $2 + \dfrac{1}{z} = 0$, then what is the value of $9 + 9z$?

(A) $-\dfrac{9}{2}$

(B) $-\dfrac{1}{2}$

(C) 0

(D) $\dfrac{9}{2}$

(E) The answer cannot be determined from the information given.

GO ON TO THE NEXT PAGE

15 In the figure above, $m + n =$

(A) 90
(B) 180
(C) $180 + y$
(D) $90 + x + y + z$
(E) $2(x + y + z)$

16 Let $wx = y$, where $wxy \neq 0$.

If both x and y are multiplied by 6, then w is

(A) multiplied by $\dfrac{1}{36}$

(B) multiplied by $\dfrac{1}{6}$

(C) multiplied by 1
(D) multiplied by 6
(E) multiplied by 36

17 The volume of a cube is less than 25, and the length of one of its edges is a positive integer. What is the largest possible value for the total area of the six faces?

(A) 1
(B) 6
(C) 24
(D) 54
(E) 150

18 The ratio of smokers to nonsmokers on a particular flight was $2 : 3$. Smoking passengers represented five more than $\dfrac{1}{3}$ of all the passengers aboard. How many passengers were on that flight?

(A) 15
(B) 25
(C) 30
(D) 45
(E) 75

GO ON TO THE NEXT PAGE

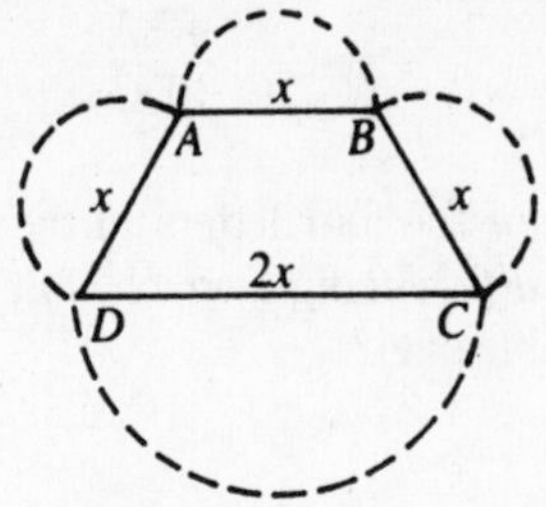

19 The quadrilateral $ABCD$ is a trapezoid with $x = 4$. The diameter of each semicircle is a side of the trapezoid. What is the sum of the lengths of the 4 dotted semicircles?

(A) 8π
(B) 10π
(C) 12π
(D) 14π
(E) 20π

20 $\dfrac{7x}{144}$ yards and $\dfrac{5y}{12}$ feet together equal how many inches?

(A) $\dfrac{7x}{12} + \dfrac{5y}{4}$

(B) $\dfrac{7x}{12} + 5y$

(C) $\dfrac{7x}{4} + 5y$

(D) $\dfrac{7x}{4} + 60y$

(E) $7x + \dfrac{5}{4}y$

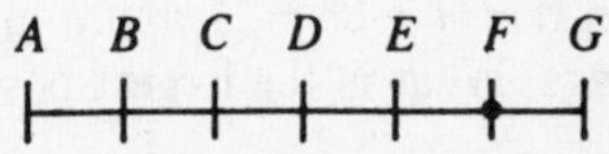

21 AG is divided into six equal segments in the figure above. A circle, not visible, with center F and radius $\dfrac{1}{5}$ the length of AG, will intersect AG between

(A) F and G
(B) E and F
(C) D and E
(D) C and D
(E) A and B

22 If $x < 0$ and $y < 0$, which of the following must always be positive?

   I. $x \cdot y$
  II. $x + y$
 III. $x - y$

(A) I only
(B) I and II only
(C) I and III only
(D) II and III only
(E) I, II, and III

GO ON TO THE NEXT PAGE ⟩

23 Given that $a + 3b = 11$ and a and b are positive integers. What is the largest possible value of a?

(A) 4
(B) 6
(C) 7
(D) 8
(E) 10

$$\begin{array}{r} AB \\ +BA \\ \hline CDC \end{array}$$

25 If each of the four letters in the sum above represents a *different* digit, which of the following *cannot* be a value of A?

(A) 6
(B) 5
(C) 4
(D) 3
(E) 2

24 The figure above is a rectangle having width a and length $a - b$. Find its perimeter in terms of a and b.

(A) $a^2 - ab$
(B) $4a - 2b$
(C) $4a - b$
(D) $2a - 2b$
(E) $2a - b$

IF YOU FINISH BEFORE TIME IS CALLED, YOU MAY CHECK YOUR WORK ON THIS SECTION ONLY. DO NOT TURN TO ANY OTHER SECTION IN THE TEST.

How Did You Do on This Test?

Step 1.   Go to the Answer Key on page 882.

Step 2.   For your "raw score," calculate it using the directions on page 87.

Step 3.   Get your "scaled score" for the test by referring to the Raw Score/Scaled Score Conversion Tables on page 90.

THERE'S ALWAYS ROOM FOR IMPROVEMENT!

Answer Key for Practice Test 5

Section 1—Verbal

1. E	8. B	15. C	22. E	29. B
2. C	9. D	16. B	23. D	30. A
3. B	10. E	17. D	24. B	
4. A	11. D	18. B	25. C	
5. B	12. C	19. C	26. E	
6. B	13. E	20. E	27. E	
7. B	14. E	21. E	28. C	

Section 2—Math

1. A	5. C	9. A	13. B	17. D	21. C	25. A
2. C	6. A	10. B	14. A	18. A	22. B	
3. B	7. D	11. D	15. E	19. B	23. D	
4. E	8. D	12. D	16. C	20. E	24. B	

Section 3—Verbal

1. A	7. D	13. B	19. B	25. C	31. B
2. E	8. B	14. A	20. C	26. B	32. C
3. E	9. A	15. D	21. E	27. A	33. A
4. C	10. B	16. E	22. B	28. C	34. B
5. D	11. C	17. E	23. B	29. D	35. D
6. E	12. B	18. C	24. D	30. C	

Section 4—Math

1. D	6. C	11. C	16. $7/18$, .388 or .389	21. 44
2. C	7. A	12. B	17. 8	22. $1/4$ or .25
3. D	8. A	13. A	18. $2/3$ or .667 or .666	23. 60
4. B	9. B	14. C	19. 60	24. 10
5. A	10. D	15. D	20. 36	25. 48

Section 5—Verbal

1. C	4. C	7. C	10. E	13. C
2. D	5. A	8. D	11. A	
3. E	6. A	9. C	12. E	

Section 6—Math

1. A	6. B
2. B	7. D
3. C	8. E
4. E	9. B
5. E	10. B

Section 7—Math

1. A	6. B	11. D	16. C	21. C
2. C	7. A	12. D	17. C	22. A
3. E	8. A	13. B	18. E	23. D
4. B	9. E	14. D	19. B	24. B
5. D	10. C	15. C	20. C	25. E

Explanatory Answers for Practice Test 5

Section 1: Verbal Ability

> As you read these Explanatory Answers, refer to "Using Critical Thinking Skills in Verbal Questions" (beginning on page 236) whenever a specific Strategy is referred to in the answer. Of particular importance are the following Master Verbal Strategies:
>
> Sentence Completion Master Strategy 1—page 245.
> Sentence Completion Master Strategy 2—page 246.
> Analogies Master Strategy 1—page 236.
> Reading Comprehension Master Strategy 2—page 263.

1. Choice E is correct. See **Sentence Completion Strategy 2.** Examine the first word of each choice. Choice (A) committees and Choice (B) tribes are incorrect because it is clear that committees and tribes cannot be equated with cities such as Athens. Now consider the other choices. Choice (E) societies . . . participated is the only choice which has a word pair that makes sentence sense.

2. Choice C is correct. See **Sentence Completion Strategy 2.** Examine the first word of each choice. Choice (A) abolished and Choice (E) discounted do not make sense because we cannot say that fossils are abolished or discounted in rock formations. Now consider the other choices. Choice (C) preserved . . . hardened is the only choice which has a word pair that makes sentence sense.

3. Choice B is correct. See **Sentence Completion Strategy 2.** Examine the first word of each choice. We eliminate Choice (A) dominated and Choice (D) cautioned because the trends do *not* dominate or caution affluence. Now consider the other choices. Choice (C) accentuated . . . depression and Choice (E) accepted . . . revolution do *not* make sentence sense. Choice (B) reflected . . . prosperity *does* make sentence sense.

4. Choice A is correct. See **Sentence Completion Strategy 1.** The word "conserve" (meaning to "protect from loss") completes the sentence so that it makes good sense. The other choices don't do that.

5. Choice B is correct. See **Sentence Completion Strategy 1.** The word "prevalent" (meaning widely or commonly occurring) completed the sentence so that it makes good sense. The other choices don't do that.

6. Choice B is correct. Since this question has the two-blank choices, let us use **Sentence Completion Strategy 2.** When we use Step 1 of Strategy 2, we find a very unusual situation in this question—the first words in all five choices make sense: "With lack of" *advice* or *control* or *opportunity* or *sympathy* or *conscience,* "anyone can develop the disease of alcoholism . . ." Accordingly, we must go to Step 2 of Strategy 2 and consider *both* words of each choice. When we do so, we find that only Choice (B) control . . . foolishly makes good sentence sense.

7. Choice B is correct. See **Sentence Completion Strategy 4.** "Because" is a *result indicator.* Since the generating system was not functioning efficiently, the use of electricity had to be *diminished* or *curtailed.*

8. Choice B is correct. See **Sentence Completion Strategy 1.** Something staple, such as bread, is in constant supply and demand. Beer, then, is considered a liquid bread by the Bavarians. Choices A, C, D, and E do not make good sense in the sentence.

9. Choice D is correct. See **Sentence Completion Strategy 1.** The word "extreme" is the most appropriate among the five choices because the forest fire season is in *full swing.* The other choices are, therefore, not appropriate.

10. Choice E is correct. An apiary houses bees. A stable houses horses. Also see **Analogy Strategy 6.**

    (Purpose relationship)

11. Choice D is correct. A foreman holds a position both of leadership and membership of a jury. A captain holds a position both of leadership and membership of a group. We have here a Part : Whole relationship. Choices B and E also express a Part : Whole relationship, but they do not include the leadership quality of the capitalized words and the Choice D words. Therefore, Choices B and E are incorrect. See **Analogy Strategy 4.**

    (Part : Whole relationship)

12. Choice C is correct. An addendum is attached to the end of the book. An epilogue is attached to the end of a play. You might have considered Choice A as correct. But a finale is *not* added; it is part of the original musical score. See **Analogy Strategy 4.**

    (Action to Object relationship)

13. A catcher on a baseball team uses a mask to protect his face from being hit by the ball. A driver of car uses the visor above the windshield to protect his eyes from direct sunlight or glare.

    (Purpose relationship)

14. Choice E is correct. A person who is contrite is not carefree. A person who is dignified is not informal.

    (Opposite relationship)

15. Choice C is correct. To taunt is to ridicule or mock while vilify is to defame or slander. To chuckle is to laugh softly while to guffaw is to laugh loudly and boisterously.

    (Degree relationship)

16. Choice B is correct. See lines 21–29: "That was why . . . until he reached bitter despair . . . the man of property could die." The "well-upholstered hell" constituted the lifestyle that almost caused him to

commit suicide. The passage shows no justification for Choices A, C, D, and E. Accordingly, these are incorrect choices.

17. Choice D is correct. Throughout paragraph 3 we see the evidences of the speaker's happiness as a result of his renouncing the "power, women and money" (lines 22–23) as well as the arrogance and intellectuality referred to in line 17. Choices A, B, and C are incorrect because, though the passage discusses these choices, they do not really *pinpoint* the relation between the third and fourth paragraphs. Choice E is incorrect because paragraph 3 does not generalize about the specific points made in paragraph 2.

18. Choice B is correct. His "complete hopelessness and despair" (lines 3–4) led to Siddhartha's decision to commit suicide. The passage does not answer the questions expressed in Choices A, C, D, and E. Therefore, these choices are incorrect.

19. Choice C is correct. From the context of the sentence and the one preceding it, we can see that the word "transitory" means short-lived.

20. Choice E is correct. The unhappiness that may result from wealth and power are brought out clearly throughout the second paragraph. In contrast, peace and quiet are likely to assure a happy life. The last paragraph demonstrates this conclusively. Although Choices A, B, C, and D are vital points, none of the choices is sufficiently inclusive to be considered the *main* idea of the passage. References to these choices follow. Choice A—lines 13–21: "He had been full of arrogance . . . brought him salvation." Choice B—lines 5–8: "Was it not his Self . . . filled him with fear?" Choice C—lines 10–11: "Too much knowledge had hindered him." Choice D—lines 19–21: "Now he understood . . . brought him salvation."

21. Choice E is correct. The word "Self" as it is used in this passage means one's own interests, welfare, or advantage; self-love. By an extension of these definitions, "Self" may be considered selfishness. See lines 5–8: "Was it not his Self . . . filled him with fear." Accordingly, Choices A, B, C, and D are incorrect.

22. Choice E is correct. See lines 21–22: "All human beings have at least four types of intelligence." Choice A is incorrect. See lines 50–52: "Persistence kept Einstein looking for the solution to the question of the relationship between the law of gravity and his special theory of relativity." Isaac Newton (1642–1727) formulated the law of gravitation. Choice B is incorrect. The passage simply states:

"The idea for the self-starting electric motor came to Nikola Tesla one evening as he was reciting a poem by Goethe and watching a sunset" (lines 30–32). Choice C is incorrect. The author indicates a span of time when he states: "The discoveries made by scientific geniuses from Archimedes through Einstein . . ." (lines 1–2). Archimedes was an ancient Greek mathematician, physicist, and inventor (287–212 B.C.), whereas Einstein was, of course, a modern scientist (1879–1955). Choice D is incorrect. The passage states: ". . . while an IQ above a certain point—about 120—is very helpful for a scientist [it] is not crucial for producing a work of genius" (lines 18–21). The passage does not specifically say that most scientists have IQ scores above 120.

23. Choice D is correct. See lines 42–44: "The scientist solves a problem by shifting from one intelligence to another, although the logical-mathematical intelligence is dominant." Accordingly, Choices A, B, C, and E are incorrect.

24. Choice B is correct. When the author describes the work experiences of Einstein and Tesla, he refers to their use of one or more of the four types of intelligence. Moreover, lines 26–28 state: "Some corroboration of these [four intelligence] categories comes from the reports of scientists who describe thought processes centered around images, sensations, or words." Choices A, C, D, and E are incorrect because the author does not refer to these choices in the passage.

25. Choice C is correct. The author indicates that great scientists use to advantage four intelligences—logical-mathematical, spatial, linguistic, and bodily-kinesthetic. See lines 22–25: "The great scientist possesses the ability to move back and forth among them—the logical-mathematical, the spatial which includes visual perception, the linguistic, and the bodily-kinesthetic." Choices B and D are brought out in the passage but not at any length. Therefore, Choices B and D are incorrect. Choice A is incorrect because the author nowhere compares the thinking of the average individual and that of the great scientist. Choice E is incorrect because, though the concepts are mentioned, they certainly are not clarified in the passage.

26. Choice E is correct. As a football star, he would certainly have to have a high level of (a) spatial intelligence [II], which involves space sensitivity as well as visual perception, and (b) bodily-kinesthetic intelligence [IV], which involves the movement of muscles, tendons, and joints. As a literature major, he would certainly have to have a high level of linguistic intelligence [III], which involves the ability to read, write, speak, and listen. Whether he would have logical-mathematical intelligence to a high degree is questionable. It follows that Choices A, B, C, and D are incorrect.

27. Choice E is correct. According to what is stated in lines 50–56, persistence is an important characteristic of the scientist. Thus the author would probably not agree with the statement in Choice E. The author would agree with the statement in Choice A: See lines 4–5. Note that although the author may not agree that IQ is what makes the scientist brilliant, he believes that *most* people feel that way. The author would agree with the statement in Choice B. See lines 30–32 and lines 55–60. The author would agree with the statement in Choice C. See lines 15–16 in the context with the rest of the passage. The author would probably not disagree with the statement in Choice D since the author does not appear to distinguish artists from scientists in their thinking process even though the passage is primarily about the scientists: See lines 9–14.

28. Choice C is correct. See lines 51–54. Note that although "persistence" is mentioned in lines 47–51, the passage states that fluid thinking may be connected to persistence, not defined as persistence. Thus Choice A is incorrect.

29. Choice B is correct. Given the context in lines 47–54, the word "paradoxically" means seemingly contradictory.

30. Choice A is correct. It can be seen in the passage that the author is intrigued by and interested in the way the scientist thinks but at the same time reports the findings very objectively.

Explanatory Answers for Practice Test 5 (continued)

Section 2: Math Ability

As you read these solutions, you are advised to do two things if you answered the Math question incorrectly:

1. When a specific Strategy is referred to in the solution, study that strategy, which you will find in "Using Critical Thinking Skills in Math Questions" (beginning on page 174).

2. When the solution directs you to the "Math Refresher" (beginning on page 291)—for example, Math Refresher #305—study the 305 Math principles to get a clear idea of the Math operation that was necessary for you to know in order to answer the question correctly.

1. Choice A is correct.

$$\sqrt{\frac{3}{\sqrt{9}}} = \sqrt{\frac{3}{3}}$$
$$= \sqrt{1}$$
$$= 1$$

(Math Refresher #430)

2. Choice C is correct.

Given:
$$\begin{array}{r} 59\triangle \\ -\ 293 \\ \hline \square 97 \end{array} \qquad \boxed{1}$$

(Use Strategy 17: Use the given information effectively.)

From $\boxed{1}$ we see that $\triangle - 3 = 7$ $\qquad \boxed{2}$
From $\boxed{2}$ we get $\triangle = 10$ $\qquad \boxed{3}$

From $\boxed{1}$ and $\boxed{3}$ we get $\triangle = 0$ in $\boxed{1}$ and we had to borrow to get 10. Thus, we have

$$\begin{array}{r} 8 \\ 5\cancel{9}\cancel{0} \\ -\ 293 \\ \hline \square 97 \end{array} \qquad \boxed{4}$$

Calculating $\boxed{4}$, we get

$$\begin{array}{r} 8 \\ 5\cancel{9}\cancel{0} \\ -\ 293 \\ \hline 297 \end{array}$$

We see that the digit represented by the $\square$ is 2.

(Logical Reasoning and Subtraction)

3. Choice B is correct. **(Use Strategy 16: The obvious may be tricky!)**

$1,000 - 1 = 999$ is *not* correct.
Neither 1 nor 1,000 is to be included.
Thus there are $1,000 - 2 = 998$ integers between 1 and 1,000.

(Logical Reasoning)

4. Choice E is correct.

Given: $\dfrac{a - b}{b} = \dfrac{1}{2}$ $\qquad \boxed{1}$

(Use Strategy 13: Find unknowns by multiplication.)

Multiply $\boxed{1}$ by $2b$. We have

$$2b\left(\frac{a-b}{b}\right) = \left(\frac{1}{2}\right)2b$$

$$2(a-b) = b$$
$$2a - 2b = b$$
$$2a = 3b \qquad \boxed{2}$$

(Use Strategy 13: Find unknowns by division.)

Dividing $\boxed{2}$ by $2b$, we get

$$\frac{2a}{2b} = \frac{3b}{2b}$$
$$\frac{a}{b} = \frac{3}{2}$$

(Math Refresher #406)

5. Choice C is correct.

Number of pounds of force	Height object is raised
3	6 feet
6	12 feet
9	18 feet

$\boxed{1}$

(Use Strategy 2: Translate from words to algebra.)

We are given that:

height raised = c (force exerted) $\boxed{2}$

Substituting $\boxed{1}$ into $\boxed{2}$, we get

$$6 = c(3)$$
$$2 = c \qquad \boxed{3}$$

Given: Height object is raised = 15 feet $\boxed{4}$
Substituting $\boxed{3}$ and $\boxed{4}$ into $\boxed{2}$, we have

$$15 = 2 \text{ (force exerted)}$$
$$7\frac{1}{2} = \text{force exerted}$$

(Math Refresher #200 and #406)

6. Choice A is correct.

Given: $a = 1, b = -2, c = -2$ $\boxed{1}$
$\dfrac{b^2 c}{(a-c)^2}$ $\boxed{2}$

Substitute $\boxed{1}$ into $\boxed{2}$. We get

$$\frac{(-2)^2(-2)}{(1-(-2))^2} =$$

$$\frac{4(-2)}{(3)^2} =$$

$$\frac{-8}{9}$$

(Math Refresher #429 and #431)

7. Choice D is correct.

Given: $\dfrac{y}{3}, \dfrac{y}{4}, \dfrac{y}{7}$ are integers. $\boxed{1}$

(Use Strategy 17: Use the given information effectively.)

If all items in $\boxed{1}$ are integers, then 3, 4, and 7 divide y evenly (zero remainder). y must be a common multiple of 3, 4, and 7. Multiplying 3, 4, and 7 we get 84.

(Math Refresher #607)

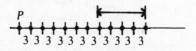

8. Choice D is correct. **(Use Strategy 11: Use new definitions carefully.)**

We are told that the points are each 3 units apart, as indicated above. We are looking for all those points that are more than 19 units away from point P. By checking the diagram we find 5 such points (marked with arrow in diagram).

(Logical Reasoning)

9. Choice A is correct.

Given: $y = 28j$ $\boxed{1}$
j is any integer $\boxed{2}$

(Use Strategy 13: Find unknowns by division.)

Divide $\boxed{1}$ by 2. We have

$$\frac{y}{2} = \frac{28j}{2}$$

$$\frac{y}{2} = 14j \qquad \boxed{3}$$

(Use Strategy 19: Factor.)

Factor the 14 in ③. We get

$$\frac{y}{2} = (2)(7)(j) \qquad \boxed{4}$$

Using ② and ④ we see that $\frac{y}{2}$ is an integer with a factor of 2.

Thus, $\frac{y}{2}$ is even.

(Math Refresher #603 and #605)

10. Choice B is correct.

Given: $\qquad\qquad\qquad\qquad$ ①
$(a + 2, a - 2) = [a]$ for all integers a. $\qquad$ ②
We need to find $(6,2)$

(Use Strategy 11: Use new definitions carefully.) Using ① and ② we have

$$a + 2 = 6 \qquad \text{and} \qquad a - 2 = 2$$
$$a = 4 \qquad\qquad\qquad a = 4 \quad \boxed{3}$$

Using ①, ②, and ③, we get

$$(6,2) = [4]$$

(Math Refresher #431 and #406)

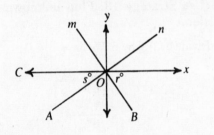

11. Choice D is correct.

Given: $\qquad\qquad m \perp n \qquad\qquad$ ①

From ① we know that $\angle AOB$ is a right angle.
Thus $\angle AOB = 90°$ $\qquad\qquad\qquad$ ②

From the diagram, we see that $\angle COx$ is a straight angle.
Thus $\angle COx = 180°$ $\qquad\qquad\qquad$ ③

(Use Strategy 3: The whole equals the sum of its parts.)

We know that $\angle COA + \angle AOB + \angle BOx = \angle COx$ $\qquad\qquad\qquad\qquad\qquad$ ④

Given: $\qquad \angle COA = s° \qquad$ ⑤
$\qquad\qquad \angle BOx = r° \qquad$ ⑥

Substituting ②, ③, ⑤, and ⑥ into ④, we get

$$s + 90 + r = 180$$
$$s + r = 90$$
$$r + s = 90$$

(Math Refresher #501, #511, and #406)

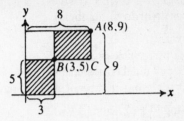

12. Choice D is correct. **(Use Strategy 17: Use the given information effectively.)**

From the given coordinates, we can find certain distances, as marked above.

Using these distances we find:
$$BC = 8 - 3 = 5 \qquad \boxed{1}$$
$$AC = 9 - 5 = 4 \qquad \boxed{2}$$

We know that Area of a rectangle = length × width $\qquad\qquad\qquad\qquad$ ③

Using the diagram and ③ we have

$\qquad$ Area of lower rectangle $= 5 \times 3 = 15 \quad \boxed{4}$

Substituting ① and ② into ③, we get

$\qquad$ Area of upper rectangle $= 5 \times 4 = 20 \quad \boxed{5}$

(Use Strategy 13: Find unknowns by addition.)

Adding ④ and ⑤ together, we get

$$\text{Total area} = 15 + 20 = 35$$

(Math Refresher #410 and #304)

13. Choice B is correct.

Given: $\quad$ Total number of students $= 2,800 \quad$ ①

(Use Strategy 2: Translate from words to algebra.)

$$\text{Number of German students} = \frac{1}{4} \times 2,800$$
$$= \frac{2,800}{4}$$
$$= 700 \qquad \boxed{2}$$

(Use Strategy 13: Find unknown by subtraction.)

Subtracting ② from ① we get

$\qquad$ Number of students
$\qquad$ not studying German =
$\qquad\qquad 2,800 - 700 =$
$\qquad\qquad\qquad 2,100$

(Math Refresher #200 and #111)

14. Choice A is correct. **(Use Strategy 2: Translate from words to algebra.)**

Given:
cost per vehicle = $y   ⬚1
Let x = number of students paying $0.40   ⬚2
Then $x + 6$ = number of students paying $0.25   ⬚3

Using ⬚1, ⬚2, and ⬚3,

We are told that: $x(\$0.40) = \$y$ ⬚4
$(x + 6)(\$0.25) = \$y$ ⬚5

From ⬚4 and ⬚5 we get

$$x(\$0.40) = (x + 6)(\$0.25)$$
$$.40x = .25x + 1.50$$
$$.15x = 1.50$$
$$x = 10 \quad ⬚6$$

Substitute ⬚6 into ⬚4. We have

$$10(\$0.40) = \$y$$
$$\$4.00 = y$$
$$\$4 = y$$

(Math Refresher #200, #406, and #431)

15. Choice E is correct.

Given: $8(679) + 679$ ⬚1

(Use Strategy 17: Use the given information effectively.)

⬚1 can be written as:

$$8(679) + 1(679) = \quad ⬚2$$
$$9(679)$$

We need to check the choices.

(Use Strategy 8: When choices must be tested start with E.)

Choice E = $6(679) + 3(679) =$
$9(679)$

This equals ⬚2.

(Common Factors)

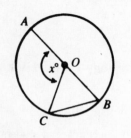

16. Choice C is correct.

Given: AB is a diameter   ⬚1
O is the center of the circle   ⬚2
$CB = OB$ ⬚3

Using ⬚2, we know that OB and OC are radii   ⬚4

From ⬚4 we get that $OB = OC$.   ⬚5

Using ⬚3 and ⬚5 together, we have

$$OB = OC = CB \quad ⬚6$$

(Use Strategy 18: Remember the equilateral triangle.)

From ⬚6, we have $\triangle OBC$ is equilateral   ⬚7

From ⬚7, we get that $\angle B = \angle C = \angle COB = 60°$ ⬚8

From ⬚1, we get $\angle AOB$ is straight angle.   ⬚9

From ⬚9, we have $\angle AOB = 180°$ ⬚10

(Use Strategy 3: The whole equals the sum of its parts.)

From the diagram we see that:

$$\angle AOC + \angle COB = \angle AOB \quad ⬚11$$

Given: $\angle AOC = x°$ ⬚12

Substituting ⬚8, ⬚10, and ⬚12 into ⬚11, we get

$$x + 60 = 180$$
$$x = 120 \quad ⬚13$$

(Use Strategy 13: Find unknowns by division.)

Divide by ⬚13 by 6. We have

$$\frac{x}{6} = \frac{120}{6}$$
$$\frac{x}{6} = 20$$

(Math Refresher #501, #508, #524, and #406)

17. Choice D is correct.

Given: Selling price of radio = $64   ⬚1
Regular price of radio = $80   ⬚2

(Use Strategy 2: Remember how to find percent discount.)

$$\text{Percent discount} = \frac{\text{Amount off}}{\text{original price}} \times 100 \quad ⬚3$$

Subtracting ⬚1 from ⬚2, we get

Amount off = $80 − $64 = $16   ⬚4

Substituting ⬚2 and ⬚4 into ⬚3, we have

$$\text{Percent discount} = \frac{\$16}{\$80} \times 100$$
$$= \frac{\$16 \times 100}{\$80} \quad ⬚5$$

(Use Strategy 19: Factor and reduce.)

Percent discount $= \dfrac{\$\cancel{16} \times \cancel{5} \times 20}{\$\cancel{16} \times \cancel{5}}$

Percent discount $= 20$ ⑥

Given: Regular price of different radio $= \$200$ ⑦

New percent discount

$\qquad = 1\dfrac{1}{2} \times$ Other radio's percent discount ⑧

Using ⑥ and ⑧, we have

$$\text{New percent discount} = 1\dfrac{1}{2} \times 20 =$$
$$= \dfrac{3}{2} \times 20$$
$$= 30 \quad ⑨$$

(Use Strategy 2: Remember how to find percent of a number.)

We know percent of a number =
percent $\times$ number. ⑩

Substituting ⑦ and ⑨ into ⑩, we have

$$\text{Amount of discount} = 30\% \times \$200$$
$$= \dfrac{30}{100} \times \$200$$

Amount of discount $= \$60$ ⑪

(Use Strategy 13: Find unknowns by subtraction.)

Subtracting ⑪ from ⑦, we have

Selling price of different radio
$= \$200 - \$60$
$= \$140$

(Math Refresher #200 and #114)

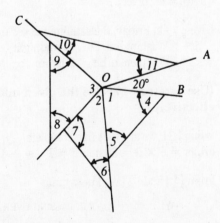

18. Choice A is correct.

$\qquad$ Given: $\angle AOB = 20°$ ①

(Use Strategy 3: The whole equals the sum of its parts.)

We know that the sum of the angles
of a triangle $= 180°$ ②

For each of the four triangles, applying ② yields:

$$\angle 8 + \angle 9 + \angle 3 = 180 \quad ③$$
$$\angle 6 + \angle 7 + \angle 2 = 180 \quad ④$$
$$\angle 4 + \angle 5 + \angle 1 = 180 \quad ⑤$$
$$\angle 10 + \angle 11 + \angle COA = 180 \quad ⑥$$

We know that the sum of all the angles about a point
$= 360°$ ⑦

Applying ⑦ to point O, we have

$$\angle 1 + \angle 2 + \angle 3 + \angle COA + \angle AOB = 360° \quad ⑧$$

Substituting ① into ⑧, we get

$$\angle 1 + \angle 2 + \angle 3 + \angle COA + 20 = 360$$
$$\angle 1 + \angle 2 + \angle 3 + \angle COA = 340 \quad ⑨$$

(Use Strategy 13: Find unknowns by addition.)

Adding ③, ④, ⑤, and ⑥, we have

$$\angle 4 + \angle 5 + \angle 6 + \angle 7 + \angle 8 + \angle 9 + \angle 10 +$$
$$\angle 11 + \angle 1 + \angle 2 + \angle 3 + \angle COA = 720° \quad ⑩$$

(Use Strategy 13: Find unknowns by subtraction.)

Subtracting ⑨ from ⑩, we get

$$\angle 4 + \angle 5 + \angle 6 + \angle 7 + \angle 8 +$$
$$\angle 9 + \angle 10 + \angle 11 = 380° \quad ⑪$$

Thus, the sum of the marked angles $= 380°$

(Math Refresher #505 and #406)

19. Choice B is correct.

$\qquad$ Given: $3a + 4b = 4a - 4b = 21$ ①

From ①, we get

$$3a + 4b = 21 \quad ②$$
$$4a - 4b = 21 \quad ③$$

(Use Strategy 13: Find unknowns by addition.)

Add ② and ③ together. We get

$$3a + \cancel{4b} = 21$$
$$+\ 4a - \cancel{4b} = 21$$
$$\overline{7a \qquad = 42}$$
$$a \qquad = 6$$

(Math Refresher #407)

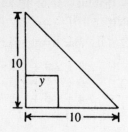

20. Choice E is correct.

We know that Area of a triangle

$$= \frac{1}{2} \times \text{base} \times \text{height} \quad \boxed{1}$$

Use the diagram, and substituting into $\boxed{1}$, we get

$$\text{Area of triangle} = \frac{1}{2} \times 10 \times 10$$
$$= 50 \quad \boxed{2}$$

(Use Strategy 2: Translate from words to algebra.)

We are told:

$$\text{Area of square} = \frac{1}{5} \times \text{Area of triangle} \quad \boxed{3}$$

We know that
Area of a square $= (\text{side})^2 \quad \boxed{4}$

Using the diagram, and substituting into $\boxed{4}$, we get

$$\text{Area of square} = y^2 \quad \boxed{5}$$

Substituting $\boxed{2}$ and $\boxed{5}$ into $\boxed{3}$, we have

$$y^2 = \frac{1}{5} \times 50$$
$$y^2 = 10 \quad \boxed{6}$$

Take the square root of both sides of $\boxed{6}$. We get

$$y = \sqrt{10}$$

(Math Refresher #200, #303, #307, and #430)

21. Choice C is correct.

$$\text{Given:} \quad \text{Print rate} = \frac{80 \text{ characters}}{\text{second}} \quad \boxed{1}$$
$$\frac{\text{Number of characters}}{\text{Page}} = 2400 \quad \boxed{2}$$

(Use Strategy 13: Find unknowns by division.)

Dividing $\boxed{2}$ by $\boxed{1}$, we have

$$\frac{2,400 \text{ characters}}{\text{page}} \div \frac{80 \text{ characters}}{\text{second}} =$$

$$\frac{2,400 \text{ characters}}{\text{page}} \times \frac{\text{second}}{80 \text{ characters}} =$$

$$\frac{2,400 \text{ second}}{80 \text{ page}}$$

$$= \frac{30 \text{ seconds}}{\text{page}} \quad \boxed{3}$$

The time for an M-page report will be

$$\frac{30 \text{ seconds}}{\text{page}} \times M \text{ pages} =$$

Time for M-page report $= 30\,M$ seconds $\boxed{4}$

(Use Strategy 10: Know how to use units.)

To change time from seconds to minutes we multiply

$$\text{by } \frac{1 \text{ minute}}{60 \text{ seconds}} . \quad \boxed{5}$$

Applying $\boxed{5}$ to $\boxed{4}$, we get

$$\begin{array}{l}\text{Time for } M\text{-page} \\ \text{report, in minutes}\end{array} = 30M \text{ seconds} \times \frac{1 \text{ minute}}{60 \text{ seconds}}$$

$$= \frac{30\,M \text{ minutes}}{60}$$

$$= \frac{M}{2} \text{ minutes}$$

(Math Refresher #201 and #121)

22. Choice B is correct.

Given: On Friday, the satellite passed over
Washington, D.C., at midnight $\boxed{1}$
Complete orbit = 5 hours $\boxed{2}$

(Use Strategy 17: Use the given information effectively.)

Using $\boxed{2}$, we see that five complete
orbits = $5 \times 5 = 25$ hours = 1 day + 1 hour $\boxed{3}$

From $\boxed{1}$ and $\boxed{2}$ we know that

DAY	TIME PASSING OVER D.C.	
Friday	7:00 P.M., midnight	$\boxed{4}$

Applying $\boxed{3}$ to $\boxed{4}$, and continuing this chart, we have

Saturday	8:00 P.M., 1:00 A.M.
Sunday	9:00 P.M., 2:00 A.M.
Monday	10:00 P.M., 3:00 A.M.
Tuesday	11:00 P.M., 4:00 A.M.
Wednesday	midnight, 5:00 A.M.

(Logical Reasoning)

23. Choice D is correct. **(Use Strategy 2: Know how to find percent of a number.)**

$$\text{Let } x = \text{price of car} \qquad \boxed{1}$$
$$\text{Given: 1st reduction} = 30\% \qquad \boxed{3}$$
$$\text{2nd reduction} = 40\% \qquad \boxed{3}$$

We know amount of discount

$$= \text{percent} \times \text{price} \qquad \boxed{4}$$

Using $\boxed{1}$, $\boxed{2}$, and $\boxed{4}$, we get

$$\text{Amount of 1st discount} = 30\% \times x$$
$$= .30x \qquad \boxed{5}$$

(Use Strategy 13: Find unknowns by subtraction.) Subtracting $\boxed{5}$ from $\boxed{1}$, we have

$$\text{Reduced price} = x - .30x$$
$$= .70x \qquad \boxed{6}$$

Using $\boxed{3}$, $\boxed{6}$, and $\boxed{4}$, we get

$$\text{Amount of 2nd discount} = 40\% \times .70x$$
$$= .40 \times .70x$$
$$= .28x \qquad \boxed{7}$$

Subtracting $\boxed{7}$ from $\boxed{6}$, we have

$$\text{Price after 2nd reduction} = .70x - .28x$$
$$= .42x \qquad \boxed{8}$$

(Use Strategy 16: The obvious may be tricky!)

Since $\boxed{8}$ = $.42x$, it is 42% of the original price of x. This is *not* the answer to the question.

Since $\boxed{8}$ is 42% of the original it is the result of a 58% discount.

The answer is 58%.

(Math Refresher #200 and #114)

24. Choice B is correct.
$$\text{Let } x = 0.393939\ldots \qquad \boxed{1}$$

(Use Strategy 13: Find unknowns by multiplication.)

Multiply $\boxed{1}$ by 100. We get

$$100x = 39.393939\ldots \qquad \boxed{2}$$

(Use Strategy 13: Find unknowns by subtraction.)

Subtract $\boxed{1}$ from $\boxed{2}$. We get

$$99x = 39$$
$$x = \frac{39}{99}$$
$$x = \frac{13}{33} \qquad \boxed{3}$$

To find the difference between $\frac{2}{3}$ and $\boxed{1}$,

we need $\frac{2}{3} - \frac{13}{33} =$

$$\frac{22}{33} - \frac{13}{33} =$$

$$\frac{9}{33} = \frac{3}{11}$$

(Math Refresher #602)

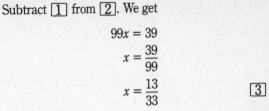

25. Choice A is correct.

$$\text{Given: Diameter of circle} = 2 \qquad \boxed{1}$$

(Use Strategy 14: Draw lines to help find the answer.)

Draw radius OD, with D the point of tangency and OB as shown above. $\qquad \boxed{2}$

(Use Strategy 18: Remember the equilateral triangle.)

Given: Triangle ACB is equilateral $\qquad \boxed{3}$

From $\boxed{2}$ we get $OD \perp AB$, since radius $\perp$ tangent at point of tangency. $\qquad \boxed{4}$
From $\boxed{4}$, we get $\angle ODB = 90°$ $\qquad \boxed{5}$
From $\boxed{3}$, we get $\angle ABC = 60°$ $\qquad \boxed{6}$

From the geometry of regular polygons, we know that OB bisects $\angle ABC$. $\qquad \boxed{7}$
From $\boxed{6}$ and $\boxed{7}$ we get $\angle DBO = 30°$ $\qquad \boxed{8}$

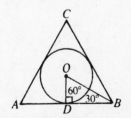

From $\boxed{5}$ and $\boxed{8}$ we have

$\triangle ODB$ is a 30–60–90 triangle

From $\boxed{1}$, we get $OD = 1$ $\qquad\boxed{9}$

(Use Strategy 18: Remember the special right triangles.)

Using $\boxed{9}$ and the properties of the 30–60–90 right triangle, we get $OB = 2, DB = 1\sqrt{3} = \sqrt{3}$ $\quad\boxed{10}$

We know $AB = 2 \times DB$ $\qquad\boxed{11}$

Substituting $\boxed{10}$ into $\boxed{11}$, we have

$$AB = 2\sqrt{3} \qquad\boxed{12}$$

We know the Area of an equilateral triangle = $\dfrac{(\text{side})^2 \sqrt{3}}{4}$ $\qquad\boxed{13}$

Substituting $\boxed{12}$ into $\boxed{13}$, we get

$$\text{Area of } \triangle ABC = \frac{(2\sqrt{3})^2\sqrt{3}}{4}$$

$$= \frac{12\sqrt{3}}{4}$$

$$= 3\sqrt{3} \qquad\boxed{14}$$

We know the Area of a circle = $\pi(\text{radius})^2$ $\quad\boxed{15}$

Substituting $\boxed{9}$ into $\boxed{15}$, we get

$$\text{Area of circle O} = \pi(1)^2$$

$$= \pi \qquad\boxed{16}$$

(Use Strategy 13: Find unknowns by subtraction.)

Subtracting $\boxed{16}$ from $\boxed{14}$, we get

Shaded area = $3\sqrt{3} - \pi$

(Math Refresher #308, #310, #508, #524, #525, and #509)

Explanatory Answers for Practice Test 5 (continued)

Section 3: Verbal Ability

As you read these Explanatory Answers, refer to "Using Critical Thinking Skills in Verbal Questions" (beginning on page 236) whenever a specific Strategy is referred to in the answer. Of particular importance are the following Master Verbal Strategies:

Sentence Completion Master Strategy 1—page 245.
Sentence Completion Master Strategy 2—page 246.
Analogies Master Strategy 1—page 236.
Reading Comprehension Master Strategy 2—page 263.

1. Choice A is correct. See **Sentence Completion Strategy 2.** Examine the first words of each choice. We eliminate Choice (C) imagined and Choice (E) intuitive. Reason: The effect of the long war was *not* imagined or intuitive (meaning knowing by a hidden sense). Now we consider Choice (B) immediate ... staring and Choice (D) delayed ... rebuilding. Neither word pair makes sense in the sentence. Choice (A) cumulative ... corrosion *does* make sense in the sentence.

2. Choice E is correct. See **Sentence Completion Strategy 3.** If you had tried to complete the sentence *before* looking at the five choices, you might have come up with any of the following words meaning "continually" or "regularly":

   constantly   always
   perpetually   persistently
             habitually

   The other choices are, therefore, incorrect.

3. Choice E is correct. See **Sentence Completion Strategy 2.** Examine the first word of each choice. Choice (D) crushes is eliminated because it is not

likely that the bee will crush the nectar from different flowers. Now consider each pair of words in the other choices. We find that Choice (E) extracts ... converts has the only word pair that makes sense in the sentence.

4. Choice C is correct. See **Sentence Completion Strategy 2.** Examine the first word of each choice. Choice (E) a futile does *not* make good sense because we do not refer to momentum as futile. Now consider the other choices. Choice (C) an increasing ... athletics is the only choice which has a word pair that makes sentence sense.

5. Choice D is correct. See **Sentence Completion Strategies 1 and 4.** The plan turned out to be impractical, unable to be logically supported. Note the root "ten" *to hold,* so "untenable" means *not holding.* Also note that the word "since" in the sentence is a *result indicator.*

6. Choice E is correct. See **Sentence Completion Strategy 1.** The word "effective" (meaning "serving the purpose" or "producing a result") makes good sense in the sentence. The other choices don't do that.

7. Choice D is correct. See **Sentence Completion Strategy 4.** The word "despite" is an opposition indicator. A strange and inevitable or *ineluctable* fate seemed to keep him helpless and unhappy, despite occasional periods of calm, peacefulness or *serenity.*

8. Choice B is correct. See **Sentence Completion Strategies 1 and 4.** Try each choice, being aware that "result" is, of course, a result indicator: Samuel Clemens chose the pen name Mark Twain.

9. Choice A is correct. See **Sentence Completion Strategy 1.** The word "versatile" means capable of turning competently from one task or occupation to another. Clearly, Choice (A) versatile is the only correct choice.

10. Choice B is correct. See **Sentence Completion Strategy 2.** Examine the first words of each choice. We eliminate Choice (C) avoided and Choice (D) realized because it does not make sense to say that Leonardo realized or avoided the Law of Gravity. Now we consider Choice (A) examined . . . colorful and Choice (E) suspected . . . mural, neither of which makes sentence sense. Choice (B) anticipated . . . anatomical is the only choice that makes sentence sense.

11. Choice C is correct. A run is a defect or damage in a stocking. A blemish is a defect or flaw on the skin—such as a pimple or blackhead. Also see **Analogy Strategy 5.** The word "run" may be a noun or a verb. It is a noun in this analogy. You might have selected Choice (D) thread : fabric, which is a Part-Whole relationship just as RUN : STOCKING is. However, we must include the idea of a defect or damage in the correct choice. Therefore, Choice D is incorrect.

    (Action to Object relationship and Part-Whole relationship)

12. Choice B is correct. A porthole is an opening that lets light into a ship. A pupil is an opening in the iris of the eye that lets light pass to the retina of the eye.

    (Part-Whole and Purpose relationship)

13. Choice B is correct. A procrastinator and delay are closely associated. A genius and creativity are closely associated.

    (Association relationship)

14. Choice A is correct. Something that is watertight does not allow water to enter. Something that is hermetic does not allow air to enter.

    (Result relationship)

15. Choice D is correct. A drizzle is a light rainfall, and a cloudburst is a heavy rainfall. A flurry is a light snowfall, and a blizzard is a heavy snowfall.

    (Degree relationship)

16. Choice E is correct. A seamstress follows a pattern to make clothing. A cook follows a recipe to make a meal. Consider also Choice (B) architect : blueprint. An architect *makes* a blueprint for someone else to follow. Therefore, Choice B is incorrect because it does not have the same relationship as the capitalized words and the Choice E words. See **Analogy Strategy 4.**

    (Action to Object and Result relationship)

17. Choice E is correct. A person may loot in order to get booty. A child may suckle in order to get milk. We have here a Purpose relationship. Choice (A) shout : attention also shows a purpose. However, attention is not a material thing such as booty and milk. Therefore, Choice A is incorrect. See **Analogy Strategy 4.**

    (Purpose relationship)

18. In this question, "pick" is a verb meaning to play an instrument by pulling at the strings of the instrument either with the fingers or with a plectrum. Just as one picks a banjo, one strums a guitar. We have here an action-object relationship. (The word "pick" may also be a verb meaning to choose. The same word may also be a noun meaning a plectrum, which is a small, thin piece of metal or plastic.) See **Analogy Strategy 5.**

    (Action to Object relationship)

19. Choice B is correct. An archipelago consists of many islands. A chorus consists of many voices. Consider Choice (A) universe : stars. The stars do *not* make up the entire universe. Some of the space of the universe consists of other matter. But the islands *do* make up the entire archipelago, and the voices *do* make up the entire chorus. So Choice A is incorrect. See **Analogy Strategy 4.**

    (Whole-Part relationship)

20. Choice C is correct. Something that is nugatory has no worth. Something that is desultory has no continuity.   **(Opposite relationship)**

21. Choice E is correct. To enervate is to deprive of strength. To incarcerate is to deprive of freedom.

    (Result relationship)

22. Choice B is correct. One who is licentious lacks morality. One who is pugnacious lacks amiability.

(Opposite relationship)

23. Choice B is correct. To glance at something is to give it cursory treatment. To delve into something is to give it thorough treatment.

(Association relationship)

24. Choice D is correct. The second paragraph states that "the other classes . . . adopted many of the outward characteristics of the aristocracy."

25. Choice C is correct. The second paragraph implies that the bourgeoisie was "rising to political power" and rivaling the power of the aristocracy.

26. Choice B is correct. The third and fifth paragraphs describe the castles as "strongholds" and "fortified houses."

27. Choice A is correct. This information is given in paragraph 3, where it states that "the Magyar armies" harried central Europe.

28. Choice C is correct. The fourth paragraph relates how "power passed into the hands of warriors invested by the monarchy and the Church with lands."

29. Choice D is correct. Paragraph 2 states, "Noblemen who became bishops or who founded new Orders helped to implant aristocratic principles . . . deep within . . . the Church."

30. Choice C is correct. Given the context of the rest of the sentence, it can be seen that Choice C is correct.

31. Choice B is correct. The last paragraph states that hunting was a rehearsal for war and it made up "for the lack of butcher's meat."

32. Choice C is correct. See paragraph 2: "Even the unarmed peasantry . . . long remained tenaciously loyal to their lords, held to their allegiance by that combination of love and fear, *amor et timor* . . ."

33. Choice A is correct. See paragraph 4: ". . . warriors . . . undertook . . . to protect the unarmed peasantry."

34. Choice B is correct. See paragraph 4: "It was recognized in theory that the Church and the monarchy were the principal powers and that they were bound by the nature of their office to ensure peace and security . . . but . . . they were too weak, too torn by internal conflicts to fulfill their obligations."

35. Choice D is correct. Given the context of the rest of the sentence, it would appear that because of the word "themselves," "retinue" must refer to humans. It is more likely that it refers to "attendants" than to "family."

898 • FOUR MORE PRACTICE SCHOLASTIC ASSESSMENT TESTS

Explanatory Answers for Practice Test 5 (continued)

Section 4: Math Ability

As you read these solutions, do two things if you answered the Math question incorrectly:

1. When a specific Strategy is referred to in the solution, study that strategy, which you will find in "Using Critical Thinking Skills in Math Questions" (beginning on page 174).

2. When the solution directs you to the "Math Refresher" (beginning on page 291)—for example, Math Refresher #305—study the 305 Math principles to get a clear idea of the Math operation that was necessary for you to know in order to answer the question correctly.

1. Choice D is correct. **(Use Strategy C: Use numbers in place of variables when a comparison is difficult.)**

Choose specific values of a and b satisfying the requirements.

EXAMPLE 1

$$a = 13 \quad \text{and} \quad b = 1$$

Thus, $a > b$

EXAMPLE 2

$$a = 1 \quad \text{and} \quad b = 13$$

Thus, $a < b$
So Choice D is the answer.

(Math Refresher #431)

2. Choice C is correct.

We know that a cube has 6 faces $\boxed{1}$

Given: Number of striped faces = 1 $\boxed{2}$
  Rest of faces are red. $\boxed{3}$

(Use Strategy 13: Find unknowns by subtraction.)

Subtract $\boxed{2}$ from $\boxed{1}$. We get

$$6 - 1 = 5$$

Thus $\boxed{3}$, Number of red faces, = 5 $\boxed{4}$

Column A	Column B	
The number of faces of the cube that are red	5	$\boxed{5}$

Substituting $\boxed{4}$ into $\boxed{5}$, we have

5 5

(Math Refresher #313)

3. Choice D is correct.

Method 1: We are given that
$$5 + m > 12 \text{ or } m > 7 \qquad \boxed{1}$$
$$5 + n > 12 \text{ or } n > 7 \qquad \boxed{2}$$

However, there is no equation relating m and n.

Method 2: **(Use Strategy C: Use numbers in place of variables when a comparison of the two columns is difficult.)** Choose specific values of m and n that satisfy $\boxed{1}$ and $\boxed{2}$.

EXAMPLE

$$m = 9 \text{ and } n = 8$$

Thus, $m > n$.

Hence, no conclusion can be drawn.

(Math Refresher #431)

4. Choice B is correct. **(Use Strategy 6: Know how to manipulate inequalities.)**

We are given that $x - y < 0$ $\boxed{1}$

Adding y to both sides of $\boxed{1}$, we get $x < y$

(Math Refresher #420)

5. Choice A is correct.

$$w > 0 \qquad \boxed{1}$$

Column A	Column B	
$\dfrac{w+3}{4}$	$\dfrac{w+6}{8}$	$\boxed{2}$

(Use Strategy D: Compare fractions by multiplying both columns by a positive number.) Multiply $\boxed{2}$ by 8. The columns become

$$2\cancel{8}\left(\frac{w+3}{\cancel{4}}\right) \qquad \cancel{8}\left(\frac{w+6}{\cancel{8}}\right)$$

$$2w + 6 \qquad\qquad w + 6 \qquad \boxed{3}$$

(Use Strategy A: Cancel like quantities from both columns by subtraction.) Subtract 6 from $\boxed{3}$. The columns become

$$2w \qquad\qquad\qquad w$$

Taking note of $\boxed{1}$, we know

$$2w > w$$

(Math Refresher #406)

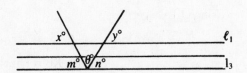

6. Choice C is correct.

Know the properties of parallel lines!

In the diagram above, we have

$$x = m \qquad \boxed{1}$$
$$y = n \qquad \boxed{2}$$

(Use Strategy 13: Find unknown expressions by addition.)

Thus, adding $\boxed{1}$ and $\boxed{2}$

$$x + y = m + n \qquad \boxed{3}$$

(Use Strategy 3: The whole equals the sum of its parts.)

Since ℓ_3 is a straight line, then

$$m + n + \theta = 180$$
$$\text{or } m + n = 180 - \theta \qquad \boxed{4}$$

Substituting $\boxed{3}$ into $\boxed{4}$

$$x + y = 180 - \theta$$

(Math Refresher #504 and #406)

7. Choice A is correct.

$$r > 3 \qquad \boxed{1}$$

Column A	Column B
The average rate when r words are typed in 3 hours	The average rate when 3 words are typed in r hours

(Use Strategy 2: Translate from words to algebra.) The columns become

$\dfrac{r \text{ words}}{3 \text{ hours}} =$	$\dfrac{3 \text{ words}}{r \text{ hours}} =$	
$\dfrac{r}{3}$ words/hour	$\dfrac{3}{r}$ words/hour	$\boxed{2}$

(Use Strategy 6: Know how to manipulate inequalities.) Divide $\boxed{1}$ by r. We get

$$\frac{r}{r} > \frac{3}{r}$$
$$1 > \frac{3}{r} \qquad \boxed{3}$$

Divide $\boxed{1}$ by 3. We get

$$\frac{r}{3} > \frac{3}{3}$$
$$\frac{r}{3} > 1 \qquad \boxed{4}$$

Combining $\boxed{4}$ and $\boxed{3}$, we get

$$\frac{r}{3} > \frac{3}{r} \qquad \boxed{5}$$

Substituting $\boxed{2}$ into $\boxed{5}$, the columns are

$$\frac{r}{3} \text{ words/hour} > \frac{3}{r} \text{ words/hour.}$$

(Math Refresher #200, #419, and #422)

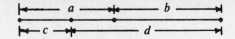

8. Choice A is correct.

From the diagram we see that

$$a > c \qquad \boxed{1}$$
$$d > b \qquad \boxed{2}$$

(Use Strategy 6: Know how to add inequalities.)

Adding $\boxed{1}$ and $\boxed{2}$, we get $a + d > b + c$

(Math Refresher #420)

9. Choice B is correct. **(Use Strategy 17: Use the given information effectively.)**

By definition of a circle, all points on the circumference are the same distance from the center. Any point inside the circle is closer to the center. Thus,

$$OA < OP$$

(Math Refresher #524 and Logical Reasoning)

10. Choice D is correct.

Column A	Column B
Area of parallelogram with a diagonal of length 6	Area of square with a diagonal of length 6

(Use Strategy 14: Draw lines to help solve the problem.)

Below is a square with a diagonal of length 6.

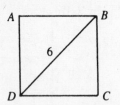

Below is a parallelogram *BEDF* with a diagonal of length 6, inside the square from above. $\boxed{1}$

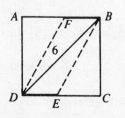

Below is square *ABCD* inside parallelogram *BEDF*, with a diagonal of length 6. $\boxed{2}$

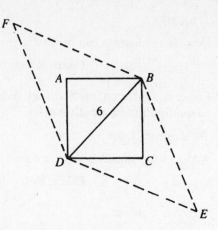

From $\boxed{1}$ it must be true that

Area of parallelogram *BEDF* with diagonal of length 6 $\Big\} < \Big\{$ Area of square *ABCD* with a diagonal of length 6.

From $\boxed{2}$ it must be true that

Area of square *ABCD* with a diagonal of length 6 $\Big\} < \Big\{$ Area of parallelogram *BEDF* with a diagonal of length 6.

Since two different relationships between the columns are possible, the relationship cannot be determined.

(Math Refresher #305 and #303)

11. Choice C is correct. **(Use Strategy 11: Use new definitions carefully.)**

Given: $x \, \textcircled{\wedge} \, y = y^4$ $\boxed{1}$

Column A	Column B
$7 \, \textcircled{\wedge} \, a$	$5 \textcircled{\wedge} \, a$

Using $\boxed{1}$, we get

$$7 \, \textcircled{\wedge} \, a = a^4 \qquad 5 \, \textcircled{\wedge} \, a = a^4$$

(Math Refresher #431)

12. Choice B is correct. **(Use Strategy 17: Use given information effectively.)**

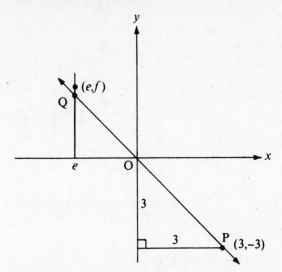

We know from the diagram that point P is (3, −3), since each leg of the right triangle is 3.

Slope of any line with points (x_1, y_1) and (x_2, y_2) is

$$\frac{y_2 - y_1}{x_2 - x_1}.$$ ⬚1

Line PO contains P (3, −3) and O (0,0). ⬚2

Substituting ⬚2 in ⬚1, the slope of PO is

$$\frac{0 - (-3)}{0 - 3}$$

$$= \frac{3}{-3}$$ ⬚3

$$= -1$$

From ⬚3 we know that every point on line PO must have x- and y-coordinates with the same value for the slope to have a value of −1. ⬚4

(Use Strategy 14: Draw lines in a diagram to make a problem easier.)

Note in our diagram that point Q has been added, as well as a line segment at x-coordinate e. Since Q is on line PO, we know from ⬚4 that the coordinates for Q are

$$x = e$$
$$y = -e$$ ⬚5

Since (e, f) is higher in the diagram than point Q, (e, f) has a greater y-coordinate. Therefore, from ⬚5, $f^2 > e^2$.

(Math Refresher #410, #416, #501, and #519)

13. Choice A is correct. **(Use Strategy 11: Use new definitions carefully.)**

In Row 1, there are 3 boxes.
In Row 2, there are 5 boxes.
In Row 3, there are 7 boxes.
Thus, in Row n, there are $2n + 1$ boxes, so that in Row 9, there are $2(9) + 1 = 19$ boxes.

You may also keep adding 2 for each new row:

Row	Number of Boxes
3	7
4	9
5	11
6	13
7	15
8	17
9	19

(Math Refresher #406 and #431)

14. Choice C is correct. **(Note: If you have to guess because you cannot solve the problem, use Strategy F: For straightforward calculations, try Choice C.)**

Here is the way to *solve* the problem:

Area of a triangle $= \frac{1}{2}$ (base)(height).

Thus,

$$\text{Area of } \triangle PQR = \frac{1}{2}(18)(h)$$
$$= 9h$$ ⬚1
$$\text{Area of } \triangle XYZ = \frac{1}{2}(6)(3h)$$
$$= 9h$$ ⬚2

From ⬚1 and ⬚2, we see that
Area of $\triangle PQR$ = Area of $\triangle XYZ$

(Math Refresher #306 and #431)

15. Choice D is correct. **(Use Strategy 2: Translate from words to algebra.)**

$$A_n + A_{n+1} = -1 + 1 \text{ or } 1 - 1$$
$$A_n + A_{n+1} = 0 \text{ in either case}$$ ⬚1
$$A_n - A_{n+1} = 1 - (-1) = 2$$ ⬚2
or
$$A_n - A_{n+1} = -1 - 1 = -2$$ ⬚3

Since ⬚1 < ⬚2 and ⬚1 > ⬚3, there are two different possible results. Thus, the answer cannot be determined.

(Math Refresher #200 and #431)

16. $\frac{7}{18}$ or .388 or .389

(Use Strategy 12: Try not to make tedious calculations.)

$$\left(\frac{1}{2} - \frac{1}{3}\right) + \left(\frac{1}{3} - \frac{1}{4}\right) + \left(\frac{1}{4} - \frac{1}{5}\right) +$$

$$\left(\frac{1}{5} - \frac{1}{6}\right) + \left(\frac{1}{6} - \frac{1}{7}\right) + \left(\frac{1}{7} - \frac{1}{8}\right) +$$

$$\left(\frac{1}{8} - \frac{1}{9}\right) =$$

$$\frac{1}{2} + \left(-\frac{1}{3} + \frac{1}{3}\right) + \left(-\frac{1}{4} + \frac{1}{4}\right) +$$

$$\left(-\frac{1}{5} + \frac{1}{5}\right) + \left(-\frac{1}{6} + \frac{1}{6}\right) + \left(-\frac{1}{7} + \frac{1}{7}\right) +$$

$$\left(-\frac{1}{8} + \frac{1}{8}\right) - \frac{1}{9} =$$

$$\frac{1}{2} + 0 + 0 + 0 + 0 + 0 + 0 - \frac{1}{9} =$$

$$\frac{1}{2} - \frac{1}{9} =$$

$$\frac{9}{18} - \frac{2}{18} =$$

$$\frac{7}{18}$$

(Math Refresher #110 and Logical Reasoning)

17. **8**

(Use Strategy 11: Use new definitions carefully.) The first five elements of the series, calculated by the definition, are

1, 2, 2, 4, 8

(Logical Reasoning)

18. $\frac{2}{3}$ or .667 or .666

(Use Strategy 2: Translate from words to algebra.)

$$p = \frac{3}{5} m \qquad \boxed{1}$$

$$q = \frac{9}{10} m \qquad \boxed{2}$$

(Use Strategy 13: Find unknowns by division of equations.)

Thus, $\dfrac{p}{q} = \dfrac{\frac{3}{5}\,\cancel{m}}{\frac{9}{10}\,\cancel{m}}$

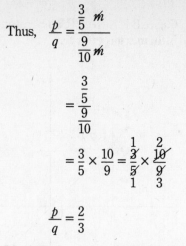

$$= \dfrac{\frac{3}{5}}{\frac{9}{10}}$$

$$= \frac{3}{5} \times \frac{10}{9} = \frac{\overset{1}{\cancel{3}}}{\cancel{5}} \times \frac{\overset{2}{\cancel{10}}}{\cancel{9}_{3}}$$

$$\frac{p}{q} = \frac{2}{3}$$

(Math Refresher #200 and #112)

19. **60**

(Use Strategy 2:

$$\text{Average} = \frac{\text{sum of values}}{\text{total number of values}}$$)

Given: $\dfrac{40 + 40 + 40 + z}{4} = 45$ $\boxed{1}$

Multiplying $\boxed{1}$ by 4,

$$40 + 40 + 40 + z = 180$$
$$120 + z = 180$$
$$z = 60$$

(Math Refresher #601 and #406)

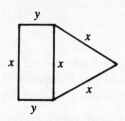

20. **36**

(Use Strategy 2: Translate from words to algebra.) When the given diagram has been labeled as above, then we know

$$3x = 39 \qquad \boxed{1}$$
$$xy = 65 \qquad \boxed{2}$$

From $\boxed{1}$ we have

$$x = 13 \qquad \boxed{3}$$

Substituting $\boxed{3}$ into $\boxed{2}$, we have

$$13y = 65$$
$$\text{or} \quad y = 5 \qquad \boxed{4}$$

The perimeter of the rectangle

$$= 2x + 2y$$
$$= 2(13) + 2(5)$$
$$= 36$$

(Math Refresher #200, #304, #308, and #431)

21. **44**

(Use Strategy 17: Use the given information effectively.)

Game		Darrin	Tom
1		69	43
2		59	60
3		72	55
4		70	68
5		78	73
Totals		348	299

We need the scores at the end of the first four games. We have been given the totals for all five games.

(Use Strategy 13: Find unknowns by subtraction.)

Darrin's Total = 348	☐1
Darrin's Game 5 = 78	☐2
Tom's Total = 299	☐3
Tom's Game 5 = 73	☐4

Subtract ☐2 from ☐1. We get
Darrin's Total for 1st four games = 348 − 78
$$= 270 \quad \boxed{5}$$

Subtract ☐4 from ☐3. We get
Tom's total for 1st four games = 299 − 73
$$= 226 \quad \boxed{6}$$

Subtracting ☐6 from ☐5, we have

Number of points Tom was behind Darrin after the first four games = 270 − 226
$$= 44$$

(Subtraction and Logical Reasoning)

22. **Choice $\frac{1}{4}$ or .25**

(Use Strategy 17: Use the given information effectively.)

The 17 slips, numbered from 1 to 17, consist of ☐1
8 even numbers (2,4,6, ... 16) and ☐2
9 odd numbers (1,3,5, ... 17). ☐3

Subtracting 5 even-numbered slips from ☐2 leaves
8 − 5 = 3 even-numbered slips. ☐4

Adding ☐3 and ☐4 we have
$$9 + 3 = 12 \text{ slips remaining} \quad \boxed{5}$$
We need $\dfrac{\text{even-numbered slips}}{\text{total numbered slips}}$ ☐6

Substituting ☐4 and ☐5 into ☐6, we have
$$\frac{3}{12} = \frac{1}{4}$$

(Math Refresher #603 and Logical Reasoning)

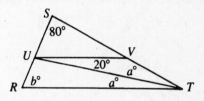

23. **60**

Given: $UV \parallel RT$ ☐1

From ☐1 we get $a = 20$, since alternate interior angles are equal ☐2

(Use Strategy 3: The whole equals the sum of its parts.) From the diagram we see that
$$\angle STR = a + a \quad \boxed{3}$$

Substituting ☐2 into ☐3, we have
$$\angle STR = 20 + 20 = 40 \quad \boxed{4}$$

We know that the sum of the angles in a triangle = 180, thus
$$\angle R + \angle S + \angle STR = 180 \quad \boxed{5}$$

We are given, in the diagram, that
$$\angle R = b \quad \boxed{6}$$
$$\angle S = 80 \quad \boxed{7}$$

Substituting ☐6, ☐7 and ☐4 into ☐5, we get
$$b + 80 + 40 = 180$$
$$b + 120 = 180$$
$$b = 60$$

(Math Refresher #504, #505, and #406)

24. **10**

(Use Strategy 2: Translate from words to algebra.)

Given: Rose's earnings = $44 ☐1
Rose's time worked = 8 days ☐2

(Use Strategy 13: Find unknowns by division.)

Dividing $\boxed{1}$ by $\boxed{2}$, we have

$$\text{Rose's daily rate} = \frac{\$44}{8 \text{ days}}$$

$$\text{Rose's daily rate} = \frac{\$11}{2 \text{ days}} \qquad \boxed{3}$$

Given: Total earnings to equal \$99 $\boxed{4}$

Substituting $\boxed{1}$ from $\boxed{4}$, we get

Amount left to be earned = \$55 $\boxed{5}$
We know
(daily rate)(days worked) = money earned $\boxed{6}$

Substituting $\boxed{3}$ and $\boxed{5}$ into $\boxed{6}$, we get

$$\left(\frac{\$11}{2 \text{ days}}\right)(\text{days worked}) = \$55$$

Multiplying $\boxed{7}$ by $\frac{2}{11}$ days, we have

$$\frac{2 \text{ days}}{11}\left(\frac{11}{2 \text{ days}}\right)(\text{days worked}) = (\overset{5}{\cancel{55}})\frac{2}{11} \text{ days}$$

$$\text{days worked} = 10 \text{ days}$$
(Math Refresher #200, #406, and #121)

25. **48**

Given: Areas of all 12 triangles are the same $\boxed{1}$
         Area of outlined region = 256 $\boxed{2}$
         Area of square $ABCD$ = 128 $\boxed{3}$

(Use Strategy 3: The whole equals the sum of the parts.)

By looking at the diagram, we observe

Area of 8 triangles (I, II, ... , VIII) = Area of Outlined Region − Area of Square $ABCD$.
Substituting $\boxed{2}$ and $\boxed{3}$ into the above, we get

Area of 8 triangles (I, ... , VIII)

$$= 256 - 128$$
$$= 128 \qquad \boxed{4}$$

Using $\boxed{1}$, we get
Area of each of the 12 triangles =
$$\frac{\text{Area of 8 triangles}}{8}$$

Substituting $\boxed{4}$ into the above, we get

Area of each of the 12 triangles = $\frac{128}{8}$

Area of each of the 12 triangles = 16 $\boxed{5}$

(Use Strategy 3: The whole equals the sum of its parts.)

Shaded Area = Area $\triangle$V + Area $\triangle$VI +
Area $\triangle$XI $\boxed{6}$

Substituting $\boxed{1}$ and $\boxed{5}$ into $\boxed{6}$, we get

Shaded Area = 16 + 16 + 16 = 48

(Logical Reasoning)

Explanatory Answers for Practice Test 5 (continued)

Section 5: Verbal Ability

As you read these Explanatory Answers, refer to "Using Critical Thinking Skills in Verbal Questions" (beginning on page 236) whenever a specific Strategy is referred to in the answer. Of particular importance is the following Master Verbal Strategy:

Reading Comprehension Master Strategy 2—page 263.

1. Choice C is correct. Throughout Passage A, the author is bringing out the fact that violence is widely shown and well received on television. For example: Line 1: "Violence is alive and well on television." Lines 4–6: ". . . as a result of . . . the horror of violence." Lines 12–13: "Violence on TV . . . in recent years." Although Choices A, B, D, and E are discussed or implied in the passage, none of these choices summarizes the content of the passage as a whole. Therefore, these choices are incorrect.

2. Choice D is correct. See lines 30–33: "The simple gunfight . . . for hundreds to die." Accordingly, Choice A is incorrect. Choices B and C are incorrect because there is no violence shown on the screen in these choices. Choice E is incorrect because the violence of a double murder by a jealous husband hardly compares in intensity with the violence of a bomb exploding in a bus carrying a busload of innocent civilians.

3. Choice E is correct. See lines 30–33: "The simple gunfight of the past . . . for hundreds to die." Choice A is incorrect because, though the statement may be true, the passage nowhere indicates that TV programs generally are different today from what they were a generation ago. Choice B is incorrect. See lines 37–38: "Many people . . . the way of the world." Choice C is incorrect. See lines 12–14: "Vio-

lence on TV . . . and more action series." Choice D is incorrect. See lines 38–41: "It is high time . . . viewing televised violence." No mention is made in the passage that broadcasting stations are doing any warning or notifying about the dangers of showing violence on TV.

4. The cruelties of our prison system are referred to in lines 63–69: ". . . just as so much of our current violence is socially acceptable . . . classes of society." The horrors of our prisons were current at the time the author wrote this article, and they are current today. The violence spoken about in Choices A, B, and D were socially acceptable at the time they occurred in the past. The question asks for an illustration of *current* "socially acceptable" violence. Accordingly, Choices A, B, and D are incorrect. Choice E, though it refers to current violence, is *not* socially acceptable. See lines 70–74: "What we have now . . . familiar 'crime in the streets.' " Therefore, Choice E is incorrect.

5. Choice A is correct. The author's definition of violence is extremely broad—including not only acts of force but also the social infliction of harm as in "exploiting women and children in textile mills and sweatshops" (lines 58–59). Passage B refers to acts of violence other than those expressed in Choices B and C. Therefore, these choices are incorrect. One

could easily cite illegal conduct on the part of the government or a citizen that is *not* of a violent nature. Therefore, Choice D is incorrect. The FBI could conceivably commit an act of violence. The author would not condone this. See lines 77–79: "But now, too, official violence . . . numerous sympathizers." Therefore, Choice E is incorrect.

6. Choice A is correct. The author of Passage B describes current violence as "acceptable neither to the authorities nor to the victims" [Item I]. Item II and Item III are not indicated anywhere in the passage. Therefore, only Choice A is correct.

7. Choice C is correct. It indicates the only form of violence that is *not* mentioned in Passage B. The following line references are given to indicate that Choices A, B, D, and E represent forms of violence that *are* mentioned in the passage. Choice A—see lines 48–49: ". . . the lawlessness . . . during Reconstruction and after." Choice B—see lines 43–44: ". . . our almost . . . against the Indians." Choice D— see lines 44–45: ". . . and all the others . . . Mexicans in Texas." Choice E—see lines 46–47: ". . . the pervasive violence of slavery."

8. Choice D is correct. The author, throughout Passage B, expresses opposition to any type of violence— whether one engages in violence or tolerates it. Therefore, Choice D is correct because the author would not approve of the violence practiced by football players. Accordingly, Choices A, B, C, and E are incorrect. Although Choice A involves violence, a person who tries to prevent a mugging is obviously opposed to the violence of the mugger.

9. Choice C is correct. In the context of the rest of the sentence in lines 2–3 and line 46, you can see that "pervasiveness" means "seeping through." Note that Choice A is incorrect because in lines 2–3, the word "variety" is used and would be redundant if repeated. This is also true for Choice B, "televised."

10. Choice E is correct. See lines 17–18, 24, and 31.

11. Choice A is correct. The author's attitude in Passage B is that violence as shown historically is "a way of life." Thus if violence were curtailed on television, it would still exist elsewhere and continue to exist.

12. Choice D is correct. Only the author of Passage A proposes a direct resolution—lines 38–41. The statement in Choice A is *true*. See lines 70–89. The statement in Choice B is *true*. See lines 29–31 and 43–69. The statement in Choice C is *true*. The author of Passage A primarily talks only about televised violence, whereas the author of Passage B refers to corporate violence, air pollution, prison violence, and the like. The statement in Choice E is *true*. See lines 38–41 and lines 42–69.

13. Choice C is correct. It can be seen from what precedes in Passage B that "polarization" must mean some very great opposing viewpoints. Don't be lured into Choice A, thinking that polarization has to do with electrical current; or Choice B, that polarization has to do with governments, since society was discussed; or Choice D, that polarization has to do with religion because religious dissent was mentioned; or Choice E, that polarization has to do with climate because we have a north and south pole.

Explanatory Answers for Practice Test 5 (continued)

Section 6: Math Ability

As you read these solutions, do two things if you answered the Math question incorrectly:

1. When a specific Strategy is referred to in the solution, study that strategy, which you will find in "Using Critical Thinking Skills in Math Questions" (beginning on page 174).

2. When the solution directs you to the "Math Refresher" (beginning on page 291)—for example, Math Refresher #305—study the 305 Math principles to get a clear idea of the Math operation that was necessary for you to know in order to answer the question correctly.

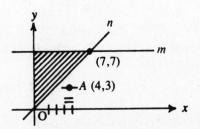

1. Choice A is correct. **(Use Strategy 17: Use the given information effectively.)** Since n goes through point O, the origin, whose coordinates are (0,0), and through (7,7), all of the points on n have the same x and y coordinates. Choice A, (4,3), is 4 units to the right of O but only 3 units up. It is below n and not in the shaded area.

    (Math Refresher #410)

2. Choice B is correct. **(Use Strategy 2: Translate from words to algebra.)** This problem tests the concepts of set union and set intersection. We can solve these types of problems with a diagram. Let

    c = set of all calculus students
    p = set of all physics students

Thus, draw the diagram:

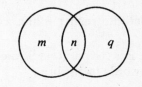

Where

m = number of students taking *only* calculus
q = number of students taking *only* physics
n = number of students taking *both* calculus and physics

Thus,

$m + n$ = number of students in calculus class
$n + q$ = number of students in physics class
$m + n + q$ = number of students taking either calculus or physics or both

We are given that

$$m + n + q = 36 \qquad \boxed{1}$$
$$n = 10 \qquad \boxed{2}$$
$$m + n = 31 \qquad \boxed{3}$$

We want to find

$$n + q \qquad \boxed{4}$$

(Use Strategy 13: Find unknowns by subtracting equations.) Subtract equation $\boxed{2}$ from equation $\boxed{3}$ to get

$$m = 21 \qquad \boxed{5}$$

Now subtract equation $\boxed{5}$ from equation $\boxed{1}$ to get

$$n + q = 15$$

(Math Refresher #406 and Logical Reasoning)

3. Choice C is correct. **(Use Strategy 2: Translate from words to algebra.)** The key is to be able to translate English sentences into mathematical equations.
    Let p = price of one frying pan
    m = price of one coffee mug
    We are given

    $$p + 2m = \$27 \qquad \boxed{1}$$
    $$p + m = \$23 \qquad \boxed{2}$$

    Subtract equation $\boxed{2}$ from equation $\boxed{1}$ to get

    $$m = \$4 \qquad \boxed{3}$$

    Substitute equation $\boxed{3}$ into equation $\boxed{2}$

    $$p + \$4 = \$23$$

    Subtract \$4 from both sides of the above equation

    $$p = \$19$$

    (Math Refresher #200, #406, and #407)

4. Choice E is correct. **(Use Strategy 2: Translate from words to algebra.)**

    Each tile is a square with perimeter = 2 feet
    Each side of the tile is $\frac{1}{4}$ (2 feet) = $\frac{1}{2}$ foot $\boxed{1}$

    The area of each tile is (Side)².
    Using $\boxed{1}$, we get area of each tile

    $$= \left(\frac{1}{2}\right)^2 = \frac{1}{4} \text{ square foot} \qquad \boxed{2}$$

    The area of the floor is $b \times h$ =
    8 feet × 6 feet =
    48 square feet $\boxed{3}$

    (Use Strategy 17: Use the given information effectively.)

    The number of tiles necessary, at minimum, to cover the floor

    $$= \frac{\text{Area of floor}}{\text{Area of 1 tile}} \qquad \boxed{4}$$

Substituting $\boxed{2}$ and $\boxed{3}$ into $\boxed{4}$ we get:
The number of tiles necessary, at minimum, to cover the floor

$$= \frac{48}{\frac{1}{4}} = \$48 \times \frac{4}{1}$$

The number of tiles necessary, at minimum, to cover the floor

$$= 192$$

(Math Refresher #200 and #303)

5. Choice E is correct.
    The only restriction is that 9 and 12 must each divide Q without a remainder. $\boxed{1}$

    (Use Strategy 7: Use numerics to help find the answer.)

    Choose specific values for Q that satisfy $\boxed{1}$.

    EXAMPLE 1

    $$Q = 36$$

    Then, Q will divide 36 and 72.

    EXAMPLE 2

    $$Q = 108$$

    Then, Q will divide neither 36 nor 72. Clearly, the answer to this question depends on the specific value of Q.

    (Math Refresher #431)

6. Choice B is correct. Since $DC \perp AC$, $\angle DCB$ is a right angle and has a measure of 90°. **(Use Strategy 3: The whole equals the sum of its parts.)** Since the sum of the angles of a $\triangle$ is 180°, we have

    $$\angle DBC + 90 + 20 = 180$$
    $$\angle DBC = 70 \qquad \boxed{1}$$

    Since $EB \perp BD$, $\angle DBE$ is a right angle and has a measure of 90° $\boxed{2}$
    (Use Strategy 3: The whole equals the sum of its parts.) The whole straight $\angle ABC$ is = to the sum of its parts. Thus

    $$\angle DBC + \angle DBE + x = 180 \qquad \boxed{3}$$

    Substituting $\boxed{1}$ and $\boxed{2}$ into $\boxed{3}$ we have

    $$70 + 90 + x = 180$$
    $$x = 20$$

    (Math Refresher #501, #505, #406, and #431)

7. Choice D is correct. **(Use Strategy 3: The whole equals the sum of its parts.)**

    Volume of rectangular solid
    = Volume of small compartment
    + Volume of larger compartment $\boxed{1}$

    Area of rectangular dividing wall
    $= l \times w$

    $39\text{cm}^2 = 13\text{cm} \times w$

    $3\text{cm} = w$ $\boxed{2}$

    $\boxed{2}$ is the height of the rectangular solid as well.

    Volume of rectangular solid $= l \times w \times h$
    $= 15\text{cm} \times 12\text{cm} \times h$ $\boxed{3}$

    Substituting $\boxed{2}$ into $\boxed{3}$, we get

    Volume of rectangular solid =
    $15\text{cm} \times 12\text{cm} \times 3\text{cm}$
    Volume of rectangular solid $= 540\text{cm}^3$ $\boxed{4}$

    Volume of small compartment
    = Area of base × height
    $= \frac{1}{2} \times 12\text{cm} \times 5\text{cm} \times 3\text{cm}$ $\boxed{5}$

    Volume of small compartment $= 90\text{cm}^3$

    Substitute $\boxed{4}$ and $\boxed{5}$ into $\boxed{1}$. We get

    $540\text{cm}^3 = 90\text{cm}^3 +$ Volume of larger compartment
    $450\text{cm}^3 =$ Volume of larger compartment

    (Math Refresher #312 and #306)

8. Choice E is correct. **(Use Strategy 17: Use the given information effectively.)**

    Given: x $\boxed{1}$
    $11 - x$ $\boxed{2}$
    $x - 4$ $\boxed{3}$

    as the lengths of the three sides of a triangle.

    We know that the sum of any two sides of a triangle is greater than the third $\boxed{4}$

    First, we use $\boxed{1} + \boxed{2} > \boxed{3}$. We have

    $x + 11 - x > x - 4$
    $11 > x - 4$
    $15 > x$ $\boxed{5}$

    Next, we use $\boxed{2} + \boxed{3} > \boxed{1}$. We have

    $11 - x + x - 4 > x$
    $7 > x$ $\boxed{6}$

    To satisfy $\boxed{6}$ and $\boxed{5}$, we choose $\boxed{6}$.

    $7 > x$, or, $x < 7$ satisfies both $\boxed{7}$

    Finally, we use $\boxed{1} + \boxed{3} > \boxed{2}$. We have

    $x + x - 4 > 11 - x$
    $2x - 4 > 11 - x$
    $3x > 15$
    $x > 5$, or, $5 < x$ $\boxed{8}$

    (Use Strategy 6: Know how to manipulate inequalities.) Combining $\boxed{7}$ and $\boxed{8}$, we get

    $5 < x < 7$

    (Math Refresher #516, #419, and #420)

9. Choice B is correct.

    Given: $\dfrac{1}{11^{20}} - \dfrac{1}{11^{21}}$ $\boxed{1}$

    (Use Strategy 12: Don't make tedious calculations. Do it the easy way.)

    Rewrite $\boxed{1}$ as $\dfrac{1}{11^{20}} - \dfrac{1}{11^{20} \cdot 11} =$

    $\dfrac{1}{11^{20}}(1) - \dfrac{1}{11^{20}}\left(\dfrac{1}{11}\right) =$

    $\dfrac{1}{11^{20}}\left(1 - \dfrac{1}{11}\right) =$

    $\dfrac{1}{11^{20}}\left(\dfrac{11}{11} - \dfrac{1}{11}\right) =$

    $\dfrac{1}{11^{20}}\left(\dfrac{10}{11}\right) =$

    $\dfrac{10}{11^{21}} =$

    (Math Refresher #429 and #409 and Subtracting Fractions)

10. Choice B is correct.

    Given: a, b are integers
    Average of a, b and 4 is 6

    $\left(\text{Use Strategy 5:}\right.$
    $\left.\text{Average} = \dfrac{\textbf{Sum of values}}{\textbf{Total number of values}}\right)$

    Using $\boxed{2}$, we have

    $\dfrac{a + b + 4}{3} = 6$ $\boxed{3}$

    (Use Strategy 13: Find unknowns by multiplication.)

Multiply $\boxed{3}$ by 3. We get

$$3\left(\frac{a + b + 4}{3}\right) = (6)3$$

$$a + b + 4 = 18$$
$$a + b = 14 \qquad \boxed{4}$$

Using $\boxed{1}$ and $\boxed{4}$, the possibilities are:

$a + b$	ab	
$1 + 13$	13	Choice A
$2 + 12$	24	
$3 + 11$	33	
$4 + 10$	40	Choice C
$5 + 9$	45	
$6 + 8$	48	Choice D
$7 + 7$	49	Choice E

Checking all the choices, we find that only Choice B, 14, is not a possible value of ab.

**(Math Refresher #601 and #406
and Logical Reasoning)**

Explanatory Answers for Practice Test 5 (continued)

Section 7: Math Ability

As you read these solutions, do two things if you answered the Math question incorrectly:

1. When a specific Strategy is referred to in the solution, study that strategy, which you will find in "Using Critical Thinking Skills in Math Questions" (beginning on page 174).

2. When the solution directs you to the "Math Refresher" (beginning on page 291)—for example, Math Refresher #305—study the 305 Math principles to get a clear idea of the Math operation that was necessary for you to know in order to answer the question correctly.

1. Choice A is correct. **(Use Strategy 2: Translate from words to algebra.)**
Let x = Amount that Greg had to start.
Then $x + 5$ = Amount that Greg has after receiving $5 from David. $\boxed{1}$

$$\$25 = \text{Amount David has.} \qquad \boxed{2}$$

We are told that Greg now has $\frac{1}{5}$ as much as David does.
This translates to:

$$\text{Greg} = \frac{1}{5}(\text{David}) \qquad \boxed{3}$$

Substituting $\boxed{1}$ and $\boxed{2}$ into $\boxed{3}$, we get

$$x + 5 = \frac{1}{5}(25)$$

$$x + 5 = \frac{1}{5} \times 5 \times 5$$

$$x + 5 = 5$$

$$x = 0$$

(Math Refresher #200 and #406)

2. Choice C is correct.
The ratio of the perimeter of the larger square to that of the smaller is

$$\frac{6 + 6 + 6 + 6}{2 + 2 + 2 + 2} = \frac{24}{8} = \frac{3}{1} \text{ or } 3 : 1$$

One can arrive at this result directly if one remembers that the ratio of the perimeters of two squares is the same as the ratio of the lengths of the sides of the two squares.

(Math Refresher #303)

3. Choice E is correct. **(Use Strategy 9: Remember the rate, time, and distance relationship.)**
Remember that rate × time = distance

$$\text{or} \qquad \text{average rate} = \frac{\text{total distance}}{\text{total time}}$$

$$\text{or} \qquad \text{average rate} = \frac{1056 \text{ feet}}{12 \text{ seconds}}$$

$$= 88 \text{ feet/second}$$

(Math Refresher #201 and #202)

4. Choice B is correct.
Given: $2z + 1 + 2 + 2z + 3 + 2z = 3 + 1 + 2$
(Use Strategy 1: Cancel numbers from both sides of an equation.)
We can immediately cancel the +1, +2, and +3 from each side.

$$\text{We get } 2z + 2z + 2z = 0$$
$$6z = 0$$
$$z = 0$$

Thus, $z + 4 = 0 + 4 = 4$

(Math Refresher #406 and #431)

5. Choice D is correct. **(Use Strategy 17: Use the given information effectively.)**

$$\frac{1}{n^2}\left(\frac{m^5n^3}{m^3}\right)^2 = \frac{1}{n^2} = (m^2n^3)^2 = \frac{m^4n^6}{n^2} = m^4n^4$$

(Math Refresher #429)

6. Choice B is correct.

$$2(w)(x)(-y) - 2(-w)(-x)(y) =$$
$$-2wxy - 2wxy =$$
$$-4wxy$$

(Math Refresher #406)

7. Choice A is correct. **(Use Strategy 2: Translate from words to algebra.)**
The sum of the $\underbrace{\text{square of } x}_{x^2}$ and the $\underbrace{\text{square of } y}_{y^2}$

So, five times that quantity is

$$5(x^2 + y^2)$$

(Math Refresher #200)

8. Choice A is correct. **(Use Strategy 11: Use new definitions carefully.)**
From the definition we get

$$2 + 6 + 7 = 5Z$$
$$15 = 5Z$$
$$3 = Z$$

(Math Refresher #431)

9. Choice E is correct. **(Use Strategy 11: Use new definitions carefully.)**
Since $W, X, Y,$ and Z are distinct digits from 0 to 9, the largest possible sum of $W + X + Y = 7 + 8 + 9 = 24.$ ☐1

By definition, $W + X + Y = 5Z$ ☐2
Substituting ☐1 into ☐2, we get

$$\text{largest value of } 5Z = 24$$

(Use Strategy 8: When all choices must be tested, start with Choice E and work backward.) Look at the choices, starting with Choice E. If $Z = 5$, then $5Z = 25$, which is larger than 24. Thus, Choice E is correct.

(Math Refresher #431 and Logical Reasoning)

10. Choice C is correct. **(Use Strategy 2: Translate from words to algebra.)** We are given

$$p > 0 \quad ☐1$$
$$q > 0 \quad ☐2$$
$$x < 0 \quad ☐3$$
$$y < 0 \quad ☐4$$

(Use Strategy 6: Know how to manipulate inequalities.)

$$p > q \text{ or } q < p \quad ☐5$$
$$x > y \text{ or } y < x \quad ☐6$$

For I: Add $-p$ to both sides of inequality ☐5:

$$q - p < 0$$

Thus, I is less than zero.

For II: From inequalities ☐2 and ☐4, $qy < 0$, and II is less than zero.

For III: The value of p and x depends on specific values of p and x:

(Use Strategy 7: Use numerics to help decide the answer.)

EXAMPLE 1

$$p = 3 \text{ and } x = -5$$
Thus, $\qquad p + x < 0$

EXAMPLE 2

$$p = 5 \text{ and } x = -3$$
Thus, $\qquad p + x > 0$
Thus, II is not always less than zero. Choice C is correct.

(Math Refresher #420, #421, and #431)

11. Choice D is correct. **(Use Strategy 2: Translate from words to algebra.)**

$$N + 6N + 9N = 16N$$

Any divisor of 16 or of N will divide $16N$.

(Use Strategy 8: When all choices must be tested, start with Choice E and work backward.) Starting with Choice E, we see that 16 divides $16N$ evenly. Choice D, however, does *not* divide $16N$ evenly. Thus we have found the answer.

(Math Refresher #200 and #431)

12. Choice D is correct.

$$\text{We are given: } x = 3a - 18 \quad \boxed{1}$$
$$5y = 3a + 7 \quad \boxed{2}$$

We need $5y - x$. $\boxed{3}$

(Use Strategy 13: Find unknown expressions by subtracting equations.) Subtracting $\boxed{1}$ from $\boxed{2}$, we get

$$5y - x = 3a + 7 - (3a - 18)$$
$$= 3a + 7 - 3a + 18$$
$$5y - x = 25$$

(Math Refresher #406)

13. Choice B is correct. **(Use Strategy 2: Translate from words to algebra.)**

Given:

$$p + pq = 4(p - pq) \quad \boxed{1}$$

(Use Strategy 13: Find unknown expressions by division.) Since $pq \neq 0$, divide $\boxed{1}$ by p.

$$1 + q = 4(1 - q) \quad \boxed{2}$$
$$\text{or} \quad 1 + q = 4 - 4q$$
$$\text{or} \quad 5q = 3$$
$$\text{or} \quad q = \frac{3}{5}$$

Thus, q has exactly one value.
Since p cannot be determined from equation $\boxed{1}$, none of the other choices is correct.

(Math Refresher #406)

14. Choice D is correct. **(Use Strategy 17: Use the given information effectively.)**

Since $2 + \frac{1}{z} = 0$, we have

$$\frac{1}{z} = -2$$
$$z = -\frac{1}{2} \quad \boxed{1}$$

We need $9 + 9z$ $\boxed{2}$

Substituting $\boxed{1}$ into $\boxed{2}$, we get

$$9 + 9\left(-\frac{1}{2}\right) = 9 - 4\frac{1}{2} = 4\frac{1}{2} = \frac{9}{2}$$

(Math Refresher #406 and #431)

15. Choice C is correct. **(Use Strategy 3: The whole equals the sum of its parts.)** From the diagram, we see that each straight angle is equal to the sum of two smaller angles. Thus,

$$m = 180 - x \quad \boxed{1}$$
$$n = 180 - z \quad \boxed{2}$$

(Use Strategy 13: Find unknown expressions by addition of equations.) Adding $\boxed{1}$ and $\boxed{2}$ we have

$$m + n = 180 + 180 - x - z \quad \boxed{3}$$

We know that the sum of the angles of a triangle $= 180$
Therefore, $y + x + z = 180$
or $y = 180 - x - z$ $\boxed{4}$
Substituting $\boxed{4}$ into $\boxed{3}$, we have

$$m + n = 180 + y$$

Accordingly, Choice C is the correct choice.

(Math Refresher #406, #505, and #501)

16. Choice C is correct.

$$\text{We are given: } wx = y \quad \boxed{1}$$
$$\text{or } w = \frac{y}{x} \quad \boxed{2}$$

(Use Strategy 2: Translate from words to algebra.) If x and y are multiplied by 6, in $\boxed{1}$, we have

$$w(6)(x) = (6)(y)$$
$$wx = y$$
$$w = \frac{y}{x} \quad \boxed{3}$$

$\boxed{2}$ and $\boxed{3}$ are the same.

Therefore $\frac{y}{x} = 1\left(\frac{y}{x}\right)$

The answer is now clear.

(Math Refresher #200 and #406)

17. Choice C is correct. **(Use Strategy 2: Translate from words to algebra.)**
We know that the volume of a cube $= e^3$
We are told that $e^3 < 25$
(Use Strategy 17: Use the given information effectively.)

Since e is a positive integer (which was given),

$$e \text{ can be: } 1 \rightarrow 1^3 = 1$$
$$2 \rightarrow 2^3 = 8$$
$$3 \rightarrow 3^3 = 27$$
$$\text{etc.}$$

For $e = 2$, the volume is 8, which is < 25
Any larger e, will have a volume > 25
Thus, area of one face $= e^2 = 2^2 = 4$
Total area $= 6(4) = 24$

(Math Refresher #202 and #313)

18. Choice E is correct. **(Use Strategy 2: Translate from words to algebra.)**

$$\text{Let } s = \text{number of smokers}$$
$$n = \text{number of nonsmokers}$$
$$\text{Then } s + n = \text{Total number of passengers.}$$

We are given: $\dfrac{s}{n} = \dfrac{2}{3}$ or $s = \dfrac{2}{3}n$ $\boxed{1}$

and: $s = \dfrac{1}{3}(s + n) + 5$ $\boxed{2}$

Substituting $\boxed{1}$ into $\boxed{2}$, we have

$$\frac{2}{3}n = \frac{1}{3}\left(\frac{2}{3}n + n\right) + 5$$

$$\frac{2}{3}n = \frac{1}{3}\left(\frac{2}{3}n + \frac{3}{3}n\right) + 5$$

$$\frac{2}{3}n = \frac{1}{3}\left(\frac{5}{3}n\right) + 5$$

$$\frac{2}{3}n = \frac{5}{9}n + 5 \qquad \boxed{3}$$

Multiplying both sides of $\boxed{3}$ by 9, we get

$$9\left(\frac{2}{3}n\right) = 9\left(\frac{5}{9}n + 5\right)$$

$$\frac{18}{3}n = 5n + 45$$

$$6n = 5n + 45$$

$$n = 45$$

$$s = \frac{2}{3}(45) = 30$$

$$s + n = 75$$

(Math Refresher #200 and #406)

19. Choice B is correct. **(Use Strategy 3: The whole equals the sum of its parts.)** The path is made up of 4 semicircles, three of diameter 4 and one of diameter 8.

[Remember circumference is $2\pi r$. Thus, $\dfrac{1}{2}$ circumference $= \dfrac{1}{2}(2\pi r)$.]
Therefore, the length of the path is

$$= \frac{1}{2}(2\pi)\left(\frac{4}{2}\right) + \frac{1}{2}(2\pi)\left(\frac{4}{2}\right) + \frac{1}{2}(2\pi)\left(\frac{4}{2}\right)$$
$$+ \frac{1}{2}(2\pi)\left(\frac{8}{2}\right)$$

$$= 10\pi$$

(Math Refresher #310 and #311)

20. Choice C is correct. **(Use Strategy 10: Know how to use units.)**

$$\frac{7x}{144} \text{ yards} = \left(\frac{7x}{144} \text{ yards}\right)\left(\frac{36 \text{ inches}}{\text{yards}}\right) =$$

(Use Strategy 19: Factor and reduce.)

$$= \frac{7x}{12 \times 12} \times 12 \times 3 \text{ inches}$$

$$= \frac{7x}{3 \times 4} \times 3 \text{ inches}$$

$$\frac{7x}{144} \text{ yards} = \frac{7x}{4} \text{ inches} \qquad \boxed{1}$$

$$\frac{5y}{12} \text{ feet} = \left(\frac{5y}{12} \text{ feet}\right)\left(12 \frac{\text{inches}}{\text{foot}}\right) =$$

$$\frac{5y}{12} \text{ feet} = 5y \text{ inches} \qquad \boxed{2}$$

(Use Strategy 13: Find unknown expressions by addition of equations.) Adding $\boxed{1}$ and $\boxed{2}$, we have

$$\frac{7x}{144} \text{ yards} + \frac{5y}{12} \text{ feet} = \left(\frac{7x}{4} + 5y\right) \text{ inches}$$

(Math Refresher #121 and #431)

$$
\begin{array}{ccccccc}
A & B & C & D & E & F & G
\end{array}
$$

21. Choice C is correct.

Given:
AG is divided into 6 equal segments $\qquad \boxed{1}$

Radius of circle, centered at $F = \dfrac{1}{5}AG$ $\qquad \boxed{2}$

(Use Strategy 14: Label unknown quantities)

Label segments with "a" as shown in above diagram.

Using $\boxed{2}$, radius of circle centered at $F = \frac{1}{5}(AG)$

$$= \frac{1}{5}(6a)$$

$$= 1\frac{1}{5}a$$

This means from the center at F, the left tip of the radius of the circle is $1\frac{1}{5}a$ from point F. Thus the circumference hits the line between D and E.

(Math Refresher #200, #419, and #524)

22. Choice A is correct.

$$\text{Given: } x < 0 \qquad \boxed{1}$$
$$y < 0 \qquad \boxed{2}$$

(Use Strategy 6: Know how to manipulate inequalities.)

Multiply $\boxed{1}$ by $\boxed{2}$, we get

$$x \cdot y > 0 \qquad \boxed{3}$$

Thus I is always positive

Adding $\boxed{1}$ and $\boxed{2}$ we get

$$x + y < 0 \qquad \boxed{4}$$

Thus II is not positive

(Use Strategy 7: Use numerics to help find the answer.)

$$\text{Let } x = -2, y = -3$$
$$\text{III becomes } x - y = -2 - (-3)$$
$$= -2 + 3$$
$$= 1 \qquad \boxed{5}$$

Now let $x = -3, y = -2$

Now let $x = -3, y = -2$

$$\text{III becomes } x - y = -3 - (-2)$$
$$= -3 + 2$$
$$= -1 \qquad \boxed{6}$$

From $\boxed{5}$ and $\boxed{6}$ we see that III is not always positive.

Using $\boxed{3}$, $\boxed{4}$ and $\boxed{7}$, we find that only Choice A, I only, is correct.

(Math Refresher #419, #425, and #431)

23. Choice D is correct.

$$\text{Given: } a + 3b = 11 \qquad \boxed{1}$$
$$a \text{ and } b \text{ are positive integers} \qquad \boxed{2}$$

(Use Strategy 17: Use the given information effectively.)

From $\boxed{1}$, we get

$$a = 11 - 3b \qquad \boxed{3}$$

From $\boxed{3}$ we see that a will be largest when b is smallest. Using $\boxed{2}$, we get

$$b = 1 \text{ is its smallest value} \qquad \boxed{4}$$

Substituting $\boxed{4}$ into $\boxed{3}$, we have

$$a = 11 - 3(1)$$
$$a = 11 - 3$$
$$a = 8$$

(Math Refresher #406 and Logical Reasoning)

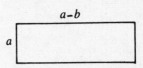

24. Choice B is correct. **(Use Strategy 2: Translate from words to algebra.)**

Perimeter of a rectangle

$$= 2(\text{length}) + 2(\text{width}) \; \boxed{1}$$

Substituting from the diagram into $\boxed{1}$, we have

$$\text{Perimeter} = 2(a - b) + 2(a)$$
$$= 2a - 2b + 2a$$
$$\text{Perimeter} = 4a - 2b$$

(Math Refresher #200, #304, and #431)

25. Choice E is correct.

$$\begin{array}{r} AB \\ + \; BA \\ \hline CDC \end{array}$$

Given: A, B, C, and D are different digits. $\boxed{1}$

The largest possible AB is 98. Thus,

$$\begin{array}{r} 98 \\ + \; 89 \\ \hline 187 \end{array}$$

Thus, the only possible value for C is 1 $\qquad \boxed{2}$

(It cannot be greater than 1 since we used the largest value of AB.)

Using $\boxed{2}$, the problem becomes

$$\begin{array}{r} AB \\ BA \\ \hline 1D1 \end{array} \qquad \boxed{3}$$

We know that the sum of $B + A$ must end in a 1. $\boxed{4}$
Using $\boxed{4}$ and $\boxed{1}$ we know $B + A = 11$ $\boxed{5}$

(Use Strategy 8: When choices must be tested, start with E and use Strategy 7: Use numerics.)

Use Choice E.

$$\text{Let } A = 2 \qquad \boxed{6}$$

Substituting $\boxed{6}$ in $\boxed{5}$, we have

$$B + 2 = 11$$
$$B = 9 \qquad \boxed{7}$$

Using $\boxed{6}$ and $\boxed{7}$, the problem becomes

$$
\begin{array}{r}
29 \\
+ \ 92 \\
\hline
121
\end{array}
\qquad \boxed{8}
$$

This cannot be, since in $\boxed{1}$, we are told $A, B, C,$ and D are different digits. But we have $D = A$.

Thus, A cannot equal 2.

(Math Refresher #431 and Logical Reasoning)

PART 10

THE SAT-II WRITING TEST*

A major feature of SAT-II, the new Writing Test, will include a direct writing sample and multiple-choice questions that require recognition of the conventions of standard written English, appropriate diction, and effective and logical expression. The complete Writing Test will be given at five Saturday and Sunday administrations per year.

The new SAT-II Writing Test will offer a number of advantages:

- An essay will provide a direct measure of writing ability;

- Essay topics will not assume any specific subject-matter knowledge;

- Revision-in-context passages present a context larger than a discrete sentence and therefore permit questions on logic, coherence, and organization;

- Revision-in-context tasks are similar to common in-class exercises in which students revise their own essays;

- Usage questions require students to recognize errors. Sentence-Correction questions require recognition of errors and selection of the correct rephrasing.

* Note: This test *does not* count toward your SAT-I score.

Content of the Writing Test

Multiple-Choice Questions: 40 Minutes, 60 Questions

- Usage

- Sentence Correction

- Revision-in-Context

Writing Exercise: 20 Minutes

Scoring the Writing Test

All essays will be scored holistically. Two readers will independently read each essay and score according to agreed-upon criteria.

Essay Reporting Service

Students may request that copies of essays be sent to high schools and/or colleges.

The Essay on the SAT-II Writing Test

Those of you who are taking the SAT-II Writing Test will be required to write an essay. Here's an example of the directions to the Essay:

SECTION 2	**Time—20 minutes** **1 Question**	**ESSAY**

Be sure to fill in the appropriate boxes at the top of the answer sheet for this section of the test. In the box labeled "TOPIC," please write the word **"Advance."**

You have 20 minutes to write an essay on the topic assigned below. DO NOT WRITE ON ANOTHER TOPIC. AN ESSAY ON ANOTHER TOPIC IS NOT ACCEPTABLE.

The essay is assigned to give you an opportunity to show how well you can write. You should, therefore, take care to express your thoughts on the topic clearly and effectively. How well you write is much more important than how much you write, but to cover the topic adequately you may want to write more than one paragraph. Be specific.

Your essay must be written on the lines provided on your answer sheet. You will receive no other paper on which to write. You will find that you have enough space if you write on every line, avoid wide margins, and keep your handwriting to a reasonable size.

Consider carefully the following quotation and the assignment below it. Then plan and write your essay as directed.

"Any advance involves some loss."

Assignment: Choose a specific example from personal experience, current events, or from your reading in history, literature, or other subjects and use this example as the basis for an essay in which you agree or disagree with the statement above. Be sure to be specific.

WHEN THE SUPERVISOR ANNOUNCES THAT 20 MINUTES HAVE PASSED, YOU MUST STOP WRITING THE ESSAY. DO NOT GO ON TO ANY OTHER SECTION IN THE TEST.

YOU MAY MAKE NOTES ON THIS PAGE, BUT YOU MUST WRITE YOUR ESSAY ON THE ANSWER SHEET.

Here are some more sample Essay topics:

Consider carefully the following statement and the assignment below it. Then, plan and write your essay as directed.

"Outrageous behavior is instructive. It reveals to us the limits of our tolerance."

Assignment: The quotation implies that those who go beyond accepted standards help us to clarify our own standards. Do you agree or disagree with the quotation? Discuss, supporting your position with examples from current affairs, literature, history, or your own experience.

Consider carefully the following quotation and the assignment following it. Then, plan and write your essay as directed.

"People seldom stand up for what they truly believe; instead they merely go along with the popular view."

Assignment: Do you agree or disagree with this statement? Write an essay in which you support your opinion with specific examples from history, contemporary affairs, literature, or personal observation.

Consider carefully the following statement and the assignment below it. Then, plan and write your essay as directed.

"Everything has its cost."

Assignment: Choose an example from literature, current affairs, history, or from personal observation in which a cause, an ideal, or an object had to be paid for at some cost. What was that cost? Was what was gained worth it, or was the cost too high? Give reasons for your position.

Important Tips on How to Write the Best Essay

Making Your Sentences Effective

What Is Style?

Many good ideas are lost because they are expressed in a dull, wordy, involved way. We often have difficulty following—we may even ignore—instructions that are hard to read. Yet we find other instructions written in such a clear and simple way that a child could easily follow them. This way of writing—the words we choose and the way we use them—we call style.

No two people write exactly alike. Even when writing about the same thing, they probably will say it differently. Some will say it more effectively than others, of course; what they say will be more easily read and understood. But there is seldom any one best way to say something. Rather, there are usually several equally good ways. This flexibility is what makes English such a rich language.

Style can't be taught; each person's style is like personality—it is unique to him or her. But we can each improve our style. Let us consider how we can improve our writing style by improving our sentences.

How to Write Effective Sentences

We speak in sentences; we write in sentences. A single word or phrase sometimes carries a complete thought, but sentences are more often the real units of thought communication.

Writing good sentences takes concentration, patience, and practice. It involves much more than just stringing words together, one after another, as they tumble from our minds. If writers aren't careful, their sentences may not mean to the reader what they want them to; they may mean what they *didn't* want them to—or they may mean nothing at all.

This section discusses five things writers can do to write better sentences—or improve sentences already written. These are:

1. Create interest
2. Make your meaning clear
3. Keep your sentences brief
4. Make every word count
5. Vary your sentence patterns

Let's consider interest first.

1. Create Interest

We can make our writing more interesting by writing in an informal, conversational style. This style also makes our writing easier to understand and our readers more receptive to our thoughts.

Listen to two men meeting in the coffee shop. One tells the other, "Let me know when you need more paper clips." But how would he have written it? Probably as follows:

Request this office be notified when your activity's supply of paper clips, wire, steel gem pattern, large type 1, stock No. 7510-634-6516, falls below 30-day level prescribed in AFR 67-1, Vol. II, Section IV, subject: Office Supplies. Requisition will be submitted as expeditiously as possible to preclude noncompliance with appropriate directives.

Judging from the formal, academic style of much of our writing, we want to *impress* rather than *express*. There seems to be something about writing that brings out our biggest words, our most complex sentences, and our most formal style. Obviously this is not effective writing. We wouldn't dare say it aloud this formally for fear someone would laugh at us, but we will write it.

WRITE TO EXPRESS

One of the best ways to make our writing more interesting to the reader and, hence, more effective is to write as we talk. Of course we can't write *exactly* as we talk, and we shouldn't want to. We usually straighten out the sentence structure, make our sentences complete rather than fragmentary or run-on, substitute for obvious slang words, and so on. But we can come close to our conversational style without being folksy or ungrammatical or wordy. This informal style is far more appropriate for the kind of writing we do and for the kind of readers we have than the old formal style. And it certainly makes better reading.

BE DEFINITE, SPECIFIC, AND CONCRETE

Another way—and one of the surest—to arouse and hold the interest and attention of readers is to be definite, specific, and concrete.

2. Make Your Meaning Clear

You do not need to be a grammarian to recognize a good sentence. After all, the first requirement of grammar is that you focus your reader's attention on the meaning you wish to convey. If you take care to make your meaning clear, your grammar will usually take care of itself. You can, however, do three things to make your meaning clearer to your reader: (1) emphasize your main ideas, (2) avoid wandering sentences, and (3) avoid ambiguity.

EMPHASIZE THE MAIN IDEAS

When we talk we use gestures, voice changes, pauses, smiles, frowns, and so on to emphasize our main ideas. In writing we have to use different methods for emphasis. Some are purely mechanical; others are structural.

Mechanical devices include capital letters, underlining or italics, punctuation, and headings. Printers used to capitalize the first letter of a word they wanted to emphasize. We still occasionally capitalize, or use a heavier type to emphasize words, phrases, or whole sentences. Sometimes we underline or italicize words that we want to stand out. Often we label or head main sections or subdivisions, as we have done in this book. This effectively separates main ideas and makes them stand out so that our reader doesn't have to search for them.

But mechanical devices for emphasizing an idea—capitalization, particularly—are often overused. The best way to emphasize an idea is to place it effectively in the sentence. The most emphatic position is at the end of the sentence. The next most emphatic position is at the beginning of the sentence. The place of least importance is anywhere in the middle. Remember, therefore, to put the important clause, phrase, name, or idea at the beginning or at the end of your sentences, and never hide the main idea in a subordinate clause or have it so buried in the middle of the sentence that the reader has to dig it out or miss it altogether.

Unemphatic: People drive on the left side instead of the right side in England.
Better: Instead of driving on the right side, people in England drive on the left.

AVOID WANDERING SENTENCES

All parts of a sentence should contribute to one clear idea or impression. Long, straggling sentences usually contain a hodgepodge of unrelated ideas. You should either break them up into shorter sentences or put the subordinate thoughts into subordinate form. Look at this sentence:

The sergeant, an irritable fellow who had been a truck driver, born and brought up in the corn belt of Iowa, strong as an ox and 6 feet tall, fixed an angry eye on the recruit.

You can see that the main idea is "The sergeant fixed an angry eye on the recruit." That he was an irritable fellow, strong as an ox, and 6 feet tall adds to the main idea. But the facts that he had been a truck driver and had been born in Iowa add nothing to the main thought, and the sentence is better without them.

The sergeant, an irritable fellow who was strong as an ox and 6 feet tall, fixed an angry eye on the recruit.

AVOID AMBIGUITY

If a sentence can be misunderstood, it will be misunderstood. A sentence that says that "The truck followed the jeep until its tire blew out" may be perfectly clear to the writer, but it will mean nothing to the reader until the pronoun *its* is identified.

MAKE SURE THAT YOUR MODIFIERS SAY WHAT YOU MEAN

"While eating oats, the farmer took the horse out of the stable." This sentence provides little more than a laugh until you add to the first part of the sentence a logical subject ("the horse"): "While the horse was eating oats, the farmer took him out of the stable." Sometimes simple misplacement of modifiers in sentences leads to misunderstanding: "The young lady went to the dance with her boyfriend wearing a low-cut gown." You can clarify this sentence by simply rearranging it: "Wearing a low-cut gown, the young lady went to the dance with her boyfriend."

3. Keep Your Sentences Brief

Sentences written like 10-word advertisements are hard to read. You cannot get the kind of brevity you want by leaving out the articles (*a, an,* and *the*). You can get brevity by dividing complex ideas into bite-size sentences and by avoiding unnecessary words and phrases and needless repetition and elaboration. Here are some suggestions that will help you to write short, straightforward sentences.

USE VERBS THAT WORK

The verb—the action word—is the most important word in a sentence. It is the power plant that supplies the energy, vitality, and motion in the sentence. So use strong verbs, verbs that really *work* in your sentences.

USE THE ACTIVE VOICE

Sentences written in the basic subject-verb-object pattern are said to be written in the *active voice*. In such sentences someone or something *does* something to the object—there is a forward movement of the idea. In sentences written in the *passive voice*, the subject merely receives the action—it has something done to it by someone or something, and there is no feeling of forward movement of the idea.

The active voice, in general, is preferable to the passive voice because it helps to give writing a sense of energy, vitality, and motion. When we use the passive voice predominantly, our writing doesn't seem to have much life, the actor in the sentences is not allowed to act, and verbs become weak. So don't rob your writing of its power by using the passive voice when you can use the active voice. Nine out of ten sentences will be both shorter (up to 25 percent shorter) and stronger in the active voice.

Let's compare the two voices:

Active: The pilot   flew   the aircraft.
(*Actor*)   (*action*)   (*acted upon*)

Passive: The aircraft was flown by the pilot.
(*Acted upon*)   (*action*)   (*actor*)

Now let's see some typical passive examples:

The committee will be appointed by the principal.
Reports have been received . . . .
Provisions will be made by the manager in case of a subway strike.

Aren't these familiar? In most of these we should be emphasizing the actor rather than leaving out or subordinating him or her.

See how much more effective those sentences are when they are written in the active voice.

The principal will appoint the committee.
We have received reports . . . .
The manager will make provisions in case of a subway strike.

AVOID USING THE PASSIVE VOICE

The passive voice always takes more words to say what could be said just as well (and probably better) in the active voice. In the passive voice the subject also becomes less personal and may seem less important, and the motion of the sentence grinds to a halt.

There are times, of course, when the passive voice is useful and justified—as when the person or thing doing the action is unknown or unimportant.

When we use the lifeless passive voice indiscriminately, we make our writing weak, ineffective, and dull. Remember that the normal English word order is subject-verb-object. There may be occasions in your writing when you feel that the passive voice is preferable. But should such an occasion arise, think twice before you write; the passive voice rarely improves your style. Before using a passive construction, make certain that you have a specific reason. After using it, check to see that your sentence is not misleading.

TAKE A DIRECT APPROACH

Closely related to passive voice construction is indirect phrasing.

It is requested . . . .
It is recommended . . . .
It has been brought to the attention of . . . .
It is the opinion of . . . .

Again this is so familiar to us that we don't even question it. But who requested? Who recommended? Who knows? Who believes? No one knows from reading such sentences!

This indirect way of writing, this use of the passive voice and the indirect phrase, is perhaps the most characteristic feature of the formal style of the past. There are many explanations for it. A psychiatrist might say the writer was afraid to take the responsibility for what he or she is writing or merely passing the buck. The writer may unjustifiably believe this style makes him or her anonymous, or makes him or her sound less dogmatic and authoritarian.

Express your ideas immediately and directly. Unnecessary expressions like *it, there is,* and *there are* weaken sentences and delay comprehension. They also tend to place part of the sentence in the passive voice. *It is the recommendation of the sales manager that the report be forwarded immediately* is more directly expressed as *The sales manager recommends that we send the report immediately.*

Change Long Modifiers

Mr. Barnes, who is president of the board, will preside.

Vehicles that are defective are . . .

They gave us a month for accomplishment of the task.

to Shorter Ones:

Mr. Barnes, the board president, will preside.

Defective vehicles are . . .

They gave us a month to do the job.

Break Up Long Sentences:

There is not enough time available for the average executive to do everything that might be done and so it is necessary for him to determine wisely the essentials and do them first, then spend the remaining time on things that are "nice to do."

The average executive lacks time to do everything that might be done. Consequently, he must decide what is essential and do it first. Then he can spend the remaining time on things that are "nice to do."

4. Make Every Word Count

Don't cheat your readers. They are looking for ideas—for meaning—when they read your letter, report, or directive. If they have to read several words that have little to do with the real meaning of a sentence or if they have to read a number of sentences to get just a little meaning, you are cheating them. Much of their time and effort is wasted because they aren't getting full benefit from it. They expected something that you didn't deliver.

MAKE EACH WORD ADVANCE YOUR THOUGHT

Each word in a sentence should advance the thought of that sentence. To leave it out would destroy the meaning you are trying to convey.

"Naturally," you say. "Of course!" But reread the last letter you wrote. Aren't some of your sentences rather wordy? Couldn't you have said the same thing in fewer words? And finally, how many times did you use a whole phrase to say what could have been said in one word, or a whole clause for what could have been expressed in a short phrase? In short, try tightening up a sentence like this:

The reason that prices rose was that the demand was increasing at the same time that the production was decreasing.

Rewritten:

Prices rose because the demand increased while production decreased.

Doesn't our rewrite say the same thing as the original? Yet we have saved the reader some effort by squeezing the unnecessary words out of a wordy sentence.

Now try this one:

Wordy: The following statistics serve to give a good idea of the cost of production.
Improved: The following statistics give a good idea of the production costs.
            or
            These statistics show production costs.

And this one:

Wordy: I have a production supervisor who likes to talk a great deal.
Improved: I have a talkative production supervisor.

In all of those rewritten sentences we have saved our reader some time. The same thing has been said in fewer words.

Of course you can be *too* concise. If your writing is too brief or terse, it may "sound" rude and abrupt, and you may lose more than you gain. You need, then, to be politely concise. What you are writing, what you are writing about, and whom you are writing for will help you decide just where to draw the line. However, the general rule, make every word count, still stands. Say what you have to say in as few words as clarity *and tact* will allow.

CONSOLIDATE IDEAS

A second way to save the reader's effort is to consolidate ideas whenever possible. Pack as much meaning as possible into each sentence *without making the sentence structure too complicated.*

Each sentence is by definition an idea, a unit of thought. Each time the readers read one of these units they should get as much meaning as possible. It takes just about as much effort to read a sentence with a simple thought as it does to read one with a strong idea or with two or three strong ideas.

There are several things we can do to pack meaning into a sentence. In general, they all have to do with summarizing, combining, and consolidating ideas.

Some people write sentences that are weak and insignificant, both in structure and thought. Ordinarily several such sentences can be summarized and the thought put into one good, mature sentence. For example:

We left Wisconsin the next morning. I remember watching three aircraft. They were F-4s. They were flying very low. I felt sure they were going to crash over a half a dozen times. The F-4 is new to me. I hadn't seen one before.

Rewritten:

When we left Wisconsin the next morning, I remember watching three F-4s, a type of aircraft I had never seen before. They were flying so low that over a half dozen times I felt sure they were going to crash.

When summarizing like this, be sure to emphasize the main action. Notice in the next example how we have kept the main action as our verb and made the other actions subordinate by changing them to verbals.

Poor: It was in 1959 that he *retired* from teaching and he *devoted* his time to *writing* his autobiography. (three verbs, one verbal)

Improved: In 1959 he *retired* from teaching to *devote* his time to *writing* his autobiography. (one verb, two verbals)

Here is an example similar to ones we might find in a directive:

Poor: The evaluation forms will be picked up from your respective personnel office. You should have these completed by 1700 hours, 18 May. They will be delivered immediately to the security section.

Notice that in the above instructions all of the actions are to be performed by the reader or "you." Now let's put these into one sentence, placing the things to be done in a series and using a single subject.

Improved: Pick up the evaluation forms from your personnel office; complete and deliver them to the security section by 1700 hours, 18 May. (The subject [you] is understood.)

The same thing can be done with subjects or predicates:

Poor: Horror stories shown on television appear to contribute to juvenile delinquency. Comic books with their horror stories seem to have the same effect. Even the reports of criminal activities which appear in our newspapers seem to contribute to juvenile delinquency.

Improved: Television, comic books, and newspapers seem to contribute to juvenile delinquency by emphasizing stories of horror and crime.

There is one more thing we can do to make our sentences better. We can vary their length and complexity. The following paragraphs suggest ways to do this.

5. *Vary Your Sentence Patterns*

We should, as a general rule, write predominantly short sentences. Similarly, we should keep our sentences simple enough for our readers to understand them easily and quickly.

But most people soon get tired of nothing but simple, straightforward sentences. So, give your reader an occasional change of pace. Vary both the length and the construction of your sentences.

VARY SENTENCE LENGTH

Some writers use nothing but short, choppy sentences ("The road ended in a wrecked village. The lines were up beyond. There was much artillery around.") In the hands of a Hemingway, from whom this example is taken, short sentences can give an effect of purity and simplicity; in the hands of a less skillful writer, choppy sentences are usually only monotonous.

The other extreme, of course, is just as bad. The writer who always writes heavy sentences of 20 to 30 words soon loses the reader. Some great writers use long sentences effectively, but most writers do not.

The readability experts suggest that, for the most effective *communication*, a sentence should rarely exceed 20 words. Their suggestion is a good rule of thumb, but sentence length should vary. And an occasional long sentence is not hard to read if it is followed by shorter ones. A fair goal for most letter-writers is an average of 21 words per sentence, or less. For longer types of writing, such as regulations and manuals, sentences should average 15 words or less. The sentences in opening paragraphs and in short letters may run a little longer than the average.

VARY SENTENCE CONSTRUCTION

Just as important as varied sentence length is variety of construction. Four common sentence categories are simple, compound, complex, and compound-complex.

A *simple sentence* consists of only one main (independent) clause:

Rain came down in torrents.
Rain and hail started falling. (Simple sentence with compound subject)
The storm began and soon grew in intensity. (Simple sentence with compound predicate)

A *compound sentence* has two or more main clauses:

Rain started falling, and all work stopped.
The storm began; all work stopped.
The storm began, the workers found shelter, and all work stopped.

A *complex sentence* has one main clause and at least one subordinate (dependent) clause. (Subordinate clauses are underlined in the following sentences.)

They were just starting their work <u>when the rain started</u>.
<u>Before they had made any progress</u>, the rain started falling.
The storm, <u>which grew rapidly in intensity</u>, stopped all work.

A *compound-complex sentence* has two or more main clauses and at least one subordinate clause. (Subordinate clauses are underlined in the following sentences.)

Rain started falling, and all work stopped <u>before they had made any progress</u>.
<u>Although the workers were eager to finish the job</u>, the storm forced them to stop, and they quickly found shelter.
They had made some progress <u>before the storm began</u>, but, <u>when it started</u>, all work stopped.

The names of the categories are really not important except to remind you to vary your sentence construction when you write. But remember that sentence variety is not just a mechanical chore to perform after your draft is complete. Good sentence variety comes naturally as the result of proper coordination and subordination when you write.

For example:

If two or more short sentences have the same subject, combine them into one simple sentence with a compound verb:

The men were hot. They were tired, too. They were also angry.
The men were hot and tired and angry.

If you have two ideas of equal weight or parallel thought, write them as two clauses in a compound sentence.

The day was hot and humid. The men had worked hard.
The men had worked hard, and the day was hot and humid.
The day was hot and humid, but the men had worked hard.

If one idea is more important than others, put it in the main clause of a complex sentence:

Poor: The men were tired, and they had worked hard, and the day was hot.

Better: The men were tired because they had worked hard on a hot day.
                 or
                 Although the day was hot and the men were tired, they worked hard.

If the adverbial modifier is the least important part of a complex sentence, put it first and keep the end position for the more important main clause:

Instead of: The men finished the job in record time, even though the day was hot and humid and they were tired.

Better: Even though the day was hot and humid and the men were tired, they finished the job in record time.

But be careful about having long, involved subordinate clauses come before the main clause. The reader may get lost or confused before getting to your main point or give up before getting to it. Also beware of letting too many modifying words, phrases, or clauses come between the subject and the verb. This is torture for the reader. The subject and the verb are usually the most important elements of a sentence; keep them close together whenever possible.

Other Types of Questions on the SAT-II Writing Test

Following are some directions and samples of some of the other question types on the SAT-II Writing Test.

Directions: The following sentences test your knowledge of grammar, usage, diction (choice of words), and idiom.

Some sentences are correct.
No sentence contains more than one error.

You will find that the error, if there is one, is underlined and lettered. Elements of the sentence that are not underlined will not be changed. In choosing answers, follow the requirements of standard written English.

If there is an error, select the one underlined part that must be changed to make the sentence correct and fill in the corresponding oval on your answer sheet.

If there is no error, fill in answer oval E.

EXAMPLE:

The other delegates and him immediately
     A   B   C
accepted the resolution drafted by the
                          D

neutral states. No error
          E

SAMPLE ANSWER

Ⓐ ● Ⓒ Ⓓ Ⓔ

Sample Questions with Answers

1. Even before he became the youngest player to win
     A
   the Wimbledon men's singles championship, Boris
               B
   Becker had sensed that his life would no longer be
        C   D
   the same. No error.
         E

2. If any signer of the Constitution was to return to life
                               A
   for a day, his opinion of our amendments would be
     B   C   D
   interesting. No error.
          E

3. The dean <u>of the college</u>, together <u>with</u> some other
      A   B
   faculty members, <u>are</u> planning a conference for
                       C
   the purpose of <u>laying</u> down certain regulations.
                    D
   <u>No error.</u>
    E

4. If one <u>lives</u> in Florida <u>one day</u> and in Iceland the
           A   B
   next, he is <u>certain</u> to feel the <u>change</u> in temperature.
                 C   D
   <u>No error.</u>
    E

5. <u>Now</u> that the stress of examinations and interviews
    A
   are over, we can <u>all</u> <u>relax</u> for a while. <u>No error.</u>
    B   C   D   E

6. The industrial <u>trend</u> <u>is</u> in the direction of <u>more</u>
                    A   B   C
   machines and <u>less</u> people. <u>No error.</u>
                  D   E

7. The American standard of living <u>is</u> still <u>higher</u>
                                     A   B
   <u>than most</u> of the <u>other countries</u> of the world.
    C   D
   <u>No error.</u>
    E

8. At last, <u>late</u> in the afternoon, a long line of flags and
    A   B
   colored umbrellas <u>were</u> seen moving <u>toward</u> the
                       C   D
   gate of the palace. <u>No error.</u>
                         E

9. Due to the failure of the air-cooling system, many in
    A
   the audience <u>had left</u> the meeting <u>before</u> the princi-
                  B   C
   pal speaker <u>arrived.</u> <u>No error.</u>
                 D   E

10. Psychologists and psychiatrists <u>will tell</u> us that it is
                                      A
    of utmost importance that a <u>disturbed</u> child <u>receive</u>
                                  B   C
    professional attention <u>as soon as</u> possible.
                             D
    <u>No error.</u>
     E

11. <u>After waiting</u> in line <u>for three hours</u>, <u>much to our</u>
     A   B   C
    disgust, the tickets <u>had been</u> sold out when we
     C   D
    reached the window. <u>No error.</u>
                          E

12. That angry outburst of <u>Father's</u> last night was so
                            A
    annoying that it resulted in our <u>guests</u> <u>packing up</u>
                                       B   C
    and leaving <u>this</u> morning. <u>No error.</u>
                  D   E

13. <u>Sharp</u> advances last week in the wholesale price of
     A
    beef <u>is</u> a strong indication of higher meat <u>costs</u> to
          B   C
    come, but so far retail prices continue <u>favorable.</u>
                                              D
    <u>No error.</u>
     E

14. An acquaintance with the memoirs of Elizabeth Bar-
    rett Browning and Robert Browning <u>enable</u> us to
                                         A
    appreciate the <u>depth of influence</u> that two people of
                     B
    talent can have <u>on</u> <u>each other.</u> <u>No error.</u>
                      C   D   E

15. The supervisor <u>was advised</u> to give the assignment
                     A
    to <u>whomever</u> he <u>believed</u> had a strong sense of
        B   C
    responsibility, and the courage <u>of</u> his conviction.
                                      D
    <u>No error.</u>
     E

16. If he <u>would have</u> <u>lain</u> quietly as instructed by the
    A   B
    doctor, he <u>might not</u> <u>have had</u> a second heart attack.
              C   D
    <u>No error.</u>
    E

17. The founder and, <u>for many years,</u> the <u>guiding spirit</u>
                      A   B
    of the "Kenyon Review" is John Crowe Ransom, <u>who</u>
                                                 C
    you must know <u>as</u> an outstanding American critic.
                  D
    <u>No error.</u>
    E

18. <u>Though</u> you may not <u>agree with</u> the philosophy of
    A   B
    Malcolm X, you must admit that he <u>had</u> tremendous
                                      C
    influence <u>over</u> a great many followers. <u>No error.</u>
              D   E

19. There is no objection to <u>him</u> joining the party
                             A
    <u>provided</u> he is willing to <u>fit in with</u> the plans of the
    B   C
    group and is <u>ready and</u> able to do his share of the
                 D
    work. <u>No error.</u>
          E

20. <u>Ceremonies</u> <u>were opened</u> by a drum and bugle corps
    A   B
    of Chinese children parading <u>up</u> Mott Street
                                 C
    in colorfulful uniforms. <u>No error.</u>
                             D   E

21. The reason <u>most</u> Americans <u>don't</u> pay much atten-
               A   B
    tion to <u>rising</u> African nationalism is <u>because</u> they
            C   D
    really do not know modern Africa. <u>No error.</u>
                                      E

22. There <u>remains</u> many reasons for the <u>animosity</u> that
          A   B
    <u>exists</u> <u>between</u> the Arab countries and Israel.
    C   D
    <u>No error.</u>
    E

23. The Federal Aviation Administration <u>ordered</u> an
                                        A
    emergency inspection <u>of several</u> Pan American
                         B
    planes <u>on account of</u> a Pan American Boeing 707
           C
    <u>had crashed</u> on Bali, in Indonesia. <u>No error.</u>
    D   E

24. A gang <u>of armed thieves,</u> directed by a young
           A
    woman, <u>has raided</u> the mansion of a <u>gold-mining</u>
           B   C
    millionaire <u>near Dublin</u> late last night. <u>No error.</u>
                D   E

25. I <u>had</u> a male <u>chauvinist pig dream</u> that the women
      A   B
    of the world <u>rose up</u> and denounced the <u>women's</u>
                 C   D
    liberation movement. <u>No error.</u>
                         E

Directions: The following sentences test correctness and effectiveness of expression. In choosing answers, follow the requirements of standard written English; that is, pay attention to grammar, choice of words, sentence construction, and punctuation.

In each of the following sentences, part of the sentence or the entire sentence is underlined. Beneath each sentence you will find five ways of phrasing the underlined part. Choice A repeats the original; the other four are different.

Choose the answer that best expresses the meaning of the original sentence. If you think that the original is better than any of the alternatives, choose it; otherwise, choose one of the others. Your choice should produce the most effective sentence—clear and precise, without awkwardness or ambiguity.

EXAMPLE

Laura Ingalls Wilder published her first book and she was sixty-five years old then.

SAMPLE ANSWER

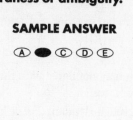

(A) and she was sixty-five years old then
(B) when she was sixty-five
(C) being age sixty-five years old
(D) upon the reaching of sixty-five years
(E) at the time when she was sixty-five

Sample Questions with Answers

26. Such of his novels as was humorous were successful.

(A) Such of his novels as was humorous were successful.
(B) Such of his novels as were humorous were successful.
(C) His novels such as were humorous were successful.
(D) His novels were successful and humorous.
(E) Novels such as his humorous ones were successful.

27. Being that the plane was grounded, we stayed over until the next morning so that we could get the first flight out.

(A) Being that the plane was grounded, we stayed over
(B) In view of the fact that the plane was grounded, we stayed over
(C) Since the plane was grounded, we stayed over
(D) Because the plane was grounded, we stood over
(E) On account of the plane being grounded, we stayed over

28. He never has and he never will keep his word.

(A) He never has and he never will
(B) He has never yet and never will
(C) He has not ever and he will not
(D) He never has or will
(E) He never has kept and he never will

29. The teacher felt badly because she had scolded the bright child who was restless for want of something to do.

(A) felt badly because she had scolded the bright child
(B) felt badly why she had scolded the bright child
(C) felt bad because she had scolded the bright child
(D) felt bad by scolding the bright child
(E) had felt badly because she scolded the bright child

30. This book does not describe the struggle of the blacks to win their voting rights that I bought.

    (A) does not describe the struggle of the blacks to win their voting rights that I bought
    (B) does not describe the black struggle to win their voting rights that I bought
    (C) does not, although I bought it, describe the struggle of the blacks to win their voting rights
    (D) which I bought does not describe the struggle to win for blacks their voting rights
    (E) that I bought does not describe the struggle of the blacks to win their voting rights

31. Barbara cannot help but think that she will win a college scholarship.

    (A) Barbara cannot help but think
    (B) Barbara cannot help but to think
    (C) Barbara cannot help not to think
    (D) Barbara can help but think
    (E) Barbara cannot but help thinking

32. In spite of Tom wanting to study, his sister made him wash the dishes.

    (A) Tom wanting to study
    (B) the fact that Tom wanted to study
    (C) Tom's need to study
    (D) Tom's wanting to study
    (E) Tom studying

33. The old sea captain told my wife and me many interesting yarns about his many voyages.

    (A) my wife and me
    (B) me and my wife
    (C) my wife and I
    (D) I and my wife
    (E) my wife along with me

34. A great many students from several universities are planning to, if the weather is favorable, attend next Saturday's mass rally in Washington.

    (A) are planning to, if the weather is favorable, attend next Saturday's mass rally in Washington
    (B) are planning, if the weather is favorable, to attend next Saturday's mass rally in Washington
    (C) are planning to attend, if the weather is favorable, next Saturday's mass rally in Washington
    (D) are planning to attend next Saturday's mass rally in Washington, if the weather is favorable
    (E) are, if the weather is favorable, planning to attend next Saturday's mass rally in Washington

35. Jane's body movements are like those of a dancer.

    (A) like those of a dancer
    (B) the same as a dancer
    (C) like a dancer
    (D) a dancer's
    (E) like those of a dancer's

36. This is one restaurant I won't patronize because I was served a fried egg by the waitress that was rotten.

    (A) I was served a fried egg by the waitress that was rotten
    (B) I was served by the waitress a fried egg that was rotten
    (C) a fried egg was served to me by the waitress that was rotten
    (D) the waitress served me a fried egg that was rotten
    (E) a rotten fried egg was served to me by the waitress

37. Watching the familiar story unfold on the screen, he was glad that he read the book with such painstaking attention to detail.

    (A) that he read the book with such painstaking attention to detail.
    (B) that he had read the book with such painstaking attention to detail.
    (C) that he read the book with such attention to particulars.
    (D) that he read the book with such intense effort.
    (E) that he paid so much attention to the plot of the book.

38. If anyone requested tea instead of coffee, it was a simple matter to serve it to them from the teapot at the rear of the table.

    (A) it was a simple matter to serve it to them
    (B) it was easy to serve them
    (C) it was a simple matter to serve them
    (D) it was a simple matter to serve it to him
    (E) he could serve himself

39. He bought some bread, butter, cheese and decided not to eat them until the evening.

    (A) some bread, butter, cheese and decided
    (B) some bread, butter, cheese and then decided
    (C) a little bread, butter, cheese and decided
    (D) some bread, butter, cheese, deciding
    (E) some bread, butter, and cheese and decided

40. The things the children liked best were <u>swimming in the river and to watch the horses being groomed by the trainer.</u>

    (A) swimming in the river and to watch the horses being groomed by the trainer.
    (B) swimming in the river and to watch the trainer grooming the horses.
    (C) that they liked to swim in the river and watch the horses being groomed by the trainer.
    (D) swimming in the river and watching the horses being groomed by the trainer.
    (E) to swim in the river and watching the horses being groomed by the trainer.

Explanatory Answers

1. Choice E is correct. All underlined parts are correct.

2. Choice A is correct. "If any signer of the Constitution *were* to return to life..." The verb in the "if clause" of a present contrary-to-fact conditional statement must have a past subjunctive form (*were*).

3. Choice C is correct. "The dean of the college... *is planning*..." The subject of the sentence (*dean*) is singular. Therefore, the verb must be singular (*is planning*).

4. Choice E is correct. All underlined parts are correct.

5. Choice B is correct. "Now that the stress... *is over*..." The subject of the subordinate clause is singular (*stress*). Accordingly, the verb of the clause must be singular (*is*—not *are*). Incidentally, *examinations* and *interviews* are not subjects—they are objects of the preposition *of*.

6. Choice D is correct. "... of more machines and *fewer* people." We use *fewer* for persons and things that may be counted. We use *less* for bulk or mass.

7. Choice C is correct. "...than *that of most* of the other countries of the world." We must have parallelism so that the word *standard* in the main clause of the sentence acts as an antecedent for the pronoun *that* in the subordinate clause. As the original sentence reads, the American standard of living is still higher than the countries themselves.

8. Choice C is correct. "... a long line of flags... *was seen*..." The subject of the sentence is singular (*line*). Therefore, the verb must be singular (*was seen*).

9. Choice A is correct. "*Because of* the failure..." Never start a sentence with *Due to*.

10. Choice E is correct. All underlined parts are correct.

11. Choice C is correct. "After waiting in line for three hours, the tickets had, *much to our disgust*, been sold out when we reached the window." Avoid squinting constructions—that is, modifiers that are so placed that the reader cannot tell whether they are modifying the words immediately preceding the construction or the words immediately following the construction.

12. Choice B is correct. "... resulted in our *guests'* packing up..." A noun or pronoun immediately preceding a gerund is in the possessive case. Note that the noun *guests* followed by an apostrophe is possessive.

13. Choice B is correct. "Sharp advances... *are*..." Since the subject of the sentence is plural (*advances*), the verb must be plural (*are*).

14. Choice A is correct. "An acquaintance with the memoirs... *enables* us..." Since the subject of the sentence is singular (*acquaintance*), the verb must be singular (*enables*).

15. Choice B is correct. "... to *whoever*... had a strong sense..." The subject of the subordinate clause is *whoever*, and it takes a nominative form (*whoever*—not *whomever*) since it is a subject. Incidentally, the expression *he believed* is parenthetical, so it has no grammatical relationship with the rest of the sentence.

16. Choice A is correct. "If he *had lain*..." The verb in the "if clause" of a past contrary-to-fact conditional statement must take the *had lain* form—not the *would have lain* form.

17. Choice C is correct. "... John Crowe Ransom, *whom* you must know as an outstanding American critic." The direct object of the subordinate clause—or of any clause or sentence—must be in the objective case and, accordingly, must take the objective form (*whom*—not *who*).

18. Choice E is correct. All underlined parts are correct.

19. Choice A is correct. "There is no objection to *his* joining... We have here a pronoun that is acting as the subject of the gerund *joining*. As a subject of the gerund, the pronoun must be in the possessive case (*his*).

20. Choice D is correct. "... of Chinese children parading *in colorful uniforms* up Mott Street." In the original sentence, *in colorful uniforms* was a misplaced modifier.

21. Choice D is correct. "The reason... is *that*..." We must say *the reason is that*—not *the reason is because*.

22. Choice A is correct. "There *remain* many reasons..." The word "There" in this sentence is an expletive or introductory adverb. The subject of the

sentence ("reasons") must agree with the verb ("remain") in number.

23. Choice C is correct. "...*because* a Pan American Boeing 707 had crashed..." The word group *on account of* has the function of a preposition. We need a subordinate conjunction (*because*) here in order to introduce the clause.

24. Choice B is correct. "...*raided* the mansion..." The past tense (*raided*)—not the present perfect tense (*has raided*)—is necessary because the sentence has a specific past time reference (*last night*).

25. Choice E is correct. All underlined parts are correct.

26. Choice B is correct. Choice A is incorrect because the plural verb ("were") is necessary. The reason for the plural verb is that the subject "as" acts as a relative pronoun whose antecedent is the plural noun "novels." Choice B is correct. Choice C is awkward. Choice D changes the meaning of the original sentence—so does Choice E.

27. Choice C is correct. Choice A is incorrect—never start a sentence with "being that." Choice B is too wordy. Choice D is incorrect because we "stayed"—not "stood." Choice E is incorrect because "on account of" may never be used as a subordinate conjunction.

28. Choice E is correct. Avoid improper ellipsis. Choices A, B, C, and D are incorrect for this reason. The word "kept" must be included since the second part of the sentence uses another form of the verb ("keep").

29. Choice C is correct. Choice A is incorrect because the copulative verb "felt" takes a predicate adjective ("bad")—not an adverb ("badly"). Choice B is incorrect for the same reason. Moreover, we don't say "felt bad why." Choice D is incorrect because the verbal phrase "by scolding" is awkward in this context. Choice E is incorrect because of the use of "badly" and because the past perfect form of the verb ("had felt") is wrong in this time sequence.

30. Choice E is correct. Choices A, B, and C are incorrect because the part of the sentence that deals with the buying of the book is in the wrong position. Choice D is incorrect because the meaning of the original sentence has been changed. According to this choice, others besides blacks have been struggling.

31. Choice A is correct. The other choices are unidiomatic.

32. Choice D is correct. Choice A is incorrect because the possessive form of the noun ("Tom's") must be used to modify the gerund ("wanting"). Choice B is too wordy. Choice C changes the meaning of the original sentence. Choice E is incorrect for the same reason that Choice A is incorrect. Also, Choice E changes the meaning of the original sentence.

33. Choice A is correct. Choice B is incorrect because "wife" should precede "me." Choice C is incorrect because the object form "me" (not the nominative form "I") should be used as the indirect object. Choice D is incorrect for the reasons given above for Choices B and C. Choice E is too roundabout.

34. Choice D is correct. Choices A, B, C, and E are incorrect because of the misplacement of the subordinate clause ("if the weather is favorable").

35. Choice A is correct. Choices B and C are incorrect because of improper ellipsis. The words "those of" are necessary in these choices. Choice D is incorrect because the "body movements" are not "a dancer's." The possessive use of "dancer's" is incorrect in Choice E.

36. Choice D is correct. The clause "that was rotten" is misplaced in Choices A, B, and C. Choice D is correct. Choice E is incorrect because in this context the passive use of the verb is not as effective as the active use.

37. Choice B is correct. Choice A uses wrong tense sequence. Since the reading of the book took place before the watching of the picture, the reading should be expressed in the past perfect tense, which shows action prior to the simple past tense. Choice B corrects the error with the use of the past perfect tense, "had read," instead of the past tense, "read." Choices C, D, and E do not correct the mistake, and Choice E in addition changes the meaning.

38. Choice D is correct. Choice A is wrong because the word "them," being plural, cannot properly take the singular antecedent "anyone." Choices B and C do not correct this error. Choice D corrects it by substituting "him" for "them." Choice E, while correcting the error, changes the meaning of the sentence.

39. Choice E is correct. Choice A contains a "false series," meaning that the word "and" connects the three words in the series—bread, butter, cheese—with a wholly different clause, instead of with a similar fourth word. The series, therefore, needs its own "and" to complete it. Only Choice E furnishes this additional "and."

40. Choice D is correct. Choice A violates the principle of parallel structure. If the first thing the children liked was "swimming" (a gerund), then the second thing they liked should be, not "to watch" (an infinitive), but "watching" (the gerund). Choice B does not improve the sentence. Choice C repeats the beginning of the sentence with the repetitious words "that they liked." Choice E simply reverses the gerund and the infinitive without correcting the error.

Revision-in-Context Passage with Questions

Directions: **Questions 1–5** are based on a passage that is one student's early draft of an essay. Because the passage is an early draft, some sentences need to be rewritten to make the ideas clearer and more precise.

Read the passage carefully and answer the questions that follow it. Some of the questions are about particular sentences or parts of sentences and ask you to make decisions about sentence structure, diction, and usage. Some of the questions refer to the entire essay or parts of the essay and ask you to make decisions about organization, development, appropriateness of language, audience, and logic. In each case, choose the answer that most effectively makes the intended meaning clear and follows the requirements of standard written English.

(1) *In more and more families, both husbands and wives work nowadays and with this there are new problems that result.* (2) *One reason there are so many two-career couples is that the cost of living is very high.* (3) *Another is because women are now more independent.*

(4) *An example of a two-career couple is Mr. and Mrs. Long.* (5) *Mrs. Long is a university professor.* (6) *Her husband works for a large corporation as a personnel counselor.* (7) *They have two children.* (8) *The Longs believe that the number of two-career couples is likely to increase.* (9) *However, society generally still expects a married woman to continue to fulfill the traditional roles of companion, housekeeper, mother, hostess.* (10) *Thus, as the Longs have experienced, conflicts arise in many ways.* (11) *When career opportunities clash, it is difficult for them to decide which career is more important.*

(12) *There are some basic things that can be done to try to solve a couple's problems.* (13) *Partners should discuss issues with each other openly.* (14) *Keep a realistic estimate on how much can be done.* (15) *Each partner must set priorities, make choices, and agree to trade-offs.* (16) *Men and women have to understand each other's feelings and be aware of this problem before they get involved.*

(SENTENCE STRUCTURE)

1. Which of the following is the best revision of the underlined portion of sentence 1 below?

   In more and more families, both husbands and wives work <u>*nowadays and with this there are new problems that result.*</u>

   (A) nowadays, a situation that is causing new problems
   (B) nowadays and this is what is causing new problems
   (C) nowadays and this makes them have new problems as a result
   (D) nowadays and with it are new problems
   (E) nowadays, they are having new problems

(USAGE)

2. Which of the following is the best revision of the underlined portion of sentence 3 below?

   Another <u>*is because women are now more independent.*</u>

   (A) is women which are
   (B) reason is that women are
   (C) comes from women being
   (D) reason is due to the fact that women are
   (E) is caused by the women's being

(SENTENCE COMBINING)

3. Which of the following is the best way to combine sentences 5, 6, and 7?

    (A) Mrs. Long, a university professor, and her husband, a personnel counselor for a large corporation, have two children.
    (B) As a personnel counselor for a large corporation and as a university professor, Mr. and Mrs. Long have two children.
    (C) Having two children are Mr. and Mrs. Long, a personnel counselor for a large corporation and a university professor.
    (D) Mrs. Long is a university professor and her husband is a personnel counselor for a large corporation and they have two children.
    (E) Mr. and Mrs. Long have two children—he is a personnel counselor for a large corporation and she is a university professor.

(PASSAGE ORGANIZATION)

4. In relation to the passage as a whole, which of the following best describes the writer's intention in the second paragraph?

    (A) To summarize contradictory evidence
    (B) To propose a solution to a problem
    (C) To provide an example
    (D) To evaluate opinions set forth in the first paragraph
    (E) To convince the reader to alter his or her opinion

(SENTENCE STRUCTURE)

5. In the context of the sentences preceding and following sentence 14, which of the following is the best revision of sentence 14?

    (A) You should keep a realistic estimate of how much you can do.
    (B) Estimate realistically how much can be done.
    (C) Keep estimating realistically about how much can be done.
    (D) They should be estimating realistically about how much it is possible for them to do.
    (E) They should estimate realistically how much they can do.

Answer Key:

1. A, 2. B, 3. A, 4. C, 5. E.

Sample Test with Answers

[1]To enter the perceptual world of whales and dolphins, you would have to change your primary sense from sight to sound. [2]Your brain would process and store sound pictures rather than visual images. [3]Individuals and other creatures would be recognized either by the sounds they made or by the echoes they returned from the sounds you made. [4]Your sense of neighborhood, of where you are, and whom you are with, would be a sound sense. [5]Sound is the primary sense in the life of whales and dolphins. [6]Vision is often difficult or impossible in the dark and murky seas. [7]Many whales and dolphins navigate and hunt at night or below the zone of illuminated water. [8]Vision depends on the presence of light, sounds can be made and used at any time of the day or night, and at all depths. [9]Sounds are infinitely variable: loud to soft, high notes to low notes, short silences to long silences, and many other combinations. [10]Sounds can be stopped abruptly in order to listen to a neighbor in the silence. [11]They can be finitely directed and pinpointed by the listener. [12]And communicating and locating by sound does not require a disruption of daily routines. [13]Whales and dolphins can keep in sound contact simply by blowing bubbles as they exhale.

1. If the passage were split into two paragraphs, the second paragraph should begin with the sentence

   (A) Many whales and dolphins navigate and hunt at night or below the zone of illuminated water.
   (B) Sounds are infinitely variable (etc.).
   (C) Sound is the primary sense in the life of whales and dolphins.
   (D) Your sense of neighborhood, of where you are, and whom you are with, would be a sound sense.
   (E) Vision is often difficult or impossible in the dark and murky seas.

2. What should be done with sentence 8?

   (A) The comma after the word *light* should be omitted and the word *and* inserted.
   (B) A semicolon should be substituted for the comma after *light*.
   (C) After the word *sounds* there should be a comma, then the word *however,* and then another comma.
   (D) The sentence should begin with the words *for instance.*
   (E) The sentence should begin with the word *whereas.*

3. Sentence 11 would be more clear if

   (A) The words *by the speaker* were added after the word *directed.*
   (B) The sentence began with *Sounds* rather than *They.*
   (C) The word *finitely* were used again before *pinpointed.*
   (D) The words *by whales or dolphins* were inserted after *directed.*
   (E) The word *always* followed the word *can.*

4. The last sentence, sentence 13, should be

   (A) omitted
   (B) left as it is
   (C) placed before sentence 12
   (D) expanded to explain that whales and dolphins are mammals and therefore exhale through lungs
   (E) changed to read: *Whales and dolphins can keep in contact with each other through sound simply by blowing bubbles as they exhale.*

Explanatory Answers

1. Choice C is correct. Choice A is incorrect because the sentence is dealing with the limitations in the use of vision in whales and dolphins, and the subject of vision has already been introduced in the previous sentence, sentence 6. Choice B is incorrect for similar reasons: The subject of sound has just been discussed in the previous sentence and it is logical that this discussion continue. All the sentences before this address themselves to the reader and explain what changes would have to occur in order for us to perceive the world as whales and dolphins do. Sentence 5 turns the discussion to whales and dolphins themselves and their use of sound. (Notice that sentence 1 says "... *you* would have to change *your primary sense* ...," and sentence 5 says "Sound is the *primary sense* in the life of *whales and dolphins.*") This is the only logical place to begin a second paragraph. Choice D is incorrect because, as it has been stated, sentences 1 through 4 address the reader and therefore belong in one paragraph. Choice E is wrong because, although it is introducing the subject of vision in whales and dolphins for the first time, it is necessary that it follow directly after sentence 5 in order to show that sound is the primary sense *because* vision is restricted in the dark and murky seas.

2. Choice E is correct. As it stands, sentence 8 contains two complete thoughts—one about vision and one about sound, separated only by a comma, which is grammatically incorrect. Although Choice A remedies this situation, it does not make clear that a *comparison* is being made between the uses of vision and hearing. This is also true of Choice B. Choice C makes the comparison clear by the use of the word *however,* but leaves the two thoughts separated only by a comma, and is therefore wrong. Choice D is wrong for two reasons: The sentence is not really giving an example of something which was stated previously, and therefore the words *for instance* do not make sense here; furthermore, the words *for instance* do not make the comparison clear, and so the sentence remains as two separate thoughts with only a comma between them. Choice E remedies the situation completely: The word *whereas* tells us immediately that a comparison is about to be made, and the first part of the sentence ("Whereas vision depends on the presence of light") is now an *incomplete* thought which must be followed by a comma and then the rest of the sentence.

3. Choice A is correct. The sentence as it stands is unclear because it would make it seem that the listener directs as well as pinpoints the sounds, whereas it is the *speaker* who directs them. Therefore Choice A is correct. There is no need for the sentence to begin with the word *sounds;* since sentence 10 began with it, the word *they* in sentence 11 clearly refers to *sounds.* Therefore Choice B does nothing to improve the sentence. Choice C is incorrect because to pinpoint means to locate precisely or exactly, and therefore it would be redundant to insert the word *finitely.* Although Choice D improves the sentence by telling us *who* directs the sounds, Choice A is better because it is the *speaker* who directs the sounds and the listener who pinpoints them, whether whale or dolphin. Choice E is wrong because it would be assumed by the reader that if sounds *can* be finitely directed and pinpointed, they would be in most cases; to say *always can* would be too extreme.

4. Choice B is correct. Sentence 13 is necessary to show that emitting and listening to sounds do not disrupt the routines of whales and dolphins, stated in sentence 12. To omit the sentence, as Choice A suggests, is incorrect. Choice B is correct; it should be left as it is. Choice C is wrong; sentence 13 explains sentence 12, and therefore needs to follow it, not precede it. Choice D is incorrect because the passage is about the use of sound by whales and dolphins, not about the fact that they are mammals. To go into an explanation of this would be to go into disproportionate detail on this one topic. Choice E is wrong for two reasons: (1) The *with each other* is understood (one has contact *with* something; otherwise it is not *contact*). (2) It also implies that whales keep in contact with dolphins and dolphins with whales, whereas what the author means is that whales and dolphins keep in contact with their own kind. To insert *with each other,* therefore, makes the sentence quite confusing.

PRACTICE PAGES

PRACTICE PAGES

PRACTICE PAGES

PRACTICE PAGES

PRACTICE PAGES

PRACTICE PAGES

PRACTICE PAGES

PRACTICE PAGES

PRACTICE PAGES

PRACTICE PAGES

PRACTICE PAGES